Fodor's

CHINA

WELCOME TO CHINA

China—old and new—is a feast for the senses. The vast, awe-inspiring landscapes run the gamut from river deltas, subtropical jungles, and deserts to pulsing megacities with space-age skylines. Tranquil palaces and fog-wrapped mountain peaks evoke the Taoist philosophers of yesteryear. Hong Kong's and Beijing's dizzying modernity exhilarates city culture vultures. Full of diverse peoples and traditions, this fast-changing country reveals its riches to travelers who seek them out, from foodies on a quest for the best dumplings to explorers trekking the Silk Road.

TOP REASONS TO GO

★ **Great Wall:** China's most iconic fortification delivers postcard-perfect views.

★ **Tiger Leaping Gorge:** Breathtaking mountain scenery rewards adventurous hikers.

★ **Architecture:** Futuristic skyscrapers vie with dynastic compounds to dazzle the eye.

★ **Food:** The vibrant flavors of authentic Chinese cuisine are a gourmand's delight.

★ **Imperial History:** Terracotta Warriors and ancient temples take you back 5,000 years.

★ **Cities:** Beijing's Olympic makeover, Hong Kong's harbor, Shanghai's Art Deco splendor.

Fodor's CHINA

Publisher: Amanda D'Acierno, *Senior Vice President*

Editorial: Arabella Bowen, *Editor in Chief*; Linda Cabasin, *Editorial Director*

Design: Tina Malaney, *Associate Art Director*; Chie Ushio, *Senior Designer*; Ann McBride, *Production Designer*

Photography: Jennifer Arnow, *Senior Photo Editor*; Jennifer Romains, *Photo Researcher*

Production: Linda Schmidt, *Managing Editor*; Evangelos Vasilakis, *Associate Managing Editor*; Angela L. McLean, *Senior Production Manager*

Maps: Rebecca Baer, *Senior Map Editor*; David Lindroth, Mark Stroud (Moon Street Cartography) *Cartographers*

Sales: Jacqueline Lebow, *Sales Director*

Marketing & Publicity: Heather Dalton, *Marketing Director*; Katherine Punia, *Publicity Director*

Business & Operations: Susan Livingston, *Vice President, Strategic Business Planning*; Sue Daulton, *Vice President, Operations*

Fodors.com: Megan Bell, *Executive Director, Revenue & Business Development*; Yasmin Marinaro, *Senior Director, Marketing & Partnerships*

Writers: Christy Choi, Sophie Friedman, Daniel Garber, Kit Gillet, Julie Grundvig, Dana Kaufman, Charley Lanyon, Maloy Luakian, Tom O'Malley, Yuan Ren, Adrian Sandiford, Dorothy So, Kate Springer, Sander Van de Moortel

Editors: Salwa Jabado (lead editor), Mark Sullivan (Hong Kong editor), Caroline Trefler (Beijing editor)

Editorial Contributors: Bethany Beckerlegge, Sophie Friedman, John Rambow, Megan Wood

Production Editor: Elyse Rozelle

9th Edition

ISBN 978-1-101-87821-7

ISSN 1070-6895

SPECIAL SALES

This book is available at special discounts for bulk purchases for sales promotions or premiums. For more information, e-mail specialmarkets@penguinrandomhouse.com

PRINTED IN THE UNITED STATES OF AMERICA

10 9 8 7 6 5 4 3 2 1

CONTENTS

Fodor's Features

MAPS

ABOUT THIS GUIDE

Fodor's Recommendations

Everything in this guide is worth doing—we don't cover what isn't—but exceptional sights, hotels, and restaurants are recognized with additional accolades. **Fodor's Choice ★** indicates our top recommendations. Care to nominate a new place? Visit Fodors.com/contact-us.

Trip Costs

We list prices wherever possible to help you budget well. Hotel and restaurant price categories from **$** to **$$$$** are noted alongside each recommendation. For hotels, we include the lowest cost of a standard double room in high season. For restaurants, we cite the average price of a main course at dinner or, if dinner isn't served, at lunch. For attractions, we always list adult admission fees; discounts are usually available for children, students, and senior citizens.

Hotels

Our local writers vet every hotel to recommend the best overnights in each price category, from budget to expensive. Unless otherwise specified, you can expect private bath, phone, and TV in your room. For expanded hotel reviews, facilities, and deals visit Fodors.com.

Top Picks	Hotels &
★ Fodor's Choice	Restaurants
	🏠 Hotel
Listings	⤴ Number of
✉ Address	rooms
✉ Branch address	🍽 Meal plans
☎ Telephone	✕ Restaurant
🖷 Fax	⟲ Reservations
⊕ Website	🏛 Dress code
✉ E-mail	▭ No credit cards
🎫 Admission fee	$ Price
⊙ Open/closed	
times	**Other**
Ⓜ Subway	⇨ See also
✛ Directions or	☞ Take note
Map coordinates	🏌 Golf facilities

Restaurants

Unless we state otherwise, restaurants are open for lunch and dinner daily. We mention dress code only when there's a specific requirement and reservations only when they're essential or not accepted. To make restaurant reservations, visit Fodors.com.

Credit Cards

The hotels and restaurants in this guide typically accept credit cards. If not, we'll say so.

EUGENE FODOR

Hungarian-born Eugene Fodor (1905–91) began his travel career as an interpreter on a French cruise ship. The experience inspired him to write *On the Continent* (1936), the first guidebook to receive annual updates and discuss a country's way of life as well as its sights. Fodor later joined the U.S. Army and worked for the OSS in World War II. After the war, he kept up his intelligence work while expanding his guidebook series. During the Cold War, many guides were written by fellow agents who understood the value of insider information. Today's guides continue Fodor's legacy by providing travelers with timely coverage, insider tips, and cultural context.

EXPERIENCE CHINA

1

WHAT'S WHERE

Numbers refer to chapters.

2 Beijing. Beijing is in massive flux, and the construction never stops. Feel the ancient pulse beneath the current clamor.

3 Beijing to Shanghai: Hebei, Shandong, Anhui, Jiangsu. Discover a cultural and natural treasure trove—Huangshan peaks are islands in a sea of clouds, and canal-laced Suzhou is the Venice of the Orient.

4 Shanghai. In the 1920s Shanghai was known as the Whore of the Orient, but we like to think of her as a classy lady who knows how to have a good time. The party stopped for a few decades after the revolution, but now Shanghai is back in swing.

5 East Coast: Zhejiang, Fujian. Fujian's Xiamen is an undiscovered pearl, with all the history, culture, and infrastructure of more popular tourist magnets. Zhejiang's Hangzhou is known for scenic West Lake, immortalized in Chinese poetry.

6 Hong Kong. A city of contrasts—east and west, old and new, work hard and play harder. Long nights of barhopping are offset by tai chi sessions at dawn.

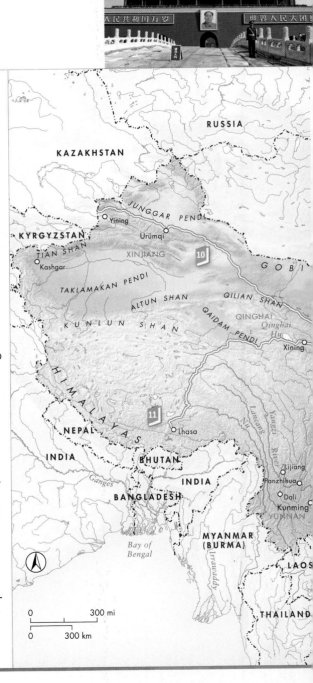

7 Pearl River Delta: Guangzhou and Shenzhen. The word "engine" is used metaphorically to describe the Pearl River delta region, but the vibrations are still palpable here in China's industrial hub.

8 Southwest: Guangxi, Guizhou, Yunnan. The mountains are high and the emperor is far away. If you're looking to take a walk on the wild tribal side, then any or all of these three regions should be high on your list.

9 Sichuan and Chongqing. China's latest industrial revolution is happening in faraway Sichuan and Chongqing, where the nearby Three Gorges Dam (in Hubei), while hotly debated, remains a stunning sight.

10 The Silk Road: Shaanxi, Gansu, Qinghai, Xinjiang. Distant and mysterious, this was ancient China's lifeline to the outside world. Visit the country's last remaining walled cities—Xi'an is fascinating for its cultural and its historical importance.

11 Tibet. The roof of the world is not the most accessible place, but that's changing thanks to the train line connecting Lhasa to major cities throughout China.

NEED TO KNOW

Capital: Beijing

Population: 1,384,694,199

Currency: Yuan Renminbi

Money: ATMs are ubiquitous in big cities; cash is king

Language: Mandarin

Country Code: 86

Emergencies: 110

Driving: On the right

Electricity: 220v/50 cycles; plugs have two flat prongs

Time: 12 hours ahead of New York

Documents: Visa required

Mobile Phones: GSM (900 and 1800 bands)

Major Mobile Companies: PCCW, China Mobile

WEBSITES

China: ⊕ www.cnto.org

Hong Kong: ⊕ www.discoverhongkong.com

State travel agency: ⊕ www.citsusa.com

GETTING AROUND

✈ **Air Travel:** The major airports are Shanghai, Beijing, Guangzhou Baiyun, and Hong Kong.

🚌 **Bus Travel:** China has expansive long-distance bus services, but rides in rural areas are not for the faint of heart.

🚗 **Car Travel:** A Chinese driver's license and residence permit are needed to rent a car.

🚆 **Train Travel:** The train network is extensive, and the high-speed CRH zoom to and from a handful of major cities. Passports are needed to buy tickets.

PLAN YOUR BUDGET

	HOTEL ROOM	MEAL	ATTRACTIONS
Low Budget	Y1000	Y49	Shanghai's Fuxing Park, free
Mid-Budget	Y1,300	Y100	Beijing's Great Wall, Y45
High Budget	Y1,800	Y350	Hong Kong's The Peak Tram and Sky Terrace, HK$80

WAYS TO SAVE

Eat local. Western meals go for Western prices, so eat Chinese food to avoid a high markup.

Book a rental apartment. In Shanghai, Beijing, and especially Hong Kong, hotels can get pricey. Rent an apartment instead, and you'll get a kitchen, too.

Go on two wheels. Avoid cabs, which can really add up, and do as the locals do by renting a bike to get around.

Hang out in the park. Walk the Bund and the French Concession in Shanghai, visiting parks where locals practice tai chi, calligraphy, and ballroom dancing.

PLAN YOUR TIME

Hassle Factor	Low. There are direct flights daily from many major U.S. cities to China. In China's big cities, the airports are well set up to accommodate foreigners. Cabs are cheap and plentiful.
3 Days	Take in Beijing's top historical sites, including the Forbidden City and Tiananmen Square. Then venture out to the Summer Palace and hike the Great Wall of China.
1 Week	Start off in Beijing, checking off its major sites. Go out to 798 to see what's happening in contemporary Chinese art. Wander the hutong, tuck into dumplings, and go boutique-hopping. From Beijing, fly to Xi'an to see the Terracotta Warriors and visit the Muslim Quarter for authentic snacks.

WHEN TO GO

High Season: China is massive with varied weather. In general, the best time to visit is spring (late March to May) and fall (September to early-November), when temperatures are in the 50s-70s°F.

Low Season: Mid-November to early March is frigid in northern and western China and cold and damp around Shanghai, but this can be a good time to visit Beijing. Avoid Chinese New Year, in late January or early February.

Value Season: June, July, and August are sweltering and humid in and around Shanghai; it's slightly cooler in Beijing and drier. In far northwest China, it's hot but dry. Hotel prices are moderate.

BIG EVENTS

January or February: Shops and restaurants close for the week of Chinese New Year and everything sells out months in advance. ⊕ www.chinesenewyears.info

January: Harbin Ice Festival is the world's largest ice and snow festival. ⊕ www.icefestivalharbin.com

March: Authors talk about Asia and China at the Shanghai and Beijing International Literary festivals.

June: The Dragon Boat Festival celebrates the poet Qu Yuan; participants eat zongzi and watch rowing competitions.

READ THIS

■ *River Town,* Peter Hessler. Memoir by a Peace Corps volunteer in Sichuan.

■ *Waiting,* Ha Jin. A love story during the Cultural Revolution.

■ *The Good Earth,* Pearl S. Buck. A farmer and his wife struggle in 1920s China.

WATCH THIS

■ *The Last Emperor.* A biopic about the life of Puyi—the last emperor.

■ *Farewell My Concubine.* Two Peking opera actors and the woman who comes between them.

■ *Lust, Caution.* Ang Lee's espionage thriller set in Hong Kong and Shanghai.

EAT THIS

■ **Xiaolongbao:** steamed soup dumplings

■ **Dandan noodles:** Sichuan noodle dish in a spicy sauce

■ **Mantou:** light, steamed buns

■ **Hongshao rou:** a classic Shanghai dish of sweet, saucy red-braised pork

■ **Peking duck:** crispy outside, tender inside, wrapped in a pancake

■ **Wonton noodles:** a mild broth studded with shrimp wontons

QUINTESSENTIAL CHINA

Art for Art's Sake

China may be careening through the 21st century at breakneck speed, but the Chinese are immensely proud of their artistic heritage and traditional folk arts have not been forgotten. Every region of China is rich in local arts and craft traditions. In the north, delicate designs are painstakingly cut from rice paper and hung from windows and doors during festivals and weddings. In the east, Suzhou is as famous for its elegant silk embroidery as it is for its gardens, and nearby Huangshan is a wonderful place to discover bamboo weaving. Yunnan is known for its ethnic batik cloth, Sichuan for its lacquer paintings, Fujian for its colorful hand puppets. Everywhere you go you'll see fluttering overhead one of China's oldest pastimes: kite flying, dating all the way back to 475 BC.

Be Moved

Getting there is often half the fun, and in China there are limitless ways to travel from point A to point B. China already has the world's longest high-speed rail network, and has plans to add many new lines in the coming years. But there's more than just trains. Sightseeing in Chongqing? Cross the Yangtze or Jialing rivers in an old-school cable car. Horses are the best way to get around in the beautiful countryside surrounding Songpan in Sichuan. If you're flying into Shanghai's Pudong Airport, take the superslick maglev train into town at speeds of more than 260 miles per hour. China's crown jewels of passenger transport belong to Hong Kong, where it's normal to get around by light rail, bus, taxi, trolley, boat—it even has the longest covered outdoor escalator system in the world.

Chinese culture is rich, diverse, and will hit you like a ton of bricks. Keep an open mind while you're traveling, because this will be an experience of a lifetime.

China Beyond the Han

The Han are far and away the dominant ethnic group in China, but there is surprising ethnic diversity, from the Muslim Uighurs in Xinjiang to the Dai and Hani of Xishuangbanna. Officially there are 56 ethnic groups, including the nomadic Mongols, which make up the great Chinese nation. Though small in number relative to the Han, the minorities have historically been a force to be reckoned with. Rulers of the last dynasty (the Qing) were Manchus. Though Chinese history is rife with examples of intertribal war and Han incursion into non-Han territory (Tibet being the latest and most famous example), the revolution, in theory, leveled the playing field. Traveling through areas less dominated by the Han Chinese offers views of the country far different from the usual Beijing–Shanghai–Three Gorges tour.

All the Tea in China

For a vast majority of the Chinese people, the day begins and ends with tea. Whether it's being savored in a delicate ceremonial porcelain cup or slurped out of a glass mason jar, you can bet that the imbiber takes tea consumption seriously. Ask a Chinese person about the best tea and the answer will very likely depend on where they're from. The highly prized Pu'er tea has a dark color and heavy, almost earthy flavor. It gets its name from the region of southern Yunnan Province where it's grown. Fujian produces the best oolong teas, thanks to the high mountains and favorable climate. Oolong is usually served with much ceremony. Perhaps the most expensive tea in China is a variant of green tea from the Longjing ("Dragon Well") region of Hangzhou. Longjing tea is served in clear glasses, so one can watch the delicate dance of the long, thin leaves as they float to the top.

IF YOU LIKE

Contemporary Art

Over the past two decades, China has experienced an explosion of state-run and private art galleries and museums, fueled by a burgeoning middle-class and creative renaissance. Chinese contemporary artists are well known for their unabashed take on hot-button issues such as the environment, corruption, materialism, and poverty, including Ai Weiwei and Cai Guo-qiang, who regularly make international headlines. Beijing is the cultural heart of the contemporary art movement but other cities are catching up—Shanghai and Guangzhou are also home to thriving avant-garde art scenes and frequently play host to local and international exhibitions.

Dashanzi 798 Art District, Beijing. This former Bauhaus-inspired warehouse complex in Beijing's Chaoyang District houses dozens of galleries and the workshops of many of the country's most established and up-and-coming artists.

Guangdong Museum of Art, Guangzhou. Calling itself the "first contemporary art museum" in Guangzhou, this cutting-edge space shows works of traditional and modern artists, with a special focus on artists from the Pearl River delta.

Power Station of Art, Shanghai. Located on the banks of Shanghai's scenic Huangpu River, this converted power plant is China's first state-run contemporary art museum. The immense industrial space hosts revolving local and international exhibits of world-class stature.

Suzhou Creek Art District, Shanghai. In a renovated factory area on Suzhou Creek, more than 120 art galleries and studios are open to the public. Some of Shanghai's top artists have studios here, including the contemporary art collective Liu Dao and world-renowned artists Zhou Tiehai and Xu Zhen.

Bicycling

In the not-too-distant past, China was known as "The Bicycle Kingdom," but as cars become more popular, the iconic sea of bicycles that once filled the avenues of Beijing and Shanghai is drying to a trickle.

But this doesn't mean that bicycling enthusiasts should lose heart. While the two-wheeled herd has thinned out considerably, you'll hardly be riding alone. Most hotels will be able to help you out with bicycle rentals, or a brand-new Flying Pigeon (the bike of China) should only set you back a few hundred yuan.

Beijing. Though notorious for its bad air and traffic gridlock, the capital is still our favorite urban bicycling ground. Its wide avenues and impossible-to-maneuver-by-car back alleyways make it an ideal city to tour by bicycle.

Chengdu. The spiciest city in China is also as flat as a Ping-Pong table, which makes it one of our favorites for exploring by bike.

Shanghai. The Pearl of the Orient is also two-wheel friendly, though you'll be asked to dismount and walk along the Nanjing pedestrian area.

Xi'an. The city center is small enough to make it perfect for exploring by bike. For a unique experience, take a spin on top of the city wall, the only one left fully intact in all of China.

Treasure Hunting

For anyone who loves to shop, China is heaven on earth. Along with the glitzy department stores found in big cities, vibrant street markets and pedestrian shopping areas are found everywhere and can be terrific places to hunt for bargains.

Every region of China has a specialty, whether silk embroidery in Suzhou, mud figures in Beijing, Longjing tea in Hangzhou, or stuffed tiger toys in Xi'an. Popular souvenirs include Chinese silk, jade, and wood carvings—travelers never come home disappointed. The rule of the land is to bargain hard and bring an extra bag for your loot.

Duolun Lu, Shanghai. Spend a pleasant afternoon strolling along Duolun Lu's pedestrian street in Shanghai's historic Hongkou District, once the home of aspiring writers Lu Xun and Mao Dun. Browse through the numerous bookstores, galleries, and curio shops, and when you're done you can relax over a cup of tea at one of the many restored teahouses.

Panjiayuan Antiques Market, Beijing. If you have a hankering for a scroll, jade bracelet, embroidery, or even a musical Mao alarm clock, this is the place. On weekends, Beijing's most popular spot for kitsch is teeming with shoppers on the lookout for a well-fought bargain. Haggle fiercely and doubt any claims that the Ming-style vase you desire is the real thing.

Suzhou Arts and Crafts Museum, Suzhou. Housed in a restored courtyard, this museum is a terrific place to purchase authentic arts and crafts, including jade, silk embroidery, and sandalwood carvings. In the adjoining workshop watch artisans at work shaping lattice fans and transforming blocks of jade into delicate figurines.

Temple Street Night Market, Hong Kong. Locals and tourists alike frequent this lively night market for its festive atmosphere and outdoor dining. Hundreds of vendors vie for your attention, selling everything from silk scarves to bamboo backscratchers. Most people come here for the party rather than the merchandise, but it's still a good spot to find a treasure or two.

Adventurous Dining

Much has been written about the cuisine of China, and for a very good reason—it's some of the best (and most varied) on the planet. Most visitors will be happy to stick with such well-known dishes as Peking duck or kung pao chicken, but for those who want a culinary walk on the wild side, might we suggest a few less well-known regional favorites?

Huangshan Stone Frog, Anhui. Stone frog soup is a delicacy of Huangshan, famous for its simple, rustic cuisine. Hefty-sized black frogs are collected from the rivers around the mountain and served in a clear soup mixed with bamboo shoots, mushrooms, and ham. Locals claim the frogs will cure bad eyesight, strengthen bones, and increase energy. What's better for a day scaling the peaks of Huangshan?

Thousand-Year-Old Eggs, Guangdong. Preserved eggs are a Cantonese specialty made from coating duck or chicken eggs in a potent mixture of lime, salt, ash, and clay for up to a month until the egg whites turn dark brown and the yolks become green, smelling faintly of ammonia. With a jelly-like consistency, this pungent delicacy is often served with congee or pickled ginger to make it less edgy.

Yak-Butter Tea, Yunnan, Tibet. This beverage is ubiquitous throughout both Tibet and the higher mountain regions of Yunnan Province. Thick and tangy, the main ingredients of yak-butter tea are yak butter, tea, and salt. Though its adherents drink it by the gallon, considering it delicious and healthy, unsuspecting imbibers have likened its flavor to melted blue cheese, or even wood polish.

Village Life

Escape from the noisy, crowded cities and explore China's many traditional villages, situated among some of the country's most idyllic scenery. Take a flat-bottomed boat down the canals of an ancient water town, explore minority cultures in China's colorful southwest, or stay overnight in a fortified Hakka village.

Hakka Roundhouses, Fujian. The massive, earth-built houses of the Hakka peoples resemble flying saucers dropped from the sky. Standing four stories high, the mushroom-shaped buildings provided protection from marauding bandits in early times and are still home to Hakka families today.

Hongcun, Anhui. Locals like to say that Hongcun is shaped like a buffalo. Wander through the cobblestone lanes and you'll get a glimpse of well-preserved Hui architecture, with detailed carvings of characters drawn from myths and folklore on the beams and lattice windows.

Kaili, Guizhou. Nestled in a magical landscape of waterfalls, caves, and rushing rivers, the town of Kaili is a wonderful jumping-off point to explore the minority cultures of the Dong and Miao communities scattered throughout the surrounding area.

Luzhi, Jiangsu. This tiny water village, with a shady, tree-lined canal snaking through the center, is most famous for its ancient stone bridges and women wearing traditional embroidered dress.

Sacred Sites

Despite taking a beating over the past century, the sacred landmarks of China's complex religious past are alive and well. Go on a spiritual pilgrimage and immerse yourself in the wonders of the country's temples, mosques, sculptures, and sacred mountains.

Great Mosque, Shaanxi. The Great Mosque in Xi'an is one of the largest in China. Situated in the city's vibrant Muslim quarter, it has been an active place of worship since the Tang Dynasty, when Xi'an (known as Chang'an) was the gateway to the Silk Road.

Lama Temple, Beijing. A heady mix of colorful mandalas, scroll paintings, and statues of deities fill the halls of this stunning Tibetan temple complex located in the heart of Beijing.

Leshan Buddha, Sichuan. Sitting at a mere 233 feet high, the mighty Leshan Buddha serenely overlooks the Dadu and Min rivers churning below. To gain a full appreciation of his awesomeness, visitors can hike down a stairway chiseled from the sheer rock face to a platform at the base and take a picture with the Buddha's toes—each is 28 feet long!

Mount Tai, Shandong. Taoist masters once brewed their elixirs of immortality atop Mount Tai's mystical pinnacles. Your ascent to the heavens will be via the mountain's 6,000 steps, taking you through strange-shaped peaks and misty wooded hills.

Getting Back to Nature

China offers the perfect opportunity to get away from it all. From the remote deserts of the northwest to the steamy bamboo groves of the south, it's easy to find places to become one with nature.

Bird Island, Qinghai. Birds are the main attraction at China's largest inland saltwater lake. Depending upon the time of year, you can expect to see egrets, sand pipers, cormorants, geese, and plenty of seagulls. The best time of year to visit is

May and June, when thousands of birds descend from the skies to breed.

Hua Shan, Shaanxi. The Taoist mountain of Hua Shan is a dream destination for the novice and avid hiker. Paths wind circuitously upwards 7,000 feet between barefaced cliffs, twisted pines, and deep gorges.

Jiuzhaiguo Nature Reserve, Sichuan. This remote nature reserve in northern Sichuan is dotted with pristine lakes, deep valleys, high mountain meadows, and scattered Tibetan settlements. It also offers an opportunity to see deer, bears, and the elusive panda, if you're lucky.

Tiger Leaping Gorge, Yunnan. This fantastic canyon, 10 miles long, with a rushing white-capped river and surrounded by towering cliffs, is a true must-see. There are opportunities for one- to two-day hikes in the rugged mountain wilderness.

Setting Sail

Did you know China invented the paddle-boat? Follow in the footsteps of Zhenghe, China's great explorer, and embrace your nautical side. Whether by canoe, river raft, or cruise ship, there are plenty of lakes, rivers, and seas to sail, all with something unique to offer.

East Lake, Shaoxing. Black-awning boats ply the waters of East Lake, a man-made quarry dating back to the Han Dynasty. The blue-gray cliffs, grottoes, and arched bridges give the lake a unique beauty and charm that have even impressed the most discriminating visitors—it's said that Emperor Shi Huangdi liked to stop here and stretch his legs.

Erhai Lake, Yunnan. Take a flat-bottomed boat across scenic Erhai Lake and watch local fishermen use trained cormorants to catch fish. Surrounding the lake are pretty Bai minority fishing villages, temples, and views of majestic Cangshan mountain in the background.

Li River, Guangxi. One of the most scenic ways to see the fantastical limestone karst of southwest China is by boat. Hire a bamboo raft and drift your way tranquilly through the lush, brilliant green landscape enjoying the panoramic vistas at every turn.

The Three Gorges River Cruise, Yangtze River. Float down the third-longest river in the world, traversing through the most stunning river scenery in China. Kick back, drink in hand, and enjoy the dramatic landscape gradually unfolding around you.

CHINA'S WORLD HERITAGE SITES

China has racked up a total of 47 United Nations World Heritage Sites. Given the country's huge tourism numbers, sites can be overrun at peak travel times, but it doesn't take much to get away from the crowds.

Forbidden City

(A) Sitting at the heart of Beijing across from Tiananmen Square, the nearly 500-year-old Forbidden City is one of the world's most impressive imperial compounds. For the emperors and their courts, this moat-encircled complex was literally their city within a city, featuring 1,000 buildings covering more than 7.8 million square feet. Today the Forbidden City is home to the Palace Museum and its world-class collection of priceless paintings, bronzes, pottery, and documents that once belonged to the Qing imperial collection.

Temple of Heaven

(B) The Temple of Heaven—known in Chinese as the Altar of Heaven—was once where Ming and Qing emperors made sacrifices to heaven. The emperor and his court visited the Temple of Heaven twice each year to perform ceremonies with the hope of ensuring a good harvest—even a minor mistake could spell disaster for China. The complex was built in the early 15th century by the Yongle Emperor, who was also behind the construction of the Forbidden City.

Great Wall

(C) The Great Wall of China is one of the country's most iconic structures, as well as one of the world's most ambitious engineering projects. Originally intended to prevent invasion by nomadic tribes north of China, the wall was an imperial obsession for more than 1,000 years, beginning in the 5th century BC. Built primarily of stone and rammed earth, the

wall stretches 5,500 miles (8,850 kilometers) from its easternmost point on the Bohai Sea to its western terminus at Lop Nur in Xinjiang.

Old Town of Lijiang

(D) The Old Town of Lijiang is renowned for its winding cobblestone streets, charming wooden homes, and clear, fish-filled mountain streams. The area has been home to the Naxi people (with their unique culture and architecture) for eight centuries. One of China's most popular destinations for domestic or international travelers, Lijiang is visited by millions each year. UNESCO has raised concerns that overcommercialization is affecting the site's heritage value, but it is still a must-visit destination for many tourists.

Yunnan Three Parallel Rivers Protected Areas

(E) Northwest Yunnan is one of the world's biodiversity hot spots, primarily owing to the steep river valleys through which the upper reaches of the Yangtze, Mekong, and Salween rivers flow. These protected areas contain unforgettable scenery, including the awe-inspiring Tiger Leaping Gorge and hundreds of varieties of rhododendrons, and rare animals such as the red panda and snow leopard.

South China Karst

(F) Spread across the southwestern regions of Yunnan, Guizhou, and Guangxi, the South China Karst area is recognized for the diversity of its limestone scenery. The Stone Forest, outside of Yunnan's capital Kunming, is the best-known site in this group, featuring stone spires and strangely shaped monoliths that boggle the mind. A stony paradise for shutterbugs, Stone Forest and the other South China Karst sites are very popular, but still large enough to allow you to find your own quiet corner to take photos or just marvel at these improbable wonders.

CHINA'S WORLD HERITAGE SITES

Emei Shan

(G) Mist-shrouded Emei Shan is located in lush southern Sichuan Province. Emei Shan is one of China's four sacred Buddhist mountains. Emei's seemingly endless stone paths are usually hiked over one or two days. Hikers on Emei go there for the luxuriant and diverse foliage, the charming, run-down monasteries, the occasional waterfall, and the gangs of Tibetan macaques roaming its slopes. Emei's peak is best seen at dawn, when the sun rises from a sea of clouds.

Mogao Caves

(H) The northwestern city of Dunhuang in Gansu Province was once an important stopover on the Silk Road that connected China with Europe via Central Asia. Along with bringing traders and goods in from the West, the Silk Road also brought Buddhism. The Mogao Caves near Dunhuang were first established more than 2,300 years ago as places for Buddhists to practice their faith. Over time, the caves grew into a complex of nearly 500 temples featuring astonishingly well-preserved Buddhist painting and architecture collected during a 1,000-year period.

Terracotta Warriors

(I) The Terracotta Army at the mausoleum of the first Qin Emperor is one of the biggest archaeological discoveries in the last half century. In 1974 farmers discovered pits with thousands of life-size statues of soldiers, horses, chariots, musicians, and acrobats—their find instantly captured China's, and the world's, imagination. The army was commissioned by Qin Shihuang, China's first emperor, and buried with him in the early 3rd century with the hope that the warriors would protect him in the afterlife. Each 6-foot-tall statue is believed to have been modeled after a living human from the emperor's time.

Potala Palace

(J) The Potala Palace is one of the world's most impressive buildings. Looking out over the valley below, its 13 stories house more than 1,000 rooms with countless shrines and statues throughout. Prior to serving as the residence of Dalai Lamas, the Potala was originally used by the historic Tibetan king Songtsen Gampo as a retreat for meditation. Its first palace was begun in the 7th century, with construction finishing in 1645. The Potala suffered during the 1959 uprising that led to the current Dalai Lama's fleeing Tibet, and also was at risk during the Cultural Revolution, but this great building still stands tall today, a monument to the greatness of Tibet's past.

Summer Palace

(K) In Beijing's northern suburbs, the Summer Palace is where many an emperor went to escape his virtual imprisonment within the city center's Forbidden City. A peaceful retreat with a tranquil lake, a hill with scenic views of the city below, and a fantastic collection of gardens, statues, and pagodas, the Summer Palace is a great place to take a break from Beijing without actually leaving the city.

Chengde Mountain Resort

(L) Beijing summers can be unbearably hot, even if you're the emperor. The Qing emperors, who were accustomed to the cooler climes of Manchuria, decided it was better to relocate their courts during the sweltering summer heat to higher, cooler ground, choosing a mountain in Chengde, Hebei Province, to serve as their summer capital. Legendary emperors, including Kangxi, Yongzheng, and Qianlong, escaped the heat while continuing to perform their imperial duties. The compound is loosely modeled on the Forbidden City, but its gardens, pagoda, and outlying temples give it a character all its own.

CHINA TODAY

Government

Mao Zedong's announcement of the establishment of the People's Republic of China on October 1, 1949, finished one turbulent chapter in Chinese history and began another. The fall of the Qing, growing incursion by foreign countries, and the devastation of World War II sandwiched between two periods of bloody civil war gave way to purges of the country's artists and intellectuals, increasing isolationism, the colossal failure of the Great Leap Forward, and the tragic chaos of the Cultural Revolution.

The last quarter century has been characterized by relative stability and growth. Since the late 1970s the sole power holder in the People's Republic of China, the Chinese Communist Party, has brought hundreds of millions out of poverty and significantly relaxed its iron grip on personal freedoms. Diplomatically, Beijing has also become an increasingly savvy power broker on the global stage, while Western powers have been distracted by war and economic woes.

The party has no shortage of challenges that threaten its mandate to rule, including widespread corruption, an increasingly vocal and media-savvy populace, environmental disasters, and a widening wealth gap. In 2014, thousands of pro-democracy advocates shut down city streets in Hong Kong protesting reforms to Hong Kong's political system that would allow direct elections, but only from cherry-picked candidates that meet Beijing's approval.

Economy

China is undergoing the greatest economic expansion the world has ever seen, with the country now the world's most important producer and consumer of just about everything. Since the launch of Paramount Leader Deng Xiaoping's reform and open policy in 1978, the Middle Kingdom has experienced roughly 10% annual GDP growth and has become the world's second-largest economy, trailing only that of the United States (for now).

China's coastal region was the early beneficiary of economic reforms, with cities such as Shanghai, Beijing, Shenzhen, and Guangzhou powering an export-focused economic model. Today the story is the awakening of markets in second- and third-tier cities as the country moves toward a consumption-driven economy.

Media

The media in China has primarily served as a government mouthpiece since 1949. Since 1999 the Internet has not only provided Chinese people with greater access to information, it has also given rise to "Netizens," Chinese who use the Internet to voice their concerns and displeasures with modern society.

Beijing's attempts to manage the Internet have drawn much criticism beyond China's borders, but that hasn't stopped the Internet from becoming a part of daily life for more and more Chinese. With more than 618 million people regularly going online, China is the world's largest Internet market.

Government attempts to control the Internet have caused some of the world's biggest companies to pull out of the country or be blocked. Google made headlines in 2010, when it shut down its Beijing operations and redirected traffic to its Hong Kong site. Sites including Facebook and Twitter were blocked in 2009, presumably owing to government concerns about the potential for social media to be used in organizing anti-government activities.

Religion

Officially an atheist country, China is home to large numbers of Buddhists, Muslims, Christians, and Taoists. Until recently, practicing any religion could lead to detention or worse, but now the country's temples, mosques, and churches are active once more—although the watchful eye of the government is never far away.

Despite its general increasing tolerance toward religion, the Chinese government has taken strong measures against groups that it considers a threat to its rule, most notably the Falun Gong, which it considered a cult and banned in 2000. Buddhists in Tibet and Uighur Muslims in Xinjiang frequently clash with police and soldiers, leading to heightened tension in those regions.

Sports

Despite its Olympic success, China has not been able to develop popular home-grown sports leagues. Men's soccer is seen as one of the country's biggest disappointments—China's national team has only once qualified for the World Cup. The national soccer league is riddled with corruption and empty seats, with most Chinese preferring to watch European matches.

Basketball is also extremely popular in China—even remote mountaintop villages have a court or two. In the late 1990s NBA games began to be broadcast on the mainland, to the delight of sports fans. Yao Ming, now retired from the Houston Rockets, was one of China's most successful athletes to play internationally. Everyone from kids to grandparents seemed to have a Chicago Bulls cap, and Michael Jordan was as recognizable as Bill Clinton. Today Kobe Bryant and a new generation of stars are being emulated by Chinese streetballers, and many former NBA players are finding second careers in the Chinese Basketball Association.

Sexual Mores

China is often thought of as a sexually conservative country, but you don't get to be the world's most populous country by being a bunch of prudes. Over the centuries Chinese society has seen it all, from polygamy to prostitutes, from eunuchs to transvestite actors.

Premarital sex in China may be discouraged, but young Chinese all over the country are engaging in sex, whether it be with a steady boyfriend or girlfriend or a drunken one-night stand. Public displays of affection in broad daylight aren't commonplace, but also not unheard-of.

Part and parcel with China's economic development has been the return of prostitution. More often than not, Chinese hotels will have on-site prostitution, and the odd international five-star occasionally gets busted for offering "special services" to guests.

Homosexuality was officially considered a mental illness in China until 2001—since then the country has become considerably more accepting of gays, lesbians, and transgendered individuals. These days nearly every major city has a few gay bars, and even straight Chinese take fashion cues from their homosexual "comrades."

Sexual relations between Chinese and foreigners are generally accepted, but there is occasional friction or unpleasantness. On the short end of China's gender-imbalance stick, some Chinese men resent foreign men and the Chinese women who date them. On the flip side of that coin, a Chinese man who is dating a foreign woman is often hailed as a stud.

FLAVORS OF CHINA

Chinese cuisine spans the entire spectrum of flavors, ingredients, and cooking styles. Almost every city or town is known for at least one or two specialty dishes. Wheat is the staple of choice in China's dry north, but in the wet, humid south rice is favored. Most large Chinese cities offer a bit of everything from around the country. There's plenty of delicious street food out there—look for stalls with a long line of locals and make sure your food is cooked while you're waiting.

Vegetables and Tofu

Vegetables are usually a part of any Chinese meal, with most varieties common to Western countries available—plus many that aren't, such as bitter melon or morning glory. Cold dishes such as pickled radishes or cucumber chunks in garlic and vinegar are a common way to start off a meal. Hot vegetable dishes can take on all forms. Many, especially leafy greens, are often simply chopped and stir-fried with just a bit of seasoning. Where you are in China often affects the cooking method of your favorite veggie. If you're hungry for potatoes in Harbin, they may be cooked with green pepper and eggplant in a red sauce, whereas in Yunnan, spicy mashed potatoes, crispy hash browns, and even potato and pumpkin soup are more common. Tofu, known in China as *doufu*, is available in a wide variety of shapes, sizes, and colors. Firm white tofu is commonly eaten in the Sichuanese style—bathed in a spicy and numbing sauce—but it is also served in soups with spinach or other greens. More adventurous eaters might try tofu with preserved eggs or "stinky tofu," which bears an aroma similar to sweaty feet. Tofu skin (*doufu pi*) is a byproduct of normal tofu production, and contains fewer impurities. It can be stir-fried with peppers or mushrooms, and is

a popular ingredient for cooking in hotpot. Vegetarians traveling in China should keep in mind that many restaurants will add small amounts of pork, ham, oyster sauce, or other non-veggie items to seemingly vegetarian dishes, including tofu. "Vegetarian" dishes may also be cooked in lard. Make sure you emphasize no meat whatsoever when ordering to maximize the chance of getting what you want.

Meat

Chinese cuisine features nearly every type of meat imaginable—nothing is too strange to consume, and there are no prohibitions on consumption of certain animals. Dog, bullfrog, rabbit, and snake are perfectly ordinary ingredients, as are all varieties of organs, including kidneys, liver, ears, and even penises. Pork and chicken are the most popular meats. Beef is also commonly consumed, but lamb tends to be found mainly only in Muslim dishes. It's difficult to find Western-style large chunks of meat—shredded, sliced, or cubed, it all comes small and chopstick-ready. Chicken is often cooked on the bone. In Beijing, Peking duck is a specialty that can't be missed—wrap it in thin pancakes with scallions and dip it in tangy sauce. Dishes from the predominantly Muslim northwest feature hearty stews. Sichuan cuisine, while too spicy for some, features some great meat dishes, including the accessible kung pao chicken. In Yunnan, the local ham is famous, and works great adding flavor to fried vegetable dishes. Iron plate beef (*tieban niurou*) is a popular fajita-style dish that can be found countrywide, and features strips of beef cooked with onion and green pepper in gravy, served on an iron hot plate. If you're into street snacks, slender kebabs of barbecued meat can be found for sale across the country, usually flavored with

chili and cumin. Yunnan takes this a step further—the province is known for its night stalls selling all manner of skewered treats.

Seafood

Fish holds a special place in Chinese cuisine—it's both a status dish and an auspicious symbol. Any banquet celebrating a festival or a special occasion will feature a fish. The fish is usually cooked and served whole, swimming in soy sauce with a dressing of scallions. In the seafaring south, superstitious eaters never turn the fish over, but eat "through" it. The quality and variety of seafood is much better on China's coast, but it is consumed countrywide, with farmed fish keeping inland diners happy. Most river or lake fish should be avoided, owing to pollution issues.

Seafood is kept alive as long as possible to preserve freshness, so don't be surprised to find yourself choosing your ingredients from tanks at the front of the restaurant or watching your fish being killed in front of you. Given this extra difficulty when ordering, Hong Kong is a great place to eat seafood. All manner of shellfish are on the menu. Generally cooking styles are simple, and focus on the flavor of the ingredients. Some diners may find shellfish less well cooked than they are used to. Shrimp is usually served with the shells on.

Shark-fin soup is one of the most expensive delicacies to be found in China, and is often served to esteemed guests or at important business banquets. Many Chinese are unaware of the massive negative impact the harvesting of shark fins is having on the oceanic ecosystem. Prior to an expensive banquet, you may want to tell your host that you do not eat shark-fin soup for environmental reasons—this can save you the social awkwardness of refusing it when it is placed before you. More progressive restaurants in China are now taking the soup off their menus.

Staple foods

As noted earlier, China's staple foods are split along a north-south divide, but that doesn't mean that people in the north don't eat rice and southerners don't enjoy a bowl of wheat noodles.

Wheat is the primary grain grown in China's north, and wheat flour is used in making a wide variety of noodles as well as dumplings, breads, and pancakes. *Lamian*—wheat noodles made fresh by an entertaining process of stretching, swinging, and smacking wheat dough— are one of the most popular noodles in China. Lanzhou-style lamian are available almost anywhere in China, and are typically served in a mutton broth with green onions and sprigs of cilantro. Stir-fried noodles (*chaomian*) are also popular, and can be made with virtually any ingredient. Xinjiang cuisine features some of the most delicious noodles found in China, ranging from chunks of diced noodles to long, flat, wide noodles and everything in between. Dumplings are a popular wheat-based staple, and can be a meal on their own. They can be prepared by boiling, steaming, or boiling and then panfrying. Steamed buns with filling (*baozi*) or without (*mantou*) are often eaten for breakfast. Steamed rice is most commonly eaten white, with other dishes piled on top of it, but many people enjoy it stir-fried with any imaginable combination of vegetables, egg, meats, or seafood. Rice noodles can be found throughout southern China, from fat spaghetti-like *mixian* to fettuccine-style *fen*, to *fensi*, a transparent noodle that resembles vermicelli.

FAQ

Will I need a visa?

Yes! Most foreign nationals traveling to China must have an entry visa. These visas are not issued upon arrival. Americans are currently charged a flat rate of $130 per visa, regardless of duration. Tourist visas vary in length from 30 days to six months, and allow for one or multiple entries over the course of their validity. The number of entries and length of stay are up to you when you fill out the application. Applications can be completed in person if you live in a city with a Chinese consulate. If not, there are many visa service centers available online that will process your application. Fees may vary, so shop around and check the Better Business Bureau if you have any questions regarding legitimacy.

What's the best way to get around?

Domestic airline services connecting cities in China have increased greatly in the past decade, and even smaller out-of-the-way cities have small airports. If you have more time, train travel is also an option. The country is crisscrossed by one of the world's most extensive railway systems, and train travel is one way to get a feel for the vastness of China. Often it is also cheaper than flying, and is very dependable. China has converted several lines between major metropolises into high-speed (or bullet) train routes. Bus routes between cities are also well established, and in rural areas are often the only way to travel between small towns. Car rental is becoming more popular, but you must first obtain a Chinese driver's license, a time-consuming and convoluted process, or you can hire a driver.

Should I take a package tour?

If you are traveling to China to see only the major tourist attractions, or are very concerned about the language differences, a package tour is the answer. However, if your travel plans allow for improvisation or you want to stray a bit off the beaten path, skip the tours. Part of the adventure of traveling is exploring the unknown, and with most packages you will be with other tourists and have little say in where you stay or eat, or how long you have to view a specific site. Also, once in China you can find any number of small tours that last from an afternoon to a few days and will help tailor your trip so it is uniquely your own.

How big is the language barrier?

For the uninitiated, Chinese can be very intimidating. The language is tonal, has no alphabet, and regional dialects vary widely. Learning a few phrases in Mandarin Chinese before you go helps tremendously. Nonetheless, interest in learning English is a national phenomenon in China, and schoolchildren are all taught English from the first grade. Tourist destinations and other places catering to foreigners will usually have at least one designated English speaker. For getting around, have the name and address of your hotel written down in Chinese characters to show to taxi drivers. Tourist sites are well marked in English. Subway maps are also written in English and Chinese.

Are any subjects off-limits?

As anywhere, be respectful. The Chinese are gregarious and curious, and you may be surprised at what they think about the rest of the world. There is no one subject that is strictly forbidden or generally considered offensive, but you may want to speak cautiously when discussing touchy

subjects like religious tolerance, Tibet, or Xinjiang.

Will my bankcard work at Chinese ATMs?

Banks in China are ubiquitous, and most ATMs accept cards with the Cirrus or Plus logos. Those with Visa or MasterCard logos are also widely accepted. This is true even in rural areas, especially if they are accustomed to foreign travelers passing through. That said, in more remote places the Bank of China is more reliable than smaller local banks. ATMs usually have an option for directions in English. If you encounter a machine with no English or that won't accept your card, chances are the bank around the corner will be more helpful.

Can I use my credit cards?

Resorts and major hotels accept credit cards, but for daily purchases like food and drink or souvenir shopping, it's best to use cash. Credit-card use is growing in China, but is by no means widespread.

Can I drink the water?

No. Tap water in China can contain any number of chemicals and/or parasites that can quickly ruin your vacation. In major cities some hotels have begun to install water-filtration systems, but even these are questionable. Bottled water is sold cheaply everywhere and remains the most reliable option. Check to make sure the cap is sealed before you buy. The boiled water or hot tea that is served in restaurants or available in your hotel room is also considered safe.

Are the toilets as bad as I've heard?

They can be. Bathrooms in hotels generally should be clean and well maintained, and many have Western-style toilets instead of the typical Asian "squat" toilet. Restrooms in restaurants, train stations, and other public places range from clean to abysmal, so be prepared. In rural areas you can often expect the worst. When going out for the day, it is always a good idea to take some toilet paper or baby wipes and hand sanitizer. Public toilets on the street charge a small admission fee, so keep some small change with you.

Should I bring any medications?

The Centers for Disease Control recommend updating your usual vaccinations and visiting a doctor or clinic that specializes in travel medicine four to six weeks before traveling to China. Of course, if you have a daily medication regime, plan accordingly. An anti-diarrhea medication may be a lifesaver, especially on long bus rides or train journeys. Also, if you suffer from motion sickness you may want to bring the proper medicine from home.

Can I trust Chinese hospitals?

For minor injuries, bumps, or bruises, and general maladies like colds or flu, Chinese hospitals are reliable, though often not up to Western standards of hygiene. Major cities usually have both Western and traditional Chinese-style hospitals, but rural areas generally have fewer medical options. Travel insurance providing medical evacuation services is highly recommended in case of serious injury or illness.

Should I be concerned about crime?

Violent crime against foreigners is almost unheard of in China. However, petty theft can be a worry when traveling on long-distance buses and trains or when staying at small guesthouses. Always keep your money, passport, and anything else you consider vital on your person when traveling, and be vigilant in crowded places.

GREAT ITINERARIES

Stretching over 3,100 miles from east to west, China is an enormous country with wildly varied geography, ranging from the mist-wrapped peaks of Huangshan in the east to the dusty Tarim Basin in the northwest, one of the lowest points on earth. To get around this vast country you'll need plenty of patience and a good sense of humor. With the development of high-speed trains, it's now easy to zip between major cities like Beijing and Shanghai, but travel to more distant destinations is generally slower and more unpredictable. Domestic flights can get you almost anywhere, though they are often more expensive than other options. Whether traveling by plane, train, or bus, it's good to book ahead, especially during Chinese New Year, when you are competing for tickets with 1.3 billion people on the move.

Lay of the Land
Beijing to Shanghai

Once home to emperors, China's capital city of Beijing presides over the heavily industrialized northeast. Hypermodern Shanghai is halfway down China's prosperous east coast and is iconic for its architecture and fashion. Suzhou lies within an arm's reach from Shanghai and is famous for its classical gardens and unique stone bridges. Upriver from Shanghai on the banks of the Yangtze, you'll find the ancient city of Nanjing, once China's southern capital. The lofty peaks of Huangshan, only a few hours by train from Nanjing, are a wonderful place to take refuge from the summer heat.

East Coast

Zhejiang is China's wealthiest province. Hangzhou, surrounded by forested hills and tea plantations, is most famous for its lovely West Lake and is a wonderful place for a biking excursion. Nestled within the Yangtze Delta, the province also has a number of charming restored waterways and villages waiting to be explored. Rugged, mountainous Fujian boasts verdant tea fields, ancient Hakka roundhouses, and unspoiled beaches. On the coast, prosperous Xiamen is worth exploring for its colonial architecture.

Hong Kong and the Pearl River Delta

Guangzhou, in Guangdong Province, is a noisy, crowded metropolis and the heart of the Pearl River delta. Scratch the surface of its frenetic exterior and you'll find a thriving art scene, fabulous food, and a rich cultural history. On the border of Hong Kong, Shenzhen is a young, fast-paced city known as much for shopping as for factories. Colorful, vibrant Hong Kong is a not-to-be-missed hodgepodge of steel and glass skyscrapers, open-air markets, luxury boutiques, and traditional temples.

The Southwest

The dramatic karst peaks and winding rivers of Guilin and Yangshuo in Guangxi Province grace so many postcards of China. Lush mountains dotted with villages surround Guiyang, Guizhou's capital. Kunming, the capital of Yunnan, is also home to many of China's ethnic groups and boasts some of the most stunning topography in China, ranging from the sweltering jungles of the Mekong Delta in the south to the dramatic snow-capped mountains of the Tibetan Plateau in the west. The province shares road connections with neighboring Myanmar and Laos and is linked by rail to Vietnam.

Sichuan and Chongqing

Southwestern Sichuan Province, known as the "rice bowl" of China, includes the

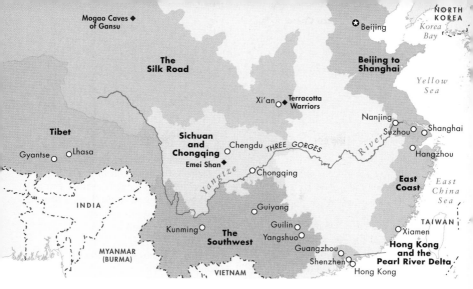

fertile Sichuan basin and is considered the country's agricultural heartland. Its capital, Chengdu, is the financial hub of the southwest, and its many rail and bus connections link eastern and western China. Outside of Chengdu is the Buddhist holy mountain of Emei Shan, famous not only for its temples but also its unruly golden monkeys. In the very center of China sits hilly Chongqing, or "Mountain City," and the best place to hop on a Three Gorges cruise along the Yangtze.

The Silk Road

In northwest China is Xi'an, long-ago capital of the Tang Dynasty. Once the most cosmopolitan city in the world, Xi'an was the terminus of the eastern Silk Road. The emblematic Terracotta Warriors are now its most famous attraction. The Mogao Caves of Gansu offer a glimpse into the most important Buddhist pilgrimage site along the Silk Road. Sweeping deserts and plains make up the Xinjiang Autonomous Region, China's largest province. Xinjiang is home to the Uyghurs, a large Muslim minority. Its capital city, Ürümqi, is an excellent place to launch explorations into the desert or westwards to the ancient Silk Road city of Kashgar.

Tibet

With its stunning snowcapped peaks, picturesque river valleys, and magnificent palaces and temples, Tibet has long-conjured up romantic visions of a windswept mountain kingdom, pristine and inaccessible. In reality, the Tibetan Autonomous Region is undergoing a massive infrastructure overhaul, and the Lhasa-Beijing railway has made it much easier to reach the Roof of the World. In Lhasa, dramatic Potala Palace is a central attraction, along with the Bhakor pilgrimage circuit. At this writing, Tibet was largely closed to foreigners because of political unrest.

Timing

Because China is so vast, the best time to visit depends on where you are traveling. In general, the most comfortable times of year are in spring or fall to avoid extreme temperatures. Summers can be unbearably hot and humid, with drenching rain and flooding. Winters in the north are bitterly cold.

Peak Season: October and May

Whatever season you go, don't travel during the rush of peak holiday times, especially the first week of October and May and during Chinese New Year.

THE CLASSIC FIRST TRIP

BEIJING, THE SILK ROAD, SICHUAN, AND SHANGHAI, 12 DAYS

This journey covers many of China's most iconic destinations. Begin in Beijing, exploring the former glory of Beijing's imperial palaces and climb the Great Wall before embarking westward to Xi'an, once the capital of the Tang Dynasty and home to China's famous Terracotta Warriors. Head southwest to Chengdu to see the world's largest Buddha before ending your visit in the bustling megacity of Shanghai, once dubbed the "Paris of the East."

Day 1: Beijing

Beijing is the cultural heart of China and the nation's top travel destination. Stay at **The Orchid,** a snug boutique hotel tucked away in one of the few remaining *hutong* areas (alleyways) of Beijing near the Drum Tower. It's a short taxi ride to the Forbidden City. It's also close to **Tiananmen Square,** where you can watch the daily flag-raising ceremony at dawn. After the flag raising, take a stroll around the square and soak in the atmosphere. And of course, a tour of the **Forbidden City** is an essential Beijing experience. Finish your day with a traditional feast at the **Li Qun Roast Duck Restaurant,** Beijing's most popular spot for Peking duck.

Day 2: The Great Wall

(Excursion will take approximately 8 hours, either by private car or tour bus)

China's greatest monument is still a must-see. Avoid the more commercial Badaling and head farther afield to the less-crowded sections of the **Great Wall** at Mutianyu, Simatai, or Jinshaling. Pack a picnic lunch and enjoy the spectacular views from the top. Tour buses leaving for the Great Wall congregate around Tiananmen Square, or you could book a private tour or hire a car and driver.

Day 3: Summer Palace and the Temple of Heaven

(Summer Palace is 45 minutes by car from Tiananmen Square, Temple of Heaven is 12 minutes by car from Tiananmen Square)

Beijing is dotted with numerous imperial palaces and pleasure gardens. Take a taxi to the city's northwestern reaches to visit the lovely **Summer Palace,** which has come to symbolize the decadence that brought about the fall of the Qing Dynasty. The **Temple of Heaven** is considered to be the perfect example of Ming Dynasty architecture, and is a great place to take a break from the frenetic pace of the capital. For dinner, try a savory bowl of traditional hand-pulled noodles at **Old Beijing Noodle King,** a short walk from the Temple of Heaven. Later in the evening, take in the colorful theatrics at the nearby Tianqiao Acrobatic Theatre.

Day 4: Shopping and Art

Beijing teems with cultural performances, fabulous restaurants, and sprawling outdoor markets. Spend the morning hunting for souvenirs at **Beijing Curio City** or the **Silk Alley Market** in the Chaoyang District. In the afternoon explore the **798 Art District,** a popular place to see Chinese contemporary art. For dinner, tuck into a bowl of steaming pork or vegetable dumplings at **Baoyuan Dumpling.**

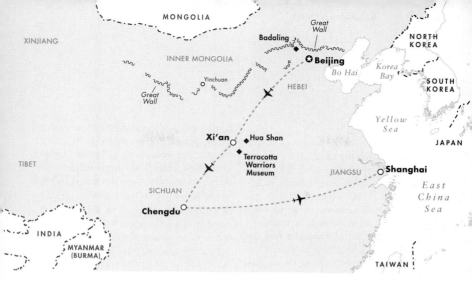

Days 5–7: Xi'an, China's Ancient Capital

(2 hours by plane from Beijing; 12 hours by train from Beijing's West Rail Station)

Xi'an was the most important city in China until the 9th century AD. Once the eastern gateway to the Silk Road, the region is a gold mine of historical treasures, most of which can be covered in just a few days. For convenience, head to Xi'an's Old City and check yourself into the **Ibis Xi'an**, which has clean and comfortable rooms. Your first day should be spent visiting Xi'an's most popular attractions, including the **Bell Tower** in the city center and the impressive **Big Wild Goose Pagoda**. Make sure to attend the Tang Dynasty dinner theater, which serves imperial cuisine and acrobatic shows every evening.

Devote your next day to visiting the **Terracotta Warriors Museum**, east of Xi'an. The life-size warriors and horses, built to protect China's first emperor in the afterlife, are part of a huge necropolis that stretches for miles. If you have the time, we also recommend a day trip to the spectacular peaks of **Hua Shan**. To get to either of these sites, book a tour or catch a public bus.

Days 8–10: Chengdu

(1½ hours by plane from Xi'an; 13 hours by train from Xi'an)

See days 15–18 of the Southern China itinerary.

Days 10–12: Shanghai

(2½ hours by plane from Chengdu; 14 hours by train from Chengdu)

See days 1–2 of the Shanghai and the Chinese Heartland itinerary.

SHANGHAI AND THE CHINESE HEARTLAND

SHANGHAI, ANHUI, JIANGSU, HUBEI, AND SICHUAN, 11–14 DAYS

Eastern China is a showcase of China's amazingly diverse topography. Much of this area lies in the fertile Yangtze basin— a misty watercolor of blues, greens and yellows, whitewashed farmhouses, and dense networks of rivers, waterways, and canals. Journey from the glittering skyscrapers of Shanghai to the wilds of Huangshan and the Yangtze River. Because of the distances covered, it's suggested to fly some legs of this trip to save time.

Day 1: Shanghai

Shanghai is all about the country's future, not its past. Catch the ultrafast train from the airport to the city center. The most convenient place for hotels is the neighborhood of Puxi, which includes the **Former French Concession,** close to most of Shanghai's most popular attractions. Stay in the delightful **Magnolia Bed and Breakfast,** a small boutique hotel south of Jing'an Park. After checking in, explore some of Shanghai's fascinating colonial history by foot or taxi. Walk through **Xintiandi,** where restored traditional houses mix with bars, boutiques, and galleries. Spend some time searching for the perfect souvenir on **Nanjing Road.** Alternatively, you could time travel through 3,000 years of Chinese art and antiquities at the **Shanghai Museum.** For dinner, head to longtime favorite **Grape** for home-style Chinese food in a friendly atmosphere.

Day 2: Paris of the East

The next day explore **The Bund** by foot, taxi, or subway. This waterfront boulevard is the city's best spot for people-watching and culinary exploration. For a bird's-eye view of China's sprawling economic capital, head across the Huangpu River to **Pudong,** where you can ascend the **Oriental Pearl Tower,** the **Jinmao Tower,** or the **Shanghai World Financial Center,** also known as the "Bottle Opener." There's also **Yu Garden,** where you can relax amid meticulous landscaping and traditional architecture. In the alleys round Yu Garden are many local restaurants serving terrific food and tea in unpretentious surroundings.

Days 3–4: Suzhou and Tongli

(Suzhou is 35 minutes by high-speed train from Shanghai; Tongli is 90 minutes by taxi from Shanghai)

Regarded in ancient times as heaven on earth, **Suzhou** retains many of its charms despite the encroaching forces of modernization. Stroll through elegant gardens and temples along the gently flowing branches of the Grand Canal.

Suzhou is close enough to work well as a day trip from Shanghai but it's highly recommended to spend the night and catch a bus the next day to **Tongli,** a restored water village. If you're staying in Suzhou, book a room at the **Pan Pacific Suzhou,** situated in a lovely garden complex. A quick walk or taxi will take you to the **Master of the Nets Gardens,** which holds Chinese opera performances on summer evenings. Also make sure to visit the iconic **Suzhou Museum,** designed by I.M. Pei. For a memorable meal, try the fragrant soup-filled dumpling at **Xichengyuan Wonton** near the Master of the Nets Gardens. After two days spent exploring Suzhou and Tongli, take the train back to Shanghai where you can catch a plane to Huangshan.

Days 5–8: Huangshan

(1 hour by plane from Shanghai to Tunxi)

One of China's best-known natural wonders, **Huangshan** (Yellow Mountain) is a breathtaking range of 72 jagged peaks punctuated by fantastically twisted pine trees and unusual rock formations. **Tunxi,** or Huangshan City, is about 40 miles from Huangshan. After landing in Tunxi, hire a taxi or take a minibus to **Tangkou** at the base of the mountain. There are numerous ways to the top, either on foot or by cable car. Spend a night at the **Baiyun Hotel,** one of the mountaintop guesthouses, before waking at dawn to watch the sun rise over an eerie sea of fog.

After visiting Huangshan, the quickest way to continue on to the Three Gorges is to return to Shanghai where you can catch a flight onwards to Yichang, in Hubei Province.

Days 9–13: Yichang and The Three Gorges

(2 hours by plane from Shanghai to Yichang)

A cruise along the **Yangtze River** through the **Three Gorges** is an unforgettable experience. Along the way you'll pass over abandoned metropolises that were humming with life only a few years ago, as well as their modern counterparts that were built on higher ground. One recommended cruise line is Victoria Cruises, which offers a range of excursions up and down the Yangtze.

The town of **Yichang** sits at the eastern entrance of the Three Gorges. Cruises will sail through the Gezhou Dam and offer excursions to the Three Gorges Dam site, Fengdu, or "Ghost City," and the Little Three Gorges before disembarking at **Chongqing**.

Day 14: Chongqing

(5 days by boat from Yichang)

After finishing a cruise along the Yangtze, **Chongqing** has enough to recommend a day or two of exploration. Built into the side of a hill, the city is a maze of steep stairways, hills, and tunnels. Most of the main tourist sites and hotels are located around the Jiefang Bei area. The convenient **Howard Johnson ITC Plaza** offers plush rooms and an excellent restaurant. After settling in, walk to **18 Steps**, one of the most curious attractions in Chongqing. Not to be missed is a ride in a cable car, where you are treated to a bird's-eye view of the Yangtze and the sprawling city below. For traditional Sichuan cuisine, head to **Xiaotian'e Sichuan Restaurant** on the banks of the Yangtze to indulge in hotpot and other fiery specialties.

SOUTHERN CHINA: CITIES AND MOUNTAINS

HONG KONG, MACAU, GUANGXI, YUNNAN, AND SICHUAN, 15–18 DAYS

With its lush geography, karst limestone peaks, and rich cultures, a visit to southern China offers opportunities to witness the country's incredible natural and ethnic diversity. Begin your trip in fast-paced Hong Kong before heading farther south to the gorgeous backcountry of Guangxi, Guizhou, and Yunnan.

Day 1: Hong Kong

Despite the city's return to Chinese rule in 1997, **Hong Kong** still feels a world away from the mainland. Get settled in at the **Lan Kwai Fong Hotel** with its amazing harbor views. When you're rested, take a ride on the Star Ferry connecting Hong Kong Island with **Kowloon.** Try dim sum at the legendary **Tim Ho Wan** in Kowloon—the coconut cream buns and shrimp dumplings are superb. Back on Hong Kong Island, don't miss the smoke-filled **Man Mo Temple** and Hong Kong's famous assortment of antiques shops and art galleries. Ride the very steep tram to the summit of **Victoria Peak,** with views of the entire harbor.

Day 2: Get out of the City

(30 minutes by express ferry to Lantau)

While the business districts clustered around the harbor feature some of the world's densest urban jungle, Hong Kong also has a relaxed natural side. **Lantau Island** is a favorite of visitors for its beaches and hiking trails. Board the ferry at the Outlying Islands Ferry Pier on Hong Kong Island. Arriving at the town of **Mui Wo,** you can catch a bus to the island's top two attractions: **Po Lin Monastery,** featuring the world's tallest outdoor bronze statue of Buddha, and **Tai O,** an old fishing village dotted with terrific seafood restaurants. For even greater solitude, take the ferry to one of the smaller **Outer Islands.**

Day 3: Macau

(1 hour by TurboJet from Hong Kong)

Even with a recent push to become Asia's Las Vegas, **Macau** is still decidedly quieter and more traditional than Hong Kong. The slower pace of development has left much of the city's colonial charm intact.

Start with a visit to **Largo do Senado** (Senate Square), paved with Portuguese-style tiles and surrounded by brightly colored colonial buildings. The city is home to two beautiful churches, **São Domingos** and **São Paulo**, the latter featuring exhibits on the early history of Asian Christianity. If you plan to stay overnight, the **Altira Macau** has breathtaking ocean views. For flavorful Macanese dishes like steamed crab and clams stewed in beer, **A Lorcha** restaurant is highly recommended.

Days 4–8: Yangshuo and Longsheng

(1½-hour flight from Hong Kong to Guilin; 90-minute bus ride or 4-hour boat ride from Guilin to Yangshuo; 3 hours by bus from Guilin to Longsheng)

The scenery in northern Guangxi is some of the most beautiful in all of China. Enchanted by dramatic groupings of sheer limestone karst mountains , visitors often find themselves loath to leave. To get to **Yangshuo,** you'll first head to Guilin, where you'll have a choice of taking the bus or the more scenic four-hour Li River Cruise. Once in Yangshuo, the **Giggling Tree** is an excellent base for exploring natural sites like **Green Lotus Peak** and **Moon Hill.** For meals, join the backpackers at **Kelly's Place** for beer and dumplings. Head back through Guilin to the town of **Longsheng,** home to the famously photogenic **Dragon's Backbone Rice Terraces** before returning to Guilin.

Days 9–14: Northwest Yunnan

(2- to 2½-hour flight from Guilin to Dali or Lijiang with connection in Kunming)

Sandwiched between the Tibetan Plateau and Myanmar, this area has long attracted foreigners with its mix of minority cultures and stunning natural beauty. **Dali,** beside the waters of Erhai Lake, is home to the Bai people, who settled here 4,000

years ago; the elegant **Three Pagodas** north of town is one of China's most iconic images. For a unique experience, book a room at the **Yunnan Inn**, owned by Chinese artist Fang Lijun. Pancakes and decent coffee at **Café de Jack** will fill you up before heading out to explore Dali's scenic **Old Town**. A three-hour bus ride north of Dali lies **Lijiang**, home of the Naxi people. **The East River Hotel** offers a tranquil location and is close to **Mishi** for grilled yak meat and beer. The highlight of the region is **Tiger Leaping Gorge,** one of the deepest river gorges in the world and a popular two-day hike.

Day 15–18: Chengdu
(1½-hour flight from Dali to Chengdu)

As the capital of Sichuan Province, **Chengdu** has long been one of China's great cultural centers. Famous for its spicy cuisine, the city also manages to maintain a pleasant atmosphere of yesteryear. Stay at the elegant **Minshan Fandian** in the center of town near People's Park. A quick taxi ride away is the remarkable **Buddhist Wenshu Monastery,** known for its peaceful tea gardens. For animal lovers, take a bus 45 minutes out of town to the **Giant Panda Breeding Research Base**. If you crave authentic Sichuan hotpot, **Shijing Shenghuo** brings the fire. No matter how little time you have available, make the three-hour bus trip south to **Leshan** to see the world's largest stone-carved Buddha. With toes the size of a small bus, the seated **Grand Buddha** is impressive, to say the least.

PEOPLE OF CHINA

People often think of China as an ancient, monolithic culture comprised of a single, massive group of genetically similar people. In actuality, China contains a rich mosaic of different cultures and ethnicities, and officially recognizes 56 distinct ethnic groups. Ranging from populations of a few thousand to 1.2 billion, each group has made a unique contribution to China's cultural diversity with its language, costume, cuisine, philosophies, and traditions.

The Han

The largest of China's ethnic groups is the **Han** people, who make up more than 90% of China's total population and around one-fifth of all humanity. They trace their origins to the Yellow River region, and take their name from the Han Dynasty, which was established in 206 BC. The Han have had the biggest impact on China's history, and every major dynasty but two—the Yuan and the Qing—has been Han.

The Zhuang

Outside of China, few people know of the **Zhuang** people, but they are China's second-largest ethnic group. The Zhuang speak a language related to Thai, and are primarily found in Guangxi, which is officially an "autonomous region" and ruled by the Zhuang, at least in theory.

The Tibetans

Tibetans—known for their unique brand of Buddhism—are the best-known ethnic group inhabiting China's more rugged geography.

The Peoples of Yunnan Province

Mountainous Yunnan Province in the country's southwest is home to the largest variety of ethnic groups, with some like the **Jinuo** and **Pumi** found nowhere else. **Tibetans, Naxi, Bai, Yi,** and **Lisu** are major ethnic groups found in the highlands of northwest Yunnan. In southern Yunnan, near the borders with Laos and Vietnam, there are ethnic **Dai, Hani,** and **Miao**, who have more in common with Southeast Asia than northern China. The Miao people are spread across Southern China, and are typically found in mountain villages.

The Mongols and Manchus

The **Mongols** and **Manchus** are the two Chinese ethnic groups that can claim to have ruled the Han. Kublai Khan founded the Yuan Dynasty in 1271, but keeping control over China and other territories proved too much for the Mongols, and the dynasty was finished just under a century later. Today Mongols in China are primarily found in Inner Mongolia in the country's north, where many still live nomadic lives on the grasslands.

The Qing Dynasty of the Manchus had more staying power, running from 1644 to 1912 and producing several notable emperors. Under Qing rule Han Chinese adopted some Manchu customs, including the long braids worn by men and the binding of women's feet. Most Manchus in China live in the northeastern provinces of Jilin, Liaoning, and Heilongjiang.

The Uighurs and The Hui

The Muslim **Uighurs** of Xinjiang in northwest China are more numerous than Tibetans, and are related to modern-day Turks—some Uighurs have blonde hair and green eyes. The **Hui** are China's largest Muslim group, and are known for being skilled businesspeople—not a big surprise, considering that they are descended from Silk Road traders. Of China's minorities, the Hui are the most widely dispersed—Hui-run Muslim restaurants can be found in virtually every city or large town.

THE AGE OF EMPIRES

When asked his opinion on the historical impact of the French Revolution, Zhou Enlai, the first Premier of Communist China, quipped, "It's too early to tell." Though a bit tongue in cheek, China does measure its history in millennia, and in its grand timeline, interactions with the West have been mere blips.

According to historical records, Chinese civilization stretches back to the 15th century BC—markings found on turtle shells carbon dated to around 1500 BC bear some similarity to modern Chinese script. China then resembled city-states rather than a unified nation. Iconic figures such as Laozi (the father of Taoism), Sun Tzu (author of the Art of War), and Confucius lived during this period. Generally, 221 BC is accepted as the beginning of Imperial China, when the city-states united under various banners.

Over the next 2,200 years (give or take a few), China alternated between periods of harmony and political upheaval. Its armies conquered new territory and were in turn conquered by external invaders (most of whom wound up themselves being assimilated).

By the early 18th century, the long, slow decline of the Qing—the last of China's Imperial dynasties—was already in progress, making the ancient nation ripe for exploitation by rising European powers. The Imperial era ended with the forced abdication of child Emperor Puyi (whose life is chronicled in Bernardo Bertolucci's The Last Emperor), and it's here that the history of modern China, first with the founding of the republic under Dr. Sun Yat-sen and then with the establishment of the People's Republic under Mao Zedong, truly begins.

Writing Appears

1500BC　　　　　　　　　　1200BC　　　　　　　　　　900BC

(left) Oracle shell with early Chinese characters. (top, right) The Great Wall stretches 4,163 miles from east to west. (bottom, right) Confucius, Lao-tzu, and a Buddhist Arhat.

circa 1500 BC

Writing Appears

The earliest accounts of Chinese history are still shrouded in myth and legend, and it wasn't until 1959 that stories were verified by archaeological findings. For millennia, people formed communities in the fertile lands of what is now central China. The first recorded Chinese characters are said to have been developed 3,500 years ago. Though sometimes referred to as the Shang Dynasty, this period was more of a precursor to modern Chinese dynasties than a truly unified kingdom.

475–221 BC

The Warring States Period

China was so far from unified that these centuries are collectively remembered as the Warring States Period. As befitting such a contentious time, military science progressed, iron replaced bronze, and weapons material improved. Some of China's greatest luminaries lived during this period, including the father of Taoism, Laozi, Confucius, and Sun-Tzu, one of the greatest military tacticians and the author of the infamous *Art of War*, which is still studied in military academies around the world.

221–207 BC

The First Dynasty

The Qin Dynasty eventually defeated all of the other warring factions thanks to their cutting-edge military technology, namely the cavalry. The Qin were also called Ch'in, which may be where the word China first originated. The first Emperor, Qin Shi Huang, unified much of the lands and established a legal code and vast bureaucracy to hold it together. The Qin dynasty also standardized the written and spoken language and introduced a common currency.

(left) Terracotta
warrior.
(top right)
Temple of Xichan
in Fuzhou

In order to protect his newly unified country, Qin Shi Huang ordered the creation of the massive Great Wall of China, which was built and rebuilt over the next 1,000 years. He was also a sculpture enthusiast and commissioned a massive army of stone soldiers to follow him into the afterlife. Buried with him, these terracotta warriors would remain hidden from the eyes of the world for two thousand years, until they were found by a farmer digging in a field just outside of Xian. These warriors are among the most important archaeological finds of the 20th century.

220–265 AD

Buddhism Arrives

Emperor Qin's dreams of a unified China fell apart, and eventually the kingdom split into three warring factions. But what was bad for stability turned out to be good for literature. The Three Kingdoms Period is still remembered in song and story. *The Romance of the Three Kingdoms* is as popular among Asian bookworms as the *Legend of King Arthur* is among Western readers. It's still widely read and has been translated into almost every language. Variations of the story have been adapted

for manga, television series, and video games.

The Three Kingdoms period was filled with court intrigue, murder, and massive battles that, while exciting to read about centuries later, weren't much fun at the time. Armies ravaged the countryside, and most people lived and died in misery. Perhaps it was the carnage and disunity of the time that turned the country into a magnet for forces of harmony; it was during this period that Buddhism took hold in China, traveling over the Himalayas from India, via the Silk Road.

Religion Diversifies

600	800	1000

(left) Statue of Genghis Khan. (top right) Dongguan Mosque in Xining, Qinghai. (bottom right) Empress Shengshen

Religion Diversifies

618–845

Chinese spiritual life continued to diversify.

Nestorian Monks from Asia Minor arrived bearing news of Christianity, and Saad ibn Abi Waqqas (a companion of the Prophet Muhammad) supposedly visited the Middle Kingdom to spread the word of Islam. During this era, Wu Zetian, onetime concubine, seized power from the Tang Dynasty and became the first (and only) woman to assume the title of emperor. She ruled for 25 years through puppet emperors and finally, for 15 years, as Emperor Shengshen.

Ghengis Invades

1271–1368

In Xanadu did Kublai Khan a stately pleasure dome decree…

Or so goes the famed Coleridge poem. But Kublai's grandfather Temujin (better known as Ghengis Khan) had bigger things in mind. One of the greatest war tacticians in history, he united the restive nomads of Mongolia's grassy plains and eventually sacked, looted, and pillaged much of the known west and most of the Chinese landmass. By the time Ghengis died in 1227, his grandson was well-tutored and ready to take on the rest of China.

By 1271, Kublai had established a capital in a land-locked city that would only much later become known as Beijing. This marks the beginning of the first (but not last) non-Han dynasty. Kublai Khan kept fighting southward and by 1279, Guangzhou fell to the Mongols, and Khan became the ultimate monarch of China. Though barbarians at heart, the Mongols must be credited for encouraging the arts and a number of early public works projects, including extending the highways and grand canals.

(left) Emperor Chengzu of the Ming Dynasty. (top right) Forbidden City in Beijing (bottom right) Child emperor Puyi.

Ming Dynasty

1368–1644

Many scholars believe that the Mongols' inability to relate with the Han is what ultimately pushed the Han to rise up and overthrow them. The reign of the Ming Dynasty was the last ethnically Han Dynasty to rule over a unified China. At its apex, the Bright Empire encompassed a landmass easily recognized as China, even by today's mapmakers. The Ming Emperors built a huge army and navy, refurbished the agricultural system, and printed many books using movable type long before Gutenberg. In the 15th century, Emperor Yongle began construction of the famous Forbidden City in Beijing, a veritable icon of China.

Also during the Ming Dynasty, China's best known explorer, Zheng He, plied the seven seas in massive treasure fleets that dwarfed in size and range the ships of Christopher Columbus. A giant both in stature and persona, Admiral Zheng (who was also a eunuch) spent two decades expanding China's knowledge of the world outside of its already impressive borders. He traveled as far as India, Africa, and (some say) even the coast of the New World.

Qing Dynasty

1644–1911

The final dynasty represented a serious case of minority rule. They were Manchus from the northeast. The early Qing dynasty was a brutal period as forces loyal to the new emperor crushed those loyal to the old. The Qing Dynasty peaked in the mid-to-late 18th century but soon after, its military powers began to wane. In the 19th century, Qing control weakened and prosperity diminished. By 1910 China was fractured, a baby sat on the Imperial throne, and the Qing Dynasty was on its deathbed.

(top left) A depiction of the Second Opium War. (bottom left) Chiang Kai-shek (top, right) Mao Zedong on December 6, 1944. (bottom, right) Dr. Sun Yat-sen.

The Opium Wars

1834–1860

European powers were hungry to open new territories up for trade, but the Qing weren't buying. The British East India Company, strapped for cash, realized they could sell opium in China at huge profits. The Chinese government quickly banned the nefarious trade and in response, a technologically superior Britain declared war. After a humiliating defeat in the first Opium War, China was forced to cede Hong Kong. Other foreign powers soon followed with territorial demands of their own.

Republican Era

1912–1949

China's Republican period was chaotic and unstable. The revolutionary Dr. Sun Yat-sen—revered by most Chinese as the father of modern China—was unable to build a cohesive government without the aid of regional warlords and urban gangsters. When he died of cancer in 1925, power passed to Chiang Kai-shek, who set about unifying China under the Kuomintang. What began as a unified group of both left- and right-wingers quickly deteriorated, and by the mid-1920s, civil war between the Communists and Nationalists was brewing.

The '30s and '40s were bleak decades for the Chinese people, caught between a vicious war with Japan and periodic clashes between Kuomintang and Communist forces. After Japan's defeat in 1945, China's civil war kicked into high gear. Though the Kuomintang were armed with superior weapons and backed by American money, the majority of Chinese people rallied behind the Communists. Within four years, the Kuomintang were driven off the mainland to Taiwan, where the Republic of China exists to the present day.

(top left) 1950s Chinese stamp with Mao and Stalin. (top right) Shenzhen (bottom left) Poster of Mao's slogans.

1949–Present

The People's Republic

On October 1, 1949, Mao Zedong declared from atop Beijing's Gate of Heavenly Peace that "The Chinese People have stood up." And so the People's Republic of China was born. The Communist party set out to overhaul China's ancient feudal system, emphasizing class struggle, redistribution of wealth, and elimination of foreign dominance. The next three decades would see a massive, often painful transformation of Chinese society from feudalism into the modern age.

The Great Leap Forward was a disaster—Chinese peasants were encouraged to cram 100 years of industrial development into as many weeks. Untenable decisions led to industrial and agricultural ruin, widespread famine, and an estimated 30 million deaths. The trauma of this period, however, pales in comparison to The Great Proletarian Cultural Revolution. From 1966–1976, fear and zealotry gripped the nation as young revolutionaries heeded Chairman Mao's call to root out class enemies. During this decade, millions died, millions were imprisoned, and much of China's accumulated religious,

historical, and cultural heritage literally went up in smoke.

Like a phoenix rising from its own ashes, China rose from its own self-inflicted destruction. In the early 1980s, Deng Xiao-ping took the first steps in reforming China's stagnant economy. With the maxim "To Get Rich is Glorious," Deng loosened central control on the economy and declared Special Economic Zones where the seeds of capitalism could be incubated. Three decades later, the nation is one of the world's most vibrant economic engines. Though China's history is measured in millennia, her brightest years may well have only just begun.

BEIJING

WELCOME TO BEIJING

TOP REASONS TO GO

★ **The Forbidden City:**
Built by more than 200,000 workers, it's the largest palace in the world and has the best-preserved and most complete collection of imperial architecture in China.

★ **Tiananmen Square.**
The political heart of modern China, the square covers 100 acres, making it the largest public square in the world.

★ **Temple of Heaven:**
One of the best examples of religious architecture in China, the sprawling, tree-filled complex is a pleasant place for wandering: watch locals practice martial arts, play traditional instruments, and enjoy ballroom dancing on the grass.

★ **Magnificent Markets:**
So much to bargain for, so little time! Visit outdoor Panjiayuan Antiques Market, the Silk Alley Market, or the Yashow Market.

★ **Summer Palace.** This garden complex dates back eight centuries, to when the first emperor of the Jin Dynasty built the Gold Mountain Palace on Longevity Hill.

1 Dongcheng District.
Dongcheng (East District) encompasses the Forbidden City, Tiananmen Square, Wangfujing (a major shopping street), the Lama Temple, and many other historical sights dating back to imperial times.

2 Xicheng District.
Xicheng (West District), west of Dongcheng, includes Beihai Park, former playground of the imperial family, and a series of connected lakes bordered by willow trees, courtyard-lined *hutong*, and lively bars.

Liuyin Park
Ditan Park
Ande Lu
Deshengmendong Dajie (2nd Ring Rd.)
Gulouwai Dajie
Andingmenwai
Hepingli Xijie
Hepingli Dongjie
Zoujiazhuang Xilu
Beitucheng Dongdong Lu
Hepingli Beijie
Andingmennei Dajie
TO ↗ BEIJING AIRPORT
Yonghegong Dajie
Andingmendong Dajie
Xianhevuan Lu
Dongzhimenwaixie Jie
Xinyunnan Lu
Liangma River
DONGZHIMEN
Jiaodaokou Dongdajie
Dongzhimennei Dajie
Dongzhimenwai Dajie
Qianhai
DONGCHENG 1
Zhangzizhong Lu
Dongsi Tiao
Gongrentiyuchangbei Lu
Beihai Park
DI'ANMEN
DONGSI
Dongsibei Dajie
Chaoyangmennei Dajie
Forbidden City
Beichizi Dajie
Wangfujing Dajie
Dongdanbei Dajie
DONGDAN
CHAOYANG 3
Jinyu
Beijingzhan
Ritan Park
Chang'an Jie
Jianguomennei Dajie
Jianguomenwai Dajie
Jianguo Lu
Tiananmen Square
Qianmen Dajie
Chongwenmenxi Dajie
Beijing Train Station
Tonghui River
QIANMEN
Zushikoudong Dajie
Guangumenwai Lu
Guanqumenbinhe Lu
City Moat
Zhushikou Dajie
CHONGWEN
Tiantan Lu
Beiwei Lu
Tiantan Park
Tiyuguan Lu
Jinsong Lu
Tiananlonan Dajie
Tiantandong Lu
Temple of Heaven
Longtan Park
0 — 1 mile
0 — 1 kilometer

GETTING ORIENTED

Laid out like a target with ring roads revolving around a bull's-eye, with **Chang'an Jie** (Eternal Peace Street) cutting across the middle, Beijing sprawls outward from the central point of the **Forbidden City.** The ring roads are its main arteries, and, along with Chang'an Jie, you will find yourself traveling them just about any time you go from one place to another aboveground. As you explore Beijing, you'll find that taxis are often the best way to get around. However, if the recently expanded subway system goes where you're headed, it's often a faster option than dealing with traffic. The city is divided into 18 municipal and suburban districts (*qu*), though most visitors will spend their time only in the central ones.

3 Chaoyang District.
Chaoyang is the biggest and busiest district, occupying the areas north, east, and south of the eastern Second Ring Road. It's home to foreign embassies, multinational companies, the Central Business District, and the Olympic Park.

4 Haidian District.
Haidian is the technology and university district. It's northwest of the Third Ring Road and packed with shops selling electronics and students cramming for the next exam.

Updated by
Kit Gillet, Tom
O'Malley,
Yuan Ren,
and Adrian
Sandiford

There's nowhere else in the world quite like Beijing. It's a modern-day megalopolis at the very core of the world's second-greatest economy, but it's also a gateway into China's imperial past and 5,000 years of history. This is a city where you can stand at the crossroads of time.

In Beijing the march to modernity may seem unrelenting at times, but the city still clings to parts of the past, including a heritage perhaps best encapsulated by the extraordinary Forbidden City. Once home to the emperors of old, it still dominates the city's center. And then, just an hour or two from downtown, stands one of the great wonders of the world: the Great Wall. Built during the Ming Dynasty to keep out the world, it's a telling contrast to the China of today.

Despite the proliferation of shiny office towers, high-rise residences, and shopping centers, there are still plenty of world-class historic sites to be discovered, including the famous rapidly disappearing *hutong*, neighborhoods formed from alleyways. Scores of the city's imperial palaces, mansions, and temples built under the Mongols during the Yuan Dynasty (1271–1368) were rebuilt during the later Ming and Qing dynasties. Despite the ravages of time and the Cultural Revolution, many of these refurbished sites are still in excellent condition.

PLANNING

WHEN TO GO

The best time to visit Beijing is spring or early fall, when the weather is pleasant and crowds are a bit smaller. Book at least one month in advance for travel during these two times of year. In winter Beijing's Forbidden City and Summer Palace can look fantastical and majestic, when the traditional tiled roofs are covered with a light dusting of snow and the venues are devoid of tourists.

Avoid the two long national holidays: Chinese New Year, which ranges from mid-January to mid-February; and National Day holiday, the first week of October, when Chinese normally get a lengthy holiday. Millions

Shoppers enjoy a sunny day in the Xidan neighborhood.

of Chinese travel during these weeks, making it difficult to book hotels, tours, and transportation.

The weather in Beijing is at its best in September and October, with a good chance of sunny days and mild temperatures. Winters are cold, but it seldom snows. Late April through June is lovely, but come July the days are hot and excruciatingly humid with a greater chance of rain. Spring is also the time of year for Beijing's famous dust storms.

GETTING AROUND

ON FOOT

Though traffic and modernization have put a bit of a cramp in Beijing's walking style, meandering remains one of the best ways to experience the capital—especially the old hutong that are rich with culture and sights.

BIKE TRAVEL

The proliferation of cars (some 1,000 new automobiles take to the streets of the capital every day, bringing the total to more than 5 million vehicles) has made biking less pleasant and more dangerous here. Fortunately, most streets have wide, well-defined bike lanes often separated from other traffic by an island. If a flat tire or sudden brake failure strikes, seek out the nearest street-side mechanic, easily identified by the bike parts and pumps. Bikes can be rented at many hotels and next to some subway stations.

SUBWAY TRAVEL

The subway is the best way to avoid Beijing's frequent traffic jams. With the opening of new lines, Beijing's subway service is increasingly convenient. The metropolitan area is currently served by 14 lines as well as an express line to the airport. The subway runs from about 5 am to midnight daily, depending on the station. Fares are Y2 per ride for any distance and transfers are free. Stations are marked in both Chinese and English, and stops are also announced in both languages. Subways are best avoided during rush hours, when severe overcrowding is unavoidable.

TAXI TRAVEL

The taxi experience in Beijing has improved significantly as the city's taxi companies gradually shift to cleaner, more comfortable new cars. In the daytime, flag-fall for taxis is Y13 for the first 3 km (2 miles) and Y2 per kilometer thereafter. The rate rises to Y3 per kilometer on trips over 15 km (8 miles) and after 11 pm, when the flag-fall also increases to Y14. At present, there's also a Y1 gas surcharge for any rides exceeding 3 km (2 miles). ⚠ **Be sure to check that the meter has been engaged to avoid fare negotiations at your destination.** Taxis are easy to hail during the day, but can be difficult during evening rush hour, especially when it's raining. If you're having difficulty, go to the closest hotel and wait in line there. Few taxi drivers speak English, so ask your hotel concierge to write down your destination in Chinese.

GOOD TOURS

Taking a tour will make it easier to sightsee without the hassle. However, if you're adventurous, you can easily explore the city on your own, even if you don't speak Chinese. You can't rely on taxi drivers to know the English names of the major tourist sites, but armed with the names in Chinese in this guide, you should have few or no problems getting around. If you do opt for an organized tour, keep in mind that a little research pays off.

GENERAL CULTURAL AND SPECIAL INTEREST TOURS

Local guides are often creative when it comes to showing you history and culture, so having an expert with you can make a big difference. Learning is the focus of Smithsonian Journeys' small-group tours, which are led by university professors. China experts also lead National Geographic's trips, but all that knowledge doesn't come cheap. WildChina is a local company with unusual trips: one of their cultural trips explores China's little-known Jewish history. The Hutong and the China Culture Center are also wonderful local resources for tours, classes, lectures, and other events in Beijing. The China Guide is a Beijing-based, American-managed travel agency offers tours that do *not* make shopping detours. Bespoke Beijing and Stretch-a-Leg Travel, and WildChina specialize in taking visitors to off-the-beaten-track locations and can offer personalized tours.

Contacts **Bespoke Beijing** ✉ B510, 107 Dongsi Bei Dajie, Dongcheng District ☎ 010/6400–0133 ✍ info@bespoke-beijing.com ⊕ www.bespoke-beijing. com ⊙ Daily 9–5. **China Culture Center** ✉ 21 Liangmaqiao Rd., inside the Drive-in Movie Theater Park, Chaoyang District ☎ 010/6432–9341, 010/8420–0671 weekends ⊕ www.chinaculturecenter.org. **The China Guide** ✉ Bldg. 7-1, Jianguomenwai Waijiaogongyu Diplomatic Compound, 8th fl., Room 81 ☎ 010/8532–1860 ✍ book@thechinaguide.com ⊕ www.thechinaguide.com ⊙ Weekdays 10–6. **National Geographic Expeditions** ☎ 888/966-8687

⊕ www.nationalgeographicexpeditions.com. **Smithsonian Journeys**
☎ 855/330–1542 in the U.S. ⊕ www.smithsonianjourneys.org. **Stretch-A-Leg
Travel** ✉ 2 Qian'gulouyuan, Jiaodaokou, Dongcheng District ☎ 010/6401–8933
✐ info@stretchaleg.com ⊕ www.stretchalegtravel.com ⊗ Weekdays 10–6.

BIKING

Cycle China offers plenty of cycling trips in and around Beijing and
beyond, such as the Great Wall. You can hire bikes from them, or take
your own. Bike China Adventures organizes trips of varying length and
difficulty all over China.

Contacts Bike China Adventures ☎ 800/818–1778 ⊕ www.bikechina.com.
Cycle China ✉ 12 Jingshan Dong Jie, Dongcheng District ☎ 139/1188–6524
⊕ www.cyclechina.com ⊗ Daily 9–6.

CULINARY

Intrepid Travel is an Australian company offering a China Gourmet
Traveler tour with market visits, cooking demonstrations, and plenty
of good eats. Imperial Tours Culinary Tour combines sightseeing with
cooking lectures and demonstrations, and lots of five-star dining.

Contacts Imperial Tours ✉ 2-2004 Wanguocheng, 1 Xiangheyuan Lu,
Dongcheng District ☎ 888/888–1970 in the U.S., 010/8440–7162 in China
⊕ www.imperialtours.net. **Intrepid Travel** ☎ 800/970–7299 in the U.S. ⊕ www.
intrepidtravel.com.

HIKING

Beijing Hikers offer multiple hikes and camping stays on and around
the Great Wall and always make sure that they leave no rubbish behind,
unlike many other companies.

Contacts Beijing Hikers ✉ 10 Jiuxianqiao Zhong Lu, Bldg. A, Suite 4012,
Chaoyang District ☎ 010/6432–2786 ⊕ www.beijinghikers.com ⊗ Weekdays
9–6.

PEDICAB TOURS

Pedicabs (basically large tricycles with room for passengers behind a
pedaling driver) were once the vehicles of choice for Beijingers laden
with a week's worth of groceries or tourists eager for a street's-eye city
tour. Today many residents are wealthy enough to bundle their purchases into taxis or their own cars, and the tourist trade has moved
on to the tight schedules of air-conditioned buses. But pedicabs have
made a big comeback in Beijing in recent years and can now be hired
near major tourist sites. A ride through the hutong near Houhai is the
most popular pedicab journey. ■TIP➔ **Be absolutely sure to negotiate the fare in advance, clarifying which currency will be used (yuan or
dollars), whether the fare is considered a one-way or round-trip (some
drivers will demand payment for a round-trip whether or not you use
the pedicab for the return journey), and whether it is for one person
or two.** Beginning in 2008, government-approved pedicab tours were
supposed to be fixed at Y35 per hour, though the actual price is often
higher. Feel free to tip your driver for good service on longer tours.
Independent pedicabs for hutong tours can be found in the small plaza
between the Drum Tower and the Bell Tower.

BEIJING'S SUBWAY

Although Beijing's subway system has grown to 17 lines, the original 2 lines provide access to the most popular areas of the capital. **Line 1** runs east and west along Chang'an Jie past the China World Trade Center, Jianguomen (one of the embassy districts), the Wangfujing shopping area, Tiananmen Square and the Forbidden City, Xidan (another major shopping location), and the Military Museum, before heading out to the far western suburbs. **Line 2** (the inner loop line) runs along a sort of circular route around the center of the city shadowing the Second Ring Road. Important destinations include the Drum and Bell towers, Lama Temple, Dongzhimen (with a connection to the airport express), Dongsishitiao (near Sanlitun and the Workers' Stadium), Beijing Train Station, and Qianmen (Front Gate), south of Tiananmen Square. Free transfers between Lines 1 and 2 can be made at either Fuxingmen or Jianguomen stations. Line 10, which forms a rough loop following the Third Ring Road, runs through the Central Business District at Guomao station (where a transfer is possible to Line 1), up toward the Sanlitun area at Tuanjiehu, and connects with the airport express line at Sanyuanqiao.

If both you and your final destination are near the Second Ring Road, on Chang'an Jie, or on the northern or eastern sides of the Third Ring Road, the best way to get there is probably by subway. It stops just about every kilometer (half mile), and you'll easily spot the entrances (with blue subway logos) dotting the streets. Each stop is announced in both English and Chinese, and there are clearly marked signs in English or pinyin at each station. Transferring between lines is easy and free, with the standard Y2 ticket including travel between any two destinations.

Subway tickets can be purchased from electronic kiosks and ticket windows in every station. Start off by finding the button that says "English," insert your money, and press another button to print. Single-ride tickets cost Y2, and you'll want to pay with exact change; the machines don't accept Y1 bills, only Y1 coins. It's also possible to buy a stored-value subway card with a Y20 deposit and a purchase of Y10–Y100.

In the middle of each subway platform you'll find a map of the Beijing subway system along with a local map showing the position of exits. Subway cars also have a simplified diagram of the line you're riding above the doors.

Trains can be very crowded, especially during rush hour, and it's not uncommon for people to push onto the train before exiting passengers can get off. Prepare to get off by making your way to the door before you arrive at your station. Be especially wary of pickpockets.

■TIP➔ Unfortunately, the subway system is not convenient for disabled people. In some stations there are no escalators, and sometimes the only entrance or exit is via steep steps.

VISITOR CENTERS

For general information, including advice on tours, insurance, and safety, call, or visit China National Tourist Office's website, as well as the website run by the Beijing Tourism Administration (BTA). ■TIP→ **The BTA maintains a 24-hour hotline for tourist inquiries and complaints, with operators fluent in English. BTA also runs Beijing Tourist Information Centers, whose staff can help you with free maps and directions in Beijing.**

Beijing Tourist Information Beijing Tourism Administration ☎ *010/8353–1111* ✉ *visitbeijingeng@163.com* ⊕ *english.visitbeijing.com.cn.*

EXPLORING

On a seemingly superhuman scale that matches its status as the capital city of the world's most populous nation, Beijing is laid out with vast expanses of wide avenues and roadways organized in an orderly pattern. There are four key districts to note. Within the Second Ring Road (which replaced Beijing's now-forgotten city walls) are **Dongcheng** (the east half of the old center) and **Xicheng** (the west half). Dongcheng is home to many notable imperial sights; Xicheng is more relaxed and laid-back, thanks to a combination of charming alleyways, parks, and lakes. The **Chaoyang** District, east of the Old City, is where the full force of contemporary China can be felt, among the skyscrapers of the Guomao business district and the main shopping and nightlife hub of Sanlitun. To the northwest is **Haidian**, the city's university and tech district, as well as the location of some of Beijing's more far-flung sights, such as the Summer Palace.

DONGCHENG DISTRICT 东城区

Feeling the weight and the power of China's history is inevitable as you stand on the Avenue of Eternal Peace, Chang'an Jie, at the crossroads of ancient and modern China. The pale expanse of Tiananmen Square, built by Mao Zedong to fit up to a million revolutionary souls, leaves even mobs of tourists looking tiny and scattered. An iconic portrait of Mao sits upon the scarlet wall of Tiananmen Gate, the serenity of his gaze belying the tumult of his reign. And beyond, the splendors of the Forbidden City await.

The soul of old Beijing lives on throughout Dongcheng District, where you'll find the city's top historic sites and idyllic hutong worth getting lost in. A day or two exploring the district will leave you feeling as if you've been introduced to the complicated character of the capital. Dongcheng is also one of the smaller districts in the city, which makes it ideal for tackling on foot or by bicycle. ■TIP→ **Note that indoor photography in many temples and sites like the Forbidden City is not permitted.**

GETTING HERE AND AROUND

Dongcheng is easily accessible by subway, with stops along most of its perimeter: Tiananmen East station to Jianguomen on Line 1 forms the south side of this district; Jianguomen to Gulou Dajie on Line 2 forms the district's north and east sides. Line 2 stops at the Lama Temple, the Ancient Observatory, Wangfujing, and Tiananmen Square. Taxi travel during peak hours (7 to 9 am and 5 to 8 pm) is difficult. At other times traveling by taxi is affordable, convenient, and the fastest option (especially at noon, when much of the city is at lunch, and after 10 pm). Renting a bike to see the sites is also a good option. Bus travel within the city is only Y1 for shorter distances and can be very convenient, but requires reading knowledge of Chinese to find the correct bus to take. Once on the bus, stops are announced in Chinese and English.

MAKING THE MOST OF YOUR TIME

Most of Dongcheng can be seen in a day, but it's best to set aside two, because the **Forbidden City** and **Tiananmen Square** will likely take the better part of one day. The climb up Coal Hill (also called Prospect Hill) in **Jingshan Park** will take about 30 minutes for an average walker. From there, take a taxi to the **Lama Temple**, which is worth a good two hours, then visit the nearby **Confucius Temple.**

TOP ATTRACTIONS

Fodor's Choice ★ **Confucius Temple** (孔庙 *Kǒngmiào*). This tranquil temple to China's great sage has endured close to eight centuries of additions and restorations. The Hall of Great Accomplishment in the temple houses Confucius's funeral tablet and shrine, flanked by copper-colored statues depicting China's wisest Confucian scholars. As in Buddhist and Taoist temples, worshippers can offer sacrifices (in this case to a mortal, not a deity). The 198 tablets lining the courtyard outside the Hall of Great Accomplishment contain 51,624 names belonging to advanced Confucian scholars from the Yuan, Ming, and Qing dynasties. Flanking the Gate of Great Accomplishment are two carved stone drums dating to the Qianlong period (1735–96). In the Hall of Great Perfection you'll find the central shrine to Confucius. Check out the huge collection of ancient musical instruments.

In the front and main courtyards of the temple you'll find a cemetery of stone tablets. These tablets, or stelae, stand like rows of crypts. On the front stelae you can barely make out the names of thousands of scholars who passed imperial exams. Another batch of stelae, carved in the mid-1700s to record the *Thirteen Classics,* which are philosophical works attributed to Confucius, line the west side of the grounds.

■TIP→ We recommend combining a tour of the Confucius Temple with the nearby Lama Temple. Access to both is convenient from the Yonghegong subway stop at the intersection of Line 2 and Line 5. You can also easily get to the Temple of Heaven by taking Line 5 south to Tiantandongmen.

The complex is now combined with the Imperial Academy next door, once the highest educational institution in the country. Established in 1306 as a rigorous training ground for high-level government officials, the academy was notorious, especially during the early Ming Dynasty

Continued on page 64

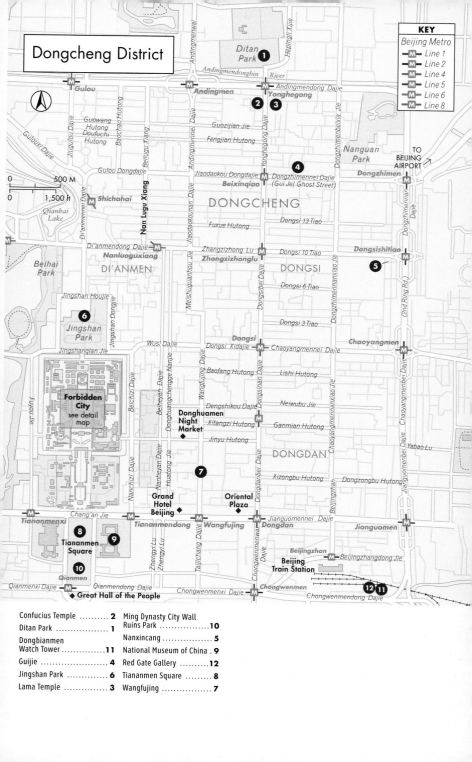

Dongcheng District

Ditan Park **1**

Ⓜ Gulou
Andingmenwai
Andingmendongbin River
Heping'li Xijie
Andingmen
Ⓜ Andingmendong Dajie
Yonghegong

2 **3**

Guowang Hutong
Doufuchi Hutong
Baochao Hutong
Beitugu Xiang
Guozijian Jie
Fengjian Hutong
Yonghegong Dajie
Dongzhimenbeixia Jie
Nanguan Park
TO BEIJING AIRPORT →

Gulouxi Dajie
Jiuguoku Dajie
Gulou Dongdajie
Andingmennei Dajie
Jiaodaokou Nanjie
Jiaodaokou Dongdajie
Dongzhimennei Dajie (Gui Jie/ Ghost Street)
Dongzhimen Ⓜ

4

Shichahai Ⓜ
Nan Lugu Xiang
Beixinqiao Ⓜ
DONGCHENG
Dongzhimennan Dajie

Qianhai Lake
Qianhai Dajie
Di'anmennei Dajie
Di'anmendong Dajie
Nanluoguxiang Ⓜ
DI'ANMEN
Fuxue Hutong
Dongsi 13 Tiao

Beihai Park
Meishuguanhou Jie
Zhangzizhong Lu
Zhangzizhonglu Ⓜ
Dongsi 10 Tiao
Dongsishitiao Ⓜ

5

Dongsi 6 Tiao
DONGSI
(2nd Ring Rd)

Jingshan Houjie
Jingshan Dongjie
Dongsi 3 Tiao

6
Jingshan Park

Jingshanqian Jie
Wusi Dajie
Dongsi Xidajie
Dongsi **Dongsi**
Chaoyangmennei Dajie
Chaoyangmen Ⓜ
Chaoyangmennanxiao Jie

Forbidden City
see detail map
Beichizi Dajie
Donghuangchenggen Nanjie
Wangfujing Dajie
Dongsinan Dajie
Baofang Hutong
Lishi Hutong
Neiwubu Jie
Chaoyangmenbei Dajie
Yabao Lu

Fuyou Jie
Beiheyan Dajie
Nanheyan Dajie
Hutong Jie
Dengshikou Dajie
Ganmian Hutong

Donghuamen Night Market ◆
Xitangzi Hutong
Jinyu Hutong
DONGDAN

7

Nanchizi Dajie
Grand Hotel Beijing ◆
Oriental Plaza ◆
Xizongbu Hutong
Dongzongbu Hutong

Chang'an Jie
Tiananmenxi Ⓜ
Ⓜ
Tiananmendong
Wangfujing
Dongdan Ⓜ
Jianguomennei Dajie
Jianguomen Ⓜ

8
Tiananmen Square
9
Zhengyi Lu
Zhengyi Lu
Taijichang Dajie
Jianguomennei
Jianguomenbei Dajie
Jianguomennei Dajie

10
Qianmen Ⓜ
Beijing Train Station
Beijingzhan Ⓜ Beijingzhangdong Jie

Qianmenxi Dajie
Qianmendong Dajie
Chongwenmenxi Dajie
Chongwenmen Ⓜ
Chongwenmennei Dajie
Chongwenmennan Dajie
Chongwenmendong Dajie

◆ **Great Hall of the People**

12 **11**

0   500 M
0   1,500 ft

THE FORBIDDEN CITY

Undeniably sumptuous, the Forbidden City, once home to a long line of emperors, is Beijing's most enduring emblem. Magnificent halls, winding lanes, and stately courtyards await you—welcome to the world's largest palace complex.

As you gaze up at roofs of glazed-yellow tiles—a symbol of royalty—try to imagine a time when only the emperor ("the son of God") was permitted to enter this palace, accompanied by select family members, concubines, and eunuch-servants. Now, with its doors flung open, the Forbidden City's mysteries beckon.

The sheer grandeur of the site—with 800 buildings and more than 8,000 rooms—conveys the pomp and circumstance of Imperial China. The shady palaces, musty with age, recall life at court, where corrupt eunuchs and palace officials schemed and bored concubines gossiped.

BUILDING TO GLORY

Under the third Ming emperor, Yongle, 200,000 laborers built this complex over the course of 14 years, finishing in 1420. Yongle relocated the Ming capital to Beijing (from Nanjing in the south) to strengthen China's northern frontier. After Yongle, the palace was home to 23 Ming and Qing emperors, until the dynastic system crumbled in 1911.

In imperial times, no buildings were allowed to exceed the height of the palace. Moats and massive timber doors protected the emperor. Gleaming yellow roof tiles marked the vast complex as the royal court's exclusive dominion. Ornate interiors displayed China's most exquisite artisanship, including ceilings covered with turquoise-and-blue dragons, walls draped with priceless scrolls, intricate cloisonné screens, sandalwood thrones padded in delicate silks, and floors of golden-hued bricks. Miraculously, the palace survived fire, war, and imperial China's collapse.

MORE THAN FENG SHUI

The Forbidden City embodies Feng Shui, architectural principles used for thousands of years throughout China. Each main hall faces south, opening to a courtyard flanked by lesser buildings. This symmetry repeats itself along a north–south axis that bisects the imperial palace, with a broad walkway paved in marble. This path was reserved exclusively for the emperor's sedan chair.

The entire complex follows the principles of Feng Shui.

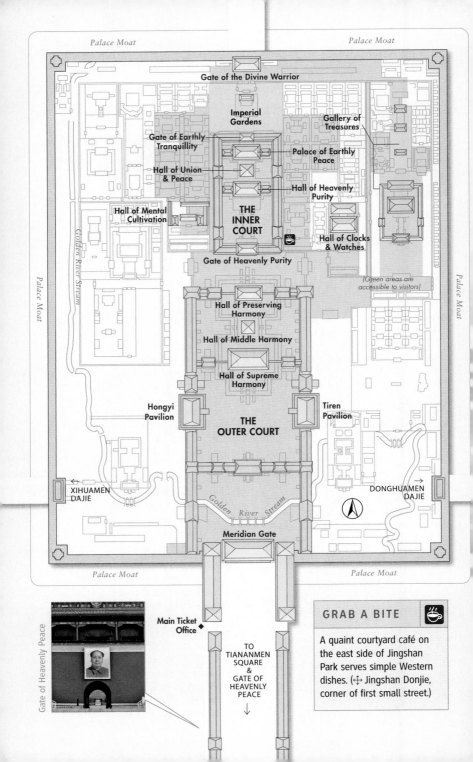

Palace Moat

Palace Moat

Gate of the Divine Warrior

Imperial Gardens

Gallery of Treasures

Gate of Earthly Tranquillity

Palace of Earthly Peace

Hall of Union & Peace

Hall of Heavenly Purity

Hall of Mental Cultivation

THE INNER COURT

Hall of Clocks & Watches

Gate of Heavenly Purity

(Green areas are accessible to visitors)

Hall of Preserving Harmony

Hall of Middle Harmony

Hall of Supreme Harmony

THE OUTER COURT

Hongyi Pavilion

Tiren Pavilion

Golden River Stream

Palace Moat

Palace Moat

← XIHUAMEN DAJIE

DONGHUAMEN DAJIE →

Golden River Stream

Meridian Gate

Palace Moat

Palace Moat

Main Ticket Office ◆

TO TIANANMEN SQUARE & GATE OF HEAVENLY PEACE ↓

Gate of Heavenly Peace

GRAB A BITE

A quaint courtyard café on the east side of Jingshan Park serves simple Western dishes. (⊕ Jingshan Donjie, corner of first small street.)

WHAT TO SEE

The most impressive way to reach the Forbidden City is through the **Gate of Heavenly Peace** (Tiananmen), connected to Tiananmen Square. The Great Helmsman himself stood here to establish the People's Republic of China on October 1, 1949.

The **Meridian Gate** (Wumen), sometimes called Five Phoenix Tower, is the main southern entrance to the palace. Here, the emperor announced yearly planting schedules according to the lunar calendar; it's also where errant officials were flogged. The main ticket office and audio-guide rentals are just west of this gate.

The central entrance of the Meridian was reserved for the emperor. The one day the empress was allowed to walk through it was her wedding day.

THE OUTER COURT

The **Hall of Supreme Harmony** (Taihedian) was used for coronations, royal birthdays, and weddings. Bronze vats, once kept brimming with water to fight fires, ring this vast expanse. The hall sits atop three stone tiers with an elaborate drainage system with 1,000 carved dragons. On the top tier, bronze cranes symbolize longevity. Inside, cloisonné cranes flank the imperial throne, above which hangs a heavy bronze ball—placed there to crush any pretender to the throne.

Take a close look at the bronze vats and you'll see the telltale scratch marks of greedy foreign soldiers who scraped the gold with their bayonets.

Emperors greeted audiences in the **Hall of Middle Harmony** (Zhonghedian). It also housed the royal plow, with which the emperor would turn a furrow to commence spring planting.

The highest civil service examinations, which were personally conducted by the emperor, were once administered in the **Hall of Preserving Harmony** (Baohedian). Behind the hall, a 200-ton marble relief of dragons, the palace's most treasured stone carving, adorns the staircase.

The Hall of Supreme Harmony was the site of many imperial weddings.

A short jaunt to the right is **Hall of Clocks and Watches** (Zhongbiaoguan), where you'll find a collection of early timepieces. It's pure opulence, with jeweled, enameled, and lacquered timepieces (some astride elephants, others implanted in ceramic trees). Our favorites? Those crafted from red sandalwood. *(additional admission cost)*

You'll see that lions in the palace live in pairs. A female lion playing with a cub symbolizes imperial fertility. A male lion, sitting majestically with a sphere beneath his paw, represents power.

Marble dragons will greet you behind the Hall of Preserving Harmony.

Emperors Throne in the Palace of Heavenly Purity

THE INNER COURT

Now you're approaching the very core of the palace. Several emperors chose to live in the Inner Palace with their families. The **Hall of Heavenly Purity** (Qianqinggong) holds another imperial throne; the **Hall of Union and Peace** (Jiaotaidian) was the venue for the empress's annual birthday party; and the **Palace of Earthly Peace** (Kunninggong) was where royal couples consummated their marriages. The banner above the throne bizarrely reads DOING NOTHING.

On either side of the Inner Palace are six western and six eastern palaces—the former living quarters of concubines, eunuchs, and servants. The last building on the western side, the **Hall of Mental Cultivation** (Yangxindian), is the most important of these; starting with Emperor Yongzheng, all Qing Dynasty emperors attended to daily state business in this hall.

AN EMPEROR CHEAT SHEET

JIAJING (1507–1567)

Ming Emperor Jiajing was obsessed with Taoism, which he hoped would give him longevity, but which also led him to ignore state affairs for 25 years. His other fixation was the pursuit of girls: his 18 concubines conspired to strangle him in his sleep, but their plot was uncovered. Nearly all of the girls, and their families, were killed.

YONGZHENG (1678–1735)

The third emperor of the Qing Dynasty, Yongzheng was tyrannical but efficient. He became emperor amid rumors that he had forged his father's will. He appeased his brothers by promoting them, but then proceeded to murder and imprison anyone who posed a challenge, including his own brothers, two of whom died in prison.

Pagoda in the Imperial Garden

FAST FACTS

Address: The main entrance is just north of the Gate of Heavenly Peace, which faces Tiananmen Square on Chang'an Jie.

Web site: www.dpm.org.cn

Open: Tues.–Sun.

UNESCO Status: Declared a World Heritage Site in 1987. You must check your bags prior to entry and also pass through a metal detector.

The Gallery of Treasures (Zhenbaoguan), actually a series of halls, has breathtaking examples of imperial ornamentation. The first room displays candleholders, wine vessels, tea sets, and a golden pagoda commissioned by Qing emperor Qian Long in honor of his mother. A cabinet on one wall contains the 25 imperial seals. Jade bracelets, golden hair pins, and coral fill the second hall; carved jade landscapes a third. *(Admission: Y10)*

HEAD FOR THE GREEN

North of the Forbidden City's private palaces, beyond the **Gate of Earthly Tranquillity**, lie the most pleasant parts of the Forbidden City: the **Imperial Gardens** (Yuhuayuan), composed of ancient cypress trees and stone mosaic pathways. During festivals, palace inhabitants climbed the Hill of Accumulated Elegance. You can exit the palace at the back of the gardens through the park's **Gate of the Divine Warrior** (Shenwumen).

■ The palace is always packed with visitors, but it's impossibly crowded on national holidays.

■ Allow 2–4 hours to explore the palace. There are souvenir shops and restaurants inside.

■ You can rent audio guides at the Meridian Gate.

CIXI (1835–1908)

The Empress Dowager served as de facto ruler of China from 1861 until 1908. She was a concubine at 16 and soon became Emperor Xianfeng's favorite. She gave birth to his only son to survive: the heir apparent. Ruthless and ambitious, she learned the workings of the imperial court and used every means to gain power.

PUYI (1906–1967)

Puyi, whose life was depicted in Bertolucci's classic *The Last Emperor*, took the throne at age two. The Qing dynasty's last emperor, he was forced to abdicate after the dynasty fell. During an attempted restoration in 1917, he held the throne for 12 days. Puyi was forced out of the Imperial City in 1924 by a warlord.

era, for the harsh discipline imposed on scholars perfecting their knowledge of the Confucian classics. The Riyong Emperors Lecture Hall is surrounded by a circular moat (although the building is rectangular in shape). Emperors would come here to lecture on the classics. This ancient campus would be a glorious place to study today with its washed red walls, gold-tiled roofs, and towering cypresses (some as old as 700 years). ⊠ *13 Guozijian Lu, off Yonghegong Lu near Lama Temple, Dongcheng District* ☏ *010/8401–1977* ⊕ *www.kmgzj.com* 🎫 *Y30* ⊙ *Daily 8:30–5* Ⓜ *Yonghegong.*

Dongbianmen Watch Tower (东便门角楼 *Dōngbiànmén jiǎolóu*). This is Beijing's last remaining Ming watchtower. Be sure to check out the Red Gate Gallery inside, which shows works by well-known contemporary Chinese artists. The gallery was set up in 1991 by Brian Wallace, an Australian who studied art history at China's Central Academy of Fine Arts. The second and third floors are devoted to the history of the Chongwen District. ⊠ *Dongbianmen Watchtower, Chongwen District* ☏ *010/6525–1005* ⊕ *www.redgategallery.com* 🎫 *Free* ⊙ *Daily 9–5.*

Forbidden City. *See the highlighted feature in this chapter.* ⊠ *Main entrance just north of the Gate of Heavenly Peace, which faces Tiananmen Square on Chang'an Jie, Dongcheng District* ☏ *010/6404–4071* 🎫 *Y40 Nov. 1–Mar. 31; Y60 Apr. 1–Oct. 31; the Hall of Clocks and Watches and the Gallery of Treasures are an additional Y10 each* ⊙ *Nov. 1–Mar. 31, daily 8:30 am–4:30; Apr. 1–Oct. 31, daily 8:30–5. Closed Mon. throughout the year*

Jingshan Park (景山公园 *Jǐngshān gōngyuán*). This park, also known as Coal Hill Park, was built around a small peak formed from earth excavated for the Forbidden City's moats. Ming rulers ordered the hill's construction to improve the feng shui of their new palace to the south. You can climb a winding stone staircase past peach and apple trees to Wanchun Pavilion, the park's highest point. On a clear day it offers unparalleled views of the Forbidden City and the Bell and Drum towers. Chongzhen, the last Ming emperor, is said to have hanged himself at the foot of Coal Hill as his dynasty collapsed in 1644. ⊠ *Jingshanqian Dajie, opposite the north gate of the Forbidden City, Xicheng and Dongcheng districts* ☏ *010/6404–4071* 🎫 *Y2* ⊙ *Daily 6 am–7 pm.*

Lama Temple (雍和宫 *Yōnghégōng*). One of the most important functioning Buddhist temples in Beijing, this much-visited Tibetan Buddhist masterpiece has five main halls and numerous galleries hung with finely detailed *thangkhas* (Tibetan religious scroll paintings). The entire temple is decorated with Buddha images—all guarded by somber lamas dressed in brown robes. Originally a palace for Prince Yongzheng, it was transformed into a temple once he became the Qing's third emperor in 1723. The temple flourished under Emperor Qianlong, housing some 500 resident monks. This was once the official "embassy" of Tibetan Buddhism in Beijing, but today only about two dozen monks live in this complex.

Don't miss **The Hall of Heavenly Kings**, with statues of Maitreya, the future Buddha, and Weitou, China's guardian of Buddhism. This hall is worth a slow stroll. In the courtyard beyond, a pond with a bronze

2

mandala represents paradise. The Statues of Buddhas of the Past, Present, and Future hold court in **The Hall of Harmony.** Look on the west wall where an exquisite silk thangkha of White Tara—the embodiment of compassion—hangs. Images of the Medicine and Longevity Buddhas line **The Hall of Eternal Blessing. In The Pavilion of Ten Thousand Fortunes** you see the breathtaking 26-meter (85-foot) Maitreya Buddha carved from a single block of sandalwood. ■ **TIP→ Combine a visit to the Lama Temple with the Confucius Temple and the Imperial Academy, which are a five-minute walk away, within the hutong neighborhood opposite the main entrance.** ✉ *12 Yonghegong Dajie, Beixinqiao, Dongcheng District* ☎ *010/6404–4499* 🚌 *Y25* ⊙ *Daily 9–4:30* Ⓜ *Yonghegong, Line 2.*

Ming Dynasty City Wall Ruins Park (明城墙遗址公园 *Míng chéngqiáng yízhǐ gōngyuán*). This rebuilt section of Beijing's old inner-city wall is a nicely landscaped area with paths full of Chinese walking their dogs, flying kites, practicing martial arts, and playing with their children. It was made using original bricks that had been snatched decades earlier, after the city wall had been torn down. At the eastern end of the park is the grand Dongbianmen Watch Tower, home to the popular Red Gate Gallery. ✉ *Dongbianmen, Dongdajie St., Chongwen District* 🚌 *Free* ⊙ *Daily, park open 24 hrs* Ⓜ *Jiandemen.*

National Museum of China (中國國家博物館 *Zhōngguó guójiā bówùguǎn*). This monumental edifice on the eastern side of Tiananmen Square showcases 5,000 years of history in immaculate surroundings. With 2 million square feet of exhibition space, it's impossible to see everything. The propaganda-heavy history sections can be safely skipped; focus instead on the ancient China section on the lower level, which houses magnificent displays of bronzes and jade artifacts. The museum also features strong shows of visiting works from abroad, such as Renaissance art from Florence and ceramics from the British Museum and the Victoria and Albert Museum. ✉ *16 Dong Chang An Jie, Dongcheng District* ☎ *010/6511–6400* ⊕ *en.chnmuseum.cn* 🚌 *Free with passport* ⊙ *Tues.–Sun. 9–5, ticket booth closes at 3:30* Ⓜ *Tiananmen East.*

Fodor's Choice
★

Red Gate Gallery (红门画廊 *Hóng mén huàláng*). This gallery, one of the first to open in Beijing, displays and sells contemporary Chinese art in the extraordinary location of the old Dongbianmen Watchtower, which dates back to the 16th century. The venue is worth a visit even if you're not interested in the art. Be aware that the subway stop listed here is about a 25-minute walk from the gallery. ✉ *1/F and 4/F, Dongbianmen Watchtower, Chongwenmen Dongdajie, Dongcheng District* ☎ *010/6525–1005* ⊕ *www.redgategallery.com* Ⓜ *Jianguomen.*

Fodor's Choice
★

Tiananmen Square (天安门广场 *Tiānānmén guǎngchǎng*). The world's largest public square, and the very heart of modern China, Tiananmen Square owes little to grand imperial designs and everything to Mao Zedong. At the height of the Cultural Revolution, hundreds of thousands of Red Guards crowded the square; in June 1989 the square was the scene of tragedy when student demonstrators were killed.

Today the square is packed with sightseers, families, and undercover policemen. Although formidable, the square is a little bleak, with no shade, benches, or trees. Come here at night for an eerie experience—it's a little like being on a film set. Beijing's ancient central axis runs right through the center of Mao's mausoleum, the Forbidden City, the Drum and Bell towers, and the Olympic Green. The square is sandwiched between two grand gates: the Gate of Heavenly Peace (Tiananmen) to the north and the Front Gate (Qianmen) in the south. Along the western edge is the Great Hall of the People. The National Museum of China lies along the eastern side. The 125-foot granite obelisk you see is the Monument to the People's Heroes; it commemorates those who died for the revolutionary cause of the Chinese people. ⊠ *Bounded by Chang'an Jie to the north and Qianmen Dajie to the south, Dongcheng District* ⊡ *Free* ☉ *Daily 5 am–10 pm* Ⓜ *Qianmen.*

DID YOU KNOW?

A network of tunnels lies beneath Tiananmen Square. Mao Zedong is said to have ordered them dug in the late 1960s after Sino-Soviet relations soured. They extend across Beijing and many have been sealed up or fallen into disrepair, though migrant workers inhabit some.

Wangfujing (王府井 *Wángfǔjǐng*). Wangfujing, one of the city's oldest and busiest shopping districts, is still lined with a handful of *laozihao*, old brand-name shops, some dating back a century, and 1950s-era state-run stores. This short walking street is a pleasant place for window-shopping. Also on Wangfujing is the gleaming Oriental Plaza, with its expensive high-end shops (Tiffany's, Burberry, Ermenegildo Zegna, and Audi among them), interspersed with Levi Jeans, Esprit, Starbucks, Pizza Hut, KFC, Häagen-Dazs, and a modern movie multiplex. ⊠ *Wangfujing, Dongcheng District.*

WORTH NOTING

Ditan Park (地坛公园 *Dìtán gōngyuán*). In "Temple of Earth Park," 105 acres of 16th-century green space, are the square altar where emperors once made sacrifices to the earth god, and the Hall of Deities. This is a lovely place for a stroll, especially if you're already near the Drum Tower or Lama Temple. ⊠ *Hepingli Xilu, just north of Second Ring Rd., Dongcheng District* ☎ *010/6421–4657* ⊡ *Y2* ☉ *Daily 6 am–9 pm.*

Guijie (簋街 *Guǐjiç*). For a nighttime-munchies cure, head to Guijie, also known as Ghost Street, which is full of restaurants serving up noodles, hotpot, and fried delights. One of the most popular dishes here is *malaxia*, or spicy crawfish. ⊠ *Dongzhimennei Dajie, Dongcheng District.*

Nanxincang (南新仓 *Nánxîncâng*). China's oldest existing granary, dating back to the Yongle period (1403–24), is now an entertainment hub of sorts, with couple of art galleries, a teahouse, and a changing lineup of bars and restaurants, including the most established of the bunch, a well-loved branch of the famed Dadong Roast Duck. The structures at Nanxincang—just 10 years younger than those of the Forbidden City—were just one of the more than 300 granaries that existed in this area during imperial days. ⊠ *Dongsi Shitiao, 1 block west of the Second Ring Rd., Dongcheng District.*

A portrait of the Great Helmsman gazes down on Tiananmen Square.

NEED A BREAK?

Donghuamen Night Market (东华门夜市 *Dōnghuāmén yèshì*). Crunchy deep-fried scorpions and other critters are sold at the Donghuamen Night Market, at the northern end of Wangfujing's wide walking boulevard. We'll admit: this is more of a place to look at and perhaps photograph food rather than devour it. In addition to standard street foods, hawkers here also serve up deep-fried starfish, plus a variety of insects and other hard-to-identify food items. Most street-market food is usually safe to eat as long as it's hot. The row of stalls makes for an intriguing walk with great photo ops. ⊠ *Donganmen Dajie, on the northern side of Wangfujing, Dongcheng District.*

XICHENG DISTRICT 西城区

Xicheng District is home to a charming combination of some of the most distinctive things that the city has to offer: cozy hutongs, palatial courtyard houses, charming lakes, and fine restaurants. For many visitors, this is one of the best areas in which to fall in love with Beijing.

The best way to do that is to take a walk or bicycle tour of the hutongs here: there's no better way to scratch the surface of this sprawling city (before it disappears) than by exploring these courtyard houses as you wander in and out of historic sites in the area.

This is also a great area for people-watching, especially along the shores of Houhai. As you wander, sample the local snacks sold from shop windows. Treats abound on Huguosi Jie (just west of Mei Lanfang's house). In the evening, relax at a restaurant or bar with a view of the lake. The lakes at Shichahai are hopping day and night.

GETTING HERE AND AROUND

Houhai and Beihai Park are conveniently reached by taxi. Line 1 subway stops include Tiananmen West, Xidan, and Fuxingmen. Line 2 makes stops from Fuxingmen to the Drum Tower (Gulou), following Xicheng's perimeter.

MAKING THE MOST OF YOUR TIME

Xicheng's must-see sites are few in number but all special. Walk around **Beihai Park** in the early afternoon. If you come to Beijing in the winter, **Qianhai** will be frozen and you can rent skates, runner-equipped bicycles, or the local favorite, a chair with runners welded to the bottom and a pair of metal sticks with which to propel yourself across the ice. Dinner along the shores of **Houhai** is a good option. Head toward the northern section for a more tranquil setting or join the crowds for a booming bar scene farther south. Plan to spend a few hours shopping at **Xidan**; this can be a great place to pick up funky, cheap gifts.

TOP ATTRACTIONS

Beihai Park (北海 *Běihǎi*). A white stupa is perched on a small island just north of the south gate of this park. Also at the south entrance is **Round City**, which contains a white-jade Buddha and an enormous jade bowl given to Kublai Khan. Nearby, the well-restored **Temple of Eternal Peace** houses a variety of Buddhas. Climb to the stupa from Yongan Temple. Once there, you can pay an extra Y1 to ascend the Buddha-bedecked **Shanyin Hall**.

The lake is Beijing's largest and most beautiful public waterway. On summer weekends the lake teems with paddleboats. The **Five Dragon Pavilion**, on Beihai's northwest shore, was built in 1602 by a Ming Dynasty emperor who liked to fish under the moon. ✉ *Weijin Jie, Xicheng District* ☏ *010/6403–1102* ⊕ *www.beihaipark.com. cn* ✆ *Y10; extra fees for some sites* ☉ *Apr.–May and Sept.–Oct., daily 6:30 am–8:30 pm; Nov.–Mar., daily 6:30 am–8 pm; June–Aug., daily 6:30 am–10 pm.*

Capital Museum (首都博物馆 *Shǒudū bówùguǎn*). Moved to an architecturally striking new home west of Tiananmen Square in 2005, this is one of China's finest cultural museums. Artifacts are housed in a multistoried bronze cylinder that dominates the building's facade, while paintings, calligraphy, and photographs of historic Beijing fill the remaining exhibition halls. The museum gets extra points for clear English descriptions and modern, informative displays. Entry is free, but tickets must be booked (via the website) in advance. ✉ *16 Fuxingmenwai Dajie, Xicheng District* ☏ *010/6337–0491* ⊕ *www.capitalmuseum.org.cn/en* ✆ *Free* ☉ *Tues.–Sun. 9–4.*

Drum Tower (鼓楼 *Gǔlóu*). Until the late 1920s, the 24 drums once housed in this tower were Beijing's timepiece. Sadly, all but one of these huge drums have been destroyed. Kublai Khan built the first drum tower on this site in 1272. You can climb to the top of the present tower, which dates from the Ming Dynasty. Old photos of hutong neighborhoods line the walls beyond the drum; there's also a scale model of a traditional

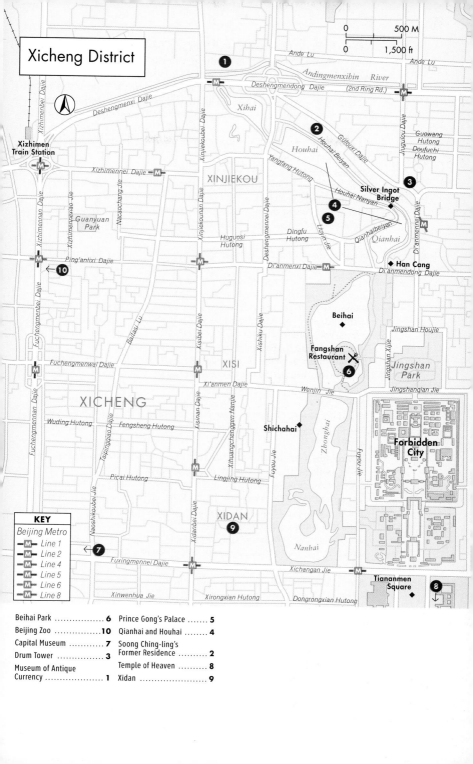

Xicheng District

Andingmenxibin River

Ande Lu

Ande Lu

0 ———— 500 M
0 ———— 1,500 ft

Xizhimenbei Dajie

Deshengmenxi Dajie

Deshengmendong Dajie

(2nd Ring Rd.)

Xizhimen
Train Station

Xihai

❶

Xinjiekoubei Dajie

Houhai

❷

Gulouxi Dajie

Jiugulou Dajie

Guowang
Hutong

Doufuchi
Hutong

Xizhimennei Dajie

Nazaochang Jie

XINJIEKOU

Yangfang Hutong

Houhai Beiyan

Silver Ingot
Bridge

❸

Guanyuan
Park

Xizhimennanxiao Jie

Houhai Nanyan

❹

❺

Huguosi
Hutong

Dingfu
Hutong

Liuyin Jie

Qianhaibeiyan

Qianhai

Ping'antixi Dajie

❿ ←

Baitasi Lu

Xinjiekounan Dajie

Deshengmennei Dajie

Di'anmenxi Dajie

Di'anmendong Dajie

Han Cang ◆

Fuchengmenbei Dajie

Xisibei Dajie

Xishiku Dajie

Beihai ◆

Jingshan Houjie

Fuchengmenwai Dajie

XISI

Fangshan
Restaurant

❻

Jingshan Xijie

Jingshan
Park

Jingshangian Jie

XICHENG

Xisinan Dajie

Xi'anmen Dajie

Wenjin Jie

Fuchengmennan Dajie

Wuding Hutong

Taipingqiao Jie

Fengsheng Hutong

Xichuangchengen Nanjie

Shichahai ◆

Fuyou Jie

Zhonghai

Fuyou Jie

Forbidden
City

Picai Hutong

Lingjing Hutong

XIDAN

❾

Naoshikoubei Jie

Xidanbei Dajie

❼ ←

Fuxingmennei Dajie

Nanhai

Xichangan Jie

Tiananmen
Square

❽ ←

KEY

Beijing Metro

Ⓜ— Line 1
Ⓜ— Line 2
Ⓜ— Line 4
Ⓜ— Line 5
Ⓜ— Line 6
Ⓜ— Line 8

Xinwenhua Jie

Xirongxian Hutong

Dongrongxian Hutong

courtyard house. The nearby **Bell Tower,** renovated after a fire in 1747, offers fabulous views of the hutongs from the top of a long, narrow staircase. The huge 63-ton bronze bell, supported by lacquered wood stanchions, is also worth seeing. In recent years, the authorities have demolished a number of historical hutong in this area, so don't be surprised if you come across serious signs of reconstruction around here. ⊠ *North end of Dianmen Dajie, Xicheng District* ☎ *010/6404–1710* 🚇 *Drum Tower Y20, Bell Tower Y20; ticket for both Y30* ⊙ *Daily 9–5* Ⓜ *Guloudajie.*

Qianhai and Houhai (前海后海 *Qiánhǎi, Hòuhǎi*). Most people come to these lakes, along with Xihai to the northwest, to stroll and enjoy the shoreside bars and restaurants. In summer you can boat or fish. In winter, sections of the frozen lakes are fenced off for skating. This daytrip is easily combined with a visit to Beihai Park or the Bell and Drum towers. ⊠ *North of Beihai Lake, Xicheng District.*

Fodor's Choice ★ **Temple of Heaven** (天坛 *Tiāntán gōngyuán*). A prime example of Chinese religious architecture, this is where emperors once performed important rites. It was a site for imperial sacrifices, meant to please the gods so they would generate bumper harvests. Set in a huge, serene, mushroom-shaped park southeast of the Forbidden City, the Temple of Heaven is surrounded by splendid examples of Ming Dynasty architecture, including curved cobalt blue roofs layered with yellow and green tiles. Construction began in the early 15th century under Yongle, whom many call the "architect of Beijing." Shaped like a semicircle on the northern rim to represent heaven and square on the south for the earth, the grounds were once believed to be the meeting point of the two. The area is double the size of the Forbidden City and is still laid out to divine rule: buildings and paths are positioned to represent the right directions for heaven and earth. This means, for example, that the northern part is higher than the south.

The temple's hallmark structure is a magnificent **blue-roofed wooden tower** built in 1420. It burned to the ground in 1889 and was immediately rebuilt using Ming architectural methods (and timber imported from Oregon). The building's design is based on the calendar: 4 center pillars represent the seasons, the next 12 pillars represent months, and 12 outer pillars signify the parts of a day. Together these 28 poles, which also correspond to the 28 constellations of heaven, support the structure without nails. A carved dragon swirling down from the ceiling represents the emperor.

Across the Danbi Bridge, you'll find the **Hall of Prayer for Good Harvests.** The middle section was once reserved for the Emperor of Heaven, who was the only one allowed to set foot on the eastern side, while aristocrats and high-ranking officials walked on the western strip. ■ TIP→ **If you're coming by taxi, enter the park through the southern entrance (Tiantan Nanmen). This way you approach the beautiful Hall of Prayer for Good Harvests via the Danbi Bridge—the same route the emperor favored.**

Directly east of this hall is a long, twisting platform, which once enclosed the animal-killing pavilion. The Long Corridor was traditionally hung

Playing with ribbons in Beihai Park

with lanterns on the eve of sacrifices. Today it plays host to scores of Beijingers singing opera, playing cards and chess, and fan dancing.

Be sure to whisper into the echo wall encircling the **Imperial Vault of Heaven**. This structure allows anyone to eavesdrop. It takes a minute to get the hang of it, but with a friend on one side and you on the other it's possible to hold a conversation by speaking into the wall. Tilt your head in the direction you want your voice to travel for best results. Just inside the south gate is the **Round Altar**, a three-tiered, white-marble structure where the emperor worshipped the winter solstice; it's based around the divine number nine. Nine was regarded as a symbol of the power of the emperor, as it's the biggest single-digit odd number, and odd numbers are considered masculine and therefore more powerful.

The Hall of Abstinence, on the western edge of the grounds, is where the emperor would retreat three days before the ritual sacrifice. To understand the significance of the harvest sacrifice at the Temple of Heaven, it's important to keep in mind that the legitimacy of a Chinese emperor's rule depended on what is known as the *tian ming*, or the mandate of heaven, essentially the emperor's relationship with the gods.

A succession of bad harvests, for example, could be interpreted as the emperor losing the favor of heaven and could be used to justify a change in emperor or even in dynasty. When the emperor came to the Temple of Heaven to pray for good harvests and to pay homage to his ancestors, there may have been a good measure of self-interest to his fervor.

The sacrifices consisted mainly of animals and fruit placed on altars surrounded by candles. Many Chinese still offer sacrifices of fruit and incense on special occasions, such as births, deaths, and weddings.

■ TIP→ **We recommend buying an all-inclusive ticket. If you only buy a ticket into the park, you'll need to pay an additional Y20 to get into each building.**

Beijing's subway Line 5 (purple line) makes getting to the Temple of Heaven particularly simple. Get off at the Tiantandongmen (Temple of Heaven East Gate) stop. This line also runs direct to the Lama Temple (Yonghegong), so combining the two sites in a day makes a lot of sense.

Automatic audio guides (Y40) are available at stalls inside all four entrances. ⊠ *Yongdingmen Dajie (South Gate), Xuanwu District* ☎ *010/6702–8866* ⊕ *en.tiantanpark.com* ⊞ *All-inclusive ticket Y35; entrance to park only Y15* ⊙ *Daily 6 am–10 pm; ticket booth closes at 4:30* Ⓜ *Tiantandongmen.*

Xidan (西单 *Xîdân*). This area teems with shopping malls and small stores selling clothing and accessories, and upwardly mobile Chinese coming to browse and buy. The glitzy 13-story Joy City mall, full of local and international brands, is a major sign of commerce's grip here. Ⓜ *Xidan.*

WORTH NOTING

Beijing Zoo (北京动物园 *Bìijîng dòngwù yuán*). Though visitors usually go straight to see the giant pandas, don't miss the other interesting animals, like tigers from the northeast, yaks from Tibet, enormous sea turtles from China's seas, and red pandas from Sichuan. The zoo started out as a garden belonging to one of the sons of Shunzhi, the first emperor of the Qing Dynasty. In 1747, the Qianlong emperor had it refurbished (along with other imperial properties, including the summer palaces) and turned it into a park in honor of his mother's 60th birthday. In 1901, the Empress Dowager gave it another extensive face-lift and used it to house a collection of animals given to her as a gift by a Chinese minister who had bought them during a trip to Germany. By the 1930s, most of the animals had died and were stuffed and put on display in a museum on the grounds. ⊠ *137 Xizhimenwai Dajie, Xicheng District* ☎ *010/6839–0274* ⊕ *www.bjzoo.com* ⊞ *Apr.–Oct. Y15, Nov.–Mar. Y10; plus Y5 for the pandas* ⊙ *Apr.–Oct., daily 7:30–6; Nov.–Mar., daily 7:30–5.*

Museum of Antique Currency (北京古代钱币博物馆 *Bìijîng gǔdài qiánbi bówùguǎn*). This museum in a tiny courtyard house (within the Deshengmen tower complex) showcases a small but impressive selection of rare Chinese coins. Explanations are in Chinese only. Also in the courtyard are coin and curio dealers. ⊠ *Deshengmen Jianlou, Bei'erhuan Zhonglu, Xicheng District* ☎ *010/6602–4178* ⊞ *Y10* ⊙ *Tues.–Sun. 9–4.*

Prince Gong's Palace (恭王府 *Gôngwángfǔ*). This grand compound sits in a neighborhood once reserved for imperial relatives. Built in 1777 during the Qing Dynasty, it fell to Prince Gong—brother of Qing emperor Xianfeng and later an adviser to Empress Dowager Cixi—after the original inhabitant was executed for corruption. With nine courtyards joined by covered walkways, it was once one of Beijing's most lavish residences. The museum offers Beijing opera and tea to visitors who pay the higher ticket price. Some literary scholars believe this was the setting for *Dream of the Red Chamber,* one of China's best-known

DID YOU KNOW?

The Temple of Heaven's overall layout symbolizes the relationship between Heaven and Earth. Earth is represented by a square and Heaven by a circle. The temple complex is surrounded by two cordons of walls; the taller outer wall is semicircular at the northern end (Heaven) and shorter and rectangular at the southern end (Earth). Both the Hall of Prayer for Good Harvests and the Circular Mound Altar are round structures on a square yard.

classical novels. ⊠ *17 Qianhai Xijie, Xicheng District* ☎ *010/8328–8149* ⊕ *www.pgm.org.cn* ✏ *Y40–Y70* ⊙ *Mid-Mar.–mid.-Nov., daily 8–4; mid.-Nov.–mid.-Mar., daily 7:30–4:30.*

Soong Ching-ling's Former Residence (宋庆龄故居 *Sòng Qìnglíng gùjû*). Soong Ching-ling (1893–1981) was the youngest daughter of Charles Soong, a wealthy, American-educated bible publisher. At the age of 18, disregarding her family's strong opposition, she eloped to marry the much older Sun Yat-sen. When her husband founded the Republic of China in 1911, Soong Ching-ling became a significant political figure. In 1924 she headed the Women's Department of the Nationalist Party. Then in 1949 she became the vice president of the People's Republic of China. Throughout her career she campaigned tirelessly for the emancipation of women, and she helped lay the foundations for many of the rights that modern-day Chinese women enjoy today. This former palace was her residence and workplace and now houses a small museum, which documents her life and work. ⊠ *46 Houhai Beiyan, Xicheng District* ☎ *010/6404–4205* ✏ *Y20* ⊙ *Daily 9–4.*

CHAOYANG DISTRICT 朝阳区

There's precious little of Beijng's ancient history found in Chaoyang District, where much of the old has been razed to make way for the blingy new. Impeccably dressed Chinese women shop the afternoons away at gleaming new malls, young tycoons and princelings park their Ferraris on the sidewalks, and everyone who's anyone congregates at the booming nightclubs filled with hip-hop music and VIP bottle service.

GETTING HERE AND AROUND

The heart of Chaoyang District is accessible via Lines 1, 2, and 10 on the subway, but the district is huge and the sites are broadly distributed. Taking taxis between sites is usually the easiest way to get around. The 798 Art District is especially far away from central Beijing, so a taxi is also the best bet (about Y30–Y50 from the center of town). Buses go everywhere, but they're slow.

MAKING THE MOST OF YOUR TIME

You can spend years lost in Chaoyang District and never get bored. There's plenty to do, but there are very few historic sights. Spend a morning shopping at **Silk Alley Market** or **Panjiayuan Antiques Market** (best on weekend mornings) and the afternoon cooling off at **Ritan Park** or **Chaoyang Park,** the latter a large and pleasant park with a lot of activities for kids. Next, head to one of the numerous bar streets for refreshments. If you like contemporary art, browse the galleries at **798 Art District.** There are a number of nice cafés here as well.

TOP ATTRACTIONS

798 Art District (798艺术区 *Qîjiübâ yìshù qû*). Chinese contemporary art has exploded in the past decade, and to see some of the finest examples of the scene look no further than 798 Art District, located in the northeast corner of the city. This was once the site of several state-owned factories, including Factory 798, that produced electronics. Beginning in 2002, artists and cultural organizations began to move

2

into the area, gradually developing the old buildings into galleries, art centers, artists' studios, design companies, restaurants, and bars. Note that most if not all of the galleries here are closed Monday.

Experimenting with classical mediums such as paint and printmaking as well as forays into new and digital media, installation, and performance art, young Chinese artists are caught between old and new, Communism and capitalism, urban and rural, rich and poor, and East and West. These conflicts set the stage and color their artistic output, with varying results. Although more and more Chinese artists are achieving international recognition, 798 still abounds with knockoffs of bad Western art and tacky Socialist Realist portraits. Nevertheless the area remains the hub of contemporary creative arts in Beijing and is definitely worth a visit if you're at all interested in the state of the arts in China.

Built in the 1950s, this factory district was a major industrial project by East German architects backed by Soviet aid. All but abandoned by the 1980s, the complex was rediscovered in the late 1990s by a small group of Beijing artists who had just been evicted from their previous haunts and were looking for a new place to set up working and living spaces. Although the scene was at first a completely DIY affair, the quality of art produced and international media attention starting from the early 2000s meant that the district government took notice. Eventually the area was declared a protected arts district, paving the way for commercial galleries, cafés, and souvenir shops. Priced out of their original studios, many working artists have decamped farther afield to the Caochangdi and Songzhuang neighborhoods. Both of these smaller areas are worth visiting, though neither is easily accessible except via taxi. Ask your hotel concierge for a detailed map or, better yet, call ahead to the galleries you're interested in visiting and get driving instructions.

798 is more accessible, however, and eminently walkable. Keep in mind that cabs are prohibited from driving into the complex, and much of the area is pedestrianized. Though it's also open Tuesday through Friday, most people visit on the weekend, when throngs of locals and foreigners congregate to see what's on display.

Many of the galleries there now are hit or miss, but establishments such as the **Ullens Center for Contemporary Arts (UCCA)** and always put on informative, challenging exhibitions. If you need to refuel, stop by At Cafe, billed as the first café in 798 and still co-owned by Huang Rui, one of the district's cofounders. ✉ *798 Art District, 2–4 Jiuxianqiao Rd., Dashanzi, Chaoyang District* ⊕ *www.798district.com.*

Ancient Observatory (北京古观象台 *Biĭjīng gǔguānxiàng tái*). This squat tower of primitive stargazing equipment peeks out next to the elevated highways of the Second Ring Road. It dates to the time of Genghis Khan, who believed that his fortunes could be read in the stars. Many of the bronze devices on display were gifts from Jesuit missionaries who arrived in Beijing and shortly thereafter ensconced themselves as the Ming court's resident stargazers. To China's imperial rulers, interpreting the heavens was key to holding onto power; a ruler knew when, say, an eclipse would occur, or he could predict the best time to plant crops. Celestial phenomena like eclipses and comets were believed to portend

Chaoyang District

TO DASHANZI

River

TO BEIJING AIRPORT

DONGZHIMEN

Xindong Lu

Xinyunnan Lu

Liangma

Dongzhimenwaixie Jie

Dongzhimennei Dajie

Dongzhimen

Dongzhimenwai Dajie

Dongzhimenwai Dajie

Nongzhaguan Beilu

National Agriculture Exhibition Center

Argiculture Exhibition Center

Chaoyanggongyuan Lu

Dongsanhuanbei Lu

Dongzhimennan Dajie

Dongsishitiao

Gongrentiyuchangbei Lu

Xindong Lu

Sanlitun Lu

Yaxiu (Yashow) Market

Gongrentiyuchangbei Lu

Tuanjiehu

Souk

(2nd Ring Rd.)

Workers' Gymnasium

Workers' Stadium

1

Nongzhanguanan Lu

Yaojiayuan Lu

Gongren Tiyuchang Nanlu

Nansanlitun Lu

Baijiazhuang Lu

(3rd Ring Rd.)

Tuanjiehu Park

Tuanjiehu Lu

Chaoyang Beilu

Chaoyangmen

Chaoyangmenwai Dajie

Dongdaqiao

Guandongdianbei Jie

Chaoyangmenwai Dajie

Hujialou

Hujialoube Jie

Jintai Xiu

Chaowaishichang Jie

Shenlu Jie

Fangcaodi Xijie

CHAOYANG

Guandongdian Nanjie

Jintaixizhao

Chaoyang Lu

Chaoyangmenbei Dajie

Ritan Beilu

Dongdaqiao Lu

Temple of the Sun

Ritan Park

3

Yabao Lu

Ritan Lu

Ritan Donglu

The Stone Boat

Guanghua Lu

Jianguomenbei Dajie

Xiushui Beijie

Guanghua Lu

Guanghua Lu

CENTRAL BUSINESS DISTRICT

Beijing Friendship Store

Xiushui Nanjie

Silk Alley Market

Guomao

Jianguomenwai Dajie

4 Jianguomen

Yonganli

Guomao

Jianguo Lu

Dongsanhuanzhong Lu

Panjiayuan Antique Market

Tonghui River

KEY
Beijing Metro
- Ⓜ Line 1
- Ⓜ Line 2
- Ⓜ Line 4
- Ⓜ Line 5
- Ⓜ Line 6
- Ⓜ Line 10

0   500 M

0   1,500 ft

2

change; if left unheeded they might cost an emperor his legitimacy—his mandate of heaven. Records of celestial observations at or near this site go back more than 500 years, making this the longest documented astronomical viewing site in the world.

The main astronomical devices are arranged on the roof. Writhing bronze dragon sculptures adorn some of the astronomy pieces at Jianguo Tower, the main building that houses the observatory. Among the sculptures are an armillary sphere to pinpoint the position of heavenly bodies and a sextant to measure angular distances between stars, along with a celestial globe. Inside, the dusty exhibition rooms shelter ancient star maps with information dating back to the Tang Dynasty. A Ming Dynasty star map and ancient charts are also on display. Most of the ancient instruments were looted by the Allied Forces in 1900, during the Boxer Rebellion, only to be returned to China at the end of World War I. ⊠ *2 Dongbiaobei Hutong, Jianguomenwai Dajie, Chaoyang District* ☏ *010/6524–2202* ⬚ *Y20* ⊙ *Tues. –Sun. 9–4* Ⓜ *Jianguomen.*

WORTH NOTING

Ritan Park (日坛公园 *Rìtán gōngyuán*). A cool oasis of water, paths and trees just west of the Central Business District, Ritan Park (also known as "Temple of the Sun Park") is a popular place to go for some peace and quiet, and is where many locals head to stretch their legs. Stop in at the Stone Boat café if you're in need of refreshment. ⊠ *Ritan Lu, northeast of Jianguomen, Chaoyang District* ☏ *010/8563–5038* ⬚ *Free* ⊙ *Daily 6 am–9 pm.*

Sanlitun (三里屯 *Sānlìtún*). The famous Sanlitun Bar Street, several blocks east of the Workers' Stadium, is known for its nightlife offerings catering to foreigners, expats, and young Chinese. Avoid the dive bars on the east side of Bar Street, however. Vics and Mix at the north gate of the Workers' Stadium are two clubs always packed with people looking for a big night out, while the bars at The Opposite House hotel are a swank respite. Taikoo Li, Beijing's hottest shopping complex, can be credited with changing the face of what was once a fairly seedy area. The Japanese-designed open-air center includes a number of international shops as well as a movie theater and some of Beijing's best restaurants and cafés, and has become the city's major hangout for the in-crowd, both local and foreign. ⊠ *Chaoyang District.*

HAIDIAN DISTRICT 海淀区

In the last decade or so Haidian has become Beijing's educational and technological center, although there's still a lot of Old Beijing left here, including the wonderful Summer Palace, with its lakes and ancient pavilions. The major IT players, including Microsoft, Siemens, NEC, and Sun, all have offices in this area, and in the Wudaokou and Zhongguancun neighborhoods you'll find kids geeking out over the latest gadgets at electronics superstores, studying in one of the many cafés, or blowing off steam at some of the area's dance clubs.

GETTING HERE AND AROUND

Subway Line 13 stops at Wudaokou, the heart of Haidian. Line 4 runs far into the northwest of the city with stops at the Summer Palace and the Old Summer Palace, though Fragrant Hills Park and the Beijing Botanical Garden are farther out still and best reached by taxi. To save money, take Line 10 to Baguo station and catch a cab from there.

MAKING THE MOST OF YOUR TIME

Because the **Summer Palace** is so large, with its lovely lakes and ancient pavilions, it makes for an entire morning of great exploring. The **Old Summer Palace** is close by, so visiting the two sites together is ideal (if you've got the energy).

Fragrant Hills Park makes for a charming outing, but keep in mind that it takes at least an hour and a half to get there from the city center. The **Botanical Garden**, with some 2,000 types of orchids, bonsai, and peach and pear blossoms, along with the **Temple of the Reclining Buddha**, is also fun, especially for green thumbs. Plan to spend most of a day if you go to either of these sites.

TOP ATTRACTIONS

Beijing Botanical Garden (北京植物园 *Bīijíng zhíwù yuán*). Sitting at the feet of the Western Hills in Beijing's northwestern suburbs, the Beijing Botanical Garden, opened in 1955, hosts China's largest plant collection: 6,000 different plant species from all over northern China, including 2,000 types of trees and bushes, more than 1,600 species of tropical and subtropical plants, 1,900 kinds of fruit trees, and 500 flower species. With its state-of-the-art greenhouse and a variety of different gardens, this is a pleasant place to explore, especially in spring, when the peach trees burst with pretty blooms. An added feature is the wonderful Temple of the Reclining Buddha, which has an enormous statue that, it's said, took 7,000 slaves to build. ✉ *Xiangshan Wofosi, Haidian District* ☎ *010/8259–8771* 💴 *Outdoor garden Y10; conservatory Y50* 🕙 *Daily 7–5 (outdoor garden)*.

Big Bell Temple (大钟寺 *Dàzhōngsì*). This 18th-century temple shields China's biggest bell and more than 400 smaller bells and gongs from the Ming, Song, and Yuan dynasties. The Buddhist temple—originally used for rain prayers—was restored after major damage inflicted during the Cultural Revolution. Before it opened as a museum in 1985, the buildings were used as Beijing No. 2 Food Factory. The bells here range from a giant 7 meters (23 feet) high to hand-sized chimes, many of them corroded to a pale green by time.

The giant, two-story bell, inscribed with the texts of more than 100 Buddhist scriptures (230,000 Chinese characters), is also said to be China's loudest. Believed to have been cast during Emperor Yongle's reign, the sound of this 46-ton relic can carry more than 15 km (10 miles) when struck forcibly. The bell rings 108 times on special occasions like Spring Festival, one strike for each of the 108 personal worries defined in Buddhism. People used to throw coins into a hole in the top of the bell for luck. The money was swept up by the monks and used to buy food. Enough money was collected in a month to buy provisions that would last for a year. ■TIP→ **You can ride the subway to the temple:**

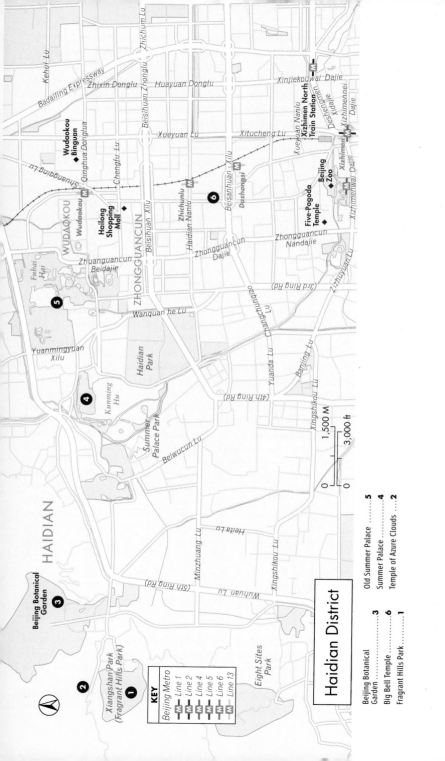

Haidian District

KEY

Beijing Metro
- Ⓜ Line 1
- Ⓜ Line 2
- Ⓜ Line 4
- Ⓜ Line 5
- Ⓜ Line 6
- Ⓜ Line 13

transfer from Dongzhimen on Line 2 to the aboveground Line 13 and go one stop north to Dazhong Si station. ⌧ *1A Beisanhuanxi Lu, Haidian District* ☎ *010/8213–2630* ☜ *Y20* ⊘ *Tues.–Sun. 9–4:30* Ⓜ *Dazhong Si.*

Fragrant Hills Park (香山公园 *Xiāngshān gōngyuán*). Once an imperial retreat, Xiangshan Park is better known as "Fragrant Hills Park." From the eastern gate you can hike to the summit on a trail dotted with small temples. If you're short on time, ride a cable car to the top. Note that the park becomes extremely crowded on pleasant fall weekends, when Beijingers turn out en masse to view the changing colors of the autumn leaves. ⌧ *Haidian District* ☎ *010/6259–1155* ☜ *Y10, one-way cable car Y60* ⊘ *Daily 6–6.*

Fodor's Choice
★

Old Summer Palace (圆明园 *Yuánmíngyuán*). About the size of New York's Central Park, this ruin was once a grand collection of palaces—the emperor's summer retreat from the 15th century to 1860, when it was looted and blown up by British and French soldiers. More than 90% of the original structures were Chinese-style wooden buildings, but only the European-style stone architecture (designed after Versailles by Jesuits and added during the Qing Dynasty) survived the fires. Many of the priceless relics that were looted are still on display in European museums, and China's efforts to recover them have been mostly unsuccessful. Beijing has chosen to preserve the vast ruin as a "monument to China's national humiliation," though the patriotic slogans that were once scrawled on the rubble have now been cleaned off.

The palace is made up of three idyllic parks: Yuanmingyuan (Garden of Perfection and Light) in the west, Wanchunyuan (Garden of 10,000 Springs) in the south, and Changchunyuan (Garden of Everlasting Spring) where the ruins are like a surreal graveyard to European architecture. Here you'll find ornately carved columns, squat lion statues, and crumbling stone blocks that lie like fallen dominoes. An engraved concrete wall maze, known as Huanghuazhen (Yellow Flower), twists and turns around a European-style pavilion. Recently restored and located just to the left of the west gate of Changchunyuan, it was once the site of lantern parties during midautumn festivals. Palace maids would race each other to the pavilion carrying lotus lanterns. The park costs an extra Y15 to enter, but it's well worth it. The park and ruins take on a ghostly beauty if you come after a fresh snowfall. There's also skating on the lake when it's frozen over. ■TIP➔ **It's a long trek to the European ruins from the main gate. Electric carts buzz around the park; hop on one heading to Changchunyuan if you feel tired. Tickets are Y5.**

If you want to save money, travel there by subway; get out at Yuanmingyuan Park Station on Line 4. ⌧ *28 Qinghua Xilu, northeast of the Summer Palace, Haidian District* ☎ *010/6262–8501* ☜ *Park Y10; extra Y15 fee for sites* ⊘ *Apr.–Oct., daily 7–6:30; Nov.–Mar., daily 7–5:30.* Ⓜ *Yuanmingyuan Park.*

Fodor's Choice
★

Summer Palace (颐和园 *Yíhéyuán*). Emperor Qianlong commissioned this giant royal retreat for his mother's 60th birthday in 1750. Anglo–French forces plundered, then burned, many of the palaces in 1860, and funds were diverted from China's naval budget for the renovations. Empress Dowager Cixi retired here in 1889. Nine years later it was here

The marble ruins of the Old Summer Palace can be found in Changchunyuan (Garden of Everlasting Spring).

that she imprisoned her nephew, Emperor Guangxu, after his reform movement failed. In 1903, she moved the seat of government from the Forbidden City to the Summer Palace, from which she controlled China until her death in 1908.

Nowadays the place is undoubtedly romantic. Pagodas and temples perch on hillsides; rowboats dip under arched stone bridges; and willow branches brush the water. The greenery is a relief from the loud, bustling city. It also teaches a fabulous history lesson. You can see firsthand the results of corruption: the opulence here was bought with siphoned money as China crumbled, while suffering repeated humiliations at the hands of colonialist powers. The entire gardens were for the Empress Dowager's exclusive use. UNESCO placed the Summer Palace on its World Heritage list in 1998.

The **Hall of Benevolent Longevity** is where Cixi held court and received foreign dignitaries. It's said that the first electric lights in China shone here. Just behind the hall and next to the lake is the **Hall of Jade Ripples**, where Cixi kept the hapless Guangxu under guard while she ran China in his name. Strung with pagodas and temples, including the impressive Tower of the Fragrance of Buddha, Glazed Tile Pagoda, and the Hall that Dispels Clouds, **Longevity Hill** is the place where you can escape the hordes of visitors—take your time exploring the lovely northern side of the hill.

Most of this 700-acre park is underwater. **Kunming Lake** makes up around three-fourths of the complex, and is largely man-made. The excavated dirt was used to build Longevity Hill. This giant body of water extends southward for 3 km (2 miles); it's ringed by tree-lined dikes, arched stone bridges, and numerous gazebos. In winter, you can skate on the ice. The less-traveled southern shore near Humpbacked Bridge is an ideal picnic spot.

At the west end of the lake you'll find the **Marble Boat**, which doesn't actually float and was built by Dowager Empress Cixi with money meant for the navy. The **Long Corridor** is a wooden walkway that skirts the northern shoreline of Kunming Lake for about half a mile until it reaches the marble boat. The ceiling and wooden rafters of the Long Corridor are richly painted with thousands of scenes from legends and nature—be on the lookout for Sun Wukong (the Monkey King). Cixi's home, in the Hall of Joyful Longevity, is near the beginning of the Long Corridor. The residence is furnished and decorated as Cixi left it. Her private theater, called the **Grand Theater Building**, just east of the hall, was constructed for her 60th birthday and cost 700,000 taels of silver.

Subway Line 4 stops at the Summer Palace. Get off at Beigongmen and take exit C for the easiest access to the north gate of the park. Otherwise, you'll have to take a taxi. It's best to come early in the morning to get a head start before the busloads of visitors arrive. You'll need the better part of a day to explore the grounds. Automatic audio guides can be rented for Y40 at stalls near the ticket booth. ⊠ *Yiheyuan Lu and Kunminghu Lu, 12 km (7½ miles) northwest of downtown Beijing, Haidian District* ☎ *010/6288–1144* ⊕ *www.summerpalace-china.com* 🎫 *Y60 summer (all-inclusive), Y50 winter (all-inclusive)* ☉ *Apr.–Oct., daily 6:30–6; Nov.–Mar., daily 7–5* Ⓜ *Beigongmen.*

WORTH NOTING

Temple of Azure Clouds (碧云寺 *Bìyún sì*). Once the home of a Yuan Dynasty official, the site was converted into a Buddhist temple in 1366 and enlarged during the 16th and 17th centuries by imperial eunuchs who hoped to be buried here. The temple's five main courtyards ascend a slope in **Fragrant Hills Park**. Although severely damaged during the Cultural Revolution, the complex has been beautifully restored.

The main attraction is the Indian-influenced **Vajra Throne Pagoda**. Lining its walls and five pagodas are gracefully carved stone-relief Buddhas and bodhisattvas. The pagoda once housed the remains of Nationalist China's founding father, Dr. Sun Yat-sen, who lay in state here between March and May 1925, while his mausoleum was being constructed in Nanjing. A hall in one of the temple's western courtyards houses about 500 life-size wood and gilt statues of arhats (Buddhists who have reached enlightenment)—each displayed in a glass case. ⊠ *Xiangshan Park, Haidian District* ☎ *010/6259–1155* 🎫 *Park Y10, temple Y10* ☉ *Daily 9–5.*

WHERE TO EAT

Since imperial times, Beijing has drawn citizens from all corners of China, and the country's economic boom has only accelerated the culinary diversity of the capital. These days, diners can find food from the myriad cuisines of far-flung regions of China, as well as just about every kind of international food.

Highlights include rare fungi and flowers from Yunnan, chili-strewn Hunan cooking from Mao's home province, Tibetan yak and *tsampa* (barley flour), mutton kebabs and grilled flatbreads from Xinjiang, numbingly spicy Sichuan cuisine, and chewy noodles from Shaanxi. And then there are ethnic foods from all over, with some—notably Italian, Japanese, and Korean—in abundance.

You can spend as little as $5 per person for a decent meal or $100 and up on a lavish banquet. The variety of venues is also part of the fun, with five-star hotel dining rooms, holes-in-the-wall, and refurbished courtyard houses all represented. Reservations are always a good idea, especially for higher-end places, so ask your hotel to book you a table.

Beijingers tend to eat dinner around 6 pm, and many local restaurants will have closed their kitchens by 9 pm, though places that stay open until the wee hours aren't hard to find. Tipping is not the custom although some larger, international restaurants will add a 15% service charge to the bill, as do five-star hotel restaurants. Be aware before you go out that small and medium venues only take cash payments or local bank cards; more established restaurants usually accept credit cards. *Use the coordinates (✣ A1) at the end of each listing to locate a site on the corresponding map.*

WHAT IT COSTS IN YUAN

	$	$$	$$$	$$$$
Restaurants	under Y100	Y100–Y150	Y151–Y200	over Y200

Prices are the average cost of a main dish at dinner or, if dinner isn't served, at lunch.

DONGCHENG DISTRICT

$ FRENCH
🍴 **Café de la Poste** (云游驿 *Yúnyóu yì*). In almost every French village or town there's a Café de la Poste, a humble hangout for a coffee, a beer, or a simple family meal. This haunt is just that: friendly service and a range of good-value bistro fare like steaks (including an excellent steak tartare), appetizers like grilled goat-cheese salad, free baskets of bread, and carafes of French wine. On weekend evenings it packs out with a pre-party expat crowd and leather-clad members of Beijing's affable motorcycle community; dancing on tables is not altogether uncommon. [$] *Average main: Y100* ✉ *58 Yonghegong Dajie, Dongcheng District* ☎ *010/6402–7047* 🌐 *www.cafedelaposte.net* 💳 *No credit cards* [M] *Yonghegong* ✣ *E2.*

$$$$ ECLECTIC Fodor's Choice ★
🍴 **Capital M.** This is one of the few restaurants in the capital with both stunning views and food worthy of the divine setting in front of Tiananmen Square. Australian-influenced classics with a Mediterranean twist are the order of the day here, served amid a vibrantly modern, muraled interior. Try the crispy suckling pig or roast leg of lamb, and save room for the famed pavlova dessert: a cloud of meringue and whipped cream sprinkled with fresh fruit. On weekends, hearty brunches and afternoon high tea are served. [$] *Average main: Y268* ✉ *2 Qianmen Pedestrian*

CHINESE CUISINE

We use the following regions in our restaurant reviews.

Beijing: As the seat of government for several dynasties, Beijing has evolved a cuisine that melds the culinary traditions of many regions. Specialties include Peking duck, *zhajiang* noodles, flash-boiled tripe with sesame sauce, and a wide variety of sweet snacks.

Cantonese: A diverse cuisine that roasts, fries, braises, and steams. Spices are used in moderation, and flavors are light and delicate. Dishes include wonton soup, steamed fish or scallops, barbecued pork, roasted goose and duck, and dim sum.

Chinese: Catchall term used for restaurants that serve cuisine from multiple regions of China.

Guizhou: The two key condiments in Guizhou's spicy-sour cuisine are *zao lajiao* (pounded dried peppers brined in salt) and fermented tomatoes (the latter used to make the region's hallmark sour fish soup (*suantangyu*).

Hunan: Chili peppers, ginger, garlic, dried salted black beans, and preserved vegetables are the mainstays of this "dry spicy" cuisine. Signature dishes include "red-braised" pork, steamed fish head with diced salted chilies, and cured pork with smoked bean curd.

Northern Chinese: A catch-all category encompassing the hearty stews and stuffed buns of Dongbei, the refined banquet fare of Shandong, Inner Mongolian hotpot, lamb and flat breads of Xinjiang, and the wheat noodles of Shaanxi Province.

Shanghainese and Jiangzhe: Cuisine characterized by rich, sweet flavors produced by braising and stewing, and the extensive use of rice wine. Signatures include steamed hairy crabs and "drunken chicken."

Sichuan (central province): Famed for bold flavors and "*mala*" spiciness created by combining chilies and mouth-numbing Sichuan pepper-corns. Dishes include kung pao chicken, mapo doufu (tofu), *dandan* noodles, twice-cooked pork, and tea-smoked duck.

Taiwanese: This diverse cuisine centers on seafood. Specialties include oyster omelets, cuttlefish soup, and "three cups chicken," with a sauce made of soy sauce, rice wine, and sugar.

Tibetan: Cuisine reliant on foodstuffs that can grow at high altitudes, including barley flour, yak meat, milk, butter, and cheese.

Yunnan (southern province): This region is noted for its use of vegetables, fresh herbs, and mushrooms in its spicy preparations. Dishes include "crossing the bridge" rice noodle soup with chicken, pork, and fish; cured Yunnan ham with Bai-style goat cheese; and steamed or grilled fish with lemongrass.

St., Dongcheng District ☎ *010/6702–2727* ⊕ *www.m-restaurantgroup. com* 🍴 *Reservations essential* Ⓜ *Qianmen* ✥ *D5.*

$ ✕**Crescent Moon** (弯弯的月亮 *Wānwānde yuèliang*). Unlike many of
ASIAN the bigger Xinjiang restaurants in town, there's no song and dance performance at this Uygur family-run spot, and none needed, as the solid cooking stands on its own merits. The heaping platters of grilled lamb skewers, *da pan ji* (chicken, potato, and green pepper stew), homemade yogurt, and freshly baked flatbreads are all terrific, as are the light and dark Xinjiang beers available here. The traditional green-and-white Islamic decor, Uygur CDs playing on the stereo, and clouds of hookah smoke lend an authentic Central Asian atmosphere to the dining experience. Ⓢ *Average main: Y60* ✉ *16 Dongsi Liutiao, Dongcheng District* ☎ *010/6400–5281* 🚫 *No credit cards* Ⓜ *Zhangzizhonglu* ✥ *E3.*

$$ ✕**Dali Courtyard** (大理 *Dàlǐ*). Yunnan Province's tranquility and bohe-
YUNNAN mian spirit are captured in this enchanting traditional courtyard house,
Fodor's Choice a 10-minute walk from the Drum and Bell towers. On breezy summer
★ nights the best seats are in the central courtyard with its overflowing greenery; these are popular, so reservations are essential. The restaurant offers only set menus for the table, starting at Y150 per person. Expect aromatic grilled fish, stir-fried Yunnan mushrooms, delicious mint-infused salads, and in-season vegetable dishes. Ⓢ *Average main: Y150* ✉ *67 Xiaojingchang Hutong, Gulou Dong Dajie, Dongcheng District* ☎ *010/8404–1430* Ⓜ *Guloudajie* ✥ *D2.*

$ ✕**Deyuan Roast Duck** (德缘烤鸭店 *Dé yuán kǎoyā diàn*). This unsung
NORTHERN Peking duck restaurant deserves a wider following. A typically lively
CHINESE dining room packs in locals for its traditional take on the capital's signature quacker, which is roasted over fruit wood, carved table-side, and sold at a price that ought to make the bigger restaurants like Quanjude and Bianyifang blush. Beijing's ruling triumvirate of traditional meat (mutton, duck, donkey) comes in many tasty forms here, and there are a wealth of appealing stir-fries and dry pot dishes that use beef, bacon, shrimp, tofu, and country vegetables. Only about a decade old and with no "time-honored" status to fall back on, Deyuan simply cooks great food at great prices. Ⓢ *Average main: Y80* ✉ *57 Dashilan Xijie, Dongcheng District* ☎ *010/6308–5371* Ⓜ *Qianmen* ✥ *C5.*

$$ ✕**Hani Geju** (哈尼个旧餐厅 *Hāní gèjiù cāntīng*). A stone's throw from
YUNNAN the Bell Tower, this cozy Yunnan restaurant boasts a trimmed down menu of southwest Chinese fare, such as authentic Bai-minority goat cheese with bacon (smoked in-house), fluffy-centered potato balls with an addictively crisp coating, zingy mint salads, and delicate rice noodle dishes. The emphasis here is on organic sourcing, moderate seasoning, and no MSG. Innovative taster platters at lunchtime means you can sample their best dishes in mini, single-serving portions. After your meal, take a stroll through the surrounding warren of hutong alleyways, some of the most atmospheric in the city. Ⓢ *Average main: Y110* ✉ *48 Zhonglouwan Hutong, Southeast of Bell Tower, Dongcheng District* ☎ *010/6401–3318* Ⓜ *Guloudajie* ✥ *D2.*

$ ✕**Jin Ding Xuan** (金鼎轩酒楼 *Jīndǐngxuān jiǔlóu*). Clad in red neon
CANTONESE after dark, this jovial dim sum restaurant offers four bustling floors of great-value dishes around the clock. Expect to wait in line at busy

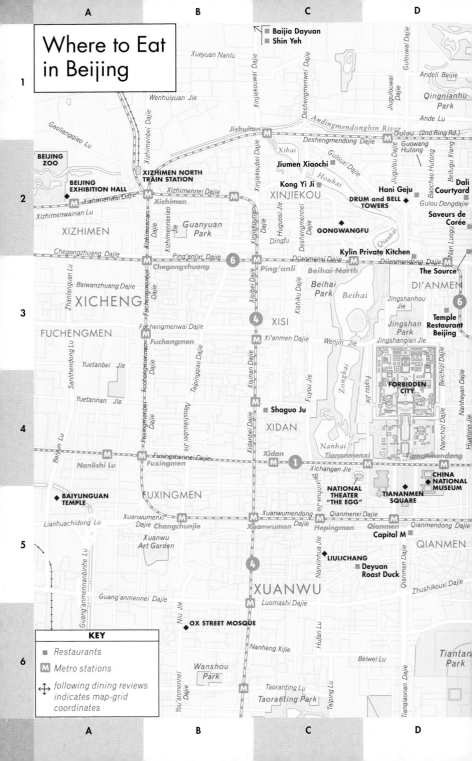

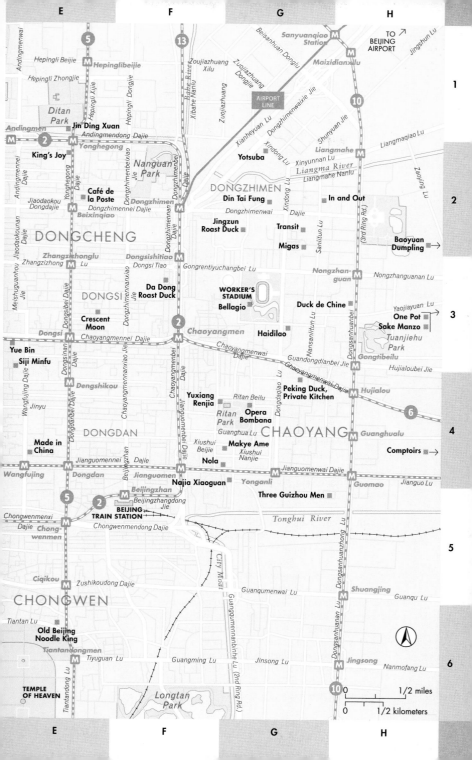

periods; once inside, keep an eye out for the cold dish and drink carts wheeling by. The menu is extensive and service is regimented—you won't go wrong with an order of shrimp dumplings, fried turnip cake with Cantonese sausage, and tender braised steak served in a clay pot. A recent addition is the "pollution menu"—new dishes that claim to counteract the effects of Beijing's smog. $ *Average main: Y70* ✉ *77 Hepingli Xijie, Dongcheng District* ☎ *010/6429–6699* Ⓜ *Yonghegong* ✛ *E1.*

$$$$

VEGETARIAN

Fodor's Choice

★

✕ **King's Joy** (京兆尹 *Jīng zhào yǐn*). The chefs at this elegantly upscale vegetarian restaurant enact miracles with tofu, mushroom, and wheat gluten. Try the sweet and sour "ribs" made from lotus root, then the rich and earthy basil-braised eggplant, and finish with glutinous rice tarts (*ai wo wo*) filled with sweet red bean paste and crunchy walnuts. The building, designed to resemble Beijing's traditional quadrangle courtyards (*siheyuan*), is enhanced by views of the Lama Temple across the street, as well as the crisp white tablecloths, fresh orchids, and harp performances inside. $ *Average main: Y250* ✉ *2 Wudaoying Hutong, Yonghegong, Dongcheng District* ☎ *010/8404-9191* Ⓜ *Yonghegong* ✛ *E2.*

$

CHINESE FUSION

✕ **Kylin Private Kitchen** (麒麟阁私房菜 *Qílín gé sīfáng cài*). The skylit, plant-strewn interior of this small hidden gem is a pleasant spot to linger over the excellent contemporary Chinese food, which often blends various styles and techniques. A highlight of the compact menu is the *zhiguo* ("paper pot") dishes, featuring fragrant shrimp or green beans served in a Japanese-style paper pot over a flame. Most diners order the *zijiangyu*, an aromatic fish stew cooked with chilies, purple ginger, and fresh Sichuan peppercorns: choose from three types of fish and three levels of spiciness. The restaurant is in a narrow alley that once housed imperial midwives during the Ming Dynasty. $ *Average main: Y100* ✉ *6 Qilin Bei Hutong, Dongcheng District* ☎ *010/6407–3516* Ⓜ *Nanluoguxiang* ✛ *D2.*

$$$

NORTHERN CHINESE

Fodor's Choice

★

✕ **Made In China** (长安壹号 *Cháng'ān yīhào*). The glassed-in kitchens at this Grand Hyatt restaurant are like theater for foodies. White-robed chefs twirl floury noodles as beautifully bronzed Peking ducks are hooked on poles out of tall brick ovens. Tradition rules when it comes to Executive Chef Jin's famous duck, and eating it is a three-stage process: skin dipped in sugar, then breast meat with scallions, and finally pancakes stuffed with leg meat, skin, hoisin, cucumber, and minced garlic. The trick, says Jin, is to roll the pancakes small enough to eat in one mouthful. $ *Average main: Y200* ✉ *Grand Hyatt, 1 Dong Chang An Jie, Dongcheng District* ☎ *010/8518–1234* ✍ *Reservations essential* Ⓜ *Wangfujing* ✛ *E4.*

$

NORTHERN CHINESE

✕ **Old Beijing Noodle King** (老北京炸酱面大王 *Lǎo Běijīng zhájiàngmiàn dàwáng*). This chain of noodle houses serves hand-pulled noodles and traditional local dishes in a lively, old-time atmosphere, with waiters shouting across the room to announce customers arriving. Try the classic *zhajiang* noodle, served in a ground-meat sauce with accompaniments of celery, bean sprouts, green beans, soybeans, slivers of cucumber, and red radish. $ *Average main: Y30* ✉ *56 Dong Xinglong Jie, Dongcheng District* ☎ *010/6701–9393* ▭ *No credit cards* Ⓜ *Chongwenmen* ✛ *E6.*

Street food is ubiquitous in Beijing; kebabs, from China's northwest, are local favorites.

$$ × Saveurs de Corée (韩香馆 *Hán xiāng guǎn*). This long-standing
KOREAN Korean restaurant, which has moved with the times, remains the best
contemporary option in the vicinity of Nanluogu Xiang. The redesigned
central courtyard is a delightful setting to sample signature fragrant
sliced beef with shiitake mushrooms, "seafood pizza" (a light frittata
with kimchi, shrimp, and squid), and the simply divine chicken soup,
made with Korean ginseng and a whole organic chicken. An adjoining
bar serves Korean-inspired cocktails heavy on soju, a Korean vodka.
Carnivores take note: the same owners run Korean barbecue restaurant
at nearby Xiang'er Hutong. $ *Average main: Y120* ✉ *20 Juer Hutong,
off Nanluoguxiang, Dongcheng District* ☎ *010/6401–6083* Ⓜ *Nan-
luoguxiang* ✛ *D5.*

$ × Siji Minfu (四季民福烤鸭店 *Sìjì mín fú kǎoyā diàn*). Here's a rare
NORTHERN thing: a local restaurant chain that insists on seasonality and says no to
CHINESE MSG. Folks line up out the door for the Peking duck, expertly roasted
so that the skin shatters while the flesh remains unctuously tender. Also
popular is the *zhajiang main*, Beijing's austere signature dish of chewy
wheat noodles topped with a rich meat sauce and crunchy vegetable
accompaniments. A traditional dessert platter includes *wandouhuang*, a
dense, sweet cake made from white peas, and *ludagun* (literally "rolling
donkey"), a sticky rice cake so named because its dusting of soybean
flour resembles a donkey that has rolled on the ground. $ *Average
main: Y90* ✉ *Donghua Hotel, 32 Dengshikou Xijie, Wangfujing Dajie,
Dongcheng District* ☎ *010/6513–5141* Ⓜ *Dengshikou* ✛ *E4.*

$$$ × The Source (都江源 *Dōujiāngyuán*). The Source dishes up dainty set
SICHUAN menus of Sichuan-inspired favorites (RMB 188 or 288 per person) in a
romantic, historic courtyard. Dishes change according to seasonality,

but you can expect several hot and cold appetizers, meat and seafood dishes, and a few surprise concoctions from the chef, all tweaked for international palates (the waitresses will ask how spicy you like your food). On a peaceful hutong intersecting busy Nanluogu Xiang, the building was once the backyard of a Qing Dynasty general referred to by the imperial court as "The Great Wall of China" for his military exploits. The grounds have been painstakingly restored; an upper level overlooks a small garden shaded by pomegranate and date trees. $ *Average main: Y188* ⊠ *14 Banchang Hutong, Kuanjie, Dongcheng District* ☎ *010/6400–3736* ⚇ *Reservations essential* Ⓜ *Nanluoguxiang* ✛ *D2.*

$$$$
MODERN
EUROPEAN
Fodor's Choice
★

✕ **Temple Restaurant Beijing.** Worship at the altar of Epicureanism and surround yourself with serenity at the city's best international fine-dining restaurant, nestled in the heart of Old Beijing. TRB (as it's also known) serves high-end European cuisine in a spacious, minimalist dining room within a fabulously restored Ming Dynasty Buddhist temple complex. The four-course tasting menu (Y458) includes dishes such as all-day braised short rib with burdock chips, and house-cured gravlax served table-side by Ignace, the most charming restaurateur in town. The wine list is excellent, with a deep focus on Champagne, Bordeaux, and Burgundy. $ *Average main: Y250* ⊠ *23 Songzhusi, Shatan Beijie, Dongcheng District* ☎ *010/8400–2232* ⊕ *www.temple-restaurant.com* ⚇ *Reservations essential* Ⓜ *National Art Museum* ✛ *D3.*

$
CHINESE

✕ **Yue Bin** (悦宾饭馆 *Yuèbīn fànguǎn*). Yue Bin was the first private restaurant to open in Beijing after the Cultural Revolution era, and its home-style cooking still attracts neighborhood residents, as well as hungry visitors from the nearby National Art Museum. The tiny, no-frills dining room is just big enough for half a dozen tables, where you'll see families chowing down on specialties such as *suanni zhouzi*, garlic-marinated braised pork shoulder; *guota doufuhe*, tofu pockets stuffed with minced pork; and *wusitong*, a spring roll filled with duck and vegetables. $ *Average main: Y50* ⊠ *43 Cuihua Hutong, Dongcheng District* ☎ *010/6524–5322* ▭ *No credit cards* Ⓜ *National Art Museum* ✛ *E3.*

XICHENG DISTRICT

$
ECLECTIC

✕ **Jiumen Xiaochi** (九门小吃). A dozen well-known restaurants, some dating back more than a century and threatened by the urban renewal of the old Qianmen business district, have found refuge in this large traditional courtyard house in Xiaoyou Hutong. Some of Beijing's oldest and most famous eateries have regrouped here under one roof, and it's become a popular tourist draw. These are our favorites: **Baodu Feng.** This vendor specializes in tripe. The excellent accompanying dipping sauce is a long-guarded family secret. You'll see upon entering that this stall has the longest line. **Chatang Li.** On offer here is *miancha*, a flour paste with either sweet or salty toppings. Miancha was created by an imperial chef who ground millet, poured boiling water into it, mixed it into a paste, and added brown sugar and syrup. The imperial family loved it, and it soon became a breakfast staple. **Niangao Qian.** This stall makes sticky rice layered with red-bean paste. It's the most popular sticky rice snack made by the Hui, or Chinese Muslims. **Yangtou Ma.**

Known for thin-sliced meat from boiled lamb's head, this shop was once located on Ox Street, in the old Muslim quarter. **Doufunao Bai.** These folks sell soft bean curd, recognized for its delicate texture. It's best topped with braised lamb and mushrooms. **En Yuan Ju.** Sample the chaogeda, which are small, stir-fried noodles with vegetables and meat. **Yue Sheng Zhai.** Line up for excellent *jiang niurou* (braised beef), *shao yangrou* (braised lamb), and *zasui tang* (mutton soup). **Xiaochang Chen.** The main ingredient of this vendor's dish is intestines, complemented with pork, bean curd, and *huoshao* (unleavened baked bread). The contents are simmered slowly in an aromatic broth. **Dalian Huoshao.** This stall serves pot stickers in the shape of old-fashioned satchels that the Chinese once wore. These pot stickers were the creation of the Yao family of Shunyi, who set up their small restaurant in the old Dong'an Market in 1876. $ *Average main: Y90* ⌂ *1 Xiaoyou Hutong, Gulou Xidajie, just off Houhai lake, Xicheng District* ✛ *C2.*

$$
SHANGHAINESE
✕ **Kong Yi Ji** (孔乙己 *Kǒngyǐjǐ*). Named for the down-and-out protagonist of a short story by Lu Xun (one of China's most famous writers), the exhaustive menu at this elegant restaurant features dishes from Lu's hometown of Shaoxing, near Shanghai. Expect light, delicate offerings such as *longjing xiaren*—plump, peeled shrimp poached in aromatic green tea until ethereally soft. Also served is a wide selection of the region's famed *huangjiu* (sweet rice wine); it comes in heated silver pots and you sip from a shallow ceramic cup. The peaceful lakeside location is a perfect launching point for an after-dinner stroll; private rooms on the second floor have balconies with lovely lake views. $ *Average main: Y110* ⌂ *Southwest shore of Houhai, Deshengmennei Dajie, Xicheng District* ☎ *010/6618–4915* Ⓜ *Shichahai* ✛ *C2.*

$
CHINESE
✕ **Shaguo Ju** (沙锅居 *Shāguō jū*). Established in 1741, this time-honored brand serves a long-standing Manchu favorite—*bairou*, or "white-meat" pork casserole, which consists of thin strips of fatty pork concealing bok choy and glass noodles below. *Shaguo* is the Chinese term for a casserole pot, and there are many others on the menu at this perennially busy restaurant. Historically, Shaguo Ju emerged as a result of ceremonies held by imperial officials and wealthy Manchus in the Qing Dynasty, which included sacrificial offerings of whole pigs. The meat offerings were later given away to the city's night watchmen, who shared the "gifts" with friends and relatives. Such gatherings gradually turned into a small business, and the popularity of "white meat" became more widespread. $ *Average main: Y60* ⌂ *60 Xisi Nan Dajie, Xicheng District* ☎ *010/6602–1126* ▭ *No credit cards* Ⓜ *Xidan* ✛ *C4.*

CHAOYANG DISTRICT

$
NORTHERN
CHINESE
✕ **Baoyuan Dumpling** (宝源饺子屋 *Bǎo yuán jiǎozi wū*). The fillings at this cheerfully homey joint go far beyond the standard pork and cabbage—the photo-filled menu includes dozens of creative filling options, including beef, lamb, seafood, smoked bean curd, noodles, and just about every vegetable you can name, many wrapped in bright skins of purple, green, and orange, thanks to the addition of vegetable juice to the dough. The minimum order for any kind of dumpling is two *liang* (100 grams, or about 10 dumplings). There's a separate menu with

a solid selection of family-style Chinese dishes—you'll see the popular *mapo doufu* (spoon-soft tofu with ground pork in a mildly spiced sauce) on many tables. $ *Average main: Y50* ⊠ *North of 6 Maizidian Jie, Chaoyang District* ☎ *010/6586–4967* ▭ *No credit cards* ✛ *H2.*

$$
TAIWANESE

✕ **Bellagio** (鹿港小镇 *Lùgǎng xiǎo zhèn*). This popular chain of glitzy, see-and-be-seen restaurants dishes up Taiwanese favorites to a largely young and upwardly mobile clientele. A delicious choice is the "three-cup chicken" (*sanbeiji*), served in a sizzling pot fragrant with ginger, garlic, and basil, and the wonderful crispy fried mixed mushrooms with XO sauce. Finish your meal with a Taiwan-style mountain of crushed ice topped with condensed milk and beans, mangoes, strawberries, or peanuts. This branch, beside the Workers Stadium, is open until 4 am, making it a favorite with Beijing's clubbers. The smartly dressed staff—clad in black and white—sport identical short haircuts. $ *Average main: Y140* ⊠ *6 Gongti Xilu, Chaoyang District* ☎ *010/6551–3533* ✛ *G3.*

$
FRENCH

✕ **Comptoirs de France Bakery** (法派 *Fǎpài*). This small chain of contemporary French-managed patisseries is Beijing's go-to spot for Gallic cakes, pastries, and tarts. A variety of other goodies are on offer, like airy macaroons, flaky croissants, sandwiches in crunchy home-baked baguettes, and savory croquettes and quiches. Beside the standard coffee options, Comptoirs has a choice of unusual hot chocolate flavors. Try the Sichuan pepper–infused variety, which has a mouth-tingling kick. $ *Average main: Y80* ⊠ *China Central Place, Bldg. 15, N. 102, 89 Jianguo Lu(just northeast of Xiandai Soho), Chaoyang District* ☎ *010/6530–5480* ⊕ *www.comptoirsdefrance.com* ▭ *No credit cards* Ⓜ *Dawanglu* ✛ *H4.*

$$$
NORTHERN
CHINESE
Fodor's Choice
★

✕ **Da Dong Roast Duck** (北京大董烤鸭店 *Běijīng Dàdǒng kǎoyā diàn*). You won't go wrong with the namesake dish at this world-famous eatery. Chef Dadong's version combines crisp, caramel-hued skin over meat less oily than tradition dictates, and is served with crisp sesame pockets in addition to the usual steamed pancakes. But the duck is only half the story. Dadong is an innovative chef and a student of many culinary styles, and his tome-like menu has some of the most original and luxe dishes in the city. Noodles are made from lobster meat, wafer-thin Kobe steaks are blow-torched table-side, and braised thorny sea cucumber is paired with a fresh lemon sorbet. Several locations offer various levels of decor and ambience; this one strikes the best balance between bling and tradition. $ *Average main: Y180* ⊠ *1–2 Nanxincang Guoji Dasha, 22 Dongsishitiao, Chaoyang District* ☎ *010/5169–0328* ⌂ *Reservations essential* Ⓜ *Dongsishitiao* ✛ *F3.*

$$
TAIWANESE
Fodor's Choice
★

✕ **Din Tai Fung** (鼎泰丰 *Dǐngtàifēng*). Taipei's best known restaurant, now with several branches in Beijing, specializes in *xiaolong bao*—steamed dumplings filled with piping hot, aromatic soup. Crafted to an exacting standard, there are several beautifully wrapped variations on the standard pork ones, such as crab, chicken, shrimp, or a luxurious pork and black truffle variety. The *dandan* noodles, vegetable dishes, fried rice, and sweet dessert dumplings are also excellent. Service is friendly and efficient, and the dining room strikes an easy balance between refined and casual. $ *Average main: Y150* ⊠ *24 Xinyuan Xili*

Zhongjie, Chaoyang District ☎ *010/6462–4502* 🌐 *www.dintaifung.com.cn* ✥ *G2.*

$$$$ CHINESE Fodor's Choice ★ 🍴 **Duck de Chine** (全鸭季 *Quányājì*). At what is hands-down the city's tastiest destination for Peking duck, the lacquered skin is simply more aromatically flavorful than the competition. Cantonese father-son chef duo Peter and Wilson Lam spent months formulizing the perfect bird, roasted for exactly 65 minutes over jujube wood. The house-made sauce is a fabulous piece of food theater, and supporting dishes—order the duck liver on toast—are largely faultless. A daily lunchtime dim sum deal is excellent value. The simplicity of the loft-like, industrial space extends to the chefs, who in slate-gray robes wheel out each duck to the sound of a gong. A bottle of Bollinger from the adjoining Champagne bar is claimed to be the perfect pairing, but the crisp prosecco, at a fraction of the price, cuts through the rich, oily duck just as well. If it's fully booked, there is a newer, larger location on Jinbao Jie. [$] *Average main: Y220* ✉ *1949 The Hidden City, Courtyard 4, Gongti Beilu, Behind Pacific Century Place, Chaoyang District* ☎ *010/6501–8881* [M] *Tuanjiehu* ✥ *H3.*

$ CHINESE Fodor's Choice ★ 🍴 **Haidilao** (海底捞 *Hǎidǐlāo huǒguō*). You can expect to wait for a table at this trendy hotpot haven, but fortunately there's plenty to do while you're in line. Enjoy a complimentary manicure or shoeshine and munch on crunchy snacks to whet your appetite for the main draw: bubbling pots of broth (spices optional), a variety of thinly sliced meat, fresh veggies, greens, mushrooms, and more for dipping, and a DIY sauce bar with loads of choices. Order the "kungfu noodles," then sit back and marvel as a waiter twirls the noodles expertly at your table. More than a dozen locations are around town. [$] *Average main: Y90* ✉ *2A Baijiazhuang Lu, Chaoyang District* ☎ *010/6595–2982* 🌐 *www.haidilao.com* ✥ *G3.*

$ YUNNAN 🍴 **In and Out** (一坐一忘 *Yīzuò yīwàng*). On a tree-lined street in the heart of Beijing's embassy district, this large, Yunnan restaurant, adorned with decorative crafts and paintings from China's southwest, serves as an excellent introduction to the light, fresh, and spicy flavors of the province. Staff in traditional dress dish up crispy potato pancakes, eggs stir-fried with fragrant jasmine flowers, tilapia folded over lemongrass and lightly grilled, and aromatic sticky rice stuffed inside long strips of bamboo. Comfy private rooms are perfect for groups; service can be rather absent at busy periods, so poke your head out of the door and holler. [$] *Average main: Y90* ✉ *1 Sanlitun Beixiaojie, Chaoyang District* ☎ *010/8454–0086* ✥ *G2.*

$ NORTHERN CHINESE 🍴 **Jingzun Roast Duck Restaurant.** Locals and foreigners alike pack out this pleasant mid-range restaurant for affordable roast duck and tasty, varied Chinese fare with a Beijing slant. The roadside patio, garlanded by twinkling Christmas lights, is a lovely spot for warm weather dining. Standout dishes include plump shrimp with lemongrass, stir-fried celery with smoked tofu, and the eye-wateringly hot Chinese mustard greens with sesame sauce. A basic wine list and local draft beer are available. To avoid disappointment, order your duck when you reserve a table. [$] *Average main: Y90* ✉ *4 Chunxiu Lu, opposite Holiday Inn Express, Chaoyang District* ☎ *010/6417–4075* ✥ *G2.*

$$ TIBETAN 🍴 **Makye Ame** (玛吉阿米 *Mǎjíāmǐ*). Fluttering prayer flags lead up to the second floor entrance of this Tibetan restaurant, where a pile of *mani* (prayer) stones and a large prayer wheel greet you. Elegant Tibetan Buddhist trumpets, lanterns, and handicrafts adorn the walls, and the kitchen serves a range of hearty dishes that run well beyond the region's staples of *tsampa* (roasted barley flour) and yak-butter tea. Try the vegetable *pakoda* (a deep-fried dough pocket filled with vegetables), curry potatoes, grilled mushrooms, and cumin-roasted lamb ribs. There are live Tibetan performances most nights. [$] *Average main: Y110* ✉ *11 Xiushui Nanjie, 2nd fl., Chaoyang District* ☎ *010/6506–9616* [M] *Jianguomen* ✥ *G4.*

$$ SPANISH Fodor's Choice ★ 🍴 **Migas** (米家思 *Mǐ jiā sī*). The fact that Beijing's hottest rooftop bar and nightclub becomes a sophisticated Spanish restaurant at mealtimes is quite the Houdini act. Most heralded for its terrific three-course lunch deal, which changes weekly, Migas is a whirlwind adventure in Spanish gastronomy, starring slow-roasted suckling pig, chicken grilled on a Josper oven, creamy cod with steamed eggplant, and "liquid bombons" with deliciously sticky fillings. Throw in complimentary baskets of home-baked bread, inventive amuse-bouches, and a funky, casual environment, and you can see why Beijing's young professionals have made this place their own. [$] *Average main: Y150* ✉ *Nali Patio, 81 Sanlitun Lu, 6th fl., Chaoyang District* ☎ *010/5208–6061* [M] *Tuanjiehu* ✥ *G2.*

$ NORTHERN CHINESE Fodor's Choice ★ 🍴 **Najia Xiaoguan** (那家小馆 *Nà jiā xiǎo guǎn*). The Manchu ruled all of China during the Qing Dynasty, but it is their roots as a semi-pastoral people living north of the Great Wall that are celebrated at this excellent restaurant. Dishes like pot-braised venison reflect the Manchu's love of hunting, and the hearty, tender ox ribs here would have been ideal fortification for the far northeast's freezing winters. Huge wooden tables, a decent wine list, and excellent service make the affordable fare here even more enjoyable; expect to wait for a table at peak times. [$] *Average main: Y90* ✉ *10 Yonganli, south of LG Twin Towers, Chaoyang District* ☎ *010/6567–3663* ✍ *Reservations essential* [M] *Yong'Anli* ✥ *G5.*

$ KOREAN 🍴 **One Pot.** Chef-owner Andrew Ahn has toned down the glamour at this excellent Korean restaurant, formerly known as Ssam, to focus on reinventing street snacks. Think *kimbap* (Korean-style sushi rolls), rich miso crab stew, and the unpronounceable *tteokbokki*—a popular street food of rice cakes and fish cakes in sweet chili sauce. The twist here is that the rice is stuffed with cheese and stewed table-side in a range of inventive sauces, such as pumpkin gravy. The tiramisu, made with a reduction of the Korean spirit *soju*, is one of the few Ssam survivors. After your meal, order a fabulous cup of coffee (the imported beans are ground table-side) to set you up for a drink or three in one of the many Sanlitun bars nearby. [$] *Average main: Y100* ✉ *Sanlitun SOHO, Gongti Beilu, Tower 2, B1–238, Chaoyang District* ☎ *010/5395–9475* [M] *Tuanjiehu* ✥ *H3.*

$$$$ ITALIAN Fodor's Choice ★ 🍴 **Opera Bombana.** Italian chef Umberto Bombana won three Michelin stars for his acclaimed Hong Kong restaurant. This Beijing franchise could be seen as a bit of a cash-in, though under the stewardship of former Sureno chef Marino D'Antonio it still makes a strong case for

being Beijing's best Italian, with delectable signatures like langoustine carpaccio, and Wagyu beef ravioli with pungent Gorgonzola sauce. It's a gorgeous dining environment, too, especially considering its location inside a high-end shopping mall. Opera Bombana is also serious about baking; grab a bag of *bomboloni* to go from the bakery counter—these sugary donuts filled with a rich lemony custard are sinfully good. $ *Average main: Y260* ✉ *Parkview Green, 9 Dongdaqiao Lu, LG2-21, Chaoyang District* ☎ *010/5690–7177* Ⓜ *Dongdaqiao* ✛ *G4.*

$$
NORTHERN CHINESE

✕ **Peking Duck, Private Kitchen** (私房烤鸭 *Guǒguǒ sīfáng kǎoyā*). Doing away with the banquet-style scene that accompanies the more traditional roast duckeries in Beijing, diners here lounge on comfortable sofas in a moderately sized, warmly lit dining room where the signature dish is made to exacting standards. The set menus, which all include succulent Peking duck, are good value and include other popular dishes such as kung pao shrimp and green beans in sesame sauce. $ *Average main: Y120* ✉ *Vantone Center, 6A Chaowai Dajie, FS2015, Chaoyang District* ☎ *010/5907–1920* ⊗ *No lunch.* Ⓜ *Dongdaqiao* ✛ *G4.*

$$
JAPANESE
Fodor's Choice
★

✕ **Sake Manzo.** As Beijing's best all-round Japanese *izakaya*-style restaurant, this is the place for frothy mugs of Asahi draft and perfectly executed dishes like beer-marinated fried chicken with vinegar, a crisp pork cutlet under a mound of diced greens, sublime soba noodles, and some of the best sushi and sashimi in the city for the price. A white-walled, bustling dining area gets the atmosphere just right; larger groups will be ushered to comfy private rooms with sunken seating. The slow-cooked pork belly in miso broth with a poached egg gets rave reviews. Ask the helpful waitstaff for sake recommendations. $ *Average main: Y140* ✉ *8A Tuanjiehu Beisitiao, Chaoyang District* ☎ *010/6436–1608* ✛ *H3.*

$
CHINESE

✕ **Three Guizhou Men** (三个贵州人 *Sāngeguìzhōurén*). The widespread popularity of Guizhou cuisine and its trademark spicy-sour flavors prompted three Guizhou artist friends to set up shop in Beijing (their paintings and sculptures decorate the dining area). There are many dishes here to recommend, but among the best are "beef on fire" (pieces of beef placed on a bed of chives over burning charcoal) accompanied by ground chilies; pork ribs; spicy lamb with mint leaves; the region's signature *suantangyu* (fish in a spicy-sour soup), and *mi doufu*, a rice-flour cake in spicy sauce. $ *Average main: Y90* ✉ *Jianwai SOHO, Bldg. 7, 39 Dong Sanhuan Zhonglu, Chaoyang District* ☎ *010/5869–0598* Ⓜ *Guomao* ✛ *G5.*

$$$
SICHUAN
Fodor's Choice
★

✕ **Transit** (渡金湖 *Dùjīnhú*). This is one of Beijing's hottest contemporary Chinese restaurants, and we're not just talking about the chilies. Located in the upscale Sanlitun Village North, this glam Sichuan establishment marries the region's famous spicy dishes with slick service and a designer interior entirely at home amid the surrounding luxury boutiques. The region's fiery classics are elegantly prepared; the *koushuiji* (cold chicken appetizer dressed in chili oil), the mouth-numbing *dandan* noodles, and the crisp stir-fried eel with chili have garnered rave reviews. Unlike most Chinese restaurants, Transit serves fabulous cocktails and has an extensive, if pricey, wine list. $ *Average main: Y160* ✉ *Sanlitun Village North, N4–36, Chaoyang District* ☎ *010/6417–9090* ✍ *Reservations essential* ⊗ *No lunch* ✛ *G2.*

$$$ JAPANESE Fodor's Choice ★ 🍴 **Yotsuba** (四叶 *Sìyè*). This tiny, unassuming restaurant serves arguably the best sushi in the city. The interior comprises a sushi counter manned by a Japanese master working continuously and silently, and two small sunken tatami-style dining areas that evoke an old-time Tokyo restaurant. The seafood is flown in from Tokyo's Tsukiji fish market; the daily chef's selection (about Y280) is a wooden board of sushi made from the best catches of the day. Reservations are a must for this dinner-only Chaoyang gem. There are three locations around town. [$] *Average main: Y200* ✉ *2 Xinyuan Xili Zhongjie, Bldg. 2, Chaoyang District* ☎ *010/6464–2365* ✍ *Reservations essential* ⊙ *No lunch* ✥ *G2.*

$ SICHUAN 🍴 **Yuxiang Renjia** (渝乡人家 *Yúxiāngrénjiā*). Of the thousands of Sichuan restaurants in Beijing, the Yuxiang Renjia chain is often the choice of Sichuan natives living in the capital. Huge earthen vats filled with pickled vegetables, hanging bunches of dried peppers and garlic, and servers in traditional garb evoke the Sichuan countryside. The restaurant does an excellent job with classics like *gongbao jiding* (diced chicken stir-fried with peanuts and dried peppers) and *ganbian sijidou* (green beans stir-fried with olive leaves and minced pork). Thirty different Sichuan snacks are served for lunch on weekends, all at very reasonable prices. There are more than a dozen locations around the city. [$] *Average main: Y70* ✉ *Lianhe Dasha, 101 Chaowai Dajie, 5th fl., Chaoyang District* ☎ *010/6588–3841* 🌐 *www.yuxiangrenjia.com* [M] *Chaoyangmen* ✥ *F4.*

HAIDIAN DISTRICT

$$$$ CHINESE 🍴 **Baijia Dayuan** (白家大宅门 *Báijiā dà zháimén*). Staff dressed in richly hued, Qing Dynasty attire welcome you at this grand courtyard house, the Bai family mansion. Bowing slightly, they'll say *"Nin jixiang"* ("May you have good fortune"). The mansion's spectacular setting was once the garden of Prince Li, son of the first Qing emperor. Cao Xueqin, the author of the Chinese classic *Dream of the Red Chamber,* is said to have lived here as a boy. Featured delicacies (ordered via an iPad) include bird's-nest soup, braised sea cucumber, abalone, and authentic imperial snacks. On weekends, diners are treated to short, live performances of Beijing opera. After dinner, explore the beautiful garden. [$] *Average main: Y250* ✉ *15 Suzhou St., Haidian District* ☎ *010/6265–4186* ✍ *Reservations essential* [M] *Suzhoujie* ✥ *C1.*

$$ TAIWANESE 🍴 **Shin Yeh** (欣叶 *Xīnyè*). The focus at this smartly appointed eatery is on authentic, fresh Taiwanese flavors. Try *caipudan,* a scrumptious turnip omelet, or the poetically named *fotiaoqiang* ("Buddha jumping over the wall"), a delicate soup full of seafood and medicinal herbs. For something a little less austere, the crisp barbecued pigeon is a lip-smacking delight; the accompanying tot of lemon juice is meant to counteract all that oil. Last but definitely not least, try the *mashu,* a glutinous rice cake rolled in ground peanuts. [$] *Average main: Y110* ✉ *Xin Zhongguancun Shopping Center, 19 Zhongguancun Dajie, 4th fl., Haidian District* ☎ *010/8248–6288* [M] *Zhongguancun* ✥ *C1.*

WHERE TO STAY

The first real wave of tourists to visit China in the early 1980s had little need for guidebooks—foreigners were only allowed to stay in ugly, state-run, Stalinist-style blocks. But times have changed. Now Beijing has it all: a glorious glut of the world's best hotel brands; cheap and breezy places to make your base; intimate boutique beauties; and historical courtyard conversions.

The main hubs for hotels are around Wangfujing (Beijing's famous shopping strip), in the vicinity of the northeast Third Ring Road, and along Chang'an/Jianguomen, one of the city's main thoroughfares that connect the Central Business District (CBD) to Tiananmen Square. This is where you'll find the city's most recognizable and reputable hotels, all of which offer luxurious rooms, international-standard facilities, and attentive service. Don't despair if you're on a budget: there are plenty of decent dwellings next to the tourist trail at a fraction of the cost.

"Location, location, location" should be your mantra when booking a Beijing hotel, especially if you're only in town for a few days. It's a big city: there's no point schlepping halfway across it for one particular hotel when a similar option is available in a more convenient area. Consider where you'll be going (Summer Palace? Forbidden City? Great Wall?), then pick your bed. Busy execs should choose wisely in order to avoid getting snarled up in Beijing's horrific traffic, which most likely means staying a little farther west near Financial Street or in the other commercial hub of Guomao (the CBD) in the east. Those in search of nightlife will want to be by Sanlitun, home to the capital's best bars and restaurants. If you're after a one-of-a-kind Beijing experience, check out the city's courtyard hotels. These distinctive lodgings are often converted *siheyuan*—traditional homes built as residential quadrangles among the hutongs. *Use the coordinates (✛ A1) at the end of each listing to locate a site on the corresponding map. Hotel reviews have been shortened. For full information, visit Fodors.com.*

WHAT IT COSTS IN YUAN			
	$	$$	$$$	$$$$
Hotels	under Y1,100	Y1,100–Y1,400	Y1,401–Y1,800	over Y1,800

Prices are for two people in a standard double room in high season.

DONGCHENG DISTRICT

$$
HOTEL
Fodor's Choice
★

3+1 Bedrooms. Modern, minimalist design—pure white interiors, freestanding bathtubs, individual courtyards—meets old Beijing at this intimate four-bedroom boutique hotel within the quaint alleyways (hutong) near the historic Drum and Bell towers. **Pros:** spacious rooms; free in-room Wi-Fi and minibar; private terraces. **Cons:** no health club; no restaurants; occasionally absent service. $ *Rooms from: Y1200* ✉ *17 Zhangwang Hutong, Jiu Gulou Dajie, Drum Tower, Dongcheng*

District ☎ *010/6404–7030* 🌐 *www.3plus1bedrooms.com* 🛏 *3 rooms, 1 suite* 🍴 *Breakfast* [M] *Gulou Dajie* ✥ *C2.*

$ HOTEL 🏨 **Double Happiness Courtyard** (北京阅微庄四合院酒店 *Běijīng yuè wēi zhuāng sìhéyuàn jiǔdiàn*). The rooms in this atmospheric warren of wooden corridors, courtyards, and rickety staircases are fairly spacious, with Chinese-style beds, wooden furniture, and small bathrooms, but it's the friendly, English-speaking service, central location, and good rates that make it so popular. **Pros:** traditional architecture; hutong location; good for families. **Cons:** dingy entrance; old-fashioned facilities; can be chilly in winter. [$] *Rooms from: Y780* ✉ *37 Dongsi Sitiao, Dongcheng District* ☎ *010/6400–7762* 🌐 *www.hotel37.com/en/index.asp* 🛏 *32 rooms, 2 suites* 🍴 *No meals* [M] *Dongsi, Line 5* ✥ *E4.*

$ HOTEL 🏨 **The Emperor** (皇家驿栈 *Huángjiā yìzhàn*). Lauded for its lovely rooftop bar with views over the Forbidden City, the Emperor's has a traditional exterior that belies guest rooms seemingly inspired by the film *2001: A Space Odyssey*: minimalist white decor, sunken beds with tube pillows, lozenge-like sofas, and minibars that rise up from concealed cabinets. **Pros:** best rooftop terrace in the city; unbeatable views of the Forbidden City. **Cons:** no elevator; limited gym facilities; far from the subway. [$] *Rooms from: Y1000* ✉ *33 Qihelou Jie, Dongcheng District* 🌐 *www.theemperor.com.cn* 🛏 *46 rooms, 9 suites* 🍴 *No meals* ✥ *D4.*

$$ HOTEL 🏨 **Grand Hotel Beijing** (北京贵宾楼饭店 *Běijīng Guìbīnlóu fàndiàn*). On the north side of Chang'an Avenue, and adjoining the ritzier Raffles, the Grand offers a decent blend of luxury and comfort without the international brand price tag. **Pros:** good location; classic decor; great rooftop views. **Cons:** some rooms in need of renovation; confusing layout; little atmosphere. [$] *Rooms from: Y1200* ✉ *35 Dongchang'an Jie, Dongcheng District* ☎ *010/6513–7788* 🌐 *www.grandhotelbeijing.com* 🛏 *214 rooms, 50 suites* 🍴 *No meals* [M] *Wangfujing* ✥ *D6.*

$$$$ HOTEL FAMILY Fodor's Choice ★ 🏨 **Grand Hyatt Beijing** (北京东方君悦酒店 *Běijīng Dōngfāngjūnyuè jiǔdiàn*). The wow factor at the this top-notch hotel—close to Tiananmen Square and the Forbidden City—comes from its huge glass facade and extraordinary lagoon-like swimming area: entwined around lush vegetation, waterfalls, and statues, it has a "virtual sky" ceiling that imitates different weather patterns. **Pros:** great dining; plenty of shopping; very impressive pool and gym. **Cons:** dull rooms; overpriced bar; Internet is extra. [$] *Rooms from: Y2200* ✉ *1 Dongchang'an Jie, corner of Wangfujing, Dongcheng District* ☎ *010/8518–1234* 🌐 *www.beijing.grand.hyatt.com* 🛏 *825 rooms, 155 suites* 🍴 *No meals* [M] *Wangfujing* ✥ *D5.*

$$$ HOTEL Fodor's Choice ★ 🏨 **Hilton Beijing Wangfujing.** Even the smallest rooms at this big-brand boutique style hotel come with walk-in wardrobes, freestanding tubs, and six-head showers, and if you can stand the very bachelor-pad brown and slate interiors, you'll reap the benefits of being just a stroll from the Forbidden City and Tiananmen Square. **Pros:** central location; quiet; huge guest rooms. **Cons:** not easy to get cabs; service can get a little strained. [$] *Rooms from: Y1800* ✉ *8 Wangfujing Dong Jie, Dongcheng District* ☎ *010/5812–8888* 🌐 *www3.hilton.com* 🛏 *197 rooms, 58 suites* 🍴 *No meals* ✥ *D5.*

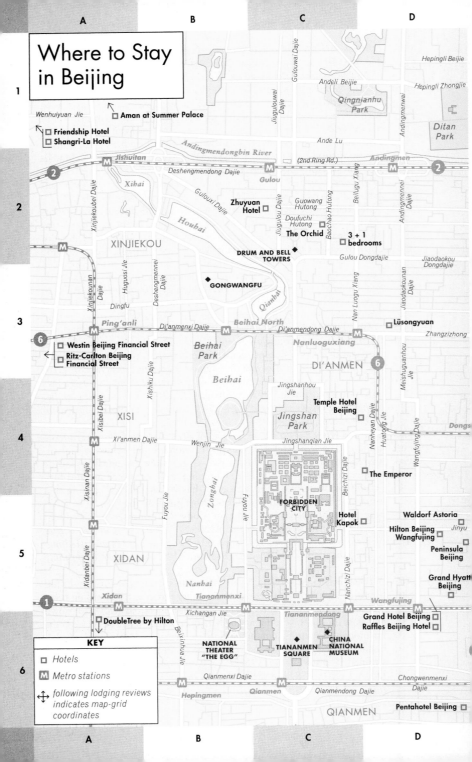

Where to Stay in Beijing

KEY

☐ Hotels

Ⓜ Metro stations

⟷ following lodging reviews indicates map-grid coordinates

$
HOTEL
FAMILY
Fodor's Choice
★

Holiday Inn Express Beijing Dongzhimen (*Běijīng dōngzhīmēn zhìxu*). Cheap and cheerful does it at this value chain close to Sanlitun (Beijing's lively nightlife center)—yes, it lacks a pool and gym, and the guest rooms are somewhat small, but everything here works, from the gleaming lobby to the surprisingly comfortable beds, while touches such as free-to-use Apple Macs next to the front desk and a games console area add a little something extra. **Pros:** cheap yet extremely modern and clean; tour operator next door; close to some great nightlife and dining. **Cons:** breakfast can be crowded (and no lunch or dinner options); small rooms; subway is a long walk away. **$** *Rooms from: Y558* ⊠ *1 Chunxiu Rd., Dongcheng District* ☏ *010/6416–9999* ⊕ *www.holidayinnexpress. com* ↩ *350 rooms* ⏽⊙⏽ *Breakfast* ✛ *G3.*

$$
HOTEL

Hotel Cote Cour (北京演乐70号 *Běijīng yǎn lè 70 hào*). This boutique courtyard hideaway claims to have once served as a rehearsal space for imperial musicians during the Ming Dynasty; renovated rooms wrap around an attractive old courtyard and feature antique pieces, comfy beds with feather duvets, and the usual Western comforts. **Pros:** central location; boutique atmosphere; English spoken. **Cons:** standard rooms a little small; expensive. **$** *Rooms from: Y1300* ⊠ *70 Yanyue Hutong, Dongcheng District* ☏ *010/6523–9598* ⊕ *www.hotelcotecourbj.com/ indexe.asp* ↩ *12 rooms, 2 suites* ⏽⊙⏽ *No meals* ✛ *E4.*

$$$$
HOTEL

Legendale (励骏酒店 *Lìjùn jiǔdiàn*). The faux European spectacle that is the Legendale screams nouveau riche, but this château-like hotel, with its sparkling chandeliers, gilded staircase, and Parisian fireplace in the lobby, is genuinely comfortable and luxurious. **Pros:** plenty of pampering; in a great neighborhood; luxurious rooms. **Cons:** high prices; vast size can make it feel empty; no traditional Chinese elements. **$** *Rooms from: Y2100* ⊠ *90–92 Jinbao St., Dongcheng District* ☏ *010/8511–3388* ⊕ *www.legendalehotel.com* ↩ *390 rooms, 81 suites* ⏽⊙⏽ *Breakfast* Ⓜ *Dengshikou* ✛ *E5.*

$
HOTEL
Fodor's Choice
★

Lüsongyuan (侣松园宾馆 *Lǚsōngyuán bīnguǎn*). The traditional wooden entrance to this delightful courtyard hotel, on the site of an old Mandarin's residence, is guarded by two *menshi* (stone lions)—this is a classic old-Beijing experience, turned over to tourism, with no attempts at modern updates or fancy design, but, rather, just a good choice for cheap, traditional living. **Pros:** convenient location; near restaurants; unfussy courtyard conversion. **Cons:** a lack of luxury; can be hard to find; carpets are in need of a clean. **$** *Rooms from: Y768* ⊠ *22 Banchang Hutong, Kuanjie, Dongcheng District* ☏ *010/6401–1116* ↩ *55 rooms* ⏽⊙⏽ *No meals* Ⓜ *Zhangzizhonglu* ✛ *D3.*

$
HOTEL
Fodor's Choice
★

The Orchid. A firm favorite among travelers looking for somewhere hip but still down-to-earth, the Orchid is a serene spot in the heart of Beijing's most vibrant hutong district, with two tiers of flower-strewn terraces, ludicrously comfy beds, a complimentary à la carte breakfast menu, and friendly staff who have an infectious love for their gentrifying neighborhood. **Pros:** great hutong location; cool interiors; some rooms with gardens. **Cons:** reservations a must; can be hard to find. **$** *Rooms from: Y800* ⊠ *65 Baochao Hutong, Gulou Dong Dajie, Gulou, Dongcheng District* ☏ *010/8404–4818* ⊕ *www.theorchid beijing.com* ↩ *10 rooms* ⏽⊙⏽ *Breakfast* Ⓜ *Guloudajie* ✛ *C2.*

2

$$$
HOTEL
Fodor's Choice
★

 Peninsula Beijing (王府半岛酒店 *Wángfǔ Bàndǎo jiǔdiàn*). Guests at the Peninsula Beijing enjoy an impressive combination of modern facilities and traditional luxury here—the guest rooms are a little small for this sort of hotel, but are superlatively well appointed, with teak and rosewood flooring, colorful rugs, and high-tech touches like custom bedside control panels that let you adjust lighting, temperature, and the flat-screen TVs; the service is excellent, as is the spa. **Pros:** close to sightseeing, restaurants, and shopping; rooms are impeccable; near the Forbidden City. **Cons:** lobby is squeezed by the surrounding luxury shopping mall; hectic; rooms could be bigger. $ *Rooms from: Y1600* ✉ *8 Jinyu Hutong, Wangfujing, Dongcheng District* ☎ *010/8516–2888* ⊕ *www.peninsula.com* ⤳ *525 rooms, 59 suites* ☉|*No meals* Ⓜ *Dengshikou* ✣ *D5.*

$$$$
HOTEL
Fodor's Choice
★

 Raffles Beijing Hotel (北京饭店莱佛士 *Běijīng fàndiàn Láifóshì*). Raffles is an iconic brand in Asia, and this property doesn't disappoint; in 2006, Singaporean designer Grace Soh restored half of what was the Beijing Hotel into its former glory (crystal chandeliers in the lobby; a broad white staircase enveloped in a royal-blue carpet) while retaining its history—service is excellent, and the location, for tourism purposes, is flawless. **Pros:** within easy walking distance of the Forbidden City; nifty location for sightseeing; switched-on staff; spacious rooms. **Cons:** pricey restaurants; not in the right part of town for business travelers; occasional problems with the pool. $ *Rooms from: Y2500* ✉ *33 Dongchang'an Jie, off Wangfujing Dajie, Dongcheng District* ☎ *010/6526–3388* ⊕ *www.raffles.com/beijing* ⤳ *171 rooms, 24 suites* ☉|*No meals* Ⓜ *Wangfujing* ✣ *D6.*

$$$$
HOTEL
Fodor's Choice
★

 The Regent (北京丽晶酒店 *Běijīng Lìjīng jiǔdiàn*). Luxurious (if businesslike) rooms, a prestigious location on the corner of ritzy Jinbao Jie close to Wangfujing, and a spectacularly soaring glass-walled lobby are reasons why the Regent is a top choice for high rollers. **Pros:** convenient location; close to the subway; spacious rooms. **Cons:** unimpressive breakfast; occasional blemishes in some rooms; check-in can be slow. $ *Rooms from: Y2250* ✉ *99 Jinbao St., Dongcheng District* ☎ *010/8522–1888* ⊕ *www.regenthotels.com* ⤳ *500 rooms, 25 suites* ☉|*No meals* Ⓜ *Dengshikou* ✣ *E5.*

$$$$
HOTEL
Fodor's Choice
★

 Temple Hotel Beijing (东景缘 *Dōng jǐng yuán*). Five hundred years in the making, this beguiling combination of boutique luxury and heritage architecture is one of Beijing's most romantic hotel experiences. **Pros:** historic buildings in hutong location; great for art lovers; exceptional. **Cons:** no gym, pool, or spa; expensive. $ *Rooms from: Y2400* ✉ *23 Shatan Beilu, Dongcheng District* ☎ *010/8401–5680* ⊕ *www.thetemplehotel.com* ⤳ *8 rooms* ☉|*No meals* ✣ *C4.*

$$$$
HOTEL
Fodor's Choice
★

 Waldorf Astoria Beijing (北京华尔道夫酒店 *Běijīng huá ěr dàofū jiǔdiàn*). No expense has been spared on this stunning, boutique-inspired hotel in central Wangfujing; the public areas have walls of Suzhou silk, staircases of gold-flecked Italian marble, and countless pieces of art, while guest rooms strike a delightful balance of contemporary style and high-tech luxury, with Apple TVs, Bose sound systems, Nespresso machines, Japanese toilets, heated bathroom floors, and a Samsung tablet beside the bed to control the lights, TV, and curtains, and also order various services. **Pros:** Beijing's most beautiful hotel; brand-new; central location. **Cons:** expensive; not much nightlife in the immediate area. *$ Rooms from: Y2500 ⊠ 5-15 Jinyu Hutong, Dongcheng District ☎ 010/8520–8989 ⊕ waldorfastoria3.hilton.com/ en/hotels/china/waldorf-astoria-beijing-bjswawa/index.html ⤴ 176 rooms* ⦿⧘ *No meals* Ⓜ *Dengshikou* ⊹ *D5.*

XICHENG DISTRICT

$$$$　　☒ **Ritz-Carlton Beijing, Financial Street** (北京金融街丽思卡尔顿酒店
HOTEL　*Běijīng Lìsīkǎ'ěrdùn jiǔdiàn*). With ample amounts of glass and chrome, the Ritz-Carlton could be mistaken for one of the many sleek office buildings that crowd this very business-oriented area; the interior is equally swish and contemporary, with smart East-meets-West decor that's up to the Ritz standard—its location, excellent amenities, and eager-to-please staff make it popular with tour groups as well as businesspeople. **Pros:** impeccable service; luxurious atmosphere; incredible Italian dining. **Cons:** far from the city's attractions; expensive; lobby lacks pizzazz. *$ Rooms from: Y2000 ⊠ 18 Financial St., Xicheng District ☎ 010/6601–6666 ⊕ www.ritzcarlton.com ⤴ 253 rooms, 33 suites* ⦿⧘ *No meals* Ⓜ *Fuchengmen* ⊹ *A3.*

$$　　☒ **Westin Beijing Financial Street** (威斯汀酒店 *Wēisītīng jiǔdiàn*). It's busi-
HOTEL　ness as usual at this worthwhile spot: comfortable rooms with plush beds, neutral tones and marble bathrooms; a plethora of amenities, including dining spots both formal and fun; and not forgetting the perhaps-to-be-expected, well-staffed executive lounge. **Pros:** sumptuous beds; high-tech gadgets; business location. **Cons:** glass between bathroom and bedroom not for the timid; gym could be bigger; not in a good spot for tourists. *$ Rooms from: Y1400 ⊠ 9B Financial St., Xicheng District ☎ 010/6606–8866 ⊕ www.westin.com/beijingfinancial ⤴ 486 rooms, 25 suites* ⦿⧘ *No meals* Ⓜ *Fuchengmen* ⊹ *A3.*

CHAOYANG DISTRICT

$$　　☒ **EAST, Beijing** (北京东隅 *Běijīng Dōngyú*). From the folks behind the
HOTEL　Opposite House, EAST is a business hotel with pizzazz, from the con-
Fodor'sChoice　temporary, light-filled guest rooms done out with oak floors and huge
　★　windows (the corner rooms have the best views), to Xian, a hip bar, lounge and music venue with delicious wood-fired pizza and a connoisseur's selection of single malts. **Pros:** a business hotel with style; impeccable service; great in-house dining and drinking. **Cons:** far from the main tourist sights (other than 798); nearby subway yet to open. *$ Rooms from: Y1250 ⊠ 22 Jiuxianqiao Lu, Jiangtai, Chaoyang District ☎ 010/8426–0888 ⊕ www.east-beijing.com ⤴ 346 rooms, 23 suites* ⦿⧘ *No meals* ⊹ *H1.*

$$$$　　☒ **Four Seasons Hotel Beijing** (北京四季酒店 *Běijīng Sìjì jiǔdiàn*). Even
HOTEL　the most modest "deluxe" rooms at the Four Seasons Beijing come
Fodor'sChoice　with state-of-the-art tech, bathtubs with city views, and clever architec-
　★　ture that seems to amplify the already generous 46 square meters (500 square feet) of living space. **Pros:** some of the best service in the city; elegant rooms; impeccable attention to detail. **Cons:** very expensive;

not particularly close to key tourist hubs; lobby feels a little cramped. [$] *Rooms from: Y3200* ✉ *48 Liangmaqiao Rd., Chaoyang District* ☎ *010/5695–8888* 🌐 *www.fourseasons.com/beijing* 🛏 *247 rooms, 66 suites* 🍴 *No meals* [M] *Liangmaqiao* ⊕ *H2.*

2

$$ HOTEL Fodor's Choice ★ **Grace Beijing** (一驿 *Géruìsī Běijīng*). Housed in a redbrick Bauhaus factory building in Beijing's 798 art district, this stylish boutique hotel mixes French-colonial and Art Deco touches, with contemporary artworks dotted throughout the stylish guest rooms, which range from boxy singles to spacious suites with freestanding tubs. **Pros:** unique art-themed hotel; on-site restaurant is excellent; perfect for visiting 798. **Cons:** far from everything else; no subway; no pool. [$] *Rooms from: Y1100* ✉ *D-Park, Jiuxianqiao Lu 2 Hao Yuan, 798 Art District, Chaoyang District* ☎ *010/6436–1818* 🌐 *www.gracehotels.com* 🛏 *30 rooms* 🍴 *Breakfast* ⊕ *H1.*

$$$$ HOTEL **Hotel Eclat** (北京怡亨酒店 *Běijīng yí hēng jiǔdiàn*). Attached to Parkview Green, Beijing's most artsy and upscale shopping mall, this playfully ultra-luxe option has "lagoon" suites with their own private swimming pools, and a fabulous art collection that includes original works by Salvador Dalí and Andy Warhol. **Pros:** excellent service; free minibar and other welcome treats; attached to shopping mall. **Cons:** expensive; not that close to sights; immediate area lacks local color. [$] *Rooms from: Y2300* ✉ *9 Dongdaqiao Lu, Chaoyang District* ☎ *010/8561–2888* 🌐 *www.eclathotels.com/beijing/default-en.html* 🛏 *74 guest rooms, 26 suites* 🍴 *No meals* [M] *Dongdaqiao, Line 6* ⊕ *G5.*

$ HOTEL **Kempinski Hotel Beijing Lufthansa Center** (凯宾斯基饭店 *Kǎibīnsījī fàndiàn*). One of the capital's older luxury hotels, the Kempinski could stand to give its guest rooms a refresh, but the facilities remain first-rate thanks to a well-equipped gym, easy access to shopping in the attached Lufthansa Center, and plenty of dining opportunities. **Pros:** excellent service; a good bar; easy access to the airport. **Cons:** some areas are in need of renovation; far from the big tourist spots. [$] *Rooms from: Y1100* ✉ *50 Liangmaqiao Lu, Chaoyang District* ☎ *010/6465–3388* 🌐 *www.kempinski.com* 🛏 *526 rooms, 114 suites* 🍴 *No meals* [M] *Liangmaqiao* ⊕ *H2.*

$$ HOTEL FAMILY **Kerry Centre Hotel** (北京嘉里中心饭店 *Běijīng Jiālǐ zhōngxīn fàndiàn*). Recently renovated, this Shangri-La–owned stalwart is now more appealing than ever, with the stylish Centro Bar joined by the excellent all-day Kerry's Kitchen, and a brand new top-of-the-range health club that has a play area just for kids. **Pros:** reasonably priced luxury; great for kids; nearby shopping. **Cons:** smallish rooms; congested area; expensive bar. [$] *Rooms from: Y1250* ✉ *1 Guang Hua Lu, Chaoyang District* ☎ *010/6561–8833* 🌐 *www.shangri-la.com/beijing/kerry* 🛏 *487 rooms, 23 suites* 🍴 *No meals* [M] *Guomao* ⊕ *H5.*

$$$ HOTEL Fodor's Choice ★ **The Opposite House** (瑜舍 *Yúshě*). In the heart of the Sanlitun nightlife district and designed by the famed architect Kengo Kuma, this exemplar of 21st-century China has a huge atrium and contemporary art in the stunning lobby, plus spacious and warm guest rooms kitted out with natural wood and Scandi-Asian minimalist chic. **Pros:** a design addict's dream; fantastic food and drink options (both within and around); unique experience. **Cons:** too trendy for some; not close to the tourist

trail; awful traffic. $ *Rooms from: Y1725* ✉ *11 Sanlitun Lu, Chaoyang District* ☎ *010/6417–6688* ⊕ *www.theoppositehouse.com* ⤢ *98 studios, 1 penthouse* ⦿ *No meals* ✛ *H3.*

$$$$ ⛏ **Park Hyatt Beijing** (北京柏悦酒店 *Běijīng Bòyuè jiǔdiàn*). An easy-to-

HOTEL   like (if costly) slice of luxury, this 63-story tower hotel offers plenty of

Fodor's Choice   pampering (just imagine your own spa-inspired bathroom with over-

★   sized rain shower, deep-soak tub, and heated floors), with large guest rooms that are a tad businesslike but packed with the obligatory modern amenities. **Pros:** spectacular views of the city; the hotel's buzzing Xue bar has a fab rooftop terrace; good location for business. **Cons:** pricey; lacks intimacy; hard area for walking around. $ *Rooms from: Y2000* ✉ *2 Jianguomenwai Dajie., Chaoyang District* ☎ *010/8567– 1234* ⊕ *beijing.park.hyatt.com* ⤢ *237 rooms, 18 suites.* ⦿ *No meals* Ⓜ *Guomao* ✛ *H6.*

$$$ ⛏ **St. Regis** (北京国际俱乐部饭店 *Běijīng guójì jùlèbù fàndiàn*). At

HOTEL   this favorite of business travelers and dignitaries, the luxurious interiors

Fodor's Choice   combine classic Chinese elegance with modern furnishings, but it's the

★   facilities that really stand out: the health club is equipped with a Jacuzzi that gets its water directly from a natural hot spring; the glass-atrium swimming pool offers a sun-drenched backstroke; and the smart, wood-paneled Press Club Bar has the air of a private club. **Pros:** grand lobby; fantastic facilities; good Asian and European restaurants. **Cons:** the little extras really add up; local area a bit tired; not many good places to eat nearby. $ *Rooms from: Y1742* ✉ *21 Jianguomenwai Dajie, Chaoyang District* ☎ *010/6460–6688* ⊕ *www.stregis.com/beijing* ⤢ *156 rooms, 102 suites* Ⓜ *Jianguomen* ✛ *F5.*

$$ ⛏ **W Beijing Chang'an** (北京長安街W 酒店 *Běijīng cháng'ān jiē W*

HOTEL   *jiǔdiàn*). The sassy Starwood brand W has finally landed in China's capital, bringing tech-laden guest rooms, comfy beds, pillow menus, and free snacks. **Pros:** brand new; hip design. **Cons:** a little farther out than the Wangfujing hotels. $ *Rooms from: Y1288* ✉ *2 Jianguuomen Nan Dajie, Chaoyang District* ☎ *010/6515–8855* ⤢ *349 rooms* ✛ *H6.*

HAIDIAN DISTRICT

$$$$ ⛏ **Aman at Summer Palace** (北京颐和安缦 *Běijīng yíhé ānmàn*). The

HOTEL   epitome of blissful indulgence, this luxury hotel (part of the famed

Fodor's Choice   Aman chain) is spread out across a series of carefully renovated ancient

★   Qing Dynasty courtyards—it even has its own private entrance to the Summer Palace—with guest rooms decorated in restful earth tones (lovely traditional wooden screens and bamboo blinds) and grounds that are positively stunning. **Pros:** right next to the Summer Palace; restaurant Naoki serves fine *kaiseki* (Japanese) cuisine; beautiful setting. **Cons:** very pricey; extremely far from downtown; too isolated for some. $ *Rooms from: Y4100* ✉ *1 Gongmen Qian St.,Summer Palace, Haidian District* ☎ *010/5987–9999* ⊕ *www.amanresorts.com* ⤢ *51 rooms, 33 suites* ⦿ *Breakfast* Ⓜ *Yiheyuan* ✛ *B1.*

$$ ⛏ **Shangri-La Hotel, Beijing** (北京香格里拉饭店 *Běijīng Xiānggélǐlā*

HOTEL   *fàndiàn*). With its landscaped gardens, luxury mall, and the addition of a more modern wing, the Shangri-La is a slice of charm for business travelers and those who don't mind being far from the city center; the

service is spot-on throughout, from the pristine rooms to the efficient check-in, while the dining options are excellent (the pick of the bunch being the superb and expensive S.T.A.Y, a French restaurant from the brain of Michelin-loved, three-starred chef Yannick Alléno). **Pros:** nice gardens; excellent amenities; great restaurants. **Cons:** far from the city center; no subway; older wing not as good as the newer one. $ *Rooms from: Y1180* ⊠ *29 Zizhuyuan Lu, Haidian District* ☎ *010/6841–2211* ⊕ *www.shangri-la.com* ☞ *670 rooms, 32 suites* ❙⊙❙ *Breakfast* ✢ *A1.*

OUTSIDE THE CITY CENTER

$$$$
RENTAL
FAMILY

🏠 **Grandma's Place (Schoolhouse Hotels)** (奶奶家 *Năinaijiā*). This two-bedroom rental cottage is part of a project that offers gorgeous self-catering stays in remote villages around the Great Wall; Grandma's Place is the pick of the bunch, created using stones salvaged from Ming and Qing Dynasty structures, as well as massive beams from an old village house, with a cozy, traditional *kang*—a brick bed heated from beneath—and a very private fruit garden and terrace that provides jaw-dropping views of the Great Wall. **Pros:** a wonderfully rustic getaway with modern comforts; views of the Great Wall; The Schoolhouse restaurant is nearby. **Cons:** guests need a car to get here; no hotel services; outside of Beijing. $ *Rooms from: Y2600* ⊠ *The Schoolhouse, 12 Mutianyu Village, Huairou District* ☎ *010/6162–6282* ⊕ *www.grandmasplaceatmutianyu.com* ☞ *2 rooms (8 homes available)* ▭ *No credit cards* ❙⊙❙ *Breakfast* ✢ *H1.*

$$$
HOTEL
Fodor'sChoice
★

🏨 **Langham Place, Beijing Capital Airport.** Airport hotels have a reputation for dullness—not so with Langham Place, a fun and funky spot next to Terminal 3 that screams style with high-tech guest rooms, luxurious marble bathrooms, and soundproofed floor-to-ceiling windows; the in-house contemporary art gallery and stylish dining options point to this hotel's playful sense of creativity. **Pros:** airport hotels are rarely this stylish; fantastic service; good facilities. **Cons:** far from the city center; overly long corridors; can feel too quiet at times. $ *Rooms from: Y1608* ⊠ *1 Er Jing Rd., Beijing Capital International Airport (Terminal 3)* ☎ *010/6457–5555* ⊕ *beijingairport.langhamplacehotels.com* ☞ *372 rooms, 67 suites* ❙⊙❙ *No meals* Ⓜ *Airport Express* ✢ *H1.*

$$$
RENTAL
FAMILY
Fodor'sChoice
★

🏡 **Shan Li Retreats.** These five village houses have been renovated into gloriously beautiful rental properties, with old wooden beams and traditional-style beds mixed with subtle modern touches, all nestled among the mountains and valleys of Huangyankou village (120 km from the city), next to crumbling Great Wall watchtowers on the hill above. **Pros:** a bucolic escape from the city; good hikes nearby; beautifully restored village homes. **Cons:** a car is required to get there; guests need to take their own food. $ *Rooms from: Y1500* ⊠ *Huangyankou Cun, Beizhuang, Miyun County* ☎ *138/1171–6326* ⊕ *www.shanliretreats.com* ☞ *5 houses* ⊙ *Closed Nov.–Mar.* ❙⊙❙ *No meals* ✢ *H1.*

NIGHTLIFE

With intimate bars, world-class cocktail lounges, happening dance halls, sports bars, and even English-style pubs, Beijing has just about every kind of experience you can imagine. Keep in mind, though, that establishments seemingly rise up overnight, and can disappear just as quickly in the breakneck pace of development that is endemic to Beijing.

DONGCHENG DISTRICT

BARS

Fodor's Choice
★

Amilal (按一拉尔 *Àn yī lā'ěr*). If you have the patience to find this cozy courtyard bar in a tiny alley, you'll be rewarded with one of the city's hidden gems. Grab a seat at one of the rough wooden tables, listen to the low-key live music that's often playing, and enjoy the laid-back hutong vibe that's so unique to Beijing. For such a small bar, there's an unexpectedly good selection of whiskies on offer, too. ⊠ *48 Shoubi Hutong, off the east end of Gulou Dongdajie, Dongcheng District* ☎ *010/8404–1416.*

Drum & Bell Bar (鼓钟咖啡馆 *Gǔzhōng kāfēiguǎn*). Situated next to the Drum and Bell Towers (hence the name), this busy bar has one of Beijing's nicest views from its roof deck (when the surrounding area is not undergoing renovation, as tends to happen around here from time to time). An all-you-can-drink deal on Sunday only serves to sweeten the deal. ⊠ *41 Zhonglouwan Hutong, next to the Drum and Bell Towers, Dongcheng District* ☎ *010/8403–3600.*

Great Leap Brewing (大跃啤酒 *Dàyuèpíjiǔ*). At Beijing's first proper microbrewery, the beers are made with ingredients such as tea and Sichuan peppercorns. The courtyard operation also hosts weekly movie screenings and the odd special event. Don't miss the bar peanuts—spicy and salty, they'll keep you going back to the bar for just one more brew. This place has been so successful, in fact, that the owners have since opened a much-larger flagship space in downtown Sanlitun (on Xinzhongjie). ⊠ *6 Doujiao Hutong, Dongcheng District* ☎ *010/5717–1399* ⊕ *www.greatleapbrewing.com.*

Mao Mao Chong (毛毛虫 *Máomáochóng*). This bar is known for top-quality infused cocktails, included a chili-infused vodka Bloody Mary and a Sichuan peppercorn Moscow Mule. Another standout is the owners' own Bangkok Hilton: Thai tea–infused Scotch, crème de cassis, bitters, syrup made from *pandanus* (screw pine) leaves, and an orange twist. The pizzas and artwork are an added reason to stop in. ⊠ *12 Banchang Hutong, Jiaodaokounan, Dongcheng District* ☎ *010/6405–5718* ⊕ *www.maomaochongbeijing.com* ⊗ *Closed Mon.*

Slow Boat Brewery Taproom (慢船啤酒厂 *Màn chuán píjiǔ chǎng*). At this sleek yet cozy taproom inside the hutongs, there are at least a dozen beers on tap at any given moment, including all-weather tipples such as pale ales and IPAs, as well as seasonal specialties (warming stouts in the winter, refreshing citrusy brews come summertime). A luxurious bonus if you're here during the frigid winter season are the heated floors. ⊠ *56 Dongsi Batiao, Dongsi Beidajie, Dongcheng District* ☎ *010/6538–5537*

2

⊕ *www.slowboatbrewery.com* ⊙ *Closed Mon.* Ⓜ *Zhangzizhong Lu (Line 5).*

Yin (饮 (皇家驿栈屋顶) *Huángjiā Yìzhàn*). The Emperor Hotel's rooftop terrace bar certainly has the "wow" factor when it comes to the view, thanks to a vista that overlooks the Forbidden City, plus there's even a hot tub on hand if you need to relax. Unsurprisingly, drink prices are high, and, more often than not, it tends to be too empty for real fun, but it can be a good place to show visitors. Befitting the design focus of the hotel, red lanterns and fashionably outfitted staff add to the classiness of the experience. If only it had a bit more buzz. ⊠ *The Emperor Hotel, 33 Qihelou Dajie, top fl., Dongcheng District* ☎ *010/6526–5566* Ⓜ *Tiananmen East.*

XICHENG DISTRICT

BARS

East Shore Live Jazz Café (东岸咖啡 *Dōng'àn kāfēi*). There's no competition: This place has the most fabulous views of Houhai lake, hands-down, and authentic jazz on stage every night. ⊠ *2nd fl., 2 Qianhai Nanyanlu, west of the Post Office on Di'anmen Waidajie, Xicheng District* ☎ *010/8403–2131.*

CHAOYANG DISTRICT

BARS

Apothecary (药剂员 *Yào jì yuán*). Like an old-fashioned pharmacist doling out carefully concocted medicinals, the bartenders at this low-key venue artfully turn all of your favorite ingredients into cocktails that will soothe the soul. Mixologist-in-chief Leon Lee is something of a local celebrity for good reason. The location (in the trendy Nali Patio complex) and the tasty bar food are bonuses. ⊠ *3/F, Nali Patio, 81 Sanlitun Beilu, Chaoyang District* ☎ *010/5208–6040* Ⓜ *Tuanjiehu.*

China Bar (北京亮酒吧 *Běijīng liàng jiǔbā*). Perched atop the 65-story Park Hyatt, this upmarket cocktail bar offers bird's-eye views of the city, smog and all. Dark and sultry, the modern Asian decor is minimalist and doesn't distract from the views, or the drinks. Cocktails are expertly mixed; Scotch purists can choose from a 20-plus strong list of single malts. ⊠ *Park Hyatt, 2 Jianguomenwai Dajie, 65th fl., Chaoyang District* ☎ *010/8567–1838* Ⓜ *Guomao.*

Face (飞色 *Fēi sè*). Stylish without being pretentious, Face has been around longer than most, and remains popular with a mature and usually well-heeled crowd. The complex holds a multitude of restaurants, but the real gem is the bar. Grab a lounge bed surrounded by silky drapes, take advantage of the happy-hour drink specials, and enjoy some premier people-watching. ⊠ *26 Dongcaoyuan, Gongti Nanlu, Chaoyang District* ☎ *010/6551–6788* ⊕ *www.facebars.com* Ⓜ *Dongdaqiao.*

Ichikura (一藏 *Yī cāng*). This tiny bar is the place to go if you're a discerning whiskey drinker—there are hundreds of varieties on offer. The dimly lit interior, minimalist decor, and hushed conversation give it an air of exclusivity—it's worthy of James Bond. Drinks are taken very seriously here, and it shows in both the quality of the alcohol and the professionalism with which it's mixed by the Japanese-led bar staff. The entrance is via stairs at the south wall of the Chaoyang Theatre. ⊠ *Chaoyang Theatre, 36 Dongsanhuan Beilu, 2nd fl., Chaoyang District* ☎ *010/6507–1107* Ⓜ *Hujialou.*

Mokihi. Tucked behind an Italian-fusion restaurant on an unassuming strip mall of establishments near Chaoyang Park, Mokihi is a perfect oasis from the hustle and bustle of everyday Beijing. Have the Japanese-trained bartenders mix up one of their signature cocktails and nibble on delightful hors d'oeuvres while engaging in quiet conversation with your drinking companions. ⊠ *C12, Haoyun Jie (Lucky St.), 3rd fl., Chaoyang District* ☎ *010/5867–0244.*

Fodor'sChoice ★ **Q Bar.** This tucked-away lounge south of the main Sanlitun drag is an unpretentious option for an evening out. The cocktails here—strong, authentic, and not ridiculously expensive—are a bit of a legend in Beijing, thanks to the involvement of Echo Sun, who has been a real pioneer on the local drinks scene. Don't be put off by the fact that it's on the top floor of a bland, 1980s-styled hotel; in the summer the terrace more than makes up for that. ⊠ *Top fl.of Eastern Inn Hotel, 6 Baijiazhuang Lu, corner of Sanlitun Nanlu and Gongti Nanlu, Chaoyang District* ☎ *010/6595–9239* ⊕ *www.qbarbeijing.com* Ⓜ *Tuanjie Hu.*

Twilight (暮光 *Mùguāng*). Opened by some of the same people involved with Apothecary in Sanlitun, Twilight is an oasis of cool in the otherwise somewhat-dry Central Business District (CBD). Have the bartender make you a perfect old-fashioned, which you can pair with one of the bar's tasty pizzas. ⊠ *Bldg. 5, Jianwai SOHO, 39 Dongsanhuan Zhonglu, 3rd fl., Chaoyang District* ☎ *010/5900–5376.*

HAIDIAN DISTRICT

BARS

Lush. The go-to hangout in the university district of Wudaokou, Lush is a home-away-from-home for many a homesick exchange student. With weekly pub quizzes, open-mike nights, and large, strong drinks, Lush is an excellent place to start the night for those in this part of town. ⊠ *2nd fl., Bldg. 1, Huaqing Jiayuan, Chengfu Lu, Haidian District* ☎ *010/8286–3566* ⊕ *www.lushbeijing.com* Ⓜ *Wudaokou.*

The Red House (色家 *Hóng jiā*). The simple, no-frills exterior here reflects the bar as a whole—bare walls warmed by a roaring fire, friendly bar staff, and a loyal crowd looking for a home away from home to booze in peace. The pizza oven never stops churning out tasty pies, a good accompaniment to the beers on tap. ⊠ *Wudaokou, Wangzhuang Lu, Haidian District* ☎ *010/6291–3350* Ⓜ *Wudaokou.*

PERFORMING ARTS

The performing arts in China took a long time to recover from the Cultural Revolution (1966–76), and political works are still generally banned or avoided. In recent years, names such as Kevin Spacey and the Royal Shakespeare Company have alighted on Beijing, reinforcing the capital's reputation as an arts destination. For culture vultures, there are avant-garde plays, chamber music, traditional Peking opera, acrobatics shows, and lots more.

As most of the stage is inaccessible to non-Chinese speakers, visitors to Beijing are more likely to hunt out the big visual spectacles, such as Beijing opera or kung fu displays. These long-running shows are tailored for travelers: your hotel will be able to recommend performances and venues and will likely be able to help you book tickets.

ACROBATICS AND KUNG FU

Chaoyang Theater (朝阳剧场 *Cháoyáng jùchǎng*). This space is the queen bee of acrobatics venues, especially designed to unleash oohs and ahhs. Spectacular individual and team acrobatic displays involving bicycles, seesaws, catapults, swings, and barrels are performed here nightly. It's touristy but fun. ⊠ *36 Dongsanhuan Beilu, Chaoyang District* ☎ *010/6507–2421* ⊕ *www.chaoyangjuchang.com* Ⓜ *Hujialou*.

Fodor's Choice **The Red Theatre** (红剧场 *Hóng jùchǎng*). If it's Vegas-style stage antics
★ you're after, the *Legend of Kung Fu* show is what you want. Extravagant martial arts—performed by dancers, not martial artists—are complemented by neon, fog, and heavy-handed sound effects. Shows are garish but also sometimes glorious. ⊠ *44 Xingfu Dajie, Dongcheng District* ☎ *010/5165–1914, 135/5252–7373* ⊕ *www.redtheatre.cn* Ⓜ *Tiantan Dong Men*.

Tianqiao Acrobatic Theater (天桥乐茶馆). The Beijing Acrobatics Troupe of China is famous for weird, wonderful shows. Content includes a flashy show of offbeat contortions and tricks, with a lot of high-wire action. There are two shows per night, usually scheduled for 5:30 and 7:15 pm, but it's best to phone ahead and check. ⊠ *5 Tianqiao Shichang Lu, east end of Beiwei Lu, Xicheng District* ☎ *010/6303–7449*.

BEIJING OPERA

Chang'an Grand Theater (长安大戏院 *Cháng'ān dàxìyuàn*). In this theater specializing in Chinese opera, spectators can choose to sit either in the traditional seats or at cabaret-style tables. Besides Peking-style opera, the theater also puts on performances of other regional styles, such as *yueju* (from Guangdong) and *chuanju* (from Sichuan). ⊠ *7 Jianguomennei Dajie, Dongcheng District* ☎ *010/6510–1309* ⊕ *www.changantheater.com* Ⓜ *Jianguomen*.

Huguang Guild Hall (湖广会馆 *Húguǎng huìguǎn*). Built in 1807, the Huguang Guild Hall was at its height one of Beijing's "Four Great" theaters. In 1925, the Guild Hall hosted Dr. Sun Yat-sen at the founding of the Chinese Nationalist Party (KMT). Today, the Guild Hall has been restored to its former glory and hosts regular opera performances. The venue also has a small museum of Peking opera artifacts. ⊠ *3 Hufang Lu, Xicheng District* ☎ *010/6351–8284* Ⓜ *Caishikou*.

Lao She Teahouse (老舍茶馆 *Lǎoshě cháguǎn*). Named for famed Beijing author Lao She, this teahouse in the Qianmen area plays host to a variety of traditional performances, including acrobatics, opera, and vaudeville shows. Dinner is served on the premises; reservations are required one day in advance for the nightly shows. ✉ *Bldg. 3, 3 Qianmenxi Dajie, Xicheng District* ☎ *010/6303–6830.*

Fodor's Choice ★ **Liyuan Theater** (梨园剧场 *Líyuán jùcháng*). The unabashedly touristy shows here are still a great time. You can first watch performers put on makeup before the show (come early) and then graze on snacks and sip tea while watching English-subtitled shows. Glossy brochures complement the crooning. ✉ *1/F, Qianmen Hotel, 175 Yong'an Lu, Xicheng District* ☎ *010/6301–6688* ⊕ *www.qianmenhotel.com/en/liyuan.html.*

MUSIC

Beijing Concert Hall (北京音乐厅 *Běijīng yīnyuètīng*). One of Beijing's main venues for Chinese and Western classical-music concerts also hosts folk dancing and singing, and many celebratory events throughout the year. The 1,000-seat venue is also the home of the China National Symphony Orchestra. ✉ *1 Bei Xinhua Jie, Xicheng District* ☎ *010/6605–7006* Ⓜ *Tiananmen West.*

Fodor's Choice ★ **Forbidden City Concert Hall** (北京中山 *Zhōngshān gōngyuán yīnyuètáng*). One of the nicest venues in Beijing, the 1,400-seat Forbidden City Concert Hall plays host to a variety of classical, chamber, and traditional music performances in plush surroundings and with world-class acoustics. Though the facilities are completely modern, concertgoers are treated to a moonlit walk through Zhongshan Park, a former imperial garden dotted with historical landmarks. ✉ *In Zhongshan Park, Xichang'an Jie, Xicheng District* ☎ *010/6559–8285* ⊕ *www.fcchbj.com* Ⓜ *Tiananmen West.*

MAO Live House. With some of the most committed gig fans in the city, and live music almost every night of the week, MAO Live House is *the* place to experience the vibrant local music scene. ✉ *111 Gulou Dongdajie, Dongcheng District* ☎ *010/6402–5080* ⊕ *www.mao-music.com* Ⓜ *Gulou Dajie.*

Poly Theater (保利剧院 *Bǎolì jùyuàn*). This is a modern shopping-center-like complex on top of Dongsishitiao subway station. One of Beijing's better-known theaters, the Poly hosts Chinese and international concerts, ballets, and musicals. ■TIP→ **If you're seeking a performance in English, this is one of your best bets.** ✉ *1/F Poly Plaza, 14 Dongzhimen Nandajie, Dongcheng District* ☎ *010/6500–1188* ⊕ *www.polytheatre.com* Ⓜ *Dongsishitiao.*

THEATER

FAMILY **China National Puppet Theater** (中国木偶剧院 *Zhōngguó guójiā mùǒujùyuà*). The shadow and hand-puppet shows at this theater convey traditional stories—it's lively entertainment for children and adults alike. This venue also attracts foreign performers, including the Moscow Puppet Theater. ✉ *1 Anhuaxili, Chaoyang District* ☎ *010/6425–4847* ⊕ *www.puppetchina.com* Ⓜ *Anhuaqiao.*

National Centre for the Performing Arts (国家大剧院. *Guójiā dàjùyuàn*). Architecturally, the giant silver dome of this performing arts complex is stunning, and its interior holds a state-of-the-art opera house, a music hall, and a theater. "The Egg," as it's been called, offers a world-class stage for national and international performers. If you don't wish to see a show, you can tour the inside of the building by paying for an entrance ticket. ⊠ *2 Xi Chang'an Jie, Xicheng District* ☎ *010/6655-0000* ⊕ *www.chncpa.org* Ⓜ *Tiananmen West.*

SHOPPING

Shopping is an integral part of any trip to Beijing. Between the hutongs, the markets, the malls, and the shopping streets, it sometimes seems like you can buy anything here.

Large markets and malls are the lifeblood of Beijing, and they're generally open from 9 am to 9 pm, though hours vary from shop to shop. If a stall looks closed (perhaps the lights are out or the owner is resting), don't give up. Many merchants conserve electricity or take catnaps when business is slack. Just knock or offer the greeting "*ni hao*" and, more often than not, the lights will flip on and you'll be invited to come in. Shops in malls have more regular hours and will only be closed on a few occasions throughout the year, such as Chunjie (Chinese New Year) and October's National Day Golden Week.

Major credit cards are accepted in pricier venues but cash is the driving force here. ATMs abound, however it's worth noting that before accepting any Mao-faced ¥100 notes, most vendors will hold them up to the light, tug at the corners, and rub their fingers along the surface. Counterfeiting is becoming increasingly sophisticated in China, and banks are reluctant to accept responsibility for ATMs that dispense fake notes.

The official currency unit of China is the yuan or *renminbi* (literally, "the people's currency"). Informally, though, the main unit of currency is called *kuai* (using "kuai" is the equivalent of saying a "buck" in the United States). On price tags, renminbi is usually written in its abbreviated form, RMB, and yuan is abbreviated as ¥. 1 RMB = 1 Renminbi = 1 Yuan = 1 Kuai = 10 Jiao = 10 Mao = 100 Fen.

If you're looking to bargain, head to the markets; Western-style shops generally go by the price tags. Stalls frequented by foreigners often have at least one employee with some degree of fluency in English. In many situations—whether or not there's a common tongue—the shop assistant will whip out a calculator, look at you to see what they think you'll cough up, then type in a starting price. You're then expected to punch in your offer (start at one third of their valuation). The clerk will usually come down a surprisingly large amount, and so on and so on. A good tip to note is that there's a common superstition in Chinese markets that if you don't make a sale with your first customer of the day, the rest of the day will go badly—so set out early, and if you know you're the first customer of the day, bargain relentlessly.

DONGCHENG DISTRICT

Strolling the old hutongs (alleyways) of Dongcheng is one of the simplest pleasures to be found in Beijing. This area is rife with them and, despite a local council that's itching to modernize, many remain relatively unscathed—and filled with households that have lived there for generations. Efforts to reinvigorate some of the hutongs have resulted in a thriving boutique culture, with Nanluoguxiang the first to receive the attentions of tourist dollars. Its bohemian mix of hipster-chic stores, silk shops, and Old China wares attracts huge interest. Next to bask in the limelight was the quieter, but no less hip, Wudaoying Hutong, opposite Lama Temple. Today both command high rents and almost as much attention as nearby Houhai. For some truly unusual finds, try exploring some of the lesser-trod tributaries off Gulou Dongdajie, such as Baochao, Fangjia, and Beiluoguxiang instead.

ART AND ANTIQUES

Beijing Postcards (北京卡片 *Běijīng Kǎpiàn*). Run by historians, this small gallery near bustling Nanluoguxiang showcases a small collection of hundred-year-old Beijing maps and photos of the Drum and Bell Tower. As well as selling postcards, reprints, and calendars, the company also runs town walks and historical talks—some of the best you'll find in the city. Check the website for upcoming events as well as a list of other stores selling its products. To visit the gallery, email or phone for an appointment. ✉ *Chaodou hutong, Dongcheng District* ☎ *156/1145–3992* ⊕ *www.bjpostcards.com* Ⓜ *Zhangzizhonglu.*

Lost & Found (失物招领 *Shīwù zhāolǐng*). Stylish and sensitive to Beijing's past, American designer Paul Gelinas and Chinese partner Xiao Miao salvage objects—whether they're chipped enamel street signs from a long-demolished hutong, a barbershop chair, or a 1950s Shanghai fan—and lovingly remove the dirt before offering them on sale in their treasure trove of a store. This branch is tucked down a tree-lined hutong where imperial exams once took place, and there's another a few doors down. ✉ *42 Guozijian, Dongcheng District* ☎ *010/6401–1855* 🕓 *Mon.–Thurs. 10:30–8, Fri.–Sun. 10:30–8:30* Ⓜ *Yonghegong* ✉ *57 Guozijian, Dongcheng District* ☎ *010/6400–1174* 🕓 *Mon.–Thurs. 10:30–8, Fri. and Sat. 10:30–8:30* Ⓜ *Yonghegong.*

CLOTHING

Mega Mega Vintage. In Gulou, the only real currency is "vintage." Fresh-from-the-factory retro T-shirts have their place, but nothing can replace leafing through the racks at Mega Mega Vintage in search of gold. Distressed denim, classic tees, leather bags, and old-style dresses crown a collection that rises high above the "frumpery" peddled by countless copycat boutiques. ✉ *241 Gulou Dong Dajie, Dongcheng District* ☎ *010/8404–5637* ⊕ *www.douban.com/group/mmvintage* 🕓 *Daily 1:30–9:30* Ⓜ *Beixinqiao.*

Plastered T-Shirts. Now over 15 years old, this store is a must-visit for anyone in search of that rarest of all things: a souvenir you'll actually use when home. Stop here for T-shirt designs that capture the nostalgic days of Old Peking, as well as retro posters, notebooks, and even thermoses from the '80s. It's fun and kitschy, and everything

costs around Y100. ⊠ *61 Nanluoguxiang Hutong, Dongcheng District* ☎ *136/8339–4452* ⊕ *www.plasteredtshirts.com* ⊙ *Daily 9:30 am–11 pm* Ⓜ *Nanluoguxiang.*

Woo (妩 *Wǔ*). The gorgeous scarves displayed in the windows here lure in passersby with their bright colors and luxurious fabrics. In contrast to those of the vendors in the markets, the cashmere, silk, and bamboo used here are 100% natural. The design and construction are comparable to top Italian designers, while the prices are much more affordable. ⊠ *110/1 Nanluoguxiang, Dongcheng District* ☎ *010/6400–5395* ⊙ *Daily 9:30 am–10 pm* Ⓜ *Nanluoguxiang.*

MALLS AND DEPARTMENT STORES

Malls at Oriental Plaza (东方广场购物中心 *Dōngfāng guǎngchǎng*). This enormous shopping complex originates at the southern end of Wangfujing, where it meets Chang'an Jie, and stretches a city block east to Dongdan Dajie. It's a true city within a city and certainly geared toward higher budgets. Some of the more upscale shops include Kenzo and Armani Exchange; ladies should check out the boutique from iconic Chinese-American designer Anna Sui for clothes, accessories, and makeup. ⊠ *1 Dongchang'an Jie, Dongcheng District* ☎ *010/8518–6363* ⊙ *Daily 10–10* Ⓜ *Wangfujing.*

MARKETS

FAMILY **Hongqiao Market** (红桥市场 *Hóngqiáo shìchǎng*). Hongqiao, or Pearl Market, is full of tourist goods, knockoff handbags, and cheap watches, but it's best known for its three stories of pearls. Freshwater, seawater, black, pink, white: The quantity is overwhelming, and quality varies by stall. Prices also range wildly, though the cheapest items are often fakes. Fanghua Pearls (No. 4318), on the fourth floor, displays quality necklaces and earrings, with photos of Hillary Clinton and Margaret Thatcher shopping there to prove it. Fanghua has a second store devoted to fine jade and precious stones. Stallholders in the market can be pushy, but try to accept their haggling in the gamelike spirit it's intended. Or wear headphones and drown them out. ⊠ *9 Tiantan Lu, east of the northern entrance to Temple of Heaven, Dongcheng District* ☎ *010/6711–7630* ⊙ *Daily 9:30–7* Ⓜ *Tiantan Dongmen.*

SILK AND FABRICS

Daxin Textiles Co. (大新纺织 *Dàxīn fǎngzhī*). For a wide selection of all types of fabrics, from worsted wools to sensuous silks, head to this shop. It's best to buy the material here and find a tailor elsewhere, as sewing standards can be shoddy. ⊠ *Northeast corner of Dongsi, Dongcheng District* ☎ *010/6403–2378* Ⓜ *Dongsi.*

XICHENG DISTRICT

Xicheng is best known as the home of the Forbidden City, but it also has a few choice shopping areas. Located to the south of Tiananmen Square, **Qianmen** might not rank high on the authenticity scale, thanks to a pre-Olympics renovation, but it still offers plenty of color (as well as brand names)—a ride on the tram down what is one of the city's oldest shopping streets is a must. To the east lies the similarly spruced-up

Dashilar area, a series of shiny hutongs (alleyways) that are a bit too clean to be real but house old-school Chinese medicine stores, silk shops, and "ancient" souvenirs aplenty.

Head northwest of the Forbidden City and you'll find Beijing's lake district of Shichahai, comprising Qianhai, Xihai, and Houhai. The latter is surrounded by a morass of hutongs that include Yandai Xiejie, a side street packed with stores and hawkers pushing jewelry, clothes, Mao-shape oddities, and plenty of stuff you don't need but simply can't resist. Meanwhile, farther west of here lies **Xidan**, a giant consumer playground swarming with high-rise malls and bustling underground markets stuffed with cheap clothing and accessories—it's the go-to place for Beijing's young and fashionable. At 13 stories, **Joy City** is the largest mall, while **Mingzhu** and **77th Street** are best for market browsing. And for those who are especially flush with cash, **Galeries Lafayette** is luxury-brand heaven, with the likes of Alexander McQueen, Jimmy Choo, and Gucci.

CHINESE MEDICINE

Tongrentang (同仁堂 *Tóngréntáng*). A first-time consultation with a Chinese doctor can feel a bit like a reading with a fortune-teller. With one test of the pulse, many traditional Chinese doctors can describe the patient's medical history and diagnose current maladies. Serving as official medicine dispenser to the Imperial Court until its collapse, Tongrentang now has branches all over the city. At its 300-year-old store in Dashilan you can browse the glass displays of deer antlers and pickled snakes, dried seahorses and frogs, and delicate tangles of roots with precious price tags of Y48,000. If you don't speak Chinese and wish to have a consultation with a doctor, consider bringing along a translator. ✉ *24 Dashilan, Qianmen, Exit C, Xicheng District* ☎ *010/6701–5895* ⊙ *Daily 8:30–5* Ⓜ *Qianmen*.

⚠ Chinese medicine can be effective, but that's unlikely to be the case when it's practiced by lab-coated "doctors" sitting behind a card table on the street corner. If you're seeking Chinese medical treatment, visit a local hospital, Tongrentang medicine shop, or ask your hotel concierge for a legitimate recommendation.

MARKETS

Baoguosi Temple Antiques Market (报国寺收藏品市场 *Bàoguósì shōucángpǐn shìchǎng*). This little-known market, atmospherically set in the grounds of Baoguosi Temple, is a smaller, more manageable version of Panjiayuan. It sees very few foreigners, and no one will speak English, but armed with a calculator, stallholders will get their point across. As well as memorabilia from the Cultural Revolution, look out for stalls that sell original photos, ranging from early-20th-century snaps to people posing with their first TVs in the 1970s. ✉ *Guanganmennei Dajie, Xicheng District* ☎ *010/8223–4583* ⊙ *Daily 9:30–4:30* Ⓜ *Caishikou*.

SILK AND FABRICS

Beijing Silk Shop (北京谦祥益丝绸商店 *Běijīng qiānxiángyì sīchóu shāngdiàn*). Since 1830, the Beijing Silk Shop has been supplying the city with bolts of quality silks and other fabrics. There are tailors on-site to whip up something special, and the second floor has ready-to-wear clothing. To reach the shop, walk all the way down Dashilan then head directly onto Dashilan West Street. ⊠ *50 Dashilan Xi Jie, Xicheng District* ☏ *010/6301–4732* ⊙ *Daily 9–8:30* Ⓜ *Qianmen.*

SPECIALTY SHOPS

Tea Street (马连道茶叶批发市场 *Mǎliándǎo cháyè chéng*). Literally a thousand tea shops perfume the air of this prime tea-shopping district, west of the city center. Midway down this near-mile-long strip looms the **Teajoy Market,** the Silk Alley of teas. Unless you're an absolute fanatic, it's best to visit a handful of individual shops, crashing tea parties wherever you go. Vendors will invite you to sit down in heavy wooden chairs to nibble on pumpkin seeds and sample their large selections of black, white, oolong, jasmine, and chrysanthemum teas. Prices range from a few kuai for a decorative container of loose green tea to thousands of yuan for an elaborate gift set. Tea Street is also the place to stock up on clay and porcelain teapots and service sets. Green and flower teas are sold loose; black teas are sold pressed into disks and wrapped in natural-colored paper. ⊠ *Maliandao Lu, Xicheng District* ✛ *South end of Maliandao Lu near Guang'anmen Waidajie* Ⓜ *Xuanwumen.*

TOYS

Three Stones Kite Store (三石斋风筝店 *Sānshízhāi fēngzhēng*). For something more traditional, go fly a kite. Here, for three generations, the same family has hand-painted butterflies and birds onto bamboo frames to delight adults and children alike. They're a far cry from the run-of-the-mill types you can find elsewhere. ⊠ *25 Di'anmen Xidajie, Xicheng District* ☏ *010/8404–4505* ⊕ *www.cnkites.com* ⊙ *Daily 10–9* Ⓜ *Shichahai.*

CHAOYANG DISTRICT

The vast Chaoyang District is *the* area to shop in Beijing, although given that it's the size of many cities, that is somewhat understating things. It stretches all the way from downtown to the airport, encompassing 798 Art District, Sanlitun, and the Central Business District areas. Its consumerist joys lie mainly in its collection of labyrinthine markets and ever more futuristic malls, with a smattering of boutiques in between. Parkview Green and Indigo are just some of the more impressive examples of shopping malls to dot this part of new-look China. Elsewhere, shopping highlights include Panjiayuan Antique Market, Silk Road Market, the indie stores of 798, and the local capitalist's mecca that is Sanlitun Village.

BOOKS

The Bookworm (书虫 *Shūchóng*). Thousands of English-language books fill the shelves at this pleasant café in the heart of Sanlitun. Read for free over a coffee or a simple bistro meal, or join the lending library for a fee. The Bookworm is also a good spot to buy new international magazines and best sellers. This is a popular venue for guest speakers, poetry readings, film screenings, and live-music performances. The kitchen offers a three-course set lunch and dinner. For a quick bite, sandwiches, salads, and a cheese platter are also available. ⊠ *4 Sanlitun Nan Lu, set* *back slightly in an alley 50 meters south of the Gongti Beilu junction, Chaoyang District* ☎ *010/6586–9507* ⊕ *www.beijingbookworm.com* ⊘ *Daily 9 am–midnight* Ⓜ *Tuanjiehu.*

CLOTHING

Fodor's Choice
★

Best New China. Showcasing an eclectic collection from more than 100 homegrown designers, Best New China makes a bold statement about China's emerging fashion. Many of the clothes, shoes, and accessories here are created by subtly tinkering with tradition—they have been given a twist of modern chic while remaining distinctly "period." The store's celebrity founder, Hong Huang, has been a driving force behind the concept, and also helped create its celebrity following. From high-fashion to simple linen and even gargoyle art, there's something for just about everyone. Prices start from under Y100 for accessories to a few thousand for clothing. ⊠ *Fl. B1, Sanlitun Village North, Chaoyang District* ☎ *010/6416–9045* ⊕ *www.brandnewchina.cn* Ⓜ *Tuanjiehu.*

UCCA Store (东八时区 *UCCA Shāngdiàn*). The 798 Art District is home to a burgeoning collection of housewares, fashion, and design shops. The most innovative of these is an offshoot of the Ullens Center for Contemporary Art (UCCA), located just one door down from the gallery. Clothes, posters, ingenious knickknacks, and artist Sui Jianguo's iconic (and pricey) "Made in China" plastic dinosaurs make it a must-visit for anyone in the area. ⊠ *798 Art District, 4 Jiuxianqiao Lu, Chaoyang District* ☎ *010/5780–0224* ⊕ *ucca.org.cn/en/uccastore* ⊘ *Daily 10–7.*

HOUSEWARES

Spin (旋 *Xuán*). This trendy ceramics shop near the 798 Art District features the work of several talented Shanghainese designers who take traditional plates, vases, and vessels and give them a unique and delightful twist. Prices are surprisingly inexpensive. ⊠ *6 Fangyuan Xilu, Lido, Chaoyang District* ☎ *010/6437–8649* ⊘ *Daily 10–7.*

JEWELRY

Shard Box Store (慎 德阁 *Shèndégé*). The signature collection here includes small to midsize jewelry boxes fashioned from the broken shards of antique porcelain. Supposedly the shards were collected during the Cultural Revolution, when scores of antique porcelain pieces were smashed in accordance with the law. Birds, trees, pining lovers, and dragons decorate these affordable ceramic-and-metal containers, which range from Y20 to Y200. ⊠ *4 Ritan Beilu, Chaoyang District* ☎ *010/8561–3712* ⊘ *Daily 9–7* Ⓜ *Yong'anli* ⊠ *2 Jiangtai Lu, near the Holiday Inn Lido* ☎ *010/5135–7638* ⊘ *Daily 9–7* Ⓜ *Sanyuanqiao.*

MALLS AND DEPARTMENT STORES

China World Mall (国贸商城 *Guómào Shāngchéng*). Nothing embodies Beijing's lusty embrace of luxury goods quite like China World Mall, which is home to a giant branch of the Hong Kong designer emporium Joyce. The average spend here must run into millions of yuan. However, for smaller budgets, there are plenty of cafés and affordable restaurants; the cinema is decent, and there's also a good ice rink for kids. The mall is open every day, from 10 am to 9:30 pm. ⊠ *1 Jianguomenwai Dajie, Chaoyang District* ☎ *010/8535–1698* Ⓜ *Guomao.*

Indigo (颐堤港 *Yítígǎng*). Located just on the edge of Dashanzi (798 Art District), this complex is one of the city's many impressive "super malls." Light, airy, and with a few new stores still not open, the malls houses brands that include the GAP, H&M, and Sephora as well as the Parisian Bread and Butter and homebred earthy fashion house JNBY; there is also a branch of the excellent Page One bookstore. The indoor garden isn't much to write home about, but a gigantic outdoor park area might be when it's finished. ⊠ *18 Jiuxianqiao Lu, Chaoyang District* ☏ *010/8426–0898* ⊕ *www.indigobeijing.com* ⊘ *Daily 10–10.*

Parkview Green, Fangcaodi (芳草地 *Fāngcǎodí*). Scattered in and around this giant, green pyramid-shaped "biodome" is a boutique hotel, a mall that doubles as a walk-through gallery, and one of the largest private collection of Salvador Dalí works on display outside Spain. For shoppers, stores by designers Stella McCartney and Mulberry rub shoulders with the likes of GAP; meanwhile a branch of the world-famous Taiwanese dumpling-slingers Din Tai Fung is always worth a visit. Even if designer knickknacks aren't your thing, stopping by just to gawk at the sheer grandiosity of it all comes highly recommended. ⊠ *9 Dongdaqiao Lu, Chaoyang District* ☏ *010/5690–7000* ⊕ *www.parkviewgreen.com/eng* ⊘ *Daily 10–10* Ⓜ *Dong Daqiao.*

The Place (世贸天阶 *Shìmào tiān jiē*). Shopping-wise you'll find all the usual suspects here—Zara, JNBY, et al—even if a lack of good dining spots ensures that you won't linger too long. However, visitors largely flock to The Place to witness its eye-wateringly gigantic LED screen, which bursts into life every hour in the evenings and shows some pretty stunning mini-movies (the meteorites are the best!) before lapsing back into screensavers and commercials. ⊠ *9 Guanghua Lu, Chaoyang District* ☏ *010/6587–1188* ⊕ *www.theplace.cn* ⊘ *Daily 10–10* Ⓜ *Jintaixizhao.*

Sanlitun Village (三里屯 Village *Sānlìtún Village*). The default destination for all expats, this fashionable complex, split into two zones, gets the nod for its great range of stores at all price points, cool architecture, and fun people-watching. Village South houses the biggest Adidas store in the world, as well as branches of Uniqlo, Steve Madden, I.T, and the busiest Apple store you'll ever see. The newer and more upscale Village North has designer stores such as Alexander Wang and Emporio Armani. There's also a good cinema and some great restaurants and bars. ⊠ *19 Sanlitun Jie, Chaoyang District* ☏ *010/6417–6110* ⊕ *www.sanlitunvillage.com* ⊘ *Daily 10–10* Ⓜ *Tuanjiehu.*

MARKETS

Fodor's Choice ★ **Panjiayuan Antiques Market** (潘家园市场 *Pānjiāyuán shìchǎng*). Every day the sun rises over thousands of pilgrims rummaging in search of antiques and curios, though the biggest numbers of buyers and sellers are on weekends. With over 3,000 vendors crowding an area of 48,500 square meters, it's a sure bet that not every jade bracelet, oracle bone, porcelain vase, and ancient screen is authentic, but most people are here for the reproductions anyway. Behold the bounty: watercolors, scrolls, calligraphy, Buddhist statues, opera costumes, old Russian SLR cameras, curio cabinets, Tibetan jewelry, tiny satin lotus-flower shoes, rotary telephones, jade dragons, antique mirrors, and infinite displays of "Maomorabilia." If you're buying jade, first observe the Chinese customers, how they hold a flashlight to the milky-green stone to test its authenticity. As with all Chinese markets, bargain with a vengeance, as many vendors inflate their prices astronomically for *waiguoren* ("outside-country people").

A strip of enclosed stores forms a perimeter around the surprisingly orderly rows of open-air stalls. Check out photographer Xuesong Kang and his **Da Kang** store (No. 63-B) for some fascinating black-and-white snaps of Beijing city life, dating from the start of the 20th century up to the present day. Also be sure to stop by the **Bei Zhong Bao Pearl Shop** (甲-007) for medium-quality freshwater pearls cultivated by the Hu family. Also here are a sculpture zoo, a book bazaar, reproduction-furniture shops, and an area stashing propaganda posters and Communist literature. Stalls start packing up around 4:30 pm, so make sure to get there on the early side. ✉ *18 Huaweili, Panjiayuan Lu, Chaoyang District* ☎ *010/6774–1869* ☉ *Weekdays 8:30–6, weekends 6–6* Ⓜ *Panjiayuan.*

Fodor'sChoice ★ **Silk Street Market** (秀水市场 *Xiùshuǐ shìchǎng*). Once a delightfully chaotic sprawl of hundreds of outdoor stalls, the Silk Alley Market is now corralled inside a huge shopping center. The government has been cracking down on an increasing number of certain copycat items, so if you're after a knockoff Louis Vuitton purse or Chanel jacket, just ask; it might magically appear from a stack of plastic storage bins. You'll face no dearth, however, of fake Pumas and Nikes or Paul Smith polos. Chinese handicrafts and children's clothes are on the top floors. Bargain relentlessly, carefully check the quality of each intended purchase, and guard your wallet against pickpockets. ✉ *8 Xiushui Dong Jie, Chaoyang District* ☎ *010/5169–9003* ⊕ *www.silkstreet.cc* ☉ *Daily 9:30–9* Ⓜ *Yong'anli.*

Yashow Market (雅秀市场 *Yǎxiù shìchǎng*). Especially popular among younger Western shoppers, Yashow is yet another indoor arena stuffed to the gills with low-quality knockoff clothing and shoes. Prices are slightly cheaper than Silk Alley, but the haggling no less essential—don't pay any more than Y50 for a pair of "Converse" sneakers. Also, don't be alarmed if you see someone sniffing the shoes or suede jackets: they're simply trying to see if the leather is real. On the third floor, **Wendy Ya Shi** (No. 3066) is the best of the many tailors on offer, with a basic suit usually starting out at around Y1,500 (including fabric) after a good haggle. ■TIP→ **The Lily Nails salon on the first floor offers inexpensive manicures and foot rubs if you need a break.** ✉ *58 Gongti Beilu, Chaoyang District* ☎ *010/6416–8699* ☉ *Daily 9:30–9* Ⓜ *Tuanjiehu.*

HAIDIAN DISTRICT

If you're in Haidian, the chances are that you're a student, Korean, or both. An abundance of universities and a large Korean population around **Wudaokou** make this a rather bustling, fun area, although it's not worth the journey for that alone—unless you have a penchant for

Inspecting the goods at the Panjiayuan Antiques Market

kimchi, cheap shots, and overcrowded dance floors. But, if you're on your way to the Summer Palace or Beijing Zoo, it's worth stopping by, if only to wind down with a massage at one of the many cheap Korean joints. Inexpensive and cheerful boutiques and restaurants are in abundance, while the usual mainstream chain stroes can be found farther east at the shopping malls in **Zhongguancun,** which is also home to Beijing's largest IT and electronics market.

ELECTRONICS

Zhongguancun Electronics City. There's little in the world of IT and electronics that can't be found in Hailong, Dinghao, and the other multistory malls around the Zhongguancun subway station. Before you buy, make sure you compare prices among a few of the stalls (literally hundreds may be offering the same product or services). Never accept the initial quote without driving a hard bargain, and don't hesitate to pit sellers' prices against each other —it's the thing to do when the competition is this intense. ⊠ *Zhongguancun Dajie, Haidian District* ☎ *010/8266–3883* ⏰ *Daily 9–7.*

SIDE TRIPS FROM BEIJING

The wonders of Beijing aren't confined to the city center. Venturing into the outskirts and beyond, you'll discover a wealth of sights that provide a further look at imperial might, offer natural delights and some refreshing relief from city crowds, and even deliver a whiff of adventure.

Of course, the Great Wall is a good starting point for any exploration, and while it isn't (as the old propagandist myth goes) visible to the naked eye from space, it's nonetheless an awesome sight. It might have failed to prevent the Manchus from invading, but few more soaring testimonies to human endeavor are more visually rewarding. You needn't stop there, though. Imperial tombs and Buddhist temples also surround the capital, with remarkable mausoleum complexes to the east near Changping and the west at Zunhua and a satisfying swath of temples in the western suburbs.

THE GREAT WALL

60–120 km (37–74 miles) north and west of Beijing.

Any visitor to Beijing should aside at least a day to visit one of the incredible sections of the Great Wall, just outside the city. Badaling is the closest to Beijing, just about an hour from the city center. The farther you get from Beijing, the more rugged the terrain, so you'll add the excitement of seeing the wall tumbling across the countryside.

⇨ *See the highlighted feature in this chapter for more about the Great Wall.*

GETTING HERE AND AROUND

The easiest and most comfortable way to visit the wall is by private car. Though taxis are occasionally willing to make the trip to more accessible sections like Badaling and Mutianyu, most hotels can arrange a four-passenger car and an English-speaking driver for eight hours at around Y500–Y700. Settle details in advance, and remember that it's polite to invite your driver to eat meals with you. To ensure your driver doesn't return to Beijing without you, pay after the trip is over.

TOURS

In addition to the tour buses that gather around Tiananmen Square, most hotels and tour companies offer trips (in comfortable, air-conditioned buses or vans) to Badaling, Mutianyu, Juyongguan, and Jinshanling. Smaller, private tours are generally more rewarding than large bus trips. Trips will run between Y400 and Y1,500 per person, but costs vary depending on the group size, and can sometimes be negotiated. Wherever you're headed, book in advance.

For further help in planning your trip to the wall, while adding a bit of adventure to the mix, consider the following:

Albatros Adventure Great Wall Marathon. Not for the faint of heart, the Great Wall Marathon (and half marathon) takes place each May and covers approximately 6.5 km (4 miles) of the Great Wall, with the rest of the course running through lovely valleys in rural Tianjin. Visitors must book through Albatros, a Danish tour company that arranges weeklong packages, or a local operator. ⊠ *Albatros, Tøndergade 16, Copenhagen, Denmark* ☎ *45/3698–9838* ⊕ *great-wall-marathon.com.*

Beijing Hikers. Arrange weekly day-treks to the wilder parts of the Great Wall throughout the year, as well as personalized tours. ☎ *010/6432 2786* ⊕ *www.beijinghikers.com.*

Beijing Service. Private guided tours by car include stops at Badaling, Mutianyu, Jinshanling, and Juyongguan for small groups of up to four

2

people. ✉ *9-6 West Block of Chang An Block, Miyun* ☎ *010/5166–7026* ⊕ *www.beijingservice.com.*

Bespoke Beijing. This firm designs private tours with English-speaking guides to suit your interests. ✉ *107 Dongsi Bei, Dongcheng District* ☎ *010/6400–0133* ⊕ *www.bespoke-beijing.com.*

CITS (China International Tour Service). The company runs bus tours to Badaling and private tours to Badaling, Mutianyu, and Jinshanling. ✉ *1 Dongdan Bei, Dongcheng District* ☎ *010/6522–2991* ⊕ *www.cits.net.*

Cycle China. This company runs good guided hiking tours of the unrestored wall at Jiankou. ✉ *12 Jingshan East St., opposite the east gate of Jingshan Park, Dongcheng District* ☎ *10/6402–5653* ⊕ *www.cyclechina.com.*

EXPLORING

Great Wall at Badaling. Only one hour by car from downtown Beijing and located not far from the Ming Tombs, the Great Wall at Badaling is where visiting dignitaries go for a quick photo op. Postcard views abound here, with large sections of the restored Ming Dynasty brick wall rising majestically to either side of the fort while, in the distance, portions of early-16th-century Great Wall disintegrate into more romantic but inaccessible ruins.

The downside is that Badaling suffers from its popularity, with tour groups flocking here en masse. This has led to its reputation as "one to be avoided" by those allergic to shoulder-bumping and being gouged by hawkers. Nevertheless, with popularity comes tourist-friendly facilities, and those with disabilities find access to the wall here to be far better than at other sections. Either take the cable car to the top or walk up the gently sloping steps, relying on handrails if necessary. On a clear day, you can see for miles across leafy, undulating terrain from atop the battlements. The admission price also includes access to the China Great Wall Museum and the Great Wall Circle Vision Theater.

A car for four people from central Beijing to Badaling should run no more than Y600 for five hours, and you can sometimes make arrangements to include a stop at the Thirteen Ming Tombs. By public transportation, trains leave Beijing North Station for Badaling Station (Y6) almost every hour from 6:12 am and take 1 hour 20 minutes. From there, it's just a 20-minute walk to the entrance to Badaling Great Wall. Or, take Line 2 on the subway to Jishuitan and walk to Deshengmen bus terminus. From there, take Bus 880 to Badaling (Y12). Be warned: private taxis hang around the station and drivers will try to convince you that it's easier to go with them. It isn't. Stick to your guns and get on that bus.

■ TIP➔ Most tours to Badaling will take you to the Thirteen Ming Tombs, as well. If you don't want a stop at the tombs—or at a tourist-trapping jade factory or herbal medicine center along the way—be sure to confirm the itinerary before booking. ✉ *Yanqing County* ⊕ *70 km (43 miles) northwest of Beijing* ☎ *010/6912–1383* ⊕ *www.badaling. cn* 🏷 *Wall Y45; cable car Y80 one-way, Y100 round-trip* ☉ *Apr.–Oct., daily 6:30–6:30; Nov.–Mar., daily 7–6.*

Continued on page 134

THE GREAT WALL

For some people, the Great Wall is the main reason for a trip to China; for any visitor to Beijing, it's a must-see. Originally intended to keep foreigners out, the world's most famous wall has become the icon of an increasingly open nation. One of the country's most accessible attractions, the Great Wall promises both breathtaking scenery and cultural illumination.

Built by successive dynasties over two millennia, the Great Wall isn't one structure built at one time, but a series of defensive installations that shrank and grew. Especially vulnerable spots were more heavily fortified, while some mountainous regions were left un-walled altogether. The actual length of the wall remains a topic of considerable debate: at its longest, some estimates say the protective cordon spans 6,437 km (4,000 miles)—a distance wider than the United States. Although attacks, age, and pillaging (not to mention today's tourist invasion) have caused the crumbling of up to two-thirds of its length, new sections are being uncovered even today.

As kingdoms scrambled to protect themselves from marauding nomads, portions of wall cropped up, leading to a motley collection of northern borders. It was the first emperor of a unified China, Qin Shi-huang (circa 259–210 BC), founder of the Qin Dynasty, who linked these fortifications into a single network. By some accounts, Qin mustered nearly a million people, or one-fifth of China's workforce, to build this massive barricade, a mobilization that claimed countless lives and gave rise to many tragic folktales.

The Ming Dynasty fortified the wall like never before: for an estimated 5,000 km (3,107 miles), it stood 26 feet tall and 30 feet wide at its base. However, the wall failed to prevent the Manchu invasion that toppled the Ming in 1644. That historical failure hasn't tarnished the Great Wall's image, however. Although China once viewed it as a model of feudal oppression, the Great Wall is now touted as the national symbol. "Love China, Restore the Great Wall," declared Deng Xiaoping in 1984. Since then large sections have been repaired and opened to visitors, turning it also into a symbol of the tension between preservation and restoration in China.

AN ETERNAL WAIT

One legend concerns Lady Meng, whose husband was kidnapped on their wedding night and forced to work on the Great Wall. She traveled to the work site to await his return, believing her determination would bring him back. She waited so long that, in the end, she turned into a rock, which to this day stands at the head of the Great Wall in the beautiful seaside town of Qinhuangdao.

MATERIALS & TECHNIQUES

■ During the 2nd century BC, the wall was largely composed of packed earth and piled stone.

■ Some sections, like those in the Taklimakan Desert, were fortified with twigs, sand, and even rice (the jury's still out on whether workers' remains were used as well).

■ The more substantial brick-and-mortar ruins that wind across the mountains north of Beijing date from the Ming Dynasty (14th–17th centuries). Some Ming mortar kilns still exist in valleys around Beijing.

VISITING
THE GREAT WALL

As a visitor to Beijing, you simply must set aside a day to visit one of the glorious Great Wall sites just outside the capital.

At Mutianyu in the mountains on a clear summer day

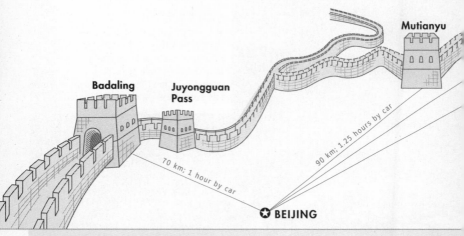

Mutianyu

Badaling

Juyongguan Pass

70 km; 1 hour by car

90 km; 1.25 hours by car

⭐ **BEIJING**

GREAT WALL SITES NEAR BEIJING

There are five Great Wall sites within relatively close proximity to the city of Beijing: depending on what you're looking for and how much time you have, there is one to fit your itinerary. Generally

Part of the Great Wall of China at Badaling

speaking, the farther you go from Beijing, the more rugged the terrain and the fewer tourists and hawkers you'll see. Badaling and Juyongguan are the most accessible sections of the Great Wall from Beijing, and these are where most of the tours go but there are tour options for all different kinds of Great Wall experiences. See the Great Wall Tours listings for some of our suggestions.

Badaling is about an hour-long drive from Beijing and is great for photo ops, with amazing postcard views.

Because it's easy to get to, though, there are often swarms of tourists, as well as lots of hawkers. The upside is that there are tourist-friendly facilities and there is better disability access here than elsewhere.

Juyongguan is also about an hour's drive from Beijing, and near Badaling. It has similarly impressive views and less crowds, but that's partly because the site has been heavily restored and feels a bit commercial.

If you're looking for a less-traveled section of the wall

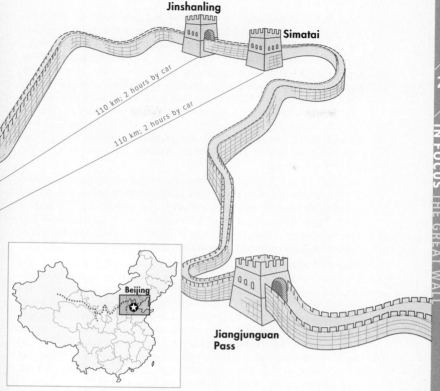

Jinshanling

Simatai

110 km; 2 hours by car

110 km; 2 hours by car

Beijing

Jiangjunguan Pass

that is still accessible from Beijing, head to fantastic **Mutianyu**. It's only slightly farther from Beijing than Badaling but significantly more spectacular. Although you'll see the occasional souvenir stand, it's much less crowded than Badaling, and you'll be able to enjoy more solitude, along with amazing views from the towers and wall. Mutianyu is definitely more about hiking than Badaling or Juyongguan. It's a strenuous hour's hike out of the parking lot, although there is a cable car that can

The Great Wall between Jinshanling and Simatai

take you up to the wall, from where there are additional trails.

Jinshanling is the most rustic and the least touristed section of the Wall that's

within easy proximity to Beijing. It's about a 2-hour drive from Beijing and most people come here on an overnight camping trip. This is an unforgettable experience if you have the time and like to camp.

Simatai is for adventure-seekers. It's remote and often precarious. It's also about a 2-hour drive from Beijing.

Great Wall at Jinshanling. The Great Wall at Jinshanling is perhaps the least tamed of the restored Great Wall sections near Beijing, as well as the least visited. Besides being the starting point for a fantastic four-hour hike toward Simatai, it also stands as one of the few sections of the Great Wall on which overnight camping trips are available. A starry night here is gorgeous and unforgettable—go with a tour group such as Cycle China or Beijing Hikers. However, some have argued that unregulated tourism such as this goes against the efforts of others to preserve the wall, so tread carefully and leave nothing behind in order to reduce your impact. If you must take a souvenir, pack a piece of charcoal and paper to make rubbings of the bricks that still bare the stamp of the date they were made.

The trip by car to Jinhshanling from central Beijing should cost around Y700 and take about two hours. By public transportation, take a train from Beijing North Train Station to Luanping and a local bus or taxi from there. Trains leave almost every hour until 8 pm. ⊠ *Jinshanling ✣ 110 km (68 miles) northeast of Beijing* ☎ *031/4883–0222* ☜ *Apr.–Oct. Y65, Nov.–Mar. Y55; overnight stays at campsite Y150* ☽ *Daily 5–7.*

Great Wall at Juyongguan. Juyongguan is a quick, easygoing alternative for those not willing to blow a whole day traveling to Mutianyu or Jinshanling, or brave the more testing, unrestored sites such as Jiankou. It's the part of the wall that runs closest to Beijing and once guarded a crucial pass to the city, repelling hordes of Mongol and, latterly, Japanese invaders. The section also lies not far from Badaling, essentially acting as an overflow for its oversubscribed neighbor. It certainly loses nothing in the comparison, boasting similarly impressive views but with far less abrasive crowds. However, Juyongguan has been heavily restored and does feel a little sterile and commercial as a result.

The main attraction here is the Cloud Platform (or "Crossing Street Tower"), which was built in 1342 during the Yuan Dynasty. In appearance, it now resembles a rather squat Arc de Triomphe. The three white Tibetan stupas that originally sat atop it were destroyed during the early Ming period, only to be replaced with a Buddhist Tai'an temple, which was later toppled by fire in 1702. Today, carvings on the inner portal depicting the Four Heavenly Kings (Buddhist gods who defend the four compass points) and some elegant script work make for fascinating viewing on the way up the pass.

The trip by car from central Beijing to Juyongguan should cost around Y450 for the round-trip and takes about an hour. By public transportation, take Line 13 on the subway to Longze. Exit the station and walk to the bus stop across the street to take Bus 58 (Y12) to Shahe; take Bus 68 at the same stop to Juyongguan Gongjiaochang and walk to the wall from there. The trip takes about 2½ hours. ⊠ *Juyongguan ✣ 59 km (37 miles) northwest of Beijing* ☎ *010/6977–1665* ☜ *Apr.–Oct. Y45, Nov.–Mar. Y28* ☽ *Apr.–Oct., daily 8–5; Nov.–Mar., daily 8:30–4:30.*

Great Wall at Mutianyu. Only slightly farther from downtown Beijing than Badaling, the Great Wall at Mutianyu is more spectacular and, despite the occasional annoyances of souvenir stands, significantly less crowded. This long section of wall, first built during the Northern Qi

2

Dynasty (6th century) and restored and rebuilt throughout history, can offer a less busy Great Wall experience, with unforgettable views of towers winding across mountains and woodlands. On a clear day, you'll swear you can see the deserts of Mongolia in the distance.

The lowest point on the wall is a strenuous one-hour climb above the parking lot. As an alternative, you can take a cable car on a breathtaking ride to the highest restored section, from which several hiking trails descend. Take a gorgeous 1½-hour walk east to reach another cable car that returns to the same parking lot. Mutianyu is also known for its toboggan run—the perfect way to end a long hike.

The trip by car from central Beijing to Mutianyu should cost around Y600 and it takes about an hour. By public transportation, take Bus 936 from Dongzhimen to Huairou bus stop. From there take a minibus to Mutianyu (Y25–Y30) or hire a taxi to take you there and back (about Y100–Y150 round-trip).

■ TIP→ For those taking a car, the road from Huairou, a suburb of Beijing, to Mutianyu follows a river upstream and is lined with restaurants selling fresh trout. In addition, Hongluo Temple is a short drive from the bottom of the mountain. ✉ *Huairou County* ✛ *90 km (56 miles) northeast of Beijing* ☎ *010/6162–6022* ✐ *Apr.–Oct. Y25; cable car Y80 one-way, Y100 round-trip* ☽ *Apr.–Oct., daily 8–5; Nov.–Mar., daily 8:30–4:30.*

Great Wall at Simatai (司马台长城 *Sīmǎtái chángchéng*). Remote and largely unrestored, this section of the Great Wall is ideal if you're seeking adventure. Near the frontier garrison at Gubeikou, the wall traverses towering peaks and hangs precariously above cliffs. Be prepared for no-handrails hiking, tough climbs, and unparalleled vistas.

The first 10 of the watchtowers is currently accessible to visitors, and the hike to the top and back is just under two hours. Alternatively, a cable car takes you two-thirds of the way up; from there it's a steep 30-minute climb to the summit.

The trip by car from central Beijng to Simitai costs about Y800 and takes about two hours. By public transportation, take the 980 or 980快 (fast bus) from Dongzhimen bus stop to Miyun, getting off at Gulou. Cross the road to the opposite bus station and transfer to Bus 51 or 38 toward Simatai and get off at Gubeikou Water town (or Gubeikou Shuizhen). Follow directions to the ticket hall where you can pick up your pre-booked online tickets for the wall.

■ TIP→ It's necessary to reserve a ticket online using a Chinese mobile number, to which a ticket code will be sent (your hotel or a travel agency can help with these arrangements). ✉ *Near Miyun, Miyun County* ✛ *120 km (75 miles) northeast of Beijing* ☎ *010/8100–9999* ⊕ *www.wtown. com* ✐ *Y40 (Y110 including Gubei Water Town); cable car, Y80 one-way, Y120 round-trip* ☽ *Apr.–Oct., daily 9–6; Nov.–Mar., daily 9–5.*

THIRTEEN MING TOMBS

48 km (30 miles) north of Beijing.

A narrow valley just north of Changping is the final resting place for 13 of the Ming Dynasty's 16 emperors (the first Ming emperor was buried in Nanjing; the burial site of the second one is unknown; and the seventh Ming emperor was dethroned and buried in an ordinary tomb in northwestern Beijing). Ming monarchs once journeyed here each year to kowtow before their clan forefathers and make offerings to their memory. These days, few visitors can claim royal descent, but the area's vast scale and imperial grandeur do convey the importance attached to ancestor worship in ancient China. A leisurely stroll down the Sacred Way, inspecting the series of charming larger-than-life statues of imperial officials and animals, is a wonderful experience. Many visitors combine a stop here with an excursion to the Badaling section of the Great Wall, which is found off the same expressway.

Zhaoling. Allow ample time for a hike or drive northwest from Changling to the six fenced-off **unrestored tombs,** a short distance farther up the valley. Here, crumbling walls conceal vast courtyards shaded by pine trees. At each tomb, a stone altar rests beneath a stele tower and burial mound. In some cases the wall that circles the burial chamber is accessible on steep stone stairways that ascend from either side of the altar. At the valley's terminus (about 5 km [3 miles] northwest of Changling), the Zhaoling Tomb rests beside a traditional walled village that's well worth exploring.

Picnics amid the ruins have been a favorite weekend activity among Beijingers for nearly a century; if you picnic here, be sure to carry out all trash. ⊠ *Changping District* ⌧ *Apr.–Oct. Y35, Nov.–Mar. Y25* ⊙ *Apr.–Oct., daily 8:30–5:30; Nov.–Mar., daily 8:30–5.*

THE WESTERN TEMPLES

20–70 km (12–43 miles) west of Beijing.

Some of China's most spectacular temples and other monuments are on wooded hillsides west of Beijing. Here you'll discover magnificent murals at Fahai Temple, about an hour's drive from the center, and Jietai, an ancient Buddhist site nearby. Tian Yi Mu is not a temple but the elaborate tomb of one of the high-ranking eunuchs who once played a vital role in affairs of state. Yunju Temple is best known for its mind-boggling collection of 14,278 minutely carved Buddhist tablets. While all these sights are in the western suburbs of Beijing, you will probably want to approach them as three separate excursions: Fahai Temple and Tian Yi Mu on one; Jietai Temple and nearby Tanzhe Temple on another; and Yunju Temple on a third. If traveling by taxi or private car, you could work visits to Fahai Temple, Tian Yi Mu, and Jietai and Tanzhe temples into one full day.

Fahai Temple (法海寺 *Fǎhǎi sì*). The stunning works of Buddhist mural art at Fahai Temple, 20 km (12 miles) west of the central city, are among the most underappreciated sights in Beijing. Li Tong, a favored eunuch in the court of Emperor Zhengtong (1436–49), donated funds to construct Fahai Temple in 1443. The project was highly ambitious: Li Tong invited only celebrated imperial and court painters to decorate the temple. As a result, the murals in the only surviving chamber of that period, Daxiongbaodian (the Mahavira Hall), are considered the finest examples of Buddhist mural art from the Ming Dynasty. Sadly, statues of various

Buddhas and one of Li Tong himself were destroyed during China's Cultural Revolution.

The most famous of the nine murals in Mahavira Hall is a large-scale triptych featuring Guanyin (the Bodhisattva of Compassion) and Wenshu (the Bodhisattva of Marvelous Virtue and Gentle Majesty) in the center, and Poxian (the Buddha of Universal Virtue) on either side. The depiction of Guanyin follows the theme of "moon in water," which compares the Buddhist belief in the illusoriness of the material world to the reflection of the moon in the water. Typically painted with Guanyin are her legendary mount Jin Sun and her assistant Shancai Tongzi. Wenshu is often presented with a lion, symbolic of the bodhisattva's wisdom and strength of will, while Poxian is shown near a six-tusked elephant, each tusk representing one of the qualities that leads to enlightenment. On the opposite wall is the *Sovereign Sakra and Brahma* mural, with a panoply of characters from the Buddhist canon.

The murals were painted during the time of the European Renaissance, and though the subject matter is traditional, there are comparable experiments in perspective taking place in the depiction of the figures, as compared with examples from earlier dynasties. Also of note is a highly unusual decorative technique; many contours in the hall's murals, particularly on jewelry, armor, and weapons, have been set in bold relief by the application of fine gold threads.

The temple grounds are also beautiful, but of overriding interest are the murals themselves. Visitors stumble through the dark temple with rented flashlights (free with your ticket). Viewing the murals in this way, it's easy to imagine oneself as a sort of modern-day Indiana Jones unraveling a story of the Buddha as depicted in ancient murals of unrivaled beauty. Fahai Temple is only a short taxi ride from Beijing's Pingguoyuan subway station. ⊠ *Moshikou Lu, Shijingshan District, Beijing* ✢ *Take an approximate Y19 taxi ride from Pinguoyuan subway station directly to the temple* ☎ *010/8871–3975* ☒ *Y20 (Y100 including Buddhist murals)* ☉ *Daily 9–4.*

Fodor's Choice **Tian Yi Mu** (北京宦官文化陈列馆（田义幕） *Tiányì mù*). Eunuchs have
★ played a vital role throughout Chinese history, frequently holding great sway over the affairs of state. Their importance, often overlooked, is celebrated in the **Beijing Eunuch Culture Exhibition Hall** and the tomb of the most powerful eunuch of all, **Tian Yi** (1534–1605). Tian Yi was only nine when he was voluntarily castrated and sent into the service of the Ming emperor Jiajing. During the next 63 years of his life, he served three rulers and rose to one of the highest ranks in the land. By the time he died, there were more than 20,000 eunuchs in imperial service. Thanks to their access to private areas of the palace, they became invaluable as go-betweens for senior officials seeking gossip or the royal ear, and such was Tian Yi's influence. It's said that upon his death the Forbidden City fell silent for three days.

Though not as magnificent as the Thirteen Ming Tombs, the final resting place of Tian Yi befits a man of high social status. Of special note are the intricate stone carvings around the base of the central burial mound. The

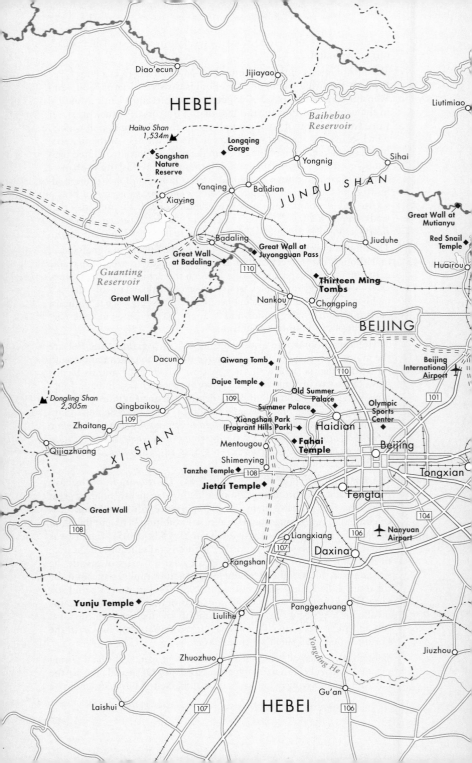

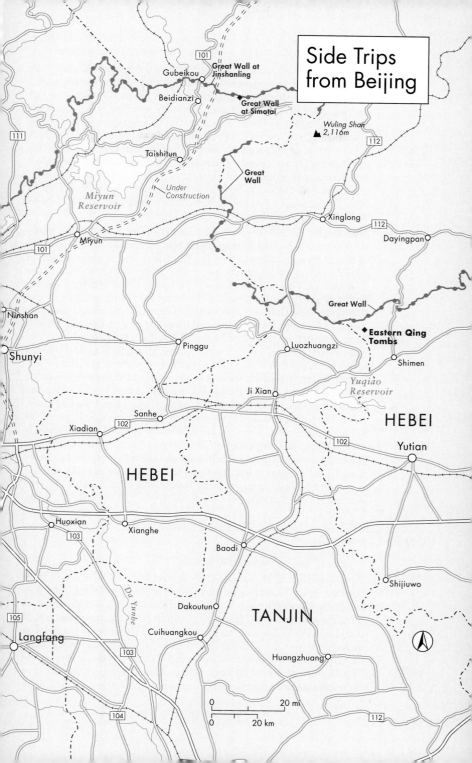

Side Trips
from Beijing

101

Gubeikou Great Wall at
Jinshanling

Beidianzi Great Wall
at Simatai

Wuling Shan
2,116m

111 112

Taishitun

Miyun
Reservoir Great
Wall

Under
Construction Xinglong 112

Miyun Dayingpan

101

Ninshan Great Wall

Shunyi Pinggu Luozhuangzi Eastern Qing
Tombs

Shimen

Ji Xian Yuqiao
Reservoir

Sanhe HEBEI

Xiadian 102

102 Yutian

HEBEI

Huoxian Xianghe

103 Baodi

Shijiuwo

Da Yunhe Dakoutun TANJIN

105 Cuihuangkou

Langfang Huangzhuang

103

0   20 mi

0   20 km

104 112

four smaller tombs on either side belong to other eunuchs who wished to pay tribute to Tian Yi by being buried in the same compound as him.

The small exhibition hall at the front of the tomb complex contains the world's only "eunuch museum" and offers some interesting background (albeit mostly in Mandarin), particularly on China's last eunuch, Sun Yaoting (1902–96). It's worth visiting, if only to see the rather gruesome mummified remains of one castrati that holds center stage—you can still make out the hairs on his chin. Another equally squirm-inducing sight is the eye-watering collection of castration equipment; keep a look out for the ancient Chinese character meaning "to castrate," which resembles two knives, one inverted, side by side. The hall and tomb are a five-minute walk from Fahai Temple; just ask people the way to Tian Yi Mu. ⊠ *80 Moshikou Lu, Shijingshan District, Beijing* ☎ *010/8872–4148* 💳 *Y8* ⊙ *Daily 9–3:30.*

Jietai Temple (戒台寺 *Jiètái sì*). The four main halls of one of China's most famous ancient Buddhist sites occupy terraces on a gentle slope up to Ma'an Shan (Saddle Hill), 35 km (22 miles) west of Beijing. Built in AD 622, the temple has been used for the ordination of Buddhist novices since the Liao Dynasty. The temple complex expanded over the centuries and grew to its current scale in a major renovation conducted by devotees during the Qing Dynasty (1644–1912). The temple buildings, plus three magnificent bronze Buddhas in the Mahavira Hall, date from this period. There's also a huge potbellied Maitreya Buddha carved from the roots of what must have been a truly enormous tree. To the right of this hall, just above twin pagodas, is the Ordination Terrace, a platform built of white marble and topped with a massive bronze statue of Shakyamuni Buddha seated on a lotus flower. Tranquil courtyards, where ornate stelae and well-kept gardens bask beneath a scholar tree and other ancient pines, add to the temple's beauty. Many modern devotees from Beijing visit the temple on weekends. Getting to Jietai and the nearby Tanzhe Temple is easy using public transportation. Take subway Line 1 to its westernmost station, Pingguoyuan. From there, take the No. 931 public bus to either temple—it leaves every half hour and the ride takes about 70 minutes. A taxi from Pingguoyuan to Jietai Temple should be Y50 to Y60; the bus fare is Y6. ⊠ *Mentougou County, Beijing* ☎ *010/6980–6611* 💳 *Y45* ⊙ *Daily 8:30–5.*

YUNJU TEMPLE

75 km (47 miles) southwest of Beijing.

Yunju Temple (云居寺 *Yúnjū sì*). To protect the Buddhist canon from destruction by Taoist emperors, the devout Tang-era monk Jing Wan carved Buddhist scriptures into stone slabs that he hid in sealed caves in the cliffs of a mountain. Jing Wan spent 30 years creating these tablets until his death in AD 637; his disciples continued his work for the next millennium into the 17th century, thereby compiling one of the most extensive Buddhist libraries in the world, a mind-boggling collection of 14,278 minutely carved Buddhist tablets. A small pagoda at the center of the temple complex commemorates the remarkable monk. Although the

The Eastern Qing Tombs are the most expansive burial grounds in China.

tablets were originally stored inside Shijing Mountain behind the temple, they're now housed in rooms built along the temple's southern perimeter.

Four central prayer halls, arranged along the hillside above the main gate, contain impressive Ming-era bronze Buddhas. The last in this row, the Dabei Hall, displays the spectacular *Thousand-Armed Avalokiteshvara.* This 13-foot-tall bronze sculpture—which actually has 24 arms and five heads and stands in a giant lotus flower—is believed to embody boundless compassion. A group of pagodas, led by the 98-foot-tall Northern Pagoda, is all that remains of the original Tang complex. These pagodas are remarkable for their Buddhist reliefs and ornamental patterns. Heavily damaged during the Japanese occupation and again by Maoist radicals in the 1960s, the temple complex remains under renovation.

Yunju Temple is 70 km (43 miles) southwest of central Beijing. By bus, take No. 917 from Tianqiao Long-distance Bus Station to Liangxiang Ximen, then change to Fangshan Bus Nos.12, 19, 31 to Yun Ju Si. ⊠ *Off Fangshan Lu, Nanshangle Xiang, Fangshan County, Beijing* ☎ *010/6138–9612* 🎟 *Y40* 🕙 *Daily 8:30–4.*

EASTERN QING TOMBS

125 km (78 miles) east of Beijing.

Modeled on the Thirteen Ming Tombs, the mausoleum complex at Zunhua, known as the Eastern Qing Tombs, replicate the Ming walkways, walled tomb complexes, and subterranean burial chambers. But they're even more extravagant in their scale and grandeur, and far less touristy.

These imposing ruins contain the remains of five emperors, 14 empresses, and 136 imperial concubines, all laid to rest in a broad valley chosen by Emperor Shunzhi (1638–61) while on a hunting expedition. By the Qing's collapse in 1911, the tomb complex covered some 18 square miles (46 square km) of farmland and forested hillside, making it the most expansive burial ground in all China.

The Eastern Qing Tombs are in much better repair than their older Ming counterparts—and considerably less crowded. Although several of the tomb complexes have undergone extensive renovation, none is overdone. Peeling paint, grassy courtyards, and numerous stone bridges and pathways convey a sense of the area's original grandeur. Often visitors are so few that you may feel as if you've stumbled upon an ancient ruin unknown beyond the valley's farming villages.

The tombs are a two- to three-hour drive from the capital and are surrounded by dramatic rural scenery, making this trip one of the best full-day excursions outside Beijing. Consider bringing a bedsheet, a bottle of wine, and boxed lunches, as the grounds are ideal for a picnic.

Fodor's Choice ★ **Yuling** (清东陵 *Qīngdōnglíng*). Of the nine tombs open to the public, Yuling is not to be missed. This is the resting place of the Qing Dynasty's most powerful sovereign, Emperor Qianlong (1711–99), who ruled China for 59 years. Beyond the outer courtyards, Qianlong's burial chamber is accessible from inside Stela Hall, where an entry tunnel descends some 65 feet (20 meters) into the ground and ends at the first of three elaborately carved marble gates. Beyond, exquisite carvings of Buddhist images and sutras rendered in Tibetan adorn the tomb's walls and ceiling. Qianlong was laid to rest, along with his empress and two concubines, in the third and final marble vault, amid priceless offerings looted by warlords early in the 20th century. ⊠ *Hebei Province, Zunhua County, Malanguan* ☏ *0315/694–0888* ✉ *Y152 (with rest of tombs)* ☉ *Daily 8:30–5.*

Fodor's Choice ★ **Dingdongling** (清东陵 *Qīngdōnglíng*). The most elaborate of the Qing tombs was built for the infamous Empress Dowager Cixi (1835–1908). Known for her failure to halt Western-imperialist encroachment, Cixi once spent funds allotted to strengthen China's navy on a traditional stone boat for the lake at the Summer Palace. Her burial compound, reputed to have cost 72 tons of silver, is the most elaborate (if not the largest) at the Eastern Qing Tombs. Many of its stone carvings are considered significant because the phoenix, which symbolizes the female, is level with, or even above, the imperial (male) dragon—a feature ordered, no doubt, by the empress herself. A peripheral hall paneled in gold leaf displays some of the luxuries amassed by Cixi and her entourage, including embroidered gowns, jewelry, imported cigarettes, and even a coat for one of her dogs. In a bow to tourist kitsch, the compound's main hall contains a wax statue of Cixi sitting Buddha-like on a lotus petal flanked by a chambermaid and a eunuch. ⊠ *Hebei Province, Zunhua County, Malanguan* ☏ *0315/694–0888* ✉ *Y152 (with rest of tombs)* ☉ *Daily 8:30–5.*

BEIJING TO SHANGHAI

Hebei, Shandong, Jiangsu, and Anhui

WELCOME TO BEIJING TO SHANGHAI

TOP REASONS TO GO

★ **Qingdao:** Hit the beach or explore the historic corners of the Bavarian-styled "Old City," with its mansions, churches, and burgeoning café culture.

★ **Huangshan:** Framed in spectral mist, Yellow Mountain's towering granite peaks have inspired artists and poets for centuries.

★ **Chengde:** Originally an imperial summer retreat, this town's magnificent temples, palaces and deer-filled parks now attract weekenders hunting for culture.

★ **Suzhou:** Discover flower-filled classical gardens in a town still threaded with ancient waterways.

★ **Qufu:** Visit the birthplace of China's foremost philosopher and spiritual thinker, the "Great Sage" Confucius.

1 Hebei. Wrapped around the nation's capital, Hebei's attractions are definitely worth a side trip. The Manchu summer retreat of Chengde puts on an almighty show of pomp and splendor, and in Shanhaiguan the Great Wall finally comes to an end at the ocean.

2 Shandong. Follow in the footsteps of emperors with a pilgrimage to Taishan, the most revered of all China's sacred mountains. For the more earthly pleasures of sun, seafood, and suds, don't miss the seaside city of Qingdao, China's water sports (and drinking) capital.

3 Jiangsu. A witness to turbulent historic events, Jiangsu abounds with mausoleums and memorials, ancient temples and palaces, and the region's finest cuisine. Nanjing was the country's capital for six dynastic periods. Nearby Suzhou and Yangzhou are renowned for their splendid gardens.

4 Anhui. It may be one of China's poorest provinces, but Anhui's wealth lies in its immaculately preserved villages and the sublime mountain scenery at Huangshan.

GETTING ORIENTED

Stretching from Hebei, which is culturally and geographically Northern China, to the more refined province of Jiangsu, this region is accessible thanks to a well-developed tourist infrastructure. All four provinces have convenient air and rail links to the major transport hubs of Beijing and Shanghai. As you travel from north to south, you can judge for yourself whether Chinese stereotypes are accurate: Northerners are viewed as typically taller and lighter skinned, raised on wheat-based foods like noodles and bread that thrive in the cool, dry climate. Southerners, on the other hand, are thought of as shorter and darker, with rice their staple of choice. The mighty Yangtze River that flows past Nanjing is sometimes taken to represent this vague cultural border.

3

Updated by Tom O'Malley

Tombs, temples, elegant gardens, and historic water towns are just the beginning of what this extraordinary region has to offer. This is where Confucius was born, where China's two great rivers and the Great Wall meet the sea, and where some of the country's most celebrated mountain landscapes have inspired pilgrimages for millennia.

Despite phenomenal development across Eastern China over the past decade, it's still possible to lose yourself in the canal-side walkways and idyllic gardens of Suzhou, the "Venice of the East," or pick a path through the cobbled streets of old Yangzhou. Eight of China's 43 UNESCO World Heritage Sites dot this region, with Anhui's villages of Xidi and Hongcun and Shandong's Qufu, Confucius's ancestral birthplace, managing to retain most of their historic and artistic character. Buy Suzhou's famous silk from the owners of the silk-spinning worms, Tsingtao beer straight from the source in Qingdao, and sample the dim-sum delights of Huaiyang cuisine at its most authentic in Yangzhou.

Everyone from Emperor Qin to Chairman Mao has tackled the trail to the summit of Tai Shan, China's most sacred Taoist mountain. And they didn't have a cable car to help them. To the south, Huangshan's mysterious peaks, fringed with spindly pines and swathed in clouds, have inspired whole schools of Chinese painting.

Travel here has never been easier. Increasingly comfortable and internationally minded lodgings are springing up everywhere. Bullet trains have slashed journey times, whisking you from one destination to the next. Remember that the pedestrian in no way has the right of way in China, and take a business card with your hotel's address in Chinese to show a taxi when returning home after a long day's sightseeing.

PLANNING

WHEN TO GO

Spring and summer is the best time to head to the coast at Qingdao and, farther north, Beidaihe and Shanhaiguan. Save the arduous ascents of Huangshan and Taishan for autumn, when the crowds and temperatures have died down.

The eastern region of China is heavily populated, and sometimes it seems like everyone takes to the road (or train, or plane). Avoid traveling during the Chinese New Year, which is based on the lunar calendar and falls between January and March. The weeklong National Day holiday at the start of October can easily be avoided with a bit of planning.

GETTING HERE AND AROUND

With the exception of Huangshan, Chengde, and Yangzhou, every destination in this chapter is now connected by the China Highspeed Rail network, by far the most convenient and comfortable way to get around. Buses are very efficient, and tickets can usually be bought the same day. Airline tickets can be purchased close to the departure date and prices are fairly consistent, assuming you avoid traveling during a Chinese holiday, when prices can skyrocket.

AIR TRAVEL

Besides the major international airports in Beijing and Shanghai, other domestic air hubs include Nanjing, Qingdao, and Shijiazhuang (the capital of Hebei Province). Unlike other areas of the country, distances between sights in this region aren't great. The main operators are Air China and China Eastern Airlines, though there are several regional carriers like Shandong Airlines and Hebei Airlines.

BUS TRAVEL

With many thousands of destinations and departures, buses can be handy for short trips, especially to destinations outside the high-speed rail network (Nanjing to Yangzhou is a good example). Buses are usually in reasonable condition and have air-conditioning, assigned seating, and reliably punctual service. Remember to bring a pair of headphones, as you can usually expect a noisy kung-fu movie playing on the video monitor. Never patronize the army of touts who work at the main bus stations; always buy your tickets from the official counters or better yet, through your hotel.

CAR TRAVEL

Hiring a car and driver gives you the freedom to explore the region at your own leisure, but it can be costly. Expect prices of at least $150 a day if you book through an international hotel, and substantially more if you want an English-speaking guide.

TRAIN TRAVEL

China's excellent high-speed rail system has made Shandong and Jiangsu more accessible than ever before, with many trains whizzing along at over 300 kph (186 mph). Tickets can usually be purchased through your hotel (strongly recommended), or online at ⊕ *www.ctrip. com* which are then couriered to your accommodation, or lastly inside the station itself, although the lines are often long and vendors can be curt with non-Chinese speakers. Buy tickets at least 24 hours ahead of when you intend to travel, or longer during peak periods. Passports are mandatory for buying tickets and boarding the train. In the event that you miss your train, go to a ticket counter —they will usually put you on the next available service for a nominal fee. Note: only holders of Chinese ID cards can use the electronic ticket machines in stations.

HEALTH AND SAFETY

Take all prescription medicine with you. For minor ailments, such as headaches and stomachaches, Chinese pharmacies are widespread and stocked with both Chinese and Western medicine. Antibiotics can be purchased easily and cheaply over the counter. Carry waterless hand sanitizer and toilet paper. Safe bottled water is widely available.

RESTAURANTS

Every locality has its own specialties—wild game in Hebei, braised chicken in Shandong, duck cooked myriad ways in Jiangsu. Try Qingdao's famous chili-fried clams, or Suzhou's sweet-and-sour river fish. Jiangsu cuisine, called Huaiyang, is considered one of China's four great cooking styles, and is light, fresh, and sweet (though not as sweet as in Shanghai). As you travel inland to Anhui, the food is famously salty, relying heavily on preserved ham and soy sauce to enhance flavors. Anhui chefs make good use of mountain-grown mushrooms and bamboo shoots. Vegetarian options, often available in or near Buddhist temples, showcase chefs who manipulate tofu, wheat gluten, and vegetables to create "mock" meat that even carnivores will appreciate.

HOTELS

Hotels in this region are improving every year, and most major cities now have a range of international luxury brands. Don't expect to find such creature comforts in smaller cities, but you will discover comfortable mid-range lodgings. English-speaking staff can be thin on the ground at cheaper Chinese-run hotels. Most places these days accept credit cards, and you'll get better rates if you book in advance. Chinese hotels are easy to book, often without prepaying, through English-language Chinese websites like ⊕ *www.ctrip.com* or ⊕ *www.elong.com* and increasingly, through global booking sites like ⊕ *www.booking. com. Hotel reviews have been shortened. For full information, visit Fodors.com.*

WHAT IT COSTS IN YUAN				
	$	$$	$$$	$$$$
Restaurants	under Y50	Y50–Y99	Y100–Y165	over Y165
Hotels	under Y1,100	Y1,100–Y1,399	Y1,400–Y1,800	over Y1,800

Restaurant prices are the average cost of a main course at dinner or, if dinner is not served, at lunch. Hotel prices are the lowest cost of a standard double room in high season.

VISITOR INFORMATION

In the bigger cities you'll find storefronts and street kiosks with signs reading "Tourist Information." However, finding someone who speaks enough English to be helpful might be difficult, as these booths cater to domestic tourists. Your best bets for in-depth assistance are larger hotels. Be polite and persistent. Write dates clearly when inquiring about tickets, speak slowly, and inspect any tickets given to you thoroughly before leaving. Look for copies of the English-language *Redstar* (Qingdao), *Map Magazine* or *The Nanjinger* (Nanjing), and *More Suzhou* in hotels, restaurants, and coffee shops.

TOURS

Group tours are always an option, but often feature unwelcome shopping stops, leaving less time to enjoy the sights. Do your research, ask questions, and if the package price seems too high or low, be skeptical. The best source of information is on Fodor's forums (⊕ *www.fodors. com*), where many travelers share the good, the bad, and the ugly, like pressured tipping, frequent shopping stops, and low-quality food.

Beijing Discovery Tours. This American-Chinese company can arrange private tours of Beijing, the surrounding sights, and beyond. The company is extremely reliable and thorough. ☎ *800/306–1264 in U.S., 130/1112–0229 ⊕ www.beijingdiscoverytours.com.*

HEBEI

Many visitors travel through Hebei without a backward glance on the way to and from the capital, but the province has several sites worth a detour. Chengde is a worthwhile stop for those whose appetites for dynastic history have been whetted by Beijing's grand imperial attractions. The town's glory days were during the 18th century, after the Qing Emperor Kangxi had made it his summer retreat and hunting ground, establishing the country's largest royal garden and a bevy of opulent Buddhist temples that dot the surrounding hillsides. The emperors may be long gone, but the town still serves as a holiday destination, now for busloads of Beijing residents. Farther south, at the seaside resorts of Beidaihe and Shanhaiguan, where the Great Wall meets the sea, foreign visitors can experience a singularly Chinese take on the seaside vacation.

CHENGDE

5 hrs (230 km [140 miles]) by train northeast of Beijing; 3 hrs by bus.

Recent development has not been particularly kind to Chengde, but the sights here are well tended, and in fine weather it's still possible to glimpse the natural beauty of this river valley that so captivated Emperor Kangxi on a hunting trip in the late 1600s. With the Wulie River gurgling through and the Yanshan Mountains providing an impressive backdrop, Chengde was deemed an ideal spot to establish a summer retreat where the emperor could escape the heat of the capital and indulge in hunting and fishing. Later Chengde would serve a crucial

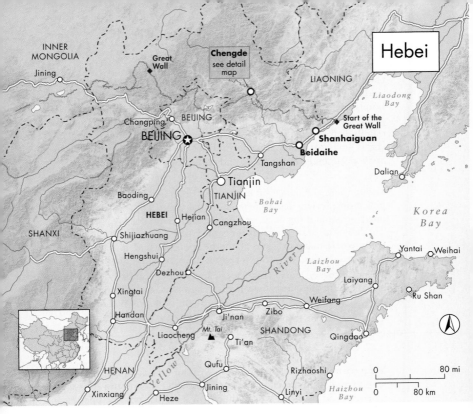

diplomatic function, its grand temples erected in honorific tribute to host visiting religious and political leaders of China's border ethnicities.

Today it is a UNESCO World Heritage Site, awarded collectively to the magnificent Mountain Resort and the Eight Outer Monasteries (though only five are open to tourists at time of writing). Although children enjoy romping through the imperial gardens, there's little else to entertain younger visitors. It's generally considered best to visit in summer or early autumn to escape the heat of cities like Beijing, but a visit during the off-season is a good way to avoid the tourist hordes, and the rather steep admission prices are reduced after the first of November.

GETTING HERE AND AROUND

BUS TRAVEL   Long-distance bus is the fastest way to get from Beijing to Chengde, but rather less comfortable than the train, since the bus often stops to pick up extra passengers along the route. Two or three services an hour leave from Sihui bus station in the east of the city (on Subway Line 1) and take between 2½ and 3½ hours (Y85) to arrive at Chengde East Bus Station, a short taxi ride from the sights.

TRAIN TRAVEL   Most travelers arrive on the K7711 direct train from Beijing, which departs from Beijing Main Rail Station at 7:56 am, arriving in Chengde at 12:31 pm. No trains run between Chengde and Beidaihe or Shanhaiguan.

Train Contact Chengde Train Station ⊠ *Chezhan Lu.*

TAXI TRAVEL   Chengde is a small city, so you shouldn't have to pay more than Y20 to get from the city center out to the temples.

SAFETY AND PRECAUTIONS

Like most Chinese cities, Chengde is a very safe place to explore. Violent crime is extremely rare, but petty theft can be a problem. Keep a close eye on your personal belongings in crowded places.

TIMING

Most of the main attractions are bunched to the north and east of the Mountain Resort, so one or two full days should be enough time to see the sights. That said, the Mountain Resort is huge, and could easily take up a full day by itself. If you want to do any hiking in the surrounding countryside, plan on three full days.

TOURS

All hotels in Chengde run tours covering the main sights during the high season. An English-speaking guide costs around Y100.

ESSENTIALS

Medical Assistance Chengde Central Hospital ⊠ *22 Xi Da Jie* ☏ *0314/202–2222.*

Visitor and Tour Info Chengde CITS ⊠ *Yun Shan Lu* ☏ *0314/206–1848.*

EXPLORING

Don't waste your energy wandering around the city itself. The massive scale of the Mountain Resort, twice as large as Beijing's Summer Palace, means you will be doing plenty of walking. Bus route 6 links the Mountain Resort with the outer temples.

TOP ATTRACTIONS

Fodor's Choice   **Mountain Resort** (避暑山庄 *Bìshǔ shānzhuāng*). Charmed by Chengde's
★   dramatic setting, pleasant climate, and plentiful game, Emperor Kangxi ordered construction of the first palaces of the Mountain Resort in 1703. Within a decade, this once sleepy settlement boasted dozens of ornate temples, pagodas, and walled grasslands spread out across 1,500 acres. By the end of the 18th century nearly 100 imperial structures had been built, with Chengde becoming the epicenter of Chinese political and cultural life whenever the emperor and his entourage decamped here from Beijing.

The Mountain Resort and its surrounding temples were more than just an imperial retreat, however. Besides luxurious quarters for the emperor and his court, great palaces and temples were constructed to house visiting dignitaries—particularly China's border groups like the Mongols and Tibetans—and to woo them with the might and wealth of the Qing empire. Not forgetting, of course, that the Qing also came from beyond the Great Wall as the pastoral Manchu. The location was useful, as Chengde lay far enough away from Beijing to host talks with border groups who wouldn't otherwise set foot in the capital. From the interconnected palaces, each built in different architectural styles, to the replicas of famous temples representing different Chinese religions and ethnic groups, everything about the resort was designed to reflect

China's diversity. In retrospect, it was as much a Qing statement of intent as it was a holiday home.

Today, the palace and its walled-off landscape of lakes, grasslands, hills, and forests dominates the center of Chengde. The steep hills in the northern half of the park, crowned by stone walls that resemble the Great Wall, afford beautiful panoramas, as does a slog up the nine-tiered pagoda in the center. Even during peak season (April to October) it rarely feels crowded. ✉ *Center of town* ☎ *0314/2029771* 🏷 *Apr.–Oct. Y120, Nov.–Mar. Y90* 🕐 *Apr.–Oct., daily 7–5; Nov.–Mar., daily 7–4:30.*

Pule Temple (普乐寺 *Pùlè sì*). The conical-roofed centerpiece of this serene hillside temple, the Pavilion of the Brilliance of the Rising Sun (*Xuguangge*), will be instantly recognizable if you've visited Beijing's Temple of Heaven. Built to host visiting Kazak, Uygher, and Kyrger dignitaries, as well as to commemorate certain Mongol tribes, Pule Temple was laid out to resemble a mandala of Tibetan Buddhism. From the south wall of the temple, it's a peaceful 40-minute walk up the hillside to Sledgehammer Rock. The Y50 ticket includes admission to Sledgehammer Rock and the lovely Anyuan Temple down the hill. ✉ *East of Mountain Resort* 🏷 *Y50* 🕐 *Apr.–Oct., daily 8–5:30; Nov.–Mar., daily 8:30–5.*

Puning Temple (普宁寺 *Pǔníng sì*). Located on the western banks of the Wulie River, this temple was built in 1755 to commemorate Emperor Qianlong's triumphant conquest of the warring Dzungar people from Xinjiang. Intended to mark a new period of peace, it was modeled after the Samye Monastery, a sacred Lamaist site in Tibet. Also known as "Big Buddha Temple," its main attraction is an awe-inspiring 72-foot-tall statue of Guanyin, a Buddhist deity of compassion. The statue is made from five types of wood, including pine, cypress, elm, and fir. ✉ *Puning Si Lu* ☎ *0314/205–8209* 🏷 *Apr.–Oct. Y80, Nov.–Mar. Y60* 🕐 *Apr.–Oct., daily 8–4:30; Nov.–Mar., daily 8:30–4.*

Putuo Zongcheng Temple (普陀宗乘之庙 *Pǔtuó zōngchéng zhīmiào*). Built from 1767 to mark Emperor Qianlong's birthday, the largest of Chengde's temples is modeled on the Potala Palace in Lhasa—it also goes by the nickname "Little Potala." A fusion of Chinese and Tibetan architectural styles, it's most impressive when viewed from the north wall of the Mountain Resort, or from the courtyard of Anyuan Temple. Inside the imposing gate is a pavilion housing three stelae, the largest inscribed in Han, Manchu, Mongolian, and Tibetan languages. The Y80 ticket includes admission to the Xumi Fushou Temple next door, a replica of the Tashilhunpo Monastery in Tibet, the traditional seat of the Panchen Lama. ✉ *Shizigou Lu* ☎ *0314/216–3072* 🏷 *Apr.–Oct. Y80, Nov.–Mar. Y60* 🕐 *Apr.–Oct., daily 8–5; Nov.–Mar., daily 8:30–4:30.*

WORTH NOTING

Sledgehammer Rock (棒槌峰 *Bàngchuí fēng*). A chairlift ride or a 35-minute hike leads from Pule Temple up through lovely hillside to this remarkable rock protrusion that spawned a local legend: if the rock should fall, so will the virility of local men. In fact, this unusual geological feature probably played a part in Emperor Kangxi choosing

154 <

Chengde

Anyuan
Temple

Chair Lift
to Club
Rock

Mountain
Resort

Ideal
Island

Western
Hospital

Honeman
Internet Café

Lizheng
Gate

Dehui
Gate

Xi Dajie

Lizhengmen Dajie

Shanxiying Jie

Dufongfu Dajie

CITS

Qinglengdon Dajie

Nanyingzi Dajie

Zhonghua Lu

Zhijinsi Jie

Wulie Lu

Wenjiagou Lu

Sushunfu Lu

Yuhua Lu

Dongzigou Lu

Xinhua Lu

Long-distance
Bus Station

Chengde
Bridge

Cunqu Lu

Chezhan Lu

Railway
Station

Shanzhuang Dong Lu

Wulie River

Huancheng Donglu

Shanzhuang Dong Lu

Huancheng Donglu

Wulie River

KEY

1 *Exploring Sights*

① *Restaurants and Hotels*

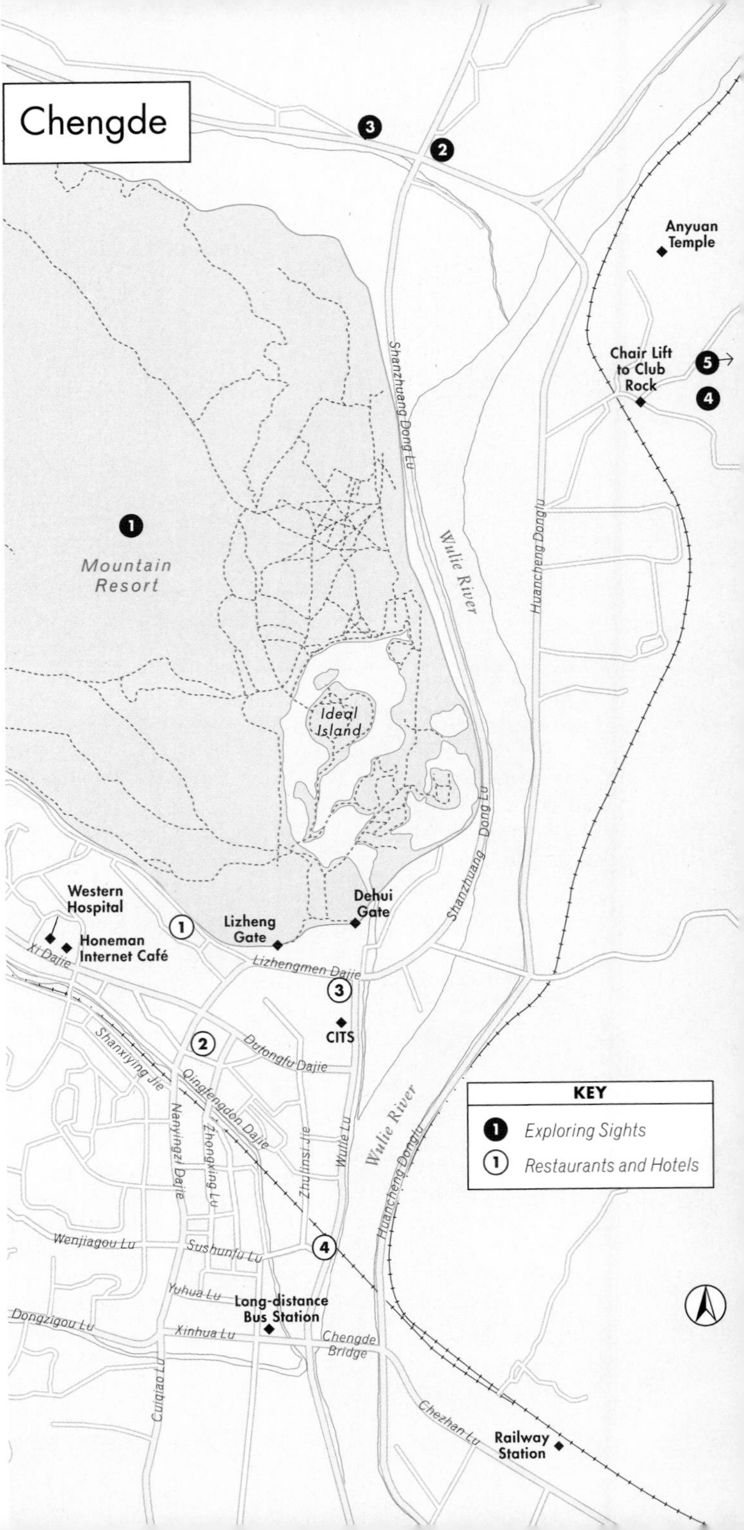

Chengde to establish his summer retreat. ✉ *Y50, includes entrance to Pule Temple and Anyuan Temple* ⊘ *Daily 8–5.*

WHERE TO EAT

Given Chengde's role as a royal hunting ground, it's no surprise that the local specialty is wild game. Spiced deer meat grilled on skewers goes for about Y5 and pheasant-and-mushroom–stuffed dumplings can be sampled at the visitor-friendly shops on the street south of the Summer Resort. Look out for hawkers selling *ludagun*, a Chengde snack of steamed sticky rice with red bean paste, rolled in soybean flour to give it its descriptive name, "donkey rolling on the ground."

$$
CHINESE

✕ **Da Qinghua.** Directly opposite the south entrance to the Mountain Resort, this cheerful place is easily spotted by its rustic wooden exterior and is a good bet if you want to sample a few local dishes. Try the delicious specialty: homemade dumplings filled with pheasant and local mushrooms. There's also a branch beside the train station, where you can grab a quick bite before catching the 19:15 express back to Beijing. $ *Average main: Y80* ✉ *Shan Zhuang Lu* ☎ *0314/2036–2222* ⊟ *No credit cards.*

$$
NORTHERN
CHINESE

✕ **Qiaojia Manchu Eight Bowls Restaurant** (金桥乔家八大碗 *Jīnqiáo qiáojiā bādà wǎn*). Be warned: a wall of deer heads greets you at the entrance to this popular restaurant, and the stuffed animal theme continues throughout. But there's no better place in town to try the variety of game dishes beloved of the Manchu people. Venison features heavily, of course, but you can try wild boar and eggplant stew, braised camel hump, and even deep-fried sparrow. The steamed deer blood curd was a recipe developed in order not to waste the blood of the kill after a hunt, and it's surprisingly tasty. If this all sounds a bit macabre, there are plenty of chicken, beef, and fish dishes, along with hearty vegetable stir-fries and warming soups. $ *Average main: Y80* ✉ *Liushuigou Lu and Zhongxing Lu intersection* ☎ *0314/203–7888.*

WHERE TO STAY

$$$
HOTEL

🏨 **Qi Wang Lou.** New management has rejuvenated this once famous villa complex beside the Mountain Resort; now genuinely luxurious, the wooden furniture-filled guest rooms and meticulously tended gardens make this the finest accommodation in town by a country mile. **Pros:** peaceful; central location; the only genuine luxury hotel in town. **Cons:** expensive; no bar. $ *Rooms from: Y1700* ✉ *1 Bei Bifengmen Dong Lu* ☎ *0314/202–7898* ⊕ *www.qiwanglou.com* ⤢ *49 rooms, 7 suites* ❍❘ *Breakfast.*

$
HOTEL

🏨 **Shenghua Hotel** (盛华大酒店 *Shènghuá dàjiǔdiàn*). The carpets at the Shenghua could do with a scrub, but a few touches like teddy bears on the beds and bathtubs serves to elevate this average but well-run hotel from its peers. **Pros:** tasty restaurant; reliable service; near train station. **Cons:** a bit far from the main sights. $ *Rooms from: Y350* ✉ *22 Wulie Lu* ☎ *0314/227–1000* ⊕ *www.shenghuahotel.com* ⤢ *111 rooms* ❍❘ *Breakfast.*

The main shopping street, Nanyingzi Dajie (parallel to the Wuli River), is a good place to stroll in the evening, when a night market stretches all the way down the street. Many of the vendors sell antiques and fun knickknacks.

BEIDAIHE

2 hrs (260 km [160 miles]) by express train east of Beijing; 3 hrs (395 km [245 miles]) by train southwest of Shenyang; 1 hr (35 km [22 miles]) by minibus southwest of Shanhaiguan.

English railway engineers came across this small fishing village in the 1890s. Not long after, wealthy Chinese and foreign diplomats were visiting in droves. After Mao Zedong came to power, the new rulers developed a taste for sea air. Today the seaside retreat has an interesting mix of beach kitsch and political posturing, with Communist party members past and present owning villas here. Beidaihe is terrifyingly crowded during the summer and practically empty the rest of the year.

GETTING HERE AND AROUND
Most visitors come directly from Beijing, and the train is the most convenient option. The train station in Beidaihe is about a 15-minute taxi ride to the beachfront.

AIR TRAVEL   Though originally scheduled for completion in 2014, Qinhuangdao Beidaihe Airport, 34 km (23 miles) from Beidaihe, is yet to open at time of writing.

BOAT AND FERRY TRAVEL   Qinhuangdao is one of the biggest harbors in China. Destinations include Dalian (14 hours), Shanghai (28 hours), Qingdao (12 hours), and Tianjin (18 hours). CITS in Qinhuangdao has prices and schedules.

Boat and Ferry Contacts Qinhuangdao CITS ✉ *100 Heping Dajie, Qinhuangdao* ☎ *0335/323-1117* ⊕ *www.cits.net.*

BUS TRAVEL   An excellent minibus service links Beidaihe, Qinhuangdao, and Shanhaiguan. Buses leave every 30 minutes. The bus station in Beidaihe is at the intersection of Heishi Lu and Haining Lu. Buy tickets on the bus.

Bus Contact Beidaihe Bus Station ✉ *Beining Lu and Haining Lu.*

TRAIN TRAVEL   Trains traveling up the coast from Beijing all pass through Beidaihe, Shanhaiguan, and Qinhuangdao. Be sure to book the faster D or G class trains.

Train Contact Beidaihe Train Station ✉ *Zhannan Da Jie.*

SAFETY AND PRECAUTIONS
The area's street food is generally safe if cooked at a high heat and not left out in the sun. Be especially careful with seafood, and only dine at crowded places where the food cannot sit for too long.

TIMING
A half day is sufficient to see what the village has to offer, but if the weather allows, it can be a great place to bicycle ride and linger for a bit longer. Many visitors like to combine a trip here with a visit to the Great Wall at Shanhaiguan.

ESSENTIALS

Medical Assistance Beidaihe Hospital ✉ *200 Lianfeng Lu* ☎ *0335/404–1624.*

Visitor and Tour Info Beidaihe CITS ✉ *Jinshan Hotel, 4 Dongsan Lu* ☎ *0335/428–6891* 🌐 *www.cits.net.*

EXPLORING

The best way to get around on a sunny day is to rent a bicycle and cruise up and down the seafront. The southern end of Haining Lu leading down to Middle Beach is the liveliest spot, with faux-European buildings delivering a healthy dose of seaside kitsch.

Lianfeng Hill Park (联峰山公园 *Liánfēngshān gōngyuán*). North of Middle Beach you'll find this lovely park, where quiet paths through a pine forest lead to the **Guanyin Temple** (Guanyin Si). Look for the aviary, known as the Birds Singing Forest. There are also good views of the sea from the top of Lianfeng Hill. ✉ *Jianqui Lu* ☎ *0335/404–1591* 🎟 *Y30* 🕒 *Daily 8–5.*

WHERE TO EAT AND STAY

In summer, seafood restaurants line the beach, and you only need to point at the most appetizing thing squirming in red buckets for the waiter to serve up a delicious fresh meal. A plateful of fresh mussels should cost about Y25, fresh crabs a little more. More good seafood restaurants are clustered on Haining Lu near the beach.

$$$ BAKERY 🍴 **Kiesslings** (起士林餐厅 *Qǐshìlín cāntīng*). Originally opened by Austrians, this popular place is actually three restaurants in one: a petite stone lodge serving Russian and Bavarian fare, an expansive dining room serving Chinese dishes, and a European-style café and bakery doing a brisk business selling freshly baked walnut cakes. The first two are situated on the grounds of the attractive Kiessling Beidaihe Hotel; the café-bakery is on the main street. Unlike most places in Beidaihe, it's open all year. [$] *Average main: Y130* ✉ *Kiessling Beidaihe Hotel, 95 Dongjing Lu* ☎ *0335/468–0000* 🌐 *www.qishilin.com.*

$ HOTEL 🏨 **Beidaihe Guesthouse for Diplomatic Missions** (北戴河外交人员宾馆 *Běidàihé wàijiāo rényuán bīnguǎn*). Catering mostly to Russian travelers, this attractive complex is made up of low-slung buildings set among cypresses and pines in a quiet spot close to its own beach. **Pros:** a classic experience; near the ocean. **Cons:** older buildings could use renovation. [$] *Rooms from: Y600* ✉ *1 Baosan Lu* ☎ *0335/428–0600* 🌐 *www.bsbdm.com.cn* 🛏 *165 rooms* 🕒 *Closed Nov.–Mar.* 🍽 *No meals.*

$ HOTEL FAMILY 🏨 **Holiday Inn Qinhuangdao Sea View.** Nicer than any hotels in Beidaihe or Shanhaiguan (but a good 15 minutes from either by cab), the pleasant rooms here overlook a sandy beach and out towards the Bohai Sea; other bonuses include a great indoor pool and, more unusually, an authentic Indian restaurant. **Pros:** international standard accommodation and service; friendly staff. **Cons:** a cab ride from Beidaihe. [$] *Rooms from: Y600* ✉ *25 Dongguang Lu, Qinghuangdao* ☎ *0335/343–0888* 🛏 *274 rooms* 🍽 *Breakfast.*

The rugged landscape around Shanhaiguan

SHANHAIGUAN

2½ hours (280 km [174 miles]) by train east of Beijing, 1 hr (35 km [22 mi]) by minibus northeast of Beidaihe; 2½ hrs (360 km [223 mi]) southwest of Shenyang.

On the northern tip of the Bohai Coast, Shanhaiguan is the end of the road for the Great Wall. After 8,850 km (5,500 miles), the massive structure plunges into the sea. During the Ming Dynasty, Shanhaiguan was fortified to prevent hordes of mounted Manchurian warriors from pushing to the south. Now local tourists swarm the town during the summer. An impressive wall still surrounds what was the Old Town, sadly razed in 2007 and rebuilt as a spiritless faux-historic tourist area.

GETTING HERE AND AROUND

Shanhaiguan-bound express trains depart from Beijing several times daily, but it's also possible to take a train to Qinhuangdao and catch a taxi for the 20-minute drive to Shanhaiguan.

AIR TRAVEL   Until Qinhuangdao Beidaihe Airport is up and running, air travel is not an option.

BUS TRAVEL   A minibus service runs from Beidaihe to Shanhaiguan, with departures every 30 minutes.

Bus Contact Shanhaiguan Bus Station ✉ *Nanguan Dajie, west side of the railway station* ☎ *0335/502–3879.*

TAXI TRAVEL   The half-hour taxi ride between Beidaihe and Shanhaiguan costs about Y80.

TRAIN TRAVEL Shanhaiguan has limited train service; it might be necessary to take a train to Qinhuangdao and transfer to a bus or taxi to Shanhaiguan.

Train Contact Shanhaiguan Train Station ✉ *Off Nanguan Da Jie.*

TIMING

Shanhaiguan has enough to keep you occupied for one day, perhaps two if you plan on doing some serious Great Wall hiking. The town comes alive in the summer, but by late October many restaurants and tourist facilities shut down for the season. The First Gate Under Heaven and Great Wall sections are open year-round, however.

ESSENTIALS

Medical Assistance Qinhuangdao Friendship Hospital ✉ *28 Jianguo Lu, Qinhuangdao* ☎ *0335/303–1222.*

EXPLORING

TOP ATTRACTIONS

First Gate Under Heaven (天下第一关 *Tiānxià dìyīguān*). The first heavy fortification along the Great Wall as it runs inland from the ocean, this mighty four-sided citadel guards the strategic Shanhai pass ("Shanhaiguan" in Chinese), around which the original town grew. Patrolling the battlements you can glimpse the Great Wall snaking up the sides of nearby mountains and grasp just how intimidating a barrier this must have presented to potential invaders. Not that it worked—the Manchus overran it in 1644, ultimately bringing down the Ming Dynasty. ✉ *Diyiguan Lu* ☎ *0335/505–1106* 🎫 *Y50, includes admission to Great Wall Museum* 🕓 *Daily 7:30–6:30.*

Great Wall Museum (长城博物馆 *Chángchéng bówùguǎn*). Housed in a Qing Dynasty–style building past the First Gate Under Heaven, the Great Wall Museum has a diverting collection of historic photographs and cases full of military artifacts, including the fierce-looking weaponry used by attackers and defenders. There are some English captions. ✉ *South of First Gate Under Heaven, Diyiguan Lu* 🎫 *Y50, includes admission to First Gate Under Heaven* 🕓 *Daily 7:30–4:30.*

Jiaoshan Great Wall (角山长城 *Jiāoshān chángchéng*). One way to leave behind the crowds at the First Gate Under Heaven is to scale the wall as it climbs Jiao Mountain, about 3 km (2 miles) from the city. The first section has been restored and fitted with handrails and ladders up the sides of the watchtowers, but you can keep climbing until you reach a more wild, authentic stretch. After that you can take a path through trees that leads to the Qixian Monastery, or continue to the top for stunning if precarious views of the mountains and lakes beyond. A chairlift operates in high season. Jiaoshan is a 10-minute taxi ride from Shanhaiguan. ✉ *Jiaoshan Lu* ☎ *0335/505–2884* 🎫 *Y30* 🕓 *Daily 7:30–5.*

Jiumenkou Great Wall (九门口长城 *Jiǔménkǒu chángchéng*). Farther from town than the Jiaoshan Great Wall, Jiumenkou is notable as the only section of the Great Wall to ford a river. Clamber up the battlements for dramatic views over the countryside. Jiumenkou is about 15 km (9 miles) north of Shanhaiguan; ask your taxi driver to wait for you for the return trip (a total of about Y100). ✉ *Zhijiu Xian* 🎫 *Y30* 🕓 *Daily 8–5.*

Old Dragon Head (老龙头 *Lǎolóngtóu*). Legend has it that the Great Wall once extended into the Bohai Sea, ending with a giant carved dragon's head. Although the structure you see today was rebuilt in the 1980s, witnessing the waves smash against the massive base is a stirring sight. The admission price gets you into several rebuilt Ming Dynasty naval barracks, but you can just skip it altogether and head directly to the beach for the best photo ops. ⊠ *1 Laolongtou Lu* ☎ *0335/515–2996* 💳 *Y50* ⊙ *Daily 8–5.*

WORTH NOTING

Mengjiangnu Miao (孟姜女庙 *Mèngjiāngnǚ miào*). About 8 km (5 miles) or 10 minutes in a taxi up the coast from Old Dragon Head is this shrine commemorating a local legend. As the story goes, a woman's husband died while building the Great Wall. She wept as she searched for his body, and in sympathy the wall split open before her, revealing the bones of her husband and others buried within. Overcome with grief, she threw herself into the sea. ☎ *0335/505–3159* 💳 *Y30* ⊙ *Daily 7–5.*

WHERE TO EAT AND STAY

$$
SEAFOOD
✕ **Wang Yang Lou** (望洋楼饭店 *Wàngyánglóu fàndiàn*). Probably the town's most upmarket option, Wang Yang Lou serves tasty local seafood and an array of family-style Chinese dishes. There's no menu—order at the open kitchen to the left of the entrance by pointing at things swimming in the tanks, or at the displayed photos of dishes themselves. The dining room itself is large but lacks much in the way of character. $ *Average main: Y70* ⊠ *51 Nanhai Xi Lu* ☎ *0335/515–5666* ▭ *No credit cards.*

$
HOTEL
▦ **Shanhai Holiday Hotel** (山海假日酒店 *Shānhǎi jiàrì jiǔdiàn*). One of the few lodgings inside the walls of the recently rebuilt "ancient city," this Qing Dynasty–styled complex offers simply furnished rooms set around a series of courtyards. **Pros:** close to the First Gate Under Heaven. **Cons:** the "ancient city" is dead in the evenings. $ *Rooms from: Y300* ⊠ *Beima Lu, beside the west gate* ☎ *0335/535–2800* ⬎ *277 rooms* ❙⊙❙ *Breakfast.*

$
HOTEL
▦ **Wanghai Vacational Village** (望海度假村 *Wànghǎi dùjiàcūn*). A short march from Old Dragon Head, this resort-style hotel is centered around a seafood restaurant that's nestled, rather unexpectedly, in a greenhouse filled with tropical flora. **Pros:** lovely restaurant; on the beach; near the Great Wall. **Cons:** outside of town. $ *Rooms from: Y300* ⊠ *1 Wanghai Lu* ☎ *0335/535–0777* ⬎ *44 rooms* ❙⊙❙ *No meals.*

SHANDONG

Around 100 million people call the Shandong region home, and an annual influx of domestic tourists considerably adds to that number. Most flock to this region for Qingdao, China's most attractive coastal city and best known for its beaches, beer (sold as "Tsingtao" in the West), and Bavarian architecture, the walled town of Qufu, home of the philosopher Confucius, and Mount Tai, the most revered of all China's sacred mountains.

JI'NAN

1½ hours (500 km [220 miles]) by bullet train south of Beijing; 2½ hours (395 km [245 miles]) by bullet train west of Qingdao.

Most famous for its 70 or so active springs, Ji'nan, nicknamed "City of Springs," is the provincial capital of Shandong. In the tourist stakes it is overshadowed entirely by its coastal rival, Qingdao, but this modern and easygoing metropolis can be a pleasant base if visiting nearby Taishan. Ji'nan's three main sights are Thousand Buddha Mountain, Daming Lake, and Baotu Spring Park. These and a handful of other attractions easily occupy visitors for a day or so.

In 1901, Ji'nan was hauled into the 20th century by the construction of a railway linking it to German-controlled Qingdao. European and Japanese companies found Ji'nan to be a convenient place to do business. A few buildings from this concession era remain in the downtown area, although they are increasingly overshadowed by new shopping centers and hotels.

GETTING HERE AND AROUND
Far and away the best way to get here from Beijing is to catch one of the many daily bullet trains, which stop at Jinan Station or the newer Jinan West Station. The trip takes between 1½ and 2 hours.

AIR TRAVEL
Regular flights link Ji'nan Yaoqiang Airport with Beijing, Shanghai, Hong Kong, and other major Chinese cities. The airport is 40 km (25 miles) northeast of downtown Ji'nan. The journey takes 45 minutes in a taxi and costs around Y100.

Air Contact Ji'nan Yaoqiang Airport ⊠ *Jichang Lu, Yaoqiang* ☎ *0531/96888.*

BUS TRAVEL
Regular buses link Ji'nan with Tai'an (one hour) and Qufu (three hours).

Bus Contacts Ji'nan Long-Distance Bus Station ⊠ *131 Jiluo Lu* ☎ *0531/96369.* **Tai'an Bus Station** ⊠ *139 Dongyue Dajie, opposite the train station, Tai'an* ☎ *0538/833-2938.* **Qufu Bus Station** ⊠ *Yulong Lu, Qufu* ☎ *537⊠/441-2554.*

TRAIN TRAVEL
Ji'nan is connected to Qufu, Tai'an, and Qingdao, and accessible from Shanghai, stopping at both Suzhou and Nanjing on route. There is no shortage of fast trains, and it's possible to buy your tickets mere minutes before getting on board, though during busy periods it pays to purchase in advance.

Train Contacts Ji'nan Train Station ⊠ *19 Chezhan Jie* ☎ *0531/8601-2520.* **Ji'nan West Train Station** ⊠ *Weihai Lu, Huayin District.* **Tai'an Train Station** ⊠ *Dongyue Dajie, Tai'an* ☎ *0538/9510-5688.*

SAFETY AND PRECAUTIONS

As in most inland Shandong cities, air pollution can be a problem, especially in hot weather.

Medical Assistance Jinan Central Hospital ⊠ *1st fl., International Department, 105 Jiefang Lu* ☎ *0531/8569-5114.*

TIMING

Ji'nan's sights are relatively close together, making one day enough time to comfortably visit them as well as walk around the city.

ESSENTIALS

Visitor and Tour Info Ji'nan CITS ⊠ *Bldg. 30, 1 Jiefang Lu, 6th fl., Ji'nan* ⊕ *www.cits.net.* **Ji'nan Tourist Service** ⊠ *86 Jingshi Lu, Ji'nan* ☎ *800/420-8858* ⊕ *www.travelshandong.us.*

EXPLORING

Ji'nan's downtown area is relatively compact. A meandering ring-shaped canal connects Baotu Spring Park with other tourist spots, eventually spilling out into Daming Lake. Tourist boats ply the waterways; an all-day pass costs Y100. The grid of streets south of the main railway station, which bear the most European influence, are well worth exploring on foot.

Baotu Spring Park (趵突泉 *Bàotūquán*). Qing Dynasty Emperor Qianlong proclaimed this the finest of Ji'nan's many natural springs gurgling north from the foothills of Taishan. The spring is most active after the summer rains, when crowds gather under pavilions to watch it frothing and gushing. The pure water is said to be ideal for making tea; try it out at the Wangheting Teahouse, just east of the spring. A small museum in the park recounts the life of Ji'nan's most prized poetess Li Qingzhao, who lived near here in the 11th century. ⊠ *Baotuquan Nan Lu, Ji'nan* 🖼 *Y40* ⊙ *Daily 7 am–9 pm.*

Burning incense at the Thousand Buddha Mountain

Daming Lake (大明湖 *Dàmíng hú*). Fed by artesian springs and garlanded by vivid banks of willows, Daming Lake has been inspiring Chinese poets and writers for 1,500 years. Surrounded by temples, pavilions, and leafy walkways, it's a pleasant spot for a stroll. There's a teahouse on top of the 50-meter tall pagoda on the island in the east of the lake. Climb up for pleasant views of Thousand Buddha Hill on clear days. ⊠ *Daming Hu Lu, Ji'nan* 🍴 *Y30* ⏰ *Daily 6:30–6.*

Nanjing Sifang Art Museum (南京四方当代美术馆 *Nánjīng sìfāng dāngdài měishùguǎn*). This museum explores Chinese art and architecture, but its main draw could be the stunningly angular design of its buildings, set in Laoshan National Park. Designed by American architect Steven Holl, it includes a gallery seemingly suspended in midair and a courtyard paved with bricks from destroyed houses in central Nanjing. ⊠ *178 Zhenzhu Lu, Nanjing* ☎ *025/6819–0789* 🌐 *www.sifangartmuseum.org.*

Sacred Heart Cathedral (洪家楼耶稣圣心主教座堂 *Jīngsìlù jiàotáng*). An interesting legacy of the German influence in Shandong is a handful of concession-era churches, this Gothic cathedral being the most impressive. Constructed around 1901 and resembling the Notre Dame in Paris, it can hold 800 worshippers. ⊠ *585 Huahong Lu, Ji'nan.*

NEED A BREAK? **Shandong Elite Teahouse** (山东名人茶馆 *Shāndōng míngrén cháguǎn*). This teahouse makes for a lovely break after climbing Thousand Buddha Mountain. The exquisite room is decorated with lattice paneling, ornate vases, and musical instruments. There are many varieties of tea to choose

from; if you're hungry, there are several small restaurants within walking distance. ✉ ***9 Qianfoshan Lu, Ji'nan*** ☎ ***0531/8296–0376.***

FAMILY **Thousand Buddha Mountain** (千佛山 *Qiānfóshān*). On the southern edge of the city is Thousand Buddha Mountain, which gets its name from the multitude of Buddha images chiseled into the lofty cliffs since the early Sui Dynasty. It is still the focus of religious festivals, although many of the original statues have been lost to history, replaced by modern reconstructions. Getting to the top of the hill requires a 30-minute walk or a cable car ride (Y25 round-trip). Either way you'll be rewarded with a good view of Ji'nan—air quality permitting. For kids, there's an excellent slide to whiz back down to the bottom. ✉ *18 Jingshiyi Lu, Ji'nan* ☎ *0531/8266–2321* 🎟 *Y30* 🕒 *Daily 6–6.*

WHERE TO EAT

$$$ VEGETARIAN 🍴 **Foshan Yuan** (佛山院素食店 *Fóshānyuàn sùshídiàn*). This comfy vegetarian restaurant specializes in dishes that look and taste remarkably like meat or fish. If sea cucumbers made from textured soy protein sounds like a gastronomic step too far, fear not: the delicious vegetable dumplings, braised mushrooms, and hearty tofu dishes are sure to satisfy. This place is a little tricky to find; locals should be able to point you in the right direction. [$] *Average main: Y105* ✉ *Foshan Yuan Xiao Qu, near Chaoshan Jie, Ji'nan* ☎ *0531/8602–7566* 💳 *No credit cards.*

$$ INTERNATIONAL 🍴 **Jenny's Cafe.** Recognizable by its bright pink sign, this centrally located eatery turns out decent salads, soups, and other light fare, but its tasty selection of cakes, coffees, and milk shakes makes it a better bet for a mid-afternoon break. There's a fully stocked bar if you need something stronger. Locals love the daintily laid tables and shabby-chic European touches. [$] *Average main: Y90* ✉ *2 Wenhua Xi Lu, Ji'nan* ☎ *0531/8260–0214* 💳 *No credit cards.*

$$ NORTHERN CHINESE 🍴 **Jufengde Restaurant** (聚丰德饭店 *Jùfēngdé fàndiàn*). This long-standing eatery is a well-liked spot to sample *Jinan lu cai*, a variation of one of the eight famous cuisines of China. The signature dish is *jiu zhuan da chang* (literally "nine turns intestine"), chewy braised spirals of pork chitterlings, but if that sounds a bit extreme, try the sweet-and-sour fried carp, or their decent local take on roast duck with pancakes. Be sure to get a side order of *youxuan*, Ji'nan's famously crispy fried bread snacks. [$] *Average main: Y70* ✉ *11 Jingwu Lu, Ji'nan* ☎ *0531/8691–6451.*

WHERE TO STAY

$ HOTEL 🏨 **C.Sohoh Business Hotel** (舜和商誉酒店 *Shùnhé shāngyù jiǔdiàn*). A short walk from the main sights, this affordable business hotel is small enough to feel intimate and welcoming, with well-maintained rooms and excellent service. **Pros:** personalized service, great location; reasonable rates. **Cons:** small rooms. [$] *Rooms from: Y380* ✉ *53 Luoyang Lu, Ji'nan* ☎ *0531/8615–1388* 🌐 *www.csohoh.com* 🛏 *125 rooms* 🍽 *Breakfast.*

$$ HOTEL 🏨 **Sheraton Ji'nan** (济南喜来登 *Jǐnán xǐláidēng jiǔdiàn*). Overlooking the enormous, lotus-shaped sports venue built to host the 11th Chinese National Games, this reliably comfortable hotel has the benefit of indoor and outdoor pools and an excellent spa. **Pros:** excellent facilities; great Japanese restaurant. **Cons:** isolated location. [$] *Rooms*

from: Y1100 ⊠ *8 Long Ao Bei Lu, Ji'nan* ☎ *0531/8162–9999* ⊕ *www.starwoodhotels.com* ⤵ *410 rooms* ⦿| *No meals.*

$ 🏨 **Sofitel Ji'nan Silver Plaza** (苏菲特银座大酒店 *Sūfēité yínzuò*
HOTEL *Dǎjiǔdiàn*). Looking somewhat like a tube of lipstick from the outside, this 49-story cylinder sits right in the center of town, boasting sleek and spacious guests rooms and a grand lobby with impressive chandeliers and marble columns. **Pros:** excellent location; eye-catching design; very good Italian restaurant. **Cons:** small bathrooms. **$** *Rooms from: Y1050* ⊠ *66 Luoyuan Dajie, Ji'nan* ☎ *0531/8606–8888* ⊕ *www.sofitel.com* ⤵ *426 rooms* ⦿| *No meals.*

NIGHTLIFE

Banjo (班卓音乐酒吧 *Bānzhuó yīnyuè jiǔbā*). This funky, eclectic bar has live music most nights of the week, attracting a mix of young locals and expats. It's conveniently located among a row of Chinese, Japanese, and Korean restaurants that are very lively at night. ⊠ *51 Foshan Jie, Ji'nan* ☎ *0531/8685–8585.*

SHOPPING

Shandong Curios City (山东古玩城 *Shāndōng gǔwàn chéng*). This cluster of small antiques shops is huddled around an attractive courtyard. Jade, jewelry, and regional antiques are beautifully displayed; expect to bargain for prices. ⊠ *283 Quancheng Lu, Ji'nan.*

SIDE TRIP TO LINGYAN TEMPLE

Shandong played a vital role in the spread of Buddhism in China. In the 4th century AD the Chinese Buddhist monk Faxian landed on the coast near present day Qingdao to decode scriptures he'd gathered on travels to India, Sri Lanka, and Nepal. Ji'nan became the center of Buddhist culture for the whole province. During the Tang and Song dynasties, the Lingyan Temple was one of the most important Buddhist temples in China.

GETTING HERE AND AROUND

Lingyan Temple is about 76 km (46 miles) south of the city. The best way to get here is to arrange a car and driver through your hotel or a travel agency.

Lingyan Temple (灵岩寺 *Língyánsì*). In a dramatic mountain setting, the 1,600-year-old Lingyan Temple is most famous for the Thousand Buddha Hall, with its cast of 40 hand-carved and painted wooden figures seated around the chamber. Unerringly lifelike, each one is distinct, from facial features to the folds of their robes. Dating back to the Song Dynasty, these are some of the finest religious sculptures in China. Several years ago, researchers cracked one of the life-sized statues open and found a full set of internal organs inside, made out of stuffed silk.

In the temple grounds, the Pagoda Forest (Da Lin) is a totemic graveyard of sculpted towers erected over centuries, each marking the passing of a prominent monk. The size and artistry of each tower points not to the status of the deceased, but the prosperity of the temple at the time. The cycle of boom and bust, it would seem, is eternal. ⊠ *Changqing District, Wande* ☎ *0531/8746–8099* ⤳ *Y40* ☉ *Daily 8–5.*

The Confucius Temple on top of the beautiful Mt. Tai

SIDE TRIP TO MOUNT TAI

A destination for pilgrims for 3,000 years, the mountain was named a UNESCO World Heritage Site in 1987. Confucius is said to have climbed up the slopes, scanned the horizon and observed: "The world is very small." Many centuries later, Mao Zedong reached the top and even more famously proclaimed: "The East is red."

GETTING HERE AND AROUND

Mount Tai is near the town of Tai'an, a major stop on the Shanghai–Beijing railway. Dozens of trains travel through Tai'an daily. By road, Tai'an is about 50 km (30 miles) south of Ji'nan. Buses to Tai'an leave Ji'nan's main bus station every 25 minutes between 5 am and 6 pm. From any spot in Tai'an, a taxi to Mount Tai (Taishan) takes less than 15 minutes and costs about Y10.

Mount Tai (泰山 *Tàishān*). Reaching 5,067 feet above sea level, Mount Tai is the most venerated of the five sacred mountains of China. It is also reputedly the most climbed peak on earth, tamed by 7,000 steps over 7.5 km (4.5 miles) from base to summit, making it accessible to anyone with a sturdy pair of shoes and a head for heights. Over the ages calligraphy has been etched into boulders and cliffs like graffiti, and temples of various faiths line the route, making a climb here a fascinating jaunt through Chinese history.

It's possible to climb the steps to the summit and back down in a day (a cinch if you use the cable car), but spending the night on the peak is also an option. The classic photo—sunrise over the cloud-hugged peaks—is actually a rare sight because of the mist. ✉ *Tai'an* 🎟 *Dec. 1–Jan. 31 Y100, Feb. 1–Nov. 30 Y125.*

WHERE TO STAY

$ 🏨 **Ramada Plaza Tai'an** (东尊华美达
HOTEL **大酒店** *Dōngzūn huáměidá dàjiǔdiàn*). Make sure to ask for a mountain-view room in this resort style hotel in the quiet foothills of Mount Tai, offering compact but comfortable rooms, soft beds, international TV channels, and thunderous showers; if you can stand to

> ### CONFUCIUS SOUVENIERS
>
> Many locals claim to be direct descendants of Confucius, and they take great pride in their heritage. Although the philosopher would have raised an eyebrow, the townspeople do a good line in Confucius-brand cookies, wine, and many other items.

miss the much-hyped sunrise, this is far better value—and provides a better night's sleep—than you'll find on the summit. **Pros:** lovely setting; great facilities; **Cons:** not on the summit; buffet breakfast just average. $ *Rooms from: Y600* ✉ *16 Yinhsheng Donglu, Tai'an* ☎ *0538/836–8888* 🛏 *328 rooms* 🍽 *Breakfast.*

$ 🏨 **Shenqi Hotel** (泰山神憩宾馆 *Tàishān shénqì bīnguǎn*). This is the
HOTEL only real hotel on the summit, and consequently it's overpriced considering its barely adequate rooms. **Pros:** perfect place to watch the sunrise. **Cons:** expensive for what you get; very basic rooms. $ *Rooms from: Y600* ✉ *10 Tian Jie, Tai'an* ☎ *0538/822–3866* 🛏 *62 rooms* 🍽 *No meals.*

SIDE TRIP TO QUFU

This sleepy provincial town is the birthplace of the country's foremost spiritual teacher and philosopher, Kong Fuzi, known to the West as Confucius. His impact was immense in China, and his code of conduct was a part of daily life here until it fell out of favor two millennia later during the Cultural Revolution. His teachings—that son must respect father, wife must respect husband, citizens must respect officials—were swept away by Mao Zedong because of their associations with the past. Qufu suffered greatly during the Cultural Revolution, with the Red Guards smashing statues and burning buildings. But the pendulum has swung back, and Confucius's teachings are back in vogue. Encircled by a Ming Dynasty wall, Qufu certainly has character, though there's little to do once the tourist sights close for the day.

GETTING HERE AND AROUND

A handful of Qufu-bound bullet trains leave Beijing each day, passing through Jinan and Tai'an on route. The trip takes about 2½ hours. Regular buses also run trips from Ji'nan to Qufu. The Qufu bus station is south of the town center at the intersection of Shen Dao and Jingxuan Lu.

EXPLORING

Confucian Forest (孔林 *Kǒng lín*). Confucius and his descendants have been buried in this tree-shaded cemetery for the past 2,000 years. Surrounded by a 10-km (6-mile) wall, Confucian Forest has more than 100,000 pine and cypress trees, jostling for space with burial mounds, grave stones, and statues commemorating generations of the Kong family. ✉ *Lindao Lu, Qufu* 🎫 *Y40* 🕘 *Daily 8–5.*

Confucius Family Mansion (孔府 *Kǒng fǔ*). Beside the east wall of the Confucius Temple is the Confucius Family Mansion. A fascinating collection of stately abodes and gardens, it dates from the 16th century and illustrates the wealth and glory once enjoyed by Confucius's descendants. When the Kong family were in residence the mansion would have been heavily guarded; trespassing was punishable by death. The tallest structure here is the four-story "refuge tower," which the family could flee to in times of trouble. ✉ *Banbi Jie, Qufu* 🎫 *Y60* 🕘 *Daily 8–5.*

WISEMAN PASS

If you want to soak up as much Confucianism as possible during your visit to Qufu, get a ticket that grants access to all three sites. That's Y185 for a ticket that covers the Confucius Temple, Confucius Family Mansion, and the Confucian Forest.

Confucius Temple (孔庙 *Kǒng miào*). Within Qufu's restored city walls, the sprawling Confucius Temple comprises 66 buildings spread across more than 50 acres, making this one of the largest palace complexes from imperial China. Like the Forbidden City, built 80 years earlier, its colonnaded halls and courtyards flow symmetrically along a central axis. The Hall of Great Achievements features mighty pillars entwined with dragons. Seek out the Apricot Platform in front, where it's said Confucius once preached beneath the shade of an apricot tree. September 28, the date of the Great Sage's birthday, is quite the party here. ✉ *Banbi Jie, Qufu* 🎫 *Y90* 🕘 *Daily 8–5.*

WHERE TO STAY

$ HOTEL 🏨 **Queli Hotel** (阙里宾馆 *Quēlǐ bīnguǎn*). In a small town lacking lodging options, this well-run but dated hotel, a short stroll from the Confucius Temple and the Confucius Family Mansion, is your best bet if you want to be close to the sights. **Pros:** prime location for attractions. **Cons:** showing its age; uninspiring rooms; hard beds. [$] *Rooms from: Y550* ✉ *1 Queli Lu, Qufu* ☎ *0537/486–6818* 🛏 *150 rooms* 🍴 *Breakfast.*

$ HOTEL Fodor's Choice ★ 🏨 **Shangri-La Qufu.** Two kilometers (1 mile) south of the old walls, this elegant new hotel set around a purpose-built lake is Qufu's first five-star accommodation, at last making the UNESCO-listed town a compelling destination for a luxury break or side trip. **Pros:** the only true luxury accommodation in town; excellent service and facilities. **Cons:** at least a 20-minute walk to the sights. [$] *Rooms from: Y900* ✉ *3 Chunqiu Lu, Qufu* ☎ *0537/505–5616* 🛏 *322 rooms* 🍴 *Breakfast.*

QINGDAO

4½ hrs (540 km [335 miles]) by bullet train southeast of Beijing; 2½ hrs by train (390 km [242 miles]) east of Ji'nan.

Qingdao has had a turbulent century, but it has emerged as one of China's most charming cities. It was a sleepy fishing village until the end of the 19th century, when Germany, using the killing of two German missionaries as a pretext, set up another European concession to take advantage of Qingdao's coastal position. The German presence lasted only until 1914, but locals continued to build Bavarian-style houses, and today a walk around the Old Town can feel like you've stumbled into a town in the Black Forest. Unlike many cities that had foreign concessions, Qingdao has recognized the historical value of these buildings and is now enthusiastic about preserving them. With its seafront promenades, winding colonial streets, and pretty parks, Qingdao is probably China's best city for strolling.

Home to the country's best-known beer, Tsingtao, Qingdao is very accommodating when it comes to alcohol consumption. (Look for beer being sold on the streets in plastic bags.) But wine drinkers should take heart, as the region is also developing a much-talked-about wine industry.

The city is a destination for golfers, its courses especially popular with traveling Koreans and Japanese.

GETTING HERE AND AROUND

A comfortable way to get to Qingdao is aboard one of the several daily bullet trains that link Qingdao to Beijing (4½ hours). Buy tickets from travel agents or through your hotel, as lines are long and there are few English speakers at the station.

The long-distance bus terminal is opposite the train station. Taxis are a cheap way to get around. Getting anywhere in town will generally cost less than Y35.

Line 1 of the new Qingdao Metro underground network should be up and running at time of publication.

AIR TRAVEL   Qingdao Liuting Airport is 30 km (19 miles) north of the city. In a taxi, the journey takes 40 minutes and costs around Y80. Direct flights link Qingdao with Osaka and Seoul, as well as Hong Kong and other major Chinese cities.

Air Contact Qingdao Liuting Airport (青岛机场 *Qīngdǎo jīchǎng*). ⊠ *Liuting* ☎ *0532/96567.*

BUS TRAVEL   Buses travel between Ji'nan and Qingdao every 20 minutes; the trip is 4–5 hours.

Bus Contact Qingdao Long-Distance Bus Station ⊠ *2 Wenzhou Lu* ☎ *0532/8371–8060.*

TRAIN TRAVEL   Direct trains link Qingdao with Ji'nan (three hours), Beijing (4½ hours), and Shanghai (6½ hours).

Train Contact Qingdao Train Station ⊠ *2 Tai'an Lu* ☎ *0532/12306.*

TIMING

Qingdao is a very pleasant seaside city. Two full days is just about enough to cram in all the sights, but the city has enough attractions to keep you happily occupied for longer.

ESSENTIALS

Boat and Ferry Contact Qingdao Ferry Terminal ⊠ *6 Xinjiang Lu, 2 km (1 mile) north of the train station* ☎ *0532/8282–5001.*

Medical Assistance International Clinic of Qingdao Municipal Hospital ✉ *5 Donghai Zhong Lu* ☎ *0532/8593–7690.*

Visitor and Tour Info Qingdao CITS ✉ *73 Xianggang Zhong Lu* ☎ *0532/8386–3960* ⊕ *www.cits.net.* **Qingdao Tourism Administration** ✉ *7 Minjiang Lu* ☎ *0532/8591–2029.*

EXPLORING
TOP ATTRACTIONS

German Governor's Residence (青岛迎宾馆 *Qīngdǎo yíng bīnguǎn*). The cookie dough–colored German Governor's Residence, transformed into a museum in 1996, was where the mustachioed governor and his aristocratic entourage wined, dined, and held sway over Qingdao for their short but influential tenure. Built in 1906 on a commanding perch over the Old City, the interior resembles a Bavarian hunting lodge, with wood paneling, glazed tile fireplaces, colored glass chandeliers, and quirky grandfather clocks. Notable Chinese guests since include Mao Zedong, Zhou Enlai, and Deng Xiaoping. English audio guides are available. ✉ *26 Longshan Lu, below Xinhao Hill Park* 🎟 *Y20* ⊙ *Daily 8:30–4:30.*

Granite Mansion (花石楼 *Huāshí lóu*). After the German Governor's Residence, the 1903 Granite Mansion is Qingdao's most famous example of concession-era German architecture. This miniature castle was built as a villa for a Russian aristocrat but soon became a fishing retreat for the governor. ✉ *18 Huanghai Lu* 🎟 *Y7* ⊙ *Daily 8–5.*

Protestant Church (基督教堂 *Jīdū jiàotáng*). Qingdao's charming Protestant Church is easy to spot: look for the ostentatious green spire resembling a medieval castle. It was built in 1910 at the southwest entrance of Xinhao Hill Park. Puff up the steps to the bell tower for sea views and to marvel at the German-engineered clock mechanism. ✉ *15 Jiangsu Lu* 🎟 *Free* ⊙ *Daily 8:30–4:30.*

St. Michael's Cathedral (青岛天主教堂 *Qīngdǎo tiānzhǔ jiàotáng*). With its towering 200-foot twin steeples and red-tile roof, St Michael's is probably Qingdao's most recognizable landmark. The classic Gothic Revival structure was built by the Germans in 1934 but was badly damaged during the Cultural Revolution. The surrounding area is worth a stroll, the streets a mix of sturdy concession buildings and contrastingly shabby modern architecture. The square in front of the cathedral is the most popular spot in town for wedding photos; an enormous "wedding banquet restaurant" is conveniently located opposite. ✉ *15 Zhejiang Lu* 🎟 *Y8* ⊙ *Mon.–Sat. 8–5, Sun. 10–5.*

FAMILY **Sun Yat-sen Park** (中山公园 *Zhōngshān gōngyuán*). The largest of the city's parks, Sun Yat-sen Park is inland from Huiquan Bay and has a number of attractions, including a small zoo, a botanical garden, and the Zhanshan Buddhist Temple. Qingdao's TV tower, a city landmark, offers striking views from its observation deck. Originally planted by the Japanese in 1915, the park contains some 20,000 cherry trees. The annual Cherry Blossom Festival is held at the end of May. ✉ *28 Wendeng Lu* ☎ *0532/8287–0564* 🎟 *Free (attractions inside cost extra)* ⊙ *Daily until nightfall.*

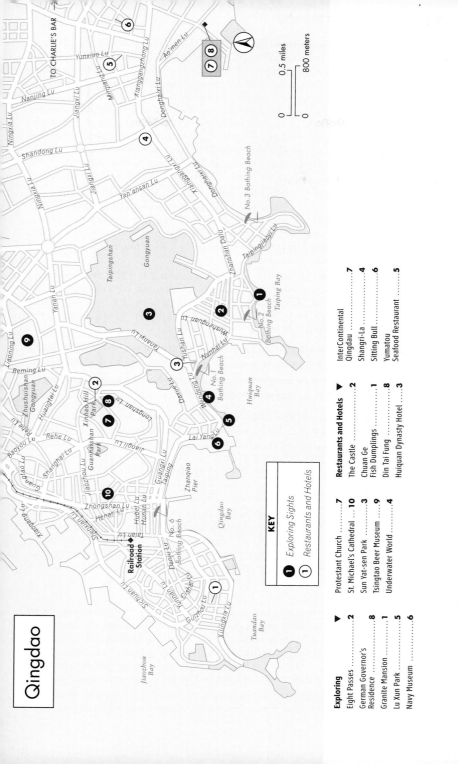

Qingdao

Exploring ▶

Eight Passes	2
German Governor's Residence	8
Granite Mansion	1
Lu Xun Park	5
Navy Museum	6
Protestant Church	7
St. Michael's Cathedral	10
Sun Yat-sen Park	3
Tsingtao Beer Museum	9
Underwater World	4

Restaurants and Hotels ▶

The Castle	2
Chuan Ge Fish Dumplings	1
Din Tai Fung	8
Huiquan Dynasty Hotel	3
InterContinental Qingdao	7
Shangri-La	4
Sitting Bull	6
Yumatou Seafood Restaurant	5

KEY

① Exploring Sights

① Restaurants and Hotels

0 — 0.5 miles

0 — 800 meters

TO CHARLIE'S BAR

Jiaozhou Bay

Tuandao Bay

Qingdao Bay

Huiquan Bay

Taiping Bay

No. 6 Bathing Beach
No. 1 Bathing Beach
No. 2 Bathing Beach
No. 3 Bathing Beach

Railroad Station

Zhanqiao Pier

Tsingtao Beer Museum (青啤博物馆 *Qīngpí bówùguǎn*). Beer fans should make a pilgrimage to the Tsingtao Beer Museum on Dengzhou Lu, also known as *Pijiu Jie* (Beer Street). The Germans established China's most famous brewery more than a century ago, and a few of the original brick buildings still remain, alongside a modern bottling plant. The old photographs, beer labels, and dioramas are of middling interest; best of all are the beer samples you can enjoy along the way. The surrounding area is lined with bars, eateries, and bottle-shaped benches where weary revelers can rest. ⊠ *56 Dengzhou Lu* 🕾 *0532/8383–3437* ⊕ *www.tsingtaomuseum.com* 🎟 *Y60* ⊗ *Daily 8:30–4:30.*

WORTH NOTING

Eight Passes (八大关 *Bādàguān*). Named after the Great Wall's eight strategic passes, this scenic area lies in between Taiping and the Huiquan Cape. Sometimes referred to as "Little Switzerland," the grounds of more than 200 European-style villas are landscaped with pine, ginkgo, and peach trees. The serene No. 2 bathing beach and Granite Mansion are also here.

Lu Xun Park (鲁迅公园 *Lǔxùn gōngyuán*). Built in 1929, this park named for the distinguished Chinese writer and revolutionary sits on the rocky coastline of Huiquan Bay. It's a lovely park, with tree-shaded paths, elegant pavilions, and rugged reefs, making for attractive sea vistas. ⊠ *1 Qinyu Lu* 🎟 *Free* ⊗ *Daily 7:30–6:30.*

NEED A BREAK?

Café Roland (朗园酒吧 *Lǎngyuán jiǔbā*). In a German-style building dating from the 1930s, Café Roland has a lovely wooden interior and a view of No. 3 Beach. Try the excellent, homemade rum-raisin ice cream. ⊠ **9 Taiping Jiao Er Lu** 🕾 **0532/8387–5734.**

Navy Museum (海军博物馆 *Hǎijūn bówùguǎn*). A short walk from the west entrance of Lu Xun Park is the Navy Museum, with an arsenal of archaic weaponry, Russian-made fighter planes, and several rusting naval vessels moored in the harbor. You can see much of it—and skip the entrance fee—by walking along the seawall to the Little Qingdao Isle with its charming lighthouse and excellent café. ⊠ *8 Lai Yang Lu* 🕾 *0532/8286–6784* 🎟 *Y50* ⊗ *Daily 8:30–5.*

FAMILY **Underwater World** (青岛海底世界 *Qīngdǎo hǎidǐshìjiè*). Located near No. 1 Beach, this family-friendly attraction features a moving platform with 360-degree views of the surrounding marine life. Four underground levels, interactive video displays, and tacky marine shows entertain the kids for hours. ⊠ *1 Laiyang Lu* 🕾 *0532/8289–2187* 🎟 *Y130* ⊗ *Daily 8–5:30.*

WHERE TO EAT

Clams, crabs, crayfish, shrimp, oysters—it's no surprise that Qingdao's specialty is seafood. A shoal of excellent seafood restaurants can be found in or around Minjiang Lu and Yunxiao Lu, where the time between choosing your catch and having it arrive steaming on your plate is about three minutes. For seafood with sea views, there are some cheap and cheerful lunch spots on Qinyu Lu just west of Lu Xun Park.

In Qingdao's seafood restaurants you're usually expected to order on entry at the row of tanks, and tell whoever's assisting you how you'd like your food cooked. Here's a quick guide: *qing zheng* means simply to steam; *xiang la* means to stir-fry with chilies, garlic, and ginger; *zha de* is deep-fried; and *hong shao* is braised in soy sauce, rice wine, and a little sugar.

GANBEI!

Qingdao International Beer Festival. The Qingdao International Beer Festival, China's biggest, has been held since 1991. The state-sponsored fun begins in mid-August, lasts for two weeks, and causes hotel prices to skyrocket. The focus is mostly on big-name brews from around the world, and you won't see any lederhosen, but it's still great fun.

$$$ MANDARIN 🍴 **Chuan Ge Fish Dumplings** (船歌鱼水饺 *Chuángē yúshuǐjiăo*). A market-fresh spread of live seafood, meats, and vegetables greets you at the entrance of this excellent eatery, a hit with well-heeled locals. Browse the live seafood (a small-sized lobster, freshly steamed, will set you back about Y220), point at the dishes you want to try, and take your seat. Don't miss the signature cuttlefish dumplings (*moyu jiaozi*) wrapped in dough dyed black from the cuttlefish ink. [$] *Average main: Y110* ✉ *39 Qutangxia Lu* ☎ *0532/8267–0026.*

$$$ SHANGHAINESE 🍴 **Din Tai Fung** (鼎泰丰 *Dĭngtàifēng*). Inside the posh Marina City Mall beside the Olympic Sailing Center, Din Tai Fung serves up its brand of precisely pleated dumplings to CBD execs and tourists staying at the InterCon nearby. The *xiaolongbao* dumplings from this renowned Taiwanese brand contain delicate fillings and scalding soup—the delicately steamed crab dumplings pair well with the ocean view. [$] *Average main: Y100* ✉ *Marina City Mall, 86 Ao'men Lu* 🌐 *www.dintaifungusa.com.*

$$ AMERICAN 🍴 **Sitting Bull** (毅牛烤排馆*Yìniú kăopái guăn*). Embracing the mantra of simplicity, Sitting Bull wows with its slow-cooked ribs with a sticky glaze, pulled-pork sandwiches, homemade bratwursts, and freshly baked cornbread. Everything here is washed down with Californian wines and draft beers from local craft brewery Strong Ale Works. A diamond in a rough retail area, the exposed-brick dining room has communal bench tables and a contemporary, laid-back vibe. [$] *Average main: Y80* ✉ *Tai Gu Square, 138 Zhangzhou Lu* ☎ *0532/8571–7103.*

$$ SEAFOOD 🍴 **Yumatou Seafood Restaurant** (渔码头海鲜舫 *Yúmătóu hăixiānfăng*). Size up your dinner at this quintessential seafood place, one of many on or around Minjiang Lu. Rows of tanks swarm with live sea creatures, with prices marked per *jin* (about 500 grams). For shellfish, this is enough for two to share. Order the Qingdao signature: a round of clams fried with chilies and garlic (*gala* in the local dialect), which pairs perfectly with a jug of fresh Tsingtao beer. Point at the scallops and ask for them to be served *suanrong fensi,* meaning steamed with garlic and vermicelli noodles. [$] *Average main: Y60* ✉ *24 Yunxiao Lu* ☎ *0532/8577–9999.*

WHERE TO STAY

$ HOTEL Fodor's Choice ★ 🏨 **The Castle** (怡堡酒店 *Yíbăo jiŭdiàn*). Sharing the same historic gardens as the German Governer's Residence, this affordable boutique hotel belies its mock-Bavarian exterior with flamboyantly designed guest rooms with huge beds, flat-screen TVs, and pretty views over the Old City. **Pros:** in the heart of the Old City; excellent service; great value. **Cons:** you might have to wait for taxis in the evening. [$] *Rooms from: Y600* ✉ *26 Longshan Lu, grounds of the German Governor's Residence* ☎ *0532/8869–1111* 🌐 *www.thecastle-hotel.com* 🛏 *50 rooms* 🍴 *Breakfast.*

$ HOTEL FAMILY 🏨 **Huiquan Dynasty Hotel** (汇泉王朝大店 *Huìquán wángcháo dàjiǔdiàn*). Looming over the city's most popular beach, this long-established hotel makes up for average rooms with the city's best ocean views, easy beach access for kids, and friendly service. **Pros:** great ocean views from some rooms; convenient beach access; English-speaking staff. **Cons:** in high season rooms don't justify price. [$] *Rooms from: Y800* ✉ *6 Nanhai Lu* ☎ *0532/8287–1122* 🛏 *405 rooms* 🍴 *No meals.*

$$ HOTEL 🏨 **InterContinental Qingdao** (青岛海尔洲际酒店 *Hǎiěr zhōujì jiǔdiàn*). Adjacent to the Olympic Sailing Center and a short walk from the Marina City shopping complex, this ultramodern hotel boasts contemporary rooms with dark wood paneling, built-in mood lighting, massive LCD TVs, and stand-alone bath tubs. **Pros:** Qingdao's most luxurious lodging; marina location; gorgeous rooms. **Cons:** among the city's priciest hotels. [$] *Rooms from: Y1300* ✉ *98 Ao Men Lu* ☎ *0532/6656–6666* 🌐 *www.intercontinental.com/Qingdao* 🛏 *422 rooms* 🍴 *No meals.*

$$ HOTEL 🏨 **Shangri-La** (香格里拉大酒店 *Xiānggélǐlā dàjiǔdiàn*). A few hundred yards from the coastline, the ever reliable Shangri-La is conveniently close to some of the best shopping and dining in town; insist on a room in the newer Valley Wing. **Pros:** convenient to beach; comfortable rooms; cozy bar. **Cons:** immediate area difficult to navigate on foot. [$] *Rooms from: Y1100* ✉ *9 Xiang Gang Zhong Lu* ☎ *0532/8388–3838* 🛏 *696 rooms* 🍴 *No meals.*

NIGHTLIFE

Most of the action takes place in the eastern part of the city. Jiangxi Lu and Minjiang Lu are two lively streets east of Zhongshan Park with a smattering of decent nightlife options.

Charlie's Bar (查理斯酒吧 *Chálǐsī jiǔbā*). A convenient base camp in Qingdao's party zone, Charlie's Bar is a laid-back establishment with a sports-pub atmosphere, a long wooden bar, and Guinness on draft. ✉ *167 Jiangxi Lu* ☎ *0532/8575–8560.*

Downtown Bar. This is the home of live music in Qingdao. Chinese rock, metal, and indie bands as well as a smattering of foreign talent play at this rough-and-ready club regularly, with cover charges starting at around Y40. ✉ *"Creative 100" Creative Industries Park, 105 Nanjing Lu, Bldg. 3* ☎ *0532/5524–7795.*

Room Lounge (入目有你 *Rùmù yǒunǐ*). Opened by a local whiskey aficionado, Room Lounge has Qingdao's best collection of single malts, as well as expertly mixed cocktails and a musical menu favoring reggae and electronic beats. The cozy, smoke-filled space attracts a discerning local crowd. Well-kept secrets aren't always easy to find—this one is on the ground floor of an apartment building. ✉ *Haihua Bldg., 1 Shandong Lu* ☎ *13905323300.*

Tsingtao Brewery Bar (青岛啤酒厂 *Qīngdǎo píjiǔchǎng jiǔbā*). At the Tsingtao Brewery Bar you can drink from the source. In front of the Tsingtao Brewery Museum, it's cavernous, brightly lit, and packed in

Qingdao has lovely seafront promenades, winding colonial streets, and pretty parks.

high season with convivial gangs of beer-swilling Chinese tourists. ✉ 56 *Dengzhou Lu* ☎ 0532/8383–3437.

SPORTS AND THE OUTDOORS

Chinese visitors come to Qingdao by the tens of thousands for the beaches. Each of the seven sandy beaches that run along the coast for more than 10 km (6 miles) has a variety of facilities ranging from changing rooms to kiosks renting inflatable toys to speedboat rides and water sports.

BEACHES

No. 1 Beach is the busiest, and in summer it can be difficult to find a place for your towel. If your goal is peace and quiet, head to **No. 2 Beach,** as fewer Chinese tourists venture out that way. In the summer, look out for the armies of brides and bridegrooms using the beaches for their wedding photos, and look out for another more recent phenomena: the facekini. This startlingly strange mask is worn by ladies to avoid getting a tanned face.

GOLF

Qingdao International Golf Club. The 18-hole Qingdao International Golf Club is 20 minutes from downtown. It has driving ranges and a fine-dining restaurant. Booking ahead, especially on weekends, is recommended—it's particularly popular with South Korean golfers who appreciate the value compared to their home country. ✉ *118 Songling Lu* ☎ 0532/8896–0001.

WATER SPORTS

The waterfront at Fushan Bay has been completely transformed with the construction of the Olympic Sailing Center. Several other places will also help you get on or in the water.

Qingdao Qinhai Scuba Diving Club. Near No. 1 Bathing Beach, the Qingdao Qinhai Scuba Diving Club is one of the few government-approved diving clubs in northern China. Diving conditions here are variable, with visibility at about

4–5 meters on a good day. All equipment is provided for PADI certification courses or guided recreational dives. ⊠ *5 Huiquan Lu* ☎ *0532/8387–7977.*

Yinhai International Yacht Club. One of the country's largest yacht clubs, Yinhai International Yacht Club has yachts of all sizes for rent, and offers lessons to beginners and more experienced sailors. The club is in the east of town, near the Olympic Sailing Center. ⊠ *30 Donghai Zhong Lu* ☎ *0532/8588–6666* ⊕ *www.yinhai.com.cn.*

SHOPPING

The north end of Zhongshan Lu has a cluster of antiques and cultural artifacts shops.

Hong Ren Tang Pharmacy (宏仁堂 *Hóngrén táng*). This traditional family-run drugstore has been operating here for more than 70 years. Inside, arcane displays and cabinets are stocked with thousands of herbs and medicines and more exotic products like antler and dried seahorses, all used to concoct Chinese medicines. Look for the English-speaking counter for foreign customers. This northern stretch of Zhongshan Lu is good for antiques, jade-carving, and other traditional businesses. ⊠ *196 Zhongshan Lu, Shinan* ☎ *0532/8282–5279.*

Qingdao Arts and Crafts Store (青岛 *Qīngdǎo*). The city's largest antiques shop is the Qingdao Arts and Crafts Store, with four floors of porcelain, scroll paintings, silk, gold, jade, and other stones. ⊠ *212 Zhongshan Lu* ☎ *0532/8281–7948.*

Taidong Night Market (台东夜市 *Táidōng yèshì*). A lively mix of clothing, footwear, household goods, and souvenir tea sets can be found at this bustling street market walking distance from the Tsingtao Beer Museum. ⊠ *Taidong Yilu, Shibei District* ⊙ *Daily 5:30 pm–10 pm.*

SIDE TRIPS FROM QINGDAO

Huadong Winery (华东百利酒庄 *Huádōng bǎilì jiǔzhuāng*). Near Laoshan is Huadong Winery, Shandong's premier vinous brand made from vines imported from France back in the 1980s. Although not as famous as the province's brewery, the 30 or so wines produced here have won a string of prizes. The wines are available for tasting and purchase by the case; call to arrange a visit—they speak English. The

beautiful scenery alone makes this a worthwhile side trip from Qingdao.
✉ *Nanlong Kou, Lao Shan, Qingdao* ☎ *0532/8881–7878*

Mount Lao (崂山 *Láoshān*). Rising to a height of more than 3,280 feet, Mount Lao (Laoshan) is just as scenic—though not as famous— as Shandong neighbor Mount Tai. A place of pilgrimage for centuries, the craggy slopes of Laoshan once boasted nine palaces, eight temples, and 72 convents. Most have been lost over the years, but those remaining are worth seeking out for their elegant architecture and stirring sea views. With sheer cliffs and cascading waterfalls, Laoshan is the source of the country's best-known mineral water (a vital ingredient in the local brew, Tsingtao). It's possible to see the mountain's sights as a day trip. Tourist buses to Laoshan leave from the main pier in Qingdao, or hop on to public Bus 304. Mount Lao is 40 km (25 miles) east of Qingdao. 🎫 *Y90* ⊙ *Daily 7–5*.

JIANGSU

Coastal Jiangsu is defined by water. This eastern province is crossed by one of the world's great rivers, the mystical Yangtze, and has a coastline stretching hundreds of miles along the Yellow Sea. Jiangsu is also home to the Grand Canal, an ancient feat of engineering. This massive waterway, the longest ancient canal in the world, with some parts dating from the 5th century BC, allowed merchants to ship the province's plentiful rice, vegetables, and tea to the north. Within the cities, daily life was historically tied to the water, and many old neighborhoods are still crisscrossed by countless small canals.

As a result of its trading position, Jiangsu has long been an economic and political center of China. The founder of the Ming Dynasty established the capital in Nanjing, and it remained there until his son moved it back north to Beijing. Even after the move, Nanjing and Jiangsu retained their nationwide importance. After the 1911 revolution, the province once again hosted the nation's capital in Nanjing.

Planning a trip in the province is remarkably easy. The cities are close together and connected by many trains and buses. Autumn tends to be warm and dry, with ideal walking temperatures. Spring can be rainy and windy, but the hills burst with blooms. Summers are infamously oppressive, hot, and humid. The winter is mild, but January and February are often rainy.

REGIONAL TOURS

Many hotels can also arrange guides and drivers, but they tend to be more expensive.

Tour Contacts Jiangsu Huate International Travel Service. This company has a number of guides who speak English. ✉ *33 Jinxiang He Lu, Nanjing* ☎ *025/8337–8695.* **Jinling Business International Travel Service.** The company has its own fleet of comfortable cars with knowledgeable drivers and offers a range of options for travelers. It can arrange trips throughout the region. ✉ *Junling Guoji Bldg., 5 Guangzhou Lu, Nanjing* ☎ *025/5186–0969.*

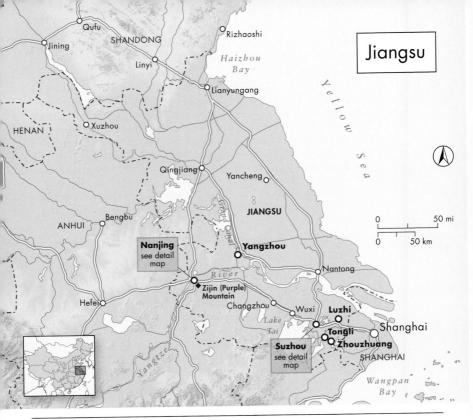

NANJING

*1½ hrs (309 km [192 miles]) by bullet train west of Shanghai; 3½ hrs
(1,039 km [646 miles]) by bullet train southeast of Beijing.*

The name *Nanjing* means Southern Capital, and for six dynastic periods, as well as during the country's brief tenure as the Republic of
China, the city was China's administrative capital. It was never as successful a capital as Beijing, and the locals chalk up the failures of several dynasties here to bad timing, but it could be that the laid-back
atmosphere of the Yangtze Delta just isn't as suited to political intrigue
as the north.

Nanjing offers travelers significantly more sites of historical importance
than Shanghai. Among the most impressive are the remnants of the
colossal Ming Dynasty city wall, built by 200,000 laborers to protect
the new capital in the 14th century. A number of important monuments, tombs, and gates reflect the glory and instability of Nanjing's
incumbency.

The city lies on the Yangtze, and the Yangtze River Bridge or the more
subdued park at Swallow Rock are great places for viewing the river.
The sheer amount of activity on the water is testimony to its continued
importance as a corridor for shipping and trade. Downtown, the streets

are choked with traffic, but the chaotic scene is easily avoided with a visit to any of the large parks. You can also take a short taxi ride to Zijin (Purple) Mountain, where quiet trails lead between Ming Tomb and the grand mausoleum of Sun Yat-sen.

GETTING HERE AND AROUND

Regular daily flights connect Nanjing with all other major Chinese cities. The airport is located just 36 km (22 miles) from the city center.

Nanjing's position on the Beijing–Shanghai high-speed railway line makes train travel a great option. Bus travel in this area of China is considerably more comfortable than elsewhere, thanks to a network of highways linking the cities and a fleet of air-conditioned coaches with comfortable seats.

Getting around a city the size of Nanjing can be a daunting task, but the easy-to-use subway system has made navigating safer and easier. Useful stops for travelers on its two lines include Sanshan Jie (Confucius Temple area), Xuanwu Gate (Xuanwu Lake and Hunan Road area), and Yunjinlu (Nanjing Massacre Memorial). Fares are inexpensive, only Y2 to Y6, depending on how many stations you travel to.

Getting around Nanjing by taxi is both fast and inexpensive, though taxi drivers generally cannot speak any English, so be prepared with the address of your destination written in Chinese. For the more adventurous, bicycles can be rented from some small hotels and tourist agencies; the city is very bicycle-friendly, with mostly flat roads and many dedicated bicycle lanes.

The best way to explore some of Nanjing's tourist destinations, once you're on Purple Mountain, is aboard the tourist buses (Y1, Y2, Y3) that run from the train station to Ming Tomb, Sun Yat-sen Botanical Gardens, Sun Yat-sen Mausoleum, and Spirit Valley Pagoda. The fare is Y3.

AIR TRAVEL Most flights from Europe or North America go through Shanghai or Beijing before continuing on to Nanjing's Lukou Airport, but there are direct flights from Asian hubs like Seoul, Singapore, Nagoya, and Bangkok. From Nanjing several flights leave daily for Shanghai, Beijing, Guangzhou, Xiamen, Wuhan, and Hong Kong; flights leave daily for Xi'an, Chengdu, and Zhengzhou.

Taxis from Nanjing Lukou Airport, 36 km (22 miles) southwest of the city, should take between 20 and 30 minutes. The fare should be between Y90 and Y130.

Air Contacts Air China ☎ *025/8449–9378* ⊕ *www.airchina.com.cn/en.*
Nanjing Lukou Airport ✉ *Lukou Jie, Jiangning District* ☎ *968–890* ⊕ *www. njiairport.com.*

BUS TRAVEL Buses are the best way to reach Yangzhou, and they leave frequently from the main long-distance bus station and take about an hour. The trip to Shanghai takes between three and four hours, and the trip to Suzhou can take as little as two hours; buses to both cities depart from the Zhongshan Nan Lu Bus Station.

Bus Contact Nanjing Long Distance Bus Station ✉ *1 Jianning Lu* ☎ *025/8553–1299.*

TRAIN TRAVEL   There are many bullet trains daily, arriving at either Nanjing Railway Station or the newer Nanjing South Railway station. Trains to Suzhou take about 90 minutes. The train to Yangzhou also takes 90 minutes, but it's a pleasant trip with the bonus of crossing the Yangtze via the Yangtze River Bridge.

Train Contact Nanjing Train Station ✉ *264 Long Pan Lu* ☎ *025/8582–2222.* **Nanjing South Train Station** ✉ *Yuxie Jie, Yuhuatai District.*

SAFETY AND PRECAUTIONS

Nanjing is a huge, crowded city, but is safe to explore day or night. Use common sense in busy places such as the metro and train stations, where petty theft is a possibility.

TIMING

Considering the massive size of the city and the sheer number of attractions, try to devote at least two to three full days exploring.

TOURS

Major hotels will often arrange a tour guide for a group. Nanjing China Travel Service can arrange almost any type of tour of the city.

ESSENTIALS

Medical Assistance International SOS Clinic ✉ *Grand Metro Park Hotel, 319 Zhongshan Dong Lu, ground fl., Xuanwu District* ☎ *025/8480–2842* ⊕ *www. internationalsos.com.*

Visitor and Tour Info Nanjing China Travel Service ✉ *12 Baixin Bldg., Baizi Ting, south of the Drum Tower* ☎ *025/8336–6582.* **Nanjing CITS** ✉ *313 Zhongshan Bei Lu* ☎ *025/8343–9898* ⊕ *www.cits.net.*

EXPLORING

TOP ATTRACTIONS

Confucian Temple (夫子庙 *Fūzǐ miào*). Overlooking the Qinhuai River, a tributary of the Yangtze, a Confucian Temple has stood on this spot for 1,000 years, give or take. The present incarnation dates back to the 1980s, rebuilt a few decades after it was destroyed by the Japanese in 1937. The surrounding area is the city's busiest shopping and entertainment district, festooned with neon at night and packed with tourists. The alleys behind the temple, once home to China's most famous district of courtesans, now house a market and curio shops. Boat rides along the Qinhuai River leave from in front of the temple every evening. ✉ *Zhongshan Lu and Jiankang Lu, on the Qinhuai River* 🚗 *Y25* ⊙ *Daily 8:30–6.*

Fodor's Choice ★   **Ming Tomb** (明孝陵 *Míng xiàolíng*). One of the largest and most important burial mounds in China, this is the final resting place of Emperor Hong Wu, the founder of the Ming Dynasty. Born a peasant and orphaned at a young age, he became a monk and eventually led the army that overthrew the Yuan Dynasty, making Nanjing his capital in 1368 and building its mighty walls. You approach the tomb along the Spirit Way, flanked by auspicious stone lions, elephants, camels, and mythical beasts. Winding paths make the area around the tomb perfect for strolling. ✉ *Mingling Lu, on Purple Mountain* 🚗 *Y70 (includes Plum Blossom Hill and Sun Yat-sen Botanical Park)* ⊙ *Daily 8–6.*

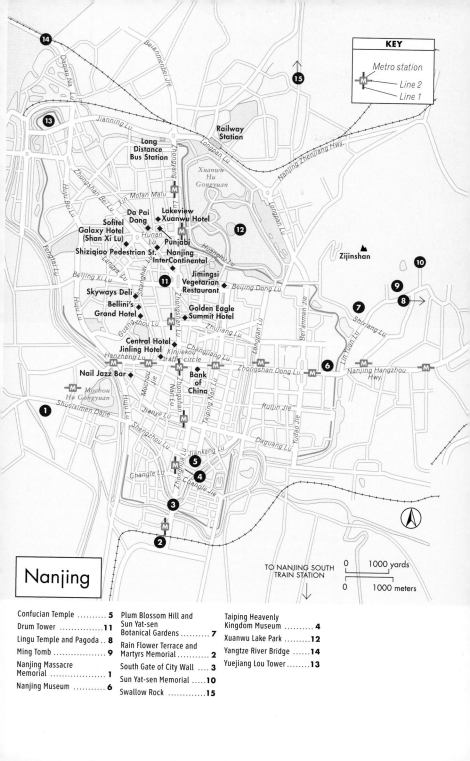

Nanjing

The Spirit Way, lined with stone camels and other auspicious animals, leads to Ming Tomb.

Nanjing Massacre Memorial (大屠杀纪念馆 *Dàtúshā jìniànguǎn*). In the winter of 1937, Japanese forces occupied Nanjing. In the space of a few days, thousands of Chinese were killed in the chaos, which became known as the "Rape of Nanjing." This monument commemorates the victims, many of whom were buried in mass graves. Be advised, this is not for the squeamish. Skeletons have been exhumed from the "Grave of Ten Thousand" and are displayed with gruesomely frank explanations as to how each lost his or her life. The memorial also displays artifacts from the Sino-Japanese reconciliation after World War II, which ended the conflict between the two countries on a less strident, more hopeful note. To get here, take the subway to Yunjinlu (Line 2). ⊠ *418 Shui Ximen Da Jie, west of Mouchou Lake Park* ☏ *025/8661–2230* ⊕ *www.nj1937.org* ✉ *Free* ☉ *Tues.–Sun. 8:30–4:30.*

Nanjing Museum (南京博物馆 *Nánjīng bówùguǎn*). After four years of renovations this huge museum has reopened with a further four exhibition halls. Attempting to make its vast collection of artifacts accessible and fun, the museum has added more dinosaur fossils for young visitors and a colorful exhibition on the Republic period after 1911. The Ming and Qing imperial porcelain collection remains one of the world's largest, and keep an eye out for what might be the museum's singular treasure—a full-sized suit of ceremonial armor made from jade tiles threaded with silver, dating back to the Eastern Han Dynasty. ⊠ *Zhongshan Dong Lu, inside Zhongshan Gate* ☏ *025/8480–2119* ⊕ *www.njmm.cn* ✉ *Free (bring passport)* ☉ *Daily 9–4:30.*

FAMILY **South Gate of City Wall** (中华门 *Zhōnghuámén*). Built as the linchpin of the city's defenses, this is less a gate than a complete fortress, with multiple courtyards and tunnels where several thousand soldiers could withstand a siege. It was rarely attacked; armies wisely avoided it in favor of the less heavily fortified areas to the north. Today, bonsai enthusiasts maintain displays in several of the courtyards. ✉ *Southern end of Zhonghua Lu, south side of city wall* 🎟 *Y25* 🕑 *Daily 8–6.*

Taiping Heavenly Kingdom Museum (太平天国历史博物馆 *Tàipíng tiānguó lìshǐ bówùguǎn*). Commemorating a fascinating period of Chinese history, this museum follows the life of Hong Xiuquan, a Christian who led a peasant revolt in 1859. He ultimately captured Nanjing and ruled for 11 years. Hong, who set himself up as emperor, claimed to be the younger brother of Jesus. On display are artifacts from the period. After browsing through the museum, stroll through the grounds of the surrounding Ming Dynasty garden compound, once the home of high-ranking Taiping officials. In the evening there are performances of opera and storytelling. ✉ *128 Zhanyuan Lu, beside the Confucian Temple* ☎ *025/8662–3024* 🎟 *Y30* 🕑 *Daily 8:30–5.*

Xuanwu Lake Park (玄武湖公园 *Xuánwǔhú gōngyuán*). More lake than park, this pleasant garden is bounded by one of the longer sections of the monumental city wall, which you can climb for a good view of the water. Purple Mountain rises in the east, and the glittering skyscrapers of modern Nanjing are reflected on the calm water. Causeways lined with trees and benches connect several large islands in the lake. Pedal-powered and battery-powered boats can be hired by the hour at a number of jetties. ✉ *Off Hunan Lu, outside the city wall* 🎟 *Y30* 🕑 *Daily 9–9.*

WORTH NOTING

Drum Tower (鼓楼 *Gǔlóu*). First built in 1382, the Drum Tower (Gulou in Chinese) gives the central city district its name. In ancient times, drums housed inside were used to signal important events, from the changing of the night's watch to an enemy attack or the even greater threat of fire. Today just one drum remains. ✉ *1 Dafang Xiang, beside Gulou People's Sq.* ☎ *025/8663–1059* 🎟 *Y20* 🕑 *Daily 8:30 –5.*

NEED A MAS-SAGE?

Shou Jia Massage (手佳盲人按摩保健中心 *Shǒujiā mángrén ànmó bǎojiàn zhōngxīn*). This health center is serious about traditional Chinese medicine. The center trains and employs the visually impaired for therapeutic massage treatments, and the friendly staff brings you endless cups of medicinal tea. ✉ *136 Chang Jiang Lu* ☎ *025/8470–2129.*

Lingu Temple and Pagoda (灵谷寺，灵谷塔 *Línggǔ sì* and *Línggǔ tǎ*). Close to the Sun Yat-sen Memorial, this temple commemorates Xuan Zang, the roving monk who brought Buddhist scriptures back to China from India. Seek out the Beamless Hall, a magnificent 14th-century structure built entirely from bricks without wood or nail to help bear its roof. Today it has been given over to propagandistic Republic-era displays. Farther up the hill is an impressive nine-story granite pagoda built in 1929 as a memorial to fallen revolutionaries. Vendors sell balloons to toss from the upper balcony. ✉ *Ta Lu, southeast of Sun Yat-sen Memorial* ☎ *025/8444–6443* 🎟 *Y80 (includes Sun Yat-sen Mausoleum)* 🕑 *Daily 8–5.*

Plum Blossom Hill and Sun Yat-sen Botanical Gardens (梅花山，中山植物园 *Méihuāshān and Zhōngshān zhíwùyuán*). March and April are the best months to visit Plum Blossom Hill, when peach, pear, plum, and cherry trees explode with color and fragrance. The rest of the year it's probably not worth a special trip. The exhibits at the botanical gardens, established in 1929, are a rewarding experience year-round for those interested in the country's flora. ⊠ *1 Shixiang Lu, northeast of Nanjing Museum* ⊡ *Y70 (includes Ming Tomb)* ⊙ *Daily 7–6.*

Rain Flower Terrace and Martyrs Memorial (雨花台，烈士陵园 *Yǔhuātái, Lièshì língyuán*). This scenic area gets its name from the legend of Yunzhang, a 15th-century Buddhist monk who supposedly pleased the gods so much with his recitation of a sutra that they showered flowers on this spot. It was put to a grim purpose in the 1930s, when the Nationalists executed thousands of their left-wing political enemies here. In 1950, after the founding of the People's Republic of China, it was transformed into a memorial park furnished with statues of heroic martyrs, soaring obelisks, and a museum. ⊠ *215 Yuhua Lu, outside Zhonghua Gate* ⊡ *Free* ⊙ *Daily 8–5.*

Sun Yat-sen Mausoleum (中山陵 *Zhōngshānlíng*). Acknowledged by both the Nationalist and Communist governments as the father of modern China, Sun Yat-sen (also known as Zhong Shan) lies buried in a delicately carved marble sarcophagus, reached by a broad set of concerte steps rising up the hillside. His final resting place is the center of a solemn and imposing monument to the ideas that overthrew the imperial system. Steep trails wind around the pine-covered scenic area, which feels a world away from Nanjing's hyperkinetic buzz. ■TIP→ **The mausoleum gets crowded on weekends, so try to come during the week.** ⊠ *Lingyuan Lu, east of the Ming Tomb* ⊡ *Y80 (includes Linggu Temple and Pagoda)* ⊙ *Daily 8–5.*

Swallow Rock (燕子矶 *Yànzijī*). North of the city, this small park overlooking the Yangtze River is worth the trip for stirring views of Asia's longest waterway. The "rock" refers to a huge boulder jutting out into the water, a spot where Tang Dynasty poet Li Bai found inspiration. To get here, take Bus 8 to the last stop. ⊠ *Northeast of Mount Mufu, on the Yangtze River* ⊡ *Y10* ⊙ *Daily 7:30–6.*

Yangtze River Bridge (长江大桥 *Chángjiāng dàqiáo*). Completed in 1968 at the height of the Cultural Revolution, this bridge was the first truly great engineering project completed solely by the Communists, touted

PEDESTRIAN STREETS

Confucius Temple Area (*Fūzǐ miào*). In the Confucius Temple Area are souvenir and shopping streets around the Qinhuai River. ⊠ *Zhongshan Lu and Jiankang Lu.*

Hunan Road. These streets are filled with snacks, shops, and restaurants. ⊠ *Hunan Lu, west of Zhongshan North Rd. and east of Zhongyang Lu.*

Xinjiekou City Center. Around the big malls and shopping centers are several bustling pedestrian streets. ⊠ *Xinjiekou, between Huaihai Lu and Zhongshan Lu.*

as a defining symbol of the spirit and ingenuity of the Chinese people. Decorated in stirring Socialist-Realist style, huge stylized flags sculpted from red glass rise from the bridge's piers, and groups of giant-size peasants, workers, and soldiers stride forward triumphantly. The Great Bridge Park lies on the southern side; from here you can take an elevator up to the top or browse a gallery of old photographs. Bus No. 1 from the Confucian Temple takes you to the bridge. ✉ *End of Daqiao Nan* 🎫 *Y15* ⏲ *Daily 7:30–5.*

Yuejiang Lou (阅江楼 *Yuèjiāng lóu*). Ming Dynasty founding emperor Hongwu wrote a poem describing his plans to have a tower built on top of Lion Mountain, from where he could gaze out at the Yangtze River. Other imperial business got in the way, and for several centuries the building remained on paper. In 2001, his dreams were realized; a gargantuan, historically accurate, and slightly sterile tower arose. The views, though, are terrific. ✉ *202 Jianning Lu* ☎ *025/5880–3977* 🎫 *Y40* ⏲ *Daily 7–5.*

3

WHERE TO EAT

For more information on bars and restaurants in Nanjing, pick up a copy of the local bilingual *Map Magazine* or *The Nanjinger* at your hotel. Printed monthly, it has the latest listings and reviews of many popular spots in the city, as well as upcoming cultural events.

$$ ITALIAN FAMILY 🍴 **Bellini** (贝丽妮意式餐厅 *Bèilìnī yìshì cāntīng*). Run by Italian hosts, the crisp Napoli-style pizzas at this contemporary Italian eatery come recommended, but you shouldn't overlook the seafood specialties and wide-ranging pasta dishes. Ingredients and cooking techniques are authentic, and regular half-price deals (particularly on Tuesdays) attract a local expat and student crowd. This is the newer, "downtown" branch; the original location is a little out of the way. [$] *Average main: Y85* ✉ *14 Nan Xiu Cun, Shanghai Lu* ☎ *025/5288–8857* 🌐 *www.bellinirestaurants.com.*

$$ MANDARIN Fodor's Choice ★ 🍴 **Da Pai Dang** (南京大牌档 *Nánjīng dàpáidǎng*). Lined with street-food-style stalls, this wildly popular dining hall has been dishing up specialties of the Yangtze wetlands since 1994. Waterfowl is the big draw; try Nanjing's famous salted duck, served sliced on the bone, or a steamer full of duck dumplings. Appetizers and soups focusing on the area's vegetables offer light relief from the more starchy offerings. Order from the picture menu (with tiny English translations) or get up and browse, pointing to what you want and giving your table number to one of the costumed attendants. There are five locations around town, but this is the original and the best. [$] *Average main: Y60* ✉ *Hunan Lu* ☎ *025/8330–5777.*

$ FAST FOOD 🍴 **Hui Wei** (回味 *Huí wèi*). Beloved by locals, Nanjing's very own fast-food chain makes for a convenient pit stop to try two regional specialties: *xiaolongbao* (soup-filled pork dumplings) and *maoxue fensi tang* (rice noodle soup with duck blood cubes). Branches are everywhere (the original is located on Hunan Lu), but the nicest location is on the causeway crossing Xuanwu Lake, where you'll find tables at the water's edge. [$] *Average main: Y20* ✉ *Along the causeway crossing Xuanwu Lake.*

$$ VEGETARIAN 🍴 **Jimingsi Vegetarian Restaurant** (鸡鸣寺百味斋茶社 *Jīmíng sì bǎiwèizhāi cháshè*). Inside the Jiming Temple, this establishment uses

wheat gluten and other ingredients to create mock pork, fish, chicken, and goose dishes. An English menu features a selection of the best offerings. Tofu threads and the Sichuan-style "fish" are recommended. This restaurant is noteworthy more for its view of the temple grounds than its food, but overall it's worth a lunch stop. [$] *Average main: Y60* ✉ *Jiming Temple, off Beijing Dong Lu, south of Xuanwu Lake Park* ☎ *025/8771–3690* 💳 *No credit cards* 🕘 *No dinner.*

$$$ INDIAN 🍴 **Punjabi** (本杰比印度料理 *Běnjiébǐ Yìndù liàolǐ*). Indian chefs slap naan dough to the sides of roaring *tandor* ovens in the open kitchen of this popular North Indian restaurant. Typically rich Punjabi dishes like butter chicken make up most of the menu, with *biryanis* (spiced rice dishes) and southern-style *dosas* (savory pancakes) toward the back. Look for the large red-and-blue sign halfway down Hunan Pedestrian Street pointing you down the alley. [$] *Average main: Y100* ✉ *2 Hunan Lu* ☎ *025/832–45421* 💳 *No credit cards.*

$$ CHINESE 🍴 **Shizi Lou** (狮子楼大酒店 *Shīzilóu dàjiǔdiàn*). Near the Shanzi Road Market, this bustling restaurant is a popular purveyor of Huaiyang cuisine, one of the "four great traditions" of Chinese cooking. Try the signature "lion's head" meatballs (*shizitou*), large and succulent orbs of pork stewed with vegetables in a clear soup, or the gut-bustingly oversized potstickers (*guotie*). If you're feeling brave, opt for a round of stinky tofu, malodorous for the uninitiated but mouthwateringly tasty. [$] *Average main: Y90* ✉ *29 Hunan Lu, near Shizi Bridge* ☎ *025/8360–7888* 💳 *No credit cards.*

$$ CAFÉ 🍴 **Skyways Deli** (云中食品店 *Yúnzhōng shípǐndiàn*). Popular with overseas students studying at Nanjing University, Skyways is the perfect antidote to oily Chinese food. This clean, user-friendly deli offers a list of sandwiches and salads that lets you choose, check, and chow in a matter of minutes. Most impressive are the bakery items, especially the chocolate-dipped coconut macaroons and the Swedish Napoleon cookies. A small grocery area offers pricy imported meats and cheeses. The owners also manage Swede and Kraut, a restaurant serving German fare, just up the road. [$] *Average main: Y70* ✉ *160 Shanghai Lu* ☎ *025/8331–7103* 💳 *No credit cards.*

WHERE TO STAY

$ HOTEL 🏨 **Central Hotel** (中心大酒店 *Zhōngxīn dàjiǔdiàn*). Steps from the heart of the city, this well-run hotel has an offbeat charm. **Pros:** good value; convenient location; nice decor. **Cons:** some rooms better than others. [$] *Rooms from: Y600* ✉ *75 Zhongshan Lu* ☎ *025/8473–3888* 🌐 *www.njcentralhotel.com* 🛏 *339 rooms* 🍽 *No meals.*

$$ HOTEL 🏨 **Fairmont Nanjing** (南京费尔蒙 *Nánjīng Nánjīng fèiěrméng*). Occupying the uppermost floors of the Jimao Tower, designed so that its 62 concertina-like stories resemble a Chinese lantern, Fairmont Beijing is Nanjing's newest international luxury hotel, with state-of-the-art rooms, a fabulous spa (try the indoor mineral pool), and fawning service. **Pros:** sparklingly new; convenient to airport. **Cons:** slightly outside the center. [$] *Rooms from: Y1100* ✉ *333 Jiangdong Zhong Lu, Jianye District* ☎ *25/8672–8888* 🌐 *www.fairmont.com/nanjing* 🛏 *284 rooms, 75 suites* 🍽 *Breakfast.*

$ **Grand Hotel** (南京古南都饭店 *Nánjīng gǔnándōu fàndiàn*). Over-
HOTEL looking the busy shopping centers in Nanjing's commercial center, the
FAMILY Grand Hotel is an affordable and reliable base for seeing the sights,
with a decent Western restaurant, babysitting service, and other family-
friendly extras. **Pros:** good for families with kids; central location; helpful staff. **Cons:** some rooms need renovations. $ *Rooms from: Y550*
✉ *208 Guangzhou Lu* ☎ *025/8331–1999* ⊕ *www.njgrandhotel.com*
⇗ *305 rooms, 11 suites* ❙○❙ *No meals.*

$$ **InterContinental Nanjing** (南京绿地洲际酒店 *Nánjīng lùdìzhōujì*
HOTEL *jiǔdiàn*). The loftiest five-star pile in town, this hotel towers above its
rivals in both height and price, although its decor and fittings—all blacks,
creams, and chromes—is geared more to the Chinese businessman than
foreign tourists. **Pros:** international luxury and service; location. **Cons:**
expensive; very businesslike. $ *Rooms from: Y1300* ✉ *1 Zhongyang
Lu, Gulou District* ☎ *025/8353–8888* ⊕ *www.intercontinental.com/
Nanjing* ⇗ *433 rooms, 37 suites* ❙○❙ *Breakfast.*

$ **Jinling Hotel** (金陵饭店 *Jīnlíng Fàndiàn*). Something of an institution,
HOTEL Nanjing's original modern five-star hotel is worth a look for its great
location in the center of town, solicitous service, and—in its newly
built tower—sparklingly modern rooms. **Pros:** luxurious accommoda-
tions; attentive service. **Cons:** expensive rates. $ *Rooms from: Y1000*
✉ *2 Xinjiekou* ☎ *025/8471–1888, 025/8472–2888* ⊕ *www.jinlinghotel.
com/English/index.aspx* ⇗ *592 rooms, 33 suites* ❙○❙ *No meals.*

$ **Lakeview Xuanwu Hotel** (南京玄武饭店 *Nánjīng xuánwǔ fàndiàn*).
HOTEL Ask for an east-facing room at this welcoming hotel and you'll be
Fodor'sChoice treated to rousing views of Xuanwu Lake and the wall surrounding
★ Nanjing's old city. **Pros:** good views; pleasant rooms; great value. **Cons:**
some outdated facilities. $ *Rooms from: Y600* ✉ *193 Zhongyang Lu*
☎ *025/8335–8888* ⇗ *258 rooms, 47 suites* ❙○❙ *No meals.*

$ **Sofitel Galaxy Hotel** (苏菲特银河大酒店 *Sūfēitèyínhé dàjiǔdiàn*). If
HOTEL you're looking for luxury, this 48-story tower remains a fine choice
Fodor'sChoice despite all the recent competition; rooms and suites are chic and under-
★ stated, with subtle oriental flourishes and all the trimmings you'd expect
from the brand, including plasma TVs and rainfall showers. **Pros:** pre-
mium facilities; great location; lovely views. **Cons:** cigarette smoke in
public areas. $ *Rooms from: Y1050* ✉ *9 Shanxi Lu* ☎ *025/8371–8888*
⊕ *www.sofitel.com/Nanjing* ⇗ *278 rooms* ❙○❙ *No meals.*

NIGHTLIFE

Nanjing is a dynamic metropolis with thousands of foreign students
and a dynamic bar scene. Get the latest updates on the ever-changing
nightlife from *Map Magazine* or *The Nanjinger*. Nanjing's nightlife
centers on the 1912 neighborhood, named for the year the Republic
of China was founded. A few dozen restaurants, bars, and clubs are
packed into several pedestrian-only blocks at the intersection of Taiping
Lu and Changjiang Lu, a 15-minute walk northeast of the city center.
For something a little more bohemian, a burgeoning café and restaurant
scene can be found along Shanghai Lu, close to Nanjing University.

Blue Marlin (蓝枪鱼 *Lánqiāngyú*). Sandwiched between glitzy night-
clubs, Blue Marlin is the place to kick off a night out. Big, brash, and
commercial, it caters to all tastes with imported beers, decent cocktails,

and finger food. Evenings bring televised sports and live music from a house band. ✉ *8 Changjiang Hou Jie* ☎ *025/8453–7376* ⊕ *www.bluemarlin.cn.*

Finnegan's Wake (芬尼根酒吧 *Fēnnígēn jiǔbā*). Expect a proper Irish (or Scottish) welcome at this beautifully designed pub, depending on which of the two owners pours your pint of Guinness or Kilkenny. Get chatting and you may well move on to one of the 70 whiskeys, best enjoyed by the fireplace in the upstairs lounge. An extensive menu includes Irish stew and the "ultimate" Dublin fried breakfast. There's live Celtic music most nights. ✉ *Off Zhongshan Nan Lu* ☎ *025/5220–7362* ⊕ *www.finneganswake.com.cn.*

Myth Bar (谜酒吧 *Mí jiǔbā*). A step above the other Nanjing watering holes, this split-level bar has evolved from an expat-oriented drinking den to a high-class, live jazz palace, with a hike in drinks prices and a sharpening up of clientele. One of the best spots in town for civilized fun. ✉ *60-6 Jiangsu Lu* ☎ *025/8330–7877.*

Nail Jazz Bar (钉子酒吧 *Dīngzi jiǔbā*). This dark and cozy bar has the look and feel of a neighborhood jazz joint—sadly, it lacks a jazz band most of the time, opting for a bored-looking singer who warbles along to a backing track. It has a friendly atmosphere and the city's most eclectic selection of bottled beers. ✉ *10 Luolang Xiang, south of the Sheraton Nanjing* ☎ *025/8653–2244* ⊕ *www.nailbar.cn.*

Prime (南京绿地洲际酒店 *Nánjīng lǜdì zhōujì jiǔdiàn*). Jiangsu's high-flyers toast their bottom line over classy cocktails on the 78th floor of the Zifeng Tower, China's third-tallest building. Nestled atop the InterContinental Nanjing, the bar boasts the city's best wine selection, with a good number available by the glass. Smog permitting, there are stunning city views across Xuanwu Lake to the leafy mound of Zhongshan Park. ✉ *InterContinental Nanjing, 1 Zhongyang Lu, 78th fl.* ☎ *025/8353–8888.*

SHOPPING

The best place to buy traditional crafts, art, and souvenirs is the warren of small shops in the center of the city. Nanjing is a convenient place to pick up many of the traditional crafts of Jiangsu—purple sand teapots, flowing silks, brocade robes, and folk paper cuttings.

Brocade Research Institute (南京云锦研究所有限公司 *Nánjīngyún jǐnyán jiūsuǒ yǒuxiàn Gōngsī*). On the UNESCO Intangible Cultural Heritage list, brocades are lavishly embroidered robes unique to Nanjing, once worn by emperors. The Brocade Research Institute is part retail outlet part workshop, where the traditional brocades are still being made today using huge, old-fashioned looms operated by two people at a time. The gift shop sells beautiful examples of the fabric. A fantastic, recently opened museum has high-tech exhibits including holographic displays, 360-degree film screenings, and even a fashion show. ✉ *240 Chating Dong Jie, behind Nanjing Massacre Memorial* ☎ *025/8651–8580.*

Chaotian Gong Antique Market (朝天宫古玩市场 *Cháotiān gōng gǔwán shìchǎng*). In the courtyard of the Confucian Temple, the Chaotian Gong Antique Market has an array of curios, from genuine antiques

高舉民族大團結旗幟　共創 21 世紀新輝煌

天下為公

DID YOU KNOW?

The Sun Yat-sen Memorial honors the father of modern China. He inspired the overthrow of the Qing Dynasty and was the first provisional president of the newly founded Republic of China in 1912. However, his real fame lies in his political philosophy, the Three Principles of the People: nationalism, democracy, and the people's livelihood.

to fakes of varying quality. A vendor's opening price can border on the ludicrous, especially with foreign customers, but some good-natured bargaining can yield success. The market is liveliest on weekend mornings. ⊠ *Zhongshan Lu and Jiankang Lu.*

Fabric Market (面料市场 *Miànliào shìchǎng*). Northwest of the Drum Tower, the Fabric Market sells silks, linen, and traditional cotton fabrics. Bargaining is necessary, but the prices are reasonable. Expect to pay Y50 to Y60 per meter of silk. Many vendors can also arrange tailoring. ⊠ *215 Zhongshan Bei Lu.*

FAMILY **Fashion Lady Mall** (时尚莱迪商城 *Shíshàng láidí shāngchéng*). This subterranean retail center contains literally hundreds of tiny shops all lit with colorful neon and hawking everything from bargain women's clothing and accessories to gems, jewelry, and beauty treatments like manicures and massages. A unique shopping experience (for the girls), it's great people-watching, too. Accessible directly from Xinjiekou subway station. ⊠ *30 Zhenghong Jie, Baixia District.*

YANGZHOU

1 hr (106 km [66 miles]) by bus northeast of Nanjing; 3½ hrs (300 km [185 miles]) by bus from Shanghai; 2 hours by train from Nanjing.

Despite rapid outward expansion, the historic center of Yangzhou has retained a laid-back feel not often found in Eastern China. Small enough to be seen in a day, its charm may encourage you to linger.

Due to its fortuitous position on the Grand Canal, Yangzhou has flourished since the Tang Dynasty. Drawing on thousands of years as a trade center for salt and silk, Yangzhou maintains a cosmopolitan feel. Indeed, some of the most interesting sites demonstrate a blending of cultures: Japanese relations are evidenced in the monument to Jian Zhen, a monk who helped spread Buddhist teachings to Japan. European influence is seen in the Sino-Victorian gardens of He Yuan, and Persian contact is preserved in the tomb of Puddahidin, a 13th-century trader and descendant of Mohammed.

GETTING HERE AND AROUND

The best way to get to Yangzhou is by bus. It lies on the Beijing–Shanghai and Nanjing–Nantong highways. Yangzhou's West Bus Station is the fastest way to get to Nanjing, while Yangzhou East Bus Station serves Suzhou and Shanghai.

AIR TRAVEL Yangzhou Taizhou Airport, which opened in 2012, is located 30 km (21 miles) northeast of the city. It has daily flights from Beijing, Chengdu, and Guangzhou.

BUS TRAVEL Frequent bus service runs between Yangzhou and Nanjing and Suzhou, and on to Shanghai. Most routes have air-conditioned buses. Yangzhou West Bus Station is about 6 km (4 miles) west of the city on Jiangyang Xi Lu. Yangzhou East Bus Station is east of the city along Yunhe Xi Lu.

Bus Contact Yangzhou West Bus Station ⊠ *Jiangyang Xi Lu* ☎ *0514/8786–1812.*

TRAIN TRAVEL   Yangzhou has a recently built train station in the western outskirts beside the Shangri-La Hotel that's only practical if you are coming from nearby Nanjing.

Train Contact Yangzhou Train Station ✉ *Wenchang Xi Lu* ☎ *0514/8554-6222.*

TOURS

Hotels are the chief source of tourist information in Yangzhou. Not only for the young, China Youth Travel in Yangzhou can put together any kind of trip, from morning boat rides around Slender West Lake to evening cruises down the Great Canal. The staff speaks English and has the most experience working with foreign travelers.

Tour Info Yangzhou China Youth Travel Agency ✉ *6 Siwangting Lu* ☎ *0514/8793-3876.*

TIMING

Many travelers explore Yangzhou as a day trip from Nanjing, which is perfectly possible, but to get the most out of the city we recommend staying at least one night.

ESSENTIALS

Medical Assistance Yangzhou No. 1 People's Hospital ✉ *45 Taizhou Lu* ☎ *0514/8790-7353.*

EXPLORING

TOP ATTRACTIONS

Da Ming Temple (大明寺 *Dàmíng sì*). Built 1,600 years ago, the Da Ming Temple is one of the more interesting Buddhist shrines in Eastern China. The main attraction is a memorial to Tang Dynasty monk Jian Zhen, who traveled to Japan to spread the teachings of Buddha. It took the determined missionary six attempts to cross the East China Sea, and cost him his eyesight. For refreshment, seek out the still-flowing Fifth Spring Under Heaven in the temple grounds. The water's high mineral content means it's great for tea, which you can sip in a small teahouse. ✉ *8 Pingshan Tang Lu, next to Slender West Lake* ☎ *0514/8734–0720* 🎫 *Y45* ⊙ *Daily 7:45–5.*

Ge Garden (个园 *Gè yuán*). With more than 60 varieties of bamboo, this lovely garden is so named because the characteristic trio of leaves on a bamboo plant look like the Chinese character *ge* (个). There are yellow stalks, striped stalks, huge treelike stands, and dwarf bamboo with delicate leaves. The place was built by a wealthy salt merchant named Huang Zhiyun, who believed bamboo represented the loyalty of a good man. As you wander the quiet avenues, note the loose bricks in the path arranged to clack under your footsteps. The garden is also accessible from an entrance on Dongguan Jie. ✉ *10 Yangfu Dong Lu, east of Yangzhou Hotel* ☎ *0514/8793–5233* ⊕ *www.ge-garden.net* 🎫 *Y40* ⊙ *Daily 7:15–6.*

Slender West Lake (瘦西湖 *Shòuxī hú*). Originally part of a river, Slender West Lake was created during the Qing Dynasty by wealthy salt merchants hoping to impress Emperor Qianlong on his many visits to Yangzhou. The park, laced with willows and dotted with pavilions, bridges, and tearooms, can be seen in an hour or savored for a half day. The **Fishing Terrace** is where the emperor decided he'd try his

The Wang's Residence was spared during the Cultural Revolution because it had been converted into a factory.

hand at angling; the merchants reportedly had their servants wade into the lake and hook a fish on each line he cast. Another mark left by the emperor is the **White Pagoda**, a dome-shaped Buddhist stupa. The emperor casually remarked that Slender West Lake only lacked a stupa to resemble Beijing's Beihai Park. By the time the sun shone through the morning mist, there was the emperor's stupa, hastily carved out of salt and convincing from a distance. A permanent structure was completed much later. It seems all the flattery had the desired effect; Yangzhou prospered as a trading center right up until the 20th century. ⊠ *28 Da Hongqiao Lu, in the northern part of the city* ☎ *0514/8733–0189* ▦ *Y100* ☉ *Daily 7–6.*

Wang's Residence (汪氏小苑 *Wāngshì xiǎoyuàn*). This was once one among dozens of private mansions belonging to Yangzhou's prosperous merchant class, but it alone made it through the ravages of the Cultural Revolution largely intact, thanks to its conversion into a factory. Keep an eye out for the exquisite wood carving, especially the crisscrossing bamboo design carved in layers out of *nanmu*, a glimmering wood now extinct in this area of China. There's even a bomb shelter in the small inner garden—a reminder of the Japanese invasion. ⊠ *14 Di Gong Di, between Taizhou Lu and Guoqing Lu* ☎ *0514/8732–8869* ▦ *Y25* ☉ *Daily 8–5:30.*

Yangzhou Museum (扬州博物馆 *Yángzhōu bówùguǎn*). Housed in an impressive building beside Mingyue Lake in the town's western suburbs, the Yangzhou Museum has seven exhibition halls packed with Chinese jade, earthenware, bronze vessels, porcelain, and paper-cutting.

✉ *Wenchang Xi Lu, Bowuguan Lu* ☎ *0514/8522–8018* 🎫 *Free* 🕑 *Daily 8:30–4:30.*

REPLANTING GARDENS

Many of the country's historic gardens have been recently pieced back together. Most were ravaged during the Cultural Revolution, when for years Red Guard troops were encouraged to smash China's heritage to pieces. To this day, China is still replanting gardens, repairing temples, and restoring historic architecture.

WORTH NOTING

Garden Tomb of Puhaddin (普哈丁墓 *Pǔhādīng mù*). The Garden Tomb of Puhaddin faces the Grand Canal, from where you climb a stairway to a graveyard of marble-slab headstones. Toward the back a garden with a charming pavilion reveals both Persian and Chinese design elements. Largely ignored by local tourists, a visit to the garden tomb is a reminder of the city's Islamic influence. ✉ *Laopai Lu at Quanfu Lu, near Jiefang Bridge* 🎫 *Y15* 🕑 *Daily 7:30–4:30.*

He Garden (何园 *Hé yuán*). In the southeast part of the Old Town, the Victorian-influenced He Garden is notable for its melding of European and Chinese architecture and landscape design. Dating from the 1880s, it differs from a traditional Chinese garden partly because of the wooden pathway linking the buildings. Other East-meets-West aspects include Victorian-style fireplaces inside the residence. ✉ *66 Xuning Men Dalu, southeast corner of the city* ☎ *0514/8723–2360* 🎫 *Y40* 🕑 *Daily 7:30–5:30.*

WHERE TO EAT

$$ CHINESE 🍴 **Fu Chun Teahouse** (富春茶社 *Fùchūn cháshè*). Busiest at breakfast, this venerable institution steams all sorts of delicious buns and dumplings. They are hungrily wolfed down by locals and tourists alike, along with cups of kui dragon tea, a light and fragrant green tea known colloquially as "Monkey King." Try the *xiefen tangbao*, oversized crabmeat dumplings from which you slurp out the rich soup through a straw. Served in bamboo steamers, the jade dumplings are filled with a local leafy vegetable. Fu Chun is also a good place to sample the dish Yangzhou gave to the world: fried rice. [$] *Average main: Y60* ✉ *35 Desheng Qiao Lu* ☎ *0514/8723–3326* 💳 *No credit cards* 🕑 *No dinner.*

$$$ EUROPEAN 🍴 **The Old Brewery** (老啤酒厂 *Lǎo píjiǔ chǎng*). With an affable Chinese-American owner, this riverside brewery and restaurant offers three varieties of home-brewed beer—note the stainless-steel tanks by the entrance. The ambitious menu has everything from pan-seared foie-gras to squid-ink risotto, but the crisp-crusted, generously topped pizzas are a safe bet. Live music plays nightly. The canal-side location is ideal for an after-dinner stroll. [$] *Average main: Y120* ✉ *128 Nantong Donglu, Guangling District* ☎ *0514/8721–5225* 💳 *No credit cards.*

WHERE TO STAY

$ HOTEL Fodor's Choice ★ 🏨 **Changle Inn** (长乐客栈 *Chánglè kèzhàn*). It's worth dragging your suitcase along the cobblestones of historic Donguang Street to reach this restored Qing Dynasty courtyard hotel in the heart of old Yangzhou, with quiet gardens and pavilions joined by lantern-lit pathways and oval "moon gates." **Pros:** directly opposite Ge Garden; gorgeous

CLOSE UP

Adopting in China

For some, the gardens, the architecture, the history, and the scenery are all secondary reasons to visit Yangzhou. Theirs is a more personal and momentous trip. On the outskirts of town there is a white-tiled compound called the Yangzhou Social Welfare Institute. This is where American parents and Chinese children come together to form families. Since Chinese law began promoting foreign adoption in 1991, there has been a huge surge in the number of families adopting from China. More than 60,000 children have been brought to the United States from China over the past 20 years, although numbers have declined in recent years due to a tightening of restrictions and an increase in domestic adoption.

Around 95% of children in orphanages are female. There persists a strong preference for boys, especially in rural areas. This is largely due to a combination of bias and traditional social structures whereby girls marry out and males help provide for the family. An unintended consequence of the One Child Policy exacerbates prejudices against women. Some Chinese parents, desperate to have a male child, take drastic measures like gender-selective abortion and even abandon their girls on the steps of orphanages.

The first wave of American-adopted Chinese girls are already teens. As they come of age, their transracial families face unique challenges as they grapple with questions of racial and cultural identity. Support groups, social organizations, and even specialized heritage tour groups address these questions and assist children in learning more about their places of birth.

---

setting; smart rooms. **Cons:** difficult to get taxis here. $ *Rooms from: Y700* ✉ *357 Dongguan Jie, opposite Ge Garden* ☎ *0514/8799–3333* ⊕ *www.yangzhoucentre-residence.com* ↝ *80 rooms* ⦿ *Breakfast.*

$ ⌺ **Ramada Plaza Yangzhou Casa** (华美达凯莎酒店 X*iefen tangbao*).
HOTEL Overlooking the Grand Canal in an enviable city-center location, the popular Ramada Plaza Yangzhou Casa sits within striking distance of Slender West Lake and Ge Garden. **Pros:** great location; modern rooms; efficient facilities. **Cons:** lengthy check-in lines. $ *Rooms from: Y600* ✉ *318 Wen Chang Zhong Lu* ☎ *0514/8780–0000* ⊕ *www.ramada.com* ↝ *204 rooms* ⦿ *No meals.*

$$ ⌺ **Shangri-La Yangzhou** (扬州香格里拉酒店 *Yángzhōu xiānggélǐlā*
HOTEL *jiǔdiàn*). Yangzhou's first international luxury lodging, the Shangri-La makes up for its out-of-center location with the city's must sumptuously appointed rooms and suites. **Pros:** excellent service; modern facilities; chic rooms. **Cons:** hidden among office buildings; a 15-minute taxi ride from the center. $ *Rooms from: Y1100* ✉ *472 Wenchang Xi Lu* ☎ *0514/8512–8888* ⊕ *www.shangri-la.com/yangzhou/shangrila* ↝ *369 rooms* ⦿ *No meals.*

NIGHTLIFE

Similar to the 1912 area in Nanjing and opposite the Old Brewery, Yangzhou's 1912 area is a collection of glitzy Chinese restaurants, bars, and karaoke dives.

SUZHOU

Approximately 60 minutes (84 km [52 miles]) by bullet train west of Shanghai; 90 minutes (217 km [135 miles]) by bullet train southeast of Nanjing; 5 hrs (1,146 km [712 miles]) by bullet train south of Beijing.

Suzhou has long been known as a center of culture, beauty, and sophistication. The "Venice of the East" produced scores of artists, writers, and politicians over the centuries, developing a local culture based on refinement and taste. Famous around the world for its meticulously landscaped classical gardens and crisscrossing waterways, Suzhou's elegance extends even to its local dialect—a Chinese saying purports that two people arguing in the Suzhou dialect sound more pleasant than lovers talking in standard Chinese.

Unlike in other cities in Eastern China, glass-and-steel office parks have been barred from the Old City, and this preservation makes Suzhou a pleasant place to explore. There is excellent English signage on the roads, and the local tourism board has even set up a convenient information center to get you on the right track.

Only an hour outside of Shanghai, the tourist trail here is well worn, and during the high season you will find yourself sharing Suzhou's gardens with packs of foreign and domestic tour groups. It's worth getting up early to hit the most popular places before the crowds descend.

GETTING HERE AND AROUND

Buses and trains to Shanghai take about an hour. Buses bound for Nanjing (two hours) and Yangzhou (three hours) depart from the North Bus Station. Frequent trains to Nanjing take 90 minutes. It's a popular route, so be sure to buy tickets in advance.

AIR TRAVEL Suzhou is served, rather inconveniently, by Shanghai's international airports, Hongqiao and Pudong. Hongqiao Airport is about 86 km (53 miles) from Suzhou, and shuttle buses run throughout the day. The trip takes less than two hours. If you are coming into Pudong, buses that make the long 120-km (74-mile) trip from the airport leave about once an hour.

Air Contacts China Eastern Airlines ✉ *115 Ganjiang Xi Lu* ☎ *0512/6522–2788* ⊕ *www.ce-air.com.* **China Southern Airlines** ✉ *943 Renmin Lu* ⊕ *www.flychinasouthern.com.*

BUS TRAVEL Bus service between Suzhou and Nanjing is frequent. Suzhou has two long-distance bus stations. The North Bus Station is beside Suzhou Railway Station; the South Bus Station is located on the South Ring Road where it meets Yingchun Lu.

Bus Contact Suzhou North Bus Station ✉ *29 Xihui Lu* ☎ *0512/6753–0686.*

TRAIN TRAVEL Trains arriving from Shanghai, Nanjing, and Beijing stop at Suzhou Railway Station or the newer Suzhou North Railway Station, a 25-minute

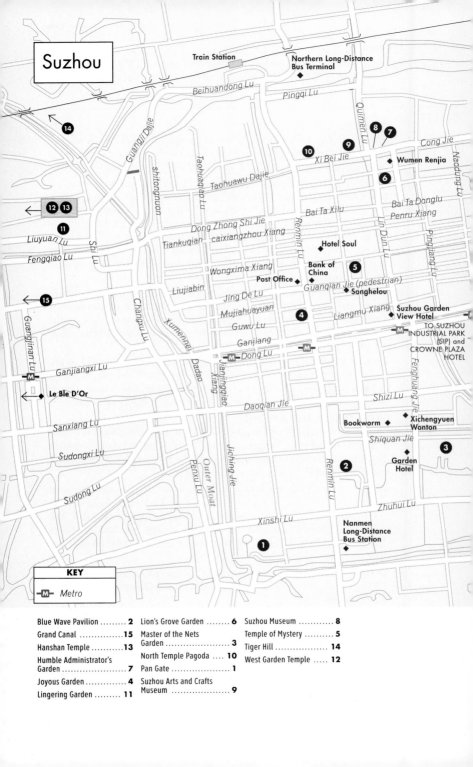

Suzhou

Train Station
Northern Long-Distance Bus Terminal

Beihuandong Lu
Pingqi Lu
Quimen Lu

Guangji Daije
Xi Bei Jie
Cong Jie
Naodung Lu

shitongnuon
Taohuaqiao Lu
Taohuawu Dajie
Wumen Renjia
Bai Ta Donglu
Penru Xiang

Dong Zhong Shi Jie
Bai Ta Xilu
Lin Dun Lu
Pingjiang Lu

Tiankuqian   caixiangzhou Xiang
Renmin Lu
Hotel Soul

Wongxima Xiang
Bank of China
Liujiabin
Jing De Lu
Post Office
Guanqian Jie (pedestrian)
Songhelou

Mujiahuayuan
Liangmu Xiang
Suzhou Garden View Hotel

Guwu Lu
Ganjiang
TO SUZHOU INDUSTRIAL PARK (SIP) and CROWNE PLAZA HOTEL

Changxu Lu
Kumennei
Dong Lu

Ganjiangxi Lu
Jianjingqiao Xiang

Le Ble D'Or
Shizi Lu
Fenghuang Jie

Sanxiang Lu
Daoqian Jie
Bookworm
Xichengyuen Wonton
Shiquan Jie

Sudongxi Lu
Renmin Lu
Garden Hotel

Sudong Lu
Penxu Lu
Outer Moat
Jiching Jie
Zhuhui Lu

Xinshi Lu
Nanmen Long-Distance Bus Station

Guangji Daije
Liuyuan Lu
Fengqiao Lu
Shi Lu
Guangjinan Lu

KEY

🚇 Metro

taxi ride from the Old City. Tickets can usually be purchased through your hotel (advisable) or at the station.

Train Contact **Suzhou Train Station** ✉ *Beihuan Xi Lu* ☏ *0512/6753-2831.* **Suzhou North Train Station** ✉ *Fulin Lu, Xiangcheng.*

TIMING

Suzhou has more than enough attractions to merit at least two full days. Gardens and other sights are spread throughout the city so traveling to and fro takes a bit of time.

ESSENTIALS

Medical Assistance **Suzhou Kowloon Hospital, International Clinic** ✉ *118 Wansheng Jie* ☏ *0512/6262-9999.*

Visitor and Tour Info **Suzhou CITS** ✉ *18 Da Jing Xiang* ☏ *0512/6511-7505* ⊕ *www.cits.net.*

EXPLORING

TOP ATTRACTIONS

Blue Wave Pavilion (沧浪亭 *Cānglàng tíng*). The oldest existing garden in Suzhou, the Blue Wave Pavilion dates back more than 900 years to the Song Dynasty. With a rambling, maze-like design, the grounds feel a little wilder than other Suzhou gardens. The central pond is surrounded by a wooden walkway; gaze into the water at the reflection of the upturned eaves of the surrounding buildings. More than 100 different latticework motifs in the windows provide visual variety as you saunter through the covered corridor that winds through the grounds. The **Pure Fragrance Pavilion** showcases Qing Dynasty furniture at its most extreme; the entire suite is created from gnarled banyan root. ✉ *3 Canlanting Jie, between Shiquan Jie and Xinshi Lu* ☏ *0512/6519-4375* ▦ *Mid-Apr.–Oct. Y20, Nov.–mid-Apr. Y15* ⊙ *Daily 7:30–5.*

Grand Canal (京杭大运河 *Jīngháng dàyùnhé*). Suzhou is threaded by a network of narrow waterways, with an outer moat surrounding its ancient center. The canals that now seem quaint were once choked with countless small boats ferrying goods between the city's merchants. All of these channels connect eventually to imperial China's main conduit of trade and travel, the **Grand Canal**, which passes through the town's southern outskirts.

Fodor'sChoice
★

Humble Administrator's Garden (拙政园 *Zhuōzhèng yuán*). More than half of Suzhou's largest garden is occupied by ponds and lakes. The garden was built in 1509 by Wang Xianjun, an official dismissed from the imperial court. He chose the garden's name from a Tang Dynasty line of poetry reading "humble people govern," perhaps a bit of irony considering the magnificent scale of his private residence. In the warmer months the pond overflows with fragrant lotuses and the garden fills with tourists. Seek out the tiny museum near the exit for an informative display on the aesthetic differences between Chinese and Western garden design. ✉ *178 Dongbei Jie, 1 block east of Lindun Lu* ☏ *0512/6751-0286* ⊕ *www.szzzy.cn* ▦ *Mid-Apr.–Oct. Y70, Nov.–mid-Apr. Y50* ⊙ *Daily 7:30–5:30.*

Lingering Garden (留园 *Liú yuán*). Windows frame yet more windows, undulating rooflines recall waves, and a closed corridor opens out into a tranquil pool in this intriguing garden. The compound provides an endless array of architectural surprises: in a corner an unexpected skylight illuminates a planted nook; windows are placed to frame bamboos as perfectly as if they were painted. The **Mandarin Duck Hall** is particularly impressive, with a picturesque moon gate engraved with vines and flowers. In the back of the garden stands a 70-foot-tall rock moved here from Lake Taihu. Occasional solo musical performances on erhu and zither enliven the halls. ⊠ *338 Liuyuan Lu, west of the moat* ☎ *0512/6557–9466* ⊕ *www.gardenly.com* ✉ *Mid-Apr.–Oct. Y40, Nov.–mid-Apr. Y30* ☉ *Daily 7:30–5.*

FAMILY **Lion's Grove Garden** (狮子林 *Shīzilín*). This garden employs countless craggy rock formations from nearby Lake Taihu to create a surreal moonscape. A labyrinth of caves surrounds a small lake; they're great fun for kids to explore, but watch for sharp edges. There's a popular local saying that if you talk to rocks, you won't need a psychologist, making this garden a good place to spend an hour. A tearoom on the second floor of the main pavilion has nice views over the lake. ⊠ *23 Yuanlin Lu, 3 blocks south of the Humble Administrator's Garden* ☎ *0512/6727–8316* ⊕ *www.szszl.com* ✉ *Y30* ☉ *Daily 8:15–5:30.*

Fodor's Choice
★ **Master of the Nets Garden** (网师园 *Wǎngshī yuán*). All elements of Suzhou style are here in precise balance: rocky hillscapes, layered planting, undulating walkways, and charming pavilions overlooking a central pond. Representing mountains, rivers, and the four seasons, it's a theme park of sorts, centuries before Walt Disney came along. It's also a fine example of how Chinese garden design creates the illusion of space, since this garden really isn't that big. To avoid the crowds, visit in the evening, when you can saunter from room to room enjoying traditional opera, flute, and dulcimer performances—as the master himself might have done. Evening performances are held from mid-March to mid-November. ⊠ *11 Kuo Jia Tou Gang, south of Shiquan Lu, east of Daichengqiao Lu* ☎ *0512/6529–3190* ⊕ *www.szwsy.com* ✉ *Mid-Apr.–Oct. Y30, Nov.–mid-Apr. Y20* ☉ *Daily 7:30–5.*

Temple of Mystery (玄妙观 *Xuánmiào guān*). One of the best-preserved Taoist complexes in Suzhou, the Temple of Mystery is a rare example of a wooden structure that has stood the test of time, with parts dating from the 12th century (it was founded in the 3rd century). Fortunately it suffered little damage in the Cultural Revolution, and retains a splendid ceiling of carefully arranged beams and braces painted in their original colors. The temple grounds back on to a large square that is now a touristy market. ⊠ *Guanqian Jie* ☎ *0512/6777–5479* ✉ *Y10* ☉ *Daily 8:30–5.*

Tiger Hill (回球 *Hǔqiū*). This hill is the burial place of the king of the State of Wu, who founded the city in 514 BC. At the top of the approach is a huge sheet of stone called **Thousand Man Rock,** where legend has it that the workers who built the tomb were thanked for their labors with an elaborate banquet. The wine, alas, was drugged, so they perished to keep the tomb's entrance a secret. Modern archaeologists think they have discovered it hidden under the artificial lake. The secret may be out, but the king's wish to rest in peace is ensured by

The Humble Administrator's Garden is the largest garden in Suzhou.

the fact that excavating the tomb would bring down the fragile Song Dynasty pagoda that stands above. The **Leaning Pagoda** is one of the most impressive monuments in Suzhou, with Persian influence evident in the arches and other architectural elements. A helpful audio guide explains many of the park's legends. ⊠ *Huqiu Lu, northwest of the city* ☎ *0512/6532–3488* ⊠ *Mid-Apr.–Oct. Y60, Nov.–mid-Apr. Y40* ☽ *Daily 7:30–5.*

WORTH NOTING

Hanshan Temple (寒山寺 *Hánshān sì*). Best known as a subject of one of the Tang Dynasty's most famous poems, which described the sound of its massive bell at midnight, this large, pristinely painted temple may leave those unfamiliar with the ancient poetry feeling a little underwhelmed. The place has the frenetic feel of a tourist attraction rather than the serenity of a temple. Literary pilgrims can line up to ring the temple bell themselves for an extra charge. ⊠ *24 Hanshan Si Nong* ☎ *0512/6533–6634* ⊠ *Mid-Apr.–Oct. Y20, Nov.–mid-Apr. Y20* ☽ *Daily 8–5.*

Joyous Garden (怡园 *Yíyuán*). The youngest garden in Suzhou, Joyous Garden was built in 1874. It borrows elements from Suzhou's other famous gardens: rooms from the Humble Administrator's, a pond from the Master of the Nets. The most unusual feature is an oversize mirror, inspired by the founder of Zen Buddhism, who stared at a wall for years to find enlightenment. The garden's designer hung the mirror opposite a pavilion, to let the building contemplate its own reflection. From April to October the garden doubles as a popular teahouse in the evening. ⊠ *343 Renmin Lu* ☎ *0512/6524–9317* ⊠ *Y15* ☽ *Daily 7:30–5.*

North Temple Pagoda (北寺塔 *Běisì tǎ*). One of the symbols of ancient Suzhou, this temple towers over the Old City. The complex has a 1,700-year history, dating to the Three Kingdoms Period. The wooden pagoda has nine levels; you can climb as high as the eighth level for what might be the best view of Suzhou. Within the grounds are the Copper Buddha Hall and Plum Garden, which, built in 1985, lack the history and complexity of Suzhou's other gardens. ⊠ *Xibei Jie and Renmin Lu, 2 blocks west of Humble Administrator's Garden* ☎ *0512/6753–1197* 🎟 *Y25* 🕑 *Mar.–Oct., daily 7:45–6.*

WORD OF MOUTH

"Once you get inside the Old Town, there are no motorized vehicles, just bikes and pedestrian traffic. Nothing really seems to be rebuilt here, so you can get a feel for the old ways of living; people still doing their laundry and washing vegetables in the canal. Stopped and had tea at a cute tea shop. Good local art here in Tongli, as well as inexpensive embroidered wall art." —quimbymoy

Pan Gate (盘门 *Pánmén*). Traffic into Old Suzhou came both by road and canals, so the city's gates were designed to control access by both land and water. This gate—more of a small fortress—is the only one that remains. In addition to the imposing wooden gates on land, a double sluice gate can be used to seal off the canal and prevent boats from entering. A park is filled with colorful flowers, in contrast to the subdued hues in the city's traditional gardens. You can also climb the **Ruiguang Pagoda**, a tall, slender spire originally built more than 1,000 years ago. ⊠ *1 Dong Dajie, southwest corner of the Old City* ☎ *0512/6526–0004* 🎟 *Panmen Gate Y40; Ruigang Pagoda Y6* 🕑 *Daily 8–4:45.*

Suzhou Arts and Crafts Museum (工艺美术博物馆 *Gōngyì měishù bówùguǎn*). This impressive collection of contemporary art is proof that Suzhou craftsmanship remains very healthy. It's just a shame that, all too often, ivory seems to be the material of choice. A highlight here is watching artists in action during high season, carving jade, cutting latticework fans from thin sheets of sandalwood, and fashioning traditional calligraphy brushes. Perhaps most amazing is the careful attention to detail of the women embroidering silk. The museum is set within attractive gardens and traditional buildings. ⊠ *58 Xibei Jie, between Humble Administrator's Garden and the North Pagoda* ☎ *0512/6753–4874* 🌐 *www.szgmb.cn* 🎟 *Y15* 🕑 *Daily 9–5.*

Suzhou Museum (苏州博物馆 *Sūzhōu bówùguǎn*). This is the most modern building to emerge amid a neighborhood of traditional architecture. The museum is the valedictory work for 90-year-old modernist master I.M. Pei. A controversy erupted over whether to allow Pei to construct the glass-and-steel structure in historical Suzhou. Like his crystal pyramid in the courtyard of the Louvre, this building thrives on juxtapositions of old and new. The museum houses historical objects from Suzhou's ancient past and an impressive collection of Ming and Qing Dynasty paintings and calligraphy. English-language docent tours cost Y100. ⊠ *204 Dongbei Jie, next to Humble Administrator's Garden*

☎ *0512/6757–5666* 🌐 *www.szmuseum.com* 🎟 *Free* ⏲ *Tues.–Sun. 9–5* ⏲ *Closed Mon.*

West Garden Temple (西园寺 *Xīyuán sì*). This temple is most notable for the **Hall of 500 Arhats** (*wubai luohan tang*), which houses 500 gold-painted statues of these Buddhist guides. Many of the carvings exhibit a playful humor: one struggling with dragons, another cradling a cat. ✉ *8 Xiwan Lu, across from Lingering Garden* 🎟 *Y30* ⏲ *Daily 7–5.*

WHERE TO EAT

Shiquan Jie is quickly becoming one of the city's restaurant hubs, with both Suzhou-style restaurants and Chinese regional cuisine from Xinjiang to Yunnan. Many offer English menus.

$$$$ CHINESE 🍴 **Songhelou** (松鹤楼 *Sònghèlóu fǎndiàn*). Ever since Emperor Qianlong, the Qing Dynasty's most famous tourist, declared the fish here a triumph, Songhelou has ridden on his yellow coattails. The most famous eatery in town, "Pine and Crane," as its name translates to in Chinese, is pricy and overhyped. That doesn't stop tourists coming in droves to chow on braised tofu with crabmeat, pork belly with cherry sauce, and other local specialties. If you find folks are queuing out the door here, try the similarly venerable Deyuelou, selling much the same Suzhou fare, across the street. [$] *Average main: Y210* ✉ *72 Taijian Nong, south of the Temple of Mystery* ☎ *0512/6770–0688.*

$$$ CHINESE Fodor's Choice ★ 🍴 **Wumen Renjia** (吴门人家 *Wúmén rénjiā*). Shelled river shrimp (*wumen xiaren*) are a light and delicate signature dish at this lovely restaurant accessed via a narrow alley north of Lion's Grove Garden. The busy kitchen also pulls off a satisfactorily crisp rendition of the region's famous *songshu guiyu* (squirrel fish), scored and fried so that the white meat fans outwards in chopstick-friendly mouthfuls. Sweet-and-sour sauce completes the experience. The traditional setting means Wumen Renjia is popular with Chinese travelers. [$] *Average main: Y130* ✉ *31 Panru Xiang, north of Lion's Grove Garden* ☎ *0512/6728–8041.*

$ SHANGHAINESE Fodor's Choice ★ 🍴 **Xichengyuan Wonton** (熙盛源馄饨 *Xīchéngyuán húntun*). Locals squeeze around tables at this simple eatery, a quick hop from the Master of the Nets Garden, to lunch on mouthwateringly zingy wonton soup and *xiaolongbao* (freshly steamed, soup-filled pork dumplings). There is no menu—order at the entrance, take a number, and find a seat. Try the pork wontons in spicy soup or go for the wontons filled with *jiecai*, a local green vegetable, and served in a fragrant clear broth. [$] *Average main: Y30* ✉ *43 Fenghuang Jie* ☎ *0512/6512–8707.*

WHERE TO STAY

$$ HOTEL 🏨 **Crowne Plaza Hotel Suzhou** (中茵皇冠假日酒店 *Zhōngyín xīngguān jiàrì jiǔdiàn*). Eight decks of spacious rooms wrap around a nautical-themed lobby bar at this ship-shaped luxury hotel on Jinji Lake; splurge on one of the Captain's Suites if you want to enjoy a soak in a private hot tub while you gaze out at the water. **Pros:** whimsical design; light-filled rooms; lovely pool. **Cons:** pricey in-room Internet access; outside the city center. [$] *Rooms from: Y1100* ✉ *68 Xinggang Lu* ☎ *512/6761–6688* 🌐 *www.crowneplaza.com* 🛏 *344 rooms* 🍽 *No meals.*

$ HOTEL 🏨 **Garden Hotel** (南园兵官 *Nányuán bīnguǎn*). After a day exploring Suzhou's many gardens, return to one of your own—10 acres, to be precise, complete with flowering trees, tranquil ponds, and colorful pagodas, with rooms spread across six low-slung buildings. **Pros:** pleasant grounds; peaceful atmosphere; great service. **Cons:** interior a little sterile; some rooms overdue for renovations. $ *Rooms from: Y700* ✉ *249 Shiquan Jie* ☎ *0512/6778–6778* ⇆ *104 rooms* ❘○❘ *No meals.*

$
HOTEL

🏨 **Hotel Soul** (苏哥利酒店 *Sūgēlì jiǔdiàn*). This centrally located design hotel is by no means the quintessential Suzhou experience, but the comfortable beds, international cable channels, and a bistro-style restaurant could be just the ticket after a long day of wandering around the city's classical gardens. **Pros:** great value; friendly service; central location. **Cons:** no historic value; gym very basic. $ *Rooms from: Y550* ✉ *27-33 Qiaosikong Xiang, east of Pingan Fang* ☎ *0512/6777–0777* ⊕ *www. hotelsoul.com.cn* ⇆ *225 rooms* ❘○❘ *No meals.*

$
HOTEL
FAMILY
Fodor's Choice
★

🏨 **Pan Pacific Suzhou** (吴宫泛太平洋酒店 *Súzhōu wúgōng táipíngyáng dàjiǔdiàn*). One of the city's more unique luxury hotels, the Pan Pacific Suzhou has a two-story stone entrance topped by a pagoda that's modeled after the neaby Pan Gate; musicians playing traditional instruments are on hand to welcome you. **Pros:** beautiful architecture; peaceful gardens; pretty pool. **Cons:** in an older part of town. $ *Rooms from: Y900* ✉ *259 Xinshi Lu* ☎ *0512/6510–3388* ⊕ *www.panpacific.com/suzhou* ⇆ *481 rooms* ❘○❘ *No meals.*

$
B&B/INN
Fodor's Choice
★

🏨 **Pingjiang Lodge** (平江客栈 *Píngjiāng kèzhàn*). This grand old mansion has a superb location next to historic Pingjiang Jie, and offers a welcome balance of period atmosphere and affordable comfort. **Pros:** quaint style; great location; affordable rates. **Cons:** service can be a little frosty; some rooms a bit dark. $ *Rooms from: Y600* ✉ *32 Niu Jia Xiang, southern end of Pingjiang Jie* ☎ *0512/6523–3888* ⇆ *50 rooms* ❘○❘ *No meals.*

$
HOTEL

🏨 **Suzhou Garden View Hotel** (苏州人家大酒店 *Súzhōu rénjià dájiǔdiàn*). Beside a canal and a short stroll to historic Pingjiang Lane, this comfortable and well-run hotel wraps around a peaceful courtyard and Suzhou-style garden. **Pros:** great value; distinctive touches. **Cons:** difficult to find a taxi; small bathrooms; poor amenities. $ *Rooms from: Y500* ✉ *66 Luo Guaqia, Lindun Lu* ☎ *0512/6777–8888* ⊕ *www.szrj-h. com* ⇆ *188 rooms* ❘○❘ *No meals.*

NIGHTLIFE

At night, the stretch of Shiquan Jie between Renmin Lu and Fenghuang Lu is home to a cluster of Irish pubs, small hole-in-the wall Chinese bars, and karaoke clubs. Storefronts change quickly—at time of writing a remarkably accurate replica of "The Drunken Clam" from U.S. TV show *Family Guy* was doing a roaring trade. In any case, you are bound to find somewhere lively and fun. A newer, more high-end nightlife area replete with bars, glitzy nightclubs, and international restaurants has developed farther out from the center on the west shore of Jinji Lake, a stroll south of the Dongfangzhimen Subway Station.

The Bookworm (老 *Lǎoshūchóng*). Visit this canal-side town house to peruse a wide selection of English-language books and magazines while sipping imported wines and beers. At night there's regular live music. ✉ *77 Gunxi Fang, off Shiquan Jie* ☎ *0512/6581–6752* ⊕ *www. suzhoubookworm.com.*

Le Ble D'or (金色三麥 *Jīnsè sānmài*). This enormous brewpub has servers garbed in Bavarian dirndls, a jarringly French name, and a self-described "American style." Occupying the entire fourth floor of a high-rise building, it's the local outpost of a popular Taiwanese chain. Three types of craft beer are brewed on the premises, and the menu includes sticky barbecue pork ribs, fried chicken, and truffle fries in portions meant for sharing. The Munich-inspired *bierkeller* interior can seat a staggering 900 people at its long tables. ⊠ *Jinhe Guoji Dasha Bldg., 34 Shishan Lu, 4th fl., East New Town* ☎ *0521/6665–5909* ⊕ *www.lebledor.com.*

STROLL INTO THE PAST

Pingjiang Lu is an ancient, well-preserved cobbled street in the center of the Old City, following the course of a narrow canal. Dating back 800 years, this north-to-south lane and its side streets feature bygone scenes of daily life. Quaint whitewashed canal-side houses with overhanging balconies and black-tiled roofs cluster under weeping willows and jasmine trees. Arched bridges reflected in the canals are picture-perfect. The area has become trendy in recent years, drawing new bars, restaurants, and art galleries, but for now the old and new coexist in relative harmony. Moreover, it's possible to duck into one of the alleyways and discover locals clinging to a way of life relatively unchanged for hundreds of years. It's here where you'll find the living echoes of old Suzhou.

SHOPPING

Districts around the major gardens and temples teem with silk shops and outdoor markets. The city's long history of wealth and culture has encouraged a tradition of elegant and finely worked craft objects. One of the best known is double-sided embroidery, where two designs are carefully stitched on both sides of a sheet of silk. The city is also famous for its finely latticed sandalwood fans. Both are available at the Suzhou Arts and Crafts Museum. The area outside the west gate of the Master of the Nets Garden has dozens of small stalls selling curios and inexpensive but interesting souvenirs.

Su Embroidery Studio (苏绣工作室 *Sūxiù gōngzuòshì*). Pick up fine examples of hand-embroidered silk as well as Suzhou double-sided embroidery at this showroom and workshop. Custom pieces can be ordered and shipped internationally. ⊠ *1902 Senso International Plaza, 98 Bei Dongwu Lu* ☎ *0512/5887–1762.*

Suzhou Cultural Relics Store. Since 1956, the Suzhou Cultural Relics Store has been selling antiques, calligraphy, jades, and other items. Prepare to bargain on price. ⊠ *1208 Renmin Lu* ☎ *0512/6523–3851.*

Suzhou Silk Museum Shop (苏州丝绸博物馆 *Sūzhōu sīchóu bówùguǎn*). Near the North Pagoda, the well-stocked Suzhou Silk Museum Shop is the main reason folks come to the Silk Museum. ⊠ *661 Renmin Lu* ☎ *0512/6753–4941.*

The canals of Tongli, one of the water villages near Suzhou.

SIDE TRIPS FROM SUZHOU: WATER VILLAGES

Centuries-old villages, preserved almost in their original state, are scattered around Suzhou. Bowed bridges span narrow canals, as traditional oared boats paddle by, creating an almost picture-perfect scene of life long past. A trip to one of these villages could well be the photographic highlight of your trip to Eastern China.

Be warned, though, that the tourist dollars flowing in may have saved these villages from the wrecking ball, but they have also changed their character to differing degrees. Those closest to the larger cities are the most swamped by tour groups. Trekking to an out-of-the-way destination can pay off by letting you find a village that, outside of high season, you might have mostly to yourself.

ZHOUZHUANG
30 km (19 miles) southeast of Suzhou

Zhouzhuang (周庄 *Zhōuzhuāng*). The most famous of the water villages is undoubtedly Zhouzhuang. Its fame is partly due to its proximity from Suzhou and Shanghai, just 45 minutes and an hour away, respectively. As a result, more than 2.5 million visitors head here each year to catch a glimpse of Old China. Its charm is reduced by the sheer number of tourists who elbow their way through the streets. Next to the "ancient memorial archway," which isn't ancient at all, is a ticket window. The entrance fee of Y100 gets you into the water-village-turned-gift shop.

Crowds aside, Zhouzhuang is fun for families. Several residences, some 500 years old, let you peek in to see what life was like in the Ming and Qing dynasties. There are several storefronts where you can see brick making, bamboo carving, and basket weaving—traditional crafts that up until recently were in widespread use throughout the countryside. The food is typical country fare, making it a nice break from the fancier cuisines of Suzhou and Shanghai. Braised pork belly, crunchy stir-fried water chestnuts, pickled vegetables, and wild greens abound. For crafts, skip the snuff bottles and teapots and opt for something you probably won't find elsewhere: homemade rice wine, rough-hewn ox-horn combs, and bamboo rice baskets.

Buses bound for Zhouzhuang depart from Suzhou's North Bus Station every 20 minutes between 7 and 5. The 90-minute trip costs Y25.

TONGLI
18 km (11 miles) southeast of Suzhou

Tongli (同里 *Tónglǐ*). The pick of the water villages is Tongli, 30 minutes from Zhouzhuang and 90 minutes from Suzhou. A number of locals still live and work here, lending this village a more authentic atmosphere than Zhouzhuang. The streets are cobbled, and the complete absence of cars makes Tongli feel like it's from a different era, provided you can get away from the crowds. Your best bet is to avoid the main thoroughfares and seek out the quaint side streets and narrow alleyways that open onto canals and bridges. Tongli is the largest of the water villages, imminently photographable, and a pleasure to explore. Near the entrance gate are several private homes offering beds, and throughout the village are tea shops and local restaurants with small tables set out in front of the canals. Hiring a boat (Y100 for up to six people) to be punted along the waterways gives a different perspective on the town. The admission fee is Y100.

The fastest buses to Tongli leave from Suzhou South Bus Station every 20 minutes between 7 and 5. The journey costs Y12. Most taxis in town will also take you; when you negotiable a fee, aim for about Y150. This is by far the fastest way to get there, and you can take the bus back.

Ancient Chinese Sexual Culture Museum (古代性文化展示 *Gǔdài xìng-wénhuà zhǎnshì*). A favorite spot in Tongli is Tuisi Garden, a slightly smaller version of the private courtyard parks found in Suzhou. Tongli is also home to the Ancient Chinese Sexual Culture Museum, housed in a former girl's school. The controversial exhibition of ancient erotic toys and artworks is the project of a retired university professor. ⊠ *Entrance to town* ☎ *0512/6332–2973* 🎫 *Y20* ⊙ *Daily 8–4:30.*

LUZHI
25 km (15 miles) east of Suzhou

Luzhi (角直 *Lùzhí*). Even farther off the beaten path than Zhouzhuang or Tongli is the water village Luzhi, roughly half an hour from Suzhou. Though it's a popular tourist destination, it remains one of the more peaceful communities in the area. Described as a "museum of bridges," the village has more than 40 in all shapes and styles. Many of the older women in the village preserve traditional customs, wearing folk headdresses and skirts.

Luzhi-bound buses leave from Suzhou's North Bus Station every 30 minutes between 6:30 am and 6:30 pm. The 40-minute ride costs Y10. ⊠ *Y100.*

Baosheng Temple (保圣寺 *Bǎoshèng sì*). Luzhi is notable for the spectacular Baosheng Temple, a yellow-walled compound built in the year 503 that is famous for its breathtaking collection of Buddhist arhats. Arranged on a wall of stone, these clay sculptures are the work of Yang Huizhi, a famous Tang Dynasty sculptor. Made more than 1,000 years ago, they depict Buddhist disciples who have gained enlightenment. The temple also features a well-preserved bell from the end of the Ming Dynasty. ⊠ *Luzhi* ☎ *0512/6501–0011* ⊠ *Free* ☉ *Daily 8–4:30.*

ANHUI

Eastern China's most rural province, Anhui has a rugged terrain that forces families to fight their hardscrabble farmland for every acre of harvest. Today it remains significantly poorer than its neighbors, with an average income half that of neighboring Zhejiang, a successful manufacturing hub. But what Anhui lacks in material wealth it makes up for in splendid natural landscape. Travelers here enjoy countryside largely untouched by the last century. Near Huangshan (Yellow Mountain), towering granite peaks loom over green fields, and broad-shouldered water buffalo plow the flooded rice paddies.

The foothills of Huangshan have a remarkable wealth of historical architecture. Tiny communities dot the landscape in Shexian and Yixian counties. Many of these villages were far enough out of the way that even the Cultural Revolution's zealous Red Guards left them alone. Today, though increasingly visited by tourists, whole villages retain their original architecture, and in some cases, generations of inhabitants.

Anhui boasts significant contributions to Chinese civilization. The province produces both the paper and ink most favored for Chinese calligraphy. Hui opera, an ancient musical form that developed in the province, was a major influence on Beijing Opera. Hui cuisine is included among China's great culinary traditions, making use of mountain vegetables and herbs, with many delicious stewed and braised dishes.

Most of the province's highlights lie in the south, best accessed from Shanghai, Hangzhou, and Nanjing.

REGIONAL TOURS
Nearby Nanjing is a good place in which to make arrangements for your travels in Anhui, particularly around Huangshan.

Jiangsu Huate International Travel Service. For organized tours, flights, and other arrangements, contact Jiangsu Huate International Travel Service. ⊠ *33 Jinxiang He Lu, Nanjing* ☎ *025/8337–8598.*

HUANGSHAN

5½ hrs (250 km [155 miles]) by train west of Nanjing; 3½ hrs by long-distance bus.

Huangshan (Yellow Mountain) is Eastern China's most dreamlike mountain landscape, where delicate songshu pines cling to the vertiginous sides of soaring granite peaks. Its mist-swathed vistas are a recurring motif in Chinese art and literature, and, tamed by tens of thousands of stone steps (and a few cable cars), are accessible to anyone with a head for heights.

3

Fodor's Choice
★

Huangshan (黄山 *Huángshān*). Eastern China's most impressive natural landscape, Yellow Mountain's peaks thrust upward through rolling seas of clouds, spindly pines clinging precipitously to their sides. A favorite retreat of emperors and poets past, its vistas have inspired some of China's most outstanding artworks and literary endeavors. So beguiling were they that centuries of labor went into constructing the paths and stone stairways, some ascending gently through virgin forest, others sharp and steep. Since 1990, the area has been designated a UNESCO World Heritage Site.

The common English translation—Yellow Mountain—is misleading. Huangshan is not a single mountain but a range of peaks stretching across four counties. To complicate matters, the name is not a reference to color. The region was originally called the "Black Mountains," but a Tang Dynasty emperor renamed it to honor Huangdi, the Yellow Emperor. And according to legend, it was from these slopes that he rode off to heaven on the back of a dragon.

The mountain is renowned for its gnarled stone formations, many sporting fanciful names to describe their shape. Some will require a stretch of the imagination, while others will leap out at you on first glance. Generations of Chinese poets and travelers have humanized these peaks and forests in this way, and left their mark on the area.

■ TIP→ **Be forewarned: Huangshan has its own weather.** More than 200 days a year, precipitation obscures the famous views. It can be sunny below, but in the mountains it's damp and chilly. That said, even on the foggiest of days the wind is likely to part the mist long enough to offer a satisfactory glimpse of the famous peaks. *Mar.–Nov. Y300, Dec.–Feb. Y150 ☉ Daily 24 hrs.*

GETTING HERE AND AROUND

Most long-distance transportation, including trains and airplanes, arrives in Tunxi, the largest city near Huangshan. Be aware, however, that Tunxi is still about an hour from the entrance to the scenic mountain area. Minibuses to Tangkou and other destinations around the base of the mountain leave from the plaza in front of Tunxi's Huangshan Railway Station, costing around Y15 to Y30. There are also plenty of taxi drivers who are happy to offer their services, usually for around Y70–Y100 per carload.

Some buses from Nanjing, Hangzhou, and Shanghai go directly to Tangkou, the entrance at the base of the mountain. The airport is close to Tunxi, about a Y15 to Y20 cab ride from the center of town.

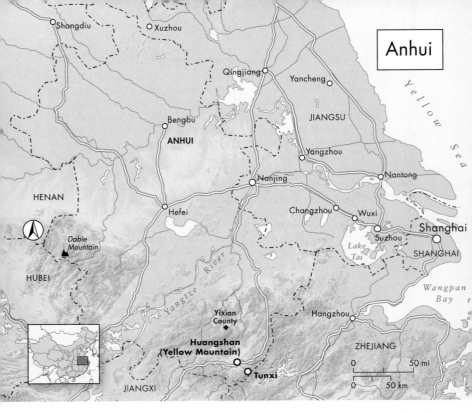

AIR TRAVEL If you plan to fly to Huangshan, you'll land at the Huangshan City Airport near Tunxi, about 60 to 90 minutes by car from the mountain. There are direct flights from Beijing, Guangzhou, Shanghai, and Ji'nan.

TAXI AND MINIBUS TRAVEL In Tunxi, minibuses and taxis that congregate around the train station will take you to Huangshan. For about Y20 they will drop you at the main gate at the bottom of the mountain or at the beginning of the climbing section.

TRAIN TRAVEL There is one overnight train from Shanghai to Huangshan Railway Station, arriving at about 9 am. From the station you can catch a minivan or taxi to Huangshan.

TIMING

Allow at least two days for a visit to Huangshan, and another day or so to see the villages around Tunxi. Thanks to the cable cars on the mountain (each trip costing Y80 per person), it is possible to take in a lot of scenery in one full day. On weekends or holidays you can expect lengthy queues at the cable cars.

TOURS

With well-signposted trails and several cable cars, tours up the mountain are unnecessary. A better bet is to get hold of a good map (the Chinese maps for sale tend to lack detail or be outdated—consider downloading one to your mobile device) and chart the paths you plan to

take. Many consider Xihai Grand Canyon loop to be the most rewarding section, with spectacular scenery and fewer visitors. It's possible to
hike down into the canyon from the summit and return via cable car.
The best place for current information about the region is the English-
language Huangshan Travel Net, run in conjunction with CTS.

ESSENTIALS

Nearly all services are 90 minutes away from the mountain area in
Tunxi.

Medical Assistance Beihai Medical Center ✉ *Huangshan Scenic Area, across
from Beihai Hotel, Huangshan Scenic Area* ☎ *0559/558–2555.* **Jade Screen
Tower First-Aid Station** ✉ *Jade Screen Tower Hotel, Huangshan Summit,
Huangshan* ☎ *0559/558–2288.*

Visitor and Tour Info Huangshan Travel Net ✉ *27 Xin'an Bei Lu, Tunxi*
☎ *0559/251–2155, 0559/251–2133* ⊕ *www.uhuangshan.com.*

EXPLORING

There are two primary hiking routes up the mountain. The Eastern
Steps, a straightforward path through forests, is both the shortest and
the easiest. The Southern Steps (some guidebooks call these the Western
Steps, which causes confusion with another set of steps used primarily by porters) require more effort, but they pay off with remarkable
scenery. The steep, winding path reveals sheer peaks and precipitous
lookouts over mist-enshrouded valleys.

Climbing up is physically taxing, but climbing down is mentally
exhausting, requiring far more concentration. If you have the time and
the leg muscles, it's nice to ascend the South Steps, where the scenery
stretches before you. The views are a good excuse to stop and catch
your breath.

EASTERN STEPS

The Eastern Steps are quicker than the Southern Steps, but the scenery
isn't as rewarding and there are fewer scenic side routes. Along the way
is a building called **Fascinating Pavilion,** most notable as a rest stop
along the way. There's a short half-hour side hike to **Pipeng,** with a
good view out over a number of the smaller eastern peaks. By the time
you reach **Cloud Valley,** the landscape that makes Huangshan famous
begins to come into view. **Beginning to Believe Peak** is the start of the
awe-inspiring landscape, and the first true majestic vista on this path.

Cloud Valley Temple Cable Car Station (云谷寺索道 *Yúngǔsì suǒdào*). The
Eastern Steps begin at the Cloud Valley Temple Cable Car Station. The
cable car takes eight minutes to traverse what takes hikers three or
more hours. Large windows provide an aerial view of the mountain
and bamboo forests below. This area was once home to several monasteries, nunneries, and temples. By the beginning of the 20th century
they had been largely abandoned, but the name Cloud Valley Temple
Area remains. ✉ *Close to Cloud Valley Temple, Huangshan* 🎫 *Y80*
🕙 *Weekdays 6:30–4:30, weekends 6:30–5.*

DID YOU KNOW?

Climbing the rough-hewn steps of Huangshan is not something you'll quickly forget. More than 60,000 steps have been carved into the side of the mountains, some as far back as 1,500 years ago.

SOUTHERN STEPS

The steep Southern Steps are by far the tougher path. However, the climb pays off with great views and some beautiful side trails. Although the Eastern Steps feel like a walk through the woods, the Southern Steps truly feel like an ascent into the clouds. The steps begin around the Hot Springs, at the **Mercy Light Temple** area. **Midway Mountain Temple** has facilities to rest, eat, and even stay overnight, but no temple. It's here that the splendor of Huangshan comes into full view. At the **Three Islands at Penglai**, a trio of peaks emerge from a sea of mist. If you're feeling energetic, a side tour of **Heavenly Capital Peak** affords spectacular views out over the rest of the range. The effort is worth a try even if it looks cloudy, because the mist can sometimes clear by the time you get to the top. This may not be the highest peak in the range, but it is one of the steepest.

> ### BE PREPARED
>
> Most paths are well maintained with good steps and sturdy handrails, but Huangshan still has sheer drop-offs and steep, uneven, rain-slicked steps. A walking stick (sturdy wooden dragon-head staffs are on sale around the mountain) will help steady your ascent. It can get very cold on the peaks, and rain can come unexpectedly. Dress in layers, and consider bringing a hooded sweatshirt to stay warm.

Jade Screen Cable Car (玉屏索道 *Yùpíng suǒdào*). The Jade Screen Cable Car runs parallel to the Southern Steps, leaving riders close to the Welcoming Guests Pine. It can close unexpectedly in inclement weather. ✉ *Huangshan* 🚡 *Y80* 🕙 *Weekdays 6:30–4:30, weekends 6:30–5.*

THE SUMMIT

The entrance to the summit area, also known as Tianhai, is announced by the **Welcoming Guest Pine**, a lone pine clinging to the edge of a cliff, one branch outstretched. Behind it a sheer stone slope rises out of the clouds. Continuing onward, you can climb **Lotus Peak**, the tallest in the province. A walk through **Turtle Cave**, an arched pathway straight through the hillside, brings the weary traveler to **Bright Top Peak**, slightly lower than Lotus, and an easier climb.

The **Xihai Grand Canyon** loop starts at the Cloud Dispelling Pavilion and ends at the Haixin Ting Pavilion. Rock formations called "Upside Down Boot" and "Lady Playing Piano" may be clumsily translated, but they are stunning. The farther along you walk, the fewer travelers you'll come across. At the southern end of the loop, near Haixin, the trail reaches the **Immortal's Walk Bridge**, a dizzying arch over the misty abyss that leads to a terrace on one of the mountain's spires. A huge landscape spreads out beneath, without a single tour group in sight.

A highlight of any trip is sunrise, visible from several places on the mountain. Most hikers arrive well after dawn, but you'll be rewarded with the spectacle of Huangshan materializing from the shadows if you arrive just before first light, weather permitting of course. A popular viewing spot near the Beihai Hotel is the **Dawn Pavilion**. There are several less crowded peaks with equally good views a little farther from the hotels. **Refreshing Terrace, Lion Peak,** and **Red Cloud Peak** all provide unobstructed views of the rising sun.

Compared to the ascent, the summit area is relatively level, but there is still a good amount of stair climbing. It takes about three to four hours to walk the full summit circle, and considerably more if you take side trails.

WHERE TO EAT

Tangkou, a village that has sprung up to serve mountain climbers, has the most for travelers, including hotels, restaurants, grocery stores, and shops to gear up for the long climb ahead. Tangkou sits near the front gate of the park, and buses run regularly to the trailheads for both the Southern and Eastern steps. If you want to take the shorter route up the Eastern Steps, the Cloud Valley Temple Area is a convenient option. The Hot Springs area is also a much more pleasant option than Tangkou.

$$ CHINESE 🍴 **Celebrity's Banquet** (喜来大酒店 *Xǐlái dàjiǔdiàn*). The best restaurant on the summit, Celebrity's Banquet inside the Xihai Hotel celebrates local culture with a range of traditional Hui dishes. Soups of dried vegetables, jellied tofu, braised pork, and a delicately flavored pumpkin soup shouldn't be missed. [$] *Average main: Y80* ✉ *Xihai Hotel, Grand Canyon Loop, Summit Area, Huangshan* ☎ *0559/558–8888.*

$$ CHINESE 🍴 **Tangzhen Hotel Restaurant** (汤镇大酒店 *Tāngzhèn dàjiǔdiàn*). This hotel is nothing to write home about, but the Hui cuisine here is especially good, attracting locals from around the area. Specialties include cured mandarin fish, home-cured pork with bamboo, and stewed dishes served in clay pots. [$] *Average main: Y80* ✉ *Tangzhen Hotel, at the main entrance to Huangshan, Tangkou* ☎ *0559/556–2665* 🌐 *www.tangzhenhotel.com* 💳 *No credit cards.*

WHERE TO STAY

Several small, basic huts can be found along the Southern Steps, but it would be better to push on to the hotels in the Summit Area. They are your only option if you want to catch the sunrise. As a bonus, you'll have the dew-drenched forests to yourself for a few hours before the latecomers arrive. Reservations are strongly recommended, especially for weekends; this is a popular destination for Chinese travelers, as well as tourists from Japan and Korea.

$ HOTEL 🏨 **Baiyun Hotel** (白云宾馆 *Báiyún bìnguǎn*). From the Yungu Cable Car station (or top of the Eastern Steps for hikers), this is the first of the four main hotels at the summit area that you'll reach; middling rooms are made up for somewhat by a good restaurant downstairs. **Pros:** good location; great restaurant. **Cons:** few amenities. [$] *Rooms from: Y950* ✉ *Summit Area, Huangshan* ☎ *0559/558–2708* 🛏 *80 rooms, 1 suite* 🍽 *No meals.*

$ HOTEL 🏨 **Beihai Hotel** (北海宾馆 *Běihǎi bìnguǎn*). With rooms set among flowering rhododendrons and azaleas, the Beihai Hotel is a decent choice for a night on the mountain; ask for a front-facing room which has better views, and don't forget to try the sauna. **Pros:** ideal location; soothing sauna. **Cons:** uninspiring decor in rooms. [$] *Rooms from: Y900* ✉ *Huangshan Scenic Area, Huangshan* ☎ *0559/556–2555* 🛏 *137 rooms, 2 suites* 🍽 *No meals.*

$ HOTEL 🏨 **Jade Screen Tower Hotel** (玉屏楼宾馆 *Yùpǐng lóu bīnguǎn*). The first proper hotel you'll reach after a long climb up the Southern Steps (or a rather quicker cable car journey), the views here are unmatched, although like most if its neighbors it has smallish and fairly basic rooms. **Pros:** great place to catch the sunrise; welcome sight after a long climb. **Cons:** limited facilities. $ *Rooms from: Y650* ⊠ *Summit Area, past Welcoming Guest Pine, Huangshan* ☎ *0559/558–2132* ⊕ *www.hsyplhotel.com* ↪ *29 rooms, 1 suite* ꙮ *No meals.*

$$
HOTEL
Fodor's Choice
★

⊡ **Xihai Hotel** (黄山西海饭店 *Huángshān xīhǎi fàndiàn*). The classiest of the four main summit hotels, you can count on comfortable and spacious doubles, a very good restaurant, adjoining café, and the best location of all. **Pros:** genuinely high-standard accommodations. **Cons:** expensive; some bathroom amenities cost extra. $ *Rooms from: Y1200* ⊠ *Xihai Scenic Area, Huangshan* ☎ *0559/558–8186* ⊕ *www.hsxihaihotel.cn/en/index.html* ↪ *180 rooms.*

TUNXI

5½ hrs (250 km [155 miles]) by train west of Nanjing; 3½ hrs by long-distance bus.

This is the gateway to the Yellow Mountain area. Apart from being a transportation hub, Tunxi also has a charming strip of shops and restaurants and is a convenient place from which to take trips to Shexian and Yixian counties, famous for their historical architecture.

GETTING HERE AND AROUND

Unless you arrive on a long-distance bus bound for Tangkou, your bus or train is probably bound for Tunxi, around 65 km (40 miles) from the mountain.

AIR TRAVEL Huangshan Tunxi International Airport, located near Tunxi, welcomes flights from Beijing, Guangzhou, Chengdu, Xian, and Shanghai. There are also roughly two flights a week from Hong Kong. Taxis to Tunxi cost Y15 to Y30.

Air Contacts Air China ⊠ *23 Huashan Lu* ☎ *0559/953–4111* ⊕ *www.airchina.com.cn/en* ⊠ *49 Huangshan Donglu* ☎ *0559/254–1222.* **Huangshan Tunxi International Airport** (黄山机场 *Huángshān jīchǎng*). ⊠ *Yingbin Dadao, west of the city* ☎ *0559/293–4111* ⊕ *www.hsairport.com.*

BUS TRAVEL Buses are a convenient way of getting to Tunxi from Zhejiang, Jiangsu, and even Shanghai. Buses that run hourly from Hangzhou take 3½ hours and cost Y65. The route takes you through some gorgeous scenery. Buses from Nanjing take around five hours and cost Y80. From Shanghai, buses take eight to nine hours and cost Y120.

Bus Contact Tunxi Bus Station ⊠ *95 Huangshan Dong Lu* ☎ *0559/256–6666.*

TRAIN TRAVEL Several trains depart daily for Nanjing (6 hours), and there are two trains each day for Shanghai (11½ hours).

Train Contact Huangshan Train Station ⊠ *Northern end of Qianyuan Beilu* ☎ *0559/211–6222.*

TIMING

Tunxi is mostly a place to spend a night before your Huangshan trek. It can also be a good place to arrange tours of the area.

TOURS

Guides can be a good idea if you are exploring the countryside around Huangshan, which is tricky to access by public transport. CTS has private village tours in Yixian county and architecture tours in Shexian county.

ESSENTIALS

Medical Assistance People's Hospital of Huangshan City ⊠ *4 Liyuan Lu, Huangshan* ☎ *0559/251–7036.*

Visitor and Tour Info CTS ⊠ *12 Qianyuan Bei Lu* ☎ *0130/1312–1152 English-language hotline* ⊕ *www.chinatravelservice.com* ✉ *1Binjiang Xi Lu* ☎ *0559/251–5303* ⊕ *www.huangshanguide.com.*

EXPLORING

Tunxi Old Street (屯溪老街 *Túnxī lǎojiē*). In Tunxi, the best place to stroll is along Old Street. The avenue is quiet during the day, but comes alive in the early evening. Shops along the way stay open until about 10 or 11. Wade through the tourist offerings and you may find some treasures.

WHERE TO EAT AND STAY

$$
CHINESE
✕ **Diyilou** (老街第一楼 *Lǎojiē dìyīlóu*). At this lively restaurant in a traditional house, the local specialties include tender bamboo shoots, four-mushroom soup, braised tofu, and a mushroom-wrapped meatball that is not to be missed. Order by pointing to plated sample dishes. Ⓢ *Average main: Y70* ⊠ *247 Tunxi Lao Jie, at Lao Jie* ☎ *0559/253–9797.*

$
HOTEL
🛏 **Crowne Plaza Huangshan Yucheng** (昱城皇冠假日酒店 *Yùchéng huángguān jiàrì jiǔdiàn*). Huangshan's first international five-star hotel, it's nevertheless great value for the quality, especially by local standards; a good bet for a night of creature comforts after you've hiked the trails and returned to Tunxi. **Pros:** reliable international brand; nice pool. **Cons:** lacks personality. Ⓢ *Rooms from: Y550* ⊠ *1 Huizhou Lu* ☎ *0800/830–1275* ⤻ *485 rooms* ⦿ *Breakfast.*

$
HOTEL
🛏 **Huashan Hotel** (華山賓館 *Huàshān bīnguǎn*). A block away from the city's main shopping district, the enormous guest rooms at this well-appointed hotel come as a pleasant surprise, even if service can be confused at times. **Pros:** great access to shopping; plenty of room to spread out. **Cons:** so-so restaurant; some rooms a little musty. Ⓢ *Rooms from: Y300* ⊠ *3 Yanan Lu* ☎ *0559/232–2888* ⤻ *186 rooms, 14 suites* ⦿ *No meals.*

$
B&B/INN
Fodor'sChoice
★
🛏 **Pig's Heaven Inn** (猪栏酒吧 *Zhūlán jiǔbā*). Wake to the crowing of roosters in this boutique hotel set in a 400-year-old stone house on the fringes of Xidi, a village an hour's drive from Tunxi. **Pros:** traditional lodging; beautiful surroundings; drivers at the ready. **Cons:** a bit far from Huangshan; staff knows very little English. Ⓢ *Rooms from: Y800* ⊠ *Renrang Li, Xidi* ☎ *0559/515–4555* ⤻ *5 rooms* ⦿ *No meals.*

SHOPPING

Sanbai Yanzhai. When shopping along Lao Jie, the best offerings are traditional calligraphy ink and paper. The best ink stones are sold at Sanbai Yanzhai. ⊠ *173 Lao Jie* ☎ *0559/253–5538.*

Stone and Bamboo Shop. The Stone and Bamboo Shop sells exquisite examples of traditional bamboo carving. ⊠ *122 Lao Jie* ☎ *0559/751–5042.*

The shops and restaurants on Old Street in Tunxi

SIDE TRIP TO SHEXIAN COUNTY

25 km (15 miles) east of Tunxi.

Shexian County has been called a living architectural art museum because of its natural beauty and array of historic buildings. Over the centuries, it has inspired philosophers, poets, and painters. Today, there is no lack of tourists, but it's a pleasant day trip from Tunxi.

GETTING HERE AND AROUND

Buses run throughout the day from the Tunxi long-distance bus station. The trip should take about 45 minutes and costs approximately Y10. Once you get to Shexian Bus Station in Huizhou Old City, you can board a minibus or take a taxi to outlying scenic spots. However, if you are traveling with several people, it's best to hire a car and driver for the day, as many of these places are quite remote and spread out.

EXPLORING

Huashan Mysterious Grottoes (华山谜窟 *Huàshān míkū*). The Huashan Mysterious Grottoes are a combination of impressive natural caves and rooms carved into rock illuminated with colored lights. No one seems quite certain when or why they were built, but it makes for a distracting excursion. ⊠ *Between Xiongcun and Tunxi* ☎ *0559/235–9888* ⊕ *www. huashanmiku.cn* ⊠ *Y70* ⊘ *Daily 7:30–6:30.*

Huizhou Old Town (惠州老城 *Huìzhōu lǎochéng*). This site boasts several examples of Huizhou architecture that speaks of the wealth of the merchants that lived here, including a centuries-old city wall and a magnificent four-sided memorial gate guarded by sculptures of frolicking lions. ⊠ *Huizhou* ☎ *0559/653–1586* ⊠ *Y80* ⊘ *Daily 7:30–6:30.*

Memorial Arches (堂樾牌楼群 *Tángyuè páilóuqún*). A recurring feature of Huizhou architecture, there are almost 100 similar memorial archways dotted throughout Shexian County, but this well-preserved row of seven is the most famous, commemorating the wealthy Bao family and representing traditional values like morality, piety, and female chastity. ⊠ *5 km (3 miles) west of Huizhou Old Town, Tangyue* 🖃 *Y100* ⊙ *Daily 7:30–5:30.*

Yuliang Village (渔梁古镇 *Yúliáng gǔzhèn*). Near Huizhou Old Town, Yuliang Village overlooks an ancient Tang Dynasty dam with water still gurgling over its sloped sides. Fishermen in wooden skiffs still make their living here. A narrow street parallel to the river is a pleasant spot for a stroll. Most families leave their doors open, allowing a peak into simple homes where pages from magazines are often used as wallpaper. Inexpensive pedicabs travel here from the Shexian Bus Station in Huizhou Old City, or you can catch Bus 1 from the train station. ⊠ *Changxi Xian, Yuliang* 🖃 *Y30* ⊙ *Daily 7:30–6:30.*

SIDE TRIP TO YIXIAN COUNTY

A pleasant day trip from Tunxi, Yixian County is the site of some beautiful and ancient rural architecture set in bucolic surroundings. Yixian County receives nearly 2.5 million visits per year, but don't let that deter you, as the UNESCO World Heritage Sites in the area are eminently photogenic.

GETTING HERE AND AROUND
To reach Yixian County, take the buses that leave from in front of Tunxi's train station. They cost about Y10 and depart every 20 minutes.

EXPLORING
Hongcun Village (宏村 *Hóngcūn*). A delicately arched bridge leads the way into Hongcun, a delightfully preserved settlement laid out to resemble a water buffalo. Two 600-year-old trees mark its horns, a lake its belly, and streams diverted for irrigation are its intestines! A number of films have used Hongcun as a location, including *Crouching Tiger, Hidden Dragon*. Several large halls and old houses are open to visit. The Salt Merchant's House is especially well preserved, with intricate decorations and carvings that fortunately survived the Cultural Revolution. ⊠ *Yi Xian, Hongcun* ☎ *0559/251–7464* 🖃 *Y80* ⊙ *Daily 6:30–6:30.*

Xidi Village (西递村 *Xīdì*). A UNESCO World Heritage Site, Xidi Village is known for its exquisite memorial gate. There were once a dozen gates, but they were destroyed during the Cultural Revolution. The existing gate was left standing as a "bad example" to be criticized. There are several houses in the village with excellent examples of brick carving and an impressive Clan Temple with massive ginkgo columns and beams. ⊠ *Off Taohuayuan Lu, Xidi* ☎ *0559/515–4030* 🖃 *Y80* ⊙ *Daily 6:30–6:30.*

SHANGHAI

WELCOME TO SHANGHAI

TOP REASONS TO GO

★ **Skyline Views:** Head to the top of the *Shanghai World Financial Center, known to locals as the* "bottle opener," the pagoda-inspired Jin Mao, or the gargantuan Shanghai Tower, and look straight into the clouds.

★ **Modern Art:** The far-flung Power Station of Art is a contemporary hub worth the trek down to the former World Expo site.

★ **People-Watching:** A strong sense of community and small living spaces push life out onto the street, where locals chit chat, play cards, exercise, ballroom dance, and stroll about.

★ **Yu Garden:** When not too crowded, the garden offers a few minutes of peace and beauty amid the clamor of the city, with rocks, trees, and walls curved to resemble dragons, bridges, and pavilions.

★ **The Bund:** This water-front promenade is lined with regal colonial buildings in 52 architec-tural styles, and it looks much as it did during Shanghai's Golden Age nearly a century ago.

1 Old City. This area was once the Chinese city where locals lived when foreigners filled the concessions.

2 Xintiandi and City Center. City Center is the larger area encompass-ing Xintiandi and People's Square. Shopping, bars, and restaurants mix together in restored *shikumen* (stone gate) houses.

3 The Bund and Nanjing Dong Lu. People come from all over China to shop on what was once the country's premier shopping street and enjoy. Shanghai's famous waterfront boulevard, the Bund.

4 Former French Concession. Whether you're an architecture fan, a photographer, or a romantic a wander through these streets is always a wonderful way to pass an afternoon.

5 Jing'an and Changning. Running west into Jing'an, Nanjing Dong (east) Lu turns into Nanjing Xi (west) Lu, and the shops go from mass market to ultra-luxury.

6 Pudong. The eastern side of the Huangpu River is home to the central business district in Lujiazui, with a trio of supertall skyscrapers.

4

GETTING ORIENTED

Shanghai is fast and tough, so bring good shoes and a lot of patience. Don't expect the grandeur of ancient sights, as you would in Beijing, but rather relish the small details like exquisitely designed Art Deco buildings or laid-back cafés. Shanghai hides her gems well, so it's important to be observant and look up and around. The crowds of people and the constant change can make travelers weary, so take advantage of the wide range of eateries and benches on which to take a break.

7 Hongkou and Putuo. Just north of the Bund, quiet Hongkou is steeped in history. Putuo, north of Jing'an, is where you'll find gallery strip M50.

8 Xujiahui, Hongqiao, and Gubei. There are a confluence of malls and few charms in Xujiahui. Hongqiao and Gubei are popular with business travelers.

Updated by Sophie Friedman

Shanghai is a city of two faces. It is home to some of the world's tallest skyscrapers, miles of luxury goods shops, and scores of trendy bars and restaurants. But look just beyond the main streets and you'll find narrow alleyways packed with traditional lane houses, where laundry billows from bamboo poles, and local communities are alive and well.

Shanghai has always been China's most Westernized city. In its heyday, Shanghai had the best nightlife, the greatest architecture, and the strongest business in Asia. Nearly a century later, after extreme tumult and political upheaval, it's back on top.

Shanghai's charm lies not in a list of must-see sites, but in quiet, tree-lined streets, the Bund's majestic colonial buildings, sweet boutiques, and a dizzying array of places to eat and drink, from literal hole-in-the-walls to celebrity chef restaurants.

Today, Shanghai has nearly 24 million people, the skyscrapers keep getting taller, the metro keeps getting longer, and the historical buildings continue to evade the wrecking ball. For how much longer is anyone's guess.

PLANNING

WHEN TO GO

The best time to visit Shanghai is early spring or early fall, when the weather is good and crowds diminish. Although temperatures are scorching and the humidity can be unbearable, summer is the peak tourist season, and hotels and transportation can get very crowded.

Avoid the two main public holidays, Chinese New Year (which ranges from mid-January to mid-February) and the National Day holiday (always the first week of October), when a billion-plus people are on the move.

CLOSE UP

A Brief Introduction to Shanghai History

Until 1842, the "City Above the Sea" was a small fishing village. After the first Opium War, the village was carved up into autonomous concessions administered concurrently by the British, French, and Americans.

With dance halls, glitzy restaurants, international clubs, brothels, opium dens, and a racetrack, Shanghai catered to the rich. The "Paris of the East" was known as a place of vice and indulgence. It was amid this glamour and degradation that the Communist Party held its first meeting in 1921.

In the '30s and '40s the city suffered raids, invasions, and occupation by the Japanese. After the war's end, Nationalists and Communists fought a three-year civil war for control of China. The Communists declared victory in 1949 and established the People's Republic of China. Between 1950 and 1980, Shanghai's industries soldiered on through periods of extreme famine and drought, reform, and suppression. Politically, the city was central to the Cultural Revolution and the Gang of Four's base. The January Storm of 1967 purged many of Shanghai's leaders, and Red Guards set out to destroy the "Four Olds": old ways of ideas, living, traditions, and thought.

In 1972, with the Cultural Revolution still going, Shanghai hosted the historic meeting between Premier Zhou Enlai and U.S. President Richard Nixon. In 1990, China's leader, Deng Xiaoping, chose Shanghai as the center of the country's commercial renaissance, and it has again become a place of hedonism and capitalism, one of China's most ideologically, socially, culturally, and economically open cities.

GETTING HERE AND AROUND

AIR TRAVEL

Shanghai's two major international airports—Pudong (PVG) and Hongqiao (SHA)—make it easy to get here from the rest of the world. Many major world cities have direct flights: United Airlines runs daily direct flights from Newark to Pudong; Delta flies direct from Pudong to Tokyo and Detroit; Turkish Airlines has daily direct flights from Istanbul. A few budget airlines, such as Air Asia, fly from Shanghai (to Kuala Lumpur for example), with most leaving from Pudong.

Airport Information Hongqiao International Airport (虹桥国际机场 *Hóngqiáo guójì jīchǎng*). ☎ 021/6268–8918 ⊕ en.shairport.com. **Pudong International Airport** (浦东国际机场 *Pǔdōng guójì jīchǎng*). ☎ 021/9608–1388 ⊕ en.shairport.com.

GROUND TRANSPORTATION Most international flights go through Pudong International Airport (PVG), which is 45 km (30 miles) east of the city, whereas many domestic routes and some flights from Hong Kong, Taiwan, Japan, and Korea operate out of the older Hongqiao International Airport (SHA), 15 km (9 miles) west of the city center.

Taking a taxi is the most comfortable way into town from Pudong International Airport. Expect to pay around Y200 to Y260 for the 45-minute trip to downtown Puxi; for a cab to Hongqiao, a western suburb, tack on Y80. Puxi is the west side of the Huangpu River and Pudong is the east side. With the exception of Pudong, all areas listed here are in Puxi. Puxi is home to Shanghai's historic center. From Pudong Airport, getting to places in Pudong takes 25–30 minutes and should cost no more than Y115. At rush hour, these times and rates can easily double; if you will be arriving between 8 and 9:30 am or 4 and 7 pm, it's best to book a car service that charges a flat rate.

For the quickest ride, catch the Maglev train, which tops out at 431 kph (268 mph). At the Longyang Lu metro station in Pudong it connects to Lines 2 and 7, which can get you downtown in about 25 minutes. It costs Y50 for a single trip (Y40 if you present your ticket from a same-day flight) and Y80 per round-trip. For a mere Y7 you can hop on metro Line 2 at Pudong International Airport, cross the platform at Guanglan Road Station, and be downtown in just over an hour. Note that the Maglev train runs 6:30 am–9:30 pm and the metro 9:30 am–9:15 pm, so these are not early-morning or late-night options.

From Hongqiao Airport, a taxi downtown will cost you Y55–Y85 and takes 30 to 40 minutes; it takes about an hour to reach Pudong. You can take metro Lines 2 and 10 from Hongqiao for Y5. A taxi from one airport to the other takes about an hour and 20 minutes and costs upwards of Y270. Metro Line 2 also connects Hongqiao Airport and Pudong Airport, making trips between the two significantly cheaper.

Many hotels offer free airport transfers to their guests. Otherwise, shuttle buses link Pudong Airport with a number of hotels (routes starting with a letter) and transport hubs (routes starting with a number) in the city center. Most shuttle buses depart every 10 to 20 minutes between roughly 7 am and midnight. Trips to Puxi take about 90 minutes and cost between Y25 and Y40. From Hongqiao Airport, Bus 925 runs to People's Square, but there's little room for luggage. It costs Y4.

The best bus for travelers going *to* Pudong Airport is the direct airport bus from Jing'an Temple. It's well known and easy to find. If you are standing in front of Jing'an temple facing West Nanjing Road, it's a few minutes' walk to your left. The bus departs every 15 minutes from the ground-level parking lot; tickets cost Y22 and can only be paid for in cash.

Ground Transportation Maglev Train ☎ *021/2890-7777* ⊕ *www.smtdc.com.*

BIKE TRAVEL

Few hotels rent bikes, but you can inquire at bike shops like Giant, where the rate is Y50 a day, plus a large refundable deposit. Giant does not rent helmets. Note that for about Y200 you can buy your own basic bike at Tesco or Carrefour. Shanghai's frenzied traffic is not for the faint of heart, though most secondary streets have wide, well-defined bike lanes. ■ TIP➔ **If you plan to do a lot of cycling during your trip, it's best to bring your own helmet.**

Bike Rental Bohdi Bikes ☎ *021/5266-9013.* **Giant Bikes** (捷安特 *Jié'āntè*). ✉ *743 Jianguo Xi Lu, French Concession* ☎ *021/6437-5041.*

BUS TRAVEL

Taking buses is possible—the stops are called out in English—but as they are often crowded, slow, and the maps are only in Chinese, it is easier to stick to the metro.

Bus Contact **Shanghai Central Long Distance Bus Station** (上海长途客运总站 *Shànghǎi chángtú kèyùn zǒngzhàn).* ✉ *1662 Zhongxing Lu, near Shanghai Railway Station, Zhabei* ☎ *021/6605-0000.*

FERRY TRAVEL

Ferries run around the clock every 10 minutes between the Bund and Pudong's terminal just south of the Riverside Promenade. The per-person fare is Y2 each way.

Ferry Contacts **China-Japan International Ferry Company** ✉ *908 Dongda-ming Lu, 18th fl., Hongkou* ☎ *021/6325-7642.* **Pudong–Puxi Ferry** ✉ *Puxi dock, Jinling Lu, at the Bund, The Bund* ✉ *Pudong dock, 1 Dongchang Lu, south of Binjiang Dadao, Pudong.* **Shanghai Ferry Company** ☎ *021/6537-5111, 021/5393-1185* ⊕ *www.shanghai-ferry.co.jp/english.*

SUBWAY TRAVEL

Shanghai's quick and efficient subway system—called the Shanghai metro—is an excellent way to get around town, and the network is growing exponentially every year. English maps and exit signs abound, and the single-ticket machines have an English option, too. In-car announcements for each station are given in both Chinese and English. Keep your ticket handy: you'll need to insert it into a second turnstile as you exit at your destination.

■TIP→ Refillable transport cards costing Y30 are available from metro stations. Add as much money as you like, and use them to pay for taxi, metro, ferry, and bus rides. The transport cards aren't discounted, but they'll save you time you would have spent joining queues and fumbling for cash. To purchase, say, *Wo yao yi zhang ka* (我要一张卡) which means "I want a card."). ■TIP→ Shanghai is a sprawling city with large districts, but the downtown area is fairly compact, and the subway reaches nearly all places you'll want to visit.

Subway Contacts **Shanghai Metro Passenger Information** ☎ *021/6437-0000* ⊕ *www.shmetro.com.*

TAXI TRAVEL

Taxis are plentiful, cheap, and easy to spot. Your hotel concierge can call for one by phone or you can hail one on the street. The available ones have a small lighted sign on the passenger side. If you're choosing a cab from a line, peek at the driver's license on the dashboard. The lower the license number, the more experienced the driver. Drivers with a number below 200,000 can usually get you where you're going. ■TIP→ Drivers don't speak English, so it's best to give them a piece of paper with your destination written in Chinese characters. (Keep a card with the name of your hotel on it handy for the return trip.) Taxis start at Y14 for the first 2.40 km; after 11 pm this jumps to Y18.

TRAIN TRAVEL

Several train stations, the newest of which is Hongqiao Railway Station, right next to Hongqiao Airport, serve Shanghai well. You can hop a train to Guangzhou (7 hours), Beijing (5 hours), Nanjing and Shaoxing (1½ hours), Hangzhou (45 minutes), Suzhou (25 minutes), as well as a few other nearby places. The G- and D-trains are the fastest and the only type you'll want to board. You'll need your passport to buy tickets, which, outside of Chinese New Year and Golden Week (first week of October) can be purchased day-of at the station.

Train Contacts Hongqiao Railway Station ✉ *Hongyu Elevated Rd. Exit, just west of Hongqiao Airport, Minhang* ☎ *021/12306.* **Shanghai Railway Station** ✉ *303 Moling Lu, Zhabei* ☎ *021/6317–9090.* **Shanghai South Railway Station** ✉ *289 Humin Lu, at Liuzhou Lu, Xujiahui* ☎ *021/5436–9511.*

HEALTH AND SAFETY

Tap water in Shanghai is safe for brushing teeth. However, it contains a high concentration of metals, so you should buy bottled water to drink. It is available at every corner store—look for FamilyMart, Kedi, AllDays, and Watsons—bottles start from Y1.50. Make sure that food has been thoroughly cooked and is served to you fresh and hot; thoroughly scrub all produce, especially before eating it raw. Shanghai's polluted air can bring on, or aggravate, respiratory problems. If you're a sufferer, bring a mask from home; 3M's N95 masks can be purchased inexpensively in the United States.

The most reliable places to buy prescription medication are the 24-hour pharmacy at the ParkwayHealth Medical Center or the Shanghai United Family Health Center. During the day, the Watson's chain is good for over-the-counter medication, but has limited selection; there are dozens of branches around town. Chinese pharmacies offer a fuller range of over-the-counter drugs and are usually open later; look for the green cross on a white sign. Pantomiming works well for things like band-aids, ace bandages, and cough medicine, so do not feel embarrassed to use hand gestures.

There is almost no violent crime against tourists in China, partly because the penalties are severe for those who are caught—China's yearly death-sentence tolls run into the thousands. Single women can move about Shanghai with little to no hassle, though as in all major cities, handbag-snatching and pickpocketing do happen in markets and on crowded buses or trains.

Shanghai is full of people looking to make a quick buck. The most common scam involves people persuading you to go with them for a tea ceremony, which is often so pleasant that you don't smell a rat until several hundred dollars appear on your credit-card bill. "Art students" who pressure you into buying work is another common scam. Avoiding such scams is as easy as refusing *all* unsolicited services—be it from taxi or pedicab drivers, tour guides, or potential "friends." Simply put: if someone is offering you something, you don't want it. It is not considered rude to ignore them.

CLOSE UP Tips to Unlocking the City

NAVIGATING THE STREETS

The Huangpu River divides Shanghai into east and west sides. The metro area is huge, but the city center is a relatively small district in Puxi, west of the river. On the east side is Pudong, which has undergone massive urbanization in the past two decades. The city is loosely laid out on a grid, and most neighborhoods are easily explored on foot. Massive construction in many neighborhoods makes pavement uneven and the air dusty, but if you can put up with this, walking is the best way to really get a feel for the city and its people. Taxis are readily available and good for traveling longer distances, and the subway network covers all of downtown and many far-flung areas.

Major east–west roads are named for Chinese cities and divide the city into *dong* (east), *zhong* (middle), and *xi* (west) sections. North–south roads divide the city into *bei* (north) and *nan* (south) segments. The heart of the city is found on its chief east–west streets—Nanjing Lu, Huaihai Lu, and Yan'an Lu overpass.

■ TIP➔ **Street signs in Shanghai are written in Chinese and English, *not* in pinyin, the transliteration**

of Chinese. When asking for directions, pinyin will guide your pronunciation; for this reason, our listings have street names written as Nanjing Xi Lu or Shiji Dadao, not West Nanjing Road or Century Avenue. Our maps, however, follow the city's street signs; they are written as West Nanjing Road, *not* Nanjing Xi Lu.

NAVIGATING VOCABULARY

Below are some terms you'll see on maps and street signs and in the names of most places you'll go:

Dong (东) is east, **xi (西)** is west, **nan (南)** is south, **bei (北)** is north, and **zhong (中)** means middle. **Jie (街)** and **lu (路)** mean street and road, respectively, **da dao (大道)** means avenue, **da (大)** means big, and **xiao (小)** means small.

Qiao (桥) or bridge, is part of the place-name at just about every entrance and exit on the ring roads. **Men (门)**, meaning door or gate, indicates a street that passed through an entrance in the fortification wall that surrounded the city hundreds of years ago. The entrances to parks and some other places are also referred to as *men*. For example, Xizhimen literally means Western Straight Gate.

If your passport is stolen, contact the U.S. Consulate immediately; consular officers can arrange an emergency passport for you and guide you through getting a new Chinese visa.

Shanghai traffic is as manic as it looks, and survival of the fittest (or the biggest) is the main rule. Cars will turn right on red, right into you. Beware of buses, which make wide turns and regularly ignore pedestrians' rights. Likewise, watch out for scooters, which will speed through lights and wildly turn corners.

Consulate United States Consulate (美国领事馆 *Měiguó lǐngshìguǎn*). ⊠ *8F, back side of Westgate Mall, 1038 W. Nanjing Rd., American Citizen Services,*

Jing'an ☎ *021/6433–6880, 021/6433–3936 after-hours emergencies, 021/3217–4650 citizen services* ⊕ *shanghai.usembassy-china.org.cn.*

Emergency Contacts **Fire** ☎ *119.* **ParkwayHealth 24-Hour Line (百汇医疗** *Bǎi huì yīliáo).* ☎ *021/6445–5999* ⊕ *www.parkwayhealth.cn.* **Police** ☎ *110, 021/6357–6666 Public Security Bureau Division for Foreigners.* **Shanghai Ambulance Service** ☎ *120.*

Medical Services **Huashan Hospital (华山医院** *Huàshān yīyuàn).* ⊠ *Foreigners' Clinic, 15F, 12 Wulumuqi Zhong Lu, Jing'an* ☎ *021/6248–9999 24-hr hotline* ⊕ *www.sh-hwmc.com.cn.* **ParkwayHealth (百汇医疗** *Bǎi huì yīliáo).* ⊠ *Shanghai Centre West Tower, 1376 Nanjing Xi Lu, Room 203, Jing'an* ☎ *021/6445–5999 24-hr hotline.* **Hongqiao Clinic** ⊠ *2258 Hongqiao Lu, Hongqiao* ☎ *021/6445–5999.* **Jinqiao Clinic** ⊠ *51 Hongfeng Lu, Pudong* ☎ *021/6445–5999.* **Shanghai East International Medical Center (上海东方联合医院** *Shànghǎi dōngfāng liánhé yīyuàn).* ⊠ *150 Jimo Lu, near Pudong Da Dao, Pudong* ☎ *021/5879–9999* ⊕ *www.seimc.com.cn.* **Shanghai United Family Hospital and Clinics (上海和睦家医院** *Shàng huà hémù jiā yīyuàn).* ⊠ *1139 Xianxia Lu, Changning* ☎ *021/400-639-3900 appointments, 021/2216–3999 24-hr hotline* ⊕ *www.unitedfamilyhospitals.com.*

Postal Services **Post Office** ⊠ *276 Bei Suzhou Lu, Hongkou* ⊠ *Shanghai Centre, East Tower, 3F, 1376 Nanjing Xi Lu, Jing'an.* ⊠ *105 Tianping Lu, French Concession*

HOURS OF OPERATION

All businesses close for Chinese New Year. Others have shortened operating hours during national holidays.

Shops: Stores are generally open daily 10 to 9; some stores stay open as late as 10 pm.

Temples and Museums: Most temples are open daily 8 to 5. Museums and most other sights are generally open 9 to 4, six days a week, with Monday being the most common closed day. Museums without permanent collections are closed during exhibition installation, so call ahead. Parks are open round the clock, and entering after dark is perfectly safe; in fact, you may be treated to the sight of a dozen seniors ballroom dancing.

Banks and Offices: Government offices are open weekdays 9 to 5, but some close for lunch between noon and 2. Most banks are open seven days a week from 9 to 6. Bank branches and CITS tour desks in hotels offer 24 hour ATMs. Many hotel currency-exchange desks stay open 24 hours.

TOURS

Tours are a nice way to unwind post-flight, and can help you get your bearings on that stressful first afternoon.

BOAT TOURS

Huangpu River boat tours afford a great view of Pudong and the Bund, but after that it's mostly ports and cranes.

Cruises from Oriental Pearl Tower. Forty-minute boat tours run day and night along the Bund from the Pearl Tower's cruise dock in Pudong. Tickets, excluding Pearl Tower admission, can be purchased at the gate

DID YOU KNOW?

Nanjing Road is the main shopping street in Shanghai and has been so for more than a century. At the start of the 20th century, the street was home to a number of franchised stores, eight big department stores, and at least one casino. Today, West Nanjing Road is lined with luxury goods shops and a long swath of East Nanjing Road is pedestrian only.

to the tower. ⊠ *Oriental Pearl Cruise Dock, 1 Shiji Dadao (Century Ave.), Pudong* ☎ *021/5879–1888* ✆ *From Y100.*

Huangpu River Cruises. Boats run nightly 6–9 pm, leaving every 30 minutes and traveling for 45–60 minutes up and down the Huangpu River to where it meets the Yangtze. You'll see barges, bridges, and factories, but not much scenery. ⊠ *501 Zhongshan Dong Er Lu, The Bund* ☎ *021/6374–4461* ✆ *From Y100.*

BUS TOURS

Gray Line Tours. On offer are half- and full-day group coach tours of Shanghai, as well as one-day trips to Suzhou, Hangzhou, and other nearby waterside towns. ⊠ *5A, 5F, 1399 Beijing Xi Lu, Jing'an* ☎ *021/6289–5221* ⊕ *www.grayline.com/shanghai* ✆ *From $58.*

Jinjiang Tours (锦江旅游公司 *Jǐnjiāng lǚyóu gōngsī*). This state-owned company runs half- and full-day group bus tours of Shanghai. Stops include the French Concession, People's Square, Jade Buddha Temple, Yu Garden, the Bund, and Xintiandi. Full-day tours include lunch, but those with dietary restrictions should pack snacks. ⊠ *191 Changle Lu, Room A101, Xuhui* ☎ *021/6445–9525* ✆ *From Y350.*

HERITAGE TOURS

Context Travel. U.S.-based Context runs small group and private walking tours in Shanghai and Beijing. Tours focusing on food, history, art, architecture, and urban planning are led by academics and experts in these fields. ☎ *215/392–0303 U.S. office* ⊕ *www.contexttravel.com* ✆ *From Y550.*

Shanghai Jewish Tours. Available daily in Hebrew or English and led by an Israeli photojournalist, this half-day tour takes you to the sites of Shanghai's Jewish history, such as the 1920 Ohel Rachel Synagogue. ⊕ *www.shanghai-jews.com* ✆ *From Y100.*

VISITOR INFORMATION

The best thing to hit Shanghai since an extended metro system is the Shanghai Call Centre (☎ 962288), where a host of English-speaking operators answer any question you have, help you communicate with taxi drivers, and provide directions to restaurants, bars, shops, and museums. There are also a number of French-, German-, and Spanish-speaking operators. Though you'll see what appear to be information kiosks on the street, bypass these; they're staffed by well-meaning college students who rarely offer valuable information.

Visitor Info Shanghai Tourist Information Services ⊠ *Yu Garden, 149 Jiujia-ochang Lu, Huangpu* ☎ *021/6355–5032.*

EXPLORING

Today beauty and charm coexist with kitsch and commercialism. From the colonial architecture of the Former French Concession to the forest of cranes and the neon-lit high-rises of Pudong, Shanghai is a city of paradox and change.

OLD CITY

Tucked away in the east of Puxi are the remnants of Shanghai's Old City. Once encircled by a thick wall, a fragment of which still remains, the Old City has a sense of history among its fast disappearing old shikumen (stone gatehouses), temples, and markets; it wasn't until 1854 that Chinese were allowed to move out of the so-called "Chinese City" and into the foreign concessions. Delve into narrow alleyways where residents still hang their washing out on bamboo poles and chamber pots remain in use. Burn incense with the locals in small temples, sip tea in a teahouse, or get a taste of Chinese snacks and street food. This is the place to get a feeling for Shanghai's past, but you'd better get there soon, as the wrecker's ball knows no mercy.

GETTING AROUND

This area could take a very long afternoon or morning, as it's a good one to do on foot. Browsing the souvenir stalls around Yu Garden might add an hour. Metro Line 10 has a Yu Garden station, and it's a 30-minute walk from Nanjing Dong Lu station on Lines 2 and 10.

TOP ATTRACTIONS

City God Temple (城隍庙 *Chénghuáng miào*). At the southeast end of the Yu Gardens bazaar stands this Taoist temple, built during the early part of the Ming Dynasty and destroyed by fire in 1924. The main hall was rebuilt in 1926, and has been renovated many times over the years. Inside are gleaming gold figures, and atop the roof you'll see statues of crusading warriors—flags raised, arrows drawn. This is a popular place for locals to light incense; expect it to be crowded around major holidays like Chinese New Year. ✉ *249 Fangbang Zhong Lu, Old City* ☎ *021/6386–8649* 🎟 *Y10* ⊙ *Daily 8:30–4.*

Long Museum (龙美术馆 *Lóng měishùguǎn*). Billionaire art collectors Liu Yiqian and Wang Wei don't do anything halfway; their Long Museum, designed by Shanghai-based firm Atelier Deshaus, is a testament to the money flowing into supporting contemporary Chinese art. The museum hosts rotating exhibitions, from Qing Dynasty paintings to a show on the past, present, and future of silver in Mexico. Long Museum is also walking distance from Yuz Museum. ✉ *3398 Longteng Dadao, near Chuanchang Lu, Old City* ☎ *021/6877–8787* ⊕ *thelongmuseum.org* 🎟 *Y50* ⊙ *Last entry 5 pm* ⊙ *Closed Mon.* ✉ *Bldg. 210, 2255 Luoshan Lu, near Huamu Lu, Pudong* ☎ *021/6877–8787*

FAMILY

Fodor'sChoice

★

Power Station of Art (上海当代艺术博物馆 *Shànghǎi dāngdài yìshù bówùguǎn*). The site of the Shanghai World Expo was a barren wasteland until this massive contemporary art museum, housed in a former power plant, opened in late 2012. It did so with a bang, opening the ninth Shanghai Biennale and simultaneously hosting an exhibition from the Centre Pompidou in Paris. Rather than a permanent collection, the museum hosts one large-scale exhibition after another. It pulls in top Chinese artists like Cai Guoqiang and is the city's home for major touring exhibitions. It is a 15-minute walk from Xizang Nan Lu metro station. ✉ *200 Huayuangang Lu, near Miaojiang Lu, Old City* ☎ *021/3110–8550* ⊕ *www.powerstationofart.org/en* 🎟 *Free; special exhibitions Y20.*

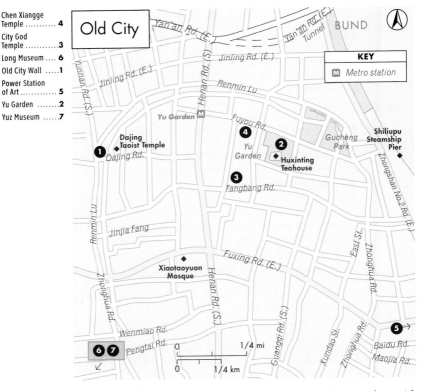

Fodor's Choice ★ **Yu Garden** (豫园 *Yù yuán*). Since the 18th century, this complex, with its traditional red walls and upturned tile roofs, has been a marketplace and social center where local residents gather, shop, and practice *qi gong* in the evenings. It is overrun by tourists and not as impressive as the ancient palace gardens of Beijing, but Yu Garden is a piece of Shanghai's rapidly disappearing past, and one of the few old sights left in the city.

To get to the garden itself, you must wind your way through the crowded bazaar. The garden was commissioned by the Ming Dynasty official Pan Yunduan in 1559 and built by the renowned architect Zhang Nanyang over 19 years. When it was finally finished it won international praise as "the best garden in southeastern China." In the mid-1800s, the Society of Small Swords used the garden as a gathering place for meetings. It was here that they planned their uprising with the Taiping rebels against the French colonists. The French destroyed the garden during the first Opium War, but the area was later rebuilt.

Winding walkways and corridors bring you over stone bridges and carp-filled ponds and through bamboo stands and rock gardens. Within the park are an **old opera stage,** a **museum** dedicated to the Society of Small Swords rebellion, and an **exhibition hall** of Chinese calligraphy and paintings. ⊠ *218 Anren Lu, bordered by Fuyou Lu, Jiujiaochang Lu, Fangbang Lu, and Anren Lu, Old City* ☎ *021/6326–0830,*

021/6328–3251 ⊕ *www.yugarden.com.cn* ✉ *Y40 (Apr. 1–June 30; Sept. 1–Nov. 30); Y30 (July 1–Aug. 31; Dec. 1–Mar. 31)* ⊘ *Daily 8:30–5.*

FAMILY

Fodor's Choice

★

Yuz Museum (余德耀美术馆 *Yúdéyào měishùguǎn*). In a former airport hanger, walking distance from the nearby Long Museum, is the Yuz Museum, brainchild of Chinese-Indonesian art collector Budi Tek. The massive, light-flooded space is perfect for showcasing installations like Maurizio Cattelan's *Untitled*, an olive tree planted in a cube of dirt, which was featured in his retrospective at New York's Guggenheim. Chinese artists get plenty of show time, too; in the same exhibition, one will find Ren Jian's painting *Stamp Collection*, six acrylic-on-canvas versions of stamps from African nations. The museum has Wi-Fi throughout, a small gift shop, and a café where you can watch the sun set. Its cement courtyard, with several sets of stairs, ramps, and a few sculptures, is a good place for kids to roam free. ✉ *35 Fenggu Lu, near the river, Old City* ☎ *021/6426–1901* ⊕ *www.yuzmshanghai.org* ✉ *Y60* ⊘ *Closed Mon.*

WORTH NOTING

Chen Xiangge Temple (陈向阁寺 *Chénxiànggé sì*). If you find yourself passing by this tiny temple on your exploration of the Old City, you can make an offering to Buddha with the free incense sticks that accompany your admission. Built in 1600 by the same man who built Yu Garden, it was destroyed during the Cultural Revolution and rebuilt in the 1990s. The temple is now a nunnery, and you can often hear the women's chants rising from the halls beyond the main courtyard. ✉ *29 Chenxiangge Lu, Old City* ☎ *021/6320–0400* ✉ *Y5* ⊘ *Daily 7–4.*

Old City Wall (上海古城墙大 *Shànghǎi gǔ chéngqiángdà*). The Old City used to be completely surrounded by a wall, built in 1553 as a defense against Japanese pirates. Most of it was torn down in 1912, except for one 50-yard-long (40-meter-long) piece that still stands at Dajing Lu and Renmin Lu. Shanghai history enthusiasts can walk through the remnants and check out the rather simple museum nearby, which is dedicated to the history of the Old City (signs are in Chinese). Stroll through the tiny neighboring alley of Dajing Lu for a lively panorama of crowded market life in the Old City. ✉ *269 Dajing Lu, at Renmin Lu, Old City* ✉ *Museum Y5* ⊘ *Daily 9–4:30.*

XINTIANDI AND CITY CENTER

Xintiandi is Shanghai's showpiece restoration project. Reproduction shikumen (stone gate houses) contain expensive bars, restaurants, and chic boutiques. On warm nights, the restaurants' outdoor tables are filled with diners watching the world go by.

Another good people-watching spot is the area around People's Square, which has some magnificent examples of historical architecture and a smattering of museums. The adjoining People's Park is a pleasant green space where it's possible to escape the clamor of the city for a while.

A nighttime view of a teahouse in Yu Garden

GETTING AROUND

People's Square metro station is the point of convergence for Shanghai's metro Lines 1, 2, and 8. The often-packed underground passageways can be confusing, so it's best to take the first exit and then find your way aboveground. Xintiandi can be reached by taking Line 10 to the Xintiandi stop or Line 1 to the Huangpi Nan Lu station, which is a block or two north of Xintiandi.

The sights in this area are divided into two neat clusters—those around People's Square and those around Xintiandi. You can easily walk between the two in 20 minutes. Visiting all the museums in the People's Square area could take a good half day. Xintiandi's sights don't take very long at all, so you could go in the afternoon, check out the museums, and then settle down for a pre-dinner drink.

TOP ATTRACTIONS

Fodor's Choice ★ **People's Square** (人民广场 *Rénmín guǎngchǎng*). Home of the Shanghai Museum, the city's enormous main square is a social center for locals. During the day, residents stroll, practice tai chi, and fly kites. In the evening, kids roller-skate and ballroom dancers hold group lessons. There is also a small amusement park. Weekends here are extremely busy, particularly on Xizang Road, and are not for the agoraphobic. ⊠ *Enter at Xizang Lu, City Center.*

Fodor's Choice ★ **Shanghai Museum** (上海博物馆 *Shànghǎi bówùguǎn*). Look past the eyesore of an exterior—this museum holds the country's premier collection of relics and artifacts. Eleven galleries exhibit Chinese artistry in all its forms: paintings, bronzes, sculpture, ceramics, calligraphy, jade, furniture of the Ming and Qing dynasties, coins, seals, and art by indigenous populations. Its bronze collection is one of the best in the world, and its dress and costume gallery showcases intricate handiwork from several of China's 55 ethnic minority groups. There are signs and an audio guide available in English. You can relax in the museum's pleasant tearoom or head to the shop for postcards, crafts, and reproductions of the artwork. ⊠ *201 Renmin Dadao, City Center* ☎ *021/6372–3500* ⊕ *www. shanghaimuseum.net/en/index.jsp* ✉ *Free, Y40 for English-language audio guide* ☉ *Daily 9–5; no entry after 4.*

Fodor's Choice ★ **Xintiandi** (新天地 *Xīntiāndì*). By World War II, more than two-thirds of Shanghai's residents lived in a shikumen, or "stone gate house." Most have been razed in the name of progress, but this 8-acre collection of stone gate houses has been transformed into an upscale shopping-and-dining complex called Xintiandi, or "New Heaven on Earth." The restaurants are busy from lunch until past midnight, especially those with patios for watching the passing parade of shoppers. ⊠ *181 Taicang Lu, bordered by Madang Lu, Zizhong Lu, and Huangpi Nan Lu, Xintiandi* ☎ *021/6311–2288* ⊕ *www.xintiandi.com.*

Shikumen Open House Museum (石库门博物馆 *Shí kù mén bówùguǎn*). Just off Xintiandi's main thoroughfare is the Shikumen Open House Museum, a beautifully restored stone gate house (shikumen) filled with furniture and artifacts collected from the other nearby shikumen (now turned shops). Exhibits explain the European influence on shikumen design, the history of the neighborhood's renovation, and future plans for the entire 128-acre project. ⊠ *House 25, Xintiandi North Block, 118 Taicang Lu, Xintiandi* ☎ *021/3307–0337* ⊕ *www. xintiandi.com* ✉ *Y20* ☉ *Daily 10:30–10:30.*

WORTH NOTING

Grand Theater (上海大剧院 *Shànghǎi dàjùyuàn*). The spectacular front wall of glass shines as brightly as the star power in this magnificent theater. Its three stages present the best domestic and international performances. The dramatic curved roof atop a square base is meant to follow the ancient Chinese philosophy that "the earth is square and the sky is round." ■TIP➔ The best time to see it is at night. ⊠ *People's Sq., 300 Renmin Dadao, City Center* ☎ *021/6386–8686* ⊕ *www.shgtheatre.com.*

Park Hotel (国际饭店 *Guójì fàndiàn*). This Art Deco structure overlooking People's Park was once the tallest hotel in Shanghai. Completed in 1934, it was known for its luxurious rooms, fabulous nightclub, and chic restaurants. Today the lobby is the most vivid reminder of its glorious past. It was an early inspiration for architect I.M. Pei (creator of the glass pyramids at the Louvre). ⊠ *People's Sq., 170 Nanjing Xi Lu, City Center* ☎ *021/6327–5225.*

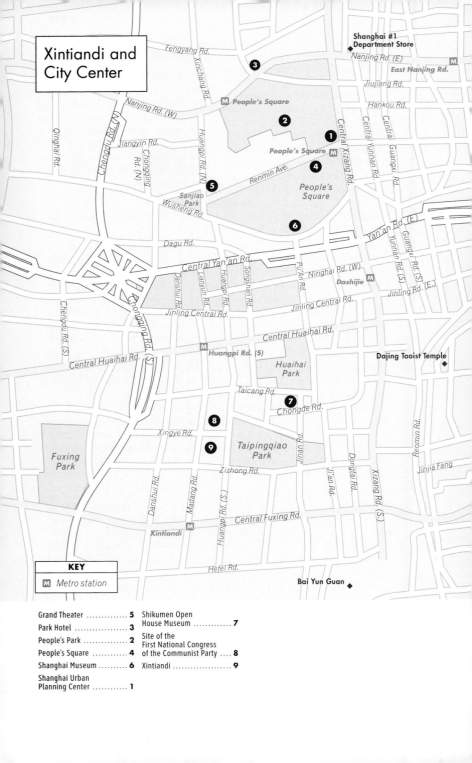

People's Park (人民公园 *Rénmín gōngyuán*). In colonial days this park was the northern half of the city's racetrack. Today the 30 acres of flower beds, lotus ponds, and trees are crisscrossed by a large number of paved paths. It's also home to the **Museum of Contemporary Art** and the **Urban Planning Exhibition Hall.** ■TIP→ **The marriage market, held in the park weekends noon–5 pm, is not to be missed.** Desperately seeking spouses for their children, the parents and grandparents of unmarried adults post flyers advertising their child's height, job, income, Chinese Zodiac sign, and more. ⊠ *231 Nanjing Xi Lu, City Center* ☎ *021/6327–1333* ✉ *Free.*

Fodor's Choice ★

Shanghai Urban Planning Center (上海城市规划中心 *Shànghǎi chéngshí guīhuà zhōngxīn*). To understand the true scale of Shanghai and its ongoing building boom, visit the Master Plan Hall of this museum. Sprawled out on the third floor is a 6,400-square-foot planning model of Shanghai—the largest of its kind in the world—showing the metropolis as city planners expect it to look in 2020. You'll find familiar existing landmarks like the Pearl Tower and Shanghai Center as well as a detailed model of the Shanghai Expo, complete with miniature pavilions. ⊠ *People's Sq., 100 Renmin Dadao (People's Ave.), City Center* ☎ *021/6372–2077* ⊕ *www.supec.org* ✉ *Y30* ☉ *Mon.–Thurs. 9–5, Fri.–Sun. 9–6, last ticket sold 1 hr before closing.*

Site of the First National Congress of the Communist Party (共产党第一次全国代表大会 *Gòngchǎndǎng dìyīcì quánguó dàibiǎo dàhuì*). The secret meeting on July 31, 1921 that marked the first National Congress was held at the Bo Wen Girls' School, where 13 delegates from Marxist, Communist, and Socialist groups gathered from around the country. The upstairs of this restored *shikumen* is a well-curated museum detailing the rise of communism in China. Downstairs lies the very room where the first delegates worked. It remains frozen in time, the table set with matches and teacups. Ironically, the site today is surrounded by Xintiandi, Shanghai's center of capitalist conspicuous consumption. ⊠ *374 Huangpi Nan Lu, City Center* ☎ *021/5383–2171* ✉ *Free, audio tour Y10* ☉ *Daily 9–4.*

THE BUND AND NANJING DONG LU

On the bank of the Huangpu River is the Bund, Shanghai's most recognizable sightseeing spot, lined with massive foreign buildings that predate 1949. Some of these buildings have been developed into lifestyle complexes with spas, restaurants, bars, galleries, and designer boutiques. The Bund is also an ideal spot for that photo of Pudong's famous skyline. Running perpendicular to the Bund, pedestrian-only

Nanjing Dong Lu is lined on both sides with shops and their glowing neon signboards. It's a popular shopping spot for locals who flock to massive outposts of American chains. Some of the adjacent streets still have a faded glamour, and some—lined with shops selling hardware or bicycle parts—are great for a peek at local life. The best time to visit Nanjing Dong Lu is at night.

GETTING AROUND

The simplest way to get here is to take metro Line 2 or 10 to Nanjing Dong Lu station, and then head east for the Bund or west for the main shopping area of Nanjing Dong Lu. Alternatively, you can take Line 1, 2, or 8 to People's Square station and walk east for about 30 minutes to the Bund or 15 minutes to Nanjing Dong Lu.

SAFETY AND PRECAUTIONS

As in any tourist area, there are pickpockets. Not so much a safety issue as an annoyance are the "art students" who press you to buy their over-priced work or those who insist on inviting you to a sham tea ceremony.

TOP ATTRACTIONS

Fodor's Choice ★ **The Bund** (外滩 *Wàitān*). Shanghai's waterfront boulevard best shows both the city's pre-1949 past and its focus on the future. Both the northern and southern ends of the Bund are constantly changing, with hotels and restaurants popping up amid scooter repair shops and hardware stores.

On the riverfront side of the Bund, Shanghai's street life is in full force. You'll find Chinese tourists as well as foreigners here, ogling the Pudong skyline. If you have blonde hair, prepare to be stopped for photos. In the morning, just after dawn, the Bund is full of people ballroom dancing, doing aerobics, and practicing kung fu, qi gong, and tai chi. The rest of the day, people walk the embankment, snapping photos of the Oriental Pearl Tower, the Huangpu River, and each other. In the evenings, lovers come out for romantic walks amid the floodlit buildings and tower. ■TIP➔ **Be prepared for the aggressive souvenir hawkers; while you can't completely avoid them, just ignore them and watch your pockets and bags.** ✉ *Zhongshan Dong Yi Lu, between Jinling Lu and Suzhou Creek, The Bund.*

Former Hong Kong and Shanghai Bank Building (浦东发展银行 *Pǔdōng fāzhǎn yínháng*). When this beautiful neoclassical structure was built by the British in 1923, it was the second-largest bank building in the world. After the building was turned into offices for the Communist Party in 1949, the beautiful 1920s Italian-tile mosaic in the building's dome was deemed too extravagant and was covered by white paint. Ironically enough, this protected it from being destroyed by the Red Guards during the Cultural Revolution. The mural was then forgotten until 1997, when the Pudong Development Bank renovated the building. If you walk in and look up, you'll see the circular mosaic in the dome—an outer circle portraying the cities where the bank had branches at the time: London, Paris, New York, Bangkok, Tokyo, Calcutta, Hong Kong, and Shanghai; a middle circle made up of the 12 signs of the zodiac; and the center painted with a large sun and Ceres,

The Bund is great for people-watching and checking out Shanghai's famous skyscrapers.

the Roman goddess of abundance. ⊠ *12 Zhongshan Dong Yi Lu, The Bund* ☎ *021/6161–6188* ⊠ *Free* ⊙ *Weekdays 9–5:30, weekends 9–5.*

Peace Hotel (和平饭店 *Hépíng fàndiàn*). This hotel at the corner of the Bund and Nanjing Dong Lu is among Shanghai's most treasured buildings. If any establishment will give you a sense of Shanghai's past, it's this one. Its high ceilings, ornate woodwork, and streamlined fixtures are still intact. Following a renovation in 2010, the hotel reopened as the Fairmont Peace Hotel, with the jazz bar, tea lounge, restaurant, shopping arcade, and ballroom all restored to their original glory, evoking old Shanghai cabarets and galas. On the mezzanine level is a small but fascinating gallery chronicling the hotel's past.

The south building, formerly the Palace Hotel (and now the Swatch Art Peace Hotel), was built in 1906. The north building, once the Cathay Hotel, built in 1929, is more famous. It was known as the private playroom of its owner, Victor Sassoon, a wealthy landowner who invested in the opium trade. Sassoon lived and entertained his guests in the copper penthouse. The hotel was rated on a par with the likes of Raffles in Singapore and the Peninsula in Hong Kong. It was *the* place to stay, see, and be seen in old Shanghai. Noël Coward wrote *Private Lives* here. ⊠ *20 Nanjing Dong Lu, The Bund* ⊕ *www.fairmont.com/peace-hotel-shanghai.*

WORTH NOTING

Bank of China (中国银行 *Zhōngguó yínháng*). British Art Deco and Chinese elements combine in this 1937 building, which was designed to be the tallest in the city. However, opium magnate Victor Sassoon insisted that no building surpass his Cathay Hotel (now the Peace

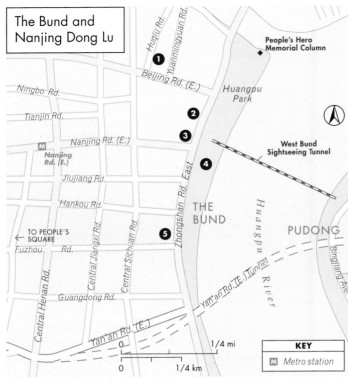

The Bund and
Nanjing Dong Lu

Hotel). Were it not for the Cathay Hotel's copper-faced pyramid roof, the bank would indeed be taller. ⊠ *23 Zhongshan Dong Yi Lu, The Bund* ☎ *021/6329–1979.*

FAMILY

Fodor's Choice

★

Rockbund Art Museum (**上海外滩美术馆** *Shànghǎi wàitān měishùguǎn*). The detailing on this 1932 Art Deco building is as enticing as the artwork inside. Rockbund has no permanent collection, which keeps things exciting. When exhibitions are being installed, the museum is closed, so check the website before you go. Exhibits come from both Chinese and international artists, and some include interactive elements. Lectures and film screenings are held often; many are in English, and some are family-friendly. On the top floor is a quiet, airy seating area and, the cherry on the sundae, the museum's roof deck. ⊠ *20 Huqiu Lu, just off Beijing Dong Lu, The Bund* ☎ *021/3310–9985* ⊕ *www. rockbundartmuseum.org* ⊠ *Y30* ⊙ *Tues.–Sun. 10–6.*

FORMER FRENCH CONCESSION

With its tree-lined streets and crumbling old villas, the Former French Concession is Shanghai's most visitor-friendly area, with ample shade and sidewalks meant to be pounded. ■TIP→ **If you're looking at a larger city map, the Former French Concession is located in Xuhui District.** The area is a wonderful place to go wandering and make serendipitous

A BRIEF HISTORY

The Bund's name is derived from the Anglo-Indian, and literally means "muddy embankment." In the early 1920s, the Bund became the city's foreign street: Americans, British, Japanese, French, Russians, Germans, and other Europeans built banks, trading houses, clubs, consulates, and hotels in styles from neoclassical to Art Deco.

As Shanghai grew to be a bustling trading center in the Yangtze Delta, the Bund's warehouses and ports became the heart of the action. With the Communist victory, the foreigners left Shanghai, and the Chinese government moved its own banks and offices here.

4

discoveries of stately architecture, groovy boutiques and galleries, or cozy cafés. Much of Shanghai's past beauty remains, although many of the old buildings are in a desperate state of disrepair. One of the major roads through this area, Huaihai Lu, is a popular shopping location, with all the big foreign chains and an assortment of local brands. Julu Lu, Fumin Lu, Fuxing Xi Lu, Yongfu Lu, and Yongkang Lu are where many of Shanghai's restaurants, bars, and clubs are located, so if you are looking for an evening out, head to this area.

GETTING AROUND

This is a lovely area to walk around, so it's best to leave cabs behind and go on foot. The only site that is at a distance is Soong Ching-ling's Former Residence, which is a bit farther down Huaihai Lu. Access it via metro Lines 10 and 11 at Jiaotong University. Any of the three Line 1 metro stops (Shaanxi Nan Lu, Changshu Lu, or Hengshan Lu) will land you somewhere in the French Concession area. Line 7 connects at Changshu Lu and Line 10 at Shaanxi Nan Lu.

TOP ATTRACTIONS

Former Residence of Dr. Sun Yat-sen (故居的孫逸仙 *Gùjū de Sūn Yìxiān*). Sun Yat-sen, the father of the Republic of China, lived in this two-story house for five years, from 1919 to 1924. His wife, Soong Qing-ling, of the illustrious Soong family, continued to live here until 1937. Today it's been turned into a museum, and tours are conducted in Chinese and English. ⊠ *7 Xiangshan Lu, French Concession* ☎ *021/6437–2954* 🔾 *¥20* ⏲ *Daily 9–4:30.*

Fuxing Park (复兴公园 *Fùxīng gōngyuán*). This European-style park, once open only to Shanghai's French residents, is one of downtown's most tranquil spots. Here you'll find people strolling hand in hand, practicing tai chi, and playing cards and mah-jongg. There is a tiny amusement park and, on weekends and holidays, art projects for kids. The open spaces double as dance floors, with elderly couples dancing away the day—tourists are welcome to join in. ⊠ *105 Fuxing Zhong Lu, enter on Sinan Lu, French Concession* ☎ *021/5386–1069* 🔾 *Free* ⏲ *Daily 6–6.*

Former French Concession

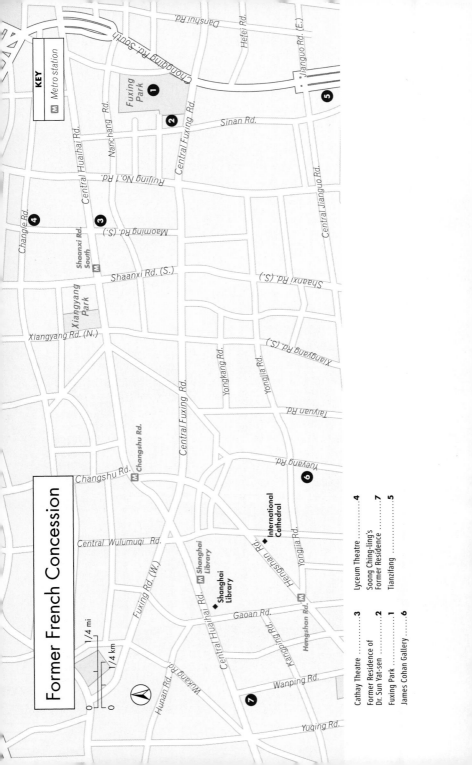

KEY

Ⓜ Metro station

Fuxing Park	**1**
Former Residence of Dr. Sun Yat-sen	**2**
Cathay Theatre	**3**
Lyceum Theatre	**4**
Tianzifang	**5**
James Cohan Gallery	**6**
Soong Ching-ling's Former Residence	**7**

Streets and landmarks labeled on map: Danshui Rd., Hefei Rd., Jianguo Rd. (E.), Chongqing Rd. South, Nanchang Rd., Central Fuxing Rd., Sinan Rd., Fuxing Park, Central Huaihai Rd., Ruijing No. 1 Rd., Maoming Rd. (S.), Changle Rd., Shaanxi Rd., Shaanxi South, Shaanxi Rd. (S.), Central Jianguo Rd., Xiangyang Park, Xiangyang Rd. (N.), Yongkang Rd., Yongjia Rd., Taiyuan Rd., Xiangyang Rd. (S.), Central Fuxing Rd., Changshu Rd., Central Wulumuqi Rd., Yueyang Rd., Fuxing Rd. (W.), Shanghai Library, Central Huaihai Rd., Hengshan Rd., International Cathedral, Yongjia Rd., Gaoan Rd., Kangping Rd., Hengshan Rd., Wanping Rd., Hunan Rd., Wukang Rd., Yuqing Rd.

1/4 mi
1/4 km

Fodor's Choice ★ **James Cohan Gallery.** The Shanghai outpost of the New York Gallery of the same name brings in big-name international artists like Fred Tomaselli as well as rising Chinese stars. Inside an old house and backed by a large, verdant garden, the gallery space has beautiful hardwood floors, big windows, and a lovely oak banister. ⊠ *Bldg. 1, 170 Yueyang Lu, French Concession* ☎ *021/5466–0825* ⊕ *www.jamescohan.com* ⊙ *Closed Mon.*

Soong Qing-ling's Former Residence (故居的宋庆龄 *Gùjū de Sòng Qìnglíng*). A daughter of the prominent Soong family, Soong Qing-ling (also known as Madame Sun Yat-sen) was first a Nationalist and then a Communist. Her sister Mei-ling married Chiang Kai-shek, who was the head of the Nationalist government from 1927 to 1949. This three-story house, built in 1920 by a German ship owner, was Soong's primary residence from 1948 to 1963. It has been preserved as it was during her lifetime; in the study are her 4,000 books and, in the bedroom, the furniture that her parents gave as her dowry. The small museum next door has some nice displays from Soong Qing-ling and Sun Yat-sen's life, including pictures from their 1915 wedding in Tokyo. ⊠ *1843 Huaihai Zhong Lu, French Concession* ☎ *021/6437–6268* ⊕ *www.shsoongchingling.com* ⊠ *Y20* ⊙ *Daily 9–4:30.*

WORTH NOTING

Cathay Theatre (国泰电影院 *Guótài diànyǐngyuàn*). The Art Deco–style Cathay Cinema was one of the first movie theaters in Shanghai. The building still serves as a theater, showing a mix of Chinese and Western films. The theater was a favorite of Shanghainese author Eileen Chang, of *Lust, Caution* fame. ⊠ *870 Huaihai Zhong Lu, at Maoming Nan Lu, French Concession* ☎ *021/5404–0415* ⊕ *www.guotaifilm.com.*

Lyceum Theatre (兰新大戏院 *Lánxīn dàxìyuàn*). In the days of Old Shanghai, the Lyceum Theatre was the home of the British Amateur Drama Club. The old stage is still in use as a concert hall. On the second floor is O Theatre, a quiet cocktail and Champagne bar open even when shows aren't on. ⊠ *57 Maoming Nan Lu, French Concession* ☎ *021/6217–8530.*

FAMILY **Tianzifang** (田子坊 *Tiánzi fāng*). If Xintiandi is the government's orderly, sanitized *shikumen* restoration project, Tianzifang is the opposite. The former residential district is a labyrinth of alleyways between redbrick lane houses. Shops, restaurants, cafés, and a few galleries fill the spaces today. There are shops selling everything from the now-ubiquitous Obamao T-shirts to leather journals and shoes, tea, and qipao dresses. ■ TIP→ You can also enter Tianzifang from the back side, at 155 Jianguo Zhong Lu. ⊠ *Enter at 210 or 248 Taikang Lu, between Ruijin Er and Sinan Lu, French Concession.*

JING'AN AND CHANGNING

Shanghai's glitziest malls are on or near the main street in this area, Nanjing Xi Lu. If you're into designer threads, luxury spas, or expensive brunches, you can satisfy your spending urges and max out your credit here. For those of a more spiritual bent, Jing'an Temple, which is as gilded as its surroundings, is one of Shanghai's largest temples and

stands in sharp contrast to its materialistic neighbors. The small Jing'an Park across the street is popular with couples. Behind the temple is an interesting network of back streets. Sandwiched between Hongqiao, Gubei, and Jing'an is Changning District, which has a number of quiet, very local neighborhoods alongside commercial hubs.

GETTING AROUND

Sights are thin in this area, but if you like international designer labels, this is where you can work the plastic, albeit at a huge markup from prices you'd find in the States. Metro Line 2 takes you to the Nanjing Xi Lu stations, and Lines 2 and 7 take you to **Jing'an Temple.** To wander the small streets behind Jing'an Temple, take Line 7 to Changshou Lu station and walk south. If you want to take a taxi afterward, joining the line at the Shanghai Centre/Portman Ritz-Carlton is a good idea, especially when it's raining.

EXPLORING

Jing'an Temple (静安寺 *Jìng'ān sì*). Originally built about AD 300, this temple has had a tumultuous history of destruction and rebuilding, with a brief stint as a plastics factory during the Cultural Revolution. What you see today dates to the 1980s. The temple's main draw is its copper Hongwu bell, cast in 1183 and weighing 3.5 tons. The gilded temple, on one of Shanghai's busiest thoroughfares, is an interesting contrast to the surrounding skyscrapers, shopping malls, and luxury boutiques. ⊠ *1686 Nanjing Xi Lu, next to the Jing'an Si subway entrance, Jing'an* ☎ *021/6256–6366* ⊲ *Y30* ⊙ *Daily 7:30–5.*

Moller Villa (马勒别墅饭店 *Mǎ lēi biéshù*). Built by Swedish shipping magnate Eric Moller in 1936, this massive villa resembles a fairy-tale castle. It's a surprising sight when you come down from the pedestrian bridge that leads from Jing'an into the French Concession. Inside is a rather gaudy hotel. ⊠ *30 Shaanxi Nan Lu, Jing'an* ☎ *021/6247–8881* ⊕ *www.mollervilla.com.*

Paramount (百樂門 *Bǎilèmén*). Built in 1933, the Paramount was considered the finest dance hall in Asia. Until 1949, the so-called "Gate of 100 Pleasures" was the place for very late, very wild nights. After the Communist Revolution, Paramount closed and reopened as Red Capitol Cinema, showing propaganda films. In 2001, it again became a dance hall, with disco balls reflecting light on its storied floor. You'll still find ballroom dancers here, but it's a much more chaste affair with an older crowd, though anyone is welcome to step on to the floor and ask for a dance. Come nightfall, the domed roof glows blue. ⊠ *218 Yuyuan Lu, Jing'an* ☎ *021/6249–8866.*

PUDONG

Shanghai residents used to say that it was better to have a bed in Puxi than an apartment in Pudong, but the neighborhood has come a long way in recent years. It's now a futuristic city of wide boulevards and towering skyscrapers topped by the Shanghai World Financial Center, fondly referred to as "the bottle-opener." Apartments here are some of the most expensive in Shanghai. Although a little on the bland side, it is home to expat compounds designed in a bizarre medley of architectural styles, international schools, and malls. However, there are a few sites here worth visiting, particularly if you have children.

GETTING AROUND

The Bund Tourist Tunnel is a strange and rather garish way of making the journey under the Huangpu River to Pudong. You might get a few laughs from the light displays. Otherwise, you can take the metro on Line 2 to Lujiazui, or catch the ferry from the Bund.

Outside of the Lujiazui metro stop and Century Park, Pudong is not a pedestrian-friendly area, as there are large, rather featureless distances between the sights. You can either take the metro to get around or jump in a cab. If you visit all the sights, you could easily spend a day out here.

TOP ATTRACTIONS

21st Century Minsheng Art Museum (21世纪民生现代美术馆 *21 Shìjì mínshēng xiàndài měishùguǎn*). Like the Power Station of Art, this sleek new museum is located on the site of Shanghai's 2010 World Expo. The museum takes its name from its sponsor, Minsheng Bank, which opened it to showcase contemporary art in all mediums, from photography to sound, by artists from China and beyond. The museum is housed in the former French expo pavilion. It is walking distance from China Art Palace. ⊠ *1929 Shibo Dadao (Expo Ave.), just off Expo Park, Pudong*

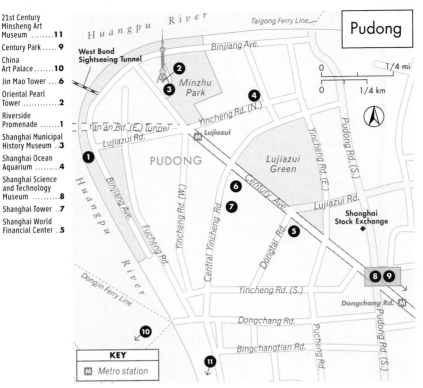

☎ *021/6105–2121* ⊕ *www.21msms.com* ✉ *Free* ⊙ *Last entrance 5:30 pm* ⊙ *Closed Mon.*

Jin Mao Tower (金茂大厦 *Jīnmào dàshà*). Rising 88 floors—eight being the Chinese number implying wealth and prosperity—this tower combines the classic 13-tier Buddhist pagoda design with postmodern steel and glass. It houses one of the highest hotels in the world—the Grand Hyatt Shanghai occupies the 53rd to 87th floors. The 88th-floor observation deck, reached in 45 seconds by two high-speed elevators, offers 360-degree views of the city. ■TIP➔ **Skip the line and instead spend what you would've shelled out for a ticket to the observation deck at the 87th-floor Cloud 9 bar.** ⊠ *88 Shiji Dadao (Century Ave.), Pudong* ☎ *021/5047–0088* ✉ *Observation deck Y100* ⊙ *Daily 8 am–10 pm.*

Oriental Pearl Tower (东方明珠塔 *Dōngfāng míngzhūtǎ*). Looking like a stucture straight out of *The Jetsons*, the Oriental Pearl Tower was built when much of Pudong was still farmland. It's especially kitschy at night when it flashes with colored lights. A museum in the base recalls Shanghai's pre-1949 history. Each with its own observation deck, the three spheres are supposed to represent pearls (as in the city's nickname, the "Pearl of the Orient"). Go to the top sphere for a 360-degree bird's-eye view of the city, or grab a drink in the tower's revolving restaurant (skip the food). ⊠ *1 Shiji Dadao (Century Ave.), Pudong*

☎ *021/5879–1888* ⊕ *www.orientalpearltower.com/en* 🚇 *Y100–Y150* ⊙ *Daily 8 am–9:30 pm.*

FAMILY **Shanghai Municipal History Museum** (上海市历史博物馆 *Shànghǎi shì lìshǐ bówùguǎn*). This impressive museum in the base of the Pearl Tower recalls Shanghai's pre-1949 history. Inside, you can stroll down a re-created Shanghai street circa 1900 or check out a streetcar that used to operate in the concessions. Dioramas depict battle scenes from the Opium Wars, shops found in a typical turn-of-the-20th-century Shanghai neighborhood, and grand Former French Concession buildings of yesteryear. ✉ *1 Shiji Dadao (Century Ave.), Pudong* ☎ *021/5879–1888* ⊕ *historymuseum.sh.cn* 🚇 *Y35* ⊙ *Daily 8 am–9 pm.*

Shanghai Tower (上海中心大厦 *Shànghǎi zhōngxīn dàshà*). When Shanghai Tower opens in the summer of 2015, it will be the country's tallest structure and the second tallest in the world (beat out by the Burj Khalifa in Dubai). The 121-story building stands more than 2,000 feet tall and houses a hotel, offices, and shops, with more than 100 elevators to serve them all. Its sky-high observation decks promise to be among the world's tallest. ✉ *Near Fucheng Lu and Lujiazui Xi Lu, Pudong.*

Shanghai World Financial Center (上海环球金融中心 *Shànghǎi huánqiú jīnróng zhōngxīn*). The iconic "bottle opener" has three observation decks, the highest of which is on the 100th floor. The Park Hyatt is housed on floors 79 to 93, giving it a loftier perch than its older sibling, the neighboring Grand Hyatt. The view from up here is a knockout; on a clear day, you can see far and wide; on an overcast day, you'll feel as though you're floating in the clouds. ■TIP→ **Consider skipping the observation decks in favor of the hotel. Afternoon tea at the 87th-floor Living Room is a treat.** ✉ *100 Shiji Dadao (Century Ave.), Pudong* ☎ *021/5878–0101* ⊕ *www.swfc-observatory.com* 🚇 *Y120– Y150* ⊙ *Daily 8 am–11 pm.*

WORTH NOTING

FAMILY **Century Park** (世纪公园 *Shìjì gōngyuán*). If you're staying in Pudong, this giant swath of green is a great place to take kids, as it has a variety of bicycles for hire, good flat paths for rollerblading, and pleasure boats. On a nice day, pack a lunch and head to the designated picnic areas, fly a kite in the open areas, or take a walk among the trees. ✉ *Huamu Lu, near Fangdian Lu, Pudong* ⊕ *www.centurypark.com. cn* 🚇 *Y10* ⊙ *Daily 7–6.*

Fodor's Choice ★ **China Art Palace** (中华艺术宫 *Zhōnghuá yìshù gōng*). Housed inside the China Pavilion at the Shanghai World Expo site, this gleaming homage to contemporary art has a whopping 27 exhibition halls. Much of the work is underwhelming, but be sure to stop by the animation hall, where you can catch shorts and feature-length films from the '50s to the '90s. The touring exhibits are often a real treat; besides a huge Picasso retrospective, the museum has hosted works from New York's Whitney Museum, London's British Museum, and Paris's Maisons de Victor Hugo. Look for works from David Hockney, Jasper Johns, and Rodin. Reservations are required, and your hotel should be able to help. ✉ *161 Shangnan Lu, Pudong* ☎ *021/6222–8822* ⊕ *artshow.eastday.*

com/zhysg 🖼 *Free; audio guides Y20 (with Y200 deposit)* 🕐 *Tues.–Sun. 9–5; last entry at 4.*

Riverside Promenade (滨江大道 *Bīnjiāng dàdào*). Although this park along the Huangpu River has a sterile atmosphere, it offers the most beautiful views of the Bund. As you stroll on the grass and concrete you get a perspective of Puxi unavailable from the west side. If you're here in the summer, you can "enjoy wading," as a sign indicates, in the chocolate-brown Huangpu River from the park's wave platform. ⊠ *Bingjiang Dadao, Pudong* 🖼 *Free.*

FAMILY **Shanghai Ocean Aquarium** (上海海洋水族馆 *Shànghǎi hǎiyáng shuǐzúguǎn*). As you stroll through the aquarium's 120-meter (394-foot) glass viewing tunnel, you may feel like you're walking your way through the seven seas—or at least five of them. The aquarium's 10,000 fish represent 300 species, five oceans, and four continents. You'll also find penguins and species representing all 12 of the Chinese zodiac symbols, such as the tiger barb, sea dragon, and seahorse. ■ TIP → **To avoid crushing crowds, do not visit on weekends or during school holidays.** ⊠ *1388 Lujiazui Ring Lu, Pudong* 📞 *021/5877–9988* ⊕ *www.sh-soa. com* 🖼 *Y160* 🕐 *Daily 9–6.*

FAMILY **Shanghai Science and Technology Museum** (上海科技馆 *Shànghǎi kējìguǎn*). This family favorite has more than 100 hands-on exhibits in its sprawling galleries. Earth Exploration takes you through fossil layers to the Earth's core for a lesson in plate tectonics. Spectrum of Life introduces you to the animal and plant kingdoms in a simulated rain forest. Light of Wisdom explains basic principles of light and sound through interactive exhibits, and simulators in AV Paradise put you in a plane's cockpit and on television. Children's Technoland has a voice-activated fountain and a miniature construction site. Two IMAX theaters and a "4-D" IWERKS theater screen larger-than-life movies, though some are in Chinese. All signs are in English. ■ TIP → **Avoid visiting on weekends and during school holidays or prepare to face massive crowds.** ⊠ *2000 Shiji Dadao (Century Ave.), Pudong* 📞 *021/6854–2000* ⊕ *www.sstm. org.cn* 🖼 *Y60* 🕐 *Tues.–Sun. 9–5:15.*

HONGKOU AND PUTUO

Although often neglected in favor of more glamorous neighborhoods, the northern Shanghai districts of Putuo and Hongkou offer interesting sites and shouldn't be ignored.

Hongkou District is relatively undeveloped and unchanged, and buildings from the past are visible behind cheap clothing stores. Shanghai's old Jewish Quarter is here, too. An area with an interesting history, Hongkou has the most sights worth seeing, as well as the lush green sweep of Lu Xun Park.

In Putuo, the old buildings and warehouses around Suzhou Creek, which feeds into the Huangpu, are slowly being turned into a hip and happening artsy area, particularly the M50 development. Also in Putuo District is another one of Shanghai's main temples, the Jade Buddha

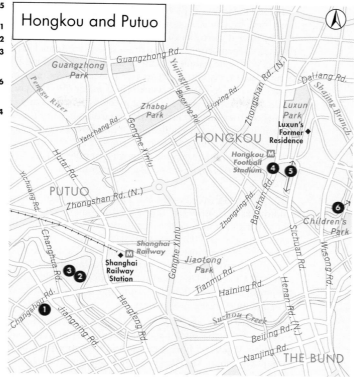

Temple, which is an easy walk from Jing'an, the district just to the south.

GETTING AROUND

For the Jade Buddha Temple and M50, you can hop off the metro Line 3 or 4 at Zhongtan Lu, and then it's a short walk to M50 and a longer one to Jade Buddha. You can take Line 3 to Dongbaoxing Lu and Hongkou Stadium for Lu Xun Park and Duolun Lu. The easiest way to get around is by taxi or on foot.

The galleries at M50 open later in the morning, so it may be best to head to some other sites first. All galleries are closed on Monday and some on Tuesday.

EXPLORING

Duolun Lu (多伦文化街 *Duōlún wénhuà jiē*). Although this road has been heavily restored, its architecture and general ambience takes you back in time to the 1930s, when the 1-km (½-mile) lane was a favorite haunt of writer Lu Xun and fellow social activists. Bronze statues of those literary luminaries dot the lawns between the villas and row houses whose ground floors are now home to cafés, antiques shops, and art galleries. As the street takes a 90-degree turn, its architecture shifts 180 degrees with the seven-story stark gray Shanghai Duolun Museum of Modern Art. ⊠ *Off Sichuan Bei Lu, Hongkou.*

Jade Buddha Temple (玉佛寺 *Yùfó sì*). Completed in 1918, this temple is fairly new by Chinese standards. During the Cultural Revolution, the monks pasted portraits of Mao Zedong on the outside walls so that the Red Guards couldn't tear them down without destroying Mao's face as well. The temple is built in the style of the Song Dynasty, with symmetrical halls and courtyards, upturned eaves, and bright yellow walls. The temple's great treasure is its 2-meter (6½-foot) seated Buddha made of white jade with a robe of precious gems, originally brought to Shanghai from Burma. Frightening guardian gods of the temple populate the halls, home to a collection of Buddhist scriptures and paintings. The temple is madness at festival times. ■TIP→ **There's a simple vegetarian restaurant serving inexpensive noodle dishes.** ✉ *170 Anyuan Lu, Putuo* ☎ *021/6266–3668* ⊕ *www.yufotemple.com* 🎫 *Y30* ⏰ *Daily 8:30–4:30.*

M50 (莫干山路 *Mògànshān lù*). This cluster of art galleries and artist studios, inside a sprawling former textile mill, sits beside Suzhou Creek. The galleries are filled almost exclusively with work by Chinese artists, but a few, like m97 Gallery, showcase foreign work. There are also a few shops selling music and art supplies and a couple of coffee shops. Don't be shy about nosing around—occasionally artists will be up for a chat. ■TIP→ **Mind the weather, as some of galleries lack heating and cooling systems.** ✉ *50 Moganshan Lu, Putuo* 🎫 *Free* ⏰ *Most galleries closed Mon. Opening times vary.*

m97 Gallery (m97画廊 *M97 huàláng*). More spacious and slightly removed from the rest of the M50 galleries, m97 specializes in photography. Works by both Chinese and foreign artists, like Dutch photographer Robert Van Der Hilst and German artist Michael Wolf are on display here. Wolf's "Life in Cities" series may be of particular interest to urbanites who have experienced the claustrophobia of city life. Tucked inside the gallery is a nook of enticing photography books for sale. ✉ *97 Moganshan Lu near Aomen Lu, 2nd fl., Putuo* ☎ *021/6266–1597.*

Ohel Moishe Synagogue and Huoshan Park (摩西会堂 *Móxī huìtáng*). Built in 1927, this synagogue, the spiritual center of Shanghai's Jewish ghetto in the '30s and '40s, now houses the Jewish Refugee Memorial Hall of Shanghai. More than 20,000 Central European refugees fled to Shanghai during World War II, and the museum has a good selection of photos and newspaper clippings. Around the corner is Huoshan Park, where a memorial tablet has been erected in honor of Israeli prime minister Yitzhak Rabin's 1993 visit. ✉ *62 Changyang Lu, Hongkou* ☎ *021/6541–5008* 🎫 *Y50* ⏰ *Mon.–Sat. 9–5.*

Shanghai Duolun Museum of Modern Art (上海多伦现代美术馆 *Shànghǎi duōlún xiàndài měishùguǎn*). Covering more than 14,400 square feet, Shanghai's first state-owned modern art gallery wraps around a metal spiral staircase that's a work of art in itself. The frequently changing exhibits are cutting-edge for Shanghai. They've showcased electronic art from American artists, examined gender issues among the Chinese people, and featured musical performances ranging from Chinese electronica to the *dombra,* a traditional Kazak stringed instrument. A tiny

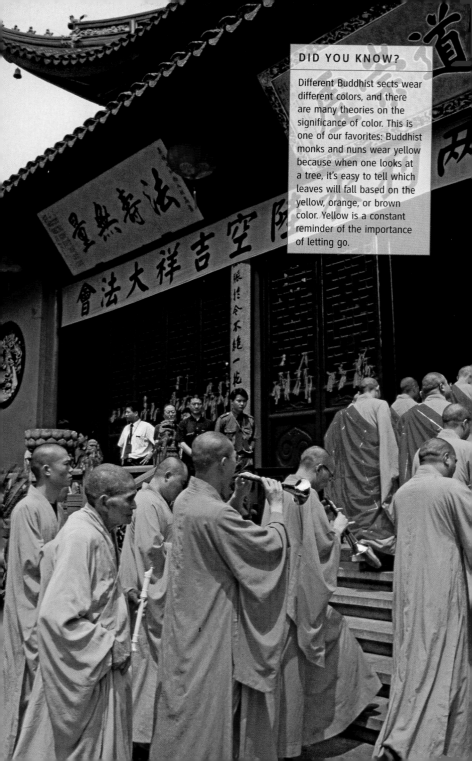

shop sells art books. ⊠ *27 Duolun Lu, Hongkou* ☎ *021/6587–2530* 🖃 *Y20* ⊗ *Sun.–Tues. 10–5.*

XUJIAHUI, HONGQIAO, AND GUBEI

Buyers throng the large malls in the shopping precinct at Xujiahui, which shines with neon and giant billboards. To the west are the districts of Hongqiao and Gubei, where expats live in high-walled compounds and drive huge SUVs. If you're feeling homesick, a visit to Hongmei Lu and its string of Western restaurants will do the trick.

GETTING AROUND

Metro Line 1 takes you right into the depths of the Grand Gateway Mall at Xujiahui. The other sights are fairly far-flung, so a taxi is a good idea. If you are going to places like the Shanghai Botanical Gardens, be prepared for a hefty fare. Otherwise, you can get off at Shanghai South Railway Station.

EXPLORING

Longhua Martyrs Cemetery (龙华烈士陵园 *Lónghuá lièshì língyuán*). It may seem tranquil now, but Longhua Martyrs Cemetery has had a bloody history. It has been the execution site of many Communists, particularly during the Guomingdang crackdown in 1927. Nowadays, it's full of large Soviet-style sculpture and immaculate lawns. The most chilling is the small, unkempt, grassy execution area accessed by a tunnel. In the 1950s, the remains of murdered Communists were found here still wearing leg irons. ⊠ *180 Longhua Xi Lu, Xujiahui* ☎ *021/6468–5995* ⊕ *www.slmmm.cn* 🖃 *Park Y1, museum Y5* ⊗ *Daily 6–5; museum 9–3:30.*

Longhua Temple (龙华寺 *Lónghúa sì*). Shanghai's largest and most active temple has as its centerpiece a seven-story, eight-sided pagoda. While the temple, which made a cameo in Spielberg's *Empire of the Sun,* is thought to have been built in the 3rd century, the pagoda dates from the 10th century; it's not open to visitors. Near the front entrance stands a three-story bell tower, where a 3.3-ton bronze bell is rung at midnight every Lunar New Year's Eve. Along the side corridors you'll find a room filled seven rows deep with small golden statues. The third hall is the most impressive. Its three giant Buddhas sit beneath a swirled red and gold dome. ⊠ *2853 Longhua Lu, Xujiahui* ☎ *021/6456–6085, 021/6457–6327* 🖃 *Y10* ⊗ *Daily 7–4:30.*

St. Ignatius Cathedral (聖依納爵主教座堂 *Shèngyī nà jué zhǔjiào zuò táng*). Just a hop from the traffic-clogged roads surrounding Xujiahui metro station and its periphery of malls is this Neo-Gothic Roman Catholic cathedral, which opened in 1910. In 1966, with the start of the Cultural Revolution, its beautiful stained-glass windows, the ceiling, and spires were destroyed by the Red Guards. The church spent the next 10 years as a state-owned grain warehouse. Finally, in the 1980s, the cathedral was restored; today it remains the headquarters of the Roman Catholic Diocese of Shanghai. ⊠ *158 Puxi Lu, Xujiahui* ☎ *21/6441–2211* ⊗ *Sat. 1–6, Sun. 2–4; Mass is held daily at 6:15 am and 7 pm.*

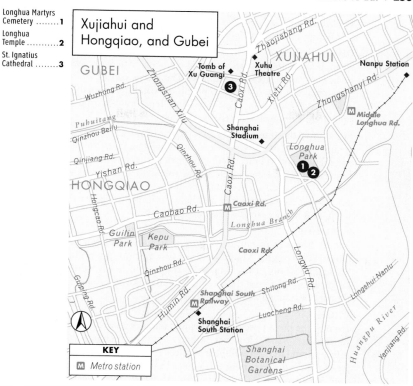

WHERE TO EAT

You'll notice that most Chinese restaurants in Shanghai have large, round tables. The reason becomes clear the first time you eat a late dinner at a local restaurant and are surrounded by jovial, laughing groups of people toasting and topping off from communal bottles of beer, sharing cigarettes, and spinning the lazy Susan loaded with food. Whether feting guests or demonstrating their wealth, hosts will order massive, showy spreads.

Shanghai's standing as China's most international city is reflected in its dining scene. You can enjoy *jiaozi* (dumplings) for breakfast, foie gras for lunch, and Korean beef for dinner. In many restaurants, it's traditional to order several dishes to share among your party for family-style dining. Tipping is not expected, but more upmarket restaurants will tack on a 10–15% service charge. Although you can eat at Chinese restaurants for less than Y50 per person, Western meals go for Western prices.

Some restaurants in Shanghai offer set lunches at a fraction of the dinner price. Check out the dining section of *City Weekend, That's Shanghai, Time Out Shanghai,* or Smartshanghai.com, all of which list dining discounts and promotions around town.

Use the coordinates (✛ B2) at the end of each listing to locate a site on the Where to Eat in Shanghai map.

ON THE MENU

Shanghainese food is fairly typical Chinese, with dark, sweet, and oily dishes served in great abundance. The plates can be quite small—it's not unusual for two diners to polish off six different dishes. The drink of choice is *huangjiu*, or yellow wine. It's a mild-tasting sweetish rice wine that pairs well with the local cuisine.

Sometimes the finest dining experience in the city can be had with a steamer basket of *xiaolongbao*—Shanghai's signature dumplings, which are small steamed buns filled with pork (or crabmeat) in broth. They're best eaten by poking a hole in the top with a chopstick—watch out, they're hot!—and sucking out the innards. Pair dumplings with a cold beer. River fish is often the highlight (and most expensive part) of the meal, and hairy crab is a seasonal delicacy.

MEAL TIMES

Dinner hours in restaurants begin at around 5 pm, but often carry on late into the night. Many of the classic restaurants popular with the Shanghainese only close after the last diners have left, which sometimes keeps them open until the wee hours of the morning. Generally, though, dinner is eaten between 6 and 11 pm.

PRICES

Even in the most upscale restaurants, main courses are unlikely to cost more than US$60. However, famous restaurants charge as much as the international market will bear—prices that often don't reflect the quality of the dining experience. If you're looking for an excellent meal and you don't care about the restaurateur's name, then exceptional dining experiences can be had for half the price.

On the street, local food can be found for supremely cheap prices (starting at less than $1 per dish). Tiny curb-side restaurants will charge slightly more. The experience of eating at a small, unknown restaurant is pure China.

SERVICE

Outside of hotel restaurants, service ranges from not great to very poor. This is not a tipping culture, so there is little incentive to perform. Keep this in mind when you're on a tight schedule.

WHAT IT COSTS IN YUAN			
	$	$$	$$$	$$$$
Restaurants	under Y100	Y100–Y150	Y151–Y200	over Y200

Restaurant prices are the average cost of a main course at dinner or, if dinner is not served, at lunch.

Cheap snacks can be found on the streets around the Old City.

OLD CITY

Narrow and crowded, the Old City is all that's left of Old China in Shanghai. The area is home to the impressive Yu Garden, and is a good place to find traditional street food. Adventurous diners should explore the side streets around Fangbang Lu in search of authentic Chinese snacks. **TIP→ At this neighborhood's eateries, with no English menu, many sellers are going to charge you the foreigner price. Unless you speak Chinese and can ask for and understand the price, be prepared to pay more than the locals. Make sure you know the price before you take a bite, even if that means for it to be written down.**

$$ TAIWANESE FAMILY 🍴 **Din Tai Fung** (鼎泰豐 *Dǐngtàifēng*). The delicate, impeccably folded *xiaolongbao* (soup dumplings) are the star attraction, and the pork and black truffle version is especially delectable. The atmosphere at this Taiwanese chain is far less chaotic than at its neighbors in and around Yu Garden, and it also has much better food. The service is very good, especially for those with children; the staff will fawn over your offspring and immediately bring over a high chair and kid-sized tableware. [$] *Average main: Y110* ✉ *168 Fangbang Zhong Lu, Old City* ☎ *021/6334–1008* ✣ *F3* [$] *Average main: Y110* ✉ *Super Brand Mall, 168 Lujiazui Xi Lu, 3rd fl., Lujiazui* ☎ *021/5047–8883* ✣ *F3.*

$$ CHINESE 🍴 **Lu Bo Lang** (绿波廊 *Lǜbōláng*). A popular stop for visiting dignitaries, Lu Bo Lang makes for a great photo op. The traditional three-story Chinese pavilion with upturned eaves sits next to the Bridge of Nine Turnings in Yu Garden. The food is good but not great, with many expensive fish choices on the menu. Among the best dishes are the crabmeat with bean curd, the braised eggplant with chili sauce, and

the sweet *osmanthus* cake, made with the sweetly fragrant flower of the same name. $ *Average main: Y150* ⊠ *115 Yuyuan Lu, Old City* ☎ *021/6328–0602* ⌕ *Reservations essential* ✢ *F3*.

XINTIANDI AND CITY CENTER

$$$ ✕ **The 5 Tables Bistro** (5桌餐厅 *5 Zhuō cāntīng*). This restaurant is small
EUROPEAN   in size but packs in plenty of personality. The friendly Singaporean owner is the sole waiter, yet no water glass goes unfilled; the service here puts fully staffed restaurants to shame. The menu is just one sheet of paper and on offer are one soup, one starter, a few mains, and two desserts. Dishes change frequently, so one week, if you're lucky, you'll be slurping up bacon potato soup; another will find you tucking eagerly into seared scallops paired with caper sauce and a vegetable puree. $ *Average main: Y175* ⊠ *210 Danshui Lu, City Center* ☎ *021/3304–1205* ⌕ *Reservations essential* ✢ *D4*.

$$$$ ✕ **Coquille.** Just south of Xintiandi is this lovely French restaurant, where
FRENCH   the scent of butter and brine waft from the kitchen. The brainchild of Californian banker-turned-restaurateur John Liu, Coquille occupies the space that was previously his mother's Vietnamese restaurant. The interior was completely overhauled, and diners now tuck into platters of seafood and slurp French onion soup seated in brasserie chairs at white marble- and dark wood-topped tables. If you can't get a table, grab a seat at the bar and watch the frenetic concocting of cocktails. $ *Average main: Y220* ⊠ *29-31 Mengzi Lu, near Xujiahui Lu, City Center* ☎ *021/3376–8127* ⌕ *Reservations essential* ☾ *Closed Mon. No lunch* ✢ *D5*.

$ ✕ **Jia Jia Tang Bao** (佳家汤包 *Jiā jiā tāng bāo*). It would be a shame to
CHINESE   leave Shanghai without trying xiaolongbao, and locals flock here in
FAMILY   droves for what are said to be the best in town. Soup dumplings are the only thing on the menu, and once the kitchen runs out the restaurant shuts down for the day. It's a proper local hole-in-the-wall, with orange plastic chairs and grimy tabletops and floors, but eating here is an authentic and delicious experience not to be missed. $ *Average main: Y20* ⊠ *90 Huanghe Lu, City Center* ☎ *021/6327–6878* ▭ *No credit cards* ☾ *No dinner* ✢ *E3*.

$ ✕ **Kabb.** Serving burgers, salads, and other standard American fare, this
AMERICAN   café in Xintiandi is best known for its outdoor seating. The food is good but without distinction, though the portions are large. The service is slightly indifferent, and the prices are rather high. However, it does fit the bill for lunch in the sun. $ *Average main: Y95* ⊠ *181 Taicang Lu, Xintiandi* ☎ *021/3307–0798* ✢ *D3*.

$$$$ ✕ **T8** (T 八 *T bā*). A veteran of the Shanghai fine dining scene, T8 has
INTERNATIONAL   garnered its share of headlines for its impressive interior and inspired
Fodor'sChoice   contemporary cuisine. The restaurant occupies a traditional shiku-
★   men house in Xintiandi and has modernized the space with raw stone floors, carved-wood screens, and imaginative lighting that transforms shelves full of glasses into a modern-art sculpture. The kitchen turns out exciting fusion dishes from fresh seasonal ingredients, so the menu changes with the seasons. $ *Average main: Y250* ⊠ *181 Taicang Lu,*

Xintiandi ☎ *021/6355–8999* 🌐 *www.t8shanghai.com* ✍ *Reservations essential* ✥ *D4.*

$$$$ CANTONESE 🍴 **Wan Hao** (万豪 *Wànháo*). Overlooking People's Square, this elegant restaurant on the 38th floor of the JW Marriott Shanghai specializes in Cantonese dishes, though the menu contains other popular options like Peking duck. The food is good without being exceptional, and the ambience is pleasant. Look to the seasonal dishes for the freshest options; the chef is always updating the menu. Servings tend to be on the small side, so expect to order several dishes per person. If you're unsure about your order, the staff is happy to help. As you'd expect, the service here is quite good. [$] *Average main: Y250* ✉ *JW Marriott Shanghai at Tomorrow Sq., 399 Nanjing Xi Lu, 38F, City Center* ☎ *021/5359–4969* 🌐 *www.marriott.com* ✥ *D2.*

4

$$ SHANGHAINESE 🍴 **Xin Jishi.** "New Jesse" is the shiny, clean version of Old Jesse, a popular if slightly run-down Shanghainese restaurant deep in the French Concession. This outpost lacks the old-world charm that the other branch has, but it has more seating and is smack bang in the middle of Xintiandi. You'll have much better luck getting a table here than at the original branch; when you do, try classics like *hongshao rou* (red-braised pork), *bao zai fan* (clay pot rice), and drunken chicken marinated in rice wine. [$] *Average main: Y150* ✉ *Xintiandi North Block, 181 Taicang Lu, Unit 2, No. 9, Xintiandi* ☎ *021/6336–4746* 🌐 *www.xinjishi.com* ✥ *D3.*

$ SICHUAN Fodor's Choice ★ 🍴 **Yu Xin Chuan Cai** (渝信川菜 *Yú xìn chuāncài*). This place offers spicy Sichuan food that is extremely popular with the locals. It's crowded and often quite smoky. Try the tea-smoked duck, and whatever you order, be sure to get rice, too. Book ahead, or be prepared to wait 30 to 60 minutes for a table. The restaurant is inside an office building; take the escalators or the elevator to the third floor. [$] *Average main: Y90* ✉ *Zhaoshangju Sq., 333 Chengdu Bei Lu, 3rd fl., City Center* ☎ *021/5298–0438* ✍ *Reservations essential* ▭ *No credit cards* ✥ *D3.*

THE BUND AND NANJING DONG LU

The Bund is the heart of modern Shanghai, with the colonial history of Puxi facing the towering steel and glass of Pudong. The stellar view of the river and Pudong has attracted some of the finest restaurant development in town. The Bund has been expanding to the south, with the opening of a handful of restaurants. Bund-side eateries are, on the whole, expensive; we've listed places where you're paying not just for the view.

$$ YUNNAN 🍴 **Lost Heaven** (话马天堂 *Huāmǎ tiāntáng*). This place serves Yunnan cuisine—Southern Chinese from the borders of Myanmar (Burma) and Vietnam, with Thai influence as well. The low-lit dining room is romantic, with traditional Yunnanese decor that transports you south to the more exotic province. The service lacks a bit, but it's still a good place for a dinner for two or for a boisterous group night out. This branch has a spacious roof deck that's popular in the summer. There's another location in the middle of the Former French Concession. [$] *Average main: Y150* ✉ *17 Yan'an Dong Lu, The Bund* ☎ *021/6330–0967*

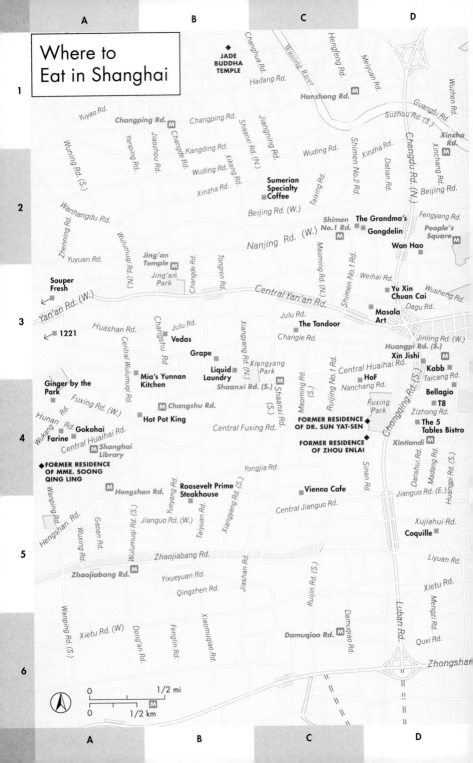

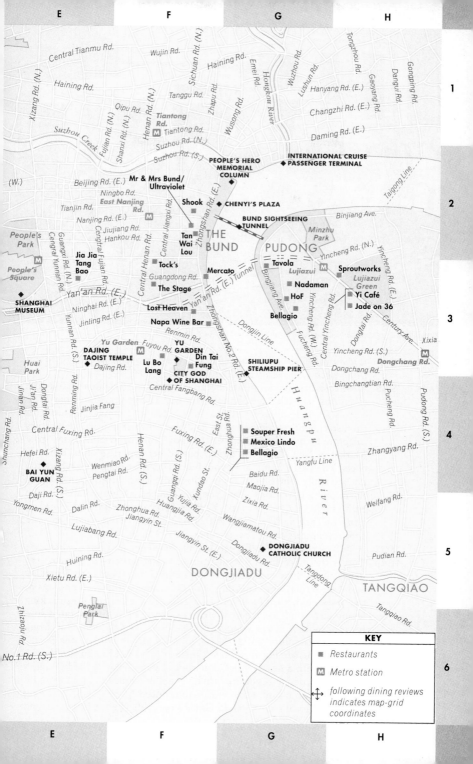

Xintiandi is a great place to hang out and watch the crowds pass by.

🌐 *www.lostheaven.com.cn ✥ F3.* $ *Average main: Y150* ✉ *38 Gaoyou Lu, French Concession* ☎ *021/6433–5126* ✥ *B4.*

$$$$ ITALIAN 🍴 **Mercato.** Prolific restaurateur Jean Georges Vongerichten's namesake restaurant has delighted Shanghai for quite a few years now, but Mercato is a whole different animal. The interior is industrial chic with iron, steel, and reclaimed wood. The black leather and wooden chairs celebrate form and function. Chef Sandy Yoon, who came from Spice Market in New York, has clearly passed her expertise on to her sous chefs. The pasta dishes are good, but the smaller plates are where the kitchen really shines: the octopus is so tender it is gobbled up in seconds, the ricotta and seasonal fruit compote reached for immediately by the entire table. $ *Average main: Y230* ✉ *Three on the Bund, 17 Guangdong Lu, 6th fl., The Bund* ☎ *021/6321–9922* 🌐 *www.jean-georges.com/restaurants/china/shanghai/mercato* ⏲ *No lunch* ✥ *F3.*

$$$$ FRENCH 🍴 **Mr & Mrs Bund** (**先生和小姐外滩的** *Xiānshēng hé xiǎojiě wàitāndé*). This is the place for a late-night bite: Shanghai-famous French chef Paul Pairet's Bund-side eatery is open until 2 am Tuesday to Thursday and 4 am Friday and Saturday. With 32 wines by the glass and inventive dishes like foie-gras crumble, a giant french fry, and lip-smacking lemon tart, you'll leave here more than satisfied. This is a popular spot for proposals. $ *Average main: Y250* ✉ *Bund 18, 18 Zhongshan Dong Yi Lu, 6F, The Bund* ☎ *021/6323–9898* 🌐 *www.mmbund.com* ✥ *F2.*

$$$$ ECLECTIC 🍴 **Napa Wine Bar.** For oenophiles, this is the best of the Bund-side restaurants, with a nearly 4,000 square-foot wine cellar in the building's basement. Luxury goods are heavily taxed in China, and that includes wine, but you'll find a few reasonably priced bottles here, including some from local Shanxi-based Grace Vineyard. The kitchen is helmed

by chef Patrick Dang, formerly of T8, and from it comes inventive dishes such as the carbonara 2013. In it, cuttlefish shavings are used in place of pasta, uni and pollock swapped in for egg and bacon. Dishes are available à la carte, but many diners go in for tasting menus, which offer the best value. $ *Average main: Y280* ✉ *Bund 22, 22 Zhongshan Dong Er Lu, 2F, The Bund* ☎ *021/6318–0057* ⊕ *www.napawinebarandkitchen. com* ⌕ *Reservations essential* ⊙ *No lunch Mon.* ✛ *F3.*

> **WORD OF MOUTH**
>
> "Walked to JiaJia Dumpling. Unfortunately, most dumplings on the menu were sold out already before noon, but the one I wanted was still available—crab and pork. The order found its way to me and I got the most delicious, delicate dumpling I've had in my life." —mmyk72

$$$$ ╳ **The Stage** (舞台餐厅 *Wŭtaí cāntīng*). Although lunch and dinner buf-
ECLECTIC fet is fairly standard stuff, this eatery is home to Shanghai's original
FAMILY gluttonous Sunday Champagne brunch. Costing Y568 (+15%) and booked three to four weeks in advance, the meal has become an insti- tution. Check it out if you feel the need for some decadent indulgence, as you'll feast on crab legs, charcuterie, plate after plate of cakes, and loads of Champagne. It runs from 11:30 to 2:30. $ *Average main: Y568* ✉ *The Westin Shanghai Bund Center, 88 Henan Zhong Lu, The-Bund* ☎ *021/6335–0577* ⊕ *www.starwoodhotels.com* ⌕ *Reservations essential* ✛ *F3.*

$ ╳ **Tock's** (淘客吃 *Táo kè chī*). This Montreal deli stands on a busy
DINER thoroughfare like a lone island of sandwiches in a sea of Chinese food.
FAMILY Proprietor Brian Tock knows a good sandwich—the Montrealer moved to Shanghai with dreams of proper smoked meat, and he has made them come true here. Pastrami is nestled between slices of rye bread and served with the requisite coleslaw, pickle, and homemade fries and this is the only place in Shanghai to get *poutine* (fries smothered in gravy and cheese curds). $ *Average main: Y80* ✉ *221 Henan Zhong Lu, The Bund* ☎ *021/6346–3735* ⊕ *www.tocksdeli.com.cn* ⊙ *Daily 11–10* ✛ *F3.*

$$$$ ╳ **Ultraviolet.** The location of this "experimental restaurant" by Paul
ECLECTIC Pairet (of Mr & Mrs Bund restaurant fame) is a secret. You meet at Mr & Mrs Bund and board a minibus bound for a location somewhere near Suzhou Creek. The 10-seat dining room at Ultraviolet is a world unto itself. Each course is paired with wraparound video projections, an appropriate song (The Beatles' "Ob-La-Di, Ob-La-Da," for example, when Pairet serves his take on fish-and-chips), and even customized scents. A place at the table will cost you a cool Y3,000. Bookings are accepted three months in advance, and you'll need to put down a deposit. $ *Average main: Y3000* ✉ *Mr & Mrs Bund, 18 Zhong-shan Dong Yi Lu, 6F, The Bund* ☎ *021/6142–5198* ⊕ *www.uvbypp. cc/bookings* ⌕ *Reservations essential* ⊙ *Closed Mon. No lunch* ✛ *F2.*

FORMER FRENCH CONCESSION

$ ╳ **Farine.** Deep in the heart of the French Concession is this faithful
BAKERY re-creation of a Parisian pâtisserie. Prices are double, even triple what you'd pay in France; such is the cost of using imported, organic French

flour. If the line out the door doesn't convince you the desserts and pastries here are divine, one bite into a buttery *pan au chocolate* or a creamy raspberry cheesecake will. The coffee is some of Shanghai's best, and what would a croissant be without an accompanying café au lait, anyway? There's one large communal table out front and two free-standing benches; on weekends the small patio is packed to the gills. [$] *Average main: Y45* ✉ *378 Wukang Lu, French Concession* ☎ *021/6433–5798* 🌐 *www.farine-bakery.com* ⊕ *A4.*

$ CAFÉ 🍴 **Ginger by the Park** (金各咖啡 *Jīngé kāfēi*). Tucked away in the Former French Concession, Ginger is a café with a strong European flavor. The servings are small for the price, but the intimate space is a good place for quiet conversations and to relax in the afternoon with a cup of coffee. For a rare tranquil Shanghai moment, have your drinks on the patio. Located in the triangle that forms what many Shanghai denizens refer to as the gay neighborhood, this is a welcoming spot for all. ■ **TIP→ The park next door makes this a good place for families, but narrow spaces and lots of steps make it difficult to bring in strollers.** [$] *Average main: Y75* ✉ *91 Xingguo Lu, near Hunan Lu, French Concession* ☎ *021/3406–0599* 🌐 *www.gingerfoods.com* ⊕ *A4.*

$$ JAPANESE 🍴 **Gokohai** (钰香海 *Yùxiānghaǐ*). Offering solid Japanese hotpot, Gokohai gives each diner a selection of meats (served in enormous, sombrero-shaped piles) and vegetables to cook in a pot full of steaming broth. Ask for the all-you-can-eat-deal for Y128, and wash it down with an Asahi beer. Meat is the star here; vegetarians will likely leave hungry. [$] *Average main: Y128* ✉ *1720 Huaihai Xi Lu, near Wuxing Lu, French Concession* ☎ *021/6471–7657* ✍ *Reservations essential* 💳 *No credit cards* 🕒 *No lunch* ⊕ *A4.*

$ SHANGHAINESE 🍴 **Grape** (葡萄园 *Pútáoyuán*). For Westerners who want to dip a toe into Shanghainese cuisine, Grape offers a convenient downtown location with an English menu, complete with photos. Dotting the menu's pages are such recognizable dishes as sweet-and-sour pork and lemon chicken, as well as delicious dishes like garlic shrimp and *jiachang doufu* (home-style bean curd). [$] *Average main: Y50* ✉ *55 Xinle Lu, French Concession* ☎ *021/5404–0486* 💳 *No credit cards* ⊕ *B3.*

$$$ CHINESE 🍴 **Hot Pot King.** The popular *huoguo,* or hotpot, is an at-the-table cooking method in which you simmer fresh ingredients in a broth. Hot Pot King continues to reign over the hotpot scene in Shanghai because of its extensive menu and refined setting. The most popular of the 17 broths is the yin-yang, half spicy red, half basic white pork-bone broth. Add in a mixture of seafood, meat, vegetables, and dumplings for a well-rounded pot, then dip each morsel in the sauces mixed table-side by your waiter. The minimalist white-and-gray interior has glass-enclosed booths and well-spaced tables, a nice change from the usual crowded, noisy joints. ■ **TIP→ Strict vegetarians won't find much on the menu.** [$] *Average main: Y160* ✉ *1416 Huaihai Lu, 2F, French Concession* ☎ *021/6473–6380* ⊕ *A4.*

$$ MODERN AMERICAN FAMILY 🍴 **Liquid Laundry** (LL创意料理，精酿酒馆 *LL chuàngyì liàolǐ, jīng niàngjiǔ guǎn*). This modern gastropub appeals to families by day and to a trendy party crowd come nightfall. During lunch and brunch, this is a good, if slightly hectic place to dine with kids, but on Friday

and Saturday nights, a DJ turns the spacious restaurant into a thumping club. The well-curated menu runs from moist rotisserie chicken to superb seared yellowtail. Crispy pizzas come straight out of the massive gilded pizza oven to your plate. Much of the beer is brewed in-house, and a rotating selection of craft beers from around the world are on tap. [$] *Average main: Y100* ✉ *Kwah Center, 1028 Huaihai Zhong Lu, 2F, French Concession* ✥ *Entrance is on Donghu Lu, just off of Huaihai; look for bank ICBC* ☎ *021/6445–9589* ✍ *Reservations essential* ✥ *B3.*

$ YUNNAN 🍴 **Mia's Yunnan Kitchen** (香所 *Xiāng suǒ*). A wall of picture windows looks out onto leafy Anfu Lu, so you can watch passersby from this simply furnished dining room. The home-style dishes include pickled mashed potatoes and *ru bing* (rectangles of panfried goat cheese). Wash everything down with a Belgian beer or one of the house juices. One or two staff members speak English. [$] *Average main: Y90* ✉ *45 Anfu Lu, French Concession* ☎ *021/5403–5266* ▭ *No credit cards* ✥ *A3.*

$$$$ STEAKHOUSE Fodor's Choice ★ 🍴 **Roosevelt Prime Steakhouse** (罗斯福顶级牛排馆 *Luósīfú dǐngjí níupaíguǎn*). Located in the historic Marshall Mansion—which was built in 1920 and takes its name from onetime Secretary of State George Marshall—this steak house offers excellent cuts of meat with a clubby ambience. The meat is USDA Prime, cooked to your specification in an imported stone oven. The steaks are not cheap, ranging in price from Y300 up to Y1,200, though regular main dishes are more reasonable. Still, this is an upmarket restaurant, and dinner for two can reach four digits. Try the mac and cheese with black truffles or the excellent Caesar salad. Note that there's a 10% service charge. [$] *Average main: Y500* ✉ *160 Taiyuan Lu, French Concession* ☎ *021/6433–8240* 🌐 *www.rooseveltsteakhouse.com* ⏲ *No lunch* ✥ *B5.*

$$ INDIAN 🍴 **The Tandoor.** Tucked away inside the Jinjiang Hotel, this is a quiet, upmarket Indian restaurant whose prices would shock anyone who's eaten at Indian restaurants in London or New York. That said, the food is excellent and the service, for Shanghai, is quite good. Don't miss the *murgh malai kebab* (tandoori chicken marinated in cheese and yogurt), or the *palak aloo* (spinach with potatoes) or the filling *dal makhani* (lentil curry). Outfitted with mirrors, Indian artwork, lots of carved wood, and Chinese characters dangling from the ceiling, the restaurant is ingeniously designed to show the route of Buddhism from India to China. [$] *Average main: Y125* ✉ *Jinjiang Hotel, South Bldg., 59 Maoming Nan Lu, French Concession* ☎ *021/6472–5494* 🌐 *www.tandoorchina.cn* ⏲ *Closed daily between 2:30 and 5:30 pm* ✥ *C3.*

$$ INDIAN 🍴 **Vedas** (度餐厅 *Dù cāntīng*). The far-too-bright lobby belies the more flatteringly lighted Vedas, where the traditional decor is dark and comfortable. The menu focuses on northern Indian cuisine, and the hand-pulled naan bread, thick and succulent curries, fiery vindaloos, and house-made chutneys are excellent. Vedas is extremely popular, and always bustling. You won't have an intimate, tranquil dining experience, but do expect spectacular food and great service. [$] *Average main: Y100* ✉ *83 Changshu Lu, 3F, French Concession* ☎ *021/6445–8100* 🌐 *www.vedascuisine.com* ✍ *Reservations essential* ✥ *B3.*

$ AUSTRIAN 🍴 **Vienna Café** (维也纳咖啡 *Weíyěnà kāfēi*). Serving up delicious house-made desserts, Vienna Café is a Shanghai institution. This place is definitely not trendy, nor is it trying to be anything other than an Austrian coffeehouse. With a wood-paneled main dining room and a tiny solarium, this is perfect setting for a hearty lunch, a weekend breakfast, or an afternoon coffee break. Indulge yourself with the Sachertorte, and never mind the effects on your waistline. Prices are higher than they would be in Europe, but Vienna Café's ambience is a rarity in the alleged Paris of the East. Ⓢ *Average main: Y95* ✉ *25 Shaoxing Lu, French Concession* ☎ *021/6445–2131* 🚫 *No credit cards* ✛ *C4.*

JING'AN AND CHANGNING

$$ ✕ **1221** (1221餐厅 *Yīrèryī cāntīng*). This stylish but casual eatery is
SHANGHAINESE a favorite with expats. The streamlined dining room is very chic, its crisp white tablecloths contrasting with the warm golden walls. Shanghainese food is the mainstay, with a few Sichuan dishes thrown in for good measure. From the extensive 26-page menu (in English, pinyin, and Chinese), you can order dishes like sliced *you tiao* (fried bread sticks) with shredded beef, a whole chicken in a green-onion soy sauce, and *shaguo shizi tou* (pork meatballs). Ⓢ *Average main: Y150* ✉ *1221 Yanan Xi Lu, Changning* ☎ *021/6213–6585, 021/6213–2441* ✍ *Reservations essential* ✛ *A3.*

$ ✕ **The Grandma's** (外婆家 *Wàipó jiā*). Serving cuisine from neighbor-
CHINESE ing Zhejiang Province, this is the ultimate cheap and cheerful Chinese
FAMILY restaurant. Crowds come for the juicy roast chicken, spicy tofu in chili oil (*mapo doufu*), and wontons bursting with pork and chives. After 6 pm you may have to wait an hour for a table. Its location in a mall, with plenty of room to run around, and the massive menu on which there's something to feed even the pickiest of eaters, make it a great spot for kids. Ⓢ *Average main: Y60* ✉ *818 Mall, 818 Nanjing Xi Lu, 7F, Jing'an* ☎ *021/5239–7225* ✍ *Reservations not accepted* 🚫 *No credit cards* ✛ *D2.*

$$ ✕ **Masala Art** (香料艺术 *Xiāngliào yìshù*). A stalwart of the Shanghai
INDIAN dining scene, Masala Art is a favorite of Indian expats. Come here for excellent breads, sublime curries, and delicious tandoor dishes, all served with a smile. Ⓢ *Average main: Y100* ✉ *397 Dagu Lu, Jing'an* ☎ *021/6327–3571* ✍ *Reservations essential* ✛ *D3.*

$ ✕ **Sumerian Specialty Coffee** (Sumerian精品咖啡 *Sumerian jīngpǐn*
CAFÉ *kāfēi*). Coffee is serious business here, as indicated by the high prices,
FAMILY the variety, and the bags of beans sitting out, but these expert brews are served without a hint of pretension. The popular Kyoto iced coffee is perfect for Shanghai's sweltering summers, and for jetlagged visitors in need of a jolt of caffeine. On the menu are assorted sandwiches, bagels from local purveyor Spread the Bagel, and a few salads. In the dessert case are cookies from local shop Strictly Cookies as well as a few cakes and tarts. Ⓢ *Average main: Y40* ✉ *415 Shaanxi Bei Lu, Jing'an* ☎ *021/135–6475–5689* ⊕ *sumeriancoffee.com* ☾ *No dinner* ✛ *C2.*

Hotpot can be found in almost every city in China.

PUDONG

$
ECLECTIC
FAMILY
✗ **HoF** (巧薈 *Qiǎo huì*). It's a mystery how owner Brian Tan stays so slim with all this tempting chocolate. Desserts are to die for; our pick of the dizzying lot is the orange chocolate mud cake with caramel and sea salt. There are savories on the menu, too, including duck confit and superb salmon rilettes. Ogle the neighboring Oriental Pearl Tower and toast to your fantastic trip with glasses of the well-priced port. $ *Average main: Y65* ⊠ *DBS Tower, B1, 1318 Lujiazui Huan Lu, Pudong* ☎ *021/5010–0800* ⊘ *Closed Sun.* ✛ *G3* $ *Average main: Y65* ⊠ *30 Sinan Lu, French Concession* ☎ *021/6093–2058* ⊘ *No dinner* ✛ *C4.*

$$$$
INTERNATIONAL
Fodor'sChoice
★
✗ **Jade on 36** (翡翠36 *Fěicuì sānshíliù*). This is a restaurant that must be experienced to be believed. Perched on the 36th floor of the Shangri-La, it offers great views of Pudong. Diners can choose from the à la carte menu, whose dishes include foie gras and pan-seared scallops, or from several set menus priced Y758–Y1,388 (not including wine pairings). The food is tops among Shanghai's French eateries, the service impeccable, and the view first-rate. It's an expensive indulgence, but worth every penny. $ *Average main: Y500* ⊠ *Pudong Shangri-La, 33 Fucheng Lu, 36th fl., Pudong* ☎ *021/6882–8888* ⌂ *Reservations essential* ⊘ *No lunch* ✛ *G3.*

$$$$
SUSHI
✗ **Nadaman.** Sleekly elegant and stylized, Nadaman is modern Japanese dining taken to its extreme. The accents of raw granite merged into a formalized designer interior reflect the restaurant's origins in modern Tokyo. With a focus on freshness and presentation, Nadaman gives diners superb cuisine with a price tag to match. The sushi is some of the finest in the city. $ *Average main: Y500* ⊠ *Pudong*

Shangri-La, 33 Fucheng Lu, 2F, Pudong ☏ *021/5888–3768* ⌂ *Reservations essential* ✛ *G2.*

$
DELI
FAMILY
Fodor'sChoice
★

✕ **Sproutworks** (豆苗工坊 *Dòumiáo gōngfāng*). From two American-born Chinese comes a menu of affordable, rotating salads, sandwiches, and sides—in the West, the concept is far from groundbreaking, but there's not yet a single other place like it in Shanghai. It's easy to stay healthy with side dishes like shredded Brussels sprouts with hazelnuts and Parmesan, but the blueberry crumb cake, brownies, and cheesecake are hard to pass up. $ *Average main: Y65* ✉ *Super Brand Mall, B2, 168 Lujiazui Lu, Pudong* ☏ *021/6890–5966* ⊕ *www.sproutworks. com.cn* ✛ *H3* $ *Average main: Y65* ✉ *185 Madang Lu, Xintiandi* ☏ *021/6339–0586* ✛ *H3.*

$$$$
ECLECTIC
FAMILY

✕ **Yi Café** (怡咖啡 *Yí kāfēi*). Serving a world of cuisines, this open-kitchen eatery is very popular with the Lujiazui business set, as well as local diners, for the quality and variety of the food. The amount of food here is staggering—sushi, pasta, curries, tandooris, Peking duck, steak, seafood, sandwiches, a salad bar, and a dessert area that'll delight the young and young at heart. This experience doesn't come cheap, at Y288 for lunch and Y368 for dinner, but if you've got a big appetite, it's worth it. Prices exclude 15% service charge. $ *Average main: Y368* ✉ *Pudong Shangri-La, 33 Fucheng Lu, 2F, Pudong* ☏ *021/6882–8888* ✛ *H3.*

XUJIAHUI, HONGQIAO, AND GUBEI

$
TAIWANESE
FAMILY

✕ **Bellagio** (百乐宫 *Bǎilègōng*). Taiwanese expats pack the dining room of Bellagio, so you know this is an authentic taste of Taiwan. Red fabric–covered chairs and black streamlined tables contrast with the white walls and decorative moldings. Waitresses with short, chic hairstyles move efficiently between the closely spaced tables. The menu includes such traditional entrées as three-cup chicken, as well as 25 noodle dishes spanning all of Southeast Asia. Save room for dessert: shaved-ice snacks are obligatory Taiwanese treats, and come in 14 varieties. The Gubei and Hongqiao branches tend to be filled with Asian expats, while the downtown outlets see more Westerners. $ *Average main: Y90* ✉ *778 Huangjin Cheng Dao, by Gubei Lu, Gubei* ☏ *021/6278–0722* ⌂ *Reservations not accepted* ✛ *G4* $ *Average main: Y90* ✉ *101 Shuicheng Nan Lu, Gubei* ☏ *021/6270–6866* ⊕ *www.bellagiocafe.com.cn* ✛ *G4* $ *Average main: Y90* ✉ *68 Taicang Lu, Xintiandi* ☏ *021/6386–5701* ⊕ *www.bellagiocafe.com.cn* ✛ *D4* $ *Average main: Y90* ✉ *DBS Tower, 1318 Lujiazui Huan Lu, B1, Pudong* ☏ *021/5015–1539* ⊕ *www. bellagiocafe.com.cn* ✛ *G3.*

$
DELI
FAMILY

✕ **Souper Fresh.** When boiled and blanched vegetables and heavy meat dishes become too much, take respite at Souper Fresh, where the prices are reasonable, the salad bar is simple but well stocked, and the desserts are worth saving room for. The atmosphere is eminently casual, and the magazine rack is filled with American and British tabloid magazines. $ *Average main: Y58* ✉ *3213 Hongmei Lu, Hongqiao* ☏ *021/3415–1677* ⊕ *www.souperfresh.com* ✛ *G4* $ *Average main: Y58* ✉ *Bldg. 4, Room 101, 99 Ronghua Xi Lu (behind Dunkin Donuts), Gubei* ☏ *021/3250–8277* ✛ *A3.*

WHERE TO STAY

Shanghai's stature as China's business capital hasn't stopped it from catering both to business and leisure travelers, especially with its handful of boutique hotels. Business hotels can be divided into two categories: modern Western-style hotels with all the latest amenities and older hotels built during the city's glory days. The latter may lack great service, modern fixtures, and convenient facilities, but they may make up for it in charm, tradition, and history.

Judging by the number of international chain hotels in Shanghai, the city has proven just how much it has opened to the outside world. Many aren't merely hotels; they're landmarks on the Shanghai skyline. Even the historic properties that make up the other half of Shanghai's hotel market feel the pressure to update their rooms and facilities.

Shanghai may have an excellent subway system and cheap, plentiful taxis, but if you want to take full advantage of Shanghai's popular tourist sights, restaurants, and nightlife, opt to stay in downtown Puxi, incorporating the quiet, leafy green Former French Concession, the historic promenade of the Bund, and the bustling shopping street of Nanjing Dong Lu. From these neighborhoods you'll have easy access to the rest of Shanghai.

Hotel reviews have been shortened. For full information, visit Fodors.com. Use the coordinates (✣ B2) at the end of each listing to locate a site on the Where to Stay in Shanghai map.

4

RESERVATIONS AND RATES

Increasing competition means there are bargains to be had, especially during the low season from November through March. Avoid traveling during the Golden Week (always the first week of October), when the city is packed and rooms and prices are at a premium. During Chinese New Year (mid-January to mid-February) there are excellent deals to be had and the city is astoundingly quiet; the downside is that *everything* is closed.

Rates quoted may or may not include breakfast, so double check online. All hotel prices listed here are based on high-season rates.

WHAT IT COSTS IN YUAN

	$	$$	$$$	$$$$
Hotels	under Y1,100	Y1,100–Y1,400	Y1,401–Y1,800	over Y1,800

Hotel prices are the lowest cost of a standard double room in high season.

XINTIANDI AND CITY CENTER

$$$$ HOTEL 🏨 **JW Marriott.** For the best views in Puxi, look no further—this futuristic 60-story tower on the edge of People's Square turns heads with its 45-degree twist, which divides the executive apartments below from the 22-story hotel above. **Pros:** fantastic location; great views; unbeatable rooftop pool. **Cons:** exterior is far more contemporary than interiors. [$] *Rooms from: Y1880* ✉ *399 Nanjing Xi Lu, City Center*

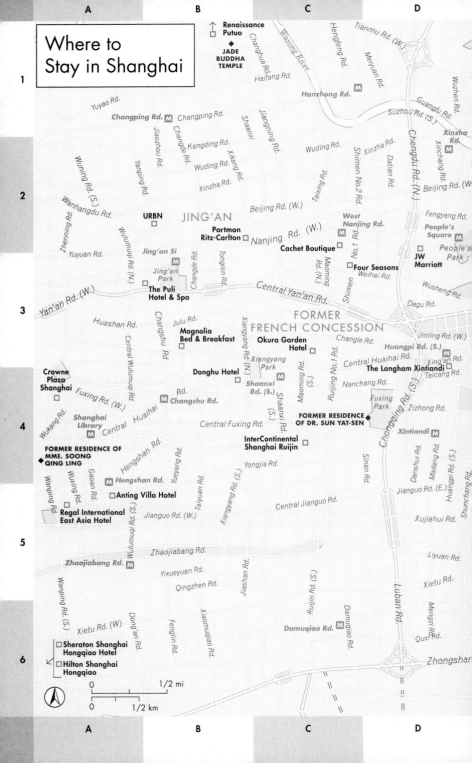

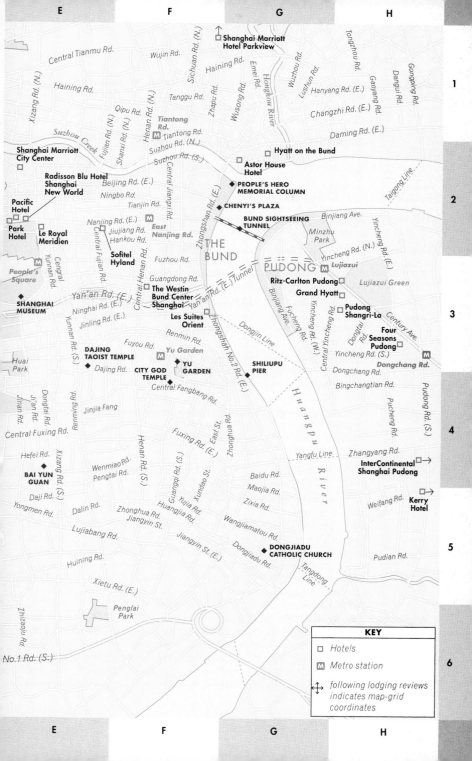

WHERE SHOULD I STAY?

	Neighborhood Vibe	Pros	Cons
Xintiandi and City Center	Xintiandi and People's Square are neighborhoods in City Center. The former has stone houses that have been converted into shops and boutiques; the latter is a large public square and park.	Xintiandi has some lovely and very quiet shaded streets, good restaurant options, and plenty of shopping. People's Square has good metro connections.	The Xintiandi complex lacks authenticity; People's Square is a madhouse.
The Bund and Nanjing Dong Lu	The Bund is quiet at night, and lined with colonial architecture. Nanjing Dong Lu is perfect for people-watching.	Sweeping views from the Bund; walking distance to sites like Xintiandi and Yu Garden; good metro access.	The area is always very crowded and chaotic on weekends.
Former French Concession	Tree-lined streets filled with restaurants, and shops are far calmer than those in other areas.	Quaint and charming streets, crumbling colonial architecture, loads of places to eat and imbibe.	Some hotels are far from the metro; major sites like the Bund are not within walking distance.
Jing'an and Changning	Where local meets expat, tree-lined streets meet traffic-jammed boulevards.	Has a nice traditional feel; plenty of restaurants and bars; good metro access.	Nanjing Xi Lu is packed with pedestrians and traffic.
Pudong	Shiny skyscrapers and office towers; large housing compounds.	Very nice hotels in China's tallest buildings; convenient to the airport; good views of the Bund.	Far from the action, especially restaurants and bars.
Hongqiao	A residential area with clusters of restaurants and malls.	Very close and convenient to Shanghai's domestic airport and main railway station.	There is little to see and do in this neighborhood.

☎ *021/5359–4969, 888/236–2427* ⊕ *www.jwmarriottshanghai.com* ⤳ *305 rooms, 37 suites* ⦿*No meals* ✛ *D3.*

$$$$ 🏨 **The Langham Xintiandi** (新天地朗廷酒店 *Xīntiāndì lǎngtíng jiǔdiàn*).
HOTEL Since it opened, The Langham Xintiandi has been receiving nothing but praise for service that's impeccable without being intrusive and rooms that are big and plush. **Pros:** unbeatable service and location; well-kept pool; modern gym. **Cons:** light sleepers may find street-facing rooms a tad noisy; staff answering the phone often seem a bit confused. ⓢ *Rooms from: Y2000* ⊠ *99 Madang Lu, Xintiandi* ☎ *021/2330–2288* ⊕ *www.xintiandi.langhamhotels.com/info/hotels_in_xintiandi.htm* ⤳ *316 rooms, 41 suites* ⦿*No meals* ✛ *D4.*

$ 🏨 **Pacific Hotel** (金门大酒店 *Jīnmén dàjiǔdiàn*). This 1926 property has
HOTEL done an admirable job of preserving its charm: the marble lobby and the downstairs bar, with leather chairs and photos from 1920s Shanghai, sweep you back to the city's glory days. **Pros:** near People's Park; lots of lovely details; great views. **Cons:** poor service; institutional bathrooms; aging property. ⓢ *Rooms from: Y500* ⊠ *People's Sq., 108 Nanjing Xi*

Lu, City Center ☎ *021/6327–6226* 🛏 *177 rooms, 5 suites* 🍴 *No meals* ⊕ *E2.*

$ HOTEL 🏨 **Park Hotel** (国际饭店 *Guójì fàndiàn*). Once Shanghai's tallest building, the 20-story Park Hotel has long since been eclipsed by other hotels whose glory days are present instead of past. **Pros:** central location; historic property; grand lobby. **Cons:** mixed service; not many amenities. [$] *Rooms from: Y872* ✉ *People's Sq., 170 Nanjing Xi Lu, City Center* ☎ *021/6327–5225* 🛏 *225 rooms, 25 suites* 🍴 *No meals* ⊕ *E2.*

$$ HOTEL 🏨 **Radisson Blu Hotel Shanghai New World** (上海新世界丽笙大酒店 *Shànghǎi xīn shìjièlìshēng dàjiǔdiàn*). A prominent landmark not only on People's Square, but also on the Shanghai skyline, the Radisson Blu is topped by what looks for all the world like a flying saucer. **Pros:** prime location; city views; distinctive architecture. **Cons:** somewhat dated decor; its location makes taxis hard to grab. [$] *Rooms from: Y1350* ✉ *People's Sq., 88 Nanjing Xi Lu, City Center* ☎ *021/6359–9999* 🌐 *www.radisson.com/shanghaicn_newworld* 🛏 *429 rooms, 91 suites* 🍴 *No meals* ⊕ *E2.*

WORD OF MOUTH

"We were really impressed by Shanghai. I expected it to be similar to Hong Kong, and it's definitely not. I loved the vibe of the city—more energetic, youthful, and cutting-edge. I love historic architecture and . . . I expected just a slew of pretty buildings on the Bund and was surprised to find interesting structures, from old to very new, all over Shanghai." —tansmets

THE BUND AND NANJING DONG LU

$$$ HOTEL Fodor's Choice ★ 🏨 **Le Royal Meridien** (上海世茂皇家艾美酒店 *Shìmào huángjiā àiměi jiǔdiàn*). Dominating the foot of the Nanjing Dong Lu pedestrian-only street, Le Royal Meridien has changed the face of Puxi hospitality. **Pros:** central location; excellent facilities; elegant rooms. **Cons:** service hiccups; annoying elevator system. [$] *Rooms from: Y1440* ✉ *505 Nanjing Dong Lu, Nanjing Dong Lu* ☎ *021/3318–9999* 🌐 *www.lemeridien.com.cn* 🛏 *646 rooms, 115 suites* 🍴 *No meals* ⊕ *E2.*

$$$$ HOTEL 🏨 **Les Suites Orient** (东方商旅精品酒店 *Dōngfāng shānglǚ jīngpǐn jiǔdiàn*). This Taiwanese-owned hotel is a favorite of ours, and not just because of its excellent location on the Bund. **Pros:** homey feeling; excellent service; great amenities. **Cons:** far from the subway. [$] *Rooms from: Y1900* ✉ *1 Jinling Dong Lu, The Bund* ☎ *021/6320–0088* 🌐 *www.lessuitesorient.com* 🛏 *43 suites* 🍴 *Breakfast* ⊕ *F3.*

$$$ HOTEL 🏨 **Shanghai Marriott City Centre** (上海雅居乐万豪酒店 *Shànghǎi yǎjūlè wànháo jiǔdiàn*). This hotel caters to business travelers, but its location two blocks north of People's Square and Nanjing Dong Lu makes it great for tourists. **Pros:** solid service; central location; reasonable rates. **Cons:** rather bland decor. [$] *Rooms from: Y1600* ✉ *555 Xizang Zhong Lu, Nanjing Dong Lu* ☎ *021/2312–9888* 🌐 *www.marriott.com* 🛏 *664 rooms, 54 suites* 🍴 *No meals* ⊕ *E2.*

$ HOTEL 🏨 **Sofitel Hyland.** Facing the pedestrian-only Nanjing Dong Lu, the Sofitel Hyland is a convenient base for shopping and exploring the city center. **Pros:** handy location; close to shopping; rooms with some nice details. **Cons:** small rooms; poor frontage. $ *Rooms from: Y800* ✉ *505 Nanjing Dong Lu, Nanjing Dong Lu* ☎ *021/6351–5888* ⊕ *www. accorhotels-asia.com* ⇄ *299 rooms, 73 suites* ⚬○⚬ *No meals* ⊹ *E2*.

$$
HOTEL
FAMILY 🖼 **The Westin Bund Center Shanghai** (上海威斯汀大饭店 *Shànghǎi wēisītīng dàfàndiàn*). With its distinctive room layouts, glittering glass staircase, and 90-plus works of art on display, the Westin Shanghai is a masterpiece near the majestic Bund. **Pros:** very attentive service. **Cons:** far from most shopping and restaurants. $ *Rooms from: Y1350* ✉ *Bund Center, 88 Henan Zhong Lu, The Bund* ☎ *021/6335–1888, 888/625–5144* ⊕ *www.westin.com/shanghai* ⇄ *570 rooms, 24 suites* ⚬○⚬ *No meals* ⊹ *F3*.

FORMER FRENCH CONCESSION

$
HOTEL 🖼 **Anting Villa Hotel** (安亭别墅花园酒店 *Āntíng biéshù huāyuán jiǔdiàn*). Although it's just two blocks from the Hengshan Road night-life district, the Anting Villa Hotel is a convenient and surprisingly quiet retreat tucked away down a small side street. **Pros:** central location; well-priced for the neighborhood. **Cons:** a little faded; can be hard to communicate. $ *Rooms from: Y650* ✉ *46 Anting Lu, French Concession* ☎ *021/6433–1188* ⊕ *www.antingvillahotel.com* ⇄ *135 rooms, 11 suites* ⚬○⚬ *No meals* ⊹ *A5*.

$
HOTEL 🖼 **Donghu Hotel** (東湖賓館 *Dōnghú bīnguǎn*). Just off the frenzied shopping street of Huaihai Lu, the Donghu Hotel remains one of Shanghai's best-preserved hotels from the city's heyday in the 1920s. **Pros:** traditional and elegant; indoor pool; a stone's throw from the subway. **Cons:** poor service; rooms in original building need refurbishment. $ *Rooms from: Y530* ✉ *70 Donghu Lu, French Concession* ☎ *021/6415–8158* ⊕ *www.donghuhotel.com* ⇄ *271 rooms, 26 suites* ⚬○⚬ *No meals* ⊹ *B4*.

$$$
HOTEL
FAMILY 🖼 **InterContinental Shanghai Ruijin.** Formerly the Morris Estate, the pre-served villas here showcases how opulently *tai-pan* (expatriate million-aire businessmen) lived in Shanghai's 1920s and '30s. **Pros:** beautiful rooms; historical grandeur; prime location. **Cons:** service is uneven; taxis can be hard to find. $ *Rooms from: Y1588* ✉ *118 Ruijin Er Lu, French Concession* ☎ *021/6472–5222* ⊕ *www.ihg.com/intercontinental/ hotels/gb/en/shanghai/shgsr/hoteldetail* ⇄ *200 rooms, 38 suites* ⚬○⚬ *No meals* ⊹ *C4*.

$
B&B/INN 🖼 **Magnolia Bed & Breakfast** (白玉兰 *Bái yùlán*). At the intersection of five tree-lined streets in the Former French Concession, the Magno-lia is a charming little B&B that's perfect if you want to be in the center of the action. **Pros:** great location; rich in character; a taste of local culture. **Pros:** it can be loud; there's no 24-hour service; there's no elevator. $ *Rooms from: Y650* ✉ *36 Yanqing Lu, French Concession* ☎ *021/5403–5306* ⊕ *www.magnoliabnbshanghai.com* ⇄ *4 rooms, 1 suite* ⚬○⚬ *Breakfast* ⊹ *B3*.

$$
HOTEL 🖼 **Okura Garden Hotel** (花园饭店 *Huāyuán fàndiàn*). A parklike set-ting in the heart of the Former French Concession makes this 33-story tower a favorite retreat, especially among Japanese travelers familiar with the Okura name. **Pros:** gorgeous surroundings; historic building; convenient to shops, restaurants, and the subway. **Cons:** you're paying more for beauty and location than service. $ *Rooms from: Y1100* ✉ *58*

Maoming Nan Lu, French Conces-sion ☎ *021/6415–1111* ⊕ *www. gardenhotelshanghai.com* ⟿ *478 rooms, 22 suites* ℃ *No meals* ✛ *C3*.

$$ 🏨 **Regal International East Asia Hotel**
HOTEL (富豪环球东亚酒店 *Fùháo huán-qiú dōngyà jiǔdiàn*). Regal is one of the few big chain hotels in the French Concession, making it a great option for people who want big-hotel service in a more local neighborhood. **Pros:** easy access to public transportation; top-notch fitness center; lots of activities for nights you want to stay in. **Cons:** on a high-traffic street. $ *Rooms from: Y1100* ⊠ *516 Hengshan Lu, French Concession* ☎ *021/6415–5588* ⊕ *www.regalhotel.com/regal-shanghai-east-asia-hotel/en/home/home.html* ⟿ *278 rooms, 22 suites* ℃ *No meals* ✛ *A5*.

> **UNIQUE SPOT**
>
> Magnolia B&B is one of Shanghai's most charming budget boutique hotels and a must if you're looking for a personalized experience that the larger hotels just can't offer.

JING'AN AND CHANGNING

$$ 🏨 **Cachet Boutique** (上海凯世精品酒店 *Shànghǎi kǎishì jīngpǐn jiǔdiàn*).
HOTEL In a handsome 1920s building on Nanjing Xi Lu hides Cachet, formerly known as JIA Shanghai. **Pros:** exquisite design and unique setting; kitchenettes; privacy. **Cons:** no pool; no business center. $ *Rooms from: Y1200* ⊠ *931 Nanjing Xi Lu, enter on Taixing Lu, Jing'an* ☎ *021/6217–9000* ⊕ *www.cachethotels.com/en/destinations/shanghai/overview* ⟿ *45 rooms* ℃ *Breakfast* ✛ *C2*.

$$ 🏨 **Crowne Plaza Shanghai** (银星皇冠假日酒店 *Shànghǎi Yínxīng*
HOTEL *huángguān jiàrì jiǔdiàn*). On the far western side of the Former French Concession, this hotel makes up for its out-of-the-way location with great service. **Pros:** good service; lots of amenities; nice pool. **Cons:** you'll need taxis to get to and from the hotel; spaces feel dated; some nonsmoking rooms still smell smoky. $ *Rooms from: Y1100* ⊠ *400 Panyu Lu, Changning* ☎ *021/6280–8888, 800/227–6963* ⊕ *www.ihg. com* ⟿ *488 rooms, 12 suites* ℃ *No meals* ✛ *A4*.

$$$ 🏨 **The Four Seasons** (四季酒店 *Sìjì jiǔdiàn*). With palm trees, babbling
HOTEL fountains, and golden-hued marble as warm as sunshine, the lobby of the Four Seasons is an elegant oasis in bustling downtown Puxi. **Pros:** impeccable service; convenient location; family programs. **Cons:** ongoing construction from the metro is loud and dusty. $ *Rooms from: Y1725* ⊠ *500 Weihai Lu, Jing'an* ☎ *021/6256–8888, 800/819–5053* ⊕ *www.fourseasons.com* ⟿ *360 rooms, 79 suites* ℃ *No meals* ✛ *C3*.

$$$$ 🏨 **The Portman Ritz-Carlton** (波特曼丽嘉酒店 *Bōtèmàn lìjiā jiǔdiàn*).
HOTEL Outstanding facilities and a prime location in the Shanghai Centre have
FAMILY made the Portman Ritz-Carlton one of the city's most desirable destinations for more than a decade. **Pros:** superb location, rooftop pool; family programs. **Cons:** staying here can feel like you're in a bubble. $ *Rooms from: Y2300* ⊠ *1376 Nanjing Xi Lu, Jing'an* ☎ *021/6279–8888, 800/241–3333* ⊕ *www.ritzcarlton.com* ⟿ *510 rooms, 68 suites* ℃ *No meals* ✛ *B2*.

4

$$$$ RESORT Fodor's Choice ★ **The PuLi Hotel & Spa.** An oasis of calm in the center of bustling Shanghai, this hotel is billed as an urban resort with an emphasis on soothing decor and relaxing amenities. **Pros:** long list of complimentary amenities; great location; quiet; popular Sunday brunch. **Cons:** service can be hit or miss; rack rates are staggeringly expensive [$] *Rooms from: Y3950* ✉ *1 Changde Lu, Jing'an* ☎ *021/3203–9999* 🌐 *www.thepuli.com/en* *193 rooms, 36 suites* 🍴 *Breakfast* ✣ *A3.*

$$$ HOTEL Fodor's Choice ★ **URBN** (雅悦酒店 *Yǎyuè jiǔdiàn*). Innovatively designed and environmentally friendly, this is Shanghai's first carbon-neutral hotel. **Pros:** eco-friendly vibe; luxe setting; quiet location. **Cons:** not terribly suitable for mobility-impaired guests. [$] *Rooms from: Y1500* ✉ *183 Jiaozhou Lu, near Beijing Xi Lu, Jing'an* ☎ *021/5153–4600* 🌐 *www.urbnhotels.com* *24 rooms, 2 suites* 🍴 *No meals* ✣ *B2.*

PUDONG

$$$$ HOTEL **Four Seasons Pudong** (浦东四季酒店 *Pǔdōng sìjì jiǔdiàn*). While its older sister is more posh, the Pudong outpost of the Four Seasons is flashy and hip. **Pros:** sleek design; prompt service; nice little terrace. **Cons:** it's a long walk to restaurants; no nearby nightlife. [$] *Rooms from: Y2300* ✉ *210 Shiji Da Dao, Pudong* ☎ *021/2036–8888* 🌐 *www.fourseasons.com/pudong* *187 rooms, 15 suites* 🍴 *No meals* ✣ *H3.*

$$$$ HOTEL **Grand Hyatt** (上海金茂君悦大酒店 *Shànghǎi jīnmàojūn yuè dàjiǔdiàn*). Views, views, views are what this hotel is all about—occupying floors 53 through 87 of the spectacular Jin Mao Tower, the Grand Hyatt's interior is defined by contemporary lines juxtaposed with Space Age grillwork and sleek furnishings and textures. **Pros:** beautiful rooms; high-tech amenities; fantastic city views. **Cons:** pricey rates; no guarantee of clear views. [$] *Rooms from: Y2000* ✉ *Jin Mao Tower, 88 Shiji Dadao (Century Ave.), Pudong* ☎ *021/5049–1234, 800/233–1234* 🌐 *www.shanghai.grand.hyatt.com* *510 rooms, 45 suites* 🍴 *No meals* ✣ *H3.*

$$$ HOTEL FAMILY **InterContinental Shanghai Pudong** (锦江汤臣洲际大酒店 *Jǐnjiāng tāngchén zhōujì dàjiǔdiàn*). The pièce de résistance of the 24-story Hotel InterContinental Pudong is a nearly 200-foot-high Italian Renaissance–inspired atrium, decorated with red Chinese lanterns, that shines natural light onto the 19 guest floors. **Pros:** well priced for its amenities. **Cons:** not the best location for exploration on foot; Wi-Fi is not free [$] *Rooms from: Y1680* ✉ *777 Zhangyang Lu, Pudong* ☎ *021/5831–8888, 800/327–0200* 🌐 *www.intercontinental.com* *317 rooms, 78 suites* 🍴 *No meals* ✣ *H4.*

$$$ HOTEL FAMILY **Kerry Hotel** (嘉里大酒店 *Jiālǐ dàjiǔdiàn*). This hotel within easy driving distance of Pudong International Airport is great if you're traveling with kids—across the street is Century Park, where tandem bikes and pleasure boats are available. **Pros:** great for kids, easy access to greenery. **Cons:** far from downtown. [$] *Rooms from: Y1700* ✉ *1388 Huamu Lu, Pudong* ☎ *021/6169–8800* 🌐 *www.shangri-la.com/shanghai/kerryhotelpudong* *843 rooms, 31 suites* 🍴 *No meals* ✣ *H5.*

$$$$ 🏨 **Pudong Shangri-La** (浦东香格里拉酒店 *Pǔdōng xiānggélǐlā jiǔdiàn*).
HOTEL   The Shangri-La occupies one of the most prized spots in Shanghai:
Fodor'sChoice   overlooking the Huangpu River, opposite the Bund, and near the
★   Pearl Tower. **Pros:** fantastic location; good restaurants; glorious views.
Cons: expensive rates; nearby restaurants are in shopping malls.
Ⓢ *Rooms from: Y2100* ⊠ *33 Fucheng Lu, Pudong* ☎ *021/6882–8888,*
800/942–5050 ⊕ *www.shangri-la.com* ⇱ *916 rooms, 65 suites* ⦿ *No*
meals ✛ *H3.*

$$$$ 🏨 **Ritz-Carlton Pudong** (上海浦东丽思卡尔顿上海世茂皇家艾美酒店
HOTEL   *Shànghǎi pǔdōng lìsīkǎ'ěrdùn Shànghǎi shìmào huángjiā ài měi jiǔdiàn*).
FAMILY   The Ritz-Carlton Pudong boasts a 55th-floor spa with staggering views
of the Huangpu River and the entire downtown skyline, an impressive
Italian restaurant, and a rooftop bar that's such a good lookout point
you may never want to leave. **Pros:** near upscale shopping; easy access
to financial center; great views. **Cons:** the only nearby restaurants are
in shopping malls. Ⓢ *Rooms from: Y2800* ⊠ *8 Shiji Dadao (Century*
Ave.), Pudong ☎ *021/2020–1888* ⊕ *www.ritzcarlton.com* ⇱ *285 rooms*
⦿ *No meals* ✛ *H3.*

HONGKOU AND PUTUO

$ 🏨 **Astor House Hotel** (浦江饭店 *Pǔjiāng fàndiàn*). The oldest Western
HOTEL   hotel in China, the Astor House does an admirable job of capturing
the ambience of Victorian Shanghai. **Pros:** gorgeous building; historic
atmosphere; close to the Bund. **Cons:** confused service; spartan furnishings; dated rooms. Ⓢ *Rooms from: Y718* ⊠ *15 Huangpu Lu, Hongkou*
☎ *021/6324–6388* ⊕ *www.pujianghotel.com/index.htm* ⇱ *127 rooms,*
3 suites ⦿ *No meals* ✛ *G2.*

$$$$ 🏨 **Hyatt on the Bund** (外滩茂悦大酒店 *Wàitān màoyuè dàjiǔdiàn*). Near
HOTEL   the banks of Suzhou Creek, the Hyatt on the Bund offers beautifully
appointed rooms in an airy and modern building. **Pros:** gorgeous facilities; views are hard to beat; short walk from the Bund. **Cons:** rather
bland neighborhood; the food underwhelms; can be difficult to get
taxis. Ⓢ *Rooms from: Y2000* ⊠ *199 Huangpu Lu, near Wuchang Lu,*
Hongkou ☎ *021/6393–1234* ⊕ *www.shanghai.bund.hyatt.com* ⇱ *600*
rooms, 31 suites ⦿ *No meals* ✛ *G2.*

$ 🏨 **Renaissance Putuo** (上海明捷万丽酒店 *Shànghǎi míngjié wànlì*
HOTEL   *jiǔdiàn*). Though it's outside the downtown district, this reasonably
priced hotel is adjacent to a station on metro Line 7, putting you four
stops from the Jing'an Temple and five from the Former French Concession. **Pros:** good value; well-appointed rooms; nice pool. **Cons:** far
from the action. Ⓢ *Rooms from: Y958* ⊠ *50 Tongchuan Lu, Putuo*
☎ *021/2219–5888* ⊕ *www.marriott.com* ⇱ *315 rooms, 15 suites* ⦿ *No*
meals ✛ *B1.*

$ 🏨 **Shanghai Marriott Hotel Parkview.** From the expansive marble lobby
HOTEL   to the elegant rooms and suites overlooking tranquil Daning Lingshi
Park, this design-conscious property has a sense of space, light, and
quiet—always welcome in Shanghai. **Pros:** fine Asian dining; impeccable service; sleek, contemporary decor. **Cons:** conference groups
can overwhelm the breakfast buffet; 30 minutes outside city center

4

[$] *Rooms from: Y925* ✉ *333 Guongzhong Xi Lu, Zhabei* ☎ *21/3669–8888* 🌐 *www.marriott.com* 🛏 *304 rooms, 13 suites* 🍴 *No meals* ✣ *F1.*

XUJIAHUI, HONGQIAO, AND GUBEI

$$ HOTEL 🏨 **Hilton Shanghai Hongqiao** (上海虹桥希尔顿酒店 *Shànghǎi hóngqiáo xī'ěrdùn jiǔdiàn*). A 20-minute drive from Hongqiao Airport, this behemoth is ideal for business travelers catching early flights. **Pros:** very close to the airport; good value. **Cons:** more geared toward business travelers; far from public transportation [$] *Rooms from: Y1350* ✉ *1116 Hongsong Dong Lu, Hongqiao* ☎ *021/3323–6666* 🌐 *www3.hilton.com* 🛏 *623 rooms, 51 suites* 🍴 *No meals* ✣ *A6.*

DRINK AND A VIEW

Check out the spectacular Vue bar at the Hyatt on the Bund and enjoy expansive vistas and a rooftop hot tub.

$ HOTEL 🏨 **Sheraton Shanghai Hongqiao Hotel** (虹桥喜来登上海太平洋大饭店 *Hóngqiáo xǐláidēng Shànghǎi tàipíngyáng dàfàndiàn*). Popular with business travelers for its location near Hongqiao Airport, this hotel is somewhat dated but a good option for those who want to be near the airport without being too far from downtown. **Pros:** beautifully decorated; reasonable rates; great for business travelers. **Cons:** far from the subway; uneven service. [$] *Rooms from: Y1000* ✉ *5 Zunyi Nan Lu, Hongqiao* ☎ *021/6275–8888, 888/625–5144* 🌐 *www.starwoodhotels.com* 🛏 *474 rooms, 22 suites* 🍴 *No meals* ✣ *A6.*

NIGHTLIFE AND PERFORMING ARTS

Fueled equally by expatriates and an adventurous population of locals, Shanghai boasts an active and diverse nightlife. Shanghai lacks the sort of performing-arts scene you'd expect from a city its size, but it's getting there. Chinese opera remains popular with an older crowd and is even enjoying resurgence with a younger audience.

NIGHTLIFE

Offerings range from world-class swank to dark and dingy dens or from young Shanghainese kids screaming experimental punk to Filipino cover bands singing "Hotel California" in a hotel basement. Prices, scenes, crowds, and ambience range just as wildly.

For an array of pleasant but pricey bars, head to **Xintiandi**, which every year sees swank new destinations debuting in its historic halls. Farther east, **The Bund** is also a good place for upscale bars.

Yongfu Lu, near Fuxing Lu, once the top destination for the city's expats, is still lined with bars, including the excellent el Coctel. A dozen blocks to the east, the tiny watering holes along **Yongkang Lu** are most popular in the summer, when the street becomes so thronged with young revelers that no vehicles can pass.

Shanghai's seedy bar strips are going the way of dial-up Internet connections. **Huashan Lu** still has a few bars for those who like their nightlife more on the wild side. They feature "fishing girls" who ask gents to give them money to buy drinks in exchange for their company (or something more). They either pocket the money or take a cut from the bar.

XINTIANDI AND CITY CENTER

BARS

Barbarossa (爸爸露沙 *Bābālùshā*). This is a popular evening destination especially with nearby office workers who come by for happy hour. The interior is straight out of *Arabian Nights*, with billowing draperies swathing the space. Usually quiet and classy, it switches to hot, hip, and hopping on weekend nights, especially in summer. It's the ambience, not the food or drink, that bring people in. ⊠ *Inside People's Park, 231 Nanjing Xi Lu, next to Shanghai Art Museum, City Center* ☎ *021/6318–0220* ⊕ *www.barbarossa.com.cn.*

Constellation (酒池星座 *Jiǔ chí xīngzuò*). The fourth sibling in the growing Constellation bar family, this branch is just south of Xintiandi, a stone's throw from the metro station. It sticks to the mini chain's tried-and-true formula of cigars, mid-volume jazz, and quality, Japanese-style cocktails. ⊠ *398 Zizhong Lu, Xintiandi* ☎ *021/6333–7009.*

de Bellotas (贝优塔 *Bèi yōu tǎ*). Tucked away outside Xintiandi proper, this quaint self-titled "jamon y vino" (ham and wine) bar has a rich hardwood ceiling, sunlight streaming through the arched windows, and thick legs of ham hanging from above the deli case. The focus is on Spanish wines, tapas, and a variety of ham, including Jamón Ibérico aged 48 months. ⊠ *68 Taicang Lu, Xintiandi* ☎ *021/6384–1382.*

TMSK (透明思考酒吧 *Tòumíngsīkǎo jiǔba*). Short for Tou Ming Si Kao, this exquisitely designed little bar is an aesthete's dream. Glisteningly modern, TMSK is stunning—as are the prices of its drinks. ⊠ *Xintiandi North Block, Unit 2, House 11, 181 Taicang Lu, Xintiandi* ☎ *021/6326–2227.*

CLUBS

M2. This is the first and founding member of the Muse group, a popular chain of clubs that, in its heydey, were four. The group is now down to this and the one on the Bund. Both play hip-hop, house, and electro and throw themed parties. M2 is loud and crowded; it's where people end up after hitting a few other drinking establishments. Both branches are popular with young locals who order bottle service and stay until the sun comes up. ⊠ *Hong Kong Plaza, 283 Huaihai Zhong Lu, 4F, City Center* ☎ *021/6288–6222.*

LIVE MUSIC

288/The Melting Pot (288阳光小筑 *288 Xiànchǎng yīnyuè ba*). With live performers of varying styles nightly, and up-and-coming rockers on weekend, this laid-back bar is a favorite with music lovers, locals, and foreigners alike. ⊠ *288 Taikang Lu, French Concession* ☎ *021/6415–8180.*

MAO Livehouse (光芒 *Guāngmáng*). To the west and south of Xintiandi is Shanghai's most active large-scale concert venue. Past performers include Thee Oh Sees, Grimes, and Gang of Four. Up-and-coming local and foreign bands regularly take to the stage, and the acts vary from heavy metal to folk. ⊠ *308 Chongqing Nan Lu, 3F, City Center* ☎ *021/6445–0086.*

KARAOKE

Karaoke is ubiquitous in Shanghai; most nights the private rooms at KTV (Karaoke TV) establishments are packed with Shanghainese crooning away with their friends. Many bars employ "KTV girls" who sing along with male patrons and serve cognac and expensive snacks. (At some establishments, KTV girls are also prostitutes.)

Cashbox Party World (钱柜KTV *Qiánguì KTV*). This giant establishment is one of Shanghai's most popular Karaoke TV (KTV) bars, and among the few that are dedicated to KTV instead of KTV girls. There's another location at 139 Xinhui Lu, right by Jade Buddha Temple. ⊠ *109 Yandan Lu, inside Fuxing Park, City Center* ☎ *021/5306–3888.*

Haoledi (好乐迪KTV *Hāolèdī KTV*). Crowded at all hours with locals of all ages crooning pop favorites, the popular Haoledi chain has branches virtually everywhere. A few of the outlets in downtown are at 180 Xizang Zhong Lu, near People's Square, and on the seventh floor of mall Metro City, at 1111 Zhaojiabang Lu in Xujiahui. ⊠ *438 Huaihai Zhong Lu, City Center* ☎ *021/6311–5858.*

THE BUND AND NANJING DONG LU

BARS

Chalet. This is the Yu Gardens outpost of a popular French Concession bar known for its deep couches and mulled wine. A neighborhood bar with laid-back atmosphere and very reasonably priced drinks, this branch of Chalet has sports on a big screen, Stella Artois on draft, and all-night happy hour every Tuesday. The menu offers surprisingly good pub grub, including de rigueur chicken strips and lighter options like a couscous salad. ⊠ *SSAW Hotel, 1F, 839 Renmin Lu, The Bund* ☉ *Daily 5 pm–2 am* ⊠ *385 Yongjia Lu, French Concession* ☎ *021/3401–0958.*

Char (上海外滩英迪格酒店 *Shànghǎi wàitān yīngdígé jiǔdiàn*). Hotel Indigo's dark, sexy rooftop bar and steak house offers panoramic views of the Pudong skyline and Huangpu River. The hotel's location on the water's edge makes for unimpeded views of the river. Snack on a charcuterie board for two as you gaze out over the water. ⊠ *Hotel Indigo, 585 Zhongshan Dong Er Lu, 29-31F, The Bund* ☎ *021/3302–9995* ⊕ *www.char-thebund.com.*

Unico (惟壹 *Wéi yī*). A Latin-inspired lounge where you can kick off your night before you go clubbing, Unico offers a dizzying array of pricey cocktails, divided up by compass coordinates. From the Caribbean, there's the El Presidente, made with rum, sweet vermouth (made in-house), and grapefruit bitters, topped with an orange twist. The music is loud enough that you can dance, but if you're not standing next to the band you can still have a conversation. Skip the lackluster food. ⊠ *Three on the Bund, 3 Zhongshan Dong Yi Lu, 2F, The Bund* ☎ *021/5308–5399.*

CLUBS

Bar Rouge. In the trendy Bund 18 complex, Bar Rouge is the destination du jour of Shanghai's beautiful people. Pouting models and visiting celebrities are among the regular clientele, as are seemingly every French expat in Shanghai. Views of Pudong are knockout, and so are drink prices. ⊠ *Bund 18, 18 Zhongshan Dong Yi Lu, 7th fl., The Bund* ☏ *021/6339–1199* ⊕ *www.bar-rouge-shanghai.com.*

M1NT. Two-parts club, one part bar, M1NT is one of the few places in Shanghai with a strict door policy. The club, on the 24th floor of an office tower, is tucked away on a quiet side street just behind the Bund. There's no set dress code, but men should not wear shorts. Although bottle service is popular, plenty of revelers stick to buying drinks and shots from the bar, whose lines can be three deep. The shark tank is partiers' favorite photo backdrop. ⊠ *318 Fuzhou Lu, 24F, The Bund* ☏ *021/6391–2811* ⊕ *www.m1ntglobal.com/club-shanghai.*

Muse on the Bund. Loud and crowded, Muse on the Bund plays hip-hop, house, and electro music and throws themed parties. When you need to chill out, there's a huge rooftop with a wading pool. Weekends see the club absolutely teeming with moneyed locals (and a smattering of expats) ordering up bottle after bottle from the top shelf. ⊠ *Yi Feng Galleria, 77 Beijing Dong Lu, 5F, The Bund* ☏ *021/5213–5228.*

LIVE MUSIC

House of Blues and Jazz (布鲁斯与爵士之屋 *Bùlǔsī yǔ juéshì zhīwū*). Decked out in memorabilia from Shanghai's jazz era of the 1930s, the House of Blues and Jazz would be a great bar even without the music, but the several nightly sets make it a must-visit, and the dark-wood paneling and low lighting, plus the requisite smoke, all add to the ambience. ⊠ *60 Fuzhou Lu, The Bund* ☏ *021/6323–2779* ⊕ *www. houseofbluesandjazz.com.*

Peace Hotel Jazz Bar (和平饭店爵士酒吧 *Hépíng fàndiàn juéshì jiǔbā*). The average age of the musicians who make up the Old Jazz Band is 80, but you wouldn't know it listening to them jam. The food and drinks on offer were inspired by what the bar served in the 1920s and '30s, when Shanghai was in its golden age and the Peace Hotel was *the* place to see and be seen. The dark wood, heavy red curtains, and warming cocktails make this bar an especially good choice for winter. ⊠ *20 Nanjing Dong Lu, The Bund* ☏ *021/6321–6888* ⊕ *www.fairmont.com/peace-hotel-shanghai/dining/thejazzbar* ⊗ *Band plays daily at 7 pm.*

FORMER FRENCH CONCESSION

BARS

Fodor's Choice ★

Cotton's (棉花酒吧 *Miánhuā jiǔbā*). This friendly, laid-back favorite moved many times before settling into the current old garden house. Busy without being loud, Cotton's is a rare place where you can have a conversation with friends—or make some new ones. The patio here is one of Shanghai's loveliest, but the food is not, so stick to drinks. ⊠ *132 Anting Lu, French Concession* ☏ *021/6433–7995* ⊕ *www.cottons-shanghai.com* ⊗ *Daily 11 am–2 am* ⊠ *294 Xinhua Lu, Changning* ☏ *021/6282–6897* ⊕ *www.cottons-shanghai.com* ⊗ *Weekdays 4 pm–midnight, weekends 11 am–midnight.*

LOCAL BREWS

Northern Chinese swear by their *baijiu*, a strong, usually sweet, clear liquor, but Shanghainese opt for milder poison. Most beloved is *huangjiu*, a brown brew from Shaoxing with a mild taste that resembles whiskey, which may explain why the latter is the most popular foreign liquor among locals. Huangjiu's quality is determined by whether it was brewed 2, 5, or 10 years ago. It is usually served warm, sometimes with ginger or dried plum added for kick.

Beer is also widely consumed; although there is a Shanghai beer brand, it is cheap, very bitter, and mostly found in the suburbs. Stores stock brands like Suntory, Reeb (yes, it's "beer" spelled backward), and Li Bo; of the three, Suntory is by far the best. Bars serve Tsingtao and imports like Tiger, Heineken, and Budweiser, which are more expensive. You'll find Sinkiang Black at Xinjiang restaurants. Craft beer can be had at Shanghai's small but strong homegrown breweries.

Fodor'sChoice **Salute.** A slice of Italy it's not, but this rustic wine bar's three ramshackle
★ rooms and quaint courtyard make for a popular date night or low-key evening spot. It's bottles only here, but by China standards, they're reasonably priced. From the kitchen come charcuterie and cheese platters, panini, and small plates of marinated vegetables. ⊠ *59 Fuxing Xi Lu, French Concession* ☏ *021/3461–9828.*

Senator Saloon. On a quiet street in the French Concession, a few blocks from the bars along Yongfu Lu, is Senator Saloon. The unmarked entrance is easy to miss, and you'd never guess there was a swinging speakeasy within. Cocktails include classics as well as contemporary concoctions. Big band music on the stereo, velvet damask wallpaper, and a pressed-tin ceiling all lend to the feeling that you've traveled back in time. ⊠ *98 Wuyuan Lu, French Concession* ☏ *021/5423–1330.*

Union Trading Co. The cocktail list here has 100-plus concoctions, some classic and some dreamt up by Texan bartender Yao Lu. The delightfully summery Witchy Woman is a mix of Campari, white rum, orgeat syrup, lime juice, orange juice, and Angostura bitters. Sop up some of the liquor with the bar's red velvet donut holes, served with a side of cream cheese frosting. An expat favorite, Union has the feeling of a neighborhood pub but the prices and service of a posh cocktail bar. ⊠ *64 Fenyang Lu, entrance is on Fuxing Lu, just west of Fenyang, French Concession* ☏ *021/6418–3077* ☾ *Closed Mon.*

CLUBS

The Apartment (汉俱 *Hàn jù*). This bumping club is packed to the gills every weekend night with throngs of sweaty young dancers grinding up against one another to Top-40 hits. The rooftop, with its own bar, is a far better option. ⊠ *47 Yongfu Lu, French Concession* ☏ *021/6437–9478.*

The Shelter (庇护所 *Bìhù suǒ*). Opened by a collective of Shanghai's leading DJs, this former bomb shelter is not for the claustrophobic. It is a favorite with Shanghai scenesters for its cheap drinks and reasonable cover charge. It's a bit musty and damp down in the basement, but that doesn't stop revelers from packing in whenever there are big-name shows. ⊠ *47 Yongfu Lu, by Fuxing Lu, French Concession* ☎ *021/6437–0400.*

LIVE MUSIC

Cotton Club (棉花俱乐部 *Miánhuā jùlèbù*). A dark and smoky jazz and blues club, the Cotton Club is an institution in Shanghai, and still one of the best places to catch live music. It's in a great neighborhood for barhopping, so head here for the 9 pm set and get your night rolling. ⊠ *1416 Huaihai Zhong Lu, corner of Fuxing Lu, French Concession* ☎ *021/6437–7110* ⊕ *www.thecottonclub.cn.*

JZ Club (爵士酒吧 *Juéshì jiǔbā*). This place is the king of Shanghai's jazz offerings. Various house bands and stellar guest performers mix it up nightly. Look for plush seating and drink prices to match. When you need a break from the noise and crowds, cool off on the roof deck. JZ Club is also the organizer of JZ Festival, which they claim is Asia's largest jazz fest. It takes place annually, over three days in mid-October, and is held outdoors at Expo Park, along the water in Pudong. ⊠ *46 Fuxing Xi Lu, French Concession* ☎ *021/6431–0269* ⊕ *www.jzclub.cn/en.*

GAY–LESBIAN BARS AND CLUBS

Eddy's (嘉侬咖啡厅 *Jiā nóng kāfēi tīng*). Flamboyant drag queen Eddy has had to move this gay bar around the city over the years, but it has found a more permanent home on this stretch of Huaihai Zhong Lu, from which the "gayborhood" spreads out. ⊠ *1877 Huaihai Zhong Lu, French Concession* ☎ *021/6282–0521.*

JING'AN AND CHANGNING

BARS

Kaiba (开巴 *Kāi bā*). Unpretentious and free of frills, Kaiba is the ideal neighborhood bar. It's been around for ages, serving Belgian brews and a few other imports. There are 30 beers on tap and snacks like house-made sausage and Belgian waffles. ⊠ *Zhong Plaza, 479 Wuding Lu, Jing'an* ☎ *021/6288–9676.*

Rhumerie Bounty. This private-themed rum bar hits just the right note when it comes to decor. The drink of choice here is Havana Club that's been soaked with fruit (lychee, pineapple, melon, etc.) so that it's ultra-sweet. Standard cocktails and beer are available as well. ⊠ *550 Wuding Lu, Jing'an* ☎ *023/6271–1406.*

Time Passage (昨天今天明天酒吧 *Zuótiān jīntiān míngtiān jiǔbā*). Shanghai favors slick nightclubs and posh wine bars, but Time Passage, whose Chinese name is "yesterday, today, tomorrow," has always been the exception. Cheap beers, friendly service, and a cool, if grungy, atmosphere makes it the best way to start—or end—a night on the town. ⊠ *183 Caojiayan Lu, near Huashan Lu, Changning* ☎ *021/6240–2588.*

UVA. Its name means "grape" in Italian, so it's no surprise that UVA is a little wine bar. Run by a pair of Italians, it offers quite good value wine by the glass and bottle. The bar is popular with couples as well as office workers who turn out for happy hour. From the kitchen come some of Shanghai's better pizzas. ⊠ *819 Shaanxi Bei Lu, Jing'an* ☎ *021/5228–0320.*

Zhong Plaza. Just off Nanjing Xi Lu, behind the West Nanjing Road metro station, is this small complex of bars and restaurants housed in lovingly restored lane houses. The buildings' tenants include Belgian beer bar **Kaiba**; cocktail bars **Starling**, **el Ocho**, and **Logan's Punch**; tapas bar **Tomatito**; cheap and cheerful restaurant **Noodle Bull**; and Turkish restaurant **Black Pepper**. ■TIP➔ **To get here, either take a cab to the corner of Nanjing Xi Lu and Taixing Lu, and walk on Taixing Lu towards Wujiang Lu, or take metro Line 2 to West Nanjing Road.** ✉ *99 Taixing Lu, off Nanjing Xi Lu, Jing'an.*

GAY–LESBIAN BARS AND CLUBS

390 Bar (酒吧 *390 Jiǔbā*). Shanghai's only gay live music venue, 390 bar is also popular with Shanghai's straight club-goers. The decor is outrageous and flaming, perfect for the space. The drinks list includes some unique cocktails, so before you try the A Clockwork Orange (made with gin and orange liqueur), fill up on a sausage and chutney made by a local British jam merchant. ✉ *390 Panyu Lu, Changning* ☎ *021/186–2124–9854* ⊕ *www.390shanghai.com.*

LIVE MUSIC

Wooden Box Cafe (木盒咖啡馆 *Mùhé kāfēi guǎn*). On a quiet lane off busy Nanjing Xi Lu, this café and bar mimics the inside of a tree house, with high ceilings and wood paneling on the rounded walls. The performers here play a variety of jazz and acoustic music, which you can listen to while sipping wine and beer (avoid the food, however). ✉ *9 Qinghai Lu, Jing'an* ☎ *021/5213–2965.*

Fodor's Choice ★ **Yuyintang** (育音堂 *Yùyīntáng*). No one has done as much to bring Shanghai rock out from the underground and into the open as has this collective. Headed by a sound engineer and former musician, the group started hosting regular concerts around town and eventually opened its own space. Shows, usually on Friday, Saturday, or Sunday nights, spotlight the latest in young Chinese music, especially punk and rock, and the occasional Western act. ✉ *851 Kaixuan Lu, enter behind metro station, Changning* ☎ *021/5237–8662* ⊕ *www.yuyintang.org* 🕑 *Shows generally start at 8 or 9 pm.*

PUDONG

BARS

FAMILY **The Brew** (嘉里大酒店 *Jiā lǐ dàjiǔdiàn*). The Kerry Hotel's microbrewery is tightly run by Kiwi brewmaster Leon Mickelson. The crisp cider is very good for those who don't love beer, while the Pilsner and IPA are the most popular among brew-heads. Shooting pool, tossing back peanuts from a tin pail, and sipping brewskies, you may well forget you're in China. On weekend afternoons, this is a family-friendly bar. ✉ *The Kerry Hotel, 1388 Huamu Lu, Pudong* ☎ *021/6169–8888.*

Cloud 9 (九重天). Perched on the 87th floor of the Grand Hyatt, Cloud 9 is among the city's loftiest bars. It has unparalleled views of Shanghai from among—and often above—the clouds. The sky-high views come with sky-high prices. Come on a clear day and ask for a table facing west, towards the Huangpu River and the Bund. ✉ *Grand Hyatt, 88 Shiji Dadao, Pudong* ☎ *021/5049–1234* ⊕ *Jiǔ chòngtiān.*

Jade on 36 (翡翠36酒吧 *Fěicuì 36 jiǔbā*). This swanky spot in the newer tower of the Pudong Shangri-La is the place for creative cocktails. Exquisite design and corresponding views (when Shanghai's pollution levels cooperate) have made Jade popular with locals. ✉ *Pudong Shangri-La, 33 Fucheng, 36th fl., Pudong* ☎ *021/6882–3636.*

HONGKOU AND PUTUO

GAY–LESBIAN BARS AND CLUBS

Lai Lai Dancehall (来来舞厅 *Láilái wǔtīng*). This is one of Shanghai's gems, a sweet, simple dance hall where local men can come three nights a week and dance to tender Chinese pop songs from an earlier time. Songs are played by a band, which sometimes dresses in drag, as does one of the owners. There are a number of regulars, and strangers aren't shy about asking for a dance, but it's all quite chaste. Foreigners are most welcome and treated no differently than locals. In general, photos are not allowed. ✉ *235 Anguo Lu, 2F, near Zhoujiazui Lu, Hongkou* ☎ *150–2174–7399* 🖃 *Y10* ⊘ *Fri.–Sun. 6–9 pm.*

LIVE MUSIC

Bandu Music (半度音乐 *Bàndù yīnyuè*). An unpretentious café and bar in the M50 art compound, Bandu sells hard-to-find CDs and occasionally holds concerts of traditional Chinese folk music. When touring the M50 galleries, this is a nice place for a break. ✉ *M50, 50 Moganshan Lu, Unit 11, 1F, Putuo* ☎ *021/6276–8267* ⊕ *bandumusic.com.*

XUJIAHUI, HONGQIAO, AND GUBEI

BARS

FAMILY **Shanghai Brewery** (上海啤酒坊 *Shànghǎi píjiǔ fāng*). It's a family affair at Shanghai Brewery, where you're equally likely to find a group of footballers and a posse of parents with toddlers in tow. There are seven house-made brews here, including a Black-Eyed Bear Stout and the sweet, summery peach beer. The food menu is all over the place, with both Western dishes and a handful of Asian options, but it's all solid. ✉ *3338 Hongmei Lu, Hongqiao* ☎ *021/6406–5919* ⊕ *shanghaibrewery.com* ✉ *19 Dongping Lu, French Concession* ☎ *021/3461–0717* ⊕ *www.shanghaibrewery.com.*

GAY–LESBIAN BARS AND CLUBS

ICON. With a capacity of 1,500 people, Shanghai's most tucked away gay bar is also its largest. Inside Shanghai Stadium, shirtless locals and expats dance all night to trance and Top-40 hits as strobe lights flash, go-go dancers thrust, and everyone is bathed in purple light. ✉ *Shanghai Stadium, Gate 7, Lingling Lu, near Xietu Lu, Xujiahui* ⊕ *www. angelshanghai.com* ⊘ *Fri. and Sat. from 10 pm.*

PERFORMING ARTS

For modern culture more in tune with Shanghai's vibe head to the Shanghai Dramatic Arts Center, which balances sumptuous historical epics with small, provocative plays examining burning social issues.

ACROBATICS

FAMILY   **ERA–Intersection of Time** (上海马戏城 *Shànghǎi mǎxì chéng*). This troupe performs more than 15 acts per show of remarkable gravity-defying stunts. Performances are held at Shanghai Circus World, a glittering, gold, 1,600-seat dome, north of the city center, in Zhabei. It's a fantastical experience, but note that the more expensive tickets are not worth the price in terms of view or comfort. The performance space is just a few minutes' walk from the metro stop of the same name. ■TIP→ It's easiest to eat dinner downtown before going to Shanghai Circus World. ⊠ *Shanghai Circus World, 2266 Gonghexin Lu, Zhabei* ☏ *021/6552–5468, 021/5665–6622* ⊕ *www.era-shanghai.com* 🎫 *Y120–Y600* ⊙ *Daily at 7:30 pm.*

Shanghai Acrobatics Troupe (上海杂技团 *Shànghǎi zájìtuán*). This troupe performs remarkable gravity-defying stunts at both the Shanghai Centre Theater, inside the Portman Ritz-Carlton and at Shanghai Circus World, a glittering, gold, 1,600-seat dome, which is north of the city center, in Zhabei. There are also performances at the Shanghai Circus World at 2266 Gonghe Xin Lu in Zhabei. ⊠ *Shanghai Centre Theater, 1376 Nanjing Xi Lu, Jing'an* ☏ *021/6279–8945 Shanghai Centre, 021/5665–3646 Circus World* 🎫 *Y150–Y280* ⊙ *Daily at 7:30 pm.*

CHINESE OPERA

Kunqu Opera Troupe (上海昆剧团 *Shànghǎi kūnjùtuán*). Kunqu opera originated in Jiangsu Province more than 400 years ago. Because of the profound influence it exerted on other Chinese opera styles, it's often called the mother of Chinese opera. Its troupe and theater are located in the lower part of the Former French Concession. ⊠ *9 Shaoxing Lu, French Concession* ☏ *021/6437–1012* 🎫 *Y30–Y280* ⊙ *Sat. at 7:15.*

Yifu Theatre (逸夫舞台 *Yìfú wǔtái*). Not only Beijing Opera but also China's other regional operas, such as Huju, Kunqu, and Yueju, are performed regularly at this theater in the heart of the city center. Considered the marquee theater for opera in Shanghai, it's just a block off People's Square. ⊠ *701 Fuzhou Lu, City Center* ☏ *021/6351–4668.*

DANCE AND CLASSICAL MUSIC

Shanghai Concert Hall (上海音乐厅 *Shànghǎi yīnyuètīng*). More than a decade ago, city officials spent $6 million to move this venerable concert hall two blocks to avoid the rumble from the nearby highway. Only then did they discover that it now sat over an even more rumbling subway line. Oops. It's the home of the Shanghai Symphony Orchestra, and hosts top-level classical musicians from around China and the world. ⊠ *523 Yan'an Dong Lu, City Center* ☏ *021/6386–9153.*

Shanghai Oriental Art Center (上海东方艺术中心 *Shànghǎi dōngfāng yìshù zhōngxīn*). This cultural powerhouse presents traditional Chinese works as well as a superb selection of Western shows. The Royal New Zealand Ballet, Munich Philharmonic Orchestra, and Netherlands Symphony Orchestra are just three among a slew of groups that have performed here. ⊠ *425 Dingxiang Lu, Pudong* ☏ *021/4006–466–406* ⊕ *en.shoac.com.cn.*

THEATER

Lyceum Theatre (兰馨大戏院 *Lánxīn dàxìyuàn*). Although the renovation of Shanghai's oldest theater sadly replaced the richly stained wood with glaring marble and glass, the design of the space makes for an intimate theater experience. The Lyceum regularly hosts drama and music from around China as well as smaller local plays and Chinese opera performances. On the second floor is cocktail and Champagne bar O Theatre, which is open even when shows aren't on. ✉ *57 Maoming Nan Lu, French Concession* ☎ *021/6217–8539.*

Fodor's Choice
★ **Shanghai Dramatic Arts Center** (上海话剧艺术中心 *Shànghǎi huàjù yìshù zhōngxīn*). The city's premier theater venue and troupe, the Shanghai Dramatic Arts Center presents an award-winning lineup of its own original pieces, plus those of other cutting-edge groups around China. It also stages Chinese-language adaptations, sometimes very inventive, of Western works, such as a festival of Samuel Beckett works reinterpreted through Chinese opera. ✉ *288 Anfu Lu, French Concession* ☎ *021/6473–4567* ⊕ *www.china-drama.com.*

SHOPPING

Shanghai is chock-a-block with places to spend money. The markup on luxury goods is extremely high in China, and even clothes at American chains are pricier here than in the States. Malls usually don't open until 10; boutiques open at 11. The upside is that chain stores tend to stay open later, with many closing at 10 pm. Independent shops close by 7:30 pm. Markets generally start earlier, at around 7:30 or 8, and close around 6. Most stores are open seven days a week.

Yu Garden, a major tourist haunt in the Old City area of Shanghai, can be overwhelming, but if you're looking for tchotchkes, hard bargaining brings rewards. Here is where you'll find imitation jade, tiny Buddha statues, costume jewelry, scarves, and the like. Also check out these streets that specialize in specific traditional products: **Fenyang Lu,** in the French Concession, and **Jinling Lu,** west of the Bund, for musical instruments; **Fuzhou Lu, between People's Square** and **the Bund,** in City Center, for books and art supplies, including calligraphy supplies; **Changle Lu** and **Maoming Lu** in the Former French Concession for *qipao* (Chinese-style dresses).

For a traditional massage, you'll find hundreds of blind massage parlors, inexpensive no-frills salons whose blind masseurs are closely attuned to the body's soft and sore spots. At the other end of the spectrum lie the hotel spas, luxurious retreats where pampering is at a premium.

XINTIANDI AND CITY CENTER

Exclusive and expensive stores are housed in reproduction traditional shikumen—stone gate houses. Your plastic will get plenty of work here, but step outside Xintiandi proper and you'll find charming streets upon which pajama-clad citizens still do their marketing.

CLOTHING AND SHOES

Shanghai Tang (上海滩 *Shànghǎitān*). This is one of China's leading fashion brands, with distinctive acid-bright silks, soft-as-a-baby's-bottom cashmere, and funky housewares. Sigh at the beautiful fabrics and gasp at the inflated prices. ✉ *181 Taicang Lu, City Center* ☎ *021/6384–1601* ⊕ *www.shanghaitang.com* ✉ *Cathay Mansion, 868 Huaihai Zhong Lu, French Concession* ☎ *021/5403–0580.*

Shanghai Trio (上海组合 *Shànghǎi zǔhé*). Chinese fabrics mixed with French flair, irresistible children's clothes and sweet little kimonos in bright colors, great utilitarian satchels that scream urban chic, and crafty necklaces are the stars of this range. This is the shop to come to when you want to spoil your precious nieces and nephews. ✉ *Xintiandi Style, 245 Madang Lu, 1st fl., Xintiandi* ☎ *021/5358–0188* ⊕ *www.shanghaitrio.com.cn.*

Uma Wang. When the Central St. Martins grad launched her eponymous line in 2005, little did she know her designs would soon be on the catwalks of London, Paris, New York, and Milan. Knitwear is Wang's signature design and, in her industrial chic shop, you'll find chunky vests, mohair dresses, and cardigans that can double as scarves. For the average shopper, the space is more gallery than viable shopping destination—as Wang's star has risen, so too have her prices; a dress now goes for more than Y3,500. ✉ *Xintiandi Style, L229, 245 Madang Lu, City Center* ☎ *021/3331–5109.*

GIFTS

Shanghai Museum Shop (上海博物馆商店 *Shànghǎi bówùguǎn shāngdiàn*). This selection of books on China and Chinese culture is impressive, and there are also some interesting children's books. Expensive reproduction ceramics are available, as are more affordable gifts like magnets, scarves, and notebooks. ✉ *Shanghai Museum, 201 Renmin Dadao, People's Sq., City Center* ☎ *021/6372–3500* ✉ *123 Taicang Lu, Luwan* ☎ *021/6384–7900.*

Zen Lifestore (钲艺廊 *Zhēng yìláng*). The porcelain goods here are truly lovely, available in an eye-popping array of colors. Designs range from delicate Chinese landscapes to modern geometric prints. You'll also find pretty candles, incense holders, and pipe-and-water-spigot candelabras (which are very cool, but a bit large to carry home). ✉ *118 Xingye Lu, City Center* ☎ *02/5382–2070* ✉ *7 Dongping Lu, French Concession* ☎ *021/6437–7390.*

JEWELRY

Amy Lin's Pearls and Jewelry (艾敏林氏珠宝 *Àimǐnlínshì zhūbǎo*). Friendly owner Amy Lin has some mystique surrounding her. It's alleged that she has sold pearls to European first ladies and American presidents. Whether or not that's just a rumor, her shop is an oasis in the chaotic sea that is Han City Fashion Plaza, i.e. the fake market—shop after shop of knockoff bags and outerwear. Here you'll find inexpensive trinkets, strings of seed pearls, and stunning Australian seawater pearl necklaces. ✉ *Han City, 580 Nanjing Xi Lu, 3rd fl., City Center* ☎ *021/5228–2372* ⊕ *www.amylinspearls.com.*

SPAS

Mandara Spa (蔓达梦水疗 *Màndámèng shuǐliáo*). With its exposed wood beams, unpolished bricks, and soothing fountains, the Mandara Spa in the JW Marriott resembles a traditional Chinese water town. Face and body treatments include the spa's signature massage, a 75-minute rubdown in which two therapists administer a blend of five massage styles: Shiatsu, Thai, Lomi Lomi, Swedish, and Balinese. ⊠ *JW Marriott, 399 Nanjing Xi Lu, City Center* ☎ *021/5359–4969* ⊕ *www. mandaraspa.com.*

THE BUND AND NANJING DONG LU

ANTIQUES

Shanghai Antique and Curio Store (上海文物商店 *Shànghǎi wénwù shāngdiàn*). A pleasant departure from the touristy shops in the area, this government-owned store is an excellent place to gauge whether you are being taken for a ride elsewhere. Goods range from small pieces of embroidery to wedding baskets (traditionally used to hold part of the bride's dowry). A sign warns that some pieces may not be taken out of the country, and we don't recommend you try and find out. ⊠ *192–246 Guangdong Lu, The Bund* ☎ *021/6321–5868.*

BOOKS AND ART SUPPLIES

Shanghai Foreign Language Bookstore. You could while away an hour or two in this massive bookstore, which has a huge selection of English-language books for children and adults. The downside here is that there's so much, it's not always organized well, and few of the clerks speak English. Still, wander the floors and you'll find new and back issues of magazines ranging from *Vogue* to *National Geographic*, and shelf upon shelf of novels and nonfiction books. Prices are higher than what you'd pay in the States but not terribly so. ⊠ *390 Fuzhou Lu, The Bund* ☎ *021/6322–3200.*

CERAMICS

Blue Shanghai White (海上青花 *Hǎishàngqīnghuā*). The eponymous colored ceramics here are designed and hand-painted by the owner and are made in Jingdezhen, once home to China's imperial kilns. Some larger pieces are made with wood salvaged from demolition sites around Shanghai. Prices start at Y75 for a cup to Y30,000 for a screen with ceramic panels. Teapots will run you Y1,000–Y2,000. ⊠ *17 Fuzhou Lu, Room 103, The Bund* ☎ *021/6323–0856* ⊕ *www.blueshanghai white.com.*

CLOTHING AND SHOES

Suzhou Cobblers (苏州臭皮匠 *Sūzhōu chòu píjiang*). Sold here are beautifully embroidered handmade shoes and slippers for men and women, with quirky designs such as cabbages. You'll also find funky bags made from rice sacks and sweet knitted toys and children's shoes and sweaters. ⊠ *17 Fuzhou Lu, Room 101, The Bund* ☎ *021/6321–7087* ⊕ *www. suzhou-cobblers.com.*

SPAS

Banyan Tree Spa. The Shanghai branch was China's first outpost of this ultraluxurious spa chain. It occupies the third floor of the Westin Shanghai. The spa's 13 chambers as well as its treatments are designed to reflect *wu sing,* the five elemental energies of Chinese philosophy: earth, gold, water, wood, and fire. Relax and choose from a menu of massages, facials, body scrubs, or indulgent packages that combine all three. ⊠ *Westin Shanghai, 88 Henan Zhong Lu, 3F, The Bund* ☎ *021/6335–1888* ⊕ *www. banyantreespa.com.*

> ### WHO ARE THE MIAO?
>
> Famous for their intricate embroidery work, the Miao are one of the oldest ethnic-minority groups in China and one of the largest groups still in Southwest China. The Miao may have existed as early as 200 BC, in the Han Dynasty. It's not only the Miao, however, who are accomplished embroidery artists. Many ethnic-minority groups in southwestern China make pieces of similar quality.

FORMER FRENCH CONCESSION

On the eastern edge of the Former French Concession, **Tianzifang**, often referred to as Taikang Lu, after the street on which it's on, is a former residential area whose redbrick lane houses are now a maze of quaint boutiques, cafés, restaurants, and bars.

CARPETS

Carpetstan (Carpetstan 手工羊毛地毯 *Carpetstan shǒugōng yángmáo dìtǎn*). The Kashgari owner here brings in all his rugs from artisans in Kashbar, Afghanistan, Samarkand, and Isfahan. The shop occasionally hosts lectures on carpets and other woven goods. ⊠ *570 Yongjia Lu, Room 313, French Concession* ☎ *021/6082–3065.*

CLOTHING AND SHOES

Charles Philip Shanghai. Italian expat Charles Philip found inspiration for his shoe line when he had a Shanghai cobbler make his then-favorite shirt into a pair of slip-ons. Today, the shoes for men and women are sold worldwide as loafers and lace-up sneakers. Shoes start online from Y1,500 but may be found for less in shops. ⊠ *101 Gao'an Lu, French Concession* ☎ *021/6422–6928* ⊕ *www.charlesphilipshanghai.com.*

Culture Matters (飞跃回力国货专售 *Fēiyuè huílì guóhuò zhuān shòu*). Feiyue sneakers are sold in Paris for €50, but in Shanghai, where they're made, you can get them starting from just Y50. Most are canvas with rubber soles, although there are a few stylish felt models and a couple in rubber that are good for rainy weather. There's another location at 47 Changle Lu, near Chongqing Lu, one block north of Huahai Lu. ⊠ *15 Dongping Lu, French Concession* ☎ *021/136-7188-2040.*

Feel (金粉世家 *Jīnfěn shìjiā*). The *qipao* may be a traditional Chinese dress, but Feel makes it a style for modern times as well with daring cutouts and thigh-skimming designs. ⊠ *Tianzifang, No. 3, Shop 110, 210 Taikang Lu, French Concession* ☎ *021/5465-4519.*

GIFTS AND HOUSEWARES

Fodor's Choice ★ **BrutCake** (BrutCake 創意製造社 *BrutCake chuàngyì zhìzuò shè*). Taiwanese designer Nicole Teng's showroom is welcoming, with comfy oversized chairs (for sale), reclaimed wood, and quirky ceramic pieces on every surface. In addition to dinnerware and ceramic lamp shades, BrutCake sells beautiful handwoven and dyed fabrics. ✉ *232 Anfu Lu, French Concession* ☎ *021/5448-8159* ⊕ *brutcake.com* ⊗ *Closed Mon.*

Harvest Studio. Drop in to watch the Miao women with their distinctive hair knots embroidering, and sometimes singing. This studio sells Miao-embroidered pillows, purses, and clothing, as well as the silver jewelry that traditionally adorns the Miao ceremonial costume. They also have a funky range of contemporary cotton and jersey pieces. ✉ *Tianzifang, Bldg. 3, Suite 118, 210 Taikang Lu, French Concession* ☎ *021/6473-4566.*

Madame Mao's Dowry (毛太设计 *Máotài shèjì*). This shop claims its covetable collection of mostly propaganda items from the '50s, '60s, and '70s is sourced from the countryside and areas in Sichuan Province and around Beijing and Tianjin. Whether they're authentic is up for debate. Shelves and racks are filled with women's clothing from local and international designers. Look for beautiful wrapping paper from Paper Tiger and dishtowels, notecards, and T-shirts from Pinyin Press, both designers based in Shanghai. Although this could be your one-stop shopping experience, remember this is communism at capitalist prices: expect to pay around Y200 for a small Revolution-era teapot and more than Y2,000 for a mirror from the same period. ✉ *207 Fumin Lu, French Concession* ☎ *021/5403-3551.*

Fodor's Choice ★ **Piling Palang** (噼呤啪啷 *Pīlìng pālāng*). Designers Judy Kim and Bing-bing Deng, who hails from Tianjin, founded their line of cheerful ceramics in Paris in 2010. Their French Concession boutique is packed with bowls, vases, plates, trays, and beautiful cloisonné tiffin carriers in a rainbow of bright colors. Some pieces cost as little as Y60, though the large items can run into the thousands. ✉ *183 Anfu Lu, French Concession* ☎ *021/6422-7577.*

SPAS

Double Rainbow Massage House (双彩虹按摩 *Shuāngcǎihóng ànmó*). With instructions clearly spelled out in English, Double Rainbow Massage House provides an inexpensive, nonthreatening introduction to traditional Chinese massage. Choose a masseur, state your preference for soft, medium, or hard pressure, then keep your clothes on for a 45- to 90-minute massage. There's no ambience, just a clean room with nine massage tables. ✉ *47 Yongjia Lu, French Concession* ☎ *021/6473-4000.*

Dragonfly (悠亭保健会所 *Yōutíng bǎojiàn huìsuǒ*). This local spa chain has claimed the middle ground between expensive hotel spas and workmanlike blind-man massage parlors. Don the suede-soft treatment robes for traditional Chinese massage or take them off for an aromatic oil massage. Dragonfly also has waxing and nail services. ✉ *218 Xinle Lu, 2nd fl., French Concession* ☎ *021/5403-6133.*

Yu Massage (愉庭保健会所 *Yútíng bǎojiàn huìsuǒ*). Expats flock to this tranquil spa, tucked inside a garden house on a quiet street in the

French Concession. The front desk staff speak English well and can help you choose one of their handful of massages. Body massages are done in private rooms; foot massages take place in a nook lined with plush recliners. Prices are very reasonable here, with an hour-long Chinese massage running Y120. ⊠ *366 Wuyuan Lu, French Concession* ☎ *021/5403–9931.*

TEA

Shanghai Huangshan Tea Company (上海黄山茶叶有限公司 *Shànghǎi huángshān cháyè yǒuxiàn gōngsī*). This tea shop sells traditional Yixing teapots as well as a huge selection of teas from across China. The higher the price, the better quality the tea, but teas costing around Y200 per 500 grams will please all but the most persnickety of tea connoisseurs. ⊠ *605 Huaihai Zhong Lu, French Concession* ☎ *021/5306–2974.*

Song Fang Maison de Thé. Parisian Florence Samson, who has lived in Shanghai for more than a decade, sells both Chinese and French tea at inflated prices, but the location in a 1930s lane house and the second-floor café, up a winding narrow staircase, make it quite charming. If you decide to purchase one of the cornflower-blue tea canisters as a souvenir, we recommend filling it up at a less expensive shop. ⊠ *227 Yongjia Lu, French Concession* ☎ *021/6433–8283* ⊕ *www.songfangtea.com.*

Wanling Tea House. British expat James and his wife Wan Ling, who hails from the tea-producing province Fujian, have built a tidy tea business in Shanghai. In addition to their Shanghai teahouse, where you can purchase a slew of teas from China and India and teapots and cups, they sell in the United Kingdom and Australia. The selection of tea here is ample, and foreigners can feel safe in the knowledge they won't be ripped off. ⊠ *Shop 15, 570 Yongjia Lu, French Concession* ☎ *021/6073–7573* ⊕ *www.wanlingteahouse.com.*

JING'AN, AND CHANGNING

GIFTS AND HOUSEWARES

Brocade Country (锦绣纺 *Jǐnxiùfǎng*). The English-speaking owner, Liu Xiao Lan, has a Miao mother and a broad knowledge of her pieces. The Miao sew their history into the cloth, and she knows the meaning behind each one. Some pieces are collector's items, and Ms. Liu has also started designing more wearable items. Antique embroidery can cost an arm and a leg, but smaller embroidery pieces are affordable and easy to slip into a suitcase. ⊠ *616 Julu Lu, Jing'an* ☎ *021/6279–2677.*

Fodor's Choice
★

Spin (旋 *Xuán*). Halfway between a gallery and a shop, Spin sells reasonably priced contemporary Chinese pottery handmade in Jingdezhen, China's pottery capital. We love the chopstick rests shaped like bone fragments and the too-cute dim sum paperweights in a little bamboo steamer. The second level has dinnerware, tea sets, and beautifully cast maple leaves that are just the right size for change or keys. ⊠ *360 Kangding Lu, Jing'an* ☎ *021/6279–2545.*

TEA

Tianshan Tea City (大不同天山茶城 *Dàbùtóng tiānshān chāchéng*). This place stocks all the tea in China, and then some. More than 300 vendors occupy three floors, but most vendors sell the same tea, so find a seller with whom you have a rapport and sit down for a taste test. You can buy such famous teas as West Lake dragon well (*longjing*) tea, from nearby Hangzhou, and Wuyi red-robe tea, as well as the tea sets to serve them in. Though the vendors encourage you to taste all their teas, as you should, they are not terribly pushy. ⊠ *520 Zhongshan Xi Lu, Changning.*

PUDONG

4

ANTIQUES

Pudong Antique Market (上海木蓝花阁家具丽 *Shànghǎi mùlán huāgé jiājù lì*). Shanghai Mulan Huage Jiajuli is more commonly known as the Pudong Antique Market, a massive dusty, musty warehouse deep into Pudong. This cavernous junkyard is filled with vintage tea tins, stone Buddhas in a range of sizes, gramophones, wooden stools, teak wardrobes, vintage toys, and assorted other antiques. Much of the furniture is in need of refurbishment, which the staff are able to do. Bargaining is encouraged, but you may not be able to bring the price down as much as you'd like. Bring a flashlight, wet wipes, and tissues. ■ TIP→ **Take metro Line 8 to Lingzhao Xincun, then take exit 1 and immediately turn left into the first lane on your left.** ⊠ *1788 Jingyan Lu, near Shangpu Xi Lu, Pudong* ☎ *021/137–0163–3804.*

MALLS

ifc Mall. Like its Hong Kong sister, this shiny mall is packed with luxury goods stores. The basement food court has everything from octopus balls to Japanese-style crepes, as well as very expensive imported groceries. The upper levels are dotted with restaurants serving varying fare, high in quality and in price. ■ TIP→ **The Lujiazui station of metro Line 2 is inside the mall.** ⊠ *8 Shiji Da Dao (Century Ave.), Pudong* ☎ *021/2020–7070.*

Super Brand Mall (正大广场 *Zhèngdà guǎngchǎng*). One of Asia's largest malls, this 10-story behemoth has a mind-boggling array of international shops and food stops, as well as a cineplex. It can be overwhelming if you don't love to shop. The basement food court has several good restaurants, including salad spot **Sproutworks**. ⊠ *168 Lujiazui Lu, Pudong* ☎ *021/6887–7888* ⊕ *www.superbrandmall.com.*

HONGKOU AND PUTUO

Duolun Lu is a pedestrian street in historic Hongkou District. Not only is it lined with examples of old architecture and home to a contemporary art gallery, its stalls and curio stores are ripe for browsing. In Putuo, **Moganshan Lu** once housed poor artists but has been developed and repackaged as M50, with galleries and a café or two making this a worthy place to while away an afternoon.

ART

Studio Rouge. A small but well-chosen collection of mainly photography and paintings by emerging and established local Chinese artists crowds this simple space. ⊠ *50 Moganshan Lu, Block 7, Putuo* ☎ *021/5252–7856.*

XUJIAHUI, HONGQIAO, AND GUBEI

Where six major shopping malls and giant electronics complexes converge, **Xujiahui** looks like it's straight out of mid-'90s Tokyo. Shop 'til you drop, or play with the gadgets and compare prices at the electronics shops.

ANTIQUES

Hu & Hu Antiques (古悦家俱 *Gùyuè jiājù*). Co-owner Marybelle Hu worked at Taipei's National Palace Museum as well as Sotheby's in Los Angeles before opening this shop with her sister-in-law Lin in 1998. The bright, airy showroom contains Tibetan chests and other rich furniture as well as a large selection of accessories, from lanterns to mooncake molds. The prices are higher than their competitors', but so is their standard of service. ⊠ *601-38 Qingxi Lu, Hongqiao* ☎ *021/3431–1212* ⊕ *www.hu-hu.com.*

EASTERN CHINA

Zhejiang and Fujian

WELCOME TO EASTERN CHINA

TOP REASONS TO GO

★ **Hangzhou Teatime:** Sip sublime *longjing* (Dragon Well) tea and stroll in the footsteps of Marco Polo at Hangzhou's romantic West Lake.

★ **Qiantang Tidal Bore:** Marvel at one of nature's most enthralling spectacles: the mighty tidal bore at the mouth of Zhejiang's Qiantang River, best seen during the fall equinox.

★ **Gulangyu:** Wander through narrow alleyways filled with a fascinating blend of Chinese and European architecture, and recharge in seaside garden pavilions on this historic, car-free island.

★ **Shaoxing Wine:** Dramatized by one of China's most famous writers, Lu Xun, Shaoxing wine is celebrated throughout the region. Potent to be sure, Shaoxing wine is de rigueur for local dining.

★ **Hakka Roundhouses:** The founder of the Republic of China, Dr. Sun Yat-sen, came from China's proud Hakka minority group, whose ancient tradition of rounded-home architecture is now treasured.

1 Hangzhou. Described by Marco Polo as the finest and noblest city in the world, Hangzhou is most famous for the beautiful West Lake. It's also a great place to shop for colorful silks and smooth longjing tea.

2 Shaoxing. Shaoxing is famed for its historic homes, literary past, pretty canals, and many traditional bridges. The well-preserved heritage areas still capture the historic atmosphere of a traditional Yangtze Delta town. Visit the stunning Bazi Bridge, which is shaped like a figure eight and was erected more than 800 years ago.

3 Ningbo. A perfect blend of old and new, this bustling seaside metropolis is the ideal place to comfortably veer off the standard tourist trail. Climb the ancient Tianfeng Pagoda to survey the busy masses and, come nightfall, head over to laowaitan (old Bund), the city's entertainment district complete with a centuries-old Portuguese church and a handful of international bars and restaurants.

4 Xiamen. With a bird's-eye view of the Taiwan Straight, Xiamen is poised to profit from the windfall of increased economic activity between Taiwan and

Mainland China. Famous for its party atmosphere and popular with young expats, Xiamen's trendy clubs and upscale restaurants are becoming as enticing as the city's sea views and botanical gardens.

5 Gulangyu. This pedestrian-only island is just a five-minute boat ride from Xiamen. The colonial mansions are leftover from Gulangyu's past as an International Foreign Settlement.

JIANGXI

Wuyi Mountain Natural Reserve

Shaowu

Sanming

Changting

Longyan

Hakka Settlements of Yongding

GUANGDONG

5

GETTING ORIENTED

With thousands of miles of coastline, the provinces of Zhejiang and Fujian form the rounded belly section of China's east coast. Indeed, their shores front the East China Sea and the South China Sea. Zhejiang Province's primary ports of call are the cities of Ningbo and Hangzhou, both of which connect conveniently to Shanghai by bus and train. Hangzhou is also famous as the southernmost city of the Grand Canal. Directly south of Zhejiang is the lush and mountainous province of Fujian. With its proximity to the Taiwan Straight, the wealthy coastal cities of Fujian are convenient to each other, but the province's mountainous interior make them a long train trip away from the rest of the region.

Updated by
Kate Springer

In Eastern China, the past's rich legacy and the challenges of, and aspirations for, China's future combine in a present that is dizzying in its variety and speed of transformation. Zhejiang and Fujian, often overlooked on the standard Beijing–Shanghai–Hong Kong tourist trail, offer some of the country's most verdant scenery and a plethora of diversions, like hiking through ancient villages, bicycling along lush tea fields, and lounging on lively beaches.

Zhejiang has always been a hub of culture, learning, and commerce. Its cities, with their elegant gardens, elaborate temples, and fine crafts, evoke the sophisticated and refined world of classical China's literati. Since the Southern Song Dynasty (1127–79), large numbers of Fujianese have immigrated to Southeast Asia. As a result, Fujian Province has strong ties to overseas Chinese. In 1979, Fujian was allowed to form in Xiamen the first Special Economic Zone (SEZ)—a testing ground for a capitalist market economy. Today, although Xiamen is a wealthy place with a vibrant economy, the city has managed to retain its old-world charm.

PLANNING

WHEN TO GO

Fall and spring are the ideal times to visit the region. Spring, especially April and May, has very comfortable temperatures, and the trees and flowers are in full bloom. Hangzhou's spectacular cherry blossoms are out in spring, dotting the gardens surrounding the West Lake. Summers are hot and muggy, and winters are short (the temperature rarely dips below zero) but miserably wet, windy, and chilly. Typhoons can strike any time from late summer through autumn. The region has a long and very pleasant fall season, with moderate weather and clear skies lasting into early December. Chinese tourists flood in during the long weekends in April, May, and June (which change according to the lunar calendar), "Golden Week" (always the first week of October), and during Chinese New Year (late January to mid-February), so avoid traveling during these times.

GETTING HERE AND AROUND

Shanghai is generally the best place to begin exploring Eastern China. It has good amenities, and with two airports and four train stations, it offers myriad connections across the country. Most major travel agents in Shanghai speak English. If you want to make Hangzhou your base, many cheap flights are available, and the list of connecting destinations is constantly growing.

AIR TRAVEL

Air travel in Eastern China is very straightforward and simple. Hangzhou's Xiaoshan International Airport is modern and well connected, and domestic flights are abundant. Hangzhou is increasingly adding more international routes, already including Amsterdam (KLM), Kuala Lumpur (AirAsia), Tokyo (Air Nippon), Seoul (Asiana Airlines), Bangkok (China Eastern Airlines), Malé (Mega Maldives), Hong Kong (Hong Kong Airlines), and Paris (Hainan Airlines). Ningbo offers direct flights to Taipei (China Eastern Airlines), Hong Kong (Dragonair), and Beijing (China Eastern Airlines). Xiamen is well connected to Jakarta (Air China), Singapore (Xiamen Airlines), Hong Kong (Dragonair), and Manila (China Southern).

BUS TRAVEL

Traveling by bus in Eastern China is a great way to get around, as even tiny cities and villages will have a station. Large cities such as Hangzhou will have several stations. Buses in Eastern China will usually be relatively new, air-conditioned vehicles, and almost always leave on time. The biggest headache you'll likely encounter is trying to navigate through the masses at the stations to buy your tickets. Ask your hotel to purchase tickets in advance, as line etiquette in China can be frustrating, especially for non-Mandarin speakers. Buses between major cities such as Hangzhou and Ningbo leave frequently, so just show up and get on the next available departure.

CAR TRAVEL

Hiring a driver is possible and, for a large group, makes far more sense than hailing cabs. Plan on paying at least $165 for an eight-hour day. Hangzhou Car Service operates an impressive fleet of international vehicles and can arrange city tours, intercity transport, and airport pickup. Since taxis are cheap and plentiful, navigating within cities is fairly easy, but it's essential to have your destinations mapped out and written down in Chinese ahead of time.

Contact Info Hangzhou Car Service ☎ *0755/2594–1385* ⊕ *www. hangzhoucarservice.com.*

TRAIN TRAVEL

Bullet trains are the easiest, quickest, and most comfortable option. For the shortest journeys, look for G- or D-coded trains, or the letters CHR (China High-Speed Rail). Shanghai to Hangzhou, for example, takes approximately an hour, and there are roughly 30 daily departures.

D-coded trains take 1 hour and 15 minutes. Slower trains are uncomfortable for long distances and best avoided.

HEALTH AND SAFETY

Many big cities have foreign doctors and clinics catering to the expatriate community. These clinics charge exponentially more than Chinese hospitals, but hygiene standards are comparable to those of North America and Western Europe. Chinese hospitals, crowded and grimy, should be used as a last resort.

Petty crime is common, especially in crowded places such as train and bus stations. Use common sense and keep an eye on your valuables. Violent crime targeting foreigners is practically nonexistent, and most visitors feel comfortable walking around any time of day.

MONEY MATTERS

Prices are negotiable at markets and even in some malls, but don't try to haggle at a supermarket or in a restaurant. Do not accept prices quoted in foreign currency, and never pay more than you think the article is really worth. Tourist markups can hit 1,000% in major attractions. Don't be afraid to tell the vendor, "*Tai gui le!*" ("too expensive") and walk away. He or she will probably call you back with a better price.

China is not a tipping country; however, tips constitute the majority of a tour guide's income.

RESTAURANTS

Zhejiang cuisine is often steamed or roasted, and has a subtle, salty flavor; specialties include yellow croaker with Chinese cabbage, sea eel, drunken chicken, and stewed chicken. In Shaoxing, locals traditionally start the day by downing a bowl or two of *huang jiu* (yellow rice wine), the true breakfast of champions. Shaoxing's most famous dish is its deep-fried *chou dofu,* or stinky tofu. Try it with a touch of the local chili sauce.

The cuisine of Fujian has its own characteristics. Spareribs are a specialty, as are soups and stews using a soy and rice-wine stock. The coastal cities of Fujian offer a wonderful range of seafood, including river eel with leeks, fried jumbo prawns, and steamed crab.

HOTELS

Hotels in this region cater to all budgets, all the way up to luxurious resorts and international chains offering every creature comfort. Besides a general lack of amenities, cheaper options may not be able to accept foreign credit cards. Family-run guesthouses are rare, as are boutique hotels. Consider a domestic chain called the Orange Hotel, with dozens of locations throughout China, including Hangzhou and Ningbo. Comfortable rooms are available from US$50 to $85 a night.

Hotel reviews have been shortened. For full information, visit Fodors. com.

WHAT IT COSTS IN YUAN				
	$	**$$**	**$$$**	**$$$$**
Restaurants	under Y50	Y50–Y99	Y100–Y165	over Y165
Hotels	under Y1,100	Y1,100–Y1,399	Y1,400–Y1,800	over Y1,800

Restaurant prices are the average cost of a main course at dinner or, if dinner is not served, at lunch. Hotel prices are the lowest cost of a standard double room in high season.

VISITOR INFORMATION

Tourist kiosks are ubiquitous in major cities and tourist destinations, but mostly cater to domestic travelers. The best sources for visitor information are the English-language city magazines like *More Hangzhou* (⊕ *www.morehangzhou.com*) and *What's On Xiamen* (⊕ *www. whatsonxiamen.com*), both of which can be found at international hotels and restaurants.

TOURS

Tour Info Seven Cups. Tea lovers should consider Seven Cups, which offers 12- to 15-day visits to tea gardens, as well as hands-on experience with the harvest and production methods of some of China's finest teas. ☎ *0520/628–2952* ⊕ *www.sevencups.com* ✉ *From US$4,550.* **Discover Fujian.** Experience the Fujian *tulou* (round earthen structures) with Discover Fujian. The company leads reasonably priced day trips, as well as four- to five-day journeys, to these ancient, circular houses. ⊠ *1118 Xiahe Lu, 10th fl., Xiamen* ☎ *0592/398–9901* ⊕ *www.discoverfujian. com* ✉ *From Y500 per person.*

ZHEJIANG

The province of Zhejiang showcases the region's agricultural prowess and dedication to nature, even as it is one of China's most populous urban regions. The capital city of Hangzhou is famous for West Lake, which is visited by millions of tourists annually. A center of culture and trade, Zhejiang is also one of China's wealthiest provinces. Hangzhou served as one of the country's eight ancient capital cities, after the Song Dynasty rulers fled from Jurchen invaders. Throughout history, the city also benefited from its position as the last stop on the Grand Canal, the conduit for supplying goods to the imperial north. Today the city's main draws are foggy West Lake, the myriad pagodas, temples, street markets, and its famous longjing tea.

Shaoxing showcases another aspect of Zhejiang life. The small-town flavor of this city-on-canals survives, despite a growing population. Several high-profile figures helped put Shaoxing on the map, including former Premier Zhou Enlai and novelist Lu Xun.

Geographically, the river basin's plains in the north near Shanghai give way to mountains in the south of the province. Besides grain, the province also is recognized in China for its tea, crafts, silk production, and long tradition of sculpture and carving.

HANGZHOU

Approximately an hour (202 km, 126 miles) southwest of Shanghai by train.

Hangzhounese are immensely proud of their city, and will often point to a classical saying that identifies it as an "earthly paradise." Indeed, for locals, Hangzhou is one of the country's most livable cities, thanks to lots of green space and plenty of parks. Though "paradise" is an exaggeration, the city manages to retain much of its historic charm despite what can be considered an overly robust tourism market. Visitors come from all over China to see West Lake, the temples, and the silk markets. Beyond the major tourist draws, there's also a small but growing mix of local shops and low-key restaurants, as well as an increasing number of fine-dines and bars, making Hangzhou a pleasant day or overnight trip.

GETTING HERE AND AROUND

Hangzhou is best accessed by train; the high-speed line takes around an hour from Shanghai. Buses will get you here from Shanghai in 3 hours or from Suzhou in 2½ hours.

AIR TRAVEL Hangzhou Xiaoshan International Airport, about 30 km (18 miles) southeast of the city, has frequent flights to Hong Kong, Guangzhou, and Beijing, which are all about two hours away. There are also flights from other major cities around the region.

Major hotels offer limousine service to the airport. Taxis to the airport cost around Y100. A bus (Y20 per person) leaves from the CAAC office on Tiyuchang Lu at least every 30 minutes between 7:30 am and 11 pm.

Air Contacts CAAC (武林门航空售票 *Wǔlín mén hángkōng shòupiào*). ✉ 390 Tiyuchang Lu ☎ 0571/8515–4259. **Dragonair** (港龍航空有限公司 *Gǎng lóng hángkōng yǒuxiàn gōngsī*). ✉ Unit 1203, Area A, Euro America Center, 18 Jiaogong Lu ☎ 400/888–6628 ⊕ www.dragonair.com. **Hangzhou Xiaoshan International Airport** (杭州萧山国际机场 *Hangzhou Xiaoshan International Airport*). ☎ 0571/96299 ⊕ www.hzairport.com.

BUS TRAVEL Hangzhou is the bus hub for the province and has several stations. The Hangzhou Passenger Transport Station (Jiubao) is the city's biggest, with several hundred departures per day to destinations like Shaoxing (1 hour), Suzhou (2½ hours), and Shanghai (3 hours). The West Bus Station (Xi Zhan) has several buses daily to Huangshan (Yellow Mountain), as well as to Yushan. About 9 km (5 miles) north of the city is the North Bus Station (Bei Zhan), where there are buses to Hubei (16 hours), Shandong (28 hours), and Beijing (32 hours). Buses are inexpensive and leave frequently, but because of traffic delays and sometimes wild driving, we do recommend high-speed trains where available.

In addition to Hangzhou's regular city buses, a series of modern, air-conditioned buses connect most major tourist sights (Y3–Y5 per trip); these are designated by a Y prefix. Bus Y9 is the main tourist link, running around West Lake to most of the major sites. Bus Y3 runs to Diamond Hill, the China National Silk Museum, and the China Tea Museum.

Bus Contacts North Bus Station (杭州汽车北站 *Hángzhōu qìchē běi zhàn*). ✉ 766 Moganshan Lu ☎ 0571/8809–3099 ⊕ *Hángzhōu qìchē běi zhàn*. **Passenger Transport Central Station (East Bus Station)** (杭州客运中心站 *Hángzhōu kèyùn zhōngxīn zhàn*). ✉ 71 Genshan Xi Lu ☎ 0571/8519–1122. **West Bus Station** (杭州汽车西站 *Hángzhōu xī qìchē zhàn*). ✉ 357 Tianmushan Lu ☎ 0571/8522–2237.

TAXI TRAVEL Hangzhou's taxi fleet ferries visitors from West Lake to far-flung sights like the Temple of the Soul's Retreat and the China Tea Museum. You'll need your destination written down in Chinese characters. Fares usually run Y30 to Y45. You can also book cabs by the hour (about Y100) or half day (Y400), and this is much easier than flagging one down. If you're hailing a cab on the street, make sure the meter is being used; many drivers will not turn on the meter or will insist that it's broken.

■TIP→ Avoid looking for a taxi between 4 and 5 pm, as virtually all drivers are finishing their shifts and refuse to pick anyone up.

TRAIN TRAVEL Travel between Shanghai and Hangzhou is very efficient. Fast trains take about an hour, while local trains take two or more. The train station can be chaotic, but hotel travel desks will often book advance tickets for a small fee. Trains also run to Suzhou (1½ hours), Nanjing (about 2 hours), and most cities in Fujian.

Train Information Hangzhou Train Station (杭州火车站 *Hángzhōu huǒchē zhàn*). ⊠ *1 Youyi Lu, near Jiangcheng Lu* ☎ *0571/9510–5105.*

RENT A BIKE

West Lake is one of East China's most pleasant places for bicycling. This path, away from car traffic, is also a quick way to move between the area's major sights. Numerous public bike-rental agencies are scattered around the lake, especially near Orioles Singing in the Willows and on Hubin Lu, down the road from the Hyatt and adjacent to a Starbucks and Dairy Queen. Rentals are free for the first hour, maxing out at Y3 per hour after three hours, between 6 am and 10 pm. A Y200 deposit and some form of identification are required, and we do not recommend using your passport as ID.

SAFETY AND PRECAUTIONS
Hangzhou is a very safe city. Even so, be cautious in crowded places, such as the train station, and keep a close eye on valuables.

TIMING
Give yourself at least two full days to explore the city. West Lake and the pagodas and gardens that dot its periphery will occupy at least a full day. Hefang Pedestrian Street, Lingyin Temple, and a variety of museums will fill another day.

ESSENTIALS
Bank Bank of China (中国银行 *Zhōngguó yínháng*). ⊠ *321 Fengqi Lu* ☎ *0571/8501–1888* ⊕ *www.boc.cn/en.*

Medical Assistance Sir Run Run Shaw Hospital International Service Clinic (学院附属邵逸夫医院国际门诊部 *Xuéyuàn fùshǔ shào yīfū yīyuàn guójì ménzhěn bù*). ⊠ *Tower 3, 3 Qingchun Lu, 5th fl.* ☎ *0571/8609–0073* ⊕ *www.srrsh-english.com.*

Visitor and Tour Info Backyard Travel. The professional and knowledgeable travel gurus at Backyard Travel offer custom-made tours. They run a three-day, two-night Ancient Water Towns of China tour (from US$795 per person), which lets you soak up the scenic surroundings in Hangzhou, Suzhou, and Wuzhen; if you want to focus on a specific city, the guides can come up with a personalized tour. ☎ *800/2225–9273* ⊕ *www.backyardtravel.com* ✉ *From US$55.* **China International Travel Service Zhejiang** ⊠ *1 Shihan Lu, next to the Hangzhou Tourism Bureau* ☎ *0571/8515–3301* ⊕ *www.cits.net.* **CITS.** You can hire a car, driver, and translator through CITS, which has two offices in the city—one near Hangzhou Railway Station, and another north of West Lake. It's relatively inexpensive, and you'll get discounts on attraction entrance fees that you wouldn't be able to negotiate yourself. Price includes private car, English-speaking guide, and admissions. ⊠ *Eastcom Mansion, 398 Wensan Lu, 10th*

A picture-perfect sunset over West Lake

fl. ☎ 0571/8505–9039 ⊕ *www.cits.net* ✉ *From Y1,040.* **Hangzhou Tourism Commission** ✉ *228 Yan'an Lu* ☎ *0571/96123* ⊕ *en.gotohz.com.*

EXPLORING

AROUND WEST LAKE

West Lake (西湖 *Xīhú*). With arched bridges stretching over the water, West Lake is the heart of Hangzhou. Originally a bay, the whole area has been built up gradually throughout the years, a combination of natural changes and human shaping of the land. The photogenic shores are enhanced by meandering paths, artificial islands, and countless pavilions with upturned roofs. Two pedestrian causeways cross the lake: **Bai** in the north and **Su** in the west. They are named for two poet–governors from different eras who invested in landscaping and developing the lake. Ideal for strolling or biking, both walkways are lined with willow and peach trees, crossed by bridges, and dotted with benches where you can pause to admire the views. ■ TIP→ **The lake's pathways are jam-packed on weekends and during holidays, particularly Golden Week (first week of October).** ✉ *Along Nanshan Lu.*

Precious Stone Hill (宝石山 *Bǎoshí shān*). The slender spire of Baochu Pagoda rises atop the romantically named Precious Stone Hill Floating in Rosy Clouds. The brick-and-stone pagoda is visible from just about anywhere on the lake. From the hilltop you can see across the lake to the city. Numerous paths from the lake lead up the hill, which is dotted with Buddhist and Taoist shrines. Several caves provide shade from the hot summer sun. ✉ *North of West Lake.*

Fodor's Choice ★ **Evening Sunlight at Thunder Peak Pagoda** (雷锋夕照 *Léifēng xīzhào*). On the southeastern shore of West Lake is the Evening Sunlight at Thunder

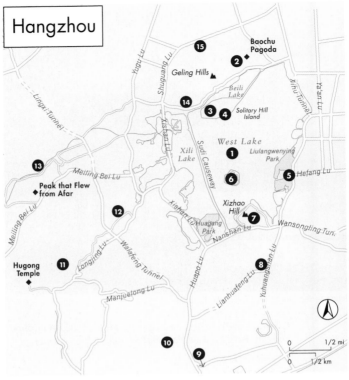

Peak Pagoda. Local legend says that the original Thunder Peak Pagoda was constructed to imprison a snake-turned-human who lost her mortal love on West Lake. The pagoda collapsed in 1924, perhaps finally freeing the White Snake. A new tower, completed in 2002, sits beside the remains of its predecessor. There's a sculpture on each level, including one that depicts the tragic story of the White Snake. The foundation dates to AD 976 and is an active archaeological site, where scientists uncovered a miniature silver pagoda containing what is said to be a lock of the Buddha's hair; it's on display in a separate hall. The view of the lake is breathtaking, particularly at sunset. ☒ *15 Nanshan Lu* ☏ *0571/8798–2111* ☐ *Y40* ⏲ *Daily 8 am–8:30 pm.*

Orioles Singing in the Willows (柳浪闻莺 *Liǔlàng wényíng*). Along the eastern bank of West Lake is Orioles Singing in the Willows, a nice park from which to watch boats traverse the water. The park comes alive during Lantern Festival, which falls on the 15th day of the first lunar month, usually in February or March. Paper lanterns are set to float on the river under the willow boughs. ☒ *11 Nanshan Lu, near intersection of Hefang Jie and Nanshan Lu.*

Solitary Hill Island (孤山 *Gūshān*). A palace for the exclusive use of the emperor during his visits to Hangzhou once stood on Solitary Hill Island, the largest island in West Lake. On its southern side is a small,

WEST LAKE IS THE BEST

There's a well-known Chinese poem that says, "Of all the lakes, north, south, east and west, the one at West Lake is the best." Start exploring where Pinghai Lu meets Hubin Lu in the northeastern part of the lake. There's a popular boardwalk with weeping willows, restaurants, and a lakeside teahouse.

Wending north, you can cross the street to ascend a small hill capped with the Baochu Pagoda. Here the views of West Lake are some of the best in the city. Once you climb

down, you can venture to the Baidi and Sudi causeways through the middle of the lake. Don't miss the classical Lingyin Temple, nestled in the nearby hills.

By night, take a guided boat from the southern shore to see one of Hangzhou's best views: the Three Pools Mirroring the Moon. When candles are set inside the trio of miniature pagodas, the glow creates a silhouette on the water resembling the moon.

carefully composed park with several pavilions and a pond. A path leads up the hill to the Xiling Seal Engraver's Society, where professional carvers design and create seals. The society's garden has one of the best views of the lake. ⊠ *Bai Causeway* 🖾 *Free* ☺ *Daily 8–dusk*

NEED A BREAK?

Cathay View Foot Massage. Reward yourself with a heavenly foot or full-body massage at Cathay View Foot Massage. For a quick respite, try the 45-minute foot massage (Y158), or settle in for a 90-minute body massage (Y228) that includes a generous spread of tea, fruit, and snacks in a cozy, dimly lit private room. This spot is just off Nanshan Lu, down a small street near the ⇨ *Crystal Orange Hotel.* ⊠ *7 Qingbo Jie, off Nanshan Lu* ☎ *0571/8768–0118.*

Three Pools Mirroring the Moon (三潭印月 *Sāntán yínyué*). Here you'll find walkways surrounding several large ponds, all connected by zigzagging bridges. Off the island's southern shore are three Ming Dynasty–era mini stone pagodas. During the Mid-Autumn Moon Festival, held in the middle of September, lanterns are lit in the pagodas, creating the reflections that give the island its name. Leisure boats from several spots around the lake, including a dock near Yue Fei's memorial, will shuttle you to the pagodas for around Y55. ⊠ *Southern side of West Lake* 🖾 *Y55, includes boat ride* ☺ *Daily 7–5:30.*

Zhejiang Provincial Museum (浙江省博物馆 *Zhéjiāng shěng bówùguǎn*). Solitary Hill Island is home to the Zhejiang Provincial Museum, which has a good collection of archaeological finds, as well as bronzes, paintings, and exhibits focusing on the province's ethnic minority groups. English signage isn't great here, but the visuals themselves are enticing. ⊠ *25 Gushan Lu* ☎ *0571/8798–0281* ⊕ *www.zhejiangmuseum.com* 🖾 *Free* ☺ *Weekdays 8:30–4:30.*

TOP ATTRACTIONS

China National Silk Museum (中国丝绸博物馆 *Zhōngguó sīchóu bówùguǎn*). From worm to weave, the China National Silk Museum explores traditional silk production, illustrating every step of the process. By the end, you'll comprehend the cost of this fine fiber made from cocoons of mulberry-munching larvae. On display are looms, brocades, and a rotating exhibit of historic robes from different Chinese dynasties. The first-floor shop has the city's largest selection of silk, and sells it by the meter. The museum is south of West Lake, on the road to Jade Emperor Hill. ⊠ *73–1 Yuhuangshan Lu* ☎ *0571/8703–5150* ⊕ *www. chinasilkmuseum.com* ⊡ *Free* ☉ *Daily 9–4:45.*

Fodor's Choice ★ **China Tea Museum** (中国茶叶博物馆 *Zhōngguó cháyé bówùguǎn*). The fascinating China Tea Museum explores all facets of China's tea culture, such as the utensils used in the traditional ceremony. Galleries contain fascinating information about the varieties and quality of leaves, brewing techniques, and gathering methods, all with good English explanations. A shop offers a wide range of teas, without the bargaining you'll encounter at Dragon Well Tea Park. ⊠ *88 Longjing Lu, north of Dragon Well Tea Park* ☎ *0571/8796–4221* ⊕ *www.teamuseum.cn* ⊡ *Free* ☉ *Tues.–Sun. 8:30–4:30.*

Dragon Well Tea Park (龙井茶园 *Lóngjǐng cháyuán*). This park is named for an ancient well whose water is considered ideal for brewing the famous local longjing (Dragon Well) tea. Distinguishing between varieties and grades of tea can be confusing for novices, especially under high pressure from the eager hawkers. It's worth a preliminary trip to the nearby tea museum to bone up on what's what. The highest quality varieties are very expensive, but once you take a sip you will taste the difference. Prices are intentionally high, so be sure to bargain. ⊠ *Longjing Lu, next to Dragon Well Temple.*

Fodor's Choice ★ **Lingyin Temple** (灵隐寺 *Língyǐn sì*). One of the major Zen Buddhist shrines in China, Lingyin Temple (Temple of the Soul's Retreat) was founded in AD 328 by Hui Li, a Buddhist monk from India. He looked at the surrounding mountains and exclaimed, "This is the place where the souls of immortals retreat," hence the name. This site is especially notable for religious carvings on the nearby **Peak Flown From Afar** (Feilai Feng). From the 10th to the 14th century, monks and artists carved more than 300 statues in and around these grottos. Uprisings, revolutions, and wars have changed the face of the shrine. The main temple was restored in 1974 following the end of the Cultural Revolution. About 5 km (3 miles) west of West Lake, the temple and carvings are among the most popular spots in Hangzhou and as such are positively teeming come weekends. ■**TIP→** To avoid crowds, visit on weekdays. ⊠ *End of Lingyin Lu* ☎ *0571/8796–8665* ⊡ *Carvings Y45, temple Y30* ☉ *Park daily 5:30–5:30, temple daily 7–5:30.*

WORTH NOTING

Dreaming of the Tiger Spring (虎跑梦泉 *Hǔ pǎo mèng quán*). According to legend, a traveling monk decided this setting would be perfect for a temple, but was disappointed to discover that there was no source of water. That night he dreamed that two tigers had ripped up the earth around him. When he awoke he was lying next to a spring. On the grounds is an intriguing "dripping wall" cut out of the mountain. Locals line up with jugs to collect the water that pours from its surface, believing that the water has special qualities—and it does. Ask someone in the temple's souvenir shop to float a coin on the surface of the water to prove it. ✉ *Hupao Lu, near the Pagoda of Six Harmonies* 🎫 *Y15* ⏲ *Daily 6–6.*

Pagoda of Six Harmonies (六和塔 *Liùhé tǎ*). Atop Moon Mountain stands the impressive Pagoda of Six Harmonies, also referred to as the Liuhe Pagoda. Those who climb to the top of the seven-story pagoda are rewarded with great views across the Qiantang River. Originally lanterns were lit in its windows and the pagoda served as a lighthouse for ships navigating the river. On the 18th day of the eighth lunar month, the pagoda is packed with people wanting the best seat to view the Qiantang Tidal Bore. On this day, the flow of the river reverses itself, creating large waves that for centuries have delighted observers. Behind the pagoda is a large park, one of our favorite family-friendly spaces in Hangzhou. The grounds house an exhibit of 100 or so miniature pagodas, representing every Chinese style. The pagoda is 4 km (2½ miles) south of West Lake. ✉ *16 Zhijiang Lu, on the Qiantang River* 🎫 *Y20–Y30* ⏲ *Daily 6:30 am–5:30 pm.*

Tomb of Yue Fei (岳飞墓 *Yuèfēi mù*). Near Solitary Hill Island stands this shrine to honor General Yue Fei (1103–42), who led Song Dynasty armies against foreign invaders. When he was a young man, his mother tattooed his back with the commandment "Repay the nation with loyalty." This made Yue Fei a hero both for his patriotic loyalty and filial piety. At the height of his success, a jealous rival convinced the emperor to have Yue Fei executed. A subsequent leader pardoned the warrior and enshrined him as a national hero. Statues of Yue Fei's accusers kneel in shame nearby. Traditionally, visitors would spit on statues of the traitors, but now a sign near the statue asks them to glare instead. ✉ *80 Beishan Lu, sest of Solitary Hill Island* ☎ *0571/8798–6653* 🎫 *Y25* ⏲ *Daily 7:30–6.*

Yellow Dragon Cave (黄龙洞 *Huánglóng dòng*). At the foot of Gem Hill is Yellow Dragon Cave, famous for a never-ending stream of water spurting from the head of a yellow dragon. Nearby are a garden, a stage for traditional Yue opera performances, and a grove in which you'll see examples of rare "square bamboo." ✉ *69 Shuguang Lu* ☎ *0571/8797–2468* 🎫 *Y15* ⏲ *Daily 8–6.*

5

Buddha sculptures on the face of the Peak Flown From Afar

WHERE TO EAT

For traditional Hangzhou food, check out Gaoyin Street (*Gāoyín Jiē*, 高银街). It's a lively strip of restaurants, snack stalls, and teahouses. Expect touts, English menus, and blazing neon signs.

$ MIDDLE EASTERN

🍴 **Dong Yi Shun** (东伊顺 *Dōngyīshùn*). All day, lines form at the take-out window for the sesame-coated naan breads and plump, well-seasoned lamb skewers. Sit inside for a large picture menu of Western Chinese and Middle Eastern dishes. The lamb-and-cheese pancake with a side order of yogurt comes highly recommended. It's a great alternative to oily Chinese dishes. Walk off the calories afterwards on neon-lit Gaoyin Street. [$] *Average main: Y45* ✉ *99 Gaoyin Jie* ☎ *0571/8780–5163* 💳 *No credit cards.*

$$$ MODERN EUROPEAN

🍴 **The Fat Duck** (肥鸭餐厅 *Féi yā cāntīng*). Tucked away in Loft 49—a converted warehouse that's now used as multipurpose artistic space—the trendy, industrial-chic restaurant feels very metropolitan. When you tire of Chinese food and crave a taste of the West, this is where to come. Naturally, duck is on the menu, as are Caesar salads, cod, and roast lamb. [$] *Average main: Y100* ✉ *No. 3, Loft 49, 49 Tongyi Lu* ☎ *0571/8831–8090.*

$$ INTERNATIONAL

🍴 **Hanyan Coffee House** (寒烟咖啡馆 *Hányān kāfēiguǎn*). On a quiet street just east of West Lake, this Himalayan café brews some of the city's best java. It's nearly impossible to pass by the curious street-side seating—picture a colorful wooden bench surrounded by potted plants, a vintage TV, and two golden Buddhas—without taking a peek inside. Inside, the eclectic space is outfitted with quilted tablecloths, comfy sofas, knit blankets, and walls stacked with books and knickknacks. Aside from coffee and a room exploding with character, you can also expect steamy teas, sandwiches, and a well-stocked bar. $ *Average main: Y50* ⊠ *128 Laodong Lu* ☎ *0571/8160–6978.*

$ ✕**Honeymoon Dessert** (滿記甜品
CAFÉ *Mǎnjì tiánpǐn*). Originally from Hong Kong, this popular dessert spot is rapidly expanding all over the mainland. Occupying a prime piece of real estate along the main drag of the West Lake area, the bright place is sleek and spotless. Trendy Hangzhou locals pack in at all hours for the inventive and exotic creations. The mango or durian pancake filled with fresh whipped cream is especially yummy. An English picture menu will help guide you. $ *Average main: Y25* ⊠ *98 Youdian Lu* ☎ *0571/8706–7050* ⊕ *www.honeymoon-dessert. com* ⊟ *No credit cards.*

$ ✕**Lingyin Si Vegetarian Restaurant** (灵隐寺面馆 *Língyǐn sì miànguǎn*).
VEGETARIAN Inside the Temple of the Soul's Retreat (Lingyin Si), this restaurant has turned the Buddhist restriction against eating meat into an opportunity to invent a range of delicious vegetarian dishes. Soy replaces chicken and beef, meaning your meal is as benevolent to your health as to the animal world. $ *Average main: Y45* ⊠ *End of Lingyin Si Lu, western shore of West Lake* ☎ *0571/8796–8665* ⊕ *www.lingyinsi.org* ⊟ *No credit cards* ☉ *Daily 9–4:30. No dinner.*

$$$ ✕**Louwailou** (楼外楼 *Lóuwàilóu*). Back in 1848, this place was a simple
CHINESE FUSION fish shack on West Lake. Business boomed and it became the most
Fodor's Choice famous restaurant in the province. With a focus on Zhejiang cuisine,
★ Louwailou specializes in lake perch, which is steamed and served with vinegar sauce. Another highlight is the classic *dongpo rou*, pork slow-cooked in yellow rice wine and tender enough to cut with chopsticks. Hangzhou's most famous dish, beggar's chicken, is wrapped in lotus leaves and baked in a clay shell. It's as good as it sounds. $ *Average main: Y150* ⊠ *30 Gushan Lu, southern tip of Solitary Hill Island* ☎ *0571/8796–9682* ⊕ *www.louwailou.com.cn.*

WHERE TO STAY

$$$$ 🛏**Amanfayun Resort** (安缦法雲酒店 *Ānmànfǎyún jiǔdiàn*). Surrounded
RESORT by tea fields, forests, and romantic courtyards, Amanfuyan tastefully re-creates the feel of a traditional Chinese village. **Pros:** luxurious spa; historic village; local touches; peaceful surroundings; nearby teahouse. **Cons:** far from city center; expensive. $ *Rooms from: Y4500* ⊠ *22 Fayun Nong* ☎ *0571/8732–9999* ⊕ *www.amanresorts.com* ⤳ *47 dwellings* ⊟❶ *No meals.*

$$$ 🛏**The Azure Qiantang** (尊蓝钱江豪华精选酒店 *Zūnlán qiánjiāng háo-*
HOTEL *huá jīng xuǎn jiǔdiàn*). Home to some of the very best views of the

FOR THE KIDS

Pagoda of Six Harmonies Garden (六和塔 *Liùhé tǎ*). One of our favorite child-friendly places is the garden behind the Pagoda of Six Harmonies in Hangzhou. Climb the stairs of the seven-story pagoda, picnic among the flower beds, and play among the miniature versions of China's most famous pagodas and temples. The pagoda is 2½ km (1½ miles) south of West Lake. ⊠ *Fuxing Jie, on the Qiantang River* ⊠ *Y20* ☉ *Daily 6:30 am–5:30 pm.*

5

Qiantang River, this luxury Starwood property aims to accentuate Hangzhou's natural beauty with big windows and a front-row seat to the tidal bore. **Pros:** excellent river views; central location; brand-new pool and fitness center. **Cons:** busy during tidal bore and holidays. $ *Rooms from: Y1600* ✉ *39 Wangjiang Dong Lu* ☎ *0571/2823–7777* ⊕ *www.theluxurycollection. com/azureqiantang* ⇔ *205 rooms* ❑ *No meals.*

$
HOTEL
Fodor's Choice
★
🏨 **Crystal Orange Hotel** (桔子水晶酒店 *Júzi shuǐjīng jiǔdiàn*). Travelers love this quirky boutique hotel so much that branches are popping up in other Chinese cities, but the Hangzhou location is a step up from the rest. **Pros:** excellent location near West Lake; bicycle rental; free Wi-Fi. **Cons:** disappointing breakfast; few amenities; limited English. $ *Rooms from: Y600* ✉ *122 Qingbo Jie* ☎ *0571/2887–8988* ⊕ *www. orangehotel.com.cn* ⇔ *113 rooms* ❑ *No meals.*

$$
HOTEL
🏨 **The Dragon** (黄龙饭店 *Huánglóng fàndiàn*). Within walking distance of Diamond Hill and the Yellow Dragon Cave, this hotel stands in quiet and attractive surroundings. **Pros:** good location; reasonable rates; free Wi-Fi. **Cons:** indifferent service; hit-and-miss English. $ *Rooms from: Y1300* ✉ *120 Shuguang Lu, at Hangda Lu* ☎ *0571/8799–8833* ⊕ *www. dragon-hotel.com* ⇔ *556 rooms* ❑ *No meals.*

$$$$
HOTEL
🏨 **Four Seasons Hotel Hangzhou at West Lake** (杭州西子湖四季酒店 *Hángzhōu xīzǐ hú sìjì jiǔdiàn*). Combining contemporary Chinese decor, modern amenities, and superlative service, the Four Seasons Hotel Hangzhou at West Lake may be the city's most luxurious retreat. **Pros:** great location; spacious rooms; beautiful landscaping. **Cons:** outdoor pool lacks privacy; heavy traffic to and from the hotel. $ *Rooms from: Y3500* ✉ *5 Lingyin Lu* ☎ *0571/8829–8888* ⊕ *www.fourseasons.com* ⇔ *73 rooms, 5 suites, 3 villas* ❑ *No meals.*

$$
HOTEL
Fodor's Choice
★
🏨 **Hyatt Regency Hangzhou** (杭州凯悦酒店 *Hángzhōu kǎi yuè jiǔdiàn*). Hangzhou's most recognizable and centrally located hotel, the Hyatt Regency combines careful service, comfortable rooms, and a great location. **Pros:** gorgeous views; good service; excellent pool. **Cons:** long check-in time; beginning to show its age; Wi-Fi costs extra. $ *Rooms from: Y1200* ✉ *28 Hubin Lu* ☎ *0571/8779–1234* ⊕ *www.hyatt.com* ⇔ *390 rooms, 22 suites* ❑ *No meals.*

$$$
HOTEL
Fodor's Choice
★
🏨 **Shangri-La Hotel Hangzhou** (杭州香格里拉饭店 *Hángzhōu xiānggélǐlā fàndiàn*). On the site of an ancient temple, the picturesque Shangri-La is a historic landmark. **Pros:** excellent location; staff speaks fluent English; free Wi-Fi. **Cons:** starting to show its age; crowded restaurants; winter fog can ruin views. $ *Rooms from: Y1500* ✉ *78 Beishan Lu* ☎ *0571/8797–7951* ⊕ *www.shangri-la.com* ⇔ *344 rooms, 38 suites* ❑ *No meals.*

CLOSE UP

The Qiantang Tidal Bore

During the autumnal equinox, when the moon's gravitational pull is at its peak, huge waves crash up the Qiantang River. Every year at this time, crowds gather at a safe distance to watch what begins as a distant line of white waves approaching. As it nears, it becomes a towering, thundering wall of water.

The phenomenon, known as a tidal bore, occurs when strong tides surge against the current of the river. The Qiantang Tidal Bore is the largest in the world, with recorded speeds of up to 25 miles an hour and heights of 30 feet. The Qiantang has the best conditions in the world to produce these tidal waves. Incoming tides are funneled into the shallow riverbed from the Gulf of Hangzhou and the bell shape narrows and concentrates the wave. People have been swept away in the past, so police now enforce a strict viewing distance.

5

$$
HOTEL

Sofitel Hangzhou Westlake (杭州索菲特西湖大酒店 *Hángzhōu suǒfēitè xīhú dàjiǔdiàn*). A stone's throw from West Lake, this high-end hotel sits in a lively neighborhood of restaurants, bars, and shops. **Pros:** great location; helpful staff; comfortable beds; free Wi-Fi. **Cons:** some mediocre views. $ *Rooms from: Y1200* ✉ *333 Xihu Dadao* ☎ *0571/8707–5858* ⊕ *www.sofitel.com* ➴ *233 rooms, 24 suites* ⊚ *No meals.*

$$$
HOTEL

Wyndham Grand Plaza Royale Hangzhou (温德姆大酒店 *Wēndémǔ dàjiǔdiàn*). With West Lake only a few steps away, this space-ship-shaped international hotel combines excellent customer service with flawless mountain, lake, city, and garden views. **Pros:** free Wi-Fi; great location; excellent customer service. **Cons:** too-firm mattresses; inconsistent restaurant service. $ *Rooms from: Y1400* ✉ *555 Fengqi Lu* ☎ *0571/8761–6888* ⊕ *www.wyndham.com* ➴ *293 rooms* ⊚ *No meals.*

NIGHTLIFE

Eudora Station (亿多瑞站 *Yìduōruì zhàn*). A more recent addition to Nanshan Road's ever-expanding foreign bar and restaurant scene, Eudora Station fills up on the weekend thanks to live music and cheap drink specials. If you're craving something familiar, the pizzas and salads are decent. ✉ *101–7 Nanshan Lu* ☎ *0571/8791–4760* ⊕ *www. eudorastation.com.*

H-Lounge (西拉酒吧 *Xīlā jiǔbā*). This intimate cocktail bar has great views from the second-story balcony, as well as an impressive range of whiskeys. The bartender can also whip up inventive cocktails inspired by Hangzhou, like the Foggy West Lake, in which Shaoxing yellow wine is mixed with tequila and a homemade syrup made with Chinese spices. ✉ *7 Paomachang Lu* ☎ *0571/8880–9701* ⊘ *Daily 7 pm–2 am.*

Fodor's Choice
★

JZ Club (黄楼酒吧 *Huánglóu jiǔbā*). For a refined night out, head to the southeastern edge of West Lake and visit this well-established jazz club with a cultured clientele. The three-story spot is known for its steady stream of talented jazz and blues performers, plus it has one of the city's best wine and whiskey lists. ✉ *6 Liuying Lu, at the intersection of Nanshan Lu* ☎ *0571/8702–8298* ⊘ *Daily 6:30 pm–2:30 am.*

Maya Bar (玛雅酒吧 *Mǎyǎ jiǔbā*). Maya Bar is known for its generous pours and a consistent Tex-Mex menu, and occasional live music has made this place popular with expats and locals for years. ✉ *94 Baishaquan Lu, near Shuguang Lu* ☏ *0571/8799–7628* ⊙ *Daily noon–2 am.*

Schanke Beer Bar (喧客德国啤酒酒吧餐厅 *Xuānkè déguó píjiǔ jiǔbā cāntīng*). For locally brewed beers and German flavors, head here. Though it may look a little out of place in modern China, the beer hall makes its own dark and wheat beers and serves some tasty sausages to boot. ✉ *Rooms 1-3 and 2-2, 32 Qingchunfang* ☏ *0571/5666–0999.*

SHOPPING

The best souvenirs to buy in Hangzhou are green tea and silk, but all sorts of wooden crafts, silk fans and umbrellas, and antiques are sold in small shops sprinkled around town. For the best longjing tea, head to Dragon Well Tea Park or the China Tea Museum.

China Silk Town (中国丝绸城 *Zhōngguó sīchóuchéng*). On either side of a nearly 4,000-foot-long pedestrian street, the stalls and shops of China Silk Town sell silk ties, pajamas, and shirts, plus silk straight off the bolt. ✉ *253 Xinhua Lu, between Fengqi Lu and Jiankang Lu* ☏ *0571/8510–0192.*

Fodor's Choice **Hefang Jie** (河坊街 *Héfāng jiē*). Also known as Qinghefang Historic ★ Block, Hefang Street (河坊街, *héfāng jiē*) is a lively, crowded pedestrian street and not to be missed on a visit to Hangzhou. Restored old buildings are beautifully illuminated at night and house tea shops, traditional apothecaries, clothing boutiques selling *qipao* (traditional silk Chinese dresses), scrolls, calligraphy, and wooden fans. Artists draw caricatures, candy makers sculpt sugar into art, blind masseurs alleviate tension, and storytellers re-create ancient Chinese legends. Start at Wushan Square and walk west. At night the glowing Chenghuang Pavilion, perched on a mountain top next to the square, is enchanting. ✉ *Hefang Jie, enter at Wushan Sq.*

Wushan Night Market (吴山夜市 *Wúshān yèshì*). The Wushan Night Market has stalls selling late-night local snacks, and you'll find accessories of every kind—ties, scarves, pillow covers—as well as knockoff designer goods and imitation antiques. It's open nightly from 7 pm. ✉ *Huixing Lu, near Renhe Lu.*

Xihu Longjing Tea Company (西湖龙井茶叶有限公司 *Xīhú lóngjǐng cháyè yǒuxiàn gōngsī*). A few blocks north of the China Tea Museum, the Xihu Longjing Tea Company has a nice selection of the famed longjing (Dragon Well) tea. ✉ *15 Longjing Lu* ☏ *0571/8796–2219.*

SHAOXING

64 km (40 miles) east of Hangzhou.

Shaoxing is alive in the Chinese imagination thanks to the famous writer Lu Xun, who set many of his classic works in this sleepy southern town. A literary revolutionary, Lu Xun broke tradition by writing in the vernacular of everyday Chinese, instead of the stiff, scholarly prose previously held as the only appropriate language for literature.

After dark on Hefang Street

Today, much of the city's charm is in exploring its narrow cobbled streets. The older sections of the city are made up of low stone houses connected by canals crisscrossed by arched bridges. East Lake is no match for the grandeur of Hangzhou's West Lake, but its bizarre rock formations and caves make for interesting tours. Shaoxing is also famous for its celebrated yellow-rice wine, used by cooks everywhere.

GETTING HERE AND AROUND

The most reliable and comfortable way to travel to Shaoxing is by train. Regular train and luxury bus services run to Shaoxing from Hangzhou and Shanghai a few times a day.

BUS TRAVEL   Hangzhou's East Bus Station has dozens of buses each day to Shaoxing. In Shaoxing, buses to Hangzhou leave from the main bus station in the north of town. Luxury buses take about an hour.

Bus Contact Shaoxing North Bus Station ⊠ *2 Jiefang Bei Lu, at Huan Cheng Bei Lu* ☎ *0571/8526–0207.*

TAXI TRAVEL   Although Shaoxing is small enough that walking is the best way to get between many sights, the city's small red taxis are relatively inexpensive. Most trips are Y15–Y30.

TRAIN TRAVEL   Trains between Hangzhou and Shaoxing take about 25 minutes, from Hangzhou's East station to Shaoxing's North station. It's a little farther out of the city than Shaoxing's Central train station, but the ultra-modern trip is an impressive example of China's sophisticated railway system. Spring for business or first-class seats for just a few more yuan (Y33–Y65).

Train Contact Shaoxing North Train Station ✉ *Zhangjian Dadao, Off Qiantao Highway* ☎ *0575/8802–2584.* **Shaoxing Train Station** (绍兴火车站 *Shàoxīng huǒchē zhàn*). ✉ *200 Chezhan Lu* ☎ *0575/8802–2584.*

TIMING

Shaoxing's major attractions can be seen in a day trip from Hangzhou, but don't rush: the city's slow pace and historic charm can fill two full days if you move at a leisurely pace.

ESSENTIALS

Bank Bank of China (中国银行 *Zhōngguó yínháng*). ✉ *225-229 Renmin Zhong Lu* ☎ *0575/8858–8858.*

Medical Assistance Shaoxing People's Hospital (绍兴市人民医院 *Shàoxīng shì rénmín yīyuàn*). ✉ *568 Zhongxing Bei Lu* ☎ *0575/8822–8888.*

Visitor and Tour Info Shaoxing Tourist Center ✉ *241 Luxun Zhong Lu* ☎ *0575/8514–5000* ⊕ *www.vintageshaoxing.com.*

EXPLORING

TOP ATTRACTIONS

Fodor's Choice ★

Bazi Bridge (八字桥 *Bāzí qiáo*). In a city of bridges, the Bazi Bridge is the finest and best known. Its long, sloping sides rise to a flat crest that looks like the character for eight, an auspicious number. The bridge is more than 800 years old, built in the Southern Song Dynasty, and is draped with a thick beard of ivy and vines. It sits in a quiet area of old stone houses with canal-side terraces where people wash clothes and chat with neighbors. ✉ *Bazi Qiao Zhi Jie, off Renmin Zhong Lu.*

Former Residence of Cai Yuanpei (蔡元培故居 *Càiyuánpéi gùjū*). The city's quiet northern neighborhoods are great places to wander, with several historic homes and temples that are now preserved as museums. The largest is Cai Yuanpei's house. Once the president of Peking University, Cai was a famous democratic revolutionary and educator during the republic, and his family's large compound is decorated with period furniture. ✉ *13 Bifei Nong, off Xiaoshan Lu* ☎ *0575/8511–0652* 🎟 *Y5* ⊘ *Daily 8–5.*

Lu Xun Native Place (鲁迅故居 *Lǔxùn gùjū*). As its name implies, Lu Xun Native Place is devoted to the literary giant and social critic Lu Xun. In this historic quarter, visit the Lu Xun Family Home (✉ *241 Luxun Zhong Lu* ☎ *0575/8513–3080* 🎟 *free entry*), where the writer was born. His extended family lived around him in a series of courtyards, and today, you can tour this traditional Shaoxing home and see some beautiful antique furniture. ■TIP→ **To avoid the crowds, visit in the morning or early evenings.** Down the street is the local school where Lu honed his writing skills, as well as a large square and a memorial that's dedicated to the famed writer. ✉ *235 Luxun Zhong Lu, 1 block east of Xianhen Hotel* ⊘ *Daily 8:30–5.*

Yanyu Tea House (雁雨茶艺馆 *Yànyǔ cháyì guǎn*). This idyllic little teahouse sits right along one of Shaoxing's famous waterways. The historic building is a little musty, but the antique furniture, artwork, drapes and meticulous tea service is an experience in itself. Ask for snacks, and you'll be rewarded with assorted bowls of fresh cherry tomatoes, dates,

CLOSE UP

What's Cooking

Shaoxing secured its place in the Chinese culinary pantheon with Shaoxing wine, the best yellow rice wine in the country. Although cooks around the world know the nutty-flavored wine as a marinade and seasoning, in Shaoxing the fermented brew of glutinous rice is put to a variety of uses, from drinking straight up (as early as breakfast) to sipping as a medicine (infused with traditional herbs and remedies). Like grape wines, Shaoxing mellows and improves with age, as its color deepens to a reddish brown. It is local custom to bury a cask when a daughter is born and serve it when she marries.

The wine is an excellent accompaniment to Shaoxing snacks such as pickled greens, baked rice cakes, and the city's most popular street food, *chou doufu* (stinky tofu). Usually paired with a bright red chili sauce, the golden-fried squares of tender tofu have a pleasant flavor and texture, if you can get past the pungent odor. Also, look for dishes made with another Shaoxing product, fermented bean curd, colloquially known as "moldy bean curd." With a flavor not unlike an aged cheese, it's rarely eaten by itself but complements fish and sharpens the flavor of meat dishes.

seeds, and regional fruits. ⊠ *Huanshan Rd., right across from a park called City Plaza* ☎ *0575/8511–5102.*

WORTH NOTING

Catholic Church of St. Joseph (St. Joseph 天主教堂 *Tiānzhǔ jiàotáng*). Near the Bazi Bridge is the bright pink Catholic Church of St. Joseph, dating from the turn of the 20th century. A hybrid of styles, the Italian-inspired interior is decorated with Bible passages written in Chinese calligraphy. ⊠ *Bazi Qiao Zhi Jie, off Renmin Zhong Lu.*

East Lake (东湖 *Dōng hú*). The narrow East Lake runs along the base of a rocky bluff rising up from the rice paddies. The crazily shaped cliffs were used as a rock quarry over the centuries, and today their sheer gray faces jut out in sheets of rock. You can hire a local boatman to take you along the base of the cliffs in a traditional black awning boat for around Y50. ⊠ *Yundong Lu, 5 km (4 miles) east of the city center* ☉ *Daily 7:30–5:30.*

Zhou Enlai Family Home (周恩来故居 *Zhōu Ēnlái gùjū*). The Zhou Enlai Family Home belonged to the first premier of Communist China, who came from a family of prosperous Shaoxing merchants. Zhou is credited with saving some of China's most important historic monuments from destruction at the hands of the Red Guards during the Cultural Revolution. The compound, a showcase of traditional architecture, houses exhibits on Zhou's life, ranging from his high-school essays to vacation snapshots with his wife. ⊠ *369 Laodong Lu* ☎ *0575/8513–3368* 🎟 *Y18* ☉ *Daily 8–5.*

One of Shaoxing's famous waterways

WHERE TO EAT

$ CHINESE 🍴 **Sanwei Jiulou** (三味酒楼 *Sānwéi jiŭlóu*). This restaurant serves up local specialties, including warm rice wine served in Shaoxing's distinctive tin kettles. Relaxed and distinctive, it's in an old restored building and appointed with traditional wood furniture. The second story looks out over the street below. [$] *Average main: Y40* ✉ *2 Lu Xun Lu* ☎ *0575/8896–8777* 💳 *No credit cards.*

$ CHINESE 🍴 **Xianheng Winehouse** (咸亨酒店 *Xánhēng jiŭdiàn*). More than 100 years old, this buzzing cafeteria is one of the most popular in town, so prepare for a crowd, especially on weekends. Lu Xun's most famous fictional character, the small-town scholar Kong Yiji, would sit on a bench here, sipping wine and eating boiled beans. The beans aren't for everyone, but they are worth a try. Also try the fermented bean curd and the pork belly with dried veggies—these local delicacies are especially good with a bowl of Shaoxing rice wine. [$] *Average main: Y50* ✉ *179 Lu Xun Zhong Lu, 1 block east of the Sanwei Jiulou* ☎ *0575/8511–6666* 💳 *No credit cards.*

$ CHINESE 🍴 **Xunbaoji Zhuangyuan Restaurant** (寻宝记状元楼 *Xúnbăo jì zhuàngyuán lóu*). Get here early or risk waiting in line for the famous Shaoxing delicacies, including ubiquitous stinky tofu, pork belly with dried vegetables, and chicken cooked in local wine. The restaurant is a little chaotic, but easy picture menus make ordering pretty painless. The surrounding historic district makes for a picturesque post-lunch stroll. [$] *Average main: Y50* ✉ *114 Cangqiaozhi Jie* ☎ *0575/8522–3317* ✍ *Reservations not accepted.*

WHERE TO STAY

$ HOTEL **New Century Grand Hotel Shaoxing** (紹興開元名都大酒店 *Shàoxīng kāiyuán míngdū dàjiǔdiàn*). A modern lodging option somewhat removed from the major sites, the New Century has contemporary rooms decorated in muted shades with pops of bright red. **Pros:** relatively new building; free Wi-Fi. **Cons:** indifferent service; limited English. [$] *Rooms from: Y588* ✉ *278 Remin Dong Lu* ☎ *0575/8809–8888* 🌐 *www.kaiyuanhotels.com* 🛏 *355 rooms* 🍴 *Breakfast.*

$$ HOTEL Fodor's Choice ★ **Xianheng Hotel** (绍兴咸亨大酒店 *Shàoxīng xiánhēng dàjiǔdiàn*). Conveniently located near many of the city's restaurants and a short walk from the Lu Xun Memorial, the Xianheng claims to be the first eco-friendly hotel in the province (though this is difficult to prove). **Pros:** centrally located; good value; free Wi-Fi. **Cons:** spotty English; some rooms need updating. [$] *Rooms from: Y1280* ✉ *179 Lu Xun Zhong Lu* ☎ *0575/8806–8688* 🌐 *en.xianhenghotel.com* 🛏 *206 rooms* 🍴 *Breakfast.*

SHOPPING

Lu Xun Zhong Lu (鲁迅中路 *Lǔxùn zhōng lù*). In addition to calligraphy brushes, and fans, scrolls, and other items decorated with calligraphy, this street has several shops selling the local tin wine pots. In the traditional way of serving yellow rice wine, the pots are placed on the stove to heat up wine for a cold winter's night. Also popular are traditional boatmen's hats, made of thick waterproof black felt.

NINGBO

150 km (95 miles) southeast of Hangzhou; 220 km (136 miles) south of Shanghai.

Ningbo is one of the country's biggest ports and most prosperous cities. It's an easy place to explore on foot. Rivers and canals flow through a city that is generously sprinkled with tranquil gardens and parks. Colonial architecture and centuries-old pagodas and temples are mixed (rather unfortunately) with featureless, Eastern Bloc apartment blocks and hideous glass and steel towers. Unlike Shanghai, Hangzhou, and Suzhou, Ningbo is not set up for tourism. This makes it a relaxing and authentic place to explore. Join the locals for bottomless cups of tea and mah-jongg in one of the many parks, or burn through some cash in the city's lively markets, ritzy shopping malls, and trendy nightclubs.

Ningbo, translated as "tranquil waves," sits at the confluence of three rivers (the Yuyao, the Fenghua, and the Yong) that eventually snake their way to the nearby sea. Ningbo's history stretches back thousands of years. In the 7th century, the Tang Dynasty developed a complicated system of canals, and trade with Japan and Korea boomed. The Portuguese, with their keen eye for location, settled in as early as the 16th century, and left behind a fair number of churches that are still in use today. More recently, during the Second World War, the Japanese bombed the city with fleas carrying the bubonic plague.

GETTING HERE AND AROUND

It's best to travel by rail, as express trains connect Ningbo with both Hangzhou (1 hour) and Shanghai (1¾ hours). If you prefer to take a bus, there is a steady stream heading to Hangzhou, Shanghai, and beyond, departing from the South Bus Station (across the street from the Asia Garden Hotel) every 10–15 minutes from 6 am to 8 pm. Be aware that buses can get stuck in traffic and that drivers are prone to somewhat reckless driving.

AIR TRAVEL A 25-minute drive from downtown is Ningbo's Lishe International Airport. There are connections to all major Chinese cities, as well as Hong Kong and Seoul. Major hotels offer free airport shuttle buses. An airport-bound bus (Y12) leaves from the CAAC office every hour from 7 am to 6 pm.

Air Contact Ningbo Lishe International Airport (宁波栎社国际机场 *Níngbō lìshè guójì jīchǎng).* ☒ *Yinzhou District* ☏ *0574/8742-7888* ⊕ *www. ningboairport.com.*

BUS TRAVEL Ningbo has five long-distance bus stations. The Ningbo Long-Distance Passenger Transport Center and the South Bus Station are the most useful for travelers. The former serves Nanjing, Suzhou, and Yangzhou, as well as Fujian and Anhui provinces, while the latter serves Hangzhou, Shanghai, Shoaxing, and Wenzhou. The North Bus Station serves counties around Ningbo, Jiangbei District, and Putuo Mountain. Buses from the East Bus Station head to many scenic areas in and around Ningbo.

Bus Contacts East Bus Station (汽车东站 *Qìchē dōng zhàn).* ☒ *707 Ningchuan Lu* ☏ *0574/8792-4570.* **Ningbo Passenger Transportation Center** ☒ *181 Tongda Lu* ☏ *0574/8709-1212.* **North Bus Station** (汽车北站 *Qìchē běi zhàn).* ☒ *122 Taodu Lu* ☏ *0574/8735-5321.* **South Bus Station** (汽车南站 *Qìchē nán zhàn).* ☒ *6 Nanzhan Xi Lu* ☏ *0574/8713-1834.*

TAXI TRAVEL Taxis are cheap and plentiful. Areas of interest are not far apart and should cost no more than Y15, with about Y45 to the airport.

TRAIN TRAVEL Ningbo's East Railway Station handles all of the express trains, including those that get you to Xiamen in about 5½ hours. The station is a Y30 taxi ride from city center.

Train Information East Railway Station (东火车站 *Dōng huǒchē zhàn).* ☒ *Fuming Nan Lu and Xingning Lu* ☏ *0574/8787-4214.*

TIMING

Ningbo has enough to occupy you for two full days, but the major attractions can be seen in one day. The city center is compact and can be explored on foot.

TOURS

The centrally located Ningbo Tourist Board is an excellent place to grab city maps, find the free English magazine *Ningbo Guide,* and get advice on attractions outside the city. The magazine is a must for foreigners, and has a map clearly labeling all the hot spots.

ESSENTIALS

Bank Bank of China (中国银行 *Zhōngguó yínháng).* ☒ *139 Yao Hang Jie* ☏ *0574/8719-6666.*

Medical Assistance Yinzhou No. 2 Hospital (鄞州第二医院 *Yínzhōu dì èr yīyuàn*). ⊠ *1 Qianhe Lu* ☎ *0574/8303-9999* ⊕ *www.yz2y.com*.

Visitor and Tour Info CAAC ⊠ *91 Xingning Lu* ☎ *0574/8742-7888* ⊕ *www.caac.gov.cn*. **Ningbo Tourist Board** ⊠ *159 Zhongma Lu, Ningbo Laowaitan Scenic Area Tourist Center, Laowaitan* ☎ *0574/8727-6116* ⊕ *www.gotoningbo.com*.

EXPLORING

Drum Tower (鼓楼 *Gǔlóu*). This huge yellow pavilion, complete with a medieval clock tower, was built in AD 821. Climb to the top for a bird's-eye view of the entire city. The tower marks the entrance to Gulou Pedestrian Street, lined with restored Ming Dynasty–style buildings. Here you'll find tiny shops, makeshift stalls, and every kind of local snack imaginable. It's an ideal spot for people-watching. ⊠ *Gongyuan Lu and Zhongshan Xi Lu* ⊡ *Free* ☉ *Daily 8–4*.

Jiangbei Catholic Church (江北天主教堂 *Jiāngběi Tiānzhǔ jiàotáng*). Home to China's highest percentage of Christians, Ningbo is also home to several active churches. Marking the beginning of the Laowaitan District, this church was built by the Portuguese in 1872 and is considered to be the best preserved in Zhejiang Province. On any given day Chinese couples can be found taking their wedding photos. ⊠ *2 Zhong Ma Lu, Laowaitan* ☎ *0574/8735–5903* ⊡ *Free*.

Moon Lake (月湖 *Yuè hú*). The lovely park that surrounds this 1,400-year-old lake is dotted with quaint teahouses and pavilions with upturned eaves. Weeping willows line crooked paths that wrap around bamboo groves. In addition to being a peaceful place for a leisurely stroll, the park is centrally located in the city center and a useful point of reference. ⊠ *Yanyue Lu, near Yaohang Jie*.

Tianfeng Pagoda (天封塔 *Tiānfēng tǎ*). Seven stories high, this ancient hexagonal structure was first built in AD 695, then destroyed and rebuilt several times over. The current building was finished in the 14th century and is surrounded by a tiny garden complete with gigantic rocks and several inviting stone benches. For a great view of the pagoda, walk directly across the street from the main entrance, enter the market, and walk up to the second floor. Continue climbing to the top for only Y5 and you'll be rewarded with panoramic cityscapes. ⊠ *Near intersection of Jiefang Nan Lu and Kaiming Jie* ⊡ *Y5 to climb* ☉ *Daily 8:30–4:30*.

Fodor's Choice ★ **Tianyi Pavilion** (天一阁 *Tiānyī gé*). Down a peaceful alley off Changchun Lu, the Tianyi Pavilion is the oldest private library in China. Built in 1596 and founded by politician Fan Qin, this spiritual place features gold-plated, wood-paneled buildings, bamboo groves, pools, and a rockery. The scholarly setting, worth a visit for the architecture alone, preserves an atmosphere of seclusion and contemplation. ⊠ *10 Tianyi Lu, west of Moon Lake* ☎ *0574/8729–3856* ⊡ *Y30* ☉ *Daily 8–5*.

Zhongshan Park (中山公园 *Zhōngshān gōngyuán*). In one of Ningbo's most delightful parks you'll find winding stone paths that snake over arched bridges and slender canals flowing past pavilions and teahouses. During the humid summer months the city's seniors fan themselves with oversized paper fans, crack sunflower seeds, gossip, and drink tea. Impromptu groups of musicians huddle together; old men play traditional Chinese instruments as women belt out ear-piercing renditions of Chinese opera. This is a wonderful place to relax and soak up the atmosphere. ✉ *Gongyuan Lu, end of the Drum Tower pedestrian street* 🎫 *Free* 🕒 *Daily sunrise–sunset.*

> ## SWEET DUMPLINGS
>
> Fodor's Choice ★ **Gang Ya Gou** (缸鸭狗 *Gāng yā gǒu*). Be sure to try the city's famous *tangyuan*, multicolored sugar dumplings served in a bowl of syrup and eaten like soup. There's no better place to sample this specialty than Gang Ya Gou, an inexpensive spot near Tianyi Square that's been operating since 1926. Also worth a try are the tofu pancakes and crabmeat dumplings. Look for the hard-to-miss logo depicting a dog and a duck fighting over a pot of rice, or simply follow the crowds. ✉ *Shop 68, Kaiming Jie* ☎ *0571/8732–0228* 🕒 *Daily 10:30 am–10 pm.*

WHERE TO EAT

$$ LEBANESE Fodor's Choice ★ 🍴 **Lebanese Restaurant** (黎巴嫩餐厅 *Líbānèn cāntīng*). On the eastern edge of Moon Lake, this Middle Eastern restaurant has consistently excellent food. One bite of the olive-oil-and-pine-nut-drizzled hummus and you'll immediately forgive the rather bland interior. A long-standing favorite with the city's Islamic community, the restaurant serves a variety of lamb kebabs, eggplant-based dips, and fresh mint yogurt, all of which are delicious. An English-language picture menu will help guide you. [$] *Average main: Y55* ✉ *320 Zhenming Lu* ☎ *0574/8731–5861* 🕒 *Daily 11 am–10 pm.*

$$$ THAI 🍴 **Nancy's Thai** (南茜泰国餐厅 *Nánqiàn tàiguó cāntīng*). A Ningbo landmark, this authentic Thai restaurant has an enormous neon sign that makes it easy to spot. The first level has a well-stocked bar with a decent selection of reasonably priced wines by the bottle. On the second floor is the dining room, where private tables are perfect for a romantic meal. Recommended dishes include the *tom kha gai* (coconut and chicken soup), *tom sum* (spicy papaya salad), and expertly seasoned curries. [$] *Average main: Y100* ✉ *103 Zhenming Lu* ☎ *0574/8731–8266.*

$ VEGETARIAN 🍴 **Vegetarian Lifestyle** (枣子树净素餐厅 *Zǎozǐ shùjìng sù cāntīng*). This outpost of one of Shanghai's best vegetarian Chinese restaurants makes ordering a breeze, thanks to an English-language picture menu. The nourishing and delicious spinach dumplings, fresh juices, and mock-meat dishes are consistently delicious. The restaurant enforces a no-smoking policy, which is highly unusual in China. [$] *Average main: Y45* ✉ *16 Liuting Jie, 2nd fl.* ☎ *0574/8730–1333* 💳 *No credit cards.*

$$$$ CHINESE 🍴 **Zhuang Yuan Lou Restaurant** (状元楼酒店 *Zhuàngyuánlóu jiǔdiàn*). Serving traditional Ningbo cuisine in an opulent setting on the Yu Yao River, Zhuang Yuan Lou has a stellar reputation for quality and freshness. Located at the western end of the He Yi shopping complex, the restaurant has gigantic red-and-gold doors and intricately carved antique furniture. Hostesses are decked out in elaborate silk dresses. If you're feeling bold, try the exotic and expensive local specialties. The steamed turtle, fried yellow-fish with fresh blueberries, and the pork ribs come highly recommended. [$] *Average main: Y200* ✉ *He Yi Shopping*

Center, Mandarin Garden Hotel, He Yi Lu ☎ *0574/2796–6666* 💳 *No credit cards.*

WHERE TO STAY

$ HOTEL 🏨 **Asia Garden Hotel** (亚洲华园宾馆 *Yàzhōu huá yuán bīnguǎn*). With a convenient location next to the South Bus Station, this expansive hotel is a short walk from Ningbo's main attractions. **Pros:** near all the main sights; cable channels in rooms; free Wi-Fi. **Cons:** could use renovations; bland breakfast; very limited English. [$] *Rooms from: Y290* ✉ *271 Ma Yuan Lu* ☎ *0574/8711–6888* 🌐 *www.asiagardenhotel.com* 🛏 *142 rooms* 💳 *No credit cards* 🍴 *Breakfast.*

$$ HOTEL Fodor's Choice ★ 🏨 **Shangri-La Ningbo** (香格里拉酒店 *Xiānggélǐlā jiǔdiàn*). Overlooking the confluence of three rivers, Ningbo's most opulent international hotel offers personalized service, first-rate facilities, and panoramic views of the city. **Pros:** sleek indoor lap pool; outdoor tennis courts; free Wi-Fi. **Cons:** mandatory bathing cap in the pool; loud lobby area; tour groups can flood the facilities. [$] *Rooms from: Y1218* ✉ *88 Yuyuan Jie* ☎ *0574/8799–8888* 🌐 *www.shangri-la.com/ningbo* 🛏 *562 rooms, 57 suites* 🍴 *No meals.*

$$$ HOTEL 🏨 **Sheraton Ningbo** (喜来登酒店 *Xǐláidēng jiǔdiàn*). Excellent customer service and a convenient location make this an ideal base from which to explore the city. **Pros:** impressive breakfast buffet; free Wi-Fi; free shuttle to Shanghai. **Cons:** busy lobby; aging facilities; smoking allowed in public areas. [$] *Rooms from: Y1400* ✉ *50 Caihong Bei Lu* ☎ *0574/8768–8688* 🌐 *www.starwoodhotels.com* 🛏 *345 rooms, 33 suites* 🍴 *No meals.*

$ HOTEL 🏨 **Sofitel Wanda.** Next to popular shopping complex Wanda Plaza, the Sofitel Wanda combines French flair and touches of Chinese culture for a sophisticated result. **Pros:** high English standards; impressive breakfast buffet; nice spa. **Cons:** inconsistent service; outside city center. [$] *Rooms from: Y750* ✉ *899 Siming Zhong Lu* ☎ *0574/2889–9888* 🌐 *www.sofitel.com* 🛏 *287 rooms, 18 suites* 🍴 *No meals.*

NIGHTLIFE

If you're looking for a fun night out, head over to Laowaitan, the city's entertainment strip and Ningbo's pint-size answer to Shanghai's Bund. It's designed to look like a mini European city, complete with cobblestone streets. Hundreds of local couples come here to take their wedding photos in the exotic setting.

Bar Constellation. One of the better bars on Laowaitan, Bar Constellation has earned a following thanks to its romantic ambience and professional pourers. The whisky list is more like a tome, with more than 150 brands, including familiar faces like Maker's Mark alongside more exotic options such as Nikka from Japan. You can even enjoy a Cuban cigar while you're at it. ✉ *72 Renmin Lu, Laowaitan* ☎ *0574/8765–8280.*

O'Reilly's Pub (奥赖利爱尔兰酒吧 *Ào lài lì ài'ěrlán jiǔbā*). For a low-key evening, head to the warm and welcoming O'Reilly's Pub, which has Guinness and Strongbow Cider on tap, a hodgepodge of Irish paraphernalia on the walls, and tasty Western bar grub. There's often live

Celtic, folk, and pop music. ✉ *46-9 Caihong Bei Lu* ☎ *0574/8770–4282* ⊕ *www.oreillysningbo.com* ☽ *Daily 10 am–2 am.*

SHOPPING

Antiques Market Curio Bazaar (宁波市范宅古玩集市 *Níngbō shì fàn-zhái gǔwàn jíshì*). You'll find small clusters of galleries and stalls here selling a variety of jade pieces and antique bric-a-brac of varying levels of authenticity. We like the beautiful Chinese scrolls with traditional watercolor paintings and the kitschy Mao-era memorabilia. Bargain hard, as prices are inflated for tourists. ✉ *85-97 Zhongshan Xi Lu.*

Gulou Pedestrian Street (鼓楼步行街 *Gǔlóu bùxíng jiē*). Head east down Zhongshan Xi Lu to Gulou (drum tower) Pedestrian Street; there's a row of restored buildings packed with everything from inexpensive DVDs to tea to ceramics, making it a decent spot to pick up souvenirs. In between the busy shops, there's the odd restaurant and nightclub. The area can get pretty crowded on weekends, but it is a great place to wander and soak up modern Chinese culture. ✉ *Gulou Pedestrian St., between Zhongshan Xi Lu and Zhongshan Park.*

Heyi Avenue (和義大道購物中心 *Héyì dàdào gòuwù zhòngxīn*). The city's poshest shopping area is Heyi Avenue, where you'll find high-end luxury chains like Gucci, Dior, Armani, Montblanc, and Swarovski. There's plenty of riverfront shopping, dining, and nightlife. This is where Ningbo's crème de la crème come to spend money on big-name brands and rich delicacies. ✉ *66 Heyi Lu.*

Tianyi Square (天一广场 *Tiānyī guǎngchǎng*). Just east of the Tian-feng Pagoda is Tianyi Square, Ningbo locals' favorite shopping and entertainment complex. It's a popular meeting point, thanks in part to plentiful outdoor seating around the central fountain, as well as a slew of electronics and fashion outlets. There's also a wide selection of fast food and low-key local restaurants—don't miss the Ningbo dumplings at Gang Ya Gou. If you need to take a break from the crowds, look for the enormous Yaohang Street Catholic Church just outside the square. ✉ *88 Zhongshan Dong Lu.*

OFF THE BEATEN PATH

Putuo Mountain. On this tiny island, only 12.5 square km (8 square miles), you'll find Putuoshan, one of China's four sacred Buddhist mountains. Legend has it that a 9th-century Japanese monk got caught in a storm, and Guanyin, the Buddhist goddess of mercy, miraculously appeared and guided him safely to the mountain. In thanks, he erected Puji Si, the area's most famous temple, of which there are more than 30. The island can easily be explored on foot and completely circumnavigated in a day. Take time to lounge on Thousand Step Beach, photograph the enormous 108-foot-high bronze Guanyin statue , eat fresh seafood, and climb Putuoshan (or take the cable car) for fabulous island vistas. The population is only between 3,000 and 4,000, about 1,000 of whom are monks and nuns. Getting to the island is fairly easy, with frequent boats leaving from Ningbo's wharf. The island can get crowded, so avoid weekends and holidays.

5

FUJIAN

One of China's most beautiful provinces, Fujian has escaped the notice of most visitors. This is because the region, though not too far off the beaten path, is usually passed over in favor of more glamorous destinations like Hong Kong or Shanghai. The city of Xiamen is beautiful, and remarkably green, with notable beaches along the coastline. Once a paradise of undisturbed colonial architecture, car-free Gulangyu island has since become a not-so-hidden gem, drawing hordes of tourists to its shores on weekends.

XIAMEN

262 km (163 miles) southwest of Fuzhou by car; 469 km (291 miles) northeast of Hong Kong by air.

Xiamen is a new city by Chinese standards, as it dates back only to the late 12th century. Xiamen was a stronghold for Ming loyalist Zheng Chenggong (better known as Koxinga), who later fled to Taiwan after China was overrun by the Qing. Xiamen's place as a dynasty-straddling city continues to this day due to its proximity to Taiwan. Some see Xiamen as a natural meeting point between the two sides in the decades-long separation. Only a few miles out to sea are islands that still technically belong to the Republic of China, as Taiwan is officially known in Mainland China.

Xiamen is today one of the most prosperous cities in China, with beautiful parks, impressive temples, and waterfront promenades that neatly complement the port city's historic architecture.

GETTING HERE AND AROUND

The best way to reach Xiamen is by plane. The city is accessible by long-distance trains and buses, but these entail much longer travel times.

AIR TRAVEL   Xiamen Gaoqi International Airport, one of the largest and busiest in China, lies about 10 km (6.2 miles) northeast of the city. A taxi from downtown should cost no more than Y40, and takes between 20 and 30 minutes, depending on traffic. Most carriers service Xiamen, which has connections to many cities in China and international destinations like Bangkok, Kuala Lumpur, Jakarta, Manila, Penang, Singapore, and Amsterdam. A popular regional carrier is Xiamen Airlines.

Air Contacts XiamenAir (厦门航空 *Xiàmén hángkōng*). ✉ *22 Dailiao Lu* ☎ *0592/222-6666* ⊕ *www.xiamenair.com.* **Xiamen Gaoqi International Airport** (厦门高崎国际机场 *Xiàmén gāoqí guójì jīchǎng*). ☎ *0592/96363* ⊕ *www.xiac.com.cn.*

BUS TRAVEL   Xiamen has luxury bus service to all the main cities along the coast as far as Guangzhou and Shanghai. There are three long-distance bus stations, including the main Hubin South Bus Station, just south of Yundang Lake.

Bus Contact Xiamen Hubin Long-Distance Bus Station (厦门湖滨长途汽车站 *Xiàmén húbīn chángtú qìchē zhàn*). ✉ *59 Hubin Nan Lu* ☎ *0592/221-5238.*

TAXI TRAVEL In Xiamen, taxis can be found around hotels or on the streets; they're a convenient way to visit the sights on the edge of town. Taxi drivers do not speak English, so make sure that all your addresses are written in Chinese. For farther-flung destinations, it is common to hire a taxi for an hour or two (about Y100 per hour) so you don't get stranded.

TRAIN TRAVEL Rail travel to Xiamen isn't as convenient as in many other cities. Aside from bullet trains from Shanghai and Hangzhou, new high-speed routes also reach Wuhan, Shenzhen, Chongqing, and Beijing, though most journeys involve changing trains at least once. The main railway station, which is about 5 km (3 miles) northeast of the port, is currently under renovation and is expected to be finished in late 2015 or early 2016. Until then, Xiamen North Station will be handling all of the bullet train traffic.

Train Contact Xiamen North Train Station (厦门北火车站 *Xiàmén bĕi huŏchē zhàn*). ⊠ *Shengguo Lu, off Hangsheng Lu* ☎ *0592/203-8888.* **Xiamen Train Station** ⊠ *Xiahe Lu* ☎ *0592/203-8888.*

TIMING

Xiamen is a very pleasant city, well worth a few days of exploring and hiking. Much cleaner and more environmentally conscious than other Chinese cities, it's a great place to recharge and take in some fresh air.

ESSENTIALS

Banks Bank of China (中国银行 *Zhōngguó yínháng*). ✉ *40 Hubin Bei Lu* ☎ *0592/506–6415.* HSBC (汇丰银行 *Huìfēng yínháng*). ✉ *189 Xiahe Lu* ☎ *0592/239–7799.*

Medical Assistance Xiamen Changgeng Hospital (厦门长庚医院 *Xiàmén chánggēng yīyuàn*). ✉ *123 Xiafei Lu, Xinjang Industrial Area* ☎ *0592/620–3456.*

Visitor and Tour Info CITS ✉ *Huajian Plaza, 78 Xinhua Lu, 3rd fl.* ☎ *0592/204–2207* ⊕ *www.citsxm.com.*

EXPLORING

TOP ATTRACTIONS

Hakka Roundhouses (客家土楼 *Kéjiā tǔlóu*). Legend has it that when these four-story-tall structures were first spotted by the American military, fear spread that they were silos for some unknown gigantic missile. They were created centuries before by the Hakka, an offshoot of the Han Chinese who settled all over southeastern China. Peppering the countryside of Yong Ding, 225 km (140 miles) northwest of Xiamen, these beautiful examples of Hakka architecture are made of raw earth, sand, brown sugar, and glutinous rice, and reinforced with bamboo and wood. Joining a tour group or hiring a private car is your best option for getting here. ✉ *Yong Ding.*

NEED A BREAK?

Hangzhou Xiaolongbao (杭州小笼包 *Hángzhōu xiǎolóngbāo*). On the northern end of Guanren Lu, which confusingly wraps around in a circle, there's a strip of food stalls that whip up delicious noodles, skewers, and dumplings. Stop into Hangzhou Dumplings (next to 26 Guanren Lu), which is easy to spot, as it has a bright red sign and is the only stall with a big tower of steamers out front. The family who runs this little hole-in-the-wall doesn't speak English, but they are friendly and happy to play charades. The steamed Hangzhou-style *xiaolongbao* (soup dumplings) are delicious, with their freshly folded shells and well-seasoned pork. ✉ *26 Guanren Lu.*

Hongshan Park (鸿山公园 *Hóngshān gōngyuán*). Built into a hillside, Hongshan Park has a small Buddhist temple, a lovely waterfall, and beautiful views of the city and the harbor. The steep park shoots straight up from a busy street, so wear comfortable shoes if you're eager to explore. ✉ *Siming Nan Lu, 1 block east of Zhenhai Lu* ✉ *Free.*

Nanputuo Temple (南普陀寺 *Nán pǔtuó sì*). Dating from the Tang Dynasty, Nanputuo Temple has roofs decorated with brightly painted clustered flowers, sinewy serpents, and mythical beasts. It has been restored many times, most recently in the 1980s, following the Cultural Revolution, with more touch-ups in recent years. Pavilions on either side of the main hall contain tablets commemorating the suppression of secret societies by the Qing Dynasty emperors. As the most important of Xiamen's temples, it is nearly always the center of a great deal of activity as monks and worshippers mix with tour groups. To get here, take Bus 1 or 2 from the port. ✉ *Siming Nan Lu, next to Xiamen University* ⊕ *www.nanputuo.com/npten* ✉ *Free entry* ☾ *Daily 5:40 am–6 pm.*

Wanshi Botanical Garden (万石植物园 *Wànshí zhíwùyuán*). Surrounding a pretty lake at the base of Wanshi Mountain, the Wanshi Botanical Garden has a fine collection of more than 6,500 species of tropical and subtropical flora, ranging from eucalyptus and bamboo trees to orchids and ferns. On either side of the winding pathways, there are smatterings of interesting rock formations, as well as a rose garden and several temples, the most notable being Heaven's Border Temple. The green oasis that is the botanical garden is a peaceful way to spend an afternoon, but be sure to wear comfy shoes as it is best explored on foot. ■ TIP➜ Hailing a cab from the main gate can be difficult: consider hiring a taxi to wait (about Y50 per hour), or hiking to Nanputuo Temple. ✉ *Huyuan Lu, off Wenyuan Lu* ☎ *Y40* ⊙ *Daily 5:30 am–6:30 pm.*

NEED A BREAK?

Coffee Map. Coffee Map is an unassuming Taiwanese-owned tea and coffee stand. The huge menu offers lots of delicious caffeinated drinks, and the tiny, air-conditioned seating area is a pleasant escape from Xiamen's oppressive summer humidity. It's down a small alley just opposite Xiamen University's main gate and near Nanputuo Temple. ✉ *Laohu Cheng Dian, off Siming Nan Lu* ☎ *0592/256–6388* ⊙ *Daily 8 am–10 pm.*

5

Xiamen University (厦门大学 *Xiàmén dàxué*). Right by Nanputuo Temple, housed in an interesting mix of modern and traditional colonial buildings, is Xiamen University. It was founded in the 1920s with the help of Chinese living abroad. ■ TIP➜ For some peace and quiet, take a stroll here in the early morning. ✉ *End of Siming Nan Lu, near Danan Lu* ⊕ *www.xmu.edu.cn* ☎ *Free entry; bring ID* ⊙ *Daily 8:30–5.*

WORTH NOTING

Hulishan Cannon Fort (胡里山砲台 *Húlǐshān pàotái*). A symbol of China's Westernization in the 19th and 20th centuries, Hulishan Cannon Fort was built with a hand from Germany. When it was constructed in 1894, during the Qing Dynasty, the fort was considered one of China's most technologically advanced fortresses, and acted as the central command of the coast. It served a major part in the defense against the Japanese in both 1900 and 1937, thanks in part to two massive 19th-century German Krupp cannons. Today, the fortress retains its east-meets-west architectural style, beautiful views of the coast, a castle, and one of the famed cannons. ✉ *2 Huandao Lu* ☎ *0592/209–9603* ☎ *Y25* ⊙ *Daily 7:30 am–6 pm.*

Overseas Chinese Museum (华侨博物馆 *Huáqiáo bówùguǎn*). In the southern part of the city, the Overseas Chinese Museum was founded by the wealthy industrialist Tan Kah Kee. With pictures and documents, personal items, and associated relics, three halls tell the story of the great waves of emigration from southeastern China during the 19th century. ✉ *493 Siming Nan Lu* ☎ *0592/208–4028* ☎ *Free entry* ⊙ *Tues.–Sun. 9:30–4.*

Zhongshan Park (中山公园 *Zhōngshān gōngyuán*). Commemorating Dr. Sun Yat-sen—who is known in Chinese as Sun Zhongshan—Zhongshan Park was built in 1927 and is centered around a bronze statue of the great man. It has a small zoo, pretty lakes, and canals you can explore

Continued on page 335

SPIRITUALITY IN CHINA

Even though it's officially an atheist nation, China has a vibrant religious life. What are the differences between China's big three faiths of Buddhism, Taoism, and Confucianism? Like much else in the Middle Kingdom, the lines are often blurred.

Walking around the streets of any city in China, it's hard to believe that only four decades ago the bulk of the Middle Kingdom's centuries-old religious culture was destroyed by revolutionary zealots, and that the few temples, mosques, monasteries, and churches that escaped outright destruction were desecrated and turned into warehouses and factories, or put to other ignoble uses. Those days are long over, and religion in China has sprung back to life. Even though the official line of the Chinese Communist Party is that the nation is atheist, China is rife with religious diversity.

Perhaps the faith most commonly associated with China is Confucianism, an ethical and philosophical system developed from the teachings of the sage Confucius. Confucianism stresses the importance of relationships in society and of maintaining proper etiquette. These aspects of Confucian thought are associated not merely with China (where its modern-day influence is dubious at best, especially in

a crowded subway car), but also with East Asian culture as a whole. Confucianism also places great emphasis on filial piety, the respect that a child should show an elder (or subjects to their ruler). This may account for Confucianism's status as the most officially tolerated of modern China's faiths.

Taoism is based on the teachings of the *Tao Te Ching,* a treatise written in the 4th century BC, and blends an emphasis on spiritual harmony with that of the individual's duty to society. Taoism and Confucianism are complementary, though to the outsider, the former might seem more steeped in ritual and mysticism. Think of it this way: Taoism is to Confucianism as Catholicism is to Protestantism. Taoism's mystic quality may be why so many westerners come to China to study "the way," as Taoism is sometimes called.

Buddhism came to China from India in the second century AD and quickly became a major force in the Middle Kingdom. The faith is so ingrained here that many Chinese openly scoff at the idea that the Buddha wasn't Chinese.

Buddhism teaches that the best way to alleviate suffering is to purify one's mind.

TIPS FOR TEMPLE VISITS

The Wenshu Monastery is a top sight in Chengdu.

Chinese worshippers are easygoing. Even at the smallest temple or shrine, they understand that some people will be visitors and not devotees. Temples in China have relaxed dress codes, but you should follow certain rules of decorum:

■ You're welcome to burn incense, but it's not required. If you do decide to burn a few joss sticks, take them from the communal pile and be sure to make a small donation. This usually goes to temple upkeep or local charities.

■ Be careful when shaking lit incense.

■ Respect signs reading no photo in front of altars and statues. Taoist temples seem particularly sensitive about photo taking. When in doubt, ask.

■ Avoid stepping in front of a worshipper at an altar or censer (where incense is burned).

■ Speak quietly and silence mobile phones inside of temple grounds.

■ Don't touch Buddhist monks of the opposite sex.

■ Avoid entering a temple during a ceremony.

TEMPLE OBJECTS

For many, temple visits are among the most culturally edifying parts of a China trip. Large or small, Chinese temples incorporate a variety of objects significant to religious practice.

INCENSE

Incense is the most common item in any Chinese temple. In antiquity, Chinese people burned sacrifices both as an offering and as a way of communicating with spirits through the smoke. This later evolved into a way of showing respect for one's ancestors by burning fragrances that the dearly departed might find particularly pleasing.

BAGUA

Taoist temples will have a bagua: an octagonal diagram pointing toward the eight cardinal directions, each representing different points on the compass, elements in nature, family members, and more esoteric meanings. The bagua is often used in conjunction with a compass to make placement decisions in architectural design and in fortune telling.

"GHOST MONEY"

Sometimes the spirits need more than sweet- smelling smoke, and this is why many Taoists burn "ghost money" (also known as "hell money" or "joss"), a scented paper resembling cash. Though once more popular in Taiwan and Hong Kong (and looked upon as a particularly capitalist superstition on the mainland), the burning of ghost money is now gaining ground throughout the country.

CENSER

Every Chinese temple will have a censer in which to place joss sticks, either inside the hall or out front. Larger temples often have a number of them. These large stone or bronze bowls are filled with incense ash from hundreds of joss sticks placed by worshippers. Some censers are ornate, with sculpted bronze rising above the bowls.

STATUES

Visitors will find a variety of statues of deities and mythical figures. Confucius is usually rendered as a wizened man with a long beard, and Taoist temples have an array of demon deities.

PRAYER WHEEL

Used primarily by Tibetan Buddhists, the prayer wheel is a beautifully embossed hollow metal cylinder mounted on a wooden handle. Inside the cylinder is a tightly wound scroll printed with a mantra. Devotees believe that the spinning of a prayer wheel is a form of prayer that's just as effective as reciting the sacred texts aloud.

According to legend, the Jade Emperor wanted to designate an animal to each calendar year. As the animals rushed to be the first to arrive, the rat snuck a ride on the ox's back. Just as the ox was about to cross the threshold, the rat jumped past him and arrived first. This is why the rat was given first place in the astrological chart. Find the year you were born to determine what your astrological animal is.

RAT

1936 · 1948 · 1960 · 1972 · 1984 · 1996 · 2008 · 2020

Charming and hardworking, Rats are goal setters and perfectionists. Rats are quick to anger, ambitious, and lovers of gossip.

OX

1937 · 1949 · 1961 · 1973 · 1985 · 1997 · 2009 · 2021

Patient and soft-spoken, Oxen inspire confidence in others. Generally easygoing, they can be remarkably stubborn, and they hate to fail or be opposed.

TIGER

1938 · 1950 · 1962 · 1974 · 1986 · 1998 · 2010 · 2022

Sensitive, and thoughtful, Tigers are capable of great sympathy. Tigers can be short-tempered, and are prone to conflict and indecisiveness.

RABBIT

1939 · 1951 · 1963 · 1975 · 1987 · 1999 · 2011 · 2023

Talented and articulate, Rabbits are virtuous, reserved, and have excellent taste. Though fond of gossip, Rabbits tend to be generally kind and even-tempered.

DRAGON

1940 · 1952 · 1964 · 1976 · 1988 · 2000 · 2012 · 2024

Energetic and excitable, short-tempered and stubborn, Dragons are known for their honesty, bravery, and ability to inspire confidence and trust.

SNAKE
1941 · 1953 · 1965 · 1977 · 1989 · 2001 · 2013 · 2025

Snakes are deep, possessing great wisdom and saying little. Snakes are considered the most beautiful and philosophical of all the signs.

HORSE
1942 · 1954 · 1966 · 1978 · 1990 · 2002 · 2014 · 2026

Horses are thought to be cheerful and perceptive, impatient and hot-blooded. Horses are independent and rarely listen to advice.

GOAT
1943 · 1955 · 1967 · 1979 · 1991 · 2003 · 2015 · 2027

Wise, gentle, and compassionate, Goats are elegant and highly accomplished in the arts. Goats can also be shy and pessimistic, and often tend toward timidity.

MONKEY
1944 · 1956 · 1968 · 1980 · 1992 · 2004 · 2016 · 2028

Clever, skillful, and flexible, Monkeys are thought to be erratic geniuses, able to solve problems with ease. Monkeys are also thought of as impatient and easily discouraged.

ROOSTER
1945 · 1957 · 1969 · 1981 · 1993 · 2005 · 2017 · 2029

Roosters are capable and talented, and tend to like to keep busy. Roosters are known as overachievers, and are frequently loners.

DOG
1946 · 1958 · 1970 · 1982 · 1994 · 2006 · 2018 · 2030

Dogs are loyal and honest and know how to keep secrets. They can also be selfish and stubborn.

PIG
1947 · 1959 · 1971 · 1983 · 1995 · 2007 · 2019 · 2031

Gallant and energetic, Pigs have a tendency to be single-minded and determined. Pigs have great fortitude and honesty, and tend to make friends for life.

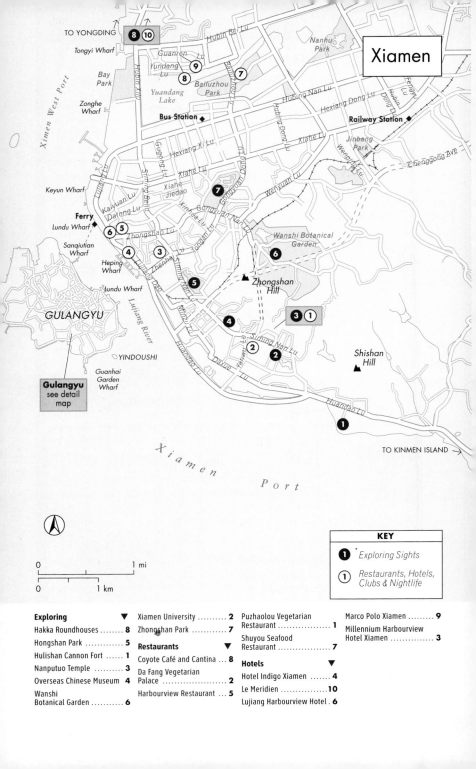

Xiamen

TO YONGDING ⑧ ⑩

Tongyi Wharf

Xiamen West Port

Bay Park

Zonghe Wharf

Guanren Lu
Yundang Lu
Yuandang Lake
⑨ Marco Polo
⑧
Baifuzhou Park

Nanhu Park

Hubin Bei Lu

Hubin Nan Lu

Hexiang Dong Lu

Bus Station ◆

Railway Station ◆

Jinbang Park

Chenggong Ave

Keyun Wharf

Hexiang Xi Lu

Xiahe Lu

Xiahe Jiedao

Gugong Lu

Siming Bei Lu

Ferry
Lundu Wharf

Kaiyuan Lu
Datong Lu

⑥ ⑤
Zhongshan Lu

④

③

Sanqiutian Wharf

Heping Wharf

Lundu Wharf

Zhenhai Lu

Kai da Lu

Gongyuan Nan Lu

Wenyuan Lu

Wanshi Botanical Garden

⑥

⑤

Zhongshan Hill ▲

GULANGYU

Lujiang River

YINDOUSHI

Guanhai Garden Wharf

Gulangyu
see detail map

Huangdao Lu

Daxue Lu

Siming Nan Lu

④

② ②

③ ①

Shishan Hill ▲

①

Huangdao Lu

TO KINMEN ISLAND →

Xiamen Port

0 ——— 1 mi
0 ——— 1 km

KEY

❶ Exploring Sights

① Restaurants, Hotels, Clubs & Nightlife

by paddleboat. The annual Lantern Festival is held here. ⊠ *Zhongshan Lu and Zhenhai Lu* ⬚ *Free.*

WHERE TO EAT

Although Xiamen is known for its fresh seafood, the city's Buddhist population means it has excellent vegetarian cuisine. Xiamen is probably the best place outside of Taiwan to experience Taiwanese cuisine, and many restaurants advertise their *Taiwan wei kou* (Taiwanese appetite) and *Taiwan xiao chi* (Taiwanese snacks).

$$ ✕ **Coyote Café and Cantina** (凯奥特咖啡馆酒馆 *Kǎiàotè kāfēiguǎn*
MEXICAN *jiǔguǎn*). The theme is heavy-handed, but Xiamen's most beloved Mexican restaurant serves steak fajitas and genuinely good burritos. Don't expect generous sides of sour cream or guacamole, but it won't matter anyway after a few well-poured margaritas. The staff members are friendly, and the alfresco seating is a nice touch. $ *Average main: Y70* ⊠ *Yang Ming Bldg., 20–22 Jianye Lu* ☎ *0592/508–0737* ⊕ *www. coyotecafe.asia* ⬚ *No credit cards.*

$ ✕ **Da Fang Vegetarian Palace** (大方素食馆 *Dà fāng sùshí guǎn*). Down
VEGETARIAN the street from Nanputuo Temple, this reasonably priced restaurant is popular with locals. Don't just come for the convenient location, though, as the restaurant has excellent food and friendly service. Try the house-special rice noodles, the mock duck, or the sizzling beef with pepper buns. The menu has English descriptions. ■ TIP➜ **To get here, turn right out of the temple's main entrance and continue for about five minutes down Siming Nan Lu until you see a yellow sign on your right.** $ *Average main: Y30* ⊠ *3 Nanhua Lu, along Siming Nan Lu* ☎ *0592/209–3236* ⬚ *No credit cards.*

$$$ ✕ **Harbourview Restaurant** (观海餐厅 *Guānhǎi cāntīng*). On the roof-
SEAFOOD top of the waterfront Lujiang Harbourview Hotel, this terrace res-
Fodor's Choice taurant has beautiful views over the bay. The Chinese chef prepares
★ delicious seafood dishes and dim sum specialties like sweet pork buns and shrimp dumplings. The à la carte menu includes English descriptions and some pictures, but you can also opt for the buffet. ■ TIP➜ **The restaurant's indoor tables fill up on weekends, but there is plenty of seating on the terrace. Aim for sundown for lovely sunset views.** $ *Average main: Y150* ⊠ *Lujiang Harbourview Hotel, 54 Lujiang Lu, 7th fl.* ☎ *0592/266–1398* ⊕ *www.lujiang-hotel.com* ⌂ *Reservations essential.*

$$ ✕ **Puzhaolou Vegetarian Restaurant** (普照楼素菜馆 *Pǔzhào lóu sù*
VEGETARIAN *càiguǎn*). The comings and goings of monks add to the atmosphere at this restaurant next to Nanputuo Temple. Popular dishes include black-mushroom soup with tofu and stewed yams with seaweed. You won't find any English translations, but there are a smattering of pictures on the menu, or you can point to dishes on other tables. ■ TIP➜ **This popular restaurants is overrun during peak hours, so head here early or prepare for a wait.** $ *Average main: Y75* ⊠ *Nanputuo Temple, 515 Siming Nan Lu* ☎ *0592/208–5908* ⊕ *www.nptveg.com* ⬚ *No credit cards.*

$$$ ✕ **Shuyou Seafood Restaurant** (舒友海鲜大酒楼 *Shūyǒu hǎixiān dà*
SEAFOOD *jiǔlóu*). Serving expensive, freshly caught seafood in a loud, boisterous setting, Shuyou is popular with locals. Downstairs, the tanks are filled with lobster, prawns, and crabs, and upstairs, diners feast on dishes cooked in Cantonese and Fujian styles. If you're in the mood for other

The Hakka Roundhouses were added to the UNESCO World Heritage List in 2008.

fare, the restaurant is also known for its excellent Peking duck and goose liver. $ *Average main: Y125* ⊠ *1 Bailuzhou Lu, near Swan Hotel Xiamen* ☎ *0592/533–0888* ⟲ *Reservations essential.*

WHERE TO STAY

$

HOTEL

🍽 **Hotel Indigo Xiamen** (廈門海港英迪格酒店 *Xiàmén hǎigǎng yīngdígé jiǔdiàn*). A boutique design hotel with colorful and comfortable rooms, Hotel Indigo's harborside location makes it a popular choice among trendy travelers. **Pros:** free Wi-Fi; good location; some rooms have private terraces. **Cons:** lobby can get noisy; some city views; spotty check-in service. $ *Rooms from: Y1000* ⊠ *16 Lujiang Lu* ☎ *0592/226–1666* ⊕ *www.ihg.com/hotelindigo* ⇆ *117 rooms, 8 suites* ❄ *No meals.*

$

HOTEL

FAMILY

🍽 **Le Meridien** (艾美酒店 *Ài měi jiǔdiàn*). With sweeping views of Xiamen Bay, this stunning property feels more like a Southeast Asian resort than a crowded Chinese metropolitan hotel. **Pros:** tropical setting; reasonable prices. **Cons:** outside the city center; slow service; in-room Wi-Fi costs extra. $ *Rooms from: Y860* ⊠ *7 Guanjun Lu* ☎ *0592/770–9999* ⊕ *www.lemeridien.com* ⇆ *314 rooms, 28 suites* ❄ *No meals.*

$$

HOTEL

Fodor's Choice

★

🍽 **Lujiang Harbourview Hotel** (鷺江宾馆 *Lùjiāng bīnguǎn*). In a nicely renovated colonial building, this hotel has an ideal location opposite the ferry pier and the waterfront boulevard. **Pros:** phenomenal location; good prices; complimentary Wi-Fi; bike rental services. **Cons:** busy pedestrian intersection; hard to hail cab; rooms on the small side. $ *Rooms from: Y1380* ⊠ *54 Lujiang Lu* ☎ *0592/202–2922* ⊕ *www.lujiang-hotel.com* ⇆ *154 rooms* ❄ *No meals.*

$ **⊞ Marco Polo Xiamen** (马可波罗
HOTEL 大酒店 *Mǎkěbōluó dàjiǔdiàn*).
Fodor's Choice Sitting pretty between the historic
★ sights and the commercial district,
the Marco Polo is one of the best
options for both business and leisure travelers. **Pros:** excellent location; helpful staff; pool and gym
on-site. **Cons:** aging facilities; free
Wi-Fi very slow. $ *Rooms from:
Y868* ⊠ *8 Jianye Lu* ☎ *0592/509–
1888* ⊕ *www.marcopolohotels.
com* ⌁ *268 rooms, 32 suites* ⦙⊙⦙ *No
meals.*

$ **⊞ Millenium Harbourview Hotel Xia-**
HOTEL **men** (厦门海景千禧大酒店 *Xiàmén hǎijǐng qiān xǐ dàjiǔdiàn*).
With an excellent location overlooking the harbor, this hotel is
a practical base. **Pros:** excellent
service; free Wi-Fi. **Cons:** can be

noisy; some rooms very dark. $ *Rooms from: Y900* ⊠ *12-8 Zhenhai
Lu* ☎ *0592/202–3333* ⊕ *www.millenniumhotels.com.cn/en/millennium
xiamen* ⌁ *329 rooms, 23 suites* ⦙⊙⦙ *Breakfast.*

NIGHTLIFE

The Zhongshan Lu pedestrian street near the ferry pier is charming in
the evening, when the colonial-style buildings are aglow with gentle
neon, but its popularity with tourists means it can be a madhouse.
Though not as romantic as it once was, this waterfront promenade is
still a popular spot for young couples walking arm in arm.

FAMILY **Bay Park** (海湾公园 *Hǎiwān gōngyuán*). This pretty park is a quiet
way to spend an evening. Walk north along the waterfront promenade,
where you'll pass by a couple of hokey, albeit popular, themed restaurants. If you're craving pizza, stop into Me & You 2 Restaurant
(⊠ *Along western promenade* ☎ *0592/221–1747*) which serves more
than 100 types of pies, plus a half-off draft beer happy hour till 8 pm
and live music nightly. Take one of the tree-lined walkways into the
center of the park and there's a nightly carnival that's great for kids, as
well as a mini street food market camped by a beautiful new overwater
footbridge that connects with the Marco Polo Hotel. ⊠ *Haiwan Park,
off Hubin Xi Lu.*

Pub Street (槟榔酒吧街 *Bīnláng jiǔbā jiē*). Make like the expats and
head to Pub Street, on Guanren Lu behind the Marco Polo Hotel, where
there are lively pubs and clubs to keep your thirst quenched. The favorite in town is the Londoner (⊠ *5-8 Guanren Lu* ☎ *0592/508–9783*),
voted the best bar for several years running, but there's something for
all tastes. Most of the bars along this leafy strip have nice outdoor
tables—particularly lovely in the spring and autumn when the humidity
has died down. ⊠ *Guanren Lu.*

SPORTS AND THE OUTDOORS

Xiamen offers some excellent hiking opportunities. Most notable of these are the hills behind the Nanputuo Temple, where winding paths and stone steps carved into the sheer rock face make for a fairly strenuous climb. For a real challenge, hike from Nanputuo Temple to the Wanshi Botanical Garden, or vice versa. If you're still in the mood for a climb after spending a few hours enjoying the garden's beautiful landscape, another more serpentine trail (a relic of the Japanese occupation) leads to Xiamen University. The hike takes the better part of an afternoon.

The area around Xiamen has decent public shores. Beachgoers abound nearly anywhere along Huandao Lu, the road that circles the island, which is also referred to as Island Ring Road.

GULANGYU

5 minutes by boat from Xiamen.

The best way to experience Gulangyu's charm is to explore its meandering streets early in the morning or late in the evening to avoid the masses. Veer off the commercial and congested tourist trail, and explore the little lanes that weave all over the island, stumbling across particularly distinctive old mansions or the weathered graves of missionaries and merchants. These quiet back alleys are fascinating to wander in, with the atmosphere of a Mediterranean city punctuated by touches of calligraphy or the click of mah-jongg tiles to remind you where you really are. And, unlike everywhere else in the country, Gulangyu does not permit cars, so you won't take your life in your hands when crossing the street.

GETTING HERE AND AROUND

Boats to the island run from early in the morning until midnight, and depart from the ferry terminal across from the Lujiang Harbourview Hotel. Electric tour buses are available on the island for Y50 per person.

BOAT AND FERRY TRAVEL Ferry service from the Xiamen Ferry dock starts at 5:45 am, with departures every 10 minutes. The trip to Gulangyu costs Y8, but the return to Xiamen is free—just be sure to hold onto your token. On a crowded day, the ferry pier can be a little difficult to navigate. Purchase a ticket at one of the counters, then board at the No. 2 Hall. Coming back, the ferry does not run after midnight, so to avoid being stranded, check the last departure time before you leave Xiamen.

No cars are allowed on Gulangyu Island.

TIMING

Gulangyu is small enough to be explored on a day trip from Xiamen, but avoid going at peak hours during the weekends or prepare for a chaotic outing. It's best to go on a weekday if possible. Moreover, accommodations are slim pickings on the island so plan to head back to Xiamen.

TOURS

The only way to explore Gulangyu is by hopping on one of the electric tour buses that ply the island or by setting out on foot. Take a morning or afternoon to climb up the narrow, winding streets to see the hundreds of colonial-era mansions (ranging from restored to ramshackle to kitschy imitations) that are the heart of this fabulous trove of late-19th- and early-20th-century architecture.

ESSENTIALS

Many sights on Gulangyu charge admission fees, but a tour aboard the island's electric bus includes admission to all sites on the tour. You can also buy a ticket for the five most-visited sites (Y100) from most ticketing counters. Island ATMs are available near major tourist sites, but it is best to do your banking before heading out.

EXPLORING

Bright Moon Garden (皓月园 *Hàoyuè yuán*). This sculpture garden on the southeastern tip of the island is a fitting seaside memorial to Zhen Chenggong, also known as Koxinga, a famous Ming general who fought to protect China from the invading Manchus. A massive stone statue of him stares eastward from a perch hanging over the sea. ⊠ *3 Zhangzhou Lu* ☎ *Y15* ⊗ *Daily 7:30–6.*

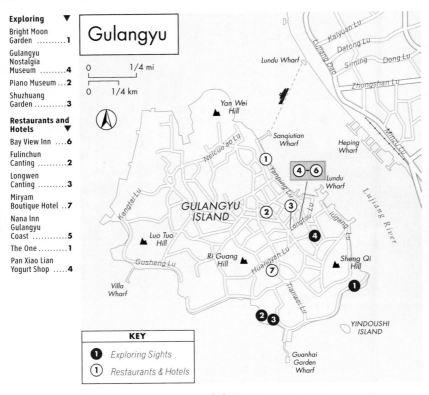

Gulangyu Nostalgia Museum (珍奇世界 *Zhēnqí shí jié*). A weirdly enjoyable mix of history and oddities, this museum, known in Chinese as Huaijiu Gulangyu Guan, is one of the country's more bizarre. Part of the museum displays the usual historical information about Fujian and Taiwan. The other part is a veritable museum of oddities, offering pickled genetic mutations like two-headed snakes and conjoined twin sheep. The room of ancient Chinese sex toys will amuse some and mystify others. ✉ *38 Huangyan Lu* ☎ *0592/206–9933* 🎟 *Y60* ⊙ *Daily 8–6.*

NEED A BREAK?

The One (一席 *Yīxí*). Right up against the main waterfront promenade, The One is a contemporary bar and café with a nice outdoor deck, trendy interiors, and a decent selection of drinks and snacks. Although servers don't speak English, the menu itself is in English. Bands perform live in the evenings when couples snag alfresco seating, though the place tends to be more of a family affair during the day. ✉ *21 Yanping Lu* ☎ *0592/400–187–1717.*

Piano Museum (钢琴博物馆 *Gāngqín bówùguǎn*). Gulangyu holds a special place in the country's musical history, thanks to the large number of Christian missionaries who called the island home in the late 19th and early 20th centuries. Gulangyu has more pianos per capita than anyplace else in China, and the Piano Museum houses more than 100 beautifully preserved instruments that were once owned by famous pianists. Tucked away up a steep hill in the Shuzhuang Garden, this charming collection is a must for any music lover. ✉ *45 Huangyan Lu* ☎ *0592/206–0238* 🎟 *Y30, included in Shuzhuang Garden ticket* ⏲ *Daily 8:15–5:45.*

> **WORD OF MOUTH**
>
> "There is a sandy beach on the offshore island of Gulang Yu (reached by regular ferry) that's quite pleasant—fine to sit on and people-watch, but no great shakes for swimming. The pleasure of the city is in just wandering through the market area, and the streets of grand mansions in various states of repair on the aforementioned island." —Alice13

Shuzhuang Garden (菽庄花园 *Shūzhuāng huāyuán*). This lovely, peaceful garden is immaculately kept and dotted with pavilions and bridges, some extending out to rocks just offshore. Built in 1913 by a wealthy Taiwanese merchant, the garden is home to several key sights, including the Piano Museum and the Twelve Grotto Heaven, which comprises 12 caves formed from multicolored sandstone. ✉ *Tianwei Lu* 🎟 *Y30* ⏲ *Daily 8–7.*

5

WHERE TO EAT

$ SEAFOOD 🍴 **Fulinchun Canting** (福林春餐厅 *Fúlínchūn cāntīng*). Serving home-style seafood cooked to order, this closet-size restaurant is almost always packed with locals during peak hours. If it comes from the sea, you'll find it here, with steamed crab, deep-fried shrimp, and whole fish served in a variety of styles. ■ **TIP→ The owners do not speak any English, but the pictures on the walls double as a menu.** [$] *Average main: Y35* ✉ *109 Longtou Lu* 💳 *No credit cards.*

$$$ SEAFOOD 🍴 **Longwen Canting** (龙文餐厅 *Lóngwén cāntīng*). Serving fresh seafood dishes, this expansive restaurant near the ferry terminal is popular with tourists. Specialties include whole steamed fish, oyster soup, and a wide variety of seafood dishes. The decor imitates a traditional Chinese interior, and on the wall, pictures are displayed to help you order without having to speak Chinese. [$] *Average main: Y125* ✉ *21 Longtou Lu* ☎ *0592/206–6369.*

$ CAFÉ 🍴 **Pan Xiao Lian Yogurt Shop** (潘小莲 *Pānxiǎolián*). This lovely little shop is easy to spot, thanks to its large orange awning and Thai-inspired exterior. It's reputed to serve the best yogurt in Xiamen. In the tiny stall, a small English menu offers a few choices, including plain homemade yogurt or yogurt topped with fresh, sweet mangoes. Walls in soothing shades of yellow serve as a canvas for massive jungle paintings. Find it underneath **Nana Inn**, on the same road as the central ferry pier. There's also another branch around the corner. [$] *Average main: Y20* ✉ *8 Longtou Lu* 💳 *No credit cards* ⏲ *Daily 9 am–10:30 pm.*

WHERE TO STAY

$ B&B/INN 🏨 **Bay View Inn** (灣景旅館 *Wānjǐng lǚguǎn*). The peppy yellow facade and white picket fence augur well for a low-key stay at the Bay View Inn. **Pros:** great location; pretty atmosphere; good café. **Cons:** can be loud; bare-bones amenities; hard beds. [$] *Rooms from: Y500* ✉ *17*

Longtou Lu ☎ *0592/206–0466* 🌐 *www.bayviewinn.cn* 🛏 *26 rooms* 🍴 *No meals.*

$ HOTEL 🏨 **Miryam Boutique Hotel** (老别墅旅馆 *Lǎo biéshù lǚguǎn*). The Victorian-era decor at this boutique hotel doesn't exactly blend in with the neighborhood, but it's hard to argue with four-poster beds, elaborate fireplaces, and sculpted gardens. **Pros:** overlooks the ocean; close to main attractions; free Wi-Fi. **Cons:** themed rooms; little English is spoken; far from pier. [$] *Rooms from: Y688* ✉ *70 Huangyan Lu* ☎ *0592/206–2505* 🌐 *www.miryamhotel.com* 🛏 *15 rooms* 🍴 *No meals.*

$ B&B/INN 🏨 **Nana Inn Gulangyu Coast** (娜娜鼓浪屿海岸旅馆 *Nànà gǔlàngyǔ hǎi'àn lǚguǎn*). Just down the street from the ferry terminal, this quirky inn has the friendly atmosphere of a hostel without the cramped quarters. **Pros:** convenient location; outdoor café; free Wi-Fi. **Cons:** basic facilities; part of a commercial complex; limited English; confusing website. [$] *Rooms from: Y360* ✉ *8 Longtou Lu* ☎ *0592/206–6396* 🌐 *www.nana123.com* 🛏 *75 rooms* 🍴 *No meals.*

HONG KONG

WELCOME TO HONG KONG

TOP REASONS TO GO

★ **Harbor views:** The skyline that launched a thousand postcards . . . See it on a stroll along the Tsim Sha Tsui waterfront, from a Star Ferry crossing the harbor, or from the top of Victoria Peak.

★ **Dim sum:** As you bite into a moist *siu mai* it dawns on you why everyone says you haven't done dim sum until you've done it in Hong Kong.

★ **Cultural immersion:** The Hong Kong Heritage Museum chronicles the city's history. On a Lantau Island hill, the 242-ton Tian Tan Buddha statue sits in the lotus position beside the Po Lin Buddhist Monastery.

★ **Shopping as religion:** At Kowloon's street markets, clothes, electronics, and souvenirs compete for space with food carts. Antiques fill windows along Hollywood Road.

★ **Horsing around:** Every year, Hong Kongers gamble billions of dollars, and the Happy Valley Racetrack is one of their favorite places to do it.

1 Hong Kong Island. It's only 78 square km (30 square miles), but it's where the action is, from high finance to nightlife to luxury shopping. The commercial districts—Western, Central, and Wan Chai—are on the north coast. Southside is home to small towns, quiet coves, and reserve areas. A 20-minute taxi ride from Central can have you breathing fresh air and seeing only greenery.

2 Kowloon. This peninsula on the Chinese mainland is just across from Central and bounded in the north by the string of mountains that give it its poetic name: *gau lung*, "nine dragons" (there are eight mountains; the ninth dragon was the emperor who named them).

3 Lantau Island. Off the west coast of Hong Kong Island lies Lantau Island. Home to the Tian Tau Buddha, Lantau is connected by ferries to Hong Kong Island and by a suspension bridge to west Kowloon.

4 New Territories. The expanse between Kowloon and the Chinese border feels far removed from urban congestion and rigor. Nature reserves (many with great trails), temples, and traditional Hakka villages fill its 200 square miles.

5 Macau. Most people visit Macau to gamble in the Cotai area, a glitzy, Vegas-like strip of hotels and casinos, and shop. But don't overlook its timeless charms and unique culture, born from centuries of both Portuguese and Chinese influence.

SHENZHEN

Lo Wu

Shek Wu Hui

Fanling

San Tin

Mai Po

Pat Heung

Shek Kong **4**

Sha Tau Kok

Luk Keng

CROOKED ISLAND

CRESCENT ISLAND

Tai Po

Tai Po Kau

Wu Kai Sha

North Channel

NEW TERRITORIES

Fo Tan

Sha Tin

Sha Tin Wai

Shak Mun

Tai Mong Tsai

Tsuen Wan

Sha Tin

Sai Kung

Sham Tseng

Shek Wan *TSING YI*

Hong Kong Heritage Museum **2**

Sha Tin Wai

Ho Chung

KAU SAI CHAU

Port Shelter

KOWLOON

Hang Hau

Yau Tong

Kennedy Town

★Star Ferry

♦ **Happy Valley Racetrack**

Tai Chik Sha

▲ HONG KONG

Victoria Peak 552m **1**

TUNG LUNG CHAU

HEI LING CHAU

Aberdeen

HONG KONG ISLAND

Shek O

Stanley

Yung Shue Wan

Sheung Sze Mun

CHEUNG CHAU

LAMMA ISLAND

PO TOI ISLANDS

South China Sea

| 0 | 3 mi |
| 0 | 3 km |

GETTING ORIENTED

Hong Kong Island and the Kowloon Peninsula are divided by Victoria Harbour. On Hong Kong Island, the central city stretches only a few kilometers south before mountains rise up. But the city really also continues several more kilometers north into Kowloon. In the main districts, luxury boutiques are a stone's throw from old hawker stalls, and a modern, high-tech horse-racing track isn't far from a temple housing more than 10,000 Buddha statues.

6

Hong Kong Island

TSIM SHA TSUI

KOWLOON

NORTH POINT

YAU TONG DISTRICT

Junk Bay

SAI YING PUN

WESTERN

Victoria Harbour

CAUSEWAY BAY

SAI WAN PO

Lei Yue Mun

Green Island

KENNEDY TOWN

SHEUNG WAN

ADMIRALTY

SHAU KEI WAN

WESTERN

CENTRAL

WAN CHAI

HAPPY VALLEY

JARDINE'S LOOKOUT

1

CHAI WAN

PEAK DISTRICT

POK FU LAM

HONG KONG ISLAND

| 0 | 1 mile |
| 0 | 1 kilometer |

Updated by Charley Lanyon, Maloy Luakian, Dorothy So, and Kate Springer

The Hong Kong Island skyline, with its ever-growing number of skyscrapers, speaks to the triumph of ambition over fate. Whereas it took Paris and London 10 to 20 generations and New York 6 to build the spectacular cities seen today, in Hong Kong almost everything you see has been built in the time since today's young investment bankers were born.

On Hong Kong Island the central city goes only a few kilometers south into the island before mountains rise up. In the main districts and neighborhoods luxury boutiques are a stone's throw from old hawker stalls.

West of Hong Kong Island you'll find Lantau Island. Lantau is connected by a suspension bridge to west Kowloon. More than 200 other islands also belong to Hong Kong.

Hong Kong's older areas—the southern side of Central, for example—show erratic street planning, but the newer developments and reclamations follow something closer to a grid system. Streets are usually numbered odd on one side, even on the other. There's no baseline for street numbers and no block-based numbering system.

PLANNING

WHEN TO GO

High season, from September through late December, sees sunny, dry days and cool, comfortable nights. January and February are mostly cool and damp, with periods of overcast skies. March and April are pleasant, and by May the temperature is consistently warm and comfortable.

June through August are the cheapest months for one reason: they coincide with the hot, sticky, and very rainy typhoon season. Hong Kong is prepared for blustery assaults; if a big storm approaches, the airwaves crackle with information, and your hotel will post the appropriate signals (a No. 10 signal indicates the worst winds; a black warning means a rainstorm is brewing). This is serious business—bamboo scaffolding and metal signs can hurtle through the streets, trees can break or fall, and large areas of the territory can flood. Museums, shops, restaurants, and transport shut down at signal No. 8, but supermarkets, convenience stores, and cinemas typically stay open.

GETTING HERE AND AROUND

AIR TRAVEL

Modern, easy to navigate, and full of amenities, Hong Kong International Airport (HKG)—also known as Chek Lap Kok, after its location—is a traveler's dream. Terminal 1, the third-largest terminal in the world, services the departures for most major airlines, as well as all arriving flights. The newer but smaller Terminal 2 handles all other airlines, including budget carriers.

The Airport Express train service is the quickest and most convenient way to and from the airport. High-speed trains whisk you to Kowloon in 21 minutes and Central in 24 minutes. Citybus runs five buses ("A" precedes the bus number) from the airport to popular destinations. They make fewer stops than regular buses (which have an "E" before their numbers). Two useful routes are the A11, serving Central, Admiralty, Wan Chai, and Causeway Bay and ending in North Point; and the A21, going to Tsim Sha Tsui, Jordan, and Mong Kok.

Taxis from the airport are reliable and plentiful. Trips to Hong Kong Island destinations cost around HK$295, while those to Kowloon are around HK$240. There is also an HK$5 charge per piece of luggage stored in the trunk.

Airport Information Hong Kong International Airport ☎ *2181–8888* ⊕ *www. hongkongairport.com.*

BOAT AND FERRY TRAVEL

With fabulous views of both sides of Victoria Harbour, the Star Ferry is so much more than just a boat. It's an iconic Hong Kong landmark in its own right, and has been running across the harbor since 1888. Double-bowed, green-and-white vessels connect Central and Wan Chai with Kowloon in less than 10 minutes, daily from 6:30 am to 11:30 pm.

Ferry Information Star Ferry ☎ *2367–7065* ⊕ *www.starferry.com.hk.*

BUS TRAVEL

An efficient network of double-decker buses covers most of Hong Kong. More intrepid visitors can take a chance on a minibus. These cream-colored vehicles seat 16 people and rattle through the city at breakneck speeds. Routes and prices are prominently displayed in front. While faster than buses, minibuses are risky if you aren't sure of your destination.

SUBWAY TRAVEL

By far the best way to get around Hong Kong is on the MTR. The network now provides all subway and train services in Hong Kong. The trains are among the cleanest in the world, with hardly any litter to be found. Eating or drinking on the trains or in the paid areas is prohibited, with fines of HK$2,000.

The five major lines are color-coded for convenience. The Island line (blue) runs along the north coast of Hong Kong Island; the Tsuen Wan line (red) goes from Central under the harbor to Tsim Sha Tsui, then

6

THE OCTOPUS CARD

The many public transportation options in Hong Kong are generally clean, safe, and inexpensive. The first step is to get an Octopus Card from any Mass Transit Railway or Airport Express station. Usable for all public transportation options, the Octopus Card is a good alternative to buying a ticket for each train trip or digging for change on the bus. The initial cost of an Octopus Card is HK$150, and you will have HK$100 available for use right away. The remaining HK$50 is a refundable deposit that provides a buffer in case you go beyond the card's value. You can top off the card at Customer Service Centres or Add Value machines at MTR stations, or at convenience stores, supermarkets, and some fast-food chains.

up to the western New Territories. Mong Kok links Tsim Sha Tsui to eastern New Kowloon via the Kwun Tong line (green). Also serving this area is the Tseung Kwan O line (purple), which crosses back over the harbor to Quarry Bay and North Point. Finally, the Tung Chung line (yellow) connects Central and West Kowloon to Tung Chung on Lantau, near the airport.

You can buy tickets from ticket machines (using coins or notes) or from English-speaking staff behind glass-windowed customer-service counters near the turnstile entrances. Fares range from HK$3.70 to HK$42.50, depending how far you travel. An alternative is the Tourist Day Pass. For HK$55, this pass allows you unlimited travel on the MTR, excluding the Airport Express, for one day. However, you cannot use the pass on other public transport or to purchase items.

TRAIN TRAVEL

The ultra-efficient MTR train network connects Kowloon to the eastern and western New Territories. Trains run every five to eight minutes, and connections to the subway are relatively quick. This is a commuter service and, like the subway, has sparkling-clean trains and stations—smoking, eating, and drinking are strictly forbidden.

Subway and Train Information MTR ☎ 2881–8888 ⊕ www.mtr.com.hk.

TRAM TRAVEL

Old-fashioned double-decker trams have been running along the northern shore of Hong Kong Island since 1904. Most routes start in Kennedy Town or Western Market, and go eastward all the way through Central, Wan Chai, Causeway Bay, North Point, and Quarry Bay to Shau Kei Wan. A branch line turns off in Wan Chai toward Happy Valley, where horse races are held in season.

Destinations are marked on the front of each tram and route maps are displayed at the stops; you board at the back and get off at the front, paying a flat rate of HK$2.30 as you leave.

Tram Information Hong Kong Tramways ☎ 2548–7102 ⊕ www.hktramways. com.

TAXI TRAVEL

Taxis are easy to find in Hong Kong, although heavy rush hour traffic in Central, Causeway Bay, and Tsim Sha Tsui means they aren't always the best option for getting around the city quickly. They're most useful other times of the day, especially after the MTR closes. Drivers usually know the terrain well, but many don't speak English; having your destination written in Chinese is a good idea.

Taxi Information Hong Kong Kowloon Taxi and Lorry Owners Association ☎ 2574-7311.

HEALTH

There are 24-hour accident and emergency services at Caritas Medical Centre, Pamela Youde Nethersole Eastern Hospital, Prince of Wales Hospital, Queen Elizabeth Hospital, and Queen Mary Hospital. Nonresidents will always be treated immediately, although they are usually charged a set fee of HK$990 for each use of the public health-care system.

PASSPORTS AND VISAS

Citizens of the United States need only a valid passport to enter Hong Kong for stays up to three months. Your passport must be valid for at least six more months. All minors regardless of age, including newborns and infants, must also have their own passports. Upon arrival, you'll have to fill in an immigrations form. Keep the departure portion of the form safe—you'll be asked to present it again for your return trip home. If you're planning to pop over the border into mainland China, you must first get a visa, although it's not necessary for Macau.

SAFETY

Hong Kong is an incredibly safe place—day and night. The police do a good job maintaining law and order, but there are still a few pickpockets about, especially in Tsim Sha Tsui and Mong Kok. Exercise the same caution you would in any large city: be aware of your surroundings, avoid crowded areas, and don't carry large amounts of cash or valuables with you.

VISITOR INFORMATION

For a guide to what's happening in Hong Kong, check out the Hong Kong Tourist Board's excellent website (⊕ *www.discoverhongkong.com/eng*).

ESSENTIALS

Consulate U.S. Consulate General ⊠ 26 Garden Rd., Central ☎ 2523-9011 ⊕ hongkong.usconsulate.gov.

Hospitals and Clinics Caritas Medical Centre ⊠ 111 Wing Hong St., Sham Shui Po, Kowloon ☎ 3408-7911 ⊕ www.ha.org.hk. **Pamela Youde Nethersole Eastern Hospital** ⊠ 3 Lok Man Rd., Chai Wan ☎ 2595-6111 ⊕ www.ha.org.hk/pyneh. **Prince of Wales Hospital** ⊠ 30-32 Ngan Shing St., Sha Tin, New Territories ☎ 2632-2211 ⊕ www.ha.org.hk/pwh. **Queen Elizabeth Hospital** ⊠ 30 Gascoigne Rd., Yau Ma Tei, Kowloon ☎ 2958-8888 ⊕ www.ha.org.hk/qeh. **Queen Mary Hospital** ⊠ 102 Pok Fu Lam Rd., Pok Fu Lam, Western ☎ 2255-3838 ⊕ www3.ha.org.hk/qmh.

Postal Services Hong Kong General Post Office ⊠ *2 Connaught Rd., Central* ☎ *2921–2222* ⊕ *www.hongkongpost.hk.* **Kowloon Central Post Office** ⊠ *405 Nathan Rd., Yau Ma Tei, Kowloon* ☎ *2928–6247* ⊕ *www.hongkongpost.hk.*

HONG KONG ISLAND

When you're on Hong Kong Island and feeling disoriented, remember that the water is always north. Central, Admiralty, and Wan Chai, the island's main business districts, are opposite Tsim Sha Tsui on the Kowloon Peninsula. West of Central are Sheung Wan and the other (mainly residential) neighborhoods that make up Western. Central backs onto the slopes of Victoria Peak, so the districts south of it—the Mid-Levels and the Peak—look down on it. Causeway Bay, North Point, Quarry Bay, Shau Kei Wan, and Chai Wan East run east along the shore after Wan Chai. Developments on the south side of Hong Kong Island are scattered: the beach towns of Shek O and Stanley sit on two peninsulas on the southeast, and industrial Aberdeen sits to the west.

WESTERN

Despite its name, the Western District is the part of Hong Kong that has been least affected by Western influence. Many of the narrow, jammed streets that climb the slopes of Victoria Peak seem to be light-years from the dazzle of Central, just a 15-minute walk down the road. Though developers are making short work of the traditional architecture, Western's colonial buildings, rattling trams, old-world medicine shops, and lively markets still recall bygone times. Western is a foodie's idea of heaven, as you'll soon discover when you step into Sheung Wan Wet Market on Queen's Road Central or browse the dried delicacies—abalone, bird's nests, sea cucumbers, mushrooms—in shops around Wing Lok Street and Des Voeux Road.

The Mid-Levels Escalator forms a handy boundary between Western and Central. Several main thoroughfares run parallel to the shore, each farther up the slope: Des Voeux Road (where the trams run), Queen's Road, Hollywood Road (where SoHo starts), and Caine Road (where the Mid-Levels begin).

As to how far west Western goes, it technically reaches all the way to Kennedy Town, where the tram lines end, but there isn't much worth noting beyond Sheung Wan.

GETTING HERE AND AROUND

The most scenic way to Sheung Wan is on a tram along Des Voeux Road. From Central or Admiralty it's probably the quickest, too: no traffic, no subway lines, or endless underground walks. There are stops every two or three blocks. The Sheung Wan MTR station brings you within spitting distance of Western Market.

TOP ATTRACTIONS

Hong Kong Museum of Medical Sciences. You can find out all about medical breakthroughs at this private museum, which is housed in an Edwardian-style building at the top of Ladder Street. The 11 exhibition galleries cover 10,000 square feet, and present information on both Western and Chinese medical practices. ✉ *2 Caine La., Western* ☎ *2549–5123* ⊕ *www.hkmms.org.hk* 💷 *HK$20* ⏱ *Tues.–Sat. 10–5, Sun. and holidays 1–5* Ⓜ *Sheung Wan, Exit A2.*

Man Mo Temple. No one knows exactly when Hong Kong Island's oldest temple was built—but the consensus is sometime between 1847 and 1862. The temple is dedicated to the Taoist gods of literature and of war: Man, who wears green, and Mo, dressed in red. The temple bell, cast in Canton in 1847, and the drum next to it are sounded to attract the gods' attention when a prayer is being offered. ✉ *124–126 Hollywood Rd., Sheung Wan, Western* ⏱ *Daily 8–6* Ⓜ *Sheung Wan, Exit A2.*

Fodor's Choice
★

University Museum and Art Gallery. Chinese harp music and a faint smell of incense float through peaceful rooms filled with a small but excellent collection of Chinese antiquities. On view are ceramics and bronzes, some dating from 3,000 BC, as well as paintings, lacquerware, and carvings in jade, stone, and wood. Some superb ancient pieces include ritual vessels, decorative mirrors, and painted pottery. The museum has the world's largest collection of Nestorian crosses, dating from the Mongol Period (1280–1368). There are usually two or three well-curated temporary exhibitions on view; contemporary artists who work in traditional mediums are often featured. The collection is spread between the T.T. Tsui Building, where there is a Tea Gallery, and the Fung Ping Shan Building, which you access via a first-floor footbridge. The museum is a bit out of the way—20 minutes from Central via Buses 3B, 23, 40, 40M, or 103, or a 15-minute uphill walk from Sheung Wan MTR—but it's a must for the true Chinese art lover. ✉ *University of Hong Kong, 90 Bonham Rd., Western* ☎ *2241–5500* ⊕ *www.hkumag.hku.hk* 💷 *Free* ⏱ *Mon.–Sat. 9:30–6, Sun. 1–6* Ⓜ *Sheung Wan.*

WORTH NOTING

Western Market. The Sheung Wan District's iconic market, a hulking Edwardian-era brick structure, is a good place to get your bearings. Built in 1906, it functioned as a produce market for 83 years. Today it's a shopping center selling trinkets and fabrics—the architecture is what's worth the visit. Nearby you'll find herbal medicine on Ko Shing Street and Queen's Road West, dried seafood on Wing Lok Street and Des Voeux Road West, and ginseng and bird's nest on Bonham Strand West. ✉ *323 Des Voeux Rd. Central, Sheung Wan, Western* ☎ *6029–2675* ⊕ *www. westernmarket.com.hk* ⏱ *Daily 10–7* Ⓜ *Sheung Wan, Exit B or C.*

CENTRAL

Shopping, eating, drinking—Central lives up to its name when it comes to all of these. But it's also Hong Kong's historical heart, packed with architectural reminders of the early colonial days. They're in stark contrast to the soaring masterpieces of modern architecture that the city is famous for. Somehow the mishmash works. With the harbor on one side and Victoria Peak on the other, Central's views—once you get high enough to see them—are unrivaled. It's a hot spot for both locals and expatriates, packed with people, sights, and life.

Shopping at the Western Market

The streets between Queen's Road Central and the harbor are laid out more or less geometrically. On the south side of Queen's Road, however, is a confusion of steep lanes. Overhead walkways connect Central's major buildings, an all-weather alternative to the chaotic streets below.

GETTING HERE AND AROUND

Central MTR station is a mammoth underground warren with a host of far-flung exits. A series of "travelators" join it with Hong Kong Station, under the IFC Mall, where Tung Chung Line and Airport Express trains arrive and depart. Rattling old trams along Des Voeux Road reliably get you into Western, or as far east as Wan Chai, with views along the way. Star Ferry vessels to Kowloon leave Pier 7 every 6 to 12 minutes.

TOP ATTRACTIONS

Central Star Ferry Pier. Take in the view of the Kowloon skyline from this pier, from which sturdy green-and-white Star Ferry vessels cross the harbor. Naturally, the views are even better from the open water. ⊠ *Pier 7, Central Ferry Pier, Man Kwong St., Central* ☎ *2367–7065* ⊕ *www. starferry.com.hk* Ⓜ *Hong Kong Station, Exit A2.*

Fodor'sChoice ★

Flagstaff House Museum of Tea Ware. All that's good about British colonial architecture is exemplified in the Flagstaff House Museum of Tea Ware's simple white facade, wooden monsoon shutters, and colonnaded verandas. Look for hundreds of delicate antique tea sets from the Tang (618–907) through the Qing (1644–1911) dynasties filling the rooms that once housed the commander of the British forces. ■ TIP➔ **Skip the lengthy, confusing tea-ceremony descriptions and concentrate on the porcelain pieces themselves.** Look out for the unadorned brownish-purple clay of the Yixing pots, whose beauty hinges on perfect form. A room on the ground floor has interactive computer stations on the history of tea. ⊠ *Hong Kong Park, 10 Cotton Tree Dr., Central* ☎ *2869–0690* ⊕ *www. lcsd.gov.hk* ▣ *Free* ⊘ *Wed.–Mon. 10–6* Ⓜ *Admiralty, Exit C1.*

FAMILY
Fodor's Choice
★

Hong Kong Park. One of the prettiest parks in the city proper, Hong Kong Park is a sprawling mix of rock gardens and leafy pathways. It's not uncommon to stumble upon locals practicing tai chi or reading in a secluded spot. This welcome respite from the surrounding skyscrapers occupies the site of a garrison called the Victoria Barracks, and some buildings from 1842 and 1910 are still standing. The park is home to the Flagstaff House Museum of Tea Ware and the Edward Youde Aviary. ⊠ *19 Cotton Tree Dr., Central* ☎ *2521–5041* ⊕ *www.lcsd.gov.hk* ▣ *Free* ⊘ *Daily 6 am–11 pm* Ⓜ *Admiralty, Exit C1.*

Mid-Levels Escalator. The unimaginatively named Mid-Levels District is halfway up the hill between the Western and Central districts and Victoria Peak. Running through it is the world's longest covered outdoor escalator, which connects to several main residential streets and walkways. Free of charge and protected from the elements, this series of moving walkways makes the uphill journey a cinch. Before 10 am the escalators only move downward, carrying an endless stream of workers and their cups of coffee. ⊠ *Next to 100 Queen's Rd. Central, Central* ⊘ *Daily 6–midnight* Ⓜ *Central, Exit D1.*

Fodor's Choice
★

Victoria Peak and the Victoria Peak Tram. As you step off the Victoria Peak Tram, you might be surprised to encounter two shopping arcades crowning Hong Kong's most prized mountaintop. But venture up the escalators to the free viewing platforms—yep, through the Peak Galleria mall—and the view will astound you. Whatever the time, whatever the weather, be it your first visit or your 50th, this is Hong Kong's one unmissable sight. Spread below you is a glittering forest of skyscrapers; beyond them the harbor and—on a clear day—Kowloon's eight mountains. On rainy days wisps of clouds catch on the buildings' pointy tops, and at night both sides of the harbor burst into color. Consider having dinner at one of the restaurants near the Upper Terminus. ■TIP➔ **Skip the Peak Tower's observation deck, which is pricey. The free sights from atop the Galleria are just as good.**

Soaring just over 1,805 feet above sea level, Victoria Peak looks over Central and beyond. The steep funicular tracks up to the peak start at the **Peak Tram Terminus,** near St. John's Cathedral on Garden Road. Hong Kong is proud that its funicular railway is the world's steepest. Before it opened in 1888, the only way to get up to Victoria Peak was to walk or take a bumpy ride in a sedan chair on steep steps. At the Lower Terminus, the Peak Tram Historical Gallery displays a replica of the first-generation Peak Tram carriage. On the way up, grab a seat on the right-hand side for the best views of the harbor and mountains. The trams, which look like old-fashioned trolley cars, are hauled the whole way in seven minutes by cables attached to electric motors. En route to the Upper Terminus, 1,300 feet above sea level, the cars pass four intermediate stations, with track gradients varying from 4 to 27 degrees.

There are well-signed nature walks around Victoria Peak, which make for wonderful respites from the commercialism. Before buying a return

6

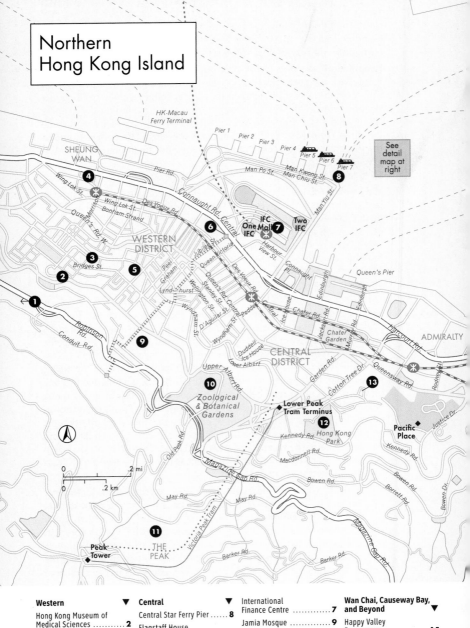

Northern Hong Kong Island

HK-Macau Ferry Terminal

SHEUNG WAN

Pier 1
Pier 2
Pier 3
Pier 4
Pier 5
Pier 6
Pier 7

See detail map at right

Man Po St.
Man Chiu St.
Man Kwong St.

Wing Lok St.
Morrison
Wing Lok St.
Bonham Strand
Queen's Rd. W.
Pier Rd.
Connaught Rd. Central
Man Yiu St.

WESTERN DISTRICT

IFC
One IFC
Mall
Two IFC

Harbour View St.

Des Voeux

Bridges St.

Peel
Graham
Lyndhurst
Wellington St.
Stanley St.
D'Aguilar St.
Wyndham St.
Queen's Rd. Central
Des Voeux Rd. Central

Queen's Rd. Central
Pedder

Connaught Pl.

Queen's Pier

Edinburgh

Chater Rd.
Ice House
Jackson Rd.
Chater

Chater Garden

Harcourt Rd.

ADMIRALTY

Robinson Rd.
Conduit Rd.

Duddell
Ice House
Lower Albert

CENTRAL DISTRICT

Garden Rd.
Cotton Tree Dr.
Queensway Rd.
Rodney

Justice Dr.

Upper Albert Rd.

Zoological & Botanical Gardens

Lower Peak Tram Terminus

Kennedy Rd.
Hong Kong Park

Pacific Place

Kennedy Rd.

Old Peak Rd.
Magazine Gap Rd.

Macdonnell Rd.

Bowen Rd.

Bowen Rd.

Borrett Rd.

Bowen Dr.

May Rd.

May Rd.

0   .2 mi
0   .2 km

Victoria Peak Tram

Magazine Gap Rd.

Peak Tower

THE PEAK

Barker Rd.

Barker Rd.

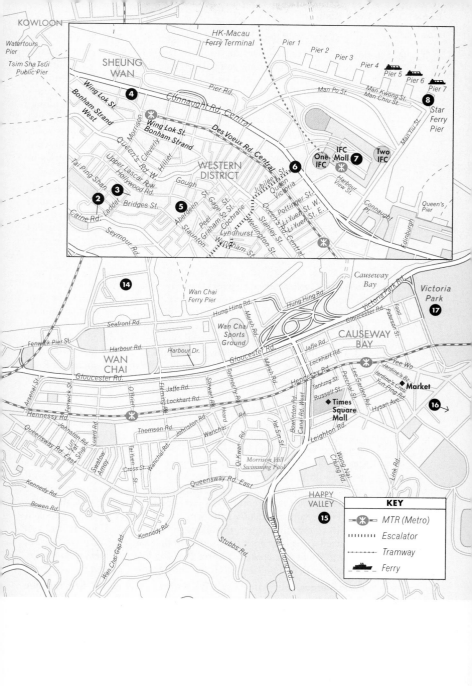

ticket on the tram or on a bus, consider taking one of the beautiful low-impact trails back to Central. You'll be treated to spectacular views in all directions on the **Hong Kong Trail,** an easygoing 40- to 60-minute paved path that begins and ends at the Peak Tram Upper Terminus. Start by heading north along fern-encroached Lugard Road. There's another stunning view of Central from the lookout, 20 minutes along, after which the road snakes west to an intersection with Hatton and Harlech roads. From here Lantau, Lamma, and—on incredibly clear days—Macau come into view. The longer option from here is to wind your way down Hatton to the University of Hong Kong campus in Western District.

Bus 15C, sometimes a red double-decker with an open top, shuttles you between the Peak Tram Lower Terminal and Central Bus Terminal near the Star Ferry Pier, every 15 to 20 minutes, for HK$4.20. ⊠ *Between Garden Rd. and Cotton Tree Dr., Central* ☏ *2522–0922* ⊕ *www.thepeak.com.hk* 🎫 *HK$28 one way, HK$40 round-trip* ⊙ *Tram daily every 10–15 mins, 7 am–midnight.*

WORTH NOTING

FAMILY **Hong Kong Zoological and Botanical Gardens.** This welcoming green space includes a children's playground and gorgeous gardens with more than 1,000 plant species, but the real attractions are the dozens of mammals housed in the zoo. If you're a fan of primates, look for rare sightings like the golden lion tamarin and the black-and-white ruffed lemur. Buses 3B, 12, and 13 run from various other stops in Central; the walk from the Central MTR stop is long and uphill. ⊠ *Albany Rd., between Robinson and Upper Albert Rds., Central* ☏ *2530–0154* 🎫 *Free* ⊙ *Daily 6 am–7 pm* Ⓜ *Central.*

International Finance Centre. One building towers above the Central skyline: Two IFC. The slender second tower of the International Finance Centre has been compared to at least one—unprintable—thing, and is topped with a clawlike structure. Designed by Argentine architect Cesar Pelli, its 88 floors top a whopping 1,352 feet. Opposite stands its dinky little brother, the 38-floor One IFC. The massive IFC Mall stretches between the two, and Hong Kong Station is underneath. If you wish to see the breathtaking views from Two IFC, visit the 55th-floor Hong Kong Monetary Authority. While there, take a quick look at exhibits tracing the history of banking in Hong Kong. Upon arrival, you may need to register your passport with the concierge. ⊠ *8 Finance St., Central* ⊕ *www.ifc.com.hk* 🎫 *Free* ⊙ *Hong Kong Monetary Authority weekdays 10–6, Sat. 10–1* Ⓜ *Hong Kong Station, Exit A2.*

Jamia Mosque. The Mid-Levels Escalator zooms by the first mosque in Hong Kong. Commonly known as the Lascar Temple, the original 1840s structure was rebuilt in 1915 and shows its Indian heritage in the perforated arches and decorative facade work. The mosque isn't open to non-Muslims, but it occupies a small, verdant enclosure that's a welcome retreat. ⊠ *30 Shelley St., above Caine Rd., Central* ☏ *2523–7743* ⊕ *www.amo.gov.hk* Ⓜ *Central, Exit D1.*

PMQ. This hip and happening area has a long history: back in the 1880s, this was the campus of the Central School, where Dr. Sun Yat-sen

A clear day on the Victoria's Peak

studied. After suffering severe damage in World War II, the area became the city's first Police Married Quarters. After standing empty for more than a decade, it reopened in 2014 as a design hub where locals could showcase their art, host workshops, arrange pop-up shops—there's even an atmospheric night market and a handful of excellent restaurants and cozy cafés. ■TIP➔ Take advantage of one of the free guided tours of the underground foundations and historic architecture. ✉ 35 Aberdeen St., SoHo, Central ☎ 2870–2335 ⊕ www.pmq.org.hk ⊙ Daily 7 am–11 pm.

WAN CHAI, CAUSEWAY BAY, AND BEYOND

The Happy Valley horse races are a vital part of Hong Kong life, so it's only fitting that they're in one of the city's most vital areas. A few blocks back from Wan Chai's new office blocks are crowded alleys where you might stumble across a wet market, a tiny furniture-maker's shop, or an age-old temple. Farther east, Causeway Bay pulses with Hong Kong's best shopping streets and hundreds of restaurants. At night the whole area comes alive with bars, restaurants, and discos, as well as establishments offering some of Wan Chai's more traditional services (think red lights and photos of seminaked women outside).

GETTING HERE AND AROUND

Both Wan Chai and Causeway Bay have their own MTR stops, but a pleasant way to arrive from Central is on the tram along Hennessy Road. If you're going beyond Wan Chai, check the sign at the front: some continue to North Point and Shau Kei Wan, via Causeway Bay, while others go south to Happy Valley.

The underground MTR stations are small labyrinths, so read the signs carefully to find the best exit. Traffic begins to take its toll on journey times to places beyond Causeway Bay, and the MTR is often the quickest way to travel.

TOP ATTRACTIONS

Fodor's Choice

★

Happy Valley Racecourse. The biggest attraction east of Causeway Bay for locals and visitors alike is this local legend, where millions of Hong Kong dollars make their way each year. The exhilarating blur of galloping hooves under jockeys dressed in bright silk jerseys is a must-see. The races make great Wednesday nights out on the town. Aside from the excitement of the races, there are restaurants, bars, and even a racing museum to keep you amused. The public entrance to the track is a 20-minute walk from Causeway Bay MTR Exit A (Times Square), or simply hop on the Happy Valley tram, which terminates right in front. ⊠ *Sports Rd. at Wong Nai Chung Rd., Happy Valley, Causeway Bay* ⊡ *HK$10* ⊙ *Wed. 6–11:30 pm during racing season* Ⓜ *Causeway Bay, Exit A.*

Victoria Park. Hong Kong Island's largest park is a welcome breathing space on the edge of Causeway Bay. It's beautifully landscaped and has recreational facilities for soccer, basketball, swimming, lawn bowling, and tennis. At dawn every morning hundreds practice tai chi chuan here. During the Mid-Autumn Festival it's home to the Lantern Carnival, when the trees are a mass of colorful lights. Just before Chinese New Year (late January to early February), the park hosts a huge flower market. On the eve of Chinese New Year, after a traditional family dinner at home, much of Hong Kong happily gathers here to shop and wander into the early hours of the first day of the new year. ⊠ *1 Hing Fat St., Causeway Bay* ☎ *2890–5824* ⊕ *www.lcsd.gov.hk* ⊡ *Free* ⊙ *24 hours* Ⓜ *Tin Hau, Exit A2.*

WORTH NOTING

Hong Kong Convention and Exhibition Centre. Land is so scarce in Hong Kong that developers usually only build skyward, but the HKCEC juts into the harbor instead. Curved-glass walls and a swooping roof make it look like a tortoise lumbering into the sea or a gull taking flight, depending on who you ask. Of all the international trade fairs, regional conferences, and other events held here, by far the most famous was the 1997 Handover Ceremony. An obelisk commemorates it on the waterfront promenade, which also affords great views of Kowloon.

Outside the center stands the *Golden Bauhinia*. This gleaming sculpture of the bauhinia flower, Hong Kong's symbol, was a gift from China. The police hoist the flag daily at 7:50 am; on the first of every month, there is an enhanced flag-raising ceremony with musical accompaniment at 7:45 am. ⊠ *1 Expo Dr., Wan Chai* ☎ *2582–8888* ⊕ *www.hkcec.com.hk* Ⓜ *Wan Chai, Exit A.*

Law Uk Folk Museum. This restored Hakka house was once the home of the Law family, who arrived here from Guangdong in the mid-18th century. It's the perfect example of a triple-*jian*, double-*lang* residence. Jian are enclosed rooms—here, the bedroom, living room, and workroom at the back. The front storeroom and kitchen are the *lang*, where the walls don't reach up to the roof, and thus allow air in. Although the museum is small, informative texts outside and displays of rural furniture and farm implements inside give a powerful idea of what rural Hong Kong was like. It's definitely worth a trip to bustling industrial Chai Wan, at the eastern end of the MTR, to see it. Photos show what the area looked like in the 1930s—these days a leafy square is the only reminder of the woodlands and fields that once surrounded this buttermilk-color dwelling. ⊠ *14 Kut Shing St., Chai Wan, Eastern* ☎ *2896–7006* ⊕ *www.lcsd. gov.hk* 🖾 *Free* ☉ *Fri.–Wed. 10–6* Ⓜ *Chai Wan, Exit B.*

KOWLOON

There's much more to the Kowloon than rock-bottom prices and goods of dubious provenance. Just across the harbor from Central, this piece of Chinese mainland takes its name from the string of mountains that bound it in the north: *gau lung,* "nine dragons" (there are actually eight mountains, the ninth represented the emperor who named them). Although less sophisticated and wilder than its island-side counterpart, Kowloon's dense, gritty urban fabric is the backdrop for Hong Kong's best museums and most interesting spiritual sights. And there's street upon street of hard-core consumerism in every imaginable guise.

Kowloon's southernmost district is Tsim Sha Tsui (TST), home to the Star Ferry Pier. The waterfront extends a few miles to TST East. Shops and hotels line Nathan Road, which runs north from the waterfront through the market districts of Jordan, Yau Ma Tei, and Mong Kok.

New Kowloon is the unofficial name for the sprawl beyond Boundary Street. The district just north is Kowloon Tong. Two spiritual sights—Wong Tai Sin and Lok Fu—are a little farther east. The tongue sticking out into the sea to the south was the runway of the old Kai Tak Airport. Kowloon City is a stone's throw west.

GETTING HERE AND AROUND

The most romantic passage from Hong Kong Island to Tsim Sha Tsui (TST) is by Star Ferry. There are crossings from Central every 6 to 12 minutes and a little less often from Wan Chai.

TST is also accessible by MTR. Underground walkways connect the station with the Tsim Sha Tsui East station on the East Rail Line, where trains depart every 10 to 15 minutes for the eastern New Territories. The Kowloon Airport Express station is amid a construction wasteland west of TST, connecting with Austin station on the West Rail. Hotel shuttles link the area to the rest of Kowloon.

The MTR is your best bet for Jordan, Yau Ma Tei, Mong Kok, and other sights in far-flung Kowloon, including Wong Tai Sin Temple, and Chi Lin Nunnery.

TSIM SHA TSUI

You'll probably come to this district hugging the waterfront at the southern tip of Kowloon (in Chinese the name means "pointed sandy mouth") to see one or more of Hong Kong's top museums. These

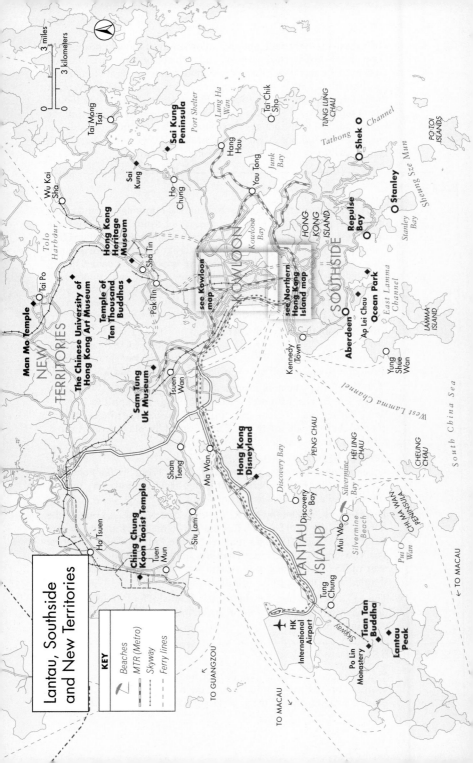

collections are within easy reach of one another amid high-rises, hotels, shops, and Kowloon Park, a coveted parcel of green space.

TOP ATTRACTIONS

Fodor'sChoice
★

Hong Kong Museum of Art. An extensive collection of Chinese art is packed inside this boxy tiled building on the Tsim Sha Tsui waterfront in Kowloon. The collections contain a heady mix of Qing ceramics, 2,000-year-old calligraphic scrolls, and contemporary canvases. It's all well organized into thematic galleries with clear, if uninspired, explanations. Hong Kong's biggest visiting exhibitions are usually held here as well. The museum is a few minutes from the Star Ferry and Tsim Sha Tsui MTR stop.

Highlights

The Chinese Antiquities Gallery is the place to head if ceramics are your thing. A series of low-lit rooms on the third floor houses ceramics from the Ming and Qing dynasties. Unusually, they're displayed by motif rather than by period: dragons, phoenixes, lotus flowers, and bats are some of the auspicious designs. Bronzes, jade, lacquerware, textiles, enamel, and glassware complete this collection of decorative art.

In the **Chinese Fine Art Gallery** you get a great introduction to Chinese brush painting, often difficult for the Western eye to appreciate. Landscape paintings from the 20th-century Guangdong and Lingnan schools form the bulk of the collection, and modern calligraphy also gets a nod.

The **Contemporary Hong Kong Art Gallery** on the second floor showcases a mix of traditional Chinese and Western techniques. Paintings account for most of the pieces from the first half of the 20th century, when local artists used the traditional mediums of brush and ink in innovative ways. Western techniques dominate later work, the result of Hong Kong artists' having spent more time abroad.

Tips

Traditional Chinese landscape paintings are visual records of real or imagined journeys—a kind of travelogue. Pick a starting point and try to travel through the picture, imagining the journey the artist is trying to convey.

There is a collection search system on the first floor, as well as a research center.

Check the website for the schedule of more detailed visits to specific galleries—they change every month. If you prefer a little more guidance, consider an English-language audio guide: it's informative, if a little dry, and it costs only HK$10. ✉ *10 Salisbury Rd., Tsim Sha Tsui* ☎ *2721–0116* ⊕ *hk.art.museum* ✉ *HK$10* ⊙ *Fri. and Mon.–Wed. 10–6, weekends 10–7* Ⓜ *Tsim Sha Tsui MTR, Exit F.*

Hong Kong Museum of History. For a comprehensive bit of history, this museum's popular Hong Kong Story should do the trick. The exhibit starts 400 million years ago in the Devonian period and makes its way all the way through to the 1997 Handover, with spectacular life-size dioramas that include village houses and a shopping street in colonial times. The ground-floor Folk Culture section offers an introduction to the history and customs of Hong Kong's main ethnic groups. Upstairs,

Kowloon

NORTHERN KOWLOON

Tai Hang Tung
Recreation
Ground
Boundary

Fa Hui
Park

TO
SHENZHEN AND
GUANGZHOU

Cheung Sha Wan Rd.

Ku Lung St.

Tai Nan St.

Lai Chi Kok Rd.

**PRINCE
EDWARD**

Prince Edward Rd. W.

Arran St.

Bute St.

Mong Kok Rd.

Fife St.

Argyle St.

Nelson St.

Shantung St.

Soy St.

Dundas St.

Pitt
Rd.

Waterloo

**MONG
KOK**

Sai Yee St.

Fa Yuen St.

Tung Choi St.

Sai Yeung St.

Nathan Rd.

Portland St.

Shanghai

Reclamation

Canton Rd.

Ferry St.

**YAU
MA TEI**

Public Sq. St.

Market St.

Kansu

Ning Po St.

Jordan Rd.

**KGV
Park**

Bowring St.

Austin Rd.

Canton Rd.

**Kowloon
Park**

Haiphong Rd.

Kowloon Park Dr.

Canton Rd.

Peking Rd.

Middle Rd.

**Star Ferry
Piers**

**Hong Kong
Cultural
Centre**

Mong Kok
KCR Station

Waterloo Rd.

Argyle St.

Yim Po Fong St.

Waterloo Rd.

Wylie Rd.

YAU MA TEI

**KING'S
PARK**

King's
Park

Wylie Rd.

King's
Park

Gascoigne Rd.

Cox's Rd.

Cheong Wan Rd.

JORDAN

**TSIM SHA
TSUI**

Kimberley Rd.

Granville Rd.

Cameron Rd.

TSIM SHA TSUI

Mody Rd.

Black
Head
Point
Garden

Chatham Rd. South

Mody
Rd.

Salisbury Rd.

Princess Margaret

Chung Hau St.

Dunbar St.

Perth St.

Argyle St.

Tin Kwong Rd.

Fat Kong St.

Sheung
Lok St.

**HO MAN
TIN**

Hong Chong Rd.

Cross-Harbour Tunnel

Salisbury Rd.

**Hung Hom
KCR Station**

**HUNG
HOM**

Wuhu St.

Bulkeley St.

Baker St.

Fat Kong St.

*Victoria
Harbour*

*Harbour
City*

0   1/4 mile

0   1/4 kilometer

KEY

⊗ *MTR (Metro)*

KCR stops

gracious stone-walled galleries whirl you through the Opium Wars and the beginnings of colonial Hong Kong. Don't miss the chilling account of life under the Japanese occupation or the colorful look at Hong Kong life in the '60s. ■TIP➔ **Unless you're with kids who dig models of cavemen and bears, skip the prehistory and dynastic galleries.**

Budget at least two hours to stroll through—more if you linger in every gallery and make use of the interactive elements. Pick your way through the gift shop's clutter to find local designer Alan Chan's T-shirts, shot glasses, and notebooks. His retro-kitsch aesthetic is based on 1940s cigarette-girl images. To get here from the Tsim Sha Tsui MTR walk along Cameron Road, then left for a block along Chatham Road South. A signposted overpass takes you to the museum. ⌧ *100 Chatham Rd. S, Tsim Sha Tsui* ☎ *2724–9042* ⊕ *hk.history.museum* ⌦ *HK$10; free Wed.* ⊗ *Mon. and Wed.–Fri. 10–6, weekends and holidays 10–7* Ⓜ *Tsim Sha Tsui, Exit B2.*

FAMILY **Kowloon Park.** These 33 acres, crisscrossed by paths and meticulously landscaped, are a refreshing retreat after a bout of shopping. In addition to playgrounds, a fitness trail, soccer pitch, aviary, and maze garden, on Sunday and public holidays there are stalls with arts and crafts, as well as a kung fu corner. ⌧ *22 Austin Rd., Tsim Sha Tsui* ☎ *2724–3344* ⊕ *www.lcsd.gov.hk* ⌦ *Free* ⊗ *Daily 5 am–midnight* Ⓜ *Tsim Sha Tsui MTR, Exit A1; Jordan, Exit C1.*

WORTH NOTING

Nathan Road. Running for several miles, this street is filled with hotels, restaurants, malls, and boutiques—retail space is so costly that the southern end is dubbed the Golden Mile. The mile's most famous tower block is ramshackle Chungking Mansions, packed with cheap hotels and Indian restaurants. The building was a setting for local director Wong Kar-Wai's film *Chungking Express*. To the left and right are mazes of narrow streets with even more shops selling jewelry, electronics, clothes, souvenirs, and cosmetics. ⌧ *Nathan Rd. between Salisbury Rd. and Boundary St., Tsim Sha Tsui* Ⓜ *Tsim Sha Tsui, Jordan, Yau Ma Tei, Mong Kok, Prince Edward.*

YAU MA TEI, MONG KOK, AND NORTHERN KOWLOON

North of Tsim Sha Tsui, the vibrant area of Yau Ma Tei teems with people and is home to several street markets. The area of Yau Ma Tei around Jordan Road blends into the neighboring district, and the Jordan MTR stop is a good place to start your exploring.

Mong Kok lives up to its Chinese name, which translates roughly as "busy corner." The neighborhood is the epicenter of Hong Kong street fashion—the trends that originate from these bustling streets are known as "MK style."

TOP ATTRACTIONS

Fodor's Choice **Chi Lin Nunnery.** Not a single nail was used to build this nunnery, which
★ dates back to 1934. Instead, traditional Tang Dynasty architectural techniques involving wooden dowels and bracket work hold everything

together. Most of the 15 cedar halls house altars to bodhisattvas (those who have reached enlightenment)—bronze plaques explain each one.

Highlights

Feng shui principles governed construction. The buildings face south toward the sea, to bring abundance; their backs are to the mountain, a provider of strength and good energy. The temple's clean lines are a vast departure from most of Hong Kong's colorful religious buildings—here painted wood and gleaming Buddha statues are the only adornments.

The **Main Hall** is the most imposing—and inspiring—part of the monastery. Overlooking the smaller second courtyard, it honors the first Buddha, known as Sakyamuni. The soaring ceilings are held up by cedar columns that support the roof—no mean feat, given that its traditionally made clay tiles make it extremely heavy.

Courtyards and gardens, where frangipani flowers scent the air, run beside the nunnery. The gardens are filled with bonsai trees and artful rockeries. Nature is also present inside: the various halls and galleries all look onto two courtyards filled with geometric lotus ponds and manicured bushes. Neighboring Nan Lian Garden, built in the same style, is adorned with pretty pavilions and more than 60 types of plant. A famous vegetarian restaurant serves up excellent set meals and dim sum. Proceeds from the restaurant fund the Chi Lin Nunnery.

Tips

Left of the Main Hall is a don't-miss hall dedicated to Avalokitesvra, better known in Hong Kong as Kwun Yum, goddess of mercy and childbearing, among other things. She's one of the few exceptions to the rule that bodhisattvas are represented as asexual beings.

Be sure to keep looking up—the latticework ceilings and complicated beam systems are among the most beautiful parts of the building. Combine Chi Lin Nunnery with a visit to Sik Sik Yuen Wong Tai Sin Temple, only one MTR stop or a short taxi ride away. ⊠ *5 Chi Lin Dr., Northern Kowloon* ☎ *2354–1888* ✉ *Free* ☉ *Nunnery daily 9–4, lotus pond garden daily 7–7* Ⓜ *Diamond Hill, Exit C2.*

Fodor's Choice **Sik Sik Yuen Wong Tai Sin Temple.** There's a practical approach to prayer at
★ one of Hong Kong's most exuberant places of worship. Here the territory's three major religions—Taoism, Confucianism, and Buddhism—are all celebrated under the same roof. You'd think that ornamental religious buildings would look strange with highly visible vending machines and LCD displays in front of them, but Wong Tai Sin pulls it off in cacophonous style. The temple was established in the early 20th century, on a different site on Hong Kong Island, when two Taoist masters arrived from Guangzhou with the portrait of Wong Tai Sin—a famous monk who was born around AD 328—that still graces the main altar. In the '20s the shrine was moved here and expanded over the years.

Start at the incense-wreathed main courtyard, where the noise of many people shaking out *chim* (sticks with fortunes written on them) forms a constant rhythm. After wandering the halls, take time out in the Good Wish Garden—a peaceful riot of rockery—at the back of the complex. At the base of the complex is a small arcade where soothsayers and palm readers are happy to interpret Wong Tai Sin's predictions for a small fee. At the base of the ramp to the Confucian Hall, look up behind the temple for a view of Lion Rock, a mountain in the shape of a sleeping lion. ■TIP→ If you feel like acquiring a household altar of your own, head for Shanghai Street in Yau Ma Tei, the Kowloon District north of Tsim Sha Tsui, where religious shops abound. ⊠ *Wong Tai Sin Rd., Northern Kowloon* ☎ *2327–8141* ⊕ *www.siksikyuen.org.hk* 💵 *Donations expected. Good Wish Garden HK$2* ⊗ *Daily 7–5:30* Ⓜ *Wong Tai Sin, Exit B2 or B3.*

Temple Street. In the heart of Yau Ma Tei, Temple Street is home to Hong Kong's biggest night market. Stalls selling kitsch of all kinds set up in the late afternoon in the blocks north of Public Square Street. Fortune-tellers, open-air cafés, and street doctors also offer their services here. ⊠ *Temple St. between Jordan Rd. and Kansu St., Yau Ma Tei* Ⓜ *Yau Ma Tei, Exit C; Jordan, Exit A.*

WORTH NOTING

Flower Market. Stalls containing local and imported fresh flowers, potted plants, and even artificial blossoms cover Flower Market Road, as well as parts of Yuen Po Street, Yuen Ngai Street, Prince Edward Road West, and Playing Field Road. ⊠ *Flower Market Rd. between Yuen Ngai St. and Yuen Po St., Mong Kok* 💵 *Free* ⊗ *Daily 7–7* Ⓜ *Mong Kok East, Exit C; Prince Edward, Exit B1.*

FAMILY **Goldfish Market.** A few dozen shops at the northern end of Tung Choi Street, starting at the intersection with Nullah Road, sell the ubiquitous fish, which locals believe to be lucky. There are other types of animals as well. ⊠ *Tung Choi St. and Nullah Rd., Mong Kok* 💵 *Free* ⊗ *Daily 10:30–10* Ⓜ *Mong Kok East, Exit C; Prince Edward, Exit B2.*

Tung Choi Street Ladies' Market. Despite the name, the stalls here are filled with no-brand clothing and accessories for both sexes. The shopping is best between Dundas and Argyle. ⊠ *Tung Choi St. between Dundas St. and Argyle St., Mong Kok* 💵 *Free* Ⓜ *Mong Kok.*

FAMILY **Yuen Po Street Bird Garden.** Adjacent to the Flower Market, this street has more than 70 stalls selling different types of twittering, fluttering birds. Pretty wooden birdcages, starting from about HK$500, are also on offer. ⊠ *Yuen Po St. between Boundary St. and Prince Edward Rd. W, Mong Kok* 💵 *Free* ⊗ *Daily 7 am–8 pm* Ⓜ *Mong Kok East, Exit C; Prince Edward, Exit B1.*

SOUTHSIDE

For all the unrelenting urbanity of Hong Kong Island's north coast, its south side consists largely of green hills and a few residential areas around picturesque bays. With beautiful sea views, real estate is at a premium; some of Hong Kong's wealthiest residents live in beautiful houses and luxurious apartments here. Southside is a breath of fresh air—literally and figuratively. The people are more relaxed, the pace is slower, and there are lots of sea breezes.

GETTING HERE AND AROUND

You can get here by bus from the center of the city, and the trip will take anywhere from 20 to 50 minutes. Note that express buses skip Aberdeen and Deep Water Bay, heading directly to Repulse Bay and Stanley. Buses run less frequently in the evening, so it's more convenient to grab a taxi (they're everywhere).

TOP ATTRACTIONS

FAMILY **Ocean Park.** Most Hong Kongers have fond childhood memories of this aquatic theme park. It was built by the omnipresent Hong Kong Jockey Club on 170 hilly acres overlooking the sea just east of Aberdeen. Highlights include the resident pandas, an enormous aquarium, and the Ocean Theatre, where dolphins and seals perform. Youngsters love thrill rides like the gravity-defying Hair Raiser. The park is accessible by a number of buses, including the 629 and 629A; get off at the stop after the Aberdeen tunnel. ■TIP➜ **If you have kids, plan to spend the whole day here.** ⊠ *Ocean Park Rd., Aberdeen, Southside* ☎ *3923–2323* ⊕ *www.oceanpark.com.hk* ✉ *HK$320* ☉ *Daily 10–7:30.*

Stanley. This peninsula town lies south of Deep Water and Repulse bays. There's great shopping in the renowned Stanley Market, full of casual clothes, cheap souvenirs, and cheerful bric-a-brac. Stanley's popular beach is the site of the Dragon Boat Races every June. To get here from Exchange Square Bus Terminus in Central, take Bus 6, 6A, 6X, 66, 64, or 260. ⊠ *Southside.*

WORTH NOTING

Aberdeen. Aberdeen's harbor contains about 3,000 junks and sampans, and each might be home to several generations of one family. During the Tin Hau Festival in April and May, hundreds more boats converge along the shore. On Aberdeen's side streets you'll find outdoor barbers hard at work and any number of dim sum restaurants serving up dishes you won't find at home. You'll also see traditional sights like the Aberdeen Cemetery, with its enormous terraced gravestones, and yet another shrine to the goddess of the sea: the Tin Hau Temple. ⊠ *Southside.*

Repulse Bay. The beach in this tranquil neighborhood is large and wide, but be warned: it's the first stop for most visitors to Southside. Two huge statues of Tin Hau—goddess of the sea—at the east end of the beach were built in the 1970s. Worshippers had planned to erect just one statue, but worried she'd be lonely. Look for a famous apartment building with a hole through it—following the principles of feng shui, the opening allows the dragon that lives in the mountains behind to readily drink from the bay. To get here, take Bus 6, 6A, 6X, 66, or 260 from Exchange Square Bus Terminus in Central. **Amenities:** food and drink; lifeguards; parking (fee); showers; toilets; water sports. **Best for:** sunset; swimming; walking. ⊠ *Beach Rd. at Seaview Promenade, Repulse Bay, Southside* ☎ *2812–2483.*

FAMILY **Shek O.** The seaside locale is Southside's easternmost village. Every shop sells the same inflatable beach toys—the bigger the better, it seems. Cut through town to a windy road that takes you to the "island" of Tai Tau Chau, really a large rock with a lookout over the South China Sea. You can hike through nearby Shek O Country Park, where the bird-watching is great, in less than two hours. To get here from Central, take the MTR to Shau Kei Wan (Exit A3), then take Bus 9 to the last stop (about 30 minutes). ⊠ *Southside.*

LANTAU ISLAND

Manic development is changing Lantau, but the island is still known as the "lungs of Hong Kong" because of the abundant forests, relative dearth of skyscrapers, and laid-back attractions—beaches, fishing villages, and hiking trails. At Ngong Ping, a mini–theme park sits at the base of the island's most famous sight, the Tian Tan Buddha. Hong Kong Disneyland sits on the northeast coast, near the airport. At 147 square km (57 square miles), Lantau is almost twice the size of Hong Kong Island, so there's room for all this development, and the island remains a welcome green getaway.

GETTING HERE AND AROUND

The speediest way to get to Lantau from Central is the MTR's Tung Chung line (HK$24), which takes about half an hour. Far more pleasant is the 35-minute ferry from Central to Mui Wo (get a window seat for the views).

TOP ATTRACTIONS

FAMILY **Hong Kong Disneyland.** Though Hong Kong's home to Mickey Mouse is tame compared with other Magic Kingdoms, it's fast bringing Mai Kei Lo Su—as the world's most famous mouse is known locally—to a mainland audience. Younger kids will find plenty of amusement, but their older siblings and parents will have to settle for just one thrill ride, Space Mountain. If you need to visit a theme park in Hong Kong, Ocean Park in Aberdeen is a better bet. ⊠ *Fantasy Rd., Lantau Island* ⊕ *park.hongkongdisneyland.com* ☜ *HK$450* ⊙ *Daily 9–9* Ⓜ *Disneyland Resort.*

Fodor's Choice **Tian Tan Buddha.** Hong Kongers love superlatives, even if making them
★ true requires strings of qualifiers. So the Tian Tan Buddha, also known as the Big Buddha, is the world's largest Buddha—that's seated, located outdoors, and made of bronze. Just know the vast silhouette is impressive. A set of 268 steep stairs lead to the lower podium, essentially forcing you to stare up at all 202 tons of Buddha as you ascend. At the top, cool breezes and fantastic views over Lantau Island await.

Highlights

Po Lin Monastery. It's hard to believe today, but from its foundation in 1927 through the early '90s, this monastery was virtually inaccessible by road. These days, it's at the heart of Lantau's biggest attraction. The monastery proper has a gaudy orange temple complex. Still, it's the Buddha people come for.

Wisdom Path. This peaceful path runs beside 38 halved tree trunks arranged in an infinity shape on a hillside. Each is carved with Chinese characters that make up the Heart Sutra, a 5th-century Buddhist prayer that expresses the doctrine of emptiness. The idea is to walk around the path—which takes five minutes—and reflect. Follow the signposted trail to the left of the Buddha.

Ngong Ping Village. People were fussing about this attraction before its first stone was laid. Ngong Ping Village is a moneymaking add-on to the Tian Tan Buddha. Walking With Buddha is intended to be a 20-minute-long educational stroll through the life of Siddhartha Gautama, the first Buddha, but it's more of a multimedia extravaganza that shuns good taste with such kitsch as a self-illuminating Bodhi tree and piped-in incense. No cost has been spared in the dioramas that fill the seven galleries—ironic, given that each represents a stage of the Buddha's path to enlightenment and the eschewing of material wealth.

Tips

You can get here on the Ngong Ping 360 gondola from a terminal adjacent to the MTR station in Tung Chung or via Bus 2 from Mui Wo or Bus 23 from Tung Chung.

The only way to the upper level, right under the Buddha, is through an underwhelming museum inside the podium. You only get a couple of feet higher up.

The booth at the base of the stairs is only for tickets for lunch—wandering around the Buddha is free.

The monastery's vegetarian restaurant is a clattering canteen with uninspiring fare. Pick up sandwiches at the Citygate Mall, Tung Chung, or eat at a restaurant in Ngong Ping Village. ⊠ *Ngong Ping, Lantau Island* ☎ *2985–5248* ⊕ *www.plm.org.hk* ✉ *Monastery and path free. Walking with Buddha: HK$40* ☉ *Buddha daily 10–5:30, monastery and path daily 8–6* Ⓜ *Tung Chung, Exit B.*

WORTH NOTING

Lantau Peak. The most glorious views of Lantau—and beyond—are from atop Lantau Peak, but at 3,064 feet, the mountaintop experience is not for the faint-hearted. The ascent up the mountain that locals call Fung Wong Shan requires a strenuous 7½-mile hike west from Mui Wo, or you can begin at the Po Lin Monastery—still a demanding two hours. You can also take Bus 23 to a trail that is closer to the summit, and climb from Stage 3 of the Lantau Trail. The most striking views are at sunrise, particularly between December and February, when the air is dry and the sky is clear. ⊠ *Lantau Island.*

THE NEW TERRITORIES

With rustic villages, incense-filled temples, green hiking trails, and pristine beaches, the New Territories are a favorite Hong Kong getaway. Sha Tin, Tuen Mun, and other "new towns" house more than half a million residents apiece, making them feel like their own cities. Even so, it's still easy to get away from the urban congestion, visit lush parks, and glimpse traditional rural life in restored walled villages and ancestral clan halls.

GETTING HERE AND AROUND

Between the bus and MTR, you can get close to many sights. Set off on the MTR from Central to Tsuen Wan; from there, taxis, buses, and minibuses will take you to places such as the Yuen Yuen Institute and

Tai Mo Shan. For Sha Tin and other spots in the east, take the MTR to Kowloon Tong; transfer to the East Rail line and head to Sha Tin station. To reach the Sai Kung Peninsula, take the MTR from Central to Choi Hung, then the green Minibus 1A to Sai Kung Town.

TOP ATTRACTIONS

Fodor'sChoice
★

Hong Kong Heritage Museum. This fabulous museum is Hong Kong's largest, yet it still seems a well-kept secret: chances are you'll have most of its 12 massive galleries to yourself. They ring an inner courtyard, which pours light into the lofty entrance hall.

Highlights

The **New Territories Heritage Hall** is packed with local history—6,000 years of it. See life as it was in beautiful dioramas of traditional villages—one on land, the other on water (with houses on stilts). The last gallery documents the rise of massive urban New Towns.

In the **T.T. Tsui Gallery of Chinese Art**, exquisite antique Chinese glass, ceramics, and bronzes fill hushed second-floor rooms. The curators have gone for quality over quantity. Look for the 3½-foot-tall terra-cotta *Horse and Rider*, a beautiful example of the figures enclosed in tombs in the Han Dynasty (206 BC–AD 220). The Tibetan religious statues and *thankga* paintings are unique in Hong Kong.

The **Cantonese Opera Heritage Hall** is all singing, all dancing, and utterly hands-on. The symbolic costumes, tradition-bound stories, and stylized acting of Cantonese opera can be impenetrable: the museum provides simple explanations and stacks of artifacts, including century-old sequined costumes that put Vegas to shame. Don't miss the virtual makeup display, where you get your on-screen face painted like an opera character's.

Kids love the **Children's Discovery Gallery,** where hands-on activities for 4- to 10-year-olds include putting a broken "archaeological find" together. The Hong Kong Toy Story charts more than a century of local toys.

Tips

Look for the audio tours in English, which are available for special exhibitions.

There's lots of ground to cover: prioritize the New Territories Heritage, the T.T. Tsui Gallery, and the Cantonese Opera Halls, all permanent displays, then move on to the temporary history and art exhibitions if time permit.

The museum is a five-minute signposted walk from Che Kung Temple station. If the weather's good, walk back along the leafy riverside path that links the museum with Sha Tin station, in New Town Plaza mall, 15 minutes away. ⊠ *1 Man Lam Rd., Sha Tin, New Territories* ☎ *2180–8188* ⊕ *www.heritagemuseum.gov.hk* ⊠ *HK$10; free on Wed.* ☉ *Mon. and Wed.–Fri. 10–6, weekends and holidays 10–7* Ⓜ *Che Kung, Exit A; Sha Tin, Exit A.*

Ten Thousand Buddhas Monastery. You climb some 400 steps to reach this temple, but look on the bright side: for each step you get about 32 Buddhas. The uphill path through dense vegetation is lined with

500 life-size golden Buddhas in all kinds of positions. Be sure to bring along water and insect repellent. Prepare to be dazzled inside the main temple, where walls are stacked with gilded ceramic statuettes. There are actually nearly 13,000 here, made by Shanghai artisans and donated by worshippers over the decades. Kwun Yam, goddess of mercy, is one of several deities honored in the crimson-walled courtyard.

Look southwest on a clear day and you can see nearby **Amah Rock,** which resembles a woman with a child on her back. Legend has it that this formation was once a faithful fisherman's wife who climbed the mountain every day to wait for her husband's return, not knowing he'd drowned. Tin Hau, goddess of the sea, took pity on her and turned her to stone.

The temple is in the foothills of Sha Tin, in the central New Territories. Take Exit B out of Sha Tin station, walk down the pedestrian ramp, and take the first left onto Pai Tau Street. Keep to the right-hand side of the road and follow it around to the gate where the signposted path starts. ■ TIP→ **Don't be confused by the big white buildings on the left of Pai Tau Road. They are ancestral halls, not the temple.** ⊠ *221 Pai Tau Village, Sha Tin, New Territories* 🖾 *Free* ☉ *Daily 9–5:30* Ⓜ *Sha Tin, Exit B.*

WORTH NOTING

The Chinese University of Hong Kong Art Museum. Located in the Institute of Chinese Studies building, the museum has paintings and calligraphy from the Qing period to modern times. There are also collections of bronze seals, carved jade flowers, and ceramics from South China. Take the East Rail line to University station, then a campus bus or taxi. ⊠ *Institute of Chinese Studies Bldg., Tai Po Rd., Sha Tin, New Territories* 🕾 *3943–7416* ⊕ *www.cuhk.edu.hk/ics/amm* 🖾 *Free* ☉ *Mon.–Sat. 10–5, Sun. 1–5* Ⓜ *University, Exit D.*

Ching Chung Koon Taoist Temple. This temple has room after room of altars filled with the heady scent of incense. On one side of the main entrance is a cast-iron bell with a circumference of about 5 feet—all large monasteries in ancient China rang such bells at daybreak to wake the monks and nuns for a day of work in the rice fields. On the other side of the entrance is a huge drum that was used to call the workers back in the evening. Inside, some rooms are papered with small pictures; the faithful pay to have these photos displayed so they can see their dearly departed as they pray. Hundreds of dwarf shrubs, ornamental fishponds, and pagodas bedeck the grounds. The temple sits adjacent to the Ching Chung MTR Light Rail station near the town of Tuen Mun. The entrance isn't obvious, so ask for directions. ⊠ *Tsing Chung Koon Rd., Tuen Mun, New Territories* 🕾 *2462–1507* Ⓜ *Siu Hong, Exit B.*

Sai Kung Peninsula. To the east of Sha Tin, the Sai Kung Peninsula is home to one of Hong Kong's most beloved nature preserves, Sai Kung Country Park. It has several hiking trails that wind through majestic hills overlooking the water. The hikes through the hills surrounding High Island Reservoir are also spectacular. Seafood restaurants dot the waterfront in Sai Kung Town as well as the tiny fishing village of Po Toi O in Clear Water Bay. At Sai Kung Town you can rent a sampan that will take you to one of the many islands in the area for a day at the beach. Take the MTR to Diamond Hill (Exit C2) and take Bus 92 to Sai Kung Town. Instead of taking the bus, you can also catch a taxi along Clearwater Bay Road, which will take you into forested areas and land that's only partially developed, with Spanish-style villas overlooking the sea. This excursion will take a full day, and you should only go if it's sunny. ⊠ *Sai Kung Peninsula, Kowloon.*

Sam Tung Uk Museum. A walled Hakka village from 1786 was saved from demolition to create this museum. It's in the middle of industrial Tsuen Wan, in the western New Territories, and its quiet courtyards and small interlocking chambers contrast with the nearby residential towers. It looks more like a large home than a village—not surprisingly, the name translates as "Three Beam House." Rigid symmetry dictated the construction: the ancestral hall and two common chambers form a central axis flanked by private areas. Traditional furniture and farm tools are on display. ■TIP→ **Head through the courtyards and start your visit in the exhibition hall at the back, where a display gives helpful background on Hakka culture and pre-industrial Tsuen Wan—explanations are sparse elsewhere. You can also try on a Hakka hat.** ⊠ *2 Kwu Uk La., Tsuen Wan, New Territories* ☎ *2411–2001* ⊕ *www.heritagemuseum. gov.hk* ⊡ *Free* ⊗ *Wed.–Mon. 10–6* Ⓜ *Tsuen Wan, Exit B3.*

WHERE TO EAT

No other city in the world boasts quite as eclectic a dining scene as Hong Kong. Opulent restaurants opened by celebrity chefs such as Gray Kunz and Joël Robuchon are just a stone's throw from humble local eateries doling out thin noodles and some of the best wonton shrimp dumplings, or delicious slices of tender barbecued meat piled atop bowls of fragrant jasmine rice.

One of the key lessons here is never judge a book by its cover—the most unassuming eateries are often the ones that provide the most memorable meals. At noodle-centric restaurants, fish-ball soup with rice noodles is an excellent choice, and the goose, suckling pig, honeyed pork, and soy-sauce chicken are good bets at the roast-meat shops. A combination plate, with a sampling of meats and some greens on a bed of white rice, is generally a foolproof way to go if you're not sure what to order. Street foods are another must-try; for just a couple of bucks, you can sample curry fish balls, skewered meats, stinky tofu, and all sorts of other delicious tidbits. If you have the chance, visit a *dai pai dong* (outdoor food stall) and try the local specialties.

MEAL TIMES

A typical Hong Kong breakfast is often congee (a rice porridge), noodles, or plain or filled buns. Most hotels serve Western-style breakfasts, however, and coffee, pastries, and sandwiches are readily available at local coffee shops and Western cafés. Lunchtime is between noon and 2 pm; normal dinner hours are from 7 until 11 pm, but Hong Kong is a 24-hour city, and you'll be able to find a meal here at any hour. Dim sum can begin as early as 7:30 am and, though it's traditionally a daytime food, you'll find plenty of specialist restaurants that serve dim sum late into the evening.

PRICES, TIPPING, AND TAX

Many restaurants in Hong Kong serve main dishes that are meant to be shared, so take this into account with respect to prices. When you get your check, don't be shocked that you've been charged for everything, including tea, rice, and those side dishes placed automatically on your table. At upmarket and Western-style restaurants tips are appreciated (10% is generous); the service charge on your bill doesn't go to the staff.

RESERVATIONS

Book ahead during Chinese holidays and the eves of public holidays, or at high-end hotel restaurants like Amber or Caprice. Certain classic Chinese dishes (especially beggar's chicken, whose preparation in a clay pot takes hours) require reserving not just a table but the dish itself. Do so at least 24 hours in advance. You'll also need reservations for a meal at one of the so-called private kitchens—unlicensed culinary speakeasies, which are often the city's hottest tickets. Book several days ahead, and be prepared to pay a deposit. Reservations are virtually unheard of at small, local restaurants.

WHAT IT COSTS IN HONG KONG DOLLARS

	$	$$	$$$	$$$$
Restaurants	under HK$100	HK$100–HK$200	HK$201–HK$300	over HK$300

Restaurant prices are the average cost of a main course at dinner or, if dinner is not served, at lunch.

HONG KONG ISLAND

Reviews are listed alphabetically within neighborhoods. Use the coordinates (✣ B2) at the end of each listing to locate a site on the Where to Eat and Stay in Hong Kong map.

WESTERN

$$$ CANTONESE Fodor's Choice ★ 🍴 **Tim's Kitchen.** Some of the homespun dishes at this restaurant require at least a day's advance notice, but the extra fuss is worth it. One signature dish pairs a meaty crab claw with winter melon—a clean and simple combo that allows the freshness of the ingredients to shine. The fist-sized crystal king prawn looks unassuming, paired with nothing but a slice of Yunnan ham on a plain, ungarnished plate. Take a bite though, and you'll be amazed at how succulent and delectably creamy it is. Word of warning—some of the more intricate dishes can get pretty pricey. But simpler (and cheaper) options are also available, such as pomelo skin sprinkled with shrimp roe, and panfried flat rice noodles. [$] *Average main: HK$300* ✉ *84–90 Bonham Strand, Sheung Wan, Western* ☎ *2543–5919* 🌐 *www.timskitchen.com.hk* ✍ *Reservations essential* [M] *Sheung Wan* ✣ *A3.*

$$$$ FRENCH 🍴 **Upper Modern Bistro.** This cool and sophisticated restaurant is a labor of love for Philippe Orrico, a protégé of revolutionary chef Pierre

Gagniare. Though classically trained in French cuisine, Orrico takes inspiration from all around the globe. Look out for Asian influences in dishes such as Brittany oysters with ponzu and squab or eggplant rolls seasoned with soy sauce. Another signature is the perfected cooked 63-degree eggs—a dish that Orrico created and serves with amazing ingredients like crabmeat and Bellota ham. $ *Average main: HK$400* ✉ *6–14 Upper Station St., Sheung Wan, Western* ☎ *2517–0977* ⊕ *www. upper-bistro.com* Ⓜ *Sheung Wan* ✛ *A2.*

$$ ✕ **Yardbird.** This bustling bi-level eatery is one of the hottest places to
JAPANESE eat. Chef-owner Matt Abergel plates perfectly cooked yakitori (Japanese-style grilled chicken) as well as a repertoire of salads and small plates designed for sharing. Definitely try the Korean fried cauliflower (here called KFC) and the liver mousse served with milk bread and crispy shallots. Drinking is another important part of the experience, so try the house-brand junmai sake or choose from the well-chosen Japanese beer and whiskey list. The only downside is that the restaurant doesn't take reservations, so arrive early or risk waiting for a table. $ *Average main: HK$150* ✉ *33–35 Bridges St., Sheung Wan, Western* ☎ *2547–9273* ⊕ *www.yardbirdrestaurant.com* ⊜ *Reservations not accepted* ◷ *Closed Sun No lunch.* ✛ *A2.*

CENTRAL

$$$$ ✕ **8½ Otto e Mezzo Bombana.** Spearheaded by Umberto Bombana (the
ITALIAN former executive chef of the Ritz-Carlton Hong Kong and often lauded
Fodor's Choice as the best Italian chef in Asia), this glitzy space delivers everything it
★ promises. The service is crisp, the wine list is extensive, and the interior is nothing less than glamorous. Most importantly, the authentic Italian food is magnificent. Bombana's famed handmade pastas live up to the hype; the cavatelli with shellfish ragout and sea urchin is particularly delicious. The mains are also solid—the Tajima short rib and beef tenderloin is excellently executed, but the seafood options fare even better. If you can't make up your mind, the degustation menu offers a neat sampling of Bombana's best. $ *Average main: HK$340* ✉ *2nd fl., Landmark Alexandra, 18 Chater Rd., Central* ☎ *2537–8859* ⊕ *www.ottoemezzobombana.com* ⊜ *Reservations essential* ◷ *Closed Sun.* Ⓜ *Central* ✛ *B3.*

$$$$ ✕ **Amber.** You'd expect the Landmark Mandarin Oriental to have a stel-
FRENCH lar restaurant, and Amber will linger in your memories for its modern style, impeccable service, and creative cuisine. Chef Richard Ekkebus's menu of creative European dishes still doesn't fail to impress. The fun begins with the amuse-bouche, which usually includes the restaurant's famous foie gras lollipops. You can then look forward to signature creations such as frogs' legs in pastry, or sea urchin set in lobster gelatin with cauliflower, caviar, and crispy seaweed waffles. If you can't make it for dinner, check out the fantastic wine-paired lunch available every weekend. $ *Average main: HK$850* ✉ *7th fl., Landmark Mandarin Oriental, 15 Queen's Rd., Central* ☎ *2132–0066* ⊕ *www. amberhongkong.com* ⊜ *Reservations essential* Ⓜ *Central* ✛ *B3.*

$$$ ✕ **Ammo.** Few places in Hong Kong have the kind of stunning gar-
ITALIAN den views that you'll find at Ammo. Housed in a former ammunition compound (hence the name) that was converted into the Asia Society

Hong Kong Center, Ammo's interiors and menus blend the old with the new and East with West, resulting in an impressive and dynamic dining experience. Dishes tout Italian roots, but you'll find plenty of Asian flourishes. Standouts include the quail salad with braised grapes and pancetta, and angel-hair pasta with uni, tomatoes, and garlic chips. Save room for dessert, because the panfried brioche is insanely satisfying. [$] *Average main: HK$300* ✉ *9 Justice Dr., Admiralty, Central* ☎ *2537–9888* 🌐 *www.ammo.com.hk* ✍ *Reservations essential* ✥ *C5.*

$$$ INTERNATIONAL FAMILY

🍴 **Café Deco.** As is often the case where there's a captive audience, dining up at the Peak Galleria mall can be unpredictable—and this huge eatery is no exception. You'll come mostly for the views, though the menu is eclectic enough to keep everyone happy. Menu options traverse four or five continents, and there's also a patisserie offering house-made desserts. Oysters and seafood are the best choices. When you book (and you must), be sure to request a table with a view, as many tables in the place have none, which defeats the purpose of coming here. [$] *Average main: HK$260* ✉ *The Peak Galleria, 118 Peak Rd., Central* ☎ *2849–5111* 🌐 *www.cafedecogroup.com* ✍ *Reservations essential* ✥ *A6.*

$$$$ CONTEMPORARY Fodor's Choice ★

🍴 **Café Gray Deluxe.** Celebrated chef Gray Kunz's restaurant offers expertly prepared modern European fare in a casual and relaxed 49th-floor locale that has stunning views of the city. A fan of fresh, seasonal ingredients, Kunz incorporates local produce into the ever-evolving menu whenever possible, and often adds Asian flavorings to excellent effect. Steak tartare shines among the lineup of stellar "first plates," which also include the signature pasta *fiore* served with tangy tomatoes and herbs. The bar boasts a fine selection of creative cocktails, so even if you can't stop by for a sit-down meal, it's worth stopping by for a cocktail and small bite. [$] *Average main: HK$450* ✉ *49th fl., The Upper House, Pacific Place, 88 Queensway, Central* ☎ *3968–1106* 🌐 *www.cafegrayhk.com* ✍ *Reservations essential* [M] *Admiralty* ✥ *C5.*

$$$ PERUVIAN

🍴 **Chicha.** Expect complex, chili-fueled flavors from Hong Kong's first Peruvian restaurant. The menu has multicultural influences, from Chinese-style *lomo saltado* (a beef, scallion, and rice stir-fry) to the Spanish paella-like *marisco jugoso* flavored with an umami sea urchin and citrus reduction. Be sure to order the ceviche (cured raw seafood) and a platter of *anticuchos* (grilled skewers) to share; the cod with ponzu miso and chili aioli is close to addictive. If you want to cap your meal off in true Peruvian fashion, finish with a pisco sour at the bar. [$] *Average main: HK$250* ✉ *26 Peel St., Central* ☎ *2561–3336* 🌐 *www.conceptcreations.hk* ✍ *Reservations essential* ✥ *A4.*

$$$$ SHANGHAINESE Fodor's Choice ★

🍴 **Fa Zu Jie.** This place is good—really, *really* good. Tucked away in a nondescript building in a hidden alley off Lan Kwai Fong, this reservations-only private kitchen plates up inventive, French-inspired Shanghainese dishes that are prepped in a polished open kitchen. The prix-fixe menu is tweaked on a regular basis, but you'll probably be treated to trademark items such as drunken quail (cooked in Chinese Hua Diao wine) served with al dente Sanuki udon noodles and plump scallops slicked in shrimp roe oil. The dining room has only a handful of tables, so try to book a few weeks in advance. [$] *Average main: HK$628* ✉ *1st*

6

fl., 20A D'Aguilar St., Central ☎ *3487–1715* ⌁ *Reservations essential* ▭ *No credit cards* ⊙ *Closed Sun. No lunch* Ⓜ *Central* ✛ *A4.*

$$$$ ✕ **L'Atelier de Joël Robuchon.** Joël Robuchon, one of the world's most
FRENCH iconic chefs, claims that his atelier (or "artist's workshop") is for contemporary casual dining. Diners sit on bar stools around a counter designed like a modern Japanese sushi bar so that everyone can watch the chefs at work in the open kitchen. Everything from the freshly baked bread to desserts is immaculately presented. Some dishes are available in small tasting portions so you can try a bit of everything. The quail with foie gras, served with the deservedly famous mashed potatoes, and the sea urchin, in a lobster jelly topped with cauliflower cream, are standouts. Those who don't want to splurge on a full meal should try the superb croissants and cakes at the salon one floor below. Ⓢ *Average main: HK$680* ⊠ *Shop 401, The Landmark, 15 Queen's Rd. Central, Central* ☎ *2166–9000* ⊕ *www.robuchon.hk* Ⓜ *Central* ✛ *B3.*

$ ✕ **Little Bao.** Slide into one of the dozen seats at the bar and tuck into the
ECLECTIC delicious *baos*—fluffy steamed buns sandwiched with all types of deli-
Fodor's Choice cious ingredients. The braised pork belly is the signature item, but we're
★ partial to the grilled chicken with Japanese pickles. Desserts are in bao form as well, with a thick slab of ice cream as the filling. Carbs aside, the rest of the menu is globally inspired and includes to-share plates such as white-pepper clams, short-rib dumplings, and truffle fries. Ⓢ *Average main: HK$90* ⊠ *66 Staunton St., Central* ☎ *2194–0202* ⊕ *www.little-bao.com* ⌁ *Reservations not accepted* ⊙ *Closed Sun. No lunch* Ⓜ *Sheung Wan* ✛ *A2.*

$$$ ✕ **Lung King Heen.** This place has made a serious case for being the
CHINESE best Cantonese restaurant in Hong Kong, especially after winning and retaining three Michelin stars every year since 2009. Where other contenders tend to get too caught up in prestige dishes and name-brand chefs, Lung King Heen focuses completely on taste. When you try barbecued suckling pig or crispy shrimp dumplings that are this divine, you'll be forced to reevaluate your entire notion of Chinese cuisine. Ⓢ *Average main: HK$300* ⊠ *4th fl., Four Seasons Hotel, 8 Finance St., Central* ☎ *3196–8880* ⊕ *www.fourseasons.com* ⌁ *Reservations essential* Ⓜ *Hong Kong* ✛ *B2.*

$ ✕ **Mak's Noodles.** Mak's may look like any other Hong Kong noodle
CHINESE shop, but this tiny storefront is one of the best known in town, with a reputation that belies its humble decor. The staff is attentive, and the menu includes a wide range of delicious dishes, such as various sauce-tossed noodles with pork. The real test of a good Cantonese noodle shop, however, is its wontons, and here they're fresh, delicate, and filled with whole shrimp. Don't miss the *sui kau*—a slightly larger and heavier dumpling that has diced mushrooms mixed in to the shrimp filling. Ⓢ *Average main: HK$40* ⊠ *77 Wellington St., Central* ☎ *2854–3810* ▭ *No credit cards* Ⓜ *Central* ✛ *A3.*

$$$$ ✕ **Restaurant Petrus.** Commanding breathtaking views atop the Island
FRENCH Shangri-La, Restaurant Petrus scales the upper Hong Kong heights of prestige, formality, and price. This is one of the city's few flagship hotel restaurants that has not attempted to reinvent itself as fusion—sometimes traditional French haute cuisine is the way to go. Likewise, the

design of the place is in the old-school restaurant-as-ballroom mode. The kitchen has a particularly good way with foie gras, and the wine list is memorable, boasting more than 1,500 vintages from some of the world's best wineries. The dress here is business casual—no jeans, sandals, or short-sleeved shirts for men. $ *Average main: HK$600* ⊠ *56th fl., Island Shangri-La, Pacific Place, Supreme Court Rd., Admiralty, Central* ☎ *2820–8590* ⊕ *www.shangri-la.com* Ⓜ *Admiralty* ✛ *C4.*

$$$ ✕**Yung Kee.** Close to Hong Kong's famous nightlife and dining dis-
CHINESE trict of Lan Kwai Fong, Yung Kee has been a local institution since it first opened as a food stall in 1942. The food is authentic Cantonese, served amid riotous decor and writhing gold dragons. Locals come here for roast goose with beautifully crisp skin and tender meat, as well as dim sum. Other excellent dishes include the "cloudy tea" smoked pork, which needs to be reserved a day in advance, and the deep-fried prawns with mini crab roe. More adventurous palates may wish to check out the thousand-year-old preserved eggs. $ *Average main: HK$250* ⊠ *32–40 Wellington St., Central* ☎ *2522–1624* ⊕ *www. yungkee.com.hk* Ⓜ *Central* ✛ *A3.*

WAN CHAI, CAUSEWAY BAY, AND BEYOND
WAN CHAI

$$$$ ✕**Bo Innovation.** The mastermind behind this renowned restaurant is
CHINESE Alvin Leung, who dubs himself the "demon chef" and has the moniker tattooed on his arm. Bo Innovation serves what he calls "X-treme Chinese" cuisine, applying molecular gastronomy, French, and Japanese cooking techniques to traditional Cantonese dishes. The beef and black-truffle *cheung fun* (steamed-rice roll) is a winner, as is the signature xiao long bao (soup dumpling). At dinner you must choose between the multicourse tasting menu, table menu, or chef's menu; à la carte dining is not available. Tables are often full on Friday and Saturday, so book in advance. $ *Average main: HK$680* ⊠ *2nd fl., J Residence, 60 Johnston Rd., Wan Chai* ☎ *2850–8371* ⊕ *www.boinnovation.com* ⌦ *Reservations essential* ☼ *Closed Sun. No lunch Sat.* Ⓜ *Wan Chai* ✛ *A4.*

$$ ✕**Liu Yuan Pavilion.** Often regarded as one of the best Shanghainese
CHINESE restaurants in town, Liu Yuan's cooking style stays loyal to tradition
Fodor's Choice with a no-fuss mentality that has worked in their favor for years. Easy
★ favorites include sweet strips of crunchy eel, panfried meat buns, and steamed *xiao long bao* dumplings plumped up with minced pork and broth. Diners also wax lyrical about the house special crispy rice soup and rice crackers smothered in salted egg yolk. Come hungry, since you'll need plenty of room to stomach all of these deliciously carby dishes. $ *Average main: HK$120* ⊠ *The Broadway, 54–62 Lockhart Rd., 3rd fl., Wan Chai* ☎ *2804–2000* Ⓜ *Wan Chai* ✛ *E4.*

$$$ ✕**Serge et le Phoque.** With its floor-to-ceiling windows and minimalist
FRENCH decor, this elegant restaurant stands out amid the clamor of Wan Chai's
Fodor's Choice street market. The kitchen serves refined, modern French cuisine, often
★ with minimalist Japanese touches. Dishes on the menu are ever-changing, but may include slow-cooked hen eggs or scallops with *yuzu kosho* (a green chili paste from Japan). Service is friendly and attentive without the stuffiness you'll find in more old-school European restaurants.

6

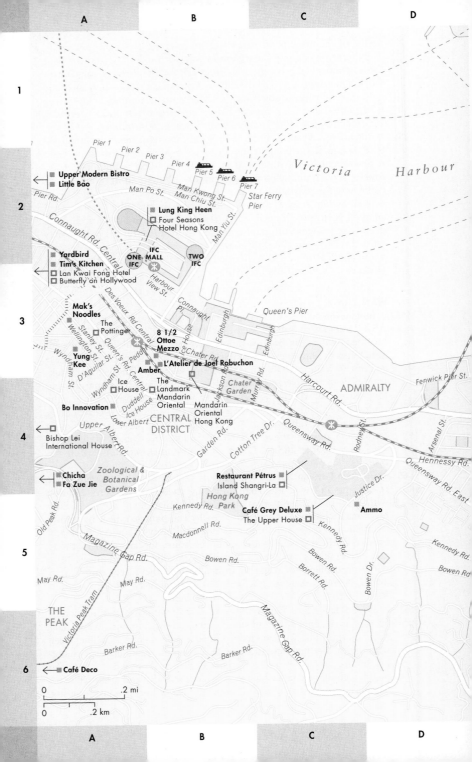

A

1

Pier 1
Pier 2
Pier 3
Pier 4

Man Po St.

◀ ■ **Upper Modern Bistro**
■ **Little Bao**

Pier Rd.

2

Connaught Rd. Central

◀ ■ **Yardbird**
■ **Tim's Kitchen**
□ **Lan Kwai Fong Hotel**
□ **Butterfly on Hollywood**

Des Voeux Rd. Central

■ **Mak's
Noodles**
□ **The
Pottinger**

Stanley St.
Wellington St.
D'Aguilar St.
Wyndham St.

■ **Yung
Kee**

Queen's Rd.

3

■ **Bo Innovation**

Duddell
Ice House St.
Lower Albert Rd.
Upper Albert Rd.

**CENTRAL
DISTRICT**

Garden Rd.

4

◀ □
**Bishop Lei
International House**

◀ ■ **Chicha**
■ **Fa Zue Jie**

*Zoological &
Botanical
Gardens*

Old Peak Rd.

Magazine Gap Rd.

May Rd.

May Rd.

5

**THE
PEAK**

Victoria Peak Tram

Barker Rd.

6

◀ ■ **Café Deco**

0 ———— .2 mi

0 ———— .2 km

A

B

Pier 5
Pier 6
Pier 7

Man Kwong St.
Man Chiu St.

**Star Ferry
Pier**

Man Yiu St.

■ **Lung King Heen**
□ **Four Seasons
Hotel Hong Kong**

**IFC
MALL**
**ONE
IFC**

**TWO
IFC**

Harbour
View St.

Connaught Pl.

House

**8 1/2
Ottoe
Mezzo**

Chater Rd.

■ **L'Atelier de Joel Robuchon**

Ice
House St.

■ **Amber**

**The
Landmark
Mandarin
Oriental**

*Chater
Garden*

**Mandarin
Oriental
Hong Kong**

Jackson Rd.

Murray Rd.

Cotton Tree Dr.

Queensway Rd.

*Hong Kong
Park*

Kennedy Rd.

■ **Restaurant Pétrus**
□ **Island Shangri-La**

Café Grey Deluxe ■
The Upper House □

Macdonnell Rd.

Bowen Rd.

Bowen Rd.

Magazine Gap Rd.

Barker Rd.

B

C

Victoria   *Harbour*

ADMIRALTY

Harcourt Rd.

Hennessy Rd.

Justice Dr.

■ **Ammo**

Kennedy Rd.

Bowen Rd.

Borrett Rd.

Bowen Dr.

C

D

Fenwick Pier St.

Queensway Rd. East

Arsenal St.

Rodney St.

Kennedy Rd.

Bowen Rd.

D

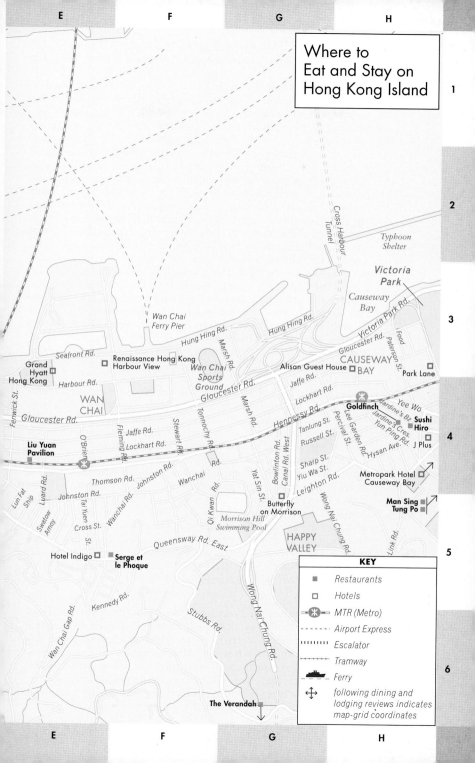

Where to Eat and Stay on Hong Kong Island

E F G H

1

2

Cross Harbour Tunnel

Typhoon Shelter

Victoria Park

Causeway Bay

3

Wan Chai Ferry Pier

Hung Hing Rd.

Hung Hing Rd.

Marsh Rd.

Victoria Park Rd.

Gloucester Rd.

Food

Paterson St.

Seafront Rd.

Renaissance Hong Kong Harbour View

Wan Chai Sports Ground

Alisan Guest House

CAUSEWAY BAY

Park Lane

Grand Hyatt Hong Kong

Harbour Rd.

Gloucester Rd.

Jaffe Rd.

Yee Wo

Goldfinch

Jardine's Bz.

Sushi Hiro

WAN CHAI

Lockhart Rd.

Hennessy Rd.

Jardine's Cres.

Yun Ping Rd.

Fenwick St.

Gloucester Rd.

Tanlung St.

Lee Garden Rd.

Percival St.

Hysan Ave.

J Plus

Liu Yuan Pavilion

O'Brien Rd.

Jaffe Rd.

Fleming Rd.

Lockhart Rd.

Stewart Rd.

Tonnochy Rd.

Marsh Rd.

Russell St.

4

Sharp St.

Metropark Hotel Causeway Bay

Thomson Rd.

Johnston Rd.

Wanchai Rd.

Wanchai

Rd.

Yat Sin St.

Bowrington Rd.

Canal Rd. West

Yiu Wa St.

Leighton Rd.

Wong Nai Chung Rd.

Link Rd.

Man Sing

Tung Po

Lun Fat

Ship

Luard Rd.

Johnston Rd.

Tai Yuen Rd.

Qi Kwan Rd.

Butterfly on Morrison

5

Swatow

Amoy

Cross St.

Morrison Hill Swimming Pool

HAPPY VALLEY

Hotel Indigo

Queensway Rd. East

Serge et le Phoque

Kennedy Rd.

Wan Chai Gap Rd.

Stubbs Rd.

Wong Nai Chung Rd.

KEY

◼ Restaurants

◻ Hotels

⊗ MTR (Metro)

- - - Airport Express

|||||| Escalator

Tramway

Ferry

↔ following dining and lodging reviews indicates map-grid coordinates

The Verandah

6

E F G H

$ *Average main: HK$300* ⊠ *Shop B2, 2 Wan Chai Rd., Wan Chai* ☎ *5465–2000* ⚞ *Reservations essential* ⊗ *No lunch* Ⓜ *Wan Chai* ✛ *E5.*

CAUSEWAY BAY

$$
STEAKHOUSE
✕ **Goldfinch Restaurant.** Travel back to the romantic 1960s as you dine at this retro restaurant. Film buffs might recognize this spot as the backdrop to renowned director Wong Kar-wai's most famous films, including *In the Mood for Love.* Like the decor, the food here has remained largely unchanged since the restaurant's heyday, and you'll find local interpretations of Western dishes, such as borscht or cream of mushroom soup and gravy-covered steaks served on sizzling iron plates. Don't come here if you're looking for an authentic steak-house experience, though: this place is strictly for those who want to relive the nostalgic charm of Hong Kong's swinging era. $ *Average main: HK$150* ⊠ *13–15 Lan Fong Rd., Causeway Bay* ☎ *2577–7981* ✛ *H4.*

$$$$
JAPANESE
✕ **Sushi Hiro.** *Uni* (sea urchin), *ikura* (salmon roe), *o-toro* (the fattiest of fatty tuna). If these words can make you drool, then you should make a beeline for Sushi Hiro, hidden in an office building but quite possibly the best place for raw fish in Hong Kong. The minimalist interior stays faithful to Japanese style, unlike at some more opulent Hong Kong restaurants. But what really draws in the Japanese crowd here is the freshness of the fish, which you can watch being filleted in front of you at the sushi bar. Dinner may get pricey, but the restaurant also does some fantastic lunch deals. $ *Average main: HK$320* ⊠ *Henry House, 42 Yun Ping Rd., 10th fl., Causeway Bay* ☎ *2882–8752* ⊕ *www.sushihiro.com.hk* Ⓜ *Causeway Bay* ✛ *H4.*

EASTERN

$
CANTONESE
Fodor'sChoice
★
✕ **Tung Po.** Arguably Hong Kong's most famous—if not most perpetually packed—indoor dai pai dong, Tung Po has communal tables large enough to fit 18 guests, and the restaurant's walls are scribbled with its ever-growing list of specials. The food is Hong Kong cuisine with fusion innovations, and you should wash everything down with a cold beer (served here in Chinese soup bowls). Try the spaghetti with cuttlefish, which is flavored with aromatic, jet-black, fresh squid ink. The seafood dishes and stir-fries are all satisfying, but it's really the atmosphere that makes Tung Po a must-visit. Owner Robby Cheung is one of the most delightful characters in the Hong Kong dining biz. Later in the evening, he'll blast the latest pop songs from the sound system. If you're lucky, you might just catch him in one of his moonwalking moods. $ *Average main: HK$95* ⊠ *2nd fl., Java Road Municipal Services Bldg., 99 Java Rd., Eastern* ☎ *2880–5224, 2880–9399* ⚞ *Reservations essential* ⊟ *No credit cards* ⊗ *No lunch* Ⓜ *North Point* ✛ *H5.*

SOUTHSIDE

$$$$
EUROPEAN
✕ **The Verandah.** You won't forget an evening at the Verandah. From the well-spaced tables overlooking the bay to the unobtrusive service to the menu of delicious classics (think French onion soup, Dover sole meunière, and tournedos Rossini), this is an unabashedly regal experience that delivers with finesse at every turn. The beautiful colonial setting is also the perfect place to enjoy a traditional English afternoon tea. Whether you're here for brunch or supper, the food doesn't disappoint, and the wine list is more reasonably priced than you might expect.

Street food in Hong Kong is cheap and delicious.

Note that sleeveless shirts and shorts aren't allowed for men during dinner. $ *Average main: HK$500* ✉ *The Repulse Bay, 109 Repulse Bay Rd., Repulse Bay, Southside* ☎ *2292–2822* ⊕ *www.therepulsebay.com* ☾ *Closed Mon. and Tues.* ✛ *G6.*

KOWLOON

Use the coordinates (✛ B2) at the end of each listing to locate a site on the Where to Eat and Stay in Kowloon map.

TSIM SHA TSUI

$$$
CHINESE
✕ **Dong Lai Shun.** This Chinese restaurant specializes in Beijing and Huai-yang cuisine and is known for its *shuan yang rou* (mutton hotpot). The restaurant offers a host of other great dishes, including traditional Peking duck and the award-winning combination of wok-fried crab-meat, rock lobster, and salted egg yolk served on rice crackers. Appetizers are particularly good—order the smoked eggs and crispy eel. Dong Lai Shun is also famous for its annual hairy crab menu, which is only available in the fall when the shelled delicacy is in season. $ *Average main: HK$250* ✉ *The Royal Garden, 69 Mody Rd., Tsim Sha Tsui* ☎ *2733–2020* ⊕ *www.rghk.com.hk* ✛ *B5.*

$$$$
CHINESE
✕ **Hutong.** It's not hard to see why Hutong is one of the hottest tables in Hong Kong: it has some of the most imaginative food in town. Its beautifully decorated dining room at the top of the dramatic One Peking Road Tower overlooks the entire festival of lights that is the Hong Kong island skyline. Best among the sensational selection of regional Chinese creations are the deboned lamb ribs and the crispy soft-shell crab with dried Sichuan peppers. Subtler dishes include fresh abalone carpaccio

Where to Eat and Stay in Kowloon

☐ W Hong Kong
☐ The Ritz-Carlton Hong Kong
■ Inakaya

KEY

■ Restaurants
☐ Hotels
Ⓜ MTR (Metro)
KCR
Ferry

following dining and lodging reviews indicates map-grid coordinates

Islam Food

Hong Chong Rd.

Hotel ICON

Cross-Harbour Tunnel

HK MUSEUM OF HISTORY

Dong Lai Shun

Mody Rd.

Cheong Wan Rd.

TSIM SHA TSUI

Chatham Rd. South

Spring Deer

Tsim Sha Tsui East Ferry Pier

Victoria Harbour

Cox's Rd.

The Luxe Manor

Kimberley Rd.

Granville Rd.

Cameron Rd.

Carnarvon Rd.

Hop Inn Carnarvon

Mody Rd.

Black Head Point Garden

Salisbury Rd.

InterContinental Hong Kong

Nathan Rd.

TSIM SHA TSUI

Austin Rd.

BP International

Haiphong Rd.

Kowloon Park

The Peninsula Hong Kong

Kowloon Park

HK MUSEUM OF ART

Yau Yuan Xiao Jui

Canton Rd.

Canton Rd.

Hutong

Marco Polo Hongkong Hotel

Star Ferry Landing

China Ferry Terminal

Harbour City

0   1/8 mile
0   1/8 kilometer

A   B   C   D

1   2   3   4   5   6

marinated in spring-onion oil, and delicate scallops tossed with pomelo. Hutong also hosts Sunday brunch, which features a limitless supply of northern Chinese specialties and free-flowing bubbly. $ *Average main: HK$368* ⊠ *28th fl., 1 Peking Rd., Tsim Sha Tsui* ☎ *3428–8342* ⊕ *www. aqua.com.hk* ➢ *Reservations essential* Ⓜ *Tsim Sha Tsui* ⊹ *C2.*

$$$$
JAPANESE

✕ **Inakaya.** On the 101st floor of the ICC building, Inakaya flaunts a jaw-dropping, bird's-eye view of the city below, but the interior of the restaurant is equally extravagant—the highlight is the specialized *robatayaki* (the Japanese equivalent to barbecue) room, which has a long counter decorated with baskets of fresh ingredients. Choose your meat or vegetables and the chefs will grill them to order and serve it the traditional way, on long wooden paddles. Because robatayaki is served in bite-sized morsels, prices can add up, but it's a fun and unique experience. If you don't want to splurge on grilled goods, Inakaya also offers other *washoku* (Japanese cuisines) such as sushi and traditional, multicourse *kaiseki* meals. $ *Average main: HK$600* ⊠ *101st fl., International Commerce Centre, 1 Austin Rd. W, Kowloon* ☎ *2972–2666* ⊕ *www.jcgroup.hk* ⊹ *B1.*

$$
CHINESE

✕ **Spring Deer.** The pastel blue and green interior make this Peking duck specialist look like something from 1950s Beijing. The crowd, too, is old-school, which only adds to the experience. You'll see locals with noodle dishes, stir-fried wok meat dishes, and so forth, but the Peking duck is the showstopper—it might be the best in town. Even the peanuts for snacking, which are boiled to a delectable softness, go above and beyond the call of duty. This place is extremely popular, so it's best to book your table at least a week in advance. $ *Average main: HK$170* ⊠ *42 Mody Rd., 1st fl., Tsim Sha Tsui* ☎ *2366–4012, 2366–5839* ➢ *Reservations essential* Ⓜ *Tsim Sha Tsui* ⊹ *C4.*

YAU MA TEI, MONG KOK, AND NORTHERN KOWLOON

$
CHINESE

✕ **Islam Food.** This halal restaurant may not be the prettiest restaurant you've ever seen, and you should expect to wait a while for a table (lines get extremely crazy during peak meal hours), but we promise that the panfried beef patties (translated as "veal goulash" on the menu) here are well worth the pilgrimage. The browned pastry packets arrive at the table piping hot and bursting with tender minced beef—good luck trying to stop at just one. Other excellent dishes include the delicious lamb brisket curry, panfried mutton dumplings, and the hot-and-sour soup. $ *Average main: HK$55* ⊠ *1 Lung Kong Rd., Kowloon City* ☎ *2382–2822, 2382–8928* ⊕ *www.islamfood.com.hk* ▭ *No credit cards* ⊹ *A6.*

$
CHINESE
Fodor'sChoice
★

✕ **Yau Yuan Xiao Jui.** This tiny storefront may look like any other noodle joint, but its humble appearance belies its culinary prowess. The restaurant serves authentic Shaanxi snacks, which can be best described as some of the heartiest and delicious chow that China has to offer. The handmade dumplings are amazing, especially if they're fattened up with lamb and scallion oil. Then there's the signature *biang biang mien*, which are extremely long and wide al dente noodle sheets designed to be anointed with chili oil, scallions, and marinated spareribs. Definitely check this place out. $ *Average main: HK$38* ⊠ *Keybond Commercial Bldg., 38 Ferry St., entrance on Saigon St., Jordan* ☎ *5300–2682* ▭ *No credit cards* Ⓜ *Jordan* ⊹ *A2.*

6

WHERE TO STAY

Whether you're a business traveler or a casual tourist, you'll inevitably be caught up with the manic pace of life in Hong Kong. Luckily, hotels are constantly increasing their efforts to provide guests with a restful haven, often bundling spectacular views of the famous skyline and harbor with chic luxury, snazzy amenities, and soothing ambience.

From budget guesthouses to gleaming towers, you're sure to find a style and site to fit your needs. Prices tend to reflect quality of service and amenities as well as location, so it's worth the effort to examine neighborhoods closely when making your choice—you may end up paying the same to stay exactly where you want to be as you would to be off the beaten path.

The rock stars of Hong Kong's hotel industry are perfectly situated around Victoria Harbour, offering unobstructed harbor views, sumptuous spas, and reputable service to compete for the patronage of business-suited jet-setters, and any visitor willing to splurge for uncompromised luxury. Farther up the hills on both Kowloon and Hong Kong Island, cozy hotels seduce travelers who simply want a safe and practical place to crash in a trendy locale.

Travelers familiar with European cities might be surprised by the lack of provenance among Hong Kong hotels—the Peninsula passes as the venerable old-timer in this brashly new city where most hotels are perched in modern towers. And the scene keeps changing: Hong Kong's continued growth as a top tourist destination and business capital means that when it comes to choice of lodging, the next big thing is always around the corner. The Ritz-Carlton, Hong Kong, recently hit the heights when it began hosting guests on the 102nd through 118th floors of the ICC tower in West Kowloon, suggesting that on the Hong Kong hotel scene the sky really is the limit.

WHAT IT COSTS IN HONG KONG DOLLARS			
$	$$	$$$	$$$$
Hotels	under HK$1,500	HK$1,500–HK$2,499	HK$2,500–HK$4,000	over HK$4,000

Hotel prices are the lowest cost of a standard double room in high season.

WHERE SHOULD I STAY?

	NEIGHBORHOOD VIBE	PROS	CONS
Western	A sprawling neighborhood with hidden alleyways, antiques shops, Chinese medicine markets, temples and hip eateries.	Western is akin to the residential extension of Central, with less traffic and similarly spectacular views. Accessible on foot, and a leisurely tram ride from Central during off-peak hours.	May require steep footwork if your destination is away from the main roads, where the trams and MTR run. Even taxis have difficulty navigating many narrow, one-way streets.
Central	A dense international finance center full of banks, shopping malls, restaurants, and footbridges above traffic. High up the escalators, Mid-Levels is an exclusive residential getaway.	Home to major luxury brands' flagship stores, as well as grand hotels, fine dining, and the famous nightlife area, Lan Kwai Fong. Mid-Levels offers quiet views from above the fray.	Congested streets by day, crowded bars by night. Mid-Levels Escalator runs uphill only after morning rush hour.
Wan Chai, Causeway Bay, and Beyond	Wan Chai hosts a strip of street-level bars in addition to the boutique Star Street area. Causeway Bay is the haven of hip young locals who come to eat, shop, and hang out in upstairs cafés.	Wan Chai has stylish restaurants, the convention center, and performing-arts venues. Causeway Bay, home to Victoria Park, is absurdly busy but conveniently situated with hotels in all price ranges.	The Wan Chai bar strip can get seedy, while Causeway Bay is extremely crowded on weekends. Eastern is mostly for business or residents.
Southside	Lower building density means more green space and fewer people, with a fishing-village atmosphere around Aberdeen.	Proximity to great beaches and treks on Hong Kong Island, as well as to Stanley Market.	Be prepared for a lot of car and bus rides along winding roads, often in slow traffic.
Lantau Island	Hong Kong's largest island hosts disparate attractions: an international airport, an outlet shopping mall, natural scenery, Hong Kong Disneyland, and AsiaWorld-Expo.	Tung Chung, at the end of the MTR line, is the point of access to the Ngong Ping cable car. Those with kids may prefer the resortlike setting inside Disneyland.	Inconvenient for exploring the rest of Hong Kong, as even Tung Chung is a half-hour MTR ride from Central.
Kowloon	The "wild" side of Hong Kong (at least according to Islanders) culminating in the commercial centers of Mong Kok and Tsim Sha Tsui.	Shopping paradise indeed, for both malls and markets. The TST promenade, including the touristy Avenue of Stars, offers postcard views of the Hong Kong skyline.	Kowloon is not everyone's idea of a holiday—outside residential areas the streets (even pedestrian) are generally noisy, crowded, and congested.

6

RESERVATIONS AND RATES

Prices vary depending on season and occupancy. Most hotels offer their best rates and special offers on their websites—look for long-stay or advanced-purchase discounts, or for that matter, last-minute booking deals. Hong Kong's high seasons are generally May through June and October through November, though rates also go up during certain holiday periods and for events such as the Hong Kong Sevens rugby tournament in March. While many hotels put on lavish breakfast buffets, breakfast is usually extra and not included in basic room rates. *Hotel reviews have been shortened. For full information, visit Fodors.com.*

HONG KONG ISLAND

Reviews are listed alphabetically within neighborhood. Use the coordinates (⌖ B2) at the end of each listing to locate a site on the Where to Eat and Stay in Hong Kong map.

WESTERN

$ **Butterfly on Hollywood.** A charming location alone is reason enough
HOTEL   to stay in one of these snug but stylishly contemporary rooms in a cozy neighborhood full of antiques shops, galleries, cafés, and up-and-coming restaurants. **Pros:** excellent location for wandering; a 10-minute walk from the hub of Hong Kong nightlife; free Wi-Fi throughout. **Cons:** cramped lobby and few hotel facilities; no views. $ *Rooms from: HK$1300* ⊠ *263 Hollywood Rd., Sheung Wan, Western* ☎ *2850–8899* ⊕ *www.butterflyhk.com* ⮃ *148 rooms* ⓧ *No meals* Ⓜ *Sheung Wan* ⌖ *A3.*

CENTRAL

$ **Bishop Lei International House.** If you've ever dreamed of living a life
HOTEL   of privilege in the Mid-Levels without having to pay through the nose
Fodor'sChoice   for it, this is your chance—all the better if you go for a slightly pric-
★   ier harbor-view room. **Pros:** unique perch near escalators, saving you countless steps up and down to SoHo and Central; good value. **Cons:** escalator runs upward-only after 10 am so lots of steps down in the morning. $ *Rooms from: HK$1200* ⊠ *4 Robinson Rd., Mid-Levels, Central* ☎ *852/2868–0828* ⊕ *www.bishopleihtl.com.hk* ⮃ *228 rooms* ⓧ *No meals* Ⓜ *Central* ⌖ *A4.*

$$$$ **Four Seasons Hotel Hong Kong.** Few comforts are neglected, with ame-
HOTEL   nities ranging from sumptuous Chinese-accented furnishings to all sorts
Fodor'sChoice   of high-tech gadgetry, but the main features are the knockout views
★   of the harbor and Victoria Peak through walls of glass. **Pros:** elite service and attention to detail; outstanding 24-hour business center. **Cons:** breakfast not included in high rates; some views are better than others. $ *Rooms from: HK$4500* ⊠ *International Finance Centre, 8 Finance St., Central* ☎ *3196–8888* ⊕ *www.fourseasons.com/hongkong* ⮃ *399 rooms* ⓧ *No meals* Ⓜ *Central* ⌖ *B2.*

$$$$ **Island Shangri-La.** A city icon towering above Pacific Place drips with
HOTEL   old-world charm and offers spacious and luxurious accommodations with an Asian twist, along with fine dining and impeccable service. **Pros:** grand lobby; beautiful pool deck with a great close-up view of the skyline; elevator access to Pacific Place Mall. **Cons:** no full-service spa. $ *Rooms from: HK$4500* ⊠ *Pacific Place, Supreme Court Rd., Admiralty, Central* ☎ *2877–3838* ⊕ *www.shangri-la.com/island* ⮃ *565 rooms* ⓧ *No meals* Ⓜ *Admiralty* ⌖ *C4.*

$ HOTEL **Lan Kwai Fong Hotel.** The scent of lemongrass and cozy feel of an old Hong Kong apartment building extend to the small but beautiful rooms enlarged by bay windows and plunging views of the surrounding cityscape. **Pros:** hotel and neighborhood have lots of character; free Wi-Fi; complimentary smartphone; some rooms have balconies. **Cons:** narrow roads surrounding the hotel are often congested. [$] *Rooms from: HK$1300* ✉ *3 Kau U Fong, Central* ☎ *3650–0000* 🌐 *www.lankwaifonghotel.com.hk* 🛏 *162 rooms* 🍴 *No meals* [M] *Sheung Wan* ✣ *A3.*

$$$$ HOTEL Fodor's Choice ★ **The Landmark Mandarin Oriental.** Some of the city's most beautifully designed and spacious rooms are equipped with massive, circular, spa-style bathtubs, the centerpieces of huge, view-filled bathrooms. **Pros:** you can't get more central in Central; elegantly appointed rooms. **Cons:** relatively small lobby; city views only. [$] *Rooms from: HK$4500* ✉ *The Landmark, 15 Queen's Rd. Central, Central* ☎ *2132–0188* 🌐 *www.mandarinoriental.com/landmark* 🛏 *113 rooms* 🍴 *No meals* [M] *Central* ✣ *B4.*

$$$$ HOTEL Fodor's Choice ★ **Mandarin Oriental Hong Kong.** Hong Kong's most famous hotel has lost none of its opulence, colonial charm, and shine over the past 50 years and is still known for spacious and luxurious accommodations and impeccable service. **Pros:** spacious, open, and beautifully designed rooms; old-world ambience at its finest; exquisite spa. **Cons:** in-room Wi-Fi isn't free. [$] *Rooms from: HK$4500* ✉ *5 Connaught Rd., Central* ☎ *2522–0111* 🌐 *www.mandarinoriental.com/hongkong* 🛏 *501 rooms* 🍴 *No meals* [M] *Central* ✣ *B3.*

$$$ HOTEL **The Pottinger.** As its name implies, The Pottinger overlooks the historic stony staircase of the same name. **Pros:** centrally located; local touches; big bathrooms; historical elements **Cons:** no pool; limited amenities; underwhelming views. [$] *Rooms from: HK$3200* ✉ *21 Stanley St., Central* ☎ *2308–3188* 🌐 *www.thepottinger.com* 🛏 *68 rooms* 🍴 *No meals* ✣ *A3.*

$$$$ HOTEL Fodor's Choice ★ **The Upper House.** Even standard rooms in this haven of stylish luxury are suites—tranquil havens of design and indulgence that feature huge window-side bathtubs, walk-in rain showers, a personal iPod touch with everything on it, free minibars, and high-end wine fridges. **Pros:** high design, and filled with works of contemporary Asian artists; feels worlds away from Central neighborhood below; incredible personalized service. **Cons:** no spa or pool; can be difficult to get a taxi. [$] *Rooms from: HK$4500* ✉ *Pacific Place, 88 Queensway, Admiralty, Central* ☎ *2918–1838* 🌐 *www.upperhouse.com* 🛏 *117 suites* 🍴 *No meals* [M] *Admiralty* ✣ *C5.*

WAN CHAI, CAUSEWAY BAY, AND BEYOND

WAN CHAI

$$$$ HOTEL FAMILY **Grand Hyatt Hong Kong.** A direct connection to the Hong Kong Convention and Exhibition Centre makes this a business-first hotel, but leisure travelers also enjoy the elegant rooms, with sweeping harbor views, and luxurious touches such as an oversized square bathtub and mirror TV. **Pros:** excellent service; extensive sports facilities; Plateau spa is a beautiful sanctuary; free Wi-Fi. **Cons:** quiet outside the hotel at night; difficult to get reservations in popular restaurant. [$] *Rooms*

from: HK$5200 ✉ *1 Harbour Rd., Wan Chai* ☎ *2588–1234* 🌐 *www.hongkong.grand.hyatt.com* 🛏 *539 rooms* 🍴 *No meals* [M] *Wan Chai, Exit A1* ✥ *E3.*

$$ HOTEL 🏨 **Hotel Indigo.** A standout boutique addition to the Wan Chai hotel scene, Hotel Indigo boasts serious architectural chops—the exterior resembles a circling dragon—as well as photogenic interiors. **Pros:** free Wi-Fi; eclectic neighborhood; panoramic views; top-notch service; convenient location. **Cons:** pricey drinking and dining options; over-air-conditioned public spaces; tiny fitness center. [$] *Rooms from: HK$2200* ✉ *242–246 Queen's Rd. E, Wan Chai* ☎ *3926–3888* 🌐 *www.ihg.com/hotelindigo* 🛏 *138 rooms* 🍴 *No meals* [M] *Wan Chai, Exit A3* ✥ *E5.*

$$$ HOTEL FAMILY 🏨 **Renaissance Hong Kong Harbour View Hotel.** These modest guest rooms in the Hong Kong Convention and Exhibition Centre complex are simply outfitted with attractive modern decor, and many have harbor views. **Pros:** great harbor views; harborside recreational garden. **Cons:** a walk from the subway but near the Star Ferry. [$] *Rooms from: HK$2800* ✉ *1 Harbour Rd., Wan Chai* ☎ *2802–8888* 🌐 *www.renaissanceharbourviewhk.com* 🛏 *857 rooms* 🍴 *No meals* [M] *Wan Chai* ✥ *E3.*

CAUSEWAY BAY

$ B&B/INN Fodor's Choice ★ 🏨 **Alisan Guest House.** Some of these no-frills rooms nestled into an old apartment building in Causeway Bay have nice views of the yachts just across Gloucester Road, and all offer cleanliness, safety, and friendly hospitality at a budget price—plus each room has the convenience of an en suite washroom and shower. **Pros:** friendly, English-speaking staff; good location; free Wi-Fi. **Cons:** small rooms and windows; basic decor; surcharge to pay with credit card. [$] *Rooms from: HK$520* ✉ *Flat A, 5th fl., Hoi To Court, 275 Gloucester Rd., Causeway Bay* ☎ *2838–0762* 🌐 *www.alisanguesthouse.com* 🛏 *25 rooms* 🍴 *No meals* [M] *Causeway Bay* ✥ *H3.*

$ HOTEL 🏨 **Butterfly on Morrison.** Standard rooms are small and housed on lower floors with no views, so consider upgrading to a larger room on the upper floors where the surrounding skyline and Happy Valley Racecourse form a dramatic backdrop. **Pros:** chic contemporary-style rooms, some with decent neighborhood views. **Cons:** few in-hotel facilities. [$] *Rooms from: HK$1300* ✉ *39 Morrison Hill Rd., Causeway Bay* ☎ *3962–8333* 🌐 *www.butterflyhk.com* 🛏 *98 rooms* 🍴 *No meals* [M] *Causeway Bay* ✥ *G5.*

$$ HOTEL Fodor's Choice ★ 🏨 **J Plus Hotel by YOO.** Designer Philippe Starck's incredible ability to blend seemingly unblendable themes makes every corner an exercise in eye candy, but it isn't all style over substance: each white-swathed room is like a mini suite, full of cozy corners and splashes of color that combine old Hong Kong, Alice in Wonderland, and everyday practicalities. **Pros:** great value for money; a design geek's dream; complimentary breakfast; kitchenettes; self-laundry facilities. **Cons:** no views. [$] *Rooms from: HK$1500* ✉ *1–5 Irving St., Causeway Bay* ☎ *3196–9000* 🌐 *www.jplushongkong.com* 🛏 *56 rooms* 🍴 *Breakfast* [M] *Causeway Bay* ✥ *H4.*

$$ HOTEL 🏨 **Metropark Hotel Causeway Bay.** The views of the skyline and adjacent Victoria Park are beautiful, whether enjoyed from the simple but effectively designed modern rooms with all the basics or the pleasant

rooftop pool. **Pros:** spectacular views for less; across from Victoria Park. **Cons:** limited facilities; small lobby; few in-room amenities. $ *Rooms from: HK$1500* ✉ *148 Tung Lo Wan Rd., Causeway Bay* ☎ *2600–1000* ⊕ *www.metroparkhotel.com* ⬦ *266 rooms* ❧ *No meals* Ⓜ *Tin Hau* ✛ *H4.*

$$ 🛏 **Park Lane.** Guest rooms are as airy as the views at this elegant land-
HOTEL mark overlooking Victoria Park, with glass-topped furnishings and glass walls that accent the open outlooks over greenery, the harbor, and the skyline. **Pros:** sprawling views; close to Causeway Bay shopping; free Wi-Fi. **Cons:** often crowded; no pool; showing its age in places. $ *Rooms from: HK$2430* ✉ *310 Gloucester Rd., Causeway Bay* ☎ *2293–8888* ⊕ *www.parklane.com.hk* ⬦ *826 rooms* ❧ *Breakfast* Ⓜ *Causeway Bay* ✛ *H3.*

KOWLOON

Use the coordinates (✛ B2) at the end of each listing to locate a site on the Where to Eat and Stay in Kowloon map.

TSIM SHA TSUI

$$ 🛏 **BP International.** These small and no-frills rooms in a modern tower
HOTEL on the north side of Kowloon Park come with a bonus: views over an extensive swath of greenery or the harbor. **Pros:** coffee shop, restaurant, and lounge on premises; self-service coin laundry. **Cons:** can get crowded with business and tour groups; few amenities. $ *Rooms from: HK$1500* ✉ *8 Austin Rd., Tsim Sha Tsui* ☎ *2376–1111* ⊕ *www.bpih.com.hk* ⬦ *529 rooms* ❧ *No meals* Ⓜ *Tsim Sha Tsui* ✛ *A3.*

$ 🛏 **Hop Inn Carnarvon.** One of the city's most charming and personable
HOTEL budget locations exudes loads of character in tidy, comfortable rooms
Fodor's Choice that are well organized and individually decorated with lots of color by
★ local artists. **Pros:** fun, beautifully original decor for budget lodgings; friendly staff; ultracool common room and outside deck; private bathrooms. **Cons:** not too many amenities, but the price is right. $ *Rooms from: HK$650* ✉ *9th fl., James S. Lee Mansion, 33–35 Carnarvon Rd., Tsim Sha Tsui* ☎ *2881–7331* ⊕ *www.hopinn.hk* ⬦ *27 rooms* ❧ *No meals* Ⓜ *Tsim Sha Tsui* ✛ *C4.*

$$$ 🛏 **Hotel ICON.** Here's a stunning design statement, from the vertical
HOTEL garden hanging above the lobby café to the stylish, panoramic lounge
Fodor's Choice on the top floor—and in between are gorgeous, view-filled guest rooms
★ outfitted with cozy woods, natural fabrics, and all the high-tech amenities. **Pros:** a designer's dream; dedication to guest experience; tranquil feel with no tour groups allowed; complimentary smartphones with free mobile data. **Cons:** surrounding area is thick with crowds at times. $ *Rooms from: HK$2600* ✉ *17 Science Museum Rd., Tsim Sha Tsui* ☎ *3400–1000* ⊕ *www.hotel-icon.com* ⬦ *262 rooms* ❧ *No meals* Ⓜ *Tsim Sha Tsui East* ✛ *B6.*

$$$ 🛏 **InterContinental Hong Kong.** Its location at the tip of the Kowloon
HOTEL Peninsula ensures panoramic, front-row harbor views from most of the
Fodor's Choice contemporary rooms, designed with Asian accents that include deep,
★ sunken tubs in the marbled bathrooms. **Pros:** exceptional views; modern design; extravagant spa. **Cons:** the Avenue of Stars just outside can get

crowded during the nightly Symphony of Lights show. $ *Rooms from: HK$3000* ⊠ *18 Salisbury Rd., Tsim Sha Tsui* ☎ *2721–1211* ⊕ *www. hongkong-ic.intercontinental.com* ↪ *503 rooms* ⦿| *No meals* Ⓜ *Tsim Sha Tsui* ✛ *D4.*

$$
HOTEL
Ⓣ **The Luxe Manor.** In the absence of views, rooms are a show in themselves, with audacious design themes (gold picture frames flying across the walls) that don't sacrifice comfort and luxury. **Pros:** a trippy experience for the eyes; close proximity to more mellow nightlife and easy shopping. **Cons:** no views; lobby feels deserted at times. $ *Rooms from: HK$1800* ⊠ *39 Kimberley Rd., Tsim Sha Tsui* ☎ *3763–8888* ⊕ *www. theluxemanor.com* ↪ *159 rooms* ⦿| *No meals* Ⓜ *Tsim Sha Tsui* ✛ *B4.*

$$
HOTEL
Ⓣ **Marco Polo Hongkong Hotel.** Spacious rooms with sweeping views of Hong Kong Island are near the shopping hub along Canton Road and linked to Harbour City's immense shopping complex. **Pros:** westward views; convenient to Star Ferry and other transport. **Cons:** full in late March during the Hong Kong Rugby Sevens tournament; boisterous crowds during German Bierfest. $ *Rooms from: HK$2300* ⊠ *Harbour City, Canton Rd., Tsim Sha Tsui* ☎ *2113–0088* ⊕ *www.marcopolohotels. com* ↪ *665 rooms* ⦿| *Some meals* Ⓜ *Tsim Sha Tsui* ✛ *D2.*

$$$
HOTEL
Fodor'sChoice
★
Ⓣ **The Peninsula Hong Kong.** Even in a city with so many world-class hotels, the Peninsula manages to stand apart from the rest, an oasis of old-world glamour—opened in 1928 and the flagship for the luxury Peninsula brand—with Kowloon and harbor views that'll make you feel like you own Hong Kong. **Pros:** legendary dining and service; state-of-the-art room facilities; tons of character; extensive on-site facilities; free Wi-Fi and VOIP calls. **Cons:** rooms are pricey. $ *Rooms from: HK$4000* ⊠ *Salisbury Rd., Tsim Sha Tsui* ☎ *2920–2888* ⊕ *www.peninsula.com* ↪ *354 rooms* ⦿| *No meals* Ⓜ *Tsim Sha Tsui, Exit L3* ✛ *D3.*

WESTERN KOWLOON

$$$$
HOTEL
FAMILY
Fodor'sChoice
★
Ⓣ **The Ritz-Carlton, Hong Kong.** From the world's highest hotel, perching on the 102nd through the 118th floors of the ICC skyscraper in West Kowloon, every large and luxurious guest room enjoys a stupendous vantage point. **Pros:** earth-shattering views; top-class service and amenities. **Cons:** pricey; surrounding Kowloon area lacks nightlife. $ *Rooms from: HK$4700* ⊠ *International Commerce Center, 1 Austin Rd. W, Kowloon City* ☎ *2263–2263* ⊕ *www.ritzcarlton.com/en/ Properties/HongKong* ↪ *312 rooms* ⦿| *No meals* Ⓜ *West Kowloon, Exit C2* ✛ *A1.*

$$$
HOTEL
Fodor'sChoice
★
Ⓣ **W Hong Kong.** A hip, young vibe prevails, but guest rooms are veritable urban oases—soundproof and spacious, alternately colorful or sleek on even and odd floors, with mood lighting, surround audiovisual systems, big mirrors, and even bigger views of the harbor. **Pros:** friendly service; spacious and colorful rooms; panoramic views; exciting bars and restaurants. **Cons:** noisy atmosphere outside rooms; removed shopping-mall location. $ *Rooms from: HK$3100* ⊠ *1 Austin Rd. W, Kowloon Station, Kowloon* ☎ *3717–2222* ⊕ *www.whotels.com/hongkong* ↪ *393 rooms* ⦿| *No meals* Ⓜ *West Kowloon* ✛ *A1.*

HONG KONG'S TOP FIVE NIGHTLIFE SPOTS

dragon-i: The door's clipboard-wielding glamazons will not make entry easy, but this remains the kingpin of the big Central clubs, and second home to the city's extravagant elite.

Fatty Crab: This New York transplant has one of the hottest bars in town, with excellent cocktails, beautiful people, and old-school hip-hop on the sound system. Try the signature Pickle Backs: a shot of bourbon followed by pickle brine.

Felix: Aqua Spirit may be trendier, but Philippe Starck–designed Felix, at the Peninsula, is an institution. The best view of the skyline is marketing currency in Kowloon, and this penthouse bar really matches its claim.

Le Jardin: This no-rules watering hole is off the beaten track near the heart of LKF. Don't let the greenery and fairy lights fool you: on a good night Le Jardin can be as wild as they come.

Solas: Stronghold of Wyndham Street's after-dark action, Solas is great if you're looking for somewhere loud and lively to meet new people over well-mixed drinks.

NIGHTLIFE

A riot of neon announces Hong Kong's nightlife districts. Clubs and bars fill to capacity, evening markets pack in shoppers looking for bargains, restaurants welcome diners, cinemas pop corn as fast as they can, and theaters and concert halls prepare for full houses.

The neighborhoods of Wan Chai, Lan Kwai Fong, Sheung Wan, and SoHo are packed with bars, pubs, and nightclubs that cater to everyone from the hippest trendsetters to bankers ready to spend their bonuses and more laid-back crowds out for a pint. Partying in Hong Kong is a way of life; it starts at the beginning of the week with a drink or two after work, progressing to serious barhopping and clubbing on the weekends. Wednesday is a big night out here, too. Work hard, play harder is the motto in Hong Kong, and people follow it seriously.

HONG KONG ISLAND

WESTERN

BARS

Club 71. This bohemian diamond-in-the-rough was named in tribute to July 1, 2003, when half a million Hong Kongers successfully rallied against looming threats to their freedom of speech. Tucked away on a terrace down a side street, the quirky, unpretentious bar is a mainstay of artists, journalists, and left-wing politicians. The outdoor area closes around midnight. ⊠ *67 Hollywood Rd., Sheung Wan, Western* ☎ *2858–7071* Ⓜ *Central.*

Fodor's Choice **Missy Ho's.** The hippest spot in Kennedy Town, Missy Ho's has made
★ a name for itself as much for the swing hanging from the ceiling and dress-up closet as for its Asian-inspired cocktails. Dark but inviting,

it's the kind of place where the bartender will urge you to enjoy tequila shots on a Tuesday night. The crowd tends to be mostly young people looking to party, but all will feel welcome. A sign that Hong Kong's nightlife epicenter is moving ever westward, the bar comes into its own on weekends when it is often full to the brim with revelers. ⊠ *Sincere Western House, 48 Forbes St., Kennedy Town, Western* ☎ *2817–3808* ⊕ *www.casteloconcepts.com.*

Fodor's Choice   **Ping Pong 129.** Housed in an old table-tennis parlor, Ping Pong 129 is one of the hottest bars in up-and-coming Sai Ying Pun. The place serves gin and tonics in oversized wine goblets and features works by local artists on the walls. It offers an array of Spanish-inspired snacks. ⊠ *Nam Cheong House, 129 2nd St., Western* ☎ *9158–1584* ⊕ *www. pingpong129.com.*

GAY AND LESBIAN SPOTS

Volume Beat. A friendly, mixed crowd of gays, lesbians, and their friends enjoys this club's free admission and open-door policy. New Arrivals Wednesdays are a staple of the scene, welcoming tourists and newbies and attracting locals with free vodka between 7 and 9 pm. Weekends are reliably hyper, with dance anthems filling the floor until the wee hours. Regular events include '70s and '80s retro nights and quiz nights. ⊠ *62 Jervois St., Sheung Wan, Western* ☎ *2799–2883* Ⓜ *Sheung Wan.*

CENTRAL

On weekends the streets of Lan Kwai Fong are liberated from traffic, and the swilling hordes from both sides of the street merge into one heaving organism. Hong Kong is proud of this très chic area, a war-ren of streets stuffed with commensurately priced restaurants, bars, and late-night boutiques. Midway between Lan Kwai Fong's madness and SoHo's bohemian glamour is Wyndham Street, home to an array of sophisticated bars, nightclubs, and restaurants and strict domain of the over 25s.

BARS

Fatty Crab. This New York transplant has become a Hong Kong hot spot because of its great cocktails and old-school hip-hop on the stereo. Snack on a pork belly bao as you mingle among the beautiful people. Fatty Crab is credited with bringing pickle-back bourbon—with a shot of pickle brine—to Hong Kong. Make sure you say hi to the own-er's dog, Bear. ⊠ *1113 Old Bailey St., Central* ☎ *2521–2033* ⊕ *www. fattycrab.com.hk* Ⓜ *Central.*

Fodor's Choice   **Globe.** In a trendy SoHo space, this British-expat hangout evokes the feel of southwest London. The owner is a beer fanatic, and the place boasts one of the best selections in Hong Kong. It's a fun and convivial spot with a mix of ages and a pretty even split between expats and locals. You can book the sectioned-off "chill-out" area to watch live sports coverage with a group of friends. Good luck trying to get the proprietors to turn on the World Series or the Super Bowl, though. Soccer and rugby reign supreme here, and you'll have to share the TV. ⊠ *45–53 Graham St., SoHo, Central* ☎ *2543–1941* ⊕ *www.theglobe.com.hk* Ⓜ *Central.*

Le Jardin. The leafy setting belies the down-and-dirty vibe at this casual bar with a terrace overlooking the colorful dining strip known locally as "Rat Alley." This refreshingly low-key bar is a little tricky to find: walk through the dining area and up a flight of steps. The place is packed on weekends. ✉ *10 Wing Wah La., Lan Kwai Fong, Central* ☎ *2877–1100* Ⓜ *Central.*

Lux. Decorated in a lush shade of red, this two-story establishment boasts a busy street-level bar with windows overlooking the crowds in Lan Kwai Fong. The daily happy hour is popular with the after-work crowd. Head upstairs and you'll find modern European fare, with signature dishes including roasted lobster spaghetti. ✉ *The Plaza, 21 D'Aguilar St., Lan Kwai Fong, Central* ☎ *2868–9538* ⊕ *www.luxhongkong.com* Ⓜ *Central.*

MO Bar. A destination for Hong Kong's big spenders, this plush bar in the Landmark Mandarin Oriental appeals to a more civilized crowd. You'll pay top dollar for the signature drinks (up to HK$200), but the striking, sleek, and supermodern interior makes it almost worthwhile. The ground-floor location means the best views will be of the other well-heeled patrons but that's ok, this is a place to be seen as much as see. ✉ *Landmark Mandarin Oriental, 15 Queen's Rd., Central* ☎ *2132–0077* ⊕ *www.mandarinoriental.com/landmark/fine-dining/mo-bar* Ⓜ *Central.*

RED Bar. Although its shopping mall location, self-service policy, and incongruous affiliation with the next-door gym may not seem appealing, once you arrive, you'll throw all your preconceived notions into the harbor. On the roof of IFC Mall, RED's outdoor terrace has breathtaking views of the city, making it a relaxing place for watching the sunset. The entire rooftop seating area is public space—a rarity in Hong Kong—so do what the locals do: buy your drinks from the CitySuper downstairs and enjoy one of the best views in the city on the cheap. ✉ *4th fl., Two IFC, 8 Finance St., Central* ☎ *8129–8882* ⊕ *www.pure-red.com* Ⓜ *Hong Kong.*

Fodor's Choice ★ **Solas.** Positioned a floor below the dance club dragon-i, this always-crowded bar is Wyndham Street's party central. Expect a mostly expat crowd of twenty- and thirtysomethings who come straight from work in their business suits. With good music—everything from electronic dance music to Katy Perry—and a well-lubricated crowd, Solas is a great place to cut loose. The interior is dark and extremely basic, but the party routinely spills into the street out front. ✉ *60 Wyndham St., SoHo, Central* ☎ *3162–3710* ⊕ *www.solas.com.hk* Ⓜ *Central.*

Staunton's Wine Bar & Cafe. Adjacent to Hong Kong's famous outdoor escalator is this popular bistro-style café and bar. As the weekend aproaches the place gets crowded, but it's still the perfect place to people-watch from the balcony. You can come for a drink at night or coffee during the day. It's also a Sunday-morning favorite for nursing hangovers over brunch. ✉ *10–12 Staunton St., SoHo, Central* ☎ *2973–6611* ⊕ *www.stauntonsgroup.com* Ⓜ *Central.*

DISCOS AND NIGHTCLUBS

Azure. Head skyward to this cosmopolitan club at the top of the Hotel LKF. The downstairs lounge features pool tables, comfy couches, and a sound track of ambient tunes. Upstairs, you can take in the harbor from the smoking terrace or dance to funky house music inside. Don't miss the excellent espresso martinis. ⊠ *29th fl., Hotel LKF, 33 Wyndham St., Central* ☎ *3518–9330* ⊕ *www.azure.hk* Ⓜ *Central.*

dragon-i. Around for more than a decade, dragon-i has lost none of its popularity, which is rare for a nightclub in Hong Kong. Have a drink on the deck or step inside the vivid red playroom, which doubles as a Chinese restaurant earlier in the day. It's the domain of the city's young, rich, and beautiful (if not necessarily classy) crowd, and attracts a busy roster of international acts and DJs. ⊠ *The Centrium, 60 Wyndham St., Central* ☎ *3110–1222* ⊕ *www.dragon-i.com.hk* Ⓜ *Central.*

Drop. This pint-size gem is *the* after-hours party spot in Central. Hidden down an alley beside a late-night food stand, its obscure location only adds to the speakeasy feel. Drop gets crowded on weekends and it can be hard to get inside, so it's best to arrive early and wait for the party to pop off. ⊠ *Basement level, On Lok Mansion, 39–43 Hollywood Rd., Central* ☎ *2543–8856* ⊕ *www.drophk.com* Ⓜ *Central.*

Oma. The owner is good friends with the people behind the now-shuttered Midnight & Co., so expect the same great electronic dance music, international DJs alongside local talent, and parties that go all night. The space is a bit of a dank hole, but thanks to the top-of-the-line sound system and strong drinks, nobody seems to notice or care. ⊠ *Basement level, Harilela House, 79 Wyndham St., Central* ☎ *2521–8815* Ⓜ *Central.*

GAY AND LESBIAN SPOTS

Propaganda. Off a quaint cobblestone street is a popular gay nightclub with an Art Deco bar area that hosts quite the flirt fest. The sunken dance floor has poles on either side for go-go boys. The place is pretty empty during the week, and on weekends the crowds arrive well after midnight. The entrance is in an alleyway called Ezra Lane, which runs parallel to Hollywood Road. ⊠ *Basement level, 1 Hollywood Rd., Central* ☎ *2868–1316* Ⓜ *Central.*

WAN CHAI

Wan Chai is the pungent night flower of the nocturnal scene, where the way of life served as inspiration for the novel *The World of Suzie Wong.* It now shares the streets with hip wine bars, salsa nights, old men's pubs, and after-parties that continue past sunrise. The seedy "hostess bars" in this neighborhood are easy to spot and avoid, with curtained entrances guarded by old ladies on stools and suggestive names in neon. But some things never change: the busiest nights are still when there's a navy ship in the harbor on an R&R stopover. Wednesday's ladies' night, with half-price drinks, is also a big draw.

BARS

Carnegie's. Named after Scottish steel baron Andrew Carnegie, whose family sailed to America in the late 1800s, this rock-and-roll bar lives up to its name. Although Carnegie himself probably didn't imagine bartop dancing at an establishment bearing his name, the Scottish owners feel that his love of music lives on in this pub. Avoid Wednesday nights, when the place is wall-to-wall teenagers in search of cheap drinks. ⊠ *53–55 Lockhart Rd., Wan Chai* ☎ *2866–6289* ⊕ *www.carnegies.net/ hongkong/* Ⓜ *Wan Chai.*

Lan Kwai Fong is Hong Kong's famous bar and dining district.

Mes Amis. In the heart of Wan Chai, this high-ceilinged bar has bifold doors that open onto the busy street corner, meaning that you won't miss any of the action outside. The perpetual crowd inside is on display to passersby outside. ✉ *83–85 Lockhart Rd., Wan Chai* ☎ *2527–6680* ⊕ *www.mesamis.com.hk* Ⓜ *Wan Chai.*

Rio. A nice alternative to the dives of Wan Chai, sophisticated Rio has a plush bar with low-key live music and a dance club complete with a light-up floor. On weekends the party runs until very late. ✉ *Hang Shun Mansion, 68–82 Jaffe Rd., Wan Chai* ⊕ *www.rioclub.hk* Ⓜ *Wan Chai.*

DISCOS AND NIGHTCLUBS
Joe Bananas. The days of all-night partying are gone: Joe Bananas has reopened as a gentler version of the boisterous place it used to be. There's almost always a live band, and the doors stay open until the wee hours. The handsome space is considered a Hong Kong landmark, and is still worth a visit. ✉ *23 Luard Rd., Wan Chai* ☎ *2537–4618* ⊕ *www. joebananas.hk* Ⓜ *Wan Chai.*

KOWLOON

Central and Wan Chai are undoubtedly the king and queen of nightlife in Hong Kong. If you're staying in a hotel, however, or having dinner across the water in Kowloon, Ashley Road and Knutsford Terrace still make for a fun night out.

BARS

Fodor's Choice ★ **Aqua Spirit.** Inside an impressive curvaceous skyscraper, this very cool bar sits on the mezzanine level of the top floor. The high ceilings and glass walls offer up unrivaled views of Hong Kong and the surrounding harbor filled with ferries and ships. Tables are placed in front of the windows so you never have to crane your neck to see the skyline. ⊠ *30th fl., One Peking, 1 Peking Rd., Tsim Sha Tsui* ☎ *3427–2288* ⊕ *www. aqua.com.hk* Ⓜ *Tsim Sha Tsui.*

Delaney's. This Irish pub has interiors that were shipped here from the Emerald Isle, and the mood is as authentic as the furnishings. Guinness and Delaney's ale (a specialty microbrew) are on tap, and there's a traditional Irish menu. The crowd includes some Irish regulars, so get ready for spontaneous outbursts of fiddling and other Celtic traditions. ⊠ *Basement fl., 71–77 Peking Rd., Tsim Sha Tsui* ☎ *2301–3980* ⊕ *www.delaneys.com.hk* Ⓜ *Tsim Sha Tsui.*

Fodor's Choice ★ **Felix.** High up in the Peninsula Hong Kong, this bar is immensely popular with visitors. It not only has a brilliant view of the island, but the dramatic interiors are by the visionary designer Philippe Starck. Another memorable feature: the men's room also has windows with great city views. If you feel like dancing, head to the dramatic Crazy Box, which has padded walls and illuminated tables. ⊠ *28th fl., Peninsula Hong Kong, Salisbury Rd., Tsim Sha Tsui* ☎ *2696–6778* ⊕ *hongkong.peninsula.com* Ⓜ *Tsim Sha Tsui.*

ARTFUL DATES

Hong Kong Arts Festival. Held each year in February and March, the Hong Kong Arts Festival's past visitors have included Mikhail Baryshnikov, Pina Bausch, and José Carreras. The focus is on performing arts. ⊕ *www. hk.artsfestival.org.*

Hong Kong International Film Festival. Asian cinema accounts for many of the 280-plus new films shown at this festival, which includes citywide exhibitions and parties in March and April. ⊕ *www.hkiff.org.hk.*

SHOPPING

It's true that the days when everything in Hong Kong was mind-bogglingly cheap are over. It *is* still a tax-free port, so you can get some good deals. But it isn't just about the savings. Sharp contrasts and the sheer variety of experiences available make shopping here very different from back home.

You might find a bargain or two elbowing your way through a chaotic open-air market filled with haggling vendors selling designer knockoffs, the air reeking of the *chou tofu* ("stinky" tofu) bubbling at a nearby food stand. But then you could find a designer number going for half the usual price in a hushed marble-floor mall, the air scented by the designer fragrances of your fellow shoppers. What's more, in Hong Kong the two extremes are often within spitting distance of each other.

HONG KONG ISLAND

WESTERN

ANTIQUES AND COLLECTIBLES

Yue Po Chai Antique Co. One of Hollywood Road's oldest shops is at the Cat Street end, next to Man Mo Temple. Its vast and varied stock includes porcelain, stone carvings, and ceramics. ⊠ *Ground fl., 132–136 Hollywood Rd., Sheung Wan, Western* ☎ *2540–4374* ⊙ *Closed Sun.* Ⓜ *Sheung Wan, Exit A2.*

ART GALLERIES

Asia Art Archive. The AAA saw it before the rest of us: contemporary Asian art is big. In 2000 the Asian Art Archive set out to address the lack of information on the emerging field and to record its growth. It provides comprehensive research resources through its website, library, and reading facilities, which are open to the public. ⊠ *11th fl., Hollywood Centre, 233 Hollywood Rd., Sheung Wan, Western* ☎ *2815–1112* ⊕ *www.aaa.org.hk* ⊙ *Closed Sun.* Ⓜ *Sheung Wan.*

Gaffer Ltd. The city's first gallery specializing in studio glass—which is gaining respect in the collecting world—has moved to the Western District and broadened its focus. The two-level gallery still hosts a backdrop of modern glass sculptures by artists from Southeast Asia, Australia, and the United States, but also showcases a variety of paintings from primarily Chinese-Australian artists. Expect everything from watercolor to abstract, pop art to traditional oil. ⊠ *Ground fl., 13 Western St., Sai Ying Pun, Western* ☎ *2521–1770* ⊕ *gaffer.com.hk* Ⓜ *Sheung Wan.*

Hanlin Gallery. For Japanese works of art, antiques, modern ceramics, and woodblocks, visit this refined gallery run by specialist Carlos Prata since 1986. His collection and expertise extend to decorative Chinese art, including fans, textiles, and silver. ⊠ *Ground fl., 185 Hollywood Rd., Sheung Wan, Western* ☎ *2522–4479* ⊕ *www.hanlingallery.com* ⊙ *Closed Sun.* Ⓜ *Sheung Wan, Exit A2.*

CLOTHING

Lee Kung Man Knitting Factory. This hole-in-the-wall shop has a surprisingly long history: it dates back to the early 1920s in Guangzhou, where the brand got its start before moving to Hong Kong. Lee Kung Man uses 1950's-era machines to make simple cotton tees and tanks, but the underwear is what brings shoppers flocking in. Despite a loyal hipster following, the store has kept prices relatively affordable, running between about HK\$80 and HK\$300 per top. Look for the signature cicada logo or the prancing deer at one of the four shops around town. ⊠ *111 Wing Lok St., Sheung Wan, Western* ☎ *2543–8579* ⊕ *leekungman.com* Ⓜ *Sheung Wan, Exit A2.*

Vivienne Tam. You know it when you walk into a Vivienne Tam boutique—the strong Chinese-motif prints and modern updates of

> ## WHY PAY RETAIL?
>
> As Central becomes Sheung Wan, a little lane called Wing Kut Street (between Queen's Road Central and Des Voeux Road) is home to costume-jewelry showrooms and wholesalers, many of whom accept retail customers and offer bargain-basement prices.

6

traditional women's clothing are truly distinct. But don't let the bold, ready-to-wear collections distract you from the very pretty accessories, which include leather bags and other items with Asian embellishments. Tam, who has seven shops here, is one of the best-known designers in Hong Kong—and, even though she's now based in New York, the city still claims her as its own. ⊠ *Shop SG03, PMQ, 35 Aberdeen St., Sheung Wan, Western* ☎ *2721–1818* ⊕ *www.viviennetam.com* Ⓜ *Central, Exit D2.*

JEWELRY AND ACCESSORIES

Chocolate Rain. The collections—dreamed up by a Hong Kong fine arts graduate—consist of pieces handcrafted from recycled materials, such as fabrics, bottle lids, paint buckets, and other funky finds. Head here for one-of-a-kind bags, unique iPhone cases, and jewelry, as well as an ever-changing array of works by the designer's friends. ⊠ *1st fl., Block A, PMQ, 35 Aberdeen St., Sheung Wan, Western* ☎ *2599–0017* ⊕ *www. chocolaterain.com* Ⓜ *Central, Exit D2.*

MARKETS

Western Market. This redbrick Edwardian-style building in the Sheung Wan District is a declared monument and the oldest existing market building in Hong Kong; when built in 1906 it was used as a produce market. These days, its classical facades are filled with kitschy commerce, with a few unmemorable shops selling crafts, toys, jewelry, and collectibles on the ground floor. Skip these and head up the escalator, where you'll find a remarkable selection of fabric: satins, silks, sequins are all here and worth a look. A more authentic experience is lunch, dinner, or high tea in the Grand Stage Ballroom Restaurant on the top floor. After a great Chinese meal you can while away the afternoon with the old-timers trotting around the room to a live band belting out the cha-cha and tango. The restaurant is also a popular spot for weddings and receptions. Visit in the evening and you're likely to snap up cashmere and chiffon while a violin sings overhead. ⊠ *323 Des Voeux Rd., Sheung Wan, Western* ☎ *6029–2675* ⊕ *www.westernmarket.com. hk* Ⓜ *Sheung Wan.*

SHOES, HANDBAGS, AND LEATHER GOODS

Fodor's Choice ★ **Select 18 and Mido Eyeglasses.** Across from the sprawling Oolaa restaurant, two of Hong Kong's best vintage hangouts are in one convenient store. Select 18 has everything from typewriters to 1970s Hermès blouses. If you can tear yourself from the heaps of jewelry and handbags, a treasure trove awaits. Tucked in back, you'll find literally thousands of retro-styled specs from Mido Eyeglasses, priced from a couple of hundred to several thousand Hong Kong dollars. The big question: tortoise-shell cat eyes or classic wayfarers? ⊠ *18 Bridges St., Sheung Wan, Western* ☎ *2858–8803* Ⓜ *Sheung Wan, Exit A2.*

Fodor's Choice ★ **Squarestreet.** You might stumble upon this local gem while wandering around Sheung Wan's evolving Po Hing Fong neighborhood. The low-key workshop and boutique features slick Scandinavian watches, shoes, luggage, and lots of handmade leather bags from Swedish designers David Ericsson and Alexis Holm. ⊠ *15 Square St., Sheung Wan, Western* ☎ *2362–1086* ⊕ *www.squarestreet.se* Ⓜ *Sheung Wan, Exit A2.*

CENTRAL
ANTIQUES AND COLLECTIBLES

Altfield Gallery. If only your entire home could be outfitted by Altfield. Established in 1980, the elegant gallery carries exquisite antique Chinese furniture, Asia-related maps and topographical prints, Southeast Asian sculpture, and decorative arts from around Asia, including silver

and rugs. Altfied Interiors, on nearby Queen's Road, features a selection of larger furniture pieces, framed art, and contemporary home accessories. ✉ *2nd fl., Shop 248-249, Prince's Bldg., 10 Chater Rd., Central* ☎ *2537–6370* ⊕ *www.altfield.com.hk* Ⓜ *Central.*

Chine Gallery. Dealing in antique furniture, artifacts, and rugs from China, this dark, stylish gallery has been around since the 1980s. It has a solid reputation among international dealers and collectors, thanks in part to its expert in-house art consultants who can help navigate the extensive collections. The company also offers a "Treasure Hunting" sourcing service to help find unique items, plus repair and maintenance services. ✉ *42A Hollywood Rd., Central* ☎ *2543–0023* ⊕ *www. chinegallery.com* Ⓜ *Central.*

Teresa Coleman Fine Arts Ltd. Specialist Teresa Coleman sells embroidered costumes from the imperial court, antique textiles, painted and carved fans, lacquered boxes, and engravings and prints in her centrally located gallery. She has a streetside shop at the same address for walk-ins, but this space is appointment only. ✉ *Ground fl., 55 Wyndham St., Central* ☎ *2526–2450* ⊕ *www.teresacoleman.com* Ⓜ *Central, Exit D2.*

ART GALLERIES

Grotto Fine Art. Director and chief curator Henry Au-yeung writes about, curates, and gives lectures on 20th-century Chinese art. His tucked-away gallery focuses exclusively on local Chinese artists, with an interest in the newest and most avant-garde works. Look for paintings, sculptures, prints, photography, mixed-media pieces, and conceptual installations. ✉ *2nd fl., 31C–D Wyndham St., Central* ☎ *2121–2270* ⊕ *www.grottofineart.com* Ⓜ *Central, Exit G.*

Hanart TZ Gallery. This is a rare opportunity to compare and contrast cutting-edge and experimental art from mainland China, Taiwan, and Hong Kong selected by one of the field's most respected authorities. Unassuming curatorial director Johnson Chang Tsong-zung also cofounded the Asia Art Archive and has curated exhibitions at the São Paolo and Venice biennials. ✉ *4th fl., Room 401, Pedder Bldg., 12 Pedder St., Central* ☎ *2526–9019* ⊕ *www.hanart.com* Ⓜ *Central, Exit D1.*

CLOTHING

A-Man Hing Cheong Co., Ltd. People often gasp at the very mention of A-Man Hing Cheong, in the Mandarin Oriental Hotel. For some it symbolizes the ultimate in fine tailoring, with a reputation that extends back to its founding in 1898. For others it's the lofty prices that elicit a reaction. Regardless, this is a trustworthy source of European-cut suits,

6

custom shirts, and excellent service. ✉ *Mezzanine, Mandarin Oriental, 5 Connaught Rd., Central* ☎ *2522–3336* Ⓜ *Central, Exit H.*

Ascot Chang. This self-titled "gentleman's shirtmaker" makes it easy to find the perfect shirt, even if you could get a better deal in a less prominent shop. Ascot Chang has upheld exacting Shanghainese tailoring traditions in Hong Kong since 1953, and now has stores in New York, Beverly Hills, Manila, and Shanghai. The focus here is on the fit and details, from 22 stitches per inch to collar linings crafted to maintain their shape. Among the countless fabrics, Italian 330s three-ply Egyptian cotton by David & John Anderson is one of the most coveted and expensive. Like many shirtmakers, Ascot Chang does pajamas, robes, boxer shorts, and women's blouses, too. It also has ready-made lines of shirts, T-shirts, neckties, and other accessories available for online ordering. Other branches are located in the IFC Mall, Elements Mall, and the Peninsula Hotel. ✉ *Shop 131, Prince's Bldg., 10 Chater Rd., Central* ☎ *2523–3663* ⊕ *www.ascotchang.com* Ⓜ *Central, Exit H.*

Barney Cheng. One of Hong Kong's best-known local designers, Barney Cheng creates haute-couture designs and prêt-à-porter collections with wit and elegance. When the Kennedy Center in Washington, D.C., hosted an exhibition titled "The New China Chic," Cheng was invited to display his works alongside those by the likes of Vera Wang and Anna Sui. His more recent pieces have drifted toward simplicity, with sophisticated cuts and exotic prints, such as alligator jackets and skirts. Cheng has made many a bride's dream dress, and his masterfully tailored evening gowns range from HK$40,000 to HK$100,000, depending on style, detailing, and fabric. Consultations are available by appointment only. ✉ *12th fl., World Wide Commercial Bldg., 34 Wyndham St., Central* ☎ *2530–2829* ⊕ *www.barneycheng.com* ⊙ *Closed Sun.* Ⓜ *Central, Exit D2.*

Blanc de Chine. Relying on word of mouth, Blanc de Chine has catered to high society and celebrities, such as actor Jackie Chan, for years. The small, refined tailoring shop neatly displays exquisite fabrics from Switzerland and Japan, lovely ready-made women's wear, menswear, and home accessories. Items here are extravagances, but they're worth every penny. ✉ *Shop 123, Prince's Bldg., 10 Chater Rd., Central* ☎ *2104–7934* ⊕ *www.blancdechine.com* Ⓜ *Central, Exit K.*

Episode. Locally owned and designed Episode collections focus on accessories and elegant clothing for working women and Hong Kong "tai tais" (a.k.a ladies who lunch). Look also for the younger, trendier Jessica collection. Though distinct, both collections pay close attention to current trends in the fashion world. Episode has a second store in Harbour City. ✉ *22nd fl., Entertainment Bldg., 30 Queen's Rd. Central, Central* ☎ *2921–2010* ⊕ *www.episode-intl.com* Ⓜ *Central, Exit D2.*

Fang Fong Projects. Fang Fong fell in love with the vintage feel of the SoHo District as a design graduate and vowed to move in. She chose a light-filled studio space to display her floaty, 1970s-inspired clothing line, with its bold prints and sexy wisps of lace and silk. She also brought her friends with her, or at least those who suited her vibe. Head here for Japanese kimono-inspired belts and for bags by U.K. brand

Dialog, which works with scrap fabric from fair trade sources. ⊠ *Shop 1, 69A Peel St., SoHo, Central* ☎ *3105–5557* Ⓜ *Sheung Wan, Exit E2.*

Hulu 10. Tucked away on historic Glenealy—center of British Hong Kong—Hulu 10 takes traditional Chinese textiles for a contemporary spin. Encased by a beautiful white brick building, the store is warm and welcoming, with dark wood floors and open space. Designed and produced locally, the garments have a throwback vibe, inspired by '60s fashion and iconic artifacts like Xian's Terracotta Warriors. Find classic Chinese tunics and silk scarves alongside more modern-looking dresses for the ladies, as well as a leaner selection of children's and menswear. ■ TIP→ **This quaint little street snakes above Lower Albert Road and can be tricky to find at first. Start from the Fringe Club at Wyndham's five-way intersection and head uphill.** ⊠ *Ground fl., 10 Glenealy, Central* ☎ *2179–5500* ⊕ *www.hulu10.com* ☉ *Closed Sun.* Ⓜ *Central, Exit D1.*

Joyce. Local socialites and couture addicts still thank Joyce Ma, the fairy godmother of luxury retail in Hong Kong, for bringing must-have labels to the city. Others may be catching up, but her Joyce boutiques are still ultrachic havens outfitted with a Vogue-worthy wish list of designers and beauty brands. Not so much a shop as a fashion institution, hushed Joyce houses the worship-worthy creations of fashion's greatest gods and goddesses. McCartney, McQueen, Oscar de la Renta: the stock list is practically a mantra. Joyce sells unique household items, too, so your home can live up to your wardrobe. The flagship store is in New World Tower. ⊠ *New World Tower, 16 Queen's Rd. Central, Central* ☎ *2810–1120* ⊕ *www.joyce.com* Ⓜ *Central, Exit G.*

Fodor'sChoice ★ **Moustache.** Brainchild of Alex Daye and Ellis Kreuger, Moustache is perched atop steep Aberdeen Street on the edge of SoHo. Find reasonably priced lightweight men's cotton shirts, Bermuda shorts, and unique finds from the owners' jaunts around Asia. The ready-to-wear garments are housed in a cozy and charismatic shop that's outfitted with an eclectic mix of maritime accents and vintage curiosities from '70s Hong Kong. You can also order locally made tailored suits and bespoke denim, but expect several weeks of production time. ⊠ *31 Aberdeen St., SoHo, Central* ☎ *2541–1955* ⊕ *www.moustachehongkong.com* Ⓜ *Sheung Wan, Exit E2.*

Fodor'sChoice ★ **Shanghai Tang.** Make your way past the perfumes, scarves, and silk-embroidered Chinese souvenirs to the second floor, where you'll find a rainbow of fabrics at your fingertips. In addition to the brilliantly hued—and expensive—silk and cashmere clothing, you'll see custom-made suits starting at around HK$30,000, including fabric. You can also have a cheongsam (a sexy slit-skirt silk dress with a Mandarin collar) made for around HK$10,000, including fabric. Ready-to-wear Mandarin suits are in the HK$15,000–HK$20,000 range. There are stores scattered across Hong Kong, including the airport's Terminal One. ⊠ *Ground–3rd fl., 1 Duddell St., Central* ☎ *2525–7333* ⊕ *www. shanghaitang.com* Ⓜ *Central, Exit D2.*

W. W. Chan & Sons Tailors Ltd. Chan is known for excellent-quality suits and shirts in classic cuts and has an array of fine European fabrics. It's comforting to know that you'll be measured and fitted by the same master tailor from start to finish. The store features a mirrored, hexagonal changing room so you can check every angle. Tailors from here travel to the United States several times a year to fill orders for their customers; if you have a suit made and leave your address, they'll let you know when they plan to visit. ⊠ *Unit B, 8th fl., Entertainment Bldg., 30 Queen's Rd. Central, Central* ☎ *2366–9738* ⊕ *www.wwchan.com* Ⓜ *Central, Exit D2.*

GIFTS AND SOUVENIRS

Mountain Folkcraft. A little old-fashioned bell chimes as you open the door to this fantastic shop filled with handicrafts and antiques from around China. Amid the old treasures, carved woodwork, rugs, and curios, are stunning folk-print fabrics. ■ TIP➜ **To reach the store from Queen's Road Central, walk up D'Aguilar Street toward Lan Kwai Fong, then turn right onto Wo On Lane.** ⊠ *Ground fl., 12 Wo On La., Central* ☎ *2523–2817* ⊕ *www.mountainfolkcraft.com* Ⓜ *Central, Exit D1.*

Tittot. This Taiwanese brand has taken modern Chinese glass art global. Glass works here are made using the laborious lost-wax casting technique, employed by artists for centuries to create a bronze replica of an original wax or clay sculpture. The collection—which includes tableware, paperweights, glass Buddhas, and jewelry—can be purchased in Lane Crawford department stores. ⊠ *Lane Crawford, IFC Mall, 8 Finance St., Central* ☎ *2118-3638* ⊕ *www.tittot.com* Ⓜ *Hong Kong, Exit A1.*

JEWELRY AND ACCESSORIES

Edward Chiu. Everything about Edward Chiu is *fabulous,* from the flamboyant way he dresses to his high-end jade jewelry. The minimalist, geometric pieces use the entire jade spectrum, from deep greens to surprising lavenders. Inspired in part by Art Deco, Chiu is also famous for contrasting black-and-white jade, setting it in precious metals, and adding diamond or pearl touches. ⊠ *Shop 2023, IFC Mall, 8 Finance St., Central* ☎ *2525–2618* ⊕ *www.edwardchiu.com* Ⓜ *Hong Kong, Exit F.*

Kai-Yin Lo. Famous for her Asian-inspired jewelry, Kai-Yin Lo combines contemporary style with ancient Chinese designs and materials such as semiprecious stones and jade. The *International Herald Tribune* has credited her with bridging the gap between fine and fashion jewelry. Sales are by appointment only. ⊠ *Block 2, Unit 3, 55 Garden Rd., Central* ☎ *2773–6009* ⊕ *www.kaiyinlo-design.com* Ⓜ *Admiralty, Exit B.*

Qeelin. With ancient Chinese culture for inspiration and *In the Mood for Love* actress Maggie Cheung as the muse, something extraordinary was bound to come from Qeelin. Its name was cleverly derived from the Chinese characters for male ("qi") and female ("lin"), and symbolizes harmony, balance, and peace. The restrained beauty and meaningful creations of designer Dennis Chan are exemplified in two main collections: Wulu, a minimalist form representing the mythical gourd as well as the lucky number eight; and Tien Di, literally "Heaven and Earth," symbolizing everlasting love. Classic gold, platinum, and diamonds mix with colored jades, black diamonds, and unusual materials for a truly unique effect. A sweeter addendum to the collection was added in the form of Bo Bo, the panda bear. The IFC Mall store is one of seven in

Hong Kong. ✉ *Shop 2059, IFC Mall, 8 Finance St., Central* ☎ *2389–8863* ⊕ *hk.qeelin.com* Ⓜ *Hong Kong, Exit F.*

Ronald Abram. Looking at the rocks in these windows can feel like a visit to a natural history museum. Large white- and rare-color diamonds sourced from all over the world are a specialty here, but the shop also deals in emeralds, sapphires, and rubies. With years of expertise, Abrams dispenses advice on both the aesthetic merits and the investment potential of each stone or piece of jewelry. ✉ *Mezzanine, Mandarin Oriental, 5 Connaught Rd., Central* ☎ *2525–1234* ⊕ *www. ronaldabram.com* Ⓜ *Central, Exit K.*

Tayma Fine Jewellery. Unusual colored "connoisseur" gemstones are set by hand in custom designs by Hong Kong–based jeweler Tayma Page Allies. The collection is designed to bring out the personality of the individual wearer, and includes oversize cocktail rings, distinctive bracelets, pretty earrings, and more. ✉ *Shop 225, 2nd fl., Prince's Bldg., 10 Chater Rd., Central* ☎ *2525–5280* ⊕ *www.taymajewellery.com* Ⓜ *Central, Exit K.*

MALLS AND SHOPPING CENTERS

Fodor's Choice ★

IFC Mall. A quick glance at the directory—Tiffany & Co., Kate Spade, Prada, Gieves & Hawkes—lets you know that the International Finance Centre isn't for the faint of pocket. Designer department store Lane Crawford chose to open its flagship store here, and J.Crew followed suit in 2014. Even the mall's cinema multiplex is special: the deluxe theaters have super-comfy seats with extra legroom and blankets for those chilled by the air-conditioning. If you finish your spending spree at sunset, go for a cocktail at RED or Isola, two posh rooftop bars with fabulous harbor views. The Hong Kong Airport Express station (with in-town check-in service) is under the mall, and the Four Seasons Hotel connects to it. ■TIP→ **Avoid the mall between 12:30 and 2, when it's flooded with lunching office workers from the two IFC towers.** ✉ *8 Finance St., Central* ☎ *2295–3308, 2295–3308 Hotline* ⊕ *www.ifc. com.hk* Ⓜ *Hong Kong, Exit F.*

SHOES, HANDBAGS, AND LEATHER GOODS

Kow Hoo Shoe Company. If you like shoes made the old-fashioned way, then Kow Hoo—one of Hong Kong's oldest, circa 1946—is for you. It also does great cowboy boots (there's nothing like knee-high calfskin!). Just be sure to make an appointment before you go. ✉ *2nd fl., Prince's Bldg., 10 Chater Rd., Central* ☎ *2523–0489* ⊕ *kowhoo.com. hk* ⊘ *Closed Sun.* Ⓜ *Central, Exit H.*

Kwanpen. Renowned for its crocodile bags and shoes, Kwanpen has acted as a manufacturer for famous brands since 1938, as well as being a stand-alone retailer. In addition to Pacific Place, it has stores in the 1881 Heritage arcade, IFC Mall, and World Trade Centre. ✉ *Shop 310, Pacific Place, 88 Queensway, Admirality, Central* ☎ *2918–9199* ⊕ *www.kwanpen.com* Ⓜ *Admiralty, Exit F.*

Lianca. This is one of those unique places that make you want to buy something even if there's nothing you need. Lianca, first and foremost a manufacturer, sells well-made leather bags, wallets, frames, key chains, and home accessories in timeless, simple designs. It's an unbranded way

6

to be stylish. ⊠ *Basement fl., 27 Staunton St., entrance on Graham St., SoHo, Central* ☎ *2139–2989* ⊕ *www.liancacentral.com* Ⓜ *Central, Exit D2.*

LIII LIII Shoes. The Chan Brothers have an illustrious history in Hong Kong and have certainly left a trail of satisfied customers in their wake; however, reviews these days speak of hit-and-miss experiences there. Prices have also shot up over the last few years (from around HK$1,500 for sandals and HK$2,300 for high heels). Still, when they are good, they are very, very good. ⊠ *1st fl., Tower 2, Shop 75, Admiralty Centre, 18 Harcourt Rd., Central* ☎ *2865–3989* Ⓜ *Admiralty, Exit A.*

Mayer Shoes. Since the 1960s, Mayer has been making excellent custom-order shoes and accessories in leather, lizard, crocodile, and ostrich. Go to them for the classic pieces for which they became famous rather than this season's "it" bag. Prices for ladies shoes start at several hundred U.S. dollars and peak at roughly US$2,000. ⊠ *Mandarin Oriental, 5 Connaught Rd., Central* ☎ *2524–3317* Ⓜ *Central, Exit K.*

WAN CHAI, CAUSEWAY BAY, AND BEYOND

CAMERAS AND ELECTRONICS

Broadway. Like its more famous competitor, Fortress, Broadway is a large electronic-goods chain. It caters primarily to the local market, so some staff members speak better English than others. Look for familiar name-brand cameras, computers, sound systems, home appliances, and mobile phones. ⊠ *7th–9th fl., Times Square, 1 Matheson St., Causeway Bay* ☎ *2506–0228* ⊕ *www.ibroadway.com.hk* Ⓜ *Causeway Bay, Exit A.*

Fodor's Choice ★ **Fortress.** Part of billionaire Li Ka-shing's empire, this extensive chain of shops sells electronics with warranties—a safety precaution that draws the crowds. It also has good deals on printers and accessories, although selection varies by shop. You can spot a Fortress by looking for the big orange sign. For the full list of outlets, visit the website. ⊠ *Times Square, Shop 719–721, 7th and 8th fl., 1 Matheson St., Causeway Bay* ☎ *2506–0031* ⊕ *www.fortress.com.hk* Ⓜ *Causeway Bay, Exit A.*

DG Lifestyle Store. An appointed Apple Center, the DG chain carries Mac and iPod products. High-design gadgets, accessories, and software by other brands are add-ons that meld with the sleek Apple design philosophy. ⊠ *Shop 903, 9th fl., Times Square, 1 Matheson St., Causeway Bay* ☎ *2506–1338* ⊕ *www.dg-lifestyle.com* Ⓜ *Causeway Bay, Exit A.*

Wanchai Computer Centre. You can find bargains on computer goods and accessories in the labyrinth of shops spanning several floors. It's not as easy to negotiate prices here as it once was, but there are technicians who can help you put together a computer in less than a day if you're rushed; otherwise, two days is normal. The starting price is around HK$3,000 depending on the hardware, processor, and peripherals you choose. This is a great resource, whether you're a techno-buff who's interested in assembling your own computer (a popular pastime with locals), or a technophobe looking for quality earphones. ⊠ *130 Hennessy Rd., Wan Chai* Ⓜ *Wan Chai, Exit A5.*

CLOTHING

45R. Around since 1978, Japanese brand 45R has garnered a reputation for ultracomfortable, exquisitely crafted jeans. Following the successes of outposts in Paris and New York, a flagship store opened on Star Street in 2008. Amid the minimalist surroundings, find heaps of its famous hand-dyed denim as well as breezy button-downs, wooly sweaters, and understated frocks. ✉ *Ground fl., Vincent Mansion, 7 Star St., Wan Chai* ☎ *2861–1145* ⊕ *www.45rpm.jp* Ⓜ *Wan Chai, Exit B2.*

Initial. This team of local designers creates simple but whimsical men's and women's clothing with a trendy urban edge. The bags and accessories strike a soft vintage tone, fitting the store's fashionably worn interiors, casually strewn secondhand furniture, and sultry jazz sound track. ✉ *The Park Lane Hong Kong, 31 Gloucester Rd., Causeway Bay* ☎ *2882–9044* ⊕ *www.initialfashion.com* Ⓜ *Causeway Bay.*

Kapok. Hip messenger bags, soft fabrics, funky watches, comfy kicks, music, stationery—Kapok has it all. This bright local favorite is a one-stop shop for classic cotton and knits. Meanwhile, its café and gallery space (just two minutes down the road on Sun Street) serves up steamy French coffee, chocolate croissants, and freshly baked cupcakes. ✉ *5 St. Francis Yard, Wan Chai* ☎ *2549–9254* ⊕ *www.ka-pok.com* Ⓜ *Wan Chai, Exit B2.*

Lu Lu Cheung. A fixture on the Hong Kong fashion scene for decades, Lu Lu Cheung creates designs that ooze comfort and warmth. In both daytime and evening wear, natural fabrics and forms are represented in practical yet imaginative ways. ✉ *Shop C, 42-48 Paterson St., Causeway Bay* ☎ *2537–7515* ⊕ *www.lulucheung.com.hk* Ⓜ *Causeway Bay, Exit E.*

Olivia Couture. The surroundings are functional, but the gowns, wedding dresses, and cheongsams by local designer Olivia Yip are lavish. With a growing clientele—including socialites looking to stand out—Yip is quietly making a name for herself and her Parisian-influenced pieces. ✉ *Ground fl., Bartlock Centre, 3 Yiu Wah St., Causeway Bay* ☎ *2838–6636* ⊕ *www.oliviacouture.com* Ⓜ *Causeway Bay, Exit A.*

Pink Martini. Step into this blush-colored boudoir for fresh young fashions with spunk, courtesy of brands like Daily Dolly and Kikka. It also has a small range of costume jewelry, clutches, and jackets, all nicely aimed at bringing out your inner girl. ✉ *Shop 2, ground fl., Bartlock Centre, 3 Yiu Wa St., Causeway Bay* ☎ *2574–1498* ⊕ *www.pinkmartini.com.hk* Ⓜ *Causeway Bay, Exit A.*

Spy Henry Lau. Local bad boy Henry Lau brings an edgy attitude to his fashion for men and women. Bold and often dark, with a touch of

CATWALK HONG KONG

Local and regional talent is showcased at Hong Kong Fashion Week, held at the Hong Kong Convention & Exhibition Centre every January and July. For more information on fashion week or featured designers such as Guo Pei, Dorian Ho, and Frankie Xie, visit ⊕ www.hkfashionweekfw.com. To read profiles of Hong Kong designers, visit ⊕ www.hkfda.org, the website of the Hong Kong Fashion Designers Association.

6

Shopping for bargains at Stanley Village Market

bling, his clothing and accessories lines are not for the fainthearted. In Central, you can visit the SoHo store at 21 Staunton Street. ⊠ *1st fl., Cleveland Mansion, 5 Cleveland St., Causeway Bay* ☎ *2317–6928* ⊕ *www.spyhenrylau.com* Ⓜ *Causeway Bay, Exit E.*

Russell Street. Gatekeeper of the up-and-coming, Russell Street aims to introduce fresh labels to Hong Kong's style savants. Taking cues from New York and London's top fashion students, as well as established international labels—think Victoria Beckham denim—the boutique showcases eclectic designs ranging from fancy furs to colorful graphic-print dresses. Among the mix of envy-inducing pieces, look for Sophie Hulme's gorgeous leather bags and lively animal print cardigans from Sibling and Sister. ⊠ *6 St. Francis Yard, Wan Chai* ☎ *2866–0800* ⊕ *www.russell-street.com* Ⓜ *Wan Chai, Exit B2.*

Sonjia by Sonjia Norman. Walk past a local garage and snoozing dogs in this old-style Hong Kong area to find the low-key atelier of Korean-English ex-lawyer Sonjia Norman. The designer crafts quietly luxurious, one-of-a-kind pieces and modified vintage clothing under the Sonjia label. Her clothes are the epitome of understated stealth wealth. An adjacent store houses Norman's home and living collection, including tableware, linens, and all kinds of cushions. ⊠ *Ground fl., 2 Sun St., Wan Chai* ☎ *2529–6223* ⊕ *www.sonjiaonline.com* Ⓜ *Wan Chai, Exit B.*

Vie. Modern and minimalist, Vie's decor is in perfect harmony with its Nordic apparel. The combination boutique and gallery on St. Francis Yard is a spinoff of Vein, and offers up a mix of Scandinavian luxury labels and home accessories. The lineup changes every four to six weeks, but you can usually find at least a dozen stalwart, simple-yet-elegant brands, including Filippa K and Won Hundred. Expect straight lines, a gray-scale palette, and unexpected splashes of color. ✉ *Shop 2, St. Francis Yard, Wan Chai* ☎ *2804–1038* ⊕ *www.bvein.com* Ⓜ *Wan Chai, Exit B2.*

JEWELRY AND ACCESSORIES

Wing On Jewelry Ltd. There's a nostalgic charm to the butterflies, birds, and natural forms fashioned from jade, pearls, precious stones, and gold here. Everything looks like an heirloom inherited from your grandmother. With on-site gemologists and artisans, and a commitment to post-sale service, this store has a long list of repeat customers. If, however, you lean toward Scandinavian aesthetics and clean lines, this probably isn't the place for you. Wing On also has a Causeway Bay branch at 459 Hennessy Road. ✉ *146 Johnston Rd., Wan Chai* ☎ *2572–2332* ⊕ *www.wingonjewelry.com.hk* Ⓜ *Wan Chai, Exit A3.*

MALLS AND SHOPPING CENTERS

Fodor's Choice ★ **Times Square.** This gleaming mall packs most of Hong Kong's best-known stores into 12 frenzied floors, organized thematically. Lane Crawford and Marks & Spencer both have big branches here, as does favored local gourmet grocer City'super. Many restaurants are located in the basement, giving way to names like Fendi and De Beers on the second floor, and mid-range options like Zara higher up. The electronics, sports, and outdoors selection is particularly good. An indoor atrium hosts everything from heavy-metal bands to fashion shows to local movie stars. ■TIP→ Among the dozen or so eateries, innovative SML (or Small Medium Large) is a good pick, thanks to its large terrace and good selection of wines. ✉ *1 Matheson St., Causeway Bay* ☎ *2118–8900 Customer Service Hotline* ⊕ *www.timessquare.com.hk* Ⓜ *Causeway Bay, Exit A.*

SOUTHSIDE

MARKETS

Fodor's Choice ★ **Stanley Market.** This was once Hong Kong's most famed bargain trove for visitors, but its ever-growing popularity means that the market in Stanley Village no longer has the best prices around. Still, you can pick up some good buys in sportswear, casual clothing, textiles, and paintings if you comb through the stalls. Good-value linens—especially appliqué tablecloths—also abound. Dozens and dozens of shops line a main street so narrow that awnings from each side meet in the middle, and on busy days your elbows will come in handy. Weekdays are a little more relaxed. One of the best things about Stanley Market is getting here: the winding bus ride from Central (routes 6, 6X, 6A, or 260) or Tsim Sha Tsui (route 973) takes you over the top of Hong Kong Island, with fabulous views along on the way. ✉ *Stanley, Southside* ⊕ *www.hk-stanley-market.com.*

KOWLOON

CLOTHING

David's Shirts Ltd. Customers have been enjoying the personalized service of David Chu since 1961. All the work is done in-house by Shanghainese tailors with at least 20 years' experience each. There are more than 6,000 imported European fabrics to choose from, each prewashed. Examples of shirts, suits, and accessories—including 30 collar styles, 12 cuff styles, and 10 pocket styles—help you choose. Single-needle tailoring; French seams; 22 stitches per inch; handpicked, double-stitched shell buttons; German interlining—it's all here. Your details, down to on which side you wear your wristwatch, are kept on file should you wish to use its mail-order service in the future. If you're in Central, The Galleria contains a second branch. ⊠ *Ground fl., Wing Lee Bldg., 33 Kimberley Rd., Tsim Sha Tsui* ☎ *2367–9556* Ⓜ *Tsim Sha Tsui, Exit B2.*

Dorfit. A longtime cashmere manufacturer and retailer, Dorfit caters to a variety of men's, women's, and children's tastes. Knitwear here comes in pure cashmere as well as blends, so be sure to ask which is which. There's a branch at 10 Wellington Street in Central, too. ⊠ *6th fl., Mary Bldg., 71–77 Peking Rd., Tsim Sha Tsui* ☎ *2312–1013* ⊕ *www.dorfit. com.hk* Ⓜ *Tsim Sha Tsui.*

Giordano. Hong Kong's version of the Gap is the most established and ubiquitous local source of basic T-shirts, jeans, and casual wear. Like its U.S. counterpart, the brand now has a bit more fashion sense and slick ad campaigns, but prices are still reasonable. Although the flagship store is in Manson House on Nathan Road, you'll have no problem finding one on almost every major street. ■ TIP➜ Its line—Giordano Concepts—offers more stylish (and pricier) urban wear in neutral colors like black, gray, and white. ⊠ *Ground fl., Manson House, 74–78 Nathan Rd., Tsim Sha Tsui* ☎ *2926–1028* ⊕ *www.giordano.com.hk* Ⓜ *Tsim Sha Tsui, Exit B1.*

Giordano Ladies. If Giordano is the Gap, Giordano Ladies is the Banana Republic, albeit with a more Zen approach. Find clean-line modern classics in neutral black, gray, white, and beige; each collection is brightened by a single highlight color, red one season, blue the next, and so on. Everything is elegant enough for the office and comfortable enough for the plane. ⊠ *1st fl., Manson House, 74–78 Nathan Rd., Tsim Sha Tsui* ☎ *2926–1331* ⊕ *www.giordanoladies.com* Ⓜ *Tsim Sha Tsui, Exit B1.*

Maxwell's Clothiers Ltd. After you've found a handful of reputable, high-quality tailors, one way to choose between them is price. Maxwell's is known for its competitive rates. It's also a wonderful place to have favorite shirts and suits copied and for straightforward, structured women's shirts and suits. It was founded by third-generation tailor Ken Maxwell in 1961 and follows Shanghai tailoring traditions, while also providing the fabled 24-hour suit upon request. The showroom and workshop are in Kowloon, but son Andy and his team take appointments in the United States, Canada, Australia, and Europe twice annually. The motto of this family business is, "Simply let the garment do the talking." ⊠ *13th fl., Maxwell Centre, 39–41 Hankow Rd., Tsim Sha Tsui* ☎ *2366–6705* ⊕ *www.maxwellsclothiers.com* Ⓜ *Tsim Sha Tsui, Exit A1.*

Mode Elegante. Don't be deterred by the somewhat dated mannequins in the windows. Mode Elegante is a favorite source for custom-made suits among women and men in the know. Tailors here specialize in European cuts. You'll have your choice of fabrics from the United Kingdom, Italy, and elsewhere. Your records are put on file so you can place orders from abroad. It'll even ship the completed garment to you almost anywhere on the planet. Alternatively, you can make an appointment with director Gary Zee, one of Hong Kong's traveling tailors, who makes regular visits to North America, Australia, Europe, and Japan. ⊠ *11th fl., Star House, 3 Salisbury Rd., Tsim Sha Tsui* ☎ *2366–8153* ⊕ *www.modeelegante.com* Ⓜ *Tsim Sha Tsui, Exit L6.*

Fodor's Choice
★
Pearls & Cashmere. Warehouse prices in chic shopping arcades? It's true. This old Hong Kong favorite is elegantly housed on both sides of the harbor. In addition to quality men's and women's cashmere sweaters in classic designs and in every color under the sun, they also sell reasonably priced pashminas, gloves, and socks, which make great gifts for men and women. In recent years the brand has developed the more fashion-focused line, BYPAC. ⊠ *Mezzanine, Peninsula Hotel Shopping Arcade, Salisbury Rd., Tsim Sha Tsui* ☎ *2723–8698* ⊕ *bypac.com* Ⓜ *Tsim Sha Tsui, Exit L4.*

Fodor's Choice
★
Sam's Tailor. Unlike many famous Hong Kong tailors, you won't find the legendary Sam's in a chic hotel or sleek mall. But don't be fooled. These digs in humble Burlington House, a tailoring hub, have hosted everyone from U.S. presidents (back as far as Richard Nixon) to performers such as the Black Eyed Peas, Kylie Minogue, and Blondie. This former uniform tailor to the British troops once even made a suit for Prince Charles in a record hour and 52 minutes. The men's and women's tailor does accept 24-hour suit or shirt orders, but will take about two days if you're not in a hurry. Founded by Naraindas Melwani in 1957, "Sam" is now his son, Manu Melwani, who runs the show with the help of his own son, Roshan, and about 57 tailors behind the scenes. In 2004 Sam's introduced a computerized bodysuit that takes measurements without a tape measure (it uses both methods, however). These tailors also make biannual trips to Europe and North America: schedule updates are listed on the website. ⊠ *Burlington House, 94 Nathan Rd., Tsim Sha Tsui* ☎ *2367–9423* ⊕ *www.samstailor.com* Ⓜ *Tsim Sha Tsui, Exit B2.*

DEPARTMENT STORES

Fodor's Choice
★
Yue Hwa Chinese Products Emporium. This popular purveyor of Chinese goods has 17 stores across Hong Kong, and the flagship one features seven floors laden with everything from clothing and housewares to traditional medicine. The logic behind its layout is hard to fathom, so go with time to rifle around. As well as the predictable tablecloths, silk pajamas, and chopsticks, there are cheap and colorful porcelain sets and offbeat local favorites like mini-massage chairs. The top floor is entirely given over to tea—you can pick up a HK$50 packet of leaves or an antique Yixing teapot stretching into the thousands. ⊠ *301–309 Nathan Rd., Jordan, Yau Ma Tei* ☎ *3511–2222* ⊕ *www.yuehwa.com* Ⓜ *Jordan, Exit A.*

JEWELRY AND ACCESSORIES

Artland Watch Co Ltd. Elegant but uncomplicated, the interior of this established watch retailer is like its service. The informed staff will guide you through the countless luxury brands on show and in the catalogs from which you can also order. Prices here aren't the best in Hong Kong, but they're still lower than at home. ⊠ *Ground fl., Mirador Mansion, 62A Nathan Rd., Tsim Sha Tsui* ☎ *2366–1074* Ⓜ *Tsim Sha Tsui.*

Sandra Pearls. You might be wary of the lustrous pearls hanging at this little Jade Market stall. But the charming owner does, in fact, sell genuine cultured and freshwater pearl necklaces and earrings at reasonable prices. Some pieces are made from shell, which Sandra is always quick to point out, and could pass muster among the snobbiest collectors. ✉ *Stall 437 and 447, Jade Market, Kansu St., Yau Ma Tei* ☎ *9485–2895* Ⓜ *Jordan, Exit A.*

TSL Jewellery. One of the big Hong Kong chains, TSL (Tse Sui Luen) specializes in diamond jewelry, and manufactures, retails, and exports its designs. Its range of 100-facet stones includes the Estrella cut, which reflects nine symmetrical hearts and comes with international certification. Although its contemporary designs use platinum settings, TSL also sells pure, bright, yellow-gold items targeted at Chinese customers. ✉ *G5–G7, Park Lane Shopper' Blvd., Nathan Rd., Tsim Sha Tsui* ☎ *2375–2661* ⊕ *www.tsljewellery.com* Ⓜ *Tsim Sha Tsui, Exit A1.*

MALLS AND SHOPPING CENTERS

Fodor's Choice ★ **Festival Walk.** Although it's located in residential Kowloon Tong, 20 minutes from Central on the MTR, reaching Festival Walk is worth the effort. After all, the mall's stores range from Vivienne Tam to Giordano (Hong Kong's take on the Gap). By day the six floors sparkle with sunlight, which filters through the glass roof. Marks & Spencer and DKNY serve as anchors; Armani Jeans and ck Calvin Klein draw the elite crowds; while Camper and agnès b. keep the trend spotters happy. Hong Kong's best bookstore, Page One, has a big branch downstairs. If you want a respite from the sometimes scorching-hot weather, Festival Walk also has one of the city's largest ice rinks, as well as a multiplex cinema. ✉ *80 Tat Chee Ave., Northern Kowloon* ☎ *2844–2200* ⊕ *www. festivalwalk.com.hk* Ⓜ *Kowloon Tong, Exit C1.*

Fodor's Choice ★ **Harbour City.** The four interconnected complexes that make up Harbour City contain almost 500 shops between them—if you can't find it here, it probably doesn't exist. Pick up a map on your way in, as it's easy to get lost. **Ocean Terminal,** the largest section, runs along the harbor and is divided thematically, with kids' wear and toys on the ground floor, and sports and cosmetics on the first. The top floor is home to white-hot department store LCX. Near the Star Ferry pier, the **Marco Polo Hong Kong Hotel Arcade** has branches of the department store Lane Crawford. Louis Vuitton, Prada, and Burberry are some of the posher boutiques that fill the **Ocean Centre** and **Gateway Arcade,** parallel to Canton Road. Most of the complex's restaurants are here, too. A cinema and three hotels round out Harbour City's offerings. ■TIP→ **Free Wi-Fi is available.** ✉ *Tsim Sha Tsui* ⊕ *www.harbourcity.com.hk* Ⓜ *Tsim Sha Tsui, Exit A1.*

MARKETS

Fodor's Choice ★ **Temple Street Night Market.** Each evening, as darkness falls, the lamps strung between the stalls of this Yau Ma Tei street market slowly light up, and the air fills with aromas wafting from myriad food carts. Hawkers try to catch your eye by flinging up clothes; Cantonese opera competes with swelling pop music and the sounds of spirited haggling; fortune-tellers and street performers add another element to the sensory overload. Granted, neither the garments nor the cheap gadgets sold here are much to get excited about, but it's the atmosphere people come for—any purchases are a bonus. The market stretches for almost a mile and is one of Hong Kong's liveliest nighttime shopping experiences. ⊠ *Temple St., Yau Ma Tei* Ⓜ *Jordan, Exit A.*

SIDE TRIP TO MACAU

Enter the desperate, smoky atmosphere of a Chinese casino, where frumpy players bet an average of five times more than the typical Vegas gambler. Sit down next to grandmothers who smoke like chimneys while playing baccarat—the local game of choice—with visiting high rollers. Then step out of the climate-controlled chill and into tropical air that embraces you like a warm, balmy hug. Welcome to Macau.

The many contrasts in this tiny enclave of 555,000 people serve as reminders of how different cultures have embraced one another's traditions for hundreds of years. Though Macau's population is 95% ethnic Chinese, there are still vibrant pockets of Portuguese and Filipino expats. And some of the thousands of Eurasians—who consider themselves neither Portuguese nor Chinese, but something in between—can trace the intermarriage of their ancestors back a century or two.

Macau's Old Town, while dominated by the buildings, squares, and cobblestone alleyways of colonial Portugal, is tinged with Eastern influences as well. In Macau you can spend an afternoon exploring Buddhist temples before feasting on a dinner of *bacalhau com natas* (dried codfish with a cream sauce), grilled African chicken (spicy chicken in a coconut-peanut broth—a classic Macanese dish), Chinese lobster with scallions, or fiery prawns infused with Indian and Malaysian flavors. Wash everything down with *vinho verde*, the crisp young wine from northern Portugal, and top it all off with a traditional Portuguese *pastel de nata* (egg-custard tart) and dark, thick espresso.

PLANNING

GETTING HERE AND AROUND

AIR TRAVEL

International flights (from Asia) come into Macau, but there are no planes from Hong Kong. Sky Shuttle offers 15-minute helicopter flights between Hong Kong's Shun Tak Centre and the Macau Ferry Terminal; they leave every 30 minutes from 9 am to 11 pm daily and cost HK$4,100 with a surcharge of HK$400 on holidays. Reservations are essential.

Contacts Macau International Airport ☎ 853/2886–1111 ⊕ www.macau-airport.com/en. **Sky Shuttle** ☎ 853/2872–7288 Macau Terminal ⊕ www.skyshuttlehk.com.

BUS TRAVEL

Public buses are clean and affordable. Trips to anywhere in the Macau Peninsula cost MOP$3.20; service to Taipa is MOP$4.20, and service to Coloane is MOP$5. Buses run from 6:30 am to midnight and require exact change upon boarding. But you can get downtown for free, via hotel or casino shuttles, from the official Border Gate crossing just outside mainland China, from the airport, and from the Macau Ferry Terminal.

FERRY TRAVEL

Ferries travel between Hong Kong and Macau every 15 minutes with a reduced schedule from midnight to 7 am. Weekday traffic is usually light, so you can buy tickets right before departure. Weekend tickets often sell out, so make reservations. You must pick up tickets at the terminal at least a half hour before departure.

Most ferries leave from Hong Kong's Shun Tak Centre (which is connected to the Sheung Wan MTR station), though limited service is available at Kowloon's Hong Kong China Ferry Terminal in Tsim Sha Tsui. In Macau most ferries disembark from the main Macau Ferry Terminal, but CotaiJet services the terminal on Taipa. The trip takes one hour each way. Buses, taxis, and free shuttles to most casinos and hotels await on the Macau side.

Contacts CotaiJet ☎ 853/2885–0595 in Macau, 2359–9990 in Hong Kong ⊕ www.cotaijet.com.mo. **TurboJET** ☎ 2859–3333 information ⊕ www.turbojet. com.hk.

TAXI TRAVEL

Taxis are inexpensive but not plentiful in Macau. The best places to catch a cab are the major casinos—the Wynn Macau, the Lisboas, the Sands Macao, and the Venetian Macao. Carry a bilingual map or ask the concierge at your hotel to write the name of your destination in Chinese. All taxis are metered, air-conditioned, and reasonably comfortable. The base charge is MOP$15 for the first 1.6 km (1 mile) and MOP$1.50 per additional 755 feet. Trips between Coloane and either the Macau Peninsula or Taipa incur respective surcharges of MOP$5 and MOP$2. Drivers don't expect a tip.

RESTAURANTS

Macau's medley of Portuguese and Cantonese cuisine—spicy and creamy Macanese interpretations of traditional Cantonese dishes such as baked prawns, braised abalone, and seafood stews—has made the peninsula one of Asia's top fine-dining destinations for decades.

Now, thanks to the spate of new casino-hotels, Macau has also become an exciting world-class culinary frontier. But Macau dining isn't all highbrow. Near the Largo do Senado, in the villages of Taipa or Coloane, wander the back alleys for *zhu-bao-bao,* a slab of fried pork on a toasted bun served with milk tea, or the signature *pasteis de nata* (custard tart): simple and delicious, and classic Macau.

IT'S GOOD TO BE JADED

The Chinese believe that jade brings luck, and it's still worn as a charm in amulets or bracelets. A jade bangle is often presented to newborns, and homes are often adorned with jade statues or other carved decorative items.

HOTELS

An influx of luxury hotels has transformed Macau into a posh place to stay. The musty three-stars are still out there, but the five-stars are generally worth the splurge. For a true Macau experience, try staying in *pousadas*, restored historic buildings that have been converted into intimate hotels with limited facilities but lots of character. *Hotel reviews have been shortened. For full information, visit Fodors.com.*

WHAT IT COSTS IN MACANESE PATACA			
	$	$$	$$$	$$$$
Restaurants	under MOP$100	MOP$100–MOP$200	MOP$201–MOP$300	over MOP$300
Hotels	under MOP$1,100	MOP$1,100–MOP$1,850	MOP$1,851–MOP$2,800	over MOP$2,800

Restaurant prices are the average cost of a main course at dinner or, if dinner is not served, at lunch. Hotel prices are the lowest cost of a standard double room in high season.

VISITOR INFORMATION

To enter Macau, Americans, Canadians, and EU citizens need only a valid passport for stays of up to 90 days. The Macau Government Tourist Office has all the information you need.

Contacts Macau Government Tourist Office (*MGTO*). ✉ *335–341, Alameda Dr. Carlos d'Assumpção* ☎ *853/2833–3000 in Macau, 8238–8680 in Hong Kong* ⊕ *www.macautourism.gov.mo.*

6

EXPLORING

Macau is a small place, where on a good day you can drive from one end to the other in 30 minutes. This makes walking the ideal way to explore winding city streets, nature trails, and long stretches of beach. Most of Macau's population lives on the peninsula attached to mainland China. The region's most famous sights are here—Senado Square, the Ruins of St. Paul's, A-Ma Temple—as are most of the luxury hotels and casinos. As in the older sections of Hong Kong, cramped older buildings stand comfortably next to gleaming new structures.

DOWNTOWN MACAU

Chances are you'll arrive at the Macau Ferry Terminal after sailing from Hong Kong. There's not much to see around the terminal itself, so hop into one of the many waiting casino or hotel shuttles and head straight downtown, less than 10 minutes away. From there it's a short walk to the city's historic center, along the short stretch of road named Avenida Almeida Ribeiro, more commonly known as San Ma Lo, which is Macau's commercial and cultural heart.

TOP ATTRACTIONS

Fodor's Choice ★ **Fortaleza da Guia** (*Guia Fortress*). This fort, built between 1622 and 1638 on Macau's highest hill, was key to protecting the Portuguese from invaders. You can walk the steep, winding road up to it or take a five-minute cable-car ride from the entrance of Flora Garden on Avenida

Sidónio Pais. From the drop-off point, follow the signs for the **Guia Lighthouse**—you can't go in, but you can get a good look at the gleaming white exterior that's lit every night. Next to it is the **Guia Chapel**, built by Clarist nuns to provide soldiers with religious services. Restoration work in 1996 uncovered elaborate frescoes mixing Western and Chinese themes. They're best seen when the morning or afternoon sun floods the chapel, which is no longer used for services. The views from here are among the best, sweeping across all of Macau. ⊠ *Guia Hill, Downtown* ☎ *853/8399–6699* ✉ *Free* ☉ *Daily 9–5:30.*

Igreja de São Domingos (*St. Dominic's Church*). The cream-and-white interior of one of Macau's most beautiful churches takes on a heavenly golden glow when illuminated for services. St. Dominic's was originally a convent founded by Spanish Dominican friars in 1587. In 1822 China's first Portuguese newspaper, *The China Bee*, was published here, and the church became a repository for sacred art in 1834 when convents were banned in Portugal. ■TIP→ **Admission to all churches and temples is free, though donations are suggested.** ⊠ *Largo de São Domingos, Downtown* ☉ *Daily 10–6.*

Fodor's Choice
★
Largo do Senado (*Senado Square*). Open only to pedestrians and paved in shiny black-and-white tiles, this has been the charming hub of Macau for centuries. Largo do Senado is lined with neoclassical-style colonial buildings painted in bright pastels. The **Edifício do Leal Senado** (Senate Building), which gives the square its name, was built in 1784 as a municipal chamber and continues to be used by the government today. An elegant meeting room on the first floor opens onto a magnificent library based on one in the Mafra Convent in Portugal, with books neatly stacked on two levels of shelves reaching to the ceiling; art and historical exhibitions are frequently hosted in the beautiful foyer and garden. ■TIP→ **Visit on a weekday to avoid the crowds, and try to come back at night, when locals of all ages gather to chat and the square is beautifully lit.** ⊠ *Downtown.*

NEED A BREAK?

Margaret's Café e Nata. Not far off the main drag but somewhat hidden down an alleyway, Margaret's Café e Nata offers a cool—albeit increasingly crowded—place to sit, outside under fans and awnings, with some of the best custard tarts in town, plus fresh juices, sandwiches, homemade tea blends, and pizza slices. ⊠ *Rua Comandante Mata e Oliveira, Downtown* ☎ *853/2871-0032.*

Leitaria i Son. Look for the small cow sign marking the out-of-the-ordinary Leitaria i Son milk bar. The decor is cafeteria-style and spartan, but the bar whips up frothy glasses of fresh milk from its dairy and blends them with all manner of juices: papaya, coconut, apricot, and more. ⊠ *Largo do Senado 7, Downtown* ☎ *853/2857-3638.*

Fodor's Choice
★
Macau Tower Convention & Entertainment Centre. Rising above peaceful San Van Lake, this 338-meter (1,109-foot) freestanding tower recalls Sky Tower, a similar structure in New Zealand—and it should, as both were designed by New Zealand architect Gordon Moller. The Macau Tower offers a variety of thrills, including the Tower Climb, which challenges the strong of heart and body with a two-hour ascent on

steel rungs 100 meters (328 feet) up the tower's mast for incomparable views of Macau and China. Other thrills include Skywalk X, an open-air stroll around the tower's exterior—without handrails; Sky-Jump, an assisted, decelerated 233-meter (765-foot) descent; and the world's highest bungee jump. More subdued attractions inside the tower include a mainstream movie theater and a revolving restaurant (the 360° Café) serving lunch, high tea, and a dinner buffet. ☒ *Largo da Torre de Macau, Downtown* ☎ *853/2893-3339* ⊕ *www.macau*

> **WORLD HERITAGE**
>
> "The Historic Centre of Macau" is one of China's 31st UNESCO World Heritage Sites. The term "center" is misleading, as the site is really a collection of churches, buildings, and neighborhoods that colorfully illustrate Macau's 400-year history. Included in it are China's oldest examples of Western architecture and the region's most extensive concentration of missionary churches.

tower.com.mo ☒ *MOP$788 for Skywalk X to MOP$1,888 for the Tower Climb; MOP$2,888 for bungee jump; photos extra.* ☉ *Observation deck, weekdays 11–7:30, weekends 11–10.*

Fodor's Choice ★ **Ruínas de São Paulo** (*Ruins of St. Paul's Cathedral*). Only the magnificent, towering facade, with its intricate carvings and bronze statues, remains from the original Church of Mater Dei, built between 1602 and 1640 and destroyed by fire in 1835. The sanctuary, an adjacent college, and Mount Fortress—all Jesuit constructions—once formed East Asia's first Western-style university. Now a tourist attraction, the ruins are the widely adopted symbol of Macau. Snack bars and shops are clustered at the foot of the site. Tucked behind the facade of São Paulo is the small **Museum of Sacred Art and Crypt,** which contains statues, crucifixes, and the bones of Japanese and Vietnamese martyrs. There are also some intriguing Asian interpretations of Christian images, including samurai angels and a Chinese Virgin and Child. ☒ *Top end of Rua de São Paulo, Downtown* ☎ *853/8399–6699* ☒ *Free* ☉ *Daily 8–5.*

Santa Casa da Misericordia (*The Holy House of Mercy*). Founded in 1569 by Dom Belchior Carneiro, Macau's first bishop, the Holy House of Mercy is the China coast's oldest Christian charity, and it continues to take care of the poor with soup kitchens and health clinics, as well as providing housing for the elderly. The exterior, with its imposing white facade, is neoclassical, but the interior is done in a contrasting opulent, modern style. A reception room on the second floor contains paintings of benefactress Marta Merop. ☒ *2 Travessa da Misericordia, Downtown* ☎ *853/2857–3938* ☒ *MOP$5* ☉ *Tues.–Sun. 10–1 and 2:30–5:30.*

Fodor's Choice ★ **Templo de A-Ma.** The tiered A-Ma Temple is one of Macau's oldest and most picturesque buildings. Properly Ma Kok Temple but known to locals as simply A-Ma, the structure originated during the Ming Dynasty (1368–1644) and was influenced by Confucianism, Taoism, and Buddhism, as well as local religions. Vivid red calligraphy on large boulders tells the story of the goddess A-Ma (also known as Tin Hau), the patron of fishermen. A small gate opens onto prayer halls, pavilions, and caves carved directly into the hillside. ☒ *Rua de São Tiago da Barra, Largo da Barra, Downtown* ☉ *Daily 7–6.*

6

WORTH NOTING

Camões Garden. Macau's most popular park is frequented from dawn to dusk by tai chi enthusiasts, palm readers, lovers, students, and men huddled over Chinese chessboards with their caged songbirds nearby. The gardens, which were developed in the 18th century, are named after Luís de Camões, Portugal's greatest poet, who was banished to Macau for several years during the 16th century. A rocky niche shelters a bronze bust of him in the park's most famous and picturesque spot, Camões Grotto. At the grotto's entrance a bronze sculpture honors the friendship between Portugal and China. A wall of stone slabs is inscribed with poems by various contemporary writers, praising Camões and Macau. In **Casa Garden**, a smaller park alongside Camões Garden, the grounds of a merchant's estate are lovingly landscaped with a variety of flora and bordered with a brick pathway. A central pond is stocked with lily pads and lotus flowers. ⊠ *13 Praça Luis de Camões, Downtown* ⊙ *Daily 6 am–10 pm.*

Fortaleza do Monte (*Mount Fortress*). On the hill overlooking the ruins of São Paulo and affording great peninsular views, this renovated fort was built by the Jesuits in the early 17th century. In 1622 it was the site of Macau's most legendary battle, when a priest's lucky cannon shot hit an invading Dutch ship's powder supply, saving the day. The interior buildings were destroyed by fire in 1835, but the outer walls remain, along with several large cannons and artillery pieces. Exhibits at the adjoining **Macau Museum** (⊙ *Daily 10–6* ⊡ *MOP$15*) take you through the territory's history, from its origins to modern development. ⊠ *Monte Hill, Downtown* ☎ *853/2835–7911* ⊕ *www.macaumuseum. gov.mo* ⊡ *Free* ⊙ *Daily 6 am–7 pm.*

Igreja de São Lourenço (*Church of St. Lawrence*). One of Macau's three oldest churches, the Church of St. Lawrence was founded by Jesuits in 1560 and has been lovingly rebuilt several times. Its present appearance dates to 1846. It overlooks the South China Sea amid pleasant, palm-shaded gardens. Families of Portuguese sailors used to gather on the front steps to pray for the sailors' safe return; hence its Chinese name, Feng Shun Tang (Hall of the Soothing Winds). Focal points of its breathtaking interior are the elegant wood carvings, striking stained-glass windows, a baroque altar, and crystal chandeliers. ⊠ *Rua de São Lourenço, Downtown* ☎ *8399–6699* ⊙ *Daily 10–5.*

Largo de Santo Agostinho. Built in the pattern of traditional Portuguese squares, St. Augustine Square is paved with black-and-white tiles laid out in mosaic wave patterns and lined with leafy overhanging trees and lots of wooden benches. It's easy to feel as if you're in a European village, far from South China. One of the square's main structures is the **Teatro Dom Pedro V**, a European-style hall with an inviting green-and-white facade built in 1859. It's an important cultural landmark for Macanese and was regularly used until World War II, when it fell into disrepair. The 300-seat venue once again hosts concerts and recitals—especially during the annual Macau International Music Festival—as well as important public events, the only times you can go inside. It does, however, have a garden that's open daily, and admission is free. **Igreja de Santo Agostinho (Church of St. Augustine)**, to one side of the

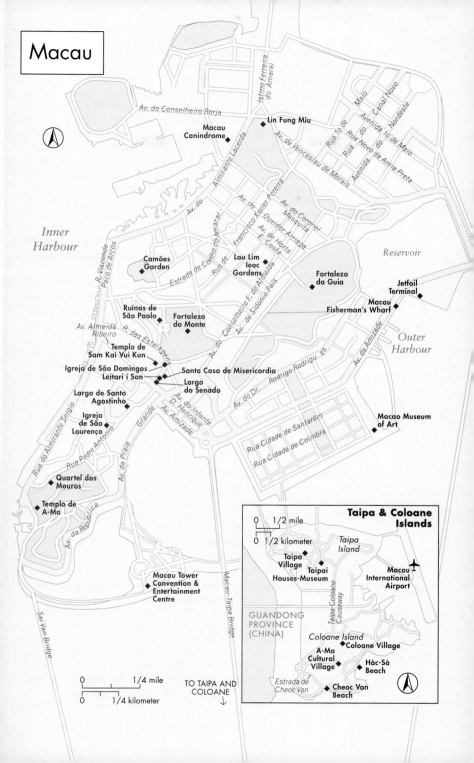

square, dates from 1591, and has a grand, weathered exterior and a drafty interior with a high turquoise-colored wood-beam ceiling (open daily 10–6). There's a magnificent stone altar with a statue of Christ on his knees, bearing the cross, with small crucifixes in silhouette on the hill behind him. The statue, called *Our Lord of Passos*, is carried in a procession through the streets of downtown on the first day of Lent. ✉ *Off R. Central, Downtown.*

Lin Fung Miu. Built in 1592, the Temple of the Lotus honors several Buddhist and Taoist deities, including Tin Hau (goddess of the sea), Kun Iam (goddess of mercy), and Kwan Tai (god of war and wealth). The front of the temple is embellished with magnificent clay bas-reliefs of renowned figures from Chinese history and mythology. Inside are several halls, shrines, and courtyards. The temple is best known as a lodging place for Mandarins traveling from Guangdong Province. Its most famous guest was Commissioner Lin Zexu, whose confiscation and destruction of British opium in 1839 was largely responsible for the First Opium War. ✉ *Av. do Almirante Lacerda, Downtown* ⏱ *Daily 7–5.*

Lou Lim Ieoc Gardens. These beautiful gardens were built in the 19th century by a Chinese merchant named Lou Kau. Rock formations, water, vegetation, pavilions, and sunlight were all carefully considered, and the balanced landscapes are the hallmark of Suzhou garden style. The government took possession and restored the grounds in the mid-1970s, so that today you can enjoy tranquil walks among delicate flowering bushes framed with bamboo groves and artificial hills. A large auditorium frequently hosts concerts and other events, most notably recitals during the annual Macau International Music Festival. Adjacent to the gardens, a European-style edifice contains the **Macau Tea Culture House,** a small museum with exhibits on the tea culture of Macau and China (🎫 *Free* ⏱ *Tues.–Sun. 9–7).* ✉ *10 Estrada de Adolfo Loureiro, at Av. do Conselheiro Ferreira de Almeida, Downtown* ☎ *853/2882–7103* 🎫 *Free* ⏱ *Daily 6–9.*

Macao Museum of Art. The large, boxy museum is as well known for its curving, rectangular framed roof as it is for its calligraphy, painting, copperware, and international film collections. It's Macau's only art museum, and has five floors of Eastern and Western works, plus important examples of ancient indigenous pottery found at Coloane's Hác-Sá Beach. ✉ *Macao Cultural Centre, Av. Xian Xing Hai, Outer Harbour* ☎ *853/8791–9814* ⊕ *www.artmuseum.gov.mo* 🎫 *MOP$5 (free Sun.)* ⏱ *Tues.–Sun. 10–6:30.*

FAMILY **Macau Fisherman's Wharf.** This sprawling complex of rides, games, and other minor attractions has a Disney-esque vibe. The centerpiece is the Roman Amphitheatre, which hosts outdoor performances, but the main draws are the lively themed restaurants on the west side: Afri-Kana (⇨ *Where to Eat)* for one, serves up Macau's best African brews and barbecues. Come for the food, and stay after dark, as Fisherman's Wharf is most active at night. ✉ *Av. da Amizade, at Av. Dr. Sun Yat-Sen, Outer Harbour* ☎ *853/8299–3300* ⊕ *www.fishermanswharf.com.mo* 🎫 *Admission free, games MOP$1–MOP$32* ⏱ *Daily 24 hrs.*

Templo de Sam Kai Vui Kun. Built in 1750, this temple is dedicated to Kuan Tai, the bearded, fierce-looking god of war and wealth in Chinese mythology. Statues of him and his two sons sit on an altar. A steady stream of people comes to pray and ask for support before they go wage battle in the casinos. May and June see festivals honoring Kuan Tai throughout Macau. ⊠ *10 Rua Sui do Mercado de São Domingos, Downtown* ⊙ *Daily 8–6.*

TAIPA

The island directly south of peninsular Macau was once two small islands that were, over time, joined by deposits from the Pearl River delta. It's connected to peninsular Macau by three long bridges. The region's two universities, horse-racing track, scenic hiking trails, and its international airport are all here.

Like downtown Macau, Taipa has been greatly developed in the past few years, yet it retains a visual balance between old Macau charm and modern sleekness. Try to visit on a weekend, so you can shop for clothing and crafts in the traditional flea market that's held every Sunday from morning to evening in Taipa Village.

TOP ATTRACTIONS

Fodor's Choice ★

Taipa Village. The narrow, winding streets are packed with restaurants, bakeries, shops, temples, and other buildings with traditional South Chinese and Portuguese design elements. The aptly named Rua do Cunha (Food Street) has many great Chinese, Macanese, Portuguese, and Thai restaurants. Several shops sell homemade Macanese snacks, including steamed milk pudding, almond cakes, beef jerky, durian ice cream, and coconut candy. ⊠ *Taipa.*

WORTH NOTING

Taipai Houses-Museum. These five sea-green buildings are interesting examples of Porto-Chinese architecture and were originally residences of wealthy local merchants. They now house changing art exhibitions. Paths lead into the beautiful adjoining **Carmel Garden,** where palm trees provide welcome shade. Within the garden stands the brilliant white-and-yellow **Nossa Senhora do Carmo** (Church of Our Lady of Carmel), built in 1885 and featuring a handsome single-belfry tower. ⊠ *Av. da Praia, Carmo Zone, Taipa* ☎ *853/2882–7103* ⊕ *housesmuseum.iacm. gov.mo* ⊠ *Museum MOP$5, free Sun.; garden free* ⊙ *Museum Tues.– Sun. 10–6; garden daily, 24 hrs.*

COLOANE

Centuries ago, Coloane was a wild place, where pirates hid in rocky caves and coves, awaiting their chance to strike at cargo ships on the Pearl River. Early in the 20th century the local government sponsored a huge planting program to transform Coloane from a barren place to a green one. Today this island is idyllic, with green hills and clean sandy beaches.

FAMILY
Fodor's Choice ★

A-Ma Cultural Village. A huge complex built in a traditional Qing Dynasty style pays homage to Macau's namesake, the goddess of the sea. The vibrancy and color of the details in the bell and drum towers, the tiled roofs, and the carved marble altars are truly awe-inspiring. It's as if you've been transported back to the height of the Qing Empire and

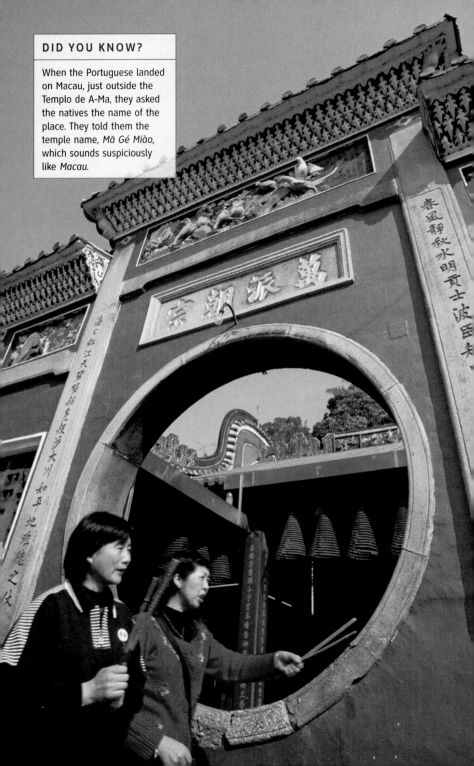

can now see temples in their true state of greatness. Other remarkable details include the striking rows of stairs leading to Tian Hou Palace at the entrance. Each row features painstakingly detailed marble and stone carvings of auspicious Chinese symbols: a roaring tiger, double lions, five cranes, the double phoenix, and a splendid imperial dragon. The grounds here also have a recreational fishing zone and an arboretum with more than 100 species of local and exotic flora.

Behind A-Ma Cultural Village, **Coloane Hill** rises 170 meters (560-feet); it is crowned by a gleaming white-marble statue of A-Ma that's 21 meters (68 feet) tall and visible from miles away. You can make the short hike up to the top or take one of the shuttle buses that leave from the base of the hill every 30 minutes. ⊠ *Off Estrada de Seac Pai Van, Coloane Island South* ⊙ *Daily 8–6.*

Fodor'sChoice **Coloane Village.** Quiet, relaxed Coloane Village is home to traditional
★ Mediterranean-style houses painted in pastels, as well as the baroque-style Chapel of St. Francis Xavier and the Taoist Tam Kung Temple. The narrow alleys reveal surprises at every turn; you may well encounter fishermen repairing their junks or a baptism at the chapel. At the village's heart is a small square adorned with a fountain with a bronze Cupid. The surrounding Macanese and Chinese open-air restaurants are among the region's best; some are the unheralded favorites of chefs visiting from Hong Kong and elsewhere in Asia. ⊠ *Coloane Island West.*

6

WHERE TO EAT

DOWNTOWN MACAU

$$ ✕ **Clube Militar de Macau** (*Macau Military Club*). Founded in 1870 as a
PORTUGUESE private military club, the stately pink-and-white structure was restored in 1995 and reopened as a restaurant. The languid old-world atmosphere perfectly complements the extensive list of traditional Portuguese dishes, such as *bacalhau dourado* ("golden cod," a specialty of fried cod and potatoes), African chicken, and *arroz de marisco* (flavored rice and seafood). Leave room for dessert—the options include Portuguese sweet rice pudding with mango, warm chestnut tart, and coconut ice cream with caramelized pineapple. $ *Average main: MOP$150* ⊠ *975 Av. da Praia Grande, Downtown* ☎ *853/2871–4000* ⊕ *www.clubemilitardemacau.net.*

$ ✕ **Dom Galo.** "Quirky" springs to mind when describing the colorful
PORTUGUESE decor, with plastic monkey puppets and funky chicken toys hanging from
Fodor'sChoice the ceilings. A wide clientele includes graphic designers, gambling-com-
★ pliance lawyers, and 10-year-old Cantonese kids celebrating birthdays. The owner is Portuguese and the food is usually spot-on, with *insalada de polvo* (octopus salad), king prawns, and steak fries served with a tangy mushroom sauce among the standouts. Pitchers of sangria are essential with any meal here. So, too, are reservations, as this place is increasingly popular with tourists. $ *Average main: MOP$100* ⊠ *Av. Sir Andars Ljung Stedt, Downtown* ☎ *853/2875–1383* ⊛ *Reservations essential.*

$$ CANTONESE Fodor's Choice ★ 🍴 **Fat Siu Lau.** Well known to both locals and visitors from Hong Kong, Fat Siu Lau has kept its customers coming back since 1903 with delicious Macanese favorites and modern creations. Try ordering whatever you see the chatty Cantonese stuffing themselves with at the surrounding tables, and you won't be disappointed. Your meal might well consist of whole curry crab, grilled prawns in a butter garlic sauce, and the famous roasted pigeon dressed in a secret marinade. Fat Siu Lau 2 is on Macau Lan Kwai Fong Street, and the newer Fat Siu Lau 3 is near the Venetian Macao—both offer the same great food albeit in more modern settings. [$] *Average main: MOP$130* ✉ *64 Rua da Felicidade, Downtown* ☎ *853/2857–3580* 🌐 *www.fatsiulau.com.mo* ✍ *Reservations essential.*

$ MACANESE 🍴 **Pastelaria Koi Kei.** Walking toward the Ruins of St. Paul's, you will likely be accosted by salespeople forcing Macanese snacks into your hands and enticing you to enter one of the street's *pastelarias*—pastry shops that serve traditional almond cakes, ginger candy, beef jerky, and egg rolls. Competition is fierce, but Pastelaria Koi Kei is one of the oldest and best. Hong Kong residents regularly haul the distinctive tan bags, heavy with snacks (in particular, the Portuguese custards), back home for friends and relatives. Other branches are on nearby Rua de São Paulo and on Rua do Cunha in Taipa. Cash is preferred. [$] *Average main: MOP$20* ✉ *70–72 Rua Felicidade, Downtown* ☎ *853/2893–8102* 🌐 *www.koikei.com.*

MACAU OUTER HARBOUR

$ AFRICAN 🍴 **AfriKana.** Macau's historical contacts with Africa, especially Angola and Mozambique, come into sharp focus in one of the few places on the peninsula where you can eat roasted coconut chicken under a thatched roof. Scores of Portuguese-speaking residents who were born in Portugal's African colonies come here for parties or cultural events. The eight thatched pavilions feature resilient colors, from dark blues to mustard yellows to sandy reds. [$] *Average main: MOP$40* ✉ *Fisherman's Wharf, Outer Harbour* ☎ *853/8299–3678* ⏲ *No lunch.*

$$$ FRENCH 🍴 **Aux Beaux Arts.** This 1930s-style Parisian brasserie in the MGM Macau is one of the trendiest restaurants around. Chinese diners are particularly fond of its fresh, catch-of-the-day seafood—the lobster is especially choice. So, too, are the French mains, such as beef tartare with french fries. Oysters and caviar are also exclusive, at prices reaching MOP$2,950 for 50 grams. In-house sommeliers are on hand to pair the latest wines with dishes. With tan wood, private booths, and a terrace, the decor is as much old French Concession Shanghai as it is old Paris. Either way, the place has raised the bar for Macau's restaurant scene. [$] *Average main: MOP$205* ✉ *MGM Macau, Av. Dr. Sun Yat Sen, NAPE, Outer Harbour* ☎ *853/8802–2319* 🌐 *www.mgmmacau.com* ⏲ *Closed Mon.*

MACAU INNER HARBOUR

$$ PORTUGUESE Fodor's Choice ★ 🍴 **A Lorcha.** Vastly popular A Lorcha (the name means "wooden ship") celebrates the heritage of Macau as an important port with a maritime-theme menu. Don't miss the signature dish, Clams Lorcha Style, with tomato, beer, and garlic. Other classics include *feijoada* (Brazilian

pork-and-bean stew), seafood paella, and perfect fire-roasted chicken. Save room for *serradura* (aka Macau sawdust pudding, made from biscuits and vanilla whipped cream). Watch for racers during the Grand Prix, as the Macanese owner Adriano is a fervent Formula fan. $ *Average main: MOP$140* ⊠ *289 Rua do Almirante Sérgio, Inner Harbour* ☎ *853/2831–3193* ⌗ *Reservations essential* ⊘ *Closed Tues.*

$$
MACANESE ✕ **Litoral.** In tastefully decorated environs with whitewashed walls and dark-wood beams, one of the most popular local restaurants offers authentic Macanese dishes that are simple, straightforward, and deliciously satisfying. Must-try dishes include the tamarind pork with shrimp paste, as well as codfish baked with potato and garlic, and a Portuguese vegetable cream soup. For dessert, try the *bebinca de leite* (coconut-milk custard) or the *pudim abade de priscos* (traditional egg pudding). Reservations are recommended on weekends. $ *Average main: MOP$180* ⊠ *261 Rua do Almirante Sergio, Inner Harbour* ☎ *853/2896–7878* ⊕ *www.restaurante-litoral.com.*

COLOANE

$$
PORTUGUESE ✕ **Restaurante Espaço Lisboa.** Occupying a converted two-story house with a small but pleasant balcony overlooking Coloane Village, this restaurant is Portuguese owned and has a Portuguese chef—so it's no surprise that it is a favorite of Portuguese residents. Menu highlights include codfish cakes, savory duck rice, monkfish rice, boiled bacalhau with cabbage, and smoked ham imported from the motherland. Take your pick from an extensive list of hearty Portuguese wines, and cap the meal by ordering homemade mango ice cream with a cherry flambé. $ *Average main: MOP$180* ⊠ *8 Rua das Gaivotas, Coloane Island West* ☎ *853/2888–2226.*

$$
PORTUGUESE
Fodor's Choice
★ ✕ **Restaurante Fernando.** Everyone in Hong Kong and Macau knows about Fernando's, but the vine-covered entrance close to Hác-Sá Beach is difficult to spot. The open-air dining pavilion and bar have attracted beachgoers for years now, and the enterprising Fernando has built a legendary reputation for his Portuguese fare. The menu focuses on seafood paired with homegrown vegetables, and diners can choose from among the bottles of Portuguese wine on display or opt for the beloved sangria. The informal nature of the restaurant fits in with the satisfying, home-style food such as grilled fish, baked chicken, and huge bowlfuls of spicy clams, all eaten with your fingers. $ *Average main: MOP$150* ⊠ *9 Praia de Hác-Sá Beach, Coloane Island South* ☎ *853/2888–2531* ⊕ *www.fernando-restaurant.com* ⌗ *Reservations not accepted* ⊟ *No credit cards.*

WHERE TO STAY

DOWNTOWN MACAU

$$
HOTEL ⛬ **Hotel Lisboa.** In Macau's infamous landmark, redolent with history and intrigue, labyrinthine hallways and salons display jade and artworks, and an ostentatiously gilded staircase leads to luxurious guestrooms with handcrafted furniture and Jacuzzi baths. **Pros:** historical interior; central location; superior restaurants; linked to the Grand Lisboa. **Cons:** older building; low ceilings; smoky casino. $ *Rooms*

from: MOP$1480 ✉ *2–4 Av. de Lisboa, Downtown* ☎ *853/2888–3888* 🌐 *www.hotelisboa.com* 🛏 *950 rooms, 50 suites* 🍴 *No meals.*

MACAU OUTER HARBOUR

$$$ HOTEL Fodor's Choice ★ 🏨 **MGM Macau.** The chic accommodations, with their muted cream, brown, and beige color palette, have everything you'd expect in the way of comfort and elegance from a luxury brand; the striking hotel around them, however, distinguishes these rooms from the rest. **Pros:** tasteful architecture; fine art; refined dining and lounge options. **Cons:** inseparable from the casino, which can get smoky and loud; high-traffic location. [$] *Rooms from: MOP$2688* ✉ *Av. Dr. Sun Yat Sen, NAPE, Outer Harbour* ☎ *853/8802–8888* 🌐 *www.mgmmacau.com* 🛏 *468 rooms, 99 suites, 15 villas* 🍴 *No meals.*

$$$ HOTEL 🏨 **Sands Macao.** The Sands Macao is nothing if not luxurious, with spacious rooms that have deep, soft carpets, large beds, and huge marble bathrooms with Jacuzzis. **Pros:** heated outdoor pool; across the street from Fisherman's Wharf. **Cons:** older property; near lots of traffic. [$] *Rooms from: MOP$2000* ✉ *203 Largo de Monte Carlo, Outer Harbour* ☎ *853/2888–3388* 🌐 *www.sands.com.mo* 🛏 *238 suites, 51 VIP suites* 🍴 *No meals.*

MACAU INNER HARBOUR

$$$$ B&B/INN Fodor's Choice ★ 🏨 **Pousada de São Tiago.** This romantic lodging's origins as a 17th-century fortress permeate every corner, from the tunnel-like entrance to the 12 modern luxury suites, each boasting a Jacuzzi bathroom and large balcony. **Pros:** all the modern comfort of a luxury hotel; complimentary minibar and Wi-Fi; intimate sunset views of the Inner Harbour. **Cons:** small pool; limited facilities. [$] *Rooms from: MOP$3000* ✉ *Fortaleza de São Tiago da Barra, Av. da República, Inner Harbour* ☎ *853/2837–8111* 🌐 *www.saotiago.com.mo* 🛏 *12 suites* 🍴 *No meals.*

TAIPA

$$$ HOTEL Fodor's Choice ★ 🏨 **Altira Macau.** Towering over northern Taipa, the Altira provides stunning sea views of the Macau Peninsula from all of its suitelike rooms, each of which also comes with a dedicated lounge, walk-in wardrobe, and circular stone bath. **Pros:** eye-popping pool; open-air rooftop bar. **Cons:** may sometimes be noisy from nearby construction; still a taxi ride from the peninsula. [$] *Rooms from: MOP$2500* ✉ *Av. de Kwong Tung, Taipa* ☎ *853/2886–8888* 🌐 *www.altiramacau.com* 🛏 *184 rooms, 24 suites, 8 villas* 🍴 *No meals.*

COLOANE

$$ RESORT FAMILY Fodor's Choice ★ 🏨 **Grand Coloane Beach Resort.** This is where you truly get away from it all: built into the side of a cliff, every room faces the ocean, and the vast private terraces are ideal for alfresco dining and afternoon naps. **Pros:** green surroundings on Hác-Sá Beach; golf-club access; free shuttles; fun for kids. **Cons:** isolated location. [$] *Rooms from: MOP$1300* ✉ *1918 Estrada de Hác Sá, Coloane Island South* ☎ *853/2887–1111, 852/2114–4368 in Hong Kong* 🌐 *www.grandcoloane.com* 🛏 *200 rooms, 8 suites* 🍴 *No meals.*

NIGHTLIFE

Old movies, countless novels, and gossip through the years have portrayed Macau's nightlife as a combustible mix of drugs, wild gambling, violent crime, and ladies of the night. Up until the 1999 handover back to mainland China, this image of Macau was mostly accurate and did much to drive away tourists. But these days you can enjoy live music and cocktails in elegant surroundings at an ever-growing range of hotels and casinos.

BARS AND CLUBS
DOWNTOWN MACAO

Bar Cristal. An antique French chandelier from the 19th century is the centerpiece of this opulent spot, designed to look like a life-size jewelry box. Order a cocktail or sample one of the many Champagnes in stock. ✉ *G/F, Encore at Wynn Macau, Rua Cidade de Sintra, Downtown* ☎ *853/8986–3663* ⊕ *www.wynnmacau.com.*

Fodor'sChoice
★

MacauSoul. Housed in a bright pink building with pine-green shutters, this lively wine bar is just steps away from the Ruins of St. Paul's Cathedral. The two British expats who manage the place have assembled a wine list that includes more than 430 Portuguese varieties, and there's a fine selection of whiskeys available as well. On the food front, look for British cheese plates, charcuterie boards, and many homemade offerings (desserts among them). Live after-dinner music plays on select dates—particularly Fridays, depending on the season. It's best to call ahead for details. ✉ *31A Rua de Sao Paulo, Travessa da Paixao, Downtown* ☎ *853/2836–5182* ⊕ *www.macausoul.com* ☾ *Closed Tues. and Wed.*

Whisky Bar. Depending on the time of day or night, this bar on the 16th floor of the StarWorld Hotel provides either upbeat cabaret entertainment or a cool moment of respite from the clinking casinos all around. Happy hour is daily from 5 to 8, and the Star Band starts playing nightly at 10:30. In addition to a full selection of the usual hard stuff, the bar has 100 different kinds of whisky, including the ultra-rare Macallan 1946. ✉ *StarWorld Hotel, Av. da Amizade, Downtown* ☎ *853/8290–8698* ⊕ *www.starworldmacau.com.*

CASINOS

Gambling is lightly regulated, so there are only a few things to remember. No one under age 18 is allowed into casinos. Most casinos use Hong Kong dollars in their gaming and not Macau patacas, but you can easily exchange currencies at cashiers. High- and no-limit VIP rooms are available on request, where minimum bets range from HK$50,000 to HK$100,000 per hand. You can get cash from credit cards and ATMs 24 hours a day, and every casino has a program to extend additional credit to frequent visitors. Most casinos don't have strict dress codes outside of their VIP rooms, but men are better off not wearing shorts or sleeveless shirts. Minimum bets for most tables are higher than those in Las Vegas, but there are lower limits for slots and video gambling.

6

Rickshaws await the gamblers leaving the Casino Lisboa, the gambling den that started it all.

DOWNTOWN MACAO

Casino Lisboa. Opened in 1970 by Dr. Stanley Ho, this iconic Macau gaming den is replete with ancient jade ships in the halls, gilded staircases, and more baccarat tables than you can shake a craps stick at. It's great for a few rounds of dai-siu—dice bets over cups of iced green tea. Most of the gamblers are from neighboring Guangdong Province, and Cantonese is the lingua franca. Other popular pastimes at this storied casino revolve around international fine-dining venues and colorful coffee shops, if you care to wander around a maze of marbled floors and low ceilings. ✉ *Av. de Lisboa, Downtown* ☎ *853/2888–3888* ⊕ *www. hotelisboa.com.*

Galaxy StarWorld. As you enter the StarWorld empire you're greeted by tall girls in high heels, while a mariachi band serenades you from across the lobby. The gaming floors are small and have a couple of Chinese-style diners if you get peckish, but the cool Whisky Bar on the 16th floor of the adjacent hotel is an atmospheric place to either begin or end your evening. The neon-blue building is just across from the Wynn Macau and down the block from the MGM Macau. Live lobby entertainment and local holiday attractions add a kitschy, friendly feel. ✉ *Av. da Amizade, Downtown* ☎ *853/2838–3838* ⊕ *www.starworldmacau.com.*

Grand Lisboa. The main gaming floor, notable for its glowing egg statue, features more than 430 tables, about 800 slot machines, and a sexy Paris cabaret show that runs every 15 minutes. The second floor has additional gambling opportunities as well as a great bar. The Grand Lisboa has a variety of dining choices, too. Options range from the baroque Don Alfonso 1890 to the Round-the-Clock Coffee Shop. If the slots have been kind, celebrate by having a divine dinner on-site at Robuchon au Dôme or The Eight: both have earned three Michelin stars. ✉ *2–4 Av. de Lisboa, Downtown* ☎ *853/2838–2828* ⊕ *www. grandlisboa.com.*

MGM Macau. A stylish part of Macau's gambling scene offers lavish lounges, Dale Chihuly glass sculptures, Portuguese-inspired architecture, and fine dining. The gambling floor itself is popular with high rollers from Hong Kong, including business tycoons who are just in for a few days. One of the owners, Pansy Ho, is the daughter of Macau's "gambling godfather," Dr. Stanley Ho; she is a high-octane business professional in her own right and a woman's classy touch shows up in this place's glitz-and-glam energy and high-society appeal. ✉ *Av. Dr. Sun Yat Sen, Downtown* ☎ *853/8802–8888* ⊕ *www.mgmmacau.com.*

Fodor's Choice
★

Wynn Macau. Listen for theme songs such as "Diamonds are Forever," "Luck Be a Lady," or "Money, Money" as Wynn's outdoor Performance Lake dazzles you with flames and fountain jets of whipping water every 15 minutes from 11 am to midnight. Inside the "open hand" structure of Steve Wynn's Macau resort, the indoor Rotunda Tree of Prosperity also wows guests with feng shui glitz. Wynn's expansive, brightly lit gaming floor, fine dining, buffet meals, luxury shops, deluxe spa, and trendy suites make this one of the more swish resorts in Macau. ✉ *Rua Cidade de Sintra, Downtown* ☎ *853/2888–9966* ⊕ *www.wynnmacau.com.*

MACAU OUTER HARBOUR

Fodor's Choice
★

Sands Macao. This was the largest casino on Earth until its sibling, the Venetian, stole the spotlight. It's also the first casino you'll see on the peninsula even before disembarking from the ferry. Past the sparkling 50-ton chandelier over the entrance, the grand gaming floor is anchored by a live cabaret stage above an open bar and under a giant screen. Several tiers are tastefully linked with escalators leading to the high-stakes tables upstairs. The friendly atmosphere and handy location, just across from Fisherman's Wharf and near the bar street in NAPE, make this a good place to warm up for your big night out. ✉ *203 Largo de Monte Carlo, Outer Harbour* ☎ *853/2888–3330* ⊕ *www.sands.com.mo.*

TAIPA

Fodor's Choice
★

Mocha at The Altira Macau. Touting itself as Macau's first "six-star" integrated resort, the Altira Macau is indeed stellar, and its casino—Mocha—is the only classy one on Taipa. Facing the glow of casinos to the north on the peninsula, it offers swank, '70s-style gaming floors decked out in browns and taupes with mod chandeliers. The selection of game play is abundant, from baccarat to straight-up slots to posh VIP gaming rooms. The VIP resort suites, fine-dining, and elegantly discreet 38 Lounge on the roof add to the overall ambience. ✉ *Av. de Kwong Tung, Taipa* ☎ *853/2886–8888* ⊕ *www.altiramacau.com.*

Fodor's Choice
★

Venetian Macao-Resort-Hotel. Twice the size of its namesake in Las Vegas, the Venetian Macao-Resort-Hotel offers ample opportunities for gaming, shopping, eating, and sleeping. Expect faux-Renaissance decoration, built-in canals plied by crooning gondoliers, live carnival acts, plenty of sheer spectacle, and more than a touch of pretension. The

35,768 square-meter (385,000-square-foot) gaming floor has some 2,000 slot machines and more than 600 tables of casino favorites. The sprawling property also includes nearly 3,000 suites, plus performance venues like the 1,800-seat Venetian Theatre and 15,000-seat Cotai Arena. It's no wonder the Venetian Macao is the must-see megacomplex that everyone's talking about. ⊠ *Estrada da Baía de N. Senhora da Esperança, Cotai* ☎ *853/2882–8888* ⊕ *www.venetianmacao.com.*

SHOPPING

Macau, like Hong Kong, is a free port for most items, which leads to lower prices for electronics, jewelry, and clothing than other international cities. But the experience is completely different, with a low-key atmosphere, small crowds, and compact areas. It is a hub for traditional Chinese arts, crafts, and even some antiques (but be aware that there are many high-quality reproductions in the mix, too). Macau's major shopping district is along its main street in the downtown area, Avenida Almeida Ribeiro, more commonly known by its Chinese name, **San Ma Lo**; there are also shops downtown on **Rua Dos Mercadores** and its side streets; in **Cinco de Outubro**; and on the **Rua do Campo.**

DOWNTOWN MACAU

DEPARTMENT STORE

New Yaohan. Originally a Japanese-owned department store, this failing facility was taken over by Macau entrepreneur Stanley Ho several years ago and transformed into a popular shopping destination for locals. "Macau's only department store" offers a good mix of shops selling household goods, clothing, jewelry, and beauty products. It also has an extensive food court, a well-stocked supermarket, and a large bakery. ⊠ *Av. Comercial de Macau, Downtown* ☎ *853/2872–5338* ⊕ *www. newyaohan.com.*

COTAI STRIP

MALLS AND SHOPPING CENTERS

Shoppes at Venetian. The Venetian Macao's vision of a gentrified megamall comes complete with cobblestone walkways, arched bridges, and working canals manned by singing gondoliers (rides are MOP$118). Its 330-plus retailers include all the big-name brands and luxury labels in fashion, accessories, gifts, services, and sporting goods. Onsite you'll also find a spa, 30 restaurants, and an international food court. Don't be surprised to see wandering stilt walkers, violinists, and juggling jesters, especially around St. Mark's Square, which hosts two to three daily live performances. The mall connects with the Shoppes at Four Seasons and Shoppes at Cotai Central, further adding to the number of upscale retail options. ⊠ *The Venetian Macao, Estrada da Baía de N. Senhora da Esperança, Cotai* ☎ *853/2882–8888* ⊕ *en.cotaistrip.com/ shopping.html.*

PEARL RIVER
DELTA

WELCOME TO PEARL RIVER DELTA

TOP REASONS TO GO

★ **Feel the buzz:** This region is the engine driving China's economic boom, and whether you're in older Guangzhou or the "instant city" of neon-lit Shenzhen, you're sure to feel the buzz of a communist nation on a capitalist joyride.

★ **Explore the ancient:** Though thoroughly modern, the Pearl River delta has not lost touch with its ancient roots. From the temples of Guangzhou to the Ming Dynasty walled city of Dapeng in Shenzhen, this is a journey through the centuries.

★ **Soak up some colonial splendor:** A slice of Guangzhou's architecture dates back to the 19th century, when European merchants amassed fortunes in the opium trade, and the buildings from which they once plied their trade still stand on quiet and leafy Shamian Island.

★ **Culinary treats:** You can sample a rich variety of foods in the Pearl River delta, from classic Cantonese fare such as dim sum to seafood fresh from the neighboring South China Sea.

1 Guangzhou. After you've adjusted to the crowds, traffic, and pollution, turn to the city's unique cuisine, sights, culture, and history, such as colonial Shamian and the nearby Baiyun Mountain, where there's a panoramic view of the city from the cable car.

2 **Shenzhen.** Come to Shenzhen to see a city that's bloomed from backwater village to major metropolis in less than three decades. Shop, dine, and head to the Overseas Chinese Town (OCT) Loft pedestrian area to take in some art and culture. The city, directly over the border from Hong Kong, offers a variety of top-notch golf courses. Its Mission Hills Golf Club is a favorite of keen local golfers.

GETTING ORIENTED

The Pearl River delta is a massive triangle. Guangzhou is at the top and Shenzhen on the east corner. We recommend beginning at one corner and making your way around. Guangzhou is fairly dense, so leave yourself two to three days in which to soak it all in before heading down to Shenzhen, where you can spend a day or two shopping, eating, and enjoying the spa before heading to Hong Kong.

7

Dongguan

KCR Rail Link

0   10 mi

0   10 km

Shenzhen Airport

Bao'an

Shekou

Dongjiaozui

Chek Lap Kok
Hong Kong Airport

Lantau Island

2 Shenzhen

HONG KONG

Tsing Yi
Kowloon

Hong Kong

Victoria Peak

Lamma Island

Po Toi

Sanmen Island

Xidan Island

Updated by
Kate Springer

History enthusiasts head to Guangzhou, Guangdong Province's ancient capital and the historic center of Cantonese culture. Gourmands flock to both Guangzhou and Shenzhen to indulge in some of the best examples of contemporary Chinese cuisine. Culture vultures take in the many temples, shrines, and museums scattered throughout the region. A visit to the Pearl River delta will quickly dismiss any lingering notions that China is still a nation bound by the tenets of Marx and Mao.

The hardworking Pearl River delta is one of China's fastest-growing and most affluent regions. With a GDP that rivals that of Saudi Arabia, Guangdong Province has been the industrial engine powering China's meteoric economic rise. All those factories, however, have turned it into one of China's more polluted areas. From the southern suburbs of Guangzhou city to the northern edge of Shenzhen, industry stretches in all directions. Tens of thousands of factories churn out the lion's share of the world's consumer products. This hyper-industry has polluted the entire area's soil, water, and air so badly that clear skies are hard to come by.

As municipal governments struggle to upgrade the quality of life for residents and visitors, pollution levels are slowly improving, as some factories are being shuttered or moved inland. Guangzhou's clean and efficient subway system continues to expand year after year. In Shenzhen, the subway system doubled in size at the end of 2011, and several new lines are under construction.

PLANNING

WHEN TO GO

The best time to go is early spring and autumn, when temperatures and humidity are much lower than in the summer, but this is complicated by a few factors. Unless you have friends in the hotel industry, don't even think about visiting Guangzhou during the twice-annual China Import and Export Fair (Canton Fair)—typically held from April 15 to May 4, as well as October 15 to November 4— when hotel prices double or triple. It's best to skip China during the Golden Week holiday (always October 1–7) when millions of locals crowd airports, hotels, and major sites. Likewise, avoid China in the two weeks before and two weeks after Chinese New Year, which falls, according to the lunar calendar, between mid January and mid February. It's at this time that the trains and buses are packed with workers headed home for the holidays and most businesses close down for the week. So what do we recommend? March, early April, September, October (excluding Golden Week), and early to mid-November.

GETTING HERE AND AROUND

The best way to get around the Pearl River delta is by train and bus. With a little assistance from your hotel, you should be just fine.

AIR TRAVEL

With Hong Kong, Macau, and Shenzhen all in such close proximity, the Pearl River delta airspace is one of the most heavily trafficked in the world. This will give you plenty of options, depending on where you are flying in from and where you want to go. Flying from another mainland city to Shenzhen or Zhuhai is usually cheaper than flying to Hong Kong or Macau. Cathay Pacific out of Hong Kong is one of the best airlines going, and can get you around the Southeast Asia region or farther abroad, while Shenzhen Airlines and China Southern Airlines are quality mainland carriers linking Shenzhen and Guangzhou with many other cities throughout China and across Asia. The major airports are Guangzhou Baiyun International Airport and Bao'an Shenzhen International Airport.

BUS TRAVEL

Bus travel through the area can often be the best way to go, although it can be complicated for the uninitiated. At the Guangzhou main railway station, where metro Lines 2 and 5 cross, you can go to the Guangdong Long-Distance Provincial Bus Station and catch buses to most other cities in the Pearl River delta. There is an English-speaking ticket window for foreigners, and all the waiting areas have the names of the destinations in pinyin. Your hotel might be able to help by writing a detailed note about where you want to go.

CAR TRAVEL

A taxi driver can be hired for around Y500–Y600 plus per day, Your hotel can also help you arrange a car service. Note that drivers will not speak English.

TRAIN TRAVEL

It is quick and easy to get from Guangzhou to Shenzhen or Hong Kong by train. Rail service has come a long way, and the Guangzhou-Kowloon line is as easy as they come. The train features comfortable seats with ample leg space. Tickets can be purchased online in advance (⊕ *www.it3.mtr.com.hk*), from travel agents, or at the station. By the end of 2017 there will be a high-speed rail train that burrows under Hong Kong's Kowloon District, cuts through Shenzhen, and terminates in Guangzhou; this should cut travel times between the two major hubs considerably.

HEALTH AND SAFETY

Overall China is quite safe, with violent crime against foreigners practically unheard of. Still, particularly in Guangzhou and Shenzhen, petty crime can be a problem. Take the usual precautions against appearing conspicuously wealthy, and carry with you only the amount of cash you need. Crowded places, such as bus and train stations, often harbor pickpockets, so keep your eyes on your bags and your wallet in your front pocket. Avoid carrying valuables in open-top bags. If you see a local wearing a backpack on the front of his or her body, it's probably a good idea to do the same.

MONEY MATTERS

ATMs abound in the developed areas of Guangzhou and Shenzhen, and most take foreign cards, so getting cash is relatively simple. A wide range of hotels and stores accept credit cards.

RESTAURANTS

Most Cantonese dishes are stir-fried or steamed, although roasted meats such as barbecued chicken and pork are also popular. A Cantonese mid-morning favorite is dim sum, consisting of bite-sized dishes like dumplings, steamed buns, and pastries. Filled with meat and vegetables, they are a perfect way to start the day, and many traditional dim sum places stop serving by mid-afternoon. In Cantonese culture, weekend dim sum is a family affair.

While Guangzhou is more of a Cantonese-food capital, you can find many other types of food in Shenzhen. Since the city is growing so quickly, most residents are from elsewhere in China, and Hunan, Sichuan, Jiangsu, and Fujian-style dishes can be found easily. Also, more specific styles of food such as Chiu Chow, with its seafood porridges and fish-ball soups, and Hakka, with its more home-style soups and excellent tofu dishes, are plentiful.

HOTELS

Over the past few years, the hotel scene in Guangzhou and Shenzhen has grown rapidly, with local hotels providing reasonably priced lodgings and international chains dominating the high end of the market. English is now spoken by at least a few staff at many mid-priced hotels, and at luxury hotels the staff often speak English well. *Hotel reviews have been shortened. For full information, visit Fodors.com.*

WHAT IT COSTS IN YUAN				
	$	$$	$$$	$$$$
Restaurants	under Y50	Y50–Y99	Y100–Y165	over Y165
Hotels	under Y1,100	Y1,100–Y1,399	Y1,400–Y1,800	over Y1,800

Restaurant prices are the average cost of a main course at dinner or, if dinner is not served, at lunch. Hotel prices are the lowest cost of a standard double room in high season.

VISITOR INFORMATION

While China is a large tourist destination, visitor information facilities are not widely available. The best place to check for the latest information is online at China-specific travel websites or on places like the Fodors.com forum.

TOURS

China Travel Service Limited (*Xiānggǎng Zhōngguó lǚxíngshè*). CTS can arrange just about any type of travel in the Pearl River delta. With more than 40 locations in and around Hong Kong, CTS has an efficient staff that can assist with everything from securing visas to booking hotel rooms. ☎ 852/2853–3533, 852/2522–0450 ⊕ *www.ctshk.com* ☉ *Weekdays 9–7, Sat. 9–5, Sun. 9:30–12:30 and 2–5.*

Splendid Tours (*Bīn fēn xíng*). Hong Kong–based Splendid Tours runs good Shenzhen and Guangzhou tours. The company can also arrange same-day service for single-entry or multiple-entry visas into China. ✉ *Sheraton Hong Kong Hotel & Towers, 20 Nathan Rd., 2nd fl., Kowloon, Hong Kong* ☎ *852/2316–2151* ⊕ *www.splendid.hk.*

GUANGZHOU

132 km (82 miles; 1½ hrs) north of Hong Kong.

The capital of Guangdong Province, Guangzhou (also known as Canton) is both a modern boomtown and an ancient port city. This metropolis of more than 13 million people has all the expected trappings of a competitive, modern Chinese city: skyscrapers, heavy traffic, efficient metro, and serious crowds. Guangzhou is an old city with a long history. Exploring its riverfront, parks, temples, and markets, one is constantly reminded of the impact its irrepressible culture, language, and cuisine have made on the world.

In the early 20th century, Guangzhou was a hotbed of revolutionary zeal, first as the birthplace of the movement to overthrow the last dynasty (culminating in the 1911 Revolution), and then as a battleground between Nationalists and Communists in the years leading to the 1949 Communist Revolution. Following Deng Xiaoping's 1978 Open Door policy, the port city was able to resume its role as a commercial gateway to China.

The Asian Games in 2010 spurred the city to extend the subway system, clean up ramshackle neighborhoods, and institute air-pollution controls. Though pollution is still a problem, Guangzhou's parks, temples,

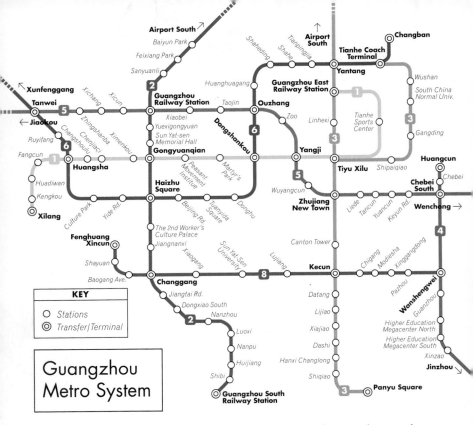

winding old-quarter backstreets, and river islets are pleasant places to explore.

GETTING HERE AND AROUND

Most travelers enter Guangzhou either by train or plane. Long-distance trains pull in at two railway stations, Guangzhou Railway Station and Guangzhou East Station. The East Station has a handy connection to the city's subway system. One-way tickets to or from Hong Kong cost Y190 or Y230 depending on the booking class. There's also a new South Railway Station, which offers high-speed trains to most of China's main cities.

Guangzhou is connected to Shenzhen, approximately 100 km (62 miles) to the south by the Guangzhou East–Shenzhen Luohu Express Train. Tickets cost Y79.50–Y99.50, depending on the class of service. There's also a 35-minute Guangzhou South–Shenzhen North link that costs Y74.50–Y200.

AIR TRAVEL Guangzhou's Baiyun International Airport currently offers at least four flights per day to Hong Kong and dozens to Beijing. The airport has direct flights to Paris, London, Singapore, Yangon (Rangoon), Bangkok, Sydney, Jakarta, Phnom Penh, and other Southeast Asia destinations, and a number of cities in North America including Los Angeles and New York.

Air Contacts China Southern Airlines (*Zhōngguó nánfāng hángkōng*). ✉ *181 Huanshi Lu, near Guangzhou Railway Station* ☏ *020/40066–95539 24-hr hotline* ⊕ *www.csair.com.* **Guangzhou Baiyun International Airport** (广州白云 国际机场 *Guǎngzhōu báiyún guójì jīchǎng*). ✉ *282 Airport Rd.* ☏ *020/3606– 6999, 020/8613–7273* ⊕ *www.baiyunairport.com.* **Zhuhai International Airport** (*Zhū hǎiguó jì jī cháng*). ☏ *0756/777–1111* ⊕ *www.zhairport.com.*

BUS TRAVEL   Guangzhou Provincial Passenger Bus Station is the largest bus station in Guangdong Province. Buses depart from here daily to neighboring Guangxi, Hunan, Fujian, and Jiangxi provinces. There are also deluxe buses to Shenzhen, Hong Kong, and Macau. The most comfortable bus from Guangzhou to Hong Kong is the deluxe, which departs from several hotels, including the China Hotel, Landmark Hotel, and Haitao Hotel. Buses also depart from the main Guangzhou Railway Station for many areas throughout Guangdong and elsewhere in China.

Bus Contacts Citybus (*Chéng bā*). ☏ *0852/2873–0818* ⊕ *www.nwstbus.com. hk.* **Guangdong Long-Distance Provincial Bus Station** (广东省汽车站 *Guǎngdōng shěng qìchē zhàn*). ✉ *145-149 Huanshi Xi Lu* ☏ *020/8666–1297.* **Guangzhou Passenger Transport Station** (广州汽车客运站 *Guǎngzhōu gōng chēzhàn*). ✉ *158 Huanshi Xi Lu* ☏ *020/8668–4259.* **Tianhe Bus Station** (天河汽车客运站 *Tiānhé qìchē kèyùn zhàn*). ✉ *633 Yanling Lu, Tianhe District* ☏ *020/3708–5070* ⊕ *www.tianhebus.com.*

SUBWAY TRAVEL   Guangzhou's ever expanding subway system is cheap, clean, and reasonably efficient. Tickets range from Y2 for short trips to Y9 for the longest leg. It's divided into nine lines that span both sides of the Pearl River, but most casual visitors will spend most of their time on Lines 1, 2, 3, and 5. The most interesting temples and shrines are within walking distance of stations along Line 1, with signs in English pointing the way.

The terminus of Line 1 is the Guangzhou East Railway Station. This area is also the heart of the Tianhe and Zhujiang New Town, Guangzhou's financial and business districts. It is also close to Beijing Pedestrian Road and Tiyuxi, the trendy shopping districts. Gongyuanqian station is the transfer point for Lines 1 and 2.

English-language subway maps are available. Make sure to ask at your hotel or pick one up at a metro station. Consider buying the Transportation Smart Card, which costs Y30 and allows you to add money as you go.

Subway Contact Guangzhou Metro (广州地铁 *Guǎngzhōu dìtiě*). ☏ *020/96891* ⊕ *www.gzmtr.com.*

TAXI TRAVEL   Although taxis in Guangzhou are cheap and plentiful, traffic can sometimes be a nightmare, as it is in most major Chinese cities. Make sure you have the name of your destination written in Chinese. Look for the dark red or blue taxis, which are considered to be trustworthy. If you take a green cab, just be extra cautious about your luggage, remember to bring change, and ask for a receipt.

TRAIN TRAVEL   About a dozen express trains (Y230 first class, Y190 second class) depart daily for Guangzhou East Railway Station from Hong Kong's Kowloon Station. The trip takes about two hours. The last train back to Hong Kong leaves at 9:32 pm. Trains between Shenzhen's Luohu

Railway Station and Guangzhou East Railway Station run every hour and cost between Y80 and Y100.

Train Contacts Guangzhou East Railway Station (广州东站 *Guǎngzhōu dōng zhàn*). ⊠ *1 Dongzhan Lu, Tianhe District* ☎ *020/6134–6222* . **Guangzhou Railway Station** (广州火车站 *Guǎngzhōu huǒchē zhàn*). ⊠ *159 Huanshi Xi Lu* ☎ *020/6135–7222*.

SAFETY AND PRECAUTIONS
Violent crime against foreigners is quite rare. However, especially in crowded train and bus stations and outside bars, foreigners can be the target of opportunists trying to separate you from your wallet.

TIMING
Two or three days in Guangzhou and one to two days in Shenzhen are probably enough to get a good taste of each city.

TOUR INFO
Guangzhou Pearl River Night Cruise (广州珠江夜游 *Guǎngzhōu zhūjiāng yè yóu*). One of the best ways to see Guangzhou is to take a nighttime Pearl River delta cruise offered by the Zhujiang Yeyou Company. The 50- to 90-minute rides pass all of the city's major sites, including Shamian Island, Ersha Island, and the Canton Tower. ⊠ *Tianzhi Wharf, Yangjiang Xi Lu, where Beijing Lu meets the river, Yuexiu District* ☎ *020/8366–1476, 40/0648–8776 booking hotline* ⊕ *www.zhujiangyeyou.com.cn* ✆ *From Y38.*

GZL International Travel Service (*Guǎng zhī lǚ guójì lǚxíngshè gǔfèn yǒuxiàn gōng si*). Guangzhou-based GZL International Travel Service has tours focusing on everything from nightlife to traditional medicine. ⊠ *1 Lejia Rd., Jichang Rd. W* ☎ *020/8633–8680, 020/8634-6903* ⊕ *www.myorientours.com.*

ESSENTIALS
Banks Bank of China (中国银行 *Zhōngguó yínháng*). ⊠ *197 Dongfeng Xi Lu* ☎ *020/8333-8080* ⊕ *www.boc.cn.***HSBC** (汇丰银行 *Huìfēng yínháng*). ⊠ *Garden Hotel, 368 Huanshi Dong Lu* ☎ *020/8313-1888* ⊕ *www.hsbc.com.cn.*

Medical Assistance Guangdong General Hospital (广东省人民医院 *Guǎngdōng xǐng rénmín yīyuàn*). ⊠ *106 Zhongshan Er Lu, Yuexiu* ☎ *020/8382-7812* ⊕ *www.e5413.com.*

EXPLORING

Guangzhou is a massive, sprawling metropolis divided into several districts and many more neighborhoods. Roughly speaking, the city is divided in half by the Pearl River, which runs from east to west and

A nighttime Zhujiang River cruise

separates the Haizhu District (a large island) from the districts in the north. Most tourist destinations are north of the Pearl River.

TOP ATTRACTIONS

Baomo Garden (宝墨园 *Bǎomò yuán*). Much more than your everyday nursery, Baomo Garden stretches across 25 acres (10 hectares) and dates back to the Qing Dynasty (1644–1911), though it was reconstructed in the late 1950s after being destroyed in the Cultural Revolution. The garden is home to more than 30 picturesque stone archways, several carp-filled lakes, and even a rose garden, but it's also known for its galleries, particularly the Treasure Hall, with its impressive collection of preserved pottery, bronze, and jade from ancient China. About an hour away from central Guangzhou by bus, or 40 minutes by taxi, Baomo Garden is a nice break from the downtown crowds. To get here, take a direct bus from the Passenger Transport Station: there are six buses a day, leaving at 8 am, 9:10 am, 10:20 am, 11:50 am, 2:20 pm, and 3:40 pm. ■ TIP➔ **No need to pack a lunch: several restaurants and teahouses on the grounds serve authentic Panyu and Cantonese cuisine.** ✉ *Zini Village, Panyu District, Guangzhou* ☎ *020/8474–6666* 💴 *Y30* ⊘ *Daily 8–6.*

Canton Tower (广州塔 *Guǎngzhōu tǎ*). Guangzhou's skyline wouldn't be as colorful without the Canton Tower, one of the world's tallest TV towers. The 112-story building outstretches even Toronto's CN Tower. Resembling a thin champagne bottle, the building turns into a kaleidoscope of color at night. There are excellent photo opportunities on the observation decks and a section of transparent floors where you can get an eagle's view of the cityscape. The tower features the world's tallest Bubble Tram , which has 16 transparent passenger cars. One revolution takes about 20 minutes. There are also two revolving restaurants and a coffee shop. ⊠ *222 Yuejiang Xi Lu, Haizhu District* ☎ *020/8933–8222* ⊕ *www.cantontower.com* ☒ *Y150–Y488* ⊙ *Daily 9 am–11 pm* Ⓜ *Canton Tower Station.*

Guangdong Museum of Art (广东美术馆 *Guǎngdōng měishùguǎn*). A trove of contemporary and classic collections, Guangdong Museum of Art regularly hosts the works of painters, sculptors, and other artists from around China and the world. There are more than 60 exhibitions a year, showcasing works from artists such as Henry Moore, one of the most celebrated English sculptors of the 20th century, and Chen Ping, who creates textured paintings inspired by politics and human suffering. The museum, which has a dozen exhibition halls and a sculpture garden, is located on Er Sha Island, next to the Xinghai Concert Hall. ⊠ *38 Yanyu Lu, Er Sha Island* ☎ *020/8735–1468* ⊕ *www.gdmoa.org* ☒ *Free* ⊙ *Tues.–Sun. 9–5.*

Guangxiao Temple (光孝寺 *Guāngxiào sì*). This is the oldest and most charming Buddhist temple in Guangzhou. The gilded wooden laughing Buddha at the entrance heralds the temple's welcoming atmosphere. A huge bronze incense burner stands in the main courtyard. Beyond the main hall, noted for its ceiling of red-lacquer timber, is another courtyard with several treasures, among them a small brick pagoda said to contain the tonsure hair of Hui-neng (the sixth patriarch of Chan Buddhism), and a couple of iron pagodas that are the oldest of their kind in China. Above them spread the leafy branches of plum trees and a banyan tree called Buddha's Tree, so named because it is said Hui-neng became enlightened in its shade. ⊠ *109 Guangxiao Lu, 2 blocks north of Ximenkou metro station, Liwan* ☒ *Y5* ⊙ *Daily 8–5* Ⓜ *Ximenkou.*

Fodor's Choice
★

Museum of the Tomb of the Nanyue King (西汉南越王博物馆 *Xīhàn nányuè wáng bówùguǎn*). In 1983, bulldozers clearing ground for the China Hotel uncovered the intact tomb of Emperor Wen, who ruled Nanyue (Southern China) from 137 to 122 BC. The tomb was restored and its treasures placed in the adjoining Nanyue Museum. The tomb contained the skeletons of the king and 15 courtiers—guards, cooks, concubines, and a musician—who were buried alive to attend him in death. Also buried were more than a thousand funerary objects, clearly designed to show off the accomplishments of the southern empire. You can walk through the remarkably compact tomb, which is built of stone slabs and located at the back of the museum up the stairs. ⊠ *867 Jiefang Bei Lu, around the corner from the China Hotel, Liwan* ☎ *020/3618–2920* ⊕ *www.gznywmuseum.org* ☒ *Y12* ⊙ *Daily 9–5:30; last admission 4:45.*

Sacred Heart Cathedral (耶稣聖心主教座堂 *Yēsū shèngxīn Zhǔjiào zuò táng*). In the heart of the old city, this Catholic church is the seat of the archbishop of the Archdiocese of Guangzhou. With gorgeous stained-glass windows and impressive high ceilings, the church is known to locals as *shíshí* (stone house) The Gothic-style cathedral was completed in 1888, and is one of the largest in Southeast Asia. Masses are popular with the city's expatriate community. ✉ *56 Yide Lu, off Yuanxi Alley, Yuexiu District* ☎ *020/8333–6761* Ⓜ *Haizhu Square.*

Fodor's Choice
★

Shamian Island (沙面岛 *Shāmiàn dǎo*). More than a century ago, the Mandarins of Guangzhou designated a 1-km (½-mile)-long sandbank outside the city walls in the Pearl River as an enclave for foreign merchants. The foreigners had previously lived and done business in a row of houses known as the Thirteen Factories, near the present Shamian, but local resentment after the Opium Wars—sometimes leading to murderous attacks—made it prudent to confine them to a protected area, which was linked to the city by two bridges that were closed at 10 every night.

The island soon became a bustling township, as trading companies from Britain, the United States, France, Holland, Italy, Germany, Portugal, and Japan built stone mansions along the waterfront. With spacious gardens and private wharves, these served as homes, offices, and warehouses. There were churches for Catholics and Protestants, banks, a yacht club, football grounds, a cricket field, and the Victory hotel.

Shamian became a fighting ground during the anti-imperialist Shakee massacre in 1925, but survived until the 1949 Revolution, when its mansions became government offices or apartment houses and the churches were turned into factories. In recent years, the island has resumed much of its old character. Many colonial buildings have been restored, and churches like Our Lady of Lourdes Catholic Church have been beautifully renovated and reopened to worshippers.

Especially worth visiting is a park with shady walks and benches that has been created in the center of the island, where local residents come to chat with friends, walk around with their caged birds, or practice tai chi. ✉ *Shamian Island.*

NEED A BREAK?

Shamian Island Blenz Coffee. Enjoy an espresso or latte in Chinese colonial splendor at this coffeehouse in a building dating back to the late Qing Dynasty. Comfy couches, strong coffee, and free Internet access are available in this café inside an old building that housed Guangzhou's U.S. Bank in the pre-revolutionary days. ✉ *46 Shamian Ave.* ☎ *020/8121-5052.*

Sun Yat-sen Memorial Hall (孙中山纪念堂 *Sūnzhōngshān jìniàn táng*). This handsome pavilion stands in a garden behind a bronze statue of Dr. Sun himself. Built in 1929–31 with funds mostly from overseas Chinese, the building is a classic octagon, with sweeping roofs of blue tiles over carved wooden eaves and verandas of red-lacquer columns. The Memorial Hall is split into four grand buildings, and includes an auditorium with seating for thousands. Worth noting are the golden characters on the front door reading *Tian Xia Wei Gong*, which translates roughly to "what is under heaven belongs to all." ✉ *259 Jiefang Lu, Yuexiu District* ☎ *020/8356-7966* 🎫 *Y10* 🕙 *Daily 8–6* Ⓜ *Sun Yat-sen Memorial Hall.*

Temple of the Six Banyan Trees (六榕寺 *Liùróng sì*). Look at any ancient scroll painting or lithograph by early Western travelers, and you'll see two landmarks rising above old Guangzhou. One is the minaret of the

Zhenhai Tower, in Yuexiu Park, was built in 1380 and later incorporated into the city wall.

mosque; the other is the 56-meter-tall (184-foot) pagoda of the Six Banyan Temple. Still providing an excellent lookout, the pagoda appears to have nine stories, each with doorways and encircling balconies. Inside, however, there are 17 levels. Thanks to its arrangement of colored, carved roofs, it is popularly known as the Flowery Pagoda. The temple was founded in the 5th century, but because of a series of fires, most of the existing buildings date from the 11th century. It was built by the Zen master Tanyu, and is still a very active place of worship, with a community of monks and regular attendance by Zen Buddhists. It was originally called Purificatory Wisdom Temple, but changed its name after a visit by the Song Dynasty poet Su Dongpo, who was so delighted by six banyan trees growing in the courtyard that he left an inscription with the characters for six banyans. ⊠ *87 Liurong Lu, south of Yuexiu Park, Liwan* ☎ *020/8339-2843* ⊠ *Y5* ⊘ *Daily 8-5* Ⓜ *Gongyuanqian.*

WORTH NOTING

Chen Clan Academy (陈家祠 *Chén jiā cí*). The Chen family is one of the Pearl River delta's oldest clans. In the late 19th century, local members who had become rich merchants decided to build a memorial temple. They invited contributions from the Chens—and kindred Chans—who had emigrated overseas. Money flowed in from 72 countries, and no expense was spared. One of the temple's highlights is a huge ridgepole frieze. It stretches 90 feet along the main roof and depicts scenes from the epic *Romance of Three Kingdoms*, with thousands of figures against a backdrop of ornate houses, monumental gates, and lush scenery. Elsewhere in the huge compound of pavilions and courtyards are friezes of delicately carved stone and wood, ceramic sculptures, fine iron castings, and a dazzling altar covered with gold leaf. The temple also houses a folk art museum and a shop that sells Chinese handicrafts. ☒ *7 Zhongshan Qi Lu, Liwan* ☎ *Y15* ⊘ *Daily 8:30–5:20* Ⓜ *Chen Clan Academy.*

Fodor'sChoice
★
Five Celestials Shrine (五仙观 *Wǔ xiān guān*). According to local legend, a quintet of gods in the form of goats blessed the city with rice and bountiful harvest. This temple was built to celebrate the origin of Guangzhou's name, which means "City of Goats." Bring your passport to gain admission. ☒ *Huifu Xi Lu, near Xianlin Lu, Yuexiu District* ☎ *020/8332–3508* ☎ *Free* ⊘ *Tues.–Fri. 9–5, weekends 8:30–5:30* Ⓜ *Gongyuanqian.*

Huaisheng Mosque (怀圣寺 *Huáishèng sì*). In the cosmopolitan era of the Tang Dynasty (618–907) a Muslim missionary named Abu Wangus, said to be an uncle of the prophet Mohammed, came to Southern China. He converted many Chinese to Islam and built this mosque in AD 627, making it one of the oldest in the world. His tomb in the northern part of the city has been a place of pilgrimage for visiting Muslims, but the mosque is his best-known memorial. A high wall encloses the mosque, which is dominated by the smooth, white minaret, which rises to 36 meters (118 feet). ☒ *56 Guangta Lu, 3 blocks southwest of the Gongyuanqian metro station, Liwan* ☎ *020/8333–3593* ⊘ *Sat.–Thurs. 8:30–5, except Muslim holy days* Ⓜ *Ximenkou.*

Qingping Market (清平市场 *Qīngpíng shìchǎng*). A busy maze of narrow streets, Qingping Market is a chaotic and colorful way to get a feel for old Guangzhou. The outdoor lanes have the most ambience, what with the overflowing knickknack stalls and traditional medicinal goods (ginseng, fungi, and the like), but there are also some newer air-conditioned indoor markets that make for a nice reprieve in the humid summertime. ☒ *Qingping Lu and Tiyun Lu* Ⓜ *Huangsha.*

FAMILY
Yuexiu Park (越秀公园 *Yuèxiù gōngyuán*). Guangzhou's largest park covers 170 rolling acres and includes landscaped gardens, artificial lakes, an Olympic-sized swimming pool, an amusement park, and playgrounds. The famous Five Rams Statue (五羊塑像 *wǔ yáng sùxiàng*) celebrates the ancient legend of the five celestials who appeared riding on goats to bring grain to the townspeople. Another must-see is the Zhenhai Tower, which has been converted into the Guangzhou Museum, where you'll find a fascinating mix of Guangzhou's archaeological findings. ☒ *Jiefang Bei Lu, across from China Hotel, Liwan* ☎ *020/8666–1950* ⊕ *www.yuexiupark-gz.com* ☎ *Free* ⊘ *Daily 6 am–11 pm* Ⓜ *Yuexiu Park.*

WHERE TO EAT

The city is well known both in and outside of China for its fresh and diverse selection of seafood, due to its close proximity to the South China Sea. Tender braised and barbecued meats are available in delicious variety, and succulent dim sum still rules the roost as the city's hometown favorite.

In addition to Chinese restaurants, Guangzhou has a number of Indian, Italian, Thai, and Vietnamese eateries as well.

Guangzhou

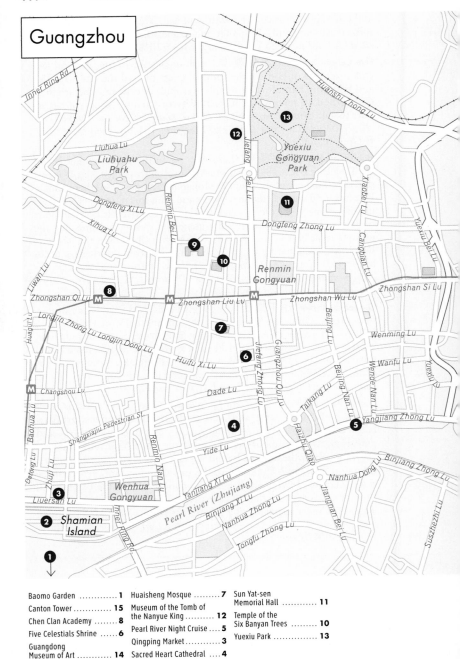

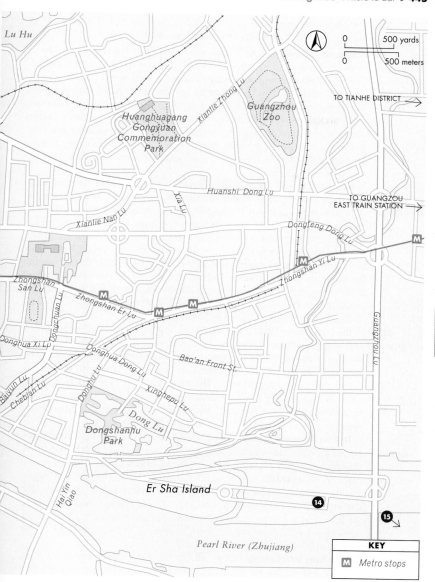

Lu Hu

0 · 500 yards
0 · 500 meters

TO TIANHE DISTRICT →

Huanghuagang
Gongyuan
Commemoration
Park

Guangzhou
Zoo

Xianlie Zhong Lu

Huanshi Dong Lu

TO GUANGZOU
EAST TRAIN STATION →

Xia Lu

Xianlie Nan Lu

Dongfeng Dong Lu

M

Zhongshan
San Lu

Zhongshan Yi Lu

M

Dongchuan Lu

Zhongshan Er Lu

M

M

Guangzhou Lu

7

Donghua Xi Lu

Donghua Dong Lu

Bao'an Front St.

Baiyun Lu

Donghu Lu

Chebian Lu

Xinghepu Lu

Dong Lu

Dongshanhu
Park

Er Sha Island

14

Hai Yin Qiao

15

Pearl River (Zhujiang)

KEY
M   Metro stops

Use the coordinates (✥ B2) at the end of each listing to locate a site on the Where to Eat and Stay in Guangzhou map.

$$ ✕ **Beiyuan Cuisine** (北园酒家 *Běiyuán jiǔjiā*). Worth a visit for the decor
CANTONESE alone, Beiyuan is a throwback to 1928, the year the restaurant opened.
Fodor's Choice The two-story dining room wraps around a traditional Chinese court-
★ yard and includes a well-manicured garden and a pond with goldfish. The restaurant's interior is jazzed up with Chinese screens, lanterns, and chandeliers. The menu—specializing in Cantonese cuisine and dim sum—is available in English, though it can be a struggle to get your hands on a copy. ⓢ *Average main: Y60* ✉ *202 Xiaobei Lu, Yuexiu District* ☎ *020/8356–3365* ⊕ *www.beiyuancuisine.com* ⚓ *Reservations essential* ✥ *E2.*

$$ ✕ **Bingsheng Pinwei** (炳勝品味 *Bǐngshèng pǐnwèi*). Take the lines out-
CANTONESE side of Bingsheng as an indication that the food here is worth the wait.
Fodor's Choice A local Cantonese favorite, Bingsheng is most famous for its *char siu*,
★ or barbecued pork. Wading through the huge picture menu (which includes English) can be a task, so look for the specialties: the chef's black barbecue pork is a signature, as well as the homemade, extra silky tofu, and enormous, piping-hot pineapple buns. People come here for lively, family-style surrounds and excellent local fare, not for the service. ■TIP➔ **Avoid the rush by getting in line by 6 pm or after 8:30 pm.** ⓢ *Average main: Y65* ✉ *168 Tianhe Dong Lu, Tianhe* ☎ *020/8751–8682* ⚓ *Reservations not accepted* Ⓜ *Shipaiqioa* ✥ *H3.*

$$$$ ✕ **The Connoisseur** (名仕阁 *Míngshì gé*). With its arched columns, gilded
EUROPEAN capitals, gold-framed mirrors, lustrous drapes, and immaculate table settings, this top-notch restaurant feels like Regency-era France. The menu has become decidedly more European as of late, with some Irish dishes making an appearance. The menu changes every six months or so. ⓢ *Average main: Y300* ✉ *Garden Hotel, 368 Huanshi Dong Lu, 3rd fl.* ☎ *020/8333–8989* ⊕ *www2.thegardenhotel.com.cn* ⚓ *Reservations essential* 🎩 *Jacket and tie* ⊗ *Closed Sun. No lunch* ✥ *F2.*

$ ✕ **Datong Restaurant** (大同酒家 *Dàtóng jiǔjiā*). Occupying all eight sto-
CANTONESE ries of an old riverfront building with an open terrace on the top floor, this restaurant is popular with locals all hours of the day, so arrive early to be guaranteed a seat. The atmosphere is chaotic and noisy, but the morning and afternoon dim sum is well worth it, especially for the low prices. Famous dishes include stewed chicken feet (delicious, we'll have you know), crispy-skin chicken, and roasted duck. ⓢ *Average main: Y40* ✉ *Nanfang Dasha, 63 Yanjiang Xi Lu, Colonial Canton* ☎ *020/8188–8447* Ⓜ *Beijing Lu* ✥ *C5.*

$$$$ ✕ **Four Seas International House** (四海一家 *Sìhǎi yījiā*). Famous for its
INTERNATIONAL massive buffet, this superkitschy colorful place offers an over-the-top
FAMILY culinary and cultural experience best (and perhaps only) appreciated by kids. It can be easy to get lost among the hundreds of food stations with varying themes, such as a sushi station shaped like treasure ship. There's no need to reserve ahead, as there are more than 1,000 tables up for grabs. ⓢ *Average main: Y168* ✉ *A2 Bldg., Wanbo Center, Yinbin Lu, 2nd fl., Panyu District* ☎ *020/3482–2266* ✥ *G6.*

$$$ ✕ **Guangzhou Restaurant** (广州酒家 *Guǎngzhōu jiǔjiā*). Earning a string
CANTONESE of culinary awards since it opened in 1935, this legendary place is one

of the best-known restaurants in town. The setting is classic Canton, with flower-filled courtyards surrounded by dining rooms of various sizes. The food is some of the finest in the city, with house specialties like "Eight Treasures," a mix of poultry, pork, and mushrooms served in a bowl made of melon. Other Cantonese dishes include duck feet stuffed with shrimp, roasted goose, and of course, dim sum. If you're staying on the eastern side of the city, there's also a branch at 112 Tiyu Dong Lu in Tianhe. ⓢ *Average main: Y125* ✉ *2 Wenchang Nan Lu, Liwan* ☎ *020/8138–0388* ✛ *B4.*

$$ ✕ **The Italian Restaurant** (小街风情意大利餐厅 *Xiǎo jiē fēngqíng yìdàlì cāntīng*). This aptly named eatery has a cheerful home-away-from-home feel, complete with flags from various countries hanging from the ceiling and beers from around the world. The food is inexpensive and good, with pizzas, pastas, and excellent bruschetta prepared by an Italian chef. Food from the menu is much better than the buffet, which is Y158 per person and lasts from 6 to 11 pm nightly. ⓢ *Average main: Y70* ✉ *Pearl River Bldg., 358-360 Huanshi Dong Lu, 3rd fl.* ☎ *020/8386–6783* Ⓜ *Taojin* ✛ *F2.*
ITALIAN

$$$ ✕ **Jiang by Chef Fei** (江-由辉师傅主理 *Jiāngyóu huīshīfù zhǔlǐ*). For fine Cantonese in a more sophisticated setting, Jiang by Chef Fei is a popular choice. The style and service here are miles away from the more casual Cantonese restaurants, and the dainty dim sum creations are equally as memorable. Chef Fei puts a contemporary twist on classic Cantonese cuisine, with creative dishes such as slow-cooked beef shank with chili sauce, Canadian red coral mussels with kale, and pan-fried goose and radish dumplings that are shaped like swans. There is also a great selection of tea and wines that you can pair with your meal. ⓢ *Average main: Y150* ✉ *Mandarin Oriental, 389 Tianhe Lu, Tianhe* ☎ *020/3808–8885* ⊕ *www.mandarinoriental.com* ✍ *Reservations essential* Ⓜ *Shipaiqiao* ✛ *H4.*
CANTONESE

$$ ✕ **Lucy's** (露丝酒吧 *Lùsī jiǔbā*). With so many cuisines represented on its menu (Asian curries, Tex-Mex favorites, British fish-and-chips, and much more), a UN think tank could happily share a table here. Steak is one of Lucy's signature dishes. A favorite among foreigners, this eatery in the old Shamian District has a lovely outdoor dining area; even the dining room has a few trees growing through the roof. A friendly and helpful staff is at your service. ⓢ *Average main: Y80* ✉ *3 Shamian Nan Jie, Shamian Island* ☎ *020/8136–6203* ▭ *No credit cards* ✛ *B6.*
ECLECTIC

$$$ ✕ **Panxi Restaurant** (泮溪酒家 *Bànxī jiǔjiā*). On the edge of Liwan Lake, this famous restaurant has a series of teahouse rooms and landscaped gardens interconnected by paths and bridges that have the feel of a Taoist temple. One room is built on a floating houseboat. Signature dishes include scallop pumpkin soup, baked crab legs, and crispy pork belly. The dim sum is highly recommended, as the restaurant is known for its beautiful presentation along with its fresh flavors. Make reservations or expect long lines. ⓢ *Average main: Y150* ✉ *151 Longjin Xi Lu, Liwan Park* ☎ *020/8172–1328* ⊕ *panxi.net.8hy.cn* ✍ *Reservations essential* Ⓜ *Zhongshanba or Changshou Lu* ✛ *A4.*
CANTONESE

$$$$ ✕ **Tang Yuan** (唐苑 *Táng yuàn*). Housed in a faux colonial-style mansion on an island in Liuhuahu Park, this restaurant's location alone
CANTONESE

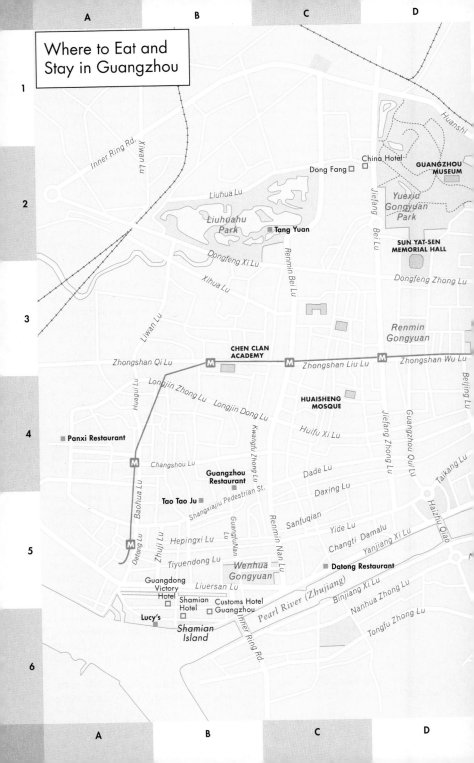

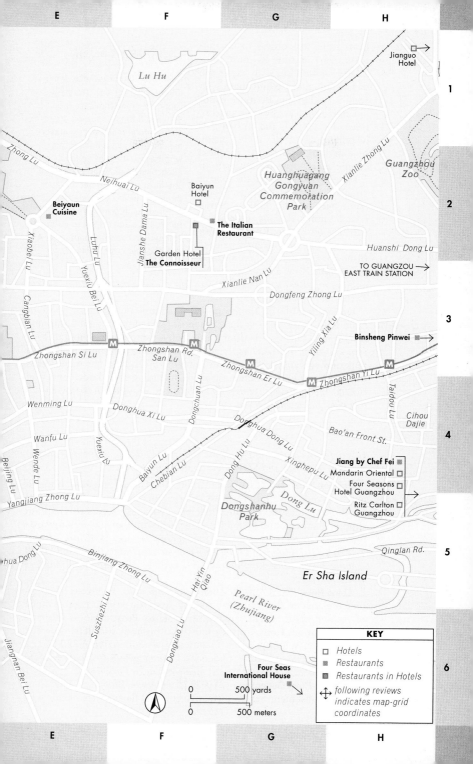

beats out most others in Guangzhou. The cuisine is pure old-school Cantonese, with expensive dishes like abalone and shark's fin soup served alongside more rational staples like crispy fried pigeon, roasted mackerel, and stuffed garlic prawns. Naturally, there's plenty of dim sum, and the "Cantonese combo plate" features a variety of roasted meats. Although the food at Tang Yuan is excellent, most people come here for the opulent dining room. A golf cart waits at the park's entrance on Liuhua Road to whisk diners to the restaurant's palatial front door. [$] *Average main: Y200* ✉ *Lihuahu Park, Dongfeng Xi Lu and Renmin Bei Lu, 2 blocks west of Yuexiu Park metro station, Yuexiu District* ☎ *020/3623–6993* ✣ *C2.*

TO YOUR HEALTH!

Good-bye Starbucks, hello Wong Chun Loong! For decades, the Loong beverage franchise has dominated the Guangzhou scene, and for good reason. Their drinks are superpopular among locals, who believe them to be thirst-quenching, healthy, and tasty. The most popular drinks are *huo ma ren,* a beverage made from crushed hemp seeds (it's the brown beverage displayed on the counter) and *yezi* (coconut milk). A cup of either costs about Y5.

$$ CANTONESE 🍴 **Tao Tao Ju** (陶陶居 *Tàotào jū*). With a name that means "house of happiness," this is one of the city's most revered traditional Cantonese restaurants. Opening its door more than a century ago, Tao Tao Ju is famous for its dim sum, especially the *nai huang bao* (buns made with milk and egg yolks). The menu, available in English, has many items that you're unlikely to find elsewhere, including tasty kudzu and frog rice. [$] *Average main: Y60* ✉ *20 Dishifu Lu, Shangxiajiu* ☎ *020/8139–6111* [M] *Huangsha* ✣ *B5.*

WHERE TO STAY

Use the coordinates (✣ B2) at the end of each listing to locate a site on the Where to Eat and Stay in Guangzhou map.

$$$ HOTEL 🏨 **Baiyuan Hotel** (广州白云宾馆 *Guǎngzhōu báiyún bīnguǎn*). Located in Guangzhou's Western Business District, this convenient hotel is ideal for both business and leisure travelers. **Pros:** easy access to premium shopping spots; close to public transportation. **Cons:** caters towards business travelers; somewhat indifferent service. [$] *Rooms from: Y1790* ✉ *367 Huanshi Dong Lu, Yuexiu District* ☎ *020/8333–3998* 🌐 *www.baiyun-hotel.com/en* 🛏 *590 rooms, 30 suites* 🍽 *Breakfast* [M] *Taojin* ✣ *F2.*

$ HOTEL 🏨 **China Hotel** (中国大酒店 *Zhôngguó dàjiǔdiàn*). Encircled by shopping esplanades, this Marriott property gives you easy access to a range of restaurants that will satisfy any appetite. **Pros:** close to subway; handy location. **Cons:** appeals mostly to business travelers; crowded and very busy lobby; aging facilities. [$] *Rooms from: Y720* ✉ *122 Liuhua Lu, Liwan* ☎ *020/8666–6888* 🌐 *www.marriottchinahotel.com* 🛏 *738 rooms, 114 suites* 🍽 *No meals* [M] *Yuexu Park* ✣ *D2.*

$ HOTEL 🏨 **Customs Hotel Guangzhou** (海关宾馆 *Hǎiguân Bînguǎn*). This four-story establishment has an attractive colonial facade that blends well with the surrounding area. **Pros:** quiet neighborhood; inexpensive; recently renovated. **Cons:** basic facilities; older style decor; very little English spoken. $ *Rooms from: Y260* ✉ *35 Shamian Lu, Shamian Island* ☎ *20/8110–2388* ⊕ *www.customshotelguangzhou.com* ⤳ *60 rooms and suites* ⎟○⎟ *No meals* ✛ *B6.*

$ 🏨 **Dongfang Hotel** (东方宾馆 *Dōngfāng bīnguǎn*). Across from Liuhua

HOTEL
Park, this conveniently located hotel caters more to local Chinese travelers but has well-priced rooms and verdant surroundings. **Pros:** spacious gardens; choice of restaurants; lovely setting. **Cons:** heavy traffic outside; hard to get a cab. $ *Rooms from: Y698* ✉ *120 Liuhua Lu* ☎ *020/8666–9900* ⊕ *www.dongfanghotelguangzhou.net* ⤳ *999 rooms, 101 suites* ⎟○⎟ *No meals* Ⓜ *Yuexiu Park* ✛ *C2.*

$$$$ 🏨 **Four Seasons Hotel Guangzhou** (四季酒店广州 *Sìjì jiǔdiàn*

HOTEL
Guǎngzhōu). You can't beat the views at the Four Seasons Hotel Guangzhou, ensconced in the 103-story Guangzhou International Finance Center. **Pros:** chic and innovative lobby lounge; spacious rooms with magnificent views; top-notch restaurants. **Cons:** pricey; busy lobby; long cab lines. $ *Rooms from: Y1880* ✉ *5 Zhujiang Xi Lu, Tianhe District* ☎ *020/8883–3888* ⊕ *www.fourseasons.com/guangzhou* ⤳ *344 rooms; 42 suites* ⎟○⎟ *No meals* Ⓜ *Huacheng Dadao* ✛ *H4.*

$$ 🏨 **Garden Hotel** (花园酒店 *Huāyuán jiǔdiàn*). In the northern busi-

HOTEL
ness suburbs, this recently renovated hotel is famous for its spectacular garden that includes an artificial hill, a waterfall, and pavilions. **Pros:** spacious premises and gardens; close to public transportation. **Cons:** impersonal service; loud, crowded common areas. $ *Rooms from: Y1188* ✉ *368 Huanshi Dong Lu, Huanshi Dong* ☎ *020/8333–8989* ⊕ *www.thegardenhotel.com.cn* ⤳ *828 rooms, 42 suites* ⎟○⎟ *No meals* Ⓜ *Taojin* ✛ *F2.*

$ 🏨 **Guangdong Victory Hotel** (广东胜利宾馆 *Guǎngdōng shènglì*

HOTEL
bīnguǎn). Originally a set of guesthouses, this refurbished hotel on Shamian Island has an old-school ambience despite its aging facilities. **Pros:** historic building; peaceful area; great view of the city from the rooftop pool. **Cons:** shabby fitness center. $ *Rooms from: Y630* ✉ *53 Shamian Bei Lu, Shamian Island* ☎ *020/8121–6688* ⊕ *www.vhotel.com* ⤳ *300 rooms, 28 suites* ⎟○⎟ *Breakfast* ✛ *B5.*

$ 🏨 **Jianguo Hotel** (广州建国酒店 *Guǎngzhōu jiànguó jiǔdiàn*). Next to

HOTEL

Fodor'sChoice
★
the Guangzhou East Railway Station, this upscale hotel offers large luxurious rooms in a sophisticated palette of soft blacks, grays, and beige. **Pros:** near subway and train stations; centrally located; clean and comfortable rooms; includes breakfast (weekdays only). **Cons:** lack of English TV channels. $ *Rooms from: Y700* ✉ *172 Linhe Zhong Lu, next to Guangzhou East Railway Station, Tianhe District* ☎ *020/8393–6388* ⊕ *www.jianguohotelgz.com* ⤳ *403 rooms, 20 suites* ⎟○⎟ *Breakfast* ✛ *H1.*

$$$$ 🏨 **Mandarin Oriental Guangzhou** (广州文华东方酒店 *Guǎngzhōu wén-*

HOTEL

Fodor'sChoice
★
huá dōngfāng jiǔdiàn). With spacious rooms, top-tier restaurants, and the Mandarin Oriental's famous service, this sophisticated address ranks firmly among the top hotels in Guangzhou. **Pros:** great location; newer property; serene spa and intimate outdoor pool; excellent restaurants and bars. **Cons:** restaurants can get crowded; taxis hard to

7

Not for the squeamish, Qingping Market is brimming with Chinese herbal medicines, dried fruits and vegetables, flowers, and seafood.

flag at peak hours. **$** *Rooms from: Y1900* ✉ *389 Tianhe Lu, Tianhe* ☎ *020/3808–8888* ⊕ *www.mandarinoriental.com* ⮎ *233 rooms, 30 suites* ⎮◯⎮ *No meals* Ⓜ *Shipaiqiao* ✛ *H4.*

$$$$ ⌕ **Ritz-Carlton Guangzhou (广州丽思卡尔顿酒店** *Guǎngzhōu lì sī kǎ'ěr*
HOTEL *dùn jiǔdiàn).* Bringing five-star luxury to Guangzhou's Pearl River New City neighborhood, the Ritz-Carlton Guangzhou is home to posh rooms with marble baths, five restaurants and a bar, and a swank spa. **Pros:** unique cuisine; bar with fine cognacs and cigars. **Cons:** books up fast during conferences. **$** *Rooms from: Y1980* ✉ *3 Xing'an Lu, Pearl River New City* ☎ *20/3813–6688* ⊕ *www.ritzcarlton.com* ⮎ *351 rooms, 35 suites* ⎮◯⎮ *Breakfast* Ⓜ *Opera House* ✛ *H5.*

$ ⌕ **Shamian Hotel (沙面宾馆** *Shāmiàn bīnguǎn).* This historical hotel was
HOTEL built in 1963 and great for visitors on a budget. **Pros:** great location and friendly staff; interesting old building. **Cons:** minimal facilities; could use renovations; very little English. **$** *Rooms from: Y368* ✉ *52 Shamian Nan Jie, Shamian Island* ☎ *020/8121–8288* ⊕ *www.gdshamianhotel. com* ⮎ *44 rooms, 1 suite* ⎮◯⎮ *No meals* Ⓜ *Huangsha* ✛ *B6.*

NIGHTLIFE AND PERFORMING ARTS

Bingjiang Xi Lu is the street for barhopping. The area is very popular with a younger crowd and has great views. For another view of the river, you can always cross the bridge to Yanjiang Xi Lu and drink at some of the bars on that side.

NIGHTLIFE
PUBS AND BARS

1920 Restaurant and Bar (1920餐厅 *1920 cāntīng*). This Bavarian-themed bar is known for its decent selection of imported wheat beers, ale (there are about a dozen), and beverages like Champagne, wine, and cocktails that are best enjoyed on the lovely, spacious outdoor patio. The atmosphere inside is chic but cozy, with a long bar and warm lighting. ✉ *Haizhu Sq., 183 Yanjiang Zhong Lu* ☏ *020/8333–6156* ⊕ *www.1920cn.com* Ⓜ *Haizhu Square.*

IN THE NEWS

Some good publications to check out for regularly updated info on ongoing cultural happenings are *Paper and That's PRD.* For online browsing, *City Weekend* (⊕ www.cityweekend.com.cn/guangzhou) is also a good resource.

Café Lounge. The Café Lounge has a mellow vibe, big comfortable bar stools, quiet tables for two, live music on weekends, and a fine selection of cigars. ✉ *China Hotel, lobby* ☏ *020/8666–6888.*

The Happy Monk (摩克咖啡厅 *Mókè kāfēitīng*). If you're looking for a low-key atmosphere and outdoor seating, head to The Happy Monk. On the drinks menu, you'll find a mix of fruity cocktails and a decent wine selection, as well as the likes of Guinness and Stella Artois on tap. The basic pub grub here isn't going to blow your mind, but the friendly ambience, tucked-away location, and funky copper-and-wood interiors make it a popular choice among locals and expats. ✉ *9 Jianshe 5th Lu, near Huale Lu, Yuexiu* ☏ *020/8376–5597* ⊕ *www.thehappymonk.com* ⊙ *Daily 10:30 am–2:30 am* Ⓜ *Taojin.*

The Loft (The Loft 酒吧 *The Loft jiǔbā*). It doesn't get much classier than the low-lit surrounds, rare whiskeys, crystal glassware, cigars and private booths at The Loft in the Mandarin Oriental. The extensive and informative whiskey list is impressive, as is the service staff's encyclopedic knowledge of each pour. The food is a draw, too, with talked-about wagyu beef *tataki*, chocolate wontons, and big, fat burgers. ■ **TIP➔** **For one of the private booths, be sure to make a reservation.** ✉ *Mandarin Oriental, 389 Tianhe Lu, Tianhe* ☏ *020/3808–8883* ⊕ *www.mandarinoriental.com* ⊙ *Daily 5 pm–1 am* Ⓜ *Shipaiqiao.*

The Paddy Field (爱尔兰餐吧 *Ài'ěrlàn cānbā*). The games of darts, pints of Guinness and Kilkenny, and football matches on a massive screen make you long for Ireland. It's a popular gathering spot for Guangzhou's expat community. ✉ *38 Huale Lu, 2nd fl., Yuexiu* ☏ *020/8360–1379* ⊕ *www.thepaddyfield.com* ⊙ *Weekdays 11:30 am–2:30 pm and 4:30 pm–2 am, weekends 11:30 am–2 am* Ⓜ *Taojin* ✉ *Lingnan Tiandi Commercial Centre, Shop XT204, 2 Xie Tian Lane, opposite the Bell Tower* ☏ *0757/8203–1023* ⊕ *thepaddyfield.com* ✉ *Fineland Tower, 28 Tiyu Dong Lu, 4th fl., Tianhe* ☏ *020/8398–6181* ⊕ *thepaddyfield.com.*

Social & Co (华菁 *Huá jīng*). Inspired by New Zealand's friendly restaurant and bar culture, Social & Co is one of the most cosmopolitan bars in Guangzhou. Indoors, there's an eclectic feel—as evidenced by kitschy garden gnomes, plump leather furniture, and polished-concrete walls—while outdoors, a spacious seating area fills up quickly for Sunday

Beijing Lu is one of Guangzhou's busiest shopping districts.

brunch (11:30 am–3 pm). On the menu, you'll find a carefully selected list of bottled beers and wine, as well as a handful of modern Aussie and New Zealand sharing plates. ⊠ *Shop 112-113, 6 Huajiu Lu, Tianhe* ☎ *020/3804-9243* ⊕ *www.socialandco.com* Ⓜ *Zhujiang New Town.*

DANCE CLUBS

Deep Anger Music Power House (咆哮 *Pàoxiào*). This cool dance club is located in a building that was a theater back in the days of Sun Yat-sen. Lounge lizards and history buffs will enjoy sipping a beer here. ⊠ *183 Yanjiang Lu* ☎ *020/8317-7158.*

Soho Bar (苏荷酒吧 *Sū hé jiǔbā*). The biggest and hippest dance and live music venue in Guangzhou, Soho Bar lets you get your jive on to house and electronica. When the sound gets to be too much, chill out on the outdoor terrace. Admission is Y50 to Y100, depending on the night. ⊠ *87 Changdi Lu* ☎ *020/8336-6611* ⊕ *www.sohobar.com.cn* Ⓜ *Haizhu Square.*

PERFORMING ARTS

Friendship Theater (友谊剧院 *Yǒuyì jùyuàn*). Operating since 1965, the Friendship Theater has hosted many art organizations from nearly 100 countries. The performance fare includes drama, theater, opera, symphony, and concerts. Almost all of the performances are in Chinese. ⊠ *696 Renmin Bei Lu, Haizhu District* ☎ *020/8666-8991* ⊕ *www. gzyyjy.com.cn* Ⓜ *Guangzhou Railway.*

Guangdong Modern Dance Company (广东现代舞团 *Guǎngdōng xiàndàiwǔ tuán*). Mainland China's first professional modern-dance company, Guangdong Modern Dance Company is regularly praised for its cutting-edge style. ⊠ *13 Shuiyinhenglu, Shaheding* ☎ *020/8704–7117* ⊕ *www.gdmdc.com.*

FAMILY **Guangzhou Puppet Art Center** (广州木偶艺术中心 *Guǎngzhōu mù'ǒu yìshù zhōngxīn*). Live puppet shows are presented every Saturday and Sunday at 10:30 am inside Guangzhou Puppet Art Center's two theaters. ⊠ *43 Hongde Lu, Haizhu District* ☎ *020/8431–0235.*

GALLERIES AND PERFORMANCE SPACES

Vitamin Creative Space (维他命艺术空间 *Wéitāmìng yìshù kōngjiān*). If eclectic art is your thing, then Vitamin Creative Space might be worth the trip, but be warned: it's located in the back of a semi-enclosed vegetable market and not easy to find even if you speak Chinese. Call ahead for directions or someone to lead you to the door. ⊠ *Xinggang Cheng, 29 Hengyi Jie, Room 301, Haizhu District* ☎ *020/8429–6760* ⊕ *www.vitamincreativespace.com/en.*

Xinghai Concert Hall (星海音乐厅 *Xīnghǎi yīnyuètíng*). Home of the Guangzhou Symphony Orchestra, Xinghai Concert Hall puts on a superb array of concerts featuring national and international performers. Next to the Guangzhou Museum of Art, the concert hall is surrounded by a fantastic sculpture garden. ⊠ *33 Qingbo Lu, Er Sha Island* ☎ *020/8735–2222* ⊕ *www.concerthall.com.cn.*

SHOPPING

Shangxiajiu Pedestrian Road is a massive warren of old shops in the heart of Old Guangzhou. There's a wide variety of street stalls selling a large selection of delicious edibles. Beijing Pedestrian Road makes no pretense at being anything other than a neon-draped pedestrian mall, similar to Beijing's Wangfujing or Shanghai's East Nanjing Road. Noisy and fun, the street is lined with cheap food stalls, cafés, and fast-food chains.

MALLS AND MARKETS

Fangsuo Commune (方所 *Fāngsuǒ*). Bookstores in China have come a long way, and now cater to the artsy and intellectual set. Located in the upscale TaiKoo Hui Mall, this bookstore offers a lot of open space, and a modish coffee bar where you can easily hook up with a laptop and latte. ⊠ *TaiKoo Hui Mall, MU35, 383 Tianhe Lu, Tianhe* ☎ *020/3868–2327* Ⓜ *Shipaiqiao.*

FAMILY **Grandview Mall** (正佳广场 *Zhèngjiā guǎng chǎng*). This megamall (one of the largest in Guangzhou) is worth a visit if you want to get a sense of Guangzhou's rapidly growing middle class. There are hundreds of stores, many of them well-known international chains including the likes of Nike, H&M, and Benefit. ⊠ *228 Tianhe Lu, Tianhe* ☎ *020/3833–0812* ⊕ *www.zhengjia.com.cn* Ⓜ *Tianhe Sports Center or Tianhenan.*

La Perle (丽柏广场 *Lìbǎi guǎngchǎng*). This upscale shopping mall sits in the city's central business district. Luxury brands include Versace, Louis Vuitton, Gucci, Furla, Fendi, and Armani. ⊠ *367 Huanshi Dong Lu, connected to Baiyuan Hotel* ☎ *020/8336–0222* ⊕ *www.laperle-global.com* Ⓜ *Taojin.*

TaiKoo Hui (太古汇 *Tàigǔ huì*). Housing more than 180 brands—both big names and new boutiques—TaiKoo Hui is one of the most sophisticated shopping experiences in Guangzhou. Look for bookstore Fang Suo, which is a great place to sit down with your laptop. The Food Garden on the third floor is also a relaxing place to grab a bite outdoors. There are a number of eateries on the mezzanine level, including the likes of Din Tai Fung, Jade Garden, and Kee Wah Bakery. ⊠ *383 Tianhe Lu, Tianhe* ☎ *020/2886–1555* ⊕ *www.taikoohui.com* Ⓜ *Shipaiqiao.*

Zhanxi Clothing Wholesale Market (站西市场 *Zhànxī shìchǎng*). At this wholesale market you can get bargains on upmarket jeans and many other kinds of casual clothing. Sellers are not as aggressive as in Beijing, however. They usually only accept orders of 100 items or more. Even if you don't need quite that many Lacoste polos, it's great fun to poke around. ⊠ *4 Zhanxi Lu, near Wangshengtang Jie* Ⓜ *Guangzhou Railway.*

SIDE TRIP TO BAIYUN MOUNTAIN

8.8 km (5.5 miles) north of central Guangzhou.

Baiyun Mountain (白云山 *Bàiyúnshǎn*). Also known as White Cloud Mountain, Baiyun Mountain gets its name from the halo of clouds that, in the days before Guangzhou was shrouded in heavy pollution, appeared around the peak following a rainstorm. The mountain is part of a 28-square-km (11-square-mile) resort area, and consists of seven parks and scenic areas, about 30 peaks, and myriad gullies. **Santailing Park** is home to the enormous Yuntai Garden, of interest to anybody with a thing for botany. **Fei'eling Park** has a nice sculpture garden, and **Luhu Park** is home to Jinye Pond, as pure and azure a body of water as you're likely to find within 100 miles. All in all, a trip to Baiyun Mountain is a good way to get out of the city center—maybe for a day of hiking—without traveling too far. The cable car is an excellent way to get an expansive view of the cityscape and take photos with the backdrop of Guangzhou's skyline. ⊕ *www.baiyunshan.com.cn* ✉ *Y5* ⏱ *Daily 9–5.*

SHENZHEN

136 km (85 miles; 1 hr 20 mins by express train, 2 hrs by express bus) from Guangzhou.

Shenzhen may be China's youngest city, but this is one metropolis that's definitely come of age. A small farming town until 1980, Shenzhen was chosen by Deng Xiaoping as an incubator in which the seeds of China's economic reform were to be nurtured. The results are the stuff of legend; a quarter century later Shenzhen is now among China's richest.

Until recently, most visitors thought of China's youngest city as a place to pass through on the way from Hong Kong to Guangzhou. But over the last several years, the city has seen a complete transformation, with zippy subways, beaming modern shopping malls, and an uptick in topnotch restaurants.

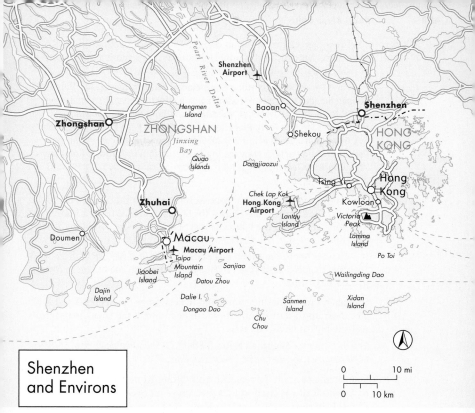

Shenzhen and Environs

GETTING HERE AND AROUND

Tens of thousands of people cross daily between Hong Kong and Shenzhen, usually over the Luohu border crossing. Over the weekends, numbers can triple. Most visitors take the East Rail Line from Kowloon to the crossing and walk into Shenzhen. Visitors can also cross at the Lok Ma Chau Station, which channels you straight into Shenzhen's Futian District, although long queues are common here.

A more expensive—but infinitely more pleasant—way is to take the ferry from Hong Kong's Central ferry pier to Shekou Harbor. Here, immigration lines are a fraction of what they can be in Luohu.

AIR TRAVEL Shenzhen's Bao'an International Airport is very busy, with flights to more than 50 cities. There is bus service between the airport and Hong Kong, as well as a ferry link between the Shenzhen and Hong Kong airports. Bus service links the Shenzhen Railway Station, via Hualian Dasha, direct to Shenzhen Airport for Y20 each way.

Air Contacts China Southern Airlines (中国南方航空 *Zhōngguó nánfāng hángkōng*). ✉ 181 Huanshi Xi Lu, Guangzhou ☏ 020/8668–2000 hotline, 400/669–5539 bookings ⊕ www.csair.cn. **Shenzhen Airport** (深圳机场 *Shēnzhèn jīchǎng*). ☏ 0755/2345–6789 ⊕ eng.szairport.com.

BOAT AND FERRY TRAVEL

The Turbojet Company runs regular ferries connecting Hong Kong, Shenzhen, Macau, and Zhuhai. One-way trips from Hong Kong to Shenzhen are around Y120–Y150.

Boat and Ferry Contacts Hong Kong-Macau Ferry Terminal (澳门码头 *Gǎngào mǎ tóu*). ⊠ *Shun Tak Centre, Connaught Rd., Sheung Wan, Hong Kong* ☎ *852/2546–3528* ⊕ *www.gov.hk/en/residents/transport/crossboundary/ ferryservices.* **Shekou Ferry Pier (Hong Kong-Macau Ferry)** ⊠ *Terminal Bldg. 1, 1 Gangwan Lu, Shekou* ☎ *0755/2669–5600* ⊕ *www.szgky.com* Ⓜ *Shekou Port.* **Shenzhen Party** ⊕ *www.shenzhenparty.com/travel.* **Turbojet Company** ⊠ *Fuyong Ferry Terminal, Airport 9th Rd., Bao'an District* ☎ *0852/2859–3333* ⊕ *www.turbojet.com.hk.*

BUS TRAVEL

Air-conditioned express buses crisscross most of the Pearl River delta region several times a day. Buses for Shenzhen leave from a number of locations, including the China Travel Service branches in Hong Kong's Central and Wan Chai districts.

Bus Contact Shenzhen Luohu Bus Station (深圳市罗湖汽车客运站 *Shēnzhèn shì luōhú qìchē kèyùn zhàn*). ⊠ *East Plaza, 1st–2nd fls., Luohu District* ☎ *0755/8232–1670.*

SUBWAY TRAVEL

Shenzhen's metro has five lines, and tickets range between Y2 and Y11. The most up-to-date information can be found at the Shenzhen Metro's website at ⊕ *www.szmc.net.*

Subway Contact Shenzhen Metro (深圳地铁 *Shēnzhèn dìtiě*). ☎ *0755/8896– 0600 customer service hotline* ⊕ *www.szmc.net.*

TRAIN TRAVEL

Shenzhen can easily be reached from Hong Kong by taking the metro to Luohu Railway Station and then crossing over the border on foot. Trains between Guangzhou East Railway Station and Shenzhen's Luohu Railway Station depart every 15 minutes and cost between Y80 and Y100.

Train Contacts Mass Transit Rail (香港地铁 *Xiānggǎng dìtiě*). ☎ *0852/2881– 8888 hotline* ⊕ *www.mtr.com.hk.* **Shenzhen Railway Station** (深圳火车站 *Shēnzhèn huǒchē zhàn*). ⊠ *1008 Jianshe Lu, Luohu District.*

SAFETY AND PRECAUTIONS

Shenzhen is safe for the most part, but keep an eye on your bags, especially in crowded spots like Luohu Station. Take care around the expat bar areas; pickpockets have been known to prey on drunken foreigners.

TIMING

Shenzhen is a good bet for a one- or two-night stay if you are looking for good food, shopping, or an expert massage. The spas remain less expensive than those in Hong Kong.

ESSENTIALS

Banks HSBC (汇丰银行 *Huìfēng yínháng*). ⊠ *Shangri-la Hotel, 1002 Jianshe Lu, Shop No. 9, Luohu District* ☎ *0755/2513–8138* ⊕ *www.hsbc.com.cn.* **Bank of China** (中国银行 *Zhōngguó yínháng*). ⊠ *Nanyang Mansion, 2002 Jianshe Lu, Luohu District* ☎ *0755/2515–6333* ⊕ *www.boc.cn.*

Medical Assistance Shenzhen People's Hospital ⊠ *1017 Dongmen Bei Lu N, Shenzhen* ☎ *0755/2553–3018, 1387 [Outpatient Dept.].* **Shenzhen Second**

AVOID THE BORDER-CROSSING CRUSH

At Luohu (the main border crossing between Hong Kong and mainland China) the masses are funneled through a three-story building. From the outside this building looks huge, but from the inside—especially when you're surrounded by a quarter of a million people waiting to be processed—the crossing is reminiscent of a scene from *Soylent Green*.

If you're going through Shenzhen on your way to Guangzhou, take the through train from Kowloon to Guangzhou. The immigration line at the Guangzhou East Station is a comparative piece of cake, even on the worst days. It's possible to buy tickets on the fly on this commuter train, but we advise booking online a day or two in advance.

If you're heading into Shenzhen, why not trade the mad crush of Luohu for an hour-long ferry ride followed by a quick trip through the much less popular border crossing at Shekou Harbor? Ferries are usually not more than half full.

Another way to get to Shenzhen is to take the East Rail Line to the Lok Ma Chau station, built by Hong Kong's MTR to make crossing the border easier for travelers. The station is expansive and efficient, though here, too, it can be quite crowded.

People's Hospital (深圳第二人民医院 *Shēnzhèn dì èr rénmín yīyuàn*). ⊠ *3002 Sungang Xi Lu, Futian District* ☎ *0755/8336–6388* ⊕ *www.szrch.com.*

7

EXPLORING

Sprawling Shenzhen is composed of numerous districts. Luohu and Futian are the "downtown" districts, with most of the major shopping areas and hundreds of hotels. A foray outside the sprawl of Shenzhen proper is worth the trip if you have the time; Yantian and Longgang are the closest destinations for beaches and atmospheric historical buildings.

Futian, Shenzhen's commercial hub, is where Shenzhen's gourmands go for a night of gastronomic pleasure. The Zhenhua Road area has scores of excellent restaurants competing for the patronage of Shenzhen's very discriminating diners. The Shekou neighborhood in the Nanshan District is known for its many outdoor bars and restaurants. It's well known by locals for for Sea World Plaza, a pedestrian mall with alfresco restaurants, low-key bars, and a completely landlocked oceangoing vessel (now transformed into a bar, hotel, and nightclub complex).

NANSHAN

TOP ATTRACTIONS

FAMILY **Window of the World** (深圳世界之窗 *Shēnzhèn shìjiè zhī chuāng*). With miniature versions of more than 130 of the world's most famous landmarks, Window of the World is one of China's biggest and busiest homegrown theme parks. Divided into five geographical areas connected by winding paths and a monorail, it includes—not at all to scale—the Taj Mahal, Mount Rushmore, the Sydney Harbor Opera House, and a 108-meter-high (354-foot-high) Eiffel Tower that can be seen from miles away. There is also a fireworks show at 9 pm on weekends and holidays. ✉ *9037 Shennan Dadao, Nanshan District* ☏ *0755/2660–8000* ⊕ *www. szwwco.com* ✎ *Y180* ⊙ *Daily 9–10:30* Ⓜ *Window of the World.*

WORTH NOTING

He Xiangning Art Museum (何香凝 美术馆 *Hé xiāngníng měishùguǎn*). The museum itself has seen better days, but this musty old building is chock-full of excellent contemporary and classical art from all over China. Not only will you find

works from young up-and-coming artists, but there are also impressive multimedia displays and sculptures. ✉ *9013 Shennan Dadao, Nanshan District* ☏ *0755/2660–4540* ⊕ *www.hxnart.com* ✎ *Free* ⊙ *Tues.–Sun. 10–5:30* Ⓜ *OCT.*

OCT Contemporary Art Terminal (OCT当代艺术中心 *OCT dāngdài yìshù zhōngxīn*). Surrounded by the OCT Loft's trendy cafés and bars, this is where you'll find works from well-regarded artists from Beijing and beyond. A cluster of exhibition halls and venues, the OCT Art Terminal hosts the Shenzhen Sculpture Biennale (usually in May) and the annual "New Works #1" exhibition, as well as artist-in-residence programs, live music, multimedia installations, and dance performances. The crown jewel is the OCT Art & Design Gallery (closed Monday), a massive glass-and-steel renovated warehouse, which champions contemporary art and aims to further graphic, fashion, and digital design in China. ✉ *Bldg. F2, Enping Jie, near Kaiping Jie and Xiangshan Dong Jie, Nanshan District* ☏ *0755/2691–5100* ⊕ *www.ocat.org.cn* ✎ *Free* ⊙ *Tues.–Sun. 10–5:30* Ⓜ *Qiaocheng East or Qiaocheng North.*

OUTER SHENZHEN

Just east of Luohu, Yantian is Shenzhen's beach district. **Dameisha** and **Xiaomeisha** are two beaches adjacent to one another, which offer sun, surf, and strange statues of colorful winged men doing what appears to be beachfront *tai chi.* Dameisha is a public beach, whereas Xiaomeisha has a Y20 admission price. Both are about 50 minutes from Luohu by taxi. **Xichong Beach,** another 30 minutes by taxi to the east, is larger and much more secluded than its neighbors close to town. These beaches are not quite up to Western standards but make for pleasant strolls.

Dapeng Fortress and the Hakka Folk Customs Museum and Enclosures are slices of ancient China; they are about an hour by taxi from the modern heart of Luohu.

TOP ATTRACTIONS

Dapeng Fortress (大鹏所城 *Dàpéng suǒchéng*). Like the rapidly disappearing *hutong* neighborhoods of Beijing, Dapeng Fortress in the Longgang District is a living museum. The Old Town contains homes, temples, shops, and courtyards that look pretty much the way they did

Don't miss the floor show at Minsk World.

when they were built over the course of the Ming (1368–1644) and Qing (1644–1911) dynasties. For the most part, the residences are occupied, the shops are doing business, and the temples are active houses of worship. Dapeng's ancient city is surrounded by an old stone wall, and entered through a series of gates. ⊠ *Pengcheng Village, Dapeng Town, Longgang District* ☎ *0755/8431–9269* ⊕ *www.szdpsc.com* 🖃 *Y20* ⊗ *Daily 8:30–6.*

Hakka Folk Customs Museum and Enclosures (客家民俗博物馆 *Kèjiā mínsú bówùguǎn*). Hakka Folk Customs Museum and Enclosures is a large series of concentric circular homes built inside an exterior wall that basically turns the whole place into a large fort. Inside the enclosure are a large number of old Hakka residences, some of which are still filled with tools and furniture left over from the Qing Dynasty. While some restoration projects elsewhere might pretty things up to the point of making the site look unreal, the opposite is true here. ⊠ *Luoruihe Village, Longgang Township, 1 Luoruihe Bei Jie, Longgang District* ☎ *0755/8429–6258* 🖃 *Y10* ⊗ *Daily 9–5.*

WORTH NOTING

Fodor'sChoice ★ **Dafen Oil Painting Village** (大芬油画村 *Dàfēn yóuhuà cūn*). If you're interested in watching art in the making, spend an afternoon at the Dafen Oil Painting Village, a small town 20 minutes by taxi from Luohu, which employs thousands of artists painting everything from originals to copies of classics. Where do all those oil paintings you find in motels come from? Visit Dafen and you'll know. It's open most days from about 10 am to 8 pm. ⊠ *Dafen Youhua Jie, near Dafen Art Museum,*

Longgang District ☎ *0755/8473–2633* ⊕ *www.cndafen.com* ⊙ *Daily 10–8.*

FAMILY   **Minsk World** (明思克航母世界 *Míngsīkè hángmǔ shìjiè*). This is Shenzhen's most popular—and perhaps strangest—tourist attraction. It's pretty cheesy but young kids might get a kick out of it. Essentially, it's a decommissioned Soviet-era aircraft carrier that a group of business executives bought in the late 1990s. Parked in perpetuity on the top deck of the ship (which is as long as three football fields placed end to end, and gets wickedly hot in the summer) are several Soviet fighter planes and helicopters. ⊠ *Haijing Lu, Dapeng Bay, Yantian District* ☎ *0755/2535–5333* 🎫 *Y130* ⊙ *Daily 9:30–7:30.*

ADVENTUROUS EATING

The Futian District's Zhenhua Road, just two blocks north of the Huaqiang metro station, is one of the more exciting food streets in Guangzhou. There are very few English menus and even less Western food, so be prepared to be adventurous. Though it's about a block away from the buzz, North Sea Fishing Village Restaurant (北海渔村, *běihǎi yúcūn*, 154 Zhenxing Lu) is a good option. The staff doesn't speak much English, but there are picture menus and live seafood in tanks out front, so you can point and choose with ease.

WHERE TO EAT

From the heavy mutton stews of Xinjiang to the succulent seafood dishes of Fujian, Shenzhen is home to thousands of restaurants existing not to please the fickle palates of visitors but to alleviate the homesickness of people pining for native provinces left behind.

$$$$
NORTHERN
CHINESE
FAMILY
Fodor'sChoice
★
 ✕ **1881** (*Yī bābā yī*). The classy decor and warm ambience are good reasons to dine at 1881, but the delicious food is what makes this one of the most popular restaurants in Shenzhen. Located inside the Grand Hyatt Shenzhen, 1881 specializes in classic Sichuan and Northern Chinese cuisines, and it's particularly well known for its wood-fired Peking duck. Also on the menu are a slew of Chinese wines and teas. ■TIP➔ **The restaurant shuts down for a few hours between lunch and dinner, so be sure to call ahead.** Ⓢ *Average main: Y200* ⊠ *Grand Hyatt Shenzhen, 1881 Bao'an Nan Lu, Luohu* ☎ *0755/2218–7338* ⊕ *www.shenzhen.grand.hyatt.com* 🍽 *Reservations essential* ⊙ *Closed 2 pm–5 pm.*

$$$
CONTEMPORARY
 ✕ **360°** (360度酒吧 *360 Dù jiǔbā*). The ultramodern vibes at 360° complement sweeping views of Shenzhen's equally modern skyline. The restaurant takes up the top two floors of the Shangri-La Hotel and offers a big selection of Western dishes in a somewhat odd picture menu. The standouts include the grilled tiger prawns with polenta, the baked scallops with XO sauce, and just about any of the steaks. Ⓢ *Average main: Y150* ⊠ *Shangri-La Hotel, 1002 Jianshe Lu, 31st fl., Luohu* ☎ *0755/8233–0888* ⊕ *www.shangri-la.com* Ⓜ *Luohu.*

$$$$
ITALIAN
 ✕ **Blue** (意大利餐厅 *Yìdàlì cāntīng*). As the name suggests, the decor here is in various shades of blue—walls, ceilings, and even the mellow lighting. The restaurant is especially well known for its expertly prepared fish dishes. If you're really in the mood for decadence, try

the dessert tray: chocolates, pastries, and several different types of mousse. [$] *Average main: Y300* ⊠ *The Venice Hotel, 9026 Shennan Lu, 3rd fl., OCT, Nanshan District* ☎ *0755/2693–6888* ⊕ *en. szvenicehotel.com* ⌖ *Reservations essential* ⊗ *No lunch* Ⓜ *Window of the World.*

$
CANTONESE

✗**Fangdu Restaurant** (芳都酒樓 *Fāngdōu jiǔlóu*). This Cantonese-style restaurant is one of the few in Shenzhen that offers the feel of a grand ballroom. Fangdu's two floors are decorated with chandeliers and opulent carpets. This is a good place to fill your stomach with decent dim sum, but be sure to get there before 2 pm—otherwise you'll be stuck with some less appealing noodle and dinner dishes. The service is friendly and speedy, but don't expect any English. [$] *Average main: Y35* ⊠ *71 Luofang Lu, Luohu* ☎ *0755/2224–3777* Ⓜ *Xinxiu.*

$$$
CONTEMPORARY

✗**Greenland Lounge** (绿涧廊大堂吧 *Lǜjiànláng dàtáng bā*). This favorite is known for its international cuisine and truly unique selection of Chinese teas. The glass-domed roof and smart-casual ambience make it a popular spot for Shenzhen's movers and shakers. Afternoon tea is highly recommended. [$] *Average main: Y100* ⊠ *Pavilion Hotel, 4002 Huaqiang Bei Lu, Futian District* ☎ *0755/8207–8888* ⊕ *www. pavilionhotel.com* Ⓜ *Huaxin.*

$$
INDIAN

✗**Little India** (小印度餐厅 *Xiǎo Yìndù*). This is definitely not your average curry house. The Nepalese chef offers cuisine from both Northern India and Nepal. The restaurant is especially well known for its tandoori dishes and its selection of naan. [$] *Average main: Y80* ⊠ *138 Mintian Lu, Futian District* ☎ *0755/8317–4827* ⊕ *www. shenzhenindianrestaurant.com* Ⓜ *Shopping Park.*

$$$
NORTHERN
CHINESE

✗**Shui Zu Yu Xiang** (水煮鱼乡 *Shuǐ zhǔ yú xiāng*). This is a hidden treasure amid Shenzhen's vast number of restaurants. It's famous for its Peking duck, said to be just as good as that in Beijing, and for its fish soups, served in hubcap-sized bowls. The catfish and pickled vegetable soup is velvety and the fish melts in your mouth. The smaller side dishes, mostly vegetables, offset the heavier fare. The waiting area in the front has birds in cages, and you're offered tea and pumpkin seeds while you wait. [$] *Average main: Y120* ⊠ *Chang'an Plaza, 1113 Shennan Dong Lu, 1st. fl, Luohu District* ☎ *0755/8230–3704, 0755/8230–3695* Ⓜ *Huangbeiling.*

$$
BAKERY

✗**Sugar Box** (糖立方 *Táng lìfāng*). This patisserie is a great place to take a break while shopping at the nearby MixC mall. Sugar Box offers a

---

TEA CULTURE

Tea enthusiasts will find everything they need and more inside the China Tea Palace (深圳中国茶宫, *Shēnzhèn zhōngguó chá gōng*) a building tucked away down an alleyway off Jingtian Bei Lu in Futian District. There is no English signage on the doorway, but look for the corridor lined with pictures of tea. There are three floors of shops selling tea, tea sets, and accessories. The stores, often family-owned, have a laid-back atmosphere. You can sample a variety of high-end teas, then join in a tea ceremony and, while you won't be overtly pressured into buying tea, the expectation is there.

7

wide variety of homemade choco-lates, cakes, and breads, as well as coffee, tea, beer, and wine. Savory items include mini sandwiches, salad, and pizza. The relaxing out-door atmosphere makes it great for people-watching and whiling away the afternoon. $ *Average main: Y60* ✉ *Grand Hyatt Shenzhen, 1881 Bao'an Nan Lu, 1st. fl, Luohu* ☎ *0755/2218–7338* ⊕ *shenzhen. grand.hyatt.com* Ⓜ *Grand Theater.*

$$ ✕ **Yokohama** (橫滨日本料理 *Héng-*
JAPANESE *bīn Rìběn liàolǐ*). Amazing views of the fishing boats and ferries of Shekou Harbor to the east and Nanshan Mountain to the north are yours at Yokohama. This is a good place to rest before taking the ferry to Hong Kong or Macau. The sashimi is the freshest around, and the other dishes are the real deal. The clientele is mostly Japanese, which is always a good sign. Try a side dish of *oshinko* (traditional Japanese pickles)—unlike many lesser Japanese restaurants in China, Yokohama takes no shortcuts with its oshinko, and offers eight different types. $ *Average main: Y70* ✉ *Nan-hai Hotel, 1 Gongye Yilu, 10th fl., Shekou District* ☎ *0755/2669–5557* Ⓜ *Shekou Gang.*

WHERE TO STAY

$$$$ ☷ **Grand Hyatt Shenzhen** (廣州富力君悅大酒店 *Guǎngzhōu fùlì jūn*
HOTEL *yuè dàjiǔdiàn*). If you're looking for a hotel that's as serious about its facilities as it is about its food, then the Grand Hyatt is for you. **Pros:** great city and river views from rooms; sprawling spa; helpful concierge service. **Cons:** convoluted elevator system; open-plan lobby gets really loud. $ *Rooms from: Y1850* ✉ *1881 Bao'an Nan Lu, Luohu District* ☎ *0755/8266–1234* ⊕ *shenzhen.grand.hyatt.com* ⤳ *439 rooms, 52 suites* ⏃⏃ *No meals* Ⓜ *Grand Theater.*

$$$ ☷ **InterContinental Shenzhen** (深圳华侨城洲际大酒店 *Shēnzhèn huáq-*
HOTEL *iáochéng zhōují dàjiǔdiàn*). A classy blend of fun and flair, the Spanish-
FAMILY themed InterContinental Shenzhen has everything from bellmen dressed in toreador costumes to a massive Pirates of the Caribbean–style ship serving as a bar and restaurant. **Pros:** eye-catching design; playful atmo-sphere. **Cons:** staff can be inattentive; crowded common areas; traffic outside. $ *Rooms from: Y1700* ✉ *9009 Shennan Lu, Nanshan Dis-trict* ☎ *0755/3399–3388* ⊕ *www.intercontinental.com* ⤳ *463 rooms, 77 suites* ⏃⏃ *No meals* Ⓜ *OCT.*

$ ☷ **Nan Hai** (南海酒店 *Shēnzhèn nánhǎi jiǔdiàn*). This hotel's retro
HOTEL space-age exterior, featuring rounded balconies that look as if they might detach from the mother ship at any moment, greets visitors arriv-ing on the ferry from Hong Kong. **Pros:** near the Hong Kong Island ferry terminal. **Cons:** dated decor. $ *Rooms from: Y759* ✉ *1 Gongye Yilu,*

One of China's youngest cities, Shenzhen City sprawls into various districts.

Shekou/Nanshan District ☎ 0755/2669–2888 ⊕ *www.nanhai-hotel. com* ⌁ *369 rooms* ⦿ *No meals* Ⓜ *She Kou Gang.*

$ ⊡ **The Pavilion** (圣廷苑酒店 *Shèngtíngyuàn jiǔdiàn*). With a great loca-
HOTEL tion in the heart of the business district and an elegant interior, the Pavilion is a solid option for an international-class hotel in Shenzhen. **Pros:**
near metro; doting service; decent dining options. **Cons:** rooms don't
have much character; aging facilities; taxi desert. $ *Rooms from: Y899*
⊠ *4002 Huaqiang Bei Lu, Futian District* ☎ 0755/8207–8888 ⊕ *www.
pavilionhotel.com* ⌁ *297 rooms and suites* ⦿ *No meals* Ⓜ *Huaxin.*

$$$ ⊡ **Shangri-La Shenzhen** (深圳香格里拉酒店 *Shēnzhèn xiānggélìlā
HOTEL jiǔdiàn*). The unbeatable location—practically straddling the border
with Hong Kong—has made the Shangri-La a popular meeting place
and a longtime landmark. **Pros:** near shopping malls; luxurious rooms.
Cons: noisy and crowded neighborhood; aging property; busy lobby.
$ *Rooms from: Y1688* ⊠ *1002 Jianshe Lu, Luohu, east side of train sta-
tion, Luohu District* ☎ 0755/8233–0888 ⊕ *www.shangri-la.com* ⌁ *522
rooms, 29 suites* ⦿ *No meals* Ⓜ *Luohu.*

$$$ ⊡ **Shenzhen Wuzhou Guest House** (五洲賓館 *Wǔzhōu bīnguǎn*). The
HOTEL word "stately" describes every aspect of the Shenzhen Wuzhou Guest
House, which was built by the municipal government to house dignitaries—the guest list includes Chinese Premier Li Keqiang—and is
now open to the public. **Pros:** a unique experience; beautifully manicured garden. **Cons:** expensive; slightly inconvenient location; limited
English. $ *Rooms from: Y1560* ⊠ *6001 Shennan Lu, Futian District*
☎ 0755/8293–8000 ⊕ *www.wuzhouguesthouse.com* ⌁ *334 rooms, 11
suites* ⦿ *No meals* Ⓜ *Futian.*

$$
HOTEL
FAMILY
Fodor's Choice
★

The Venice Hotel Shenzhen (深圳威尼斯酒店 *Shēnzhèn wēinísī jiǔdiàn*). The theme is pure Italian Renaissance, right down to the Venetian gondolier uniforms worn by the staff, and the wide spiral staircases and long hallways give the place an M.C. Escher aura. **Pros:** near metro; good restaurants; butler service; walking distance to theme parks. **Cons:** heavy-handed Italy theme; flaky Wi-Fi; some rooms a little musty. $ *Rooms from: Y1100* ⊠ *9026 Shennan Lu, across from Window of the World metro station, OCT, Nanshan District* ☎ *0755/2693–6888* ⊕ *en.szvenicehotel.com* ↷ *375 rooms and suites* �’○❘ *No meals* Ⓜ *Window of the World.*

> **FORE!**
>
> Although manufacturing is undoubtedly the Pearl River delta's raison d'être, golfing may well come in as a close second with a dozen courses.

NIGHTLIFE

Shenzhen's nightlife scene comes to a boil in two major areas: Coco Park in the Futian District (a flashy crowd) and Shekou in the Nanshan District (a bit more laid-back). Over the past couple of years, a handful of cool spots have also been popping up in the OCT Loft area.

BARS AND CLUBS

Bionic Brewery (百优酿 *Bǎi yōu niàng*). One of the only craft breweries in Shenzhen, Bionic Brewery serves up its own batches of pale ales and wheat beers, alongside guest taps from other local brewers. The taproom is a lot of fun, with plenty of seating, colorful decor, and reasonable prices—drafts cost about Y30– Y 40. ■TIP→ **It's only open on weekends, so plan ahead.** ⊠ *100-1 Jinhe Lu, around corner from Rose Café, Nanshan District* ☎ *0186/6587–4574* ⊕ *bionicbrew.com* ⊙ *Fri. and Sat. 5 pm–midnight, Sun. 5–10 pm* Ⓜ *Window of the World.*

Fool Heaven (福天堂 *Fú tiāntáng*). It's more of a stylish craft beer store than a bar, but Fool Heaven sells more than 100 types of craft beers from all over the world at great prices, ranging from about Y12 to Y60. It's self-serve, so you can take your purchases outside and enjoy the spacious outdoor seating area. If beer's not your jam, you can also find under-the-radar vodkas, wines, and whiskeys, along with coffee and tea. ⊠ *Coco Park, Zhongxin Er Lu at Fuhua Yi Lu, Futian District* ☎ *0755/137–9827–4737* Ⓜ *Shopping Park or Futian.*

Fodor's Choice
★

OCT Loft (华侨城创意文化园 *Huáqiáochéng chuàngyì wénhuà yuán*). A revamped industrial space with OCT Contemporary Art Terminal, cool studios, and shops, the leafy OCT Loft promenade is peppered with trendy alfresco cafés that are popular for evening drinks. For a relaxed night out, look for La Patisserie or LSD Party, which is an Italian café-cum-gallery (*not* a drug den). Better yet, for a memorable musical experience, time your visit with the annual Jazz Festival, usually in October. ⊠ *Off Kaiping Jie, near Xiangshan Dong Jie, Futian District* ☎ *0755/2693–4531* ⊕ *www.octloft.cn* Ⓜ *Qiaocheng East or Qiaocheng North.*

Terrace (露台 *Lù tái*). The Filipino house band rocks the joint almost every night at the Terrace, but you can also find blues, reggae, and other music here all week. If you need a rest from dancing, slip outside to the balcony for a cocktail and a view over Sea World Square. To sit near the band, expect to pay a weekend minimum charge of Y500 per table. ✉ *Sea World Sq., Taizi Lu, near Minghua Lu, Shekou District* ☎ *0755/2682–9105* ⊕ *www.theterrace.com.cn* Ⓜ *Sea World.*

True Color (本色酒吧 *Běnsè jiǔbā*). One of the coolest party scenes in Shenzhen, True Color attracts international DJs. Music is generally trance or house, and the party usually doesn't break up until dawn. ✉ *Dongmen Golden World, 1 Dongyuan Lu, 4th fl., Luohu District* ☎ *0755/8227–4834* Ⓜ *Science Museum.*

V Bar (Ⅴ 吧 *V bā*). Without a doubt the hottest nightspot in the OCT, V Bar boasts a holographic globe hovering over a circular bar. It's the only bar in town with an attached swimming pool. ✉ *The Venice Hotel, 9026 Shennan Lu, OCT, Nanshan District* ☎ *0755/2693–6888* ⊕ *en.szvenicehotel.com* ⊘ *Daily 8 pm–2 am* Ⓜ *Baishizhou.*

Viva Club (喂哇俱乐部 *Wēiwa jùlèbù*). From salsa to hip-hop, you can dance the night away inside this hot spot or enjoy a drink on the outdoor patio while you mingle with Shenzhen's young professional crowd. Tell your taxi driver "Gòuwù gōngyuán, 购物公园" (Coco Park). ✉ *Coco Park Shopping Park, 140 Futian Lu, Futian District* ☎ *755/2531–3765* Ⓜ *Shopping Park.*

SHOPPING

CITIC City Plaza (深圳中信大厦 *Shēnzhèn zhōngxìn dàshà*). Constantly adding new stores, this upscale shopping has more than 100 big brand shops, including Japanese department stores Seibu and Jusco. There's also a food court on the lower level that's not a bad place to take a break over some coffee or a bowl of noodle soup. The pedestrian square outside comes alive at night, with a smattering of bars and eateries for all types. ✉ *1093 Shennan Lu* ☎ *0755/2598–8999* Ⓜ *Science Museum.*

Dongmen Shopping Plaza. This sprawling pedestrian plaza has large shopping centers for inexpensive knockoff name-brand watches, shoes, bags, cosmetics, and clothes, as well as plenty of smaller outdoor shops. If you're into people-watching, grab a cup of bubble tea and soak up the sights. ■TIP➔ **Watch your pockets and bags, as this place can get crowded.** ✉ *Laojie metro station, exit A, Luohu District.*

Luohu Commercial City (*Luóhú shāngyè chéng*). Luohu Commercial City is a stalwart of Shenzhen's mixed-bag shopping. Its location (straddling the Hong Kong–Shenzhen border) makes it a good place to do last-minute shopping for pirated DVDs, and knockoffs of just about any name brand you can think of. On the third and fourth floors, there are some inexpensive places to get clothes tailored (store owners can mail items to you) and curtains made. It's a colorful and chaotic experience, one that is true to Shenzhen, but do be warned that here are some of the most aggressive touts you're likely to find in the city. ✉ *Adjacent to the*

Hong Kong Border Crossing/Luohu metro station, just off Yumincun Lu ⊗ *Daily 10–10.*

The MixC (华润中心 *Huárùn zhōngxīn*). Connected to the Grand Hyatt, this high-end shopping mall houses a long list of luxury brands, including Cartier, Prada, Louis Vuitton, Armani, and Burberry. Should you need a break, the pleasant outdoor plaza is home to a smattering of popular cafés and bars. ⊠ *1881 Bao'an Nan Lu, Luohu District* ☎ *0755/8266–8266* ⊕ *www.themixc.com* Ⓜ *Grand Theater.*

SPORTS AND THE OUTDOORS

GOLF

Mission Hills Golf Club (观澜湖高尔夫會 *Guānlán hú gāo'ěrfū huì*). Widely considered by golfers to be one of the top courses and clubs in Southern China, Mission Hills Golf Club has 12 18-hole courses (2 of which offer nighttime playing), as well as a top-notch clubhouse, spa, a tennis court, five restaurants, and an outdoor pool. There is a shuttle service between Hong Kong and the golf club; see website for schedule. ⊠ *1 Mission Hills Lu, Bao'an District* ☎ *0755/2802–0888* ⊕ *www.missionhillschina.com* ⊗ *Daily 6 am–dark.*

Sand River Golf Club (沙河高尔夫球会 *Shāhé gāo'ěrfū qiú huì*). Part of the Palm Springs International Club, Sand River Golf Club offers a gorgeous 27-hole course that was designed by legendary South African golfer Gary Player, and is floodlighted for night playing. Other facilities include a large driving range and various resort amenities. Prices during the week start at about Y1,600 for a round, and go up to Y2,400 on the weekends. ■ TIP➔ **The language barrier is high here, so plan ahead by having your requests written down in Chinese.** ⊠ *1 Baishi Lu, Nanshan District* ☎ *0755/2690–0111* ⊕ *www.srgc.cn/en* ⊗ *Daily 6–10:30.*

8

THE SOUTHWEST

Guangxi, Guizhou, and Yunnan

WELCOME TO
THE SOUTHWEST

TOP REASONS
TO GO

★ **Lose yourself in Lijiang:** Treasured by the Chinese and home to a UNESCO World Heritage Site, the winding cobblestone lanes of Lijiang beckon to all.

★ **Lush Xishuangbanna rain forests:** Hugging the borders of Laos and Myanmar, this small city in Yunnan is home to the Dai ethnic group, who make you feel far from the rest of China.

★ **Trek Tiger Leaping Gorge:** Explore the deepest gorge in the world, and one of the most scenic spots in all of Yunnan, and possibly China.

★ **Guizhou's eye-popping Huangguoshu Falls:** Travel to the Baishui River in Guizhou, where the largest waterfall in China plummets 230 feet.

★ **Cycling around Yangshuo:** Snake your way through this strange lunar landscape of limestone karsts.

1 Guangxi. Having inspired countless paintings and poems in the past, the spectacular karst scenery of Guilin and Yangshuo today inspires travelers who are in search of an unforgettable Chinese experience. Capital city Nanning is being groomed as China's gateway to Vietnam. This is officially the Guangxi Zhuang Minority Autonomous Region, not a province.

2 Guizhou. Off the beaten path, this fascinating province is known for its undulating mountains, terraced fields, traditional villages, frequent festivals, and China's largest waterfall, Huangguoshu. More than a third of the population is made up of Dong, Hui, Yao, Zhuang, and Miao (known outside China as the Hmong) peoples.

GETTING ORIENTED

Southwest China can be summed up in one word: diversity. The regions of Guangxi, Guizhou, and Yunnan offer some of China's most singular travel experiences. Guilin and Yangshuo in Guangxi are surrounded by otherworldly karst mountains and idyllic rivers. Qianling Park in Guizhou's capital, Guiyang, has a beautiful Buddhist temple, hundreds of monkeys, and amazing city views. Stretching between Tibet and Vietnam, Yunnan Province's geographic, biological, and ethnic variety is unparalleled anywhere else in China. This part of the world must be seen to be believed.

3 Yunnan. The ancient towns of Lijiang and Dali offer glimpses into the centuries-old traditions of the Naxi and Bai ethnic groups. For a more rugged experience, hike through the breathtaking Tiger Leaping Gorge. If a slow boat on the Mekong appeals, head south to Jinghong and chill out in the tropics.

Updated by
Sander Van de
Moortel

The southwestern provinces are among the most alluring destinations in the country. This region lays claim to some of the most breathtaking scenery in all of China—from the moonscape limestone karsts and river scenery of Yangshuo, to China's mightiest waterfall in Guizhou, to Yunnan's tropical rain forests and spectacular Tiger Leaping Gorge.

Yunnan is home to almost a third of China's ethnic minorities. In 1958 Guangxi became an autonomous region in an attempt to quell the friction between the Zhuang minority and the ethnic Han majority. Yunnan, Guangxi, and Guizhou represent the complex tapestry of China's ethnic groups.

In Kunming, Dali, and villages around Yunnan, the Yi and Bai peoples hold their Torch Festivals on the 24th day of the sixth lunar month. They throw handfuls of pine resin into bonfires, lighting the night sky with clouds of sparks. The Dai Water Splashing Festival in the rain forests of Xishuangbanna on the 22nd day of the third lunar month is liquid pandemonium. Its purpose is to wash away the sorrow of the old year and refresh you for the new.

Dali has two festivals of note: the Third Moon Fair (middle of third lunar month) during which people from all around Yunnan come to Dali to sell their wares; and the Three Temples Festival (usually May). The Sister's Meal Festival, celebrated in the middle of the third lunar month by Miao people throughout Guizhou, is dedicated to unmarried women. During the great rice harvest, special brightly colored dishes are made, and at nightfall there's much ado about courtship, dancing, and old-fashioned flirting. The Zhuang Singing Festival turns Guangxi's countryside into an ocean of song. On the third day of the third lunar month, the Zhuang gather and sing to honor Liu Sanjie ("Third Sister Liu"), the goddess of song. Singing "battles" ensue between groups who sing—often improvising—at each other until one group concedes.

PLANNING

WHEN TO GO

When you are packing for travel in Southwest China, think of the region as three distinct zones separated by altitude. Steamy tropical lowlands spread across the southern halves of Yunnan and Guangxi. The mountainous highlands of central and northwest Yunnan are characterized by intense sun, long rainy seasons, and cold winters. Somewhere in between are the cloudy mountain scenes found throughout Guizhou and northern Guangxi. Each zone requires a different packing strategy.

In summer the monsoon rains can be heavy, so keep abreast of weather reports as you travel. Temperatures don't get as hot as the tropics or as cold as the highlands, but summers can be quite hot in Guilin and Yangshuo, and winters in Guiyang can be cold enough for snow. The best time of year is spring, in April or early May. Winter months can be surprisingly cold (except in southern Guangxi and Yunnan), and the summertime heat is stifling. Mid-September can also be a comfortable time to travel. The falls at Huangguoshu are at their best in the rainy season from May through October.

GETTING HERE AND AROUND

With new roads, faster trains, and more airports every year, traveling around Southwest China is becoming increasingly convenient. If you're short on time, flying within the region is the best option, with most flights taking an hour or less. If you're not in a hurry, trains and buses are a cheap and scenic option.

AIR TRAVEL

Southwest China's air network is constantly expanding, with most popular travel destinations served by their own airports. China Eastern Airlines is the dominant carrier in the region. Kunming, Guilin, Nanning, Jinghong, and Guiyang all have international airports, and cities such as Lijiang and Dali are reachable by air.

BUS TRAVEL

Traveling around Southwest China by bus is a good way to cover the shorter distances in your travels. The regional bus network is efficient and is primarily served by luxury coaches. Keep in mind that in general there is no English spoken on buses here.

CAR TRAVEL

There are no legal car-and-driver services, only buses and taxis.

HEALTH AND SAFETY

Gastrointestinal problems are the main health concern in this part of the country—make sure that your food is cooked thoroughly in a hygienic environment. A rating system, giving restaurants grades from A to C, is intended to help you find the better places. However, A ratings are only awarded to those who pay, so don't turn up your nose at a B restaurant. Altitude sickness can be a problem if you're flying into northwest Yunnan; make sure to take it easy for the first day or two after arriving.

MONEY MATTERS

Money can be changed in major hotels, at the Bank of China, and in Kunming airport.

In all cities in this chapter, bank cards on the VISA, MasterCard, Cirrus, or Plus systems can be used at ATMs displaying their respective logos. ABC, Bank of China, and ICBC are your best bets. When traveling to remote parts of the region, have cash on hand, as ATMs accepting foreign cards are rare, and that includes those belonging to the above banks.

RESTAURANTS

In addition to great Chinese food, usually on the spicier side, Southwest China is home to a rainbow of ethnic cuisines, with Dai, Bai, and Tibetan being some of the most notable. Yunnan has the most diverse culinary offerings, which even include some breads and cheeses. Wild mushrooms are available every May through September.

HOTELS

Locally run hotels in Southwest China's larger cities offer adequate service and amenities for a reasonable price, but don't expect an English-speaking staff. There is a growing number of international luxury hotels in Kunming, Guiyang, and Nanning that offer personal service and well-regarded restaurants. Cities like Dali, Lijiang, and Yangshuo have plenty of comfortable and cheap small hotels and guesthouses where you can get home-cooked local meals. *Hotel reviews have been shortened. For full information, visit Fodors.com.*

WHAT IT COSTS IN YUAN			
$	**$$**	**$$$**	**$$$$**
Restaurants	under Y50	Y50–Y99	Y100–Y165	over Y165
Hotels	under Y1,100	Y1,100–Y1,399	Y1,400–Y1,800	over Y1,800

Restaurant prices are the average cost of a main course at dinner or, if dinner is not served, at lunch. Hotel prices are the lowest cost of a standard double room in high season.

VISITOR INFORMATION

This part of China has virtually nothing in the way of useful English-language tourist information. Cafés and guesthouses are usually good places to ask about travel in the region.

TOURS

Although they can be cheaper, Chinese package tours tend to be noisy, crowded, and aimed at getting you to buy junk. In Southwest China's larger cities, hotels are the most convenient places to make transportation arrangements. In travel hot spots such as Yangshuo, Lijiang, and Dali there are plenty of English-speaking travel agents.

China Minority Travel. One of the oldest travel agencies in Southwest China, China Minority Travel offers tours exploring virtually every corner of Southwest China. ⊕ *www.china-minority-travel.com* ✉ *From Y1800 for 2–4 people.*

WildChina Travel. This company specializes in unique itineraries in Yunnan, Guizhou, and Guangxi, and can create journeys tailored to specific interests. Prices vary greatly depending on number of days, destination, and options. About $3,000 per person for a 10-day custom tour with

Watching a Dragon Boat race at the Water Splashing Festival in Xishuangbanna

driver is a good estimate. ⊠ *Oriental Place, 9 Dongfang Dong Lu, Room 801, Chaoyang, Beijing* ☏ *010/6465–6602* ⊕ *www.wildchina. com* ✉ *From Y2100.*

GUANGXI

Known throughout China for its fairy-tale scenery, Guangxi has rivers, valleys, and stone peaks that have inspired painters and poets for centuries. From the distinctive terraced rice fields of Longsheng, which resemble a dragon's spine, to the karst rock formations that surround Guilin and Yangshuo and rise from the coastal plain in the south, Guangxi is quite possibly the most picturesque of China's regions.

A significant portion of Guangxi's population consists of ethnic minorities: the Dong, Gelao, Hui, Jing, Miao, Shui, Yao, Yi, and, in particular, the Zhuang people, who constitute about a third of the province's population. Guangxi has often seen conflict between these indigenous peoples and the Han, who established their rule only in the 19th century. Today it is one of five autonomous regions, which, in theory, have an element of self-government.

The climate is subtropical and affected by seasonal monsoons, with long, hot, humid, and frequently wet summers and mild winters. Guangxi is one of the most popular travel destinations in China.

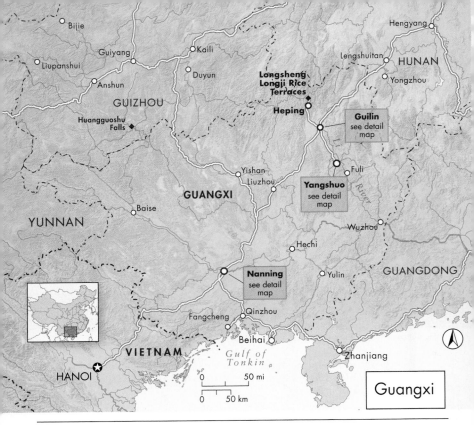

GUILIN

500 km (310 miles; 11 hrs by train) northwest of Guangzhou; 1,675 km (1,039 miles; 11 hrs by high-speed train) southwest of Beijing.

Guilin has the good fortune of being situated in the middle of some of the world's most beautiful landscapes. This region of limestone karst hills and mountains, rising almost vertically from the earth, has a dreamy, hypnotic quality. They were formed 200 million years ago, when the area was under the sea. As the land beneath began to push upward, the sea receded, and the effects of the ensuing erosion over thousands of years produced this sublime scenery.

Architecturally, the city lacks charm, having been heavily bombed during the Second Sino-Japanese War and rebuilt in the utilitarian style popular in the 1950s. Still, the river city is replete with beautiful parks and bridges, and has a number of historic sites that make it worthy of exploration. It's also a good base from which to explore northern Guangxi.

GETTING HERE AND AROUND

AIR TRAVEL About 28 km (17 miles) southwest of the city center, Guilin Liangjiang International Airport has flights to cities throughout China as well as throughout Asia. An airport shuttle bus, which operates daily from

6:30 am to 8 pm, runs between the airport and the Aviation Building at 18 Shanghai Lu, across from the main bus station. The cost is Y20 per person.

Air Contact Guilin Liangjiang International Airport ☎ 0773/284–5114.

BUS TRAVEL The main bus station in Guilin is just north of the train station on Zhongshan Nan Lu. Short- and long-distance buses connect Guilin to nearby cities, including Yangshuo, Liuzhou, and Nanning. For Longsheng, you need the Qingtan Bus Station. Long-distance sleeper coaches travel to cities throughout the Pearl River delta.

Bus Contact Guilin Bus Station ✉ *Off Zhongshan Nan Lu* ☎ *0773/386–2358.*

TRAIN TRAVEL Guilin is linked by daily rail service with most major cities in China. Most long-distance trains arrive at Guilin's South Railway Station.

Train Contact Guilin Railway Station ✉ *Off Zhongshan Nan Lu* ☎ *0773/216–4842.*

SAFETY AND PRECAUTIONS

Like most cities in Southwest China, Guilin is generally safe, but one should be careful when crossing the street, as pedestrians don't get much respect from drivers.

TIMING

Although it is increasingly overshadowed by nearby Yangshuo, Guilin is a pleasant city that's well worth a stop. Most of the sights can be taken in within a couple of days.

ESSENTIALS

Banks Bank of China ✉ *5 Shanhu Bei Lu* ☎ *0773/285–9910.*

Medical Assistance Guilin People's Hospital ✉ *12 Wenming Lu* ☎ *0773/282–7626.*

Public Security Bureau PSB Guilin ✉ *16 Shi Jia Yuan Rd.* ☎ *0773/582–9930.*

Visitor and Tour Info China International Travel Service ✉ *11 Binjiang Lu* ☎ *0773/286–6789.*

EXPLORING

TOP ATTRACTIONS

Elephant Trunk Hill (象鼻山 *Xiàngbí shān*). On the banks of the river in the southern part of the city, Elephant Trunk Hill takes its name from a rock formation arching into the water like the trunk of an elephant. Nearby is a grotto covered in poetic inscriptions inspired by the beauty of the place, some by the greatest poets of the Song Dynasty. ✉ *Binjiang Lu, across from Golden Elephant Hotel* ☎ *0773/258–6602* 🎫 *Y75* ☉ *Daily 8–5:30.*

Peak of Solitary Beauty (独秀峰 *Dúxiù fēng*). The 492-foot Peak of Solitary Beauty, with carved stone stairs leading to the top, offers an unparalleled view of Guilin—and a short but intense workout for your legs. It's one of the attractions of the **Prince City Solitary Beauty Park** (*Jing Jiang Wang Cheng*). Surrounded by an ancient wall, outside of which vendors hawk their wares, sits the heart of Old Guilin. Inside are the decaying remains of an ancient Ming Dynasty palace built in 1393 and

8

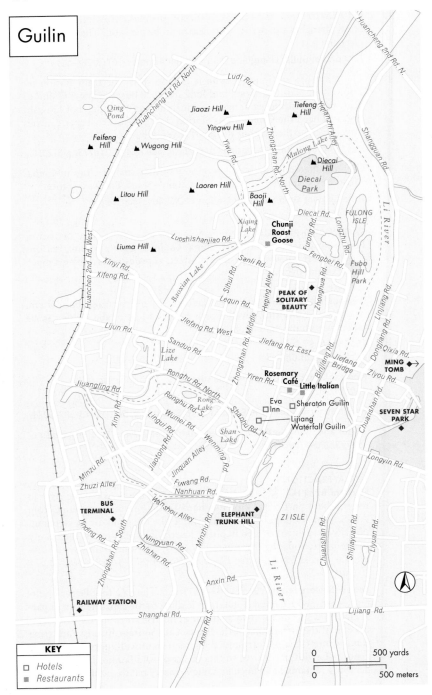

Guilin

Qing Pond

Huancheng 1st Rd. North

Ludi Rd.

Huancheng 2nd Rd. N.

Jiaozi Hill

Yingwu Hill

Tiefeng Hill

Feifeng Hill

Wugong Hill

Huanzhi Alley

Shangguan Rd.

Zhongshan North

Mulong Lake

Diecai Hill

Li River

Litou Hill

Laoren Hill

Diecai Park

Baoji Hill

Diecai Rd.

FULONG ISLE

Xiqing Lake

Chunji Roast Goose

Furong Rd.

Longzhu Rd.

Liuma Hill

Luoshishanjiao Rd.

Sanli Rd.

Heping Alley

Fengbei Rd.

Fubo Hill Park

Huanchen 2nd Rd. West

Xinyi Rd.

Xifeng Rd.

Buoxian Lake

Sihui Rd.

Lequn Rd.

PEAK OF SOLITARY BEAUTY

Zhonghua Rd.

Lijun Rd.

Jiefang Rd. West

Sanduo Rd.

Lize Lake

Zhongshan Rd. Middle

Jiefang Rd. East

Bijiang Rd.

Jiefang Bridge

Dongjiang Rd.

Qixia Rd.

Ziyou Rd.

MING TOMB →

Jiuangling Rd.

Ronghu Rd. North

Ronghu Rd. S.

Rong Lake

Yiren Rd.

Rosemary Café

Little Italian

Chuanshan Rd.

SEVEN STAR PARK

Xinyi Rd.

Lingui Rd.

Wumei Rd.

Jiaotong Rd.

Wenming Rd.

Shanhu Rd. N.

Eva Inn

Sheraton Guilin

Lijiang Waterfall Guilin

Shan Lake

Jinquan Alley

Minzu Rd.

Zhuzi Alley

Fuwang Rd.

Nanhuan Rd.

Longyin Rd.

Wanshou Alley

BUS TERMINAL

Yinding Rd.

Zhongshan Rd. South

Ningyuan Rd.

Zhishan Rd.

Minzhu Rd.

ELEPHANT TRUNK HILL

ZI ISLE

Li River

Chuanshan Rd.

Shijiayuan Rd.

Liyuan Rd.

RAILWAY STATION

Shanghai Rd.

Anxin Rd.

Anxin Rd. S.

Li River

Lijiang Rd.

KEY

□ Hotels
■ Restaurants

| 0 | 500 yards |
| 0 | 500 meters |

Guilin's Confucius temple. Sun Yat-sen lived here for a few months in the winter of 1921 (a fact duly noted on the wall by the outside gate). Cixi, the former empress dowager of China, inscribed the character for "longevity" on a rock within these walls. ✉ *2 blocks north of Zhengyang Lu Pedestrian Mall* 🎫 *Y88* 🕘 *Daily 7:30–6:30.*

Seven Star Park (七星公园 *Qīxīng gōngyuán*). This park gets its name from the arrangement of its hills, said to resemble the Big Dipper. At the center of this huge park is **Putuo Mountain** (Putuoshan), atop which sits a lovely pavilion housing a number of famous examples of Tang calligraphy. Indeed, calligraphy abounds on the side of this hill, mostly the work of Ming Dynasty Taoist philosopher Pan Changjing. Nearby is **Seven Star Cliff** (Qixing Dong), with several large caves open for exploration. The largest contains rock formations that are thought to resemble a lion with a ball, an elephant, and other figures. An inscription in the cave dates from AD 590. Seven Star Park also contains the Guilin City Zoo, only worth a stop if you have kids in tow. It costs an additional Y30. ✉ *East side of the Li River, 1 km (½ mile) east of downtown Guilin* ☎ *0773/581–4342* 🎫 *Y75* 🕘 *Daily 6 am–8 pm.*

WORTH NOTING

Ming Tomb (靖江王陵 *Jìngjiāngwáng líng*). East of downtown is the tomb of Zhu Shouqian, the nephew of the first Ming emperor, who founded a principality here. It makes a pleasant excursion by bicycle, and its gates combine with the surrounding hills to make for good photo opportunities. To get here, take Jiefang Dong Lu east about 9 km (5 miles). ✉ *Jiefang Dong Lu* ☎ *0773/589–7276* 🎫 *Y130* 🕘 *Daily 8:30–5:30.*

8

WHERE TO EAT

Guilin's notable local dishes are limited to horse meat and rice noodles, though freshwater fish is also popular with locals. The Zhengyang Lu pedestrian street has the best variety of dining spots.

$$ CANTONESE

🍴 **Chunji Roast Goose** (椿记烧鹅 *Chūn jì shāo é*). If you're ready for a truly local experience, look no further than Chunji Roast Goose. No surprises here: this Cantonese restaurant serves exactly what it says on the facade. Done in a style reminiscent of Beijing duck, the geese are roasted in a charcoal oven, until the skin is crispy and the meat deliciously succulent. A quarter serves two. Good, local food in China often comes with a noisy environment, and that's true here, so be prepared to share your table with others, or come early to avoid the crowds. Although the waitstaff do their utmost to serve everyone, few of them speak more than a few words of English. **TIP→ Try the durian cakes. While the fruit may be an acquired taste, you just might acquire it quickly here.** [$] *Average main: Y60* ✉ *2 Zhongshan Rd., inside Zhongshan Hotel* ☎ *0773/280–6188.*

$ ITALIAN

🍴 **Little Italian** (唐纳德 *Tángnàdé*). This little restaurant may have the best Western food in Guilin. The menu is straightforward: pizza, pasta, and sandwiches that are made when you order. The cozy urban decor creates an ideal environment for reading a book, checking your email, or planning the next step in your trip. Most of the young, friendly

The Zhuang and the Miao

The Zhuang are China's largest minority population, totaling more than 18 million. Most Zhuang are in Guangxi Zhuang Autonomous Region (where they constitute more than 85% of the population), Guizhou, Yunnan, and Guangdong provinces. The Zhuang language is part of the Tai-Kadai family, related to Thai and the language spoken by their fellow Chinese minority the Dai. Historically, the Zhuang have had almost constant friction with China's Han majority, but that's improved since the Guangxi Zhuang Autonomous region was established in 1958. In many ways the Zhuang are becoming assimilated into the dominant Han Chinese culture, but they have still preserved part of their strong culture and its music and dance traditions. Clothing varies from region to region, but mostly consists of collarless embroidered jackets buttoned to the left, loose wide trousers or pleated skirts, embroidered belts, and black square headbands.

The Miao are also a large minority group spread across much of southern China. Throughout their history, the Miao have had to deal with Han China's southward expansion, which drove them into marginal, chiefly mountainous areas in southern China and northern areas of Myanmar, Thailand, Laos, and Vietnam (where they are known as the Hmong). Living in such isolated regions, the Miao group developed into several subsets, including Black, Red, Green, and Big Flowery Miao. Most of China's nearly 10 million Miao are in Guizhou Province, where local markets feature their intricate and expert craftsmanship, especially jewelry, embroidery, and batik. The Miao are also renowned for their festivals, particularly the Lusheng festival, which occurs from the 11th to the 18th of the first lunar month. Named after a Miao reed instrument, Lusheng is a week of lively music, dancing, horse races, and bullfights. The Guizhou city of Kaili is the center of Miao festivals, hosting more than 120 each year.

staff speaks English. $ *Average main: Y45* ✉ *1–4, 18 Binjiang Lu* ☎ *0773/311–1068.*

$ × **Rosemary Cafe** (迷迭香 *Mídiéxiāng*). Just a hop, skip, and a jump
INTERNATIONAL away from the Sheraton Hotel, the Rosemary Cafe has outside seating in the middle of a calm pedestrian street, making it a nice place to while away an evening. It may not have the most inspired decor, but don't let that deceive you: the Western menu includes delicious burritos and salads, which you can wash down with a glass of freshly pressed pineapple juice. $ *Average main: Y45* ✉ *1–3 Yiren Lu* ☎ *0773/281–0063.*

WHERE TO STAY

$ 🛏 **Eva Inn** (四季春天酒店 *Sìjì chūntiān jiǔdiàn*). At what's the best
HOTEL budget hotel in town, the rooms are modern, with all the necessities.
Fodor'sChoice **Pros:** great location; good value; pleasant views. **Cons:** rooms could be
★ a bit bigger. $ *Rooms from: Y300* ✉ *66 Binjiang Lu, on west bank of Li
River* ☎ *0773/283–0666* ⊕ *eng.evainn.com* ➦ *113 rooms* ⊗ *No meals.*

$ 🛏 **Lijiang Waterfall Guilin** (漓江大瀑布酒店 *Líjiāng dàpùbù jiǔdiàn*).
HOTEL With a privileged perch overlooking the river, this luxury hotel has

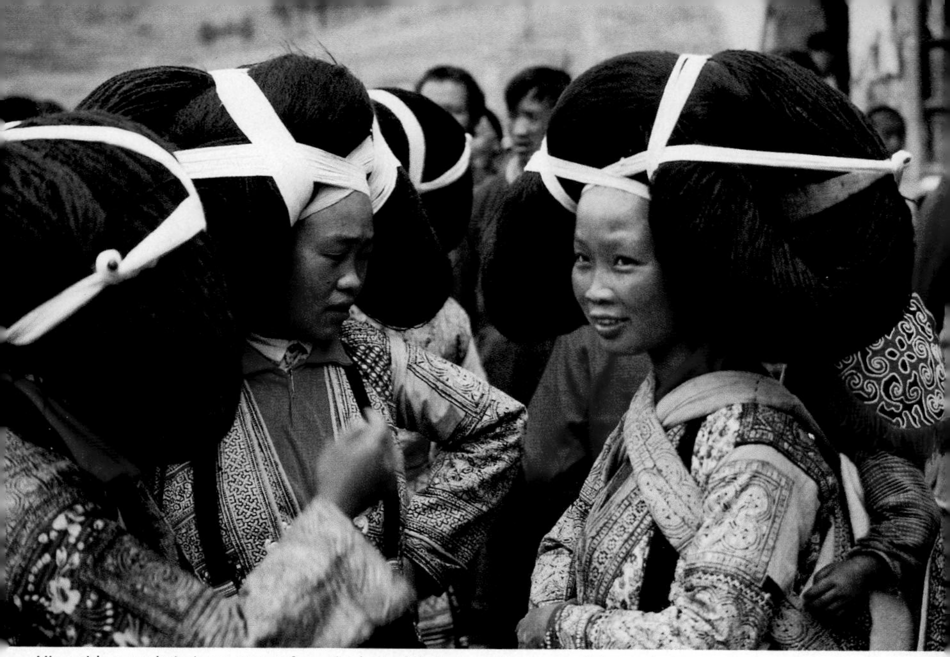

Miao girls wear hairpieces woven from the hair of their ancestors on special occasions.

breathtaking views of Elephant Trunk Hill and Seven Star Park. **Pros:** reasonable rooms for reasonable rates. **Cons:** occasionally chaotic due to conferences. [$] *Rooms from: Y680* ✉ *1 Shanhu Bei Lu, southern end of Zhengyang Lu Pedestrian St.* ☎ *0773/282–2881* 🌐 *www.waterfallguilin.info/en/index.html* 🛏 *651 rooms, 23 suites* 🍴 *No meals.*

$$$$ HOTEL **Sheraton Guilin** (贵林喜来登饭店 *Guìlín xǐláidēng fàndiàn*). Easily the most elegant hotel in town, the Sheraton Guilin welcomes you with a chic lobby with a sunny atrium and glass elevators that whisk you upstairs. **Pros:** plenty of creature comforts; good restaurants; English-speaking staff. **Cons:** slightly overpriced. [$] *Rooms from: Y2000* ✉ *15 Binjiang Lu, on west bank of Li River* ☎ *0773/282–5588* 🌐 *www.sheraton.com/guilin* 🛏 *391 rooms, 17 suites* 🍴 *No meals.*

NIGHTLIFE AND PERFORMING ARTS

Back Garden Irish Pub (后园爱尔兰酒吧 *Hòu yuán Àiʼěrlán jiŭbā*). Refurbished in mid-2014, this bar offers occasional live music, a well-stocked bar, and a friendly owner. Guinness is available in bottles, but not on tap—yet. It's the only bar in Guilin worth visiting. ✉ *Mingcheng Hotel, Zhengyang Lu* ☎ *773/280–3869.*

HEPING DISTRICT

120 km (74 miles; 3 hrs by bus) northwest of Guilin.

The town of Heping, which administrates the villages and surrounding area, is the gateway to Longsheng's terraced rice fields. Ping'an, about 10 km (6 miles) northeast of Heping, up a winding drive along a river and up a mountain, is where the most impressive scenery is, although the entire area makes for a great visit.

DID YOU KNOW?

Most of the magnificent Longji terraced fields were built about 500 years ago, during the Ming Dynasty. They're called Dragon's Backbone because the peaks of the mountain range resemble the backbone of the dragon, and the water-filled terraces shimmer like a dragon's scales. If you stand at the summit, you can see the dragon's backbone curving off to the horizon.

CLOSE UP

Guangxi's Silver-Toothed Touts

Aggressive touts are a fact of life for Western travelers in modern-day China. Guangxi Province is known for the tenacity of its touts—mostly older tribal women with silver teeth (as is the local custom). To these wandering merchants a Western traveler is a coin purse with legs.

It's not uncommon for half a dozen of these women to surround you at any given site, shouting "water" and "postcard." They'll follow you around until you buy something from each of them.

It's hard for travelers to maintain equilibrium when confronted with a gaggle of old women who seem doggedly intent on turning a hiking trip around, say, the Longsheng Rice Terraces into a no-win trinket-buying binge. Polite "no, thank you's" can soon escalate into expletive-laden tirades, possibly leading to remorse for cursing a poverty-stricken old woman.

What's worse, it accomplishes nothing. No sooner will the last bitter word leave your lips than someone will thrust a pack of commemorative postcards at you and shout "10 yuan!"

Consider the purchasing of minor souvenirs or unwanted sodas as part of the experience; keep a few yuan handy for just that, and deal with it smilingly. Failing that, you can always run. But remember, these old women know all the shortcuts, and you'll tire out and need to buy a beverage anyway. And maybe some postcards as well.

GETTING HERE AND AROUND

Buses are the best way to get to Heping town. The only alternative to a bus is to pay a premium to retain a taxi's services for the day, which will set you back at least Y500.

Buses heading to Heping from Guilin's Qintan Bus Station leave every 15 minutes and take about two hours (Y20). The express bus back to Guilin departs from Longsheng every two hours.

SAFETY AND PRECAUTIONS

If you're hiring a cab to take you to Heping, avoid making the trip at night, as the road is full of sharp corners and is not well lit. To avoid a sprain, make sure your shoes have plenty of ankle support if you plan on hiking in the rice terraces.

TIMING

The Longsheng (aka Longji) Rice Terraces make for a fulfilling day trip from Guilin, but shutterbugs may want to catch the terraces at sunrise and sunset over the course of two or three days to maximize the chance of getting that perfect shot.

TOURS

Travel plans in Longsheng are best arranged in Guilin, because Longsheng doesn't have many suitable tour companies. The stretch of Binjiang Lu south of the Sheraton has several English-speaking travel agencies.

EXPLORING

Longsheng Longji Rice Terraces (龙胜龙脊梯田 *Lóngshèng lóngjí tītián*). These terraced rice fields cut into the hills make a mesmerizing pattern of undulating color. Amazing for their scale as well as their beauty, they're called the "Dragon's Backbone" because the peaks of the mountain range resemble the backbone of the dragon, and the water-filled terraces shimmer like a dragon's scales. They've been worked for generations, by rice farmers from the local Yao, Dong, Zhuang, and Miao communities, who build their houses in villages on the hills. 🎫 *Y90.*

WHERE TO EAT AND STAY

$ ✕ **Li Qing Restaurant** (丽晴饭店 *Lìqíng fàndiàn*). In addition to well-
CHINESE   known Chinese dishes, this extremely popular restaurant serves a number of less-common dishes, such as bamboo stuffed with sticky rice, or stir-fried mountain vegetables. $ *Average main: Y25* ✉ *Ji Lu, Ping'an* ☎ *0773/758–3048* ▭ *No credit cards.*

$$$$ 🏨 **Li'an Lodge** (理安山庄 *Lǐ'ān shānzhuāng*). Perched atop a mountain
B&B/INN   and peeking through the morning mist, a stay at Li'an Lodge is the ulti-
Fodor's Choice   mate way to immerse yourself in stylish Chinese style without sliding
★   into kitsch. **Pros:** absolutely unique; magnificent location. **Cons:** food geared toward a Western palate; only accessible on foot (but sedan chair and porters are available). $ *Rooms from: Y1850* ✉ *Ping'an* ☎ *0773/758–3318* ⊕ *www.lianlodge.cn* 🛏 *16 rooms* 🍽 *No meals.*

$ 🏨 **Li Qing Guesthouse** (丽晴客栈 *Lìqíng kèzhàn*). In the village of
B&B/INN   Ping'an, the Li Qing Guesthouse is run by sisters Liao Yan Li and Liao Yan Qing. **Pros:** friendly staff; reasonable rates; popular restaurant. **Cons:** can be noisy on weekends; 15 meters from road, and can only be reached on foot. $ *Rooms from: Y200* ✉ *Ji Lu, Ping'an* ☎ *0773/758–3048* 🛏 *30 rooms* 🍽 *No meals.*

8

YANGSHUO

70 km (43 miles; 90 mins by bus) south of Guilin.

Yangshuo has taken center stage as Guangxi's top tourist destination. At the heart of the city is West Street, a pedestrian mall extending to the Li River. Many visitors are content to spend a few days eating, drinking, and gazing over the low-slung traditional structures facing toward the fang-shaped peaks that surround the town. Yangshuo is a major destination for adventure travel, and the countryside is filled with opportunities for biking, hiking, rock climbing, and caving.

Keep in mind that Yangshuo is part and parcel of the Southeast Asia backpacker circuit that was forged in the 1970s, and remains well trodden to this day. The main drag throbs with the cacophony of Hong Kong canto-pop, reggae, hip-hop, and classic rock. In restaurants competing for the tourist trade you can order everything from lasagna to enchiladas to pad thai.

GETTING HERE AND AROUND

Arriving via train or airplane means traveling via Guilin. You can also get from Guilin to Yangshuo by bus or minibus, or via a costly but pleasant boat trip.

AIR TRAVEL   Guilin Liangjiang International Airport is the gateway to Yangshuo. Taxis from Guilin Airport to Yangshuo cost around Y250.

BOAT TRAVEL   The boat from Guilin takes approximately four hours. At Y380 for a round-trip ticket, it's much costlier than other modes of travel, but the trip is pleasant and scenic. Tickets are available from any of the countless travel agents in Guilin.

BUS TRAVEL   Departing from the Guilin Train Station, express luxury buses travel between Guilin and Yangshuo every half hour between 7 am and 8 pm. The trip in air-conditioned and smoke-free buses takes just under two hours and cost Y18.

Bus Contact Yangshuo Bus Station ⊠ *Pantao Lu, across from Yangshuo Park* ☎ *0773/882–2188.*

SAFETY AND PRECAUTIONS
Yangshuo is quite safe, but it is worth being extra careful if cycling outside of town, where cars tend to be faster and not always willing to yield much road space.

TIMING
Two or three days is enough time to take in Yangshuo's town and surrounding areas.

TOURS
If getting wet and muddy underground is your idea of a good time, look no farther than Water Cave, the deepest and largest underground grotto in the area. Accessible only by flat-bottom boat, it includes a mud bath and a number of crystal clear pools perfect for washing off. Tours can be arranged through any of the travel agencies in the Xi Jie area. There are also several Chinese locals walking the streets with pictures of tour suggestions. While their quality cannot be guaranteed, some of them actually have interesting tour ideas which may include a visit to local homes. Most tours start at Y150.

ESSENTIALS
Bank Bank of China ⊠ *93 Pantao Lu* ☎ *0773/95588.*

Public Security Bureau PSB Yangshuo ⊠ *Chengbei Lu* ☎ *0773/882–2262.*

Visitor and Tour Info China International Travel Service ⊠ *43 Xianqian St., near Pantao Lu* ☎ *0773/882–7102.* **Yangshuo Insider.** This newcomer to the Yangshuo and Guilin travel scene is worth seeing about short but engaging tours and activities. For instance, you could attend a tai chi session, learn to cook Chinese food, raft the Li River, or head on a trip to one of Yangshuo's many scenic areas. ⊠ *28 Shi Ban Qiao* ☎ *159/7740–4338* ⊕ *www.yangshuo-insider. com* ▨ *From Y100 for group tours.*

EXPLORING
Moon Hill (月亮山 *Yuèliàng shān*). Probably the most popular destination in Yangshuo, Moon Hill is named after the large hole through the center of this karst peak. Amazing vistas are at the top of the several trails that snake up the hill's side. ⊠ *Yangshuo–Gaotian Lu* ▨ *Y15* ⊗ *Daily 6 am–7:30 pm.*

Yangshuo Park (阳朔公园 *Yángshuò gōngyuán*). In the center of town, Yangshuo Park is where older people come to play chess while children

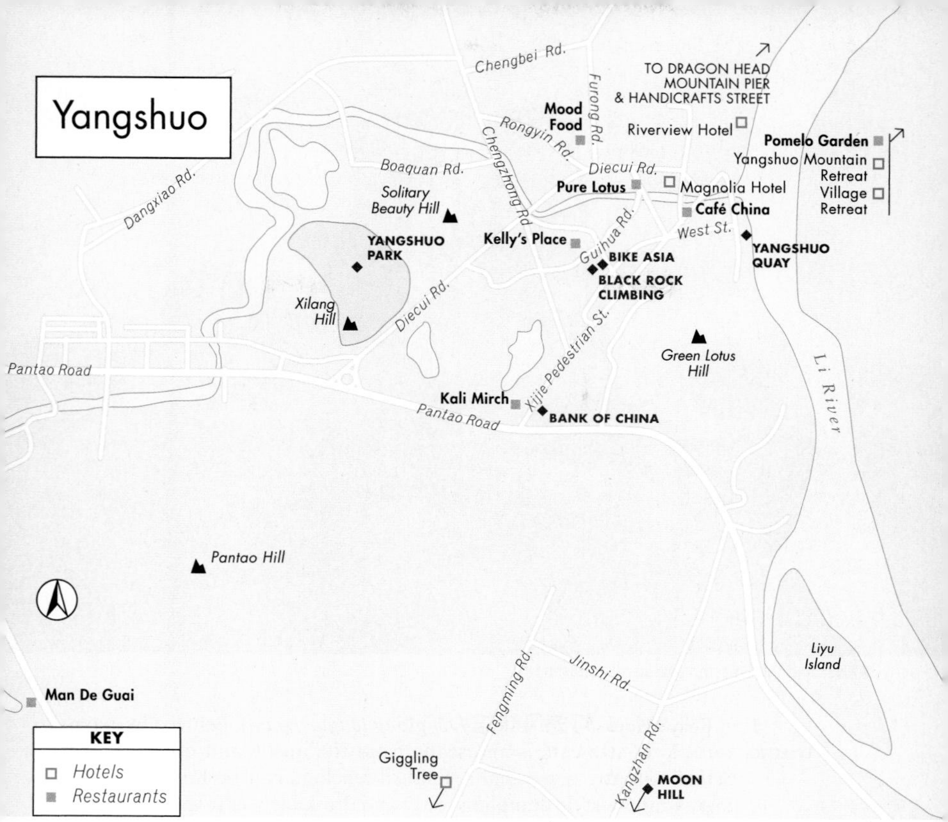
Yangshuo
Chengbei Rd.
TO DRAGON HEAD MOUNTAIN PIER & HANDICRAFTS STREET
Furong Rd.
Mood Food
Rongyin Rd.
Riverview Hotel
Pomelo Garden
Yangshuo Mountain Retreat
Village Retreat
Chengzhong Rd.
Boaquan Rd.
Diecui Rd.
Pure Lotus
Magnolia Hotel
Café China
West St.
Dangxiao Rd.
Solitary Beauty Hill
YANGSHUO PARK
Kelly's Place
Guihua Rd.
BIKE ASIA
BLACK ROCK CLIMBING
YANGSHUO QUAY
Xilang Hill
Diecui Rd.
Xijie Pedestrian St.
Green Lotus Hill
Li River
Pantao Road
Kali Mirch
BANK OF CHINA
Pantao Road
Pantao Hill
Liyu Island
Jinshi Rd.
Fengming Rd.
Kangzhan Rd.
Man De Guai
KEY
Hotels
Restaurants
Giggling Tree
MOON HILL

scamper about in small playgrounds. The park has a number of statues and ponds worth seeing, and Yangshuo Park Peak has a small pagoda offering excellent views of the surrounding town. For a more intense climb with even better views, ascend the television tower across the street from the park's entrance. ✉ *Diecui Lu, at Pantao Lu* 🎫 *Free* ⏲ *Daily.*

WHERE TO EAT

$ ECLECTIC 🍴 **Café China** (原始人咖啡厅 *Yuánshǐ rén kāfēi tīng*). On a cozy corner on bustling West Street, Café China serves addictive rotisserie chicken made from a highly guarded local recipe. The kitchen roasts between 12 and 18 chickens each night, so in-the-know diners call at least an hour in advance. One whole chicken will set you back Y50. In addition, the kitchen also turns out shepherd's pie and sandwiches on baguettes. [$] *Average main: Y35* ✉ *34 Xi Jie* ☎ *0773/882–7744* 💳 *No credit cards.*

$$ INDIAN 🍴 **Kali Mirch Indian Cuisine** (黑胡椒印度餐厅 *Hēihújiāo yìndù cāntīng*). Kali Mirch's spices and chefs come directly from India, and it's a delicious option if you're looking to take a break from Chinese food and approximations of Western food. The tandoori chicken, curry mutton, palak paneer, and pulao rice are but a few of the solid dishes here; the outdoor tables are a good place for people-watching. [$] *Average main: Y60* ✉ *Sunshine 100, West St.* ☎ *137/373–96451* 💳 *No credit cards.*

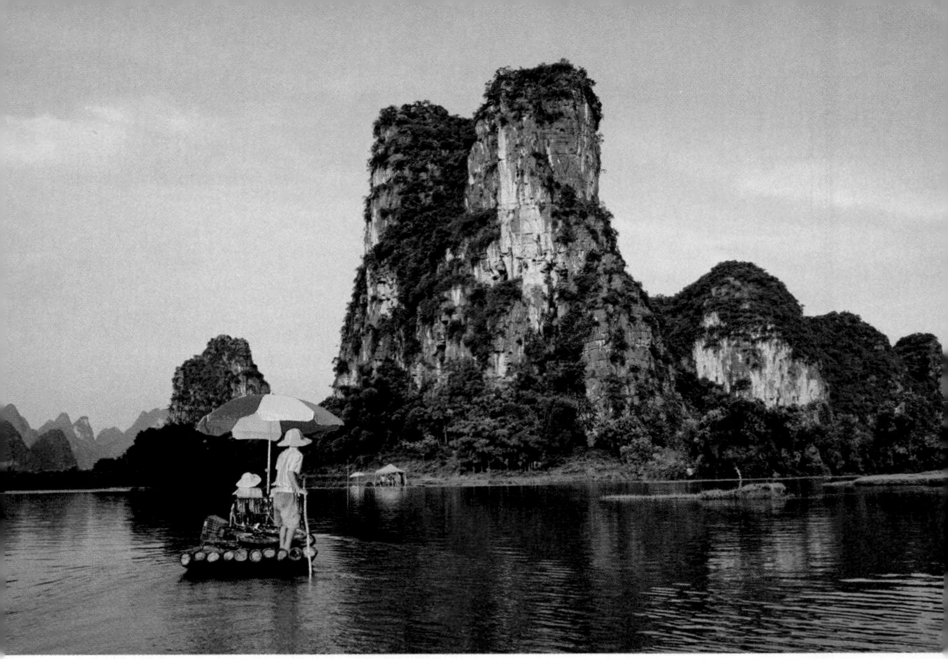

Li River and the limestone karsts of Yangshuo

$ 🍴 **Kelly's Place** (灯笼风味馆 *Dēnglóng fēngwèiguǎn*). Beloved by expats, ECLECTIC this closet-size café is an escape from the hustle and bustle of West Street. On any given night, English teachers can be found sampling tasty Chinese-style dumpling soups and drinking beer in the cobblestone pavilion. [$] *Average main: Y35* ✉ *43 Guihua Lu, 1 block north of Xi Jie* ☎ *0773/881–3233* 💳 *No credit cards.*

$ 🍴 **Man De Guai** (满得拐 *Mǎn de guǎi*). Popular with locals but unknown CHINESE to most travelers, this family-owned restaurant serves an amazing array of local dishes, with a focus on fish from the Li River. There are no English menus, but the owners will bring you into the kitchen and let you pick out what you want. It is hard to find: look for it on the small street two blocks north of the bus station, next to the large statue of Guanyin, the Buddha of Compassion. [$] *Average main: Y25* ✉ *40 Jingfeng Lu* ☎ *0773/881–1456* 💳 *No credit cards.*

$ 🍴 **Mood Food Energy Café.** Whether you believe in good karma or not, VEGETARIAN Mood Food Energy Café is a great destination for excellent vegetarian and vegan food, as well as juices. The cuisine is eclectic, with Mexican wraps and Indian soups sharing the same the menu. If you're just thirsty or looking for a treat, why not have a power shake or spoon away at a tapioca dessert? Inside and outside are conceived as an oasis of peace, so you can attempt to align your chakras as you refuel for the day. [$] *Average main: Y40* ✉ *8 Furong Rd.* ☎ *189/7868–6637.*

$ 🍴 **Pomelo Garden** (罗马假日柚子山庄 *Luómǎ jiàrì yòuzi shānzhuāng*). INTERNATIONAL A 20-minute walk from Yangshuo's center, the Village Retreat is an excellent place to enjoy a healthy breakfast, filling lunch, or a romantic dinner with views of the surrounding scenery. Trained by European masters, the chef clearly understands how Western food ought to taste—without neglecting the Chinese menu. You may find yourself astonished by signature dishes such as sirloin steak served with Belgian-style fries. Finish your meal with coffee or a milk shake and a piece of their magnificent chocolate cake. $ *Average main: Y45* ⊠ *Village Retreat, Shi Ban Qiao Village* ☎ *073/888–8766* ⊕ *www.yangshuo-village-retreat.com.*

$ ✕**Pure Lotus** (暗香疏影素菜馆 *Ànxiāngshūyǐng sùcàiguǎn*). This vege-
CHINESE tarian restaurant serves a variety of mouthwatering creations, including almond rolls, crispy tofu skin in a spicy sauce, and a vegetarian version of the famous Shanghainese *shizi tou* (meatballs). The zen-like interior adds to the calm atmosphere, helping diners forget about the hubbub outside. The staff is helpful, there's an English menu, and the prices are very affordable. $ *Average main: Y45* ⊠ *Magnolia Hotel, 7 Die Cui Lu* ☎ *0773/881–8995* ⊕ *www.yangshuomagnolia.com/purelotus.htm* ▭ *No credit cards.*

WHERE TO STAY

$ ⌂**The Giggling Tree.** Among the karst mountains outside of Yangshuo,
B&B/INN the Giggling Tree is one of China's coolest guesthouses. **Pros:** beautiful
FAMILY views; quiet countryside; good food. **Cons:** a bit remote. $ *Rooms from:*
Fodor'sChoice *Y250* ⊠ *Aishanmen Village* ☎ *136/6786–6154* ⊕ *www.gigglingtree.com*
★ ↪ *23 rooms* ▭ *No credit cards* ⍰*No meals.*

$ ⌂**Magnolia Hotel** (白玉兰酒店 *Báiyùlán jiǔdiàn*). Built around a tradi-
HOTEL tional courtyard, the Magnolia welcomes you with a glass-roofed lobby overlooking a lovely carp pond. **Pros:** comfortable rooms; lovely views; good value. **Cons:** uninspiring decor; noisy area of town. $ *Rooms from:* *Y300* ⊠ *7 Diecui Lu* ☎ *0773/881–9288* ⊕ *www.yangshuomagnolia. com* ↪ *29 rooms, 1 suite* ⍰*No meals.*

$ ⌂**Riverview Hotel** (望江楼客栈 *Wàngjiānglóu kèzhàn*). With its curva-
HOTEL ceous tile roof and balconies with stunning views of the Li River, this is one of the town's nicest budget hotels. **Pros:** comfortable rooms; tasty restaurant; river views. **Cons:** slightly isolated from the rest of town. $ *Rooms from: Y300* ⊠ *15 Binjiang Lu* ☎ *0773/882–2688* ⊕ *www. riverview.com.cn* ↪ *52 rooms* ⍰*Breakfast.*

$ ⌂**Village Retreat** (罗马假日柚子山庄 *Luómǎ jiàrì yòuzi shānzhuāng*).
B&B/INN In Shi Ban Qiao, a village around 20 minutes walking from Yangshuo's
FAMILY center, sits one of the town's more eccentric hotels, which was once
Fodor'sChoice owned by a Beijing millionaire. **Pros:** great views; excellent restau-
★ rant; superb value. **Cons:** eclectic decor doesn't appeal to everyone. $ *Rooms from: Y278* ⊠ *Shi Ban Qiao Village* ☎ *0773/888–8766* ⊕ *www.yangshuo-village-retreat.com* ↪ *13 rooms, 4 suites, 1 pent-house, 1 chalet* ⍰*No meals.*

$ ⌂**Yangshuo Mountain Retreat** (阳朔胜地渡假山庄 *Yángshuò shèngdì dù*
RESORT *jiǎ shānzhuāng*). Far away from the hubbub of Yangshuo, the Yangshuo
FAMILY Mountain Retreat is one of the area's most relaxing places to stay. **Pros:** quiet atmosphere; some of the best views around. **Cons:** too remote for some. $ *Rooms from: Y350* ⊠ *Gaotian Town* ☎ *773/877–7091* ⊕ *www.yangshuomountainretreat.com* ↪ *29 rooms* ⍰*No meals.*

8

NIGHTLIFE

The Alley (阿里酒吧 *Ālǐ jiǔbā*). With its impressive selection of beers and spirits, the Alley also happens to serve excellent bar food, including steak, burgers, and pizza. Open until late, it's an excellent place for those seeking a quiet hangout. ✉ *Guihua Lu* ☎ *0136/678–66922.*

SPORTS AND THE OUTDOORS

BIKING

Bike Asia. Cheaply made mountain bikes are available all over Yangshuo for about Y10 per day. For a better-quality ride, Bike Asia rents all sizes for Y70 per day. The company also leads short trips to the villages along the Li River that start at Y240, including lunch by the river. In the evening, the shop turns into a bar popular with expats called the Rusty Bolt. ✉ *8 Guihua Lu* ☎ *0773/882–6521* ⊕ *www.bikeasia.com.*

BOATING

Starting as a humble spring at the top of Mao'er Mountain, the majestic Li River snakes through Guangxi, connecting Yangshuo to many other towns along the way. One of the country's most scenic—and less polluted—rivers, its banks are lined with stone embankments where people practice tai chi. Several local companies offer rides on bamboo rafts along the river. You can bargain with them at the stone quay at the end of West Street.

ROCK CLIMBING

Black Rock Climbing. Yangshuo is the undisputed rock-climbing capital of China. Run by an American-Chinese couple, Black Rock is the go-to place for guided climbs suited for all skill levels. The crew are among the most experienced in China and will take care of all necessary equipment and transportation. Half-day climbs are Y260 per person; a full day will set you back Y500. ✉ *19 Guihua Lu* ☎ *137/3773–4124* ⊕ *www.blackrockclimbing.net* ✉ *From Y260.*

SHOPPING

West Street is filled with shops selling everything from tourist junk to high-quality handicrafts. Also explore Dragon Head Mountain Pier Handicrafts Street, a cobblestone street running along the river. You can bargain merchants down to half the original asking price or even less.

NANNING

350 km (217 miles; 2½ hrs by train) southwest of Guilin; 440 km (273 miles; 13 hrs by train) southeast of Guiyang; 600 km (372 miles; 12 hrs by train) west of Guangzhou.

Built along the banks of the Yong River, Nanning is the capital of Guangxi Zhuang Autonomous Region. The city isn't a major tourist draw, but it is a pleasant place to stop for a day or two. Many travelers come here for a visa before continuing into Vietnam.

GETTING HERE AND AROUND

Nanning is most accessible by bus if you're are already in Guangxi. For anything beyond, it's a flight or an overnight train.

AIR TRAVEL Nanning Wuxu International Airport is 31 km (19 miles) southwest of the city and has flights throughout China, including to Guilin.

Air Contact Nanning Wuxu International Airport ☎ *0771/209–5114.*

BUS TRAVEL There are frequent buses between Nanning and Guilin, taking at least four hours. There is no direct service from Yangshuo.

Bus Contact Nanning Bus Station ✉ *186 Minzu Ave.* ☎ *0771/242–4529.*

TRAIN TRAVEL Nanning's train station is at the northwestern edge of town, and offers frequent service to Guilin. The fastest routes take five hours.

Train Contact Nanning Railway Station ✉ *North end of Chaoyang Lu* ☎ *0771/243–2468.*

SAFETY AND PRECAUTIONS

Nanning is a quiet and safe city, but some areas can be poorly lit at night—make sure you watch where you're going after sundown.

TIMING

Nanning doesn't have much going on tourism-wise, but is an otherwise pleasant city with nice parks.

ESSENTIALS

Banks Bank of China ✉ *39 Gu Cheng Lu* ☎ *0771/281–1267.*

Medical Assistance Nanning First People's Hospital ✉ *89 Qixing Lu* ☎ *0771/263–6206.*

Public Security Bureau PSB Nanning ✉ *9 Lu Ban Rd., Xi Xiang Tang* ☎ *110, 0771/385–0565.*

Visitor and Tour Info China International Travel Service ✉ *40 Xinmin Lu* ☎ *0771/280–4391.*

EXPLORING

Guangxi Zhuang Autonomous Region Museum (广西壮族自治区博物馆 *Guǎngxī zhuàngzú zìzhìqū bówùguǎn*). This museum focuses on Guangxi's numerous ethnic minorities. In the back are magnificent full-size reconstructions of houses, pagodas, and drum towers set among attractive pools and bridges. A collection of more than 300 bronze drums made by local people is also on display. ✉ *34 Minzu Dadao* ☎ *0771/281–0907* ⊕ *www.gxmuseum.com* 🏷 *Free* ⏱ *Tues.–Sun. 8:30 am–5:30 pm.*

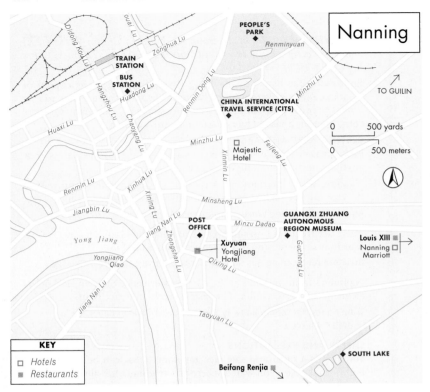

People's Park (人民公园 *Rénmín gōngyuán*). This park surrounding White Dragon Lake has some 200 species of rare trees and flowers. Here you'll find the remains of fortifications built by a warlord in the early part of the 20th century. ✉ *1 Renmin Dong Lu* 🎫 *Free* 🕓 *Daily 8:30–6.*

South Lake (南湖 *Nánhú*). South Lake covers more than 200 acres. A bonsai exhibit and an orchid garden are in the surrounding park, which is encircled by a wide path that's ideal for strolling or jogging. ✉ *Gucheng Lu* 🎫 *Free* 🕓 *Daily.*

WHERE TO EAT

$ ✕ **Beifang Renjia** (北方人家 *Běifāng rénjiā*). Tired of the local rice noo-
CHINESE dles? This is where many transplants from northeastern China come to dine on traditional *dongbei cai*. A large dumpling menu is complemented by a full range of northeastern favorites, such as moo shu pork and *disanxian* (eggplant, potatoes, and green peppers in a brown sauce). Wash it all down with a cold Harbin beer. The staff is friendly, and the menu has photos and descriptions in English. 💲 *Average main: Y25* ✉ *Hong Men Hotel, 6 Huichun Lu, 3rd fl.* 🕾 *0771/530–4263* 🚫 *No credit cards.*

$$ ✕ **Louis XIII** (路易十三西餐厅 *Lùyì shísān xī cāntīng*). Louis XIII is
INTERNATIONAL Chinese-run but nevertheless cooks up quality Western as well as Chinese dishes. The menu even features a pizza with the infamous durian,

which is a pleasant surprise—if you like durian. A second major draw is its setting, which is downright cozy and a bit classy. $ *Average main: Y50* ☒ *1 Yuanhu Lu* ☎ *0771/570–0278* ▭ *No credit cards.*

$
CHINESE
✕ **Xuyuan** (旭园 *Xùyuán*). Inside what was once the residence of General Huang Xuchu, this much-acclaimed restaurant serves excellent version of classic dishes, such as cold beef slices drenched in lemon juice, pork rolls, and roast duck. The menu includes plenty of pictures for easy ordering. The restaurant accommodates guests in private dining rooms, so noise levels are kept relatively low. $ *Average main: Y30* ☒ *53 Mingde Jie, next to the Yongjiang Hotel* ☎ *0771/280–8228.*

WHERE TO STAY

$
HOTEL
Fodor's Choice
★
🏨 **Majestic Hotel** (明园新都酒店 *Míngyuán xīndū jiǔdiàn*). Close to the main square, this luxury hotel is efficiently run. **Pros:** professional staff; well-outfitted gym; pleasant pool. **Cons:** in a tough place to catch a cab; not much of interest in the immediate vicinity. $ *Rooms from: Y450* ☒ *38 Xinmin Lu* ☎ *0771/211–8988* ⇲ *290 rooms* ⏣ *Breakfast.*

$
HOTEL
🏨 **Nanning Marriott** (鑫伟万豪酒店 *Xīnwěiwànháo jiǔdiàn*). This Marriott is in an eye-catching cylindrical tower, in the city's northeastern reaches, and close to the local convention center. **Pros:** good service; high-tech touches; good for business travelers. **Cons:** far from the city center. $ *Rooms from: Y1050* ☒ *131 Minzu Dadao* ☎ *0771/536–6688* ⊕ *www.nanningmarriott.com* ⇲ *328 rooms* ⏣ *No meals.*

$
HOTEL
🏨 **Yongjiang Hotel** (邕江宾馆 *Yōngjiāng bīnguǎn*). With nice views of the bridge crossing the Yongjiang River, this is one of Nanning's most venerable luxury hotels. **Pros:** central location; reasonable rates; excellent service. **Cons:** pool not open all year round; a little impersonal. $ *Rooms from: Y385* ☒ *1 Linjiang Lu* ☎ *0771/218–0888* ⊕ *www.yongjianghotel.com* ⇲ *130 rooms* ⏣ *No meals.*

8

GUIZHOU

With its undulating mountains, terraced fields, and traditional villages, Guizhou is among China's most interesting provinces. It has less tourism infrastructure than neighboring Guangxi or Yunnan, so Guizhou attracts visitors intent on heading off the beaten path.

More than a third of Guizhou's population belongs to one of a dozen ethnic minorities, including the Dong, Hui, Yao, Zhuang, and Miao (known in the west as the Hmong) peoples. The countryside is sprinkled with villages dominated by impressive towers—most notably those of the Dong. The province is known for its festivals, and it's hard to travel through Guizhou without running into at least one celebration.

FESTIVALS

Since the province is comprised of various ethnic groups—including the Dong, Hui, Yao, Zhuang, and Miao peoples—Guizhou is a gallery of traditional customs. Festivals are held throughout the year in Guiyang and elsewhere in the province. Many of these festivals are named after the dates on which they're held. These dates are according to a lunar calendar, so the festival called Eighth Day of the Fourth Month is not on April 8, but on the eighth day of the fourth lunar month (usually sometime in May).

Siyueba. Similar to Mardi Gras (but without the drinking or bawdy behavior), Siyueba, which translates as Eighth Day of the Fourth Month, is a major holiday in the region. During it the Miao, Buyi, Dong, Yao, Zhuang, Yi, and others in the province celebrate spring. Guiyang is a great place to check it out—the area around the fountain in the city center erupts with music, dancing, and general merrymaking.

Liuyueliu. An important traditional festival of Guiyang's Buyi population, Liuyueliu (Sixth Day of the Sixth Month) is held in midsummer, as the name implies. When it's held, thousands of Buyi people from the region gather on the banks of the Huaxi River. As the story goes, a beautiful Buyi maiden embroidered an image of mountains and rivers of immense beauty. It was so inspiring that a miscreant plotted to steal it, and on the sixth day of the sixth lunar month he sent his minions to take it by force. The maiden cast her embroidery into the air, where it was transformed into the beautiful mountains and rivers seen here today.

Miao Bullfight Festival. Among the Miao people who live in and around Kaili, a "bullfight" is a contest between the bulls themselves. This festival traditionally takes place between the planting of rice seedlings and their harvest a few months later, usually between the sixth and eighth lunar months. Owners of bulls meet beforehand to size up the competition prior to agreeing to the fight. The atmosphere on fight day is lively, with drinking, music, and exchanging of gifts. Fireworks entice the bulls into combat until one falls down or runs away.

Sister's Meal Festival. An important fertility festival among the Miao people, Sister's Meal Festival is when unmarried women harvest rice from the terraced fields and prepare a special dish of sticky rice colored blue, pink, and yellow. Men arrive to serenade the women, and the women offer gifts of rice wine and small packets of rice wrapped in cloth. In the evening, women dress up for a night of dancing.

REGIONAL TOURS

Dylan Gu. Fluent in English, Mandarin, Miao, and Dong, this tour guide knows Guizhou like the back of his hand. He is happy to custom-tailor an excursion to meet your needs. ⊠ *26 Fengqingyuan, Kaili* ☎ *0137/655–505–010 mobile* ✉ *miaoguide@163.com* ✉ *From Y400 for small group tours.*

WildChina Travel/Guizhou Tours. Founded by a native of neighboring Yunnan Province, WildChina Travel runs several high-end tours that either pass through Guizhou or are entirely dedicated to the province. Most focus on the province's incredible minority cultures and include village homestays. Tour prices vary highly depending on destination and options, but roughly $2,000 per person for a seven-day trip with driver is a good estimate. ☎ *0106/465–6602* ⊕ *www.wildchina.com* ✉ *From Y2100 per day person.*

Continued on page 502

FOR ALL THE TEA IN CHINA

Legend has it that the first cup dates from 2737 BC, when *Camellia sinensis* leaves fell into water being boiled for Emperor Shennong. He loved the result, tea was born, and so were many traditions.

Historically, when a girl accepted a marriage proposal she drank tea, a gesture symbolizing fidelity. Betrothal gifts were known as "tea gifts," engagements as "accepting tea," and marriages as "eating tea." Today the bride and groom kneel before their parents, offering cups of tea in thanks.

Serving tea is a sign of respect. Young people proffer it to their parents or grandparents; subordinates do the same for their bosses. Pouring tea also signifies submission, so it's a way to say you're sorry. When you're served tea, show your thanks by tapping the table with your index and middle fingers.

And forget about adding milk or sugar. Not only is most Chinese tea best without it, but why dilute and sweeten a beverage long known by herbalists to be good for you? Even modern medicine acknowledges that tea's powerful antioxidants reduce the risk of cancer and heart disease. It's also thought to be such a good source of fluoride that Mao Zedong eschewed toothpaste for a green-tea rinse. Smiles, everyone.

In China, tea was first discovered by the Emperor Shennong.

HISTORICAL BREW

Tea preparation is a careful affair.

THE RISE AND FALL OF EMPIRES

Tea has a long and tumultuous history, making and breaking empires in both the East and the West. Bricks of tea were used as currency, and Chinese statesmen kept rebellious northern nomads in check by refusing to sell it to them.

Rumor has it that tea caused the downfall of the Song Empire. Apparently, tea-whisking was Emperor Huizong's favorite pastime: he was so obsessed with court tea culture that he forgot all about trivial little matters like defense. The country became vulnerable to invasion and fell to the Mongols in 1279.

Genghis preferred *airag* (fermented mare's milk), but after the Mongol's defeat, the drink of kings returned with a vengeance to the court of the Ming Dynasty (1368–1644). Tea as we know it today dates to this period: the first Ming emperor, Hongwu, set the trend of using loose-leaf tea by refusing to accept tea tribute gifts in any other form.

TEA GOES INTERNATIONAL

The first Europeans to encounter the beverage were navigators and missionaries who visited China in the mid-16th century. In 1610, Dutch traders began importing tea from China into Europe, with the Portuguese hot on their heels. It was initially marketed as a health drink and took a while to catch on. By the 1640s, tea had become popular among both the Dutch and Portuguese aristocracy, initially the only ones who could afford it.

Although we think of tea as a quintessentially British drink, it actually arrived in America two years before it appeared in Britain. When the British acquired New Amsterdam (later New York) in 1664, the colony consumed more tea than all the British isles put together.

Tea was available in Britain from about 1554 onward, but Brits were wary of the stuff at first. What tipped the scales in tea's favor was nothing less than celebrity product endorsement. King

All types of tea come from one plant.

Charles II married the Portuguese princess Catherine of Braganza in 1662. She arrived in England with tea and fine porcelain tea ware in her dowry and a healthy addiction to the stuff. Members of the royalty were the 16th century's trendsetters: tea became the thing to drink at court; pretty soon the general public was hooked, too.

TEMPEST IN A TEAPOT

Tea quickly became a very important—and troublemaking—commodity. Religious leaders thought the drink sinful and doctors declared it a health risk. In Britain, ale brewers were losing profits, and pressure groups successfully persuaded the government to tax tea at 119%. On top of all this, the immensely powerful British East India Company held the monopoly on tea importation.

Tea's value skyrocketed: by 1706, the retail price of green tea in London was equivalent to $300 for 100 g (3.5 oz), far beyond the reach of normal people. Tea smuggling quickly became a massive—and often cutthroat—business. To make sought-after tea supplies stretch even further, they were routinely mixed with twigs, leaves, animal dung, and even poisonous chemicals.

Back in the New World, Americans were fed up with paying taxes that went straight back to Britain. Things came to a head when a group of patriots dressed as Native Americans peacefully boarded British ships in Boston harbor and emptied 342 chests of tea into the water. The act came to be known as the Boston Tea Party and was a vital catalyst in starting the American Revolution.

The War of Independence wasn't the only war sparked by tea. In Britain, taxes were axed and, as tea was suddenly affordable for everyone, demand grew exponentially. But China remained the world's only supplier, so that by the mid-19th century, tea was causing a massive trade deficit. The British started exporting opium into China in exchange for tea, provoking two Opium Wars. In the 1880s, attempts to grow tea in India were finally successful and Indian tea began to overtake Chinese tea on the market.

These days, over 3.2 million metric tons of tea are produced annually worldwide. After water, tea is the world's favorite drink. Though Britain and Ireland now consume far more tea per capita than China, tea is still a regular presence at the Chinese table and is inextricably bound to Chinese culture.

ANCIENT TRADE ROUTES

The Ancient Tea and Horse Caravan Road, also known as the Southern Silk Road, is a trade corridor dating back to the Tang Dynasty (618–907). The 4,000-km route emerged more than 1,200 years ago and was actually still in use until recently.

Back in the heyday of the Caravan Road, Xishuangbanna, Dali, Lijiang, and many other parts of Yunnan were important outposts on the route. Tea, horses, salt, medicinal herbs, and Indian spices all featured prominently in this massive network.

During World War II, the route was used to smuggle supplies from India into the interior of Japanese-occupied China.

DRINKING IN THE CULTURE

The way tea was prepared historically bears little resemblance to the steep-a-teabag method many westerners employ today. Tea originally came in bricks of compressed leaves bound with sheep's blood or manure. Chunks were broken, ground into a powder, and whisked into hot water. In the first tea manual, *Cha Jing (The Way of Tea)*, Tang-dynasty writer Lu Yu describes preparing powdered tea using 28 pieces of teaware, including big brewing pans and shallow drinking bowls.

The potters of Yixing (near Shanghai) gradually transformed wine vessels into small pots for steeping tea. Yixing pottery is ideal for brewing: its fine unglazed clay is highly porous, and if you always use the same kind of tea, the pot will take on its flavor.

Today the most elaborate Chinese tea service—which requires only two pots and enough cups for all involved—is called *gong fu cha* (skilled tea method). Although you can experience it at many teahouses, most people consider it too involved for every day. They simply brew their leaf tea in three-piece lidded cups, called *gaiwan*, tilting the lid as they drink so that it acts as a strainer.

THE CEREMONY

1 Rinse teapot with hot water.

2 Fill with black or oolong to one third of its height.

3 Half-fill teapot with hot water and empty immediately to rinse leaves.

4 Fill pot with hot water, let leaves steep for a minute; no bubbles should form.

5 Pour tea into small cups, moving the spout continuously over each, so all have the same strength of tea.

6 Pour the excess into a second teapot.

7 Using the same leaves, repeat the process up to five times, extending the steeping time slightly.

Green Tea leaves in a Chinese gaiwan

TEA TIMELINE

Japanese tea ceremony

350 AD	"Tea" appears in Chinese dictionary.
618–1644	Tea falls into and out of favor at Chinese court.
7th c.	Tea introduced to Japan.
1610–1650	Dutch and Portuguese traders bring tea to Europe.
1662	British King Charles II marries Portugal's Catherine of Braganza, a tea addict. Tea craze sweeps the court.
1689	Tea taxation starts in Britain; peaks at 119%.

HOW TEA IS MADE

Chinese tea is grown on large plantations and nearly always picked by hand. Pluckers remove only the top two leaves. A skilled plucker can collect up to 35 kg (77 lbs) of leaves in a day; that's 9 kg (almost 20 lbs) of tea, or 3,500 cups. After a week, new top leaves will have grown, and bushes can be plucked again. Climate and soil play an important role on a tea plantation, much as they do in a vineyard. But what really differentiates black, green, and oolong teas is the way leaves are processed.

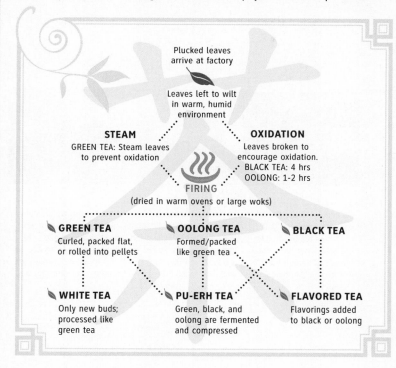

Plucked leaves arrive at factory

Leaves left to wilt in warm, humid environment

STEAM
GREEN TEA: Steam leaves to prevent oxidation

OXIDATION
Leaves broken to encourage oxidation.
BLACK TEA: 4 hrs
OOLONG: 1-2 hrs

FIRING
(dried in warm ovens or large woks)

GREEN TEA
Curled, packed flat, or rolled into pellets

OOLONG TEA
Formed/packed like green tea

BLACK TEA

WHITE TEA
Only new buds; processed like green tea

PU-ERH TEA
Green, black, and oolong are fermented and compressed

FLAVORED TEA
Flavorings added to black or oolong

Boston Tea Party

1773	Boston Tea Party: Americans dump 342 chests of tea into Boston Harbor, protesting British taxes.
1784	British tea taxes slashed; consumption soars.
1835	Tea cultivation starts in Assam, India.
1880s	India and Ceylon produce more tea than China.
1904	Englishman Richard Blechynden creates iced tea at St. Louis World's Fair.
1908	New York importer Thomas Sullivan sends clients samples in silk bags—the first tea bags.
2004	Chinese tea exports overtake India's for the first time since the 1880s.

TYPES OF TEA

The universal word for tea comes from a single Chinese character, pronounced "te" (Xiamen dialect) or "cha" (Cantonese and Mandarin). Some teas are simply named for the region that produces them (Yunnan or Assam); others are evocatively named to reflect a particular blend. Some are transliterated (like Keemun); others translated (Iron Goddess of Mercy).

	BLACK	PU-ERH	GREEN
Overview	It's popular in the West so it makes up the bulk of China's tea exports. It has a stronger flavor than green tea, though this varies according to type.	Pu-erh tea is green, black, or oolong fermented from a few months to 50 years and formed into balls. Pu-erh is popular in Hong Kong, where it's called Bo Le.	Most tea grown and consumed in China is green. It's delicate, so allow the boiling water to cool for a minute before brewing to prevent "cooking" the tea.
Flavor	From light and fresh to rich and chocolatey	Rich, earthy	Light, aromatic
Color	Golden dark brown	Reddish brown	Light straw-yellow to bright green
Caffeine per Serving	40 mg	20–40 mg	20 mg
Ideal Water Temperature	203°F	203°F	160°F
Steeping Time	3–5 mins.	3–5 mins.	1–2 mins.
Examples	Dian Hong (chocolatey aftertaste; unlike other Chinese teas, can take milk). Keemun (Qi Men; mild, smoky; once used in English breakfast blends). Lapsang Souchong (dried over smoking pine; strong flavor). Yunnan Golden (full bodied, malty).	Buying Pu-erh is like buying wine: there are different producers and different vintages, and prices vary greatly.	Bi Luo Chun (Green Snail Spring; rich, fragrant). Chun Mee (Eyebrow; pale yellow; floral). Hou Kui (Monkey Tea; nutty, sweet; floral aftertaste). Long Ding (Dragon Mountain; sweet, minty). Long Jing (Dragon's Well; bright green; nutty).

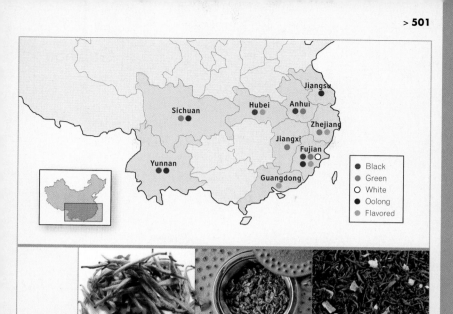

Black
Green
White
Oolong
Flavored

	WHITE	OOLONG	FLAVORED
Overview	The rare white tea is made from the newest buds, picked unopened at day-break and processed like green tea. Small batches mean high prices. It's a tea for refined palates.	Halfway between green and black tea, this tea is more popular in China than elsewhere. The gong fu cha ceremony best re-veals its complexities.	Petals, bark, and other natural ingredients are added to black or green tea to create these brews. Earl Grey is black tea scented with bergamot (a recipe supposedly given to the tea's 18th-century namesake by a Mandarin). Jasmine tea is green tea dried with jasmine petals. Others include lychee congou and rose congou: black tea dried with lychee juice or rose petals. Flavor, color, caffeine content, and ideal preparation depend on the tea component of the blend. Don't con-fuse flavored teas with the caffeine-free herbal teas made from herbs, roots, and blossoms (e.g., chamomile, peppermint, rosehips, licorice, ginger).
Flavor	Very subtle	Aromatic, lighter than black tea	
Color	Very pale yellow	Pale green to pale brown	
Caffeine per Serving	15 mg	30 mg	
Ideal Water Temperature	185°F	203°F	
Steeping Time	4–15 mins	1–9 mins.	
Examples	Bai Hao Yin Zhen (Silver Needle; finest white tea; sweet and very delicate, anti-toxin qualities). Bai Mu Dan (White Peony; smooth and refreshing).	Da Hong Pao (Scarlet Robe; comes from only 4 bushes; full bodied, floral). Tie Guan Yin (Iron Goddess of Mercy; legend has it a farmer repaired statue of the god-dess, who rewarded him with the tea bush shoot; golden yellow; floral).	

GUIYANG

350 km (217 miles; 11½ hrs by the fastest train) northwest of Guilin; 425 km (264 miles; 12 hrs by train) northwest of Nanning; 850 km (527 miles; 19½ hrs by train) northwest of Guangzhou; 1,650 km (1,023 miles; 26½ hrs by train) southwest of Beijing.

The capital is a pleasant place to begin an exploration of the province. Like most cities in China, Guiyang is fast losing its older buildings, but even in the heart of downtown enough remain to make a short stay here worthwhile. The main streets of the sprawling city are Zunyi Lu, Ruijin Lu, Zhonghua Lu, and Yan'an Lu.

GETTING HERE AND AROUND

AIR TRAVEL   Guiyang Airport lies 15 km (9 miles) to the southeast of the city. There are direct flights between Guiyang and most of China's main cities.

Air Contact Guiyang Airport ☎ *0851/549–8908.*

BUS TRAVEL   Guiyang East Passenger Terminal, the city's main long-distance bus station, has been relocated to the remote airport district southeast of the city. Luckily, the smaller bus station on Jiefang Lu just north of Guiyang's train station still has regular bus service to Anshun (2 hours), Kaili (2 hours), and other destinations around Guizhou and the rest of China.

Bus Contact **Guizhou Stadium Bus Station** ✉ *Jiefang Lu, 1 block north of the train station* ☎ *0851/579–3381.*

TRAIN TRAVEL Direct trains link Guiyang with Chongqing (9 hours), Guilin (12 hours), Kunming (10 hours), Liuzhou (8 hours), Nanning (12 hours), and Shanghai (26 hours). The train station is at the southwest edge of the city, at the southern end of Zunyi Lu.

Train Contact **Guiyang Railway Station** ✉ *Zunyi Lu* ☎ *0851/818–1222.*

SAFETY AND PRECAUTIONS

The biggest threat to personal safety in Guiyang is the frenetic traffic. Use the city's numerous pedestrian tunnels whenever possible, and never expect drivers to follow traffic rules or exercise sound judgment. Be careful with your valuables and stay vigilant for pickpockets and bag snatchers.

TIMING

A day or two is enough time to visit most of the sights and sample some local delicacies.

ESSENTIALS

Bank **Bank of China** ✉ *347 Ruijin Nan Lu* ☎ *0851/581–3814.*

Public Security Bureau **PSB Guiyang** ✉ *7 Xintian Ave., North Section* ☎ *0851/676–5230.*

Visitor and Tour Info **China International Travel Service** ✉ *1 Hequn Lu* ☎ *0851/593–6767.*

EXPLORING

TOP ATTRACTIONS

FAMILY **Qianling Mountain Park** (黔灵山公园 *Qiánlíngshān gōngyuán*). Dominating this 740-acre park is a 4,265-foot-high mountain that has fine views of the town from its western peak. The park itself has a bit of everything, including thousands of plants and a collection of birds and monkeys (many of which roam freely through the park). ✉ *187 Zaoshan Lu, 2½ km (1 mile) northwest of city* ☉ *Y5* ✆ *Daily 6:30 am–10 pm.*

Unicorn Cave (麒麟洞 *Qílín dòng*). Discovered in 1531, Unicorn Cave was used as a prison for the two Nationalist generals, Yang Hucheng and Chang Xueliang, who were accused of collaborating with the Communists when Chiang Kai-shek was captured at Xi'an in 1937. ☉ *Y5.*

Underground Gardens (地下公园 *Dìxià gōngyuán*). In this poetically named cave, 1,925 feet below the ground, a path weaves its way past the various rock formations, which are lit up to emphasize their similarity with animals, fruits, and other living things. ✉ *25 km (15 miles) south of Guiyang* ☎ *0851/511–4014* ☉ *Free* ✆ *Daily 9–5.*

WORTH NOTING

FAMILY **Hebin Park** (河滨公园 *Hébīn gōngyuán*). Filled with bamboo groves, Hebin Park sits on the banks of the Nanming River. In many ways it's the archetypical Chinese park, with senior citizens practicing tai chi in the pavilions, young couples strolling hand in hand, and the

Huangguoshu Falls, the largest of a series of nine waterfalls

omnipresent sound of music and public announcements playing from loudspeakers. For children, there's a Ferris wheel and other rides. ✉ *Ruijin Nan Lu* 🎫 *Free* 🕐 *Daily 5 am–midnight.*

WHERE TO EAT

Every province has a number of dishes that locals point to with pride. In Guizhou this is unquestionably *suan tang yu,* or fish in a sour soup. It combines a mouth-numbing number of herbs, spices, and local vegetables to make a dish that is at once spicy and savory. Another wonderfully named dish is *lian ai doufu guo,* or "the bean curd in love," which is especially popular with couples. It's a strip of vegetable- or meat-stuffed tofu toasted to a golden brown and sprinkled with sesame oil.

$ CAFÉ ✗ **Highlands Coffee** (高原咖啡 *Gāoyuán kāfēi*). Understated decor, comfy seating, and high-quality imported coffee turned into tasty beverages by skilled baristas are the highlights here. There are also savory panini on homemade bread, as well as a wide selection of teas, smoothies, and desserts. The affable American owner, who's often here, always tries to make visitors feel at home. The smoking area is separated from the rest of the dining area. $ *Average main: Y30* ✉ *1 Liudong Jie, Bo'ai Lu* ☎ *0851/582–6222* ⊕ *www.highlands-coffee.com.*

$$$ SEAFOOD Fodor's Choice ★ ✗ **Old Kaili Sour Fish Restaurant** (老凯俚酸汤鱼 *Lǎo kǎilǐ suāntāngyú*). Sour fish soup, Guiyang's signature dish, is the specialty at this venerated local joint. Choose a fish from the tanks, select your other ingredients, and mix your own sauce. The soup—an import from the city of Kaili—and the fish will then be cooked at your table. If it's too spicy, remember that a bit of white rice—*not* water—is one good method for dousing culinary flames. There are no reservations, so expect to

have to wait in line a bit on weekends or holidays. There's a another branch on nearby Shengfu Bei Jie. $ *Average main: Y150* ⊠ *55 Shengfu Lu* ☎ *0851/584–3665* ⌕ *Reservations not accepted* ▭ *No credit cards* ☉ *No lunch.*

WHERE TO STAY

$ 🛏 **Amber Hotel** (时光驿 *Shíguāng yì*). A 10-minute walk from the city
B&B/INN center, this tasteful boutique hotel has unique and spacious rooms fur-
Fodor's Choice nished with dark wood and natural stone. **Pros:** exceptional value; very
★ comfortable rooms. **Cons:** slightly outside the center. $ *Rooms from: Y300* ⊠ *47 Dongshan Lu* ☎ *0851/688–0777* ↩ *32 rooms* ▭ *No credit cards* ⦿ *No meals.*

$ 🛏 **Nenghui Jiudian** (能辉酒店 *Nénghuī jiǔdiàn*). With a central location,
HOTEL cozy accommodations, and reasonable prices, this handsome, modern hotel offers lot of bang for the yuan. **Pros:** close to the sights; nice rooms; bargain rates. **Cons:** noisy part of town. $ *Rooms from: Y450* ⊠ *38 Ruijin Nan Lu* ☎ *0851/589–8888* ↩ *125 rooms* ⦿ *Breakfast.*

$$ 🛏 **Sheraton Guiyang Hotel** (喜来登贵阳酒店 *Xǐláidēng guìyáng jiǔdiàn*).
HOTEL Among the city's best lodgings, this chain hotel has everything a high-end traveler needs, and more: a full-service spa, a bar with amazing city views, great international dining, and an attentive staff. **Pros:** excellent city views; near a pretty park; soothing spa. **Cons:** a bit impersonal. $ *Rooms from: Y1392* ⊠ *49 Zhonghua Nan Lu* ☎ *0851/588–8888* ⊕ *www.sheraton.com/guiyang* ↩ *335 rooms, 41 suites* ⦿ *Breakfast.*

SIDE TRIP TO HUANGGUOSHU FALLS

These falls are at their best from May through October and are set in lush countryside, where you'll find numerous villages. To avoid switching buses en route at the city of Anshu, book a tour with a local agency or at your hotel.

Fodor's Choice **Huangguoshu Falls** (黄果树瀑布 *Huángguǒshù pùbù*). The Baishui River
★ tumbles over nine sets of rocks, creating nine waterfalls over a course of 2 km (1 mile). At the highest point, Huangguoshu Falls drops an eye-popping 230 feet, making it the tallest in China. You can enjoy them from afar or by wading across the Rhinoceros Pool (Xiniu Jian) to the Water Curtain Cave (Shuilian Dong) hidden behind the main falls. Seven kilometers (4½ miles) downstream is the **Star Bridge Falls** (*Xingqiao Pu*). ⊠ *160 km (99 miles) southwest of Guiyang* ☎ *400/683–3333* ⊕ *www.hgscn.com* ✉ *Y180* ☉ *Daily dawn–dusk.*

KAILI

200 km (124 miles; 3 hrs by train) east of Guiyang.

The capital of the Qian Dongnan Miao and Dong Autonomous Region, Kaili serves as the starting point for a journey to the Miao and Dong villages that dominate eastern Guizhou. More than two-thirds of the population is Miao, and their villages are along the eastern and northeastern outskirts of Kaili. The Dong communities are to the southeast.

Outside town the local villages are of great interest. To the north is the Wuyang River, which passes by many mountains, caves, and Miao villages. At **Shibing** you can take boat rides through spectacular limestone gorges and arrange stops at these towns. South of Kaili are the Dong villages of **Leishan, Rongjiang,** and **Zhaoxing.** The latter village, set in a beautiful landscape, is known for its five drum towers.

GETTING HERE AND AROUND
The fastest way to get from Guiyang to Kaili is often by bus, which can take as little as two hours. The train takes about three hours.

BUS TRAVEL From the long-distance bus station just north of the Guiyang Train Station, Kaili-bound buses depart every 20 minutes or so. Buses usually don't leave until they're full. Tickets are about Y60.

Bus Contact Kaili Bus Station ⊠ *25 Wenhua Bei Lu.*

TRAIN TRAVEL Kaili's small train station is three hours from Guiyang. Trains passing through Kaili connect to Guilin, Kunming, Beijing, Shanghai, and much of the rest of China.

Train Contact Kaili Train Station ⊠ *237 Qingjiang Lu* ☎ *0855/381–2222.*

SAFETY AND PRECAUTIONS
Kaili remains relatively poor and off the beaten path: take special care, especially if out alone at night. Also keep an eye on the city's taxi drivers, who frequently refuse to start their meters and try to charge highly inflated rates for short rides.

TIMING
Though the sites in Kaili could conceivably occupy a day's time, the city is better viewed as a stepping-off point for multiday tours of the surrounding countryside and its scenic ethnic villages.

TOURS
Tour operator WildChina offers trips that take travelers from Guiyang to Kaili via several minority villages. Guizhou can sometimes be difficult for tourists to navigate, particularly for non-Chinese speakers: this tour offers a hassle-free and off-the-beaten-path look at Guizhou minority culture, with English-speaking guides.

ESSENTIALS
Bank Bank of China ⊠ *46 Beijing East Rd.* ☎ *0855/822–6503.*

EXPLORING

Drum Tower (鼓楼 *Gǔlóu*). This tower in Jinquanhu Park is the Dong people's gathering place for celebrations. ⊠ *Jinquanhu Park.*

Minorities Museum (州民族博物馆 *Zhōu mínzú bówùguǎn*). This museum displays arts, crafts, and relics of the local indigenous peoples. ⊠ *5 Guangchang Lu* 🎟 *Y10* ☉ *Mon.–Sat. 9–5.*

WHERE TO STAY

$ **Guotai Dajiudian** (国泰大酒店 *Guótài dàjiǔdiàn*). With a downtown
HOTEL location and comfortable guest rooms, the Guotai Dajiudian compares favorably with flashier options that have appeared on the outskirts of town. **Pros:** ideal location; reasonable rates; cozy rooms. **Cons:** restaurant service can be slow. $ *Rooms from: Y250* ⊠ *6 Beijing Dong Lu* ☎ *0855/826–9818* 🛏 *73 rooms* ⊟ *No credit cards* 🍽 *No meals.*

YUNNAN

Hidden deep in southwestern China, Yunnan is one of the country's most fascinating provinces. Its rugged and varied terrain contains some of China's most beautiful natural scenery, as well as the headwaters of three of Asia's most important rivers: the Yangtze, Mekong, and Salween. Stunning mountains, picturesque highland meadows, and steamy tropical jungles are inhabited by Bai, Dai, Naxi, Hani, and dozens of other ethnic groups, many of which live only in Yunnan.

Yunnan sits atop the Yunnan-Guizhou Plateau, with the Himalayas to the northwest and Myanmar, Laos, and Vietnam to the south. Yunnan was central to the Ancient Tea and Horse Caravan Route, an important trade route that connected China with the rest of Southeast Asia for thousands of years. Today Yunnan is one of the top travel destinations in China, with Lijiang, Dali, and Jinghong getting most of the attention. Countless lesser-known but equally amazing places are scattered throughout the province.

Roughly the size of California, Yunnan is becoming increasingly accessible to the outside world. More convenient air travel makes it possible to have breakfast by the Mekong in Jinghong and dinner overlooking the old mountain town of Lijiang the same day. Despite this, Yunnan still has plenty of places that are off the beaten path.

REGIONAL TOURS

China Minority Travel. This company offers tours of Yunnan that include the province's lesser-known gems, including Yuanyang, Lugu Lake, and Zhongdian. The agency has been organizing Yunnan tours for more than a decade. Multiple-day treks, family-oriented tours, and custom itineraries are all available. ✉ *Dali* ⊕ *www.china-minority-travel.com* ✉ *From Y1800.*

Zouba Tours. If you're longing to venture off the beaten track in Yunnan, this is a good tour option. Staff here have lived and traveled in Yunnan for years, and they can help you break cultural barriers with local minority cultures. The company offers fully customizable trips focusing on natural, cultural, and culinary experiences with pretty much any means possible: by car, by bike, or on foot. ✉ *Dali* ☎ *0152/8814–5939* ⊕ *www.zoubatours.com* ✉ *From Y800.*

KUNMING

400 km (248 miles; 7 hrs by train) southwest of Guiyang; 650 km (403 miles; 17½ hrs by train) southwest of Chengdu; 1,200 km (744 miles; 24 hrs by train) west of Guangzhou.

With its cool mountain air and laid-back locals, Kunming is one of China's most comfortable big cities, and is an ideal base for Yunnan travels. It's one of the few cities in the country that regularly has blue skies, and is nicknamed the "Spring City." Despite this moniker, weather can be gray and soggy during the summer monsoon season and chilly in January and February.

Kunming is changing rapidly as the city is transforming into China's gateway to Southeast Asia. But despite the disappearance of the Old City and increasingly congested traffic, Kunming remains a relaxed and somewhat idiosyncratic metropolis.

GETTING HERE AND AROUND

AIR TRAVEL An architectural highlight of the city, the new international airport is about 30 km (19 miles) east of the city center. Taxis take 30 to 40 minutes and cost Y120 to Y180, depending on traffic. Kunming is a busy air hub, with flight links all over China, as well as direct routes to Southeast Asia, Nepal, India, and the United Arab Emirates, among other areas.

Air Contact Kunming Airport ✉ *Changshui* ☎ *0871/6735–8125* ⊕ *www. newkma.com.*

BUS TRAVEL Kunming has five long-distance bus stations: the north, east, south, west, and northwest stations. All buses bound for Dali, Lijiang and Shangri-la depart from the west station; buses to Laos depart from the south station; and buses to Guangxi Province and the Yunnan-Vietnam border crossing at Hekou depart from the east station.

Bus Contact West Bus Transit Station ✉ *Chunyu Lu, at Yining Lu* ☎ *0871/6532–7326.*

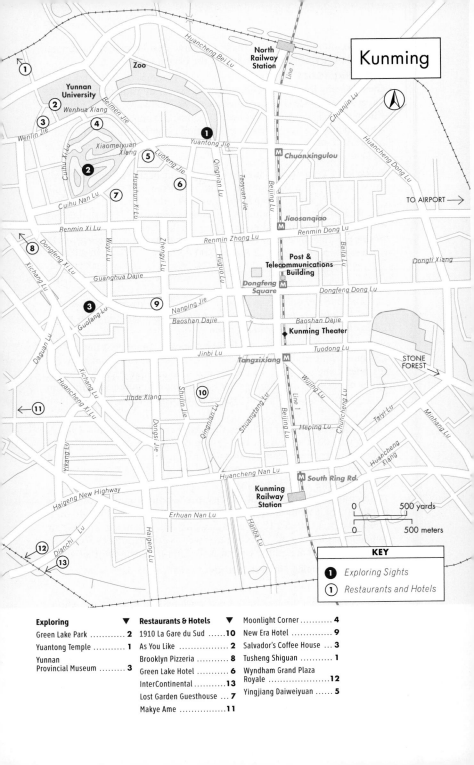

Kunming

Zoo

North Railway Station

Yunnan University

Wenhua Xiang

Bemen Jie

Xiaomeiyuan Xiang

Yuantong Jie

Chuanxingulou

Luofeng Jie

TO AIRPORT

Jiaosanqiao

Renmin Xi Lu

Renmin Zhong Lu

Renmin Dong Lu

Dongti Xiang

Guanghua Dajie

Post & Telecommunications Building

Dongfeng Square

Dongfeng Dong Lu

Nanping Jie

Baoshan Dajie

Baoshan Dajie

Kunming Theater

Jinbi Lu

Tangzixiang

Tuodong Lu

STONE FOREST

Jinde Xiang

Shulin Jie

Heping Lu

Huancheng Nan Lu

South Ring Rd.

Kunming Railway Station

Erhuan Nan Lu

Dianchi Lu

| 0 | | 500 yards |
| 0 | | 500 meters |

KEY

1 *Exploring Sights*

(1) *Restaurants and Hotels*

CAR TRAVEL If you need a car and driver while you're in Kunming, make arrangements through your hotel.

TRAIN TRAVEL The main station is at the southern end of Beijing Lu. There are day and overnight trains to both Dali (6 to 8 hours) and Lijiang (9 hours), as well as other Southwest China destinations.

Train Contact Kunming Train Station ✉ *Beijing Lu* ☎ *0871/6534–9414, 0871/6351–1534.*

METRO In 2014 metro Lines 1 and 2 began service. They act as one line, connecting southern University City in the district of Chenggong to the northern bus station. Line 3, running east–west, is supposed to open in 2015, although that date may change. The shorter Line 6 links the eastern bus station to the airport; this will eventually connect to Line 3.

SAFETY AND PRECAUTIONS

Watch out for pickpockets, especially on crowded city buses. When riding overnight on long-distance buses be careful with your valuables, as thieves sometimes steal money and electronics from sleeping passengers. Bus drivers sometimes employ a ticket system to ensure that the luggage you take is indeed yours.

Negotiate Kunming's frenetic traffic carefully, and watch out for noiseless electric scooters, which, not unlike other vehicles, often illegally travel in the wrong direction. Kunming drivers frequently ignore pedestrian right-of-way laws.

TIMING

A day or two in Kunming should suffice for most travelers.

TOURS

No group tours of Kunming are recommended, as most spend more time in shops than at attractions.

ESSENTIALS

Bank Bank of China ✉ *515 Beijing Lu* ☎ *0871/6319–2910.*

Medical Assistance Kunming First People's Hospital ✉ *504 Qingnian Lu* ☎ *0871/6318–8200.*

Public Security Bureau PSB Kunming ✉ *118 Tuodong Rd.* ☎ *110, 0871/6314–3436.*

Visitor and Tour Info GoKunming ⊕ *www.gokunming.com.* **Kunming Tourism Authority** ✉ *17 Dongfeng Dong Lu, 8th fl.* ☎ *0871/6314–9748* ⊕ *www.kmta. gov.cn.*

EXPLORING

Fodor's Choice ★ **Green Lake Park** (翠湖公园 *Cuìhú gōngyuán*). Filled with willow- and bamboo-covered islands connected by stone bridges, Green Lake Park is a favorite gathering place for Kunming's older residents, who begin to congregate in the park for singing and dancing in the late morning and stay until the gates close at 11 pm. In summer the lake is filled with pink and white lotus blossoms. In winter the park fills with migrating seagulls from Siberia, attracting large crowds. The lake was once part of Dianchi Lake, but it was severed from that larger body of water in the 1970s. ✉ *Cuihu Nan Lu* 🎫 *Free* 🕐 *Daily 7 am–11 pm.*

8

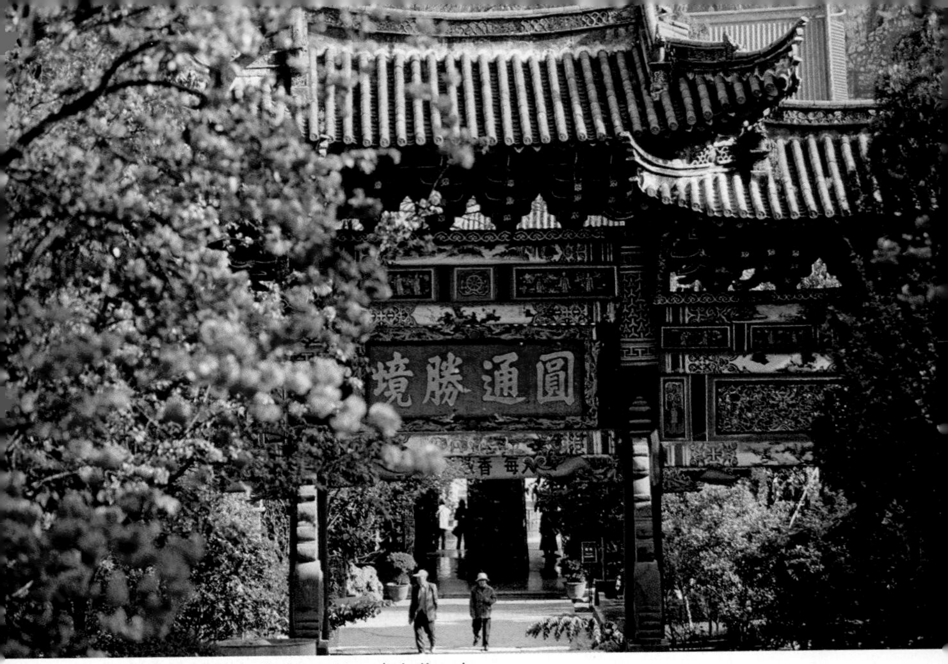

The Yuantong Temple is the largest temple in Kunming.

Yuantong Temple (圆通寺 *Yuántōng sì*). The largest temple in the city, Yuantong Temple dates back some 1,200 years to the Tang Dynasty. The compound consists of a series of gates leading to the inner temple, which is surrounded by a pond brimming with fish and turtles. The chanting of worshippers in the serene environment makes it hard to believe you're in the middle of a big city. In the back of the compound a temple houses a statue of Sakyamuni (the Buddha), a gift from the king of Thailand. ✉ *30 Yuantong Jie* 🎟 *Y6* 🕒 *Daily 8–5.*

Yunnan Provincial Museum (云南省博物馆 *Yúnnánshěng bówùguǎn*). The museum focuses primarily on the Dian Kingdom, which ruled much of Yunnan from 1000 BC to 1 BC. Most of what you'll see here is more than 2,000 years old. Exhibits have good English captions. ✉ *118 Wuyi Lu* ☎ *0871/6362–9328* 🌐 *www.ynbwg.cn* 🎟 *Free* 🕒 *Tues.–Sun. 8–5:30.*

WHERE TO EAT

$$
YUNNAN
Fodor's Choice ★

🍴 **1910 La Gare du Sud** (1910火车南站 *Yījiǔyī líng huǒchē nánzhàn*). Inside a renovated railroad station, this restaurant has outdoor seating and a historic atmosphere that are just as appealing to the menu full of tasty Yunnan dishes. The structure was built in the early 20th century by French colonists, and was once the terminus of the 535-mile railroad linking Hanoi to Kunming. Try some fried *rubing* (a local goat cheese), a spicy salad of chrysanthemum greens, or grilled tilapia. Don't pass up anything made with Yunnan's prized cured ham. The English portion of the menu is somewhat confusing, though pictures of most of the options help pick up the slack. [$] *Average main: Y60* ✉ *8 Houxin Jie* ☎ *0871/6316–9486* 💳 *No credit cards.*

$ **× As You Like** (有佳面包店 *Yǒujiā*
VEGETARIAN *miànbāo diàn*). Tucked away in
an alley off bustling Wenlin Jie,
As You Like is a quaint vegetarian restaurant and deli. The freshly
baked bread, healthy salads, and
all kinds of pastries will make your
mouth water, and the pizzas are
some the best around. It's in an
old house, so tall people will have
to mind their heads, but the food
more than makes up for it. $ *Av-
erage main: Y45* ⊠ *5 Tianjundian
Xiang, up the alley next to Dune
Cafe* ☎ *0871/6541–1715* ▭ *No
credit cards.*

$$ **× Brooklyn Pizzeria** (布鲁克林
PIZZA 披萨店 *Bùlǔkèlín pīsàdiàn*). Pop-
FAMILY ular with locals and expats alike,
this place stands for quality pizza
and other American-style snacks
and fast food, such as meatball
sandwiches and a range of salads. Pizza can be ordered per slice or
as a whole, with massive sizes for groups. For somewhere with such
broad appeal, the drink menu is unsurprisingly extensive, including
several craft beers from around the world. $ *Average main: Y60* ⊠ *11
Hongshan Dong Lu, Backstreet Block, Bldg. 12-6/8, a bit down the
road from McDonald's* ☎ *0871/6533–3243* ⊕ *www.kunmingpizza.com*
▭ *No credit cards* ☾ *Closed Wed.*

$$ **× Makye Ame** (玛吉阿米 *Mǎjí āmǐ*). As much a cultural experience as
TIBETAN a culinary adventure, Makye Ame is known for its Tibetan and Indian
song-and-dance performances. The shows are enjoyable, but can be
hard on the eardrums. For a quieter meal, ask for one of the rooms in
the back or in the cozy teahouse upstairs. Food-wise, Makye Ame serves
a large variety of Tibetan dishes, including stone-cooked yak, *malai
kafta* (large potato and cashew balls in a curried yogurt sauce), and an
incomparable platter of *xianggu* (shiitake mushrooms). A cold Lhasa
beer or some homemade yogurt wine rounds out one of the city's more
memorable meals. $ *Average main: Y60* ⊠ *Huapu Rd., 2nd fl., behind
Yimen Hotel* ☎ *0871/6833–6300* ▭ *No credit cards* ☾ *No lunch.*

$$$ **× Moonlight Corner** (*Yuèliàng wān*). With Thai owners, Thai chefs, and
THAI imported Thai ingredients, Moonlight Corner is arguably the best
restaurant of its kind in China. Try favorites such as Thai barbecued
chicken, pineapple fried rice, green papaya salad, or grilled fish, or go
for lesser-known gems such as lemongrass salad. Wash it all down with
Thai-style iced tea. This spot on the north side of Green Lake Park
has been booming with locals and foreigners since it opened. If the
sun is out, sit out front and enjoy one of the neighborhood's best park
views. $ *Average main: Y160* ⊠ *16 Cuihu Dong Lu* ☎ *0871/6513–8088*
⊕ *www.moonlightcorner.com* ▭ *No credit cards.*

BIKING KUNMING

Although traffic may seem a bit
daunting at first, Kunming is one
of the best cities in China for
biking. Small brown signs point
to historical and cultural sights.
The signs are in Chinese, but just
follow the arrows. Explore the
winding lanes at Green Lake Park;
heading south, you'll find pockets
of Old Kunming, including parks,
temples, and pagodas.

Xiong Brothers Bike Shop.
Decent rental bikes are available
here for about Y40 per day. Group
tours, conducted in Chinese, leave
Saturday morning at 9. ⊠ *51
Beimen Jie* ☎ *0871/6519–1520.*

8

CLOSE UP

Yunnan Cuisine

Dian cuisine is the term for Han Chinese cuisine found in Yunnan, especially around Kunming. Dian-style dishes are similar to Sichuan dishes and tend to favor spicy and sour flavors. Rice is a staple here, as is a type of rice noodle called *mixian*. A favorite dish is *guoqiao mixian*, a boiling broth served with raw pork and vegetables that all cook in the bowl. *Qiguo ji* (steampot chicken), another trademark Dian-style dish, uses a special earthenware pot to steam chicken and vegetables into a savory soup.

One thing that sets Dian cuisine apart from that of the rest of China is its use of dairy products. *Rubing* is a mildly flavored cheese made from goat's milk, and is typically fried and served with dried chili peppers or sugar. It is a little drier and less pungent than most other goat cheese. *Rushan*, or "milk fan," is a long strip of a cheese that is spread with a salty or sweet sauce. Wrapped around a chopstick, it makes a handy snack.

Street barbecue is a major part of the Yunnan culinary experience. Every kind of meat and vegetable is on offer, as well as quail eggs, *chou doufu* (stinky tofu), and *ou* (lotus root filled with sticky rice). Most restaurants in Yunnan close early, but barbecue stands stay open until the wee hours, making them a good place for a late-night snack. As for the morning after, a Yunnan breakfast is incomplete without *shao erkuai* (grilled rice pancakes with sweet or savory fillings and optional *youtiao*, a fried dough stick), often sold at mobile grills.

$ CAFÉ FAMILY Fodor's Choice ★ 🍴 **Salvador's Coffee House** (萨尔瓦多咖啡馆 *Sà'ěrwǎduō kāfēi guǎn*). Regularly packed to capacity and brewing some of Kunming's best coffee using a custom blend of Yunnan beans, Salvador's also has an extensive food menu. About half of its ingredients are organic, and more are being added regularly, with the goal of becoming one of the few entirely organic eateries in China. Popular main dishes include burritos, quesadillas, and falafel. The place has Wi-Fi and comfy sofas for lounging, along with outdoor seating ideal for people-watching on bustling Wenhua Xiang. [$] *Average main: Y45* ✉ *76 Wenhua Xiang* ☎ *0871/6536–3525* 🌐 *www.salvadors.cn* 💳 *No credit cards.*

$ YUNNAN Fodor's Choice ★ 🍴 **Tusheng Shiguan** (土生食馆 *Tǔshēng shíguǎn*). Without a doubt the best organic Chinese restaurant in town, Tusheng Shiguan is a must for anyone who wants to try the finest Yunnan cuisine. Don't miss the *erkuai* (rice pancakes), the *fuzhu* (a tofu-skin dish whose misleading name translates to "rotten bamboo") or the ginger beef dish, and ask which vegetables are in season. The inside and outside seating is comfortable, and the service is most hospitable. Make sure to order rice if you're having spicy dishes, and try a small jug of the home-brewed corn liquor. [$] *Average main: Y35* ✉ *Loft Jinding 1919 Complex, 15 Jindingshan Lu* ☎ *0871/6542–0010* 💳 *No credit cards.*

$ YUNNAN Fodor's Choice ★ 🍴 **Yingjiang Daiweiyuan** (盈江傣味园 *Yíngjiāng dǎiwèiyuán*). This often hectic eatery may be the best place in Kunming to enjoy Dai cuisine, which is known for its liberal use of chili peppers. If you want to go straight for the heat, try the *gui ji* or "ghost chicken," a cold salad that is slightly sour and extremely spicy. Tamer options include pineapple rice, fennel omelets, dried beef, wild mushrooms, fried fish, and tapioca with cookies in coconut milk. Dai cuisine features many dishes and ingredients that are foreign even to coastal Chinese residents. There are other branches of this chain throughout town. $ *Average main: Y40* ⌂ *Cuihu North Rd., Xiansheng Po intersection* ☎ *0871/512–2251* ▭ *No credit cards.*

WHERE TO STAY

$$$ ⌂ **Green Lake Hotel** (翠湖宾馆 *Cuìhú bīnguǎn*). Adjacent to Green Lake
HOTEL Park, this is one of Kunming's most elegant lodgings, with comfortably furnished guest rooms that are a pleasant blend of traditional design and modern style. **Pros:** great location; good service; comfortable rooms. **Cons:** many staff members speak little or no English. $ *Rooms from: Y2277* ⌂ *6 Cuihu Nan Lu* ☎ *0871/6515–8888* ⊕ *www.greenlakehotel kunming.com* ⤳ *301 rooms, 6 suites* ◎ *Breakfast.*

$ ⌂ **InterContinental Kunming** (昆明洲际酒店 *Kūnmíng zhōujì jiǔdiàn*). If
HOTEL you're in Kunming only to relax, and noisy streets and busy traffic hold
Fodor's Choice little appeal, then the international chain hotel is an exceptional option.
★ **Pros:** absolutely beautiful; quiet location. **Cons:** remote. $ *Rooms from: Y980* ⌂ *5 Yijing Rd, near Dianchi Lake* ☎ *400/886–2255* ⊕ *www.ihg. com/intercontinental* ⤳ *541 rooms* ◎ *Breakfast.*

$ ⌂ **Lost Garden Guesthouse** (一丘田七号客栈 *Yīqiūtián qīhào kèzhàn*).
B&B/INN If you manage to book a room in this always-packed guesthouse, you'll find yourself a stone's throw from Green Lake. **Pros:** close to Green Lake; personal service; cozy touch. **Cons:** basic furnishings; common areas shared with diners from outside. $ *Rooms from: Y160* ⌂ *7 Yi Qiu Tian* ☎ *0871/6511–1127* ⊕ *www.lostgardenguesthouse.com* ⤳ *14 rooms* ◎ *No meals.*

$ ⌂ **New Era Hotel** (新纪元大酒店 *Xīnjìyuán dàjiǔdiàn*). Conveniently
HOTEL located on Kunming's central pedestrian area, the New Era Hotel has well-furnished rooms with views on the west mountains and the crawling crowd below. **Pros:** great location; excellent value; sensational breakfast. **Cons:** impersonal; busy area. $ *Rooms from: Y520* ⌂ *1 Dongfeng West Rd., on Nanping Sq.* ☎ *0871/6362–4999* ⊕ *www. erahotel.com* ⤳ *315 rooms* ◎ *Breakfast.*

$$$ ⌂ **Wyndham Grand Plaza Royale** (昆明七彩云南温德姆至尊豪廷大酒店
HOTEL *Kūnmíng qīcǎi yúnnán wēndémǔ zhìzūn háo tíng dàjiǔdiàn*). Without
Fodor's Choice a doubt the city's most luxurious hotel, the Wyndham Grand Plaza
★ Royale brings taste and style to everything from the grand lobby to the soothing spa to the selection of six globe-trotting restaurants. **Pros:** attentive staff; excellent restaurants; tasteful touch to everything. **Cons:** far from the city center; views disturbed by construction. $ *Rooms from: Y1600* ⌂ *569 Dianchi Lu* ☎ *0871/6817–7777* ⊕ *www.wyndham. com* ⤳ *374 rooms* ◎ *Breakfast.*

8

NIGHTLIFE AND PERFORMING ARTS

NIGHTLIFE

When evening falls, Kunming's locals as well as its growing expat population congregate at the bars, cafés, and restaurants of Wenlin Jie and Wenhua Xiang. After midnight, the clubs and bars around the Kundu Night Market attract the crowds.

Alei Lounge Club & Tapas Bar (ALEI酒廊·精致小点 *ALEI jiǔláng jīngzhì xiǎodiǎn*). Alei is the best place to enjoy mix drinks and tapas. The interior is posh, but the atmosphere is unpretentious. ⊠ *3 A1 Bldg., Zheng Yi Fang* ☎ *0871/6836–9099.*

Chapter One. This Western-style bar attracts a largely Chinese clientele and offers a decent selection of drinks and snacks at very acceptable prices. It's very popular with locals in the evenings, when the outdoor terrace is packed to the brim. And there's an all-you-can-eat brunch buffet for Y40 every day at 11 am; although the Western food's quality can vary, as the cooks are still finding their way, the Chinese food is impeccable. ⊠ *20 Wenlin Jie* ☎ *0871/6533–1151.*

Moondog (月亮狗 *Yuèliàng gǒu*). Open until the wee hours, this bar on a side street from bustling Kundu has Kunming's widest selection of whiskeys. It's a favorite with expats for foosball, cards, and other games. ⊠ *138-5 Wacang Nan Lu* ☎ *0158/8714–6080.*

O'Reilly's Irish Pub (O'Reilly's爱尔兰酒吧 *O'Reilly's àiěrlán jiǔbā*). Run by a trio who claims never to have set foot on Irish soil, O'Reilly's Irish Pub has cold Guinness on tap, as well as a remarkable selection of Belgian ales. The obligatory pub grub is very good. The northern bar, at 13 Beichen Pedestrian Street, is quieter than the southern one, which can get quite rowdy when the local rugby team is in. ⊠ *119 Beimen St.* ☎ *0871/6561–5661* ⊕ *www.oreillys.cn.com.*

PERFORMING ARTS

Dynamic Yunnan (云南映象 *Yúnnán yìngxiàng*). Chinese dance legend Yang Liping has retired, but the Yunnan native's award-winning dance and musical production, Dynamic Yunnan, still plays to full-capacity crowds, nightly at 8:30. It's an impressive fusion of the storytelling, songs, and dances of local indigenous groups. ⊠ *Kunming Arts Theatre, 132 Dongfeng Xi Lu, near Xiao Xi Men* ☎ *087/6313–0033* ☒ *From Y180.*

Livstone House (石榴 *Shíliú*). Founded by the Yunnanese prodigy Liu Lifen, Livstone House often buzzes with activity, with art exhibit and theater productions and other performances. ⊠ *Loft Jinding 1919 Complex, 15 Jindingshan Bei Lu* ☎ *0871/6538–5159.*

Mu Yu Studio (木鱼摄影棚 *Mùyú shèyǐng péng*). A small art studio and bar hidden off Wenlin Jie, Mu Yu Studio is where Kunming's creative crowd gathers to exhibit an eclectic collection of art. ⊠ *202 Wenlin Jie, enter through the gate* ☎ *0135/7705–6433.*

SHOPPING

If you're looking for a good deal on tea, look no further than the wholesale tea market at the southeast corner of Beijing Lu and Wujing Lu. Within the market you'll find an amazing variety of green teas, black

Kunming's Flying Tigers

Despite being in the hinterland of Southwest China, Kunming played a crucial role in World War II by preventing Japanese forces from taking control of all of China. At the center of this role was the American Volunteer Group, best known by its local nickname *feihu*, or the Flying Tigers, because of the shark faces painted on their fuselages.

The group of around 300 American servicemen was led by the mysterious Claire L. Chennault. A retired captain in the U.S. Air Force, Chennault first came to Kunming in 1938, when Madame Chiang Kai-shek, wife of the country's leader, asked him to organize a Chinese air force to counter the relentless attacks from the Japanese, who were busily bombing much of China with little opposition.

Supply routes to China's capital were being taken out one after another, leaving just one road. Chennault argued that a group of American pilots could defend this crucial supply artery, as well as push the Japanese out of the region.

The Flying Tigers were tenacious fighters. They swept through much of China to combat the constant bombing by Japanese forces. Their record was second to none in World War II. They had more than 50 enemy encounters and were never defeated.

teas, flower teas, and herbal teas. It's a wholesale market, but vendors will sell you small quantities.

Qianju Jie, near the intersection of Wenlin Jie and Wenhua Xiang, is one of the more popular shopping streets in the city.

Bird and Flower Market (花鸟市场 *Huāniǎo shìchǎng*). For all kinds of trinkets and oddities, head to the Bird and Flower Market. Consisting of a bunch of street stalls along Jingxing Jie, this market is the ultimate place to sharpen your haggling skills—and perhaps find that one special gift for the folks back home. ⊠ *Jingxing Jie, off Zhengyi Lu, nearby Nanping square.*

Mandarin Books (漫林书苑 *Mànlín shūyuàn*). This is one of the best foreign-language bookstores in all of Yunnan. ⊠ *52 Wenhua Xiang 9–10* ☎ *0871/6551–6579* ⊕ *www.mandarinbooks.cn.*

STONE FOREST (SHILIN)

125 km (78 miles) southeast of Kunming.

This cluster of dark-gray limestone formations, twisted into odd shapes, makes a memorable side trip—it's one of the most interesting sites near Kunming.

GETTING HERE AND AROUND

There are several ways to get here, the best being a car and driver. One can be arranged through your hotel and should cost between Y500 and Y600. Stone Forest–bound buses depart every 15 to 30 minutes from Kunming's East Bus Station, and cost about Y20 round-trip. This trip takes at least four hours, as the driver makes numerous stops at

8

souvenir stands and junk stores along the way.

EXPLORING

Stone Forest (石林 *Shílín*). The forest's groups of karst, first formed 270 million years ago, have been given names to describe their resemblance to creatures real (turtles) or mythological (phoenixes). Walking through the park you'll find plenty

of Sani women eager to act as guides and sell you their handicrafts. The main trail became rather commercialized, but there are plenty of similar formations in other parts of the park. ⊠ *Shilin* ☎ *Y175* ⏱ *24 hrs.*

DALI

250 km (155 miles; 5 hrs by bus; 6 hrs by train) northwest of Kunming; 140 km (87 miles; 3 hrs by bus; 2 hrs by train) south of Lijiang.

This rustic town is one of those rare places that feel completely cut off from the rest of the world but still has high-speed Internet access. It's perched at the foot of the towering Cangshan Mountains and overlooks lovely Erhai Lake. The typically sunny weather, sleepy artistic atmosphere, and gorgeous sunsets have made it one of Yunnan's most popular destinations

Home to the Bai people, Dali has been inhabited for more than 4,000 years, serving as a major rice-production base for the region. Today tourism is rejuvenating the town. The upside of its building boom is a greater variety of restaurants and hotels; the downside is that the Old Town is constantly being demolished and reconstructed. A planned high-speed rail link with Kunming means now is the time to see Dali before it changes even more.

GETTING HERE AND AROUND

AIR TRAVEL There are multiple daily flights from Kunming to Dali. Dali's airport is at the southern tip of Erhai Lake. Taxis between the airport and the Old Town cost Y90 and take just under an hour.

Air Contact Dali Airport ☎ *0872/242–8915.*

BUS TRAVEL Buses from Kunming to Dali take five hours and cost Y110. Most drop you off in "New Dali," the nondescript city of Xiaguan. From there, a 25-minute cab ride gets you to the Old Town. It should cost Y40 to Y60, depending on the time of day and your haggling skills.

TRAIN TRAVEL Trains between Kunming and Dali cost around Y100, but the trip takes six hours, about one hour longer than taking a bus. However, there's an overnight train from Kunming that drops you in Dali at 6 am, so it can be a good way to save on time as well as on lodging.

Train Contact Xiaguan Train Station ⊠ *Dianyuan Lu, Xiaguan.*

The Stone Forest in Yunnan is a UNESCO World Heritage Site.

SAFETY AND PRECAUTIONS
Several solo hikers have died in the mountains above Dali in recent years. If you do any hiking beyond the paved tourist paths—do so with at least one other person.

TIMING
Most of the major sites in and around Dali can be enjoyed within two or three days. Many travelers find themselves arriving in Dali with ambitious itineraries, but end up staying to enjoy the town's lazy vibe.

FESTIVALS
Yi and Bai Torch Festival. One of the more exciting festivals in Southwest China is the Torch Festival, celebrated by both the Yi and Bai minorities on the 24th day of the sixth lunar month, which falls in June or July). Dali's Old Town is one of the best (and worst) places to catch the festival. Many local children like to frighten travelers with the flames, especially on Foreigner Street. Anyone who wants to see the festival without worrying about getting singed by pyromaniac children might want to go to Xizhou—the first town north of Dali.

TOURS
China Minority Travel lets you explore the villages surrounding Erhai Lake. Expect to pay around Y2,000 for two to four people, including a guide, transportation, and lunch.

ESSENTIALS
Medical Assistance Dali First Municipal People's Hospital ⊠ *217 Tai'an Lu* ☎ *0872/212-4462.*

Dali and the Nanzhao Kingdom

The idyllic scenery belies Dali's importance as the center of power for the Nanzhao Kingdom. The easily defensible area around Erhai Lake was the kingdom's birthplace, which began as the Bai- and Yi-dominated Damengguo in 649. Almost a century later, Damengguo was expanded to include the six surrounding kingdoms ruled by powerful Bai families. This expansion was supported by the ruling Chinese Tang Dynasty, and the kingdom was renamed Nanzhao.

The primarily Buddhist Nanzhao Kingdom was essentially a vassal state of the Tang Dynasty until AD 750, when it rebelled. Tang armies were sent in 751 and 754 to suppress the insurgents, but they suffered humiliating defeats. Emboldened by

their victories, Nanzhao troops helped the kingdom acquire a significant amount of territory. Before reaching its high point with the capture of Chengdu and Sichuan in 829, the Nanzhao Kingdom had expanded to include all of present-day Yunnan, as well as parts of present-day Burma, Laos, and Thailand.

Although the capture of Chengdu was a major victory for Nanzhao, it appears to have led directly to its decline. The Tang Dynasty couldn't stand for such an incursion and sent large numbers of troops to the area. They eventually evicted Nanzhao forces from Sichuan by 873. About 30 years later the Nanzhao leaders were finally overthrown, ending the story of their meteoric rise and fall.

Banks Bank of China ✉ 427 Fuxing Lu ☎ 0872/267–1620. **ICBC** ✉ 304 Fuxing Lu ☎ 0872/267–0263.

Public Security Bureau PSB Dali ✉ Off Hongwu Lu ☎ 110.

EXPLORING

Dali's Old Town, called Dali Gucheng, is surrounded by attractive reconstructions of the old city wall and gates. Go to the wall's southwest corner and take the stairs to the top for a great view of the city and the surrounding mountains. Outside the bustling center of the Old Town are countless little alleys lined with old Bai-style homes.

Dali has two popular pedestrian streets, Huguo Lu and Renmin Lu, both of which run east–west, or uphill–downhill. Huguo Lu, better known as Foreigner Street, is lined with the cafés that made Dali famous in the 1990s, but the street has begun to lose its luster. High rents and cutthroat competition have taken a toll on quality and service. Nightlife is concentrated on Renmin Lu.

Three Pagodas (三塔寺 *Sān tǎ sì*). The most famous landmark in Dali, the Three Pagodas appear on just about every calendar of Chinese scenery. The largest, 215 feet high, dates from AD 836 and is decorated on each of its 16 stories with Buddhas carved from local marble. The other two pagodas, also richly decorated, are even more elegant. When the water is still, you can ponder their reflection in a nearby pool. A massive Chan Buddhist Temple has been built behind the pagodas. The

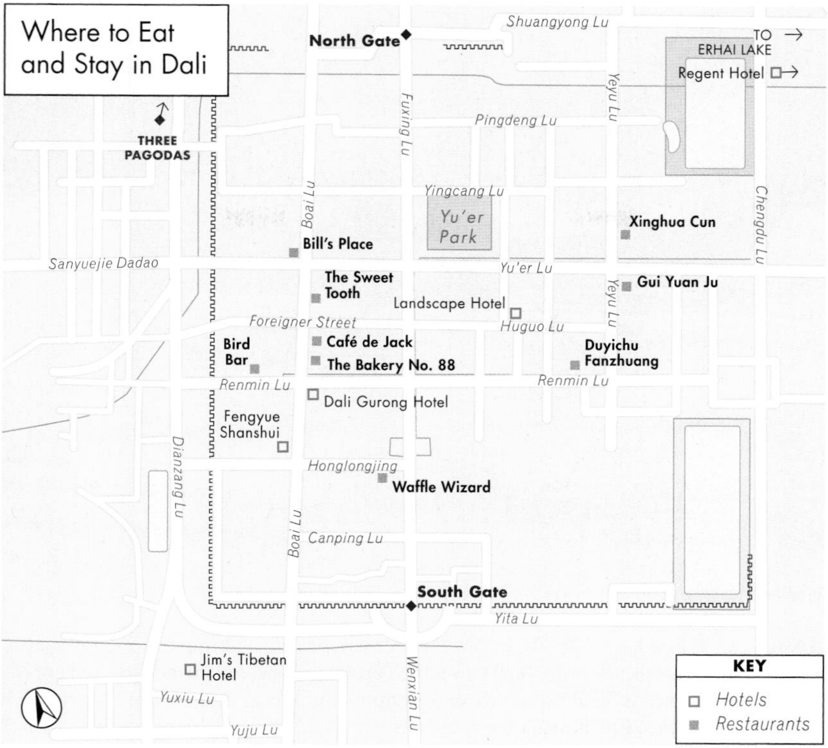
Where to Eat and Stay in Dali
North Gate
Shuangyong Lu
TO ERHAI LAKE
Regent Hotel
Yeyu Lu
Fuxing Lu
Pingdeng Lu
THREE PAGODAS
Boai Lu
Yingcang Lu
Yu'er Park
Chengdu Lu
Xinghua Cun
Bill's Place
Sanyuejie Dadao
Yu'er Lu
The Sweet Tooth
Gui Yuan Ju
Landscape Hotel
Foreigner Street
Huguo Lu
Bird Bar
Café de Jack
The Bakery No. 88
Duyichu Fanzhuang
Renmin Lu
Dali Gurong Hotel
Fengyue Shanshui
Dianzang Lu
Honglongjing
Waffle Wizard
Canping Lu
South Gate
Yita Lu
Jim's Tibetan Hotel
Yuxiu Lu
Yuju Lu
Wenxian Lu
KEY
Hotels
Restaurants

pagodas are a 20-minute walk from the Old Town. ✉ *1 km (½ mile) north of Dali Gucheng* 🎫 *Y128* 🕒 *Daily 7 am–8 pm.*

WHERE TO EAT

For a taste of authentic local Bai dishes like *paojiao zhurou* (pork with pickled peppers) or *chao rubing* (fried goat cheese), try any of the local restaurants on Renmin Lu just east of Fuxing Lu. Most of these restaurants lack English menus, but they generally have their ingredients on display.

$ CAFÉ 🍴 **The Bakery No. 88** (88号西点店 *Bābāhào xīdiǎndiàn*). The dessert counter here has some of Dali's best cakes, which can be enjoyed with a coffee and a book on the second floor if you're after somewhere quiet. It's one of the best places in town for good Western food and take-away stuffed baguettes. [$] *Average main: Y30* ✉ *52 Bo'ai Lu* ☎ *0872/267–9129.*

$ ECLECTIC 🍴 **Bill's Place** (火柴人 *Huǒchái rén*). From the rooftop, you are treated to some of the most splendid views of the Old Town. The main dining area, accessible from the street through a small door and a flight of stairs, features a little balcony with tables for two, perfect for a romantic tête-à-tête. The focus of the kitchen is on Italian and Mexican cuisine, with some very tasty fajitas and burritos. [$] *Average main: Y40* ✉ *105 Bo'ai Lu, corner of Renmin Lu* ☎ *0872/251–8323.*

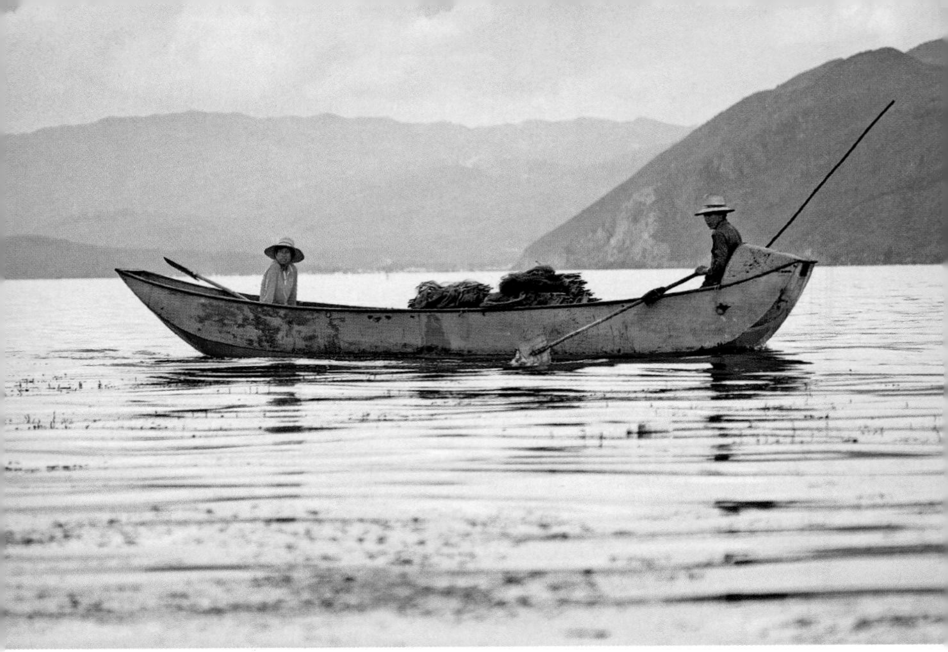

Bai fishermen on Erhai Lake

$ CAFÉ
🍴 **Bird Bar** (鸟吧 *Niǎo bā*). For a taste of one of Yunnan's major cash crops, head to the Bird Bar, which grows, roasts, and grinds its own coffee beans. The owner's love for antique buildings clearly shines through in the coffeehouse's cozy, old-fashioned interior. [$] *Average main: Y38* ✉ *22 Renmin Lu* ☎ *0872/266–1843* 🌐 *www.birdbardali.com.*

$ ECLECTIC
🍴 **Café de Jack** (樱花园西餐厅 *Yīnghuā yuán xīcāntīng*). A longtime favorite specializing in Western and Chinese classics as well as some local Bai specialties, Café de Jack serves good breakfast, lunch, and dinner—and the strongest cup of coffee in Yunnan. All three floors are a bit different: the first floor feels like a bar, the second floor is more like a restaurant, and the rooftop is a perfect place to kick back with a beer. Catch up with the rest of the world via computer terminals or Wi-Fi. [$] *Average main: Y45* ✉ *82 Bo'ai Lu* ☎ *0872/267–1572.*

$ NORTHERN CHINESE
🍴 **Duyichu Fanzhuang** (独一处饭庄 *Dúyīchù fànzhuāng*). Hidden inside a leaning shack, this little dumpling palace wraps the best *jaozi* in Dali and the surrounding region. Other dishes are on offer, depending on what's available in the local markets. The menus have been kindly translated into English by expat regulars, but they don't mention the selection of splendid house-made liquor. The owners both hail from China's freezing northeastern reaches. [$] *Average main: Y15* ✉ *Renmin Lu, across from Mayana Restaurant* 💳 *No credit cards.*

$$ KOREAN
🍴 **Gui Yuan Ju** (桂苑居 *Guì yuàn jū*). A bit removed from the crowds, Gui Yuan Ju is the city's best bet for Korean food. Dishes include Korean hotpot, barbecued meats, and lots of other Korean specialties, to be enjoyed from a relaxing albeit somewhat dull dining area. [$] *Average main: Y55* ✉ *189 Yeyu Lu* ☎ *0872/267–1889.*

$ ✕**The Sweet Tooth** (甜点屋 *Tiāndiǎnwū*). Dali's expat community
MEXICAN indulges in its love of pastries at this low-profile little eatery. Surprisingly enough, it also cooks up some of the best Mexican food in town. The prices are more than reasonable, but the seating is limited. $ *Average main: Y35* ✉ *52 Bo'ai Lu* ☎ *0872/266–3830* .

$ ✕**Waffle Wizard** (比利时挖福饼 *Bǐlìshí wā fú bǐng*). Here you'll find
CAFÉ authentic Belgian waffles topped with whipped cream, ice cream, or just a dusting of powdered sugar. If you don't have a sweet tooth, sip a cold Belgian ale while you watch the people stroll past. It's easy to miss, as this place is no more than a cutaway in the street with some chairs out front. The Wi-Fi is a plus. $ *Average main: Y20* ✉ *Corner of Honglongjing Lu and Fuxing Lu* ☎ *137/0060–6575* ⊕ *www.wafflewizard.com.*

$ ✕**Xinghua Cun** (杏花村 *Xìnghuā cūn*). In business for decades, Xinghua
YUNNAN Cun is a no-nonsense Chinese restaurant with the usual revolving-top tables and a counter filled with all kinds of homemade liquor. If you look past the spartan decor, you'll notice what this place does best: tasty Yunnanese and local Bai dishes, all served with a smile. The menus are in Chinglish, but ordering is easily done by pointing at pictures. $ *Average main: Y35* ✉ *Yeyu Lu* ☎ *0872/267–0082.*

WHERE TO STAY

$ ⌂**Dali Gurong Hotel** (古榕会馆 *Gǔ róng huìguǎn*). One of the most
HOTEL pleasant hotels in Dali's Old Town, the upscale Dali Gurong offers
Fodor's Choice spacious and well-furnished rooms in a cluster of villas in a park-like setting. **Pros:** luxurious feel; helpful staff; central location. **Cons:**
★ somewhat expensive for the area. $ *Rooms from: Y880* ✉ *59 Bo'ai Lu* ☎ *0872/268–5999* ⊕ *www.dlgrhotel.com* ↻ *61 rooms* ❙❍❙*Breakfast.*

$ ⌂**Fengyue Shanshui** (风月山水客栈 *Fēngyuè shānshuǐ kèzhàn*). Owned
HOTEL by the acclaimed Chinese artist Fang Lijun, this guesthouse is in a class by itself. **Pros:** unique style; great views; quiet at night. **Cons:** rooms may feel a little empty; often booked solid; staff does not speak English. $ *Rooms from: Y200* ✉ *3 Honglongjing* ☎ *0872/266–3741* ↻ *17 rooms, 1 suite* ▭ *No credit cards* ❙❍❙ *No meals.*

$ ⌂**Jim's Tibetan Hotel** (吉姆藏式酒店 *Jímǔ zàng shì jiǔdiàn*). Outside
B&B/INN the south gate, this quiet lodging is ideal if you want to avoid the
FAMILY hubbub of Dali's Old Town. **Pros:** kid-friendly vibe; unique interior. **Cons:** a bit dusty; a little far from the sights. $ *Rooms from: Y300* ✉ *13 Yuxiu Lu* ☎ *0872/267–7824* ⊕ *www.jims-tibetan-hotel.com* ↻ *15 rooms* ❙❍❙*Breakfast.*

$ ⌂**Landscape Hotel** (兰林阁酒店 *Lánlíngé jiǔdiàn*). With exits on both
HOTEL Huguo and Yu'er roads, the Landscape Hotel is probably the most centrally located place to stay in town. **Pros:** doesn't get any more central; great courtyards. **Cons:** average rooms. $ *Rooms from: Y880* ✉ *96 Yu'er Lu* ☎ *0872/266–6188* ⊕ *www.lanlinge.com/a/English* ↻ *202 rooms, 4 suites* ❙❍❙ *No meals.*

$ ⌂**Regent Hotel** (风花雪月大酒店 *Fēnghuāxuěyuè dà jiǔdiàn*). Littered
HOTEL with luxury artifacts, the Regent might seem a little unnecessary when compared to the highly affordable options in the Old Town. **Pros:** good quality and excellent service. **Cons:** feels isolated from the Old Town.

8

$ *Rooms from:* Y880 ✉ *Yu'er Lu and Da-Li First Class intersection* ☎ *0872/266–6666* ⊕ *www.regenthotel.cn* ⇥ *599 rooms* ⦶ *Breakfast.*

NIGHTLIFE

Bad Monkey (坏猴子 *Huàihóuzi*). One of the town's oldest establishments, this is Dali's most popular watering hole. In addition to an extensive bar, Bad Monkey brews its own beer, with every batch selling out quickly. Drinks aside, the kitchen stays open until early morning and cooks up decent fish-and-chips and pizzas. There's live music almost every night. ✉ *74–76 Renmin Lu* ⊕ *www.badmonkeybar.com.*

Kaki Cafe (柿子树咖啡馆 *Shìzǐshù kāfēi guǎn*). Tucked away in an alley off busy Renmin Lu, this is a café by day that gets a bit more lively at night, when the bottles come out. There's a standard selection of drinks, completed with the obligatory Belgian ales. This is an excellent place if you are after a quiet spot. ✉ *164 Huguo Lu, off Renmin Lu* ☎ *0872/536–5688.*

September Bar (九月 *Jiǔyuè*). With its jazzy atmosphere, loungy decor, and wall of wine bottles behind the bar, September Bar is a nice alternative if you're seeking a more intimate environment. There's regular live music and a selection of Belgian and German beers. ✉ *225 Renmin Lu* ☎ *0136/8878–3009.*

Sun Island (太阳岛 *Tàiyáng dǎo*). One of Old Town's most pleasant bars, the civilized Sun Island draws a crowd that's young, alternative, and mostly Chinese. Grab a seat at the wooden bar and strike up a conversation with the friendly staffers. ■TIP→ **For a local specialty, ask for the plum wine—it's actually plum liquor—on the rocks.** ✉ *324 Renmin Lu.*

SHOPPING

Foreigner Street is lined with Bai women who have been selling the same jewelry, fabrics, and Communist kitsch for two decades. Don't be afraid to walk away when bargaining; vendors will often drop their prices at the last minute.

Bo'ai Lu and Renmin Lu are peppered with a variety of shops featuring outdoor clothing and equipment; handicrafts from India, Nepal, and Southeast Asia; as well as Chinese antiques. Fuxing Lu, aimed primarily at Chinese tourists, is where you'll find local teas, specialty foods, and, most prominently, jade. Much of it is of low quality, so buy only if you know something about jade.

SIDE TRIPS FROM DALI

Fodor's Choice
★

Cangshan (苍山 *Cāngshān*). With a peak that rises to more than 4,500 meters (14,765 feet), "Green Mountain" can be seen from just about anywhere in Dali. A 16-km (10-mile) path carved into the side of the mountain offers spectacular views of Dali and the surrounding villages. There are also several temples, grottoes, and waterfalls just off the main trail. To get to the footpath, follow Yu'er Lu to the foot of the mountain. If you don't want to climb, there are two cable cars to take you up the mountain.

Erhai Lake (洱海湖 *Ěrhǎi hú*). Almost any street off Fuxing Lu will bring you to the shore of Erhai Lake. from which you can marvel at the looming Cangshan peaks. You may catch a glimpse of fishermen with teams

The Old Town in Lijiang at dusk

of cormorants tied to their boats. In good weather, ferries are a wonderful way to see the lake and the surrounding mountains. The ferries cost between Y30 and Y70 (depending on your ability to bargain). More interesting—and cheaper—is hiring fishermen to paddle you wherever you want to go. Boats depart from the village of Zhoucheng.

DID YOU KNOW?

The cormorants used by fishermen on Erhai Lake have a collar around their necks that prevents them from swallowing the fish they have caught.

Shaping. This town sits on the lake's northern shore, and can be most easily reached by boat or by hiring a car and driver. Its market, held every Monday morning, is the most popular in the area.

Wase. Wase has a popular area market featuring Bai clothing. The town is on the opposite side of the lake from Dali and can be reached by car or boat. Wase also has some inexpensive places to stay if you want to spend the night in a lake village.

Xizhou (喜洲 *Xǐ zhōu*). Among the prettiest towns in the area is Xizhou, about 20 km (12 miles) north of Dali. It has managed to preserve a fair amount of its Bai architecture. The daily morning market and occasional festivals of traditional music attract a fair number of tourists from Dali. Minibuses leave from Dali's west gate and cost Y7.

LIJIANG

150 km (93 miles; 3 hrs by bus; 2 hrs by train) north of Dali; 320 km (198 miles; 7 hrs by bus; 8 hrs by train) northwest of Kunming; 550 km (341 miles; 20 hrs by bus) southwest of Chengdu.

Lijiang is probably the most famous travel destination in Yunnan, as its Old Town is a UNESCO World Heritage Site. At the base of majestic Jade Dragon Snow Mountain, Lijiang is home to the Naxi people, who are related to Tibetans but have their own language and culture.

Lijiang's Old Town is a labyrinth of winding alleys, fish-filled streams, and old Naxi houses with tile rooftops. Traditional Naxi singing and dancing are on display nightly at Sifang Jie, the square in Old Town's center.

GETTING HERE AND AROUND

AIR TRAVEL   There are multiple daily flights from Kunming. The airport is 48 km (30 miles) south of Lijiang. A Y20 bus from the airport takes you to the edge of the Old Town. A taxi to the Old Town will run you Y80.

Air Contact Lijiang Airport ☏ *0888/517–3081.*

BUS TRAVEL   Lijiang's main bus station is on Xianggelila Dadao. Trips from Kunming take just over eight hours.

Bus Contact Lijiang Travel Bus Station ✉ *329 Changshui Lu* ☏ *0888/512–5492.*

TRAIN TRAVEL   There are day and night trains from Kunming. The ride takes eight hours and costs about Y150 for a berth. A train from Dali takes two hours and costs Y34. Don't expect much in the way of views, as most of the route goes through tunnels.

SAFETY AND PRECAUTIONS

Lijiang gets a lot of foot traffic, which has made the cobbled paths in the Old Town quite slippery. Also, if taking a taxi, make sure they use the meter, as some drivers may try to pull a fast one.

Visiting Tiger Leaping Gorge during rainy weather is not advised, as large rocks regularly come crashing down. The higher trail is relatively safe from such peril, but it can be slippery. Make sure you wear good shoes.

TIMING

Lijiang is good for two or three days of taking in the Old Town and surrounding areas. If you're feeling active, head to Tiger Leaping Gorge or Lugu lake for two to three days.

TOURS

Lijiang has plenty of English-language signs in the Old Town, and tour guides aren't needed on Jade Dragon Snow Mountain or in Tiger Leaping Gorge. If you want to hike the surrounding mountains, however, a guide is strongly recommended.

ESSENTIALS

Bank Bank of China ✉ *Changshui Lu.*

Medical Assistance Lijiang People's Hospital ✉ *Fuhui Lu* ☏ *0888/518–5053.*

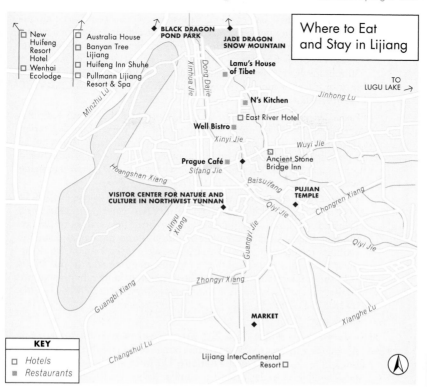

New Huifeng Resort Hotel
Wenhai Ecolodge

Australia House
Banyan Tree Lijiang
Huifeng Inn Shuhe
Pullmann Lijiang Resort & Spa

BLACK DRAGON POND PARK

JADE DRAGON SNOW MOUNTAIN

Lamu's House of Tibet

TO LUGU LAKE →

Jinhong Lu

N's Kitchen

East River Hotel

Well Bistro

Xinyi Jie

Wuyi Jie

Prague Café
Sifang Jie

Ancient Stone Bridge Inn

Baisuifang

PUJIAN TEMPLE

VISITOR CENTER FOR NATURE AND CULTURE IN NORTHWEST YUNNAN

Chongren Xiang

Qiyi Jie

Jinyu Xiang

Guangyi Jie

Qiyi Jie

Guangbi Xiang

Zhongyi Xiang

Xinhua Jie

Dong Dajie

Minzhu Lu

Huangshan Xiang

MARKET

Xianghe Lu

Changshui Lu

Lijiang InterContinental Resort

KEY
□ Hotels
■ Restaurants

Where to Eat and Stay in Lijiang

8

Public Security Bureau PSB Lijiang ✉ Fuhui Lu ☎ 110.

Visitor and Tour Info China International Travel Service ✉ Lifang Shangxia, Xianggelila Ave, 3rd fl. ☎ 0888/516–0782.

EXPLORING

With so many shops and markets selling the same things, much of Lijiang's Old Town feels more like a Special Economic Zone than a UNESCO-protected site. However, it's still possible to get away for an interesting stroll. Helpful English maps available around town help you navigate the maze. ■**TIP→ Most sites in and around Lijiang are free for holders of a "maintenance ticket," available for Y80 from most hotels and attractions.**

Black Dragon Pool Park (黑龙潭公园 *Hēilóngtán gōngyuán*). Outside the Old Town, Black Dragon Pool Park has a tranquil pavilion where locals come to play cards and drink tea. The park is one of the most popular places to photograph nearby Jade Dragon Snow Mountain. The park is home to the Dongba Research Institute Museum (*Dōngba wénhuà bówùguǎn*), devoted to Naxi Dongba culture. ✉ *Xinde Lu* ☎ *Y80* ⊙ *Daily 6:30 am–8 pm.*

Jade Dragon Snow Mountain (玉龙雪山风景区 *Yùlóng xuěshān fēngjǐng qū*). Towering majestically over Lijiang, the 18,360-foot Jade Dragon

Snow Mountain is one of China's most spectacular peaks. The mountain's jagged, snow-covered face is one of the defining sights of a trip to Lijiang. The well-maintained road to the scenic area passes numerous villages and has fine views of the valley. The park entrance is about a 30-minute drive from Old Town. Taxis should cost around Y40 one way, or Y100 or more if you want the driver to wait for you. 🎫 *Y130* 🕐 *Daily 7–5.*

Puxian Temple (普贤寺 *Pǔxián sì*). If you can find it, the Puxian Temple is a tranquil place to get away from the crowds. At the temple's vegetarian restaurant, try the *jidoufen,* a bean concoction that can be eaten hot as a porridge or cold and cut up like noodles. The ubiquitous *baba* bread is also quite good. Wash it all down with a pot of Tibetan tea, made with yak butter. ✉ *76 Qi Yi Jie* 🎫 *Free* 🕐 *Daily 8–6.*

Visitor Center for Nature and Culture in Northwest Yunnan (**滇西北自然与文化之窗暨绿色旅游推广中心** *Diān xīběi zìrán yǔ wénhuà zhī chuāng jì lǜsè lǚyóu tuīguǎng zhōngxīn*). This small but fascinating museum highlights the region's cultural and biological diversity. Exhibits include one in which villagers were given cameras to document their daily lives. Another compares photos taken in the 1920s with those taken more recently. The museum is funded by the Nature Conservancy. ✉ *42 Xianwen Xiang, at Guangyi Jie* ☎ *0888/511–5969* 🎫 *Free* 🕐 *Daily 9–6.*

WHERE TO EAT

$$ CHINESE 🍴 **Lamu's House of Tibet** (西藏屋西餐厅 *Xīzàngwū xīcāntīng*). The traditional Tibetan decor, pleasant atmosphere, and helpful staff make this one of Lijiang's better dining options. The kitchen serves Tibetan, Chinese, and Naxi cuisine, as well as familiar dishes like lasagna and french fries. [$] *Average main: Y50* ✉ *56 Jishan Xiang, Xinyi Jie* ☎ *0888/511–5776* 💳 *No credit cards.*

$$ ECLECTIC 🍴 **N's Kitchen** (二楼小厨 *Èrlóu xiǎochú*). Norman's Kitchen, or simply N's Kitchen, serves a classic selection of Western food at reasonable prices. Diners eat on the second floor, from which vantage point they can watch tourists leisurely stroll by. Also available are bus tickets and tourist and hiking information. [$] *Average main: Y55* ✉ *17 Jishan Xiang, 2nd fl.* ☎ *0888/512–0060.*

$$ CAFÉ 🍴 **Prague Café** (布拉格咖啡馆 *Bùlāgé kāfēiguǎn*). A favorite with expats, this bright, sunny eatery serves international favorites like Japanese-style *katsu don* (pork cutlets in a savory sauce). This is also the town's top choice for fresh bread, good coffee, and, especially, American-style breakfasts. It's a nice place to hang out with a cup of tea or a beer at night. There's a good book collection and free Internet access. [$] *Average main: Y50* ✉ *80 Mishi Xiang, at Xinyi Jie* ☎ *0888/512–3757* 💳 *No credit cards.*

$ CAFÉ 🍴 **Well Bistro** (井卓咖啡馆 *Jǐngzhuō kāfēiguǎn*). This second-story eatery serves a nice variety of international food at reasonable prices. It's in a pretty setting, away from the hustle and bustle of the town square. The coffee is very good, and it's a top choice for breakfast. This is one of the best places in town to hunker down with a hot drink and a good book on a cold or rainy day. [$] *Average main: Y40* ✉ *32 Mishi Xiang, at Xinyi Jie* ☎ *0888/518–6431* 💳 *No credit cards.*

Naxi Music of Lijiang

The Naxi culture is rich in artistic elements—the Naxi pictographs, architecture, Dongba shamans, and, not least of all, the music. It is a complex and intricate musical blending of Han and Naxi musical traditions that has commonly served as entertainment, as well as a measuring stick for Confucian social relationships. Naxi musicians and members of social clubs related to the music were considered to be of a higher status than the average Naxi villager.

Today Naxi music, with its 500 years of history, is a sonic time capsule, giving us the opportunity to hear songs dating as far back as the Tang, Song, and Yuan Dynasties. Most of the Naxi-inhabited counties around Lijiang feature their own orchestras specializing in the two extant versions of Naxi music: Baisha fine music and Dongjing music. A third type, Huangjing music, fell out of practice over the centuries and has since been lost.

THE ROOTS OF RHYTHM

Legend has it that Baisha fine music developed as a result of Kublai Khan's gratitude for Naxi assistance during his conquest of Yunnan during the Yuan Dynasty. The Khan is believed to have left a group of his best musicians and their musical canon with the Naxi in Lijiang. Baisha fine music is one of the grander Chinese musical styles, with large orchestras including the Chinese flute, the lute, and the zither.

Dongjing music came to this region from central China during the Ming and Qing dynasties, and is based on Taoist classics. It is the better preserved of the two musical styles, most likely because the Naxi incorporated more of their indigenous music into it.

BEAUTY IS IN THE EAR OF THE BEHOLDER

Naxi orchestras have their own standards for what makes for a quality Naxi musical experience, the key factor being age. In the eyes of the Naxi, the older the musicians, the better. Perhaps this is because fewer and fewer are learning the traditional styles. The musicians' instruments are also old, often much older than the septuagenarians playing the music—the craftsmanship 100 years ago was better than today. Naxi orchestras refuse to play any modern music. They only jam to centuries-old tunes.

For many travelers, Naxi music is an aural step back in time. Others find it screechy and grating. You can catch a show at a number of venues in Lijiang's Old Town and the new city. The most famous groups are the Baihua and Dayan orchestras. Tickets can typically be purchased starting at Y100 at most hotels and guesthouses.

WHERE TO STAY

$
HOTEL
Ancient Stone Bridge Inn (大石桥 *Dàshíqiáo kèzhàn*). Two of the rooms in this guesthouse look directly out over a brook crossed by a pair of bridges. **Pros:** good location; inexpensive rates. **Cons:** in slight need of a renovation. $ *Rooms from: Y580* ⊠ *71 Wuyi Jie Xingrenxia* ☎ *0888/518–4001, 0135/7839–4460* ⇗ *10 rooms* ▭ *No credit cards* ⭐ *No meals.*

$
B&B/INN

🏠 **Australia House** (澳洲部落客栈 *Àozhōu bùluò kèzhàn*). Run by a warm Greek-Australian owner and his Chinese family, this boutique hotel on a quiet side street in Shuhe offers nice rooms similar to the ones found elsewhere in the area, though each has its own unique touch. **Pros:** warm owners; peaceful location. **Cons:** a bit remote; certain guest areas a bit claustrophobic. **$** *Rooms from: Y580* ✉ *52/7 Dongkang Jie, Shuhe* ☎ *0888/518–8671* 🛏 *20 rooms* ⦿ *Breakfast.*

$$$
RESORT

🏠 **Banyan Tree Lijiang** (悦榕庄 *Yuèróng zhuāng*). The area's only luxury resort, the Banyan Tree is made up of villas designed to resemble traditional courtyard houses. **Pros:** nearly perfect service; upscale accommodations; breathtaking scenery. **Cons:** very expensive for the area. **$** *Rooms from: Y1500* ✉ *Yuerong Lu, Shuhe* ☎ *0888/533–1111* ⦿ *www.banyantree.com* 🛏 *55 villas* ⦿ *No meals.*

$
HOTEL

🏠 **East River Hotel** (东河客栈 *Dōnghé kèzhàn*). Well hidden in the maze of streets in Old Town, the East River Hotel offers some of the area's most comfortable rooms. **Pros:** quiet atmosphere; idyllic courtyard. **Cons:** hard to find. **$** *Rooms from: Y380* ✉ *44 Mishi Xiang, off Xinyi Jie* ☎ *0888/515–1668* ⦿ *www.ljdhkz.com* 🛏 *40 rooms* ⊟ *No credit cards* ⦿ *No meals.*

$
B&B/INN

🏠 **Huifeng Inn Shuhe** (回峰客栈 *Huífēng kèzhàn*). With each room uniquely decorated to represent one of Yunnan's many different ethnic minorities, the Huifeng Inn is one of the most remarkable hotels in Lijiang. **Pros:** splendid interior design; nice swimming pool. **Cons:** low ceilings. **$** *Rooms from: Y680* ✉ *56 Jiewei Alley, near to Old Sifang Sq., Shuhe* ☎ *0888/511–7879* ⦿ *lijianghuifeng.taobao.com* 🛏 *16 rooms* ⦿ *No meals.*

$$
RESORT
FAMILY

🏠 **Lijiang InterContinental Resort** (丽江和府皇冠度假酒店 *Lijiāng héfǔ huángguàn dùjià jiǔdiàn*). Filling the gap between the small hotels and guesthouses in the Old Town and the ultraluxurious Banyan Tree, the Lijiang InterContinental was the beginning of a wave of international five-stars moving into Lijiang. **Pros:** comfortable; high level of service. **Cons:** a bit removed from the Old Town; reception understaffed. **$** *Rooms from: Y1280* ✉ *276 Xianghe Lu* ☎ *888/558–8888* ⦿ *www.ichotelsgroup.com* 🛏 *270 rooms* ⦿ *Breakfast.*

$
B&B/INN
Fodor's Choice
★

🏠 **New Huifeng Resort Hotel** (新回峰度假酒店 *Xīn huífēng dùjià jiǔdiàn*). Although calling it a "resort" may be a bit misleading, the New Huifeng offers plenty of peace and quiet. **Pros:** great views; swimming pool; unique architecture. **Cons:** some low ceilings, so mind your head. **$** *Rooms from: Y780* ✉ *30 Zhonghe Cun, Shuhe* ☎ *131/506–75155* 🛏 *34 rooms* ⦿ *Breakfast.*

$$$$
RESORT
Fodor's Choice
★

🏠 **Pullman Lijiang Resort & Spa** (丽江铂尔曼度假酒店 *Lìjiāng bó ěr màn dùjià jiǔdiàn*). With a hard-to-beat location, the Pullman Lijiang Resort offers views of the Jade Dragon Snow Mountain so beautiful that is has a dedicated viewing area. **Pros:** stupefying views; ultimate comfort;

efficent service. **Cons:** expensive; almost clinically perfect. $ *Rooms from: Y1880* ⊠ *Entrance to Shuhe Old Town* ☏ *0888/530–0111* ⊕ *www.pullmanhotels.com/7231* ⤳ *130 villas* ⏐⏐ *Breakfast.*

$ ⊡ **Wenhai Ecolodge** (文海生态旅馆 *Wénhǎi shēngtài lǚguǎn*). One of
B&B/INN the country's first "green" resorts, Wenhai Ecolodge is in the mountain valley that is home to Lake Wenhai, a seasonal lake that appears between July and March. **Pros:** fascinating for nature lovers; gorgeous setting. **Cons:** remote location; rougher than some travelers can handle; no private bathrooms. $ *Rooms from: Y120* ⊠ *Lake Wenhai* ☏ *139/888–26672* ⊕ *www.northwestyunnan.com/wenhai_ecolodge.htm* ⤳ *12 rooms* ⊟ *No credit cards* ⏐⏐ *All meals.*

NIGHTLIFE AND PERFORMING ARTS

Traditional Naxi music and dancing can be found in the town square at Sifang Jie beginning in the afternoon and lasting into the evening.

Lijiang Impression (印象丽江 *Yìnxiàng Lìjiāng*). The city's most impressive cultural event is Lijiang Impression, a music and dance performance that makes full use of the spectacular location. There are four performances a day, and admission is Y190 to Y260, depending on how close you want to be to the front. ⊠ *Ganhai Scenic District* ☏ *0888/888–8888.*

Mountain Spirit Show (丽水金沙 *Lìshuǐ jīnshā*). At the Meeting Hall of Lijiang, the Mountain Spirit Show offers fire eating and other extraordinary feats. The 8 pm performances cost around Y190. ⊠ *Minzu Lu.*

Stone The Crows (乌鸦飞了酒吧 *Wūyā fēile jiǔbā*). Run by an eccentric Irishman, Stone The Crows offers some interesting cocktails and a selection of imported beer. Pub grub is also available, if the staff is in the mood. ⊠ *134-2 Wenzhi Alley, Yangshuo* ☏ *0131/5066–2289.*

TIGER LEAPING GORGE

91 km (57 miles; 2½ hrs by car) north of Lijiang.

Above a river that winds along for about 16 km (10 miles), this gorge is home to some of China's most breathtaking mountain scenery. The best time to visit is the dry season, from October through May.

GETTING HERE AND AROUND

The easiest way to get to the Gorge is by hiring a car. If you're interested in hiking the gorge, the easiest way to get started is to take the 8:30 am or 9 am bus on Xianggelila Avenue to Qiaotou and hike toward Daju. The trip takes about two hours.

Fodor's Choice **Tiger Leaping Gorge** (虎跳峡 *Hǔtiàoxiá*). The deepest gorge in the world
★ is hard to forget once you've seen it in person, and it makes an excellent trekking destination. If you're hiking along the upper trail, the 40-km (25-mile) route can be finished in a day or two. The upper trail connects the towns of Qiaotou in the west and Daju in the east, and there is a ferry across the river near Daju. The easiest way to tackle the walk from Lijiang is to take the 8:30 am or 9 am bus on Xianggelila Ave to Qiaotou and hike toward Daju.

There are several guesthouses in the gorge, scattered at distances to accommodate hikers at any stage of their trek. All offer food, hot

8

Black Dragon Pool Park with Jade Dragon Snow Mountain in the distance

showers, and beds for Y20 to over Y100, depending on season and weather. Many of the guesthouses have expanded and upgraded accommodations in the past couple of years, so there is more selection and even some higher-end rooms for Y150. The guesthouses have put up signs and arrows to let hikers know how much farther until the next lodging. If you don't mind not hiking the whole gorge, stop in Walnut Garden, where you can take one of the regular buses back to Lijiang. If you continue to Daju, there are only two buses a day to Lijiang, at 8:30 am and 1 pm. Also remember that the road connecting Daju to Lijiang goes through the Jade Dragon Park and tickets cost around Y220 per person just to go through. Daju is a very pleasant—though quiet, because of the road fee—town that offers basic rooms for around Y50 a night.

For those only interested in seeing the point that gives the gorge its name, the river's narrowest point, which a tiger is supposed to have leaped across to evade a hunter, there are two options: the prettier one is on the Lijiang side of the gorge, includes a nice 4-km (3-mile) walk along a path cut out of the cliff side, and costs Y50 to enter; the Shangri-La side can be reached directly by minivan but will include a few hundred steps down to where the water rages most fiercely. The entrance fee costs Y70, which also includes the rest of the gorge. Most hotels will also gladly arrange tours in minivans—expect to pay more than Y140 per person each way. ✉ Y70.

Lugu Lake (泸沽湖 *Lúgū hú*). If you have a few days to spare, Lugu Lake is a great getaway from Lijiang. The lake straddles the border of Sichuan and Yunnan provinces and is dotted with dreamy little towns belonging mostly to the Mosuo, a matriarchal subgroup of the ubiquitous Naxi. Exploring the Lake's 80 km (50 miles) of stunning lake and mountain scenery is possible by bus, but biking and hiking provide better views.

Buses taking about five hours depart each morning from Lijiang. Tickets that grant entrance to the area are Y80, and a car ticket can set you back another Y30 for one day. An airport, currently slated to open by 2016, may turn this into a major tourist hot spot. ⊠ *Lugu Lake.*

XISHUANGBANNA REGION

380 km (238 miles; 8 hrs by bus, 10 at night) southwest of Kunming; 400 km (250 miles; 12 hrs by bus) south of Dali.

Jinghong is the capital of southern Yunnan's Xishuangbanna Dai Autonomous Region, which borders Laos and Myanmar. Xishuangbanna is home to the Dai, a people related to the Thai and the Lao. Like their cousins to the south, they love very spicy food.

The city sits on the banks of the muddy Mekong, although this stretch of the legendary river is known locally as the Lancang. This is where China meets Southeast Asia; it looks and feels more and more like Laos or Thailand the farther you travel from Jinghong. Even inside the city the architecture, the clothing, and the barbecue seem much more like what you'd find in Vientiane or Chiang Mai.

Jinghong has experienced a tourism explosion, with the city completely filling up with visitors from all over China and hotel prices skyrocketing during the holidays. Thousands of apartments have been constructed to accommodate China's rich, who head here in winter. It has its own international airport, connecting it to Kunming and other major cities. But despite the increase in economic activity, the pace of life in Jinghong still moves about as fast as the Mekong.

GETTING HERE AND AROUND

AIR TRAVEL Jinghong's international airport has service to and from Kunming, Chengdu, Beijing, and Shanghai, as well as destinations in Thailand. The international terminal is about 15 minutes west of the city center. From the airport, take the Number 1 bus into town for Y2, or opt for a taxi for Y30.

Air Contact Xishuangbanna International Airport (*JHG*). ☎ *0691/215–9129.*

BUS TRAVEL Jinghong's three main bus stations are Jinghong Bus Station, north of Zhuanghong Lu on Mengle Avenue; Banna Bus Station, just north of the intersection of Mengle Avenue and Xuanwei Avenue; and the Jinghong South Bus Station, at the intersection of Mengle Avenue and Menghai Road. The former two both have services to Kunming and Dali. For shorter routes, head to Banna Bus Station. The South Station has connections to Laos and the Thai border.

Bus Contacts Banna Bus Station ⊠ *3 Minhang Lu* ☎ *0691/212–4427.* **Jinghong Bus Station** ⊠ *14 Mengle Dadao* ☎ *0691/212–2487.* **Jinghong South Bus Station** ⊠ *77 Menghai Lu* ☎ *0691/213–7105.*

SAFETY AND PRECAUTIONS

Be sure to drink plenty of water—Jinghong gets hot, and dehydration is a risk as you explore town.

TIMING

Spend a day exploring downtown Jinghong, and add an extra day or two if you plan to tour out to the surrounding countryside.

FESTIVALS

The Dai Water Splashing Festival. The Dai Water Splashing Festival is held in Dai-inhabited areas of southern Yunnan, including the cities of Jinghong and Ruili. Originally, water was poured gently upon the backs of family members to wash away the sins of the past year and provide blessings for the coming year. Today it has become a water war, replete with squirt guns, buckets of ice water, and other weapons. It is quite a bit of fun, and a great way to cool off. Just remember to leave any cameras, watches, and mobile phones back in your room, as foreigners are a beloved target.

TOURS

Tours organized by Sara Lai and Stone Chen from Forest Café are your best bet for a tailored English-language tour of Xishuangbanna.

ESSENTIALS

Medical Assistance Xishuangbanna People's Hospital ⊠ *48 Galan Zhong Lu* ☏ *0691/214–6801.*

Bank Bank of China ⊠ *65 Galan Zhong Lu* ☏ *0691/212–3187.*

Public Security Bureau PSB Jinghong ⊠ *106 Xuanwei Dadao* ☏ *110.*

Visitor and Tour Info China International Travel Service ⊠ *Galan Zhong Lu* ☏ *0691/212–8589.* **Forest Cafe** (森林咖啡屋 *Sēnlín kāfēi*). This company organizes hikes throughout the region. ☏ *691/898–5122* ⊕ *www.forest-cafe.org* ⊙ *Daily 9–8.*

EXPLORING

Even a short walk around Jinghong reveals its colorful mix of Dai, Han Chinese, Thai, and Burmese influences. It's small enough that you can cover most of it on foot in a day. Bordered by the Lancang River to the east, the city quickly begins to thin out as you head west. Once you spot the new city area, marked with dozens of high-rises, it's about time to turn back.

Lancang River (澜沧江 *Láncāngjiāng*). The Lancang River is the name of the Mekong River in China, where it originates before flowing through Southeast Asia. It is easiest to access the river from Jinghong at the Xishuangbanna Bridge. The southern bank is lined with bars and really livens up at night.

Manting Park (曼听公园 *Màntīng gōngyuán*). On the southeastern edge of Jinghong is Manting Park, where you can have a closer look at some of the area's indigenous plants. Also worth exploring is the large peacock aviary. The park is especially lively around mid-April, when people gather to celebrate the Water Splashing Festival. ⊠ *35 Manting Lu* ☏ *0691/216–1061* ☐ *Y40* ⊙ *Daily 7:30–7:30.*

Xishuangbanna Tropical Flower and Plant Garden (西双版纳热带花卉园 *Xishuāngbǎnnà rèdài huāhuì yuán*). With a well-designed layout, this is one of China's finest gardens, and an interesting place to spend several hours among fragrant frangipani, massive lily pads, drooping jackfruit, and thousands of other colorful and peculiar plants. Don't walk through too fast, or you'll miss out on some of the more unique plants, such as *tiaowu cao*, or "dancing grass," which actually stands up if you sing at it. Each plant's placard features English and Latin names. ✉ *99 Xuanwei Dadao* 🎫 *Y40* 🕒 *Daily 7:30–6.*

WHERE TO EAT

$$ YUNNAN 🍴 **Foguang Yuan** (佛光园 *Fóguāng yuán*). Behind a school and a police station, Foguang Yuan is a true oasis of peace and quiet. The restaurant is actually several dining areas built around a patch of jungle. The traditional architecture and tropical setting merit a visit, but the restaurant also serves an excellent array of Dai and Chinese classics. English menus are available, but they aren't necessarily up to date. If in doubt, you can always venture into the kitchen and point to what looks good. [$] *Average main: Y50* ✉ *2 Jiaotong Xiang, near Yiwu Lu* ☎ *0691/213–8608* 💳 *No credit cards.*

$ INTERNATIONAL 🍴 **Meimei Café** (美美咖啡厅 *Měiměi kāfēitīng*). This is a good place to compare notes with other travelers, as many people come here to buy tickets, book tours, or get travel information. One of the few places in Jinghong with an English-speaking staff, Meimei Café serves Western and Chinese favorites, as well as great coffee and juices. Open from early morning to late at night, the terrace is a splendid place to enjoy the sunrise. [$] *Average main: Y45* ✉ *2 Menglong Lu* ☎ *0691/216–1221* 💳 *No credit cards.*

$ FRENCH 🍴 **Mekong Café** (湄公咖啡馆 *Méigōng kāfēiguǎn*). Opened by a Frenchman who was once a hotel chef and his Chinese wife, Mekong Café is a favorite with all sorts of travelers. Backpackers, expats, couples as well as locals gather on its large front and back patios to enjoy afternoon dessert, delicious French cuisine, Chinese classics, or simply a drink to recover from the Jinghong heat. The chef's exquisite carpaccio salad is also great value for money. Like the Meimei Café, Mekong also offers various travel services and tours. [$] *Average main: Y30* ✉ *F1-104 Kingland International, Menglong Lu* ☎ *0691/216-2395* 🌐 *www.mekongcafe.cn.*

WHERE TO STAY

$$$$ RESORT FAMILY 🏨 **Anantara Xishuangbanna Resort & Spa** (西双版纳安纳塔拉度假酒店 *Xīshuāngbǎnnà ānnàtǎlā dùjìa jiǔdiàn*). On the banks of the Luosuo River, this luxury resort is in Menglun, about 60 km (37 miles) from Jinghong. **Pros:** perfect service; great views; sparkling pool. **Cons:** expensive. [$] *Rooms from: Y2000* ✉ *Country Rd. 009, Menglun* ☎ *691/893–6666* 🌐 *xishuangbanna.anantara.com* 🛏 *80 rooms, 23 villas* 🍽 *Breakfast.*

$ HOTEL 🏨 **Crown Hotel** (皇冠大酒店 *Huángguàn dàjiǔdiàn*). In the heart of Jinghong, the Crown Hotel has several low-slung buildings in a parklike setting with a lily-leaf-shaped swimming pool. **Pros:** central location; night market nearby; good value. **Cons:** wired Internet only. [$] *Rooms*

8

CLOSE UP

Naxi and Bai Ethnic Minorities

NAXI

Living primarily in the area around Lijiang and neighboring Sichuan, the Naxi culture is unique, even when compared with other minority groups in China. The society is traditionally matriarchal, with women dominating relationships, keeping custody of children, and essentially running the show. Some Naxis practice Buddhism or Taoism, but it is the shamanistic culture of the Dongba and Samba that set their spiritualism apart from other groups. The Dongba (male shamans) and Samba (female shamans) serve their communities as mediators, entering trancelike states and communicating with the spirit world in order to solve problems on earth. Naxi script, like Chinese script, is made up of ideograms. These pictographs are vivid representations of body parts, animals, and geography used to express concrete and abstract concepts. Despite numbering fewer than 300,000, the Naxi are one of the better-known ethnic groups in China.

BAI

The Bai, also known as the Minjia, are one of the more prominent minorities in Yunnan, although they are also found in Guizhou and Hunan provinces. Primarily centered around Dali prefecture, the Bai are known for their agricultural skills and unique architecture style. The Bai also have some of the most colorful costumes, particularly the rainbow-colored hats worn by women. The Bai, along with the Yi people, were part of the Nanzhao Kingdom, which briefly rose to regional dominance in Southwest China and Southeast Asia during the Tang Dynasty, before giving way to the Kingdom of Dali. The Dali region and the Bai have essentially been a part of the Chinese sphere of influence since the Yuan Dynasty, during which the Yuan's Mongolian armies conquered the area in the 13th century. The Bais' highly productive rice paddies were seen as an asset by the Yuan, who let them operate under relative autonomy. Today the Bai and their festivals, including the Third Moon Festival and Torch Festival, are major attractions for domestic and international tourists.

---

from: Y350 ⊠ *70 Mengle Dadao* ☎ *0691/219–9888* ⊕ *www.newtgh.com* ↪ *121 rooms* ⦿| *No meals.*

$$
RESORT
Fodor's Choice
★

🖼 **Yourantai** (悠然台 *Yōurán tái*). The "Terrace of Serenity" more than lives up to its name. **Pros:** excellent atmosphere; gorgeous setting; amazing mattresses. **Cons:** minimum stay required; steps to climb. 💲 *Rooms from: Y1280* ⊠ *2 Galan North Rd.* ☎ *138/8793–4096* ⊕ *www.yourantai.com* ↪ *6 rooms* ▬ *No credit cards* ⦿| *Breakfast.*

SHOPPING

On Zhuanghong Lu in the northern part of town, there's a handicrafts market filled with Burmese jade jewelry and goods from Vietnam and Thailand. Assume that much of it is counterfeit. There is a small but vibrant night market on Mengla Lu outside the Crown Hotel. Genuine Pu'er tea can be safely bought from the tea shop in the Golden Zone hotel.

The future leaders of the Naxi people.

SIDE TRIPS FROM JINGHONG

Ganlan Basin (橄榄坝 *Gǎnlǎn bà*). One of the more scenic areas of Xishuangbanna is this valley 37 km (23 miles) from Jinghong. Locals still live in bamboo huts in the beautiful rain forest. The area is famous in Yunnan for its tropical flowers and its millions of butterflies.

Sanchahe Nature Reserve. One of China's first serious attempts at ecotourism, the 900-acre Sanchahe Nature Reserve is home to wild elephants. Two hours north of Jinghong, the park also features a butterfly farm and a cable car that offers breathtaking views. Lodging is in "tree houses" about 25 feet above ground—a unique place to spend a night.

Xishuangbanna Tropical Botanical Garden (西双版纳热带植物园 *Xīshuāngbǎnnà rèdài zhíwùyuán*). The nearest large town in the area, Menglun, is the location of China's largest botanical garden. With a gorgeous setting on a peninsula in the Luosuo River, the garden holds more than 13,000 tropical and subtropical plant species and a section of dense, unspoiled tropical rain forest. A museum tells about the local flora and fauna, and well as the humans that have inhabited the region. Families enjoy the humid and fragrant air of the tropics, picnicking in pavilions, and observing rare plants and animals. Visits can take anywhere from a few hours to an entire day (there are restaurants and places to stay overnight). Electric buses help you explore, and hop-on, hop-off tickets are available for Y100. ■TIP→ Buses only run until 6 pm, so start at the eastern park and make your way back toward the entrance. Menglun is about 60 km (37 miles) east of Jinghong, a trip that takes about 90 minutes by bus. Or you can take a cab. ⊠ *Menglun* 🖂 *Y100.*

CLOSE UP

Dai and Yi Ethnic Minorities

DAI

Related to Thais and speakers of languages belonging to the Tai-Kadai family, the Dai seem much more Southeast Asian than Chinese. In China they are primarily located in the Xishuangbanna, Dehong, and Jingpo regions of southern Yunnan, but can also be found in Myanmar, Laos, and Thailand. They practice Theravada Buddhism, the dominant form of Buddhism in Southeast Asia. The linguistic, cultural, and religious connections with Southeast Asia give Dai-inhabited regions a decidedly un-Chinese feel. Within China, they are most famous for their spicy and flavorful food and their Water Splashing Festival (water is used to wash away demons and sins of the past and bless the future). Many grow rice and produce such crops as pineapples, so villages are concentrated near the Mekong (Lancang) and Red (Honghe) rivers. The Dai population here has ebbed and flowed with China's political tide, and many are now returning after the turmoil of the 1960s and '70s.

YI

Descendants of the Qiang people of northwestern China, the Yi (aka Sani) are scattered across southwestern China in Yunnan, Sichuan, and Guizhou provinces as well as Guangxi Zhuang Autonomous Region. The largest concentration of the more than 6.5 million Qiang descendants are in Sichuan's Liangshan region. They live in isolated, mountainous regions and are known for being fierce warriors. Notable traits include their syllabic writing system, ancient literature, and traditional medicine—all of which are still being used today. The Yi also sport extravagant costumes that vary according to geographical region. Massive black mortarboard-style hats, blue turbans, ornate red headdresses, and other headwear complement brilliantly colored vests and pants. Their language is part of the Tibeto-Burman language family and similar to Burmese. Some Yi also live in Vietnam, where they are called the Lolo.

Yiwu (易武 *Yì wǔ*). Once one of the starting points of the ancient tea and horses trade route to Tibet, this village has an Old Town featuring the houses of the "tea lords" of yesteryear. The Old Town is hidden away behind the school on a hill and makes for very pleasant investigation for an hour or two. Yiwu's higher altitude also means that it's a great way to get away from the Jinghong heat. All around the area are tea plantations you can stroll around. Several buses to Yiwu leave from Jinghong daily. ⊠ *Yiwu.*

SICHUAN AND CHONGQING

WELCOME TO SICHUAN AND CHONGQING

TOP REASONS TO GO

★ **Emeishan:** Hike 10,000 feet to the top of one of China's holy mountains and a UNESCO World Heritage Site.

★ **Giant Panda Breeding Research Base:** Stroll through the bamboo groves, bone up on the latest in genetic biology and ecological preservation, and check out cute baby pandas.

★ **Horseback riding in Songpan:** Marvel at the raw beauty of northern Sichuan's pristine mountain forests and emerald-green lakes from the backs of these gentle beasts.

★ **Liquid fire:** Savor some of the spiciest food on the planet in Chongqing's many hotpot restaurants.

★ **An engineering miracle or madness:** Enjoy a lazy riverboat ride through the surreal Three Gorges, and stand in awe of one of China's latest engineering feats, the mighty Three Gorges Dam.

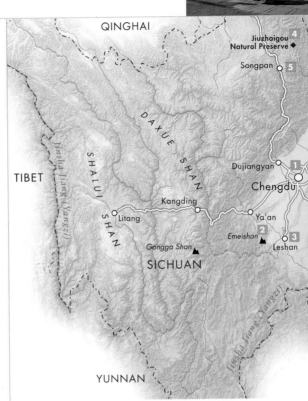

1 Chengdu. Sichuan's financial capital and culinary hub is home to more than 14 million people who speak Sichuan'hua', the charming Southwestern drawl, which is described as a lazy version of the standard Mandarin. While bent on modernizing and no longer the laid-back character she once was, the capital city still retains small pockets of tranquility if you know where to look.

2 Emeishan. One of China's holy mountains, it has almost 50 km (31 miles) of paths leading to the summit. Take time out to enjoy the lush mountains around Emeishan, which also produce some of the world's best tea.

3 Leshan. Leshan is the home of the Giant Buddha, the world's largest Buddhist sculpture, carved into a mountainside.

GETTING ORIENTED

If you're after a China experience where the cuisine is fiery and pandas can be found in the forests gnawing on bamboo, Sichuan Province in Southwestern China is a good bet. Smack-dab in the middle of Sichuan, the capital city of Chengdu is becoming increasingly easier to navigate, thanks to its subway system and plentiful taxis. It's also acclaimed for its many outdoor gear shops that can equip one for any of Sichuan's local and neighboring natural wonders. For those interested in witnessing the mighty Three Gorges Dam, the city of Chongqing, 240 km (150 miles) southeast of Chengdu, is where the best Yangtze tour boats begin their journey downriver.

GANSU

SHAANXI

Three Gorges Reservoir **7**

Wanzhou THREE GORGES

HUBEI

Jinyun Mountian CHONGQING

Neijiang **6** Fengdu

Dazu Chongqing

Yibin Luzhou

HUNAN

GUIZHOU

0   50 mi
0   50 km

9

4 **Jiuzhaigou Nature Preserve.** Nestled between the snowcapped peaks of the Aba Autonomous Prefecture in northern Sichuan lies the Jiuzhaigou Reserve, a UNESCO World Heritage Site and magical wonderland of turquoise.

5 **Songpan.** This historical town has Tang Dynasty buildings in the Old Town.

6 **Chongqing.** Formerly part of Sichuan proper,

Chongqing is its own exploding municipality with more than 25 million residents. Chongqing's meandering alleys will appeal to those who love getting lost in crowded, hilly, and twisting streets.

7 **The Three Gorges.** Riverboat cruises along the Yangtze between narrow cliffs from Fengjie to Yichang offer spectacular scenery.

Updated by
Daniel Garber
and Dana
Kaufman

Renowned for spicy, mouth-numbing cuisine, giant pandas, and fiery tempers, Sichuan is one of China's most interesting and influential provinces. Chongqing is known as China's "mountain city." Vast and modern, while still retaining many of its old buildings—for now—Chongqing features a fascinating balance of modern Chinese dynamism and Sichuan spice.

With a population of more than 100 million, Sichuan is known for its people's proud, independent spirits. One of the most famous Sichuanese ever, former paramount leader of China Deng Xiaoping, was purged from the Communist Party twice before taking control and launching the reforms that have converted the country from economic pariah to the second-largest economy in the world.

Often referred to as Szechuan cooking in the West, Sichuan's cuisine is famous in China for its liberal use of the chili pepper as well as the curious, numbing flavor of the *huajiao*, also known as the Sichuan pepper. Popular dishes such as twice cooked pork, kung pao chicken, and the ubiquitous hotpot originated in this part of the country.

The variety of ingredients found in Sichuan cooking are a reflection of the province's diverse topography. The eastern half of Sichuan is dominated by the Sichuan Basin, an area of high agricultural output that in dynastic times was fought over by rival kingdoms. Heading westward, the basin gives way to mountains that become increasingly awe-inspiring as Han Sichuan yields to the province's Tibetan regions.

Sichuan's capital of Chengdu is currently one of the country's most evolving cities. During the day, leisure-loving residents sip on tea and crack sunflower seeds while chatting or playing mah-jongg. When the sun goes down, there is plenty of amazing food to sample along with one of China's best live music scenes waiting afterward.

Once the capital of Sichuan—and China—the megacity of Chongqing sits to the east of the province and now answers directly to Beijing. With the completion of the Three Gorges Dam, which allows seagoing barges to make it all the way to Chongqing, the city is now changing faster than ever in its new role as Western China's seaport.

PLANNING

WHEN TO GO

Chengdu and eastern Sichuan are hot and humid, with temperatures of 35° to 50°F in winter and 75° to 85°F in summer. Chongqing, known as one of China's Three Furnaces, is infamous for its broiling summer temperatures—sometimes over 100°F. The western plateau is cold but intensely sunny (bring sunscreen and sunglasses). In winter temperatures drop to −15°F. Summers are around 65°F.

GETTING HERE AND AROUND

Traveling in and out of Sichuan and Chongqing has never been more convenient. The rapid modernization of the two cities and their surrounding rural areas has changed what was once a difficult area for traveling into a corridor of connectivity within and without the region.

AIR TRAVEL

Chengdu and Chongqing are both modern cities with international airports serving regional, national, and international destinations. Since the launch of a high-speed rail link, the two cities are no longer connected by flights. Sichuan Airlines is the largest local airline and serves smaller destinations throughout the province, including Jiuzhaigou. A brand-new domestic passenger terminal in Chengdu was just completed to handle the increasing passenger volume. New international routes are constantly being added to Chengdu including direct flights to Bangkok (Thai Airlines), Amsterdam (KLM), Abu Dhabi (Etihad), and Vancouver (Sichuan Airlines).

BUS TRAVEL

Taking buses around Sichuan is a convenient and economical option for short-distance travel, including Leshan. It is worth keeping abreast of the weather situation in western Sichuan, as heavy rains in the area can cause large—occasionally fatal—landslides that can close roads for days.

TRAIN TRAVEL

Chengdu and Chongqing are both major hubs in China's national rail network. The two cities are connected by a bullet train that takes about two hours. It's usually possible to buy tickets at the station on the day you want to travel if you don't mind a bit of pushing and long lines. Reserve at least two weeks in advance if you plan to travel during major Chinese holidays. It is highly recommended to avoid travel during the Chinese New Year, usually celebrated each year around late Janaury/early February, as the spectacular crush of people make all forms of travel (planes, trains, and especially buses) difficult and unpleasant.

MONEY MATTERS

Banks and ATMs are plentiful in cities and tourist destinations throughout this region. Even smaller, local Chinese banks have plentiful ATMs with the VISA logo. Most ATMs have a Y3,000 daily limit. It is advisable to secure sufficient cash before going into remote areas, just in case.

RESTAURANTS

Eating out in Sichuan and Chongqing can be a boisterous affair, with the tables surrounding you filled with loud, animated diners. Almost anything in these parts comes with some serious spice, so if you can't take the heat it's worthwhile to learn the phrase *bu lade* (boo-lah-duh, meaning "not spicy"). In addition to great Sichuan cuisine, Chengdu and Chongqing also have a growing number of international restaurants.

HOTELS

Chinese-run hotels in Sichuan and Chongqing offer adequate accommodations at a reasonable price, but the staff usually won't speak English. There are more and more international five-star hotels in Chengdu and Chongqing. In destinations such as Jiuzhaigou and Ciqikou, guesthouses are also an option. *Hotel reviews have been shortened. For full information, visit Fodors.com.*

CHONGQING NOODLES

Southern China was not always known for its noodles, as such fare was traditionally the domain of northerners. But during the mass migrations south and west over the past century, noodle culture has been introduced to the Mountain City. Now Chongqing has some of the tastiest bowls anywhere in the nation. Chongqing noodles come in all varieties, and there are too many noodle stands to count.

WHAT IT COSTS IN YUAN				
	$	**$$**	**$$$**	**$$$$**
Restaurants	under Y50	Y50–Y99	Y100–Y165	over Y165
Hotels	under Y1,100	Y1,100–Y1,399	Y1,400–Y1,800	over Y1,800

Restaurant prices are the average cost of a main course at dinner or, if dinner is not served, at lunch. Hotel prices are the lowest cost of a standard double room in high season.

VISITOR INFORMATION

Chengdu and Chongqing don't offer much useful English-language visitor information, but five-star hotels, Western cafés, and guesthouses are good places to ask around. The centrally located Shangri-La Hotel produces a highly useful city map including all the major tourist attractions along with color pictures and directions in Mandarin for taxi drivers.

SICHUAN

Throughout history, Sichuan has been known as the "Storehouse of Heaven," due not only to its abundance of flora and fauna, but also to its varied cuisine, culture, and customs. Today, however, its major cities are bathed in a semi-permanent, gray haze of pollution, largely in part due to the abundance of chemical-spewing plastic and electronics factories.

Geographically, it's dominated by the Sichuan Basin, which covers much of the eastern part of the province. The Sichuan Basin—also known as

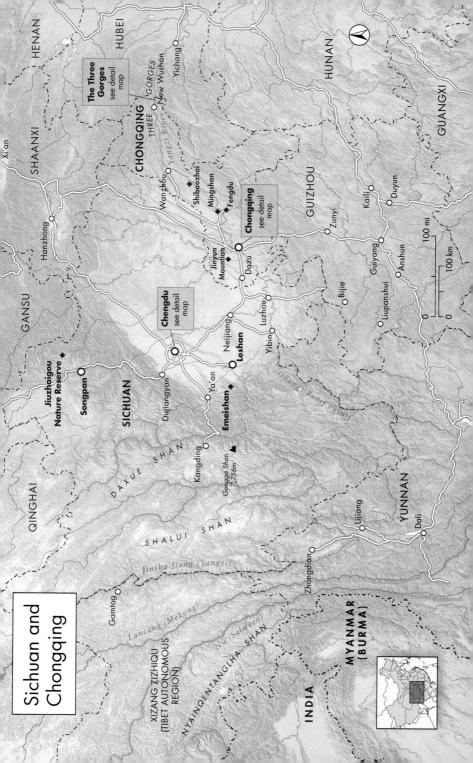

Sichuan and Chongqing

The Three Gorges
see detail map

Chengdu
see detail map

Chongqing
see detail map

HENAN
HUBEI
SHAANXI
GANSU
QINGHAI
XIZANG ZIZHIQU
(TIBET AUTONOMOUS REGION)
SICHUAN
CHONGQING
GUIZHOU
HUNAN
GUANGXI
YUNNAN
MYANMAR (BURMA)
INDIA
NYAINQENTANGLHA SHAN

Xi'an
Hanzhong
Yichang
New Wushan
Wanzhou
Shibaozhai
Mingshan
Fengdu
Jinyun Mountian
Dazu
Zunyi
Biijie
Guiyang
Anshun
Kaili
Duyun
Liupanshui
Chongqing
Luzhou
Yibin
Neijiang
Leshan
Ya'an
Emeishan
Dujiangyan
Songpan
Jiuzhaigou Nature Reserve
Kangding
Gongga Shan 7756m
Lijiang
Dali
Zhongdian
Gamlog

THREE GORGES
Yangzi River
Jinsha Jiang (Yangzi)
Lancang (Mekong)
Nu Salween
DAXUE SHAN
SHALUI SHAN

100 mi
100 km

Plight of the Panda

Mysterious, endangered, and cuddly are a few of the monikers typically associated with China's best-known symbol. Given China's recent economic reforms, pandas face a mixed future. On the one hand, economic growth and overpopulation along with polluted air and water sources, are increasingly affecting their habitat. On the other hand, more state and international resources are pouring into special research institutes like Sichuan's Panda Breeding Research Base which has recently had success in regards to breeding. In addition, China's pandas are now used as political capital through what's being called "Panda Diplomacy" as certain foreign countries preferential to Beijing are being rewarded with a giant panda. What will be the ultimate fate of these stoic creatures? It's hard to say. One thing is certain though: those who visit ecological panda preserves are part of the solution.

the Red Basin because of the reddish sandstone that predominates in the region—accounts for almost half its area. On all sides the province is surrounded by mountains: the Dabashan in the northeast, the Wushan in the east, the Qinghai Massif in the west, and the Yunnan and Guizhou plateaus in the south.

Sichuan's relative isolation made communication with the outside world difficult and fostered the development of valley, plains, and mountain cultures with distinct characteristics. The Tibetans living deep in the foothills of the Himalayas share space with Qiang, Hui, and Han settlers. In the mountains to the south toward Yunnan, there are dozens of peoples living side by side, such as the Yi, Naxi, Mosu, Miao, and Bai. These cultures all have their own religions and philosophies, with Buddhism and Taoism the dominant religions in the area.

The mountain of Emeishan is a pilgrimage site for millions of Buddhists, as is the Great Buddha in nearby Leshan. In Songpan, north of the capital city of Chengdu, Muslims, Buddhists, Christians, and Taoists live alongside each other in relative harmony, although recently anger and resentment directed at Han Chinese has sparked a string of self-immolations among Sichuan's Tibetan Buddhist monks. One of China's most famous national parks is in Jiuzhaigou, far to the north in Aba Prefecture. The natural springs, dense forests, dramatic cliffs, and sprawling waterfalls make Jiuzhaigou Nature Reserve one of the country's most popular tourist destinations.

CHENGDU

240 km (149 miles; 2 hrs by train) northwest of Chongqing; 1,450 km (900 miles; 25 hrs by train) southwest of Beijing; 1,300 km (806 miles; 27 hrs by train) northwest of Hong Kong.

Home to more than 14 million people, Chengdu is what you want it to be: while some visitors seek out the pulsating nightlife, others are happy to while away the days strolling through the city's many parks

China's cuddly symbol, the endangered giant panda

or sipping tea and cracking sunflower seeds in one of its multitude of tea gardens.

Upon arrival, you may be a bit disappointed. Much of the traditional architecture of the charming Old Town has been razed to make room for uninspired, communist-era apartment blocks and modern high-rises. The city has been torn in half, literally, for the last several years as new expressways, additional subways lines, a modern airport, and gleaming office towers push locals' tolerance and pollution levels sky-high.

Despite the rush to modernize, there is still much to see in terms of history and culture. Temples and memorials demonstrate Chengdu's position as the cosmopolitan capital of Western China. The city is also the world's great center for Sichuan cooking, famous for its spicy, mouth-numbing peppers, which many believe to be the best in China. Chengdu has too many good restaurants to list, and the hole-in-the-wall around the corner may serve the tastiest Sichuan dishes you'll eat.

All roads into Southwest China lead through Chengdu. As the gateway to Tibet, this city is the place to secure the permits and supplies needed for your trip there. Journeys south to Yunnan or north to Xi'an pass through here as well. Lying in the middle of Sichuan Province, Chengdu is also a good base for excursions to the scenic spots dotting Sichuan. ■TIP→ Like many big cities in China, Chengdu suffers from pollution. Bring eyedrops, antibacterial wipes, and possibly even a face mask.

GETTING HERE AND AROUND
Chengdu is the transportation hub of Western China. Bus, train, and plane connections are as convenient as they get in China.

Chengdu is built along a main north–south artery and surrounded by three ring roads. Cheap taxis (flag fall starts at Y9, or Y10 from 10 pm until 6 am) and the ever-expanding subway system are the best ways to get around (fares range depending on distance traveled, starting at Y2). If you are on foot, many of the city's sights are within walking distance of Tian Fu Plaza.

AIR TRAVEL Chengdu Shuangliu International Airport (CTU) is about 16 km (10 miles) southwest of the city. From here you can fly to Beijing (2½ hours), Guangzhou (2 hours), Kunming (1 hour), Shanghai (2½ hours), and practically every major domestic destination. Keep in mind Chinese airports, including CTU, has one of the world's worst on-time performance rating records, so it is advised to double-check delays online before heading to the airport. There is an expanding list of international connections.

Bus service links the airport terminal and downtown Chengdu, with Bus 303 traveling to the center of town. Taxis should cost about Y55.

Air Contact Chengdu Shuangliu International Airport ☎ *028/8520–5555* ⊕ *www.cdairport.com.*

BUS TRAVEL There are three main bus stations in Chengdu. The Xinnanmen Bus Station, in the city center, has buses to almost every town in Sichuan. The Wuguiqiao Bus Station, east of the city, is used mainly for travelers to Chongqing or Yibin. The Chadianzi Bus Station, in the northwestern part of the city, has buses to destinations in the mountains to the north and west (including Jiuzhaigou and Songpan).

Bus Contacts Chadianzi Bus Station. This bus station is the only one in Chengdu where buses depart for Jiuzhaigou National Park. There is very little English ability at most bus stations throughout Sichuan. ✉ *3rd Ring Rd., 5th Section* ☎ *028/870–6610.* **Wuguiqiao Bus Station** ✉ *194 Yinghui Rd.* ☎ *028/8471–6144.* **Xinnanmen Bus Station** ✉ *57 Linjiang Rd.* ☎ *028/8543–3609.*

TRAIN TRAVEL Chengdu sits on the Kunming–Beijing railway line, and connections are reliable. A high-speed railway was recently completed linking Shanghai to Chengdu, traveling through Nanjing and Wuhan and reaching speeds of 350 kph (217 mph). The Chengdu Railway Station is in the northern part of the city. The Chengdu East Railway Station, now accessible by subway Line 2, is where all the bullet trains arrive and depart. It's a Y20 cab ride from Tianfu Plaza.

Train Contact Chengdu Railway Station ✉ *Second Ring Rd., 3rd North Section* ☎ *028/8337–2608.* **Chengdu East Railway Station** ✉ *Chengdu, Jinjiang District* ☎ *028/8513–6245.*

SAFETY AND PRECAUTIONS

Stay alert for vehicles on both streets and sidewalks, and do not assume that drivers will follow traffic laws. Pedestrians do *not* have the right-of-way, so be extra careful crossing the street. Pickpockets, bag-snatchers, and other thieves can also be a problem. Stay alert on the street and while riding trains and buses, and don't leave valuables unsecured in hotel rooms.

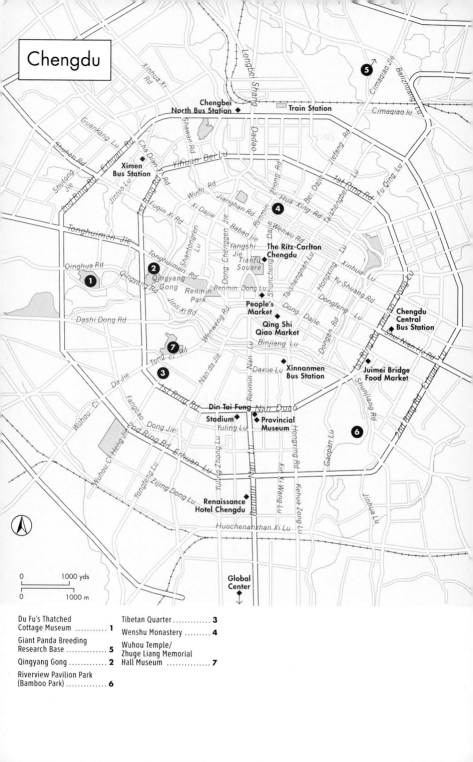

Chengdu

Medical Assistance **Chengdu Medical Center/Parkway Health.** This modern clinic is staffed with English-speaking doctors and at least one rotating Western doctor. Most international insurance is accepted. ⊠ *Chengdu No. 1 People's Hospital, 18 Wanxiang Bei Lu* ☎ *028/8331–7899* ⊕ *www.parkwayhealth.cn.* **For emergency medical assistance.** Anywhere in China, dial 120; for all other emergencies call 110. ⊠ *PSB; Foreigner's Police, Wenwu Rd., part of Xinhua Dong Rd., 40 Wenmiaohou St.* ☎ *110, 028/8674–4683.*

TIMING

Chengdu deserves at least a few days, but travelers coming from remote areas of China may wish to stay longer to take a break in the city's increasingly cosmopolitan atmosphere.

TOURS

A good resource for package and individual tours in Chengdu and throughout Sichuan is the tour agency Intowestchina.

ESSENTIALS

Bank **Bank of China** ⊠ *35 Middle Renmin Rd., 2nd Section* ⊕ *www.boc.cn.*

Consulate **U.S. Consulate** ⊠ *4 Lingshiguan Rd., Wu Hou Ci* ☎ *028/8558–3992* ⊕ *chengdu.usembassy-china.org.cn.*

Visitor and Tour Info **Into West China Holiday Travel.** This comprehensive company can offer very simple packages, from a visit to the Panda Breeding Center to more remote places in Sichuan and beyond. ⊠ *71 Qinglong St., Qingyang District* ☎ *028/8151–1098* ⊕ *www.intowestchina.com.*

EXPLORING

TOP ATTRACTIONS

Du Fu's Thatched Cottage Museum (杜甫草堂 *Dùfǔ cǎotáng*). This museum is named for the famous poet Du Fu (AD 712–770) of the Tang Dynasty, whose poetry continues to be read today. A Manchurian, he came to Chengdu from Xi'an and built a small hut overlooking the bamboo- and plum tree–lined Huanhua River. During the four years he spent here he wrote more than 240 poems. After his death the area became a garden; a temple was then added during the Northern Song Dynasty (960–1126). A replica of his cottage now stands among several other structures, all built during the Qing Dynasty. Some of Du Fu's calligraphy and poems are on display here. ⊠ *37 Qinghua Rd.* ☎ *028/8731–9258* ⊕ *www.dfmuseum.org.cn* 🎫 *Y60* ☉ *Daily 8–6.*

FAMILY **Giant Panda Breeding Research Base** (大熊猫博物馆 *Dàxióngmāo bówùguǎn*). The Giant Panda Breeding Research Base is worth the 45-minute drive (from the center of Chengdu) to walk the peaceful bamboo groves, snap pictures of the lolling pandas, and catch a glimpse of the tiny baby pandas that are born with startling regularity. Crews of scientists help pandas breed and care for the young in a safe, controlled environment. Guests can also briefly hold a baby or juvenile giant panda for a donation to the center of Y2,000. ■ TIP→ **Visit early in the morning, when the pandas are most active.** To get here, book a driver through your hotel for Y300 to Y400 round-trip. A taxi will cost about Y80 each way depending how well you bargain. ⊠ *26 Jiefang Rd.* ☎ *028/8351–0033* ⊕ *www.panda.org.cn/english* 🎫 *Y58* ☉ *Daily 8–5.*

The Wenshu Monastery in Chengdu

Qingyang Gong (青羊宫 *Qīngyáng gōng*). Built during the Tang Dynasty, Qingyang Gong is the oldest Taoist temple in the city, and one of the most famous in China. Six courtyards open out onto each other before arriving at the sculptures of two goats, which represent one of the earthly incarnations of Lao Tzu (the legendary founder of Taoism). If you arrive mid-morning, you can watch the day's first worshippers before the stampede of afternoon pilgrims. The temple grounds are filled with nuns and monks training at the Two Immortals Monastery, the only such facility in Southwest China. A small teahouse is on the premises. ✉ *9 1st Ring Rd., 2nd Section* ☎ *028/8776–6584* 💲 *Y5* ⏰ *Mar.–Sept., daily 8–6; Oct.–Feb., daily 8–5.*

Fodor'sChoice ★ **Wenshu Monastery** (文殊院 *Wénshū yuàn*). Named after Manjusri, the bodhisattva of transcendent wisdom, Wenshu Monastery is one of the most important (and well-perserved) Zen Buddhist monasteries in China, and has been around almost as long as the religion itself. It was originally constructed during the Sui Dynasty, around the same time as Zen Buddhism's emergence in China. The monastery and accompanying temples have since been destroyed several times, most notably during the Ming Dynasty, after which the monks are said to have continued sitting among the ruins chanting sutras. It is notable for hundreds of antique statues crafted from a variety of materials that have survived upheavals of times past better than the actual buildings. The attractive 11-tiered Thousand Buddha Peace Pagoda is actually a rather late addition—it was built in 1988 based on an original Sui Dynasty pagoda. ✉ *15 Wenshu Yuan St., off Renmin Middle Rd.* 💲 *Free* ⏰ *Daily 8:30–6.*

9

Wuhou Temple. The Wuhou Temple (武侯祠 *Wǔhòu cí*) complex houses the **Zhuge Liang Memorial Hall Museum**, a shrine to the heroes that made the Shu Kingdom legendary during the Three Kingdoms Period. The temple here was constructed in AD 221 to entomb the earthly remains of Shu Emperor Liu Bei. During the Ming Dynasty, Liu Bei's subjects were also housed here, most notably Zhuge Liang. Liu Bei's most trusted adviser during the Three Kingdoms Period, Zhuge Liang is a legendary figure in Sichuan, and in some respects more honored than his master. The temple burned during the wars that toppled the Ming Dynasty and was rebuilt in 1671–72 during the Qing Dynasty. The main shrine, Zhaolie Temple, is dedicated to Liu Bei; the rear shrine, Wu Hou Temple, to Zhuge Liang. There is also the Sworn Brotherhood Shrine, which commemorates Liu Bei, Zhang Fei, and Guan Yu's "Oath in the Peach Garden." The Sichuan Opera performs here nightly from 7:30 to 10. The Y180 ticket is expensive, but the face-changing, fire-breathing, lyre-playing ensemble may help justify the price tag. ✉ *231 Wuhou Ci Da St.* ☎ *028/8555–2397* ⊕ *www.wuhouci.net.cn* ✆ *Y60* ⊙ *Daily 8–9.*

WORTH NOTING

Fodor's Choice ★ **Riverview Pavilion Park (Bamboo Park)** (望江楼公园 *Wàngjiānglóu gōngyuán*). The four-story wooden pavilion in Riverview Pavilion Park, dating from the Qing Dynasty, offers splendid views of the Fu River. The poet Xue Tao, who lived in Chengdu during the Tang Dynasty, was said to have spent time near the river, from which she apparently drew water to make paper for her poems. The pavilion stands amid more than 150 species of bamboo, a plant revered by the poet. ■TIP→ **A perfect place to stroll early mornings while the older population practice tai chi and the "Chinese yo-yo".** Don't rush out before enjoying a cup of inexpensive, Y10, Mao Feng green tea (a local specialty grown in the nearby mountains). It is the perfect escape to the messy city! ✉ *30 Wangjiang Rd.* ☎ *028/8522–3389* ⊕ *www.wangjianglou.com* ✆ *Y20* ⊙ *Daily 6:30 am–8:30 pm.*

Fodor's Choice ★ **Tibetan Quarter** (小拉萨 *Xiǎolásà*). Chengdu's tiny Tibetan Quarter is a fascinating place to explore. Shop for colorful Tibetan clothing and art, including religious objects such wooden beads, Buddhist prayer flags, and Tibetan scrolls. Make sure to bargain hard. If you can't make it to Tibet, stop for a cup of salty yak milk tea at one of the many restaurants lining the main drag. ✉ *Wuhuoci Heng St., Wu Hou Ci.*

WHERE TO EAT

In Chengdu, hotpot is easy to find. A walk down just about any street will turn up at least one restaurant serving this local specialty: a boiling vat of chili oil, red peppers, and mouth-numbing spices into which you dip duck intestines, beef tripe, chicken livers, or (for the less adventurous) bamboo shoots and mushrooms.

$$$$
CHINESE
✕ **Din Tai Fung Dumpling Restaurant** (鼎泰丰 *Dǐngtàifēng*). This Taiwanese-started unpretentious dumpling shop has received rave reviews since the 1980s, and it currently operates in more than 10 countries, including the United States. The famed "xiao long bao," perfectly crafted pork dumplings, are a must. The menu is in English with pictures, making the pointing game very easy. Creative dishes to suit both meat lovers and

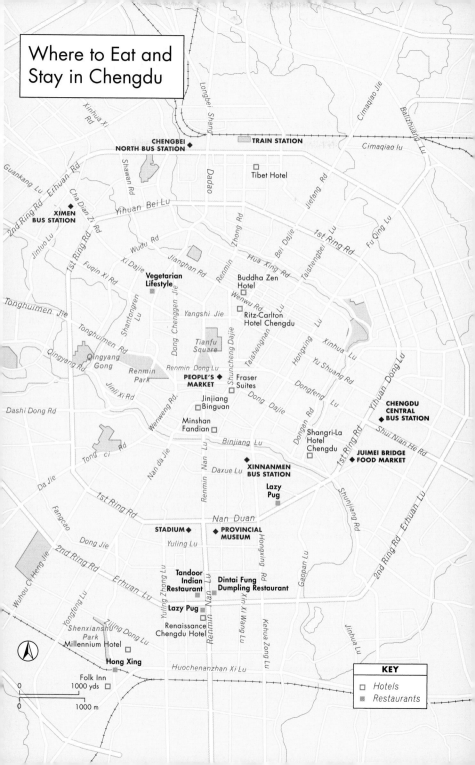

Where to Eat and Stay in Chengdu

KEY
- ☐ Hotels
- ■ Restaurants

TRAIN STATION

CHENGBEI NORTH BUS STATION

Tibet Hotel

Xinhua Xi Rd

Longbei Shang

Cimaqiao Jie

Balizhuang Lu

Cimaqiao lu

Guankang Lu

2nd Ring Rd
Erhuan Rd

XIMEN BUS STATION

Cha Dian Zi Rd

Shawan Rd

Yihuan Bei Lu

Dadao

Jiefang Rd

Zhong Rd

Bei Dajie

1st Ring Rd

Taishengbei Lu

Fu Qing Lu

Jinluo Lu

1st Ring Rd

Fuqin Xi Rd

Wudu Rd

Jianghan Rd

Hua Xing Rd

Buddha Zen Hotel

Vegetarian Lifestyle

Tonghuimen Jie

Tonghuimen Rd

Shantongren Lu

Dong Chengen Jie

Yangshi Jie

Wenwu Rd

Ritz-Carlton Hotel Chengdu

Taishengnan

Hongxing Lu

Xinhua Lu

Yu Shuang Rd

Qingyang Gong

Renmin Park

Tianfu Square

Shuncheng Dajie

Renmin Dong Lu

PEOPLE'S MARKET

Fraser Suites

Dongfeng Lu

CHENGDU CENTRAL BUS STATION

Qingyang Rd

Jinli Xi Rd

Jinjiang Binguan

Dong Dajie

Dongan Rd

Yihuan Dong Lu

Dashi Dong Rd

Wenweng Rd

Minshan Fandian

Binjiang Lu

Shangri-La Hotel Chengdu

Shui Nian He Rd

1st Ring Rd

JUIMEI BRIDGE FOOD MARKET

Tong ci

Nan da Jie

Renmin Nan Lu

Daxue Lu

XINNANMEN BUS STATION

Shunjiang Rd

2nd Ring Rd
Erhuan Lu

Da Jie

Lazy Pug

1st Ring Rd

Nan Duan

Nan Nan Lu

Hongxing Rd

Gaopan Lu

Fangcao

Dong Jie

STADIUM

Yuling Lu

PROVINCIAL MUSEUM

2nd Ring Rd

Erhuan Lu

Wuhou Ci Heng Jie

Yongfeng Lu

Ziiing Dong Lu

Yuling Zhong Lu

Nan Lu

Tandoor Indian Restaurant

Dintai Fung Dumpling Restaurant

Xin Xi Wang Lu

Kehua Zong Lu

Jinhua Lu

Shenxianshu Park

Millennium Hotel

Lazy Pug

Renaissance Chengdu Hotel

Hong Xing

Folk Inn

Huochenanzhan Xi Lu

0   1000 yds

0   1000 m

N

vegetarian palates are widely available. It is an ideal place to dine for its spotless hygiene standards, which cannot be promised in many Chinese restaurants in the city. It is located in a new mall, Raffles, which has plenty of Western stores. $ *Average main: Y200* ⊠ *Raffles Mall, Renmin South Rd., 4th Section, Wu Hou Ci* ☎ *028/0892–82882* ⊕ *www.dintaifung.com.cn* ☖ *Reservations not accepted* ⊘ *Daily 11 am–10 pm.*

$$
SICHUAN

✕ **Hong Xing** (红杏酒家 *Hóngxìng jiǔjià*). Eat like a local at Hong Xing, where Sichuan cuisine is done consistently well. The useful picture menu has amusing English translations and makes ordering a pointing game. With a dining room that resembles an enormous ballroom, you'll feel like you're crashing a wedding reception. Favorites on offer include eggplant with garlic and ginger, pork with peanuts and peppers, or the house signature dish called Hong Xing Ji, which is tender bits of chicken floating in a sea of sesame oil topped with peanuts and mouth-numbing pebbles of Sichuan peppercorns. There are lots of unique vegetarian options, including shredded white bamboo. $ *Average main: Y80* ⊠ *137 Ziwei Dong Lu* ☎ *028/8517–5388* ▭ *No credit cards.*

$$$
SICHUAN

✕ **Huang Cheng Lao Ma** (皇城老妈 *Huáng chéng lǎomǎ*). Run by artists, this amazing restaurant occupies a massive brick-and-stone building with sculpted pillars flanking either side and a facade depicting scenes from old Chengdu. The hotpot comes in the traditional spicy varieties, as well as a *qing tang,* or "soft soup," style without the spices. You can also opt for those prepared with wild mushrooms or seafood. There are often photo exhibitions from local artists. $ *Average main: Y100* ⊠ *20 3rd Section, 2nd Ring Rd., Wu Hou Ci* ☎ *028/8513–9999* ⊕ *www.hclm.net* ▭ *No credit cards.*

$$
MODERN
AMERICAN
Fodor's Choice
★

✕ **Lazy Pug** (懒巴哥西餐厅 *Lǎnbāgè xǐcāntīng*). Chengdu's only American-owned restaurant and bar, the Lazy Pug serves the city's most authentic dishes you will no doubt be craving from home. Barbecue brisket and pulled pork sandwiches along with the steak fajitas are standout dishes. Great blues music and the owner's travel photos decorating the brick walls will make you feel like you've momentarily stepped out of China. There's a long list cocktails, beer, and wine hard to find elsewhere. Sunday brunch is a hit with the city's large expat community. $ *Average main: Y80* ⊠ *Renaissance Chengdu Hotel, 48 Ren Min South Rd., 4th Section* ☎ *028/13881782604* ⊕ *www.thelazypug.com* ▭ *No credit cards* ⊘ *Closed Mon.*

$$$
INDIAN

✕ **Tandoor Indian Restaurant** (天都里印度餐厅 *Tiāndùlǐ Yìndù cāntīng*). Just a couple of blocks southwest from the American Consulate and across the street from the Bookworm Cafe, this northern Indian restaurant serves Chengdu's best Indian fare. The decor, a sophisticated combination of wood and mirrors, makes a meal here seem like a special occasion. Tandoor is named after the traditional clay oven used in India, so it's no surprise the grilled meats and chicken are consistently tender and delicious. $ *Average main: Y100* ⊠ *34 S. Renmin Rd., 4th Section, behind the Sunjoy Inn, Wu Hou Ci* ☎ *028/8555–1958* ⊕ *www.tandoorchina.cn.*

$$$
CHINESE

✕ **Vegetarian Lifestyle** (成都素食的生活方式 *Chéngdū sùshíde shēnghuó fāngshì*). All famous Chinese dishes can be found on this restaurant's user-friendly picture menu, from Peking duck to Sichuan numbing

CLOSE UP

Chengdu's Green Tea

Not many people know that some of the best green tea comes from the mountains of western Sichuan. In Chengdu, the art of drinking tea is taken very seriously and almost every local is passionate about their chosen favorite leaf.

Chengdu's most celebrated green tea, grown row upon row on Sichuan's Emei Mountain (Emeishan), is called Zhuye qing (Bamboo Leaf Green). Slightly bitter, crisp, and earthy in flavor, Zhu Ye Qing is also the name of a ritzy tea franchise with several outlets in Chengdu and generous sample tastings.

If you want to sample some good tea, head to People's Park, Wenshu Temple, or the recently redeveloped *kuan xiangzi* and *zhai xiangzi* (wide and narrow alley) area. Another interesting experience is to wander the fragrant alleys of Chengdu's Northside Tea Market (五块石茶叶市场 Wǔkuàishí cháyè shìchǎng), a wholesale tea market featuring tea from all over China along with an incredible selection of tea utensils including teapots, pickers, boilers, scoopers, and patterned glasses. You'll no doubt be invited to sample a variety of different teas. Remember that buying is optional, and bargaining is expected and part of the fun.

peppercorns and chicken. Well, mock chicken, but it tastes so close to real chicken, and sometimes better, even the biggest carnivore would enjoy dining here. Ultraclean and friendly service can be expected. Very creative veggie dishes include a mushroom hotpot and mango mushrooms! It is more of a lunch spot as the atmosphere is simple and no alcohol is served. $ *Average main: Y120* ⊠ *27 Qinglong St., Qingyang District* ☎ *028/8628–2848* ⊟ *No credit cards.*

$$$
SICHUAN

✕ **Yang Yang Restaurant** (杨杨餐馆 *Yángyáng cānguǎn*). This *New York Times*-raved-about restaurant offers what is considered Sichuan "soul food". Mouthwatering dishes are created from simple ingredients such as eggplant and potatoes. Yang Yang is a perfect place to sample many dishes in a lively, authentically Sichuanese environment. From the sweet-and-sour pork to thinly sliced beef soaked in chili oil, the menu is tourist-friendly, complete with pictures. $ *Average main: Y100* ⊠ *32 Jin Yuan Xiang, Wu Hou Ci* ☎ *028/8523–1394* ⊟ *No credit cards.*

WHERE TO STAY

$
HOTEL

🏨 **Buddha Zen Hotel** (成都圆和圆佛禅文化酒店 *Fóshēnwénhuà jiǔ diàn*). Drawing inspiration from the nearby Wenshu Zen Buddhist monastery, this boutique hotel has carefully designed antique wooden decorations, a peaceful courtyard, wonderful staff, and good food. **Pros:** good location; crisp service; reasonable prices. **Cons:** street can be noisy; hard beds. $ *Rooms from: Y700* ⊠ *B6-6 Wenshu Fang, near Wenshu Temple* ☎ *028/8692–9898* ⊕ *www.buddhazenhotel.com* ⇗ *35 rooms* ⫟ *No meals.*

$
HOTEL

🏨 **Folk Inn** (同档次酒店 *Fújīn fàndiàn*). In the southern part of Chengdu near leafy Shen Xian Shu Park, this boutique hotel has temple-style architecture and antique wooden furniture that give it plenty of

9

character. **Pros:** plenty of charm; reasonable rates; near a pretty park. **Cons:** staff doesn't speak English; hard beds. $ *Rooms from: Y500* ✉ *63 Shenxianshu South Rd.* ☎ *028/8123–8888* ⌂ *98 rooms, 12 suites* ⑪ *No meals.*

$$$
HOTEL
⌂ **Fraser Suites** (成都仁恒辉盛阁国际公寓 *Rènhéng huǐshènggé guójī gōngyù*). This Singaporean-managed skyscraper in the heart of downtown puts you within walking distance of Tian Fu Square; it's also a two-minute walk to the nearest subway station, so getting around the city is a breeze. **Pros:** great location; luxe rooms; English-speaking staff. **Cons:** expensive rates; lack of dining options. $ *Rooms from: Y1500* ✉ *111 Zhihui St.* ☎ *028/8516–6999* ⊕ *chengdu.frasershospitality.com* ⌂ *360 residences* ⑪ *Breakfast.*

$
HOTEL
⌂ **Jinjiang Binguan** (锦江宾馆 *Jǐnjiāng bīngguǎn*). For years this was the city's best hotel—foreign dignitaries and bigwigs from Beijing could always be found milling around the lobby. **Pros:** great riverside location; large rooms; next to subway. **Cons:** no longer the best in town. $ *Rooms from: Y900* ✉ *80 Renmin Nan Rd., 2nd Section* ☎ *028/8550–6666* ⊕ *www.jjhotel.com* ⌂ *456 rooms* ⑪ *No meals.*

$$
HOTEL
⌂ **Millennium Hotel** (新东万千喜大酒店 *Xíndǒng wānqián huàn dǎjiǔdiàn*). Located south of the city center in the Tongzilin residential district, this hotel faces a slender park that's a great place to watch elderly couples practice tai chi while their grandchildren fly homemade kites. **Pros:** great amenities; adjoining multilevel Starbucks Coffee; peaceful location. **Cons:** disappointing breakfast buffet; long waits for taxis. $ *Rooms from: Y1100* ✉ *41 Shenxianshu Rd.* ☎ *028/8512–7777* ⊕ *www.millenniumhotels.com.cn* ⌂ *359 rooms* ⑪ *All meals.*

$
HOTEL
⌂ **Minshan Fandian** (岷山饭店 *Mǐnshān fàndiàn*). This elegant hotel seems out to prove a point: a locally owned lodging can match and even outdo the international chains. **Pros:** great value; excellent service; city center. **Cons:** noisy streets outside. $ *Rooms from: Y800* ✉ *55 Renmin South Rd., 2nd Section* ☎ *028/8558–3333* ⊕ *www.minshan.com. cn* ⌂ *370 rooms, 13 suites* ⑪ *No meals.*

$
HOTEL
⌂ **Renaissance Chengdu Hotel** (万丽酒店 *Wànlì jiǔdiàn*). Recently bought by Marriott (formerly called the Master) this hotel is now up to international standards. **Pros:** location; price. **Cons:** facilites; not near temples and other tourist attractions. $ *Rooms from: Y1000* ✉ *48 S. Renmin Rd., 4th Section, Wu Hou Ci* ☎ *028/8887–8888* ⊕ *www.marriott.com* ⌂ *368 rooms and suites* ⑪ *Breakfast.*

$$$
HOTEL
⌂ **The Ritz-Carlton Chengdu** (成都富力丽思卡尔顿酒店). The Ritz is the newest and by far the poshest new address in Chengdu. **Pros:** great dining options; very comfortable rooms. **Cons:** obnoxious, loud locals; not located near any other "foreign" friendly dining. $ *Rooms from: Y1800* ✉ *269 Shuncheng Ave., Qingyang District* ☎ *28/8358–8888* ⊕ *www. ritzcarlton.com* ⌂ *353 rooms and suites* ⑪ *Multiple meal plans.*

$$
HOTEL
Fodor's Choice
★
⌂ **Shangri-La Hotel Chengdu** (香格里拉大酒店 *Xiǎnggēlǐlā dǎjiǔdiàn*). Opulent style and exceptional service are hallmarks of the Singapore-based Shangri-La chain, and the Chengdu property delivers both. **Pros:** great service; good restaurants, soothing spa. **Cons:** slightly inconvenient location, aging a bit. $ *Rooms from: Y1400* ✉ *9 Binjiang Dong*

Rd. ☎ *028/8888–9999* 🌐 *www.shangri-la.com* 🛏 *593 rooms* 🍴 *No meals.*

$ HOTEL 🏨 **Tibet Hotel** (成都西藏饭店 *Xīzàng fàndiàn*). Located near the train station, this inexpensive hotel is a good option for those planning trips to Tibet. **Pros:** good value; handy travel office. **Cons:** far from many dining and nightlife areas. [$] *Rooms from: Y380* ✉ *10 Renmin North Rd.* ☎ *028/8318–3388, 800/886–5333* 🌐 *www.tibet-hotel.com* 🛏 *238 rooms, 22 suites* 🍴 *No meals.*

NIGHTLIFE

Zhai Xiangzi, or Narrow Alley, is a pedestrian street packed with restaurants, bars, and shops, all built in traditional Chinese-style architecture complete with ornate entrance gates, tiny pavilions, and narrow walkways. Flanked by the parallel Kuan Xiangzi and Jing Ziangzi (Wide Alley and Well Alley), it is popular among tourists and locals alike. Foreign-owned bars catering to the city's expats can be found in the maze of commercial units tucked next to the Renaissance Hotel on Renmin South Road, only a minute walk directly east from the Tong Zi Lin Subway stop. For a more local experience, visit the cluster of bars running along the river on Wangjiang Lu.

Bookworm (老书虫咖啡 *Lǎoshùchóng kāfēi*). South of the U.S. Consulate you'll find the Bookworm, a relaxed haven for thousands of the city's expats to drink, eat, and browse through more than 1,000 books. It's the only place in the city to buy English language books, travel guides, and magazines. An annual literary festival (usually held in March) draws famous authors like humorist David Sedaris. The Worm is also a great place to enjoy a pint of Guinness or decent imported wine as well as decent Western and Asian dishes. ✉ *Yujie Dong Jie 2–7, off Renmin South Rd.* ☎ *028/8552–0117* 🌐 *www.chengdubookworm.com.*

Kuan Zhai Xiang Zi (Wide and Narrow Alleys) (宽窄巷子). The gentrified ancient alleys of the Qing Dynasty is now a walking street packed with restaurants, bars, shops, and one of the city's many Starbucks outlets—all built in a traditional Chinese style. It is popular among tourists and locals alike. Although the priciest drinks in the city, it is all set in a beautiful setting.

9

Underground Pub (随到酒吧 *Suìdǎo jiǔbā*). Tucked away in Jiu Yan Qiao, one of the city's biggest areas for nightclubs, this small and smoky British-owned bar draws in a good mix of young locals and expats. The beer list is constantly expanding, and offers Chengdu's largest selection of Belgian beers. The place is also gay friendly. ✉ *Tai Ping Nan Xin Jie, Jiu Yan Qiao* ☎ *028/135–4022–1774* 🌐 *www.undergroundchengdu.com.*

SHOPPING

The main shopping street is Chunxi Lu, east of Tianfu Square. It's nearly always jam-packed with people, especially on weekends. Near Wenshu Monastery, Wenshu Fang is another of the city's pedestrian streets lined with traditional-style architecture. Many shops selling flavorful tea and local handicrafts can be found here.

New Century Global Centre (世界纪的全球中心 *Chéngdù shǐjiè jīde quánqiú zhòngxǐn*). Nothing says modern China quite like this gigantic, tacky super-structure currently holding the "biggest freestanding building in the world" title. China is no stranger to superlatives and this stands as a reminder by the government of just how economically powerful China, and particularly Chengdu, has become. One can shop, sleep, swim, and ice skate without leaving. The Paradise Island Water Park even provides artificial sunlight. The massive structure designed by a British-Iraqi architect has also become a huge embarrassment to the Communist Party due to reminders of

> **EMEISHAN'S TEA**
>
> Emeishan is part of a range that stretches from Ya'an in the north to Xichang in the south. These mountains produce some of the world's best green tea. Emei's local tea is called Zhu Ye Qing (Jade Bamboo Leaf), and there are several types and grades. It's possible to buy organic Zhu Ye Qing around the mountain and in more than a dozen ultra-sleek shops in Chengdu.

the widespread corruption, as the billionaire financier was convicted of embezzlement and since vanished. A place to visit once and never again. ✉ *1700 Tianfu Ave. N, Chengdu.*

Song Xian Qiao Antique and Art Market (送仙桥 *Sóngxiān qiǎo*). A good place to shop for souvenirs is Song Xian Qiao Antique City, the country's second-largest antiques market, with more than 500 separate stalls selling everything from Mao-era currency to fake Buddha statues to wonderful watercolor paintings. It's near Du Fu's Cottage and Wu Hou Temple. The market does not get into full swing until late morning. There are several noodle shops and teahouses surrounding the market and river. ■ TIP➔ **Always counter offer with less than half the asking price and proceed from there.** ✉ *416 Qingyang Shang Jie.*

EMEISHAN

100 km (62 miles) southwest of Chengdu.

This 10,000-foot mountain is a famous Buddhist pilgrimage site, dotted with temples. You can hike the 25 miles of stone staircase to the Golden Summit of Emeishan in two to three days. It's a difficult climb—the stairs up the mountain somehow make it seem more arduous. On the first day, hike until a bit before nightfall and walk into one of the temples along the way to sleep for Y20 to Y40 per person. Most hikers can reach the summit by nightfall of the second day or sometime on the third day. Stay a night near the top of the mountain and rise early: the clouds that often obscure views during the day are bathed in a breathtaking amber color at sunrise.

The most common route to the top is past Long Life Monastery. This route takes you past the Elephant Bathing Pool, once used by Bodhisattva Puxian to wash the grime off his white elephant. Once you ascend from here you will be mostly free of the madding crowd. A recommended route down is the long shoulder of the mountain past Magic Peak Monastery, where the scenery is beyond compare. Sharing a simple meal with monks in the courtyard and then staying the night in the monastery is magical.

The Wannian monastery at Emeishan

For an easier pilgrimage, take advantage of the Y40 minibus service from the Mount Emeishan Tourist Transportation Center below Declare Nation Temple up to the Leidong Terraces, from where your climb will take about two hours. To avoid climbing altogether, ride the cable car (Y70 round-trip) to the summit from Jieyin Dian.

Regardless how you ascend, the best times to climb are in the spring or fall. Bring a change of clothes for the sweaty part of the journey and a warm jacket for the summit. Water and food are available on the mountain, carried by pipe-puffing porters to the stalls along the way.

GETTING HERE AND AROUND

Most people get to Emeishan Town via a shuttle bus from Chengdu or Leshan, but you can also take the train. The trip from Chengdu takes about two to three hours by bus or three hours by train. Inexpensive public buses travel between destinations, but schedules vary and stops are often unmarked.

BUS TRAVEL   There are departures from Chengdu's Xinnanmen station every half hour and from Leshan every hour on the hour between 7 am and 6 pm. One-way tickets cost between Y35 and Y45, and the trip takes two hours. Also departing from Leshan are buses that travel directly to Emeishan's Baoguo Si. They depart every half hour between 9 and 5 for about Y10.

Most buses coming from Chengdu and Leshan bypass Emei altogether and head directly for the base of the mountain.

A Kunming-bound train from the Chengdu North Railway Station passes through Emeishan Town; it takes two to three hours and costs about Y40.

Train Contact Emeishan Railway Station (乐山城峨眉山城火车站). ✉ *Emeishan* ☎ *083/3516–8609.*

SAFETY AND PRECAUTIONS

The biggest threat here is the unpredictable weather on top of the mountain, so bring warm clothes and dress in layers. Also, be careful of falls or twisted ankles on the slippery stone staircases that run up the mountain.

> **EMEISHAN'S MONKEY TROUBLE**
>
> The mountain's wily golden monkeys have been known to steal items (such as cameras) and hang them in trees. They will try to surround you, screaming, pointing, and jumping in an intimidating manner. Walk quickly through the band before they can increase in number and avoid making eye contact.

Medical Assistance Emeishan Renmin Hospital ✉ *94 Santaishan Jie* ☎ *083/3553–4524, 083/3552–2725.*

TIMING

Climbing the mountain from base to peak and back again can take anywhere from three to six days, depending on your fitness level. A day of relaxation and recovery for tender joints and muscles will likely be in order afterward. Taking a shuttle bus most of the way and then transferring to a chairlift requires as little as a day.

TOURS

Relatively clear English signage makes organized tours of Emeishan unnecessary, but guides can be booked through hotels in Emeishan Town, the cluster of hotels and restaurants at the base of the mountain.

ESSENTIALS

Bank Agricultural Bank of China ✉ *Near Baoguo Monastery* ☎ *083/3559–3397.*

Visitor and Tour Info Emeishan Travel Agency ✉ *94 Ningshan Rd.* ☎ *083/3552–4244.*

EXPLORING

Emeishan (峨眉山 *Éméishān*). The 10,000-foot-high Emeishan (literally translated as Lofty Eyebrow Mountain) in southern Sichuan is one of China's holiest Buddhist pilgrimage sites. The temples here survived the Cultural Revolution better than most others in China, due in part to courageous monks. Still, of the hundreds of temples that once were found here, only 20 remain. Today it is one of the better-known tourist attractions in the country. ■TIP→ **A bamboo walking stick is very useful when ascending the mountain. It's also a good way to scare off the fearless gangs of Tibetan macaques that inhabit the area.**

WHERE TO EAT AND STAY

$ ✕ **Emei Kaoyu** (峨眉烤鱼 *Éméi kǎoyú*). Set among several other decent restaurants on "Good Eats Street," Emei Kaoyu lays out a variety of fresh vegetables every day. After you've have selected your favorites, the cooks turn them into delicious stir-fries. Try fiddlehead ferns fried with local bacon. The street is just up the hill from the bus station at the base of the mountain. $ *Average main: Y35* ⊠ *Haochi Jie* ☎ *138/0813–5338* ▤ *No credit cards.*

$ 🏨 **Baoguo Monastery** (报国寺 *Bàoguó sì*). This monastery at the foot of **HOTEL** the mountain is one of the many accommodations available to those journeying to the Golden Summit. **Pros:** monastic experience; handy location; reasonable rates. **Cons:** pretty basic. $ *Rooms from: Y75* ⊠ *Baoguo Si* ⇖ *30 rooms* ▤ *No credit cards* ❍⏐ *No meals.*

$ 🏨 **Teddy Bear Hotel** (小熊咖啡 *Xiǎoxióng kāfēi*). Despite its odd name **HOTEL** and spartan decor, the Teddy Bear is one of the few hotels in town with an English-speaking staff. **Pros:** free maps and information; congenial owners; Wi-Fi connections. **Cons:** hard beds. $ *Rooms from: Y250* ⊠ *43 Baoguosi Lu* ☎ *0833/559–0135* ⊕ *www.teddybear.com.cn* ⇖ *40 rooms* ▤ *No credit cards* ❍⏐ *No meals.*

LESHAN

165 km (102 miles; 3 hrs by bus) south of Chengdu.

Leshan is famous for the Great Buddha, carved into the mountainside at the confluence of the Dadu, Qingyi, and Min rivers. The Great Buddha—a UNESCO World Heritage Site—was initiated by the monk Haitong in 713, but he didn't live to see its completion in 803. The statue, blissfully reclining, has overlooked the swirling, choppy waters for 1,200 years and is the world's largest Buddhist sculpture

GETTING HERE AND AROUND

BUS TRAVEL Leshan-bound buses leave from Chengdu's Xinnanmen station every 30 minutes between 7:30 and 7:30. Buses from Chongqing leave every hour from 6:30 to 6:30. From Leshan's Xiao Ba Bus Station, take public bus Line 13 directly to the Great Buddha's main gate.

TRAIN TRAVEL The train trip between Chengdu and Leshan takes between 1½ and 2½ hours and costs Y8 to Y109.

SAFETY AND PRECAUTIONS

Watch out for slippery paths, and make sure you're well hydrated for long walks in the steamy forested park that surrounds the Great Buddha.

Medical Assistance Leshan Renmin Hospital (乐山人民医院). ⊠ *76 Baita Jie* ☎ *0833/211–9310.*

TIMING

One day is sufficient to see the Buddha and the surrounding park and pavilions.

TOURS

Boats at a dock about 1,500 feet up the river from the main gate will take you for a bumpy ride to within camera distance of the Giant Buddha. The 40-minute trip is Y40 per person. From the boat you will be able to see two heavily eroded guardians that flank the main statue.

ESSENTIALS

Bank Bank of China ⊠ *35 Huangjiashan* ☎ *0833/212–5246.*

9

DID YOU KNOW?

The Giant Buddha of Leshan has a sophisticated, built-in drainage system of hidden gutters and channels embedded on the head, arms, behind the ears, and in the clothes. This helps displace rainwater and cut back on erosion.

EXPLORING

Giant Buddha (乐山大佛极 Lèshān *dàfó*). Rising 233 feet, this is the tallest stone Buddha and among the tallest sculptures in the world. The big toes are each 28 feet long. A monk who wished to placate the rivers that habitually took local fishermen's lives started the construction of the Giant Buddha in AD 713. The project took more than 90 years to complete, and it had no noticeable effect on the waters. It's possible to clamber, via a stairway hewn out of rock, down to the platform where the feet rest. ☎ *0833/230–2121* 🌐 *whc.unesco.org* 🎫 *Y95 (includes Wu You Temple)* 🕒 *Daily 8–5:30.*

Wu You Temple (乌尤寺 *Wūyóu sì*). There are several temples and pagodas in the park that houses the Giant Buddha, including this Ming Dynasty structure with a commanding view of the city. You might find yourself staring at the lifelike figures and wondering about the people who served as the models. 🎫 *Y95 (includes Giant Budhda)* 🕒 *Daily 8–5:30.*

WHERE TO EAT

$$ SICHUAN FAMILY

🍴 **Deng Qiang** (邓蕸饭店 *Dèngqiǎng fàndiàn*). This always-packed family-run restaurant near the river is only a five-minute walk from the Giant Buddha. Local Sichuan dishes, including Leshan's famous cold chicken in a spicy sauce, can be sampled here. Consistently delicious food, a friendly staff, and a laid-back atmosphere make Deng Qiang by far the best choice in the town. [$] *Average main: Y50* ✉ *158 Binjiang Lu Xia Duan* ☎ *0833/212–5110* 💳 *No credit cards.*

JIUZHAIGOU NATURE PRESERVE

350 km (217 miles; 8–10 hrs by bus) north of Leshan; 225 km (140 miles; 4–6 hrs by bus) northwest of Chengdu.

Forget the noisy, crowded and polluted metropolises of Chengdu and Chongqing and brace yourself for nature at its most majestic. In Northern Sichuan on the Tibetan Plateau, Jiuzhaigou is a UNESCO World Heritage Site overflowing with distinctive blue, green, and turquoise-colored lakes, multilevel waterfalls, and fascinating Tibetan Villages.

GETTING HERE AND AROUND

AIR TRAVEL

You can fly from Chengdu to Jiuhuang Huanglong Airport, one hour south of Jiuzhaigou in Huanglong (1 hour, about Y650). Your hotel should arrange a transfer; otherwise a shuttle bus will cost Y45.

Air Contact Jiuzhaigou Huanglong Airport ☎ *0837/724–3700* 🌐 *www.jzairport.com.*

BUS TRAVEL

Several buses a day (Y158 per person, 9–10 hours) shuttle passengers from Chengdu's Xinnanmen Bus Station or Chadianzi Bus Station. Overnight buses are also available, allowing you the chance to get some rest before tackling the park. However, the day buses have a better reputation for safety and you won't miss the incredible mountain scenery.

TIMING

The park can be seen in one day, although it is a hectic day. If you want to go camping and explore sites outside the national park, three days should suffice. Although the scenery is spectacular at any time of the year, it is important to remember that more than 1.5 million people visit every year and its highly advised to completely avoid the Chinese holiday season.

TOURS

If you want to experience Jiuzhaigou as the Chinese do, sign up with any of the numerous package tours in Chengdu and Chongqing. A word to the wise: be prepared to be herded along by a guide armed with a flag and a bullhorn. General information on tours from Chengdu and Chongqing is available from China Travel Service.

ESSENTIALS

Visitor and Tour Info China Travel Service ☎ 028/6866–3866, 028/6866–3138 ⊕ www.chinatravelservice.com. **Jiuzhaiguo Park Office** ☎ 0837/773–9753 ⊕ www.jiuzhai.com.

EXPLORING

Exploring the park is made easier by frequent ranger stations and signs in English. As you explore the Y-shaped Jiuzhaigou Nature Reserve, your first stop will undoubtedly be the Zaru Valley, on your left. Deeper in the valley you'll pass the stunning Shunzheng Terrace Waterfall before you reach Mirror Lake and Nuorilang Falls. On the right side of this path you'll find the fabled Nine Villages, where it is possible to have a meal with the locals.

From Mirror Lake, veer left to the Zechawa Village, an impossibly beautiful small Tibetan community. From the village, the path travels through a temperate rain forest interspersed with dozens of turquoise-colored pools. At the far end of the left branch of the Y is Long Lake, a beautiful and peaceful place. Down the right branch of the Y is a series of amazing small lakes, including Five Flower Lake and Arrow Bamboo Lake, crisscrossed by wooden walkways.

Fodor's Choice ★ **Jiuzhaigou Nature Reserve** (九寨沟自然保护区 *Jiǔzhàigōu zìrán bǎohùqū*). High among the snowcapped peaks of the Aba Autonomous Prefecture of northern Sichuan lies the Jiuzhaigou Nature Reserve, a spectacular national park filled with lush valleys, jagged peaks, a dozen large waterfalls, and most famously, a collection of iridescent lakes and pools. Jiuzhaigou has become one of the country's most popular tourist destinations, with more than 1.5 million people visiting every year. This UNESCO World Heritage Site preserve's cerulean and aqua pools are among the most beautiful in the world, and the park's raw natural beauty has been compared to Yellowstone National Park. Also similar to Yellowstone are the crowds—throngs of Chinese tourists descend daily on this 800-km (497-mile) stretch of lush forests, piercing peaks, languid lakes, and clear pools. Jiuzhaigou is a natural reserve and a collection of villages, mostly of Tibetan and Qinang origin. (The name Jiuzhaigou means Nine Villages.) The park shelters 76 mammal species, including pandas, black bears, and deer. The climate is wet in the spring and fall, very snowy and cold in the winter, and bright and warm in the summer. ☎ 0837/773–9753 ⊕ *www.jiuzhai.com* ✉ *Apr.–mid-Nov. Y220, mid-Nov.–Mar. Y80* ☉ *Apr.–mid-Nov., daily 7–6; mid-Nov.–Mar., daily 8–5.*

A bridge in Songpan

WHERE TO EAT AND STAY

Did someone say yak? Jiuzhaigou, or "nine village gully," refers to the nine Amdo Tibetan tribes who inhabit the area and your perfect excuse to try Tibetan cuisine. Near the main gate of Jiuzhaigou Reserve you'll find restaurants selling dried yak, cured yak, pickled yak, smoked yak, fried yak, and—well, you get the point. Sample the *sampas* (barley-and-yak-butter tea cakes).

$$$
HOTEL
Intercontinental Resort Jiuzhai Paradise (九寨沟天堂洲际大酒店 *Jiǔzhàigòu tiāntàngzhōu guójì dàjiǔdiàn).* The region's most luxurious lodging, the Intercontinental Resort Jiuzhai Paradise is tucked away in a valley 20 km (12 miles) from the Jiuzhaigou Nature Reserve. **Pros:** stunning location; amazing architecture; plush rooms. **Cons:** less-than-stellar food and service. $ *Rooms from: Y1500* ⊠ *Near Jiuzhaigou Nature Preserve* ☎ *0837/778–9999* ⊕ *www.intercontinental.com* ⇱ *1,020 rooms, 131 suites* ⫯⊙*No meals.*

$$$
RESORT
Sheraton Jiuzhaigou Resort (九寨沟喜来登国际大酒店 *Jiǔzhàigōu xǐláidēng guójì dàjiǔdiàn).* The region's first luxury hotel, the Sheraton Jiuzhaigou Resort sits about 1,000 feet from the mouth of the Jiuzhai Valley. **Pros:** top-notch service; hard-to-beat location; plush rooms. **Cons:** some dated decor. $ *Rooms from: Y1500* ⊠ *Jiuzhaigou Scenic Spot* ☎ *800/810–3088* ⊕ *www.sheraton.com/jiuzhaigou* ⇱*482 rooms, 20 suites* ⫯⊙*No meals.*

9

SONGPAN

350 km (217 miles; 8–10 hrs by bus) northwest of Chengdu.

Songpan has experienced quite a mini-construction boom over the past decade, with better transport connections and more accommodation options offering travelers a bit of comfort along with plenty of fresh mountain air. The ancient village of Songpan was once an important military post built during the Tang Dynasty (AD 618–907). Although horseback riding through the surrounding countryside is the major draw, Songpan's unique mix of local cultures provides plenty of local color including Tibetan, Qiang, Han, and Hui.

GETTING HERE AND AROUND

AIR TRAVEL Don't be fooled by the name of Songpan's Jiuzhaigou Huanglong Airport—it's about 88 km (55 miles) from Jiuzhaigou. Aggressive cabbies compete to take you on the 60-minute trip to Songpan (Y100).

BUS TRAVEL Buses from Chengdu's Chadianzi bus station shuttle passengers daily (8 hours), with several buses departing between 6:30 am and 9:30 am. Tickets cost Y123. From Songpan to Jiuzhaigou its another two to three hours. Tickets cost Y28.

SAFETY AND PRECAUTIONS

When hiring a car to go between Songpan and Jiuzhaigou, do not switch cars midway through the journey, as both drivers will try to claim your agreed-upon fare. At an elevation of almost 10,000 feet, altitude sickness can be a serious issue. Remember to take any physical activity slow, and stay hydrated.

WHERE TO EAT AND STAY

$ ✕ **Emma's Kitchen.** On the main drag not far from the bus station,
CHINESE Emma's Kitchen serves both Western and Chinese fare. The prices are reasonable, and the very friendly staff speaks English. The proprietor is a great source of information about the area. With no actual address, simply go about 30 meters from the bus station, then turn left onto the main road. Ⓢ *Average main: Y40* ⊠ *Main road, near the bus station* ☎ *0837/723–1088* ▭ *No credit cards.*

$ ⌂ **Old House Hotel** (老房子 *Lǎofángzǐ*). Also known as the Guyun Inn,
B&B/INN this guesthouse has a café with good coffee and online access. **Pros:** convenient location; helpful staff. **Cons:** small rooms. Ⓢ *Rooms from: Y200* ⊠ *Shunjiang Lu, near the bus station* ☎ *0837/723–1368* ⌁ *15 rooms* ▭ *No credit cards* ⦿ *No meals.*

CHONGQING AND THE YANGTZE RIVER

Called the Mountain City (also the name of the local beer), Chongqing is the major jumping-off point for the Three Gorges cruise down the Yangtze River. The classic novel *The Three Kingdoms* takes place along this stretch of the river, and the cliffs are lined with caves and tombs dating back to the Yellow Emperor. The controversial Three Gorges Dam is now complete, and the water level is steadily rising—millions of people have been displaced, entire villages swamped, and countless historical artifacts lost forever—but China needs energy, and the western regions need a reliable inland port, therefore the dam stays.

DID YOU KNOW?

Chongqing is the heart of the Ba Yu Culture—vibrant, colorful, and proud—with its own version of Sichuan Opera, its own cuisine, and a history of rebelliousness. The Chongqingese are known for their directness and fiery tempers.

CHONGQING

240 km (149 miles; 4 hrs by bus) southeast of Chengdu; 1,800 km (1,116 miles; 3 hrs by plane) southwest of Beijing; 1,025 km (636 miles; 34 hrs by train) northwest of Hong Kong.

With a layout reminiscent of Hong Kong and a distinct Sichuanese vibe, Chongqing is one of the most interesting and dynamic cities in Western China. The "Mountain City," as it is known, is much more three-dimensional than your average Chinese metropolis, so prepare for plenty of hills and stairs. By Western standards, Chongqing is not a sophisticated place, and this is precisely the reason it is so captivating. Wander off the main pedestrian and shopping drags, get lost in its alleys and local neighborhoods, and dive right in. One of the world's most massive cities, Chongqing is raw and unforgiving. If you want a taste of the real modern China, skip dressed-up Shanghai and sanitized Beijing and head directly into the beating heart of the dragon.

The central peninsula area of Yuzhong District, between the Jialing River to the north and the Yangtze River to the south, is the most interesting and dynamic area of Chongqing. Within Yuzhong, most of the action is centered around the Jiefang Bei (Liberation Monument) area, where you will find the bulk of Chongqing's top hotels, restaurants, bars, and clubs. It is essential to wander off Jiefang Bei to immerse yourself in this thriving metropolis.

9

GETTING HERE AND AROUND

Chongqing is smack-dab in the middle of China, connected by rail, bus, and plane to every major city in the country. Chongqing's Jiangbei International Airport is among the busiest in the region, with daily flights to all major cities in China. For trips to Chengdu, the high-speed rail link is the best bet.

Chongqing's light-rail line from the city center to the zoo in the south is worth the Y10 round-trip ticket price. The two stations in the city center (Jiao Chang Kou and Lin Jiang Men) are easily accessible from Jiefang Bei. The line curves north to the Jialing River—above ground—and goes through six riverside stations before it heads south to the terminal station at the zoo.

AIR TRAVEL Traffic permitting, Chongqing's Jiangbei International Airport is a 40-minute drive north by taxi from the city center. The airport has flights to every major domestic, and some international hubs, mostly within Asia, including Bangkok (Air Asia) and Doha (Qatar Air). A new direct route just opened, connecting Chongqing to Europe via Helsinki (Finn Air).

BOAT AND
FERRY TRAVEL
Boats go on the Yangtze from Chongqing all the way to Shanghai (seven days), but the most popular route is the cruise downstream from Chongqing to Yichang or Wuhan (three to four days) or upstream from Wuhan to Chongqing. Most major sights, including the Three Gorges and Three Little Gorges, lie between Chongqing and Yichang. Tourist boats offer air-conditioned cabins with a television and private bath.

> **WORD OF MOUTH**
>
> "If you're planning a trip to Jiuzhaigou and Huanglong, and flying directly from Chengdu, please give yourself a lot of time to acclimate before going to Huanglong." —rkkwan

BUS TRAVEL
The shared train and bus station may be the most inconvenient, crowded, and annoying station in the world. Once your taxi has maneuvered through the corrugated tin walls and piles of baggage, finding your bus or train is not hard, however.

Chongqing to Chengdu is a well-trodden path. The bus departs every hour, takes five to six hours, and costs Y120. Buses are viable options as far as Yibin, but trains are recommended for all other destinations.

CAR TRAVEL
A taxi is often the most convenient way to navigate the winding roads and long distances. Meters start at Y5, and even long cab rides tend to be much cheaper than they would be elsewhere in China. There is a Y3 fuel surcharge added to every fare.

TRAIN TRAVEL
Trains leave Chongqing every minute for every conceivable city in China. If you're going to Chengdu, the ultramodern high-speed rail link has cut the travel time from four hours to just two hours. A hard seat on the train is Y98 and a soft seat is Y117.

SAFETY AND PRECAUTIONS

Despite its size, Chongqing is a very safe city in terms of crime. But with all the construction and demolition taking place above street level, it is worth being careful where you walk when on the sidewalk due to falling debris. In addition, manic Chongqing taxi drivers are a major hazard, whether you're a passenger or a pedestrian on the street. Always remember to buckle up and use the subway whenever possible.

TIMING

You could easily stay in Chongqing for a week without seeing everything, but most of the sights of interest in and around the city can be visited within three or four days. Avoid the brutal summers when Chongqing morphs into a furnace and come visit in the spring or the fall when the climate is pleasant.

TOURS

Chongqing Dongfang Travel Service ⊠ *5 Chaoqiang Rd.* ☎ *0236/371–0326.*

ESSENTIALS

Bank Bank of China ⊠ *218 Zhong Shan Yi Rd., YuZhong District* ☎ *023/6388-9453.*

Train Contact Cai Yuan Ba Bus and Train Station ⊠ *Off of Nan Qu Rd.* ☎ *023/6168-1114.*

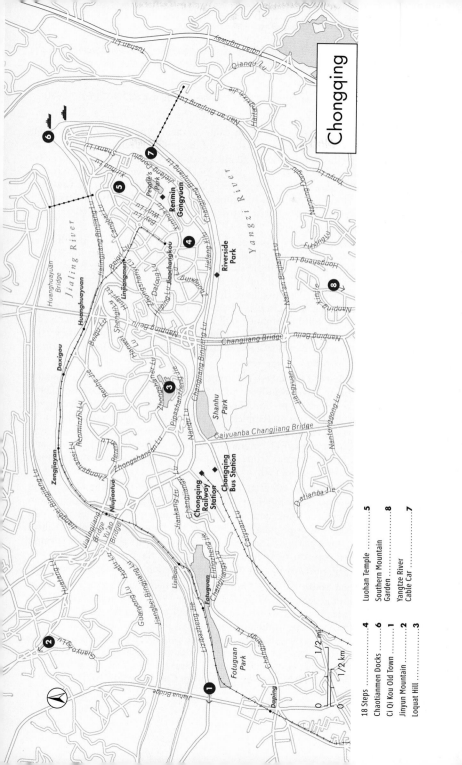

Chongqing

0   1/2 km
0   1/2 mi

Medical Assistance Global Doctor ✉ *Hilton Hotel, 139 Zhong Shan San Rd., Room 701, YuZhong District* ☎ *023/8903-8837* ⊕ *www.globaldoctor.com.au* ⊙ *Weekdays 9–6.*

Visitor and Tour Info CITS ✉ *151 Jiefangbei Zourong Rd.* ☎ *023/6372-7120.*

EXPLORING

Be sure to ride on both of the cable cars that dangle above the city. One links the north and south shores of the Jialing River, from Cangbai Lu to the Jinsha Jie station, and gives excellent views of the docks, the city, and the confluence of the Jialing and Yangtze rivers. The other crosses the Yangtze itself, and starts off of Xinhua Lu, just west of the Chongqing Hotel. Ideal for taking photos of the city and the two rivers, it's a good opportunity to rise above it all and get a grip on the city.

TOP ATTRACTIONS

18 Steps. 18 Steps is one of the coolest places in the city, literally and figuratively. The neighborhood is just south of the Liberation Monument, and hasn't changed since the early 20th century. The name refers to the steps leading from the upper level of Jie Fang Bei down to the slums below. The infamous 18 Steps tunnel, the scene of horrible carnage during WWII, serves as a congregation point for the whole neighborhood. Find the tunnel, pull up a mat, and sip tea while the locals stare at you incredulously. At the top of the steps is a teahouse with a treasure trove of WWII memorabilia. ✉ *Jie Fang Bei District, south of the Liberation Monument.*

Ci Qi Kou Old Town. Perched in the western part of the city overlooking the Jialing River, this district dates back to the late Ming Dynasty. There is a main drag with dozens of souvenir and snack shops, including the peaceful Baolun Si Temple, which dates back 1,500 years. If you do stay until late into the evening, head down the alleys off the main drag and have a bowl of "night owl noodles." They're spicy, meaty, and filling. The taxi ride from downtown takes approximately 30 minutes and costs around Y30.

Jinyun Mountain (缙云山 *Jìnyúnshān*). Just north of the city, Jinyun Mountain has some pretty views and a smattering of pavilions from the Ming and Qing dynasties. Three contain imposing statues: the Giant Buddha, the Amitabha Buddha, and the famous general of the Three Kingdoms period, Guan Yu. The park also has a set of **hot springs**, where you can swim in a pool or soak in the private cubicles. ✉ *50 km (30 miles) by bus north of the city, Beibie* ☎ *Y15* ⊙ *Daily 8:30–6.*

Luohan Temple (罗汉寺 *Luóhàn sì*). Originally built about 1,000 years ago, then rebuilt in 1752 and again in 1945, the Luohan Temple is a popular place of worship, and a small community of monks is still active here. One of the main attractions is the 500 lifelike painted clay arhats—Buddhist disciples who have succeeded in freeing themselves from the earthly chains of delusion and material greed. At the back of the temple you can order tea, get a massage, and enjoy a vegetarian lunch. ✉ *7 Luohan Si, across from Carrefour* ☎ *Y10* ⊙ *Daily 8–5.*

Continued on page 577

A CULINARY TOUR OF CHINA

For centuries the collective culinary fragrances of China have drifted far beyond its borders and tantalized the entire world. Now with China's arms open to the world, a vast variety of Chinese flavors—from the North, South, East, and West—are more accessible than ever.

In dynasties gone by, a visitor to China might have to undertake a journey of a thousand li just to feel the burn of an authentic Sichuanese hotpot, and another to savor the crispy skin and juicy flesh of a genuine Beijing roast duck. Luckily for us, the vast majority of regional Chinese cuisines have made successful internal migrations. As a result, Sichuanese cuisine can be found in Guangzhou, Cantonese dim sum in Urumuqi, and the cumin-spiced lamb-on-a-stick, for which the Uigher people of Xinjiang are famous, is now grilled all over China.

Four corners of the Middle Kingdom

Before you begin your journey, remember, a true scholar of Middle Kingdom cuisine should first eliminate the very term "Chinese food" from their vocabulary. It hardly encompasses the variety of provincial cuisines and regional dishes that China has to offer, from succulent Shanghainese dumplings to fiery Sichuanese hotpots.

To guide you on your gastronomic journey, we've divided the country's gourmet map along the points of the compass—North, South, East, and West. Bon voyage and bon appétit!

Following the revolution, it was hard to find authentic Chinese cuisine.

NORTH

THE BASICS

Cuisine from China's Northeast is called dongbei cai, and it's more wheat than rice based. Vegetables like kale, cabbage, and potatoes are combined with robust, thick soy sauces, garlic (often raw), and scallions.

Even though many Han Chinese from southern climates find mutton too gamey, up north it's a regular staple. In many northern cities, you can't walk more than a block without coming across a small sidewalk grill with yang rou chua'r, or lamb-on-a-stick.

NOT TO BE MISSED

The most famous of all the northern dishes is Peking duck, and if you've ever had it well prepared, you'll know why Beijingers are proud of the dish named for their city.

As far back as the 15th century it was an Imperial dish, reserved for royalty. Like many such delicacies, it's likely the recipe was smuggled out of the Forbidden City by cooks or servants, eventually finding its way into restaurants.

Peking duck sliced table-side.

A bit different from the "crispy duck" eaten in Cantonese-style restaurants around the globe, proper Peking duck should have skin that's both brittle and yielding. Getting there is a meticulous, multi-day process, but the real key is the date-infused liquid poured into the duck cavity, which is sealed, and the bird is then hung over the fire. Full of fruity juice, the meat will steam gently from the inside as the flames in the oven lick and crackle the skin.

THE CAPITAL CITY'S NAMESAKE DISH

A perfectly prepared duck

Scallions

Soy based hoisin sauce

Pancakes

SOUTH

9

(left) Preparing for the feast. (top right) Dim sum as art. (bottom right) Place your order.

THE BASICS

The dish most associated with Southern Chinese cuisine is dim sum, which is found in great variety and abundance in Guangdong province, as well as Hong Kong and Macau. Bite-size dim sum is usually eaten early in the day. Any good dim sum place should have dozens of varieties. Some of the most popular dishes are *har gao*, a shrimp dumpling with a rice-flour skin, *siu maai*, a pork dumpling with a wrapping made of wheat flour, and *chaa-habao*, a steamed or baked bun filled with sweetened pork and onions. Adventerous eaters should order the chicken claws. Trust us, they taste better than they look.

> The Cantonese saying *"fei qin zou shou"* roughly translates to *"if it flies, swims or runs, it's food."*

For our money, the best southern food comes from Chaozhou (Chiuchow), a coastal city only a few hours' drive north of its larger neighbors. Unlike dim sum, Chaozuo cuisine is extremely light and understated. Deep-fried bean curd is also a remarkably fresh Chaozuo dish.

NOT TO BE MISSED

One Chaozuo dish that appeals equally to the eye and the palate is the plain-sounding mashed vegetable with minced chicken soup. The dish is served in a large bowl, and resembles a green-and-white yin-yang. As befitting a dish resembling a Buddhist symbol, a vegetarian version substituting rice gruel for chicken broth is usually offered.

SOUTHWEST AND FAR WEST

Southwest

THE BASICS

When a person from the Southwest asks you if you like spicy food, consider your answer well. Natives of Sichuan and Hunan take the use of chilies, wild pepper, and garlic to blistering new heights. These two areas have been competing for the "spiciest province in China" title for centuries. The penchant for fiery food is likely due to the weather—hot and humid in the summer and harshly cold in the winter. But no matter what the temperature, if you're eating Sichuan or Hunan dishes, be prepared to sweat.

Southwest China shares some culinary traits with both Southeast Asia and India. This is likely due to the influences of travelers from both regions in centuries past. Traditional Chinese medicine also makes itself felt in the regional cuisine. Theory has it that sweating expels toxins and equalizes body temperature.

As Chairman Mao's province, Hunan has a number of dishes with revolutionary names. The most popular are red-cooked Hunan fish *(hongshao wuchangyu)* and red-cooked pork *(hongshao rou)*, which was said to have been a personal favorite of the Great Helmsman.

Sichuan pepper creates a tingly numbness.

NOT TO BE MISSED

One dish you won't want to miss out on in Sichuan is *mala zigi*, or "peppery and hot chicken." It's one part chicken meat and three parts fried chilies and a Sichuanese wild pepper called *huajiao* that's so spicy it effectively numbs the tongue. At first it feels like eating Tiger Balm, but the hot-cool-numb sensation produced by crunching on the pepper is oddly addictive.

KUNG PAO CHICKEN

One of the most famous Chinese dishes, Kung Pao chicken (or gongbao jiding), enjoys a legend of its own.

Though shrouded in myth, its origin exemplifies the improvisational skills found in any good Chinese chef. The story of Kung Pao chicken has to do with a certain Qing Dynasty era (1644–1911) provincial governor named Ding Baozhen, who arrived home unexpectedly one day with a group of friends in tow. His cook, caught in between

shopping trips, had only the chicken breast and a few vegetables he was planning to cook for his own dinner. The crafty chef diced the chicken into tiny bits and fried it up with everything he could find in the cupboard—some peanuts, sugar, onion, garlic, bits of ginger, and a few handfuls of dried red peppers—and hoped for the best.

(top left) Tibetan dumplings. (center left) Uyghur-style pilaf. (bottom left) Monk stirring tsampa barley. (right) Juggling hot noodles in the Xinjiang province.

Far West

THE BASICS

Religion is the primary shaper of culinary tradition in China's Far West. Being a primarily Muslim province, chefs in Xinjiang don't use pork products of any kind. Instead, meals are likely to be heavy on spiced lamb. Baked flat breads coated in sesame seeds are a specialty. Whole lamb roasted on a spit, fine spicy tomato salads, and lightly spiced mutton and vegetable soups are also favorites.

NOT TO BE MISSED

In Tibet, climate is the major factor dictating cuisine. High and dry, the Tibetan plateau is hardly suited for rice cultivation. Whereas a Han meal might include rice, Tibetan cuisine tends to include tsampa, a ground barley usually cooked into a porridge. Another staple that's definitely an acquired taste is yak butter tea. Dumplings, known as *momo,* are wholesome and filling. Of course, if you want to go all out, order the yak penis with caterpillar fungus.

EAST

(top left) Cold tofu with pork and thousand-year-old eggs. (top right) Meaty dumplings. (bottom right) Letting off the steam of Shanghai: soup dumplings. (bottom left) Steamed Shanghai hairy crabs.

THE BASICS

The rice, seafood, and fresh vegetable-based cooking of the southern coastal provinces of Zhejiang and Jiangsu are known collectively as huiyang cai. As the area's biggest city, Shanghai has become a major center of the culinary arts. Some popular dishes in Shanghai are stir-fried freshwater eels and finely ground white pepper, and red-stewed fish—a boiled carp in sweet and sour sauce. Another Shanghai favorite are xiaolong bao, or little steamer dumplings. Similar to Cantonese dim sum, xiaolong bao tend to be more moist. The perfect steamed dumpling is meant to explode in your mouth in a juicy burst of meat.

NOT TO BE MISSED

Drunken anything! Shanghai chefs are known for their love of cooking with wine. Dishes like drunken chicken, drunken pigeon, and drunken crab are all delectable meals cooked with prodigious amounts of Shaoxing wine. People with an aversion to alcohol should definitely avoid these. Another meal not to be missed is hairy freshwater crabs, which only come into season in October. One enthusiast of the dish was 15th-century poet and essayist Li Yu, who wrote of the dish in near-erotic terms. "Meat as white as jade, golden roe . . . to use seasoning to improve its taste is like holding up a torch to brighten the sunshine."

Southern Mountain Garden (重庆南山公园 *Chóngqìng nánshān gōngyuán*). Southern Mountain is the highest point in the city, and at 935 feet it's the most popular place from which to view Chongqing. For a thousand years Nan Shan has been the route over which travelers and traders of medicine, tea, spices, and silk entered the city and headed on to Sichuan. The best place to enjoy the views and the feel of the mountain is in this very traditional Chinese garden with oddly shaped rocks and bonsai trees. ✉ *101 Nanshan Gongyuan Rd.* 🎟 *Y30* ⏲ *Daily 8–5.*

Fodor's Choice ★ **Yangtze River Cable Car** (电缆车 *Diànlǎnchē*). The Yangtze River Cable Car is a great way to experience the enormous scale of the city, sky, and mountains and a bird's eye-view of Chongqing, one of the world's biggest cities. Ideal for taking photos of the city and the two rivers, it's a good opportunity to rise above it all and get a grip on the massive scale of the metropolis. ✉ *Jiefang Dong Rd., west of the Chongqing Hotel* 🎟 *Y2* ⏲ *Daily 7 am–10 pm.*

WORTH NOTING

Chaotianmen Docks (朝天门码头 *Cháotiānmén mǎtóu*). Not as busy and bustling as once upon a time, Chaotianmen Docks lets you get a glimpse of China at work. Here you can witness the merging of the muddy-brown Yangtze River and the blue-green Jialing River. Chaotianmen Square has great skyline views. ✉ *Shaanxi Rd.*

Loquat Hill (枇杷山 *Pípáshān*). The 804-foot Loquat Hill has great views of the river below. At night, enjoy the city lights. There's also a small park with no entrance fee. ✉ *Zhongshan Er Rd.* 🎟 *Free* ⏲ *Daily 8–7.*

WHERE TO EAT

$$ MEXICAN 🍴 **Cactus Tex-Mex** (仙人墨西哥餐厅 *Xiānrèn Móxīgē fàndiàn*). Anyone craving something other than mouth-numbing local dishes will be thrilled to find this American-owned Tex-Mex restaurant. The menu is what you'd expect: enchiladas, quesadillas, and burgers and wings thrown in for good measure. Sip from your favorite of the premium tequilas and watch locals mingle with expats or take in views of the Yangtze River. [$] *Average main: Y80* ✉ *9F Hong Ya Dong, YuZhong District* ☎ *29/348–729–387* 🌐 *www.cactustexmex.com* 💳 *No credit cards.*

$ CAFÉ 🍴 **Nenlu Tea** (嫩绿茶 *Nēnlǜ chá*). Slick and comfortable, this modern teahouse is the city's answer to Starbucks. With several locations dotted around the city (with the Jiabin Lu branch boasting awesome river views), Nenlu is the perfect place to escape the heat, crowds, and general pandemonium of navigating the hilly streets. Loose-leaf teas from around the world and creative drink options make this place worth the visit. [$] *Average main: Y30* ✉ *88 Jiabin Lu, Hong Ya Cave* ☎ *023/6373–4860* 🌐 *www.nenlu.com.*

$$ SICHUAN 🍴 **Qiqi Shanyu Hot Pot** (琪琪上虞火锅 *Qíqí shàngyú huǒguò*). If you ask a local about classic Chongqing-style hotpot, you might be steered to this restaurant. Sure enough, it serves up a highly authentic version of the city's signature dish. The big pot of broth is served hot, and soon comes to a boil over a burner in the center of your table. Choose from tofu, vegetables, or raw shaved beef and mutton and cook them by placing them in the broth. Qiqi Shanyu has all the classic ingredients, but also has a few tricks up its sleeve, such as compartmentalized pots

Damming the Yangtze

Nearly a century ago, Chinese leader Sun Yat-sen first proposed damming the Three Gorges area of the Yangtze River, a project that subsequently appealed to Chiang Kai-shek and even the invading Japanese, both of whom prepared plans for the project.

CONSTRUCTION AND BENEFITS

It wasn't until the 1990s under the Communist government that China began building the world's largest power generator, the Three Gorges Dam. In addition to power generation, the dam's locks are big enough to handle containerized sea barges, allowing Chongqing to be the world's farthest inland seaport.

Construction of the main body of the Three Gorges Dam was finished in 2006, and the 26th generator was installed in 2008. Eight additional generators bring total power generation capacity to an unmatched 22.5 gigawatts.

Even in China, the sheer scale of this project is staggering. The $26-billion dam is more than 600 feet high and a mile wide. By 2010 it had an installed capacity of 18.2 gigawatts and was able to generate 80,000 gigawatt-hours of power annually.

As with any infrastructure project of its scope, the dam has been controversial from the beginning, with critics focusing on its massive social, cultural, and environmental costs.

REPERCUSSIONS

The reservoir created by the flooding of the Three Gorges area was preceded by the forced relocation of more than 1.2 million people. Many of these people are now migrant workers in nearby cities.

The rising river levels also resulted in the submerging of many significant and valuable relics and buildings dating back to the beginning of Chinese civilization. Although some artifacts and buildings were moved uphill, it is widely acknowledged that the flooding of the gorges incurred major cultural losses.

It is the environmental impact of the dam project that has attracted the most negative publicity, with serious potential ramifications both upstream and downstream from the dam.

Behind the dam, millions of acres of forest were drowned, and landslides have become a bigger problem than before. The reduced ability of the Yangtze to flush itself clean of wastewater and other pollution has led to the reservoir's containing higher levels of pollution than the river did before damming.

Downstream, it is the lack of sediment that threatens riverbanks, which could become more prone to flooding. The economic dynamo of Shanghai, which is built on the river's floodplain, could also become more vulnerable to inundation after being deprived of normal silt deposits.

While disaster has been averted so far, heavy rains have provided a jittery first major test for the dam, which almost filled to capacity. There are also concerns about cracks already appearing in the dam and its seismological impact.

for cooking different ingredients with different cooking times. Unusual but highly recommended ingredients include duck and eel. $ *Average main: Y85 ✉ Zourong Plaza, 69 Linjiang Rd., 2nd fl. ☎ 023/6379–9369 ▭ No credit cards.*

$$$ ✕ **Xiaotian'e Sichuan Restaurant** (重庆小天鹅 *Chóngqìng xiǎotián'é*). **SICHUAN** Some of Chongqing's most authentic Sichuanese dishes are served in this restaurant on the bank of the Yangtze. An after-dinner stroll along the banks of the river is a great cap to the meal. A house specialty is water-boiled fish slices: the "water" actually has liberal amounts of oil, dried chilies, whole Sichuan peppercorns, and other spices that create an explosion of flavor. If you want a seat overlooking the river, try to beat the dinner rush and arrive by 6 pm. $ *Average main: Y100 ✉ 88 Jiabin Rd., 11th fl. ☎ 023/6303–9958 ▭ No credit cards.*

WHERE TO STAY

$$ 🏨 **Hilton Chongqing** (重庆希尔顿酒店 *Chóngqìng xiǎotián'é*). In a leafy, **HOTEL** quiet neighborhood near Lianglukou Stadium, the Hilton Chongqing has plush rooms with the firmest beds in town and fabulous bathrooms. **Pros:** modern design; nice views; helpful staff. **Cons:** not very close to shopping. $ *Rooms from: Y1100 ✉ 139 Zhongshan San Rd. ☎ 023/8903–9999 ⊕ www.hilton.com.cn ⤶ 400 rooms, 35 suites* ¶❍¶ *No meals.*

$$ 🏨 **InterContinental Chongqing** (]重庆洲际大酒店 *Chóngqìng zhōu jí* **HOTEL** *dàjiǔdiàn*). With one of the city's top breakfast buffets and a trio of top-notch restaurants, the InterContinental is a favorite with locals and visitors. **Pros:** convenient downtown location; lots of amenities; plush rooms. **Cons:** upper-level views tend to be obscured. $ *Rooms from: Y1200 ✉ 101 Minzu Rd. ☎ 023/8906–6888 ⊕ www.intercontinental. com ⤶ 308 rooms, 30 suites* ¶❍¶ *No meals.*

$$ 🏨 **JW Marriott** (重庆JW万豪酒店 *JWwǎnhào jiǔdiàn*). Just off the **HOTEL** city's main drag, this gleaming glass tower puts you within walking distance of virtually anywhere near Liberation Monument. **Pros:** great location; elegant rooms; good pool. **Cons:** poor breakfast buffet; some air-conditioning problems. $ *Rooms from: Y1200 ✉ 77 Qing Nian Rd., YuZhong District ☎ 023/6388–8888 ⊕ www.marriotthotels.com ⤶ 428 rooms, 32 suites* ¶❍¶ *No meals.*

$$ 🏨 **Le Méridien Chongqing** (艾美大酒店 *Ǎi méi dàjiǔdiàn*). Successfully **HOTEL** blending French hospitality and Chinese architectural flourishes, the **Fodor's Choice** upscale Le Méridien Chongqing is truly a gem. **Pros:** spacious rooms; ★ great design; stellar service. **Cons:** not in the center of town. $ *Rooms from: Y1200 ✉ 10 Jiang Nan Rd., Nan An District ☎ 023/8638–8888 ⊕ www.lemeridien.com/chongqingnanan ⤶ 288 rooms, 31 suites* ¶❍¶ *No meals.*

$ 🏨 **Radisson Blu** (雷迪森酒店 *Ruīdǐsà jiǔdiàn*). For the price, this is an **HOTEL** excellent option in downtown Chongqing. **Pros:** comfortable rooms; great location. **Cons:** predictable design. $ *Rooms from: Y500 ✉ 22 Nan Bin Rd., Nan An District ☎ 023/8866–8888 ⊕ www.radissonblu. com ⤶ 280 rooms, 28 suites* ¶❍¶ *No meals.*

$ 🏨 **Somerset JieFangbei Chongqing** (重庆盛捷解放碑服务公寓 *Shèngjié* **HOTEL** *jiéfàngbēi*). This sleek hotel's prime location makes it easy to see the best of the city. **Pros:** great location; modern feel; memorable river

9

One of the Victoria cruise ships sailing through the Qutang Gorge

views. **Cons:** often fully booked. $ *Rooms from: Y700* ⊠ *108 Minzu Rd., YuZhong District* ☎ *023/8677–6888* ⊕ *www.somerset.com* ↩ *157 rooms* ⦿| *No meals.*

PERFORMING ARTS

Fodor'sChoice
★
Hong Ya Cave (洪崖洞 *Hóngyá dòng*). This complex overlooks the Jialing River and has a brightly lit waterfall and paved streets built right into the mountainside. The main attraction is the Ba Yu Theater, a rather cheesy performance of Chongqing customs and folklore. The historical aspects of Ba Yu culture have been dumbed down, but the costumes, choreography, and the bit on the Devil Town of Fengdu make it an evening well spent. There are plenty of foot massage places and a sprinkling of Western restaurants, one of the best being Cactus Tex Mex. ⊠ *56 Cangbai Rd., south bank of the Jialing River* ☎ *023/6303–9968.*

SHOPPING

Carrefour (家乐福超市 *Jiālèfú chāoshì*). Near Chaotianmen Port, Carrefour is the largest foreign-owned department store chain in China. The France-based giant sells everything from congee to caviar, plus there's a decent import section with all the goodies from back home. ⊠ *Cangbai Rd.* ☎ *023/6378–8852.*

SIDE TRIP TO DAZU

Fodor'sChoice
★
Baoding Shan (保定山 *Bǎodìngshān*). A UNESCO World Heritage Site, these Buddhist caves rival those at Datong, Dunhuang, and Luoyang. The sculptures, ranging from teeny-tiny to gigantic, contain unusual domestic details, as well as purely religious works. There are two major sites at Dazu—Bei Shan and Baoding Shan. Work at the caves began

in the 9th century during the Song and Tang Dynasties, and continued for more than 250 years.

Baoding Shan is the more impressive of the two sites, where the carvings were completed according to a plan. Here you will find visions of hell reminiscent of similar scenes from medieval Europe; the Wheel of Life; a magnificent 100-foot reclining Buddha; and a gold statue of the 1,000-armed goddess of mercy.

The best way to reach Dazu is to book a tour from Chongqing. Every agency offers the Dazu tour for between Y220 and Y250, which includes transportation, lunch, and admission. You could also go on your own, but you won't save much. Minibuses departing from Chongqing's Liberation Monument cost Y180 to Y230 round-trip. ✉ *Mar.–Dec. Y180, Jan. and Feb. Y130* ⊗ *Daily 8–6.*

WHERE TO STAY

$ 🏨 **Dazu Binguan** (大足兵官 *Dàzú bīngguǎn*). If you find yourself stay-
HOTEL   ing overnight in Dazu, your best bet is this serviceable but unimaginative hotel. **Pros:** prime location. **Cons:** uncomfortable beds. 💲 *Rooms from: Y250* ✉ *350 Longgang Zhong Rd.* ☎ *023/4372–1888* 🛏 *132 rooms* 🍽 *No meals.*

THE THREE GORGES

The third-longest river in the world after the Amazon and the Nile, the Yangtze cuts across 6,380 km (3,956 miles) and seven provinces before flowing out into the East China Sea. After descending from the mountain ranges of Qinghai and Tibet, the Yangtze crosses through Yunnan to Sichuan, winding its way through the lush countryside between Sichuan and Hubei before flowing northward toward Anhui and Jiangsu. Before the 20th century, many lost their lives trying to pass through the fearsome stretch of water running through what is known as the Three Gorges—the complicated system of narrow cliffs between Fengjie, in Sichuan, and Yichang, in Hubei.

The spectacular scenery of the Three Gorges—Qutang, Wu, and Xiling—has survived the rising waters of the newly dammed Yangtze River. A trip through the Three Gorges offers a glimpse of the new China moving full steam ahead. Almost all of the cities and towns in the area are in the middle of a construction and tourism boom. The Yangtze itself has endless streams of passenger and cargo boats moving up and downstream.

While there is no doubt that much of the charm has been diminished by the flooding of the area, the Gorges are still scenic and fascinating. Sitting on deck and taking in the moon and stars on a clear night while heading downstream is a great way to escape the hustle and bustle of Chinese cities.

BOAT TOURS

Riverboat rides essentially come in two forms: luxury and domestic. Domestic cruises are much cheaper and have few amenities. No matter which option you choose, book ahead, as berths are limited.

9

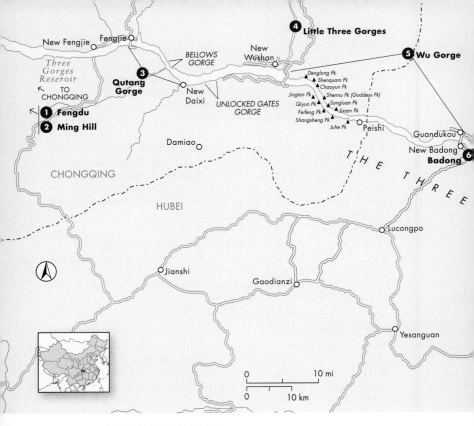

LUXURY CRUISE BOATS

The foreign-owned ships, such as the Victoria Series boats, are big, quadruple-decker liners and by far the most comfortable option. In addition to spacious decks from which to soak up the breathtaking views, many boats are equipped with a gym, a ballroom, a business center with Internet connection, and bars and restaurants. There are also a few shops in case you run out of film or other necessities. The ticket price includes the admission cost for most of the sites along the way, except the Little Three Gorges. A one-way package tour ranges from Y3,793 to Y4,583, and the boats themselves are divided into three-, four-, and five-star service.

DOMESTIC BOATS

These less expensive, less luxurious boats are divided into four classes. Suites offer almost all of the amenities of Luxury Cruise Boats and are available for Y2,084 each way. First class sleeps two people and costs Y1,042 each way. Spartan rooms come with two beds, a private bathroom, TV, and air-conditioning. Second and third classes, costing Y503 and Y347 each way, have bunk beds, shared bathrooms that aren't always kept clean, and limited views. The domestic boats usually serve good Chinese food, depending on the class you choose.

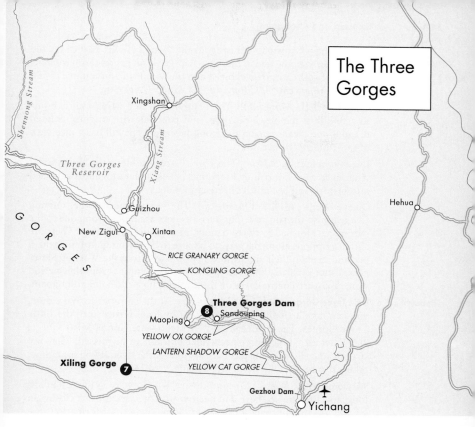

The tour operators have been consolidated into one company called Chongqing Port International Travel Service, and most tours get booked through them. Offices can be found throughout the Chaotianmen District. Prices range from Y476 for the least expensive tour to Y4,600 for the costliest.

Contact Chongqing Port International Travel Service ✉ *18 Xinyi St., Chaotianmen, Yu Zhong District, Chongqing* ☎ *023/6310–0595.*

HYDROFOIL

This option is used by those returning from Yichang to Chongqing, who don't want to do the whole trip over again in reverse. Prices vary, but currently it is Y280 from Yichang to Chongqing and takes about six hours. You have to get off at Wanxian and take a bus back into Chongqing. This costs Y120 and takes another 3½ hours. If you're pressed for time, an airport in Yichang has daily flights to Chongqing and Chengdu, along with less frequent flights to Beijing, Shanghai, and Guangzhou.

SIGHTS EN ROUTE

Fodor'sChoice **Fengdu "Ghost City"** (丰都魔鬼城 *Fēngdū*). Also known as Guicheng or
★ the "city of devils," this city on the banks of the Yangtze is filled with temples, buildings, and statues depicting demons and devils. During the Tang Dynasty, the names of two local princely families, Yin (meaning "hell") and Wang (meaning "king"), were linked through marriage,

making them known as Yinwang, or the "king of hell." Part of the old city has been submerged in the Three Gorges Dam project. You can take a series of staircases or a cable car to the top of the mountain. ⊠ *160 km (100 miles) east of Chongqing* 🚟 *Y80* ⊙ *Daily 6–6.*

Ming Hill (岷山 *Mingshan*). The bamboo-covered Ming Hill is home to a Buddhist temple, a pavilion, and pagodas with brightly painted dragons and swans emanating from the eaves. The hill has a nice view of the Yangtze River.

Three Gorges (三峡 *Sānxiá*). The Three Gorges lie along the fault lines of what once were flourishing kingdoms. Those great kingdoms vanished into history and became, collectively, China.

Qutang Gorge (瞿塘峡 *Qūtángxiá*). The westernmost gorge, Qutang Gorge is also the shortest. The currents here are quite strong due to the natural gate formed by the two mountains, Chijia and Baiyan. There are cliff inscriptions along the way, so be sure to have your guide point them out and explain their significance. Several are from the Warring States period more than 2,000 years ago. Warriors' coffins from that period were discovered in the caves on these mountains, and some still remain.

Fodor's Choice
★
Little Three Gorges (小三峡 *Xiǎo sānxiá*). At the entrance to Wu Gorge, you can take a smaller boat navigated by local boatmen to the Little Three Gorges. These three gorges—Dragon Gate Gorge, Misty Gorge, and Emerald Gorge—are spectacular and not to be missed. They are striking and silent, rising dramatically out of the river. If you have time, take a trip to the Old Town of Dachang. 🚟 *Y240.*

Wu Gorge (巫峡 *Wūxiá*). The impressive Wu Gorge is 33 km (20 miles) long. Its cliffs are so sheer and narrow that they seem to be closing in on you as you approach in the boat. Some of the cliff formations are noted for their resemblances to people and animals. Most notable is the Goddess Peak, a beautiful pillar of white stone.

Badong (巴东 *Bādōng*). At the city of Badong, just outside the eastern end of Wu Gorge, boats leave for Shennongjia on the Shennong River, where you can take in the costumes and traditions of Tujia and Miao ethnic minorities.

Xiling Gorge (西岭峡 *Xīlíngxiá*). About 66 km (41 miles) long, Xiling Gorge is the longest and deepest of all the gorges, with cliffs that rise up to 4,000 feet. It is undoubtedly the most peaceful and contemplative leg of the journey.

Three Gorges Dam (长江三峡大坝 *Chángjiāng sānxiá dàbá*). Xiling Gorge ends at the Three Gorges Dam. Nothing that you've seen or read about this project can possibly prepare you for its massive scale. Sit back in awe as the boat approaches this great dam and then slowly slips down the locks into the lower reaches of the river. 🚟 *Y180.*

THE SILK ROAD

Shaanxi, Gansu, Quinghai, and Xinjiang

WELCOME TO THE SILK ROAD

TOP REASONS TO GO

★ **Terracotta Warriors:** Take in one of the nation's most haunting and memorable sites—the vast life-size army of soldiers, built to outlast death.

★ **Discover Dunhuang:** Satisfy your inner archaeologist at the magnificent Mogao caves and scale the shifting slopes of Singing Sand Mountain.

★ **Seek Solace at Kumbum Monastery:** Visit one of the six great monasteries of the Tibetan Buddhist sect known as Yellow Hat, reputedly the birthplace of the sect's founder, Tsong Khapa.

★ **Tour Turpan:** Discover the ruins of the ancient city-states Jiaohe and Gaochang, destroyed by Genghis Khan and his unstoppable Mongol hordes.

★ **Kashgar and the Karakorum Highway:** Explore Central Asia's largest and liveliest bazaar before heading south to the snowcapped Pamir Mountains and crystal-clear Karakul Lake.

1 Shaanxi. Visit the tomb of China's first emperor and its army of thousands of Terracotta Warriors in Xian. Shaanxi is the starting point of the fabled Silk Road that brought silks and spices from China to Rome more than two millennia ago.

2 Gansu. Arid and mountainous, Gansu has served as a corridor to the West for thousands of years. Heralded sites include the Mogao Grottoes, Singing Sand Mountain, and the remote Labrang Monastery.

GETTING ORIENTED

There was no single "Silk Road," but scores of trading posts that formed an overland trade network that linked China, Central Asia, and Europe. The current "Silk Road" received its moniker from German scholar Baron Ferdinand von Richtofen in the mid-19th century, when the Chinese section of the route stretched to Xian in Shaanxi Province. After passing through the famed Jade Gate, which divided China from the outside world, it webbed out in three directions to several key cities in Xinjiang: Ürümqi in the north, Korla in the center, Hotan in the south, and Kashgar in the west.

3 Qinghai. Away from the industrialized cities, on the vast open plains, seminomadic herders clad in brown robes slashed with fluorescent pink sashes still roam the grasslands.

4 Xinjiang. Chinese in name only, Xinjiang is a land of vast deserts and ancient Silk Road settlements, including legendary Kashgar. The region is populated by Uyghurs, China's largest minority group.

10

Updated by
Christy Choi

The Silk Road spans from far Western China's snowcapped mountains, scorching deserts, and glassy lakes to the thriving metropolis that is Xian. It may not be the bustling trade route it once was, but the area still remains alive and kicking. While the area is one of the most isolated and less-traveled parts of China, it remains one of the most interesting culturally, as a locus where people from Tibet, Kazakhstan, the Han Chinese, and others continue to mix and mingle. There's no shortage of monasteries, mosques, bustling markets, and historical sites to visit, although much of Kashgar's Old City has been and continues to be demolished by Chinese authorities.

The history of the Silk Road starts in 138 BC, when Emperor Wudi of the Han Dynasty sent a caravan of 100 men to the west, attempting to forge a political alliance with the Yuezhi people living beyond the Taklamakan Desert. The mission was a failure, and only two men survived the 13-year return journey, but they brought back with them to Chang'an (present-day Xian) tales of previously unknown kingdoms: Samarkand, Ferghana, Parthia, and even Rome. More important, they told stories about the legendary Ferghana horse, a fast and powerful creature said to be bred in heaven. Believing that this horse would give his armies a military advantage over the Huns, Emperor Wudi sent a number of large convoys to Central Asia in order to establish contact with these newly discovered kingdoms—and to bring back as many horses as possible. These envoys of the Han emperor were the first traders on the Silk Road.

The extension of the Silk Road beyond Central Asia to the Middle East and Europe was due to another ill-advised foreign excursion, this time on the part of the Roman Empire. In 55 BC Marcus Licinius Crassus led an army to the east against Parthia, in present-day Syria. The battle was one of Rome's greatest military defeats, but some of the survivors were able to obtain Chinese silk from the Parthians. Back in Rome, wearing silk became the fashion, and for the first time in history a trade route was established covering the 5,000-mile journey between East and West.

It might seem odd today, but the two empires knew very little about the origins of their precious cargo. The reason for this common ignorance was the complicated supply chain that transported goods over the Silk Road. No one merchant made the entire journey, but wares were instead brought from kingdom to kingdom, switching hands in the teeming bazaars of wealthy oasis cities along the way.

Over time, the Silk Road became less important due to the opening of sea routes, and was dealt a deathblow by the isolationist tendencies of the Chinese Ming Dynasty in the 14th century. Yet today the Silk Road is being resurrected to transport the modern world's most precious commodity: oil. China's rapid development has created an almost insatiable appetite for energy resources. In the last few years, pipelines have been completed from Kazakhstan and Xinjiang to Shanghai.

PLANNING

WHEN TO GO
The best time to visit is from early May to late October, when it's warm and the land is in bloom with grasses and flowers. It's also high tourist season, when many festivals take place.

In spring, wildflowers make a colorful, riotous appearance on the mountain meadows, rolling grasslands, and lush valleys.

Dry, sunny summers provide blue skies and long days, optimal for exploring and photographing the region. Afternoons, however, can be insufferably hot, and most tourists follow the locals' lead in taking a midday siesta. Clear skies last usually through October, while winter brings subfreezing temperatures and a dearth of travelers. Although solitude may have its charms, a few sights close for the off-season. Note that Xian suffers from severe pollution which is at its worst in winter, when coal is burned for fuel.

10

GETTING HERE AND AROUND
Xian, the capital of Shaanxi Province, is also the area's main travel hub. You can board trains and buses to most corners of the region and planes to just about anywhere in the country. To avoid long and back-breaking journeys by bus, it's worth flying at least occasionally, and with tickets often heavily discounted there's not always a huge price difference. The train is also more comfortable than buses and extremely efficient—and with the great scenery, time passes quickly.

AIR TRAVEL
Air China, China Southern, and Hainan Airlines are the main airlines that fly to Xian and Lanzhou from major cities in China. From Ürümqi there are daily flights from Kashgar, Hami, Korla, and Hotan. Tickets are easy to come by, frequently at discounted rates. Daily flights are also available from Hong Kong via Cathay Pacific and Dragonair.

BUS TRAVEL

Spectacular scenery and time for contemplation are the rewards for taking bus journeys. The negatives include long journeys, regular breakdowns, and, often, smoking on board. In Xinjiang, long-distance bus routes crisscross the province, and from Ürümqi there are sleeper buses for the 24-hour journey to Kashgar (flying is often a similar price). In addition, there are handy tourist buses from Ürümqi to Heavenly Lake and from Xian city out to the Terracotta Warriors.

WOMEN'S WEAR

Many places along the Silk Road have large Muslim communities, and it's courteous to dress appropriately when there. Women will feel less conspicuous in Xinjiang if they dress as most locals do and wear long trousers and cover their shoulders. Scarves aren't necessary, but they can be good protection against dust.

CAR TRAVEL

It's simple to hire a car and driver in major tourist destinations such as Xian, Ürümqi, Kashgar, and Turpan; ask your hotel or contact a local travel agency. It's unlikely that your driver will speak English, so agree on your destination beforehand and whether tolls and other sundry costs are included in the price. Expect to pay around Y900 a day for a modern car.

TRAIN TRAVEL

Shaanxi and Gansu provinces are well connected to major cities in the rest of China, with direct trains from Beijing and Shanghai to Xian, Lanzhou, and Dunhuang. Xinjiang and Qinghai are more isolated, though there are trains from all the above cities to Xining and Ürümqi. From Xining and Lanzhou, there's daily service to Lhasa in Tibet. The trip takes around 24 hours, and you must book in advance and secure a Tibet Travel Permit. From Ürümqi there is regular service to Kashgar, Korla, Hotan, Turpan, and Hami, as well as Almaty in Kazakstan.
■TIP→ For all train travel, save yourself the hassle and ask your hotel or travel agency to book your ticket.

HEALTH AND SAFETY

In an emergency, your first stop should be a good hotel. Even if you are not a guest, or if you don't speak Chinese or have a Chinese friend to call on, get a hotel involved to arrange treatment and provide translation. Emergency services operators do not speak English.

TRAVELING IN THE DESERT

Things change quickly from uncomfortable to dangerous in the intense heat of northwest China's expansive deserts. Temperatures in the summer reach 100°F (37.8°C), with some areas—the depression around Turpan in particular—soaring to 122°F (50°C). Many of the sites you'll be visiting are remote and lack even the most basic facilities.

In conditions like these, it's unwise to travel without abundant water, as well as strong sunscreen, sunglasses, hand sanitizer, a good hat, toilet paper, and some heat-resistant snacks (dried fruit and nuts). Buy frozen plastic bottles of water in the morning and they'll stay cool until lunchtime.

MONEY MATTERS

You can use foreign bank cards at some places in all major cities in the region, including Xian, Ürümqi, and Lanzhou. Credit cards are not accepted outside of big hotels. The farther away you get from metropolitan areas, the less likely it is that your card will work in a local ATM. Have a supply of cash to avoid getting stranded. Traveler's checks can be cashed and foreign currency converted at Bank of China branches and major hotels. Tipping is unnecessary in restaurants and hotels: some more expensive hotels will add a service charge, but there is no need to add anything extra.

RESTAURANTS

Restaurants vary from street-side stalls to modern restaurants with air-conditioning and English menus, though don't expect cutting-edge style and ambience in any of the eateries in this part of the country.

The cuisine in Shaanxi revolves around noodles and *jiaozi* (dumplings) rather than rice, and lamb is the meat of choice. A Xian Muslim specialty is *yang rou pao mo*, a spicy lamb soup poured over broken pieces of flat bread. Other popular Muslim street foods are *heletiao* (buckwheat noodles marinated in soy sauce and garlic) and *roujiamo* (pita bread filled with beef or pork and topped with cumin and green peppers).

Gansu and Qinghai don't offer many culinary surprises, but in Xinjiang, where temperatures can reach scorching levels, you'll find a variety of local ices, ice cream, and *durap* (a refreshing mix of yogurt, honey, and crushed ice). ⚠ While delicious, ices might not be as hygienic as you'd like. Traditional Uyghur dishes like *bamian* (lamb and vegetables served over noodles) and *kevap* (spicy lamb kebabs) are ubiquitous, and often washed down with fresh pomegranate juice. Grapes from Turpan and melons from the oasis town of Hami are famous throughout China.

HOTELS

Cities that see a regular influx of tourists, such as Xian and Ürümqi, offer the full spectrum of lodging options. The more remote the area, the fewer the choices, and standards are lower than you might be used to; also, don't expect your credit cards to be accepted. There are almost no boutique options in the region, though in Kashgar there are some dusty hotels that have historic interest, remnants from when the city was a center for trade between the east and west. *Hotel reviews have been shortened. For full information, visit Fodors.com.*

WHAT IT COSTS IN YUAN			
	$	**$$**	**$$$**	**$$$$**
Restaurants	under Y50	Y50–Y99	Y100–Y165	over Y165
Hotels	under Y1,100	Y1,100–Y1,399	Y1,400–Y1,800	over Y1,800

Restaurant prices are the average cost of a main course at dinner or, if dinner is not served, at lunch. Hotel prices are the lowest cost of a standard double room in high season.

10

Travelers should use guidebooks, travel agencies, and online forums like Fodors.com for information. As in the rest of China, official tourist information is hard to come by.

TOURS

CITS. The Xian branch of the state-run travel service gets good reviews, thanks to the friendliness of its young, well-trained staff. Its tours might be more expensive, but they include nicer cars and smaller groups. Tours head to key Silk Road destinations. ⊠ *48 Chang'an Bei Lu, Xian* ☎ *029/8669–2066* ⊕ *www.chinabravo.com* ✉ *Tours from US$70.*

Sino NZ Tourism Group. Run out of Xian Apartment Guesthouse, this tour agency offers walking tours of downtown Xian. Price depends on the size of your group and includes all admissions, English-speaking guide, transportation, and lunch. ⊠ *Hong Cheng Guoji Apartment Complex, Bldg. A, 15 Xihuamen Jie, Xian* ☎ *152–9159–8650 mobile phone (no area code)* ⊕ *www.xianapartmentshq.com* ✉ *From Y300.*

SHAANXI

Shaanxi has more often than not been the axis around which the Chinese universe revolved. It was here more than 6,000 years ago that Neolithic tribes established the earliest permanent settlements in China. In 221 BC the territories of the Middle Kingdom were unified here under the Qin Dynasty (from which the name "China" is derived). Propitiously located at the eastern terminus of the famed Silk Road, Shaanxi later gave birth to one of the ancient world's greatest capitals, Chang'an, a city enriched financially and culturally by the influence of foreign trade.

But nothing lasts forever: as the Silk Road fell into disuse and China isolated itself from the outside world, Shaanxi's fortunes declined. Flood, drought, and political unrest among the province's large Muslim population made Shaanxi a very difficult place to live for most of the past 1,000 years. It's only since the founding of the People's Republic in 1949 that the area has regained some of its former prominence, both as a center of industry and as a famed travel destination.

XIAN

2 hrs by plane or 6 hrs by high-speed train southwest of Beijing; 11 hrs by fast train west of Shanghai.

Many first-time visitors to Xian are seeking the massive terra-cotta army standing guard over the tomb of China's first emperor. Xian was known in ancient times as Chang'an (meaning Long Peace), and was one of the largest and most cultured cities in the world. During the Tang Dynasty—considered by many Chinese to be the nation's cultural pinnacle—the city became an important center for the arts. Not surprisingly, this creative explosion coincided with the height of trade on the Silk Road, bringing Turkish fashions to court and foreigners from as far away as Persia and Rome. Although the caravan drivers of yesteryear

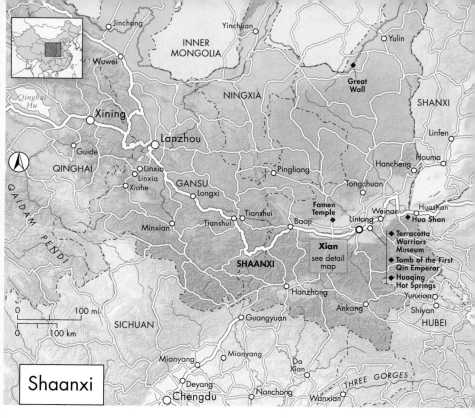

Shaanxi

have long since turned to dust, their memory lives on in the variety of faces seen in Xian.

GETTING HERE AND AROUND

AIR TRAVEL Although Xian's Xianyang Airport is an inconvenient 47 km (29 miles) northwest of the city center in neighboring Xianyang, it has daily flights to and from Beijing, Shanghai, Hong Kong, Guangzhou, Chengdu, Kunming, Dunhuang, and Ürümqi. International destinations include Japan, South Korea, Singapore, and Thailand. If your hotel doesn't arrange transportation, taxis will try to squeeze every last yuan out of your wallet. Taxis run on a meter, but drivers will often try and charge you a flat fare. Outside of rush hour, expect to pay between Y85 and Y130, depending on the type of vehicle and how far into the city you're going; fuel costs are what accounts for some of the price range. Buses are a far more economical option, costing Y27 and running every 30 minutes. There are six routes to choose from, with Route 1 to the Bell Tower and 2 to the train station the most useful—make sure you have the name of your destination in Chinese.

Air Contact Xian Xianyang International Airport ☎ 029/8879–8450.

BUS TRAVEL Just about every bus in Xian passes through the traffic circle around the Bell Tower. So long as you have your destinations written out in Chinese and you know what number bus to take and where to get off, riding the bus in Xian is not difficult, and is far less expensive than taking taxis.

The long-distance bus station on Jiefang Lu, across the street and just west of the train station, has buses to Lanzhou, Xining, and other destinations throughout Shaanxi and Henan. Tourist destinations like the Terracotta Warriors Museum are served from the parking lot between the train station and the Jiefang Hotel.

Bus Contact Xian Bus Station (西安汽车站 *Xī'ān qìchē zhàn*). ✉ 354 *Jiefang Lu* ☎ 029/8742–7420.

CAR TRAVEL Because so many of the sights lie outside the city proper, hiring a taxi or a car and driver gives you the freedom to depart when you like instead of waiting for the rest of the tour. Prices start at about Y800 per day, but vary widely based on the type of vehicle and whether you need an English-speaking guide. Every major hotel can arrange car services. Note that during rush hour finding a taxi may be near impossible. If you're desperate, do what the locals do and hail an already occupied cab. If you're going in the same direction, they'll take you. Expect to pay the amount on the meter minus the amount on the meter when you boarded. Some drivers may charge the full amount.

TRAIN TRAVEL The train station lies on the same rail line as Lanzhou. Those arriving in Xian by train disembark north of the old city walls. The train station is close to most hotels; a taxi should cost less than Y12. The foreigners' ticket window, on the second floor above the main ticket office, is open daily 8:30 to 11:30 and 2:30 to 5:30. It sometimes closes without explanation. For a small booking fee, hotels and travel agencies can get tickets. It's easy enough to get tickets yourself by checking the schedule online and then going to the ticket window armed with the name of your destination in Chinese and what time you want to go. Be prepared to pay in cash.

Train Contacts Xian Railway Station (西安火车站 *Xī'ān huǒchē zhàn*). ✉ 151 *Huancheng Bei Lu* ☎ 029/12306 ⊕ www.12306.cn.

SAFETY AND PRECAUTIONS
All normal precautions here apply, especially when it comes to pickpocket prevention at tourist destinations.

TREASURES OF SHAANXI

Shaanxi gave birth to 13 major Chinese dynasties, including the Zhou, Qin, Han, and Tang states. The Tang is considered China's Golden Age. Consider first hitting the Shaanxi History Museum. Once you've steeped yourself in its chronology, local "must-see" destinations like Xian's Drum Towers, Muslim Quarter, and Great Goose Pagodas will make much more sense. So, too, will the awe-inspiring army of Terracotta Warriors at the tomb of China's first emperor. True fans of history can even make the trip to China's own Valley of the Kings near Xianyang.

TIMING

If you're in a rush, you can in two days see the main city and take a day trip to the Warriors. However, Xian is one of China's more appealing cities, and a few days' stay will reveal the unique ambience of the city's Muslim quarter and great food.

TOURS

Most hotels offer their own guided tours of the area, usually dividing them into eastern area, western area, and city tours. Most tour operators have English-language tour guides.

Be sure to check more than one company to confirm that you're being charged the going rate. Bargaining may get you a much better deal. One of the best places to comparison shop is on the second floor of the Bell Tower Hotel, where several tour companies vie for your business. Try Golden Bridge first, but there are other good options.

EASTERN TOUR By far the most popular option from Xian, tours that head east of the city usually visit the Tomb of the First Qin Emperor, the Terracotta Warriors Museum, and the Huaqing Hot Springs, all in the town of Lintong. Many tours also stop at the Banpo Matriarchal Clan Village in eastern Xian. The China International Travel Service (CITS) offers this tour for around Y550, which includes all admission tickets and an English-speaking guide. The journey takes most of the day; plan on leaving after breakfast and returning in time for dinner. Bring your own snacks and drinks.

If you don't want a guide, you're better off taking Bus 306 (travel Bus No. 5), which leaves constantly from the parking lot between the Xian train station and the Jiefang Hotel. The 60-minute journey costs Y8; you can buy tickets on the bus. The Terracotta Warriors are the last stop. To travel between any of the sites in Lintong, a taxi should cost between Y10 and Y15 (although some drivers ask foreigners for Y20). To get back to Xian, simply wait along the road for a bus headed to the city.

WESTERN TOUR Less popular than the eastern tour, this excursion varies wildly from operator to operator. Find out what you're getting for the money. Amateur archaeologists and would-be tomb raiders will hardly be able to tear themselves away from the sites in what's been called China's own Valley of the Kings; others will appreciate some of the relics, but may tire of what appear to be mounds of dirt or holes in the ground. There is no English-language signage.

Of the 18 imperial tombs on the plains west of Xian, a list of the best should include the Qianling Mausoleum, resting place of Tang Dynasty Empress Wu Zetian, China's only female sovereign. A number of her relatives—many sentenced to death by her own decree—are entombed in the surrounding area. The tomb of Prince Yi De contains some beautifully restored frescoes. Other stops on the western tour might include the Xianyang City Museum in Xianyang and the Famen Temple in Famen. Sino NZ Tourism Group offers a customizable western tour. For an individual traveler, expect to pay around Y1,000 for a one-day tour, inclusive of car, guide, and admissions fees. The larger the group,

10

The Bell Tower in Xian

the lower the price per person. Plan on spending the whole day visiting these sites.

ESSENTIALS

Bank Bank of China (汇丰银行 *Huìfēng yínháng*). ⊠ *107 Dong Dajie* ☎ *029/8741-5624* ⊕ *www.hsbc.com.cn* ✉ *157 Jiefang Lu* ☎ *029/8742-5916* ⊕ *www.hsbc.com.cn* ✉ *21 Xianning Xi Lu* ☎ *029/8249-2382.*

Internet Hai An Xian Internet Bar (海岸西安网吧 *Hǎi'àn Xī'ān wǎngba*). ⊠ *232 Jiefang Lu* ☎ *029/8741-0555* 🖰 *Y4 per hr* ⊙ *Daily 8 am–midnight.*

Medical Assistance Ambulance ☎ *120.* **Police** ☎ *110.* **Shaanxi Provincial People's Hospital** (陕西省人民医院 *Shǎnxī shěng rénmín yīyuàn*). ⊠ *256 Youyi Xi Lu* ☎ *029/8525-1331.*

Visitor and Tour Info Golden Bridge Travel ⊠ *Bldg. 3, Anding Guangchang, off Xi Da Jie, 5th fl., Rooms A503 and A505* ☎ *029/8763-9810* ⊕ *www. trip51168.com.*

EXPLORING

TOP ATTRACTIONS

Bell Tower (钟楼 *Zhōnglóu*). Xian's most recognizable structure, the Bell Tower was built in the late 14th century in what was then the center of the city. It's still good a reference point—the tower marks the point where Xi Dajie (West Main Street) becomes Dong Dajie (East Main Street) and Bei Dajie (North Main Street) becomes Nan Dajie (South Main Street). To reach the tower, which stands isolated in the middle of a traffic circle, use any of eight entrances to the underground passageway. Once inside the building, you'll see Ming Dynasty bells on display. Concerts are given six times daily (9:10, 10:30, 11:30, 2:30, 3:30, and 4:30). For Y5 you can make your own music by ringing a copy of the large iron bell that gives the tower its name. Don't miss the panoramic views of the city from the third-floor balcony. ✉ *Junction of Dong Dajie, Xi Dajie, Bei Dajie, and Nan Dajie* ⊕ *www.xazgl.com/ ewzjj.asp* ☎ *Y35; Y50 includes admission to Drum Tower; Y17 for students with valid ID* ☉ *Daily 8:30–6.*

Big Wild Goose Pagoda (大雁塔 *Dàyàn tǎ*). This impressively tall pagoda lies 4 km (2½ miles) southeast of South Gate, on the grounds of the still-active Temple of Thanksgiving (Da Ci'en Si). The pagoda was constructed adjacent to the Tang palace in the 7th century to house scriptures brought back from India by a monk Xuan Zang. It's been rebuilt numerous times since then, most recently during the Qing Dynasty, in Ming style. A park and huge plaza surround the temple, and locals gather here after work to fly kites, stroll hand in hand, and practice calligraphy. There is a popular water-fountain show synchronized to music at noon and 9 pm. The main entrance gate to the temple is on the plaza's southern edge. ✉ *Yanta Lu* ☎ *029/8552–7958* ☎ *Y50; additional Y40 to climb the pagoda* ☉ *Daily 9–5.*

Drum Tower (鼓楼 *Gǔlóu*). Originally built in 1384, this 111-foot-high Ming Dynasty building—which used to hold the alarm drums for the imperial city—marks the southern end of Xian's Muslim Quarter. Various ancient drums are on display inside the building, and concerts are given daily at 9:10, 10:30, 11:30, 2:30, 3:30, and 4:30. After passing through the tower's massive base, turn left down a small side street called Huajue Xiang to find everything from shadow puppets to Mao memorabilia—truly a souvenir heaven. After clearing that gauntlet, you'll find yourself deep inside the Muslim Quarter at the entrance to the Great Mosque. ✉ *Beiyuanmen, 1 block west of the Bell Tower* ☎ *Y35; Y50 includes admission to Bell Tower* ☉ *Apr.–Oct., daily 8:30 am–9:30 pm; Nov.–Mar., daily 8:30–6.*

Fodor's Choice
★

Forest of Stone Tablets Museum (碑林博物馆 *Bēilín bówùguǎn*). Head here for a glimpse into what the ancient Chinese deemed important enough to set in stone. As the name suggests, there is no shortage of historical stone tablets, with content ranging from descriptions of administrative projects and old maps to artistic renditions of landscape, portraiture, and calligraphy. The garden complex and former Confucian temple house one of the world's first dictionaries and a number of Tang Dynasty classics as well as the epitaphs of nobility. One tablet, known as the Nestorian Stela, dates from AD 781 and records the interaction between the Chinese emperor and a traveling Nestorian priest. After presenting the empire with translated Nestorian Christian texts, the priest was allowed to open a church in Xian. Non-Chinese speakers may feel frustrated that they can't read all the tablets, as only a few translations are available, but the complex is well worth the visit for history, anthropology, and culture buffs. ✉ *15 Sanxue Jie at the end of Wenhua Jie* ☎ *029/8721–0764* ⊕ *www.beilin-museum.com* ☎ *Mar.–Nov. Y75, Dec.–Feb. Y50* ☉ *Mar.–Nov., daily 8–6:45; Dec.–Feb., daily 8:15–5:15.*

10

Great Mosque (西安大清真寺 *Xī'ān dà Qīngzhēnsì*). This lushly land-scaped mosque with four graceful courtyards may have been established as early as AD 742, during the Tang Dynasty, but the remaining buildings date mostly from the 18th century. Amazingly, it was left standing during the Cultural Revolution. Stone tablets mark the various pavilions, often bearing inscriptions in both Chinese and Arabic. Look above the doors and gates: there are some remarkable designs, including three-dimensional Arabic script that makes the stone look as malleable as cake frosting. Non-Muslims are not allowed in the prayer hall, as the mosque is still an active place of worship. At times local Muslim couples dressed to the nines in brightly colored traditional garb come to take wedding pictures. The place is a bit hard to find, but wandering the **Muslim Quarter** surrounding the mosque is a treat, particularly for foodies. The bustling streets are the center of the city's Hui (Chinese Muslim) community. Navigate narrow streets and alleys filled with endless knickknack and food stalls. Spicy mutton kebabs and chicken wings grilling on coal spits, piles of walnuts, chili powder, dates and other dried foods, and vendors squeezing out pomegranate juice are staples along the way. Step into any well-populated restaurant and try anything from cold sesame noodles to panfried dumplings to *yang rou pao mo*, the local specialty of crumbled bread in a rich lamb broth. To get to the mosque, after passing through the Drum Tower, follow a small curving market street called Huajue Xiang on the left. (You'll see an English sign posted on a brick wall next to the street's entrance reading "Great Mosque.") When you reach a small intersection, the mosque's entrance is on the left. ✉ *30 Huajue Xiang* 🚊 *Y25* ⊙ *May–Sept., daily 8–7; Oct.–Apr., daily 8–5.*

Fodor's Choice
★
Shaanxi History Museum (陕西历史博物馆 *Shǎnxī lìshǐ bówùguǎn*). Although museums in China are often underwhelming, this is a notable exception. The works in this imposing two-story structure, built in 1991, range from crude Paleolithic stone tools to gorgeously sculpted ceramics from the Tang Dynasty. Get close to several Terracotta Warriors taken from the tombs outside town on display. The exhibits, which have English descriptions, leave no doubt that China once had the world's most advanced culture. The museum is free; a limited number of tickets are handed out in the morning and the afternoon. Arrive early, and bring your ID. To avoid crowds, start at the top floor and work your way down. English audio guides are available, and some local companies provide excellent guides who can tell you backstories about the artifacts and the people and places they belonged to. ✉ *91 Xiaozhai Dong Lu* ☎ *029/8525–4727* ⊕ *www.sxhm.com* 🚊 *Free (excluding unless for special exhibitions)* ⊙ *Tues.–Sun.: Mar. 16–Nov. 14, 8:30–6; Nov. 15–Mar. 15, 9–5:30.*

South Gate and City Walls (南门 (永宁门) *Nánmén (yǒngníng mén)*). Also known as Yongning Gate, this is the most impressive of the 13 gates leading through Xian's 39-foot-high city walls. This was the original site of Tang Dynasty fortifications; the walls you see today were built at the beginning of the Ming Dynasty, and they include the country's only remaining example of a complete wall dating to this dynasty. Head up to top to watch the sunset, or even a bike ride around the city fortifications. Biking the entire 13.7-km (8.5-mile) route atop the walls takes about 90 minutes. Rental bikes are Y45 for 100 minutes, and you must put down a Y200 deposit. Open-air electric cars cost Y80. ⊠ *Nan Dajie near Yongningmen metro station* ☎ *Y54* ⊘ *Apr.–Oct., daily 8 am–10 pm; Nov.–Mar., daily 8–8.*

WORTH NOTING

Banpo Matriarchal Clan Village (半坡博物馆 *Bànpō bówùguǎn*). About 5 km (3 miles) east of the city are the remains of a 6,000-year-old Yang-shao village, including living quarters, a pottery-making center, and a graveyard. The residents of this matriarchal community of 200 to 300 people survived mainly by fishing, hunting, and gathering, although there is ample evidence of attempts at animal domestication and orga-nized agriculture. The small museum contains stone farming and hunt-ing implements, domestic objects, and pottery inscribed with ancient Chinese characters. The archaeological site has captions in English. Unless you're interested in documenting one of China's great tourist oddities, avoid the awful model village that sits in a state of semi-disrepair toward the rear of the property. ⊠ *155 Banpo Lu, off Chang-dong Lu* ☎ *029/8351–2807* ⊕ *www.bpmuseum.com* ☎ *Mar.–Nov. Y65, Dec.–Feb. Y45* ⊘ *Daily: Mar.–Nov., 8–5:30; Dec.–Feb., 8–4.*

Culture Street (Shuyuanmen) (文化街 (书院门) *Wénhuà jiē (Shūyuàn mén)*). Take a stroll along this leafy boulevard lined with galleries, shops, and few cafés. Mostly clear of the city's traffic save for a hand-ful of tuk-tuks or "beng beng che" as the locals call them, the cobbled streets run along the southern end of the old city walls and feature beautifully restored buildings with traditional Ming architecture. Start near Heping Lu and walk towards the South Gate and you'll pass by the Forest of the Stone Tablets Museum. Not too far after, you'll find the Guanzhong Academy, built in 1609. Take a peek through the gates, as entrance is forbidden. ⊠ *1 block north of South Gate.*

Fodor's Choice
★

Small Goose Pagoda (小雁塔 *Xiǎoyàn tǎ*). Once part of the 7th-century Jianfu Temple, this 13-tier pagoda was built by Empress Wu Zetian in 707 to honor her predecessor, Emperor Gao Zong. Much less impos-ing than the Big Goose Pagoda, the smaller pagoda housed Buddhist texts brought back from India by the pilgrim Yiqing in the 8th century. A tremendous earthquake in 1555 lopped off the top two stories of what was originally a 15-story structure; climbing to the top lets you examine the damage. The Xian Museum (free admission, ID required) is part of the same complex, and shows how the ancient capital changed over the centuries. On the grounds is also giant bell visitors can ring for good luck—for a price. The whole park offers good people-watching opportunities, and is very peaceful compared to other Xian attractions, making it a good place to take a break. ⊠ *72 Youyi Xi Lu, west of Nan-guan Zhengjie* ☎ *029/8523–8032* ⊕ *www.xabwy.com* ☎ *Y30 to climb the pagoda* ⊘ *Daily 9–5.*

AROUND XIAN

Famen Temple (法门寺 *Fǎmén sì*). Originally built in the 3rd century AD, the temple was the site of an amazing find during renovations in 1981. A sacred crypt housing four of Sakyamani Buddha's finger

10

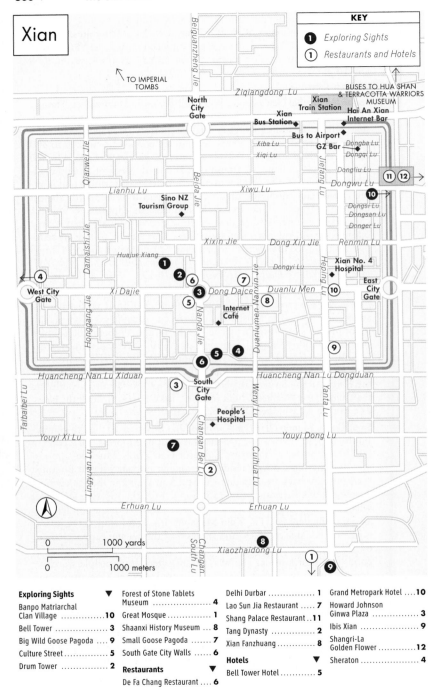

Xian

KEY

- **1** *Exploring Sights*
- (1) *Restaurants and Hotels*

TO IMPERIAL TOMBS

BUSES TO HUA SHAN & TERRACOTTA WARRIORS MUSEUM

Beiguanzheng Jie

Ziqiangdong Lu

North City Gate

Xian Train Station

Xian Bus Station

Hai An Xian Internet Bar

Bus to Airport

Qianwei Jie

Xiba Lu

GZ Bar

Dongba Lu

Xiqi Lu

Dongqi Lu

Lianhu Lu

Beida Jie

Jielang Lu

Dongliu Lu

Dongwu Lu

11 **12**

Sino NZ Tourism Group

Xiwu Lu

10

Dongsi Lu

Dongsan Lu

Donger Lu

Damaishi Jie

Xixin Jie

Dong Xin Jie

Renmin Lu

Huajue Xiang

1

2 **6**

7

Dongyi Lu

Xian No. 4 Hospital

East City Gate

West City Gate

4

Xi Dajie

3

Dong Dajie

Duanlu Men

8

Heping Lu

10

Honggang Jie

5

Internet Café

Nanda Jie

Duanlumen Nanjie

5 **4**

9

Huancheng Nan Lu Xiduan

6

Huancheng Nan Lu Dongduan

3

South City Gate

Taibaibei Lu

Wenyi Lu

Yanta Lu

People's Hospital

Youyi Xi Lu

7

Lingyuan Lu

Changan Bei Lu

2

Cuihua Lu

Youyi Dong Lu

Erhuan Lu

Erhuan Lu

0   1000 yards

0   1000 meters

Changan South Lu

Xiaozhaidong Lu

8

(1)

9

bones was discovered to hold more than 25,000 coins and 1,000 sacrificial objects of jade, gold, and silver. Many of these objects are now on display in the on-site museum. The temple is in Famen, 125 km (80 miles) west of Xian. ☒ *Famen* ☎ *0917/525–4002* ⊕ *www.famensi. com* ☒ *Y120* ☉ *Daily: Mar.–Oct., 8–5:30; Nov.–Feb., 8:30–5.*

Huaqing Hot Springs (华清池 *Huáqīng chí*). A pleasure palace

during the Tang Dynasty and later the living quarters of General Chiang Kai-shek during the Chinese Civil War, this destination gets mixed reviews from visitors. Despite the name, the hot springs are often out of action, leaving visitors to wander around the garden. You'll probably be happier spending your time on **Lishan,** the small mountain directly behind Huaqing Hot Springs. It was on these slopes that Chiang was captured, and it has China's first beacon tower and a number of small temples. It was also thought to be the spot where the Emperor Xuanzong and his consort Yang Guifei came for their romantic escapes. If you are here in the evening (8:30 pm), catch the light-and-sound show that uses the mountain as a backdrop. The attraction is 30 km (19 miles) east of Xian. ☒ *38 Huaqing Lu, Lintong* ☎ *029/8381–2003* ⊕ *www.hqc.cn* ☒ *Dec.–Feb. Y80, Mar.–Nov. Y110* ☉ *Dec.–Feb., daily 7:30–6:30; Mar.–Nov., daily 7–6.*

Fodor's Choice
★

Huashan (华山 *Huáshān*). A few hours east of Xian lies one of China's five sacred mountains, a traditional watercolor come to life. The 7,218-foot mountain has stunning scenery, Taoist temples, pines reminiscent of a Dr. Seuss creation, and sheer granite walls that rise shockingly out of the surrounding plains. The five peaks of Huashan reminded ancient visitors of flower petals, hence the name; translated it means "Flower Mountain." Climbing the mountain is not a trip for the fainthearted: unless you're an Olympic athlete, hiking the main trail to the highest South Peak will take a good seven to nine hours, some of it along narrow passes on sheer cliffs. Thankfully, there are cable-car rides to North and West Peak that bring you most of the way up the trail. Don't worry about looking like a wimp; there's plenty of climbing left to do from the cable-car terminal. While once the place was for hermits, as mountain paths have been improved and access made easier the lower peaks can get crowded. Thrill-seekers can walk the plank path, a narrow wooden ledge built around a cliff side thousands of meters above ground level, dubbed the most dangerous trail in the world.

From Xian you can take a D train (Y45) or G train (Y62) to Huashan North Station, situated 5 km (3 miles) from the park entrance; frequent minibuses (Y10) link the two. A better choice might be one of the coaches that leave hourly every morning from the parking lot in front of the Jiefang Hotel, across from the train station. You may or may not be asked to provide your passport information when you buy a ticket.

10

Continued on page 609

THE
TERRACOTTA
WARRIORS

In 1974, Shaanxi farmers digging a well accidentally unearthed one of the greatest archaeological finds of the 20th century— the Terracotta Warriors of Chinese Emperor Qin Shihuang. Armed with real weapons and accompanied by horses and chariots, the more than 8,000 soldiers buried in Qin's tomb were to be his garrison in the afterlife.

(top) Statues depict different military units. (right) Note how the faces differ. Each one is sculpted to be unique.

DID YOU KNOW?

The thousands of life-size soldiers include charioteers, cavalrymen, archers, and infantrymen. They're all arranged according to rank and duty—exactly as they would have been for a real-life battle. Each one has individual facial features, including different mustaches, beards, and hairstyles.

UNCOVERING AN ARMY

WHO WAS QIN SHIHUANG?

After destroying the last of his rivals in 221 BC, Qin Shihuang became the first emperor to rule over a unified China. He established a centralized government headquartered near modern day Xianyang in Shaanxi Province. Unlike the feudal governments of the past under which regional officials developed local bases of power, the new centralized government concentrated all power in the hands of a godlike emperor.

Unfortunately for Qin Shihuang's potential heirs, the emperor's inexhaustible hunger for huge engineering projects created high levels of public unrest. These projects, including a precursor to the Great Wall, his own massive tomb, and numerous roads and canals, required the forced labor of millions of Chinese citizens. In 210 BC, Qin died from mercury poisoning during a failed attempt at making himself immortal. Only four years later, his son was overthrown and killed, bringing an ignominious end to China's first dynasty.

A THANKLESS JOB

The construction of Qin Shihuang's gargantuan tomb complex—which includes the Terracotta Warriors—was completed by more than 700,000 workers over a period of nearly 40 years. The warriors themselves are believed to have been created in an assembly line process in which sets of legs and torsos were fired separately and later combined with individually sculpted heads. Most workers were unskilled laborers; skilled craftsmen completed more delicate work such as the decoration of the tomb and the molding of heads. The soldiers were then painted with colored lacquer to make them both more durable and realistic. It's believed that all of the workers were buried alive inside the tomb (which hasn't yet been excavated) to keep its location and treasures a secret and protect it from grave robbers.

DISCOVERING THE WARRIORS

Only five years after the death of Qin Shihuang, looting soldiers set fire to the thick wooden beams supporting the vaults. As wood burned and the structure became unsound, beams and earthen walls came crashing down onto the statues, crushing many soldiers and burying all. In many ways, though, the damage to the vaults was a blessing in disguise. The buried Terracotta Warriors were forgotten to history, but the lack of oxygen and sunlight preserved the figures for centuries.

Since its rediscovery, only a part of the massive complex has been excavated, and the process of unearthing more warriors and relics continues. No one is sure just how many warriors there are or how far the figures extend beyond the already excavated 700-foot-by-200-foot section. For the time being, most excavation work has stopped while scientists attempt to develop a method of preserving the figures' colored lacquer, which quickly deteriorates when exposed to oxygen.

(top) Warriors were once painted in bright colors.

IN FOCUS THE TERRACOTTA WARRIORS

10

VISITING THE WARRIORS

Be sure to walk around to the rear of Vault 1, which contains most of the figures that have already been unearthed. There you can see archaeologists reassembling the smashed sodiers. Vaults 2 and 3 contain unreconstructed warriors and their weapons and give you an idea of how much work went into presenting Vault 1 as we see it today.

CIRCLE VISION THEATER

Before heading to the vaults, stop by this 360-degree movie theater and learn how the army was constructed, destroyed, forgotten, and then rediscovered. Although the film is cheesy, it's nonetheless entertaining and informative. It gives a sense of what the area may have been like 2,200 years ago.

VAULT 1

Here you'll find about 6,000 warriors, although only 1,000 have been painstakingly pieced together by archaeologists. The warriors stand in their original pits and can only be seen from the walkways erected around the digs. Those in the front ranks are well shaped and fully outfitted except for their weapons, whose wooden handles have decayed over the centuries (the chrome-plated bronze blades were still sharp upon excavation). Walk around to the rear of the vault where you can see terracotta warriors in various states of reconstruction.

Archaeologists have puzzled together almost 1,000 statues, including warriors, chariots, horses, officials, acrobats, strongmen, and musicians. The tallest statues are also the highest in rank; they are the generals.

COLORATION

The colored lacquers that were used not only gave the terracotta soldiers a realistic appearance, but also sealed and protected the clay. Unfortunately, upon exposure to oxygen, these thin layers of color become extremely brittle and flake off or crumble to dust. Chinese scientists are devising excavation methods that will preserve the coloration of warriors unearthed in the future.

Ready on one knee with bow in hand, these archers are poised to rise and fire a deadly salvo at a moment's notice.

Every cavalry rider is accompanied by a life-size terracotta horse.

VISITING THE WARRIORS

(top) Statues were made in pieces and then assembled. (right) The statue of an officer. (opposite page) The cavalry horses.

VAULT 2

This vault offers a glimpse of unreconstructed figures as they emerge from the ground. It has remained mostly undisturbed since 1999 when archaeologists found the first tricolor figures—look closely and you can still see pink on the soldiers' faces and patches of dark red on their armor. As with ancient Greek sculptures, the warriors were originally painted in lifelike colors and with red armor. Around the sides of the vault, you can take a close-up look at excellent examples of soldiers and their weaponry in glass cases.

VAULT 3

Sixty-eight soldiers and officers in various states of reconstruction stand in what appears to be a military headquarters. Although the condition of the warriors are similar to those in Vault 2, there is one unique figure: a charioteer standing at the ready, though his wooden chariot has been lost to time.

EXHIBITION HALL

Near Vault 3, an imposing sand-colored pavilion houses two miniature bronze chariots unearthed in the western section of Qin Shihuang's tomb. Found in 1980, these chariots are intricately detailed with ornate gold and silver ornamentation. In the atrium leading to the bronze chariots, look for a massive bronze urn—it's one of the treasures unearthed by archaeologists in their 1999 excavation of an accessory pit near the still-sealed mausoleum. Other artifacts on display including Qin Dynasty tricolor pottery and Qin jade carvings.

HOW TO VISIT THE WARRIORS

GETTING THERE
Practically every hotel and tour company in Xian arranges bus trips to the Terracotta Warriors as part of an Eastern Tour package. If you aren't interested in having an English-speaking guide for the day, you can save a lot of money by taking one of the cheap buses (Y8 one-way) that leave for the town of Lintong from the parking lot between Xian's train station and the Jiefang Hotel. The ride to the Terracotta Warriors Museum should take less than two hours. ☉ *Mar.–Nov., daily 8:30–5:30; Dec.–Feb., daily 8:30–5* 🎫 *Mar.–Nov. Y150, Dec.–Feb. Y120. Price includes movie, access to 3 vaults, and entrance to the Exhibition Hall* ☎ *029/8139–9001 (main office), 029/8139–9126 (ticket office).*

VISITING TIPS
Cameras: You can shoot photographs and videos inside the vaults, a change from previous years when guards brusquely confiscated film upon seeing your camera. You still can't use a flash or tripod, however.

Souvenirs: You can buy postcards and other souvenirs in the shops outside the vaults and the Circle Vision Theater. Alternatively, you can face the fearsome gauntlet of souvenir hawkers outside the main gates; miniature replica Terracotta Warriors can be found here for as little as Y1 each. If you're intimidated by the aggressive touts, however, there's nothing available here that you can't get back in Xian. So be strong, don't look them in the eyes, and most important, never stop walking.

Time: You'll likely end up spending two to three hours touring the vaults and exhibits at the Terracotta Warriors Museum. The time spent here will probably be part of a long day-tour visiting a number of sites—the Hauqing Hot Springs and possibly the Banpo Matriachal Clan Village—clustered around the small city of Lintong, east of Xian.

Tours can be arranged for around Y400, but it might be better to head over on your own so you don't waste time waiting around, and have more time on the mountain. ■TIP➡ **On a rainy day, bring a raincoat or buy one there, don't bring an umbrella. Gusts of wind can come out of nowhere, and you could be yanked off balance while hiking the narrow trails. The danger is so real that locals go far as to call them death umbrellas.** 🎫 *Mar.–Nov. Y180, Dec.–Feb. Y100* ☉ *Mar.–Nov., daily 7–7; Dec.–Feb., daily 9–5.*

Fodor's Choice ★ **Terracotta Warriors Museum** (兵马俑博物馆 *Bīngmǎyǒng bówùguǎn*). Discovered in 1974 by farmers digging a well, this UNESCO World Heritage Site includes more than 7,000 Terracotta Warriors standing guard over the tomb of Qin Shihuang, the first emperor of a unified China. The warriors, more than 1,000 of which have been painstakingly pieced together, come in various forms: archers, infantry, charioteers, and cavalry. Relics are still being unearthed, and some are being left underground until archaeologists find a way to preserve the painted surface, which as of now disintegrates when it comes to contact with outside air. In 2010, 114 extra warriors were discovered in Pit One. Incredibly, each of the life-size statues is unique, including different

CLOSE UP

Raiders of the Lost Tomb

Qin started construction on his enormous, richly endowed tomb, said to be boobytrapped with automatic crossbows, almost as soon as he took the throne. According to ancient records, this underground palace contained 100 rivers of flowing mercury as well as ceilings inlaid with precious stones and pearls representing the stars and planets. Interestingly enough, mercury levels in the area's soil are much higher than normal, indicating that there may be truth to those records. Though the site of the tomb was rediscovered to the east of Xian in 1974 (soon after the Terracotta Warriors were unearthed), the government didn't touch it because it lacked

the sophisticated machinery needed to excavate safely. Authorities also executed any locals foolish enough to attempt a treasure-seeking foray. In 1999, archaeologists finally began excavations of the area around the tomb and unearthed some fabulous treasures. They've only scratched the surface, however. Most of the tomb still lies buried. In fact, no one is even certain where its main entrance—reportedly sealed with molten copper—is located. Authorities have delayed further excavations until the tomb can be properly preserved rather than risk damaging what may be China's greatest archaeological site.

mustaches, beards, hairstyles, and even wrinkles. An exhibition hall displays artifacts unearthed from distant sections of the tomb, including two magnificently crafted miniature bronze chariots. Allow yourself at least three hours if you want to study the warriors in detail. The site is 30 km (19 miles) east of Xian in the town of Lintong. ⊠ *Lintong* ☎ *029/8139–9001* ⊕ *www.bmy.com.cn* ✉ *Mar.–Nov. Y150, Dec.–Feb. Y120* ⏰ *Mar.–Nov., daily 8:30–5:30; Dec.–Feb., daily 8:30–5.*

Tomb of the First Qin Emperor (秦始皇陵 *Qínshǐhuáng líng*). The tomb—consisting mainly of a large burial mound—may pale compared to the Terracotta Warriors Museum, but history buffs will enjoy it. According to ancient records, the underground palace took more than 40 years to build, and many historians believe the tomb contains a wealth of priceless treasures, though perhaps we will never know for sure. You can climb to the top of the burial mound for a view of the surrounding countryside, although most visitors hurry off to see the Terracotta Warriors Museum after watching a mildly amusing ceremony honoring the emperor who united China. The tomb is in Lintong, 30 km (19 miles) east of Xian, by the Terracotta Warriors Museum. ⊠ *Lintong* ✉ *Nov–Mar. Y150, Apr.–Oct. Y120; includes admission to the Terracotta Warriors Museum* ⏰ *Apr.–Oct., daily 7–7; Nov.–Mar., daily 8–6.*

WHERE TO EAT

$$
CHINESE
FAMILY

✕ **De Fa Chang Restaurant** (德发长饺子馆 *Défāchǎng jiǎozi guǎn*). If you think dumplings are just an occasional snack food, think again. De Fa Chang, one of Xian's most famous restaurants, is known for its dumpling banquet. Do try the panfried *guotie*, stuffed with pork and chives, and the *suan tang shuijiao*, dumplings in spicy and sour soup. For the dumpling banquet, head upstairs and choose between the preset menus.

The buffet is not open in the afternoon between lunch and dinner, but considerably cheaper à la carte dishes can be found downstairs. Order at the counter or just grab a plate as a cart passes by your table and be ready to pay on the spot. The restaurant can be a bit tricky to find; walk along the front of the building facing Xi Dajie, past the shops selling trinkets and antiques to the end of the row. $ *Average main: Y60* ⊠ *3 Xi Dajie, north side of Bell Tower Sq.* ☎ *029/8721–4060* ⊟ *No credit cards.*

$$
INDIAN

✕ **Delhi Darbar** (新德里餐厅 *Xīndélǐ cāntīng*). For a break from Chinese food, try this place, which is run by Indian expats. The fluffy naan bread is a must-order alongside the warm, fragrant curries. Although the service needs some polishing, the staff are good at handling requests for vegetarian dishes, of which there are also enough on the menu to ensure everyone leaves satisfied. $ *Average main: Y80* ⊠ *3 Yanta Xi Lu, near Big Wild Goose Pagoda* ☎ *029/8525–5157* ⊟ *No credit cards.*

$
**NORTHERN
CHINESE**

✕ **Lao Sun Jia Restaurant** (孙老家饭庄 *Lǎosūnjiā fàn zhuāng*). This traditional, family-run affair has been serving some of the best local Islamic lamb and beef specialties since 1898; it's become so popular that it's grown into a small Xian chain. The decor isn't special, but the food is popular with Xian's large Muslim community. A few famous offerings, such as the roasted leg of lamb or the spicy mutton spareribs, are pricey, but most dishes are inexpensive. Try *yang rou pao mo*—the servers will bring you flatbread which you tear up into small pieces and place into a bowl, which they then take and cook in lamb broth. Ask for an English menu. $ *Average main: Y30* ⊠ *364 Dong Dajie, near the corner of Duanlu Men* ☎ *029/8742–1858* ⊟ *No credit cards.*

$$$
CANTONESE

✕ **Shang Palace Restaurant** (香宫 *Xiāng gōng*). All of Xian's top hotels have elegant eateries, but Shang Palace deserves special mention for its Cantonese and Sichuan dishes, which are authentic and approachable. On the menu, classics like honey-barbecued pork and stir-fried chili chicken sit alongside less familiar dishes; note that drinks are pricey. Try the thick spicy noodles, a delicious local specialty. The hotel employs a noodle master. On some evenings as you dine, musicians pluck away in traditional costumes. Most of the staff speaks some English. $ *Average main: Y150* ⊠ *Shangri-La Golden Flower Hotel, 8 Changle Xi Lu* ☎ *029/8323–2981, 029/8322–1199.*

$$$$
CHINESE
Fodor'sChoice
★

✕ **Tang Dynasty** (西安唐乐宫 *Xī'ān tánglègōng*). Don't confuse the cuisine served in the Tang Dynasty's popular dinner theater with the specialties available at the separate restaurant. While the former serves mediocre fare, the latter specializes in Tang Dynasty–imperial cuisine—a taste you're not likely to find back home at your local Chinese restaurant. Locals praise the abalone and other fresh fish dishes as the finest in Xian. You can reserve either for dinner and the show (Y500) or just the show (Y220), which starts every night at 8:30 pm. $ *Average main: Y180* ⊠ *75 Changan Bei Lu* ☎ *029/8782–2222* ⊕ *www. xiantangdynasty.com.*

$$
CHINESE

✕ **Xian Fanzhuang** (西安饭庄 *Xī'ān fànzhuāng*). This restaurant at the Xian Hotel specializes in Shaanxi snacks with a Muslim flavor, as well as "small eats"—street food spruced up for the visitor. Business executives and T-shirt-clad college students alike head to the bustling

10

first-floor dining room for the all-you-can-eat buffet, a bargain at Y25. An adjacent entrance leads to a second-floor restaurant, where more exotic and expensive dishes—algae flavored with orchid, for example—are prepared. An English menu is available, but don't expect high-quality service. $ *Average main: Y60* ⊠ *Xian Hotel, 298 Dong Dajie* ☎ *029/8727–3185* ▭ *No credit cards.*

WHERE TO STAY

$ ▧ **Bell Tower Hotel** (钟楼饭店 *Zhōnglóu fàndiàn*). Directly across from
HOTEL   the Bell Tower, this centrally located hotel puts you within walking distance of many tourist sights. **Pros:** excellent location; clean rooms. **Cons:** absence of character; rooms dated and showing wear; hotel restaurants are mediocre; lacks facilities. $ *Rooms from: Y798* ⊠ *110 Nan Da Jie* ☎ *029/8760–0000* ⊕ *www.belltowerhotelxian.cn* ↴ *300 rooms, 11 suites* ⋔ *Breakfast.*

$ ▧ **Grand Metropark Hotel Xian** (阿房宫维景国际大酒店 *Āfáng gōng*
HOTEL   *wéi jǐng guójì dàjiǔdiàn*). Although there are newer luxury properties, people return to the Grand Metropark because of its friendly staff, most of whom speak some English, and its central location. **Pros:** walking distance to the city's sights; ample breakfast spread. **Cons:** breakfast overpriced if not included in room rate; music in the atrium lobby can be annoying when you're trying to fall asleep. $ *Rooms from: Y599* ⊠ *158 Dong Dajie* ☎ *029/8723–1234* ⊕ *www.metroparkhotels.com* ↴ *315 rooms, 22 suites* ⋔ *No meals.*

$ ▧ **Howard Johnson Ginwa Plaza** (金花豪生国际大酒店 *Jīnhuā háoshēng*
HOTEL   *guójì dàjiǔdiàn*). Though dated, this HoJo offers good value for money in a hotel that sits just outside the city walls near the south gate and the Yongningmen metro station. **Pros:** convenient to city wall; breakfast buffet has plenty of Western options. **Cons:** nothing individual about this place; language barriers with staff; no Wi-Fi in rooms. $ *Rooms from: Y708* ⊠ *18 Huancheng Nan Lu (Xi Duan)* ☎ *029/8818–1111* ⊕ *www.ginwaplaza.com* ↴ *198 rooms* ⋔ *No meals.*

$ ▧ **Ibis Xian** (西安宜必思酒店 *Xī'ān yíbìsī jiǔdiàn*). The best bargain in
HOTEL   Xian's Old City is part of the French budget hotel chain Ibis. **Pros:** great location; friendly service. **Cons:** unappealing breakfast; roadside rooms can be a bit noisy at night. $ *Rooms from: Y220* ⊠ *59 Heping Lu* ☎ *029/8727–5555* ⊕ *www.accorhotels.com* ↴ *220 rooms* ⋔ *Breakfast.*

$ ▧ **Shangri-La Golden Flower** (西安金花大酒店 *Xī'ān jīn huā dàjiǔdiàn*).
HOTEL   The older of the two Shangri-La's in Xian, this remains one of the city's
Fodor'sChoice   most luxurious hotels. **Pros:** spacious rooms; excellent room service.
★   **Cons:** layout is confusing, rooms beginning to show age. ■ **TIP→** Make sure your cab driver knows you're going to the Golden Flower Hotel, and not the Shangri-La, or else you many find yourself at the newer Shangri-La all the way across town to the east. $ *Rooms from: Y660* ⊠ *8 Changle Xi Lu* ☎ *029/8323–2981, 800/8942–5050 in U.S.* ⊕ *www.shangri-la.com* ↴ *368 rooms, 13 suites, 34 apartments* ⋔ *No meals.*

$ ▧ **Sheraton Xian Hotel** (喜来登西安大酒店 *Xǐláidēng Xī'ān dàjiǔdiàn*).
HOTEL   This is a joint venture with high-quality standards, among them truly comfortably beds and front-desk staff who speak English well. **Pros:** glitzy and well-fitted bathrooms; excellent buffet breakfast. **Cons:** located in an uninteresting commercial part of town. $ *Rooms from:*

Y988 ⊠ *262 Fenghao Dong Lu* ☎ *029/8426–1888* ⊕ *www.starwood hotels.com* ⌐ *365 rooms, 61 suites* ⦸ *No meals.*

NIGHTLIFE AND PERFORMING ARTS

One of the busiest parts of town in the evening, the Muslim Quarter is where crowds converge to shop, stroll, and eat virtually every night of the week. Street-side chefs fire up the stoves and whip up tasty dishes, vendors ply the crowded lanes peddling their wares, and locals and tourists alike jostle in the frenetic pace.

GZ Groovz Jazz Club (GZ爵士酒吧 *GZ juéshì jiŭbā*). The only jazz bar in Xian, GZ Groovz is worth seeking out for its nightly live music and cheap beers. ⊠ *Dong Qi Dao Xiang, near He Ping Gate* ☎ *133/5920–7823.*

Tang Dynasty (唐代 *Táng dài*). In a city where the list of nightlife options isn't terribly long, the song and dance performance at Tang Dynasty makes for a fun if slightly cheesy evening. Dinner starts at 7 pm, shows begin at 8:30 pm, and for the meal you have a choice between the dumpling banquet (Y400) and the Tang Dynasty Dinner (Y500). You may be able to get a better deal through travel agencies that often have offices in hotel lobbies. If you're already familiar with Chinese song and dance, give this a miss. ⊠ *75 Chang'an Bei Lu* ☎ *029/8782–2222* ⊕ *www.xiantangdynasty.com.*

SHOPPING

Predictably, Xian is overloaded with terra-cotta souvenirs. There is more to buy than terra-cotta souvenirs, however. The shops are filled with carved jade, calligraphy, and Shaanxi folk paintings.

Huajue Xiang Market (化觉巷市场 *Huàjué xiàng shìchăng*). In the alley leading to the Great Mosque, the Hua Jue Xiang Market is one of the best places to find souvenirs. From embroidered bags and trinkets to lamps and musical wooden frogs, all kinds of wares are available for sale. Expect the antique you're eyeing to be fake, no matter how vehemently the vendor insists that your find is "genuine Ming Dynasty." ⊠ *Huajue Xiang right by the Great Mosque, Lian Hu district.*

10

GANSU

Gansu is the long, narrow province linking central China with the desert regions of the northwest. For centuries, as goods were transported through the region, Gansu acted as a conduit between China and the Western world. As merchants made their fortunes from silk and other luxuries, the oasis towns strung along the Silk Road became important trade outposts of the Middle Kingdom. But beyond the massive fortress at Jiayuguan lay the end of the Great Wall, the oasis of Dunhuang, and then perdition. Gansu was the edge of China.

What has long been the poorest province in China is essentially dry, rugged, and barren. The decline of the Silk Road brought terrible suffering and poverty, from which the area has only recently begun to recover as tourism boosts the local economy. Over the last few years, protests at Labrang Monastery have led to travel restrictions. The area around

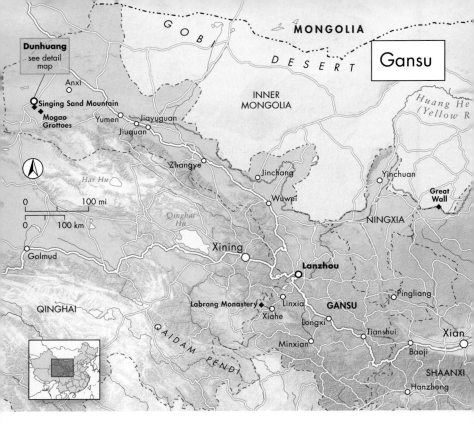

Xiahe was closed off to foreign tourists in late 2012, but at the time of writing it is open again to foreigners. Check with your travel agent for up-to-date information.

REGIONAL TOURS

John's Information Cafè. There aren't a lot of choices when it comes to tours in Gansu, but this café owned by the affable John Hu offers tours to Dunhuang and the Mogao Caves led by English-speaking guides. Prices depend on the number of people traveling and some tours exclude admissions. The company can also arrange tours of Lanzhou. ✉ *21 Mingshan Lu, Dunhuang* ☎ *0998/258–1186* ⊕ *www.johncafe. net* ✉ *From Y200.*

LANZHOU

8 hrs by train northwest of Xian; 21 hrs by train southeast of Ürümqi; 2½ hrs by train east of Xining; 18 hours by train from Beijing.

Built on the banks of the Yellow River, the capital of Gansu extends along the base of a narrow gorge whose walls rise to 5,000 feet. A city with a long history, Lanzhou has been nearly ruined by rampant industrialization, and is now one of the world's most polluted urban areas. Though air quality is getting better, in winter the city can be filled with smog.

The ethnic mix of the city's population makes the place interesting for a few hours, but plan to stay here only as long as it takes to arrange transportation to somewhere more pleasant, like Xiahe or Dunhuang.

GETTING HERE AND AROUND

AIR TRAVEL The city's Zhongchuan Airport is 67 km (42 miles) north of town. From Lanzhou there are daily flights to Dunhuang, Beijing, Guangzhou, Shanghai, Chengdu, Ürümqi, and Xian. A public bus costing Y30 per person takes over an hour to reach the airport from the China Northwest Airlines office at 512 Donggang Xi Lu.

Air Contacts Lanzhou Zhongchuan Airport (兰州中川机场 *Lánzhōu zhōngchuān jīchǎng*). ☎ 0931/816-8464 ⊕ www.lzzcairport.com.

BUS TRAVEL Long-distance buses arrive at the East Station (汽车东站 *Qìchē dōng zhàn*) on Pingliang Lu, north of the train station. Leaving the city can be a bit more complicated. Buses to major destinations like Xian, Xining, Jiayuguan, and Dunhuang usually leave from the East Station, while smaller destinations are served by the West Station (汽车西站 *Qìchē xī zhàn*). Buses to Xiahe depart from the South Station (汽车南站 *Qìchē nán zhàn*).

Buses originating in Lanzhou often require foreigners to show proof of travel insurance bought from the Chinese company PICC (The People's Insurance Company of China—a monstrously large insurance company) before purchasing tickets. It's unclear why this regulation exists, or why there's usually at least one daily bus to each destination that doesn't require the paperwork. You should be able to purchase insurance with your bus ticket, but this is often not the case. For peace of mind, head straight to the main PICC office on the north side of Qingyang Lu, just east of Jingning Lu. They'll know why you're there. A two-week policy costs Y40. At this writing, you were required to show two photocopies of your visa and passport details.

Bus Contacts Lanzhou East Bus Station (兰州汽车东站 *Lánzhōu qìchē dōng zhàn*). ✉ 129 Pingliang Lu, 1 block from the train station ☎ 0931/841-8411. **Lanzhou South Bus Station** (兰州汽车南站 *Lánzhōu qìchē nán zhàn*). ✉ 34 Langongping Lu, Qi Li He ☎ 0931/291-4066. **Lanzhou West Bus Station** (兰州汽车西站 *Lánzhōu qìchē xi zhàn*). ✉ 456 Xijin Dong Lu ☎ 0931/291-9537.

TRAIN TRAVEL The train station (兰州火车站 *Lánzhōu huǒchē zhàn*) is at the southern end of Tianshui Lu, 1 km (½ mile) south of the city's main hotels. With few trains originating here, buying sleeper tickets in Lanzhou can be difficult; your best bet is to buy tickets early, or hope for an upgrade once onboard.

Train Contact Lanzhou Train Station (兰州火车站 *Lánzhōu huǒchē zhàn*). ✉ 373 Huochezhan Dong Lu where Pingliang Lu and Tianshui Nan Lu meet ☎ 0931/12306 ⊕ www.12306.cn.

10

SAFETY AND PRECAUTIONS

Heavy rains in the past few years have led to mudslides that caused 1,500 deaths. It pays to check with a tour company before venturing out to isolated locations or in adverse weather regions. There can also be friction between ethnic Tibetans and Han Chinese in some areas.

TIMING

Lanzhou's appeal is limited; stay only as long as you need to arrange transportation to the province's other worthier attractions.

TOURS

Gansu Western Travel Service offers a day trip to Thousand Buddha Temple and Grottoes that includes all transportation and insurance for Y1,300 for a one-person tour. The larger the group, the lower the price per person. The company also has tours to Xiahe, including a five-day trip that visits the spectacularly beautiful Tibetan temples at Langmusi on the border with Sichuan. A basic two-day tour from Lanzhou costs between Y600 and Y850 per person, including hotel.

ESSENTIALS

Bank Bank of China (中国银行 *Zhōngguó yínháng*). ✉ *525 Tianshui Nan Lu* ☎ *0931/841–0884.*

Visitor and Tour Info Gansu Western Travel Service ✉ *Lanzhou Hotel, 486 Donggang Xi Lu* ☎ *0931/841–6321, 138–9331–8956 mobile phone, no area code.*

EXPLORING

Five Springs Mountain Park (五泉山公园 *Wǔ quánshān gōngyuán*). Sip tea among ancient temples and take in impressive views of the city from this pretty park. The five springs that gave the place its name, unfortunately, have dwindled to a trickle. ✉ *103 Wuquan Dong Lu* ☎ *0931/824–3247* ☉ *Daily 6 am–7 pm.*

Fodor'sChoice
★
Gansu Provincial Museum (甘肃省博物馆 *Gānsù shěng bówùguǎn*). The most famous item in this excellent museum's collection is the elegant bronze "Flying Horse," considered a masterpiece of ancient Chinese art. Other notable objects include a silver plate documenting contact between China and Rome more than 2,200 years ago, and wooden tablets used to send messages along the Silk Road. Not all exhibits have information in English. Admission is free but you'll need your passport. ✉ *3 Xijin Xi Lu, near the train station* ☎ *0931/233–9131* ⊕ *www.gansumuseum.com* 🖃 *Free* ☉ *Tues.–Sun. 9–5.*

White Pagoda Mountain Park (白塔山公园 *Báitǎshān gōngyuán*). Laid out in 1958, the park covers the slopes on the Yellow River's north bank. It's more of a carnival than a place to relax, but it's a great place for people-watching. ✉ *Enter at Zhongshan Qiao, the bridge extending over the Yellow River* ☎ *0931/836–0800* 🖃 *Y8* ☉ *Daily 6 am–7:30 pm.*

WHERE TO EAT

Many of the best restaurants in Lanzhou are found in its upscale hotels; one to try is Zhong Hua Yuan in the Lanzhou Hotel, where an English menu is available. Another place to find a good meal is along Nongmin Xiang Lu, a street that runs behind the Lanzhou Hotel. This is a great

The Great Prayer Festival at the Labrang Monastery

place to try *roujiamo*, a small sandwich filled with onion, chili, and flash-fried lamb, pork, or beef.

$ ✕ **Chuanwei Wang** (川味王 *Chuānwèi wáng*). You can often tell a good
SICHUAN restaurant by the lack of empty tables; at mealtimes, this Sichuanese eatery is always packed. There's no English menu, but pictures of almost every dish make ordering simple. If you're stuck, order *gongbao jiding* (a.k.a. authentic kung pao chicken), a slightly spicy dish of chicken stir-fried with peanuts. **$** *Average main: Y40* ⊠ *16 Nongmin Xiang* ☎ *0931/887–9879* 🚫 *No credit cards.*

$ ✕ **Ma Zilu Beef Noodles** (马子禄牛肉面 *Mǎzilù niúròumiàn*). This lively
CHINESE canteen opens at the crack of dawn and has some of the most fragrant, toothsome beef noodles in Lanzhou. There are a few other options as well; eye other people's tables to see what's good. The downstairs is set up like a cafeteria, where you can take what you want and grab a seat. Upstairs is a dining room with air-conditioning and table service. **$** *Average main: Y15* ⊠ *86 Da Zhong Xiang* ☎ *931/845–0505* ⊕ *www. mzlnrm.com* 🕙 *Closed after 2 pm.*

$$ ✕ **Xinhai Restaurant** (鑫海大酒店 *Xīnhǎi dàjiǔdiàn*). Xinhai is surpris-
CHINESE ingly affordable and offers Cantonese and Sichuan dishes in addition to Lanzhou specialties such as braised beef and hand-pulled noodles. There's a picture menu in Chinese only and one without pictures in English. **$** *Average main: Y80* ⊠ *69 Jinchang Bei Lu* ☎ *0931/886–1678* 🚫 *No credit cards.*

10

WHERE TO STAY

$$ HOTEL 🏨 **Crowne Plaza Lanzhou** (皇冠假日酒店 *Huángguàn jiàrì jiǔdiàn*). Located close to the Gansu International Convention and Exhibition Center, this modern hotel is a little removed from the city center but offers solid service and good views of the neighboring Yellow River. **Pros:** attentive staff; good breakfast buffet. **Cons:** difficult to get a taxi back to the hotel; staff don't speak much English; small gym. [$] *Rooms from: Y1250* ✉ *1 Beibinhe Dong Lu* ☎ *0931/871–1111* 🌐 *www.ihg.com* 🛏 *440 rooms* 🍴 *Breakfast.*

$ HOTEL 🏨 **Jinjiang Sun Hotel** (锦江阳光酒店 *Jǐnjiāng yángguāng jiǔdiàn*). From the marble floors in the lobby to the plush furnishings, this 25-story tower houses one of Lanzhou's top hotels. **Pros:** excellent value; reception staff speak English. **Cons:** expensive Internet; business-center facilities are sparse; in a commercial part of town. [$] *Rooms from: Y490* ✉ *589 Donggang Xi Lu* ☎ *0931/880–5511* 🌐 *www.jinjianghotels.com* 🛏 *236 rooms* 🍴 *No meals.*

$ HOTEL 🏨 **Lanzhou Hotel** (兰州饭店 *Lánzhōu fàndiàn*). Built in 1956, this concrete behemoth's Sino-Stalinist exterior hides a modern if drab interior. **Pros:** a local landmark that's easy to find. **Cons:** even the no-smoking rooms smell smoky. [$] *Rooms from: Y588* ✉ *486 Donggang Xi Lu at the corner of Tianshui Zhong Lu* ☎ *0931/841–6321* 🌐 *www.lanzhouhotel.com* 🛏 *467 rooms, 1 suites* 🍴 *No meals.*

SIDE TRIPS FROM LANZHOU

Fodor's Choice ★ **Labrang Monastery** (拉卜楞寺 *Lābǔléng sì*). In the remote town of Xiahe, the monastery is a little piece of Tibet along the Gansu-Qinghai border. A world away from Lanzhou, Xiahe has experienced a dizzying rise in the number of travelers over the past decade. Even Tibetan monks clad in traditional fuchsia robes now surf the Internet, play basketball, and listen to pop music. Despite the encroaching modernity, Xiahe is still a wonderful place, attracting large numbers of pilgrims who come to study and to spin the 1,147 prayer wheels of the monastery daily, swathed in their distinctive costume of heavy woolen robes tied with brightly colored sashes.

The Labrang Monastery is the largest Tibetan lamasery outside Tibet. Founded in 1710, it once had as many as 4,000 monks, a number much depleted due in large part to the Cultural Revolution, when monks were forced to return home and temples were destroyed. Though the monastery reopened in 1980, the government's continued policy of restricted enrollment has kept the number of monks down to about 1,500. There are guided tours daily at 10:15 am and 3:15 pm.

There are two ways to reach Xiahe: by public bus or by private tour. Buses for Xiahe leave from Lanzhou's South Station (汽车南站 *Qìchē nán zhàn*) in the morning (6:30 and 7:30) and afternoon (2 and 3) and take about four hours. Make sure to purchase tickets in advance, as some departures require travel insurance. Have two photocopies of your visa and passport information on hand in case they are required.

■ TIP→ **As of this writing, the monastery is open to tourists. However, it has been closed in the recent past due to political uprisings, so as you plan your trip, keep tabs on the news.** ✉ *2 km (1 mile) west of* long-distance bus station, Xiahe ⌂ *Y40* ☉ *Daily sunrise–sunset.*

Fodor's Choice
★ **Thousand Buddha Temple and Grottoes** (炳灵寺 *Bīnglíng sì*). One of the best day trips is the Thousand Buddha Temple and Grottoes, about 80 km (50 miles) from Lanzhou. More commonly known by its Chinese name *Bingling Si*, it's filled with Buddhist paintings and statuary, including an impressive 89-foot-tall Buddha carved into a cliff face.

The canyon that holds the Thousand Buddha Temple runs along one side of the Yellow River. The journey through a gorge lined by water-sculpted rocks is spectacular. When the canyon is dry you can

travel 2½ km (1½ miles) on foot or by four-wheel-drive vehicle to see the small community of Tibetan lamas at the Upper Temple of Bingling. However, it's much easier to book a tour. Gansu Western Travel Service offers a popular day trip that includes all transportation, insurance, and entrance fee (Y1,300 for a one-person tour; Y340 if you join a group tour of 14 people). ⌂ *Y50* ☉ *July–Nov., daily 8–5.*

DUNHUANG

17 hrs by bus or 14 hrs by train northwest of Lanzhou; 6 hrs by bus west of Jiayuguan.

A small oasis town, Dunhuang was for many centuries the most important Buddhist destination on the Silk Road. Just outside of town, beyond the towering dunes of Singing Sand Mountain, you can see the extraordinary caves of the Mogao Grottoes, considered the world's richest repository of Buddhist art.

Buddhism entered China via the Silk Road, and as Dunhuang was the point of entry to the Chinese world, it was not long before a temple was established here. By AD 366, the first caves were being carved and painted at the Mogao oasis. Work continued until the 10th century, after which they were left undisturbed for nearly 1,000 years.

Adventurers from Europe, North America, and other parts of Asia began plundering the caves at the end of the 19th century, yet most of the statuary and paintings remain. By far the most astounding find was a "library cave" filled with more than 45,000 forgotten sutras and official documents. The contents were mostly sold to Sir Aurel Stein in 1907, and when translated they revealed the extent to which Dunhuang was an ancient melting pot of cultures and religions.

10

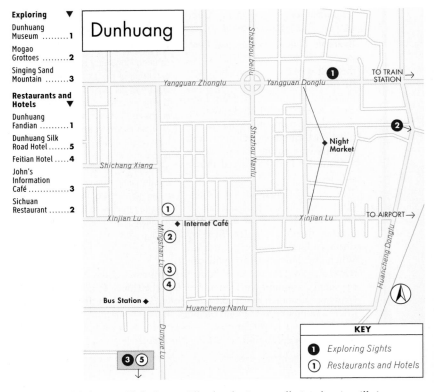

Dunhuang

Shazhou beilu

Yangguan Zhonglu   Yangguan Donglu   **TO TRAIN STATION**

1

Shazhou Nanlu

2

♦ **Night Market**

Shichang Xiang

Internet Café ♦   Xinjian Lu   **TO AIRPORT →**

Xinjian Lu

Mingshan Lu

Huancheng Donglu

1

2

3

4

Bus Station ♦

Huancheng Nanlu

Dunyue Lu

3 **5**

KEY

1 *Exploring Sights*

1 *Restaurants and Hotels*

Today you'll find a rapidly developing small city that is still, in some ways, a melting pot; tourists from across the globe converge upon Dunhuang to visit one of the most impressive sites in all of China.

GETTING HERE AND AROUND

The best way to get around tiny Dunhuang is by bicycle, and you can easily hire one from rental places around town.

AIR TRAVEL   The easiest way to reach Dunhuang is by air, with regular flights from Beijing, Xian, Lanzhou, and Ürümqi. Dunhuang's airport is 13 km (8 miles) east of town, on the road to the Mogao Grottoes. A taxi ride from the airport costs Y20 to Y30.

Air Contact Dunhuang Airport (敦煌机场 *Dūnhuáng jīchǎng*). ⊠ *13 km (8 miles) east of Dunhuang, near the Mogao Crottoes* ☎ *0937/886–6133.*

BUS TRAVEL   Buses from Lanzhou, Turpan, and Jiayuguan depart frequently for Dunhuang.

Bus Contact Dunhuang Bus Station (敦煌汽车站 *Dūnhuáng qìchē zhàn*). ⊠ *24 Mingshan Lu* ☎ *0937/882–2174.*

TRAIN TRAVEL   Dunhuang's train station is 13 km (8 miles) northeast of the town and serves Lanzhou, Xian, and Jiayuguan. A better-connected station, with services to Beijing and Shanghai, is in the small town of Liuyuan, 120 km (74 miles) away. Taxis from Liuyuan to Dunhuang cost Y120, or you can hop aboard one of the buses that leave hourly for Y15 from the main bus station.

Train Contacts Liuyuan Train Station (柳园火车站 *Liǔyuán huǒchē zhàn*). ✉ *215 Guo Dao, Jiuquan* ☎ *0902/713-0222.* **Dunhuang Train Station** (敦煌火车站 *Dūnhuáng huǒchē zhàn*). ✉ *314 Sheng Dao* ☎ *0937/12306* ⊕ *www.12306.cn.*

SAFETY AND PRECAUTIONS

Dunhuang is an expensive place to visit, as admission costs quickly add up. Taxi drivers often charge extortionate prices to take you out into the desert; never take their

opening offer! Likewise, don't get into a taxi if you've been arguing with the driver, or you may wind up stranded in the desert.

TIMING

Aim to spend at least two days in Dunhuang: one day to see the Mogao Caves and Singing Sand Mountain, and the other to spend time in the town itself.

TOURS

If you only have time for one trip out of town, head to the Mogao Grottoes (Y20 for the round-trip bus fare). Don't bother with a tour to Singing Sand Mountain, as it's easy enough to reach on your own by taxi. If you're able to spend an extra day in town, take a tour of sites relating to ancient Dunhuang.

ESSENTIALS

Bank Bank of China (中国银行 *Zhōngguó yínháng*). ✉ *310 Yangguan Zhong Lu* ☎ *0937/882-2684.*

Visitor and Tour Info CITS ✉ *857 Mingshan Bei Lu* ☎ *0937/595-5316, 138/0937-2266 mobile phone (no area code)* ⊕ *www.cits.net.*

EXPLORING

Dunhuang Museum (敦煌博物馆 *Dūnhuáng bówùguǎn*). The museum, which got shiny new digs in late 2013, displays objects recovered from nearby Silk Road fortifications such as reclining Buddhas, sumptuous wall paintings, and sculptures. If you've visited the Jade Gate or Yang-guan Pass, you may enjoy seeing what's been found. ✉ *1390 Mingshan Bei Lu* ✉ *Free* ⊙ *Daily 8 am–1 pm and 2 pm–6 pm.*

Fodor's Choice
★

Mogao Grottoes (莫高窟 *Mògāo kū*). The magnificent Buddhist grottoes lie southeast of Dunhuang. At least 40 of the 700 caves—dating from the Northern Wei Dynasty in the 4th century AD to the Five Dynasties in the 10th century AD—are open to the public. Which caves are open on a given day depends on the whim of local authorities, but you shouldn't worry too much about missing something. Everything here is stunning. You'll almost certainly visit the giant seated Buddhas in caves 96 and 130, the Tang Dynasty sleeping Buddha in cave 148, and the famous

10

"library" in caves 16 and 17, where 45,000 religious and political documents were uncovered at the turn of the 20th century. A flashlight is a useful item for your visit. Note that photographs are not allowed.

This is one site where you should hire an English-speaking guide. At a cost of Y20, your understanding of the different imagery used in each cave will increase immeasurably. Tours in English take place about three times a day in high season, so you may have to wait to join one. Be sure to verify that the tour is of the same two-hour duration and covers the same number of caves

A TOP ATTRACTION

China is promoting the Mogao Caves as one of the country's top attractions. The number of visitors jumped from 26,000 in 1979 to 680,000 in 2011. To protect the precious relics, the Dunhuang Academy built a new state-of-the-art visitor center to enhance understanding of the historic site. The avant-garde building opened to the public in October 2014. Only 6,000 visitors per day are allowed into the caves.

(8–10) as the Chinese tours. After the tour, you'll have time to wander around and revisit any unlocked caves. A fine museum contains reproductions of eight caves not usually visited on the public tour. A smaller museum near the Library Cave details the removal of artifacts by foreign plunderers. If you have a deep interest in the cave art, you may be able to pay extra to visit other caves that are sealed off to the general public. Ask at the ticket office.

To get here, take a taxi (Y60–Y80 round-trip) or take the half-hour bus ride that departs from Xinjian Lu, near the corner with Minshan Lu. The bus runs from 8:30 am to 7 pm, and tickets cost Y8 each way. The CITS branch at the Feitan Hotel offers a daily bus service, leaving Dunhuang at 8 am and returning at noon. A round-trip costs Y20. ✉ *25 km (17 miles) southeast of Dunhuang* ☎ *0937/882–5000* ✉ *May–Oct. Y180 with guided tour, Nov–Apr. Y100 with guide* ⊙ *Daily 8:30–6 (tickets sold until 3:30 pm).*

Singing Sand Mountain (鸣沙山 *Míngshāshān*). South of Dunhuang, the oasis gives way to desert. Here you'll find a gorgeous sweep of sand dunes, named for the light rattling sound that the sand makes when wind blows across the surface. At 5,600 feet above sea level, the half-hour climb to the summit is difficult but worth it for the views, particularly at sunset. Nestled in the sand is **Crescent Moon Lake** (月牙泉 *Yuèyá quán*), a lovely pool that by some freak of the prevailing winds never silts up. Camels, sleds, and various flying contraptions are available at steep prices; try your bargaining skills. ✉ *Mingshan Lu, 5 km (3 miles) south of town* ✉ *Y120* ⊙ *Daily 8–5.*

WHERE TO EAT

Dunhuang's night market is a 10-minute walk from the most popular hotels. Located between Xinjian Lu and Yangguan Dong Lu, it's worth a visit for cold beer and flavorful lamb kebabs. Small restaurants are clustered together on Mingshan Lu in the center of town.

$$
AMERICAN
✕ **John's Information Café.** Cool off after a full day of sightseeing on this trellised patio with an ice-cold beer and plate of noodles. Another

The dramatic landscape of Qinghai

option is to come early in the day for a Western-style breakfast and a cup of joe. The restaurant can arrange overnight camel rides for Y700 per person, as well as trips to Yadan National Park and other destinations. [$] *Average main: Y60* ✉ *21 Mingshan Lu, north of the Feitian Hotel* ☎ *0998/258–1186* 🌐 *www.johncafe.net* 💳 *No credit cards.*

$ SICHUAN 🍴 **Sichuan Restaurant** (四川餐厅 *Sìchuān cāntīng*). Delicious Sichuanese classics like chicken with peanuts, sweet-and-sour pork, and spicy fried potato strips are available here at very cheap prices. There's an English menu, but prices are much higher than on the Chinese menu. [$] *Average main: Y20* ✉ *21 Mingshan Lu* 💳 *No credit cards.*

10

WHERE TO STAY

$ HOTEL 🏨 **Dunhuang Fandian** (敦煌饭店 *Dūnhuáng fàndiàn*). If you're looking for something mildly luxurious, this lodging in the center of town will fit the bill. **Pros:** central location; excellent value. **Cons:** some noise from a local nightclub if you're on a low floor; Chinese breakfast options only; no elevator. [$] *Rooms from: Y200* ✉ *16 Mingshan Lu, Xiyu Rd.* ☎ *0937/885–2999* 🛏 *98 rooms* 🍽 *No meals.*

$ HOTEL Fodor's Choice ★ 🏨 **Dunhuang Silk Road Hotel** (敦煌山庄 *Dūnhuáng shānzhuāng*). This cross between a Chinese fortress and an alpine lodge is the most interesting place to stay in Dunhuang, and possibly in the whole of the province. **Pros:** rooftop terrace; good hotel food. **Cons:** touts approach guests all the time. [$] *Rooms from: Y960* ✉ *Dunyue Lu near Wenchang Nan Lu* ☎ *0937/888–2088* 🌐 *www.dunhuangshanzhuang.com* 🛏 *255 rooms, 20 suites* 🍽 *Breakfast.*

$ HOTEL 🏨 **Feitian Hotel** (飞天宾馆 *Fēitiān bīnguǎn*). Dunhuang's most popular budget hotel has a variety of clean, comfortable rooms, and is smack-dab in the middle of town. **Pros:** inexpensive rates. **Cons:** basic rooms; large deposits required upon check-in. [$] *Rooms from: Y140* ✉ *21 Mingshan Lu, ½ block north of the bus station* ☎ *0937/882-2337* 🌐 *www.dunhuangfly.com* 🛏 *90 rooms* 💳 *No credit cards* 🍴 *No meals.*

QINGHAI

A remote and sparsely populated province on the northeastern border of Tibet, Qinghai's sweeping grasslands locked in by icy mountain ranges are relatively unknown to most Chinese people, who tend to think of the province as their nation's Siberia, a center for prisons and work camps. Yet Qinghai shares much of the majestic scenery of Xinjiang, combined with the rich culture of Tibet.

The opening of the railway linking Tibet with the rest of China led to an influx of travelers to Qinghai, one of the last major stops before the train arrives in Lhasa. Many hoped that tourism would improve Qinghai's struggling economy, but restrictions on travel to Tibet also brought the number of foreigners traveling through this stunning region to a dramatic halt in 2008. Happily, the region is once again open for independent travel.

Visitors to the region should take in a few of Qinghai's must-see sites. Xining, the compact capital city, has some charming Tibetan flair. On the northwest edge of the city is the famed Tulou Temple, a solemn Taoist destination also known as the North Monastery. The Kumbum Monastery is a testament to Tibetan tranquillity. For a truly heavenly display, crane your neck skyward at the aptly named Bird Island on Qinghai Lake, several hundred miles to the west of Xining.

REGIONAL TOURS

CITS. The local branch of China's state-run travel service offers tours of the city as well as to Bird Island. It's intended for international tourists, but the office has few staffers who speak limited English. ✉ *Xining Guesthouse, 215 Qiyi Lu, Xining* ☎ *0971/613-3847* 🌐 *www.qhcits.cn.*

Tibetan Connections. This locally owned tour company offers off-the-beaten-track hikes, camping trips, and tours to Tibet and Nepal. Prices generally include car and guide; the larger the group, the lower the cost per person. ✉ *Lete Youth Hostel, Guoji Cun Apartments, Bldg. 5, Jiancai Xiang near Cuinan Lu, 15th fl., Xining* ☎ *186-9725-9259 mobile phone (no area code)* 🌐 *www.tibetanconnections.com* 🎟 *From Y,1200.*

XINING

3 hrs by train or bus west of Lanzhou; 24 hrs by train northeast of Lhasa.

Its name means "peace in the west," so it's no surprise that Xining started out as a military garrison in the 16th century, guarding the empire's western borders. It was also an important center for trade between China and Tibet. A small city by Chinese standards, with a population slightly more than 2.2 million, Xining is no longer cut off from the rest of China, but the city still feels remote. A far-flung

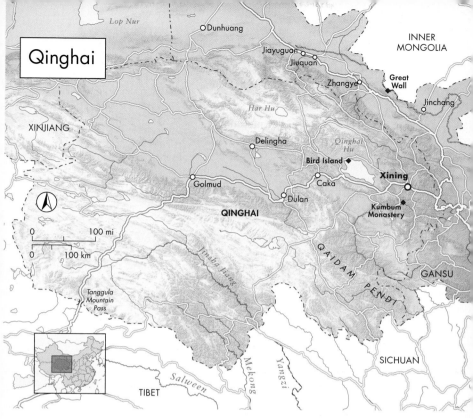

metropolis wedged between dramatic sandstone cliffs, Xining is populated largely by Tibetan and Hui peoples.

For travelers, Xining is a convenient base for visits to the important Kumbum Monastery, which sits just outside the city, and the stunning avian sanctuary of Bird Island, 350 km (217 miles) away on the shores of China's largest saltwater lake. Tibet-bound trains stop in Xining, so this could be a good place to acclimatize to the high altitude.

GETTING HERE AND AROUND

Xining Caojiabao Airport is 30 km (19 miles) east of the city. Shuttle buses costing Y25 per person can get you to or from the airport in about 40 minutes. If you're traveling with someone else, a taxi (Y80–Y100) is a better option. If you arrive by train or bus, a taxi should be around Y10.

AIR TRAVEL Daily flights link Xining with Beijing, Shanghai, Chengdu, Guangzhou, Xian, and Shenzhen. There is less frequent service to Lhasa, Ürümqi, Qingdao, and Golmud.

Air Contact Xining Caojiabao Airport (西宁机场曹家堡机场 *Xīníng cáojiā bǎo jīchǎng*). ⊠ *30 km (19 miles) east of Xining, Haidong* ☎ *0971/818–8222.*

BUS TRAVEL Tickets for the long, bumpy bus ride to Lhasa can be purchased from any travel agent. Tickets for the journey to Lanzhou (3 hours) and

Xian (15 hours) are available at the long-distance bus station, a few minutes north of the train station. If your next stop is Dunhuang, but you don't want to backpedal to Lanzhou, take the bus to Jiuquan in Gansu and get a connection farther west; the mountain scenery and small Tibetan villages along the way are spectacular.

Bus Contact Xining Main Bus Station (西宁汽车站 *Xíníng qìchē zhàn*). ✉ *Jianguo Lu, just across the river from the train station* ☎ *0971/812–3110.*

TRAIN TRAVEL   The train to Lhasa runs every day, but foreign travelers need to arrange permits and book a tour before they can buy train tickets for the 24-hour journey. You can also travel by train to Beijing, Shanghai, Lanzhou, Guangzhou, and Chengdu.

Train Contact Xining Railway Station (西宁火车站 *Xíníng huǒchē zhàn*). ✉ *Northern end of Jianguo Lu* ☎ *0971/719–2222.*

SAFETY AND PRECAUTIONS
The standard advice for travelers applies here; beware of pickpockets and be on the lookout for taxi drivers with "broken meters."

TIMING
Xining is not a place to linger, as there are other, more appealing cities in the region. Spending a night here to explore and see the city's sights is enough.

TOURS
Xining's more upscale hotels have travel offices that can help you arrange expensive private tours with English-speaking guides to Kumbum Monastery or Bird Island. For less expensive tours, contact Tibetan Connections or consider the services of an enterprising individual like Niu Xiaojun, who speaks good English and has been leading foreigners to off-the-beaten-path destinations for years.

ESSENTIALS
Medical Assistance Qinghai People's Hospital (青海省人民医院 *Qīnghǎi xīng rénmín yīyuàn*). ✉ *2 Gonghe Lu* ☎ *0971/817–7911.*

Visitor and Tour Info Niu Xiaojun ☎ *131–9579–1105 mobile phone (no area code)* 🛄 *Tours from Y200.*

EXPLORING
Although most travelers don't come to see Xining, there are a few sights in and around the city.

Dongguan Mosque (东关清真大寺 *Dōngguān qīngzhēn dàsì*). This is one of the largest mosques in all of China and illustrates the ethnic diversity of Xining. Built in the 14th century, its green-and-white dome and two tall minarets see some 40,000 to 50,000 people for Friday prayers. ✉ *Dongguan Jie near Ledu Lu* 🎫 *Y30* 🕒 *Daily 8–noon and 2–5* 🕒 *Closed to tourists Fri. 10–noon.*

Tulou Temple (**土楼寺** *Tŭlóu sì*). Xining's most important site is the Taoist Tulou Temple or North Monastery, at the northwest end of town. Construction on this series of mountainside cloisters and pavilions began more than 1,700 years ago during the Northern Wei Dynasty. Climbing the stairs to the white pagoda at the top gives you a view of the entire city sprawled out beneath you. To get here, take a taxi. ✉ *Beichan Lu* 🎫 *Y10* 🕒 *Daily 8:30–6.*

AROUND XINING

Fodor's Choice ★ **Kumbum Monastery** (**塔尔寺** *Tă'ĕr sì*). The magnificent Kumbum Monastery lies 25 km (15 miles) southwest of Xining. One of the six great monasteries of the Tibetan Buddhist sect known as Yellow Hat—and reputedly the birthplace of the sect's founder, Tsong Khapa—construction began in 1560. A great reformer who lived in the early 1400s, Tsong Khapa formulated a new doctrine that stressed a return to monastic discipline, strict celibacy, and moral and philosophical thought over magic and mysticism. Tsong's followers have controlled Tibetan politics since the 17th century. Still a magnet for Tibetan pilgrims and, more recently, waves of tourists, Kumbum boasts a dozen prayer halls, an exhibition hall, and monks' quarters (look out for the yak-butter sculptures). No photos are allowed. Public buses (Y6) to Huangzhong depart frequently from Zifang Jie Bus Station. Get off at the last stop and walk 2 km (1 mile) uphill, or take the shuttles (Y2) to the monastery's gates. Taxis from Xining will run you around Y35. ✉ *Huangzhong* ☎ *0971/223–2357* 🌐 *www.kumbum.org* 🎫 *Y80* 🕒 *Daily: winter, 8:30–5:30 pm; summer, 7:30–6:30 pm.*

WHERE TO EAT

$$ INTERNATIONAL 🍴 **Black Tent** (**黑帐篷藏吧** *Hēi zhàngpéng cángbā*). This place serves great Tibetan, Indian, and Nepali food. The friendly Tibetan waitstaff all hail from Anmo and add to the already-warm atmosphere. On the menu, which is in Tibetan and English, are plump *momo* (dumplings), a must-order. The restaurant is in Wenmiao Square, a small bar street not far from the Xingwang Hotel. [$] *Average main: Y50* ✉ *Wenmiao Square, Wenhua Jie near Xingwang Hotel, 3rd fl.* ☎ *187/9715–2326 mobile phone (no area code)* 💳 *No credit cards.*

$$ ITALIAN 🍴 **Casa Mia.** If you think it's impossible to get delicious wood-fired pizzas or hearty pastas in Xining, think again. Managed by a local Chinese woman, this eatery is financed by several European expats who wanted a place to satisfy their cravings for Italian cooking. With free wireless Internet and real espresso, the place is very popular among expats. Menus are in English and Chinese, and the staff speak English. [$] *Average main: Y60* ✉ *10–4 Wu Si Xi Lu* ☎ *0971/631–5180* 💳 *No credit cards.*

$ AMERICAN 🍴 **Elite's Cafe.** Like manna from heaven, Jesse Hoffman's café serves proper American fare, like juicy steaks, best washed down with Belgian beer, and pizzas that'll make anyone who's been on the Silk Road for a while dive in with joy. For a bit of spice, the menu offers a few Thai dishes. If you're interested in meeting other foreigners, Elite's is the place to go. $ *Average main: Y75* ⊠ *Bldg. 2, 37 Xiguan Da Dao* ☎ *138–9747–2199 mobile phone (no area code)* ▭ *No credit cards.*

$$$
CAFÉ
✗ **Greenhouse Coffee.** With free Wi-Fi and waitstaff who speak English, this is a great place to hunker down and plan your next steps on the Silk Road. The coffee here is better than at most of Xining's hotels, and will cost you less. The menu appeals to Westerners with panini, pizza, soups, and desserts such as carrot cake with proper cream cheese icing. $ *Average main: Y100* ⊠ *222-22 Banshan Huayuan, Xiadu Dajie* ☎ *0971/820–2710* ⊕ *www.greenhousecoffee.cn* ▭ *No credit cards.*

$$
ASIAN
✗ **Jianyin Revolving Restaurant** (建银宾馆旋转餐厅 *Jiànyín bīnguǎn xuánzhuǎn cāntīng*). Perched atop the 28-story Jianyin Hotel, this slowly revolving restaurant may not serve the finest Asian cuisine, but the food is really beside the point. People come here for the spectacular views of the city. There's no minimum, so sipping a cup of tea while enjoying the scenery or playing cards is perfectly acceptable. $ *Average main: Y60* ⊠ *Jianyin Hotel, 55 Xida Jie near the southeast corner of the central square* ☎ *0971/826–1885* ▭ *No credit cards.*

WHERE TO STAY

$
HOTEL
⊞ **Qinghai Hotel** (青海宾馆 *Qīnghǎi bīnguǎn*). Although the outside looks drab, this hotel's lobby is decked out in tapered columns, fountains, marble sculptures, and ornate wall decor. **Pros:** central location. **Cons:** staff speak limited English; the temperature in the rooms cannot be adjusted. $ *Rooms from: Y1000* ⊠ *158 Huanghe Rd.* ☎ *0971/614–8999* ⊕ *www.qinghaihotel.com* ⇗ *391 rooms* ⦿❘ *Breakfast.*

$$$
HOTEL
⊞ **Yinlong Hotel** (银龙酒店 *Yínlóng jiǔdiàn*). This ultramodern hotel is considered the finest lodging between Xian and Ürümqi, but standards seem to have fallen recently. **Pros:** central location; good-quality hotel restaurants; Wi-Fi in rooms. **Cons:** expensive buffet breakfast; small gym; dearth of English-speakers. ■ **TIP→ During low season (winter), rooms start from Y680.** $ *Rooms from: Y1780* ⊠ *38 Huanghe Lu* ☎ *0971/616–6666* ⊕ *www.ylhotel.net* ⇗ *316 rooms* ⦿❘ *No meals.*

SHOPPING

Visitors interested in Tibetan handicrafts will want to stroll through Xining's street markets.

Jianguo Lu Wholesale Market (建国路批发市场 *Jiànguó lù pīfā shìchǎng*). This market sells everything from traditional Tibetan clothing to favorite local foods. ⊠ *Jianguo Lu, opposite the main bus station, near Binhe Dong Lu.*

SIDE TRIP FROM XINING

Fodor's Choice
★
Bird Island (鸟岛 *Niǎo dǎo*). Bird Island is the main draw at Qinghai Hu, China's largest inland saltwater lake. The name Bird Island is a misnomer: it was an island until the lake receded, connecting it to the shore. The electric-blue lake is surrounded by rolling hills covered with yellow rapeseed flowers. Tibetan shepherds graze their flocks here as wild yaks roam nearby. Beyond the hills are snowcapped mountains. An estimated nearly 100,000 birds breed at Bird Island, including egrets, speckle-headed geese, and black-neck cranes; sadly, the numbers have been much depleted because of the country's efforts to suppress the spread of avian flu. There are two viewing sites: spend as little time as

Wenshu Hall in the Kumbum Monastery

possible at Egg Island in favor of the much better Common Cormorant Island, where you can see birds flying at eye-level from the top of a cliff. The best months to see birds are May and June.

To get to Bird Island, either contact a tour agency or catch a tourist bus from Xining Railway Station for Y35 each way. If you opt for a tour, make sure that you're not headed to the much closer tourist trap known as Qinghai Hu 151. ✉ *350 km (215 miles) northwest of Xining* 🚌 *Mid-Apr.–mid-Aug. Y100, mid-Aug.–mid-Apr. Y60; Y15 for eco-sightseeing bus* ☉ *Daily 7:10 am–6 pm.*

XINJIANG

The vast Xinjiang Uyghur Autonomous Region, covering more than 1.6 million square km (640,000 square miles), is China's largest province. Even more expansive than Alaska, it borders Mongolia, Russia, Kazakhstan, Kyrgyzstan, Tajikistan, Afghanistan, and Pakistan. Only 41% of Xinjiang's 21.8 million inhabitants are Han Chinese. About 43% are Uyghur (a people of Turkic origin), and the remainder are mostly Kazakhs, Hui, Kyrgyz, Mongols, and Tajiks.

Xinjiang gets very little rainfall except in the northern areas near Russia. It gets very cold in winter and very hot in summer, especially in the Turpan Basin, where temperatures often soar to 122°F. Visitors usually forgive the extreme weather, however, as they're charmed by the locals and awed by the rugged scenery, ranging from the endless sand dunes of the desert to the pastoral grasslands of the north.

Long important as a crossroads for trade with Europe and the Middle East, Xinjiang has nevertheless seldom come completely under Chinese control. For more than 2,000 years the region has been contested and divided by Turkic and Mongol tribes who—after setting up short-lived empires—soon disappeared beneath the shifting sands of time. In the 20th century, Uyghurs continued to resist Chinese rule, seizing power from a warlord governor in 1933 and claiming the land as a separate republic, which they named East Turkestan. China tightened its grip after the 1949 revolution, however, encouraging Han settlers to emigrate to the province to dilute the Uyghur majority, thus increasing ethnic tensions. In the last few years these tensions have blown up into full-scale social unrest. In 2008 and 2009 Uyghurs took to the streets in Ürümqi Kashgar, and Hotan, protesting that they were not free to practice their religious beliefs. More than 200 people were killed. Chinese authorities say that the vast majority of the dead were Han Chinese, while Uyghur groups claim that a significant proportion of the dead were demonstrators shot by the police. Tensions boiled over again in 2010, when a Uyghur man detonated explosives in a crowd of police officers, resulting in at least seven casualties.

Renewed unrest means tightened security in the area but, as of this writing, no travel restrictions have been imposed on foreign tourists.

DID YOU KNOW?

In the 1980s, archaeologists discovered dozens of tombs in various parts of Xinjiang, with bodies that had been buried for about 3,000 years yet remained remarkably preserved thanks to the arid desert climate. Many of the mummies, believed to be forefathers of the Uyghurs, had northern European features, including fair hair and skin.

REGIONAL TOURS

CYTS. Based in Ürümqi, this English-speaking tour agency offers interesting tailor-made tours to sights across the province, from two-day tours to Heavenly Lake to multistop trips to Turpan and Kashgar. Prices include car and driver, English-speaking guide, and entrance fees. The larger the group, the lower the price per person. ⊠ *Hong Yan Bldg., 50 Wenyi Lu, 3rd fl., Room 17, Ürümqi* ☎ *0991/232–1170* ⊠ *From Y,1000.*

Uyghur Tour & Travel Center. This excellent tour company based in Kashgar organizes tours of the Silk Road, as well as more unusual destinations like traditional Uyghur villages. It can arrange cars to take you along the Karakorum Highway at prices significantly lower than the competition, and goes out of its way to tailor tours to your requirements. Not many people come to this part of China, so prearranged group tours are not common. ⊠ *Qinibagh Hotel, 144 Seman Lu, Kashgar* ☎ *0998/298–1073, 133–9977–3311 mobile phone (no area code)* ⊕ *www.uighurtour.com* ⊠ *From Y1,000.*

ÜRÜMQI

35 hrs by train, 4 hrs by plane from of Beijing.

Xinjiang's capital and largest city, Ürümqi is at the geographic center of Asia, and has the distinction of being the most landlocked city in the world. It's a new city by Chinese standards, little more than barracks for Qing Dynasty troops when it was built in 1763. Once a sleepy trading post, Ürümqi has grown to be a sprawling city, with more than 2.7 million inhabitants. Yet despite this modernization, Ürümqi manages to conjure up the past, especially in the Uyghur-populated area near the International Grand Bazaar.

10

GETTING HERE AND AROUND

AIR TRAVEL

Many people fly to Ürümqi from Beijing, Shanghai, Hong Kong, or Xian to begin a journey on the Silk Road. The airport is 20 km (12 miles) north of the downtown area, and can be reached in about 30 minutes by taxi (Y50–Y60). Shuttle buses are Y20.

Air Contacts Ürümqi Diwopu International Airport (乌鲁木齐地窝堡国际机场 *Wūlǔmùqí de wō bǎo guójì jīchǎng*). ⊠ *16 km (10 miles) northwest of Ürümqi, Diwopu* ☎ *0991/380–1453* ⊕ *www.xjairport.com.*

BUS TRAVEL

Long-distance buses are often the only way to travel in Xinjiang if you don't want to wait a day or two for the next available train. Every city in the region is served at least daily by buses from Ürümqi. There's even bus service to Almaty, Kazakhstan.

It's usually a straightforward affair buying tickets from the only station in town, but Ürümqi is more complicated. Unless you're going to Hotan

The Xinjiang Uyghur Autonomous Region

or Altai—which have their own separate bus stations—your best bet is to first look for tickets at Nianzigou Station (碾子沟客运站 *Niǎnzi gōu kèyùn zhàn*). If you don't like what's available there, or if your destination is Kashgar or Turpan, head to the South Station (汽车南站 *Qìchē nán zhàn*).

Buses (Y25 each way) leave for Heavenly Lake (Tianchi Hu) at 9 am from the north gate of Renmin Park. They usually leave the lake at 6 pm and arrive back in Ürümqi at 7:30 pm. Be careful to get on a regular bus rather than a tour bus that will take you to minor attractions on the way, limiting your time at the lake.

Bus Contacts Ürümqi Nianzigou Long-Distance Bus Station (乌鲁木齐碾子沟客运站 *Wūlūmùqí niǎnzi gōu kèyùn zhàn*). ⊠ *49 Heilongjiang Lu* ☎ *0991/587–8898, 0991/528–2443.* **Ürümqi South Bus Station** (乌鲁木齐南汽车站 *Wūlūmùqí nán qìchē zhàn*). ⊠ *Xinhua Nan Lu, near Shengli Lu* ☎ *0991/286–6635.*

TRAIN TRAVEL Those arriving by train will find themselves about 2 km (1 mile) southwest of the city center.

Train Contact Ürümqi Train Station (乌鲁木齐火车站 *Wūlūmùqí huŏchē zhàn*). ⊠ *Qiantangjiang Lu near the Outer Ring Rd.* ☎ *0991/794–5222.*

MONEY MATTERS
In China, there's no place more difficult to run out of money than in off-the-beaten-track Xinjiang. ■**TIP→** There are ATMs in Ürümqi and Kashgar, and nearly all accept international credit cards and debit cards. Most banks will also exchange currency and traveler's checks. Many businesses will accept only cash or Chinese bank cards.

Bank Bank of China (中国银行
Zhōngguó yínháng). ✉ *1 Jiefang Nan Lu*
☎ *0991/283–4222.*

SAFETY AND PRECAUTIONS

There remains a heavy police presence following incidents of political unrest. Tourists may be stopped by security personnel but, as of this writing, there are no travel restrictions. As always, be sure to secure your valuables when in public places.

TIMING

While there is plenty to see in Ürümqi, it's fair to say that Xinjiang's best attractions are out of the capital. If the clock is ticking, spend no more than two days enjoying Ürümqi's sights before heading farther afield.

WHAT TIME IS IT?

A constant source of confusion for travelers in Xinjiang is figuring out the time. Uyghurs often refer to unofficial Xinjiang time, whereas Han Chinese use standard Beijing time (which applies to all of China and doesn't follow daylight saving time). If in doubt, ask. No matter what time is spoken, you can count on everything in Xinjiang starting two hours later than in Beijing. That is, lunch in Kashgar is usually eaten at 2 pm Beijing time.

TOURS

Ürümqi is a popular place to begin a tour of Xinjiang's vast desert expanses. Travel agencies are happy to let you pick and choose from a list of destinations. A four-wheel-drive vehicle will cost around Y1,300 per day.

ESSENTIALS

Internet Dragon Netbar ✉ *190 Wuyi Lu.*

Medical Assistance Chinese Medicine Hospital of Ürümqi
(乌鲁木齐市中医医院 *Wūlǔmùqí shì zhōngyī yīyuàn).* ✉ *590 Youhao Nan Lu*
☎ *0991/451–1380* ⊕ *www.wlmqszyyy.com.*

Visitor and Tour Info CITS ✉ *33 Renmin Lu* ☎ *0991/282–1427* ⊕ *www.*
*xinjiangtour.com/english.***Grassland Travel Service** ✉ *2 Renmin Gongyuan Bei*
Jie, southwest of People's Park entrance ☎ *0991/584–1116.*

EXPLORING

International Grand Bazaar (国际大巴扎 *Guójì dàbā zhā).* The streets around the bazaar were once full of donkey carts and flocks of sheep. Men in embroidered skullcaps and women in heavy brown wool veils remain, preserving this bustling Central Asian street market. You can bargain for Uyghur crafts, such as decorated knives, colorful silks, and carved jade. Small shops are tucked into every nook and cranny. The international bazaar itself has been heavily expanded, and now includes a newly built minaret, which you can climb for Y20. The stalls, while interesting enough, are aimed firmly at tourists; more authentic options are the streets nearby that are filled with traditional ironmongers and Islamic butcher shops. ✉ *Jiefang Nan Lu, Near Tianchi Lu.*

Red Mountain Park (红山公园 *Hóngshān gōngyuán).* This park gives you a picture-perfect view of the snowcapped Heavenly Mountains (*Tianshan*). An array of incongruously grouped objects—including an

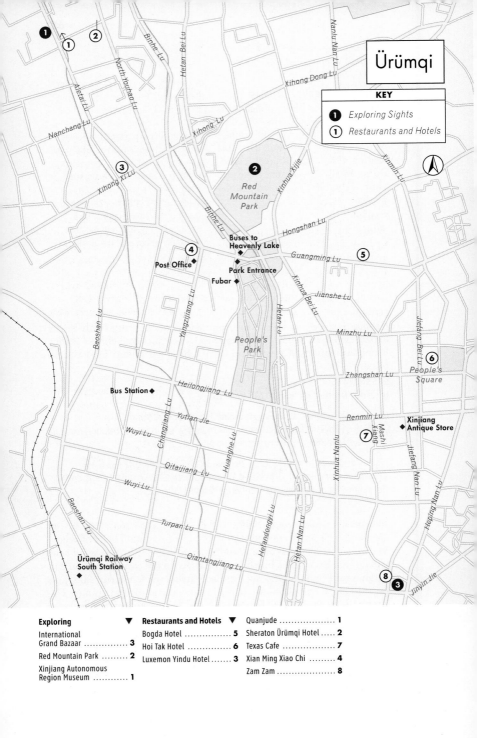

Ürümqi

KEY
- **1** Exploring Sights
- (1) Restaurants and Hotels

Red Mountain Park

Buses to Heavenly Lake
Post Office ◆
Park Entrance ◆
Fubar ◆

People's Park

Bus Station ◆

People's Square

Xinjiang Antique Store

Ürümqi Railway South Station ◆

CLOSE UP

China's Muslims

UYGHUR

The Muslim Turkic people known as Uyghurs (pronounced "WEE-grs") are one of China's largest—and in the eyes of Beijing, most troublesome—minority groups. Uyghurs mostly live in northwest China's Xinjiang, an "autonomous region" that is one of the most tightly controlled parts of the country after Tibet. Uyghurs are descendants of nomadic Turkic Central Asian tribes. Their language, food, music, dance, clothing, and other customs have little or no relation to those found elsewhere in China. Yet despite a population of nearly 10 million people, most foreigners have never heard of them or their troubled independence movement. Protests and occasional violence in the region during the late 1990s brought a severe crackdown from Beijing; limits were placed on religious education and hundreds of suspected Uyghur separatists were executed. The attacks of September 11, 2001, gave the Chinese government further leverage to oppress Uyghurs in the name of fighting terrorism.

HUI

Identifiable by their brimless white caps and head scarves, the Hui are descendants of Middle Eastern traders who came to China via the Silk Road, settling down with Chinese wives after their conversion to Islam. Over a thousand years' time, the Middle Eastern influence on the Hui appearance became diluted, but it is still very easy to distinguish between the different facial features of the Hui and Han Chinese. Because of cultural differences associated with their Islamic faith, the Hui tend to associate with others in their largely Muslim neighborhoods. The Hui reject eating several kinds of meat that can be popular with Han Chinese, including pork, horse, dog, and several types of birds. In what could be seen as a form of respect by the business-savvy Han Chinese, the Hui are generally considered to be shrewd business-people, perhaps a nod to their being descendants of foreign traders.

eight-story pagoda built by the emperor in 1788 to suppress an evil dragon—are reached via a long set of stairs. Arrive in the early evening for the pleasure of seeing the cityscape bathed in the setting sun's golden light. Ignore the cheap carnival rides near the entrance. The park is hard to find, and few tourists venture here, so take a taxi. ⊠ *Enter on Ximin Xi Lu* ☎ *0991/885–5671* ✉ *Free* ☉ *Daily 10 am–11 pm.*

Fodor's Choice **Xinjiang Autonomous Region Museum** (新疆自治区博物馆 *Xīnjiāng*
★ *zìzhìqū bówùguǎn*). Don't miss the perfectly preserved mummies at this superb museum, located 4 km (2½ miles) northwest of the city center. The mummies—including the 4,000-year-old Beauty of Loulan—were excavated from tombs in various parts of Xinjiang. In addition, the museum has a well-executed exhibition on the region's ethnic minorities. If you are lucky, one of the museum's English-speaking guides will accompany you. There's no extra charge, and it's well worth asking. ⊠ *585 Xibei Lu, 1 block west of the Sheraton* ☎ *0991/453–4453* ✉ *Free* ☉ *Tues.–Sun. 10–6.*

10

Chinese Muslim children

WHERE TO EAT

Ürümqi is a good place to have your first taste of Uyghur cuisine.

$$$ NORTHERN CHINESE 🍴 **Quanjude** (全聚德 *Quánjùdé*). This outpost of the famous Beijing Peking duck restaurant serves up a variety of food from that capital and Northeastern China. The menu differs a little from the Beijing branches, but the duck is the same. Beyond Peking duck, expect to find crispy, juicy panfried dumplings, spicy meat stews, thick-cut noodles, and steamed root vegetables. There is a lunch buffet from 1:30 to 3:30 and a dinner buffet from 7:30 to 10:30 pm. [$] *Average main: Y110* ✉ *338 Beijing Nan Lu* ☎ *991/366–1066, 991/382–2523* 💳 *No credit cards.*

$$ INTERNATIONAL FAMILY 🍴 **Texas Cafe** (得克萨斯西餐厅 *Dékèsàsī xī cāntīng*). For a little slice of the American Southwest when in far Western China, stop off at the Texas Cafe. This the only place within a few hundred miles where you'll find Tex-Mex. Satisfy your burrito craving or tuck into burgers, pasta, pizza, and the holy grail of a Western restaurant in China—coffee. All-day breakfast, free Wi-Fi, and a library make this one of the most comfortable places in Ürümqi to do some trip planning. [$] *Average main: Y50* ✉ *55 Mashi Xiang Putao Changlang* ☎ *0991/281–0025* 🌐 *texascafe.weebly.com* 💳 *No credit cards.*

$ CHINESE 🍴 **Xian Ming Xiao Chi** (西安名小吃 *Xī'ān míng xiǎochī*). If you need a change from Uyghur fare, this cheap and cheerful fast-food joint offers tasty snacks from Xian. Do as the locals do when the temperature rises: try a cooling plateful of cold noodles with cucumber called *liang pi*. Say *bu la* if you don't want your noodles to be spicy. Other specialties include *rou jia mo*, or burger-style pork sandwiches—made from a

CLOSE UP

The Jade Road

The residents of Xinjiang are apt to point out that the Silk Road isn't the first road they knew. That honor goes to the "Jade Road," which was established nearly 7,000 years ago. Running from Hotan into today's Qinghai and Gansu provinces, the Jade Road was the artery for Xinjiang's legendary white jade trade. Primarily mined from the Hotan River, Xinjiang jade comes in a number of hues, although small white stones with a reddish-brown exterior are the most highly valued.

Sensuous and smooth to the touch, this "mutton fat jade" is cloudy with translucent qualities. Chinese emperors have craved it for centuries. Good places to hunt around for all manner of jade in Ürümqi include the swirling International Grand Bazaar and the Xinjiang Antique Store.

Visitors who wish to know more about this region's heady history of jade, silk, and more should visit the Xinjiang Autonomous Region Museum.

---

meat rarely served in this part of the world. $ *Average main: Y30* ✉ *61 Yangzijiang Lu* ☎ *0991/451–5668* ▭ *No credit cards.*

$ ✕ **Zam Zam.** Near the International Bazaar, this smart Uyghur eatery
NORTHERN looks as though it should be very pricey. The ornate room is outfitted
CHINESE with carved wood and Arabic-style arches, and the staff is smartly attired. The excellent food is the best bargain in town. Few of the waiters speak Mandarin, let alone English, but there is a picture menu: point to the pilaf or the lamb dumplings. No alcohol is served. $ *Average main: Y30* ✉ *423 Heping Nan Lu* ☎ *0991/843–0555* ▭ *No credit cards.*

WHERE TO STAY

$ ⊞ **Bogda Hotel** (博格达宾馆 *Bógédá bīnguǎn*). A good budget option,
HOTEL this hotel has rooms that are cleaner and more comfortable than those offered in similarly priced lodgings. **Pros:** good selection of tours available; convenient to banks and restaurants. **Cons:** noisy lobby; little English spoken. $ *Rooms from: Y200* ✉ *253 Guangming Lu* ☎ *0991/886–3910* ⇆ *280 rooms* ▭ *No credit cards* ⍟ *Breakfast.*

$ ⊞ **Hoi Tak Hotel** (信达海德酒店 *Xìndá hǎidé jiǔdiàn*). Popular with
HOTEL Chinese tour groups and Hong Kong business travelers, this gleaming
Fodor's Choice white tower offers first-rate views of the snowcapped Heavenly Moun-
★ tains (*Tiashan*). **Pros:** the staff speak English; rooms are good value; free Wi-Fi. **Cons:** removed from main attractions. $ *Rooms from: Y700* ✉ *1 Dongfeng Lu, west side of People's Sq.* ☎ *0991/232–2828* ⊕ *www. hoitakhotel.com* ⇆ *318 rooms, 38 suites* ⍟ *No meals.*

$ ⊞ **Luxemon Yindu Hotel** (银都酒店 *Yíndū jiǔdiàn*). The Yindu is testa-
HOTEL ment to the influx of cash that has transformed Ürümqi over the past decade. **Pros:** comfortable rooms; staff speak enough English to communicate; breakfast buffet offers enough Western options. **Cons:** bad location for exploring the sights. $ *Rooms from: Y800* ✉ *179 Xihong Xi Lu* ☎ *0991/453–6688* ⊕ *www.luxemonyindu.com* ⇆ *308 rooms* ⍟ *Breakfast.*

$$ ⊞ **Sheraton Ürümqi Hotel** (喜来登酒店 *Xǐláidēng jiǔdiàn*). Very popular
HOTEL with both well-heeled business and leisure travelers, this luxury hotel

10

pampers you with an indoor pool illuminated with skylights and one of the better hotel gyms you'll find in Ürümqi. **Pros:** keen staff; relatively family-friendly; proper gym. **Cons:** inconvenient for Ürümqi's sights. [$] *Rooms from: Y1380* ✉ *669 Youhao Bei Lu* ☎ *0991/699–9999* 🌐 *www.starwoodhotels.com* 🛏 *380 rooms, 22 suites* 🍴 *No meals.*

NIGHTLIFE

As with most Chinese cities, every other block in Ürümqi is blighted by high-price karaoke parlors and blaring discos. But there are plenty of quieter places to order a bottle of cold beer, with the best options on Renmin Gongyuan Bei Jie.

Fubar (福吧 *Fúbā*). Fubar is the real thing: a tavern serving imported beer and authentic pub grub. The pizza is especially noteworthy, as are the fish-and-chips. This is the best place in Ürümqi to relax after a day exploring the city. The owners are happy to dispense free travel advice. ✉ *40 Gongyuan Bei Jie* ☎ *0991/581–4698.*

Fodor's Choice ★ **International Grand Bazaar Banquet Performance** (国际大巴扎宴会演出 *Guójì dàbā zhā yànhuì yǎnchū*). This entertaining song-and-dance performance is preceded by a ho-hum buffet that unsuccessfully tries to capture the delights of Uyghur cuisine. Never mind the food, as this is your best chance to see Uyghur, Uzbek, Kazakh, Tajik, Tartar, and even Irish dancing all in one eye-popping evening. Make reservations through your hotel. ✉ *Jiefang Lu, near Heping Nan Lu* ☎ *0991/855–6000* 🎫 *Y260–Y399.*

SHOPPING

The International Grand Bazaar is the best place to go for Uyghur items like embroidered skullcaps, brightly colored carpets, and hand-carved knives. If it's inexpensive gifts you're after, you'll find them

Xinjiang Antique Store (新疆古玩店 *Xīnjiāng gǔwàn diàn*). This shop has a good selection of Chinese bric-a-brac, including jade, jewelry, carpets, and porcelain. As all items come with a state-certified export certificate, you won't have to worry about getting your purchase through customs. There is a smaller branch inside the Xinjiang Autonomous Region Museum. ✉ *39 Jiefang Nan Lu, south of Renmin Lu* ☎ *0991/282–5161.*

SIDE TRIP FROM ÜRÜMQI

Fodor's Choice ★ **Heavenly Lake** (天池 *Tiānchí*). After a three-hour ride from Ürümqi you'll reach what it quite possibly the prettiest lake in China, surrounded by snow-sprinkled mountains. The water is crystal clear with a sapphire tint. In summer, white flowers dot the hillsides. Unfortunately, tourism is leaving its ugly footprint. The lake's southern shore is crowded with tour groups posing for snapshots with Mount Bogda in the background. To better appreciate the lake's natural beauty, arrive before the hordes, or stay until after the last bus has departed.

Kazakh families still set up traditional felt tents along the shores of Heavenly Lake from early May to late October, bringing their horses, sheep, and cashmere goats. The Kazakh people have a long history as horse breeders and are known to be skilled riders.

From Ürümqi, day-tour buses to Heavenly Lake leave at 9 am from a small street beside the north gate of People's Park (Heilongjiang Lu near

Gongyuan Bei Ji). Expect to pay around Y25 each way after bargaining plus the Y100 entrance fee to the lake. You'll have from about noon to 6 pm to explore the lake, arriving back in the city at 8 pm. Tickets—usually available up until the bus leaves—can be purchased near the buses. ✉ *Ürümqi* ✉ *Apr.–Oct. Y100, Nov.–Mar. Y40.*

TURPAN

2½–3 hrs by bus southeast of Ürümqi.

Turpan, which means "the lowest place" in Uyghur, lies in a desert basin at the southern foot of the Heavenly Mountains. Part of the basin lies 505 feet below sea level, the hottest spot in China and the second-lowest point in the world after the Dead Sea. In summer, temperatures can soar to more than 122°F (50°C), so come prepared with lots of water and sunscreen.

Turpan's claim to fame is its location between the ruins of two spectacular ancient cities, Jiaohe and Gaochang. Most visitors don't linger in Turpan, as the best five sites can easily be visited in a single day, but there are other attractions. Surrounded by some of the richest farmland in Xinjiang, Turpan's vineyards are famous for producing several varieties of candy-sweet raisins popular throughout China.

GETTING HERE AND AROUND

Too close to Ürümqi to have its own airport, Turpan is an inconvenient 60 km (38 miles) south of the nearest train station in Daheyan. A high-speed train link to the town itself is under construction, but no date has been given for its completion. If you arrive by train, head to the city via a taxi (Y40) or public bus (Y7.50). The bus trip from Ürümqi takes 2½ hours. Buses leave every 25 minutes from 7:30 am to 8:30 pm and cost Y45. The terminal is in the center of town on the north side of Laocheng Lu.

Leaving Turpan is more difficult than arriving: one bus daily departs at noon for Kashgar. For any other destination, you'll have to head back to Ürümqi.

SAFETY AND PRECAUTIONS

The harsh, dry climate is probably the biggest danger; temperatures here have reached 50°C (122°F) in the height of summer, and have fallen to −28.9°C (−20°F) in winter. Drink plenty of water in hot months, slather on that sunscreen, and stay in the shade.

TIMING

An overnight stay is enough to see the sights that lie on the outskirts of town.

10

TOURS

You could join an organized group tour around Turpan, but you'll likely spend too much time in annoying tourist traps. With a slightly more expensive taxi tour you can choose your own itinerary and spend hours roaming the ruins of Jiaohe and Gaochang. In the off-season you may be able to secure a taxi for the day for as little as Y150, although prices of Y250 are more common during the summer.

ESSENTIALS

Bus Contact Turpan Bus Station (Passenger Transport Center) (吐鲁番汽车站 *Tǔlǔfān qìchē zhàn*). ✉ *264 Laocheng Lu* 📞 *0995/852-2325.*

Train Contact Turpan Railway Station (吐鲁番火车站 *Tǔlǔfān huǒchē zhàn*). ✉ *Near Yanguan Jie, Daheyan* 📞 *0995/12306.*

EXPLORING

Emin Minaret (苏公塔 *Sūgōng tǎ*). Emin Minaret is Turpan's most recognizable image, often featured in tourist brochures. Built in 1777, it commemorates a military commander who suppressed a rebellion by a group of aristocrats. The 141-foot conical tower is elegantly spare, with bricks arranged in 15 patterns. This complex lies 4 km (2½ miles) from the city center at the southeast end of town. To get here, head east on Laocheng Xi Lu and turn right on the last paved road before you reach farmland. ✉ *Off Laocheng Xi Lu* 💴 *Y50* 🕐 *Daily 8–8.*

Karez Irrigation System (坎儿井灌溉系统 *Kǎn'erjǐng guàngài xìtǒng*). The remarkable 2,000-year-old system allowed the desert cities of the Silk Road to flourish despite an unrelentingly arid environment. In the oasis cities of Turpan and Hami, 1,600 km (990 miles) of underground tunnels brought water—moved only by gravity—from melting snow at the base of the Heavenly Mountains. You can view the tunnels at several sites around the city. Most tour guides take visitors to the largely educational Karez Irrigation Museum. Despite being described as the "underground Great Wall," most visitors are completely underwhelmed by what are essentially narrow dirt tunnels. ✉ *888 Xincheng Lu, on the city's western outskirts* 💴 *Y40* 🕐 *Daily 8–7.*

AROUND TURPAN

Fodor'sChoice ★ **Ancient City of Jiaohe** (交河故城 *Jiāohé gù chéng*). On an island at the confluence of two rivers, these impressive ruins lie in the Yarnaz Valley west of Turpan. The city, established as a garrison during the Han Dynasty, was built on a high plateau, protected by the natural fortification of cliffs rising 100 feet above the rivers. Jiaohe was governed from the 2nd to the 7th century by the kingdom of Gaochang, and occupied later by Tibetans. Despite destruction in the 14th century by Mongol hordes, large fragments of actual streets and buildings remain, including a Buddhist monastery and Buddhist statues, a row of bleached pagodas, a 29-foot observation tower, and a prison. Guards will make sure you stay on the marked paths. As at the Ruins of Gaochang, there's almost no shade, so arrive early with an umbrella in tow. ✉ *8 km (5 miles) west of Turpan* 💴 *Y40* 🕐 *Daily dawn–dusk.*

Fodor'sChoice ★ **Bezeklik Thousand Buddha Caves** (柏孜克里克千佛洞 *Bǎizīkèlǐ kèqiān fú dòng*). In a breathtaking valley inside the Flaming Mountains is

The Thousand Buddha Caves outside Turpan

this ancient temple complex, built between the 5th and 9th century by slaves whose entire lives went into the construction. Many of the fine examples of Buddhist sculpture and wall frescoes were destroyed after Islam came to the region in the 13th century. Other sculptures and frescoes, including several whole murals of Buddhist monks, were removed by 20th-century archaeologists like German Albert von Le Coq, who shipped his finds back to Berlin. Although they remain a feat of early engineering, the caves are in atrocious condition. Go just to see the site itself and the surrounding valley, which is magnificent. The views of the scorched, lunar landscape leading up to the site, which clings to one flank of a steep, scenic valley, make the trip worth the effort. Avoid the nearby Buddha Cave constructed in 1980 by a local artist; it isn't worth an additional Y20. ✉ *35 km (22 miles) east of Turpan* ☎ *Y40* ⊙ *Daily dawn–dusk.*

Fodor's Choice
★

The Ruins of Gaochang (高昌故城 *Gāochāng gù chéng*). These fascinating city ruins lie in a valley south of the Flaming Mountains. Legend has it that a group of soldiers stopped here in the 1st century BC on their way to Afghanistan, found that water was plentiful, and decided to stay. By the 7th century the city was the capital of the kingdom of Gaochang, which ruled more than 21 other towns, and by the 9th century the Uyghurs had moved into the area from Mongolia, establishing the kingdom of Kharakojam. In the 14th century Mongols destroyed the kingdom, leaving only the ruins seen today. Only the city walls and a partially preserved monastery surrounded by muted, almost unrecognizable crumbling buildings remain, an eerie and haunting excursion into the pages of history. Despite repeated plundering of the site, in the early 1900s German archaeologists were able to unearth manuscripts, statues, and frescoes in superb condition. To make the best of your time here, take a donkey cart (time to use your bargaining skills—Y25 is a fair price) to the monastery in the rear right corner; from there you can walk back toward the entrance through the ruins. There is little shade, so go early and bring an umbrella. ✉ *30 km (19 miles) east of Turpan* 🎫 *Y60* ⏲ *Daily dawn–dusk.*

WHERE TO EAT

Most visitors stick to the restaurants in and around the Turpan Hotel on Qingnian Lu, a pleasant side street shaded by grapevines. The bazaar across from the bus station is a good place to grab lunch for Y10–Y15. A lively night market with rows of kebab stands and spicy hotpot stalls is on Gaochang Lu, a 10-minute walk north from the Turpan Hotel, next to the huge public square and near the China Post building.

$$ AMERICAN 🍴 **John's Information Café.** Part of a small family-run chain that operates in destinations along the Silk Road, this popular tourist hangout is far from authentic, but people flock here for the familiar Western fare and rock-solid travel advice. The tours are good, but check carefully to see what's included. John's also offers bike hire and laundry services. [$] *Average main: Y50* ✉ *Qingnian Lu, rear of the Turpan Hotel* ☎ *0998/258–1186* 🌐 *www.johncafe.net* 💳 *No credit cards.*

$$ WESTERN CHINESE 🍴 **Muslim Restaurant** (清真餐厅 *Qīngzhēn cāntīng*). Like most hotel restaurants in the region, this one inside Turpan Hotel is poorly lighted and lacks ambience, but it does have a hearty variety of standard Uyghur dishes: lamb, noodles, and vegetables. [$] *Average main: Y50* ✉ *Turpan Hotel, 1695 Qingnian Nan Lu* ☎ *0995/856–8888* 💳 *No credit cards.*

WHERE TO STAY

$ HOTEL 🏨 **Jiaotong Hotel** (交通宾馆 *Jiāotōng bīnguǎn*). This budget option, whose rooms have been renovated, isn't a bad place to stay, despite noise from the bus station in the rear and the bazaar across the street. **Pros:** bargain rates; convenient for early buses. **Cons:** bad water pressure; occasional power outages. [$] *Rooms from: Y260* ✉ *230 Laocheng Xi Lu, next to the bus station* ☎ *0995/625–8008* 🛏 *100 rooms* 💳 *No credit cards* 🍽 *Breakfast.*

$ HOTEL 🏨 **Turpan Hotel** (吐鲁番宾馆 *Tǔlǔfān bīnguǎn*). This study in basic geometry has definitely seen better days, but rooms are relatively clean and large, the restaurant is good, and the gift shops are handy. **Pros:** offers good discounts; friendly staff. **Cons:** if you can't get a discount, better values are available elsewhere; Chinese breakfast options only. [$] *Rooms from: Y280* ✉ *1695 Qingnian Nan Lu, south of Laocheng Lu, near the Royal Garden* ☎ *0995/856–8888* 🛏 *200 rooms, 4 suites* 🍽 *No meals.*

KASHGAR

24 hrs by train or 1½ hours by plane southwest of Ürümqi.

Kashgar, the westernmost city in China, is closer to Baghdad than Beijing. More than 3,400 km (2,100 miles) west of the capital, the city has been a center of trade between China and the outside world for at least

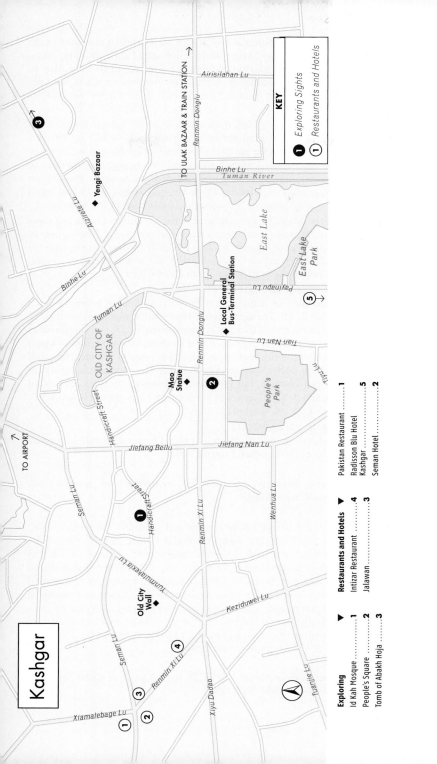

Kashgar

TO AIRPORT ↗

TO ULAK BAZAAR & TRAIN STATION ↑

Airisilahan Lu

Binhe Lu
Tuman River

East Lake

East Lake Park

Payinap Lu

Binhe Lu

Aiziiete Lu

◆ **Yengi Bazaar**

Tuman Lu

OLD CITY OF KASHGAR

◆ **Mao Statue**

◆ **Local General Bus-Terminal Station**

Renmin Donglu

Tian Nan Lu

People's Park

Jiefang Beilu

Jiefang Nan Lu

Handicraft Street

Seman Lu

Handicraft Street

Renmin Xi Lu

Wenhua Lu

◆ **Old City Wall**

Yumulakexia Lu

Keziduwei Lu

Xiyu Dadao

Xiamalebage Lu

Renmin Xi Lu

Tuanjie Lu

KEY

1 *Exploring Sights*

① *Restaurants and Hotels*

Exploring ▶
Id Kah Mosque **1**
People's Square **2**
Tomb of Abakh Hoja **3**

Restaurants and Hotels ▼
Intizar Restaurant **4**
Jalawan **3**

Pakistan Restaurant **1**
Radisson Blu Hotel
Kashgar **5**
Seman Hotel **2**

2,000 years. Today Kashgar is a hub for merchants coming in over the Khunjerab Pass from Pakistan and the Torugart Pass from Kyrgyzstan. When these two treacherous mountain passes are open from May to October, Kashgar becomes a particularly colorful city, abuzz not only with curious Western tourists but also with visitors from every corner of Central Asia.

Despite an increasing Han presence in central Kashgar (symbolized by one of the largest Mao statues in the country), the city is still overwhelmingly Uyghur. A great deal of modernization has taken place here since the railway from Ürümqi arrived in 1999. Beijing is showering the city with attention and money to boost the local economy and placate Kashgar's Uyghur population. There are still clashes, which has led to a heavy security presence, but the area is safe enough for foreigners.

Much of the city's Uyghur architecture has been demolished, but there are still some traditional houses with ornately painted balconies, as well as large remaining sections of the Old City. Most visitors come to Kashgar for the amazing Sunday Market, the largest bazaar in Central Asia and one of the best photo ops in all of China.

GETTING HERE AND AROUND

Daunted by the long train journey from Ürümqi, many tourists headed for Kashgar by air. The airport is 13 km (8 miles) north of the city center; a taxi to your hotel shouldn't cost more than Y35, and shuttle buses are Y15. Trains between Ürümqi and Kashgar (25 or 32 hours) depart three times a day; the slow train is half the price of the fast train, but you'll have to do without air-conditioning. The train station is 10 km (6 miles) east of town, not far from the livestock market. Taxis from here cost about Y15. Kashgar's long-distance bus station is just north of People's Park on Yingbin Da Dao.

SAFETY AND PRECAUTIONS

Tensions between local Uyghurs and Han Chinese remain, but tourists are not subject to any travel restrictions.

TIMING

Allow two or three days if possible, and try to time your stay to include the famous Sunday Market.

TOURS

Kashgar is a tourist-friendly city, so you shouldn't have any trouble arranging tours. Uyghur Tour and Travel Center, in the lobby of the Overseas Chinese Hotel, offers a "money-back guarantee." It has received high marks from travelers for years. A day tour of sites within Kashgar will cost around Y700 per person for a group of four and Y1,000 for a solo traveler. The price includes a car, guide, and admission tickets. If you're interested in spending a night in the area's only 1,000-star hotel—the nearby Taklamakan Desert—the agency can arrange an all-inclusive overnight camel trek for Y1,300 per person for a group of four or Y3,300 for an individual traveler.

ESSENTIALS

Air Contact Kashgar Airport (喀什机场 *Kāshí Jīchǎng*). ✉ *Yingbin Dadao* ☎ *0998/2922–600, 0998/2927–118.*

Bus Contact Kashgar International Bus Station (喀什國際汽車站 *Kāshi guójì qìchē zhàn*). ⌧ *Yingbin Da Dao* ☎ *0998/296-3630.*

Police Kashgar Public Security Bureau ⌧ *127 Youmulake Xiehai'er Lu, south of the Qinibagh Hotel* ☎ *0998/282-2028.*

Medical Assistance Kashgar First People's Hospital (喀什地区第一人民医院 *Kāshi dìqū dì yī rénmín yīyuàn*). ⌧ *120 Yingbin Da Dao* ☎ *0998/296-2337* ⊕ *www.xjkshospital.com.*

Train Contact Kashgar Train Station (喀什火车站 *Kāshi huǒchē zhàn*). ⌧ *Near Tianshan Dong Lu* ☎ *0998/12306.*

Visitor and Tour Info CITS ⌧ *Qinibagh Hotel, 144 Seman Lu* ☎ *0998/298-3156* ⊕ *www.xinjiangtour.com/english.* **Uyghur Tour and Travel Center** ⌧ *Qinibagh Hotel, 144 Seman Lu, at Renmin Lu* ☎ *0998/298-1073* ⊕ *www.uighurtour.com.*

EXPLORING

Id Kah Mosque (艾提尕尔清真寺 *Ài tí gǎ ěr Qīngzhēnsì*). Start your tour of the city with a visit to the center of Muslim life in Kashgar. One of the largest mosques in China, the ornate structure of yellow bricks is the result of many extensions and renovations to the original mosque, built in 1442 as a prayer hall for the ruler of Kashgar. The main hall has a ceiling with fine wooden carvings and precisely 100 carved wooden columns. When services aren't being held, you are free to wander the quiet shaded grounds and even to enter the prayer hall. As this is an active site of worship, dress modestly. ⌧ *Just off Jiefang Bei Lu, near Nuo'er Beixi Lu* ☎ *Y20* ☽ *Daily dawn–dusk.*

People's Square (人民广场 *Rénmín guǎngchǎng*). If you happen to forget which country Kashgar is in, chances are you aren't standing in this square. A statue of Mao Zedong—one of the largest in China—stands with his right arm raised in perpetual salute. The statue is evidence of an unspoken rule in China that directly relates the size of a Mao tribute to its distance from Beijing; the only Mao statue larger than this one is in Tibet. ⌧ *Renmin Lu, between Jiefang Nan Lu and Tian Lu.*

Tomb of Abakh Hoja (香妃墓 *Xiāng fēi mù*). About 5 km (3 miles) northeast of the city lies one of the most sacred sites in Xinjiang. The sea-green tiled hall that houses the tomb—actually about two dozen tombs—is part of a massive complex of sacred Islamic structures built around 1640. Uyghurs named the tomb and surrounding complex after Abakh Hoja, an Islamic missionary believed to be a descendant of Mohammed, who ruled Kashgar and outlying regions in the 17th century. Excavations of the glazed-brick tombs indicate that the first occupant was Abakh Hoja's father, who is buried here along with Abakh Hoja and many of their descendants.

The Han, who prefer to emphasize the site's historical connection to their dynastic empire, call it the Tomb of the Fragrant Concubine. When the grandniece of Abakh Hoja was chosen as concubine by the Qing ruler Qianlong in Beijing, Uyghur legend holds that she committed suicide rather than submit to the emperor. In the Han story, she dutifully went to Beijing and spent 30 years in the emperor's palace, then asked to be buried in her homeland. Either way, her alleged tomb was excavated

10

in the 1980s and found to be empty. The tomb is a bit difficult to locate, so take a taxi. ✉ *Aizirete Lu* 🎟 *Y30* ⏲ *Daily 8–5.*

WHERE TO EAT

$ NORTHERN CHINESE Fodor's Choice ★

🍴 **Intizar Restaurant** (银提扎尔快餐厅 *Yíntízhā'ěr kuài cāntīng*). Frequented by locals and outfitted with wooden paneling and chandeliers, Intizar is the most formal of Kashgar's Uyghur restaurants. It offers a range of Uyghur cuisine, and the menu is translated into English, including helpful descriptions of each dish. For those tired of typical Uyghur fare, Muslim-friendly stir-fry dishes are also available. Alcohol is not allowed on the premises. [$] *Average main: Y30* ✉ *33 Renmin Xi Lu, near Wenzhou Hotel* 💳 *No credit cards.*

$ MIDDLE EASTERN

🍴 **Jalawan** (吉乌兰美食 *Jíwūlán měishí*). It's very easy to join the crowds of locals relaxing at this restaurant, especially underneath the (admittedly) fake trellises of grapes around a fountain. The staff will hand you an English-language menu whose prices are a few yuan higher than on the Chinese-language menu, but when it's all so cheap, you can't complain too much. Try the *lao hu cai,* or tiger salad, an evocatively named dish of cucumber chilies and tomatoes, or the pilaf with a cooling bowl of yogurt. [$] *Average main: Y30* ✉ *Seman Lu, on the roundabout opposite the Seman Hotel* 💳 *No credit cards.*

$$ AMERICAN

🍴 **Karakorum Café** (喀拉昆仑咖啡厅 *Kā lā kūnlún kāfēi tīng*). If it's Western food you're craving, head straight to this expat-run café—after weeks of eating noodles, you'll feel it's a veritable breath of fresh air on the Silk Road. The banana smoothies go down well, as does the roast eggplant focaccia. The friendly manager will give you travel advice if asked. [$] *Average main: Y60* ✉ *87 Seman Lu, opposite the Qinibagh Hotel's entrance gate* ☎ *0998/282–2669* 🌐 *www.crowninntashkorgan.com* 💳 *No credit cards.*

$ MIDDLE EASTERN

🍴 **Pakistan Restaurant** (巴基斯坦西餐厅 *Bājīsītǎn xī cāntīng*). Foreign restaurants are rare in Kashgar, so this dirt-cheap curry joint is a welcome addition. This is where the city's Pakistani residents while away their evenings playing cards and sipping tea. There's an English menu, but its function seems to be primarily illustrative—we visited twice and got the wrong dishes both times (in both cases they were delicious). Particularly good were the curries. There are no chopsticks here, as everything is scooped up using delicious *roti* (flat bread). Hot chai served with milk is the best way to wash down your meal. This restaurant's sign is covered by a large tree, but it's directly opposite the Seman Hotel's rear entrance. [$] *Average main: Y30* ✉ *Seman Lu, opposite the Seman Hotel's rear entrance* 💳 *No credit cards.*

$ SICHUAN

🍴 **Xiao Bei Dou** (小北斗 *Xiǎo běidǒu*). When you've grown tired of mutton, head here for the best Sichuan-style dishes in Kashgar. Classic selections like sweet-and-sour pork (*tangcu liji*), chicken with peanuts (*gongbao jiding*), and scallion pancakes (*conghuabing*) are all well prepared. There's plenty of cold beer in the refrigerator, and the second-floor covered terrace is perfect on a warm summer evening. An English menu is available, but the selection is limited. [$] *Average main: Y20* ✉ *285 Seman Lu, east of the Seman Hotel* 💳 *No credit cards.*

WHERE TO STAY

$ ▦ **Radisson Blu Hotel Kashgar** (喀什深业丽笙酒店 *Kāshénshēnyèlì shēng*
HOTEL   *jiǔdiàn*). Located 10 minutes by cab from the city center, this stylish
new addition to Kashgar is a bit of luxury in the far western reaches of
China. **Pros:** some staff speak English; free Wi-Fi in rooms. **Cons:** not
walking distance from downtown. Ⓢ *Rooms from: Y788* ⊠ *2 Duolaite
Bage Lu* ☎ *0998/268–8888* ⊕ *www.radissonblu.com/hotel-kashgar*
⤳ *261 rooms* ❖| *Breakfast.*

$ ▦ **Seman Hotel** (色满宾馆 *Sèmǎn bīnguǎn*). Built in 1890 as the Rus-
HOTEL   sian consulate, this edifice served as a center of political intrigue for
many years. **Pros:** near some excellent restaurants; competitive prices
from the lobby tour agencies. **Cons:** musty bathrooms in the cheaper
rooms and dorms. Ⓢ *Rooms from: Y80* ⊠ *170 Seman Lu, at Renmin
Lu* ☎ *0998/258–2129* ⊕ *semantour.com* ⤳ *168 rooms* ❖| *No meals.*

SHOPPING

Handicraft Street (手工艺品街 *Shǒu gōngyìpǐn jiē*). Running alongside
the Id Kah Mosque is a narrow lane known as Handicraft Street. In
either direction you'll find merchants selling everything from bright
copper kettles to wedding chests to brass sleigh bells. ⊠ *Wusitang Boyi
Lu near Jiefang Bei Lu.*

Sunday Market (星期天大巴扎 *Xīngqítiān dàbā zhā*). Kashgar's famous
Sunday Market consists of two bazaars with a distance of almost 10
km (6 miles) between them. The **Yengi Bazaar** on Aizilaiti Lu (Aize-
rete Road), about 1½ km (1 mile) northeast of the city center, is open
every day, but on Sunday the surrounding streets overflow with vendors
hawking everything from boiled sheep's heads to sunglasses. In the
covered section you can bargain for decorative knives, embroidered
fabrics, and all sorts of Uyghur-themed souvenirs. Behind the bazaar,
rows of sleepy donkeys nod off in the bright sunlight, their carts lined
up neatly beside them. For the best photos, however, you'll need to
head over to the **Ulak Bazaar,** a 10-minute taxi ride east. Essentially a
livestock market, farmers here tug recalcitrant sheep through the streets,
scarf-shrouded women preside over heaps of red eggs, and old Uyghur
men squat over baskets of chickens, haggling over the virtues and vices
of each hapless hen. In the market for a camel? You can buy one here.
On the outskirts of the market you can get an old-world-style straight-
razor shave from a Uyghur barber or grab a bowl of *laghman* noodles,
knowing that it's flavored with meat that is very, very fresh.

Uyghur Musical Instruments Workshop (维吾尔民族乐器制作销售店
Wéiwú'ěr mínzú yuèqì zhìzuò xiāoshòu diàn). At this shop you can watch
the owner or his apprentice working on Uyghur string instruments—
stretching snakeskin or inlaying tiny bits of shell to make a Uyghur
guitar called a *ravap*. ⊠ *272 Kumudai'erwazha* ☎ *133/6488–8194.*

SIDE TRIPS FROM KASHGAR

Fodor'sChoice   **Karakorum Highway** (喀喇昆仑公路 *Kā lǎ kūnlún gōnglù*). The Kara-
★   korum Highway (KKH), a spectacular road winding across some of
the most dramatic and inhospitable terrain on Earth, traces one of the
major ancient silk routes, from Kashgar south for 2,100 km (1,300
miles) through three great mountain ranges over the Khunjerab Pass

10

(the highest border crossing in the world) into Pakistan. The journey can be hair-raising in part because of rock- and mudslides and in part because of daredevil driving.

At an altitude of 3,600 meters (11,800 feet), **Karakul Lake** is surrounded by mountains which remain snow-covered throughout the year, with the 7,800-meter (25,600-foot) peak of **Muztagata,** the "Father of the Ice Mountains," dominating the landscape. Arriving at the lake, you'll practically be assaulted by would-be hosts on camelback, horseback, and motorcycle. Avoid the expensive yurts near the entrance and head back along the road to the more secluded yurts, where it is possible to stay with a local family for Y50 including simple meals. Standard food will be limited to bread and butter, tea, and fried rice dishes, but there is an expensive Chinese restaurant. Toilet facilities in this area are some of the worst in China, and there are no showers, but the area's beauty makes it worthwhile. Tour the lake via camel, horse, or motorbike, or just walk around, which will take about three hours. Bring warm clothing even in the summer, as it can be downright chilly: during our visit in July, we were applying sunscreen in the morning and battling sleet in the afternoon.

Any travel agent can arrange tours to Karakul Lake, but most people make the breathtaking journey by public bus. At the time of this writing, permits are not required, but this may change. However, bring your passport or you'll be turned back at a border checkpoint in Gezcun or at one of the other checkpoints that have sprung up along the way. Buses headed for Tashkurgan, two hours south of the lake, leave Kashgar's long-distance bus station on Xiyu Dadao every morning at 9:30 Beijing Time (the bus station operates on Xinjiang time, off by two hours). You'll have to pay the full price of Y51 for your ticket even though you're not traveling the full distance. Buses reach the lake in about four hours. To catch the bus back, wait by the side of the highway and flag it down—the bus returning to Kashgar from Tashkurgan passes the lake between 11 am and 1 pm. A seat should only cost Y40, but enterprising drivers may demand Y50. Either way, the bus is much cheaper than private tours, which will set you back about Y600 per day.

TIBET

The Rooftop of the World

WELCOME TO TIBET

TOP REASONS TO GO

★ **Barkhor:** Tibetan Buddhism's holiest pilgrimage circuit, the Barkhor is both the heart of Old Lhasa and one of the liveliest people-watching spots in all of China.

★ **Potala Palace:** Towering over Lhasa, this impressive palace of the Dalai Lamas was once the world's tallest structure, and is still a wonder.

★ **Ganden Monastery:** The most remote of the capital's three great monasteries, Ganden offers stunning views of the Lhasa River valley and surrounding Tibetan farmland from a height of 14,764 feet.

★ **Gyantse Dzong:** The site of fierce fighting between Tibetan and British troops in 1904, this fortress is one of the few remaining symbols of Tibetan military power.

★ **Everest Base Camp:** Stand in awe beneath the world's tallest mountain.

1 Lhasa. Despite the city's rapid modernization, Lhasa is still one of China's must-visit destinations. From the crowded back alleys of the Barkhor to the imposing heights of the Potala Palace, a mix of Westerners, local Tibetans, Nepalese, and Han Chinese give this city an atmosphere unlike any other place in the world.

2 Gyantse. Past the sapphire waters of Yamdrok Tso and endless fields of golden highland barley, this small city is the gateway to southern Tibet and the Himalayas. An abandoned fortress high above town is testament to the area's former military importance, while the unique architecture at Pelkor Chode Monastery speaks to the city's history as a melting pot of religious denominations.

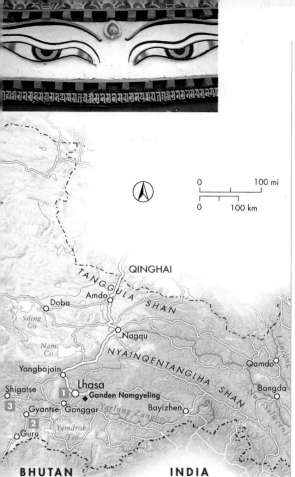

QINGHAI

TANGGULA SHAN

Doba
Amdo

Siling
Co

Nagqu

Nam
Co

NYAINQENTANGLHA SHAN

Yangbajain

Shigatse

Lhasa
◆ Ganden Namgyeling

Gyantse Gonggar Yarlung Zangbo Bayizhen

Guru Yamdrok
Tso

Qamdo

Bangda

BHUTAN   **INDIA**

0 _____ 100 mi
0 _____ 100 km

GETTING ORIENTED

The Tibetan plateau is more than twice the size of France, sandwiched between two Himalayan ridges whose peaks reach an altitude of nearly 9 km (5½ miles). With the opening of the world's highest rail line and significantly improved roads, Tibet is more accessible than ever—once you get the required permits, that is. Lhasa is the best base from which to take day trips to the fertile Kyi-chu Valley or longer jaunts into the southwestern highlands of Tsang to visit Gyantse, Shigatse, and the Everest region. Every hotel and tour operator can arrange four-wheel-drive jeeps with a driver and/or a guide. Tibet is currently undergoing massive infrastructure improvements, and many roads that were once as bumpy as the steep mountain passes have been flattened into perfect stretches of blacktop.

3 Shigatse. Tibet's second-largest city, Shigatse is the traditional capital of the Tsang region and home to the Panchen Lama's seat of power at Tashilhunpo Monastery. The ruined fortress on a hill above town has been rebuilt based on old photographs, but its concrete construction stands as one of the most glaring symbols of the modern world's encroachment on an ancient and sacred land.

4 Everest Base Camp. You may have trouble breathing when you first see the majestic peaks of the Himalayas, and not only because of the high altitude. The roof of the world is a spectacular place, with roaring snowmelt rivers feeding Tibetan farms and fields of wildflowers below.

Updated by
Kit Gillet

Tibet is all you've heard and everything you've imagined: a land of intense sunshine and towering snowcapped peaks, where crystal-clear rivers and sapphire lakes irrigate terraced fields of golden highland barley. The Tibetan people are extremely religious, viewing their daily toil and the harsh environment surrounding them as challenges along the path to life's single goal, the attainment of spiritual enlightenment. The region's richly decorated monasteries, temples, and palaces—including the Potala Palace—were not constructed by forced labor, but by laborers and artisans who donated their entire lives to the accumulation of good karma.

The death, destruction, and cultural denigration of Tibet that accompanied the Chinese invasion in the early 1950s changed this land forever, as did the Cultural Revolution in the late 1960s. Yet the people remain resilient. Colorfully dressed pilgrims still bring their offerings of yak butter to the temples, and monks work with zeal to repair the damage done to their monasteries. Many young Tibetans, attracted by the wealth and convenience brought by development, have abandoned their ancestors' traditional ways. Coca-Cola, fast food, and pulsing techno music are popular in Lhasa. Yet the changes have not lessened Tibet's allure as a travel destination. Unfortunately, however, tourism has been ever more tightly controlled since violent riots in 2008, during which protestors railed against the central government's influence over religious practice in the region. Tibetans have also been protesting years of government policies encouraging migration of majority Han Chinese to Tibet, which has stoked ethnic tensions. As the region's infrastructure is built up, Tibet's GDP is growing at 12% every year, and its small towns are quickly turning into cities; people looking for job opportunities naturally gravitate here. With seven packed trains arriving every day in Lhasa, Han Chinese almost certainly outnumber Tibetans in some areas. Still, while the Barkhor in Lhasa and the area around Tashilhunpo Monastery in Shigatse are Tibetan islands in otherwise increasingly Han cities, much of the region remains relatively free of Han Chinese influence.

> **WORD OF MOUTH**
>
> "Since the railroad and the railcars are all new, and since the speed was limited on the permafrost at 100 kph (62 mph), the ride was very smooth, and I had no problem getting to sleep at all."
> —rkwan

PLANNING

WHEN TO GO

Choosing when to visit Tibet is a matter of balancing your tolerance for extreme weather with your tolerance for tourist hordes, as well as keeping an eye on the current permit situation. The busiest months for tourists are July and August, but pleasant weather is common from May through October. However, bear in mind that Tibet can be abruptly closed to non-Chinese travelers during national holidays, such as the May 1st holiday and the October holiday. If you come at the beginning or end of the high season you'll have plenty of breathing space to take in the golden roofs of Tibet's monasteries and the icy peaks of the Himalayas. You may want to schedule your trip to coincide with one of Tibet's colorful celebrations, including the Birth of Buddha Festival (end of May), the Holy Mountain Festival (end of July), the Yogurt Festival (August), and the Bathing Festival (September). If you travel to Tibet in the off-season, many hotels and restaurants may be closed. Whenever you visit, warm clothing, sunglasses, and sunscreen are essentials for the high-altitude climate.

GETTING HERE AND AROUND

PASSPORTS AND VISAS

A visa valid for the People's Republic of China is required. You will also need a Tibet Tourism Bureau (TTB) travel permit, which is arranged by the travel agent who books your tour or transportation to Lhasa. Travel by train or plane without a permit is next to impossible—on Internet forums you may hear of the odd person who claims to have managed it, but it's more than likely that you will be refused boarding with no refund. It used to be possible to travel by train with a photocopy of your TTB, but now many officials are demanding to see the original. By plane, the original is required.

In 2013, the Tibet Tourism Bureau (TTB) relaxed its regulations on travel through the region. It no longer requires that you be a part of a group of five or more, so independent travel is once again possible. It also allows people of different nationalities to travel together. Although, in 2014 Norwegian and French citizens had some difficulties receiving permits. All travel still must be booked through local agencies.

Some regions remain out of reach. The Chamdo region has been closed since 2008, which makes overland travel from the provinces of Sichuan and Kunming impossible. At this writing Mt. Kailash was also closed, but contact your travel agent for the latest information regarding access. The TTB requires that you pay a deposit to your travel agency's account. The amount varies from Y500 to Y1,000, depending on the length of the tour.

AIR TRAVEL

In line with the government's ambitious infrastructure plans for Tibet, there are now five airports, with another one, Nagqu Dagring, due to open in 2015. When finished, Nagqu Dagring Airport will be the world's highest airport, at an altitude of 4,436 meters (14,554 feet). Currently, nine domestic airlines fly into Gonggar Airport, about 95 km (59 miles) from Lhasa, connecting Tibet with most major Chinese mainland cities and Hong Kong. Air China connects Kathmandu and Lhasa. The airport is renowned for having terrible facilities and humorless guards, so don't expect much. Tibet also has smaller airports in Chamdo, Shigatse, Nyingchi, and Ngari prefectures. These have frequent flights to Lhasa and less frequent flights to other nearby Chinese cities. Security on flights bound for Lhasa is much tighter than on other internal flights—expect to be thoroughly searched.

BUS TRAVEL

There are buses in Tibet, of the rickety, bone-shaking sort, but they tend to cater to locals only. Drivers are often very reluctant to pick up foreign travelers. In Lhasa it's easier, but you will be expected to have your tour guide with you. Most visitors hire a land cruiser to get around once outside of Lhasa.

CAR TRAVEL

A car and driver is usually included in tour packages. Travel costs are high because distances are large and gas is expensive.

TRAIN TRAVEL

Provided you have a TTB permit, you can travel on the world's highest railway to Tibet. This means that you should book a tour that includes your train trip. Air-conditioned trains, complete with oxygen masks because of the altitude, arrive several times a week from Beijing, Shanghai, Guangzhou, and Xian to Lhasa. Every passenger has to sign a health waiver saying they're fit to travel. The rail link is not without its controversies—some argue that the train encourages Han migration, and that its construction has had a tremendous environmental impact.

RESTAURANTS

It's fair to say that no one travels to Tibet for its food. Tsampa is Tibet's staple food, which is barley flour mixed with salted butter tea. It's accompanied by an odd serving of meat, vegetables, and dairy products. Lhasa has Tibet's best dining options, so make the most of the competitive market of hybrid restaurants that serve Chinese, Indian, Nepali, Tibetan, and Western fare. Most have sprung up from backpacker haunts serving perennially favorite dishes, from banana pancakes to yak burgers to chicken masala.

Because all your meals are usually included in your tour package, we do not list individual restaurants in this guide.

HOTELS

Hotel options in Lhasa have improved significantly in recent times. There are a smattering of boutique hotels and a couple of international-brand properties. Many of the more expensive hotels even equip their rooms with oxygen machines to ease the effects of altitude sickness. Tibetan guesthouses are staffed by locals and are more personable, but some of the shared bathing facilities at the lower-end options can be archaic. Outside of Lhasa, standards are much lower, so be prepared to rough it.

All your accommodations are usually included in your tour package, so we do not list individual lodgings in this guide.

TOURS

Foreign travelers are required to book a tour when securing a Tibet Travel Bureau permit. Agents should advise you on the latest changes to travel restrictions and permit requirements. Typically, the cost of an organized tour for a week runs $1,000 to $2,000 per person. When booking a tour, be sure to get confirmation in writing, with details about your hotel and meal arrangements.

Popular tours include the 2-day trip to Nam Tso Lake (Y1,000–Y1,500), the 2-day trip to Samye Monastery (Y800–Y2,500), and, when open, the 12-day trip to sacred Mount Kailash (Y7,000–Y14,000).

VISITOR INFORMATION

Travelers are at the mercy of private travel agents, guidebooks, and online travel forums for the most up-to-date information on Tibet. State-run travel bureaus do exist, but are often downright unhelpful. Such travel agencies as Tibetan Connections and Snow Lion Tours are very knowledgeable and offer great service.

LHASA

14 hrs by train south of Golmud; 43 hrs by train southwest of Beijing; 2 hrs by plane west of Chengdu; 5 hrs by plane southwest of Beijing.

The capital of Tibet is a treasure trove of monasteries, palaces, and temples. Geographically, the city is divided into a Chinese Quarter to the west and a Tibetan Quarter to the east. The Chinese neighborhood is where you'll find older hotels and Norbulingka Summer Palace. The more colorful Tibetan Quarter is full of small guesthouses, laid-back restaurants, bustling street markets, and Jokhang Temple. There is also a small Muslim Quarter to the southeast of the Barkhor. The winding lanes in and around the Barkhor are immensely walkable and a great way to rub shoulders with the locals. Don't worry about getting lost: most of the thoroughfares are circular; if you follow the pilgrims, you'll make it back to the circuit.

GETTING HERE AND AROUND

With the opening of the railway line, travelers can now travel easily and cheaply to Tibet from almost anywhere in China. You'll need a Tibet Travel Bureau permit to purchase a train ticket, and this should be arranged by your tour group. The gleaming Lhasa Train Station is

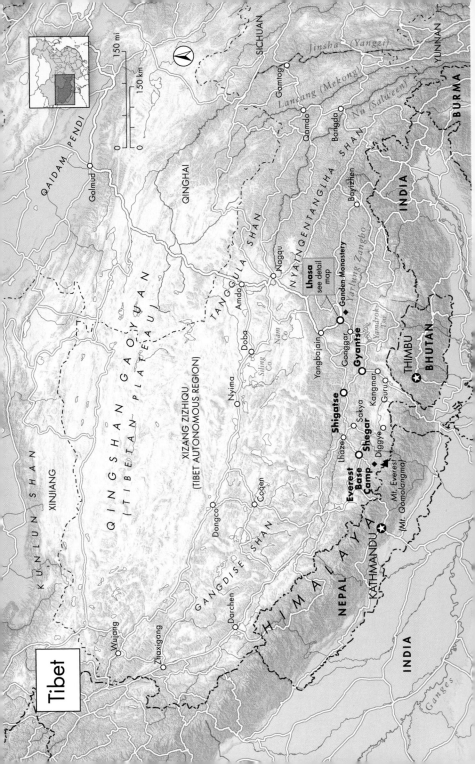

15 to 20 minutes southwest of the city center by taxi (Y50).

AIR TRAVEL Booking an airline ticket to Lhasa also requires a Tibet Tourism Bureau permit. Even if you can buy a ticket without the permit, it's highly unlikely that you will be allowed to board.

Air China, Sichuan Airlines, China Southern Airlines, and China Eastern Airlines are some of the nine airlines with frequent service to Lhasa. The easiest direct route is from Chengdu, which has as many as 10 daily flights during the summer months for about Y1,500 each way. Flights to Lhasa depart from Beijing (5 hrs), Guangzhou (5 hrs), Xi'an (3½ hrs), Chongqing (3 hrs), and Chengdu (2 hrs). The airport is about 60 km (37 miles) southwest of Lhasa, which takes about 45 minutes by taxi (Y180) or more than an hour by shuttle bus (Y25).

ABOUT THE WEATHER

From November to January, temperatures become frightfully cold (−10°F), but the climate is dry and the skies are blue. Many tourist sites in Lhasa shorten their opening hours in winter months. From June to August highs reach 80°F, although it can feel hotter. Summer sees a bit of rain, and occasionally roads will be closed to popular tourist destinations, including the Everest Base Camp. The best touring conditions occur from mid-April through May, as wildflowers bloom and snow begins to melt. September through early November, with its mild weather, is another good option.

If you are coming from Kathmandu, the nonstop flights made four times a week will give you fantastic views of the Himalayas. You must show your permit from the Tibet Tourism Bureau when you check in.

BUS TRAVEL Intercity bus travel is not only long and uncomfortable, but not encouraged for foreigners in almost all of Tibet. You can, however, take the pilgrim buses that leave every day at 6:30 am from Barkhor Square headed to Ganden Monastery. You can also travel to Shigatse from Lhasa Bus station at Jinzhu Lu.

CAR TRAVEL When you book a tour, the package will include a car and driver and all the necessary permits. If you're headed to Nepal, make sure you arrange a visa in Lhasa before your departure.

TRAIN TRAVEL The train line to Lhasa has rewritten many of the world's records for extreme engineering. It's the world's highest railway, with more than 966 km (600 miles) of track above 13,000 feet, reaching above 16,500 feet in several locations. The line is also home to the world's highest railway station, which at Tangu-la Pass sits at almost 17,000 feet.

The train is comfortable and inexpensive, with free oxygen supplies beneath every seat to combat altitude sickness. Traveling by rail is also the perfect way to see the vast uninhabited expanse of the northern Qinghai-Tibet Plateau, with yaks and antelopes roaming the hills.

SAFETY AND PRECAUTIONS

■ TIP→ Don't talk politics with Tibetans. If they speak out against the government they may be charged with treason and receive a 20-year jail term. Public Security Bureau personnel are everywhere, sometimes

CLOSE UP

Lhasa Express

One of history's most audacious engineering projects, the rail line to Lhasa began construction in 2001 after more than 30 years of delays. Chairman Mao first proposed the railroad in the 1960s, along with other infrastructure projects now being realized, like the massive Three Gorges Dam on the Yangtze River. The list of technical challenges confronting the rail line was daunting, as more than 966 km (600 miles) of track needed to be constructed at an altitude of more than 13,000 feet, topping out at Tangula Pass near 17,000 feet. Much of the track rests on semi-frozen and constantly shifting permafrost. The line also crosses through six protected environmental reserves, home to endangered species like the Tibetan antelope and the snow leopard.

Swiss engineers, experts on frozen terrain, said the project was impossible, but the Chinese government was having none of it. The first passenger train, carrying President Hu Jintao and a host of other dignitaries, rolled into Lhasa's shiny new station on July 1, 2006.

The cultural implications of the railroad to ethnic Tibetans—already a minority in their own land—are obvious. The migration of Han Chinese will continue to expand as the traditional Tibetan way of life in many areas rapidly declines in the face of modernization. Politically, the railroad is another firm sign from Beijing that they have no intention of ever letting Tibet break off into a separate political entity; in fact, plans to extend the railway to Tibet's second-largest city, Shigatse, and over the Himalayas to Kathmandu in Nepal are being developed.

However, the railway isn't completely negative for the locals. A large number of Tibetans make their livelihood from tourism, which has increased dramatically since the opening of the line. The relatively cheap, quick, and comfortable ride by train has also made it possible for Tibetans working and studying in faraway parts of China to return home and visit their families during holidays, something that was nearly impossible when the only practical way to reach Lhasa was an expensive flight.

---

in uniform, sometimes in civilian clothes or even in monks' robes. Beware of the charming Tibetan who may be a secret policeman trying to entrap you into giving him a photograph of the Dalai Lama. You could be detained or even deported. PSB offices are in all towns and many of the smaller townships.

TIMING

At a minimum, aim to spend four nights in Lhasa: this allows enough time to acclimatize to the altitude as well as see the main attractions such as Jokhang Temple, Potala Palace, and the Sera and Drepung monasteries.

TOURS

Foreign travelers to Tibet have to purchase tours along with their airline or train tickets, as is required by Chinese law. Once you're here, you may be able to book additional one-day tours through your original

The golden spires of the Jokhang Temple in Lhasa

travel agent. The city is overflowing with travel agencies, mostly geared toward Chinese tourists. A good local agency is Tibet FIT Travel.

ESSENTIALS

Air Contact Gongga Airport (贡嘎机场 *Gòng gā jīchǎng*). ✉ *101 Provincial Rd., Gonggar County* ☎ *0891/621-6465, 0891/618-2220.*

Bank Bank of China ✉ *7 Linkuo Xi Lu, Lhasa* ☎ *0891/682-8547, 0891/683-5311* ✉ *20 Beijing Dong Lu, Lhasa* ☎ *089/632-6263.*

Medical Assistance TAR People's Hospital (拉萨第一人民医院 *Lāsà dì yī rénmín yīyuàn*). ✉ *18 Linkuo Bei Lu, northeast of Potala Palace, Lhasa* ☎ *0891/632-2200.*

Train Contact China Tibet Tourism Bureau (西藏自治区旅游局 *Xīzàng zìzhìqū lǚyóu jú*). ✉ *3 Luobulingka Lu, Lhasa* ☎ *0891/683-4315* ⊕ *en.xzta.gov.cn/en/index.html* ☉ *Daily 8:30–6:30.*

Visitor and Tour Info Access Tibet Tour ✉ *Room 8110, Lhasa Chaoyang Grand Hotel, 81 Beijing Xi Lu* ☎ *028/8756-1114* ⊕ *www.accesstibettour.com.* **Snow Lion Tours** ✉ *27 Linju Lu* ☎ *971-816-3350 mobile phone* ⊕ *snowliontours.com.* **Tibet FIT Travel** ✉ *Snowlands Hotel, 4 Zangyiyuan Lu* ☎ *0891/634-9239* ⊕ *www.tibetfit.com.* **Tibet Guru** ⊕ *www.tibetguru.com.* **Tibetan Connections** ☎ *97182-03271 mobile phone* ⊕ *www.tibetanconnections.com.*

EXPLORING

Your main axis of orientation in Lhasa is Beijing Lu, a street that stretches from the Barkhor in the east to as far as Drepung Monastery in the west, passing right in front of the Potala Palace. The easiest way to get from site to site is by taxi, with journeys between most locations in the city costing no more than Y10. Pedicabs are also available, but agreeing on a price before you hop on is essential; most trips should cost about Y10. Many of the most popular attractions are concentrated in and around the Barkhor area, so walking is always an option.

TOP ATTRACTIONS

Ani Tsangkung Nunnery (阿尼仓姑寺 *Ā ní cāng gū sì*). This small, colorful convent has a livelier atmosphere than what you'll find at Lhasa's monasteries. Beaming nuns encourage you to wander through the courtyards, listen to their chanting, and watch them make ornamental butter flowers. There's a simple outdoor restaurant—popular at lunchtime—where nuns serve up inexpensive bowls of noodles and *momos* (dumplings). The chief pilgrimage site is the meditation hollow where Songtsen Gampo concentrated his spiritual focus on preventing the flood of the Kyi River in the 7th century. You're free to take photos here without charge—an option not available at many monasteries. ⊠ *Linkuo S Alley, southeast of Jokhang Temple* ☎ *0891/665–0832* 🏷 *Y40* ⊙ *Daily 8–5:30.*

Barkhor (八廓 *Bākuò*). Circling the walls of the Jokhang Temple, the Barkhor is not only Tibetan Buddhism's holiest pilgrimage circuit but also the best spot in Lhasa for people-watching. Look for monks sitting before their alms bowls while the faithful constantly spin their prayer wheels. Unless you want to shock the devout with your blatant disregard for tradition, flow with the crowd in a clockwise direction. This wide pedestrian street is also souvenir central, crammed with stalls where vendors sell prayer shawls, silver jewelry, wall hangings, and just about anything that screams "I've been to Tibet!" Don't even think about paying what the vendors ask; many of the items can easily be bargained down to less than a quarter of the original price. ⊠ *Bakuo St.*

Fodor's Choice ★ **Jokhang Temple** (大昭寺 *Dàzhāo sì*). This temple is the most sacred building in Tibet. From the gentle flicker of a butter-lamp light dancing off antique murals, statues, tapestries, and *thangkhas* (scroll paintings) to the air thick with incense and anticipation as thousands of Tibetans pay homage day and night, the temple contains a plethora of sensory delights. Most likely built in 647 during Songtsen Gampo's reign, the Jokhang stands in the heart of the Old Town. The site was selected by Queen Wengcheng, a princess from China who became Songtsen

Lhasa

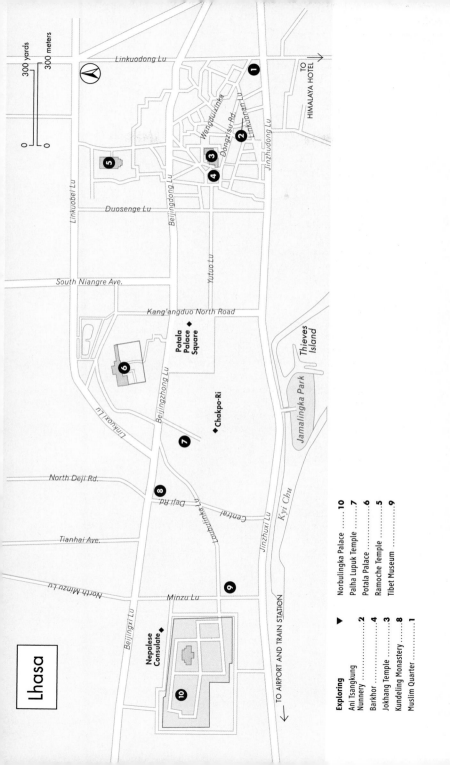

300 yards
300 meters

Linkuodong Lu

TO
HIMALAYA HOTEL

Wengdukuka

Dongzisu Rd.

Linkuonan Lu

Linkuobei Lu

Jinzhudong Lu

Duosenge Lu

Beijingdong Lu

Yutuo Lu

South Niangre Ave.

Kang'anguo North Road

Potala
Palace
Square

Beijingzhong Lu

◆ Chakpo-Ri

Linkuoxi Lu

North Deji Rd.

Deji Rd.

Tianhai Ave.

Linkuohuka Central

Jinzhuxi Lu

Kyi Chu

Thieves
Island

Jamalingka Park

North Minzu Lu

Minzu Lu

Beijingxi Lu

Nepalese
Consulate ◆

TO AIRPORT AND TRAIN STATION

Exploring
Ani Tsangkung	
Nunnery **2**	Norbulingka Palace **10**
Barkhor **4**	Palha Lupuk Temple **7**
Jokhang Temple **3**	Potala Palace **6**
Kundeling Monastery **8**	Ramoche Temple **5**
Muslim Quarter **1**	Tibet Museum **9**

Gampo's second wife. His first wife, Princess Bhrikuti from Nepal, financed the building of Jokhang. In her honor, and in recognition of Tibet's strong reliance on Nepal, the Jokhang's main gate faces west, toward Nepal. Among the bits remaining from the 7th century are the four door frames of the inner temple, dedicated to different deities. ⚠ Remember that photos are not allowed inside the buildings without a Y90 photo permit.

GETTING AROUND

Taxis are plentiful in Lhasa. Y10 will get you almost anywhere within the city limits. Getting to Drepung Monastery will cost about Y40. Minibuses ply a fixed route, with fares of around Y2. Bicycle rickshaws are also available for short trips, and normally cost Y3, although they're famous for trying to charge foreigners higher prices.

Over the centuries, renovations have enlarged the Jokhang to keep it the premier temple of Tibet. Its status was threatened in the 1950s when the Chinese Army shelled it and the Red Guards of the Cultural Revolution ransacked it. During this period, the temple was used for various purposes, including as a pigsty. Much of the damage has since been repaired, but a portion of it has been lost forever.

Before entering the Inner Jokhang, you should walk the Nangkhor Inner Circuit in a clockwise direction. It's lined with prayer wheels and murals depicting a series of Buddhist scenes. Continue on to the large Entrance Hall, whose inner chapels have murals depicting the wrathful deities responsible for protecting the temple and the city. Straight ahead is the inner sanctum, the three-story **Kyilkhor Thil,** some of whose many columns probably date from the 7th century, particularly those with short bases and round shafts.

The chapels on the ground floor of the Kyilkhor Thil are the most rewarding. The most revered chapel of the inner hall is **Jowo Sakyamuni Lhakhang,** opposite the entrance. Inside rests a bejeweled statue of Jowo Rinpoche—representing the Buddha at age 12—surrounded by adoring disciples. It was brought to Tibet by Queen Wengcheng and somehow has survived, despite a history of being plastered over and buried in sand. On busy days you may wait in line to enter this shrine, but it's worth it. On the second floor there are a number of small chapels, although many are closed to visitors. Before you leave, climb the stairs next to the main entrance up to the Jokhang's ornately decorated golden roof. You'll be rewarded with sweeping views of the Barkhor, the Potala Palace, and the snowcapped mountains beyond Lhasa. ✉ *Barkhor* ☎ *0891/632–3129* 🎫 *Y85* 🕐 *Daily 7–noon and 3–6:30, but tourists can visit only in the afternoon.*

Kundeling Monastery (功德林寺 *Gōngdélín sì*). This monastery is often overlooked by tourists, so it's less crowded than others around Lhasa. If you arrive in the morning, climb to a second-floor chapel to see monks chanting, beating drums, and playing long bronze prayer trumpets. This temple also contains examples of sand painting, in which millions of colorful grains of sand are arranged in a complex pattern over the course of hours or even days. ⊠ *Beijing Zhong Lu and Deji Lu, west of the Potala Palace* ☎ *0891/685–1973* 🎫 *Y10* ⊙ *Daily 9–8.*

Muslim Quarter (穆斯林小区 *Mùsīlín xiǎoqū*). In perhaps the most Buddhist of cities, the Muslim Quarter—centered on Lhasa's Great Mosque—is a bit of an anomaly. The district was originally intended for immigrants arriving from Kashmir and Ladakh. The Great Mosque (Da Qingzhen Si) with its green minaret was completed in 1716, but very little of the original structure remains. The area is now primarily of interest for its distinct atmosphere, thanks to its Hui Muslim residents and the large concentration of pork-free halal restaurants. ⊠ *Lingkor Nan Lu, west of Lingkor Dong Lu.*

Palha Lupuk Temple (鲁普岩寺 *Lǔpǔyán sì*). Religious rock paintings dating from as early as the 7th century can be seen at this grotto-style temple. On the third floor you'll find an entrance to a cave with sculptures carved into the granite walls, mostly by Nepalese artists more than a millennium ago. Very few tourists visit, so if you're looking to escape the crowds, head here. ⊠ *Beijing Zhong Lu, south face of Iron Mountain* 🎫 *Y20* ⊙ *Daily 9–8.*

Fodor's Choice
★
Potala Palace (布达拉宫 *Bùdálā gōng*). The awesome sight that is the Potala Palace is quite rightly considered a wonder of the world. However, virtually nothing remains of the original 11-story Potala Palace, built in 637 by Songtsen Gampo. What you see today is a 17th-century replacement. The Fifth Dalai Lama, anxious to reestablish the importance of Lhasa as the Tibetan capital, employed 7,000 workers and 1,500 artisans to resurrect the Potala Palace on the 7th-century foundation. The portion called the White Palace was completed in 1653. The Red Palace was not completed until 1694, 12 years after the Dalai Lama's death (which was kept secret by the regent in order to prevent interruption of the construction). The Potala Palace has been enlarged since then, and has been continually renovated. Once the headquarters of Tibet's theocracy, the vast complex is now a museum and a UNESCO World Heritage Site.

The Potala Palace was the world's tallest building before the advent of modern skyscrapers. Towering above the city from the slopes of Mount Marpori, the structure is 384 feet high; its 1,000 rooms house some 200,000 images. The outer section, the White Palace, was the seat of government and the winter residence of the Dalai Lama until 1951. Inside you can pass through the Dalai Lama's spartan quarters. On either side of the palace are the former offices of the government. The Red Palace, looming above the White Palace, is filled with murals that chronicle Buddhist folklore and ancient Tibetan life. Interspersed among the chapels are eight spectacular tombs covered in nearly 5 tons of gold. These bejeweled rooms contain the remains of the Fifth through 13th Dalai Lamas.

Only 2,300 visitors are allowed in each day. Your ticket allows you up to 90 minutes at the site. To limit the number of visitors, starting in 2012 the ticket price almost doubled. ⚠ **The legions of Chinese soldiers don't take kindly to being photographed. If they spot you taking pictures in their direction, they're likely to approach and want to see your** camera. ✉ *35 Beijing Zhong Lu* ☏ *0891/682–2896* ⊕ *www.potala palace.cn* 🎫 *May–Oct. Y200, Nov.–Apr. Y100* 🕐 *May–Oct., daily 8–4; Nov.–Apr., daily 8:30–3.*

DID YOU KNOW?

Underneath the 13-story, 1,000-room fortress of the Potala Palace are the dungeons, inaccessible to tourists. Justice could be harsh—torture and jail time were the punishments for refusing to pay taxes, displaying anger, or insulting a monk. The worst place to be sent was the Cave of Scorpions, where prisoners were the targets of stinging tails.

ALTITUDE ALERT

At 12,000 feet, shortness of breath and mild headaches are common during the first few days in Lhasa. These symptoms can be managed by use of a small oxygen canister, herbal remedies, or an aspirin or two. Drink plenty of water. Severe altitude sickness should immediately be brought to the attention of a physician.

WORTH NOTING

Norbulingka Palace (罗布林卡宫 *Luóbùlínkǎ gōng*). The Seventh Dalai Lama (1708–57), a frail man, chose to build a summer palace on this site because of its medicinal spring, and later moved his whole government here from the Potala Palace. Successive Dalai Lamas expanded the complex, adding additional palaces, a debating courtyard, a pavilion, a library, and a number of landscaped gardens, which are at their best in summer months. The most recent addition, built by the current Dalai Lama between 1954 and 1956, is an ornate two-story building containing his private quarters. It turned out to be the place from which, disguised as a soldier, he fled to India on March 17, 1959, three days before the Chinese massacred thousands of Tibetans and fired artillery shells into every building in the complex.

The repair work in the aftermath of the March 1959 uprising is not of high caliber, and much of Norbulingka feels run-down. That said, a collection of the Dalai Lama's carriages and automobiles housed in the **Changsam Palace** are worth a look. More fascinating are the personal effects of the current Dalai Lama housed in the **New Summer Palace,** including his radio and phonograph. You can even peek into the Dalai Lama's bathroom. No photos are allowed inside, unfortunately. There is also a small zoo full of pitiable animals, which is worth avoiding. ✉ *21 Luobulingka Lu* ☏ *0891/682–2644* 🎫 *May–Oct. Y80, Nov.–Apr. Y60* 🕐 *Mon.–Sat. 9–noon and 3–6.*

Ramoche Temple (小昭寺 *Xiǎozhāo sì*). This temple was founded by Queen Wengcheng at the same time as the Jokhang Temple. Its three-story structure dates from the 15th century. Despite restorations in the 1980s, it lost much of its former grandeur after the Chinese used it to house the Communist Labor Training Committee during the Cultural Revolution.

The Ramoche Temple was intended to house the most revered statue of Jowo Rinpoche. A threat of a Chinese invasion in the 7th century induced Queen Wengcheng to hide the statue in the Jokhang Temple.

Prayer flags are sold in front of the Jokhang, Tibet's holiest temple.

Some 50 years later it was rediscovered and placed within the Jokhang Temple's main chapel. As a substitute, Jokhang reciprocated with a Nepalese statue of Jowo Mikyo Dorje—representing Buddha as an eight-year-old—richly layered in gold and precious stones. It was decapitated during the Cultural Revolution and its torso lost in Beijing. Both head and body were found in 1984, put back together again, and placed in a small chapel at the back of the Ramoche Temple's inner sanctum. Be sure to climb to the temple's roof for a spectacular view of the Potala Palace perched high above the rooftops of Lhasa. ⊠ *Xiao Zhao Si Lu, off the north side of Beijing Dong Lu* ☎ *0891/633–6163* 🎫 *Y20* 🕙 *Daily 9–5.*

Tibet Museum (西藏博物馆 *Xīzàng bówùguǎn*). For the Chinese interpretation of Tibetan history, politics, and culture, visit this modern museum. The Y20 personal audio guide provides commentary on important pieces from prehistoric times, Chinese dynasties, and traditional Tibetan life. If you are a scholar of history, you may find some of the explanations intriguing. It often hosts temporary Tibetan art exhibitions. ⊠ *Corner of Luobulingka Lu and Minzu Nan Lu, across from Norbulingka Palace* ☎ *0891/681–2210* 🎫 *Free* 🕙 *Tues.–Sun. 9–1 and 2–6.*

NIGHTLIFE AND PERFORMING ARTS

Ganglamedo (冈拉梅朵咖啡吧 *Gānglāméiduǒ kāfēi bā*). If you're looking for a quiet spot near the Barkhor to enjoy a drink or a cup of tea after a long day, try Ganglamedo, across from the Yak Hotel. The bar

The Tibetans

They live primarily on the Tibet-Qinghai Plateau, but they also make their homes in southern Gansu, western and northern Sichuan, and northwestern Yunnan. Their culture is influenced both by Tibet's extreme geography and their unique interpretation of Buddhism, the line between the two often blurred by a "sacred geography," which deifies many of the region's mountains and lakes. Compared with other forms of Buddhism, Tibetan Buddhism (also known as "Lamaism") places far more emphasis on the physical path to enlightenment. This is why the sight of pilgrims prostrating around the base of a sacred mountain or temple for days or weeks on end is a common one in the region.

When Tibet was annexed (or "liberated") by China in 1959, their supreme spiritual leader the Dalai Lama fled in disguise to India, where he set up a Tibetan government-in-exile in Dharamsala, which became known as "little Lhasa." Since then the Dalai Lama has become an international celebrity and has succeeded in making the struggle for Tibetan independence a focus of global attention,

drawing strong condemnation—and brutal crackdowns—from Beijing. Few people realize that the Dalai Lama has actually for many years no longer insisted on independence, but a more moderate form of autonomy like that enjoyed by Hong Kong and Macau. Yet despite international pressure—and perhaps even because of the attention—there seems little hope that Tibet's status will change in the near future.

Meanwhile, Tibet continues to modernize at full speed, with seemingly every road between Lhasa and Mount Everest being upgraded simultaneously. The rail link between Beijing and Lhasa completed in 2006 has promoted "Hanification," or a major increase in the Han Chinese population. It's estimated that 60%–70% of the population in Lhasa is Han Chinese. With only 2.5 million Tibetans living in the Tibet Autonomous Region—and 800 million impoverished Han Chinese nationwide looking for a better way of life—it's only a matter of time before ethnic Tibetans become a small minority in their own homeland.

stocks a wide range of liquors. ⊠ *127 Beijing Dong Lu* ☎ *0891/633–3657* ⊕ *www.ganglamedo.com.*

Tibet Shol Opera Troupe. Tibetan operas are performed by the Tibet Shol Opera Troupe in a theater at the Himalaya Hotel. Tickets cost Y100, and reservations are required. ⊠ *Himalaya Hotel, 6 Linkuo Dong Lu* ☎ *0891/632–1111.*

SHOPPING

ARTS AND CRAFTS

For souvenirs varying from prayer flags to jewel-encrusted horse bridles, stop by one of the hundreds of open-air stalls and small shops that line the roads leading to the Jokhang Temple. Bargain in a tough but friendly manner, and the proprietors may throw in extra items for luck. Many of the goods come from around Tibet and Nepal.

Dropenling. For quality Tibetan handicrafts, visit Dropenling, down an alley opposite the Muslim Quarter's main mosque. Unlike those at other souvenir shops, all the products here are made by Tibetans, and all profits are returned to the local community. ⊠ *11 Chak Tsal Gang Lu* ☎ *0891/636–0558* ⊕ *www.tibet craft.com.*

Tanva Carpet Workshop (毯华手工 地毯 *Tǎnhuá shǒugōng dìtǎn*). On the road between Lhasa and Gongga Airport is the Tanva Carpet Workshop. The artisans here use handspun Tibetan highland wool to make both traditional and contemporary carpets using natural dyes. Even if you're not buying, it's interesting to see the whole carpet-making process from start to finish. Tanva makes the carpets that are sold in Torana stores in Beijing and Shanghai. Call ahead to arrange a visit. ☎ *1398/990–8681* ⊕ *www.toranahouse.com.*

OUTDOOR EQUIPMENT

Third Pole (第三极 *Dì sān jí*). West of the Potala Palace, the Third Pole can outfit you with everything you'll need to enjoy the great outdoors, from good hiking shoes to walking sticks to sunglasses. ⊠ *6 Luobulingka Lu* ☎ *0891/682–0549.*

Toread (探路者 *Tàn lù zhě*). A Chinese clothing chain, Toread features a wide selection of genuine outdoor equipment, as well as warm clothing if you're planning a trip to the mountains. ⊠ *182 Beijing Zhong Lu* ☎ *0891/682–9365* ⊕ *www.toread.com.cn.*

> ### WORD OF MOUTH
>
> "Remember, just about everything you do in Lhasa requires lots of walking and uphill. Potala Palace is incredibly taxing, even if you are in great shape. So, too, with the other monasteries. We saw lots of people really struggling with breathing. It is very hard work in the high altitude." —Don

AROUND LHASA

Many of Lhasa's best sites are clustered around the city center, but three of the most important are more remote. This trio of monasteries (Drepung Monastery, Ganden Monastery, and Sera Monastery) are known as the "three pillars of Tibetan Buddhism," having all been founded by religious patriarch Tsongkhapa at the beginning of the 15th century. All three are worth the effort it takes to reach them (especially Ganden Monastery, 90 minutes east of Lhasa) and should be part of any tour of Lhasa.

Drepung Monastery (哲蚌寺 *Zhébàng sì*). The largest of the Gelugpa monasteries was the residence for lesser lamas. Founded in 1416, it was enlarged in the 16th century by the Second Dalai Lama. By the era of the Fifth Dalai Lama it had become the largest monastic institution in the world, with 10,000 residents. During the Cultural Revolution it suffered only minimally, because the Army used the building as its headquarters and therefore didn't ransack it as much as other temples. The monastery was reopened in 1980, although the number of resident monks has been severely depleted.

Festivals and Celebrations

Try to time your visit with one of the brilliantly colorful traditional Tibetan festivals. Dancing monks whip up a frenzy to dispel the evil spirits of the previous year at the Year End Festival on the 29th day of the 12th lunar month. The first week of the first lunar month includes Losar (New Year Festival), when Lhasa is filled with Tibetan drama performances, incense offerings, and locals promenading in their finest wardrobe. Grand butter lanterns light up the Barkhor circuit during the Lantern Festival on the 15th of the first month. On the seventh day of the fourth month you can join the pilgrims in Lhasa or Ganden to mark the Birth of Sakyamuni (the Buddha), or you may want to wait until the 15th for the celebrations of Saga Dawa (Sakyamuni's enlightenment) and join the pilgrims who climb the Drepung Monastery to burn juniper incense. Picnics at the summer palace of Norbulingka

are common during the Worship of the Buddha in the second week of the fifth month. During Shötun (Yogurt Festival) in the first week of the seventh month, immerse yourself in the operas, masked dances, and picnics from Drepung, about 6½ km (4 miles) out of Lhasa, to Norbulingka. During the festival, giant thangkas of the Buddha are unveiled in Drepung Monastery, and Tibetan opera troupes perform operas at Norbulingka.

The Tibetan calendar is the same as the lunar calendar, so exact dates as they relate to the Western calendar are only published a year in advance. The approximate dates are as follows: Tibetan New Year (February); the Butter Lantern Festival (late February/early March); the Birth of Buddha Festival (late May/early June); the Holy Mountain Festival (late July/early August); the one-week Yogurt Festival (August); and the Bathing Festival (September).

The monastery's most important building is the Tshomchen, whose vast assembly hall, the **Dukhang**, is noteworthy for its 183 columns, atrium ceiling, and ceremonial banners. Chapels can be found on all three floors, as well as on the roof. In the two-story **Buddhas of Three Ages Chapel** (Düsum Sangye Lhakhang), at the rear of the Dukhang on the ground floor, the Buddhas of past, present, and future are each guarded by two bodhisattvas. ⊠ *Southern slope of Genpeiwuzi Mountain, 8 km (5 miles) west of Lhasa, Lhasa* ☎ *0891/686–0011* ✆ *Y55* ⊗ *Daily 9–1 (afternoon often closed to visitors).*

Fodor's Choice
★ **Ganden Monastery** (甘丹寺 *Gāndān sì*). If you have time for only one side trip from Lhasa, this rambling monastery with ocher-colored walls is your best bet. It was established in 1409 by Tsongkhapa, the founder of the Gelugpa sect, and its abbot is chosen on merit rather than heredity. Of the six great Gelugpa monasteries, Ganden was the most seriously damaged by the Chinese during the Cultural Revolution. Since the early 1980s, Tibetans have put tremendous effort into rebuilding the complex; some 300 monks are now in residence. Pilgrims come daily from Lhasa to pay homage to the sacred sites and religious relics.

The monastery comprises eight major buildings. The most impressive structure is the **Gold Tomb of Tsongkhapa** (Serdhung Lhakhang) in

the heart of the complex, easily recognized by the recently built white *chorten,* or small shrine, standing before the red building. On the second floor is the chapel of **Yangchen Khang,** with the new golden chorten of Tsongkhapa. The original from 1629, made of silver and later gilded, was the most sacred object in the land. In 1959 the Chinese destroyed it, although brave monks saved some of the holy relics of Tsongkhapa, which are now inside the new gold-covered chorten. Be careful walking around this shrine: the buttery wax on the floor is thick and slippery.

A path that circumambulates the monastery starts from the parking lot. From the path, which leads to the spot where Tsongkhapa was cremated in 1419, you'll be treated to breathtaking views of the Lhasa River valley. You'll need about an hour to complete the circuit. Photo permits cost Y20 extra. ⊠ *Tibet–Sichuan Hwy., 36 km (22 miles) southeast of Lhasa, Lhasa* ⊠ *Y45* ☉ *Daily 9–4.*

Nechung Monastery (乃琼寺 *Nǎiqióng sì*). Many people skip this 12th-century monastery, but that's a big mistake. With a strong focus on beasts, demons, and the afterlife, Nechung is unlike anything else you'll see in Tibet. Murals on the monastery's walls depict everything from humans being dismembered by dogs and vultures to demons wearing long belts of human skulls and engaged in passionate sexual intercourse. Until 1959 this monastery was home to the highly influential Nechung Oracle. Every important decision by a Dalai Lama is made after consulting this oracle, which currently resides in Dharamsala as a member of the government-in-exile. The monastery is 1 km (½ mile) southeast of Drepung Monastery. ⊠ *Off Beijing Xi Lu, 8 km (5 miles) west of Lhasa, Lhasa* ⊠ *Y25* ☉ *Daily 9–4.*

Sera Monastery (色拉寺 *Sèlā sì*). This important Gelugpa monastery, founded in 1419, contains numerous temples filled with splendid murals and icons. Originally it was a hermitage for Tsongkhapa and a few of his top students. Within a couple hundred of years it housed more than 5,000 monks.

On the clockwise pilgrimage route, start at the two buildings that will take up most of your visit. **Sera Me Tratsang,** founded in 1419, has a *dukhang* (assembly hall) rebuilt in 1761 with murals depicting Buddha's life. Among the five chapels along the north wall, the one with its exterior adorned with skeletons and skulls is unforgettable. The complex's oldest surviving structure, **Ngagpa Tratsang,** is a three-story college for tantric studies. Here you'll find statues of famous lamas and murals depicting paradise.

Continue to the four-story-high **Sera Je Tratsang,** where Manjashuri, the God of Wisdom, listens to monks engaged in philosophical debate in a courtyard just beyond the temple walls. The extremely animated debates—during which emphatic hand movements signify agreement or disagreement—take place daily starting at 3 am. Whatever your feelings are about the excitement of debates, this is one you don't want to miss. ⊠ *At the base of Mt. Phurbuchok, 5 km (3 miles) north of Lhasa, Lhasa* ☎ *0891/638–3639* ⊠ *Y50* ☉ *Daily 9–5.*

11

TSANG PROVINCE

The Tibetan province of Tsang includes some of the region's most important historic sites outside of Lhasa, but it's also rich in stunning scenery and dotted with small villages and terraced barley fields filled with brightly decorated yaks. This is your chance to get out of the city and experience rural Tibet,

> ## RUSTIC CUISINE
>
> Outside the capital, the variety of food leaves something to be desired, but in areas commonly visited by tourists you should be able to find a simple meal.

where life seems to have changed little over the past 100 years.

TOURS

If you're trying to find the majestic valleys and towering peaks that Tibet conjures up in the imagination, a journey through Tsang should be part of your itinerary. Travel agencies offer customized tours typically lasting five to eight days taking you to famous places: the brilliant blue waters of Yamdrok Tso Lake, the Dzong Fortress and Pelkor Chode Monastery in Gyantse, the Tashilhunpo Monastery in Shigatse, and the Base Camp below the world's highest peak at Mount Everest.

GYANTSE

6 hrs (180 km [110 miles]) by jeep southwest of Lhasa over the Yong-la Pass; 1½ hrs (90 km [55 miles]) southeast of Shigatse.

With small villages of stone houses beside fields of highland barley, Gyantse feels far removed from Lhasa, although the drive is only about six hours. Home to two of Tsang's most impressive sights—the massive tiered Gyantse Kumbum at Pelkor Chode Monastery and the Gyantse Dzong where British soldiers defeated Tibetans in 1904—Gyantse is an essential stop on the journey toward Everest. Tourist dollars have transformed what was once a small village into a small village bustling with hotels, restaurants, and Internet cafés. However, the sites remain impressive, and the journey to get here over the Yong-la Pass is unforgettable.

GETTING HERE AND AROUND

Coming from Lhasa, don't let your driver take the longer but faster route through Shigatse to reach Gyantse—insist on being taken via the dirt road over the Yong-la Pass, where the views are absolutely stunning. Few tourists take this route, and the locals will be genuinely surprised to see you. Once in Gyantse, don't feel the need to rush on to Shigatse the same day; you can spend the night and see the sights in the morning without significantly throwing off your touring schedule.

SAFETY AND PRECAUTIONS

At 12,959 feet above sea level, visitors to Gyantse may find the altitude difficult to handle. Take it easy and seek medical assistance if necessary.

TIMING

Most visitors spend a full day and night in Gyantse in preparation for Everest Base Camp and to allow enough time to see the town's attractions.

Kumbum is one of Tibet's largest stupas.

EXPLORING

Gyantse is easily navigable on foot. The Pelkor Chode Monastery is 10 minutes' walking northwest of the fortress; both can easily be visited and toured over the course of about three hours.

Gyantse Dzong (江孜镇 *Jiāngzī xiàn*). In the 14th and 15th centuries Gyantse rose to political power along with the rise of the Sakyapa monastic order. To get an idea of the amount of construction during this period, make the steep 20-minute climb to the top of this old fortress on the northern edge of town. The building isn't in great shape, but you'll be treated to staggering views of the town and the surrounding Nyang Chu Valley. Signs reading "Jump Off Cliff" aren't making a suggestion, but pointing to the location where Tibetan warriors jumped to their deaths rather than surrender to British troops in 1904. The best way to see everything here is to wind around the fortress clockwise toward the top, using the long concrete staircase to descend. Be careful, as there's a slippery bit of concrete at the bottom of the stairs. The **Anti-British Imperialist Museum,** just inside the front gate, is worth a visit for a distorted yet amusing account of the British invasion, sprinkled with obvious propaganda. ⊠ *North end of Yingxiong Lu, Gyantse, Tsang* ☎ *0892/817–2263* ✑ *Y40* ⏱ *Daily 9–6:30.*

Fodor's Choice
★

Pelkor Chode Monastery (白居寺 *Báijū sí*). One of the few multidenominational monastic complexes in Tibet—housing Gelugpa, Sakyapa, and Bupa monks—Pelkor Chode is home to the **Gyantse Kumbum.** Built in 1427, this building's glittering golden dome and four sets of spellbinding eyes rising over uniquely tiered circular architecture make it one of the most beautiful in Tibet. Inside there are six floors, each a labyrinth

11

A Once-Mighty Empire

CLOSE UP

The Tibet Autonomous Region (TAR) bears only a passing resemblance to what was once a massive empire that encompassed all of Tibet, Qinghai (except for the area around Xining), western Sichuan, and parts of northern Yunnan. Historically, despite their modern-day reputation for being a peaceful people, Tibetans were known as fierce warriors and feared by their neighbors. They even sacked the Chinese capital of Chang'an, now Xi'an, in the 8th century.

When the Mongols conquered China in the 13th century and founded the Yuan Dynasty, they also took control of Tibet, adopting Tibetan Buddhism as their official religion. This relationship came back to haunt Tibetans—it was used by China's successive dynasties and governments to legitimize the nation's claim to Tibet. In 1950, with almost 10 years of experience fighting first the Japanese and then the Nationalist government, the People's Liberation Army entered Tibet and quickly crushed all resistance.

of small chapels adorned with Nepalese-influenced murals and statues. A steep ladder at the rear of the fifth floor provides access to the roof. Impressive in itself, you'll appreciate this complex even more after you've seen it from the heights of Gyantse Dzong. ⊠ *Northwest end of Pelkor Lu, Gyantse, Tsang* ☎ *0892/817–2105* ✆ *Y60* ☉ *Daily 9–7.*

SHIGATSE

4½ hrs (280 km [170 miles]) west of Lhasa by jeep; 1½ hrs (90 km [55 miles]) northwest of Gyantse; 6 hrs (240 km [150 miles]) northeast of Shegar.

Tibet's second-largest city, Shigatse, is the traditional capital of Tsang and home to the Tashilhunpo Monastery, Tibet's largest functioning monastic institution. The Tsang kings once ruled over the region from the fortress north of town. Most people spend only a day in Shigatse, visiting the monastery and wandering up and down the city's Walking Street, a tourist-friendly section of Qingdao Lu. The city is divided up into a traditional Tibetan quarter and brand-new Chinese town. Shigatse is quite pleasant, but you didn't travel all the way to Tibet to see another unremarkable city.

GETTING HERE AND AROUND

The perfectly smooth road from Lhasa to Shigatse travels alongside the picturesque Tsangpo River beneath the towering walls of Nimo Gorge. Rather than stopping in Shigatse the first time you pass through, consider visiting the city on the way back from Everest Base Camp. Driving from Gyantse all the way to Shegar in a single day will maximize the time you have to spend at the mountain by getting a significant chunk of driving out of the way.

SAFETY AND PRECAUTIONS

Shigaste saw some major rioting during the disturbances in 2008, and there has been a police and army presence here and at Tashilhunpo Monastery ever since.

TIMING

A day is sufficient to walk around the town and see the monastery.

EXPLORING

Everything of interest to foreign visitors, including most hotels and restaurants, is on the stretch of road between the monastery and the fortress, namely Walking Street, which you can recognize by the Chinese-style gates on either end.

Tashilhunpo Monastery (扎什倫布寺 *Zhāshílúnbù sì*). One of the six great Gelugpa institutions, this monastery is the seat of the Panchen Lama and one of the few religious sites in Tibet not destroyed during the Cultural Revolution. The Chapel of Maitreya houses an 85-foot-high statue of the Future Buddha—the largest in the world—covered with 600 pounds of gold. More than 1,000 more images are painted on the surrounding walls. You will also be able to visit the Panchen Lama tombs, many of which are lined with photos and sculptures of their later reincarnations. The beautiful stupa of the 10th Panchen Lama, built in 1990 after his death in 1989, is topped with a remarkable likeness of his unmistakable fat, jocular face done in pure gold. As this is the largest functioning monastery in Tibet, the police presence can be a bit heavy at times, especially since the 2008 riots. Refrain from discussing politics or the Dalai Lama. Camera fees are Y75 per temple. Don't try to take unauthorized photos, as monks here have been known to manhandle those unwilling to pay for a snapshot. ⊠ *7 Jijilangka Rd., Xigaze, Tsang* ☎ *0892/882–5220* 🎫 *Y80* ⊗ *Daily 9–5 (closed to tourists noon–2).*

SHEGAR

6 hrs (240 km [150 miles]) southwest of Shigatse; 3½ hrs (110 km [70 miles]) northeast of Rongbuk Monastery and Everest Base Camp.

There isn't much of anything to see in Shegar—which also goes by the name New Tingri—a town so small that its two intersecting streets don't even have names. Nevertheless, it's the best place to spend the night before heading down to Rongbuk Monastery for the hike to Everest Base Camp. Supplies in Shegar are more expensive than in Shigatse, but the gouging here is nothing compared to what you'll find closer to Everest.

GETTING HERE AND AROUND

The long drive from Shigatse to Shegar is necessary if you want to maximize your time at Everest Base Camp. On the way to Mount Everest, you'll encounter a border area checkpoint about 15 minutes outside of town, so don't forget to bring your passport. About 45 minutes later you'll reach Bang-la Pass on the Friendship Highway, with perhaps the world's best view of the Himalayas. On a clear day you can see 4 of the world's 10 highest peaks, including Everest, Lhotse, Makalu, and Cho Oyu.

The scenery is more spectacular than the accommodations at Everest Base Camp.

SAFETY AND PRECAUTIONS

The standard advice at being at this altitude applies here; if you feel very ill, you must descend to a lower level immediately.

TIMING

Most visitors here will be very anxious to reach Everest Base Camp as soon as they can, and there is no need to hang out here for more than a night to get acclimatized.

EVEREST BASE CAMP

14 hrs (670 km [420 miles]) southwest of Lhasa by jeep; 3 hrs (110 km [70 miles]) southwest of Shegar (New Tingri).

"Because it's there," mountaineer George Mallory quipped in 1922 when asked why he wanted to climb the tallest mountain on the planet. The fabled peak is located in the world's highest national park, Qomolangma Nature Reserve, which is a visual delight that alone is worth the trek from Lhasa. After the monsoon rains in June the hillsides are covered with a variety of blooming flowers and butterflies. Even from April to June the light snow blanketing the rugged ground and along babbling brooks is striking.

GETTING HERE AND AROUND

If you only have eyes for Everest, you can make it here from Lhasa and back in three days. But you spend about 10 hours driving every day, skip all the sights along the way, and hang out for only an hour or so at Everest Base Camp. Most people make this a five-day trip. Not included in the price of your tour will be the Y180 per person entrance fee for the national park, plus Y400 per land cruiser or Y600 per van, usually split among the passengers, and an extra Y180 for the guide's admission. You are not allowed to drive directly to the Base Camp. There is a parking lot very close to Rongbuk Monastery, and mini-buses (Y25) take you from the lot the rest of the way. Have your passport with you.

SAFETY AND PRECAUTIONS

As everywhere in Tibet, altitude sickness is common here, and your body needs time to recover. Roughly one out of every 20 visitors needs to be flown out and back down to lower altitudes. If you become ill, you will want to be evacuated to Lhasa as soon as possible. Also, proper clothing and sunscreen are essential. Bring antibacterial hand wash, since it doesn't require water.

TIMING

Your time at Everest Base Camp is very much dependent on the weather; it can be demoralizing to travel so far and not see the highest mountains in the world because of cloud cover. With this in mind, it's worth planning to stay for at least a couple of days. The best time to enjoy the area is April, May, and June. Avoid traveling here from October to April, as it's cold. July and August is the rainy season, and it's almost impossible to see Mount Everest though the mist.

TOURS

Snow Lion Tours and Tibetan Connections run several tours that include a trip to Everest Base Camp. Trekking tours are possible but they are not cheap. An eight-day tour can cost you Y2,000 per day (including accommodations, food, transportation, camping gear, entrance fees, and English-speaking guide).

Rongbuk Monastery (绒布寺修道院 *Róngbù sì xiūdàoyuàn*). You can visit the world's highest monastery, Rongbuk Monastery, on your way to Base Camp. There were once 500 monks living here, but now there are only 20 monks and 10 nuns, who delight in the company of visitors. It is 8 km (5 miles) along a dirt road from the monastery to Base Camp. The 15-minute drive from the monastery is no longer officially allowed, but plenty of jeeps get through with a little cajoling and perhaps a bit of cash. It's more thrilling, however, to make the three-hour walk, even if it is just to say that you trekked the Everest region. Horse-drawn carts are also available for Y30 per person one way, making the trip in about an hour. ⊠ *Zhufeng Rd., Everest Base Camp, Tsang* ✉ *Y35.*

UNDERSTANDING CHINA

CHINA AT A GLANCE

VOCABULARY

MENU DECODER

CHINA AT A GLANCE

FAST FACTS

- Capital: Beijing
- National anthem: "March of the Volunteers"
- Type of government: Communist
- Administrative divisions: 23 provinces (including Taiwan), 5 autonomous regions, 4 municipalities, 2 special administrative regions (Hong Kong and Macau)
- Independence: October 1, 1949
- Constitution: December 4, 1982
- Legal system: A mix of custom and statute, largely criminal law, with rudimentary civil code
- Voting: 18 years of age
- Legislature: Unicameral National People's Congress; 2,987 members elected by municipal, regional, and provincial people's congresses to serve five-year terms; the last elections were in 2013.
- Population: 1.384 billion; the largest in the world
- Population density: 138 people per square km (361 people per square mile)
- Median age: Female 37.5, male 35.8
- Life expectancy: Female 77.43, male 73.09
- Infant mortality rate: 14.79 deaths per 1,000 live births
- Literacy: 95.1%
- Language: Standard Chinese or Mandarin (official), Yue (Cantonese), Wu (Shanghainese), Minbei (Fuzhou), Minnan (Hokkien-Taiwanese), Xiang, Gan, Hakka dialects
- Ethnic groups: Han Chinese 92%; Zhuang, Uygur, Hui, Yi, Tibetan, Miao, Manchu, Mongol, Buyi, Korean, and other nationalities 8%
- Religion: Officially atheist, but Taoism, Buddhism, Christianity, and Islam are practiced.
- Discoveries and Inventions: Decimal system (1400 BC), paper (100 BC), seismograph (AD 100), compass (200), matches (577), gunpowder (700), paper money (800), movable type (1045)

GEOGRAPHY AND ENVIRONMENT

- Land area: 9.3 million square km (3.6 million square miles), the fourth-largest country in the world, and slightly smaller than the United States
- Coastline: 14,500 km (9,010 miles) on the Yellow Sea, the East China Sea, and the South China Sea
- Terrain: Mostly mountains, high plateaus, deserts in west; plains, deltas, and hills in east
- Islands: Hainan, Taiwan, many smaller islands along the coast
- Natural resources: Aluminum, antimony, coal, hydropower, iron ore, lead, magnetite, manganese, mercury, molybdenum, natural gas, petroleum, tin, tungsten, uranium, vanadium, zinc
- Natural hazards: Droughts, earthquakes, floods, land subsidence, tsunamis, typhoons
- Environmental issues: Air pollution (greenhouse gases, sulfur dioxide particulates), especially from China's reliance on coal, which is used to generate 68% of the country's electric power. Acid rain is another consequence of burning high-sulfur coal, particularly in the north. Deforestation, soil erosion, and economic development have destroyed one-fifth of agricultural land since 1949. Water pollution from untreated wastes and water shortages are other problems.

"China is an attractive piece of meat coveted by all . . . but very tough, and for years no one has been able to bite into it."

— Zhou Enlai,

Chinese Premier, 1973

ECONOMY

- Currency: Yuan
- Exchange rate: Y6.14=$1
- GDP: $7.7 trillion
- Inflation: 2.6%
- Per capita income: Y60,176 ($9,800)
- Unemployment: 4.1%
- Workforce: 797.6 million (agriculture 33.6%; industry 30.3%; services 36.1%)
- Debt: $10.72 trillion
- Major industries: Armaments, automobiles, cement, chemical fertilizers, coal, consumer electronics, food processing, footwear, iron and steel, machine building, petroleum, telecommunications, textiles and apparel, toys
- Agricultural products: Barley, cotton, fish, millet, oilseed, peanuts, pork, potatoes, rice, sorghum, tea, wheat
- Exports: $2.21 trillion
- Major export products: electrical and other machinery, including data processing equipment, apparel, textiles, iron and steel, optical and medical equipment
- Export partners: U.S. 16.7%; Hong Kong 17.4%; Japan 6.8%; South Korea 4.1%
- Imports: $1.95 trillion
- Major import products: Chemicals, iron and steel, machinery and equipment, mineral fuels, plastics
- Import partners: Japan 8.3%; South Korea 9.4%; U.S. 7.8%; Germany 4.8%; Australia 4.8%

POLITICAL CLIMATE

Since the Chinese Communist Party (CCP) took control of the government in 1949, it has shown little tolerance for outside views. Other major political parties are banned and the government is quick to crack down on movements that it doesn't approve of, most recently the Falun Gong. China's size and diversity complicate national politics, with party control weaker in rural areas, where most of the population lives. Successful politicians have sought support from local and regional leaders and must work to keep influential nonparty members from creating a stir.

The decade-long struggle for democracy that ended in the bloody Tiananmen Square protests of 1989 remains a sore point for the CCP, who often blame internal dissent on foreign agitators and continually remind the population that political stability is essential for China's economic growth. There is increasing frustration among the Chinese people over political corruption at the local and national levels, prompting urgent calls for government reform. Always alert to domestic discontent, the Chinese government maintains tight control over media, Internet, and other forms of communication to prevent dissent.

DID YOU KNOW?

- There are 54.4 million Christians in China.
- China has more navigable waterways (68,350 miles) than any country in the world.
- China has approximately 3.4 million active military personnel.
- One in five people in the world are Chinese.
- During the Holocaust, Shanghai was the only port that would accept Jews without an entry visa or passport.
- Every day, China consumes 1.7 million pigs.
- China's national anthem was originally the theme song of the 1935 Chinese movie *Sons and Daughters in a Time of Storm*.

CHINESE VOCABULARY

	CHINESE	ENGLISH EQUIVALENT	CHINESE	ENGLISH EQUIVALENT
Consonants				
	b	**b**oat	p	**p**ass
	m	**m**ouse	f	**f**lag
	d	**d**ock	t	**t**ongue
	n	**n**est	l	**l**ife
	g	**g**oat	k	**k**eep
	h	**h**ouse	j	and **y**et
	q	**ch**icken	x	**sh**ort
	zh	ju**dge**	ch	chur**ch**
	sh	**sh**eep	r*	**r**ead
	z	see**ds**	c	do**ts**
	s	**s**eed		
Vowels				
	ü	**You**	ia	**y**a**rd**
	üe	y**ou** + **e**	ian	**yen**
	a	f**a**ther	iang	**young**
	ai	K**i**te	ie	**yet**
	ao	n**ow**	o	**a**ll
	e	**ea**rn	ou	g**o**
	ei	D**ay**	u	w**oo**d
	er	c**ur**ve	ua	w**a**ft
	i	y**ie**ld	uo	w**a**ll
	i (after z, c, s, zh, ch, sh)	**th**und**er**		

MANDARIN CHINESE

Mandarin Chinese is the official language of China, called by the Chinese *Putonghua* or "the common language." Beijing dialect is considered the standard form and is spoken on TV, radio, and taught in the schools. Most of the Chinese population speaks Mandarin, except in the south and westernmost provinces, where Cantonese, Uighur, or Tibetan are commonly spoken. In addition to the languages spoken by ethnic minorities, there are eight major dialects in China, including Mandarin, Cantonese, Shanghainese, Fuzhou, Minnan, Xiang, Gan, and Hakka, which all have their own subdialects.

PINYIN

The Romanization of Chinese is called *Pinyin* and it's commonly seen on street signs, in train and bus stations, and on the subways. Many Chinese don't understand Pinyin so it's necessary to always carry a language phrasebook with Chinese characters.

WORD ORDER

The basic Chinese sentence structure is the same as in English, following the pattern of subject-verb-object:

He took my pen.

s   v   o

Tā ná le wǒ de bǐ.

s   v   o

NOUNS

There are no articles in Chinese, although there are many "counters," or "measure words," which are used when a certain number of something is specified. Various attributes of a noun—such as size, shape, or use—determine which counter is used with that noun. Chinese does not distinguish between singular and plural.

a pen   yìzhī bǐ

a book   yìběn shū

VERBS

Chinese verbs are not conjugated, and they do not have tenses. Instead, a system of word order, word repetition, and the addition of a number of adverbs serves to indicate the tense of a verb, whether the verb is a suggestion or an order, or even whether the verb is part of a question. Tāzaì ná wǒ de bǐ. (He is taking my pen.) Tā ná le wǒ de bǐ. (He took my pen.) Tā yǒu méi yǒu ná wǒ de bǐ? (Did he take my pen?) Tā yào ná wǒ de bǐ. (He will take my pen.)

TONES

In English, intonation patterns can indicate whether a sentence is a statement (He's hungry.), a question (He's hungry?), or an exclamation (He's hungry!). In Chinese, words have a particular tone value, and these tones are important in determining the meaning of a word. In the following examples, the words look similar but each is said with one of the four tones found in standard Chinese: mā (high, steady tone) means mother; má (rising tone, like a question) means fiber; mǎ (dipping tone) means horse; and mà (dropping tone) means swear.

PHRASES

You don't need to master the entire Chinese language to spend a week in China, but taking charge of a few key phrases in the language can aid you in just getting by.

	ENGLISH	PINYIN
Common Greetings		
	Hello/Good morning	Nǐ hǎo/Zǎoshàng hǎo
	Good evening	Wǎnshàng hǎo
	Good-bye	Zàijiàn
	Title for a married woman or an older unmarried woman	Tàitai/Fūrén
	Title for a young and unmarried woman	Xiǎojiě
	Title for a man	Xiānshēng
	How are you?	Nǐ hǎo ma?
	Fine, thanks. And you?	Hěn hǎo. Xièxiè. Nǐ ne?
	What is your name?	Nǐ jiào shénme míngzi?
	My name is…	Wǒ jiào…
	Nice to meet you	Hěn gāoxìng rènshì nǐ
	I'll see you later.	Huítóu jiàn.
Polite Expressions		
	Please.	Qǐng.
	Thank you.	Xièxiè.
	Thank you very much.	Duōxiè.
	You're welcome.	Búkèqi
	Yes, thank you.	Shì de, xièxiè.
	No, thank you.	Bù, xièxiè.
	I beg your pardon.	Qǐng yuánliàng.
	I'm very sorry.	Hěn baòqiàn.
	Pardon me.	Dùibùqǐ.
	That's okay.	Méi shénme.
	It doesn't matter.	Méi guānxi.
	Do you speak English?	Nǐ huì shuō Yīngyǔ ma?
	Yes.	Shì de.
	No.	Bù.
	Maybe.	Bù yī dìng
	I can speak a little.	Wǒ néng shuō yī diǎnr.
	I understand a little.	Wǒ dǒng yì diǎnr.
	I don't understand.	Wǒ bù dǒng.
	I don't speak Chinese very well.	Wǒ Zhōngwén shuō de bù hǎo.
	Would you repeat that, please?	Qǐng zài shuō yíbiàn?

ENGLISH	PINYIN
I don't know.	Wǒ bù zhīdaò.
No problem.	Méi wèntí.
It's my pleasure.	Méi guānxi.

Needs and Question Words

ENGLISH	PINYIN
I'd like...	Wǒ xiǎng...
I need...	Wǒ xūyào...
What would you like?	Nǐ yaò shénme?
Please bring me...	Qǐng gěi wǒ...
I'm looking for...	Wǒ zài zhǎo...
I'm hungry.	Wǒ è le.
I'm thirsty.	Wǒ kǐukě.
It's important.	Hěn zhòngyào.
It's urgent.	Hěn jǐnjí.
How?	Zěnmeyàng?
How much?	Duōshǎo?
How many?	Duōshǎo gè?
Which?	Nǎ yí gè?
What?	Shénme?
What kind of?	Shénme yàng de?
Who?	Shuí?
Where?	Nǎli?
Where is the bathroom?	Cèsuǒ zài nǎr?
When?	Shénme shíhòu?
What does this mean?	Zhè shì shénme yìsi?
What does that mean?	Nà shì shénme yìsi?
How do you say... in Chinese?	...yòng Zhōngwén zěnme shūo?

At the Airport

ENGLISH	PINYIN
Where is...	...zài nǎr?
customs?	hǎigūan
passport control?	hùzhào jiǎnyàn
the information booth?	wènxùntái
the ticketing counter?	shòupiàochù
the baggage claim?	xínglǐchù
the ground transportation?	dìmìan jiāotōng
Is there a bus to the city?	yǒu qù chéng lǐ de gōnggòng

	ENGLISH	PINYIN
		qìchē ma?
	Where are ...	...zài nǎr?
	the international departures?	guójì hángběn chūfě diǎn?
	the international arrivals?	guójì hángběn dàodá diǎn?
	What is your nationality?	Nǐ shì něi guó rén?
	I am an American.	Wǒ shì Měiguó rén.
	I am Canadian.	Wǒ shì Jiěnádà rén.
At the Hotel, Reserving a Room		
	I would like a room...	Wǒ yào yí ge fángjiān.
	for one person	yìjiān dānrén
	for two people	yìjiān shuāngrén
	for tonight	jīntīan wǎnshàng
	for two nights	liǎng gè wǎnshàng
	for a week	yí ge xīngqī
	Do you have a different room?	Nǐ hái yǒu biéde fángjiān ma?
	with a bath	dài yùshì de fángjiān
	with a shower	dài línyù de fángjiān
	with a toilet	dài cèsuǐ de fángjiān
	with air-conditioning	yǒu kōngtiáo de fángjiān
	How much is it?	Duōshǎo qián?
	My bill, please.	Qǐng jiézhàng.
At the Restaurant		
	Where can we find a good restaurant?	Zài nǎr kěyǐ zhǎodào yìjiě hǎo cānguǎn?
	We'd like a(n)...restaurant.	Wǒmen xiǎng qù yì gè... cānguǎn.
	elegant	gāo jí
	fast-food	kuàicān
	inexpensive	piányì de
	seafood	hǎixiān
	vegetarian	sùshí
	café	kāfēi diàn
	A table for two	liǎng wèi
	Waiter, a menu, please.	Fúwùyuán, qǐng gěi wǒmen càidān.
	The wine list, please.	Qǐng gěi wǒmen jiǔdān.

ENGLISH	PINYIN
Appetizers	kāiwèi cài
Main course	zhǔ cài
Dessert	tiándiǎn
What would you like?	Nǐ yào shénme cài?
What would you like to drink?	Nǐ yào hē shénme yǐnliào?
Can you recommend a good wine?	Nǐ néng tuījiàn yí ge hǎo jiǔ ma?
Wine, please.	Qǐng lǎi diǎn jiǔ
Beer, please.	Qǐng lǎi diǎn píjiǔ.
I didn't order this.	Wǒ méiyǒu diǎn zhè gè.
That's all, thanks.	Jiù zhèxie, xièxiè.
The check, please.	Qǐng jiézhàng.
Cheers!/Bottoms Up!	Gānbēi!
To your health!	Zhù nǐ shēntì jiànkāng.

Out on the Town

Where can I find...	Nǎr yǒu...
an art museum?	yìshù bówùguǎn?
a museum of natural history?	zìránlìshǐ bówùguǎn?
a history museum?	lìshǐ bówuguǎn?
a gallery?	huàláng?
interesting architecture?	yǒuqù de jiànzhùwù?
a church?	jiàotáng?
the zoo?	dòngwùyuán?
I'd like...	Wǒ xiǎng...
to see a play.	kàn xì.
to see a movie.	kàn diànyǐng.
to see a concert.	qù yīnyuèhuì.
to see the opera.	kàn gējù.
to go sightseeing.	qù guānguāng.
to go on a bike ride.	qí zìxíngchē.

Shopping

Where is the best place to go shopping for...	Mǎi...zuì hǎo qù nǎr?
clothes?	yīfu?
food?	shíwù?
souvenirs?	jìniànpǐn?

ENGLISH	PINYIN
furniture?	jiājù?
fabric?	bùliào?
antiques?	gǔdǐng?
books?	shūjí?
sporting goods?	yùndòng wùpǐn?
electronics?	diànqì?
computers?	diànnǎo?

Directions

Excuse me. Where is…	Duìbùqǐ… zài nǎr?
the bus stop?	qìchēzhàn?
the subway station?	dìtiězhàn?
the restroom?	xǐshǒujiān?
the taxi stand?	chūzū chēzhàn?
the nearest bank?	zuìjìn de yínháng?
the hotel?	lü˘guǎn?
To the right	Zài yòubiān.
To the left.	Zài zuǐbiān.
Straight ahead.	Wǎng qián zǒu.
It's near here.	Jiùzài zhè fùjìn.
Go back.	Wǎng huí zǒu.
Next to…	Jǐnkào…

Time

What time is it?	Xiànzài jǐdiǎn?
It is noon.	Zhōngwǔ.
It is midnight.	Bànyè.
It is 9 am	Shàngwǔ jiǔ diǎn.
It is 1 pm	Xiàwǔ yì diǎn.
It is 3 o'clock.	Sān diǎn (zhōng).
5:15	Wǔ diǎn shíwǔ fēn.
7:30	Qī diǎn sānshí (bàn).
9:45	Jiǔ diǎn sìshíwǔ.
Now	Xiànzài
Later	Wǎn yì diǎnr
Immediately	Mǎshàng
Soon	Hěn kuài

ENGLISH	PINYIN
Days of the Week	
Monday	Xīngqī yī
Tuesday	Xīngqī èr
Wednesday	Xīngqī sān
Thursday	Xīngqī sì
Friday	Xīngqī wǔ
Saturday	Xīngqī liù
Sunday	Xīngqī rì (tiān)
Modern Connections	
Where can I find...	Zài nǎr kěyǐ shǐ yòng...
a telephone?	diànhuà?
a fax machine?	chuánzhēnjī?
an Internet connection?	guójì wǎnglù?
How do I call the United States?	Gěi Měiguó dǎ diànhuà zěnme dǎ?
I need...	Wǒ xūyào...
a fax sent.	fā chuánzhēn.
a hookup to the Internet.	yǔ guójì wǎnglù liánjiē.
a computer.	diànnǎo.
a package sent overnight.	liányè bǎ bāoguǒ jìchū.
some copies made.	fùyìn yìxiē wénjiàn.
a DVD player	yǐngdié jī
an overhead projector and markers.	huàndēngjī he biāoshìqì.
Emergencies and Safety	
Help!	Jiùmìng a!
Fire!	Jiùhuǐ a!
I need a doctor.	Wǒ yào kàn yīshēng.
Call an ambulance!	Mǎshàng jiào jiùhùchē!
What happened?	Fāshēng le shénme shì?
I am/My wife is/My husband is/	Wǒ/Wǒ qīzi/Wǒ zhàngfu/
My friend is/Someone is...	Wǒ péngyǒu/Yǒu rén...
having a heart attack.	bìng de hěn lìhài.
choking.	yēzhù le.
losing consciousness.	yūndǎo le.
about to vomit.	yào ǒutùwù le.

ENGLISH	PINYIN
having a seizure.	yǒu fābìng le.
stuck.	bèi kǎ zhù le.
I can't breathe.	Wǒ bù néng hūxī.
I tripped and fell.	Wǒ bàn dǎo le.
I cut myself.	Wǒ gē shěng le.
I drank too much.	Wǒ jiǔ hē de tài duō le.
I don't know.	Wǒ bù zhīdào.
I've injured my…	Wǒ de…shòushěng le.
head	tóu
neck	bózi
back	bèi
arm	gē bèi
leg	tuǐ
foot	jiǎo
eye(s)	yǎnjīng
I've been robbed.	Wǒ bèi qiǎng le.

Numbers

0	Líng
1	Yī
2	Èr, liǎng
3	Sān
4	Sì
5	Wǔ
6	Liù
7	Qī
8	Bā
9	Jiǔ
10	Shí
11	Shíyī
12	Shí'èr
13	Shísān
14	Shísì
15	Shíwǔ
16	Shíliù
17	Shíqī

ENGLISH	PINYIN
18	Shíbā
19	Shíjiŭ
20	Èrshí
21	Èrshíyī
22	Èrshí'èr
23	Èrshísān
30	Sānshí
40	Sìshí
50	Wŭshí
60	Liùshí
70	Qīshí
80	Bāshí
90	Jiŭshí
100	Yìbăi
1,000	Yìqiān
1,100	Yìqiān yìbăi
2,000	Liăngqiān
10,000	Yíwàn
100,000	Shíwàn
1,000,000	Băiwàn

MENU DECODER

ENGLISH	PINYIN	CHARACTERS
beef	niúròu	牛肉
beer	píjiǔ	啤酒
braised (in soy sauce)	hóng shāo	红烧
braised pork	hóng shāo zhūròu, hóng shāo ròu	红烧猪肉，红烧肉
bread	miànbāo	面包
butter	huángyóu	黄油
cabbage	bāoxīncài	包心菜
carrot	húluóbo	胡萝卜
celery	qíncài	芹菜
chicken	jī	鸡
chicken meat (boneless)	jīròu	鸡肉
cold	lěng	冷
coffee	kāfēi	咖啡
cucumber	huángguā	黄瓜
delicious	hǎochī	好吃
dessert	tiándiǎn	甜点
dim sum	diǎnxīn	点心
duck	yā	鸭
egg(s)	dàn	蛋
fish	yú	鱼
food	shíwù	食物
fruit	shuǐguǒ	水果
ham	huǒtuǐ	火腿
hot, spicy	là	辣
ice cream	bīngjilíng	激冰凌
juice	guǒzhī	果汁
lobster	lóngxiā	龙虾
meat	ròu	肉
milk	niúnǎi	牛奶
mustard	jièmo	芥末
noodles	miàntiáo	面条
Peking duck	Běijīng kǎoyā	北京烤鸭
pepper	hújiāo	胡椒

ENGLISH	PINYIN	CHARACTERS
pork	zhūròu	猪肉
pork chop(s)	zhūpái	猪排
potatoes	mǎlíngshǔ/tǔdòu	马铃薯/土豆
roast	kǎo	烤
roast chicken	kǎo jī	烤鸡
salad	shālā	沙拉
salt	yán	盐
shrimp	xiā	虾
soda	sūdǎ shuǐ	苏打水
soup	tāng	汤
sour	suān	酸
soy sauce	jiàngyóu	酱油
spare ribs	páigǔ	排骨
spicy	là	辣
steak	niúpái	牛排
steamed	qīng zhēng	清蒸
steamed fish	qīng zhēng yú	清蒸鱼
stir-fried	chǎo	炒
sugar	táng	糖
tea	chá	茶
vegetables	shūcài	蔬菜
wine, alcohol	jiǔ	酒

Excerpted from Living Language Complete Chinese.

TRAVEL SMART
CHINA

GETTING HERE AND AROUND

Make no mistake: This is one HUGE country. China's efficient train system is a great way of getting around, especially with the high-speed rail lines linking major cities like Beijing, Guangzhou, and Shanghai. The growing network of domestic flights is also a good option, although high-speed rail can be cheaper and faster, saving you the two-hour check-in time at most airports.

China's capital, Beijing, is in the northeast, while the financial capital of Shanghai is halfway down the east coast. The historic city of Nanjing is upriver from Shanghai; head much farther inland and you'll hit the erstwhile capital Xi'an, home to the Terracotta Warriors.

Limestone mountains surround the Guilin area, in southern China. The region's hubs cluster in the dynamic Pearl River delta region: Guangzhou, capital of Guangdong Province, and Shenzhen, an industrial boomtown on the border with Hong Kong. Though part of China, Hong Kong is a Special Administrative Region, and functions as if it were another country.

Smack bang in the middle of China is Sichuan Province. Its capital, Chengdu, is a lively financial center and an important transport hub connecting eastern and western China. Kunming is the capital of the southwestern province of Yunnan. Once the gateway to the Southern Silk Road, it now leads into the bordering countries of Myanmar, Laos, and Vietnam.

Despite ongoing international controversy, Tibet, in the far west of the country, remains a Special Autonomous Region. Its capital, Lhasa, the historic center of Tibetan Buddhism, is a mind-blowing 3,650 meters (11,975 feet) above sea level in the northern Himalayas.

Vast deserts and grassy plains make up much of northwest China. Here the autonomous Xinjiang region is home to a largely Muslim population. Its capital city, Ürümqi, is the world's farthest inland city. Nei Mongol, or Inner Mongolia, is a great swath of (mostly barren) land that runs across much of northern China.

Maps with street names in Pinyin are available in most Chinese cities, though they're not always up to date. A few crucial words of Chinese can help decode street names. *Lu* means road, *jie* means street, *dalu* is a main road, and *dajie* is a main street. Those endings are often preceded by a compass point: *bei* (north), *dong* (east), *nan* (south), *xi* (west), and *zhong* (middle). These distinguish different sections of long streets. So, if you're looking for Beijing Xi Lu, it's the western end of Beijing Road.

TRAVEL TIMES FROM BEIJING		
To	By Air	By Train
Shanghai	2¼ hours	5–20 hours
Xi'an	2 hours	5–19 hours
Guangzhou	3 hours	9–29 hours
Hong Kong	3¾ hours	24–27 hours
Guilin	3¼ hours	22–27 hours
Kunming	3¼ hours	38–47 hours
Nanjing	1¼ hours	3–15 hours
Lhasa	6 hours	45 hours
Ürümqi	4 hours	34 hours
Chengdu	3¾ hours	25–31 hours

▌ AIR TRAVEL

Beijing, Shanghai, and Hong Kong are China's three major international hubs. You can catch nonstop or one-stop flights to Beijing from New York (13¾ hours), Chicago (13–14 hours), San Francisco (11½–12½ hours), Los Angeles (11½–13 hours), London (10½–11½ hours), and Sydney (14–16 hours). Though most airlines say that reconfirming your return flight is unnecessary, some local airlines cancel your seat if you don't reconfirm.

Contacts Airline and Airport Links.com. Airline and Airport Links.com has links to the websites of many of the world's airlines and airports. ⊕ *www.airlineandairportlinks.com.*

Airline Security Issues Transportation Security Administration. The Transportation Security Administration website answers almost every question about U.S. airline security and travel regulations that you may have. ⊕ *www.tsa.gov.*

AIR PASSES

If you are flying to China on a SkyTeam airline (Delta, for example), consider the Go Greater China Pass, which covers 148 destinations in China, including Hong Kong, Macao, and Taiwan. After you purchase your international ticket to mainland China or Taiwan on a SkyTeam member airline, you can take between 3 and 16 flights within China on China Airlines, China Southern, China Eastern, or Xiamen Airlines. If you are a member of a frequent-flier program, these flights will count toward miles. The price of the pass is between $270 and $1,300, depending upon the distance you plan to fly.

Beijing, Xiamen, and Hong Kong are three of the cities included in the One-World Alliance Visit Asia Pass. Cities are grouped into zones, and a flat rate is levied for each flight based on the zone in which the city is located. It doesn't include flights from the United States, however. Inquire through American Airlines, Cathay Pacific, or any other OneWorld member. It won't be the cheapest way to get around, but you'll be flying on some of the world's best airlines.

Air Pass Info Go Greater China Pass ☎ 800/221–1212 ⊕ *www.skyteam.com/ en/flights-and-destinations/travel-passes/ go-china.* **Visit Asia Pass** ☎ 800/233– 2742 ⊕ *www.oneworld.com/flights/ single-continent-fares/visit-asia.*

AIRPORTS

Beijing Capital International Airport (PEK) is Northern China's main hub, 20 miles northeast of the Beijing city center. Plans are underway to have a new airport built in Beijing by October 2018 that will handle domestic flights. Shanghai has two airports: Pudong International Airport (PVG) is newer and flashier than Hongqiao International Airport (SHA), but Hongqiao is more efficient and closer to downtown. The main hub in southern China is the sleek and modern Hong Kong International Airport (HKG), also known as Chek Lap Kok.

There are also international airports at Guangzhou (CAN), Kunming (KMG), Xiamen (XMN), Shenzhen (SZX), Xi'an (XIY), Chengdu (CTU), and Guilin (KWL), among others.

Clearing customs and immigration in China can take a while, especially in the morning, so arrive at least two hours before your scheduled flight time.

While you're wandering through Chinese airports, someone may approach you offering to carry your luggage, or even just give you directions. Be aware that this "helpful" stranger will almost certainly expect payment. Many of the X-ray machines used for large luggage items aren't film-safe, so keep film in your carry-on if you're still using a nondigital camera.

Airport Information Beijing Capital International Airport ☎ 010/6454–1100 ⊕ *en. bcia.com.cn.* **Chengdu Shuangliu International Airport** ☎ 028/8520–5555 ⊕ *www. cdairport.com.* **Guangzhou Baiyun International Airport** ☎ 020/3606–6999 ⊕ *www. guangzhouairportonline.com.* **Guilin Liangjiang International Airport** ☎ 0773/284– 5114. **Hong Kong International Airport** ☎ 852/2261–2727 ⊕ *www.hongkongairport. com.* **Kunming Changshui International Airport** ☎ 871/96566 ⊕ *www.kmgairport.com.* **Shanghai Hongqiao International Airport** ☎ 021/96990 ⊕ *www.shanghaiairport.com.* **Shanghai Pudong International Airport**

☏ 021/96990 ⊕ en.shairport.com/pudongair. html. **Shenzhen Bao'an International Airport** ☏ 0755/2777–2000 ⊕ eng.szairport. com. **Xiamen Gaoqi International Airport** ☏ 0592/570–6078.**Xi'an Xianyang International Airport** ☏ 029/0500–2327 ⊕ www.xxia. com.cn/en.

FLIGHTS

TO AND FROM CHINA

Air China is China's flagship carrier. It operates nonstop flights from Beijing and Shanghai to various North American and European cities. Although it once had a sketchy safety record, the situation has improved dramatically, and it is now part of the Star Alliance of airlines worldwide. Don't confuse it with the similarly named China Airlines, which is operated out of Taiwan.

Air Canada has daily flights to Beijing and Shanghai from Toronto, and daily flights to Hong Kong from Toronto, Calgary, Edmonton, and Vancouver. Cathay Pacific flies to Beijing via Hong Kong. China Eastern and China Southern airlines fly from China to the West Coast of the United States. Japan Airlines and All Nippon fly to Beijing via Tokyo. United flies to Beijing and Shanghai.

WITHIN CHINA

Air China is the major carrier for domestic routes, flying to more than 180 cities in China. Its main rivals are China Southern and China Eastern. Smaller Shanghai Airlines has a growing number of national routes, mostly out of Shanghai.

The service on most Chinese airlines is on a par with low-cost American airlines—be prepared for limited legroom, iffy food, and possibly no personal TV. Always arrive at least two hours before departure, as chronic overbooking means latecomers just don't get on. In southern China typhoons often ground airplanes, so be prepared for delays if you are traveling between July and October.

You can make reservations and buy tickets for flights within China through airline websites or with travel agencies. It's

FOOT MASSAGE

Foot-massage spas are all the rage in China, but if you thought this was a new trend brought on by an upwardly mobile (and naturally more footsore) Chinese populace, think again. While Western medicine sees the foot as mere locomotion, practitioners of traditional Chinese reflexology think that bodily health is reflected in the sole. Each organ is connected to a specific reflex point on the foot. With precise and skillful manipulation of these points, vital functions can be stimulated, toxins eliminated, blood circulation improved, and nerves soothed. If your masseur is skilled, he'll be able to give you a fairly accurate health diagnosis after just a few minutes of looking at your feet. A smoker? Have indigestion? Sleeping poorly? Your feet tell all.

worth contacting a travel agency to compare prices.

Airline Contacts Air China ☏ 800/882–8122 ⊕ www.airchina.com. **China Eastern** ☏ 626/583–1500 ⊕ www.flychinaeastern.us. **China Southern** ☏ 888/338–8988 ⊕ www.fly chinasouthern.com.

▌ BIKE TRAVEL

Bicycles are still the primary form of transport for millions of Chinese people, although the proliferation of cars and smog make biking in the cities a chore. Large cities like Beijing, Chengdu, Xi'an, Shanghai, and Guilin have well-defined bike lanes, often separated from other traffic. Travel by bike is common in the countryside around places like Guilin, for locals and tourists alike. Locals don't use gears much—take your cue from them and just roll along at a leisurely pace. Note that bikes have to give way to motorized vehicles at intersections. If a flat tire or sudden brake failure strikes, seek out the nearest street-side mechanic (they're everywhere), easily identified by their bike parts and pumps.

In major cities, some lower-end hotels and hostels rent bikes. Street-side bike rental stations are also proliferating. Otherwise, inquire at bike shops, hotels, or even corner shops. The going rental rate is Y15 to Y30 a day, plus a refundable deposit. You will usually be asked to leave some form of ID. Check the seat and wheels carefully. Most rental bikes come with a lock, but they're usually pretty low quality. Instead, leave your wheels at an attended bike park—peace of mind costs a mere Y0.50. Helmets are nearly unheard of in China, though upmarket rental companies catering to foreign tourists usually stock them. They charge much more for their bikes, but they're usually in better condition.

If you're planning a lot of cycling, note that for about Y150 to Y200 you can buy your own basic bike, though expect to pay three or four times that for a mountain bike with all the bells and whistles or for a "Flying Pigeon," the classic heavy-duty model.

BIKES IN FLIGHT

Most airlines accommodate bikes as luggage, provided they are dismantled and boxed; check with individual airlines about packing requirements. Some airlines sell bike boxes, which are often free at bike shops, for about $20 (bike bags can be considerably more expensive).

Tour Operators Backroads. U.S.-based Backroads has China bike tours suitable for families to Beijing, Xi'an, and southern China. ☏ 800/462–2848 ⊕ www.backroads. com ✉ *From $5,498.* **Bike China Adventures.** Bike China Adventures organizes trips of varying length and difficulty all over China. ☏ 800/818–1778 ⊕ www.bikechina.com ✉ *From $2,500.*

▌ BOAT TRAVEL

Trains and planes are fast replacing China's boat and ferry services. The China-Japan International Ferry Company operates the Shanghai Ferry Boat that has a weekly ferry every Tuesday to Kobe or Osaka. The company maintains an English-language website with timetables.

Four- to seven-day cruises along the Yangtze River are the most popular, and thus the most touristy of the domestic boat rides. Both local and international companies run these tours, but shop around, as prices vary drastically. *See Chapter 9 for detailed information on Yangtze River cruises.*

Ferry Information China-Japan International Ferry Company ✉ *908 Dongdaming Lu, Shanghai* ☏ *021/6325–7642* ⊕ *www. shinganjin.com/index_e.php.*

▌ BUS TRAVEL

China has some reasonably comfortable long-distance buses running between most major cities. These luxury coaches are equipped with air-conditioning, soft seats, and screens playing nonstop movies, usually at deafening levels. Bring earplugs if you can't stand the noise.

Though securing a bus seat is easier than on a train, buying tickets can be complicated if you don't speak Chinese—you may end up on one of the cramped, old-fashioned buses, much like school buses (or worse). The conditions on sleeper buses are especially dire. Taking a train or an internal flight is much easier and safer, especially in rural areas where bad road conditions make for dangerous rides. Bus breakdowns are also frequent.

Big cities often have more than one bus terminal, and some companies have their own private depots. Buses usually depart and arrive punctually, and service is frequent. To avoid hassles, buying tickets through your hotel is usually worth the small surcharge.

▌ CAR TRAVEL

Driving yourself is not a possibility in mainland China, as the only valid driver's licenses are Chinese ones. International Driver's Permits (IDP) are not recognized by Chinese authorities. However, this restriction should be cause for relief, as city traffic is terrible, drivers manic and maniacal, and getting lost inevitable for first-timers. Conditions in Hong Kong aren't much better, but you can drive there using a U.S. or international license.

A far better idea is to put yourself in the experienced hands of a local driver. All the same, consider your itinerary carefully before doing so—in big cities, taking the subway or walking is often far quicker. Reserve the car for excursions farther afield.

The quickest way to arrange for a car and driver is to flag down a taxi. If you're happy with a driver you've used for trips around town, ask if you can hire him for the day. After some negotiating, expect to pay between Y350 and Y600, depending on the type of car. Most hotels can make arrangements for you, though they often charge you double that rate.

Another alternative is American car-rental agency Avis, which includes mandatory chauffeurs as part of all rental packages. A car and driver usually cost Y740 to Y850 ($118 to $136) per day. The company's headquarters are in Shanghai, with locations in Beijing, Hong Kong, Shanghai, Guangzhou, Shenzhen, and Chengdu.

Information Avis ☏ *021/6229-1118* ⊕ *www. avischina.com.*

▌ TRAIN TRAVEL

China's enormous rail network is one of the world's busiest. Though crowded, trains are usually safe, efficient, and run strictly to schedule. The high-speed rail system makes getting around the country very easy. In 2012, the Beijing–Guangzhou line opened, cutting travel time between the two cities from 30 hours to about 9 hours. At 1,428 miles, the line is the longest in the world.

There are certain intricacies to buying tickets, which usually have to be purchased in your departure city. You can buy most tickets up to 18 days in advance;

3 to 4 days ahead is usually enough time, except during the three national holidays—Chinese New Year (two days in mid-January–February), Labor Day (May 1), and National Day (October 1).

The cheapest place to purchase tickets is the train station, where they only accept cash and English is rarely spoken. In larger cities like Shanghai or Beijing, there is a special ticket window for foreigners with a staff that speaks some English. There are also train booking offices scattered around most cities. Fighting the crowds in train stations can be a headache—most travel agents or hotels will book your tickets for a small surcharge. Consider it money well spent! Travel China Guide has an online booking service that caters to foreigners. The company will deliver the tickets to your hotel or arrange for you to pick them up at the train station. Avoid the scruffy-looking individuals who try to sell you tickets outside the stations—these tickets are inevitably fake and could land you in trouble with the authorities.

The train system offers a glimpse of old-fashioned socialist euphemisms. There are four classes, but instead of first class and second class, in China you talk about hard and soft. Hard seats (*yingzuo*) are often rigid benches guaranteed to numb the buttocks within seconds; soft seats (*ruanzuo*), common on short day trips, are more like the seats in long-distance American trains. For overnight journeys, the cheapest option is the hard sleeper (*yingwo*), open bays of six bunks, in two tiers of three. They're cramped, but not uncomfortable; though you share the toilet with everyone in the wagon. Bedding is provided but you might want to take your own. Soft sleepers (*ruanwo*) are more comfortable: the closed compartments have four beds with bedding. Trains between Beijing, Shanghai, Hong Kong, and Xi'an also have a deluxe class, with only two berths per compartment and private bathrooms. The nonstop Z-series trains are even more luxurious. Train types are identifiable by the letter preceding the route number: Z is for nonstop, T is for a normal express, and C, G, and D are high-speed trains.

Overpriced dining cars serve meals that are often inedible, so do as the locals do and use the massive thermoses of boiled water in each compartment for your own noodles or instant soup. Trains are always packed, but you are guaranteed your designated seat, though not always the overhead luggage rack. When you board a train, the staff will take away your ticket and give you a plastic card with your seat or bed number. When you disembark you give the plastic card to the attendant and receive your ticket back. Note that theft on trains is increasing; on overnight trains, sleep with your valuables or keep them on the inside of the bunk.

You can find out just about everything about Chinese train travel at Seat 61's comprehensive website. China Highlights has a searchable online timetable for major train routes.

Information China Highlights ⊕ *www. chinahighlights.com.* **Seat 61** ⊕ *www.seat61. com/china.htm.* **Travel China Guide** ⊕ *www. travelchinaguide.com/china-trains.*

TRANS-SIBERIAN RAILWAY

The most dramatic Chinese train experience is the six-day trip between Beijing and Moscow, often referred to as the Trans-Siberian railway, though that's actually the service that runs between Moscow and Vladivostok. Two weekly services cover the 8,047 km (5,000 miles) between Moscow and Beijing. The Trans-Manchurian is a Russian train that goes through northeast China, whereas the Trans-Mongolian is a Chinese train that goes through the Great Wall and crosses the Gobi Desert. Both have first-class compartments with four berths or luxury two-berth compartments. Trains leave from Beijing Station—the cheapest place to buy tickets, though it's easier to get them through CITS.

ESSENTIALS

GREETINGS

Chinese people aren't very touchy-feely with one another, even less so with strangers. Stick to handshakes and low-key greetings when first meeting local people. Always use a person's title and surname until you're invited to do otherwise. In a group, greet the eldest person first as a sign of respect.

SIGHTSEEING

By and large, the Chinese are a rule-abiding bunch. Follow their lead and avoid doing anything signs advise against. Although you won't be banned from entering any sightseeing spots for reason of dress, you'd do well to avoid overly skimpy or casual clothes.

China is a crowded country; pushing, nudging, and line-jumping are commonplace. It may be hard to accept, but avoid overreacting (even verbally) if you're accidentally shoved.

OUT ON THE TOWN

It's a great honor to be invited to someone's house, so explain at length if you can't go. Arrive punctually with a small gift for the hosts; remove your shoes outside if you see other guests doing so. Eating lots is the biggest compliment you can pay the food (and the cook).

Smoking is one of China's greatest vices. No-smoking sections in restaurants used to be nonexistent, but they are becoming more common in cities like Beijing and Shanghai.

Holding hands in public is OK, but keep passionate embraces for the hotel room.

DOING BUSINESS

Time is of the essence when doing business in China. Make appointments well in advance and be extremely punctual, as this shows respect. Chinese people have a keen sense of hierarchy in the office: if you're visiting in a group, the senior member should lead proceedings.

Suits are still the norm in China, regardless of the outside temperature. Women should avoid plunging necklines, heavy makeup, overly short skirts, and high heels. Pants are completely acceptable. Women can expect to be treated as equals in business dealings.

Never say anything that will make people look bad, especially in front of superiors. Avoid being pushy or overly familiar when negotiating: respect silences in conversation, and don't hurry things or interrupt someone who is speaking. When entertaining, local businesspeople may insist on paying: after a slight protest, accept graciously.

Business cards are a big deal: not having one is like not having a personality. If possible, have yours printed in English on one side and Chinese on the other (your hotel can usually arrange this in a matter of hours). Proffer your card with both hands and receive the other person's in the same way, then read it carefully and make an admiring comment.

Many gifts, like clocks and cutting implements, are considered unlucky in China. Food—especially presented in a showy basket—is always a good gift choice, as are imported spirits. Avoid giving four of anything, as the number is associated with death. Offer gifts with both hands, and don't expect people to open them in your presence.

LANGUAGE

Nearly everyone in mainland China speaks Putonghua (*putōnghuà*, the "common language") another name for Mandarin Chinese. It's written using ideograms, or characters; in 1949 the government introduced a phonetic writing system that uses the Roman alphabet. Known as Pinyin, it's widely used to label public buildings and station names. Even if you don't speak or read Chinese, you can easily compare Pinyin names with a map.

In Hong Kong the main language spoken is Cantonese, although many people also speak English. There are many other local Chinese dialects. Some use the same characters as Putonghua for writing, but the pronunciation is so different as to be unintelligible to a Putonghua speaker. There are several non-Chinese languages (such as Mongolian, Uyghur, and Tibetan) spoken by China's ethnic minorities.

Chinese grammar is simple, but a complex tonal system of pronunciation means it usually takes a long time for foreigners to learn Chinese. Making yourself understood can be tricky; however, the Chinese will appreciate your making the effort to speak a few phrases understood almost everywhere. Try "Hello"—"*Ní hǎo*" (nee how); "Thank you"—"*Xiè xiè*" (shee-yeh shee-yeh); and "Good-bye"—"*Zài jiàn*" (dzai djan). When pronouncing words written in Pinyin, remember that "q" and "x" are pronounced like "ch" and "sh," respectively; "zh" is pronounced like the "j" in "just"; "c" is pronounced like "ts."

At times, the language barrier may feel formidable, especially outside of the big cities. To make things easier, carry the business card of your hotel with you with the name and address written in Chinese characters to show to taxi drivers or to people on the street if you get lost. In addition to your translator, dictionary, or phrasebook, always have a small notebook and pen with you to write things down for people or even to communicate through stick drawings. Many Chinese, especially students, may not understand spoken English but their reading comprehension can be quite high. In restaurants, it's perfectly acceptable to point at other people's dishes or in casual establishments to go into the kitchen and point at the ingredients you like. Even Chinese do this! In shops, calculators and hand gestures do most of the talking. Never be afraid to ask for help and try not to get too frustrated—remember, a smile and some pantomime go a very long way.

For learning Chinese at home or on your mobile device, Living Language Complete Chinese is highly recommended.

Living Language Complete Chinese ⊕ *www.livinglanguage.com.*

ACCOMMODATIONS

Location is the first thing you should consider. Chinese cities are usually big, and there's no point schlepping halfway across town for one particular hotel when a similar option is available more conveniently.

In major urban centers, many four- or five-star hotels belong to familiar international chains, and are usually a safe—if pricey—bet. You can expect swimming pools, Internet access, and business services. Hard-as-a-board beds are a trademark of Chinese hotels, even in luxury chains.

Locally owned hotels with four stars or fewer have erratic standards both inside and outside big cities, as bribery plays a big part in star acquisition. However, air-conditioning, color TVs, and private bathrooms are the norm for three to four stars, and even lone-star hotels have private bathrooms, albeit with a squatter toilet. All hotels, from pricey to cheap, will provide you with an electric kettle or a thermos for making tea.

When checking into a hotel, make sure your room isn't above or below the karaoke room, usually located on the second or third floor. Otherwise you may be in for some sleepless nights.

APARTMENT AND HOUSE RENTALS

There's an abundance of furnished properties for short- and long-term rentals in Beijing, Guangzhou, Hong Kong, Shanghai, and some other cities. Prices vary wildly. At the top end are luxury apartments and villas, usually far from the city center and accessible by (chauffeur-driven) car. Usually described as "serviced apartments" or "villas," these often include gyms and pools, and rates are usually well over $2,000 a month.

There are a lot of well-located mid-range properties in new apartment blocks. They're usually clean and nicely furnished, and rents start at $500 a month. What you get for your money fluctuates, so shop around. For longer, cheaper stays, there are normal local apartments. These are firmly off the tourist circuit and often cost a third of the price of the mid-range properties. The plumbing and electricity may not be up to code, and amenities may be lacking. It helps to bring a Chinese friend along to negotiate on your behalf.

Property sites like Asian Expat, Move and Stay, and Sublet.com have hundreds of apartments in major cities. The online classified pages in local English-language magazines or on expat websites are good places to look for cheaper properties.

Contacts Asia Expat ⊕ *www.asiaxpat.com.* **Move and Stay** ⊕ *www.moveandstay.com.* **Sublet.com** ⊕ *www.sublet.com.*

HOMESTAYS

Single travelers can arrange homestays (often in combination with language courses) through the Lotus Educational Foundation. Rates vary according to your length of stay, starting at about $200 a week. Make sure to ask for references before handing over your hard-earned cash.

Contacts Lotus Educational Foundation ☎ *408/996–1929* ⊕ *www.lotuseducation.org.*

HOTELS

When checking into a hotel, you need to show your passport—the desk clerk records the number before you're given a room. In smaller hotels outside of the big cities, unmarried couples may occasionally have problems staying together in the same room, but simply wearing a wedding band is one way to avoid this complication. Friends or couples of the same sex, especially women, shouldn't have a problem getting a room together. It's normal for hotels to post "visitor hours" for nonguests.

All hotels listed have private bath unless otherwise noted. Remember that water is a precious resource in China so use it accordingly.

■ BUSINESS SERVICES AND FACILITIES

Your hotel (or a mid- to high-end hotel nearby) is the best place to start looking for business services, including translation. Most are up to speed with the needs of business travelers, and if they don't offer a service they can put you in touch with a company that does. Regus and the Executive Centre are international business-services companies with several office locations in Beijing, Shanghai, and Hong Kong. They provide secretarial services, meeting and conference facilities, and office rentals.

Contacts Executive Centre ☎ *852/2297–2292* ⊕ *www.executivecentre.com.* **Regus** ☎ *400/120–1205* ⊕ *www.regus.cn.*

■ COMMUNICATIONS

INTERNET

In China's major cities you shouldn't have any trouble getting online. Wi-Fi is growing exponentially—most hotels offer it for free. Many also have computer terminals in their business centers that you can use if you didn't bring along a laptop. Internet cafés are ubiquitous in big cities, and are rapidly spreading to smaller destinations.

Known as *wang ba* in Chinese, they're not usually signposted in English, so ask your hotel to recommend one nearby. Prices (and cleanliness) vary considerably, but start at about Y3 to Y10 per hour.

Remember that there is strict government control of the Internet in China. Authorities frequently shut down Internet cafés, citing "spiritual pollution." There's usually no problem with accessing your email, but you may be unable to access news sites and even some blogs. To get around the restrictions, you can subscribe to a Virtual Private Network or use proxy servers to access certain sites. AnchorFree offers a free service called Hotspot Shield, although it includes annoying pop-up ads. More reliable VPN services, like those from WiTopia, cost about $50 a year for safe, fast surfing. If you're going to be in China for a while, investing in a VPN is worthwhile.

PHONES

The country code for China is 86; the city code for Beijing is 10, and the city code for Shanghai is 21. Hong Kong has its own country code: 852. To call China from the United States or Canada, dial the international access code (011), followed by the country code (86), the area or city code, and the eight-digit phone number.

Numbers beginning with 800 within China are toll-free. Note that a call from China to a toll-free number in the United States or Hong Kong is a full-tariff international call. If you need to call home, use your computer and a service like Skype. Be sure to download the U.S. version of Skype, because the Chinese TOM-Skype is constantly monitored by the government.

CALLING WITHIN CHINA

The Chinese phone system is cheap and efficient. Local calls are usually free, and long-distance rates are very low. Calling from your hotel room is a good option, as hotels can only add a 15% service charge.

Chinese phone numbers have eight digits—that's usually all you need to dial these when calling somewhere within the city. To call another city, dial 0, the city code, and the eight-digit phone number.

For directory assistance, dial 114. If you want information for other cities, dial the city code followed by 114 (this is considered a long-distance call). For example, if you're in Beijing and need directory assistance for Shanghai, dial 021–114. The operators do not speak English, so if you don't speak Chinese you're best off asking your hotel for help.

CALLING OUTSIDE CHINA

To make an international call from within China, dial 00 (the international access code) and then the country code, area code, and phone number. The United States country code is 1.

IDD (international direct dialing) service is available at all hotels, post offices, major shopping centers, and airports. Simply dial 108 (the local operator) and the local access codes from China: 811 (southern China) or 888 (northern China) for AT&T, 12 for MCI, and 13 for Sprint. Dialing instructions in English will follow.

Access Codes AT&T Direct ☎ *800/874–4000, 108-888 from northern China, 108-11 from southern China* ⊕ *www.att.com/ esupport/traveler.jsp?tab=2.* **MCI World-Phone** ☎ *800/444–4444, 108-12 from China* ⊕ *consumer.mci.com/international.* **Sprint International Access** ☎ *800/793-1153, 108-13 from China* ⊕ *www.sprint.com/ international.*

CALLING CARDS

Calling cards are a key part of the Chinese phone system. There are two kinds: the IC card (integrated circuit; *aicei ka*), for local and domestic long-distance calls on pay phones; and the IP card (Internet protocol; *aipi ka*) for international calls from any phone. You can buy both at post offices, convenience stores, and street vendors.

IC cards come in denominations of Y20, Y50, and Y100, and can be used in any pay phone with a card slot—most urban pay phones have them. Local calls using them cost around Y0.30 a minute, and less on weekends and after 6 pm.

IP cards come with face values of Y20, Y30, Y50, and Y100. The going rate for them might be half that, so bargain with the vendors. To use IP cards, first dial a local access number. You then enter a card number and a PIN, and finally the phone number, complete with international dial codes. There are countless different card brands; China Mobile, China Unicom, and China Telecom are usually reliable.

CELL PHONES

If you have a tri-band GSM or a CDMA phone, pick up a local SIM card (*sim ka*) from any branch of China Mobile or China Unicom: there are often branches at international airports. You'll be presented with a list of possible phone numbers, with varying prices—an "unlucky" phone number (one with lots of 4s) could be as cheap as Y50, whereas an auspicious one (full of 8s) could fetch Y300 or more. You then buy prepaid cards to charge minutes onto your SIM—do this straightaway, as you need credit to receive calls. Local calls to landlines cost Y0.25 per minute, and Y0.60 to cell phones. Rates can vary depending on the services you sign up for or add to your SIM. International calls from cell phones are very expensive.

Remember to bring an adapter for your phone charger. You can also buy cheap handsets from China Mobile—if you're planning to stay even a couple of days this is probably cheaper than renting a phone.

Contacts Cellular Abroad. Cellular Abroad rents and sells GMS phones and SIM card packages that work in many countries. ☏ *800/287–5072* ⊕ *www.cellularabroad.com.* **Mobal.** Mobal rents cell phones and sells GSM phones (starting at $49) that will operate in 170 countries. Per-call rates vary throughout the world. ☏ *888/888–9162* ⊕ *www.mobal.com.*

▌ CUSTOMS AND DUTIES

Except for the usual prohibitions against narcotics, explosives, plant and animal material, firearms, and ammunition, you can take anything into China that you plan to take away with you. Cameras, video recorders, GPS equipment, laptops, and the like should pose no problems. However, China is very sensitive about printed matter deemed seditious, such as religious, pornographic, and political texts, especially articles, books, and pictures of Tibet or Xinjiang. All the same, small amounts of English-language reading matter aren't generally a problem. Customs officials are for the most part easygoing, and visitors are rarely searched. It's not necessary to fill in customs declaration forms, but if you carry in a large amount of cash, say several thousand dollars, you should declare it upon arrival.

You're not allowed to remove any antiquities dating to before 1795. Antiques from between 1795 and 1949 must have an official red seal attached—quality antiques shops know this and arrange it.

U.S. Information U.S. Customs and Border Protection ☏ *877/227–5511* ⊕ *www.cbp.gov.*

▌ EATING OUT

In China meals are really a communal event, so food in a Chinese home or restaurant is always shared—you usually have a small bowl or plate and take food from central platters. Although Western-style cutlery is often available, it won't hurt to brush up on your use of chopsticks, the utensil of choice.

The standard eating procedure is to hold the bowl close to your mouth and shovel in the contents without any qualms. Noisily slurping up soup and noodles is the norm. Place bones or seeds in a small dish or on the table beside your bowl. It's considered bad manners to point or play with your chopsticks, or to place them on top of your rice bowl when you're finished eating (place the chopsticks horizontally on the table or plate). Avoid leaving your chopsticks standing up in a bowl of rice—they look like the two incense sticks burned at funerals.

If you're invited to a formal Chinese meal, be prepared for great ceremony, endless toasts and speeches, and a grand variety of elaborate dishes. Your host will be seated at the "head" of the round table, which is the seat that faces the door. Wait to be instructed where to sit. Don't start eating until the host takes the first bite, and then simply help yourself as the food comes around, but don't take the last piece on a platter. Always let the food touch your plate before bringing it up to your mouth; eating directly from the serving dish is bad form.

MEALS AND MEALTIMES

Food is a central part of Chinese culture, and so eating should be a major activity on any trip to China. Breakfast is not usually a big deal—congee, or rice porridge (*zhou*), is the standard dish. Most mid- and upper-end hotels do big buffet spreads, whereas café chains in major cities serve lattes and croissants.

Snacks are a food group in themselves. There's no shortage of street stalls selling grilled meats, bowls of noodle soup, and the ubiquitous *baozi* (steamed buns stuffed with meat or veggies). Many visitors are hesitant to eat from stalls—you'd be missing out on some of the best nibbles

around, though. Pick a place where lots of locals are eating to be on the safe side, and bring along your own chopsticks.

The food in hotel restaurants is usually acceptable but vastly overpriced. Restaurants frequented by locals always serve tastier fare at better prices. Don't pass by establishments without an English menu—a good phrase book and lots of pointing can usually get you what you want.

If you're craving Western food (or sushi or curry), rest assured that big cities have plenty of international chain restaurants. Most higher-end Chinese restaurants have a Western menu, but you're usually safer sticking to the Chinese food.

Meals in China are served early: breakfast until 9 am, lunch between 11 and 2, and dinner from 5 to 9.

Unless otherwise noted, the restaurants listed in this guide are open daily for lunch and dinner.

PAYING

At most restaurants you ask for the bill (*mai dan*) at the end of the meal, as you do back home. At cheap noodle bars and street stands you often pay up front. Only very upmarket restaurants accept credit cards.

RESERVATIONS AND DRESS

Regardless of where you are, it's a good idea to make a reservation if you can. In some places (Hong Kong, for example), it's expected. We only mention them specifically when reservations are essential (there's no other way you'll ever get a table) or when they are not accepted. For popular restaurants, book as far ahead as you can (often 30 days), and reconfirm as soon as you arrive. (Large parties should always call ahead to check the reservations policy.) We mention dress only when men are required to wear a jacket or a jacket and tie.

WINES, BEER, AND SPIRITS

Forget tea, today the people's drink of choice is beer. Massively popular among Chinese men, it's still a bit of a no-no for Chinese women, however. Tsingtao, China's most popular brew, is a 4% lager that comes in liter bottles and is usually cheaper than water. Many regions have their own local breweries, and international brands are available.

When you see "wine" on the menu, it's usually referring to sweet fruit wines or distilled rice wine. The most famous brand of Chinese liquor is Maotai, a distilled liquor ranging in strength from 35% to 53% proof. Like most firewaters, it's an acquired taste.

There are basically no licensing laws in China, so you can drink anywhere, and at any time, provided you can find a place to serve you.

▍ELECTRICITY

The electrical current in China is 220 volts and 50 cycles alternating current (AC), so most American appliances can't be used without a transformer. A universal adapter is especially useful in China, as wall outlets come in a bewildering variety of configurations: two- and three-pronged round plugs, as well as two-pronged flat sockets. Although blackouts are rare in Chinese cities, villages occasionally lose power for short periods of time.

Consider making a small investment in a universal adapter, which has several types of plugs in one lightweight, compact unit. Most laptops and cell-phone chargers are dual voltage (i.e., they operate equally well on 110 and 220 volts), so require only an adapter. These days the same is true of small appliances such as hair dryers. Always check labels and manufacturer instructions to be sure.

Contacts Walkabout Travel Gear. Walkabout Travel Gear has a good coverage of electricity; search for "adapters." ☎ 800/852–7085 ⊕ www.walkabouttravelgear.com.

▍EMERGENCIES

If you lose your passport, contact your embassy immediately. Embassy officials can also advise you on how to proceed in case of other emergencies. The staff at your hotel may be able to provide an interpreter if you need to report an emergency or crime to doctors or the police. Most police officers and hospital staff members don't speak English, though you may find one or two people who do.

Ambulances generally offer just a means of transport, not medical aid; taking a taxi is quicker, and means you can choose the hospital you want to go to. Where possible, go to a private clinic catering to expats—prices are sky-high, but their hygiene and medical standards are better. Most have reliable 24-hour pharmacies.

U.S. Embassy and Consulate United States Consulate ⊠ Citizen Services, Westgate Mall, 1038 W. Nanjing Rd., 8th fl., Jing'an, Shanghai ☎ 021/3271–4650, 021/8531–4000 after-hours emergencies ⊕ shanghai.usembassy-china.org.cn. **United States Embassy** ⊠ 55 Anjialou Lu, Chaoyang District, Beijing ☎ 010/8531–3000, 010/8531–4000 emergencies ⊕ beijing.usembassy-china.org.cn. **United States Citizens Services** ⊠ 4 Ling Shiguan Rd., Chengdu ☎ 028/8558–3992, 010/8531–4000 after-hours emergencies ⊕ chengdu.usembassy-china.org.cn/service.html ⊠ 43 Hua Jiu Rd., Zhujiang New Town, Tianhe, Guangzhou ☎ 020/3814–5775 in Guangzhou, 010/8531–4000 after-hours emergencies in Guangzhou ⊕ guangzhou.usembassy-china.org.cn/service.html.

General Emergency Contacts Ambulance ☎ 120. **Fire** ☎ 119. **Police** ☎ 110.

▍HEALTH

The most common types of illnesses are caused by contaminated food and water. Especially in developing countries, drink only bottled, boiled, or purified water and drinks; don't drink from public fountains or ask for beverages with ice. You should even consider using bottled or boiled water to brush your teeth. Make sure food has been thoroughly cooked and is served to you fresh and hot; avoid vegetables and fruits that you haven't washed (in bottled or purified water) or peeled yourself. If you have problems, mild cases of traveler's diarrhea may respond to Imodium (known generically as loperamide) or Pepto-Bismol. Be sure to drink plenty of fluids; if you can't keep fluids down, seek medical help immediately. Tap water in major cities like Beijing and Shanghai is safe for brushing teeth, but buy bottled water to drink and check to see that the bottle is sealed.

Infectious diseases can be airborne or passed via mosquitoes and ticks and through direct or indirect physical contact with animals or people. Some, including Norwalk-like viruses that affect your digestive tract, can be passed along through contaminated food. If you are traveling in an area where malaria is prevalent, use a repellant containing DEET and take malaria-prevention medication before, during, and after your trip as directed by your physician. Condoms can help prevent most sexually transmitted diseases, but they aren't absolutely reliable, and their quality varies from country to country. Speak with your physician and/or check the CDC or World Health Organization websites for health alerts, particularly if you're pregnant, traveling with children, or have a chronic illness.

SHOTS AND MEDICATIONS

No immunizations are required for entry into China, but it's a good idea to be immunized against typhoid and Hepatitis A and B before traveling, as well as to get routine tetanus-diphtheria and measles boosters. In winter a flu vaccination is also smart, especially if you're infection-prone or are a senior citizen. ■TIP➜ In summer months malaria is a risk in tropical and rural areas, especially Hainan and Yunnan provinces—consult your doctor four to six weeks before your trip, as preventive treatments vary. The risk of contracting malaria in cities is small.

Health Warnings National Centers for Disease Control & Prevention (*CDC*). ☎ 800/232–4636 International Travelers' Health Line ⊕ www.cdc.gov/travel/destinations/china.htm. **World Health Organization** (*WHO*). ⊕ www.who.int.

SPECIFIC ISSUES IN CHINA

At China's public hospitals, foreigners need to pay fees to register, to see a doctor, and then for all tests and medication. Prices are cheap compared to the fancy foreigner clinics in major cities, where you pay $100 to $150 just for a consultation. However, most doctors at public hospitals don't speak English, and hygiene standards out of the major cities can be low—all the more reason to take out medical insurance.

Hong Kong has excellent public and private health care. Foreigners have to pay for both, so insurance is a good idea. Even for lesser complaints, private doctors charge a fortune: head to a public hospital if money is tight. In an emergency you'll always receive treatment first and get the bill afterward—Y570 is the standard ER charge.

The best place to start looking for a suitable doctor is through your hotel concierge, then the local Public Security Bureau. If you become seriously ill or are injured, it is best to fly home, or at least to Hong Kong, as quickly as possible. In Hong Kong, English-speaking doctors are widely available.

Pneumonia and influenza are common among travelers returning from China—talk to your doctor about inoculations before you leave. If you need to buy prescription drugs, try to go to the pharmacies of reputable private hospitals or to bigger chain stores like Watsons.

OVER-THE-COUNTER REMEDIES

Most pharmacies in big Chinese cities carry over-the-counter Western medicines and traditional Chinese medicines. You usually need to ask for the generic name of the drug you're looking for, not a brand name. Acetaminophen—or Tylenol—is often known as paracetomol in Hong Kong. In big cities reputable pharmacies like Watsons are always a better bet than no-name ones.

▌ HOURS OF OPERATION

Most banks and government offices are open weekdays 9 to 5 or 6, although closed for lunch (sometime between noon and 2). Some bank branches keep longer hours and are open Saturday (and occasionally Sunday) mornings. Many hotel currency-exchange desks stay open 24 hours. Museums open from roughly 9 to 6, six or seven days a week. Everything in China grinds to a halt for the first two or three days of Chinese New Year (sometime in mid-January to February), and opening hours are often reduced for the rest of that season.

Pharmacies are open daily from 8:30 or 9 to 6 or 7. Some large pharmacies stay open until 9 or even later. Shops and department stores are generally open daily 8 to 8; some stores stay open even later in summer, in popular tourist areas, or during peak tourist season.

HOLIDAYS

National holidays in mainland China include New Year's Day (January 1); Spring Festival aka Chinese New Year (late January/early February); Qingming Jie (April 4); International Labor Day (May 1); Dragon Boat Festival (late May/early June); anniversary of the founding of the Communist Party of China (July 1); anniversary of the founding of the Chinese People's Liberation Army (August 1); and National Day—founding of the People's Republic of China in 1949 (October 1); Chongyang Jie or Double Ninth Festival (ninth day of ninth lunar month). Hong Kong celebrates most of these festivals, and also has public holidays at Easter and for Christmas and Boxing Day (December 25 and 26).

MAIL

Sending international mail from China is extremely reliable. Airmail letters to any place in the world should take 5 to 14 days. Express Mail Service (EMS) is available to many international destinations. Letters sent within any city arrive the next day, and mail to the rest of China takes a day or two longer. Domestic mail can be subject to search, so don't send sensitive materials such as religious or political literature, as you might cause the recipient trouble.

Service is more reliable if you mail letters from post offices rather than mailboxes. Buy envelopes here, too, as there are standardized sizes in China. You need to glue stamps onto envelopes, as they're not self-adhesive. Most post offices are open daily between 8 am and 7 pm; many keep longer hours. Your hotel can usually send letters for you, too.

You can use the Roman alphabet to write an address. Do not use red ink, which has a negative connotation. You must also include a six-digit zip code for mail within China. Sending airmail postcards costs Y4.50 and letters Y5 to Y7.

Long-term guests can receive mail at their hotels. Otherwise, the best place to receive mail is at the American Express office. Most major Chinese cities have American Express offices with client-mail service. Be sure to bring your American Express card, as the staff will not give you the mail without seeing it.

SHIPPING PACKAGES

It's easy to ship packages home from China. Take what you want to send *unpacked* to the post office—everything will be sewn up officially into satisfying linen-bound packages, a service that costs a few yuan. You have to fill in lengthy forms—enclosing a photocopy of receipts for the goods inside isn't a bad idea, as they may be opened by customs along the line. Large antiques stores often offer reliable shipping services that take care of customs in China.

International courier services operating in China include DHL, Federal Express, and UPS—next-day delivery for a 1-kilogram (2.2-pound) package starts at about Y300. Your hotel can also arrange shipping parcels, but there's usually a hefty markup.

Express Services DHL ☎ *800/810–8000* ⊕ *www.cn.dhl.com/en.html.* **FedEx** ☎ *800/463–3339* ⊕ *www.fedex.com.* **UPS** ☎ *800/820–8388* ⊕ *www.ups.com.*

ITEM	AVERAGE COST
Cup of coffee at Starbucks	Y27–Y35
Glass of local beer	Y15
Cheapest subway ticket	Y3
Starting rate for taxi ride in Beijing or Shanghai	Y10
Set lunch in a cheap restaurant	Y30
Half-hour foot massage	Y50
Movie ticket	Y99

▌ MONEY

China is a cheap destination by most North Americans' standards, but expect your dollar to do more for you in smaller cities than in pricey Shanghai or Beijing. The exception to the rule is Hong Kong, where eating and sleeping prices are on a par with those in the United States.

In mainland China, the best places to convert your dollars into yuan are your hotel's front desk or a branch of a major bank, such as Bank of China, CITIC, or HSBC. These charge standardized government rates—anything cheaper is illegal, and thus risky. You need to present your passport to change money.

Prices throughout this guide are given for adults. Substantially reduced fees are almost always available for children, students, and senior citizens.

Although credit cards are gaining ground in China, for day-to-day transactions cash is definitely king.

Currency Conversion Google ⊕ *www.google.com.* **Oanda.com** ⊕ *www.oanda.com.* **XE.com** ⊕ *www.xe.com/cc.*

ATMS AND BANKS

Your own bank will probably charge a fee for using ATMs abroad; the foreign bank you use may also charge a fee. Nevertheless, you'll usually get a better rate of exchange at an ATM than you will at a currency-exchange office or even when changing money in a bank.

■**TIP➔ PINs with more than four digits are not recognized at ATMs in many countries. If yours has five or more, remember to change it before you leave.**

ATMs are widespread in major Chinese cities. The most reliable ATMs are at HSBC, which also have the highest withdrawal limit, which offsets transaction charges. Of the Chinese banks, your best bet for ATMs is the Bank of China, which accepts most foreign cards. That said, machines frequently refuse to give cash for mysterious reasons—move on and try another. On-screen instructions appear automatically in English.

ATMs are everywhere throughout Hong Kong—most carry the sign ETC instead of ATM. Subway stations are a good place to look.

CREDIT CARDS

American Express, MasterCard, and Visa are accepted at most hotels and a growing number of upmarket stores and restaurants. Diners Club is less widely accepted.

It's a good idea to inform your credit-card company before you travel. Otherwise, the credit-card company might put a hold on your card owing to unusual activity—not a good thing halfway through your trip. Record all your credit-card numbers—as well as the phone numbers to call if your cards are lost or stolen—in a safe place, so you're prepared should something go wrong. Both MasterCard and Visa have general numbers you can call (collect if you're abroad) if your card is lost, but you're better off calling the number of your issuing bank, since MasterCard and Visa usually just transfer you to your bank; your bank's number is usually printed on your card.

If you plan to use your credit card for cash advances, you'll need to apply for a PIN at least two weeks before your trip. Although it's usually cheaper (and safer) to use a credit card abroad for large purchases (so you can cancel payments or be reimbursed if there's a problem), note that some credit-card companies *and* the banks that issue them add substantial percentages to all foreign transactions, whether they're in a foreign currency or not. Check on these fees before leaving home, so there won't be any surprises when you get the bill.

■TIP➔ **Before you charge something, ask the merchant whether or not he or she plans to do a dynamic currency conversion (DCC). In such a transaction the credit-card processor (shop, restaurant, or hotel, not Visa or MasterCard) converts the currency and charges you in dollars. In most cases you'll pay the merchant a 3% fee for this service in addition to any credit-card company and issuing-bank foreign-transaction surcharges.**

Dynamic currency conversion programs are becoming increasingly widespread. Merchants who participate in them are supposed to ask whether you want to be charged in dollars or the local currency, but they don't always do so. And even if they do offer you a choice, they may well avoid mentioning the additional surcharges. The good news is that you *do* have a choice. And if this practice really gets your goat, you can avoid it entirely thanks to American Express; with its cards, DCC simply isn't an option.

Cards American Express
] in the U.S., 336/393–1111
d ⊕ www.americanexpress.
☎ 800/234–6377 in the

U.S., 514/881–3735 collect from abroad ⊕ www.dinersclub.com. **MasterCard** ☎ 800/307–7309 in the U.S., 636/722–7111 collect from abroad, 800/110–7309 in China ⊕ www.mastercard.com. **Visa** ☎ 800/847–2911 in the U.S., 303/967–1096 collect from abroad, 800/711–2911 or 110-2911 in China ⊕ www.visa.com.

CURRENCY AND EXCHANGE

The Chinese currency is officially called the yuan (Y), and is also known as *renminbi* (RMB), or "People's Money." You may also hear it called *kuai,* an informal expression like "buck."

Old and new styles of bills circulate in China, and many denominations have both coins and bills. The Bank of China issues bills in denominations of 1 (burgundy), 2 (green), 5 (brown or purple), 10 (turquoise), 20 (brown), 50 (blue or occasionally yellow), and 100 (red). There are 1-yuan coins, too. The yuan subdivides into 10-cent units called *jiao* or *mao*; these come in bills and coins of 1, 2, and 5. The smallest denomination is the *fen,* which comes in coins (and occasionally tiny notes) of 1, 2, and 5. Counterfeiting is rife in China, and even small stores inspect notes with ultraviolet lamps. Change can be a problem—don't expect much success paying for a Y3 purchase with a Y100 note.

Exchange rates in China are fixed by the government daily, so it's equally good at branches of the Bank of China, at big department stores, or at your hotel's exchange desk. Any lower rates are illegal, so you're exposing yourself to scams. A passport is required. Hold on to your exchange receipt, which you need to convert your extra yuan back into dollars.

In Hong Kong the only currency used is the Hong Kong dollar, divided into 100 cents. Three local banks (HSBC, Standard Chartered, and the Bank of China) all issue bills and each has its own designs. At this writing the Hong Kong dollar was pegged to the U.S. dollar at approximately 7.76 Hong Kong dollars to 1 U.S. dollar.

There are no currency restrictions in Hong Kong. You can exchange currency at the airport, in hotels, in banks, and through private money changers scattered through the tourist areas. Banks usually have the best rates, but as they charge a flat HK$50 fee for non-account holders, it's better to change large sums infrequently. Currency-exchange offices have no fees, but they offset that with poor rates. Stick to ATMs whenever you can.

■TIP→ **Even if a currency-exchange booth has a sign promising no commission, rest assured that there's some kind of huge, hidden fee. (Oh...that's right. The sign didn't say no** *fee.***) And as for rates, you're almost always better off getting foreign currency at an ATM or exchanging money at a bank.**

GENERAL REQUIREMENTS FOR MAINLAND CHINA	
Passport	Must be valid for six months after date of arrival
Visa	Required for U.S. citizens ($140)
Required Vaccinations	None
Recommended Vaccinations	Hepatitis A and B, typhoid, influenza, booster for tetanus-diphtheria
Driving	Chinese driver's license required

■ PACKING

Most Chinese people dress for comfort, so you can plan to do the same. There's little risk of offending people with your dress: Westerners tend to attract attention regardless of their attire. Fashion capitals Hong Kong and Shanghai are the exceptions to the comfort rule: slop around in flip-flops and worn denims and you *will* feel that there's a neon "tourist" sign over your head. Opt for your smarter jeans or pants for sightseeing there.

Sturdy, comfortable walking shoes are a must: go for closed shoes over sandals, as

WORD OF MOUTH

"Our China experience was full of surprises at every turn, random kindness from strangers, and beauty that I'm still trying to process. I often felt I was wandering around in a dream." —Partmtn

dust, rain and toe-stomping crowds make them impractical. Northern Chinese summers are dusty and baking hot, so slacks, capris, and sturdy shorts are best. A raincoat, especially a light Goretex one or a fold-up poncho, is useful for an onset of rainy weather, especially in Southern China. During the harsh winters, thermal long johns and thick socks are a lifesaver—especially in low-star hotel rooms.

That said, in urban centers you can prepare to be unprepared: big Chinese cities are a clothes shopper's paradise. If a bulky jacket's going to put you over the airline limit, buy one in China and leave it behind when you go. All the other woollies—and silkies, the local insulator of choice—you'll need go for a song, as do brand-name jackets. Scarves, gloves, and hats, all musts, are also easy to find.

Most good hotels have reliable overnight laundry services, though costs can rack up on a long trip. Look outside your hotel for cheaper laundries, and bring some concentrated travel detergent for small or delicate items. Note that it's often cheaper to buy things than have your own laundered, so if you're even a little interested in shopping, consider bringing an extra, foldable bag for carting purchases home.

Keep packets of tissues and antibacterial hand wipes in your day pack—paper isn't a feature of many Chinese restrooms, and you often can't buy it in smaller towns. A small flashlight with extra batteries is also useful. The brands in Chinese pharmacies are limited, so take adequate stocks of your potions and lotions, feminine-hygiene products (tampons are especially hard to find), and birth control. All of these things are easy to get in Hong Kong.

You may also want to bring along a face mask to protect yourself from dust and pollution, especially in the smoggy winter months.

In your carry-on luggage, pack an extra pair of eyeglasses or contact lenses and enough of any medication you take to last a few days longer than the entire trip.

If you're planning a longer trip or will be using local tour guides, bring a few inexpensive items from your home country as gifts. Popular gifts are candy, T-shirts, and small cosmetic items such as lipstick and nail polish—double-check that none were made in China. Be wary about giving American magazines and books as gifts, as these can be considered propaganda and get your Chinese friends in trouble.

■ PASSPORTS AND VISAS

All U.S. citizens, even infants, need a valid passport with a tourist visa stamped in it to enter China (except for Hong Kong, where you only need a valid passport). It's always best to have at least six months' validity on your passport before traveling to Asia.

Getting a tourist visa to China (known as an "L" visa) in the United States is straightforward. Standard visas are for single-entry stays of up to 30 days, and are valid for 90 days from the day of issue (*not* the day of entry), so don't get your visa too far in advance. The cost for a tourist visa issued to a U.S. citizen is $140; citizens of other countries can expect to pay between $30 and $90.

Travel agents in Hong Kong can also issue visas to visit mainland China—though regulations can change during times of unrest. Note: The visa application will ask your occupation. The Chinese government doesn't look favorably upon those who work in publishing or the media. People in these professions routinely give "teacher" as their occupation. Before you go, contact the embassy or consulate of the People's Republic of China to gauge the current mood. If you

want to go to Tibet, every foreign visitor must have a Tibet Travel Permit and travel with an organized tour approved by the Tibet Tourism Bureau. Travel agencies in China can arrange this.

Hong Kong Travel Agents China Travel Service. China Travel Service has 34 branches in Hong Kong and Macau. ☒ *78-83 Connaught Rd., Hong Kong* ☎ *852/2998-7888* ⊕ *ctshk. com/english/index.htm.*

Children traveling with only one parent do not need a notarized letter of permission to enter China. However, as these kinds of policies can change, being overprepared isn't a bad idea.

Under no circumstances should you overstay your visa. To extend your visa, stop by the Entry and Exit Administration Office of the local branch of the Public Security Bureau a week before your visa expires. The office is known as the PSB or the Foreigner's Police; most are open weekdays 9 to 11:30 and 1:30 to 4:30. The process is extremely bureaucratic, but it's usually no problem to get a month's extension on a tourist visa. You need to bring your registration of temporary residency from your hotel and your passport, which you generally need to leave for five to seven days (so do any transactions requiring it beforehand). If you are trying to extend a business visa, you'll need the above items as well as a letter from the business that originally invited you to China saying it would like to extend your stay for work reasons. Rules are always changing, so you will probably need to go to the office at least twice to get all your papers in order.

Chinese Visa Information Chinese Consulate ☎ *212/868-2078* ⊕ *www.nyconsulate. prchina.org.* **Chinese Embassy Visa Office** ☎ *202/495-2266* ⊕ *www.china-embassy.org/ eng.*

RESTROOMS

Public restrooms abound in mainland China—the street, parks, restaurants, department stores, and major tourist attractions are all likely locations. Most charge a small fee (usually less than Y1), but seldom provide Western-style facilities or private booths. Instead, expect squat toilets, open troughs, and rusty spigots; WC signs at intersections point the way to these facilities. Toilet paper is a rarity, so carry tissues and antibacterial hand wipes. The restrooms in the newest shopping plazas, fast-food outlets, and deluxe restaurants catering to foreigners are generally on a par with American restrooms. In Hong Kong, public restrooms are well maintained. Alternatively, dip into malls or the lobby of big international hotels to use their facilities.

SAFETY

There is little violent crime against tourists in China, partly because the penalties are severe for those who are caught—China's yearly death-sentence tolls run into the thousands. Single women can move about without too much hassle. Handbag-snatching and pickpocketing do happen in markets and on crowded buses or trains—keep an eye open and your money safe, and you should have no problems. Use the lockbox in your hotel room to store any valuables, but always carry your passport with you for identification purposes.

China is full of people looking to make a quick buck. The most common scam involves people persuading you to go with them for a tea ceremony, which is often so pleasant that you don't smell a rat until several hundred dollars appear on your credit-card bill. "Art students" who pressure you into buying work is another common scam. The same rules that apply to hostess bars worldwide are also true in China. Avoiding such scams is as easy as refusing *all* unsolicited services—be it from taxi or pedicab drivers, tour guides, or potential "friends."

■TIP→ Distribute your cash, credit cards, IDs, and other valuables between a deep front pocket, an inside jacket or vest pocket, and a hidden money pouch. Don't reach for the money pouch once you're in public.

Chinese traffic is as manic as it looks, and survival of the fittest (or the biggest) is the main rule. Crossing streets can be an extreme sport. Drivers rarely give pedestrians the right-of-way, and don't even look for pedestrians when making a right turn on a red light. Cyclists have less power but are just as aggressive.

The severely polluted air of China's big cities can bring on, or aggravate, respiratory problems. If you're a sufferer, take the cue from locals, who wear surgical masks, or a scarf or bandanna as protection.

TAXES

There is no sales tax in China or Hong Kong. Mainland hotels charge a 5% tax; bigger, joint-venture hotels also add a 10% to 15% service fee. Some restaurants charge a 10% service fee.

TIME

The whole of China is 8 hours ahead of London, 13 hours ahead of New York, 14 hours ahead of Chicago, and 16 hours ahead of Los Angeles. There's no daylight saving time, so subtract an hour in summer.

Time Zones Timeanddate.com. Timeanddate.com can help you figure out the correct time anywhere in the world. ⊕ *www.timeanddate.com/worldclock.*

TIPPING

Tipping is a tricky issue in China. It's officially forbidden by the government, and locals simply don't do it. In general, follow their lead without qualms. Nevertheless, the practice is beginning to catch on, especially among tour guides, who often expect Y10 a day. Official CTS representatives aren't allowed to accept tips, but you can give them candy, T-shirts, and other small gifts. You don't need to tip in restaurants or in taxis.

In Hong Kong, hotels and major restaurants usually add a 10% service charge; this money rarely goes to waiters and waitresses. Add on up to 10% more for good service. Tipping restroom attendants is common, but it is generally not the custom to leave an additional tip in taxis and hair salons.

▐ TOURS

Most guided tours to China take in three or four major cities, often combined with a Yangtze River cruise or a visit to far-flung Tibet. You get a day or two in each place, with the same sights featured in most tours. If you want to explore a given city in any kind of depth, you're better doing it by yourself or getting a private guide.

Shopping stops plague China tours, so inquire before booking as to when, where, and how many to expect. Although you're never obliged to buy anything, they can take up big chunks of your valuable travel time, and the products offered are always ridiculously overpriced. Even on the best tours, you can count on having to sit through at least one or two.

Not all of the companies we list include air travel in their packages. Check this when you're researching your trip.

Recommended Companies China Focus Travel. China Focus is a reputable, long-standing agency with small group tours to China's most famous attractions, including the Yangtze River and Yunnan Province. ☎ *800/868–7244* ⊕ *www. chinafocustravel.com* ✉ *From $1,700.*

Overseas Adventure Travel. Small groups and excellent guides are what Overseas Adventure Travel takes pride in. ☎ *800/ 955–1925* ⊕ *www.oattravel.com* ✉ *From $167.*

Pacific Delight. Pacific Delight is known for its corporate and family tours around North and Southeast Asia. ☎ *800/221– 7179* ⊕ *www.pacificdelighttours.com* ✉ *From $1,600.*

R. Crusoe & Son. This offbeat company organizes unique small group or tailor-made private tours. ☎ *800/585–8555* ⊕ *www.rcrusoe.com* ✉ *From $6,990.*

Ritz Tours. The Ritz Tours is an agency offering mid-range "China Deluxe" and luxury "China Premiere" tours to China's most famous landmarks. ☎ *888/ 345–7489* ⊕ *www.ritztours.com* ✉ *From $420.*

SPECIAL-INTEREST TOURS
CULTURE

Local guides are often creative when it comes to history and culture, so having an expert with you can make a big difference.

Contacts National Geographic Expeditions. China experts lead National Geographic's trips, though all that knowledge doesn't come cheap. ☎ *888/966–8687* ⊕ *www. nationalgeographicexpeditions.com* ✉ *From $5,750.*

Smithsonian Journeys. Learning is the focus of Smithsonian Journeys' small-group tours, which are led by university professors. ☎ *855/330–1542* ⊕ *www. smithsonianjourneys.org* ✉ *From $5,169.*

Wild China. This Beijing-based company offers some of the most unusual trips around, including visits to ethnic minority groups, Tibet, and little-known Xinjiang Province. ☎ *888/902–8808* ⊕ *www. wildchina.com* ✉ *From $1,100.*

CULINARY

Contacts Artisans of Leisure. Artisans of Leisure's culinary tour takes in Shanghai and Beijing from the cities' choicest establishments, with prices to match. ☎ *800/ 214–8144* ⊕ *www.artisansofleisure.com* ✉ *From $9,000.*

Imperial Tours. Imperial Tours Culinary Tour combines sightseeing with cooking lectures and demonstrations, and lots of five-star dining. ☎ 888/888–1970 ⊕ www. imperialtours.net ✉ From $1,000.

Intrepid Travel. Intrepid Travel offers a "Real Food Adventure Tour" which includes market visits, cooking demonstrations, and lots of eating at down-to-earth restaurants. ☎ 800/970–7299 ⊕ www.intrepidtravel.com ✉ From $1,100.

GOLF

Contacts China Highlights. China Highlights organizes short golf packages that combine sightseeing with golfing in Beijing, Shanghai, Kunming, Guangzhou, and Guilin. ☎ 800/268–2918 ⊕ www. chinahighlights.com ✉ From $720.

HIKING

Contacts Wild China. Wild China offers one-of-a-kind hiking expeditions to the remote mountain areas of Sichuan and Yunnan provinces. ☎ 888/902–8808 ⊕ www.wildchina.com ✉ From $4,000.

▮ VISITOR INFORMATION

For general information before you go, including advice on tours, insurance, and safety, call or visit the website of the China National Tourist Office.

The two best-known Chinese travel agencies are the state-run China International Travel Service (CITS) and China Travel Service (CTS), both under the same government ministry. Although they have some tourist information, they are businesses, so don't expect endless resources if you're not purchasing a tour or flight. In theory, CTS offices offer local sightseeing tours, and CITS arranges packages from overseas; in reality, their services overlap.

The Hong Kong Tourism Board has heaps of online information about events, sightseeing, shopping, and dining in Hong Kong. They also organize tour packages from the United States, and local sightseeing tours.

Contacts China International Travel Service ☎ 626/568–8993 ⊕ www.citsusa. com. **China National Tourist Office**

☎ 212/760–8218 ⊕ www.cnto.org. **China Travel Service** ☎ 800/899–8618 ⊕ www. chinatravelservice.com. **Hong Kong Tourist Board** ⊕ www.discoverhongkong.com.

ONLINE TRAVEL TOOLS

The websites listed in this guide are in English. If you come across a Chinese-language site you think might be useful, copy the URL into Google, then click the "Translate this page" link. Translations are literal, but generally work for finding out information like opening hours or prices.

ALL ABOUT CHINA

The excellent *China Digital Times* tracks China-related news and culture. The Oriental List has extremely reliable information about travel in China. A detailed database on Chinese art, film, literature, and more is available at China Culture. Information about all of Hong Kong's arts and cultural programs is available at the Hong Kong Leisure and Cultural Services Department.

China Digital Times ⊕ www.chinadigital times.net.

China Culture ⊕ www.chinaculture.org.

Hong Kong Leisure and Cultural Services Department ⊕ www.lcsd.gov.hk.

The Oriental List ⊕ www.datasinica.com.

BUSINESS

China Business Weekly is published by the *China Daily* newspaper.

China Business Weekly ⊕ www.chinadaily. com.cn/english/bw/bwtop.html.

LOCAL INSIGHT

Asia Expat gives advice and listings from foreigners living in Beijing, Hong Kong, Guangzhou, and Shanghai. Asia City is an online version of quirky weekly rags that give the lowdown on everything happening in Shanghai and Hong Kong.

Asia Expat ⊕ www.asiaxpat.com.

Asia City ⊕ www.asia-city.com.

NEWSPAPERS

China Daily is the leading English-language daily. The English edition of China's most popular—and most propagandistic—daily is called the *People's Daily*. Hong Kong's leading English-language daily is the *South China Morning Post.*

China Daily ⊕ *www.chinadaily.com.cn.*

People's Daily ⊕ *www.english.peopledaily. com.cn.*

South China Morning Post ⊕ *www.scmp. com.*

GREAT CHINESE READS

Big Name Fiction: 2012 Nobel Peace Prize winner Mo Yan's *The Garlic Ballads; A Thousand Years of Good Prayers* by Li Yiyun; *The Civil Servant's Notebook* by Wang Xiaofang; *Northern Girls* by Sheng Keyi; Gao Xingjian's *Soul Mountain.*

China 101: *Tiger Head, Snake Tales* by Jonathan Fenby; *The New Emperors* by Kerry Brown; *China in Ten Words* by Yu Hua.

About Mao: Dr. Li Zhisui's *The Private Life of Chairman Mao; Jung Chang's Mao The Unknown Story; Great Leap Forward* edited by Chuihua Judy Chang, Jeffrey Inaba, Rem Koolhaas, Sze Tsung Leung.

INDEX

PHOTO CREDITS

Front cover: Masterfile (Royalty-Free Division) [Description: Statues of terracotta soldiers in a row, Xi'An, Shaanxi Province, China]. 1, Boaz Rottem/age fotostock. 2-3, Alvaro Leiva / age fotostock. 5, lu linsheng/iStockphoto. Chapter 1: Experience China. 8-9, Walter Bibikow / age fotostock. 10, Holly Peabody, Fodors.com member. 11 (left), Hong Kong Tourism Board. 11 (right), DK.samco/Shutterstock. 14, Iain Masterton / age fotostock. 15, SEUX Paule / age fotostock. 16, Brian Jeffery Beggerly/Flickr. 17, Hong Kong Tourism Board. 19, Hotel G Beijing. 20 (left), Jarno Gonzalez Zarraonandia/iStockphoto. 20 (top), fotohunter/Shutterstock. 20 (bottom), Jonathan Larsen/Shutterstock. 21 (top left), Hung Chung Chih/Shutterstock. 21 (bottom left), Peter Mukherjee/iStockphoto. 21 (right), loong/Shutterstock. 22 (left), silverjohn / Shutterstock. 22 (top right), Holger Mette/iStockphoto. 22 (bottom right), SIHASAKPRACHUM / Shutterstock. 23 (top left), richliy/Shutterstock. 23 (bottom left), Hung Chung Chih/Shutterstock. 23 (right), Ivan Walsh/Flickr. 24, John Leung/Shutterstock. 25 (left), Eastimages/ Shutterstock. 25 (right), gary718/Shutterstock. 26, Marc van Vuren/Shutterstock. 27 (left), Gretchen Winters, Fodors.com member. 27 (right), Steve Slawsky. 28, Sze Kit Poon/iStockphoto. 29 (left), oksana. perkins/Shutterstock. 29 (right), Andrew Kerr/Shutterstock. 38, bbobo, Fodors.com member. 39, qingqing/Shutterstock. 40 (left), Kowloonese/Wikimedia Commons. 40 (top right), Daniel Shichman & Yael Tauger/Wikimedia Commons. 40 (bottom right), Wikimedia Commons. 41 (left), Hung Chung Chih/ Shutterstock. 41 (right), rodho/Shutterstock. 42, (left), Chinneeb/Wikimedia Commons. 42 (top right), B_cool/Wikimedia Commons. 42 (bottom right), Imperial Painter/Wikimedia Commons. 43 (left and bottom right), Wikimedia Commons. 43 (top right), Joe Brandt/iStockphoto. 44 (top left, bottom left, and top right), Wikimedia Commons. 44 (bottom right), K.T. Thompson/wikipedia.org. 45 (top left), Wikimedia Commons. 45 (bottom left), ImagineChina. 45 (right), tomislav domes/Flickr. 46, TAO IMAGES/age fotostock. Chapter 2: Beijing. 47, TAO IMAGES/age fotostock. 48, claudio zaccherini/ Shutterstock. 49 (left), yxm2008/Shutterstock. 49 (right), Johann 'Jo' Guzman, Fodors.com member. 50, sanglei slei/iStockphoto. 51, TAO IMAGES/age fotostock. 58, lu linsheng/iStockphoto. 59 (top), TAO IMAGES/age fotostock. 59 (bottom), Bob Balestri/iStockphoto. 60, Lance Lee I AsiaPhoto.com/ iStockphoto. 61 (left), Jiping Lai/iStockphoto. 61 (right 1), May Wong/Flickr. 61 (right 2), William Perry/iStockphoto. 61 (right 3), bing liu/iStockphoto. 61 (right 4), William Perry/iStockphoto. 62 (bottom left and right), Wikimedia Commons. 62 (top), Helena Lovincic/iStockphoto. 63 (top), rehoboth foto/Shutterstock. 63 (bottom left and right), Wikimedia Commons. 67, P. Narayan/age fotostock. 71, Jose Fuste Raga/age fotostock. 73, Lim Yong Hian/Shutterstock. 81, TAO IMAGES/age fotostock. 89, TAO IMAGES/age fotostock. 94, patrick frilet/age fotostock. 111, Werner Bachmeier/age fotostock. 114-15, Sylvain Grandadam/age fotostock. 118, Christian Kober/age fotostock. 125, TAO IMAGES/ age fotostock. 128, Luoxubin I Dreamstime.com. 129, Wikimedia Commons. 130-31, Liu Jianmin/age fotostock. 132 (top), Eugenia Kim/iStockphoto. 132 (bottom), Alan Crawford/iStockphoto. 133, Chris Ronneseth/iStockphoto. 141, JTB Photo/age fotostock. Chapter 3: Beijing to Shanghai. 143, Steve Vidler/age fotostock. 144, Chi King/Flickr. 145 (left), www.seefarseeeast.com/Flickr. 145 (right), Gina Smith/iStockphoto. 146, suecan1/Flickr. 153, richliy/Shutterstock. 158, View Stock/age fotostock. 163, David Lyons/age fotostock. 166, Karl Johaentges/age fotostock. 175, Bjmcse I Dreamstime.com. 182, nozomiiqel/Flickr. 189, Charles Bowman / age fotostock. 192, JTB Photo/age fotostock. 199, White Star / Spierenb/age fotostock. 204, suecan1/Flickr. 210, Karl Johaentges/age fotostock. 215, hxdyl/Shutterstock. Chapter 4: Shanghai. 217, Lucas Vallecillos/age fotostock. 218, claudio zaccherini/Shutterstock. 219, Hel080808 Dreamstime.com. 220, Augapfel/Flickr. 227, Gaby Wojciech / age fotostock. 232, claudio zaccherini/Shutterstock. 237, Jennifer Arnow. 240-41, Pixattitude I Dreamstime.com. 251, SALDARI/age fotostock. 255, Karl Johaentges/age fotostock. 260, JTB Photo/age fotostock. 265, Hippo/age fotostock. Chapter 5: Eastern China. 293, TAO IMAGES/age fotostock. 294, Jon Mullen/ iStockphoto. 295 (left), robert van beets/iStockphoto. 295 (right), hxdbzxy/Shutterstock. 296, China National Tourist Office. 303, SuperStock/age fotostock. 308, JTB Photo/age fotostock. 312, TAO IMAGES/age fotostock. 314, JTB Photo/age fotostock. 317, JTB Photo/age fotostock. 328, SuperStock/ age fotostock. 329 (top), TAO IMAGES/age fotostock. 329 (bottom), Mark52/Shutterstock. 330, Shigeki Tanaka/age fotostock. 331 (left), Yuan yanwu - Imaginechina. 331 (top right), Huiping Zhu/ iStockphoto. 331 (bottom right), richliy/Shutterstock. 336, Christian Kober/age fotostock. 339, Shigeki Tanaka/age fotostock. Chapter 6: Hong Kong. 343, Hemis / Alamy. 344, Hong Kong Tourism Board. 345, Ella Hanochi/iStockphoto. 346, Laoshi/iStockphoto. 352, Amanda Hall / age fotostock. 357, Dallas & John Heaton / age fotostock. 369, Raga Jose Fuste / age fotostock. 381, BrokenSphere/wikipedia. org. 395, Fumio Okada / age fotostock. 406, Hong Kong Tourism Board. 420, Steve Vidler / age fotostock. 426, Christian Goupi / age fotostock. Chapter 7: Pearl River Delta. 429, José Fuste Raga/age fotostock. 430, J Aaron Farr/Flickr. 431 (left), Hector Joseph Lumang/iStockphoto. 431 (right), Mission Hills. 432, Rüdiger Meier/Wikimedia Commons. 439, View Stock/age fotostock. 442, Charles Bow-

NOTES